Introducing

the

Prentice Hall Library

featuring the

Penguin

Literature Library

WITHDRAWN

Hundreds of titles from
the world's foremost publisher
of classic and contemporary
favorites, from
Beowulf to *Black Hawk Down*

CALIFORNIA TEACHER'S EDITION

PRENTICE HALL LITERATURE

Timeless Voices, Timeless Themes

THE BRITISH TRADITION

VOLUME II

Copyright © 2002 by Pearson Education, Inc., Upper Saddle River, New Jersey 07458.
All rights reserved. Printed in the United States of America. This publication is protected by copyright, and permission should be obtained from the publisher prior to any prohibited reproduction, storage in a retrieval system, or transmission in any form or by any means, electronic, mechanical, photocopying, recording, or likewise. For information regarding permission(s), write to: Rights and Permissions Department.

ISBN 0-13-0587842

3 4 5 6 7 8 9 10 06 05

Upper Saddle River, New Jersey
Glenview, Illinois
Needham, Massachusetts

PRENTICE HALL LITERATURE

Timeless Voices, Timeless Themes

THE BRITISH TRADITION

Upper Saddle River, New Jersey
Glenview, Illinois
Needham, Massachusetts

Copyright © 2002 by Pearson Education, Inc., Upper Saddle River, New Jersey 07458.
All rights reserved. Printed in the United States of America. This publication is protected by copyright, and permission should be obtained from the publisher prior to any prohibited reproduction, storage in a retrieval system, or transmission in any form or by any means, electronic, mechanical, photocopying, recording, or likewise. For information regarding permission(s), write to: Rights and Permissions Department.

ISBN 0-13-054808-1

5 6 7 8 9 10 06 05 04

PRENTICE HALL LITERATURE

Timeless Voices, Timeless Themes

COPPER

BRONZE

SILVER

GOLD

PLATINUM

THE AMERICAN EXPERIENCE

THE BRITISH TRADITION

ACKNOWLEDGMENTS

Grateful acknowledgment is made to the following for copyrighted material:

Angel Flores, c/o Barbara Dederick "Eternity" by Arthur Rimbaud from *An Anthology of French Poetry From Nerval to Valery in English Translation with French Originals,* edited by Angel Flores. Reprinted by permission of Barbara Dederick for the Estate of Angel Flores.

Ballantine Books, a division of Random House, Inc. "Homeless" from *Living Out Loud* by Anna Quindlin. Copyright © 1987 by Anna Quindlen. Copyright © 1987 by Anna Quindlen.

Georges Borchardt, Inc. "The First Year of My Life" from *The Stories of Muriel Spark.* Copyright © 1985 by Copyright Administration. Reprinted by permission of Georges Borchardt, Inc., for the author.

Brown University Scholarly Technology Group "The Victorian Web Overview" by George P. Landow from www.stg.brown.edu.

Cambridge University Press, North American Branch Excerpt from "Letter to Thomas Flower Ellis from Thomas Babington Macaulay on the Passing of the Reform Bill" written in 1831, from *The Selected Letters of Thomas Babington Macaulay,* ed. Thomas Pinney, 5 vols. (Cambridge: Cambridge University Press, 1974–80)

Agencia Literaria Carmen Barcells, S.A. and University of Texas Press "Sonnet LXXXIX" and "Sonnet LXIX" from *100 Love Sonnets: Cien Sonetos de Amore,* by Pablo Neruda, translated by Stephen Tapscott. Copyright © 1959 by Pablo Neruda. Copyright © 1986 by the University of Texas Press.

Carol Publishing Group "The Lorelei" by Heinrich Heine from *The Poetry and Prose of Heinrich Heine,* edited by Frederic Ewen. Copyright © 1948, 1976 by The Citadel Press. Used by arrangement with Carol Publishing Group.

(Acknowledgments continue on page R40, which constitutes an extension of this copyright page.)

CONTRIBUTING AUTHORS

The contributing authors guided the direction and philosophy of *Prentice Hall Literature: Timeless Voices, Timeless Themes*. Working with the development team, they helped to build the pedagogical integrity of the program and to ensure its relevance for today's teachers and students.

Kate Kinsella

Kate Kinsella, Ed.D., is a faculty member in the Department of Secondary Education at San Francisco State University. A specialist in second-language acquisition and adolescent reading and writing, she teaches coursework addressing language and literacy development across the secondary curricula. She has taught high-school ESL and directed SFSU's *Intensive English Program* for first-generation bilingual college students. She maintains secondary classroom involvement by teaching an academic literacy class for second-language learners through the University's *Step to College* partnership program. A former Fulbright lecturer and perennial institute leader for TESOL, the California Reading Association, and the California League of Middle Schools, Dr. Kinsella provides professional development nationally on topics ranging from learning-style enhancement to second-language reading. Her scholarship has been published in journals such as the *TESOL Journal*, the *CATESOL Journal*, and the *Social Studies Review*. Dr. Kinsella earned her M.A. in TESOL from San Francisco State University and her Ed.D. in Second Language Acquisition from the University of San Francisco.

Kevin Feldman

Kevin Feldman, Ed.D., is the Director of Reading and Early Intervention with the Sonoma County Office of Education (SCOE). His career in education spans thirty-one years. As the Director of Reading and Early Intervention for SCOE, he develops, organizes, and monitors programs related to K–12 literacy and prevention of reading difficulties. He also serves as a Leadership Team Consultant to the California Reading and Literature Project and assists in the development and implementation of K–12 programs throughout California. Dr. Feldman earned his undergraduate degree in Psychology from Washington State University and has a Master's Degree in Special Education, Learning Disabilities and Instructional Design from U.C. Riverside. He earned his Ed.D. in Curriculum and Instruction from the University of San Francisco.

Colleen Shea Stump

Colleen Shea Stump, Ph.D., is a Special Education supervisor in the area of Resources and Inclusion for Seattle Public Schools. She served as a professor and, since 1993, as chairperson for the Department of Special Education at San Francisco State University. She continues as the lead consultant in the area of collaboration for the California State Improvement Grant and travels the state of California providing professional development training in the areas of collaboration, content literacy instruction, and inclusive instruction. Dr. Stump earned her doctorate at the University of Washington, her M.A. in Special Education from the University of New Mexico, and her B.S. in Elementary Education from the University of Wisconsin–Eau Claire.

Joyce Armstrong Carroll

In her forty-year career, Joyce Armstrong Carroll, Ed. D., has taught on every grade level from primary to graduate school. In the past twenty years, she has trained teachers in the teaching of writing. A nationally known consultant, she has served as president of TCTE and on NCTE's Commission on Composition. More than fifty of her articles have appeared in journals such as *Curriculum Review, English Journal, Media & Methods, Southwest Philosophical Studies, English in Texas,* and the *Florida English Journal.* With Edward E. Wilson, Dr. Carroll co-authored *Acts of Teaching: How to Teach Writing* and co-edited *Poetry After Lunch: Poetry to Read Aloud.* She co-directs the New Jersey Writing Project in Texas.

Edward E. Wilson

A former editor of *English in Texas,* Edward E. Wilson has served as a high-school English teacher and a writing consultant in school districts nationwide. Wilson has served on both the Texas Teacher Professional Practices Commission and NCTE's Commission on Composition. Wilson's poetry appears in Paul Janeczko's anthology *The Music of What Happens.* With Dr. Carroll, he co-wrote *Acts of Teaching: How to Teach Writing* and co-edited *Poetry After Lunch: Poetry to Read Aloud.* Wilson co-directs the New Jersey Writing Project in Texas.

CALIFORNIA PROGRAM ADVISORS

The California program advisors provided ongoing input throughout the development of *Prentice Hall Literature: Timeless Voices, Timeless Themes.* Their valuable insights ensure that the perspectives of the teachers throughout California are represented within this literature series.

Dawn Akuna
Teacher of Reading
Harriet Eddy Middle School
Elk Grove, CA

Kathy Allen
English Language Arts Teacher
Palos Verdes Intermediate School
Palos Verdes, CA

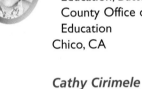

Maxine K. Bigler
Associate Director, Region II, Migrant Education, Butte County Office of Education
Chico, CA

Cathy Cirimele
Teacher of English
Bullard High School
Fresno, CA

Jesse L. Culbert
English Teacher
Willowbrook Middle School
Compton, CA

Terry Day
English and Speech Teacher
Downey High School
Modesto, CA

Yvonne Divans-Hutchinson
Language Arts Teacher
King/Drew Magnet High School of Medicine and Science
Los Angeles, CA

Diane Erickson
Teacher of English
Oxford Academy
Cypress, CA

Cynthia Hardy Gayle
Assistant Principal
Rancho del Rey Middle School
Chula Vista, CA

Joe Glover
Language Arts/ELD Teacher
Mesa Intermediate School
Palmdale, CA

Jeannette Hampton
Literacy Coordinator for Sacramento City USD, Retired
Fern Bacon Basic Middle School
Sacramento, CA

Carleen Hemric
Language Arts Teacher
Pershing Middle School
San Diego, CA

Kimberly Wise Johnson, M.Ed.
English Teacher
Arcade Fundamental Middle School
Sacramento, CA

Keith R. Jones
English/Social Studies Teacher
Elmhurst Middle School
Oakland, CA

Karen Kessinger
Teacher of English
San Bernardino High School
San Bernardino, CA

Gail Catherine Kidd
Language Arts Teacher
Center Middle School
Azusa, CA

Alan J. Leonard
English Instructor, Retired
Anaheim, CA

Catherine C. Linn, Ph.D.
Teacher of Literature and Writing
Palm Springs High School
Palm Springs, CA

Karen Lopez
English Teacher
William S. Hart High School
Newhall, CA

Robert Lopez
ELL Instructor
Gage Middle School
Huntington Park, CA

Celia Monge Mana
Language Arts Teacher
Horace Mann Middle School
San Francisco, CA

Kathleen Marshall
English Teacher
Stagg High School
Stockton, CA

Peggy P. Moore
Middle School Educator, Retired
Bayshore School District
Daly City, CA

Akiko Morimoto
Language Arts Teacher
Washington Middle School
Vista, CA

Dewhanne Nyivih
Former English Teacher
Marshall Fundamental High School
Pasadena, CA

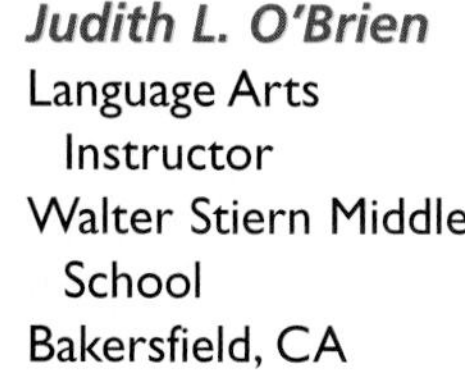

Judith L. O'Brien
Language Arts Instructor
Walter Stiern Middle School
Bakersfield, CA

Ann Okamura
Teacher of English
Laguna Creek High School
Elk Grove, CA

Judy Plouff
Language Arts/Social Studies Teacher
Sherman Oaks Center for Enriched Studies
Reseda, CA

Jan Reed
English Curriculum Specialist, Retired
Garden Grove USD
Garden Grove, CA

Marian Reimann
Assistant Principal, Curriculum and Instruction
Sutter Middle School
Winnetka, CA

Lynne Richter
Teacher of English
Fulton Middle School
Van Nuys, CA

Maureen Rippee
English Instructor
Wilson High School
Long Beach, CA

Meredith Ritner
Language Arts Teacher
Alieso Viejo Middle School
Alieso Viejo, CA

Sharon Schiesl
Language Arts Teacher
Mendez Fundamental Intermediate School
Santa Ana, CA

Carol J. Schowalter
Language Arts Teacher
El Roble Middle School
Claremont, CA

Cheryl Spivak
Language Arts/Reading Intervention Teacher
Portola Middle School
Tarzana, CA

Peggy Todd Stover
Teacher of English
Independence High School
San Jose, CA

Michael C. Sullivan
Language Arts Teacher
Pacifica High School
Garden Grove, CA

Sandra Sullivan
Language Arts Teacher
Garden Grove High School
Garden Grove, CA

Vanna Turner
Language Arts Teacher
Albert Einstein Middle School
Sacramento, CA

Linda Valdez
English Teacher
Camarillo High School
Camarillo, CA

Sonia Wilson
English Teacher
Steve Garvey Junior High School
Lindsay, CA

Mary Jo Wynne
Language Arts/Social Studies Teacher
Assumption of the Blessed Virgin Mary School
Pasadena, CA

UNIT 1

From Legend to History: The Old English and Medieval Periods (A.D. 449–1485)

PART 1 Earthly Exile, Heavenly Home

PART 2 Focus on Literary Forms: The Epic

PART 3 A National Spirit

PART 4 Perils and Adventures

Skills Workshops

UNIT 2

Celebrating Humanity: The English Renaissance Period (1485–1625)

PART 1 Lovers and Their Lines

PART 2 The Influence of the Monarchy

PART 3 Focus on Literary Forms: Drama

Skills Workshops

UNIT 3

A Turbulent Time: The Seventeenth and Eighteenth Centuries (1625–1798)

PART 3 The Ties That Bind

PART 4 Focus on Literary Forms: The Essay

Skills Workshops

UNIT 4

Rebels and Dreamers: The Romantic Period (1798–1832)

PART 2 Focus on Literary Forms: Lyric Poetry

A Closer Look

(continued)

Rebels and Dreamers: The Romantic Period (1798–1832) (continued)

PART 3 The Reaction to Society's Ills

UNIT 5

Progress and Decline: The Victorian Period (1833–1901)

(continued)

Progress and Decline: The Victorian Period (1833–1901) (continued)

PART 3 The Empire and Its Discontents

PART 4 Gloom and Glory

Skills Workshops

UNIT 6

A Time of Rapid Change: The Modern and Postmodern Periods (1901–Present)

PART 1 Waking From the Dream

(continued)

A Time of Rapid Change: The Modern and Postmodern Periods (1901–Present) (continued)

PART 2 Conflicts Abroad and at Home

PART 3 Focus on Literary Forms: The Short Story

Part 4 From the National to the Global

Skills Workshops

Resources

Comparing Literary Works

Reading Informational Materials

Connections

Literature Around the World

Writing Workshops

Listening and Speaking Workshops

Assessment Workshops

UNIT 4 Rebels and Dreamers (1798–1832)

Two Men Observing the Moon, Caspar David Friedrich, Staatl. Kunstsammlungen, Neue Meister, Dresden, Germany

Unit Objectives

1. To read selections from the Romantic period in English literature
2. To apply a variety of reading strategies, particularly interactive reading strategies, appropriate for reading these selections
3. To analyze literary elements
4. To use a variety of strategies to build vocabulary
5. To learn elements of grammar; usage, and style
6. To use recursive writing processes to write in a variety of forms
7. To develop listening and speaking skills
8. To express and support responses to various types of texts
9. To prepare, organize, and present literary interpretations

Meeting the Objectives

With each selection, you will find instructional materials through which students can meet these objectives. Further, you will find additional practice pages for reading strategies, literary analysis, vocabulary, and grammar in the **Selection Support: Skills Development Workbook** in your **Teaching Resources.**

Background

Art

Two Men Observing the Moon, Caspar David Friedrich

The German painter Caspar David Friedrich (1774–1840) is one of the most emotionally expressive painters of the Romantic period. Call students' attention to details like the nearly uprooted tree; the burning moon; and the two men, whose comradely pose seems at odds with the harsh landscape. To help students link the art to the focus of Unit 4, "Rebels and Dreamers," ask this question:

- Literature of the period often focuses on dreams and the imagination. What elements of this painting strike you as dreamlike?
  Answer: The coppery mist and burning moon are dreamlike, as is the tree's eerie attitude.

UNIT FEATURES

Connections	Reading Informational Materials
Every unit contains a feature that connects literature to a related topic, such as art, science or history. In this unit, students will sample engaging commentary on social conditions in early-nineteenth century England through Emma Thompson's skillful dramatization of Jane Austen's *Sense and Sensibility.* Use the information and questions on the Connections page to help students enrich their understanding of the selections presented within the unit.	These selections will help students to analyze and evaluate informational texts, such as workplace documents, technical directions, and consumer materials. They will expose students to the organization and features unique to non-narrative texts. In this unit, students learn to read book reviews and analyze an author's basic assumptions about literature.

“Come forth into the light of things,
Let Nature be your teacher.”

— William Wordsworth, *from* “The Tables Turned”

ASSESSMENT RESOURCES

- **Selection Support: Skills Development Workbook**
- **Formal Assessment**
- **Open Book Tests**
- **Performance Assessment and Portfolio Management**
- **Extension Activities**

Assessing Student Progress

Listed below are tools that are available to measure the degree to which students meet the unit objectives.

Informal Assessment

The questions in the Review and Assess sections are a first-level response to the concepts and skills presented with the selections. Students' responses provide a brief, informal measure of their grasp of the material. These responses can indicate where further instruction and practice are needed. Follow up with the practice pages in **Selection Support: Skills Development Workbook.**

Formal Assessment

The **Formal Assessment** booklet contains Selection Tests and Unit Tests.

- Selection Tests measure comprehension and skills acquisition for each selection or group of selections.
- Each Unit Test provides students with thirty multiple-choice questions and five essay questions designed to assess students' knowledge of the literature and skills taught in the unit.

The **Open-Book Tests** ask students to demonstrate their ability to synthesize and communicate information from selections or groups of selections.

To assess student writing, you will find rubrics and scoring models in the **Performance Assessment and Portfolio Management** booklet. In this booklet, you will also find scoring rubrics for listening and speaking activities.

Alternative Assessment

The **Extension Activities** booklet contains writing activities, listening and speaking activities, and research and technology activities that are appropriate for students with different ability levels. You may also use these activities as an alternative measure of students' growth.

Using the Timeline

The Timeline can serve a number of instructional purposes, as follows:

Getting an Overview

Use the Timeline to help students get a quick overview of themes and events of the period. This approach will benefit all students but may be especially helpful for visually oriented students, English language learners, and those less proficient in reading. (For strategies in using the Timeline as an overview, see the bottom of this page.)

Thinking Critically

Questions are provided on the facing page. Use these questions to have students review the events, discuss their significance, and examine the *so what* behind the *what happened.*

Connecting to Selections

Have students refer to the Timeline when beginning to read individual selections. By consulting the Timeline regularly, they will gain a better sense of the period's chronology. In addition, they will appreciate the world events that gave rise to these works of literature.

Projects

Students can use the Timeline as a launching pad for projects like these:

- **Relate Literature to History** As students read material in this unit, have them record allusions or facts linked to events on the Timeline. In a notebook, they should list any events they can find on the Timeline that are connected in some way to each item in their notes. At the end of the class's time with this unit, have the class compile the notes of individual students and construct a "Literature in History" Timeline.
- **Report on a Scientific Advance** Have students scan the Timeline for an invention, scientific experiment, or other advance in knowledge that interests them, research the advance and its significance, and then report on their findings to the class.

Timeline 1798–1832

1798 | 1804 | 1810

British Events

- **1798 William Wordsworth** and **Samuel Taylor Coleridge** publish *Lyrical Ballads.*
- **1801** Act of Union creates United Kingdom of Great Britain and Ireland.
- **1801** Union Jack becomes official flag. ▼
- **1803** J.M.W. Turner's *Calais Pier* exhibited in London.

- **1805** Battle of Trafalgar.
- **1807** Thomas Moore writes *Irish Melodies.*

- **1812 Byron** publishes *Childe Harold's Pilgrimage.*
- **1813 Jane Austen** publishes *Pride and Prejudice.* ◄
- **1814** George Stephenson constructs first successful steam locomotive. ▼
- **1815** John MacAdam constructs roads of crushed stone.

World Events

- **1799** France: Napoleon becomes head of revolutionary government.
- **1799** Egypt: Rosetta Stone, key to deciphering hieroglyphics, discovered.
- **1802** Haiti: Toussaint L'Ouverture leads rebellion against French rule.
- **1803** United States: Louisiana Territory purchased from France.
- **1804** Germany: Beethoven composes *Symphony No. 3.*
- **1804** France: Napoleon crowns himself emperor.

- **1807** United States: Fulton's steamboat navigates Hudson River. ▲
- **1810** South America: Simón Bolivar leads rebellions against Spanish rule.
- **1812** United States: War with Britain declared.
- **1813** Mexico: Independence declared.
- **1815** Belgium: Napoleon defeated at Waterloo.

ENRICHMENT: History Connection

Timeline: 1798–1832	Key Events
To give students an overview of the period, indicate the span of dates in the upper left-hand corner. Next, point out that the Timeline is divided into specifically British Events (on top) and World Events (on bottom). Have them practice scanning the Timeline across, looking both at the British Events and the World Events. Finally, point out that the events in the Timeline often represent beginnings, turning points, and endings.	Have students name a technological advance. **Possible response:** In 1815, John MacAdam constructs roads of crushed stone. Then, have them note evidence of new social trends. **Possible response:** In 1832, the First Reform Act gave more people the right to vote. Ask students to formulate a theme linking these trends. **Possible response:** People's common needs and rights were being addressed.

British and World Events

1816 | 1822 | 1828 | 1832

■ **1818 Mary Wollstonecraft Shelley** publishes *Frankenstein or the Modern Prometheus.* ▲

■ **1819** Peterloo Massacre in Manchester.

■ **1819 Percy Bysshe Shelley** writes "Ode to the West Wind."

■ **1820 John Keats** publishes "Ode on a Grecian Urn."

■ **1825** Horse-drawn buses begin operating in London.

■ **1825** John Nash begins rebuilding of Buckingham Palace.

■ **1827** System for purifying London water installed.

■ **1829** Robert Peel establishes Metropolitan Police in London.

■ **1830** Liverpool-Manchester railway opens. ▲

■ **1831** Michael Faraday demonstrates electromagnetic induction. ◀

■ **1832** First Reform Act extends voting rights.

■ **1816** France: René Läennec invents stethoscope.

■ **1819** United States: Washington Irving writes "Rip Van Winkle."

■ **1819** First steamship crosses Atlantic.

■ **1821** Greece: War with Turkey begins.

■ **1821** Germany: Heinrich Heine publishes *Poems.*

■ **1823** Russia: Aleksandr Pushkin begins writing *Eugene Onegin.*

■ **1825** Russia: Bolshoi Ballet founded.

■ **1826** Germany: Mendelssohn composes *Overture to A Midsummer Night's Dream.*

■ **1826** United States: James Fenimore Cooper publishes *The Last of the Mohicans.*

■ **1830** France: Stendhal publishes *The Red and the Black.*

■ **1831** United States: Edgar Allan Poe publishes *Poems.*

■ **1831** France: Victor Hugo publishes *The Hunchback of Notre Dame.*

Analyzing the Timeline

1. **(a)** Name two technological improvements in this period. **(b)** What do these improvements suggest about the state of life before this time? **[Hypothesize]**
   Answer: **(a)** MacAdam constructed roads of crushed stone (1815); a water purification system was installed in London (1827). **(b)** These changes suggest that such public matters as transportation and sanitation were primitive and may not have been systematically supervised.
2. **(a)** Name a change in English political life after 1817. **(b)** What does this change suggest about the nature of government? Explain. **[Speculate]**
   Answer: **(a)** The First Reform Act extended voting rights (1832). **(b)** This change suggests that government was growing more democratic.
3. **(a)** What nation's affairs dominated the European scene prior to 1816? **(b)** Speculate about how these events may have affected Britain. **[Speculate]**
   Answer: **(a)** French affairs (specifically, the rise of Napoleon) dominated Europe. **(b)** France can obstruct Britain's most direct route to Europe, the English Channel. Turmoil in France, and hostility toward Britain, would hinder British trade.
4. **(a)** What general trends are evident in the United States in this period? **(b)** Speculate about relations with Britain during this time, citing events to support your conclusions. **[Connect]**
   Answer: **(a)** The United States was expanding and had grown powerful enough to close off new European colonization (the Louisiana Territory was purchased in 1803); it had an active literary life, with publications by Irving (1819) and others. **(b)** Relations were poor; the two countries fought in 1812.
5. **(a)** Name three events suggesting that Britain suffered from popular unrest in the years after 1816. **(b)** Speculate about the issues that sparked this unrest. **[Speculate]**

continued

Continued from right column

Answer: **(a)** A "massacre" occurred in 1819; a police force was established in 1829; and the First Reform Act extended voting rights in 1832. **(b)** Commoners may have been agitating for political rights, laborers for fair pay and better conditions.

▶Critical Viewing

1. What does the dress of the men manning an early steam engine (1814) suggest about their occupation? **[Speculate]**
   Answer: Their top hats and collars suggest that they are the designers of the engine, not men employed to run it.
2. What does the book cover suggest about *Frankenstein's* (1818) popularity? **[Infer]**
   Answer: The cover is modern and done in a "mass-market" style, suggesting that the novel was popular long after it was written.

Literature of the Period

- For an early, sympathetic view of the human cost of the Industrial Revolution, refer students to Blake's "The Chimney Sweeper," p. 643.
- Though Wordsworth and Coleridge became more conservative, their poetic heirs continued the tradition of Romantic radicalism. Refer students to Shelley's "Men of England," p. 771.
- For a sympathetic view of the rioting Luddites—from an aristocrat, no less, and one whose district they had terrorized—refer students to Byron's "Speech to Parliament: In Defense of the Lower Classes," p. 768. (Byron's speech as a young man did not go unremembered; at his funeral, thousands of working-class people lined the streets to honor him.)

▶Critical Viewing

Possible response: The massed crowd of figures at the bottom of the painting, who have perhaps spilled out of a ship, and the turmoil of the sails suggest chaos. Participating in a sea battle must have been an overwhelming experience, involving confused sights and noises.

Rebels and Dreamers

THE ROMANTIC PERIOD (1798–1832)

Historical Background

After nearly a century of progress in science and industry, the faith of poets in reason was eroded. Whereas eighteenth-century poets had celebrated the power of human understanding—their most bitter satire could say no more than "humanity is unreasonable"—Wordsworth marked the end of the century with the warning, "Our meddling intellect / Misshapes the beauteous forms of things— / We murder to dissect."

In the ensuing period, which was named the Romantic Period by historians during the late 1800s, nearly all the attitudes and tendencies of eighteenth-century classicism and rationalism were redefined or changed dramatically. To understand how these changes occurred, it is necessary to examine not only the impact of events in Britain, but also the effects of the social and political upheaval that began taking place in other parts of the world.

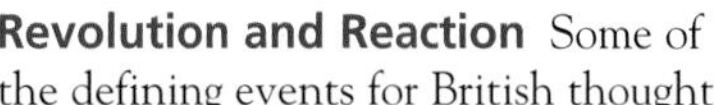

The Battle of Trafalgar, October 21, 1805, J.M.W. Turner, The Granger Collection, Ltd.

▲ **Critical Viewing** The Romantic painter J.M.W. Turner depicted the defeat of the French fleet by the British at Trafalgar. Using the details in this painting, describe the experience of participating in a sea battle. **[Speculate]**

Revolution and Reaction Some of the defining events for British thought and politics at the end of the eighteenth century took place not in England but in France. The French Revolution began on July 14, 1789, when a mob stormed the Bastille, a Paris prison for political prisoners. The successful revolutionaries placed limits on the powers of King Louis XVI, established a new government, and approved a document called the Declaration of the Rights of Man and of the Citizen, which affirmed the principles of "liberty, equality, and fraternity." France became a constitutional monarchy.

In England, the ruling class felt threatened by the events in France, which seemed to strike at the roots of social order. Most intellectuals, including such important writers of the Romantic Age as William Wordsworth, at first enthusiastically supported the revolution and the democratic ideals on which it was based.

ENRICHMENT: Social Studies Connection

Exporting the French Revolution

Explain to students that the French Revolution quickly became an international force. In the 1789 Declaration of the Rights of Man, the French revolutionaries state their basic principles. All men had by nature a right to liberty, property, and security. All were declared equal before the law—the privileges of aristocrats were suspended. In 1793, the revolutionaries added a clause stating that liberty was a human cause, not just a French one, and that every king ruled by usurping the people's liberty—kings were criminals against all humanity.

As Napoleon's troops swept through Europe, he reformed the governments of the conquered countries, replacing the remains of feudal society with an order based on wealth, merit, and equality, creating modern-style administrative bureaucracies, and redefining national boundaries to resemble today's. Ask students to speculate what Europe might be like today if Napoleon had not been so successful at war. **Possible responses:** Kings might still rule: people might not have basic rights.

The Reign of Terror As royalists, moderates, and radicals jockeyed for power, the French Revolution became more and more chaotic. In 1792, France declared war against Austria and Prussia, touching off an invasion by troops from those countries. Fuming with patriotic indignation, a radical group called the Jacobins gained control of the French legislative assembly, abolished the monarchy, and declared the nation a republic. Mobs attacked and killed many prisoners—including former aristocrats and priests—in the bloody "September massacres."

Within weeks, the revolutionaries had tried and convicted Louis XVI on a charge of treason and sent him to the guillotine early in 1793. The Jacobins, under the leadership of Maximilien de Robespierre, then began what is called the Reign of Terror. Over the course of about a year, they sent some 17,000 royalists, moderates, and even radicals to the guillotine—including, finally, Robespierre himself.

At the same time, France's new "citizen army" was making war across Europe in the name of liberty. In 1793, France declared war on Britain. Thus began a series of wars that would drag on for twenty-two years.

British Reaction The September massacres and the Reign of Terror were so shocking that even those Britons who had sympathized with the French

Close-up on History

The Napoleonic Wars

Britain's battles with France took a new turn after 1799, when a military leader named Napoleon Bonaparte seized control of France. Napoleon had grandiose plans for French expansion, and he was a brilliant military leader. After a brief break in Franco-British hostilities from 1802 to 1803, war resumed in earnest.

Napoleon, who had declared himself emperor of France, planned an invasion of Britain, but he had to abandon the plan after a British fleet under Lord Nelson defeated the French and Spanish fleets at the Battle of Trafalgar, off Spain, in 1805. Napoleon's armies had fought well against Britain's European allies, however, and by 1807 they controlled almost all of Europe as far east as the borders of Russia.

In 1812, Napoleon finally overextended himself by invading Russia. There, his armies were defeated by a combination of factors: the hardships of the Russian winter, the vastness of the landscape, and the strategic retreats of the Russian army, which involved the destruction of goods and property that the French might use. At the same time, Napoleon was experiencing reverses in the west. His forces were defeated in the Peninsular War (1808–1814) in Portugal and Spain, and, in 1814, British and allied armies closed in on him and forced him to abandon his throne.

Napoleon was not finished, however. Exiled to the Mediterranean island of Elba, he plotted to return, and, in 1815, he escaped to France. Resuming his rule for a period known as the Hundred Days, he met final defeat on the battlefield at Waterloo, Belgium, in 1815. His victorious opponent was the Duke of Wellington, the British hero of the Peninsular War.

Background

Social Studies

Arthur Wellesley, Duke of Wellington and Horatio Nelson, Lord Nelson, were among the greatest heroes of their time. Nelson cut his teeth in naval service during the American Revolution. When he destroyed a French squadron at the mouth of the Nile in 1798, he became a celebrity. He was adored by the British people, but his love for Lady Hamilton soon plunged him into scandal. Nelson guaranteed his place in British history when, at the Battle of Trafalgar, he crippled the combined French and Spanish fleet, thereby averting an invasion of Britain. Wounded during that battle, he held onto life until he heard that fifteen enemy ships had been captured. His last words were, "Now I am satisfied. Thank God I have done my duty."

Wellington led a small force to victory in the Peninsular Wars. By 1814, he had pushed the French out of Portugal and Spain. When Napoleon was defeated once and for all at Waterloo, it was Wellington who led the British forces. Wellington's military prowess made him one of the most respected men in Europe.

CUSTOMIZE INSTRUCTION FOR UNIVERSAL ACCESS

For Less Proficient Readers	For English Learners	For Advanced Readers
Define the word *romantic* for the students. Encourage students to add to this definition based on personal experience. Explain that the period in this unit is "the Romantic Age." Have students work together while reading Rebels and Dreamers to uncover connections between their own definitions and the trends that defined the period.	Inform the students that this period is called "the Romantic Age." Have them define the word *romantic,* using the dictionary if necessary. Then, have them add to their definition by reading Rebels and Dreamers.	Using a definition of *romantic,* challenge students to predict the life of a rebel or a dreamer in the Romantic age. Have them compare and contrast their original perceptions with the knowledge they acquire reading Rebels and Dreamers.

Background
Science

The railroad, which had its beginnings in the early nineteenth century, was to change the face of the nation. Businesses could ship materials and products more quickly, more reliably, and in greater quantities than ever before. Better transportation encouraged industry to grow even faster. By the middle of the century, extensive, fast travel was available even to the poor—Parliament decreed that certain trains take passengers for only a penny per mile. Horse-drawn rail-cars were first used in coal mines. The first steam-powered locomotive, built in 1814, ran at five miles per hour. By the 1850s, trains would average speeds around 20 miles per hour—quadruple their original speed.

Ask students to speculate about how life might have changed for the average Briton when passenger service began on trains.
Possible response: Students may answer that families spread out more, or that it became easier to maintain relations over a distance.

Background
Music

Romanticism influenced music throughout Europe for several decades. As a child, German Romantic composer Felix Mendelssohn read Shakespeare's plays, and at age seventeen he composed an overture to *A Midsummer Night's Dream.* Seventeen years later, he wrote incidental music for the play. Romantic music was often meant to suggest a mood and setting. Play Mendelssohn's "Scherzo" on the **Listening to Literature Audiocassettes.** Ask students to describe the feelings and images the music evokes.

▶Critical Viewing

Answer: **(a)** The dress of the woman in the foreground suggests that concerns of safety and efficiency did not define life in the factory; her long skirts might become entangled in a machine or slow down her movements. The man's open collar suggests informality. **(b)** The man is performing some duty of oversight; the woman may be fixing the machine; others appear to be weaving.

Power Loom, Anonymous, 18th Century

▲ **Critical Viewing** Early cotton mills employed mostly women and children. (a) What does the clothing of the workers in this picture suggest about factory conditions of the time? (b) Describe the tasks that you see being performed. **[Draw Conclusions]**

Revolution now turned against it. Conservative Britons demanded a crackdown on reformers, whom they denounced as dangerous Jacobins. Adding to British alarm was the success of France's new "citizen army," which had expelled the Austrian and Russian invaders and then set out to "liberate" other European nations from despotic rule. British leaders did not want France or any other nation to win dominance on the European continent. The Tory government, led by William Pitt (the Younger), outlawed all talk of parliamentary reform outside the halls of Parliament, banned public meetings, and suspended certain basic rights. Liberal-minded Britons had no political outlet for their hopes and dreams. Many turned to literature and art instead.

Society's Problems Throughout the long wars with France, Britain's government ignored the problems caused by the Industrial Revolution—overcrowded factory towns, unpleasant and unsafe working conditions in the factories, and long working hours for low pay. The working class grew steadily larger and more restless. In the factory towns of northern England, workers protested in the violent Luddite Riots (1811–1813) the loss of jobs to new machinery. Some attempted to organize into unions.

Britain's government claimed to be following a hands-off policy, but in fact it sided openly with factory owners against workers, even helping to crush the workers' attempts to form unions. In Manchester, mounted soldiers charged a peaceful mass meeting of cotton workers and killed several of them in what came to be known as the Peterloo Massacre (1819). To many, it seemed that British society was splitting into two angry camps—the working classes, who demanded reform, and the ruling classes, who fiercely resisted reform.

A new generation of Tories emerged in the 1820s, and a trickle of reforms began. A law was passed in 1824 permitting Britain's first labor unions to organize, and in 1829 the Catholic Emancipation Act restored economic and religious freedoms to Roman Catholics.

The trickle grew into a stream following a Whig victory in the election of 1830. The Reform Bill of 1832 brought sweeping changes to British political life. By extending voting rights to the small but important middle class (males only), this law threatened the traditional dominance of landowning aristocrats in Parliament. Moreover, in 1833 Parliament passed the first law governing factory safety. In that same year, it also abolished slavery.

ENRICHMENT: Social Studies Connection
Political Thought: Burke and Bentham

Explain to students that Edmund Burke's *Reflections on the French Revolution* (1790) is an important statement of conservative ideas. Burke (1729–1797) opposed the revolutionaries' assumption that society could be judged by abstract principles such as "reason" and "liberty." Governments, Burke thought, are not created but grow, and so they evolve ways to meet people's needs. A nation's traditions, however "irrational," represent a kind of inherited wisdom.

In strong contrast to Burke, Jeremy Bentham (1748–1832) argued that actions, including the laws passed by government, should be judged by the standard of "utility" alone—that is, by their usefulness in satisfying people's interests. A rational government was one which created the greatest pleasure for the greatest number. Bentham's principles, known as Utilitarianism, influenced numerous reformist politicians.

Ask students whether Burke's or Bentham's ideas apply better to today's society. Invite advanced students to find out more about these ideas.

Literature of the Period

The Beginnings of Romanticism British Romantic writers responded to the climate of their times. Their new interest in the trials and dreams of the common people and their desire for radical change developed out of the democratic idealism that characterized the early part of the French Revolution. Their deep attachment to nature and to a pure, simple past was a response to the misery and ugliness born of industrialization. For the Romantics, the faith in science and reason, so characteristic of eighteenth-century thought and literature, no longer applied in a world of tyranny and factories.

Rousseau and Goethe Many of the ideas that influenced the British Romantics, though, first arose on continental Europe well before the turn of the century. Swiss-born writer Jean-Jacques Rousseau (1712–1778), a leading philosopher of eighteenth-century France, saw society as a force that, throughout history, deformed and imprisoned an originally free human nature. "Man is born free," he wrote, "and everywhere he is in chains." His ideas influenced both American and French revolutionaries.

A group of later eighteenth-century writers and artists living in German-speaking Europe began incorporating Rousseau's ideas into poetry, fiction, and drama. The most famous of this group, Johann Wolfgang von Goethe (1749–1832), found in the German literature of the Middle Ages a primitive simplicity much in keeping with Rousseau's ideas and values. These works, not unlike the Anglo-Saxon *Beowulf,* were filled with myth, adventure, and passion. The Romantic Movement takes its name from this interest in medieval romances. Goethe's own works show a new attention to feelings and express an ideal of self-fulfillment and growth through experience.

Tea Time, David Emil

▲ **Critical Viewing** By the early 1800s, tea was truly a national drink, popular with all classes. Which details illustrate how relaxing the custom of drinking tea can be? **[Interpret]**

The Romantic Age in British Poetry Romanticism was a movement that affected not only literature but also all the other arts. In music, it produced such brilliant European composers as Germany's Ludwig van Beethoven (1770–1827) and Austria's Franz Schubert (1797–1828), but there was no one of comparable stature in Britain. In painting, Romanticism influenced the intensely personal and warmly spontaneous rural landscapes of Britain's John Constable (1776–1837) and the dramatic seascapes of J.M.W. Turner (1775–1851). However, it is for literature, especially poetry, that Britain's Romantic Age is most famous.

Wordsworth and Coleridge William Wordsworth (1770–1850) provided an early statement of the goals of Romantic poetry in the preface to *Lyrical Ballads* (1798), a collaboration with his friend Samuel Taylor Coleridge

▶Critical Viewing

Answer: The chaos in the foreground of the painting contrasts strongly with the relaxed face of the tea-drinker and the clean white tablecloth next to her.

Historical Background

Comprehension Check

1. Name two developments in France affecting Britain during the period.
   Answer: The French Revolution led to fear in Britain of social unrest; France declared war on Britain in 1793.
2. How did British intellectuals respond to the first stages of the French Revolution?
   Answer: Many supported the Revolution's democratic ideals.
3. **(a)** What direction did the French Revolution take after its first stages? **(b)** How did the British respond to this new development?
   Answer: **(a)** A radical group called the Jacobins began a Reign of Terror in which they guillotined their opponents. **(b)** British conservatives used the Terror to justify suppressing dissent; even former sympathizers turned against the French.
4. **(a)** What new troubles came to Britain as a result of the Industrial Revolution? **(b)** What was the government's initial response?
   Answer: **(a)** Workers agitated for better working conditions, higher pay, and shorter hours. **(b)** The government helped suppress the worker's movement.
5. What reforms did Parliament eventually bring about?
   Answer: Parliament legalized labor unions, restored the rights of Catholics, and extended the vote to middle-class males.

continued

continued from right column

Critical Thinking

1. For those who thought society had corrupted natural human goodness, the French Revolution was compelling. Explain. **[Connect]**
   Answer: The Revolution looked like an attempt to remake society "from the ground up, " returning to fundamental values.
2. **(a)** How did the French Revolution affect the British movement for reform? **[Interpret]** **(b)** Explain how this result might have led to a new passion in the arts. **[Speculate]**
   Answer: **(a)** Conservatives used the French Terror to justify suppressing reformers. **(b)** People may have turned to art as an outlet for the idealism thwarted in politics.
3. Middle-class reformers often allied themselves with working class radicals. Explain how such alliances led the government to give the middle class the vote. **[Speculate]**
   Answer: The government hoped to end its support of more radical reforms.

▶Critical Viewing

Possible response: Students may say that the stark image of decay—the consequence of time's passing or human folly—would inspire Romantic writers with thoughts of nature's power over human works.

➔⬅ POINT/COUNTERPOINT

Remind students that Wordsworth has become Britain's most famous Romantic poet by capturing nature's beauty and transposing it to the written word. Then, ask the following questions.

1. How could such a famous poet be considered a visionary by one observer, a country gentleman by the next?
   Answer: One critic shares Wordsworth's vision of nature and man unified; the other examines the historical conditions under which one might arrive at such a vision.
2. Is it possible that Wordsworth is both a country gentleman and a visionary poet?
   Possible response: The fact that nature had to be tamed before a Wordsworth could arise does not mean his vision is not compelling.
3. What would each critic say about Wordsworth's abilities if he were born in this era?
   Possible response: One might say his vision is even more neccessary today, when unity with nature is even further off. The other might say that his "vision" was an attempt to flee contemporary social reality, in which "nature" is likely to be encountered through a television screen.

(1772–1834). The preface defined poetry as "the spontaneous overflow of powerful feelings" and explained that poetry "takes its origin from emotion recollected in tranquility." An emphasis on the emotions, then, was central to the new Romantic poetry.

Equally important was subject matter. The new poetry, said Wordsworth, dealt with "incidents and situations from common life" over which the poet throws "a certain coloring of imagination, whereby ordinary things should be presented . . . in an unusual way."

Finally, Wordsworth's preface spoke about incorporating human passions with "the beautiful and permanent forms of nature." An emphasis on nature would become another important characteristic of British Romantic verse.

The Romantic view of nature was quite different from that of most eighteenth-century literature. Nature was not a force to be tamed and analyzed scientifically; rather, it was a wild, free force that could inspire poets to instinctive spiritual understanding.

Lyrical Ballads was cooly received at first, but with time, it came to be regarded as the cornerstone of Britain's Romantic Age. Also with time, Wordsworth and Coleridge became respected members of Britain's literary establishment. Their political thinking, deeply marked by events in France, grew more conservative, and their literary ideas began to seem less radical than they once had.

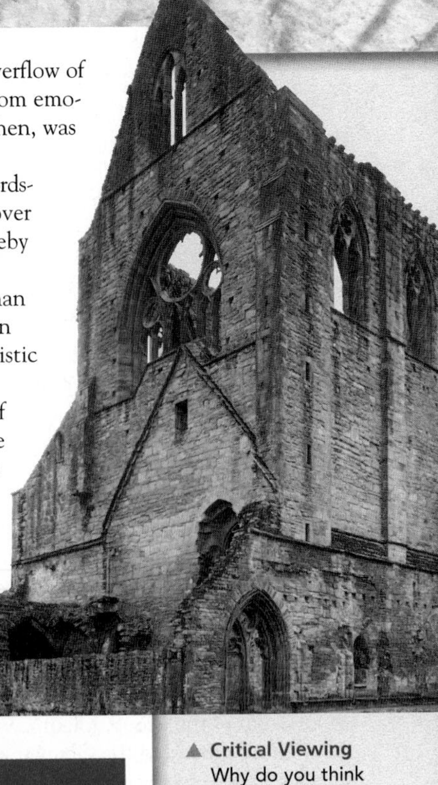

▲ **Critical Viewing** Why do you think that ruins like these appealed to Romantic writers? **[Speculate]**

Point /Counterpoint

Wordsworth, Visionary Poet or Comfortable Country Gentleman?

Was Wordsworth a poet with a revolutionary new vision of the natural world or a country gentleman who merely appreciated a tamed landscape? Two critics express these opposite perspectives on Britain's most famous Romantic poet.

Visionary Poet

"Wordsworth's 'philosophic' . . . poems . . . give us a clear and comprehensive expression of what we today so strikingly lack—an organic, unitary vision of man and nature, of the human mind, the earth, and the heavens, all activated by one spirit, all in harmonious relationship. . . ."

—George W. Meyer, *Major British Writers*

Country Gentleman

"Wordsworth's 'Nature' is of course a Nature freed of wild beasts and danger by eons of human work, a Nature in which the poet, enjoying a comfortable income, lives on the products of industrialism even while he enjoys the natural scene 'unspoilt' by industrialism."

—Christopher Caudwell, *Illusion and Reality*

ENRICHMENT: Social Studies Connection

J. M. W. Turner's *Frosty Morning*

The Romantic movement in literature found echoes in the other arts. The painter J. M. W. Turner (1775–1851) was noted for his depictions of scenes at sea as well as landscapes. His emphasis on the effects of light at the expense of objects suggest, perhaps, a perception of the spirit in nature comparable to Wordsworth's—"A presence that disturbs me with the joy / Of elevated thoughts . . . / Whose dwelling is the light of setting suns . . ."

Show students Turner's *Frosty Morning,* on p. 59 of the **Fine Art Transparencies, Vol. 1.** Ask the following questions:

1. How does the composition isolate the sky?
   Answer: The people are screened off from the sky.
2. Describe the trees' role in the composition.
   Answer: The trees join sky and earth, but also emphasize the emptiness of the sky.

The Second Generation of Romantic Poets Wordsworth and Coleridge blazed the way for a new generation of British Romantic poets—the so-called "second generation" of poets, which included George Gordon, Lord Byron; Percy Bysshe Shelley; and John Keats. Coming of age during the Napoleonic Era, these younger poets rebelled even more strongly than did Wordsworth and Coleridge against the British conservatism of the time. All three died abroad after tragically short lives, and their viewpoints were those of disillusioned outsiders.

George Gordon, Lord Byron Byron (1788–1824) was a member of the House of Lords. Although critics responded unfavorably to his early poetry, Byron persisted and finally achieved success when he published the first two cantos of *Childe Harold's Pilgrimage* (1812). Handsome, egotistical, and aloof, Byron became the darling of elegant society, but not for long. Shocked by his radical politics and scandalous love affairs, London hostesses began to shun him, and Byron left Britain in 1816, never to return.

A Writer's Voice

George Gordon, Lord Byron, and the Byronic Hero

The critic Northrop Frye declared that Byron "probably had more influence outside England than any other English poet except Shakespeare." One source of this influence was the mysterious "Byronic hero," a role model for young readers and an influence on novelists like Balzac.

In this description of the Byronic hero by Frye, you may recognize features that still characterize today's heroes of literature and film: "an inscrutable figure with hollow cheeks and blazing eyes, wrapped in a cloud of gloom, full of mysterious and undefined remorse, an outcast from society . . . he will not brook questioning, though he himself questions all established social standards, . . ."

This hero appears in various forms throughout Byron's tales in verse and his verse dramas. At the beginning of *A Dramatic Poem, Manfred*, for example, the protagonist, despite his accomplishments, feels no satisfaction and does not love anyone or anything.

Philosophy and science, and the springs
Of wonder, and the wisdom of the world,
I have essay'd,° and in my mind there is — °Tried
A power to make these subject to itself—
But they avail° not: I have done men good — °Help
And I have met with good even among men—
But this avail'd not: I have had my foes,
And none have baffled°, many fallen before me— — °Hindered
But this avail'd not:—Good, or evil, life,
Powers, passions, all I see in other beings,
Have been to me as rain unto the sands,
Since that all-nameless hour. I have no dread,
And feel the curse to have no natural fear,
Nor fluttering throb, that beats with hopes or wishes,
Or lurking love of something on the earth. . . .

Literature of the Period

Challenge students to find a passage in a selection that reflects an insight, description, or idea from Rebels and Dreamers. Have them read the passage aloud to the class and explain how it relates to Rebels and Dreamers. Students giving the presentation should then be prepared to answer questions about the passage.

Literature of the Period

1. What views about nature and science did the Romantics reject?
 Answer: The Romantics rejected the eighteenth-century view that nature was to be understood and mastered; they had lost faith in science's power to improve life.
2. Name two figures that influenced British Romantics, and their nationalities.
 Answer: Rousseau, a Swiss-born Frenchman, and Goethe, a German, influenced the British Romantics.
3. **(a)** Name two poets prominent in the early Romantic movement in England. **(b)** What role did they think feeling had in poetry?
 Answer: **(a)** William Wordsworth and Samuel Taylor Coleridge were two prominent early Romantics. **(b)** According to Wordsworth, poetry was the result of feeling—its "spontaneous overflow" recollected "in tranquility."
4. **(a)** What form of prose flourished and was transformed during the period? **(b)** Where did readers encounter works in this form?
 Answer: **(a)** The essay flourished and was transformed. **(b)** Readers encountered essays in periodicals.
5. Name two important genres of novels from the period.
 Possible responses: Gothic novels, novels of manners, and historical romances were all important forms of the period.

▶Critical Viewing

Answers:

1. **(a)** About 10 years passed between Byron's Grand Tour and his meeting with the Shelleys in Pisa (1810; 1820). **(b)** Shelley died in the Gulf of Spieza, off Italy, in 1822; Byron died in Missolonghi, in Greece, in 1824.

Percy Bysshe Shelley Byron's friend Shelley (1792–1822) was also an aristocrat and political radical, more consistently radical, in fact, than Byron. In poems such as "Song to the Men of England" (1819), Shelley urged England's lower classes to rebel. Like Byron, Shelley was shunned for his radical ideas; he left Britain for good in 1818. In his lifetime, he did not attain the fame that Byron did. Yet, he is now remembered for the fervor he brought to lyric poetry in such intensely personal and emotional verses as "To a Skylark" (1820).

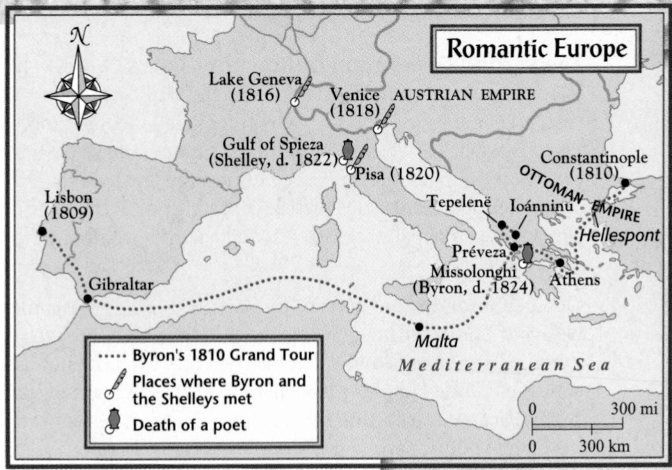

Romantic Europe

N
Lake Geneva (1816)
Venice (1818)
AUSTRIAN EMPIRE
Gulf of Spieza (Shelley, d. 1822)
Pisa (1820)
Constantinople (1810)
OTTOMAN EMPIRE
Lisbon (1809)
Tepelenë
Ioánninu
Hellespont
Préveza
Missolonghi (Byron, d. 1824)
Athens
Gibraltar
Malta
Mediterranean Sea
Byron's 1810 Grand Tour
Places where Byron and the Shelleys met
Death of a poet
0 300 mi
0 300 km

▲ **Critical Viewing** The second generation of Romantics traveled and lived in Europe. (a) How many years passed between Byron's Grand Tour of Europe and his move to Pisa? (b) When and where in Europe did Shelley and Byron die? **[Read a Map]**

John Keats Keats (1795–1821), the third great figure in the second generation of Romantic poets, was also a master of lyrical poetry. Unlike Byron and Shelley, Keats was born outside upper-class society, the son of a London stable keeper. Keats trained to be a doctor but abandoned his medical career to pursue his passion for poetry.

He produced many of his greatest poems in a burst of creativity during the first nine months of 1819—works like *The Fall of Hyperion* and "Ode on a Grecian Urn." In many of these poems, Keats tried to reconcile the eternal, and therefore almost inhuman, beauty of art with the realities of human suffering. The famous line at the end of "Ode on a Grecian Urn"—"Beauty is truth, truth beauty"—represents one response to this dilemma, but it is not a final answer for Keats. Unfortunately, Keats contracted tuberculosis. Hoping to recuperate in a warmer climate, he traveled to Italy, where he died at the age of twenty-five.

The Romantic Age in British Prose Poetry was the dominant literary form during the Romantic Age, but many significant prose works also appeared, mainly in the form of essays and novels. This was a dry period for drama—only two theaters were licensed to produce plays, and they tended to feature popular spectacles rather than serious plays. However, Byron and Shelley did write closet dramas, or verse works intended to be read rather than produced on stage.

Lamb, Hazlitt, and De Quincey British readers of the Romantic Age could find brilliant literary criticism and topical essays in a variety of new periodicals. *The London Magazine,* although it appeared from only 1820 to 1829, attracted major contributions from the three greatest essayists of the era: Charles Lamb (1775–1834), William Hazlitt (1778–1830), and Thomas De Quincey (1785–1859). Lamb, in particular, transformed the informal essay of the eighteenth century into a more personal, more introspective Romantic composition.

ENRICHMENT: Literature Connection

Romantic Essayists

Both Thomas de Quincey and William Hazlitt were early admirers of Wordsworth and Coleridge. The young De Quincey was so impressed by the *Lyrical Ballads* that he moved to the Lake District to be near Wordsworth. *Recollections of the Lake Poets* records his friendship and eventual estrangement from Wordsworth and Coleridge. Hazlitt also wrote a memoir of the early Romantics entitled *My First Acquaintance with the Poets.*

Mary Shelley Unlike the Romantic poets, the novelists of the Romantic Age did not make a sharp break with the past. The Gothic novel first appeared in the middle of the eighteenth century. It featured a number of standard ingredients, including brave heroes and heroines, threatening scoundrels, vast eerie castles, and ghosts. The fascination of the Romantics with mystery and the supernatural made such novels quite popular during the Romantic Age. One of the most successful was *Frankenstein, or the Modern Prometheus* (1818), written by Shelley's wife Mary Wollstonecraft Shelley (1797–1851).

Jane Austen The Romantic novel of manners continued in the tradition of earlier writers by turning a satirical eye on British customs. The most highly regarded writer of novels of manners was Jane Austen (1775–1817), whose works include *Sense and Sensibility* (1811) and *Pride and Prejudice* (1813). Her incisive portrayals of character and her social satire are more reflective of the classical sensibility of the eighteenth century than of the notions of the new Romantic age.

Sketch for Hadleigh Castle, John Constable

▲ **Critical Viewing** John Constable (1776–1837) is a painter linked with the Romantics. What mood does Constable create with the clouds in this scene? Why? (b) How is this mood related to the beliefs of Romanticism? Explain. **[Interpret]**

Sir Walter Scott Passionately devoted to his native Scotland, Sir Walter Scott (1771–1832) used his knowledge of Scottish history to create what amounted to a new literary form, the historical novel. It was characterized by a focus on historical events and settings, with attention to local flavor and regional speech. It also featured a Romantic treatment of realistic themes.

The close of Britain's Romantic Age is usually considered to be the year 1832, the year that the First Reform Bill was passed. However, the ideas of Romanticism remained a strong influence on following generations of writers. In fact, even today we can detect elements of Romanticism in many major works of contemporary fiction and poetry, as well as in television dramas, movies, and popular songs.

Critical Thinking

1. Wordsworth notes that poetry is created through the recollection of emotion "in tranquility." How does this idea qualify his definition of poetry as a "spontaneous overflow of powerful feelings"? **[Analyze]**
   Answer: Poetry for Wordsworth is not an immediate expression of feeling like a yell; the feelings in poetry are filtered through the poet's recollection on them.
2. Some Romantic poets rejected traditional "poetical" language, turning instead to common speech. Speculate about the reason for this choice. **[Speculate]**
   Possible response: The Romantics chose a common style to communicate their feelings clearly.
3. Describe a contemporary trend that hearkens back to Romantic ideas. Explain the connection.
   Answers: The environmental movement (for its valuing of "innocent" nature) and the "me generation" (for its emphasis on expressing feelings) hearken back to Romantiscm.

▶Critical Viewing

(a) Possible response: Constable may have wanted to create a mood of grandeur and tumult, suggesting freedom. The clouds have a restless, shapeless look, as if they might have been blown up by the storm. **(b)** The beliefs of Romanticism in the power of feeling and nature are reflected in the wild, dynamic look of nature and erasure of human presense (the ruins) in the painting.

Critical Thinking

1. **(a)** Give an example of an English word that you have heard that "sounds" foreign. **(b)** At what point in its history does a borrowed word stop sounding foreign? **(c)** What significance can "foreign-sounding" words have that familiar words do not? **[Speculate]**
   Answer: **(a)** Students may name foreign phrases that have been adopted into English, such as *déjà vu*. They may also name new slang words. **(b)** When people use the word frequently enough, it stops sounding foreign.
   (c) "Foreign-sounding" words can signify class, or pretension to it; they can suggest mystery.
2. Name another way in which languages adjust to new ideas and things. **[Analyze]**
   Answer: New words are formed by combining two or more old words; adjectives and nouns are formed from the name of the person associated with an idea or invention.

▶Critical Viewing

1. **(a)** Name two kinds of things that predominate among the things named in the chart.
   (b) Explain why nouns naming such things are common among the words English borrows from other languages. **[Hypothesize]**
   Answers: **(a)** Food and animals predominate. **(b)** English speakers adopted the local names of animals and foods not also native to England.
2. **(a)** What populated continents do not appear in the chart?
   (b) What does this absence indicate about England's relations with those continents at this time? **[Infer]**
   Answers: **(a)** Europe and North and South America do not appear. **(b)** England was not then colonizing them.

Answers

Activities

1. Students' searches may turn up more borrowed than native words. Many of these words will have Latin origins.
2. Students may find that there is a greater preponderance of native English words in the passage they analyze.

THE CHANGING ENGLISH LANGUAGE

The Romantic Age

BY RICHARD LEDERER

THE SUN NEVER SET ON THE BRITISH EMPIRE

During the Romantic Age, Britannia ruled the waves and English ruled much of the land. Great Britain's smashing conquests in the Napoleonic Wars at the beginning of the nineteenth century—culminating in Nelson's famous victory at Trafalgar in 1805—established an undisputed naval supremacy. This, in turn, gave Great Britain control over most of the world's commerce. As British ships traveled throughout the world, they left the language of the mother country in their wake but also came home from foreign ports laden with cargoes of words from other languages freighted with new meanings for English speakers.

The following are words that became part of the English language as a result of England's great economic expansion.

Country	Borrowed Words
India	*bandanna, bungalow, calico, cashmere, china, cot, curry, juggernaut, jungle, loot, nirvana, polo, punch* (beverage), *thug,* and *verandah*
Asia	*gingham, indigo, mango,* and *typhoon*
New Zealand	*kiwi*
Australia	*boomerang* and *kangaroo*
Africa	*banana, boorish, chimpanzee, gorilla, gumbo,* and *zebra*

WORDS, WORDS, WORDS

The biggest and fattest unabridged English dictionaries hold more than 600,000 words, compared to German in second place with 185,000 words, and then Russian and French at 130,000 and 100,000. One reason we have accumulated the world's largest and most varied vocabulary is that English continues to be the most hospitable and democratic language that has ever existed, unique in the number and variety of its borrowed words. Although Anglo-Saxon is the foundation of the English language, more than seventy percent of our words have been imported from other lands, ancient and modern, far and near. No wonder Ralph Waldo Emerson waxed ecstatic about "English speech, the sea which receives tributaries from every region under heaven" and Dorothy Thompson, employing a more prosaic metaphor, referred to "that glorious and imperial mongrel, the English language."

ACTIVITIES

1. Open your dictionary at random and examine the etymology of the words listed at the top of fifteen pages. Record the earliest source for each word. Words noted as *AS* or *OE* are native; the rest are borrowed. What is the ratio of native versus borrowed words? Among the borrowed words, what percentage are derived from Latin? from Greek? from French? from other languages? Compare your results with those of your classmates and discuss the implications.
2. Now choose a passage from a newspaper or magazine. Analyze the first thirty words of that passage in the manner described above. Do you notice a different ratio of native to borrowed words? Discuss your conclusions regarding random dictionary entries versus the words in actual sentences.

ENRICHMENT: Social Studies Connection

The American Influence

Explain to students that English also picked up a good number of words through the earlier British colonial experience in North America. Pilgrims and other early settlers picked up words such as *squash, moose,* and *raccoon* from the Native Americans they met. Sometimes, they named the new plants and animals they saw by combining old words in a descriptive fashion: *eggplant* and *bullfrog* are two such results. As time went on, isolation from England ensured that Americans would speak in a language of their own.

Ask students to reconstruct how new words enter their own vocabulary.
Possible responses: Students may respond that they pick up words that their friends use.

Fantasy and Reality

Hummingbird Hunters, 1884, James Farrington Gookins, Shelden Swope Art Museum, Terre Haute, Indiana

E INSTRUCTION FOR UNIVERSAL ACCESS

the selections in this part, keep in mind these factors:

rt Burns and Joanna Baillie

nay prove difficult to read and

find subject matter amusing

am Blake

-read poems

ı Christianity important in understand-

Introduction to *Frankenstein*

- Short, real-life account
- High-interest story of how *Frankenstein* came to be written

"The Oval Portrait"

- Short, gripping narrative
- Upper-level vocabulary

Selection Planning Guide

The selections that follow may be described as wild imaginings or as glimpses of real life. Each straddles the line between fantasy and reality.

The poems of Robert Burns take a down-to-earth view of life, presented through fanciful addresses to two animals he encounters. William Blake's poems, as well as his personal beliefs and philosophies, are strange but compelling combinations of reality and fancy.

Mary Shelley's Introduction to *Frankenstein,* for example is the author's true account of how she came to write the popular novel. Imbedded in the account, however, are the author's remembrances of her fantastic dreams and visions that she claims inspired the tale of horror.

Finally, Edgar Allan Poe's "The Oval Portrait" explores the fragile, sometimes indistinguishable line between reality and fantasy.

Background

Art

Hummingbird Hunters, James Farrington Gookins

In this richly colored and intricately detailed painting, tiny people hunt for hummingbirds among flower buds in a lavish garden setting. Apart from their miniature size, the artist portrays the people in realistic fashion, with true-to-life features and gestures. The flowers, too, contain exquisite, realistic detail. The painting presents an interesting and unusual blend of realistic and fantastic elements.

Use these questions for discussion:

1. If you could choose one word to describe this painting, what word would you choose?
   Possible responses: Words might include *lush, flowery, pixie-like,* and *vibrant.*
2. Is this painting more realistic or more fantastic? Explain.
   Possible responses: The painting depicts a fantasy setting. The manner in which the setting and characters are painted is realistic.

To a Mouse ✦ To a Louse ✦ Woo'd and Married and A'

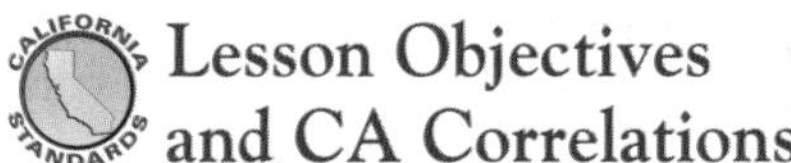

Lesson Objectives and CA Correlations

1. **To analyze and respond to literary elements**
   - Literary Analysis: Dialect **R 3.3**
   - Comparing Literary Works **R 3.2**
2. **To read, comprehend, analyze, and critique a poem**
   - Reading Strategy: Translating Dialect
   - Reading Check Questions
   - Review and Assess Questions
   - Assessment Practice (ATE)
3. **To develop word analysis skills, fluency, and systematic vocabulary**
   - Vocabulary Development Lesson: Anglo-Saxon Suffix *-some* **R 1.2**
4. **To understand and apply written and oral language conventions**
   - Spelling Strategy **LC 1.2**
   - Grammar and Style Lesson: Interjections **LC 1.1**
5. **To understand and apply appropriate writing and research strategies**
   - Writing Lesson: Comparison of Characters **W 1.9**
   - Extension Activity: Multimedia Presentation **W 1.7**
6. **To understand and apply listening and speaking strategies**
   - Extension Activity: Dialect Reading **LS 1.9**

STEP-BY-STEP TEACHING GUIDE	PACING GUIDE
PRETEACH	
Motivate Students and Provide Background	
Use the Motivation activity (ATE p. 624)	5 min.
Read and discuss author and background features (SE/ATE pp. 624, 630) [A]	5 min.
Introduce the Concepts	
Introduce the Literary Analysis and Reading Strategy (SE/ATE p. 625) [A]	15 min.
Pronounce the vocabulary words and read their definitions (SE p. 625)	5 min.
TEACH	
Monitor Comprehension	
Informally monitor comprehension by circulating while students read independently or in groups [A]	15 min.
Monitor students' comprehension with the Reading Check notes (SE/ATE pp. 627, 629, 633)	as students read
Develop vocabulary with Vocabulary notes (SE pp. 627, 629, 632, 633; ATE p. 632)	as students read
Develop Understanding	
Develop students' understanding of dialect with the Literary Analysis annotations (SE p. 632; ATE pp. 631, 632) [A]	5 min.
Develop students' ability to translate dialect with the Reading Strategy annotations (SE/ATE p. 627)	5 min.
ASSESS	
Assess Mastery	
Assess students' mastery of the Reading Strategy and Literary Analysis by having them answer the Review and Assess questions (SE/ATE p. 635)	15 min.
Use one or more of the print and media Assessment Resources (ATE p. 637) [A]	up to 45 min.
EXTEND	
Apply Understanding	
Have students complete the Vocabulary Development Lesson and the Grammar and Style Lesson (SE p. 636) [A]	20 min.
Apply students' understanding of the characters in the poems using the Writing Lesson (SE/ATE p. 637) [A]	45 min.
Apply students' understanding using one or more of the Extension Activities (SE p. 637)	20–90 min.

ACCELERATED INSTRUCTION:
Use the strategies and activities identified with an [A].

UNIVERSAL ACCESS
● = Below-Level Students
▲ = On-Level Students
■ = Above-Level Students

Time and Resource Manager

Reading Level: Challenging, Challenging, Average
Average Number of Instructional Days: 4

RESOURCES		
PRINT	**TRANSPARENCIES**	**TECHNOLOGY**
• **Beyond Literature,** Cross-Curricular Connection: Social Studies, p. 28 ▲ ■		• **Interest Grabber Video,** Tape 4 ● ▲ ■
• **Selection Support Workbook:** ● ▲ ■ Literary Analysis, p. 132 Reading Strategy, p. 131 Build Vocabulary, p. 129	• **Literary Analysis and Reading Transparencies,** pp. 55 and 56 ● ▲ ■	
		• **Listening to Literature** ● ▲ ■ Audiocassettes, Side 15 Audio CDs, CD 9
• **Literary Analysis for Enrichment** ■		
• **Formal Assessment:** Selection Test, pp. 138–140 ● ▲ ■ • **Open Book Test,** pp. 82–84 ● ▲ ■ • **Performance Assessment and Portfolio Management,** p. 20 ● ▲ ■ • PRENTICE HALL ASSESSMENT SYSTEM ● ▲ ■	• PRENTICE HALL ASSESSMENT SYSTEM ● ▲ ■ Skills Practice Answers and Explanations on Transparencies	• **Test Bank Software** ● ▲ ■ • **Got It! Assessment Videotapes,** Tape 3 ● ▲
• **Selection Support Workbook:** ● ▲ ■ Grammar and Style, p. 130 • **Writing and Grammar,** Diamond Level ● ▲ ■ • **Extension Activities,** p. 28 ● ▲ ■	• **Daily Language Practice Transparencies** ● ▲ • **Writing Models and Graphic Organizers on Transparencies,** p. 85 ● ▲ ■	• **Writing and Grammar iText CD-ROM** ● ▲ ■ ***Take It to the Net*** www.phschool.com

BLOCK SCHEDULING: Use one 90-minute class period to preteach the selections and have students read them. Use a second 90-minute class period to assess students' mastery of skills and have them complete one of the Extension Activities.

PRETEACH

Step-by-Step Teaching Guide for pp. 624–625

Motivation

Inform students that before Robert Burns and Joanna Baillie, only complex, classic language was considered to be appropriate for poetry. Burns and Baillie broke with tradition, writing their poetry in the Scottish dialect—in the language of the people. Much like rap stars of today, who write their songs in the vernacular of urban youth, Burns and Baillie used the vernacular of the Scottish people in their poetry.

Interest Grabber Video

As an alternative, play "'To a Mouse': Robert Burns" on Tape 4 to engage student interest.

❶ Background

More About the Authors

Robert Burns was one of seven children born to a farmer and his wife near Alloway in Ayrshire. He was a voracious reader, who read as much literature—particularly Shakespeare—as he could. Burns's spare time in his childhood was devoted to helping his family as a ploughman on their farm. In 1785, Burns's financial and domestic problems became so acute that he considered emigrating to Jamaica, but instead he continued to write prolifically, sent his poems to a publisher, and met immediate success upon their publication in 1786.

Scottish playwright and poet Joanna Baillie is best known for her *Plays on the Passions,* in which each drama shows the effects of one particular passion. *Basil,* on the subject of love, and *De Montfort,* on the subject of hatred, were the most successful. The dramas garnered Baillie a great deal of attention, most notably in a friendship with Sir Walter Scott, but they also were heavily criticized. Baillie's most revered drama, *The Family Legend,* based on a Scottish feud, established her as a literary success and was produced in 1810.

Prepare to Read

❶ To a Mouse ◆ To a Louse ◆ Woo'd and Married and A'

Robert Burns (1759–1796)

Known as "The Voice of Scotland," Robert Burns wrote his first verse when he was fifteen. It was a love poem to a girl named Nellie, who was helping the Burns family with the harvest on their farm in Scotland. "Thus with me," Burns later wrote, "began Love and Poesy."

Poor But Learned Beginnings Burns was born at Alloway, in Ayrshire. Although poverty kept him from a full formal education, with his father's encouragement he read widely, studying the Bible, Shakespeare, and Alexander Pope. His mother, though herself illiterate, instilled in him a love of Scottish folk songs, legends, and proverbs.

Literary Triumph In 1786, Burns published his first collection of poems, *Poems, Chiefly in the Scottish Dialect,* through a small local press. The collection, which included "To a Mouse," was a huge success, applauded by critics and country folk alike. The new literary hero was invited to the Scottish capital, where he was swept into the social scene and hailed as the "heaven-taught plowman." When he died, thousands of people from all social levels followed his coffin to the grave.

A Lasting Contribution Although Burns died while just in his thirties, having suffered for years from a weak heart, his brief career resulted in a lasting contribution to literature. Burns's poems, written for the most part in dialect, are marked by their natural, direct, and spontaneous quality. Burns certainly drew on the ballad tradition of Scotland, but while some of the poet's work had its origins in folk tunes, "it is not," as critic James Douglas writes, "easy to tell where the vernacular ends and the personal magic begins."

Joanna Baillie (1762–1851)

When Joanna Baillie's (bā´ lēz) *Plays on the Passions* was published anonymously in 1798, it created a great literary sensation in London. Debates raged over which famous man of letters had written the plays. It was not until 1800 that the true author was revealed—an unassuming thirty-eight-year-old Scottish woman named Joanna Baillie. Even her literary friends were astounded, and she became an instant celebrity.

A Gregarious Tomboy Born in Lanarkshire, Scotland, the daughter of a minister, young Joanna Baillie was a tomboy who loved horseback riding and who resisted the stern moral education given by her father. She blossomed when she and her sister, Agnes, were sent away to boarding school in 1772. Joanna Baillie became an outgoing leader who led the other girls on boisterous outdoor adventures and staged plays that she herself wrote.

A Spinster's Life in London When Baillie's father died in 1778, the family depended on the kindness of a wealthy uncle for support. He provided the two sisters with a lifetime income. When their brother married in 1791, the sisters and their mother started a household of their own. They began a busy social life amid London's bustling literary scene, welcoming many important writers of the day into their home.

Success and Critical Acclaim With Baillie's literary success, the two sisters were able to travel, and they often returned to Scotland to visit Sir Walter Scott, who helped in the production of Baillie's plays. Best known in her day for her dramatic works, Baillie also wrote poetry. Like her fellow Scot Robert Burns, she wrote poems in the dialect of her homeland, many of them on nature and rustic manners.

TEACHING RESOURCES

The following resources can be used to enrich or extend the instruction for pp. 624–625.

Motivation

Interest Grabber Video, Tape 4

Background

Beyond Literature, p. 28

Take It to the Net

Visit www.phschool.com for background and hotlinks for the selections.

Literary Analysis

Literary Analysis and Reading Transparencies, Dialect, p. 56

Reading

Literary Analysis and Reading Transparencies, Translating Dialect, p. 55

Selection Support: Reading Strategy, p. 131; Build Vocabulary, p. 129

BLOCK SCHEDULING: Resources marked with this symbol provide varied instruction during 90-minute blocks.

Preview

Connecting to the Literature

If a poem is written in your language, then, in a sense, it belongs to you. These poets write in Scottish dialect to give poetry back to Scotland.

❷ Literary Analysis

Dialect

Dialect is the language, and particularly the speech habits, of a specific social class, region, or group. A dialect may vary from the standard form of a language in grammar, in pronunciation, and in the use of certain expressions. In literature, dialect helps achieve these goals:

- Establishing character, mood, and setting
- Adding "texture" or charm for readers who do not speak the dialect

By writing in dialect, Burns and Baillie broke with tradition and gave their poetry to the common folk who spoke that dialect. Note, however, the poetic effect of the dialect even for those who do not speak it.

Comparing Literary Works

Using dialect was just one way in which late-eighteenth-century poets returned poetry to the common people. Poets like Burns and Baillie also introduced subjects drawn from everyday life, such as the mouse in Burns's "To a Mouse." This shift was part of the artistic rebellion known as Romanticism.

Before Romanticism, poets devoted their "serious" poetry to "lofty" topics, such as the fate of kings. The Romantics greatly expanded the range of subjects considered suitable for poetry, and many wrote poems based on the everyday experiences of common folk. Compare the results Burns and Baillie achieve. Ask yourself, does an "everyday" subject limit the poet's message, or does the poet reach a general truth?

❸ Reading Strategy

Translating Dialect

You may not know Scottish dialect, but you may be able to interpret words in dialect using context, by referencing a footnote, or even by noticing a resemblance to a Standard English word. Use a chart like the one shown to help you translate the Scottish dialect in the poems.

Footnotes	*sleekit*[3]
	3. sleek
Context	*saunt <u>an' sinner</u>*
	saunt = saint
Word Similarities	*dinna*
	do not
Missing Letters	*woo'd, a'*
	wooed, all

Vocabulary Development

dominion (də min′ yən) *n.* rule; authority (p. 627)

impudence (im′ pyo͞o dəns) *n.* lack of shame; rudeness (p. 629)

winsome (win′ səm) *adj.* having a charming appearance or way (p. 632)

discretion (di skresh′ ən) *n.* good judgment; prudence (p. 633)

inconstantly (in kän′ stənt lē) *adv.* changeably; in a fickle way (p. 633)

❷ Literary Analysis

Dialect

- Explain to students that in this lesson they will focus on dialect, a form of a language spoken in a specific region or by a given group.
- Explain that dialect may vary from standard language in grammar and pronunciation; point out to students that dialect helps establish character, mood, and setting.
- Read the instruction about dialect together as a class. Call students' attention to the way in which Burns and Baillie used dialect in their verse.
- Use the instruction for Comparing Literary Works to review with students how a poem written in dialect that treats common subject matter might appeal to various audiences.
- Use the Dialect transparency in **Literary Analysis and Reading Transparencies,** p. 56 to show students how to compare dialect with standard language.

❸ Reading Strategy

Translating Dialect

- Explain to students that they can interpret Scottish dialect using context, footnotes, or its resemblance to standard English.
- Use the graphic organizer on p. 625 with students to model translating dialect.
- Have students practice the skill using the Translating Dialect transparency in **Literary Analysis and Reading Transparencies,** p. 55.

Vocabulary Development

Pronounce each vocabulary word for students, and read the definitions as a class. Have students identify any words with which they are already familiar.

CUSTOMIZE INSTRUCTION FOR UNIVERSAL ACCESS

For Less Proficient Readers	For English Learners	For Advanced Readers
Model for students how to translate dialect using the graphic organizer on p. 625. Then, have students read the first two stanzas of "To a Mouse" as a group with teacher guidance, pointing out unfamiliar words as they go. As dialect words are identified, write them on the board, and have students practice translating them.	Students may have difficulty with words in dialect that differ from the standard English language they have studied. Explain to them that many of the words used in dialect sound similar to standard English words. Have students practice reading dialect words with teacher guidance in the first two stanzas of "To a Mouse."	Explain to students that dialect consists of everyday expressions and informal phrases. Have students independently read the first two stanzas of "To a Mouse." Encourage students to write their own translations of words and phrases in dialect in their notebook to aid their comprehension.

 ***E-Teach***

Visit E-Teach at www.phschool.com for teachers' essays on how to teach, with questions and answers.

TEACH

Step-by-Step Teaching Guide for pp. 626–634

CUSTOMIZE INSTRUCTION
For Bodily/Kinesthetic Learners

Encourage these students to lend their expertise to the class by reenacting the scene between the speaker and the mouse described in the first stanza of "To a Mouse."

1 About the Selection

The unexpected encounter with a field mouse, whose home he has inadvertently destroyed with his plow, prompts the sympathetic speaker to apologize to the mouse. However, in the final two stanzas, the speaker uses the incident to generalize on the similarities between the mouse's situation and that of human beings. Just as the mouse's plans for a winter home have come to nothing, so too do humans' plans often come undone.

2 ▶Critical Viewing

Answer: The mouse's timid, almost cute face might have inspired Burns's poem, because it suggests the vulnerability and sympathetic qualities of the animal.

1 To a Mouse

On Turning Her up in Her Nest with the Plow, November, 1785

Robert Burns

Background

Before Robert Burns published his poetry, works of literature were almost always modeled on the classics, in which structure, grammar, and vocabulary were polished and complex. Robert Burns ignored these conventions and boldly put poetry in the hands of the people, writing in their language, Scottish dialect, and using common folk as subject matter.

2 ▼ Critical Viewing What facial qualities of a mouse might have inspired Burns's poem? **[Hypothesize]**

TEACHING RESOURCES

The following resources can be used to enrich or extend the instruction for pp. 626–634.

Literary Analysis

- **Selection Support:** Literary Analysis, p. 132
- **Interest Grabber Video,** Tape 4

Reading

- **Listening to Literature Audiocassettes,** Side 15 ■
- **Listening to Literature Audio CDs,** CD 9 ■

■ **BLOCK SCHEDULING:** Resources marked with this symbol provide varied instruction during 90-minute blocks.

3

Wee, sleekit,[1] cow'rin', tim'rous beastie,
O, what a panic's in thy breastie!
Thou need na start awa sae hasty,
Wi' bickering brattle![2]
I wad be laith[3] to rin an' chase thee
Wi' murd'ring pattle![4]

I'm truly sorry man's dominion
Has broken Nature's social union,
An' justifies that ill opinion,
Which makes thee startle,
At me, thy poor, earth-born companion,
An' fellow-mortal!

I doubt na, whyles,[5] but thou may thieve;
What then? poor beastie, thou maun[6] live!
A daimen icker in a thrave[7]
'S a sma' request:
I'll get a blessin' wi' the lave,[8]
And never miss't!

Thy wee bit housie, too, in ruin!
4 Its silly wa's[9] the win's are strewin'!
An' naething, now, to big[10] a new ane,
O' foggage[11] green!
An' bleak December's winds ensuin',
Baith snell[12] an' keen!

Thou saw the fields laid bare and waste,
An' weary winter comin' fast,
An' cozie here, beneath the blast,
Thou thought to dwell,
Till crash! the cruel coulter[13] past
Out through thy cell.

That wee bit heap o' leaves an' stibble,
Has cost thee mony a weary nibble!

---

1. **sleekit** sleek.
2. **Wi' . . . brattle** with a quick pattering sound.
3. **wad be laith** would be loath.
4. **pattle** paddle for cleaning a plow.
5. **whyles** at times.
6. **maun** must.
7. **A . . . thrave** an occasional ear of grain in a bundle.
8. **lave** rest.
9. **silly wa's** feeble walls.
10. **big** build.
11. **foggage** rough grass.
12. **snell** sharp.
13. **coulter** plow blade.

dominion (də min′ yən) *n.* rule; authority

Reading Strategy
Translating Dialect Use context clues to determine the meaning of "win's" in line 20.

5 **Reading Check**
How does the speaker uncover the mouse?

3 Critical Thinking

Infer

- Have students read the first stanza of the poem.
- Encourage students to use the notes to aid their understanding of Scottish dialect.
- Ask students: Judging from what Burns says to the mouse, how did the mouse react to having her nest plowed up?
  Answer: The mouse may be trembling and its heart may be racing ("O, what a panic's in thy breastie!"). Startled, it has at least attempted, if not succeeded, in fleeing ("Thou need na start awa sae hasty").

4 Reading Strategy

Translating Dialect

- Tell students that they should be able to understand many unfamiliar dialect words from context.
- Have them follow the Reading Strategy instructions on p. 627: Use context clues to determine the meaning of "win's" in line 20.
  Answer: Students should see that "win's" is dialect for "winds."

5 Reading Check

Answer: The speaker uncovers the mouse when he turns up her nest with a plow.

CUSTOMIZE INSTRUCTION FOR UNIVERSAL ACCESS

For Special Needs Students	For Less Proficient Readers	For Gifted/Talented Students
Have students read aloud a section from "To a Mouse" with teacher guidance. Then ask students to redescribe the action in each line. For students who are struggling with comprehension, and to stimulate interest in the life of Robert Burns, play **Interest Grabber Video,** Tape 4.	Students may have difficulty appreciating the humor and compassion shown by the speaker in "To a Mouse." Have students read from the poem silently as they listen to **Listening to Literature Audio CDs,** CD 9. Then, guide students in a close reading of the poem in which they translate words in dialect, line by line.	Have students write the mouse's "response" to the speaker of "To a Mouse." Ask students to reread what Burns's speaker says regarding the lessons that he has learned from the incident and write a creative reply by the mouse expounding her own philosophy on the interaction between human beings and animals.

Answers for p. 628

Review and Assess

1. Possible responses: Some students may say they would feel compassion, whereas others may say they would be unmoved.
2. **(a)** The speaker has plowed up its home. **(b)** The speaker is not concerned with the grain the mouse steals. **(c)** Possible response: Students may say that the speaker forgives theft for survival, as he expresses in lines like: "I doubt na, whyles, but thou may thieve; / What then? poor beastie, thou maun live!"
3. **(a)** The mouse's attempt to prepare for winter has been undone by the speaker's plow. **(b)** "The best laid schemes o' mice an' men / Gang aft a-gley." **(c)** Possible response: The best-contrived ideas of all creatures often go awry: We cannot control the future.
4. **(a)** The speaker compares the mouse's absorption in the present with the human ability to regret the past and fear the future. **(b)** Possible responses: Students may point out that taking responsibility for the past and planning for the future are part of human dignity, though they involve suffering beyond what animals experience. Some may agree that the mouse's ignorance of past and future is a blessing because of the worry it saves the mouse.
5. Possible response: Students may value foresight as part of freedom, though it leads to more anxiety.
6. Possible response: Students may feel that dialect adds a folksy, country element of wisdom to the poem; others may find the dialect translation impedes their enjoyment of the poem's meaning.

Now thou's turned out, for a' thy trouble,
    But[14] house or hald,[15]
To thole[16] the winter's sleety dribble,
    An' cranreuch[17] cauld!

But, Mousie, thou art no thy lane,[18]
In proving foresight may be vain:
The best laid schemes o' mice an' men
    Gang aft a-gley,[19]
An' lea'e us nought but grief an' pain,
    For promised joy.

Still thou art blest, compared wi' me!
The present only toucheth thee:
But, och! I backward cast my e'e
    On prospects drear!
An' forward, though I canna see,
    I guess an' fear!

---

14. **But** without.
15. **hald** property.
16. **thole** withstand.
17. **cranreuch** (krən´ rəkh) frost.
18. **no thy lane** not alone.
19. **Gang aft a-gley** go often awry.

Review and Assess

Thinking About the Selection

1. **Respond:** How would you have reacted to the plight of the mouse? Explain.
2. **(a) Recall:** For what reason does the speaker apologize to the mouse? **(b) Infer:** How does the speaker feel about the grain the mouse steals? **(c) Interpret:** What does the speaker's reaction show about his ideas of justice?
3. **(a) Infer:** What has happened to the mouse's attempt to prepare for winter? **(b) Interpret:** Which two famous lines in the poem express the poem's theme? **(c) Paraphrase:** Restate the theme in your own words.
4. **(a) Interpret:** What comparison does the speaker draw between himself and the mouse in the last stanza? **(b) Evaluate:** Do you agree with the speaker about the mouse's advantage? Explain.
5. **Apply:** What value do you place on foresight? Explain.
6. **Evaluate:** Does dialect add to the quality of folk-wisdom in the poem, or does it distract from the meaning? Explain.

ENRICHMENT: History Connection

The Romantic Movement

Burns is a forerunner of the Romantic Movement in art and literature. In reaction to the Age of Enlightenment's emphasis on the intellect, the Romantic Movement favored taking the imagination and emotions as a guide. Unlike the previous age, in which nature was often seen as something to be conquered, Romantics viewed nature as a source of truths with which people should try to harmonize. Hence, Burns apologizes for man's intrusion with the plow into nature's "social union."

❻ # To a Louse

On Seeing One on a Lady's Bonnet at Church

Robert Burns

❼ 

The Bow, Talbot Hughes, Warrington Museum and Art Gallery, Great Britain

❽ **◀ Critical Viewing** Does this lady's pose and costume link her to the lady in the poem? Explain. **[Connect]**

Ha! whare ye gaun, ye crowlin' ferlie![1]
Your impudence protects you sairly:[2]
I canna say but ye strunt[3] rarely,
 Owre gauze and lace;
Though faith! I fear ye dine but sparely
 On sic a place.

impudence (im′ pyōō dəns) *n.* lack of shame; rudeness

❾ **✔ Reading Check** Where is the louse crawling?

1. **crowlin' ferlie** crawling wonder.
2. **sairly** wondrously.
3. **strunt** strut.

❻ About the Selection

In "To a Louse," Burns sees a louse (the singular form of *lice,* a parasite like a flea) on the bonnet of a well-dressed lady and uses the incident to satirize conceited behavior.

❼ Background

Art

The Bow, by Talbot Hughes

This painting depicts a fashionable woman who is tying a bow around her neck. Point out to students that the woman is elaborately costumed and made up according to the dictates of fashion of the times.

Use these questions for discussion:

1. How well does the subject of this painting fit the description of the lady in "To a Louse"?
 Answer: Like the lady in the poem, the lady in the painting wears delicate lace, ribbons, a bonnet, and possibly gauze. However, the bonnet lacks the balloon shape of a Lunardi.
2. Burns's poem suggests there is a difference between how we see ourselves and how others see us. Judging from the woman's expression, how do you think she sees herself? How might others see her?
 Answer: She appears to make an effort to appear well-groomed and seems quite satisfied with the results. Other people might see her as filled with vanity and a false sense of superiority.

❽ ▶ Critical Viewing

Answer: Yes, the dainty manner in which the lady ties her bow and her primping pose suggest a self-importance like that of the woman in the poem. Her costume, with its frills and bows, also seems similar to the costume worn by the woman in the poem.

❾ ✔ Reading Check

Answer: The louse is crawling across the clothing of a well-dressed lady.

CUSTOMIZE INSTRUCTION FOR UNIVERSAL ACCESS

For Less Proficient Readers	For Gifted/Talented Students
Tell students that a new TV series called *The Robert Burns Show* is scheduled to air next fall. The producers have hired them to plan an animated short for the premiere, which will be based on "To a Mouse" or "To a Louse." Have students select a poem and develop a storyboard for it. Students should break the poem into segments, create an illustration for each segment, and write the corresponding lines from the poem beneath each scene.	Tell students that a new TV series called *The Robert Burns Show* is scheduled to air next fall. The producers have hired them to choreograph and score an interpretation of "To a Mouse." Have students analyze the poem to determine how to effectively stage both the action and the speaker's commentary. Students should then assign roles, select music and other effects, rehearse, and then stage their interpretation.

10 Background

The Literature of Scotland

The Scottish dialect is an offshoot of the Northumbrian dialect of Anglo-Saxon, the forerunner of modern English spoken from A.D. 500 to 1100. Scottish dialect has a strong Norse element in vocabulary and in vowel and consonant sounds. Over time, Gaelic, French, and Dutch linguistic elements were mixed in.

The Scottish dialect entered medieval literature in the works of John Barbour (1325?–1395), Robert Henryson (1420/30–*c.* 1506), William Dunbar (1460/65–*c.* 1530), and others. Many of these poets were influenced by the English poet Geoffrey Chaucer.

Political union between Scotland and England began with James I (1566–1625). James, already king of Scotland, became king of England as well in 1603. By the 1700s, the Scottish dialect had been displaced by English as Scotland's major language for written works. Allan Ramsay (1686–1758), Burns, and others revived the dialect, nicknamed "Lallans," in the eighteenth century.

11 Critical Thinking

Analyze

- Have a student volunteer read aloud the bracketed passage. Encourage students to use the footnotes and context to understand the Scottish dialect.
- Then, ask students: What literary convention is Burns using here to give humor to his poem?
  Answer: Burns is using a combination of exaggeration (description of the louse and of the speaker's threats) and personification (speaking to the louse as if it had human qualities). This stanza has a trace of mock-heroic style, which students may know from Chaucer's "The Nun's Priest's Tale" (p. 119) or Pope's *The Rape of the Lock* (p. 532).

Ye ugly, creepin', blastit wonner,[4]
Detested, shunned by saunt an' sinner,
How dare ye set your fit[5] upon her,
    Sae fine a lady?
Gae somewhere else, and seek your dinner
    On some poor body.

Swith![6] in some beggar's haffet[7] squattle;[8]
There ye may creep, and sprawl, and sprattle[9]
Wi' ither kindred, jumping cattle,
    In shoals and nations:
Whare horn nor bane[10] ne'er dare unsettle
    Your thick plantations.

Now haud[11] ye there, ye're out o' sight,
Below the fatt'rels,[12] snug an' tight;
Na, faith ye yet![13] ye'll no be right
    Till ye've got on it,
The vera tapmost, tow'ring height
    O' Miss's bonnet.

11
My sooth! right bauld ye set your nose out,
As plump and gray as onie grozet;[14]
O for some rank, mercurial rozet,[15]
    Or fell,[16] red smeddum,[17]
I'd gie you sic a hearty dose o't,
    Wad dress your droddum![18]

I wad na been surprised to spy
You on an auld wife's flannen toy;[19]
Or aiblins some bit duddie boy,[20]
    On's wyliecoat;[21]

4. blastit wonner blasted wonder.
5. fit foot.
6. swith swift.
7. haffet locks.
8. squattle sprawl.
9. sprattle struggle.
10. horn nor bane comb made of horn or bone.
11. haud hold.
12. fatt'rels ribbon ends.
13. Na, faith ye yet! "Confound you!"
14. onie grozet (gräz´ it) any gooseberry.
15. rozet (räz´ it) rosin.
16. fell sharp.
17. smeddum powder.
18. Wad . . . droddum "would put an end to you."
19. flannen toy flannel cap.
20. Or . . . boy or perhaps on some little ragged boy.
21. wyliecoat (wī´ lē kōt´) undershirt.

10 *The Literature of Scotland*

Burns's dialect poems were part of a long struggle over Scottish identity. From the late thirteenth century to the middle of the sixteenth century, the Lowlands area of Scotland—Burns's native region—frequently warred with England. A distinctive culture blossomed in the region, yielding famous ballads such as "Barbara Allan."

Yet, Lowlands culture was a close cousin to that of the English, and influences across the border were strong. Scotland united with England in 1707, and the important Scottish authors of the time, such as economist Adam Smith, wrote in English as the English spoke it.

As Scotland grew closer to England politically, though, there was a backlash—Scotland was swept by a literary enthusiasm for things distinctly Scottish. In the poems of Burns, Baillie, and others, as well as in a new passion for collecting the old ballads, the Scottish past reasserted itself even as it faded.

But Miss's fine Lunardi![22] fie,
How daur ye do't?

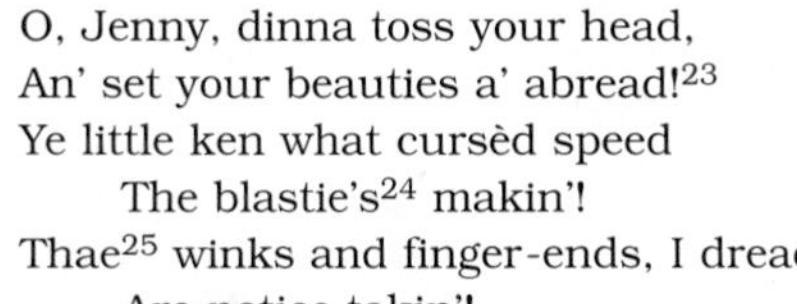

O, Jenny, dinna toss your head,
An' set your beauties a' abread![23]
Ye little ken what cursèd speed
The blastie's[24] makin'!
Thae[25] winks and finger-ends, I dread,
Are notice takin'!

O wad some Pow'r the giftie gie us
To see oursels as ithers see us!
It wad frae monie a blunder free us
And foolish notion:
What airs in dress an' gait wad lea'e us,
And ev'n devotion!

---

22. **Lunardi** balloon-shaped bonnet, named for Vincenzo Lunardi, a balloonist of the late 1700's.
23. **abread** abroad.
24. **blastie's** creature's.
25. **Thae** those.

Review and Assess

Thinking About the Selection

1. **Respond:** Did this poem make you laugh? Why or why not?
2. **(a) Recall:** What is the louse doing? **(b) Recall:** What does the speaker command it to do instead? **(c) Interpret:** What social assumptions about cleanliness does the speaker's command reflect?
3. **(a) Draw Conclusions:** What impression of Jenny does the speaker create? **(b) Analyze:** How do the references to her clothing and the contrast between her and "some poor body" contribute to this impression?
4. **(a) Infer:** In the lines 37–42, why does the speaker warn Jenny against tossing her head? **(b) Infer:** What is the reaction of others in the church to Jenny's gesture? **(c) Draw Conclusions:** Why is the contrast between this gesture and the progress of the louse particularly embarrassing?
5. **(a) Interpret:** Paraphrase the generalization that the speaker makes in the last stanza. **(b) Evaluate:** Do you agree that we would profit if we could "see oursels as ithers see us"? Explain.
6. **Make a Judgement:** Do you think caring about the impression we make on others is foolish vanity? Explain.

CUSTOMIZE INSTRUCTION FOR UNIVERSAL ACCESS

For Special Needs Students	For Less Proficient Readers	For Advanced Readers
Have students read the final stanzas of the poem with teacher guidance. For students who have difficulty analyzing how dialect can reinforce or enhance subject matter in "To a Louse," use the Dialect transparency on p. 56 of **Literary Analysis and Reading Transparencies** to model how effective dialect functions.	Have students read the final stanzas of the poem in small groups. Remind them that Burns is using dialect to convey attitudes effectively. Ask each group to discuss why Burns wrote about an insect crawling on someone's hat in dialect instead of Standard English. Students should then share their ideas in a round-table discussion.	Have students write essays in which they compare Burns's poems "To a Mouse" and "To a Louse." Students should consider the author's use of language in each poem, as well as his themes, rhythm, and rhyme. Direct students to www.phschool.com for more information on Burns and his poetry.

12 Literary Analysis

Dialect and Subject Matter

- Have students reread "To a Louse" in pairs.
- Ask students to note moments of embarrassment or potential embarrassment in the poem.
- Then, ask students, Do you think poets should write about trivial, embarrassing moments in life? Why or why not?
  Possible response: Students may feel that all of life is worthy of being explored in poetic form. Others may add that Burns discovers a deep message in a trivial scene.

Answers for p. 631

Review and Assess

1. Possible response: Students may say that the image of a fancy lady with a louse on her head made them laugh.
2. **(a)** The louse is crawling on a well-dressed lady's clothing. **(b)** The speaker commands it to go crawl on some poor beggar. **(c)** Beggars are expected to be dirty; well-dressed ladies are not.
3. **(a)** Jenny is vain and wants others to admire her. **(b)** Her "fatt'rels, snug and tight" and other finery show that she has dressed to show off; along with the condescending references to the "beggar" who is better suited to be a louse's meal, they reinforce impressions of her snobbery and vanity.
4. **(a)** The speaker warns her not to toss her head and send the louse elsewhere on her body. **(b)** Others in the church notice and point ("winks and finger-ends"). **(c)** Jenny is about to toss her head in order to draw attention to her beautiful hair, but the louse crawling on her bonnet will make the gesture ridiculous.
5. **(a)** The speaker says that if we could see ourselves as others see us, that ability would free us from making embarrassing mistakes. **(b)** Possible responses: Students may agree that we would profit because we would not waste time with foolish vanity.
6. Possible response: Self-respect demands that we care to some extent about how others see us; vanity is an excessive concern with appearances.

13 About the Selection

"Woo'd and Married and A'" offers insight into the motives for marriage. The poem begins with the bride sorrowing over her lack of finery and possessions and the prospect of marrying someone who has no more wealth than she. The bride's parents chastise the bride, declaring that she is fortunate to find anyone to marry her at all, given her poverty. The bridegroom, though, knows how to manage her anxiety: He proclaims that the bride herself is wealth enough for him. Pleased by the flattery, she gives up her worrying and goes off to be married.

14 Vocabulary Development

Anglo Saxon Suffix *-some*

- Call students' attention to the word *winsome,* a word that means "having a charming, attractive appearance or manner." Explain to students that the Anglo-Saxon suffix *-some* means "tending to" or "tending toward being."
- Have students suggest other words that contain this suffix, and list them on the chalkboard. Possible responses: *awesome, tiresome, handsome, worrisome*
- Have students define these words using the meaning of the suffix.

15 Literary Analysis

Dialect

- Review with students that dialect is often used to establish character, mood, and setting, and to add charm and "texture."
- Then, ask students the Literary Analysis question on p. 632: What feeling or qualities does the use of dialect add to the mother's advice to her daughter?
  Answer: Students should recognize that the dialect enriches the mother's remarks by suggesting an entire way of life. Expressions such as "tak your wheel" (l. 17)—a reference to spinning thread—add to the reader's impression of the life of these poor farming folk. The unique words and pronunciations emphasize the fact that the mother is steeped in this way of life and helps the reader identify her as a distinctive personality. In this way, the use of dialect adds sincerity and force to the mother's indignation.

13 Woo'd and Married and A'

Joanna Baillie

14

The bride she is winsome and bonny,
Her hair it is snooded[1] sae sleek,
And faithfu' and kind is her Johnny,
Yet fast fa' the tears on her cheek.
New pearlins[2] are cause of her sorrow,
New pearlins and plenishing[3] too;
The bride that has a' to borrow
Has e'en right mickle[4] ado.
Woo'd and married and a'!
Woo'd and married and a'!
Is na' she very weel aff
To be woo'd and married at a'?

15

Her mither then hastily spak,
"The Lassie is glaikit[5] wi' pride;
In my pouch I had never a plack[6]
On the day when I was a bride.
E'en tak to your wheel and be clever,
And draw out your thread in the sun;
The gear[7] that is gifted it never
Will last like the gear that is won.
Woo'd and married and a'!
Wi' havins and toucher[8] sae sma'!
I think ye are very weel aff
To be woo'd and married at a'."

winsome (win′ səm) *adj.* having a charming appearance or way

Literary Analysis
Dialect What feelings or qualities does the use of dialect add to the mother's advice to her daughter?

1. **snooded** bound up with a ribbon.
2. **pearlins** lace trimmings.
3. **plenishing** furnishings.
4. **mickle** much.
5. **glaikit** foolish.
6. **plack** farthing; a small coin equal to one fourth of a penny.
7. **gear** wealth or goods.
8. **havins and toucher** possessions and dowry.

ENRICHMENT: Cultural Connection

Marriage

The institution of marriage is an important tradition in many cultures, fostered by spiritual and secular societies alike. In some cultures, marriage is a fairly informal event. In other societies, marriage is characterized by a highly complex series of ritual behaviors and gestures that begin with courtship—the indication of romantic interest—and concludes with the marriage ceremony itself. As in Baillie's poem, though, most cultures allow a place for a humorous view of marriage.

Some societies still have arranged marriages in which the bride and groom have little say in their choice of a spouse, and their families make the ultimate decision. Other societies sponsor the use of matchmakers to determine the appropriate partner for a single man or woman. Still others encourage single men and women to find their own partner or spouse and make their own plans to wed.

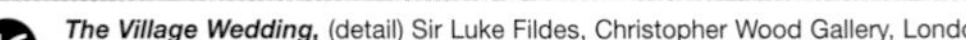

16 *The Village Wedding,* (detail) Sir Luke Fildes, Christopher Wood Gallery, London

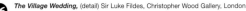

"Toot, toot," quo' her gray-headed faither,
"She's less o' a bride than a bairn,[9]
She's ta'en like a cout[10] frae the heather,
Wi' sense and discretion to learn.
Half husband, I trow, and half daddy,
As humor inconstantly leans,
The chiel maun be patient and steady[11]
18 That yokes wi' a mate in her teens.
A kerchief sae douce[12] and sae neat
O'er her locks that the wind used to blaw!
I'm baith like to laugh and to greet[13]
When I think of her married at a'!"

Then out spak the wily bridegroom,
Weel waled[14] were his wordies, I ween,
"I'm rich, though my coffer be toom,[15]

9. **bairn** child.
10. **cout** colt.
11. **The chiel maun . . . steady** The man must be patient and steady.
12. **douce** respectable.
13. **greet** weep.
14. **waled** chosen.
15. **toom** empty.

17 **▲ Critical Viewing**
Compare and contrast the setting and costumes in this painting with the scene described in the poem. **[Compare and Contrast]**

discretion (di skresh´ ən) *n.* good judgment; prudence

inconstantly (in kän´ stənt lē) *adv.* changeably; in a fickle way

19  **Reading Check**
What is the father's opinion of his daughter?

CUSTOMIZE INSTRUCTION FOR UNIVERSAL ACCESS

For English Learners	For Gifted/Talented Students
Explain to students that the words used in the poem "Woo'd and Married and A'" are difficult for most English-speakers. Have students work in pairs to make a list of words and phrases in the poem that they find difficult. Encourage students to use the footnotes and context wherever possible to define each word or phrase on their lists. For each word, include an example of its use from the poem, and explain what the word means in that context.	If possible, have students work in groups of four, reenacting the various figures in the poem "Woo'd and Married and A'." Have students plan a presentation in which each member of the group recites the portion of the poem relevant to the character he or she chooses to portray. (The student who takes the role of the bride should read the first and last paragraphs and any narrative lines.) You may want to refer students to Extension Activity 7 for a variation on this activity. (**Extension Activities,** p. 29)

16 Background

Art

The Village Wedding, (detail) by Sir Luke Fildes

Sir Luke Fildes (1844–1927) began his career as a magazine illustrator in London. He illustrated Dickens's last novel, *Edwin Drood,* before turning to painting in the 1870s. His paintings are part of the social realism movement, which seeks to truly depict both the beauty and the evils of contemporary life.

Fildes's works were very popular and were often made available as engravings. He was knighted in 1906. Use these questions for discussion:

1. Which moment in the poem could the painting be used to represent?
   Possible response: Students may say the painting captures the last stanza, in which the bride blushes, smiles, and looks down bashfully.
2. Judging from the expressions of the people in the painting, was this wedding solemn or festive?
   Possible response: Students may point out that the bride and groom seem serious and solemn, whereas the surrounding guests seem more happy and animated.

17 ▶Critical Viewing

Answer: The village setting depicted in the painting parallels the humble surroundings suggested indirectly in the poem. The dress of the groom and those following him appear to be finer than one might expect in the scene in the poem.

18 Critical Thinking

Interpret

- Read the bracketed passage aloud to students.
- Then ask them: What does the father's use of the word *yokes* in line 32 suggest about his attitude toward marriage?
  Answer: Yoking is the process of joining two animals, such as oxen, with a heavy collar so they can work together. The father's choice of words implies that he sees marriage as a chore or task.

19 Reading Check

Answer: The father thinks his daughter is foolish and immature.

ASSESS

Answers for p. 634

Review and Assess

1. **(a)** The bride is sad because she does not have fine clothes or furnishings. **(b)** Possible response: Students should agree that the mother is not at all sympathetic to her daughter's unhappiness; some students may find the bride's father sympathetic, since he both treasures and is amused by his daughter's childlike character and is "baith like to laugh and to greet [weep]" (l. 35) at the thought of her marriage. Others may note simply that he is not sympathetic, since he finds her attitude unrealistic.
2. **(a)** The bridegroom responds to his bride's unhappiness by saying that her company and beautiful eyes are wealth enough for him. **(b)** The bridegroom's words cause the bride to blush and content her. **(c)** Possible response: The bridegroom, described as "wily" (l. 37), is a clever diplomat and, perhaps, an optimist.
3. **(a)** The bridegroom succeeds in changing the bride's outlook. **(b)** The final stanza suggests the marriage will be a happy one, since the bride and bridegroom are happy with each other, despite their lack of wealth, and the bridegroom knows how to soothe and flatter his bride.
4. Possible response: Students may think that the poet is unkind to the young bride because she shows the bride's worries put to rest with a little flattery, suggesting that the bride is vain and empty-headed. Others may feel that the poet shows real insight into the bride's personality and motives and that the overall cheerfulness of the poem makes the portrayal realistic, not unkind.

Wi' the blinks o' your bonny blue e'en.[16]
I'm prouder o' thee by my side,
Though thy ruffles or ribbons be few,
Than if Kate o' the Croft were my bride
Wi' purfles[17] and pearlins enow.
Dear and dearest of ony!
Ye're woo'd and buikit[18] and a'!
And do ye think scorn o' your Johnny,
And grieve to be married at a'?"

She turn'd, and she blush'd, and she smiled,
And she looked sae bashfully down;
The pride o' her heart was beguiled,
And she played wi' the sleeves o' her gown.
She twirled the tag o' her lace,
And she nipped her boddice sae blue,
Syne blinkit sae sweet in his face,
And aff like a maukin[19] she flew.
Woo'd and married and a'!
Wi' Johnny to roose[20] her and a'!
She thinks hersel very weel aff
To be woo'd and married at a'!

16. **e'en** eyes.
17. **purfles** embroidered trimmings.
18. **buikit** "booked"; entered as married in the official registry.
19. **maukin** hare.
20. **roose** praise.

Review and Assess

Thinking About the Selection

1. **(a) Recall:** Why is the bride unhappy at the beginning of the poem? **(b) Infer:** Does either parent seem sympathetic to the daughter's unhappiness? Explain.
2. **(a) Recall:** How does the bridegroom respond to his bride's unhappiness? **(b) Analyze Cause and Effect:** Describe the effect the bridegroom's words have on his young bride. **(c) Draw Conclusions:** How would you describe the personality of the bridegroom?
3. **(a) Recall:** Which speaker succeeds in changing the bride's outlook? **(b) Draw Conclusions:** Judging from the final stanza, do you think the marriage will be a happy one? Explain.
4. **Make a Judgement:** Do you think the poet is unkind to the young bride, or does she show insight into people? Explain.

ASSESSMENT PRACTICE: Reading Comprehension

Critical Thinking **(For more practice, see Test Preparation Workbook, p. 35.)**

Many tests require students to draw conclusions based upon evidence provided in a passage. Use the following sample test item:

"Toot, too," quo her gray-headed faither,
"She's less o' bride than a bairn,
She's ta'en like a cout frae the heather,
Wi' sense and discretion to learn.
Half husband, I trow, and half daddy
As humor inconstantly leans,
The chiel maun be patient and steady

What conclusion can you draw about the groom?

A He will be cared for by his bride.
B He is handsome.
C He is wild and inconstant.
D He will have to guide his impulsive bride.

Point out that lines 29 and 31 state that the bridegroom will be *half husband . . . and half daddy* and must *be patient and steady.* Students should then see that *D* is the correct answer.

Review and Assess

Literary Analysis

Dialect

1. What does the use of **dialect** in the poems by Burns suggest about the speaker's social status?
2. What does dialect contribute to the setting of Joanna Baillie's "Woo'd and Married and A'"?
3. Find at least two examples in "To a Mouse" of the following pronunciation patterns for Scottish English: (a) Final consonants are dropped, and (b) the letter *o* is replaced by either *ae* or *a*.
4. How would the overall effect of these poems have been different if they had been written in Standard English?

Comparing Literary Works

5. Using a chart like the one shown, analyze the subject matter of the poems in this grouping.

Poem	Subject	Message

6. (a) Which poem conveys the message that applies most generally? Explain. (b) Which poem conveys a message that applies only to some people? Explain.
7. Do you think the use of everyday subjects in these poems limits the messages they convey? Explain.
8. What subject matter would you be surprised to find in poetry today? Explain.

Reading Strategy

Translating Dialect

9. List and define ten words in dialect that appear in these poems. For each, explain the techniques you used to arrive at a definition.
10. Choose one stanza from a Burns or Baillie poem, and translate it into Standard English.

Extend Understanding

11. **History Connection:** What difficulties might dialect present to historians? Explain.

Quick Review

Dialect is the form of a language spoken by a particular social class, region, or group. It differs from the standard language in pronunciation, vocabulary, or grammar.

To **translate dialect** into Standard English, read footnotes, notice context clues, look for similarities to words you know, and fill in missing letters in words.

Take It to the Net

www.phschool.com

Take the interactive self-test online to check your understanding of these selections.

Answers for p. 635

Review and Assess

1. The speaker's language suggests that he is one of the common folk, someone who is in touch with the basics of life.
2. The dialect of "Woo'd and Married and A'" emphasizes the humble, rural setting of the poem.
3. **(a)** Examples include *cow'rin'* (line 1), *strewin'* (line 20), and *comin'* (line 26). **(b)** Examples include *sae* for "so," (line 3), *ane* for "one" (line 21), and *aft* for "oft" (line 40).
4. Possible responses: The poetry would lose some of its warmth; the characters would not seem as true-to-life.
5. Possible response: "To a Mouse": Subject: uprooting of a mouse's nest; Message: The best considered plans can go awry. "To a Louse": Subject: a louse crawling on a lady's bonnet; Message: If we could see ourselves as others do, we would act less foolishly. "Woo'd . . . ": Subject: a young bride-to-be is upset about her lack of rich adornments; Message: Love can make up for material lacks.
6. **(a)** Possible response: Because all people make plans or anticipate the future in some way, the message of "To a Mouse," which concerns the uncertainty of such plans, applies most generally. **(b)** Possible response: Because the message of "Woo'd . . ." directly concerns the psychology of a wedding, it may be seen as applying only to some situations.
7. Possible responses: Yes, because the everyday subjects of the poems prevent them from addressing truths from exceptional situations such as war or tragic love; no, because both poets succeed in drawing general truths from their subjects.
8. Students should support their answers with a generalization about the standards or tastes of contemporary culture.
9. Possible responses: *beastie* = animal; *naething* = nothing; *stibble* = stubble; *gaun* = gone; *strunt* = strut; *havins and toucher* = possessions and dowry; *bairn* = child; *cout* = colt;

continued

continued from right column

douce = respectable; *greet* = weep

For each response, students should explain the techniques they used.

10. Possible translation: Stanza 1 of "To a Mouse": Poor little, scared thing! You're terrified of me! You don't need to run away from me. I would never chase you.
11. Possible response: Historians might have trouble deciphering records of events in a region if they do not understand its dialect.

ENRICHMENT: Further Reading

Other Works by the Authors

Works by Robert Burns

Poems and Songs

The Glenriddell Manuscripts

Works by Joanna Baillie

Joanna Baillie: Poems, 1790

Take It to the Net

Visit www.phschool.com for more information on the authors.

EXTEND

Answers for p. 636

❶ Vocabulary Development

Word Analysis

1. *Handsome* means tending toward being attractive.
2. *Lithesome* means tending toward being supple.
3. *Worrisome* means tending to trouble.
4. *Awesome* means tending to awe.
5. *Tiresome* means tending to exhaust (someone or something).

Spelling Strategy

1. discretion
2. possession
3. omission

Concept Development: Synonyms

1. b
2. a
3. c
4. b
5. a

❷ Grammar

1. What then? Poor beastie, thou maun live!
2. Ha! Whare ye gaun, ye crowlin' ferlie!
3. Though faith! I fear ye dine but sparely. . . .
4. My sooth! right bauld ye set your nose out, . . .
5. O, Jenny, dinna toss your head, . . .

Writing Application

Possible response: Wow! I can't believe that I glued myself to my brother. We were building a model together. He was about to put the wrong piece in place. I reached over to snatch it from him, when—slorp!—the epoxy covering both his hand and mine bonded instantly!

Integrate Language Skills

❶ Vocabulary Development Lesson

Word Analysis: Anglo-Saxon Suffix *-some*

Baillie calls the bride in her poem *winsome*, meaning "charming." The Anglo-Saxon suffix *-some* means "tending to" or "tending toward being." Literally, *winsome* means "tending to win over or to delight." Using this meaning of the suffix and a dictionary, define each word below.

1. handsome
2. lithesome
3. worrisome
4. awesome
5. tiresome

Spelling Strategy

The suffix that sounds like *shun* at the end of a word may be spelled *tion, ssion,* or *cion*. The spelling *ssion* is used when a related verb ends in *-mit* or *-ess*: *permit/permission* and *confess/confession*. In your notebook, correctly complete the spelling of each word including the *shun* sound.

1. discre__ 2. posse__ 3. omi__

Concept Development: Synonyms

Synonyms are words that share the same, or nearly the same, meaning. In your notebook, write the letter of the word that is the best synonym of the word from the vocabulary list on page 625. Then, use a dictionary to explain any differences in meaning between the synonyms in each pair.

1. dominion: (a) incapability, (b) rule, (c) pride
2. impudence: (a) rudeness, (b) shyness, (c) test
3. winsome: (a) competitive, (b) bold, (c) attractive
4. discretion: (a) disappointment, (b) good judgment, (c) gratitude
5. inconstantly: (a) changeably, (b) emptily, (c) sadly

❷ Grammar and Style Lesson

Interjections

Interjections are words or phrases expressing emotion that function independently of a sentence. A comma separates a mild interjection from the rest of the sentence. An exclamation mark follows a stronger interjection. A question mark is used when the interjection takes the form of a question.

Examples: O, what a panic's in thy breastie!

But, och! I backward cast my e'e. . . .

Practice Identify the interjection in each line, and correctly punctuate the sentence.

1. What then poor beastie, thou maun live!
2. Ha whare ye gaun, ye crowlin' ferlie!
3. Though faith I fear ye dine but sparely. . . .
4. My sooth right bauld ye set your nose out, . . .
5. O Jenny, dinna toss your head, . . .

Writing Application Write a short paragraph about a funny incident. Use at least two interjections, punctuated correctly.

WG Prentice Hall Writing and Grammar Connection: Chapter 17, Section 4

TEACHING RESOURCES

The following resources can be used to enrich or extend the instruction for pp. 636–637.

Vocabulary

- **Selection Support:** Build Vocabulary, p. 129
- **Vocabulary and Spelling Practice Book** (Use this booklet for skills enrichment.)

Grammar

- **Selection Support:** Grammar and Style, p. 130
- **Writing and Grammar,** Diamond Level, p. 394
- **Daily Language Practice Transparencies** ■

Writing

- **Writing and Grammar,** Diamond Level, p. 317 ■
- **Writing and Grammar iText CD-ROM**
- **Writing Models and Graphic Organizers on Transparencies,** p. 85

■ **BLOCK SCHEDULING:** Resources marked with this symbol provide varied instruction during 90-minute blocks.

❸ Writing Lesson

Comparison of Characters

Burns and Baillie paint brilliant miniature portraits of Scottish common folk. In an essay, compare the vain churchgoer in Burns's "To a Louse" with the moping young bride in Baillie's "Woo'd and Married and A'."

Prewriting Jot down notes on the two characters, identifying similarities and differences between them.

Drafting Choose a method of organization and follow it consistently as you draft. For instance, you might compare each character point by point, focusing first on social position and then on basic attitudes.

Revising Mark up your draft, highlighting details about one character in one color and details about the other in another color. If the pattern of highlights shows that you have departed from your chosen form of organization, reorganize passages. If you have more highlights of one color than of another, consider adding details for better balance.

Model: Revising to Better Balance Comparisons

The young bride is clearly emotional. Upset as she is about her poverty, she is easily reassured by the groom's flattery—which has nothing to do with money. *She seems to be driven by vanity, just like the vain churchgoer in Burns's poem.*

The added sentence balances the discussion of the two characters in this paragraph.

Prentice Hall Writing and Grammar Connection: Chapter 14, Section 4

❹ Extension Activities

Listening and Speaking With a group, prepare an **authentic dialect reading** of the poems in this group.

1. Listen to recordings of Burns's poetry.
2. Mark a photocopy of the poems with the correct pronounciations of words in dialect.
3. Rehearse, offering one another suggestions about pronunciation, expression, and gestures.

When you have prepared throughly, present your readings to the class. **[Group Activity]**

Research and Technology Assemble a **multimedia presentation** about Scotland that includes photographs, recordings, and maps. Make photocopies, and code each piece of art to indicate in which part of your presentation you might use it (for example, use **L** for land and **H** for history). To organize your visuals, start a folder for each category. Share your work with classmates.

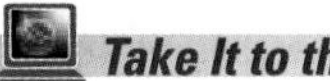

Take It to the Net www.phschool.com

Go online for an additional research activity using the Internet.

❸ Writing Lesson

- Remind students that Burns and Baillie include revealing details about the churchgoer Jenny in "To a Louse" and the bride in "Woo'd and Married and A'," respectively. Then, explain to students that they will write comparisons of characters in their poems.
- Encourage students to jot down notes about similarities and differences between the two women.
- Use the Writing Lesson to guide students in developing their comparison of characters.
- Use the Exposition: Comparison-and-Contrast rubric in **Performance Assessment and Portfolio Management,** p. 20, to evaluate students' comparisons.

❹ Listening and Speaking

- Read the Listening and Speaking lesson as a class, then divide students into groups and have them decide which poem they want to recite.
- Encourage students to practice the dialect words in the poem they have chosen, and to listen to recordings of the poem in **Listening to Literature Audiocassettes,** Side 15.

CUSTOMIZE INSTRUCTION For Universal Access

To address different learning styles, use the activities suggested in the **Extension Activities** booklet, p. 29.

- For Verbal/Linguistic Learners, use Activity 5.
- For Musical/Rhythmic Learners, use Activity 6.
- For Interpersonal Learners, use Activity 7.

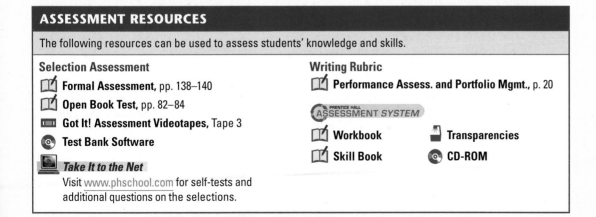

ASSESSMENT RESOURCES

The following resources can be used to assess students' knowledge and skills.

Selection Assessment

- **Formal Assessment,** pp. 138–140
- **Open Book Test,** pp. 82–84
- **Got It! Assessment Videotapes,** Tape 3
- **Test Bank Software**

Take It to the Net

Visit www.phschool.com for self-tests and additional questions on the selections.

Writing Rubric

- **Performance Assess. and Portfolio Mgmt.,** p. 20

PRENTICE HALL ASSESSMENT SYSTEM

- **Workbook**
- **Skill Book**
- **Transparencies**
- **CD-ROM**

The Lamb ✦ The Tyger ✦ The Chimney Sweeper ✦ Infant Sorrow

Lesson Objectives and CA Correlations

1. **To analyze and respond to literary elements**
   - Literary Analysis: Symbols **R 3.4**
   - Comparing Literary Works **R 3.2**
2. **To read, comprehend, analyze, and critique a poem**
   - Reading Strategy: Using Visuals as Key to Meaning
   - Reading Check Questions
   - Review and Assess Questions
   - Assessment Practice (ATE)
3. **To develop word analysis skills, fluency, and systematic vocabulary**
   - Vocabulary Development Lesson: Word Analysis: Latin Root *-spir-* **R 1.2**
4. **To understand and apply written and oral English language conventions**
   - Spelling Strategy **LC 1.2**
   - Grammar and Style Lesson: Commonly Confused Words: *rise* and *raise* **LC 1.1**
5. **To understand and apply appropriate writing and research strategies**
   - Writing Lesson: Comparative Literary Analysis **W 1.3**
   - Extension Activity: Advertisement **W 1.8**
6. **To understand and apply listening and speaking strategies**
   - Extension Activity: Musical Reading **LS 1.10**

STEP-BY-STEP TEACHING GUIDE	PACING GUIDE
PRETEACH	
Motivate Students and Provide Background	
Use the Motivation activity (ATE p. 638)	5 min.
Read and discuss author and background features (SE/ATE pp. 638, 640) **A**	5 min.
Introduce the Concepts	
Introduce the Literary Analysis concept and the Reading Strategy (SE/ATE p. 639) **A**	15 min.
Pronounce the vocabulary words and read their definitions (SE p. 639)	5 min.
TEACH	
Monitor Comprehension	
Informally monitor comprehension by circulating while students read independently or in groups **A**	10 min.
Monitor students' comprehension with the Reading Check notes (SE/ATE pp. 641, 643)	as students read
Develop vocabulary with Vocabulary notes (SE pp. 640, 641; ATE p. 641)	as students read
Develop Understanding	
Develop students' understanding of symbols with the Literary Analysis annotations (SE/ATE p. 643) **A**	5 min.
Develop students' ability to use visuals as a key to meaning with the Reading Strategy annotations (ATE p. 639)	5 min.
ASSESS	
Assess Mastery	
Assess students' mastery of the Reading Strategy and Literary Analysis concepts by having them answer the Review and Assess questions (SE/ATE p. 645)	15 min.
Use one or more of the print and media Assessment Resources (ATE p. 647) **A**	up to 45 min.
EXTEND	
Apply Understanding	
Have students complete the Vocabulary Development Lesson and the Grammar and Style Lesson (SE p. 646) **A**	20 min.
Apply students' knowledge of placement for emphasis using the Writing Lesson (SE/ATE p. 647) **A**	45 min.
Apply students' understanding using one or more of the Extension Activities (SE p. 647)	20–90 min.

A **ACCELERATED INSTRUCTION:**
Use the strategies and activities identified with an .

UNIVERSAL ACCESS
● = Below-Level Students
▲ = On-Level Students
■ = Above-Level Students

Time and Resource Manager

Reading Level: Easy, Easy, Average, Easy
Average Number of Instructional Days: 4

RESOURCES		
PRINT	**TRANSPARENCIES**	**TECHNOLOGY**
• **Beyond Literature,** Humanities Connection: Fine Art, p. 29 ▲ ■		• **Interest Grabber Video,** Tape 4 ● ▲ ■
• **Selection Support Workbook:** ● ▲ ■ Literary Analysis, p. 136 Reading Strategy, p. 135 Build Vocabulary, p. 133	• **Literary Analysis and Reading Transparencies,** pp. 57 and 58 ● ▲ ■	
		• **Listening to Literature** ● ▲ ■ Audiocassettes, Side 15 Audio CDs, CD 9
• **Literary Analysis for Enrichment** ■	• **Fine Art Transparencies, Volume 2,** Art Transparency 9 ● ▲ ■	
• **Formal Assessment:** Selection Test, pp. 141–143 ● ▲ ■ • **Open Book Test,** pp. 85–87 ● ▲ ■ • **Performance Assessment and Portfolio Management,** p. 25 ● ▲ ■ • Prentice Hall Assessment System ● ▲ ■	• Prentice Hall Assessment System ● ▲ ■ Skills Practice Answers and Explanations on Transparencies	• **Test Bank Software** ● ▲ ■ • **Got It! Assessment Videotapes,** Tape 3 ● ▲
• **Selection Support Workbook:** ● ▲ ■ Grammar and Style, p. 134 • **Writing and Grammar,** Diamond Level ● ▲ ■ • **Extension Activities,** p. 29 ● ▲ ■	• **Daily Language Practice Transparencies** ● ▲ • **Writing Models and Graphic Organizers on Transparencies,** pp. 45–56 and 85–92 ● ▲ ■	• **Writing and Grammar iText CD-ROM** ● ▲ ■ ***Take It to the Net*** www.phschool.com

BLOCK SCHEDULING: Use one 90-minute class period to preteach the selections and have students read them. Use a second 90-minute class period to assess students' mastery of skills and have them complete one of the Extension Activities.

PRETEACH

Step-by-Step Teaching Guide for pp. 638–639

Motivation

Write the word pairs *good/evil; right/wrong;* and *heaven/hell* on the chalkboard. Introduce the class to William Blake's belief that pure opposites such as these were ultimately false. The truth, in Blake's vision, involved overturning these simple terms to find a new vision of life. In works such as *The Marriage of Heaven/Hell*, Blake reinterpreted what conventional people in his day called evil—pride and desire—as ultimately innocent—the affirmation of energy. Through such strategies, Blake sought a unified vision of life, free from hypocrisy, shame, and self-righteousness. Have students identify oppositions in the poems as they read and note ways in which Blake's work challenges them.

Interest Grabber Video

As an alternative, play "'The Tyger': Mysterious Tigers" on Tape 4 to engage student interest.

❶ Background

More About the Author

William Blake is remembered today as a visionary who anticipated nineteenth-century developments in poetry and philosophy. His works are a record of his own evolving personal mythology.

Blake's radical views tended to set him apart from others. For instance, he was charged in 1803 with high treason for having "uttered seditious and treasonable expressions" against the king. Although he was acquitted, the wound left by the experience never fully healed.

Romantic poet William Wordsworth is reported to have said at Blake's death: "There was no doubt that this poor man was mad, but there is something in the madness of this man which interests me more than the sanity of Lord Byron and Walter Scott." Modern critics tend to see in Blake's extreme statements and complex images, not madness, but irony and a deliberate effort to outrage. Perhaps Blake sought to shock readers and so jolt them free of the grip of preconceived ideas.

Prepare to Read

❶ The Lamb ◆ The Tyger ◆ The Chimney Sweeper ◆ Infant Sorrow

William Blake (1757–1827)

"I must create a system or be enslaved by another man's." So spoke William Blake, an artist and poet who strove in his work to break free from the patterns of thought that defined common experience. As if to underscore the difference between his views and the ordinary, he claimed that mystical visions were the source of his inspiration.

Finding His Way Blake's visions began when, at the age of four, he thought he saw God at his window. Four years later, Blake said, he saw a tree filled with angels. While Blake's "spells" might have seemed a cause for concern, Blake's parents were followers of the mystical teachings of Emanuel Swedenborg, a Swedish spiritualist. They believed that their son had a "gift of vision" and did all they could to nurture this gift.

Blake's father was a poor Londoner who owned a small hosiery shop. He sent Blake to drawing school, and Blake pursued his own education at home through wide reading. Already well educated by the age of twelve, Blake wrote some of the simple, eloquent poems that became part of a collection entitled *Poetical Sketches* (1783). He became an engraver's apprentice and then went on to study at the Royal Academy.

Striking Out on His Own Formal study did not last long, however. The president of the Academy, noted painter Sir Joshua Reynolds, discouraged Blake's original style and pushed him toward more conventional work. The rebellious Blake left the school and eventually set up his own print shop. He was to live most of his days eking out a living as an engraver, barely making enough to support himself and his wife, Catherine.

Innocence and Experience When Blake was thirty-two, he published *Songs of Innocence*, a series of poems that he had composed when he was younger. The poems explored his favorite themes—the destiny of the human spirit and the possibility of renewing our perceptions. In these poems, Blake suggested that by recapturing the wonderment of childhood, we can achieve the goal of true self-knowledge and integration with the world. To print the collection, he developed a unique process whereby the words and illustrations were etched onto metal plates and then printed on paper. Blake often painted in colors and details on each page by hand. The result was a true integration of text and picture. Because the process was time consuming, few books could be produced. To support himself, Blake worked for other authors as an illustrator and sold what he could of his own works for one pound per copy. He also continued to write, and in 1794 he brought out a companion to *Songs of Innocence*, entitled *Songs of Experience*.

A Mature Vision Exploring the darker side of life, *Songs of Experience* reflected Blake's growing disillusionment and more mature vision. He came to believe that a return to innocence was not, at least by itself, sufficient for people to attain true self-awareness: They must also recognize and accept the parts of themselves that religion and morality teach them to reject. Thus, Blake's credo was that there must be a union of opposites, or a fusion of innocence and experience.

An Unrecognized Genius Blake's talent was barely recognized by his peers or by the public during his lifetime. It was only late in his life that a small group of admiring painters sought him out. Despite the lack of recognition, Blake filled his seventy years with constant creative activity. Years after his death, he came to be regarded as one of the most important poets of his time.

TEACHING RESOURCES

The following resources can be used to enrich or extend the instruction for pp. 638–639.

Motivation

Interest Grabber Video, Tape 4

Background

Beyond Literature, p. 29

Take It to the Net

Visit www.phschool.com for background and hotlinks for the selections.

Literary Analysis

Literary Analysis and Reading Transparencies, Symbols, p. 58

Reading

Selection Support: Reading Strategy, p. 135; Build Vocabulary, p. 133

Literary Analysis and Reading Transparencies, Using Visuals as a Key to Meaning, p. 57

BLOCK SCHEDULING: Resources marked with this symbol provide varied instruction during 90-minute blocks.

Preview

Connecting to the Literature

For a child, the tooth-fairy story can be a cherished belief. When such beliefs are disproved, a child may experience sadness, even mistrust, before finding a new, mature confidence. Like such a child, Blake passes from the innocence of "The Lamb" to the darker awareness of "The Tyger."

2 Literary Analysis

Symbols

In literary works, a **symbol** is a word, image, or idea that represents something else. Often, a symbol is something tangible, or solid, that stands for and helps readers understand something intangible, like an emotion. A symbol appears in the following line from Blake:

And wash in a river and shine in the Sun.

Washing "in a river" symbolizes the Christian rite of baptism, in which a believer is cleansed of sin. To help you interpret Blake's symbols, use a graphic organizer like the one shown.

Association		Association
Meek		
	Symbol Lamb	
Association		**Association**
		Innocent

Comparing Literary Works

Using symbols, Blake defines a unique **poetic vision** or philosophy—a comprehensive view of life, the world, and our ordinary perceptions. In the poems that follow, you will be struck by the extreme contrasts this vision includes. As you read, compare the aspects of life that Blake explores through symbols:

- The world seen from the perspective of "innocence" versus the world seen from the perspective of "experience"
- Suffering seen from "above"—suffering one rises beyond—versus suffering one is trapped inside

3 Reading Strategy

Using Visuals as a Key to Meaning

When you read literature, such as these poems, that is accompanied by illustrations, **use the visuals as a key to meaning.** Look closely at the details of Blake's illustrations, and consider how they support or add to the author's words.

Vocabulary Development

vales (vālz) *n.* valleys; hollows; depressed stretches of ground (p. 640)

symmetry (sim′ ə trē) *n.* balanced form; the beauty resulting from such balance (p. 641)

aspire (ə spīr′) *v.* have high ambitions; yearn or seek after (p. 641)

CUSTOMIZE INSTRUCTION FOR UNIVERSAL ACCESS

For Less Proficient Readers	For English Learners	For Advanced Readers
Model for students how to read symbols using the Symbols transparency on p. 58 of **Literary Analysis and Reading Transparencies.** Then, have students read the first two stanzas of "The Lamb" as a group. As they identify symbols, write them on the transparency, and have students list their associations.	Students may have difficulty with symbolic imagery. Explain to them that symbols are images that represent other things, as the eagle represents the United States. Tell students they will read a poem about a lamb, and ask them to name some associations they have with lambs. Then have students read "The Lamb" with teacher guidance.	Model for students how the meaning of symbols can be inferred using the graphic organizer on p. 639 or the Symbols transparency on p. 58 of **Literary Analysis and Reading Transparencies.** Then, have students read "The Lamb" independently, using graphic organizers to explore the meaning of the symbols in the poem.

2 Literary Analysis

Symbols

- Explain to students that in this lesson they will concentrate on symbols—words, images, or ideas that represent a set of associated things or ideas.
- Tell students that symbols are usually concrete images. A rose, an eagle, and balance scales are all concrete images—they are perceived through the senses. Each stands, though, for something abstract or not perceivable through the senses: a rose stands for love or mystery, an eagle for honor as well as the United States, the scales for justice.
- Read the note about symbols as a class. Call students' attention to the clarity and simplicity of the image that Blake uses as a symbol.
- Use the instruction for Comparing Literary Works to review with students how Blake uses symbols to convey different visions of the world, such as the perspective of innocence versus the perspective of experience.
- Use the Symbols transparency in **Literary Analysis and Reading Transparencies,** p. 58, to show students how to make associative connections between symbols and their referents.

3 Reading Strategy

Using Visuals as a Key to Meaning

- Remind students that Blake illustrated most of his collections of poetry using a process of printing and painting he himself devised.
- Explain that illustrations that accompany literature are keys to the meaning of the works.
- Have students practice the skill of using visuals to understand meaning using the Use Visuals as a Key to Meaning transparency in **Literary Analysis and Reading Transparencies,** p. 57.

Vocabulary Development

Pronounce each vocabulary word for students, and read the definitions as a class. Have students identify any words with which they are already familiar.

TEACH

Step-by-Step Teaching Guide for pp. 640–644

CUSTOMIZE INSTRUCTION For Visual/Spatial Learners

Encourage these students to diagram the position and movement of figures or the various locations in Blake's poems. Ask them to note symmetries or imbalances revealed by their diagrams.

❶ About the Selection

In this light, bright-sounding poem, a child talks to a little lamb about their creator, and both child and lamb emerge as symbols of innocence.

❷ Background

Art

Illustrated manuscript of "The Lamb," William Blake

A boy converses with a sheep. He stands outside the simple hut of a shepherd, with a thatched roof and open window. The vines and leaves that encircle the poem and illustrations create a pastoral frame for the scene. Use this question for discussion:

Why do you think the boy is shown with his arms outstretched?
Answer: He may be feeding the lamb; perhaps he is instructing the lamb or explaining something to it, as in the poem. The gesture expresses the harmonious relationship between child and lamb, and between humanity and nature, depicted in the poem.

❸ ▶Critical Viewing

Answer: Nature appears innocent, harmonious, and unthreatening, as can be inferred from the trust shown between the lamb and the boy.

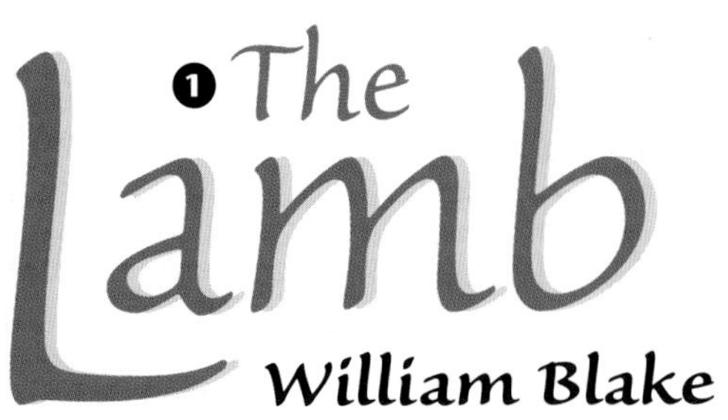

❶ The Lamb

William Blake

❷

From a manuscript of "The Lamb" by William Blake, Lessing J. Rosenwald Collection, Library of Congress, Washington, D.C.

Background

Blake illustrated his poems with striking, integrated designs. These illustrations seem to swirl through the words and become part of their meaning. Blake claimed that many of the images he drew as illustrations were likenesses of his inner visions. They have a childlike feeling and are very different from the strict, formal styles of his time.

Little Lamb who made thee
Dost thou know who made thee
Gave thee life & bid thee feed.
By the stream & o'er the mead;
Gave thee clothing of delight,
Softest clothing wooly bright;
Gave thee such a tender voice,
Making all the vales rejoice!
Little Lamb who made thee
Dost thou know who made thee

Little Lamb I'll tell thee,
Little Lamb I'll tell thee!
He is called by thy name,
For he calls himself a Lamb:
He is meek & he is mild,
He became a little child:
I a child & thou a lamb,
We are called by his name.
Little Lamb God bless thee.
Little Lamb God bless thee.

❸ ▲**Critical Viewing**
What view of nature is expressed by the style of Blake's drawing? **[Infer]**

vales (vālz) *n.* valleys; hollows; depressed stretches of ground

TEACHING RESOURCES

The following resources can be used to enrich or extend the instruction for pp. 640–644.

Literary Analysis
Selection Support: Literary Analysis, p. 136;

Reading
Listening to Literature Audiocassettes, Side 15 ■
Listening to Literature Audio CDs, CD 9 ■

Extension
Fine Art Transparencies, Volume 2, Art Transparency 9

■ **BLOCK SCHEDULING:** Resources marked with this symbol provide varied instruction during 90-minute blocks.

❹ The Tyger

William Blake

Tyger Tyger, burning bright,
In the forests of the night;
What immortal hand or eye,
Could frame thy fearful <u>symmetry</u>?

In what distant deeps or skies
Burnt the fire of thine eyes!
❺ | On what wings dare he <u>aspire</u>?
What the hand, dare seize the fire?

symmetry (sim′ ə trē) *n.* balanced form; the beauty resulting from such balance

aspire (ə spīr′) *v.* have high ambitions; yearn or seek after

❻

From a manuscript of "The Tyger" by William Blake, The Metropolitan Museum of Art

❼ ◀**Critical Viewing** Compare and contrast the tiger's expression with the poem's image of the animal. **[Compare and Contrast]**

❽ ✓**Reading Check** Who does the speaker ask the tiger about?

CUSTOMIZE INSTRUCTION FOR UNIVERSAL ACCESS

For Special Needs Students	For Gifted/Talented Students
Have students examine and discuss Blake's illustration of a tiger on p. 641. Then, have students read a section from "The Tyger" with teacher guidance. Ask students to visualize each line as they reread the entire poem to themselves. For students who are struggling with comprehension of Blake's poem, or to stimulate interest, play **Interest Grabber Tape 4:** "'The Tyger': Mysterious Tigers."	Remind students that Blake created art to illustrate his poetry. Show them Transparency 9 in **Fine Art Transparencies,** vol. 2, Blake's illustrated title page for *Songs of Innocence.* Encourage them to review Blake's work. Then, tell them that their assignment is to reverse the process and choose an illustration or painting they like and write a poem about it. Have them compare their results with Blake's illustrated poetry.

❹ About the Selection

The voice of this poem shares the chanting, nursery-rhyme quality of the voice in "The Lamb," but the scene is wilder and grimmer. Darkness replaces light, night replaces day, and experience replaces innocence. Like "The Lamb," this poem asks about the creator and the creature. It measures the character of the tiger's creator against the ferocity and power of the tiger, suggesting that the creator of the tiger has burning, passionate energy. Unlike "The Lamb," it leaves its questions about the creator unanswered.

❺ Vocabulary Development

Latin Root *-spir-*

- Call students' attention to the word *aspire* and its definition. Explain to students that *aspire* contains the Latin root *-spir-* meaning "breath" or "life." To aspire to something is to "live" for it.
- Have students suggest other words and phrases that contain this Latin root, and list them on the chalkboard.
  Possible responses: *inspire, respiration, spirit, perspiration*
- Have students look up any unfamiliar words in a dictionary.

❻ Background

Art

Illustrated manuscript of "The Tyger," William Blake

This engraving of a tiger shows a strong-looking animal, with muscular haunches and a stance that prepares it to pounce or run. Its eye appears to "burn bright" with an intense yellow light. Use this question for discussion:

What effect do the tree branches have on the layout of this poem?
Answer: The branches divide the poem into stanzas or pairs of stanzas. The tree is an otherworldly color, outlined in the tiger's orange. It unifies text and illustration and adds to the dark mood of the poem.

❼ ▶Critical Viewing

Answer: The tiger's expression in the illustration—perhaps a mischievous smile—seems far less threatening than its image in the poem.

❽ ✓Reading Check

Answer: The speaker asks about the creator of the tiger.

❾ Critical Thinking

Interpret

- Have a student volunteer read the bracketed passage.
- Then, ask students: What figure of speech is used in these lines? To what do the lines refer?
  Answer: The lines give human qualities to the stars (personification). They may refer to Lucifer's rebellion against heaven.

Answers for p. 642

Review and Assess

1. **(a)** The speaker asks the lamb who made it and whether it knows who made it. **(b)** The speaker extends these questions by asking about each detail of the lamb's appearance as endowed by its creator. **(c)** The lamb grazes, is soft, and has a tender voice.
2. **(a)** The speaker calls himself a child. **(b)** The speaker, like the lamb and the lamb's creator, is a child and presumably "meek and mild." **(c)** The speaker has knowledge, and the lamb does not.
3. **(a)** The question asked is "What immortal hand or eye, / Could frame thy fearful symmetry?" **(b)** This question suggests that the tiger is fierce. **(c)** The question suggests that the motives or vision of the creator of a creature as fierce as the tiger are difficult to understand.
4. **(a)** The questions are "Did he smile his work to see?" and "Did he who made the Lamb make thee?" **(b)** Blake is asking whether or not the same creator who made an innocent lamb is capable of making a fierce tiger, or how two such disparate forces can be part of the same world.
5. **(a)** The questions in the poem are never answered. **(b)** Possible response: Students may say that Blake hoped to provoke the reader to reconsider his or her ideas about the nature of creation.
6. Possible responses: Students may say that the world is a tiger, a realm of appetite and danger. Others may say that the world is a lamb, innocent of what is done to it. Others may feel that the world combines both appetite and innocence.

And what shoulder, & what art,
Could twist the sinews of thy heart?
And when thy heart began to beat,
What dread hand? & what dread feet?

What the hammer? what the chain,
In what furnace was thy brain?
What the anvil? what dread grasp,
Dare its deadly terrors clasp?

❾
When the stars threw down their spears
And water'd heaven with their tears:
Did he smile his work to see?
Did he who made the Lamb make thee?

Tyger, Tyger burning bright,
In the forests of the night:
What immortal hand or eye,
Dare frame thy fearful symmetry?

Review and Assess

Thinking About the Selections

1. (a) **Recall:** What two questions does the speaker ask at the beginning of "The Lamb"? (b) **Analyze:** How does the speaker extend these questions into a description of the lamb? (c) **Interpret:** Sum up the characteristics of the lamb.
2. (a) **Recall:** How does the speaker of "The Lamb" identify himself? (b) **Infer:** What does the speaker have in common with the lamb and the lamb's creator? (c) **Deduce:** Considering the opening of the second stanza, what is an important difference between the speaker and the lamb?
3. (a) **Recall:** What question is asked in the first stanza of "The Tyger"? (b) **Interpret:** What does this question suggest about the tiger's nature? (c) **Draw Conclusions:** What does this question suggest about the tiger's creator?
4. (a) **Recall:** What two questions are asked in stanza 5 of "The Tyger"? (b) **Draw Conclusions:** What deeper question about the creator is Blake asking in this stanza?
5. (a) **Analyze:** Are the questions in the poem ever answered? (b) **Synthesize:** What does this fact suggest about Blake's purpose in writing "The Tyger"?
6. **Apply:** Do you think the world is best viewed as a lamb, as a tiger, as both, or as neither? Explain.

ENRICHMENT: History Connection

Labor Laws

Throughout history, children have been put to work in various forms of labor. For many families, the economic necessities outweighed the burden on the child who was put to work. During the Industrial Revolution in England, children were used in factories regularly. Small children also did the work of cleaning accumulations of flammable soot out of chimneys because they could easily climb into the chimneys and scrape them clean, as described in Blake's poem, "The Chimney Sweeper."

Today, in the United States, strict labor laws prevent the regular employment of children. This was not always the case in this country, where children used to be employed in labor-intensive industries. In many other countries, child labor laws are not as strict. Work that can be done by small fingers and hands, such as weaving of rugs and tapestries, continues to be done by underage workers in countries around the world.

⑩ # The Chimney Sweeper

William Blake

When my mother died I was very young,
And my father sold me while yet my tongue,
Could scarcely cry weep weep weep weep.
So your chimneys I sweep & in soot I sleep.

There's little Tom Dacre, who cried when his head
That curl'd like a lambs back, was shav'd, so I said.
Hush Tom never mind it, for when your head's bare,
You know that the soot cannot spoil your white hair.

And so he was quiet, & that very night,
As Tom was a sleeping he had such a sight,
That thousands of sweepers Dick, Joe, Ned & Jack
Were all of them lock'd up in coffins of black

⑪
And by came an Angel who had a bright key,
And he open'd the coffins & set them all free.
Then down a green plain leaping laughing they run
And wash in a river and shine in the Sun.

Then naked & white, all their bags left behind,
They rise upon clouds, and sport in the wind.
And the Angel told Tom if he'd be a good boy,
He'd have God for his father & never want joy.

And so Tom awoke and we rose in the dark
And got with our bags & our brushes to work.
Tho' the morning was cold, Tom was happy & warm,
So if all do their duty, they need not fear harm.

Literary Analysis
Symbols What might the Angel in line 13 symbolize?

⑫ **Reading Check**
Why does Tom Dacre cry?

⑩ About the Selection

Conventional religious beliefs pervade this short poem about the miseries suffered by child laborers. Tom Dacre and the speaker are young children forced to work as chimney sweepers. Tom is upset when his head is shaved. The Speaker reassures him, and that night Tom dreams that an angel tells him that if he is good, God will provide.

⑪ Literary Analysis

Symbols

- Have students read lines 13–20 to themselves.
- Review with students the definition of symbols as concrete images meant to represent other, intangible things.

Monitor Progress Ask students the Literary Analysis question on p. 643: What might the Angel in line 13 symbolize?
Possible responses: The Angel may symbolize God's forgiveness of sin or St. Peter, who is said to stand at the gates of Heaven with a key.

Reteach If students have difficulty answering the question, have them list various associations with the idea of an angel or of entry to Heaven. Explain that many of their associations come from the same treasury of common meanings on which poets draw, and so they can indicate a poet's symbolic meaning.

- Ask students to identify any other symbols in this passage and explain their meaning.
Possible responses: The "bright key" may symbolize forgiveness or the resurrection; the coffins may symbolize death of the body or the death-in-life of earthly suffering; the "green plain" may symbolize Heaven; "wash in a river" suggests baptism or spiritual cleansing; the Sun may symbolize God or His love.

⑫ Reading Check

Answer: Tom Dacre cries because his head is shaved.

CUSTOMIZE INSTRUCTION FOR UNIVERSAL ACCESS

For English Learners	For Advanced Readers
As students read "The Chimney Sweeper," have them practice saying aloud any portions of the text or words they don't know. Explain to students who are having difficulty identifying symbols in the poem that they should look at each noun in the poem and make a list of associations with that word.	Tell students that Blake's poem "The Chimney Sweeper" depicts children working under cruel and inhumane conditions in Britain during the Industrial Revolution. Have students work in small groups to create a script for a short news segment about child labor that might have been aired if television had existed in early nineteenth-century Britain.

ASSESS

⓭ About the Selection

Like "The Tyger," this is a song of experience. Turning the stereotype of the joy of new life on its head, this poem presents a newborn that is not received with joy and that struggles, fights, and sulks.

Answers for p. 644

Review and Assess

1. **(a)** The child's mother died, and his father sold him. **(b)** These events suggest that chimney sweeps were abandoned by their families who had to give them up out of economic necessity, which suggests that their lives were unhappy.
2. **(a)** Tom dreams that thousands of chimney sweeps are released from black coffins by an angel, and they run down a plain and wash in a river in the sun.
   (b) Tom's dream supports the last line of the poem. If he "does his duty" as a chimney sweep, the last line says, he will go to heaven and never fear harm, as the dream suggests. **(c)** Possible response: Blake does not stand firmly behind this lesson in the poem; the misery of the chimney sweepers' lives described in the poem makes the idea that they should do their "duty" to find happiness in heaven seem ironical or unjust.
3. **(a)** The mother groaned and the father wept; at first, the child struggles and cries. **(b)** The moment was not a very joyous one.
4. **(a)** The speaker is bound in the sense that it depends on others for its needs and does not control a "dangerous world." **(b)** The infant's dependency and powerlessness reflects humanity's general dependency and powerlessness over fate.
5. The infant's final reaction, to sulk, is typical of the way in which people deal with frustration.
6. Possible responses: Readers may be inspired to challenge religious apologies for earthly sorrow by "The Chimney Sweeper." "Infant Sorrow" may prompt readers to rethink ideas of freedom and responses to constraint.

⓭ Infant Sorrow

William Blake

My mother groand![1] my father wept.
Into the dangerous world I leapt,
Helpless, naked, piping loud;
Like a fiend hid in a cloud.

Struggling in my father's hands,
Striving against my swaddling bands;
Bound and weary, I thought best
To sulk upon my mother's breast.

1. **groand** groaned; an example of Blake's often eccentric spelling.

Review and Assess

Thinking About the Selections

1. **(a) Recall:** How does the child in the first stanza of "The Chimney Sweeper" become a chimney sweep? **(b) Interpret:** What do these events suggest about the life of chimney sweeps?
2. **(a) Recall:** Describe Tom's dream. **(b) Interpret:** Connect the dream with the final line. **(c) Evaluate:** Does Blake stand firmly behind the lesson in the final line? Explain.
3. **(a) Recall:** In "Infant Sorrow," what are the reactions of the parents and the child to the child's birth? **(b) Interpret:** What do these reactions indicate about the moment?
4. **(a) Intepret:** Aside from the tight "swaddling bands," in what larger sense is the speaker bound? **(b) Generalize:** What general truth about human life does the infant's predicament suggest?
5. **Evaluate:** Is the infant's final reaction characteristic of the way people deal with frustration? Explain.
6. **Compare and Contrast:** How does each poem inspire readers to rethink assumptions about life and death?

ASSESSMENT PRACTICE: Reading Comprehension

Critical Reasoning (For more practice, see Test Preparation Workbook, p. 30.)

Many tests require students to judge the relevance of facts in a writer's argument. Have students read "The Chimney Sweeper" and then ask them the following question to show students how to identify a fact that does not support a writer's argument.

Which of these does **not** support Blake's message about the life of a chimney sweep?

A Chimney-sweeping was dangerous.
B Some chimney sweepers were quite content.
C Children were forced to work as chimney sweepers.
D Chimney sweepers were not well paid.

Lead students to recognize that Blake's intention is to portray the life of a chimney sweep as a miserable one. Choice *A, C,* and *D* support this message. Students should determine that *B* is the correct answer.

Review and Assess

Literary Analysis

Symbols

1. (a) In "The Lamb," what associations does the lamb have for Blake? (b) Identify two ideas that the **symbol** of the lamb represents.
2. (a) What might the images of fire in "The Tyger" symbolize? (b) The speaker in "The Tyger" asks who made the tiger. What does the existence of the tiger imply for Blake?
3. (a) How does the symbolism of "The Lamb" add to your understanding of the second stanza of "The Chimney Sweeper"? (b) What might the "bright key" in "The Chimney Sweeper" symbolize?

Comparing Literary Works

4. Compare the ways the idea of creation, an important part of Blake's **poetic vision,** is used in "The Lamb" and "The Tyger." Consider how this idea helps to express contrary views of the world.
5. (a) Using a chart like the one shown for each poem, compare the contrasting ideas of suffering in "The Chimney Sweeper" and "Infant Sorrow." (b) Does the ending of each poem confirm or challenge these ideas? Explain.

Who Is Suffering?	Why?	Is the Suffering Unjust?	Suggested Solution	Is the Solution Adequate?

Reading Strategy

Using Visuals as a Key to Meaning

6. (a) **Using visuals as a key,** explain in what way the mood of the illustration for "The Lamb" relates to the poem. (b) Compare Blake's picture of a tiger to the tiger in the poem.
7. In general, do illustrations enhance your understanding and enjoyment of a literary work? Why or why not?

Extend Understanding

8. **World Events Connection:** "The Chimney Sweeper" addresses the issue of child labor. In what form does the problem exist today?

Quick Review

Symbols are words, images, or ideas that represent something else, such as an emotion or an abstract concept.

A poet's **poetic vision** is a view of the world, shaped by specific and sometimes opposed traditions, problems, experiences, and values.

When a literary work is accompanied by illustrations, **use the visuals as a key to meaning** by comparing details in the illustrations with details in the text.

Take It to the Net

www.phschool.com

Take the interactive self-test online to check your understanding of these selections.

ENRICHMENT: Further Reading

More Works by William Blake

Other *Songs of Innocence*
"Infant Joy"; "Laughing Song"; "A Cradle Song"; "Nurse's Song"

Other *Songs of Experience*
"The Fly"; "A Poison Tree"; "London"; "The Human Abstract"

Take It to the Net

Visit www.phschool.com for more information on William Blake.

Answers for p. 645

Review and Assess

1. **(a)** The lamb has associations of innocence, purity, mildness, and meekness. **(b)** The symbol of the lamb represents innocence and Christ.
2. **(a)** Images of fire in "The Tyger" might symbolize hell, evil, appetite, or destruction. **(b)** The existence of the tiger implies that for Blake the creator is responsible for evil as well as good in the world.
3. **(a)** The symbolism of "The Lamb," with its descriptions of the lamb's soft fleece, helps one see that the description of Tom Dacre's hair curling like a lamb's symbolizes his innocence. The fact that this hair is shaved suggests that his innocence has been injured. **(b)** Possible response: The bright key in "The Chimney Sweeper" might symbolize eternal life.
4. In both poems, the character of the creator is reflected in his creations. In "The Lamb" he appears "meek and mild"; "The Tyger" suggests that the creator of the tiger may be terrifying.
5. **(a)** Sample response: "Chimney Sweeper": Who Is Suffering?: Tom Dacre; Why?: He must work as a chimney sweeper, and his hair has been cut; Suffering Unjust?: Yes, because Tom is forced to work as a chimney sweep; Suggested Solution: Do his duty to go to heaven; Is Solution Adequate?: No, because Tom's situation is still unjust. **(b)** Possible response: The end of "The Chimney Sweeper" challenges the idea that Tom's suffering will be improved by the prospect of heaven. The end of "Infant Joy" reiterates the idea that life is difficult and that there is not much that can be done about it.
6. **(a)** The mood of the illustration, like the mood of the poem, is calm and peaceful. **(b)** The tiger's expression in the illustration does not bear out the terrifying or awesome nature of the tiger in the poem; its muscular body might suggest power, however.

continued

Answers continued

7. Possible response: Most students will say that illustrations enhance understanding because they convey a single, vivid impression immediately, where the text requires the reader to synthesize details.
8. Possible response: Students may know of other countries where child labor is common in particular industries, such as rug weaving.

EXTEND

Answers for p. 646

❶ Vocabulary Development

Word Analysis: Latin Word *-spir-*

1. *Respiration* is the act of breathing.
2. A *respirator* is a machine that enables someone to breathe.
3. *Transpiration* is the act of "breathing out" vapor or moisture through pores.
4. *Aspirate* is to articulate sound so as to produce an audible breath.
5. A *spiracle* is a breathing hole.
6. A *spirometer* is an instrument for determining breathing capacity of lungs.

Fluency: Words in Context

1. They traveled through *vales* and over hills.
2. The *symmetry* of the animal's body made it look graceful and powerful.
3. The students *aspire* to attend a top college.

Spelling Strategy

1. aspire
2. symmetry
3. thy
4. sinews

❷ Grammar and Style

1. raise
2. rose
3. raised
4. to rise *or* risen
5. raised

Writing Application

1. Possible response: The chimney sweep raises his head to look up the chimney before he begins his work. He rises early to begin work before dawn. He hopes to raise enough money by his labors to help raise his brothers and sisters and to rise in life.

Integrate Language Skills

❶ Vocabulary Development Lesson

Word Analysis: Latin Root *-spir-*

In "The Tyger," Blake uses the word *aspire*, meaning "to yearn or seek after." *Aspire* contains the Latin root *-spir-*, meaning "breath" or "life." When you aspire to something, you "live for it." Many scientific words that have to do with breathing contain the root *-spir-*. Look up the meaning of each word below. Give a definition incorporating the meaning of *-spir-*.

1. respiration
2. respirator
3. transpiration
4. aspirate
5. spiracle
6. spirometer

Fluency: Words in Context

Use words from the vocabulary list on page 639 to replace each italicized item.

1. They traveled through *valleys* and over hills.
2. The *formal balance* of the animal's body made it look graceful and powerful.
3. The students *desire* to attend a top college.

Spelling Strategy

Both the letter *i* and the letter *y* can represent either the short *i* sound or the long *i* sound in words. Complete each word using an *i* or a *y*.

1. asp__re
2. s__mmetry
3. th__
4. s__news

❷ Grammar and Style Lesson

Commonly Confused Words: *rise* and *raise*

Blake describes children's spirits that "rise upon clouds." ***Rise*** means "to go up" or "to get up." It is sometimes confused with the verb ***raise,*** which means "to lift or elevate." *Raise* is always followed by a direct object, a noun or pronoun that tells who or what is raised. *Rise* never takes a direct object.

> I rise early in the morning.
>
> He raises a question about the tiger.

The forms of *rise* are as follows:

rise, rose, risen

The forms of *raise* are as follows:

raise, raised, raised

Practice In your notebook, write the correct form of *rise* or *raise* to complete each sentence. Remember that *rise* never takes an object, while *raise* always does.

1. You can __?__ your grades by studying.
2. His grade-point average __?__ last semester.
3. We __?__ money for our school at the silent auction.
4. I have __?__ early every day this week.
5. Have you ever __?__ the flag on the flagpole?

Writing Application Write a paragraph about the plight of chimney sweepers. Use forms of both *rise* and *raise* at least two times in your paragraph, choosing the correct word each time.

WG Prentice Hall Writing and Grammar Connection: Chapter 25, Section 2

TEACHING RESOURCES

The following resources can be used to enrich or extend the instruction for pp. 646–647.

Vocabulary

- **Selection Support:** Build Vocabulary, p. 133
- **Vocabulary and Spelling Practice Book** (Use this booklet for skills enrichment.)

Grammar

- **Selection Support:** Grammar and Style, p. 134
- **Writing and Grammar,** Diamond Level, p. 646 ■
- **Daily Language Practice Transparencies** ■

Writing

- **Writing and Grammar,** Diamond Level, p. 317 ■
- **Writing Models and Graphic Organizers on Transparencies,** pp. 45–56 and 85–92
- **Writing and Grammar iText CD-ROM**

■ **BLOCK SCHEDULING:** Resources marked with this symbol provide varied instruction during 90-minute blocks.

❸ Writing Lesson

Comparative Literary Analysis

"The Lamb" and "The Tyger" explore the same subject from different points of view. Write a comparative analysis exploring the connection between the view presented in each poem and the period of Blake's life in which it was written.

Prewriting Review the biographical information on page 638. Develop a thesis statement on the relationship you find between each poem and the period of Blake's life in which it was written.

Drafting Begin with an introduction that includes your thesis statement. Then, support your thesis by elaborating on your comparison of the poems and their connection to Blake's life.

Revising Review your essay, circling particularly striking details or ideas. Consider moving these details to the beginning or end of a paragraph to add emphasis.

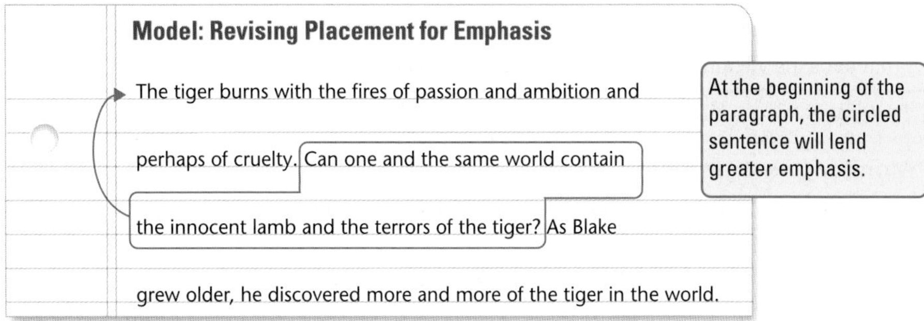

Model: Revising Placement for Emphasis
The tiger burns with the fires of passion and ambition and
perhaps of cruelty. Can one and the same world contain
the innocent lamb and the terrors of the tiger? As Blake
grew older, he discovered more and more of the tiger in the world.
At the beginning of the paragraph, the circled sentence will lend greater emphasis.

Prentice Hall Writing and Grammar Connection: Chapter 14, Section 4

❹ Extension Activities

Listening and Speaking A number of composers have set Blake's poems to music. Follow their example, and prepare a **musical reading** of Blake's poetry.

1. Choose one or two poems to set to music. Read each poem aloud, analyzing the mood.
2. Find music that creates a mood similar to that expressed in each poem.

Present your reading, introducing the piece by explaining your choice of music.

Research and Technology Choose a product, and generate an **advertisement** for it. Center your advertisement on a single visual symbol, like Blake's Tyger, that represents one or more of the attributes you wish your audience to associate with the product. Use a word-processing program to lay out your final ad.

Take It to the Net www.phschool.com

Go online for an additional research activity using the Internet.

ASSESSMENT RESOURCES

The following resources can be used to assess students' knowledge and skills.

Selection Assessment

- **Formal Assessment,** pp. 141–143
- **Open Book Test,** pp. 85–87
- **Got It! Assessment Videotapes,** Tape 3
- **Test Bank Software**

Take It to the Net
Visit www.phschool.com for self-tests and additional questions on the selections.

Writing Rubric

- **Performance Assess. and Portfolio Mgmt.,** p. 25

PRENTICE HALL ASSESSMENT SYSTEM

- **Workbook**
- **Skill Book**
- **Transparencies**
- **CD-ROM**

Lesson Support for p. 647

❸ Writing Lesson

- Remind students that in both poems, Blake suggests conclusions about the creator of the world based on his creations.
- Use the Writing Lesson to guide students in preparing comparative literary analyses of "The Lamb" and "The Tyger."
- Tell students that "The Lamb" appeared in *Songs of Innocence* and "The Tyger" in *Songs of Experience*. Review with students biographical material on p. 638 to learn more about the period in Blake's life when he composed each work.
- Guide students in developing their comparison of the two poems in the context of Blake's life.
- Use the Response to Literature rubric in **Performance Assessment and Portfolio Management,** p. 25, to evaluate students' analyses.

❹ Research and Technology

- Have students work in small groups to produce an advertisement centered on a single visual symbol.
- Ask students to think of the effective uses of symbols in commercials they know.
- Have each group choose a product, list the qualities they would want purchasers to associate with their chosen product, and find a few symbols that capture all or many of the qualities they have listed.
- Have students present their advertisements to their classmates.

CUSTOMIZE INSTRUCTION
For Universal Access

To address different learning styles, use the activities suggested in the **Extension Activities** booklet, p. 29.

- For Visual/Spatial and Verbal/Linguistic Learners, use Activity 5.
- For Bodily/Kinesthetic Learners, use Activity 6.
- For Interpersonal Learners, use Activity 7.

Introduction to *Frankenstein*

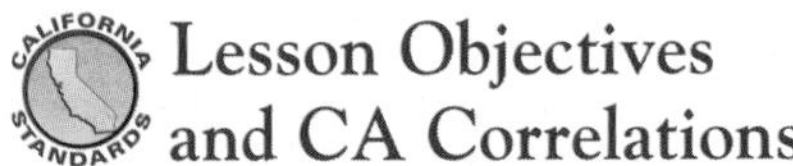

Lesson Objectives and CA Correlations

1. **To analyze and respond to literary elements**
   - Literary Analysis: The Gothic Tradition **R 3.1**
   - Connecting Literary Elements: The Romantic Movement **R 3.7**
2. **To read, comprehend, analyze, and critique nonfiction**
   - Reading Strategy: Predicting
   - Reading Check Questions
   - Review and Assess Questions
   - Assessment Practice (ATE)
3. **To develop word analysis skills, fluency, and systematic vocabulary**
   - Vocabulary Development Lesson: Related Words: *phantasm* and *fantasy* **R 1.2**
4. **To understand and apply written and oral language conventions**
   - Spelling Strategy **LC 1.2**
   - Grammar and Style Lesson: Past Participial Phrases **LC 1.1**
5. **To understand and apply appropriate writing and research strategies**
   - Writing Lesson: Essay Comparing and Contrasting Impressions of a Work **W 1.3**
   - Extension Activity: Science Report **W 1.8**
6. **To understand and apply listening and speaking strategies**
   - Extension Activity: Radio Play **LS 1.10**

STEP-BY-STEP TEACHING GUIDE	PACING GUIDE
PRETEACH	
Motivate Students and Provide Background	
Use the Motivation activity (ATE p. 648)	5 min.
Read and discuss author and background features (SE pp. 648, 651; ATE p. 651) [A]	5 min.
Introduce the Concepts	
Introduce the Literary Analysis and Reading Strategy concepts (SE/ATE p. 649) [A]	15 min.
Pronounce the vocabulary words and read their definitions (SE p. 649)	5 min.
TEACH	
Monitor Comprehension	
Informally monitor comprehension by circulating while students read independently or in groups [A]	15 min.
Monitor students' comprehension with the Reading Check notes (SE/ATE pp. 651, 653)	as students read
Develop vocabulary with Vocabulary notes (SE pp. 651, 652, 653, 654; ATE p. 653)	as students read
Develop Understanding	
Develop students' understanding of the Gothic tradition with the Literary Analysis annotations (SE/ATE p. 652) [A]	5 min.
Develop students' ability to predict with the Reading Strategy annotations (SE/ATE p. 652)	5 min.
ASSESS	
Assess Mastery	
Assess students' mastery of the Reading Strategy and Literary Analysis by having them answer the Review and Assess questions (SE/ATE p. 655)	15 min.
Use one or more of the print and media Assessment Resources (ATE p. 657) [A]	up to 45 min.
EXTEND	
Apply Understanding	
Have students complete the Vocabulary Development Lesson and the Grammar and Style Lesson (SE p. 656) [A]	20 min.
Apply students' ability to organize details using the Writing Lesson (SE/ATE p. 657) [A]	45 min.
Apply students' understanding of the selection using one or more of the Extension Activities (SE p. 657)	20–90 min.

ACCELERATED INSTRUCTION:
Use the strategies and activities identified with an [A].

UNIVERSAL ACCESS
● = Below-Level Students
▲ = On-Level Students
■ = Above-Level Students

Time and Resource Manager

Reading Level: Challenging
Average Number of Instructional Days: 4

RESOURCES		
PRINT	**TRANSPARENCIES**	**TECHNOLOGY**
• **Beyond Literature,** Cross-Curricular Connection: Science, p. 30 ▲ ■		• **Interest Grabber Video,** Tape 4 ● ▲ ■
• **Selection Support Workbook:** ● ▲ ■ Literary Analysis, p. 140 Reading Strategy, p. 139 Build Vocabulary, p. 137	• **Literary Analysis and Reading Transparencies,** pp. 59 and 60 ● ▲ ■	
		• **Listening to Literature** ● ▲ ■ Audiocassettes, Side 16 Audio CDs, CD 9
• **Literary Analysis for Enrichment** ■	• **Fine Art Transparencies, Volume 2,** Art Transparency 3	
• **Formal Assessment:** Selection Test, pp. 144–146 ● ▲ ■ • **Open Book Test,** pp. 88–90 ● ▲ ■ • **Performance Assessment and Portfolio Management,** p. 20 ● ▲ ■ • PRENTICE HALL ASSESSMENT SYSTEM ● ▲ ■	• PRENTICE HALL ASSESSMENT SYSTEM ● ▲ ■ Skills Practice Answers and Explanations on Transparencies	• **Test Bank Software** ● ▲ ■ • **Got It! Assessment Videotapes,** Tape 3 ● ▲
• **Selection Support Workbook:** ● ▲ ■ Grammar and Style, p. 138 • **Writing and Grammar,** Diamond Level ● ▲ ■ • **Extension Activities,** p. 30 ● ▲ ■	• **Daily Language Practice Transparencies** ● ▲ • **Writing Models and Graphic Organizers on Transparencies,** pp. 85–92 ● ▲ ■	• **Writing and Grammar iText CD-ROM** ● ▲ ■ ***Take It to the Net*** www.phschool.com

BLOCK SCHEDULING: Use one 90-minute class period to preteach the selection and have students read it. Use a second 90-minute class period to assess students' mastery of skills and have them complete one of the Extension Activities.

PRETEACH

Step-by-Step Teaching Guide for pp. 648–649

Motivation

Elicit from the class examples of urban myths, tales of alien abductions, or ghost stories. (Examples include stories of alligators in the sewers, of a man abducted for his kidneys, and of aliens landing in Roswell, New Mexico.) Then, inform students that two young literary rebels, Percy Bysshe Shelley and Lord Byron, along with nineteen-year-old Mary Shelley and Byron's friend Polidori indulged in the very same sort of brainstorming activity while vacationing in Italy. The result of the session was Mary Shelley's masterpiece, *Frankenstein,* which in one fell swoop helped create both the genre of modern science fiction and the genre of modern horror stories.

Interest Grabber Video

As an alternative, play "'Introduction to *Frankenstein*': Student Response" on Tape 4 to engage student interest.

1 Background

More About the Author

Mary Wollstonecraft Shelley wrote several works with Gothic or science fiction premises. *The Last Man,* a novel set in the future, is narrated by Lionel Verney, who begins life as a young shepherd boy and finds himself after many wanderings as the sole survivor in the ruined grandeur of Rome in the year 2100. Many of her short stories also use Gothic and science-fiction elements; they are published in *The Keepsake.*

Shelley's contribution to literature also includes her efforts to preserve the work of her husband, Percy Bysshe Shelley. After his death, she edited his poems, essays, and letters.

Prepare to Read

1 Introduction to *Frankenstein*

Mary Wollstonecraft Shelley (1797–1851)

Perhaps you have sat around on a rainy day with your friends exchanging thrilling "tales of terror." The classic Gothic novel *Frankenstein* was born from just such an entertainment. One day in 1816, Mary Shelley, her husband (the poet Percy Bysshe Shelley), the poet Lord Byron, and another friend challenged one another to write ghost stories. Mary Shelley's contribution, a horrific tale of the creation of a monster, eventually became the full-length novel *Frankenstein.*

When *Frankenstein* was first published in 1818, it was praised by the novelist Sir Walter Scott as an "extraordinary tale" in which the author revealed "uncommon powers of poetic imagination." Since then, *Frankenstein* has thrilled countless readers and has been interpreted and reinterpreted by generations of filmmakers.

Literary and Political Legacy Writing was in Mary Shelley's blood: Her mother, Mary Wollstonecraft Godwin (who died at Mary's birth), wrote one of the first feminist books ever published, *A Vindication of the Rights of Woman* (1792). Her father, William Godwin, was a leading reformer, author, and political philosopher who attracted a following of gifted thinkers and disciples. As a child, Mary Shelley knew some of the most famous writers of the day, including the poet Samuel Taylor Coleridge and the essayist Charles Lamb.

Exile From Her Father's House Four years after his wife's death, Godwin married a widow, Mary Jane Clairmont, whom his daughter grew to resent bitterly. Although Mary Shelley adored her father, it was agreed that to ease the situation in the tense household, the girl, now fourteen would go to live in Dundee, Scotland, in the home of William Baxter, her father's friend. After two years in Scotland, she returned to her father's home in London.

Love and Loss Upon her return, Mary Shelley (then still named Godwin) met her future husband, Percy Bysshe Shelley. Shelley was a radical young poet who had become William Godwin's admirer after reading his book *Political Justice.* Mary Godwin, only sixteen, fell in love with her father's follower. The two ran away together to the continent and later married.

Eventually, the couple settled in Italy, where they lived blissfully for an all-too-short time. (Their great friend, Lord Byron, also lived in Italy at the time.) Within a few years, the Shelleys suffered the death of two of their children. Then, tragedy struck again. In 1822, only eight years after Mary Shelley had first met him, Percy Shelley drowned, leaving the twenty-four-year-old Mary and their two-year-old son penniless.

A Career of Her Own After Percy's death, Mary returned to England, where she continued writing to support herself and her son. She produced other novels, including: *Valperga* (1823) and *The Fortunes of Perkin Warbeck* (1830), which are historical works; *The Last Man* (1826), a tale of a great plague that destroys the human race; the autobiographical *Lodore* (1835); and *Falkner* (1837), a mystery tale. *The Last Man* is believed by many to be her best work, although she is usually remembered for *Frankenstein.*

A Lasting Legacy At the age of forty-eight, Mary Shelley became an invalid. She died six years later of a brain tumor. It is ironic that Shelley, author of a work warning of the dangers of technology, died in the opening year of The Great Exhibition, a fair celebrating technological progress. In *Frankenstein,* Shelley dramatically questioned the cost of technology to the human soul—a theme writers continue to explore today.

TEACHING RESOURCES

The following resources can be used to enrich or extend the instruction for pp. 648–649.

Motivation

Interest Grabber Video, Tape 4

Background

Beyond Literature, p. 301

Take It to the Net

Visit www.phschool.com for background and hotlinks for the selections.

Literary Analysis

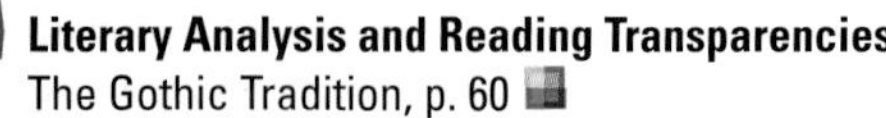

Literary Analysis and Reading Transparencies, The Gothic Tradition, p. 60

Reading

Selection Support: Reading Strategy, p. 139; Build Vocabulary, p. 137

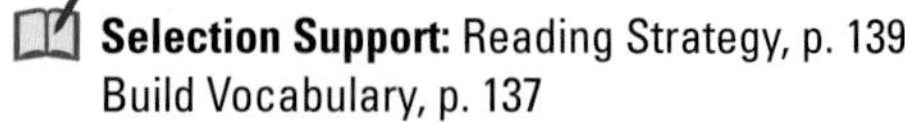

Literary Analysis and Reading Transparencies, Predicting, p. 59

BLOCK SCHEDULING: Resources marked with this symbol provide varied instruction during 90-minute blocks.

Preview

Connecting to the Literature

When Mary Shelley heard speculations about where the science of her time was going, she could not sleep—her mind was filled with visions. With these imaginings, Mary Shelley tapped into deep fears of technology and ensured the success of her novel *Frankenstein.*

❷ Literary Analysis

The Gothic Tradition

The novel *Frankenstein* is a classic example of **Gothic literature,** a form of literature in which events take the reader from the reasoned order of the everyday world into the dark and dreadful world of the supernatural. Gothic literature, popular in the late eighteenth and early nineteenth centuries, is set in dark, mysterious castles, dark towers, eerie monasteries with underground passages, or other places with a disquieting, mysterious atmosphere. As you read, note Gothic characteristics of Shelley's writing.

Connecting Literary Elements

In a Gothic novel, the "spell" of reason is broken as the characters plunge deeper into the supernatural. The popularity of this form in the late 1700s was part of the new **Romantic Movement** in literature. The Romantics rejected the idea that reason could explain everything and pledged their faith in the powers of nature and the imagination. For the Romantics, the imagination, unlike reason, had these traits:

- It was a creative force comparable to that of nature.
- It was the fundamental source of morality and truth, enabling people to sympathize with others and to picture the world.

As you read, notice how Shelley's account of the creative process reflects the high value the Romantics placed on the imagination.

❸ Reading Strategy

Predicting

Involved readers naturally try to **predict,** or make reasoned guesses about, what will happen next in a literary work. As you read, use a chart like the one shown to make, check, and, if necessary, revise predictions.

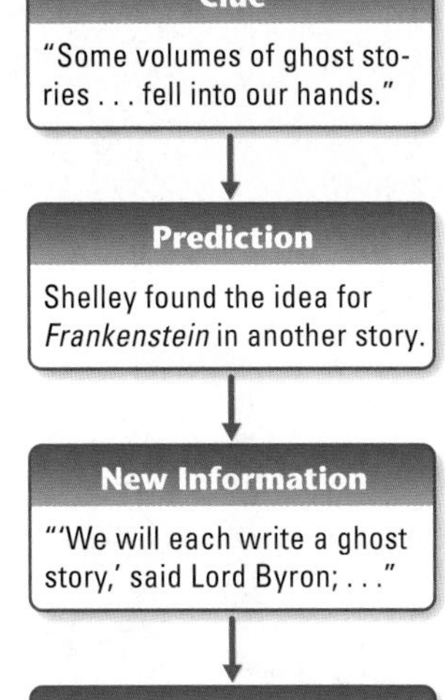

Clue
"Some volumes of ghost stories . . . fell into our hands."
Prediction
Shelley found the idea for *Frankenstein* in another story.
New Information
"'We will each write a ghost story,' said Lord Byron; . . ."
Revision
She found her idea while working on the contest that the stories inspired.

Vocabulary Development

appendage (ə pen′ dij) *n.* something added on (p. 651)

ungenial (un jē′ nyəl) *adj.* disagreeable; characterized by bad weather (p. 651)

acceded (ak sēd′ id) *v.* yielded (to); agreed (p. 652)

platitude (plat′ ə to͞od′) *n.* statement lacking originality (p. 652)

phantasm (fan′ taz′ əm) *n.* supernatural form or shape; ghost; figment of the imagination (p. 653)

incitement (in sīt′ mənt) *n.* act of urging; encouragement (p. 654)

❷ Literary Analysis

The Gothic Tradition

- Explain to students that in this lesson they will concentrate on the Gothic tradition in literature, a genre featuring supernatural events.
- Tell students that Gothic literature is often set in castles, dark passages, towers, and other places with mysterious atmospheres. The name *Gothic* describes the style of architecture used in many European castles, and the literary tradition was given this name for its use of such castles as settings.
- Use the instruction for Connecting Literary Elements to review with students how Mary Shelley's Gothic novel was in keeping with the Romantic rejection of reason in favor of imagination.

❸ Reading Strategy

Predicting

- Remind students that they often predict what will happen in a literary work by paying attention to the progress of the story and the motives of its characters. It is through prediction, for instance, that they might judge an ending dull (it fit predictions too readily) or surprising (it was different from their predictions.)
- Review with students the graphic organizer on p. 649 to show them how to use clues to make predictions about what will happen next.
- Have students practice this skill using the Predicting transparency on p. 59 of **Literary Analysis and Reading Transparencies.**

Vocabulary Development

Pronounce each vocabulary word for students, and read the definitions as a class. Have students identify any words with which they are already familiar.

CUSTOMIZE INSTRUCTION FOR UNIVERSAL ACCESS

For Less Proficient Readers	For English Learners	For Advanced Readers
Explain to students that all texts include details or "clues," that enable readers to predict what will happen next. Model for students how to predict using the graphic organizer on p. 649 and the Predicting transparency on p. 59 of **Literary Analysis and Reading Transparencies.**	Have students read the first three paragraphs of the selection with teacher guidance, repeating any words that give them difficulty. Point out that the title of the selection indicates that Shelly is telling the story of her novel *Frankenstein.* Ask students to predict the outcome of the ghost story contest for Mary Shelley, given this title.	Students should be comfortable with the idea that texts contain information that may enable them to predict what will occur next in the plot. Explain that students should read the "Introduction to *Frankenstein"* as detectives, searching for relevant "clues" that will enable them to predict what will happen next.

E-Teach

Visit E-Teach at www.phschool.com for teachers' essays on how to teach, with questions and answers.

TEACH

Step-by-Step Teaching Guide for pp. 650–654

CUSTOMIZE INSTRUCTION
For Interpersonal Learners

Explain to students that Mary Shelley got her idea for *Frankenstein* from a conversation she overheard. Have students take turns "overhearing" a conversation between two partners. Then, have them discuss ways in which their imaginations filled in details in the overheard conversations.

❶ About the Selection

The nature of a writer's inspiration has been the subject of wonder and speculation since the days of ancient Greece. In this introduction to her novel *Frankenstein,* Mary Shelley offers readers firsthand insight into the process. She reports her emotionally charged reactions to her own idea, as well as the events leading up to her inspiration.

❷ Background

Art

A View of Chamonix and Mt. Blanc
by Julius Schnorr von Carolsfeld

Julius Schnorr von Carolsfeld (1794–1872) was a German Nazarene painter. The Nazarenes were a group of Viennese artists who sought a return to the art of the early Renaissance. They occupied an abandoned monastery in Rome and worked as artist-monks.

Von Carolsfeld painted *A View of Chamonix and Mt. Blanc* in 1824. Beautifully detailed, it is a moonlit view of a famous glacier-covered mountain and a small village in the French Alps. As is common in German Romanticism, the scene takes on a mysterious feeling, in part because of the extreme realism. Use this question for discussion:

What relationship does this Romantic painting suggest between people and nature?
Answer: The human figure and the houses in the valley seem almost insignificant beside the mountains and the trees, suggesting that human beings are a tiny part of a much larger natural universe.

❷

❶ Introduction to Frankenstein

Mary Wollstonecraft Shelley

TEACHING RESOURCES

The following resources can be used to enrich or extend the instruction for pp. 650–654.

Literary Analysis

Selection Support: Literary Analysis, p. 140

Reading

Listening to Literature Audiocassettes, Side 16

Listening to Literature Audio CDs, CD 9

Extension

Fine Art Transparencies, Volume 2,
Art Transparency 3 (Show students the interior of Wells Cathedral as an example of the Gothic style in medieval architecture. This architectural style lent its name to Gothic literature, which is often set in such architectural surroundings.)

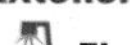

BLOCK SCHEDULING: Resources marked with this symbol provide varied instruction during 90-minute blocks.

A View of Chamonix and Mt. Blanc, Julius Schnorr von Carolsfeld, Austrian Gallery, Vienna

Background

In Greek mythology, Prometheus was one of the Titans—a race of giants who were said to have existed before humans and who engaged the gods in battle. Later myths say Prometheus created the first human beings. During the Romantic Era, Prometheus drew renewed attention. Percy Bysshe Shelley wrote a verse play about Prometheus entitled *Prometheus Unbound.* The complete title of Mary Shelley's novel about a doctor who attempts to create a man is *Frankenstein, or the Modern Prometheus.*

The Publishers of the Standard Novels, in selecting *Frankenstein* for one of their series, expressed a wish that I should furnish them with some account of the origin of the story. I am the more willing to comply, because I shall thus give a general answer to the question, so very frequently asked me: "How I, then a young girl, came to think of, and to dilate upon, so very hideous an idea?" It is true that I am very
4 averse to bringing myself forward in print; but as my account will only appear as an appendage to a former production, and as it will be confined to such topics as have connection with my authorship alone, I can scarcely accuse myself of a personal intrusion. . . .

In the summer of 1816, we[1] visited Switzerland, and became the neighbors of Lord Byron. At first we spent our pleasant hours on the lake or wandering on its shores; and Lord Byron, who was writing the third canto of *Childe Harold,* was the only one among us who put his thoughts upon paper. These, as he brought them successively to us, clothed in all the light and harmony of poetry, seemed to stamp as divine the glories of heaven and earth, whose influences we partook with him.

But it proved a wet, ungenial summer, and incessant rain often confined us for days to the house. Some volumes of ghost stories, translated from the German into French,[2] fell into our hands. There was "The History of the Inconstant Lover,"[3] who, when he thought to clasp the bride to whom he had pledged his vows, found himself in

3 ◀ Critical Viewing Based on the second paragraph of her essay, do you think Shelly might have liked this painting? Why?

appendage (ə pen′ dij) *n.* something added on

ungenial (un jēn′ yəl) *adj.* disagreeable; characterized by bad weather

5 ✓Reading Check What has the author set out to explain?

1. **we** Mary Shelley, her husband Percy Bysshe Shelley, and their two children.
2. **volumes . . . French** *Fantasmagoriana,* or *Collected Stories of Apparitions of Specters, Ghosts, Phantoms, Etc.,* published anonymously in 1812.
3. **"The History . . . Lover"** The true name of the story is "The Dead Fiancée."

3 ▶ Critical Viewing

Answer: Shelley may have found this painting appealing, because it shows the Alps off to great effect, and she has fond memories of her time there.

4 Critical Thinking

Speculate

- Have students read the bracketed passage.
- Encourage them to use their prior background knowledge of the expectations of women at the time to help them understand this passage in the proper historical context.
- Then ask students: Why do you suppose Shelley does not like the idea of bringing herself "forward in print"?
  Answer: Many authors prefer to let their work speak for itself. By commenting on the work, Shelley may fear that it will appear that she is making excuses for her work or showing too great pride in it, rather than letting a reader judge the work for him- or herself. In addition, the society of the time discouraged women from asserting themselves.

5 ✓Reading Check

Answer: The author set out to explain how she wrote such a terrifying novel at such a young age.

CUSTOMIZE INSTRUCTION FOR UNIVERSAL ACCESS

For Special Needs Students	For Gifted/Talented Students
Review with students their understanding of the various elements of the Gothic tradition. Then, have students read the descriptions of ghosts stories in the "Introduction to *Frankenstein*" with teacher guidance. Ask students to focus on aspects of these stories that seem especially Gothic. For students who are struggling with comprehension of Shelley's work, or to stimulate interest, have them listen to the selection on **Listening to Literature CD,** CD 9.	Remind students that Shelley described in detail the scene she imagined, which inspired her to write *Frankenstein.* Encourage students to illustrate one aspect of Shelley's imaginings that is especially "Gothic" in its mood. Review with students their understandings of the Gothic tradition for additional guidance. Have students display their Gothic art to the rest of the class.

6 Literary Analysis

The Gothic Tradition

- Review with students elements of the Gothic tradition, including a dark, mysterious, foreboding atmosphere and a setting that might include ruined castles and towers.
- Then, ask students the Literary Analysis question on p. 652: What elements of the Gothic tradition are incorporated in the image of a shape "lost beneath the shadow of the castle walls"?
  Answer: The setting includes a castle, typical of the Gothic tradition. In addition, the concealment of a figure in the shadows adds the mysterious threatening atmosphere characteristic of the genre.

Monitor Progress Have students identify other Gothic characteristics of the tales described by Shelley.
Possible responses: Students may note that the supernatural elements in the stories, including the ghosts in both stories and the curse on the family in the second, are characteristic of the Gothic genre.

Reteach If students have difficulty answering the question, discuss with them more recent examples of—or examples of contemporary spoofs of—the Gothic, such as Stephen King novels or the television show *The Munsters.*

7 Reading Strategy

Predicting

- Remind students that they can make predictions based on prior knowledge and on clues the work they are reading provides.
- Then, ask them the Reading Strategy question on p. 652: By what means do you think Shelley will find a story idea?
  Possible responses: Students may say that Shelley might draw on the dreariness of her environment to develop a story idea; others may say that she will expand on ideas discussed with her friends. They should note, though, that the course of her account makes it unlikely that Shelley will next report that she was inspired by one of the ghost stories she has already discussed.

the arms of the pale ghost of her whom he had deserted. There was the tale of the sinful founder of his race,[4] whose miserable doom it was to bestow the kiss of death on all the younger sons of his fated house, just when they reached the age of promise. His gigantic, shadowy form, clothed like the ghost in Hamlet, in complete armor but with the beaver[5] up, was seen at midnight, by the moon's fitful beams, to advance slowly along the gloomy avenue. The shape was lost beneath the shadow of the castle walls; but soon a gate swung **6** back, a step was heard, the door of the chamber opened, and he advanced to the couch of the blooming youths, cradled in healthy sleep. Eternal sorrow sat upon his face as he bent down and kissed the foreheads of the boys, who from that hour withered like flowers snapped upon the stalk. I have not seen these stories since then, but their incidents are as fresh in my mind as if I had read them yesterday.

"We will each write a ghost story," said Lord Byron; and his proposition was acceded to. There were four of us.[6] The noble author began a tale, a fragment of which he printed at the end of his poem of Mazeppa. Shelley, more apt to embody ideas and sentiments in the radiance of brilliant imagery, and in the music of the most melodious verse that adorns our language, than to invent the machinery of a story, commenced one founded on the experiences of his early life. Poor Polidori had some terrible idea about a skull-headed lady, who was so punished for peeping through a keyhole—what to see I forget—something very shocking and wrong of course; but when she was reduced to a worse condition than the renowned Tom of Coventry,[7] he did not know what to do with her, and was obliged to despatch her to the tomb of the Capulets,[8] the only place for which she was fitted. The illustrious poets also, annoyed by the platitude of prose, speedily relinquished their uncongenial task.

I busied myself to *think of a story*—a story to rival those which had excited us to this task. One which would speak to the mysterious fears of our nature and awaken thrilling horror—one to make the reader dread to look round, to curdle the blood, and quicken the **7** beatings of the heart. If I did not accomplish these things, my ghost story would be unworthy of its name. I thought and pondered—vainly. I felt that blank incapability of invention which is the greatest misery of authorship, when dull Nothing replies to our anxious invocations. *Have you thought of a story?* I was asked each morning, and each morning I was forced to reply with a mortifying negative. . . .

Many and long were the conversations between Lord Byron and Shelley, to which I was a devout but nearly silent listener. During one of these, various philosophical doctrines were discussed, and among

Literary Analysis
The Gothic Tradition What elements of the Gothic tradition are incorporated in the image of a shape "lost beneath the shadow of the castle walls"?

acceded (ak sēd′ id) *v.* yielded (to); agreed

platitude (plat′ ə to͞od′) *n.* statement lacking originality

Reading Strategy
Predicting By what means do you think Shelley will find a story idea?

4. **the tale . . . race** "Family Portraits."
5. **beaver** hinged piece of armor that covers the face.
6. **four of us** Byron, the two Shelleys, and John William Polidori, Byron's physician.
7. **Tom of Coventry** "Peeping Tom" who, according to legend, was struck blind for looking at Lady Godiva as she rode naked through Coventry.
8. **tomb of the Capulets** the place where Romeo and Juliet died.

ENRICHMENT: Science Connection

Contemporary Research on Life

Mary Shelley describes Dr. Frankenstein as "the pale student of unhallowed arts" whose experiments "mock" the Creator. The uneasy reaction of modern critics to developments such as cloning and genetic engineering shares a good deal with Shelley's reaction to her own vision. When human beings reshape the character of life, their actions challenge our sense that life is a gift. Without this sense, humanity seems dangerously arrogant to some. Defenders of such research emphasize the value of inquiry and of improving the quality of life.

others the nature of the principle of life and whether there was any probability of its ever being discovered and communicated. They talked of the experiments of Dr. Darwin♦ (I speak not of what the Doctor really did or said that he did, but, as more to my purpose, of what was then spoken of as having been done by him), who preserved a piece of vermicelli in a glass case till by some extraordinary means it began to move with voluntary motion. Not thus, after all, would life be given. Perhaps a corpse would be reanimated: galvanism[9] had given token of such things. Perhaps the component parts of a creature might be manufactured, brought together, and endued with vital warmth.

Night waned upon this talk, and even the witching hour had gone by, before we retired to rest. When I placed my head on my pillow, I did not sleep, nor could I be said to think. My imagination, unbidden, possessed and guided me, gifting the successive images that arose in my mind with a vividness far beyond the usual bounds of reverie. I saw—with shut eyes but acute mental vision—I saw the pale student of unhallowed arts
9 kneeling beside the thing he had put together. I saw the hideous phantasm of a man stretched out, and then, on the working of some powerful engine, show signs of life and stir with an uneasy, half vital motion. Frightful must it be, for supremely frightful would be the effect of any human endeavor to mock the stupendous mechanism of the Creator of the world. His success would terrify the artist; he would rush away from his odious handiwork, horror-stricken. He would hope that, left to itself, the slight spark of life which he had communicated would fade; that this thing, which had received such imperfect animation, would subside into dead matter; and he might sleep in the belief that the silence of the grave would quench forever the transient existence of the hideous corpse which he had looked upon as the cradle of life. He sleeps; but he is awakened; he opens his eyes; behold the horrid thing stands at his bedside, opening his curtains, and looking on him with yellow, watery, but speculative eyes.

I opened mine in terror. The idea so possessed my mind, that a thrill of fear ran through me, and I wished to exchange the ghastly image of my fancy for the realities around. I see them still: the very room, the dark parquet,[10] the closed shutters, with the moonlight struggling through, and the sense I had that the glassy lake and white high Alps were beyond. I could not so easily get rid of my hideous phantom: still it haunted me. I must try to think of something else. I recurred to my ghost story—my tiresome unlucky

9. **galvanism** use of electric current to induce twitching in dead muscles.
10. **parquet** (pär kā′) flooring made of wooden pieces arranged in a pattern.

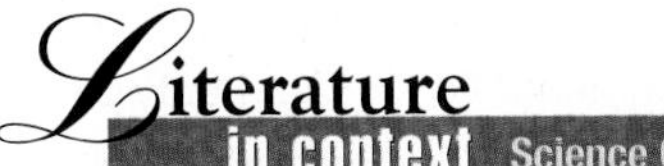

Literature in context Science Connection

8 ♦ ***The Romantics and Science***
As Shelley's Introduction suggests, the Romantics had a two-sided relationship with science. They rejected the eighteenth-century view that the universe could be explained as if it were a giant machine. Fascinated by nature, however, they eagerly read about the new sciences of life. The "Dr. Darwin" referred to by Shelley is the physician, botanist, and poet Erasmus Darwin (1731–1802), grandfather of the Charles Darwin who pioneered the theory of evolution. Erasmus Darwin wrote, "Organic forms with chemic changes strive, / Live but to die, and die but to revive." This sentiment fit well with the Romantic vision of nature as a productive power that is eternally changing, like the larva that have turned into butterflies in the photograph.

phantasm (fan′ taz′ əm) *n.* supernatural form or shape; ghost; figment of the imagination

10  **Reading Check**
That night, what does Mary Shelley imagine?

8 Background

The Romantics and Science

- Erasmus Darwin spent part of his life in Lichfield, England, where he built a botanical garden for which "the general design . . . is to enlist imagination under the banner of science." In 1791, he published a long poem, *The Botanic Garden,* written in heroic couplets in imitation of Pope. In the poem, the goddess of Botany descends to earth and explores various natural phenomena. He also published a book of prose, *Zoonomia,* in which he discusses animal life. His most famous work, perhaps, *The Temple of Nature,* was published after his death. Darwin bases his vision of life on an evolutionary principle similar to the principles of his grandson Charles Darwin.

9 Vocabulary Development

Related Words: *phantasm* and *fantasy*

- Call students' attention to the word *phantasm,* a word that means "supernatural form or shape; figment of the imagination." Explain to students that *phantasm* is related to the word *fantasy.*
- Have students suggest other words and phrases that are similar to *phantasm* or *fantasy.* Possible responses: *phantom, phantasmagoric, fantastic*
- Have students look up any unfamiliar words in a dictionary.

10 Reading Check

Answer: Mary Shelley imagines a pale student scientist kneeling beside the body he has perhaps dug up or stitched together from corpses as well as his terror when it comes to life.

CUSTOMIZE INSTRUCTION FOR UNIVERSAL ACCESS

For English Learners	For Advanced Readers
As students read, have them look up unfamiliar words in the dictionary. Help them identify cases in which context helps their comprehension. Encourage students to rely on context as much as possible as they read further, checking only crucial words in the dictionary.	Have interested students read a segment of Mary Shelley's *Frankenstein.* Then, ask them to prepare book reviews in which they compare *Frankenstein* to Shelley's description of it in her introduction to the work. Ask students to address whether or not Frankenstein's monster is as hideous as Shelley leads readers to believe that he is, and how *Frankenstein* compares with other ghost stories or novels they have read.

ASSESS

Answers for p. 654

Review and Assess

1. Possible responses: Students may say they share Shelley's interest in ghost stories because they like feeling the dread the stories elicit; other students may say that they dislike them because they are unbelievable.
2. **(a)** The bad weather that summer, and the access to other ghost stories, inspired the four to write their own. **(b)** Shelley has trouble inventing a story; Byron and her husband are frustrated writing in prose, while Polidori is not a skilled writer, and his plot is not gripping.
3. **(a)** Shelley's idea for a story comes from a discussion she overhears between Byron and her husband about the possibility of creating artificial life. **(b)** The intensity of Mary Shelley's vision suggests that she finds Dr. Darwin's experiments deeply disturbing for their implications about human power over life.
4. **(a)** The relationship between student and monster is different from that between Creator and humanity because the student does not have complete wisdom about or love for the monster, while the Creator has perfect wisdom about and love for creation. **(b)** The similarity between these relationships might be "supremely frightful," because it suggests that godlike power had been granted to mere human beings; it also suggests the idea that the creator of humanity might be undependable, or even that humanity is alone in the universe.
5. Mary Shelley has a great admiration for her husband's talents, even crediting him for *Frankenstein*'s success. She also seems to be aware of his limitations, as evidenced by her frank assessment of his failure to write a ghost story.
6. Possible response: Students may say that Shelley's dread of science is borne out by inventions such as nuclear weapons and by the possible problems presented by new technologies such as cloning.

ghost story! O! if I could only contrive one which would frighten my reader as I myself had been frightened that night!

Swift as light and as cheering was the idea that broke in upon me. "I have found it! What terrified me will terrify others, and I need only describe the specter which had haunted my midnight pillow." On the morrow I announced that I had *thought of a story*. I began that day with the words, *It was on a dreary night of November*, making only a transcript of the grim terrors of my waking dream.

At first I thought but of a few pages—of a short tale—but Shelley urged me to develop the idea at greater length. I certainly did not owe the suggestion of one incident, nor scarcely of one train of feeling, to my husband, and yet but for his incitement, it would never have taken the form in which it was presented to the world. From this declaration I must except the preface. As far as I can recollect, it was entirely written by him.

incitement (in sit′ mənt) *n.* act of urging; encouragement

And now, once again, I bid my hideous progeny go forth and prosper. I have an affection for it, for it was the offspring of happy days, when death and grief were but words, which found no true echo in my heart. Its several pages speak of many a walk, many a drive, and many a conversation, when I was not alone; and my companion was one who, in this world, I shall never see more. But this is for myself: my readers have nothing to do with these associations.

Review and Assess

Thinking About the Selection

1. **Respond:** Do you share Shelley's interest in ghost stories? Why or why not?
2. (a) **Recall:** What special set of circumstances inspired the four friends to attempt to write ghost stories?
   (b) **Compare and Contrast:** Compare the difficulty Shelley has with the reason her companions give up their efforts.
3. (a) **Recall:** What gives Shelley her idea for a story?
   (b) **Connect:** What does the intensity of her vision suggest about her reaction to Dr. Darwin's experiments?
4. (a) **Compare and Contrast:** Why is the relationship between student and monster in her vision both similar to and different from the relationship between the Creator and humanity?
   (b) **Draw Conclusions:** Why might the similarities of these relationships be "supremely frightful"?
5. **Synthesize:** What does the selection reveal about the relationship between Shelley and her husband?
6. **Make a Judgment:** In your opinion, has later history borne out Shelley's dread of science? Explain.

ASSESSMENT PRACTICE: Reading Comprehension

Critical Reasoning (For more practice, see Test Preparation Workbook, p. 28.)

Many tests require students to evaluate the assumptions on which an author's argument is based. The first step in mastering this skill is to identify assumptions. Use the following sample item to teach students how to identify an implied assumption. Write this text from the selection on the board:

> Frightful it must be, for supremely frightful would be the effect of any human endeavor to mock the stupendous mechanism of the Creator of the world.

The assumption behind this statement is

A the re-creation of life is an imitation of God's work.
B God would punish anyone who attempted to create life.
C it is natural for humans to want to play God.
D humans are frightened by science.

Lead students to recognize that the correct answer is *A*. The statement's logic is not supported by the other choices.

Review and Assess

Literary Analysis

The Gothic Tradition

1. Which characteristics of the **Gothic tradition**—horror, supernatural elements, medieval elements—do the ghost stories described by Shelley in her third paragraph share? List examples in a chart like the one shown.

Gothic Characteristic	Example in Shelley

2. In which passage does Shelley describe a connection between the world of reason and a terrifying supernatural world?
3. Explain why Shelley's idea for *Frankenstein* fits the Gothic tradition.
4. Compare the ingredients of Gothic tales with those used in current horror movies and books.

Connecting Literary Elements

5. (a) How does Shelley respond to the discussion of Darwin's experiments? (b) How does her experience echo the idea of the **Romantic imagination**—a power similar to nature's creative force?
6. (a) Contrast Shelley's first efforts to find an idea with her final inspiration. (b) How does this contrast reflect the Romantic contrast between reason and imagination?
7. What "truth" does Shelley's imagined vision suggest about the dangerous possibilities of science?

Reading Strategy

Predicting

8. Explain whether you were able to **predict** how Shelley would be affected by the discussion of Darwin's experiments.
9. Based on clues in the Introduction, predict the theme of *Frankenstein*. Explain your reasoning.

Extend Understanding

10. **Science Connection:** What scientific experiments today are comparable to Darwin's? Explain, indicating whether you find such experiments as horrifying as Shelley found Darwin's to be.

Quick Review

Literature in the **Gothic tradition** makes extensive use of medieval and supernatural elements, often depicting horrifying events set in gloomy castles.

In the **Romantic** view, the **imagination** is a creative force comparable to the force of nature. It functions independently of reason.

To **predict,** use clues in the text to make informed guesses about what will happen next.

Take It to the Net

www.phschool.com

Take the interactive self-test online to check your understanding of the selection.

Answers for p. 655

Review and Assess

1. Both stories feature supernatural elements: Both feature ghosts, one of which delivers a supernatural kiss of death.
2. Possible response: Shelley's description of the scientist's discovery of the creature he animated connects the world of reason—the scientific work of the student, which resembles Dr. Darwin's work—and a world of nightmarish horror.
3. Because *Frankenstein* creates effects of horror by taking readers from the world of reason and science to the world of monsters and terror, it is considered a Gothic tale.
4. Possible response: Students may observe that science-fiction elements, rather than ghosts and medieval ruins, figure prominently in modern tales of horror.
5. **(a)** Shelley responds to the discussion by vividly fantasizing about the implications of the experiments and, eventually, by writing *Frankenstein.* **(b)** Shelley describes herself as "possessed" by her own imagination when she has her vision. Just as nature produces beings freely out of itself, without deliberation or judgment, Shelley's imagination produces a story without her conscious, rational involvement.
6. **(a)** Shelley's initial efforts to find an idea were fruitless. Her inspiration did not involve conscious effort yet gave her a fertile idea. **(b)** This contrast reflects the Romantic contrast between reason and the imagination, because Shelley was only able to arrive at the idea for her story and so create something new when her imagination took over from her powers of reasoning.
7. Possible response: Students may say that science, according to Shelley, may lead to a terrifying unsettling of humanity's place in creation, with humanity attempting to play the role of God.
8. Possible response: Students should explain why they were not able to predict the effect of the discussion on Shelley.

continued

Answers continued

9. Possible response: Students may say that the theme is probably the damage done when humanity tries to play God.
10. Possible response: Students may mention genetic engineering. They should explain whether they find such technology horrifying, and why or why not.

ENRICHMENT: Further Reading

Other Works by Mary Shelley

Valperga

Lodore

Falkner

The Last Man

Take It to the Net

Visit www.phschool.com for more information on Mary Shelley.

EXTEND

Answers for p. 656

❶ Vocabulary Development

Related Words: *phantasm* and *fantasy*

1. *Phantom* means "a ghost"; like a *fantasy*, a phantom is an appearance without substance.
2. *Phantasmagoric* means "dreamlike or of a rapidly changing sequence of appearances"; like a *fantasy*, it refers to appearances without reality.

Spelling Strategy

1. concede
2. proceed
3. precede

Concept Development: Synonyms

1. c
2. c
3. c
4. b
5. b
6. c

❷ Grammar and Style

1. (These,) as he brought them successively to us, clothed in all the light . . . of poetry, . . .
2. . . . he advanced to the couch of (the blooming youths,) cradled in healthy sleep.
3. (His gigantic, shadowy form,) clothed like the ghost in *Hamlet*, in complete armor. . . .
4. (The illustrious poets) also, annoyed by the platitude of prose, . . .
5. He would hope that, left to itself, (the slight spark of light) which he had communicated would fade; . . .

Writing Application

Possible response: In Shelley's dream she saw an inventor beholding his monstrous creation. She saw the inventor, terrified by his own creation, bend low to the monster, stretched out like a sleeping giant.

Integrate Language Skills

❶ Vocabulary Development Lesson

Related Words: *phantasm* and *fantasy*

Shelley uses the word *phantasm*, meaning "supernatural form or shape" or "figment of the imagination," to describe her monster. *Phantasm* and the more familiar word *fantasy* are related. Based on this connection, define the following terms, explaining how each relates to the word *fantasy*.

1. phantom
2. phantasmagoric

Spelling Strategy

In most words ending with the sound *seed*, the sound is spelled *cede*, as in *accede*. Three English words end in *ceed: exceed, proceed,* and *succeed*. In your notebook, fill in the letters that spell the *seed* sound in the following words.

1. con____ 2. pro____ 3. pre____

Concept Development: Synonyms

For each numbered word, write the letter of the word that is closest to it in meaning.

1. appendage: (a) offspring, (b) fragment, (c) addition
2. ungenial: (a) friendly, (b) cruel, (c) disagreeable
3. acceded: (a) defied, (b) broken, (c) agreed
4. platitude: (a) innovation, (b) cliché, (c) statement
5. phantasm: (a) reality, (b) illusion, (c) creation
6. incitement: (a) deterrent, (b) apparition, (c) motivation

❷ Grammar and Style Lesson

Past Participial Phrases

Shelley frequently uses past participial phrases. A **past participial phrase** includes a past participle—a verbal form usually ending in *-ed*—plus its modifiers and complements. The phrase functions as an adjective and modifies a noun or pronoun.

In this example, the underlined past participial phrase modifies *stories*:

> Some volumes of ghost stories, translated from the German into French, fell into our hands.

By using past participial phrases, writers can convey much information in a single sentence. Instead of writing a series of short sentences, they can combine ideas in a single sentence to vary sentence length.

Practice Identify the participial phrase in each passage. Then, indicate the word it modifies.

1. These, as he brought them successively to us, clothed in all the light . . . of poetry, . . .
2. . . . he advanced to the couch of the blooming youths, cradled in healthy sleep.
3. His gigantic, shadowy form, clothed like the ghost in *Hamlet*, in complete armor. . . .
4. The illustrious poets also, annoyed by the platitude of prose, . . .
5. He would hope that, left to itself, the slight spark of life which he had communicated would fade; . . .

Writing Application Using at least two past participial phrases, describe Shelley's vision.

WG Prentice Hall Writing and Grammar Connection: Chapter 19, Section 2

TEACHING RESOURCES

The following resources can be used to enrich or extend the instruction for pp. 656–657.

Vocabulary

- **Selection Support:** Build Vocabulary, p. 137
- **Vocabulary and Spelling Practice Book** (Use this booklet for skills enrichment.)

Grammar

- **Selection Support:** Grammar and Style, p. 138
- **Writing and Grammar,** Diamond Level, p. 446
- **Daily Language Practice Transparencies** ■

Writing

- **Writing and Grammar,** Diamond Level, p. 178 ■
- **Writing and Grammar iText CD-ROM**
- **Writing Models and Graphic Organizers on Transparencies,** pp. 85–92

■ **BLOCK SCHEDULING:** Resources marked with this symbol provide varied instruction during 90-minute blocks.

❸ Writing Lesson

Essay Comparing and Contrasting Impressions of a Work

You've probably seen the story of Dr. Frankenstein and his monster depicted in movies. Write an essay in which you compare the impressions you had of *Frankenstein* before you read Shelley's Introduction with your impressions afterwards.

Prewriting To gather and organize details, use a chart like the one shown. First, list points you want to compare. Then, note your impressions of each before and after reading Shelley's Introduction.

Model: Organizing Details

Impressions: The Monster	
Before Reading	**After Reading**
Scary and strong, but gentle inside	

Drafting Decide how to present the details in your chart. One possibility is to describe all of your impressions before reading and then to describe all of your impressions after reading. Another approach is to use one paragraph to compare and contrast your impressions of the monster and another to compare and contrast your impressions of Dr. Frankenstein.

Revising Reread the body of your essay to make sure its organization is logical. Then, be sure your closing paragraph summarizes how your impressions did or did not change.

WG *Prentice Hall Writing and Grammar Connection: Chapter 9, Section 3*

❹ Extension Activities

Listening and Speaking Stories such as *Frankenstein* were once broadcast on radio. In a group, re-create a horror story as a **radio play.**

1. Collaborate on a script.
2. Select effective background music and sound effects.
3. Choose actors and rehearse the play.

Tape-record your performance, and play it for the class. **[Group Activity]**

Research and Technology Mary Shelley was horrified at the idea of a scientist reconstituting life. Today, animals are cloned in laboratories. Prepare a **science report** on the process of cloning. Add graphics to your word-processed report to help explain the process.

www.phschool.com

Go online for an additional research activity using the Internet.

Lesson Support for p. 657

❸ Writing Lesson

- Remind students that comparing and contrasting impressions of a work requires providing details that show similarities and differences.
- Use the Writing Lesson to guide students in preparing their comparing and contrasting impressions of *Frankenstein* before they read Shelley's Introduction with their impressions afterwards.
- Review the model with students to aid them in organizing details in their essays.
- Use the Exposition: Comparison-and-Contrast Essay rubric in **Performance Assessment and Portfolio Management,** p. 20, to evaluate students' essays.

❹ Research and Technology

- Read the Research and Technology assignment together as a class.
- Ask students to write down what they know of cloning and discuss it with a partner.
- Then, have students use the Internet or resources in the school library to prepare a science report on the process of cloning.
- Have students present their reports to their classmates.

CUSTOMIZE INSTRUCTION For Universal Access

To address different learning styles, use the activities suggested in the **Extension Activities** booklet, p. 30.

- For Visual/Spatial Learners, use Activity 5.
- For Interpersonal Learners, use Activity 6.
- For Intrapersonal Learners, use Activity 7.

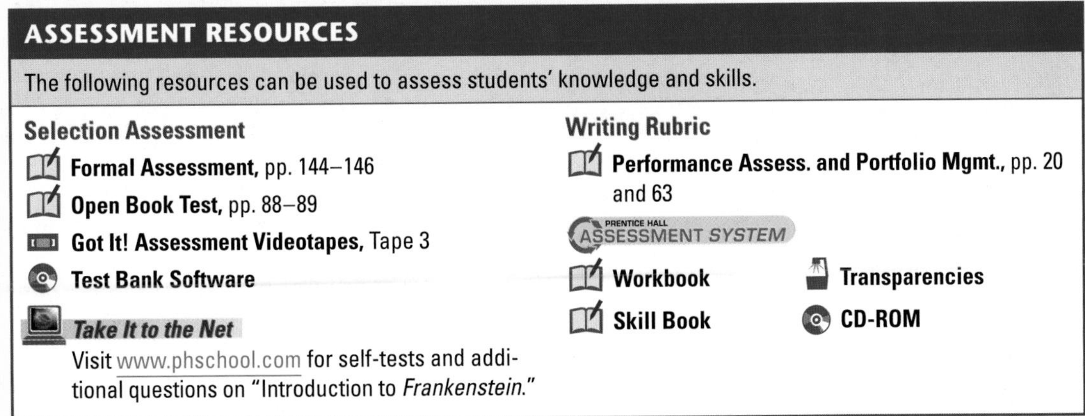

ASSESSMENT RESOURCES

The following resources can be used to assess students' knowledge and skills.

Selection Assessment

- **Formal Assessment,** pp. 144–146
- **Open Book Test,** pp. 88–89
- **Got It! Assessment Videotapes,** Tape 3
- **Test Bank Software**

Take It to the Net

Visit www.phschool.com for self-tests and additional questions on "Introduction to *Frankenstein*."

Writing Rubric

- **Performance Assess. and Portfolio Mgmt.,** pp. 20 and 63

PRENTICE HALL ASSESSMENT SYSTEM

- **Workbook**
- **Skill Book**
- **Transparencies**
- **CD-ROM**

Objectives

1. To understand the connection between fantasy and reality in the Romantic Movement and its progression into other cultures and countries
2. To understand how the artists' use of fantasy in fictional works delicately crosses the line into reality to accentuate the story and keep the reader in suspense

Connections

Edgar Allan Poe often took a realistic setting and "haunted it, " endowing it with spirits of the past, with characters weighed down by deep secrets and missions, and with supernatural effects. He sometimes also blurred the line between reality and fantasy as characters or plot slowly but inexorably crossed over the borders of reality or, as in "The Oval Portrait," the borders of life itself. Have students read "The Oval Portrait" and try to identify where the author crosses from reality to fantasy.

Fantasy and Reality

- The reality of everyday people became commonplace in the writings of the Romantic era. Prior to this time, writers focused on imaginary settings and lofty figures of which one could only dream. This revelation that the ordinary could be extraordinary led to the exploration of mystery and the supernatural.
- Ask students to name tales of the supernatural with which they are familiar. (*Carrie*, by Stephen King; "The Monkey's Paw," by W. W. Jacobs; and "The Tell-Tale Heart," by Edgar Allan Poe may come to mind.) Then, ask students why these stories remain so popular. Possible response: Each new generation of readers still values the thrills these stories provide.
- Point out that because these stories are based in reality with real settings and characters, the supernatural or fantastic occurrences are all the more thrilling.
- Inform students that the story they are about to read was written by Edgar Allan Poe, a master of blurring the lines between the actual and the fantastic.

CONNECTIONS

Literature Around the World

Fantasy and Reality

A Gothic Explosion Although the Romantic Movement led writers to focus on the experience of the common people, it also inspired them to explore more fantastic realms. The popularity of Gothic stories like Mary Shelley's *Frankenstein* reached beyond England into other cultures and countries. One of the masters of the Gothic tradition is the American writer Edgar Allan Poe.

The Oval Portrait

EDGAR ALLAN POE

The chateau into which my valet had ventured to make forcible entrance, rather than permit me, in my desperately wounded condition, to pass a night in the open air, was one of those piles of commingled gloom and grandeur which have so long frowned among the Apennines,[1] not less in fact than in the fancy of Mrs. Radcliffe.[2] To all appearance it had been temporarily and very lately abandoned. We established ourselves in one of the smallest and least sumptuously furnished apartments. It lay in a remote turret of the building. Its decorations were rich, yet tattered and antique. Its walls were hung with tapestry and bedecked with manifold and multiform armorial trophies, together with an unusually great number of very spirited modern paintings in frames of rich golden arabesque.[3] In these paintings, which depended from the walls not only in their main surfaces, but in very many nooks which the bizarre architecture of the chateau rendered necessary—in these paintings my incipient delirium, perhaps, had caused me to take deep interest; so that I bade Pedro to close the heavy shutters of the room—since it was already night—to light the tongues of a tall candelabrum which stood by the head of my bed—and to throw open far and wide the fringed curtains of black velvet which enveloped the bed itself. I wished all this done that I might resign myself, if not to sleep, at least alternately to the contemplation of these pictures, and the perusal of a small volume which had been found upon the pillow, and which purported to criticize and describe them.

Long—long I read—and devoutly, devotedly I gazed. Rapidly and gloriously the hours flew by, and the deep midnight came. The position of the candelabrum displeased me, and outreaching my hand with

Thematic Connection
What details make the setting seem fantastic?

1. **Appennines** (ap′ ə nīnz) mountain range located in Italy.
2. **Mrs. Radcliffe** Ann Radcliffe (1764–1823), English novelist.
3. **arabesque** (ar′ ə besk′) complex and elaborate design.

difficulty, rather than disturb my slumbering valet, I placed it so as to throw its rays more fully upon the book.

But the action produced an effect altogether unanticipated. The rays of the numerous candles (for there were many) now fell within a niche of the room which had hitherto been thrown into deep shade by one of the bed-posts. I thus saw in vivid light a picture all unnoticed before. It was the portrait of a young girl just ripening into womanhood. I glanced at the painting hurriedly, and then closed my eyes. Why I did this was not at first apparent even to my own perception. But while my lids remained thus shut, I ran over in mind my reason for so shutting them. It was an impulsive movement to gain time for thought—to make sure that my vision had not deceived me—to calm and subdue my fancy for a more sober and more certain gaze. In a very few moments I again looked fixedly at the painting.

Elizabeth Beale Bordley, Gilbert Stuart, Courtesy of the Museum of American Art of the Pennsylvania Academy of the Fine Arts, Philadelphia, Bequest of Elizabeth Mifflin

▲ Critical Viewing
Does this portrait, like the one in the story, capture "Life" itself? Explain. **[Connect]**

That I now saw aright I could not and would not doubt; for the first flashing of the candles upon that canvas had seemed to dissipate the dreamy stupor which was stealing over my senses, and to startle me at once into waking life.

The portrait, I have already said, was that of a young girl. It was a mere head and shoulders, done in what is technically termed a vignette[4] manner; much in the style of the favorite heads of Sully.[5] The arms, the bosom and even the ends of the radiant hair, melted imperceptibly into the vague yet deep shadow which formed the background of the whole. The frame was oval, richly gilded and filigreed in *Moresque*.[6] As a thing of art nothing could be more admirable than the painting itself. But it could have been neither the execution of the work, nor the immortal beauty of the countenance, which had so suddenly and so vehemently moved me. Least of all, could it have been that my fancy, shaken from its half slumber, had mistaken the head for that of a living person. I saw at once that the peculiarities of the design, of the *vignetting*, and of the frame, must have instantly dispelled such idea—must have prevented even its momentary entertainment. Thinking earnestly upon these points, I remained, for an hour perhaps, half sitting, half reclining, with my vision riveted upon the portrait. At length, satisfied with the true secret of its effect, I fell back within the bed. I had found the spell of the picture in an absolute *life-likeliness* of expression, which at first startled, finally confounded, subdued and appalled me. With deep and reverent awe I replaced the candelabrum in its former position. The cause of my deep agitation being thus shut from view, I sought eagerly the volume which discussed the paintings and their histories. Turning to the number which designated the oval portrait, I there read the vague and quaint words which follow:

✓ Reading Check
What does the narrator find so disturbing about the portrait?

4. ***vignette*** (vin yet′) *n.* picture or photograph with no definite border.
5. **Sully** Thomas Sully (1783–1872), American painter born in England.
6. ***Moresque*** (mô resk′) decoration characterized by intricate tracery and bright colors.

Background

The Double

- Explain to students that the theme of the double is a major one in literature around the world.
- Doubles may take the form of portraits or statues, or actual people who are identical to another character. Works by the Russian writer Fyodor Dostoevsky and Nikolai Gogol directly address this theme, as do numerous science-fiction movies and television programs.
- A confrontation with a double calls into question the very nature of a person's identity, Psychoanalyst Otto Rank argued that the double in stories, myths, and dreams represents the individual's death.
  Ask students the following question:
  In what sense is art a double of life?
  Possible response: Art imitates life, but unlike life, what it represents does not change.

Thematic Connection

Answer: Details such as "rich, yet tattered" antiques and tapestries amidst paintings in elaborately designed frames in the small apartment in the turret of the building, far from others, make the setting seem fantastic.

▶Critical Viewing

Possible responses: Yes, the woman in the portrait appears lifelike because of her natural pose and the gentle colors that mimic reality; no, the woman seems too "posed" and two-dimensional to be lifelike.

Reading Check

Answer: The narrator finds that the portrait is so lifelike and vivid that it seems as if the woman is in the room with him.

ENRICHMENT: Art

***Elizabeth Beale Bordley,* Gilbert Stuart**

The American painter Gilbert Stuart (1755–1828), who painted the portrait on p. 659, spent much of his early career in London, England, where he was influenced by such master portraitists as Joshua Reynolds and Thomas Gainsborough. He moved back to the United States in 1793 and painted luminaries such as George Washington. Stuart painted Washington several times, but perhaps his most famous portrait of him is the Athenaeum Portrait, which hangs in the Boston Museum of Fine Arts.

Use this question for discussion:

Does the portrait on p. 659 show life, death, or death-in-life? **Possible response:** Because her pose is stiff, while her coloring is lifelike, the portrait might be said to present what Poe calls death-in-life.

Answers

Connections to Literature Around the World

1. Students should mention that Shelley's *Frankenstein* and Poe's tale involve ambitious "creators" searching for perfection.
2. **(a)** Possible response: Students may note that each poet tries to capture some aspect of life, and that Burn's detailed descriptions of the minutiae of life come close to "freezing" Life. In all cases, though, the poet's figurative language and generalizations add more to the picture than "Life itself." **(b)** Possible response: No, the poems themselves are not uncanny, but they would become so if the reader experienced something in life directly resembling what they describe.

"She was a maiden of rarest beauty, and not more lovely than full of glee. And evil was the hour when she saw, and loved, and wedded the painter. He, passionate, studious, austere, and having already a bride in his Art; she a maiden of rarest beauty, and not more lovely than full of glee: all light and smiles, and frolicksome as the young fawn: loving and cherishing all things: hating only the Art which was her rival: dreading only the pallet and brushes and other untoward instruments which deprived her of the countenance of her lover. It was thus a terrible thing for this lady to hear the painter speak of his desire to portray even his young bride. But she was humble and obedient, and sat meekly for many weeks in the dark high turret-chamber where the light dripped upon the pale canvas only from overhead. But he, the painter, took glory in his work, which went on from hour to hour and from day to day. And he was a passionate, and wild and moody man, who became lost in reveries; so that he would not see that the light which fell so ghastlily in that lone turret withered the health and the spirits of his bride, who pined visibly to all but him. Yet she smiled on and still on, uncomplainingly, because she saw that the painter, (who had high renown), took a fervid and burning pleasure in his task, and wrought day and night to depict her who so loved him, yet who grew daily more dispirited and weak. And in sooth some who beheld the portrait spoke of its resemblance in low words, as of a mighty marvel, and a proof not less of the power of the painter than of his deep love for her whom he depicted so surpassingly well. But at length, as the labor drew nearer to its conclusion, there were admitted none into the turret; for the painter had grown wild with the ardor of his work, and turned his eyes from the canvas rarely, even to regard the countenance of his wife. And he *would* not see that the tints which he spread upon the canvas were drawn from the cheeks of her who sat beside him. And when many weeks had passed, and but little remained to do, save one brush upon the mouth and one tint upon the eye, the spirit of the lady again flickered up as the flame within the socket of the lamp. And then the brush was given, and then the tint was placed; and, for one moment, the painter stood entranced before the work which he had wrought; but in the next, while he yet gazed, he grew tremulous and very pallid, and aghast, and crying with a loud voice, 'This is indeed *Life* itself!' turned suddenly to regard his beloved:—*She was dead!*"

Edgar Allan Poe

(1809–1849)

Poe's real-life troubles must have inspired his dark imaginings. An orphan before he was three years old, he was taken in by the Allans, a prosperous family in Richmond, Virginia. Poe quarreled with his foster father, John Allan, and was eventually disowned.

Poe's writing career was a mixture of literary success and financial failure. He won recognition as a poet, critic, and short-story writer while earning a meager living as a magazine editor in Richmond, Philadelphia, and New York City.

Connecting Literature Around the World

1. In what way do both this tale and Shelley's *Frankenstein* address the theme of excessive ambition?
2. (a) Do any of the poems in this section try to "capture" life as the artist in Poe's story does? Explain. (b) Might any of the poems be as disturbing to a reader as the "life-like" portrait is to Poe's narrator? Explain.

ENRICHMENT: Further Reading

Other Works by the Author

"The Masque of the Red Death"
"The Black Cat"
Eight Tales of Terror
"The Tell-Tale Heart" and Other Writings

PART 2

Focus on Literary Forms: Lyric Poetry

The Wanderer over the Sea of Clouds, Caspar David Friedrich, Kunsthalle, Hamburg

Lyric poems express a writer's thoughts and feelings. The ancient Greeks, who set this type of poem to lyre music, gave the lyric its name. Romantic poets of the nineteenth century devoted themselves to lyric poetry, "singing" about nature and society's injustices.

Selection Planning Guide

The selections in this section present the lyric poetry of the English Romantic poets Wordsworth, Coleridge, Byron, Shelley, and Keats. In their works, these poets examine humanity's relationship with nature, explore realms of the imagination and of feeling, and contemplate the notions of freedom, beauty, truth, reality, fame, and justice.

Background

Art

The Wanderer Over the Sea of Clouds, 1818, by Caspar David Friedrich

This dramatic oil-on-canvas painting of a man standing alone to ponder a fog-covered landscape is emblematic of the Romantic writer contemplating his or her relationship with nature.

Although Caspar David Friedrich was German-born, he studied at the Royal Academy in Copenhagen, Denmark. Many of his paintings, like *The Wanderer,* were landscapes or seascapes capturing human isolation and suggesting people's ultimate impotence against nature's overwhelming force.

Use these questions for discussion:

1. What elements of the painting suggest the Romantics' several views of nature?
   Possible responses: The light and beauty of the landscape suggest the Romantics' optimistic views about nature, while the dark jagged rocks suggest the Romantics' sense of nature's dangerous powers.
2. How does the central figure's posture reflect Romantic attitudes toward nature and society?
   Possible responses: The central figure has his back to the viewer —the human world—and faces or embraces the landscape. In much the same way, Romantics turned away from society and toward the natural world.

CUSTOMIZE INSTRUCTION FOR UNIVERSAL ACCESS

When assigning the selections in this part, keep in mind these factors:

Poetry of William Wordsworth
- Complex syntax may challenge some readers

Poetry of Samuel Taylor Coleridge
- Archaic and poetic words may pose difficulties for students

Poetry of George Gordon, Lord Byron
- Highly musical poetry
- Students will enjoy the satiric humor of "Don Juan"

Poetry of Percy Bysshe Shelley
- Most students will find the political undercurrents compelling
- Students may benefit by reading the odes in sentences

Poetry of John Keats
- Short sonnets that are accessible
- The imagery in the odes will appeal to most students

"The Lorelei"
- Story-like lyric is easy to read and understand

Haiku
- Very short, accessible poems

Poetry of William Wordsworth

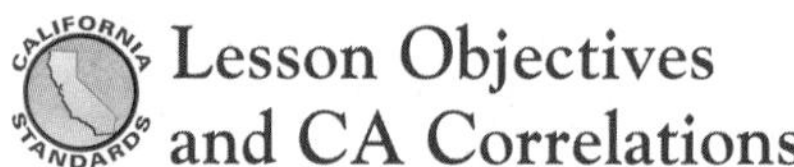

Lesson Objectives and CA Correlations

1. **To analyze and respond to literary elements**
   - Literary Analysis: Romanticism and the Lyric **R 3.1**
   - Comparing Literary Works **R 3.3**
2. **To read, comprehend, analyze, and critique a poem**
   - Reading Strategy: Using Literary Context **R 3.7**
   - Reading Check Questions
   - Review and Assess Questions
   - Assessment Practice (ATE)
3. **To develop word analysis skills, fluency, and systematic vocabulary**
   - Vocabulary Development Lesson: Word Analysis: Forms of *anatomize* **R 1.2**
4. **To understand and apply written and oral language conventions**
   - Spelling Strategy **LC 1.2**
   - Grammar and Style Lesson: Present Participial Phrases **LC 1.1**
5. **To understand and apply appropriate writing and research strategies**
   - Writing Lesson: Response to Criticism **W 1.3**
   - Extension Activity: Cultural Analysis **W 1.6**
6. **To understand and apply listening and speaking strategies**
   - Extension Activity: Photo Essay Presentation **LS 1.8, 1.10**

STEP-BY-STEP TEACHING GUIDE	PACING GUIDE
PRETEACH	
Motivate Students and Provide Background	
Use the Motivation activity (ATE p. 662)	5 min.
Read and discuss author and background features (SE pp. 662, 664, 665, 667, 672; ATE pp. 662, 664, 665, 669) [A]	10 min.
Introduce the Concepts	
Introduce the Literary Analysis and Reading Strategy concepts (SE/ATE p. 663) [A]	15 min.
Pronounce the vocabulary words and read their definitions (SE p. 663)	5 min.
TEACH	
Monitor Comprehension	
Informally monitor comprehension by circulating while students read independently or in groups [A]	35 min.
Monitor students' comprehension with the Reading Check notes (SE/ATE pp. 667, 669, 673, 675)	as students read
Develop vocabulary with Vocabulary notes (SE pp. 669, 672, 673, 674, 675, 676; ATE p. 674)	as students read
Develop Understanding	
Develop students' understanding of romanticism and the lyric with the Literary Analysis annotations (SE/ATE pp. 667, 668, 671, 672) [A]	5 min.
Develop students' understanding of literary context with the Reading Strategy annotations (SE/ATE pp. 668, 670)	5 min.
ASSESS	
Assess Mastery	
Assess students' mastery of the Reading Strategy and Literary Analysis concepts by having them answer the Review and Assess questions (SE/ATE p. 677)	15 min.
Use one or more of the print and media Assessment Resources (ATE p. 679) [A]	up to 45 min.
EXTEND	
Apply Understanding	
Have students complete the Vocabulary Development Lesson and the Grammar and Style Lesson (SE p. 678) [A]	20 min.
Apply students' ability to give subtle, nuanced interpretations using the Writing Lesson (SE/ATE p. 679) [A]	45 min.
Apply students' understanding using one or more of the Extension Activities (SE p. 679)	20–90 min.

ACCELERATED INSTRUCTION:
Use the strategies and activities identified with an [A].

UNIVERSAL ACCESS
● = Below-Level Students
▲ = On-Level Students
■ = Above-Level Students

Time and Resource Manager

Reading Level: Challenging, Challenging, Average, Average
Average Number of Instructional Days: 4

RESOURCES		
PRINT	**TRANSPARENCIES**	**TECHNOLOGY**
• **Beyond Literature,** Cross-Curricular Connection: Social Studies, p. 31 ▲ ■		• **Interest Grabber Video,** Tape 4 ● ▲ ■
• **Selection Support Workbook:** ● ▲ ■ Literary Analysis, p. 146 Reading Strategy, p. 145 Build Vocabulary, p. 143	• **Literary Analysis and Reading Transparencies,** pp. 61 and 62 ● ▲ ■	
• **Adapted Reader's Companion** ● • **Reader's Companion** ● • **Authors In Depth,** Diamond Level, p. 124 ■		• **Listening to Literature** ● ▲ ■ Audiocassettes, Side 16 Audio CDs, CD 9
• **English Learner's Companion** ● ▲ • **Literary Analysis for Enrichment** ■	• **Fine Art Transparencies, Volume 1,** Art Transparency 17 ● ▲ ■	
• **Formal Assessment:** Selection Test, pp. 152–154 ● ▲ ■ • **Open Book Test,** pp. 91–93 ● ▲ ■ • **Performance Assessment and Portfolio Management,** pp. 25 and 92 ● ▲ ■ • PRENTICE HALL ASSESSMENT SYSTEM ● ▲ ■	• PRENTICE HALL ASSESSMENT SYSTEM ● ▲ ■ Skills Practice Answers and Explanations on Transparencies	• **Test Bank Software** ● ▲ ■ • **Got It! Assessment Videotapes,** Tape 3 ● ▲
• **Selection Support Workbook:** ● ▲ ■ Grammar and Style, p. 144 • **Writing and Grammar,** Diamond Level ● ▲ ■ • **Extension Activities,** p. 31 ● ▲ ■	• **Daily Language Practice Transparencies** ● ▲ • **Writing Models and Graphic Organizers on Transparencies,** pp. 45–56 ● ▲ ■	• **Writing and Grammar iText CD-ROM** ● ▲ ■ ***Take It to the Net*** www.phschool.com

BLOCK SCHEDULING: Use one 90-minute class period to preteach the selection and have students read it. Use a second 90-minute class period to assess students' mastery of skills and have them complete one of the Extension Activities.

PRETEACH

Step-by-Step Teaching Guide for pp. 662–663

Motivation

To prepare students for Wordsworth's emotional link to nature, take a nature walk with students, either physically or with pictures or slides, through a beautiful natural setting. Have students note both the details of the scenes and their own emotional responses. Discuss how the emotions evoked by nature could inspire social or political views. Explain to students that the poetry of William Wordsworth is noted for its focus on nature and that his understanding of his own life, of poetry, and of politics all flow from his relationship with nature.

Interest Grabber Video

As an alternative, play "*The Prelude:* The French Revolution" on Tape 4 to engage student interest.

1 Background

More About the Author

De Quincey wrote of Wordsworth in 1835: "Up to 1820 the name of Wordsworth was trampled underfoot; from 1820 to 1830 it was militant; from 1830 to 1835 it has been triumphant."

As De Quincey's remark suggests, the critics' reception of Wordsworth shifted dramatically over those fifteen years. Wordsworth's choice of subjects—the rural poor, flowers—and his simple, passionate language had offended early reviewers. At best they saw his artistic decisions as a self-conscious, even precious, rejection of good taste. Some may have looked on Wordsworth with distaste for his initially radical political views. Despite such obstacles, and despite what some critics see as a decline in his creative powers after 1807, Wordsworth's fame and popularity grew. In 1843, his success became official: He was named poet laureate. Wordsworth died in 1850, shortly after the publication of a final revised text of his works.

Prepare to Read

1 Poetry of William Wordsworth

William Wordsworth (1770–1850)

Writing poetry may seem like a quiet, meditative activity, a matter of words, not deeds—hardly the scene of upheavals and crises. Yet in 1798, a revolution shook the world of poetry. In that year, William Wordsworth took generations of assumptions about the proper style, words, and subject matter for a poem and calmly put them aside.

A Revolution in Poetry In the 1802 Preface to *Lyrical Ballads*, a collection of Wordworth's and Samuel Taylor Coleridge's works, Wordsworth announced, "There will . . . be found in these volumes little of what is usually called poetic diction; as much pains has been taken to avoid it as is ordinarily taken to produce it; . . ."

Gone were the flowery language, the wittily crafted figures of speech, the effusive praise, and the tragic complaints that had defined poetry in the past. In their place, Wordsworth offered an intensified presentation of ordinary life and nature using common language. Wordsworth's revolution took literature in a dramatic new direction, building the movement known as Romanticism.

The Lake District Wordsworth's revolution was rooted in his early love for nature. Born in the beautiful Lake District of England, Wordsworth spent his youth roaming the countryside. In later years, too, he found peace and reassurance in the gentle hills and serene lakes of this landscape. This region of northwestern England became the cradle of the Romantic Movement, inspiring many personal commentaries and poetic tributes.

Revolution and Love By the time Wordsworth was thirteen, both his parents had died. Nonetheless, he was able to pursue his education and entered Cambridge University in 1787. After graduating, he traveled through Europe, spending considerable time in France. There, he embraced the ideals of the newly born French Revolution—ideals that stressed social justice and individual rights. Growing emotionally as well as intellectually, Wordsworth fell in love with Annette Vallon.

Disillusionment and Crisis Wordsworth's involvement with the Revolution and with Vallon ended abruptly when lack of funds and family pressure forced him to return home. Two months later, in 1793, England declared war on France, and the Revolution became increasingly violent. His dreams of liberty betrayed, Wordsworth lapsed into a depression. His beloved sister, Dorothy, and fellow poet Samuel Taylor Coleridge helped him through this crisis.

From Politics to Art In 1798, Wordsworth published *Lyrical Ballads* with Coleridge. With the publication of this work, Wordsworth translated his revolutionary hopes from politics to literature. His democratic ideals appeared in his use of the language of ordinary people rather than specialized "poetic" words. The "ballads" showed how the lives and experiences of ordinary people, when properly viewed, were really *extra*ordinary.

Poetry and Autobiography Critics agree that Wordsworth's greatest work is his autobiography in poetry, *The Prelude*. Wordsworth completed a version of this poem in 1799, which he expanded considerably by 1805. As he wrote to a friend, *The Prelude* told the story of "the growth of my own mind." The poem is not always factually accurate, but, as noted by critic Stephen Gill, in its combination of "satire and narrative, description and meditation, the visionary and the deliberately banal," it was unique.

Eventually, Wordsworth's radical new approach to poetry gained acceptance, while he himself grew more conservative in his politics. A new generation of Romantics, more radical than Wordsworth and Coleridge, arose. Wordsworth's position was secure, however: We remember him as the father of English Romanticism.

TEACHING RESOURCES

The following resources can be used to enrich or extend the instruction for pp. 662–663.

Motivation

Interest Grabber Video, Tape 4

Background

Beyond Literature, p. 31

Take It to the Net

Visit www.phschool.com for background and hotlinks for the selections.

Literary Analysis

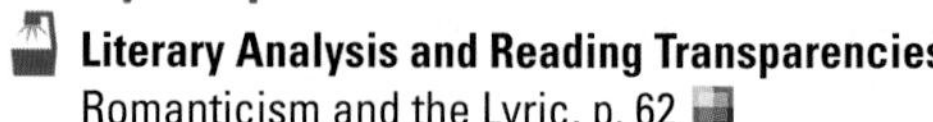

Literary Analysis and Reading Transparencies, Romanticism and the Lyric, p. 62

Reading

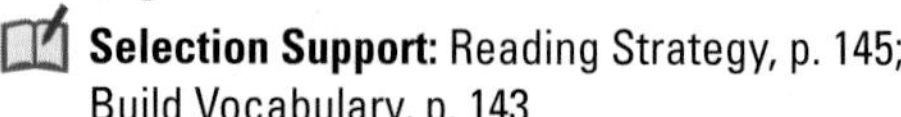

Selection Support: Reading Strategy, p. 145; Build Vocabulary, p. 143

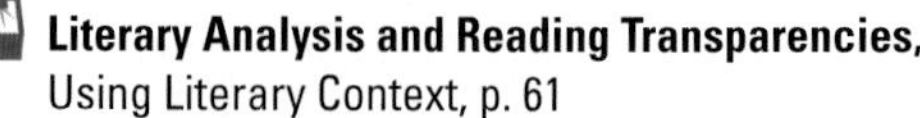

Literary Analysis and Reading Transparencies, Using Literary Context, p. 61

BLOCK SCHEDULING: Resources marked with this symbol provide varied instruction during 90-minute blocks.

Preview

Connecting to the Literature

Rock music and recycling belong to modern America, not eighteenth-century England. Yet Wordsworth's poems show a resemblance to rock's celebration of individual feeling and to environmentalists' respect for nature.

2 Literary Analysis

Romanticism and the Lyric

Romanticism was a late-eighteenth-century European literary movement. While the earlier Neoclassical writers, such as Pope and Johnson, favored reason, wit, and outward elegance, the works of many Romantic poets include these elements:

- Simplicity or directness of language
- The expression of spontaneous, intensified feelings
- Profound responses to nature, in which nature appears to reflect the soul and contemplation of nature leads to a deeper awareness of self

English Romanticism began with William Wordsworth. The **lyric,** a poem in which a single speaker expresses personal emotions and observations, was particularly suited to his vision.

Comparing Literary Works

The Romantics adopted a new, freer **diction,** or choice of words. As you read, you will notice that Wordsworth's poetry favors simple words but that his work also relies heavily on abstract terms. Compare the different types of words Wordsworth chooses—whether specific and concrete like *sycamore* or abstract like *a sense sublime*. Evaluate whether he succeeds in forging a new style that appeals to the ear, heart, and mind.

3 Reading Strategy

Using Literary Context

Literary context is the climate of literary practices and assumptions that influence a writer. Wordsworth is one of those rare writers who brings about a change in literary context. Use a chart like the one shown to identify details and qualities in his work that were revolutionary at the time.

Literary Context: Romanticism
Celebration of Common Folk
Love of Nature
Admiration for French Revolution
Loss of Faith in Reason

Vocabulary Development

recompense (rek′ əm pens′) *n.* payment in return for something (p. 669)

roused (rouzd) *v.* stirred up (p. 672)

presumption (prē zump′ shən) *n.* audacity (p. 673)

anatomize (ə nat′ ə mīz′) *v.* to dissect in order to examine structure (p. 674)

confounded (kən found′ id) *adj.* confused; mixed together indiscriminately; bewildered (p. 674)

sordid (sôr′ did) *adj.* dirty (p. 675)

stagnant (stag′ nənt) *adj.* motionless; foul (p. 676)

CUSTOMIZE INSTRUCTION FOR UNIVERSAL ACCESS

For Special Needs Students	For Less Proficient Readers	For English Learners
Have students read the adapted version of "Tintern Abbey" in the **Adapted Reader's Companion.** This version provides basic-level instruction in an interactive format with questions and write-on lines. Completing the adapted version will prepare students to read the selection in the Student Edition.	Have students read "Tintern Abbey" in the **Reader's Companion.** This version provides basic-level instruction in an interactive format with questions and write-on lines. After students finish the selection in **Reader's Companion,** have them complete the questions and activities in the Student Edition.	Have students read the adapted version of "Tintern Abbey" in the **English Learner's Companion.** This version provides basic-level instruction in an interactive format with questions and write-on lines. Completing the adapted version will prepare students to read the selection in the Student Edition.

2 Literary Analysis

Romanticism and the Lyric

- Tell students that in this lesson they will focus on Romanticism, a literary movement in Europe in the late eighteenth century. The Romantics moved away from the Neoclassical emphasis on reason, wit, and proportion and wrote poetry characterized by direct language, spontaneous expression of feeling, and deep responses to nature.
- Explain that many Romantic poets wrote lyric poems, or works in which a single speaker expresses personal emotions and observations.
- Use the instruction for Comparing Literary Works to review with students the definition of diction and to prepare them to identify what is distinctive in Wordsworth's diction.
- Use the Romanticism and the Lyric transparency in **Literary Analysis and Reading Transparencies,** p. 62, to show students how to identify aspects of Romanticism and distinguish them from Neoclassical elements.

3 Reading Strategy

Using Literary Context

- Remind students that the phrase *literary context* encompasses the background of literary practices and assumptions that influence a writer, including assumptions about proper poetic form, language, and subject matter.
- Explain that Wordsworth brought about a change in the literary context with his work, and he helped to establish Romanticism.
- Have students practice interpreting literary context with the Using Literary Context transparency in **Literary Analysis and Reading Transparencies,** p. 61.

Vocabulary Development

- Pronounce each vocabulary word for students and read the definitions as a class. Have students identify any words with which they are already familiar.

 ***E-Teach***

Visit E-Teach at www.phschool.com for teachers' essays on how to teach, with questions and answers.

Background

The Social Function of Poetry

- Explain to students that literature has had different social functions in different periods. For instance, in the seventeenth century, poets like John Donne wrote poetry in the hope of catching the attention of an aristocrat who would employ them or contribute to their support. Such a relationship was called patronage.
- In such a context, rivalry for the favor of patrons was a key factor in the writing of poetry.
- Increasing literacy and the growth of the middle class, who had the time and money for reading, widened the audience for poetry. Poets no longer needed patrons.
- By the nineteenth century, literary circles like that of the Romantics were an important part of literature. Friendships among critics, magazine editors, and poets were more likely to have an effect on poetry than relations between a poet and a wealthy patron.
- In earlier times, the idea that writing poetry was in itself a valuable occupation was not well-established. The seventeenth-century poet Ben Jonson was perhaps the first to claim professional dignity for poets. By the nineteenth century, though, Wordsworth could claim the respect of others simply for being a poet.

Use the following question for discussion:

Writers who wrote for patrons often wrote poems praising their patrons or showing off their own wit. How might poetry written for a literary circle differ in content from poetry written for a patron? **Possible response:** Because a literary circle would focus on literary quality, poets writing for a literary circle might concentrate on developing new poetic effects. They might see their efforts in terms of achieving beauty or insight, rather than amusing a reader.

A Closer Look

Poetry and Friendship in the Romantic Age

> . . . I have been on a visit to Wordsworth's at Racedown. . . . Wordsworth is a very great man, the only man *at all times* and *in all modes of excellence* I feel myself inferior. . . . (Samuel Coleridge, in a letter to Robert Southey, 1797)

Great art is not created in a vacuum. In ancient Greece, great works of art and intellect were born within communities of artists and thinkers, the result of apprenticeship and debate. Hundreds of years later, in the Renaissance city of Florence, Italy, artists gathered in schools and workshops produced breathtaking achievements in the visual arts and architecture. In Elizabethan England, Shakespeare, spurred on by his competition with rival playwright Ben Jonson, reached new heights of dramatic art. Like these earlier flowerings of creative activity, the Romantic movement was sparked and nurtured by social relationships. Where apprenticeship and rivalry had urged past artists to higher achievements, friendship was a dominant force pushing Romantic poets to make their breakthroughs.

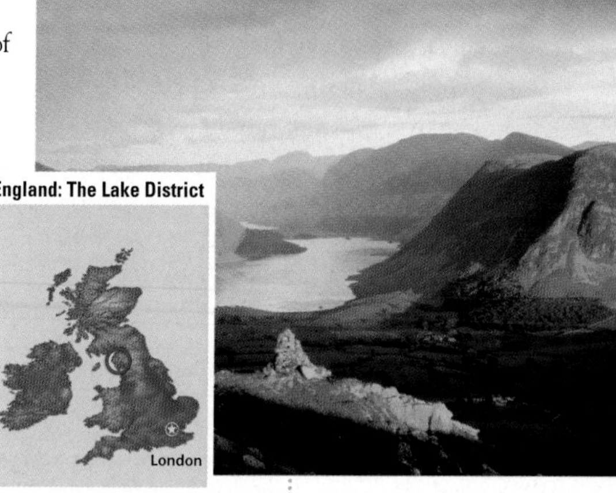

A Paradox There is a paradox here. Of all poetry, that of the British Romantics might seem likeliest to be the product of solitary writers. With their emphasis on subjective responses to nature, on their own emotions, and on radical social views, Romantic writers might seem to have had little use for society and community.

An Inspiring Friendship In fact, a strong network of friendships helped create the poetic vision of the age. The friendship between William Wordsworth and Samuel Taylor Coleridge lies at the center of the new movement in poetry. Their friendship was one of great intensity. Both men, of course, loved poetry, which they discussed with enthusiasm. They were also both fierce partisans of the French Revolution in its early days. Lovers of nature, they shared the joy of walking in the hills of England's Lake District, where Wordsworth lived with his sister Dorothy. Coleridge visited them frequently and at times lived nearby.

Complementary Talents When the two poets lived near enough to each other, they met and talked every day. Wordsworth's understanding of himself as a poet became increasingly clear to him, perhaps owing to what he described as "the power [Coleridge] possessed of throwing out in profusion grand, central truths from which might be evolved the most comprehensive systems." Coleridge, a voracious reader who delved deeply into philosophy,

ENRICHMENT: Visual Arts Connection

The Art of the Landscape

Like the Lake District Poets, Romantic painters turned new attention on nature. Landscape painting had evolved from backgrounds in paintings of religious subjects in the Renaissance to carefully composed idyllic views during the seventeenth century. With John Constable (1776–1837) and J.W.M. Turner (1775–1851), the landscape took on new life. Constable, who sketched for hours outdoors, often focused on the sky, while Turner concentrated on atmospheric effects of light. Just as Wordsworth's true subject was his own soul, Constable and Turner painted landscapes laden with emotion.

helped expand his friend's intellectual life. As a writer he worked very quickly, inspiring more spontaneity from the deliberately paced Wordsworth.

While Coleridge made his mark on Wordsworth, he also fell under Wordsworth's spell. Wordsworth was a great observer of nature and everyday life. He was also an astute reader. It was he who suggested that Coleridge center "The Rime of the Ancient Mariner" around a crime at sea. Friendship with Wordsworth heightened Coleridge's own poetic powers. It is no accident that his greatest poetry was written during their years of deepest friendship.

The Lake Poets Coleridge and Wordsworth were at the center of a circle of poets and writers, often referred to as the Lake Poets because of their attachment to England's Lake District and its natural beauty. The circle included Charles Lamb, Thomas de Quincey, William Hazlitt, and Robert Southey (see the chart for more information). Dorothy Wordsworth, too, was a key member of the circle. Her descriptive journals of her life and travels with her brother and Coleridge fed the imaginations of both poets, and provide a sense of the life they shared, as this quotation suggests:

> *Saturday, 4th October* 1800.—A very rainy, or rather showery and gusty, morning; for often the sun shines. . . . Coleridge came in while we were at dinner, very wet. We talked till twelve o'clock. He had sat up all the night before, writing essays for the newspapers. . . . Exceedingly delighted with the second part of [Coleridge's poem] *Christabel.*

Later Years The friendship between Wordsworth and Coleridge broke down around 1810, owing in part to Coleridge's reliance on painkillers. They were never fully reconciled. Even so, nearly twenty-five years after their break, Wordsworth would say, on the occasion of Coleridge's death, that Coleridge was "the most *wonderful* man he had ever known." This tradition of friendship was carried on by the next generation of Romantics as well, most notably in the friendship between Percy Bysshe Shelley and Lord Byron.

◄▼ **Critical Viewing** What connection can you make between the beauty of the scene in the photograph on the previous page and the information in the chart? **[Connect]**

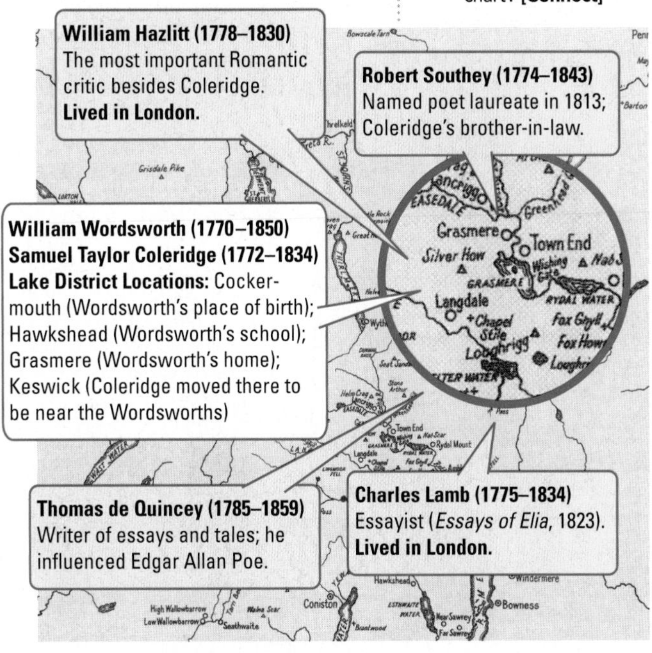

William Hazlitt (1778–1830)
The most important Romantic critic besides Coleridge.
Lived in London.
Robert Southey (1774–1843)
Named poet laureate in 1813; Coleridge's brother-in-law.
William Wordsworth (1770–1850)
Samuel Taylor Coleridge (1772–1834)
Lake District Locations: Cockermouth (Wordsworth's place of birth); Hawkshead (Wordsworth's school); Grasmere (Wordsworth's home); Keswick (Coleridge moved there to be near the Wordsworths)
Thomas de Quincey (1785–1859)
Writer of essays and tales; he influenced Edgar Allan Poe.
Charles Lamb (1775–1834)
Essayist (*Essays of Elia*, 1823).
Lived in London.
Grasmere
Town End
Silver How
Langdale
Hawkshead
Coniston
Bowness

Lake District Writers and Their Visitors

Background

Romantic Relationships

The friendships among the Lake District writers had significant consequences beyond the literary. Coleridge married Sara Fricker, for instance, under the influence of Southey, whose sister-in-law she was. The marriage ended unhappily. De Quincey, moved by Wordsworth's and Coleridge's poetry, sent Coleridge a donation and struck up a friendship with the Wordsworths. He moved to their Lake District cottage when they left for a home nearby.

Use this question for discussion:

Why might friendship encourage artists?

Possible responses: Friends will strive to distinguish themselves in each other's eyes and will encourage one another.

Critical Thinking

1. Compare the virtues that Wordsworth and Coleridge found in each other.
   Answer: Wordsworth admired Coleridge's philosophical penetration and was influenced by his spontaneity; Coleridge was influenced by Wordsworth's love of nature and literary advice.
2. What weaknesses might the two have had?
   Possible response: Wordsworth was perhaps overcautious: He was not as intellectually able as Coleridge and was a slower writer. Coleridge was perhaps too restless: His knack for grand statements and his drug abuse suggest that he was a dreamer.
3. What effect might the fact that they lived far from London have had on their work?
   Possible response: They were freed from some pressures to conform to fashion and could create their own style.

►Critical Viewing

Possible response: Its beauty helps explain why Wordsworth lived in the region from childhood on and why others joined him there.

CUSTOMIZE INSTRUCTION FOR UNIVERSAL ACCESS

For Less Proficient Readers	For Gifted/Talented Students	For Advanced Readers
Have students read A Closer Look. Then, have them read "Lines Composed a Few Miles Above Tintern Abbey," p. 666, to identify passages concerning Wordsworth's relationship with his sister Dorothy. Then, have students share passages and discuss the friendship of the two.	Have students read A Closer Look. Then, have them read "Tintern Abbey," p. 666, to identify passages showing what Wordsworth most valued in nature. Have them then produce illustrations or musical compositions capturing these aspects of nature and share them with the class.	Have students read A Closer Look, "Tintern Abbey," p. 666, and "Kubla Khan," p. 710. Have them compare the role of the memory in Wordsworth's poem with the role of fantasy in Coleridge's, relating their comparison to the poets' friendship. They should share their essays with the class.

TEACH

Step-by-Step Teaching Guide for pp. 666–676

CUSTOMIZE INSTRUCTION
For Musical/Rhythmic Learners

Have these students read "Tintern Abbey" with musical and rhythmic elements of the poem in mind. Point out that the poem has the tone of a passionate conversation—a number of lines read like exclamations, while others might be whispered. Then, ask them to deliver dramatic readings of sections of the poem for the class, emphasizing Wordsworth's dramatic cadences.

❶ About the Selection

This poem perfectly illustrates Wordsworth's belief in nature as a healer and teacher. In it, he speaks to his much-loved sister, Dorothy, hoping to share his profound joy in returning to Tintern Abbey after a five-year absence. The poem explores the soothing and uplifting effect the memory of his first visit has had during his absence. Wordsworth then turns to considering his childhood relation to nature, a relation in which heart and landscape were united in an immediate and spontaneous joy. In contrast, the adult Wordsworth detects in nature a sublime, inexpressible presence—"a motion and a spirit"—that unites all things. He hopes that his sister will share his feelings for the place and that, in the future, she will remember his devotion to nature and their visit to the Abbey.

❶ *Lines Composed a Few Miles Above Tintern Abbey*

William Wordsworth

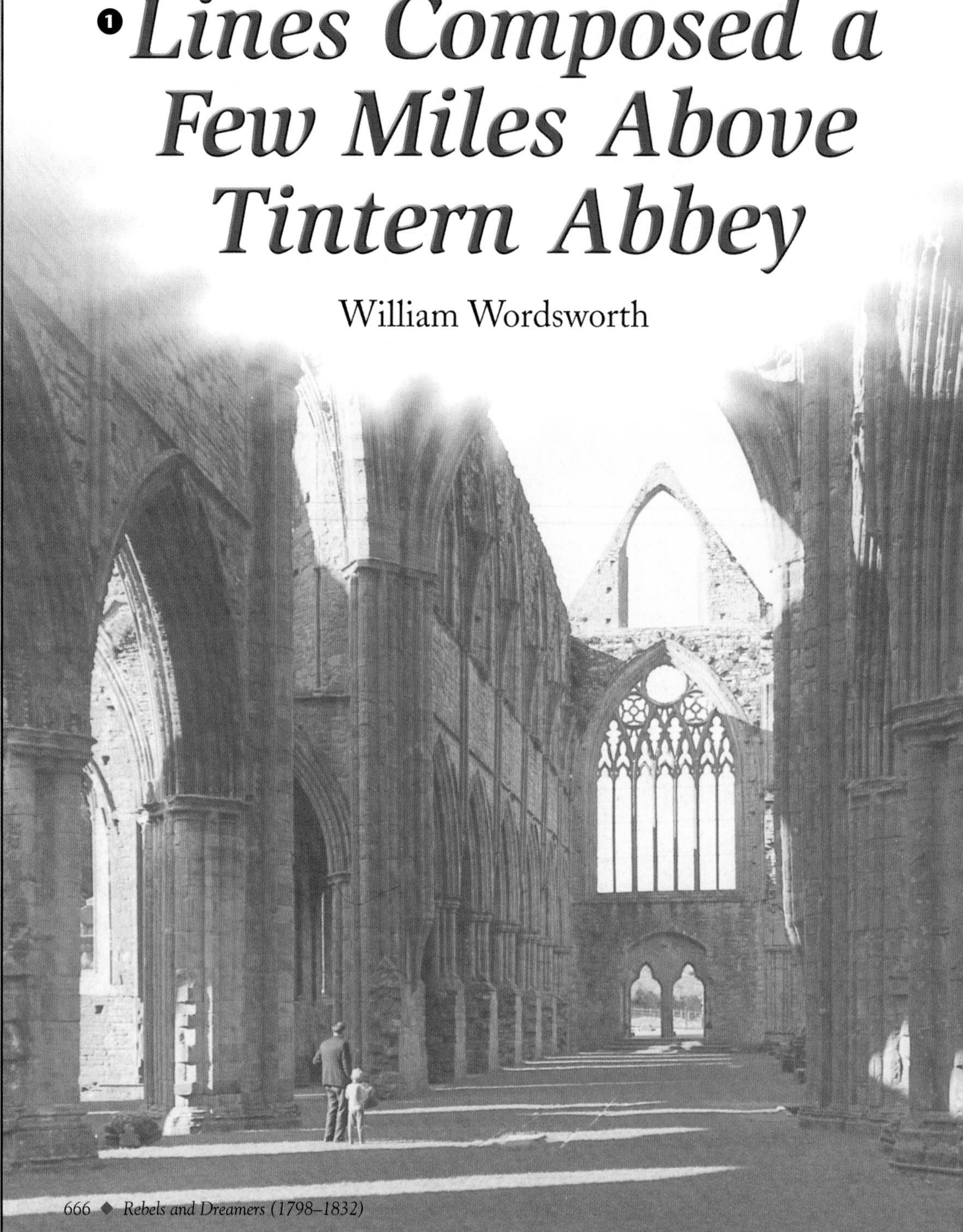

TEACHING RESOURCES

The following resources can be used to enrich or extend the instruction for pp. 664–676.

Literary Analysis

- **Selection Support:** Literary Analysis, p. 146

Reading

- **English Learner's Companion**
- **Adapted Reader's Companion**
- **Reader's Companion**
- **Listening to Literature Audiocassettes,** Side 16 ■
- **Listening to Literature Audio CDs,** CD 9 ■

Extension

- **Authors In Depth,** The British Tradition (The collection includes nine additional selections by William Wordsworth for extended reading.)
- **Fine Art Transparencies, Volume 1,** Transparency 17 (Have students read through line 49 of the poem. Display Art Transparency 17. Discuss contrasts in the moods created by poem and painting.

■ **BLOCK SCHEDULING:** Resources marked with this symbol provide varied instruction during 90-minute blocks.

Background

This poem was written in 1798 during Wordsworth's second visit to the valley of the River Wye and the ruins of Tintern Abbey, once a great medieval church, in Wales. Wordsworth had passed through the region alone five years earlier. This time he brought his sister along to share the experience. Of this visit and the poem it inspired, Wordsworth wrote, "No poem of mine was composed under circumstances more pleasant for one to remember than this."

❸

Five years have past; five summers, with the length
Of five long winters! and again I hear
These waters, rolling from their mountain springs
With a soft inland murmur. Once again
Do I behold these steep and lofty cliffs,
That on a wild secluded scene impress
Thoughts of more deep seclusion; and connect
The landscape with the quiet of the sky.
The day is come when I again repose
Here, under this dark sycamore, and view
These plots of cottage ground, these orchard tufts,
Which at this season, with their unripe fruits,
Are clad in one green hue, and lose themselves
'Mid groves and copses. Once again I see
These hedgerows, hardly hedgerows, little lines
Of sportive wood run wild: these pastoral farms,
Green to the very door; and wreaths of smoke
Sent up, in silence, from among the trees!
With some uncertain notice, as might seem
Of vagrant dwellers in the houseless woods,
Or of some hermit's cave, where by his fire
The hermit sits alone.
                                        These beauteous forms,
Through a long absence, have not been to me
As is a landscape to a blind man's eye:
But oft, in lonely rooms, and 'mid the din
Of towns and cities, I have owed to them
In hours of weariness, sensations sweet,
Felt in the blood, and felt along the heart;
And passing even into my purer mind,
With tranquil restoration—feelings too
Of unremembered pleasure: such, perhaps,
As have no slight or trivial influence
On that best portion of a good man's life.
His little, nameless, unremembered, acts

Literary Analysis
Romanticism and the Lyric How do the sensory observations Wordsworth includes reflect what you know about Romanticism?

❷ ◀ **Critical Viewing**
What elements in this photograph help it capture awe and excitement comparable to Wordsworth's on his return to the Wye? **[Connect]**

❹ ✓ **Reading Check**
Name two sights that strike Wordsworth on his return to the Wye.

❷ ▶ Critical Viewing

Answer: The presence of the man and the child in the foreground suggest the excitement of discovery and rediscovery that characterizes Wordsworth's return to the Wye, since the man may be returning to the scene while he is introducing the child to it. The diffuse light flooding the upper part of the photograph might suggest the sublime, nearly inexpressible sentiments Wordsworth associates with the natural scenes around the Wye.

❸ Literary Analysis

Romanticism and the Lyric

- Review with students what they know about Romanticism, including its use of simple language, its spontaneous expression of feelings, and its response to nature.
- Then, ask students the Literary Analysis question on p. 667: How do the sensory observations Wordsworth includes reflect what you know about Romanticism?
  Possible response: Students may note Wordsworth's loving attention to the general feeling of the scene—the cliffs that deepen the sense of seclusion—as well as to specific details such as the sycamore and unripe fruits. Along with the almost ecstatic tone of his wonder at returning, these details reflect the heartfelt response to nature characteristic of Romantics.

▶ **Monitor Progress** Have students identify other Romantic elements in this stanza.

❹ ✓ Reading Check

Possible responses: Wordsworth is struck by the steep and lofty cliffs, the greenery, and the lines of hedgerows.

CUSTOMIZE INSTRUCTION FOR UNIVERSAL ACCESS

For Less Proficient Readers	For English Learners	For Advanced Readers
Guide students as they read the first stanza as a group. Have students note details that reveal the way in which Wordsworth was changing the literary context. Enter each detail on the transparency in **Literary Analysis and Reading Transparencies,** p. 61, and have students interpret them.	Guide students as they read the first stanza as a group. Have them guide you in sketching on the chalkboard the scene described. Label each part of the drawing, inviting students to use context to define unfamiliar terms. Then, ask them what this description shows about the changing literary context.	Have students read the first stanza of "Tintern Abbey" independently. When they are done, ask them to write paragraphs in which they describe and interpret any evidence of the changes Wordsworth introduced into the literary context of the time.

❺ Literary Analysis

Romanticism and the Lyric

- Read aloud the bracketed passage to students. Review with students their understanding of the Romantic concept of a deep sympathy between the inner being of people and nature.
- Then ask students the Literary Analysis question on p. 668: How do the images in lines 40–49 reflect Romantic ideas of the relation between nature and the soul?
  Answer: The speaker reports that the memory of natural scenes worked to lighten his mood, leaving him so tranquil that he became "a living soul." In this mood, he feels he is able to "see into the life of things"—showing that nature can inspire insight. In both the deep effect of nature on the speaker and in the insight it gives, students should note a bond between nature and soul.

❻ Reading Strategy

Using Literary Context

- Remind students that literary context is the climate of opinions and traditional beliefs that inform a poet's vision.
- Ask students the Reading Strategy question on p. 668: What changing attitude about the importance of reason is reflected in Wordsworth's contrast of childhood with adulthood?
  Answer: Childhood, as Wordsworth describes it, is a time "before" reason, when his experience of nature is direct and without reflective thought. The value he gives this experience has to do with the quality of the relationship with nature, though. The contrast between the adult's possession of reason and the child's lack of it is less important than the changing quality of the speaker's experience of nature. This shift shows that, for Wordsworth, reason is no longer of central importance.

Of kindness and of love. Nor less, I trust,
To them I may have owed another gift,
Of aspect more sublime; that blessed mood,
In which the burthen[1] of the mystery,
In which the heavy and the weary weight
Of all this unintelligible world
Is lightened—that serene and blessed mood,
In which the affections gently lead us on—
Until, the breath of this corporeal frame[2]
❺ And even the motion of our human blood
Almost suspended, we are laid asleep
In body, and become a living soul;
While with an eye made quiet by the power
Of harmony, and the deep power of joy,
We see into the life of things.

If this
Be but a vain belief, yet, oh! how oft—
In darkness and amid the many shapes
Of joyless daylight; when the fretful stir
Unprofitable, and the fever of the world,
Have hung upon the beatings of my heart—
How oft, in spirit, have I turned to thee,
O sylvan[3] Wye! thou wanderer through the woods,
How often has my spirit turned to thee!

And now, with gleams of half-extinguished thought,
With many recognitions dim and faint,
And somewhat of a sad perplexity,
The picture of the mind revives again;
While here I stand, not only with the sense
Of present pleasure, but with pleasing thoughts
That in this moment there is life and food
For future years. And so I dare to hope,
Though changed, no doubt, from what I was when first
I came among these hills; when like a roe[4]
I bounded o'er the mountains, by the sides
❻ Of the deep rivers, and the lonely streams,
Wherever nature led: more like a man
Flying from something that he dreads, than one
Who sought the thing he loved. For nature then
(The coarser pleasures of my boyish days,
And their glad animal movements all gone by)
To me was all in all—I cannot paint

Literary Analysis
Romanticism and the Lyric How do the images in lines 40–49 reflect Romantic ideas of the relation between nature and the soul?

Reading Strategy
Using Literary Context What changing attitude about the importance of reason is reflected in Wordsworth's contrast of childhood with adulthood?

1. **burthen** burden.
2. **corporeal** (kôr pôr′ ē əl) **frame** body.
3. **sylvan** (sil′ vən) wooded.
4. **roe** type of deer.

ENRICHMENT: Cultural Connection

Views of Nature

A person's view of nature is strongly influenced by his or her culture. Native American cultures, for example, recognize humans' dependence on nature and strive to maintain a harmonious relationship with it.

Traditional Eastern cultures also seek to integrate human existence gracefully with nature. For example, traditional Japanese architecture is always conceived in relation to surrounding landscape and changing seasons. Rock gardens, pools, and streams serve to integrate the human artifice and natural forms. Asian methods of agriculture, such as the rice paddy, adapt farming to the terrain at hand as simply as possible.

Western cultures, on the other hand, frequently demonstrate in their technology, architecture, and agriculture a view of nature as a challenging force that must be defended against for safety or harnessed to serve human goals. At the same time, Western culture from the Romantics on recovered in nature a domain of innocence and truth, a vision that has led many Westerners to investigate the view of nature in other cultures.

What then I was. The sounding cataract
Haunted me like a passion; the tall rock,
The mountain, and the deep and gloomy wood,
Their colors and their forms, were then to me
An appetite; a feeling and a love,
That had no need of a remoter charm,
By thought supplied, nor any interest
Unborrowed from the eye. That time is past,
And all its aching joys are now no more,
And all its dizzy raptures. Not for this
Faint[5] I, nor mourn nor murmur; other gifts
Have followed; for such loss, I would believe,
8 Abundant recompense. For I have learned
To look on nature, not as in the hour
Of thoughtless youth; but hearing oftentimes
The still, sad music of humanity,
Nor harsh nor grating, though of ample power
To chasten and subdue. And I have felt
A presence that disturbs me with the joy
Of elevated thoughts; a sense sublime
Of something far more deeply interfused,
Whose dwelling is the light of setting suns,
And the round ocean and the living air,
And the blue sky, and in the mind of man;
A motion and a spirit, that impels
All thinking things, all objects of all thought,
And rolls through all things. Therefore am I still
A lover of the meadows and the woods
And mountains; and of all that we behold
From this green earth; of all the mighty world
Of eye, and ear—both what they half create,
And what perceive; well pleased to recognize
In nature and the language of the sense,
The anchor of my purest thoughts, the nurse,
The guide, the guardian of my heart, and soul
Of all my moral being.

Nor perchance,
If I were not thus taught, should I the more
Suffer[6] my genial spirits[7] to decay;
For thou art with me here upon the banks
Of this fair river; thou my dearest Friend,[8]
My dear, dear Friend, and in thy voice I catch
The language of my former heart, and read

5. **Faint** lose heart.
6. **Suffer** allow.
7. **genial spirits** creative powers.
8. **Friend** his sister Dorothy.

7 ***The Evolution of the Self***

On returning to the Wye, Wordsworth discovers his own deeper self in experiences of nature bound together by memory. His discovery contributed to a new, Romantic idea of the self. For the Romantics, the self was a journey of self-discovery, not a collection of personal quirks or facts. The Romantic poet set out to recover his or her deeper self through nature, memory, and lyric poetry. For the Romantics, writing a poem became an act of self-definition and discovery.

This Romantic idea of the self—always divided yet always recovering itself—inspired later works such as Tennyson's *In Memoriam, A. H. H.* Centuries later, Wordsworth's vision of the self and its journey still resonates in modern culture.

recompense (rek´ əm pens´) *n.* payment in return for something

9  **Reading Check**

What natural sights inspire in Wordsworth a sense of the unity of things—of "something far more deeply interfused, . . ."?

7 Background

The Evolution of the Self

Wordsworth's poetic use of psychology had an antecedent in prose: In the seventeenth century, Burton's *Anatomy of Melancholy* explored various emotional conditions in a larger inquiry. But Wordsworth's personal revelations initiated a kind of revelatory writing that allowed confessional poets two centuries later to incorporate personal details into their work. Wordsworth's willingness to focus on himself—to explore his own despair, his grief, and his joy apart from the conventional situations of love and rivalry in earlier lyric poetry—was a dramatic departure.

Most important, though, in the evolution of our culture's idea of the self is the fact that he presents memory and the repetition of past states of the soul as defining himself. Through acts of poetic introspection, Wordsworth discovers or creates himself, apart from social roles and definitions.

8 Critical Thinking

Interpret

- Have students read lines 83–93 to themselves. Ask them to pay careful attention to Wordsworth's ideas of maturity.
- Then, ask them: How does Wordsworth feel about the changes maturity has brought to his attitudes about nature? **Possible response:** Wordsworth feels that he has lost a vital joy in nature since he has grown up but refuses to mourn for it. It has been replaced by a new sense of the unity of things.

9 Reading Check

Answer: The "light of setting suns," the "round ocean," the "living air," "the blue sky," and the "mind of man" inspire in Wordsworth a sense of the unity of things.

CUSTOMIZE INSTRUCTION FOR UNIVERSAL ACCESS

For Special Needs Students	For Less Proficient Readers
Have students read "Tintern Abbey" stanza by stanza in small groups with teacher guidance. Discuss each shift in time, place, or the speaker's age as the poem unfolds. Have students identify the major contrasts between each experience in the poem.	Readers may not recognize that Wordsworth's descriptions in "Tintern Abbey" are rich in appreciation for its natural beauty and what it evokes in him. Have them think of a natural area they have observed that brings out heightened emotions. Then ask them to write a brief poem that describes the place and the emotions they feel when they visit it. Have students compare their poems to Wordsworth's "Tintern Abbey." Direct them to **Extension Activities,** p. 31, Activity 1, for additional guidance.

⑩ Background

Art

Tintern Abbey, watercolor, by Joseph Mallord William Turner

This painting by Wordsworth's contemporary shows Tintern Abbey. J.M.W. Turner (1775–1851) is known as a premier British landscape painter. He began exhibiting his work at the early age of fifteen, later studying at the Royal Academy. Turner then made a walking tour of England, painting watercolors of regional scenes, including this one. Use this question for discussion:

Why might ruins have been so attractive to Romantics such as Wordsworth and Turner?

Possible responses: Ruins suggest something no longer present and so create a sense of grandeur, comparable to Wordsworth's "sense sublime." They also reflect the power of nature over human works.

⑪ ▶Critical Viewing

Answer: Students should recognize that Turner's painting shares many qualities with Wordsworth's descriptions in the poem—the delicate treatment of light falling on Tintern Abbey, and the opening of the ruins onto the blue sky, as if revealing the infinite behind the enclosures of human artifice, evoke the elevated spirit of Wordsworth's experience of nature.

⑫ Reading Strategy

Using Literary Context

- Remind students that the Romantic focus on the power of nature was a departure from the Neoclassical preoccupation with knowledge, order, and elegance.

Monitor Progress Ask students the Reading Strategy question on p. 670: Many Neoclassical poets personified nature in a conventional way as a goddess. What makes Wordsworth's personification in lines 122–134 more personal?

Answer: Wordsworth's personification of nature presents her as having a personal bond with her admirers. She will not "betray" them, as long as they faithfully love her. This personal bond gives the personification more concreteness than one might expect in Neoclassical poetry.

⑩

Tintern Abbey, J. M. W. Turner, British Museum

⑪ ◀**Critical Viewing** Compare the appreciation of light and sky shown by Romantic painter J.M.W. Turner with Wordsworth's descriptions in the poem. **[Connect]**

My former pleasures in the shooting lights
Of thy wild eyes. Oh! yet a little while
May I behold in thee what I was once,
My dear, dear Sister! and this prayer I make
Knowing that Nature never did betray
The heart that loved her; 'tis her privilege,
Through all the years of this our life, to lead
From joy to joy; for she can so inform
The mind that is within us, so impress
With quietness and beauty, and so feed
With lofty thoughts, that neither evil tongues,
Rash judgments, nor the sneers of selfish men,
Nor greetings where no kindness is, nor all
The dreary intercourse of daily life,
Shall e'er prevail against us, or disturb
Our cheerful faith, that all which we behold
Is full of blessings. Therefore let the moon
Shine on thee in thy solitary walk;
And let the misty mountain winds be free
To blow against thee: and, in after years,
When these wild ecstasies shall be matured

⑫

Reading Strategy
Using Literary Context Many Neoclassical poets personified nature in a conventional way as a goddess. What makes Wordsworth's personification in lines 122–134 more personal?

ENRICHMENT: Science Connection

Psychology and the Child

In "Tintern Abbey," Wordsworth points to a decisive change between childhood and adulthood, an idea that was an invention of his time. In this spirit, psychologists today study the development of children into adults. Maturational theorists see the development of the nervous system as key. Behaviorists study the way children learn skills through reinforcement. Cognitive psychologists see the motor of development in a child's successful solution of increasingly complex problems. Psychoanalysts, following Sigmund Freud, hold that the structure of the adult personality depends on the repression of childhood fantasies.

Into a sober pleasure; when thy mind
Shall be a mansion for all lovely forms,
Thy memory be as a dwelling place
For all sweet sound and harmonies; oh! then,
If solitude, or fear, or pain, or grief,
Should be thy portion, with what healing thoughts
Of tender joy wilt thou remember me,
And these my exhortations! Nor, perchance—
If I should be where I no more can hear
Thy voice, nor catch from thy wild eyes these gleams
Of past existence—wilt thou then forget
That on the banks of this delightful stream
We stood together; and that I, so long
A worshipper of Nature, hither came
Unwearied in that service: rather say
With warmer love—oh! with far deeper zeal
Of holier love. Nor wilt thou then forget,
That after many wanderings, many years
Of absence, these steep woods and lofty cliffs,
And this green pastoral landscape, were to me
More dear, both for themselves and for thy sake!

Literary Analysis
Romanticism, the Lyric, and Diction Does Wordsworth use simple or difficult words to describe old age? Are they specific or general?

Review and Assess

Thinking About the Selection

1. **(a) Recall:** How long has it been since the poet visited Tintern Abbey? **(b) Infer:** At what time of year does the poet make his second visit to the area? How do you know?
2. **(a) Recall:** How have the poet's memories of his first visit helped him? **(b) Interpret:** In line 36 of the poem, the poet mentions "another gift" that his contact with this rural scene bestowed upon him. Briefly describe this gift.
3. **Compare and Contrast:** Explain the difference in the poet's attitude on his first and on his second visit to Tintern Abbey.
4. **(a) Summarize:** What wish for his sister does the poet express toward the end of the poem? **(b) Connect:** What connection can you see between this wish, Wordsworth's thoughts in lines 22–31, and his hopes in lines 62–65? **(c) Draw Conclusions:** Is memory as important a force in the poem as nature? Explain.
5. **Evaluate:** Does Wordsworth express a deep truth about our relationships with nature, or are his reactions exaggerated? Support your answer.
6. **Take a Position:** Do you agree with Wordsworth's ideas about our relationship with nature? Why or why not?

CUSTOMIZE INSTRUCTION FOR UNIVERSAL ACCESS

For Less Proficient Readers	For Advanced Readers
Some students who have read "Tintern Abbey" in its entirety with teacher guidance and reinforced various skills may still have difficulty with comprehension. You may want to consider using the **Got It! Video,** Tape 3 to assess what information they have retained from their reading and to determine what aspects of the poem they still need to study.	After students have completed reading "Tintern Abbey," have them reread the section in which Wordsworth discusses his sister. Then, have students write short stories in which they describe a day in the life of Dorothy and William Wordsworth. Encourage students to use as many details from the poem as possible. Direct students to **Extension Activities,** p. 31, Activity 3 for more instruction.

13 Literary Analysis

Romanticism, the Lyric, and Diction

- Review the definitions of diction as word choice.
- Read the bracketed passage aloud, asking students to note Wordsworth's diction.
- Then, ask students the Literary Analysis question on p. 671: Does Wordsworth use simple or difficult words to describe old age? Are they specific or general?
  Answer: Students should recognize that Wordsworth describes old age using simple words that are general, rather than specific. Examples include: *matured, sober, pleasure,* and *mansion for all lovely forms.*

Answers for p. 671

Review and Assess

1. **(a)** It has been five years. **(b)** The time of year is summer. We learn this from the "unripe fruits" in line 12.
2. **(a)** These memories have soothed him and encouraged his kindness. **(b)** This other gift is a state of harmony with the world in which he sees into "the life of things" (lines 48–49).
3. On his second visit, to his pleasure is added a "sad perplexity" (line 60) and a new pleasure at the thought that his present experience will nourish him when he remembers it.
4. **(a)** He wishes that his sister will be helped by the memory of their visit. **(b)** In each case, the memory of nature has, or it is hoped will have, an inspiring effect. **(c)** Possible response: Memory is as important as nature in the poem; nature has a powerful effect through the recollection of its beauty, not through its immediate presence.
5. Possible responses: Some students may say that he has shown nature's powerful effects; others may say that he mystically exaggerates our ordinary appreciation of nature.
6. Possible responses: Students may agree with his ideas on the basis of their own appreciation of nature; others may say that Wordsworth does not address all aspects of our relationship with nature, such as the threat it can pose.

14 About the Selection

"The Prelude" is Wordsworth's lament over the failure of the French Revolution to live up to its early possibilities and rebuild society on just and rational principles. The poem describes the excitement stirred up by the original promise of the Revolution, the eventual corruption of its ideals, and the poet's struggle with the implications of the atrocities committed in the name of Revolution.

15 Literary Analysis

Romanticism and the Lyric

- Remind students that Romanticism reflected the poetic discovery of elevated feelings and truths in the world of common experience.
- Ask students the Literary Analysis question on p. 672: What connection can you find between the spirit described in these lines and the spirit of Wordsworth's "rebellion" against old styles of poetry?
  Answer: Students should recognize that Wordsworth's enthusiasm for "youth" and for the discovery of romance in the ordinary are motivations both for a new style in poetry and for social change. Just as the Revolution transformed the dry stuff of the law into something out of a fairy tale—by transforming the law people could transform the world to fit human nature—so Wordworth's new style transformed the dry, artificial verse of the past into a means of expressing more basic truths about human experience.

14 from The Prelude

William Wordsworth

Background

In 1790, Wordsworth witnessed the early, optimistic days of the French Revolution. The country seemed on the verge of achieving true freedom from outdated, oppressive feudal institutions. Caught up in the revolutionary fervor, Wordsworth felt he was seeing "France standing on the top of golden hours." The war between England and France (declared in 1793) and the violent turn taken by the French Revolution, known as the Reign of Terror (1793–1794), dashed Wordsworth's hopes.

O pleasant exercise of hope and joy!
For mighty were the auxiliars which then stood
Upon our side, us who were strong in love!
Bliss was it in that dawn to be alive,
But to be young was very Heaven! O times,
In which the meager, stale, forbidding ways
Of custom, law, and statute, took at once
The attraction of a country in romance!
When Reason seemed the most to assert her rights
When most intent on making of herself
15 A prime enchantress—to assist the work,
Which then was going forward in her name!
Not favored spots alone, but the whole Earth,
The beauty wore of promise—that which sets
(As at some moments might not be unfelt
Among the bowers of Paradise itself)
The budding rose above the rose full blown.
What temper at the prospect did not wake
To happiness unthought of? The inert
Were roused, and lively natures rapt away!
They who had fed their childhood upon dreams,
The play-fellows of fancy, who had made
All powers of swiftness, subtlety, and strength
Their ministers,—who in lordly wise had stirred
Among the grandest objects of the sense,
And dealt with whatsoever they found there
As if they had within some lurking right
To wield it;—they, too, who of gentle mood
Had watched all gentle motions, and to these

Literary Analysis
Romanticism and the Lyric What connection can you find between the spirit described in these lines and the spirit of Wordsworth's "rebellion" against old styles of poetry?

roused (rouzd) *v.* stirred up

ENRICHMENT: Literature Connection

Nature and Literature

Wordsworth's fascination with nature and its beneficial effects on his spirit was echoed in the writings of two American writers, Ralph Waldo Emerson and Henry David Thoreau, known as the American Romantics for the compatibility of their views with those of Wordsworth and Coleridge. Emerson and Thoreau, also known as Transcendentalists, lived in New England in the mid-nineteenth century and were advocates of the same kinds of appreciation of nature that Wordsworth sponsored in his writings. Both men stressed nature's ability to restore the human soul; Emerson believed in something called an "Oversoul," a spiritual unity among all beings that could be experienced by immersing oneself in nature, similar to Wordsworth's disturbing "presence." Thoreau abandoned life among other people and retreated for a year to a cabin in the woods near Walden Pond where he sought out the peace of nature that Wordsworth so eloquently describes in "Tintern Abbey."

16

Storming of the Bastille, 14 July 1789, Anonymous, Chateau, Versailles, France

17 ◀ **Critical Viewing** Compare and contrast the impression of the French Revolution conveyed by this poem to the one conveyed by this picture. **[Compare and Contrast]**

Had fitted their own thoughts, schemers more mild,
And in the region of their peaceful selves;—
Now was it that *both* found, the meek and lofty
Did both find helpers to their hearts' desire,
And stuff at hand, plastic as they could wish,—
Were called upon to exercise their skill,
Not in Utopia,—subterranean fields,—
Or some secreted island, Heaven knows where!
But in the very world, which is the world
Of all of us,—the place where, in the end,
We find our happiness, or not at all!

. . .

But now, become oppressors in their turn,
Frenchmen had changed a war of self-defense
For one of conquest, losing sight of all
Which they had struggled for: now mounted up,
Openly in the eye of earth and heaven,
The scale of liberty. I read her doom,
With anger vexed, with disappointment sore,
But not dismayed, nor taking to the shame
Of a false prophet. While resentment rose
Striving to hide, what nought could heal, the wounds
Of mortified presumption, I adhered
More firmly to old tenets, and, to prove
Their temper, strained them more; and thus, in heat
Of contest, did opinions every day
Grow into consequence, till round my mind
They clung, as if they were its life, nay more,
The very being of the immortal soul.

. . . .

presumption (prē zump′ shən) *n.* audacity

18 ✓ **Reading Check** To which two kinds of people did the Revolution appeal?

16 Background

Art

Storming of the Bastille, 14 July 1789, Anonymous

This painting illustrates an important event in the French Revolution. On July 14, 1789, an angry mob protesting actions by King Louis XVI seized control of the long-hated Bastille prison, a symbol of royalty's absolute power. Many of the prisoners in the Bastille had been held without trial or legal cause. July 14 has since been celebrated as a French national holiday. *The Storming of the Bastille, 14 July 1789,* vividly captures the mob's assault on the prison. Use these questions for discussion:

1. How might Wordsworth respond to the scene depicted in the painting?
   Answer: He might have responded with enthusiasm for the spirit of liberation and democracy it represented.
2. How does the painting add to the poem's impact?
   Answer: It explains some of the context and creates a visual image of revolutionary fervor.

17 ▶ Critical Viewing

Answer: Students should note that the painting depicts the violence and suffering that was involved in the revolution, whereas this portion of "The Prelude" reveals the philosophical torment that resulted from the failure of the revolutionaries to live up to their ideals.

18 ✓ Reading Check

Answer: The Revolution appealed both to people "who had fed their childhood upon dreams" of ordering the world and to contemplative people who had adapted their thoughts to "all gentle motions."

CUSTOMIZE INSTRUCTION FOR UNIVERSAL ACCESS

For Less Proficient Readers	For Gifted/Talented Students	For Advanced Readers
Have students read from "The Prelude" with teacher guidance. Encourage students to focus on Wordsworth's feelings about the French Revolution. Direct students who are having difficulty understanding the context of the work to *"The Prelude:* The French Revolution" on **Interest Grabber Video,** Tape 4.	Have students read "The Prelude" in small groups and devise "Before" and "After" posters in which they express how Wordsworth felt before and after he was disillusioned with the French Revolution. Students may want to illustrate these changes in opinion and include quotes from the poem that suggest Wordsworth's changing views.	In "The Prelude," Wordsworth describes how his feelings toward the French Revolution changed. Have students write poems in which they describe something from their lives about which they have changed their opinions. Then, have them compare their poems with an excerpt from "The Prelude."

⑲ Vocabulary Development

Forms of *anatomize*

Word Analysis:

- Call students' attention to *anatomize*, a word that means "to dissect in order to examine structure." Explain to students that *anatomize* is related to the noun *anatomy* and the adjective *anatomical;* all of them come from the same Greek root.
- Have students suggest other related words, and list them on the chalkboard. Possible responses: *anatomist, atom, atomism*
- Have students look up any unfamiliar words in a dictionary.

Answers for p. 674

Review and Assess

1. **(a)** He characterizes it with the phrase "O pleasant exercise of hope and joy!" **(b)** This reaction reflects basic values of freedom and social equality. **(c)** Reason seemed to serve high ideals in the Revolution.
2. **(a)** The French became "oppressors," conquering other regions. **(b)** At first, Wordsworth tried to justify continued faith in the Revolution; in the end, he lost all feeling of conviction.
3. **(a)** When he turned aside from Nature's way, he became so misguided by maxims and creeds that he had to give up all of his convictions. **(b)** Wordsworth resolves his conflict by giving up his attempts to explain and justify. **(c)** Wordsworth learns to distrust reason and to place faith in his heart guided by nature.
4. Possible responses: Students may feel that Wordsworth has given up his political hopes too easily; he might have retained these hopes even while condemning the turn taken by the French Revolution.

I summoned my best skill, and toiled, intent
⑲ To anatomize the frame of social life,
Yea, the whole body of society
Searched to its heart. Share with me, Friend! the wish
That some dramatic tale, endued with shapes
Livelier, and flinging out less guarded words
Than suit the work we fashion, might set forth
What then I learned, or think I learned, of truth,
And the errors into which I fell, betrayed
By present objects, and by reasonings false
From their beginnings, inasmuch as drawn
Out of a heart that had been turned aside
From Nature's way by outward accidents,
And which are thus confounded, more and more
Misguided, and misguiding. So I fared,
Dragging all precepts, judgments, maxims, creeds,
Like culprits to the bar; calling the mind,
Suspiciously, to establish in plain day
Her titles and her honors; now believing,
Now disbelieving; endlessly perplexed
With impulse, motive, right and wrong, the ground
Of obligation, what the rule and whence
The sanction; till, demanding formal *proof*,
And seeking it in every thing, I lost
All feeling of conviction, and, in fine,
Sick, wearied out with contrarieties,
Yielded up moral questions in despair.

anatomize (ə nat´ ə mīz´) *v.* to dissect in order to examine structure

confounded (kən found´ id) *adj.* confused; mixed together indiscriminately; bewildered

Review and Assess

Thinking About the Selection

1. **(a) Recall:** With what phrase does the speaker describe the early days of the French Revolution? **(b) Generalize:** What basic values does his reaction reflect? **(c) Interpret:** What role did reason seem to play in the Revolution?
2. **(a) Recall:** What change in the course of the French Revolution caused a conflict in Wordsworth? **(b) Interpret:** What two reactions to this turn of events does Wordsworth describe?
3. **(a) Interpret:** What does Wordsworth say happened to him when his heart "had been turned aside / From Nature's way"? **(b) Interpret:** At the end of the excerpt, how has Wordsworth resolved his conflict? **(c) Draw Conclusions:** What change in his attitude toward reason does this experience bring about?
4. **Make a Judgment:** Do you think Wordsworth has given up political hopes too easily? Explain.

ENRICHMENT: Music Connection

Romantic Music

The Romantic movement was not confined to literature, as the J.M.W. Turner painting on p. 670 demonstrates. Music was also deeply affected by Romantic ideals, reverberating with new emotional significance. Composers such as Ludwig van Beethoven, Johannes Brahms, Robert Schumann and his wife, pianist Clara Schumann, and Felix Mendelssohn created works ranging from symphonies to chamber music to *lieder* (popular songs).

Like Wordsworth's poetry, Romantic music often reflected social events. For example, Beethoven's Symphony No. 3, originally entitled *Great Symphony for Napoleon Bonaparte,* was written in response to Napoleon Bonaparte's dramatic efforts to save the French Revolution. When Bonaparte made himself Emperor, betraying French democratic ideals, an angry and disappointed Beethoven changed the symphony's name.

20 The World Is Too Much with Us

William Wordsworth

The world is too much with us; late and soon,
Getting and spending, we lay waste our powers:
Little we see in Nature that is ours;
We have given our hearts away, a sordid boon![1]
This Sea that bares her bosom to the moon;
The winds that will be howling at all hours,
And are upgathered now like sleeping flowers;
For this, for everything, we are out of tune;
It moves us not.—Great God! I'd rather be
A Pagan suckled in a creed outworn;
So might I, standing on this pleasant lea,[2]
Have glimpses that would make me less forlorn;
Have sight of Proteus[3] rising from the sea;
Or hear old Triton[4] blow his wreathèd horn.

1. **boon** favor.
2. **lea** meadow.
3. **Proteus** (prō´ tē əs) in Greek mythology, a sea god who could change his appearance at will.
4. **Triton** in Greek mythology, a sea god with the head and upper body of a man and the tail of a fish.

21 **▲ Critical Viewing**
Do you agree with Wordsworth that an image such as this one "moves us not"? Explain. **[Make a Judgment]**

sordid (sôr´ did) *adj.* dirty

22 **Reading Check**
According to the speaker, in what way do we "lay waste our powers"?

20 About the Selections

In these sonnets, Wordsworth criticizes attitudes prevalent in the society of his day. In "The World Is Too Much With Us," he laments the materialism and preoccupation with business that have blinded people to the wonder of being. Wordsworth offers as contrast pagan society, which saw nature not as a mass of "resources" but as the manifestation of the gods.

Wordsworth wrote "London, 1802" (p. 676) after a brief return visit to France. The contrast between what he called the "vanity and parade" of London life and the "desolation" after the revolution in France moved him to blast what he saw as the self-absorption and falseness of the English.

21 ▶ Critical Viewing

Possible responses: Some students will say that the moon does move us emotionally; others will note that Wordsworth is pointing out that, as a society, we do not appreciate nature as deeply as cultures that personify its forces.

22  Reading Check

Answer: We lay waste our powers in "getting and spending."

CUSTOMIZE INSTRUCTION FOR UNIVERSAL ACCESS

For Advanced Readers

Refer students who wish to do more in-depth analysis of Wordsworth and his lyric poetry to **Authors In Depth: The British Tradition,** which contains nine additional poems, including the following:

- "Strange Fits of Passion I Have Known," p. 127
- "Lucy Gray," p. 132
- "We Are Seven," p. 134
- "The Solitary Reaper," p. 137
- "It Is a Beauteous Evening, Calm and Free," p. 138

Have students form discussion groups after reading these selections and present reports to the class.

ASSESS

Answers for p. 676

Review and Assess

1. Possible response: Students might describe ways in which the false values of commercialism at the holidays or the press of a busy schedule can diminish the quality of experience.
2. **(a)** People waste their powers by "getting and spending." **(b)** "The world" means material concerns.
3. **(a)** According to the speaker, we are out of tune with the moonlit, calm sea and with nature generally. **(b)** Being out of tune with nature means that we live in a world that is cold and sterile; we do not find things of human value and significance in nature ("Little we see in Nature that is ours," line 3). **(c)** He envisions the relation to nature implied in pagan religion, in which nature appears personified, its powers rendered in human terms.
4. **(a)** England is stagnant, lacking in "inward happiness," and filled with selfish, mediocre people. **(b)** This condition results from the fact that the English lack "manners, virtue, freedom, power." **(c)** Milton's moral vision and example would help restore England to its former ways.
5. Both poems deplore society's lack of vision. In "The World," the problem is with our relation to nature; in "London, 1802," the problem is in people's relations with themselves and one another. In both cases, we have fallen away from our full potential.
6. Possible responses: Students may agree that the materialism in modern American culture, like that in the English culture Wordsworth critiques, deprives us of a truly rich experience of nature. Students may also agree that, like England in Wordsworth's assessment, virtue has declined in modern America, as demonstrated, for instance, by frequent scandals reported on the news.

Milton![1] thou should'st be living at this hour:
England hath need of thee: she is a fen[2]
Of stagnant waters: altar, sword, and pen,
Fireside, the heroic wealth of hall and bower,
Have forfeited their ancient English dower
Of inward happiness. We are selfish men;
Oh! raise us up, return to us again;
And give us manners, virtue, freedom, power.
Thy soul was like a Star, and dwelt apart:
Thou hadst a voice whose sound was like the sea:
Pure as the naked heavens, majestic, free,
So didst thou travel on life's common way,
In cheerful godliness; and yet thy heart
The lowliest duties on herself did lay.

stagnant (stag′ nənt) *adj.* motionless; foul

1. **Milton** seventeenth-century English poet John Milton.
2. **fen** (fen) *n.* area of low, flat, marshy land.

Review and Assess

Thinking About the Selections

1. **Respond:** When have you felt that "The world is too much with us"?
2. **(a) Recall:** In "The World Is Too Much with Us," what activities cause people to exhaust their "powers"? **(b) Interpret:** What does the speaker mean by the "world"?
3. **(a) Recall:** According to the speaker, with what are we "out of tune"? **(b) Interpret:** Why is being out of tune with these experiences such a loss? **(c) Interpret:** What relationship with nature does the poet envision at the end of the sonnet?
4. **(a) Recall:** According to "London, 1802," what is England like? **(b) Analyze:** What lacks or missing qualities have caused this condition? **(c) Interpret:** How would Milton's return help?
5. **Compare and Contrast:** How are the problems criticized in the two poems similar? How are they different?
6. **Apply:** Do Wordsworth's criticisms of England also apply to modern America? Explain.

ASSESSMENT PRACTICE: Critical Reading

Critical Reasoning **(For more practice, see Test Preparation Workbook, p. 31.)**

Many tests require students to judge the relevance of facts in a writer's argument. Use the following sample item.

These waters, rolling from their mountain springs
With a soft inland murmur. Once again
Do I behold these steep and lofty cliffs,
That on a wild secluded scene impress
Thoughts of more deep seclusion; and connect
The landscape with the quiet of the sky.

Which of these facts would **not** reinforce the mood Wordsworth is trying to create?

A There is a lark singing in the hedgerows.
B Wordsworth can clearly see the mountains.
C Wordsworth is wearing new boots.
D There is dew beading the grass.

Lead students to recognize that Wordsworth is emphasizing the beauty of nature. *C*, which has nothing to do with this theme, is the correct answer.

Review and Assess

Literary Analysis

Romanticism and the Lyric

1. Identify a passage from the poems that illustrates Wordsworth's idealized view of nature.
2. Find a passage that reflects the **Romantic** belief in the dignity and importance of ordinary people and their language.
3. Romantic **lyrics** focused on the speaker's personal development. What lessons from Wordsworth's growth might readers adopt?

Comparing Literary Works

4. Using a chart like the one shown, find examples in the poems of **diction** that is specific and simple, abstract but simple, or abstract and difficult. Then, summarize your results.

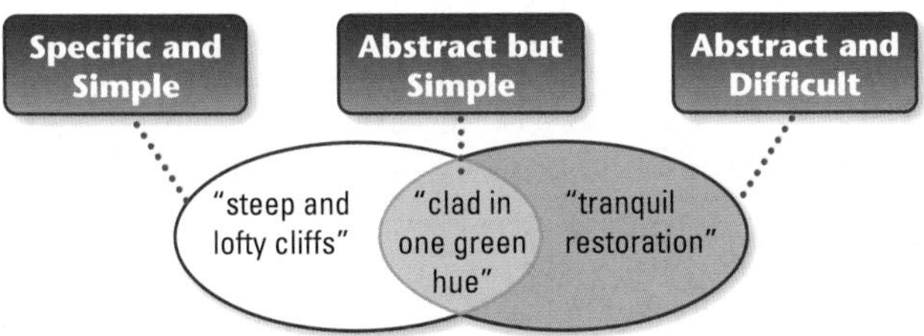

5. Wordsworth's subjects in these poems range widely, from natural scenes to politics to modern life. Does his diction vary to match his subject? Support your answer with details from the poems.

Reading Strategy

Using Literary Context

6. Imagine that you are a Neoclassical writer—a sociable city-dweller who writes polished, witty, rational verse. Explain how you might react to lines 76–80 of "Tintern Abbey."
7. (a) What do the hopes described in *The Prelude* tell you about the Romantic **literary context**? (b) What do lines 66–84 suggest about Romantic dissatisfaction with the Neoclassical context?

Extend Understanding

8. **Cultural Connection:** Would Wordsworth have appreciated modern technology such as computers and the Internet? Explain.

Quick Review

Romanticism was a literary movement that favored the expression of spontaneous feeling, simple diction, reverence for nature, self-awareness, and a celebration of common people.

A **lyric poem** expresses the observations and feelings of a single speaker.

Diction is a writer's word choice. It may favor abstract or concrete words, simple or difficult words, and common or specialized words.

To **use literary context,** connect what you are reading to the climate of literary practices and assumptions that influenced the author.

 ***Take It to the Net***

www.phschool.com

Take the interactive self-test online to check your understanding of these selections.

ENRICHMENT: Further Reading

Other Works by William Wordsworth

Lyrical Ballads

The Excursion

The Borderers

The River Duddon

 ***Take It to the Net***

Visit www.phschool.com for more information on William Wordsworth.

Answers for p. 677

Review and Assess

1. Possible response: Wordsworth's idealized feeling for nature is revealed in these lines: "And I have felt / A presence that disturbs me with the joy / Of elevated thoughts; a sense sublime / Of something far more deeply interfused, / . . . / A motion and a spirit, that impels / All thinking things, all objects of all thought, / And rolls through all things. . . ." ("Tintern Abbey," lines 93–102)
2. Possible response: Wordsworth's appreciation of ordinary language is seen in phrases such as "My dear, dear Friend, . . ." ("Tintern Abbey," line 116).
3. Possible response: Students may say that in both "Tintern Abbey" and "The Prelude" Wordsworth shows that losses or changes can lead to growth, a lesson readers may find valuable.
4. Specific and Simple: ". . . I again repose / Here, under this dark sycamore, ..."; Abstract but Simple: "The anchor of my purest thoughts . . ."; Abstract and Difficult: "A motion and a spirit, that impels / All thinking things . . ."
5. Possible response: Wordsworth's diction is fairly consistent in all four poems. Students should quote passages to support their arguments.
6. Possible response: Students may say that the Neoclassical writer would respond with puzzlement at lines that treat nature emotionally. The writer would view Wordsworth's style with disdain, since it does not use the refined vocabulary or neat, formally polished expressions of ideas that Neoclassical writers valued.
7. **(a)** These lines suggest that political idealism, youthful enthusiasm, and a desire for change, all passions stirred by the French Revolution, were important elements of this context. **(b)** Romantic hopes and dreams could not be satisfied through reliance on reason, and the Romantics rejected the central importance of reason in the Neoclassical view.

continued

Answers continued

8. Possible responses: Wordsworth probably would not have appreciated the way in which computers remove us from nature, but he might approve of the leisure-time they make possible and the information they provide, which help us enjoy nature.

EXTEND

Answers for p. 678

❶ Vocabulary Development

Word Analysis: Forms of *anatomize*

1. b
2. c
3. a
4. d

Concept Development: Synonyms

1. e
2. c
3. g
4. d
5. b
6. a
7. f

Spelling Strategy

1. criticized
2. advertise
3. recognizing

❷ Grammar and Style

1. calling for social change and praising nature; Romantics
2. Hoping to change the world; they
3. trying to locate modern-day Romantics; you
4. advocating a return to nature and the land; works
5. reflecting the clash of technology and nature; irony

Writing Application

Possible response: Wanting to see more of my natural surroundings, I wandered into the woods in my backyard. The first thing I noticed was a small squirrel digging a hole and burying acorns.

Integrate Language Skills

❶ Vocabulary Development Lesson

Word Analysis: Forms of *anatomize*

The verb *anatomize,* meaning "cut into constituent parts" or "dissect," comes from the Greek word *atomos,* meaning "that which cannot be cut further; the smallest part." When Wordsworth tries to "anatomize" society, he tries to "dissect," or analyze, it into the parts that make it up. Several scientific words come from this Greek word. In your notebook, match each word with its meaning.

1. anatomy
2. atom
3. anatomist
4. atomism

a. one who studies the structure of the body
b. the study of parts
c. the smallest part into which something can be divided
d. the theory that the world is made of tiny, indivisible particles

Concept Development: Synonyms

For each numbered word, write the letter of the word that is closest to it in meaning.

1. roused	a. audacity
2. sordid	b. dissect
3. stagnant	c. dirty
4. confounded	d. perplexed
5. anatomize	e. stirred
6. presumption	f. reward
7. recompense	g. foul

Spelling Strategy

In Standard American English, the suffix *-ize* is common, as in the word *anatomize*. The suffix *-ise* is used in only about thirty common words, including *exercise*. Correct each misspelled word below.

1. criticised 2. advertize 3. recognising

❷ Grammar and Style Lesson

Present Participial Phrases

A **present participial phrase** consists of a verb form ending in *-ing* and its complements and modifiers. The entire phrase functions as an adjective. In this example, the phrase modifies the pronoun *I*.

So might I, standing on this pleasant lea, . . .

By using present participial phrases, writers place their readers in the middle of an action that is already underway, drawing them in.

Practice Identify the present participial phrase in each sentence, and tell the word it modifies.

1. Today's world is full of Romantics calling for social change and praising nature.
2. Hoping to change the world, they write and take action.
3. You can search the Internet if you are trying to locate modern-day Romantics.
4. Essayists publish works on the Web advocating a return to nature and the land.
5. The irony of "Romanticism on the Web," reflecting the clash of technology and nature, is acknowledged by many.

Writing Application Write a paragraph about an experience you have had with nature. Use two or more present participial phrases. Circle the phrases and underline the noun or pronoun each modifies.

WG *Prentice Hall Writing and Grammar Connection: Chapter 19, Section 2*

TEACHING RESOURCES

The following resources can be used to enrich or extend the instruction for pp. 678–679.

Vocabulary

- **Selection Support:** Build Vocabulary, p. 143
- **Vocabulary and Spelling Practice Book** (Use this booklet for skills enrichment.)

Grammar

- **Selection Support:** Grammar and Style, p. 144
- **Writing and Grammar,** Diamond Level, p. 446
- **Daily Language Practice Transparencies**

Writing

- **Writing and Grammar,** Diamond Level, p. 315
- **Writing and Grammar iText CD-ROM**
- **Writing Models and Graphic Organizers on Transparencies,** pp. 45–56

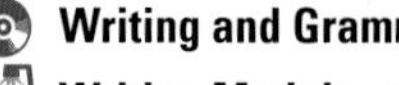

BLOCK SCHEDULING: Resources marked with this symbol provide varied instruction during 90-minute blocks.

❸ Writing Lesson

Response to Criticism

Author Thomas Wolfe defined the true Romantic feeling as "not the desire to escape life, but to prevent life from escaping you." In an essay, explain whether or not Wordsworth's poetry is captured by this definition.

Prewriting Discuss Wolfe's claim with a partner. Then, look in Wordsworth's poems for lines that reflect the desire "to prevent life from escaping you." If you cannot find any, you might challenge Wolfe's claim.

Drafting Begin your essay by relating Wolfe's quotation to Wordsworth's poetry. As you draft, organize your examples in logical order, and use quotations to support your evaluation.

Revising Review the lines of poetry you have analyzed, and circle key words they include. Add sentences to your draft if necessary to explain finer shades of meaning in these key words.

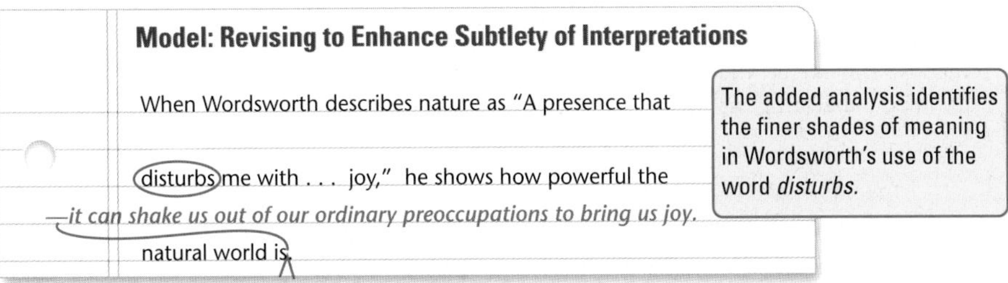

Model: Revising to Enhance Subtlety of Interpretations
When Wordsworth describes nature as "A presence that
disturbs me with . . . joy," he shows how powerful the
natural world is
—it can shake us out of our ordinary preoccupations to bring us joy.
The added analysis identifies the finer shades of meaning in Wordsworth's use of the word *disturbs.*

Prentice Hall Writing and Grammar Connection: Chapter 14, Section 3

❹ Extension Activities

Listening and Speaking The Romantic Movement affected arts other than literature. With two classmates, research Romanticism in the arts and assemble a **photo essay presentation.**

1. Use informal expressions for liveliness and technical language for precision.
2. Provide captions explaining each example.

Share your photo essay in an oral presentation, such as a slide show. **[Group Activity]**

Research and Technology Write a **cultural analysis** connecting Romanticism with the ecology movement. Develop a research strategy to find out about an active environmental group. In your analysis, identify Romantic influences in the group's statements.

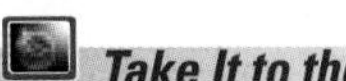

www.phschool.com

Go online for an additional research activity using the Internet.

Lesson Support for p. 679

❸ Writing Lesson

- Explain that in this lesson, students will write responses to a critic's observation about Wordsworth.
- Remind students that the foundation of a response to criticism is evidence in the text that supports or disproves the critical observation to which it responds.
- Remind students to include quotations from Wordsworth's poems to support their thesis statements.
- Use the Writing Lesson to guide students in developing their responses to criticism.
- Use the Response to Literature rubric in **Performance Assessment and Portfolio Management,** p. 25, to evaluate students' essays.

❹ Listening and Speaking

- Have students work in groups of three to research how the Romantic Movement affected arts other than literature.
- Read the Listening and Speaking Lesson with students.
- Then, have them conduct research to prepare a photo essay presentation with a script.
- Encourage them to organize their research efforts. First, they might divide up nonliterary arts, such as music and painting. Then, they should identify important names and trends using reference works that provide a survey of the movement. Selecting among these names and trends, they should then perform additional research to flesh out their understanding of the movement and acquire visual and audio material to incorporate into their presentation.

CUSTOMIZE INSTRUCTION
For Universal Access

To address different learning styles, use the activities suggested in the **Extension Activities** booklet, p. 31.

- For Visual/Spatial Learners, use Activity 5.
- For Musical/Rhythmic Learners, use Activity 6.
- For Verbal/Linguistic Learners, use Activity 7.

ASSESSMENT RESOURCES

The following resources can be used to assess students' knowledge and skills.

Selection Assessment

- **Formal Assessment,** pp. 152–154
- **Open Book Test,** pp. 91–93
- **Got It! Assessment Videotapes,** Tape 3
- **Test Bank Software**

Take It to the Net

Visit www.phschool.com for self-tests and additional questions on the selections.

Writing Rubric

- **Performance Assessment and Portfolio Management,** pp. 25 and 92

PRENTICE HALL ASSESSMENT SYSTEM

- **Workbook**
- **Transparencies**
- **Skill Book**
- **CD-ROM**

Objectives

1. To read book reviews for greater insight into literary works
2. To understand the reviewer's assumptions in a book review
3. To identify a reviewer's scale of value and form an opinion about his or her judgments

About Book Reviews

- Have students read "About Book Reviews." Then, ask students what other responses there are to literature besides book reviews.
  Possible response: Answers include essays, journal entries, journal articles.
- Next, have students discuss the various responses to literature.
- Ask students what the purposes are behind responses to literature.
  Possible response: Some purposes are to inform, to instruct, and to inspire.

Reading Strategy

Analyzing a Writer's Basic Assumptions

- Ask students to define the word *assumption.*
  Answer: An assumption may be a fact taken for granted or a guiding principle.
- Tell students that often how one acts or reacts to something is based on assumption.
- Ask students what assumptions are based on.
  Possible response: Assumptions are often based on previous knowledge or experience of the thing or situation in question. Assumptions come from one's culture, relation to family and friends, and education.
- Then, ask students how assumptions, when applied to a literary work, lead to a measurement of its value—a judgment of the work.
  Possible response: Assumptions include the critical criteria by which one typically evaluates a work. One reader may use the values *boring/exciting.* Another may use the values *superficial/deep.*
- Tell students that isolating terms in a review indicating positive or negative values will help them evaluate a reviewer's assumptions about literature.

READING INFORMATIONAL MATERIALS

Book Reviews

About Book Reviews

A **response to literature** is a piece of writing that discusses a reader's reaction to a work. A response might show why a story is moving, point out the beauties of a poem, or analyze the short-comings of a play. One type of response to literature is a book review. **Book reviews** include these elements:

- A report of the reviewer's reactions to and insights into a work
- General observations about works of this type
- Insight into the relationship of the work reviewed to the writer's life or other works, past, present, or to come
- A recommendation about the work to readers

Reading Strategy

Analyzing a Writer's Basic Assumptions

A good book reviewer uses a rich set of assumptions about what is important or valuable in literary writing. Applying these assumptions to a book, the critic can measure its value. To understand these measurements and, ultimately, to make up your own mind about the work, identify a reviewer's scale of values, **analyzing his or her assumptions**. Begin with these questions:

1. To what general ideas, such as originality or good taste, does the reviewer repeatedly refer?
2. What are the more powerful evaluative terms the reviewer uses? Look for words like *compelling* or *sentimental*.
3. Which of these ideas and terms does the reviewer take in a positive sense? Which in a negative sense?
4. Do any of these ideas or terms come in pairs of opposites that could define a scale of values, from best to worst?

As you read, use a chart like the one shown to analyze Jeffrey's scale of poetic values.

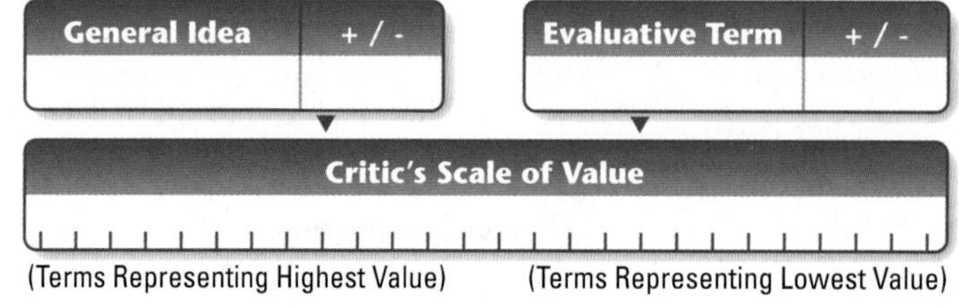

Early Reviews of Wordsworth

Francis Jeffrey

Book reviews,

The Edinburgh Review, 1807 and 1814

Jeffrey describes a distinctive general characteristic he has found in the poetry of Wordsworth and others. He offers an insight into the sources of this characteristic.

Through the use of terms such as *freedom, originality, authority, vulgar,* and *plebeian,* Jeffrey defines two scales of value: high-class versus vulgar, individuality versus polish.

With Mr. Wordsworth and his friends, it is plain that their peculiarities of diction[1] are things of choice, and not of accident. They write as they do, upon principle and system; and it evidently costs them much pains to keep *down* to the standard which they have proposed to themselves. They are, to the full, as much mannerists,[2] too, as the poetasters[3] who ring changes on the commonplaces of magazine versification; and all the difference between them is, that they borrow their phrases from a different and scantier *gradus ad Parnassum.*[4] If they were, indeed, to discard all imitation and set phraseology, and to bring in no words merely for show or for meter—as much, perhaps, might be gained in freedom and originality, as would infallibly be lost in allusion and authority; but, in point of fact, the new poets are just as great borrowers as the old; only that, instead of borrowing from the more popular passages of their illustrious predecessors, they have preferred furnishing themselves from vulgar ballads and plebeian nurseries.

. . .

Long habits of seclusion, and an excessive ambition of originality, can alone account for the disproportion which seems to exist between this author's taste and his genius; or for the devotion with which he has sacrificed so many precious gifts at the shrine of those paltry idols which he has set up for himself among his lakes and his mountains. Solitary musings, amidst such scenes, might no doubt be expected to nurse up the mind to the majesty of poetical conception (though it is remarkable, that all the greater poets lived, or had lived, in the full current

1. **diction** (dik′ shən) *n.* choice of words; style of expression.
2. **mannerists** artists using an exaggerated or artificial style.
3. **poetasters** (pō′ ət as′ tərz) *n.* inferior poets.
4. ***gradus ad Parnassum*** (grā′ dəs ad pär nas′ oom) *n.* dictionary for writing poetry (Latin for "step to Parnassus," mountain of Apollo and the Muses, deities of the arts).

Early Reviews of Wordsworth

- Remind students that Jeffrey's review uses early-nineteenth-century British English. Tell them to look up all unknown words in their dictionary.
- Have students read the selection, including the footnotes, and tell them to pay close attention to the call-out boxes accompanying the selection.
- Remind students to identify the general ideas up for discussion as they read the selection.
- Have students note down the terms that indicate measurements of value. Remind them that these words point to the reviewer's ultimate assumptions about literature.
- Ask students what label Jeffrey gives Romantic writers because of their "peculiarities of diction." **Answer:** He calls them "mannerists," meaning that, despite their claim to spontaneity, they actually have decided consciously to draw attention to their poetry by using nonpoetic language.
- Then, ask them if this is a positive or negative term. **Answer:** It is a negative term, since it means that their style is artificial.
- Next, ask students how the label *mannerist* relates to the second call-out box and its corresponding passages. **Possible response:** By calling Romantic writers mannerist—their use of language is not original but an artificial construct—Jeffrey is setting up his critique of Wordsworth's taste: His choice of "vulgar" subjects and language is in poor taste.

CUSTOMIZE INSTRUCTION FOR UNIVERSAL ACCESS

For English Learners	For Gifted/Talented Students	For Advanced Readers
Most of these students will have difficulty with the language in the selection. Guide students through the difficult diction and syntax. You may wish to pair these students up with Advanced Readers and have them answer the **Check Your Comprehension** and **Applying the Reading Strategy** questions on p. 683 together.	Have these students form a group and use a talk-show format to present an interview between Wordsworth and a book critic to the rest of the class. Students may work on the script together. Have them discuss two or more poems that they have read in class.	Have these students read work by other Romantic poets and write a short review on a poem or essay comparing their judgments with Jeffrey's. Then, have them present their work to the class.

Early Reviews of Wordsworth (continued)

- Call students' attention to the first call-out box on p. 682. Ask them to define *tact*.
  Answer: Tact is a sense of propriety, or a sense of what to do or say to maintain good relations.
- Ask students to summarize what Jeffrey says about genius.
  Possible response: Although tact cannot replace genius, the genius of a writer's work cannot be recognized and received without tact—a consideration of the reading public and of the experience of past artists.
- Have students read the second call-out box. Ask: Why does Jeffrey call attention to Wordsworth's early work?
  Possible response: Jeffrey may wish to relate to the reader that Wordsworth's quest for originality in his earlier work and, subsequently, the pitfalls of this route, is no passing fancy: it is based "upon principle and system."

Quarterly Magazines

The quarterly *The Edinburgh Review*, in which Jeffrey's reviews were first published, was a significant cultural institution. Founded in 1802 in Edinburgh, Scotland, by Jeffrey (who served as its editor), Sydney Smith, and others, the *Review* published numerous important writers, including the Romantic critic William Hazlitt. Ask students: Why is the cultural commentary published in such journals significant?
Possible responses: Such periodicals help shape readers' tastes; they open up debate on the arts.

of society), but the collision of equal minds—the admonition of prevailing impressions—seems necessary to reduce its redundancies, and repress that tendency to extravagance or puerility, into which the self-indulgence and self-admiration of genius is so apt to be betrayed, when it is allowed to wanton, without awe or restraint, in the triumph and delight of its own intoxication. That its flights should be graceful and glorious in the eyes of men, it seems almost to be necessary that they should be made in the consciousness that men's eyes are to behold them,—and that the inward transport and vigor by which they are inspired, should be tempered by an occasional reference to what will be thought of them by those ultimate dispensers of glory. An habitual and general knowledge of the few settled and permanent maxims, which form the canon[5] of general taste in all large and polished societies—a certain tact, which informs us at once that many things, which we still love and are moved by in secret, must necessarily be despised as childish, or derided as absurd, in all such societies—though it will not stand in the place of genius, seems necessary to the success of its exertions; and though it will never enable anyone to produce the higher beauties of art, can alone secure the talent which does produce them, from errors that must render it useless. Those who have most of the talent, however, commonly acquire this knowledge with the greatest facility; and if Mr. Wordsworth, instead of confining himself almost entirely to the society of the dalesmen[6] and cottagers and little children, who form the subjects of his book, had condescended to mingle a little more with the people that were to read and judge of it, we cannot help thinking that its texture might have been considerably improved: at least it appears to us to be absolutely impossible, that anyone who had lived or mixed familiarly with men of literature and ordinary judgment in poetry, (of course we exclude the coadjutors[7] and disciples of his own school) could ever have fallen into such gross faults, or so long mistaken them for beauties. His first essays we looked upon in a good degree as poetical paradoxes—maintained experimentally, in order to display talent, and court notoriety;—and so maintained, with no more serious belief in their truth, than is usually generated by an ingenious and animated defense of other paradoxes. But when we find that he has been for twenty years exclusively employed upon articles of this very fabric, and that he has still enough of raw material on hand to keep him so employed for twenty years to come, we cannot refuse him the justice of believing that he is a sincere convert to his own system. . . .

Here Jeffrey makes a general observation on the ingredients for successful poetry: genius guided by tact.

Jeffrey relates the work that he is reviewing to the author's earlier work, giving the reader a more general sense of Wordsworth as a writer.

5. **canon** (kan´ ən) *n.* group of established, basic rules.

6. **dalesmen** simple farmers.
7. **coadjutors** (ko aj´ ə tərz) *n.* assistants.

Check Your Comprehension

1. Judging from this review, what details of Wordsworth's poetry made his work revolutionary at the time?
2. According to Jeffrey, what aspects of Wordsworth's life shaped the style and content of his poetry?
3. Summarize the advice Jeffrey might give Wordsworth.

Applying the Reading Strategy

Analyzing a Writer's Basic Assumptions

Answer the following questions to determine the scale of critical values that Jeffrey applies to Wordsworth's poetry.

1. (a) Does Jeffrey agree that Wordsworth's poetry has originality? Explain. (b) Summarize the relationship Jeffrey sees between originality and self-indulgence or "intoxication."
2. What does Jeffrey see as the foundation for good poetry: originality and genius, which are the properties of an individual, or tact and polish, which represent an agreement in taste among many people? Support your answer.

Activity

Writing a Review

Francis Jeffrey was not the first person and will not be the last to write an essay on Wordsworth's poems. Read or review William Wordsworth's "Lines Composed a Few Miles Above Tintern Abbey" (p. 666). Write your own review of this poem. As you write, determine whether the poem suffers from the faults ascribed to the Romantics by Jeffrey or whether Jeffrey's assumptions left him unable to appreciate Wordsworth's poetry.

Comparing Informational Materials

Compare Jeffrey's review from the early 1800s with a contemporary view of Wordsworth's poetry. Write an essay answering these questions: Are the scale of critical values similar in both reviews? Did tastes shift significantly from the time of one essay to the time of the other? Use the chart to help you compare the critiques presented in the two reviews.

	Jeffrey's Review	Contemporary Review
Similarities		
Differences		

Amswers for p. 683

Check Your Comprehension

1. His use of diction from ordinary speech and his references to nature and rural existence made Wordsworth's work revolutionary at the time.
2. Wordworth's rural surroundings and isolation from other, cultured people shaped his poetry.
3. Possible response: Your work would surely improve, Mr. Wordsworth, if you would come in from the country and mix with men of letters and your reading public who, after all, are the ones capable of judging it.

Applying the Reading Strategy

1. **(a)** Jeffrey says Wordsworth's poetry has originality.
   (b) Possible response: In Jeffrey's view, originality is valuable in the case of genius, but in most cases it is just an idea people use to excuse their egotistical attachment to their own efforts, however defective.
2. Jeffrey believes that genius and originality cannot exist independent from an awareness of the people's taste. It is necessary to be around like minds for constructive feedback so as to check one's tendency toward deluded self-centeredness and ideas that lack relation to public discourse. Thus tact is the foundation of good poetry.

Activity

Tell students to be firm in their positive or negative opinions of Wordsworth's poem. Remind them to formulate a clear, brief thesis statement and to gather pertinent details from the poem for their review.

continued

Answers continued

Comparing Informational Materials

- Tell students to find a contemporary review comparable in length and substance to Jeffrey's review.
- Remind students of essay structure: introduction, thesis statement, body, and conclusion.

The Rime of the Ancient Mariner ✦ Kubla Khan

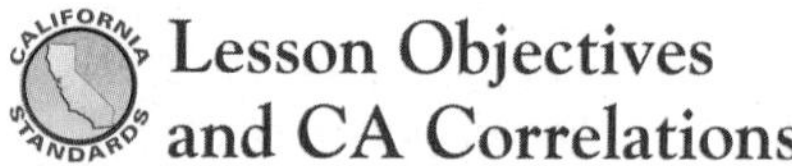

Lesson Objectives and CA Correlations

1. **To analyze and respond to literary elements**
   - Literary Analysis: Poetic Sound Devices **R 3.3**
   - Comparing Literary Works **R 3.1**
2. **To read, comprehend, analyze, and critique a poem**
   - Reading Strategy: Analyzing Poetic Effects **R 3.4**
   - Reading Check Questions
   - Review and Assess Questions
   - Assessment Practice (ATE)
3. **To develop word analysis skills, fluency, and systematic vocabulary**
   - Vocabulary Development Lesson: Latin Root *-journ-* **R 1.1**
4. **To understand and apply written and oral language conventions**
   - Spelling Strategy **LC 1.2**
   - Grammar and Style Lesson: Inverted Word Order **LC 1.1**
5. **To understand and apply appropriate writing and research strategies**
   - Writing Lesson: Analysis of a Symbol **W 1.9**
   - Extension Activity: Evaluation of a Literary Friendship **W 1.6**
6. **To understand and apply listening and speaking strategies**
   - Extension Activity: Dramatic Reading **LS 1.9**

STEP-BY-STEP TEACHING GUIDE	PACING GUIDE
PRETEACH	
Motivate Students and Provide Background	
Use the Motivation activity (ATE p. 684)	5 min.
Read and discuss author and background features (SE/ATE pp. 684, 686, 705) A	10 min.
Introduce the Concepts	
Introduce the Literary Analysis and Reading Strategy concepts(SE/ATE p. 685) A	15 min.
Pronounce the vocabulary words and read their definitions (SE p. 685)	5 min.
TEACH	
Monitor Comprehension	
Informally monitor comprehension by circulating while students read independently or in groups A	35 min.
Monitor students' comprehension with the Reading Check notes (SE/ATE pp. 687, 691, 693, 697, 701, 703, 705, 707, 711)	as students read
Develop vocabulary with Vocabulary notes (SE pp. 690, 697, 704, 708, 711; ATE p. 697)	as students read
Develop Understanding	
Develop students' understanding of poetic sound devices with the Literary Analysis annotations (SE/ATE pp. 687, 688, 690, 693, 694, 696, 698, 700, 703, 704, 706, 711) A	5 min.
Develop students' understanding of poetic effects with the Reading Strategy annotations (SE/ATE pp. 688, 690, 692, 693, 694, 696, 697, 701, 706, 707, 708, 711)	5 min.
ASSESS	
Assess Mastery	
Assess students' mastery of the Reading Strategy and Literary Analysis concepts by having them answer the Review and Assess questions (SE/ATE p. 713)	15 min.
Use one or more of the print and media Assessment Resources (ATE p. 715) A	up to 45 min.
EXTEND	
Apply Understanding	
Have students complete the Vocabulary Development Lesson and the Grammar and Style Lesson (SE p. 714) A	20 min.
Apply students' ability to use vivid and precise language using the Writing Lesson (SE/ATE p. 715) A	45 min.
Apply students' understanding using one or more of the Extension Activities (SE p. 715)	20–90 min.

ACCELERATED INSTRUCTION:
Use the strategies and activities identified with an A.

UNIVERSAL ACCESS
● = Below-Level Students
▲ = On-Level Students
■ = Above-Level Students

Time and Resource Manager

Reading Level: Average, Easy
Average Number of Instructional Days: 4

RESOURCES		
PRINT	**TRANSPARENCIES**	**TECHNOLOGY**
• **Beyond Literature,** Cross-Curricular Connection: Science, p. 32 ▲ ■		• **Interest Grabber Videos,** Tape 4 ● ▲ ■
• **Selection Support Workbook:** ● ▲ ■ Literary Analysis, p. 150 Reading Strategy, p. 149 Build Vocabulary, p. 147	• **Literary Analysis and Reading Transparencies,** pp. 63 and 64 ● ▲ ■	
• **Adapted Reader's Companion** ● • **Reader's Companion** ●		• **Listening to Literature** ● ▲ ■ Audiocassettes, Side 17 Audio CDs, CD 10
• **English Learner's Companion** ● ▲ • **Literary Analysis for Enrichment** ■	• **Fine Art Transparencies, Volume 2,** Art Transparencies 10 and 11 ● ▲ ■	
• **Formal Assessment:** Selection Test, pp. 155–157 ● ▲ ■ • **Open Book Test,** pp. 94–96 ● ▲ ■ • **Performance Assessment and Portfolio Management,** p. 25 and 92 ● ▲ ■ • PRENTICE HALL ASSESSMENT SYSTEM ● ▲ ■	• PRENTICE HALL ASSESSMENT SYSTEM ● ▲ ■ **Skills Practice Answers and Explanations on Transparencies**	• **Test Bank Software** ● ▲ ■ • **Got It! Assessment Videotapes,** Tape 3 ● ▲
• **Selection Support Workbook:** ● ▲ ■ Grammar and Style, p. 148 • **Writing and Grammar,** Diamond Level ● ▲ ■ • **Extension Activities,** p. 32 ● ▲ ■	• **Daily Language Practice Transparencies** ● ▲ • **Writing Models and Graphic Organizers on Transparencies,** pp. 99–102 ● ▲ ■	• **Writing and Grammar iText CD-ROM** ● ▲ ■ ***Take It to the Net*** www.phschool.com

BLOCK SCHEDULING: Use one 90-minute class period to preteach the selections and have students read them. Use a second 90-minute class period to assess students' mastery of skills and have them complete one of the Extension Activities.

PRETEACH

Step-by-Step Teaching Guide for pp. 684–685

Motivation

Ask students if they can describe how a child who has broken something might behave. Elicit other examples of guilty behavior from students. Note that guilt introduces a division between the person who feels guilt and others, expressed, for instance, in the person's inability to meet the gaze of others. Explain that in "The Rime of the Ancient Mariner," Coleridge has developed a vivid, fantastical vocabulary of images with which to explore the divisions and isolation created by guilt.

Interest Grabber Video

As an alternative, play "'Kubla Khan': The Silk Road" on Tape 4 to engage student interest.

1 Background

More About the Author

As the youngest son of a vicar Coleridge was initially destined for a religious career. Already well-read when he arrived at Cambridge University, he found too little to challenge him there and fell into a dissolute lifestyle. Eventually, he enlisted briefly in the army under an assumed name. Following the collapse of his plans with Robert Southey to set up a colony in Pennsylvania, Coleridge edited a radical Christian journal, *The Watchman*, which ran for ten issues. The end of his marriage, his increasing dissipation from abuse of laudanum (an opium preparation), and the breakup of his friendship with the Wordsworths marked the lowest phase in Coleridge's life. Yet he still managed to give inspiring lectures and to produce such masterful works as his *Biographia Literaria*, in which he elaborates his principles of criticism and his basic philosophy, and his *Notebooks*, in which he details his daily life, thoughts, and dreams. In the realm of theory, Coleridge is most famous for his conception of the imagination, which he took to be a formative principle shaping perception and which he distinguished from the more superficial fancy, or power of association and elaboration.

Prepare to Read

1 The Rime of the Ancient Mariner ◆ Kubla Khan

Samuel Taylor Coleridge (1772–1834)

The poetry of Samuel Taylor Coleridge stands at the place where real life slips into dreams and facts are reborn as fantasies. More than any other Romantic poet, he dared to journey inward—deep into the world of the imagination. His explorations came at a price, though. The imagination that fed his poetry also allowed him to avoid a reckoning with his own serious problems, including poor health and self-doubt.

Early Fantasies Coleridge was born in Ottery St. Mary on the Devon coast of England, the last of ten children. At an early age, he developed the habit of retreating into a world of books and fantasy. Even as a child, his response to literature was powerful. After reading an intense tale from the *Arabian Nights*, for example, he recalled feeling "haunted by specters whenever I was in the dark." When he was nine, his father died, and Coleridge was sent to school in London. Later, he went to Cambridge University, where he became a riveting public speaker, mesmerizing audiences with his originality and intelligence.

Utopian Plans At Cambridge, Coleridge's hunger for new ideas led him into radical politics. He became a friend of the poet Robert Southey. Inspired by the early promise of the French Revolution, the two men planned to form a settlement in Pennsylvania based on their utopian political ideas. The plan collapsed, however, when Southey's aunt refused to fund their project.

A Literary Breakthrough In 1795, Coleridge and his wife, Sara Fricker, moved to Somerset, where he became a friend of poet William Wordsworth. In 1798, the two poets published *Lyrical Ballads*, a joint collection of their works. The four poems that make up Coleridge's contribution to the volume deal with spiritual matters and include his masterpiece "The Rime of the Ancient Mariner." The collection of poems slowly gained critical attention. In the end, it caused a revolution in poetic style and thought, firmly establishing the movement known as Romanticism.

Twin Poles Coleridge and Wordsworth represented two opposing sides of the movement. While Wordsworth explored the language and experience of common people in natural settings, Coleridge often celebrated the strange and the exotic. Both, however, were committed to reaching truths about the human soul deeper than those conventional poetry could express.

Success and Difficulty As Coleridge's fame grew, he suffered increasingly from asthma and rheumatism and began to rely heavily on painkillers, which dulled his creative powers. Seeking to improve his health by visiting warmer climates, he spent two years in Malta and then traveled through Italy. His journey brought him little relief from pain and contributed to the collapse of his marriage. When he returned to England in 1806, Coleridge separated from his wife and moved near the Wordsworth family. By 1810, however, even this friendship was shattered. Wordsworth felt that the poet was irresponsible, and the two men never regained their close connection.

Throughout these dark days, Coleridge kept writing on many subjects and gave lectures on Shakespeare and Milton. Visits with Coleridge had a great impact on the young crop of Romantics writing at that time. Mary Shelley, the author of *Frankenstein*, often described her admiration for Coleridge's groundbreaking poetic works.

A Romantic Legacy Perhaps Coleridge's greatest legacy is his insight into the power of imagination in literature and life, a power that shapes reality and enables freedom. A magical blend of thought and emotion lies at the heart of his works, in which the unreal (but true) becomes compellingly real.

TEACHING RESOURCES

The following resources can be used to enrich or extend the instruction for pp. 684–685.

Motivation

Interest Grabber Videos, Tape 4

Background

Beyond Literature, p. 32

Take It to the Net

Visit www.phschool.com for background and hotlinks for the selections.

Literary Analysis

Literary Analysis and Reading Transparencies, Poetic Sound Devices, p. 64

Reading

Selection Support: Reading Strategy, p. 149; Build Vocabulary, p. 147

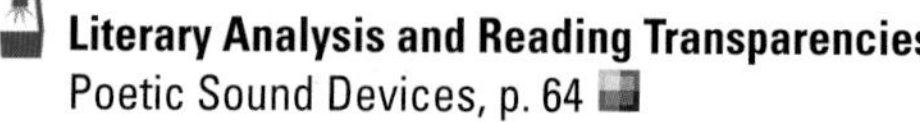

Literary Analysis and Reading Transparencies, Analyzing Poetic Effects, p. 63

BLOCK SCHEDULING: Resources marked with this symbol provide varied instruction during 90-minute blocks.

Preview

Connecting to the Literature

Like your own dreams, these poems will sweep you off to fantasy realms where truths of life—such as courage, beauty, and redemption—stand out vividly.

❷ Literary Analysis

Poetic Sound Devices

Romantic poetry like that of Coleridge achieves some of its emotional effect and beauty through **poetic sound devices,** including the following:

- **Alliteration** is the repetition of a consonant sound at the beginnings of words: "The fair breeze blew, the white foam flew, . . ."
- **Consonance** is the repetition of similar final consonant sounds in stressed syllables with dissimilar vowel sounds: "a frightful fiend / Doth close behind. . . ."
- **Assonance** is the repetition of a vowel sound in stressed syllables with dissimilar consonant sounds: "The western wave was all aflame."
- **Internal rhyme** is the use of rhymes within a poetic line: "With heavy thump, a lifeless lump, . . ."

Comparing Literary Works

Poetic sound devices give poetry a flavor all its own. So, too, does the **language of fantasy** in which Coleridge builds his dream world. For instance, in "The Rime of the Ancient Mariner," he uses archaic words—terms no longer in common use—such as *eftsoons* ("immediately"). In "Kubla Khan," he uses exotic-sounding place-names, such as Xanadu. As you read, compare the various ways in which Coleridge uses words to emphasize the difference between poetry and everyday speech, creating a contrast between fantasy-world and reality.

❸ Reading Strategy

Analyzing Poetic Effects

Analyzing poetic effects, such as sound devices, will help you appreciate poetry. As you read, use a chart like the one shown. Find examples of alliteration, consonance, assonance and internal rhyme and identify their effects.

Passage

The ship drove fast, loud roared the blast, / And southward aye we fled.

Sound Device

1. Internal rhyme: "fast / blast"
2. Assonance: "loud / southward"

Image

Ship fleeing the storm

Effect of Sound on Image

1. Rhyme emphasizes speed and abruptness.
2. Assonance fits the howling of the wind

Vocabulary Development

averred (ə vʉrd′) *v.* stated to be true (p. 690)

sojourn (sō′ jʉrn) *v.* stay for a while (p. 697)

expiated (eks′ pē āt′ id) *v.* atoned; made amends for, especially by suffering (p. 704)

reverence (rev′ ər əns) *n.* deep respect (p. 708)

sinuous (sin′ yo͞o əs) *adj.* bending; winding (p. 711)

tumult (to͞o′ mult′) *n.* noisy commotion (p. 711)

❷ Literary Analysis

Poetic Sound Devices

- Tell students that in this lesson they will focus on poetic sound devices in the work of Coleridge.
- Review with students that *alliteration* is repetition of a *consonant* sound at the beginnings of words; *consonance* is the repetition of consonant sounds at the end of nonrhyming, stressed syllables; *assonance* is repetition of a vowel sound in stressed syllables with different consonant sounds; and *internal rhyme* is the use of rhymes within a poetic line.
- Use the instruction for Comparing Literary Works to review with students the use of the language of fantasy in Coleridge's poetry. Explain that Coleridge's extensive use of sound devices already makes his language sound different from ordinary speech, an effect he intensifies with his use of archaic or exotic words.

❸ Reading Strategy

Analyzing Poetic Effects

- Explain that poetic effects such as sound devices create pleasure in themselves. For instance, Coleridge's use of sound devices creates a pleasing music in his poetry.
- Add that such poetic effects can also enhance meaning, as shown in the example in the graphic organizer on p. 685.
- Have students practice analyzing poetic effects using the Poetic Effects transparency in **Literary Analysis and Reading Transparencies,** p. 63.

Vocabulary Development

- Pronounce each vocabulary word for students and read the definitions as a class. Have students identify any words with which they are already familiar.

CUSTOMIZE INSTRUCTION FOR UNIVERSAL ACCESS

For Special Needs Students	For Less Proficient Readers	For English Learners
Have students read the adapted version of "The Rime of the Ancient Mariner" in the **Adapted Reader's Companion.** This version provides basic-level instruction in an interactive format with questions and write-on lines. Completing the adapted version will prepare students to read the selection in the Student Edition.	Have students read "The Rime of the Ancient Mariner" in the **Reader's Companion.** This version provides basic-level instruction in an interactive format with questions and write-on lines. After students finish the selection in **Reader's Companion,** have them complete the questions and activities in the Student Edition.	Have students read the adapted version of "The Rime of the Ancient Mariner" in the **English Learner's Companion.** This version provides basic-level instruction in an interactive format with questions and write-on lines. Completing the adapted version will prepare students to read the selection in the Student Edition.

 ***E-Teach***

Visit E-Teach at www.phschool.com for teachers' essays on how to teach, with questions and answers.

TEACH

Step-by-Step Teaching Guide for pp. 686–712

CUSTOMIZE INSTRUCTION
For Visual/Spatial Learners

To help students visualize the action in the poem, have them trace a map of the South Pacific and Antarctic regions and draw the ship's path using data from the first 95 lines of the poem.

1 About the Selection

This poem vividly illustrates the torments guilt can create and the horror of complete isolation from society. The central character, the ancient Mariner, recounts the tale of his crime against life—the killing of an albatross—and the physical and emotional punishments his action sets in motion. The Mariner's struggle to redeem himself and escape his isolation captures the interdependence of humanity and nature, the necessity for respect, order, and mercy among all living creatures, and the healing power of love.

2 Background

Art

Engraving for "The Rime of the Ancient Mariner," 1875, by Gustave Doré

This illustration depicts the shooting of the albatross, capturing the instant just prior to the arrow's strike.

Doré, who was born in Strasbourg, France, near the German border, moved to Paris in 1847. His woodcut illustrations for the work of writers such as Honoré de Balzac firmly established Doré's fame. Use this question for discussion:

> What elements in the engraving capture the setting of the poem?
> Answer: Elements that capture the setting include icicles on the rigging, the drifting ice, and the grayish sky.

3 ▸Critical Viewing

Possible response: The arrow headed toward the bird creates tension, while the drifting ice and blurry background make a gloomy atmosphere.

1 THE RIME OF THE ANCIENT MARINER

Samuel Taylor Coleridge

2

Engraving by Gustave Doré for "The Rime of the Ancient Mariner" by Samuel Taylor Coleridge

3 ▲ **Critical Viewing** Identify two elements in this engraving that create a gloomy, suspense-filled atmosphere. **[Analyze]**

Background

Coleridge used dreams as the basis of many of his great poems. "The Rime of the Ancient Mariner" was based on a dream reported by his friend John Cruikshank. Starting with the dream as raw material, Coleridge and Wordsworth began to elaborate upon it. Wordsworth suggested that the act that would drive the entire poem was a crime committed at sea. Using this idea and his own lively imagination, Coleridge wrote a poem that has chilled and enthralled audiences to this day. (The margin notes to the left of the poem were written by the poet.)

TEACHING RESOURCES

The following resources can be used to enrich or extend the instruction for pp. 686–712.

Literary Analysis

Selection Support: Literary Analysis, p. 150

Reading

Reader's Companion

English Learner's Companion

Listening to Literature Audiocassettes, Side 17 ■

Listening to Literature Audio CDs, CD 10 ■

Extension

Fine Art Transparencies, Volume 2, Transparencies 10 and 11. As students reflect on the power of nature in "The Ancient Mariner," display John Constable's *The Haywain* and J.W.M. Turner's *Wreck of a Transport Ship* to suggest the contrasting faces of nature in the Romantic imagination.

■ **BLOCK SCHEDULING:** Resources marked with this symbol provide varied instruction during 90-minute blocks.

Argument

How a Ship having passed the Line[1] was driven by storms to the cold Country towards the South Pole: and how from thence she made her course to the tropical Latitude of the Great Pacific Ocean; and of the strange things that befell: and in what manner the Ancyent Marinere came back to his own Country.

Part I

An ancient Mariner meeteth three Gallants bidden to a wedding feast and detaineth one.

It is an ancient Mariner,
And he stoppeth one of three.
"By thy long gray beard and glittering eye,
Now wherefore stopp'st thou me?"

"The Bridegroom's doors are opened wide,
And I am next of kin;
The guests are met, the feast is set:
May'st hear the merry din."

He holds him with his skinny hand,
"There was a ship," quoth he.
"Hold off! unhand me, graybeard loon!"
Eftsoons[2] his hand dropped he.

The Wedding Guest is spellbound by the eye of the old seafaring man and constrained to hear his tale.

He holds him with his glittering eye—
The Wedding Guest stood still,
And listens like a three years' child:
The Mariner hath his will.

The Wedding Guest sat on a stone:
He cannot choose but hear;
And thus spake on that ancient man,
The bright-eyed Mariner.

"The ship was cheered, the harbor cleared,
Merrily did we drop
Below the kirk,[3] below the hill,
Below the lighthouse top.

The Mariner tells how the ship sailed southward with a good wind and fair weather till it reached the Line.

"The Sun came up upon the left,
Out of the sea came he!
And he shone bright, and on the right
Went down into the sea.

1. **Line** Equator.
2. **Eftsoons** immediately.
3. **kirk** church.

Literary Analysis
Poetic Sound Devices What examples of internal rhymes and assonance can you find in lines 5–8?

5 Reading Check
What effect does the ancient Mariner have on the Wedding Guest?

4 Literary Analysis

Poetic Sound Devices

- Review with students the definitions of internal rhyme (the use of rhyme within a poetic line) and assonance (the repetition of a vowel sound in stressed syllables with different consonant sounds).
- Have students read lines 5–8 to themselves, and then have a student volunteer read the lines aloud.
- Then, ask students the Literary Analysis question on p. 687: What examples of internal rhymes and assonance can you find in lines 5–8?
  Answer: The internal rhyme is *met/set*. There is assonance in *next/guests/met* (or *set*).

5 Reading Check

Answer: The Mariner has a hypnotic effect on the Wedding Guest. The Wedding Guest is spellbound by his eye and cannot choose but listen to him.

CUSTOMIZE INSTRUCTION FOR UNIVERSAL ACCESS

For Less Proficient Readers	For English Learners	For Advanced Readers
Model for students how to analyze sound devices, using the Poetic Effects transparency in **Literary Analysis and Reading Transparencies,** p. 63. Have volunteers read a few stanzas aloud while the class listens just to the sound. Discuss the general qualities of the sound, and then have students identify sound devices in these stanzas.	Use the transparency on p. 63 of **Literary Analysis and Reading Transparencies** to show students how to identify sound devices. Then, have students read the first stanza of the poem as a group. Have students sound out any difficult words as they identify poetic devices.	Review with students their understanding of poetic devices by asking them to define the terms *assonance, consonance, internal rhyme,* and *alliteration.* Have students practice identifying these poetic devices in "The Rime of the Ancient Mariner" using the Poetic Effects transparency in **Literary Analysis and Reading Transparencies,** p. 63.

6 Literary Analysis

Poetic Sound Devices and the Language of Fantasy

- Have students read lines 37–40 to themselves. Ask them to identify any words with which they are not familiar.
- Then, ask students the Literary Analysis question on p. 688: What archaic word-form appears in lines 37–40?
  Answer: Students should recognize that the use of "spake" instead of "spoke" is archaic.

7 Reading Strategy

Analyzing Poetic Effects

- Read aloud the bracketed passage to students. Ask students to listen carefully to the vowel sounds as you read.

Monitor Progress Ask students the Reading Strategy question on p. 688: Find two lines in this verse that contain the long and the short sound of the same vowel. What emphasis does this alternation create?
Possible response: Students may say that the alternation of long and short sounds of the vowel *a* in line 53 ("mast-high, came") and the alternation of long and short sounds of the vowel *e* in line 54 ("As green as emerald") create a wave-like movement; the contrast tends to emphasize the words with the long sound of the vowel—*came* and *green*.

Reteach If students have difficulty with the question, have a volunteer read the stanza out loud. Classmates should volunteer suggestions for which words to emphasize. As the volunteer adapts his or her reading to these suggestions, the class should evaluate which pattern of emphasis best reflects to music of the vowel sounds in the line. Then, have students discuss how this pattern of emphasis contributes to the meaning.

"Higher and higher every day,
Till over the mast at noon[4] —"
The Wedding Guest here beat his breast,
For he heard the loud bassoon.

The Wedding Guest heareth the bridal music; but the Mariner continueth his tale.

The bride hath paced into the hall.
Red as a rose is she;
Nodding their heads before her goes
The merry minstrelsy.

The Wedding Guest he beat his breast,
Yet he cannot choose but hear;
And thus spake on that ancient man
The bright-eyed Mariner.

The ship driven by a storm toward the South Pole.

"And now the Storm blast came, and he
Was tyrannous and strong:
He struck with his o'ertaking wings,
And chased us south along.

"With sloping masts and dipping prow,
As who pursued with yell and blow
Still treads the shadow of his foe,
And forward bends his head,
The ship drove fast, loud roared the blast,
And southward aye[5] we fled.

"And now there came both mist and snow.
And it grew wondrous cold;
And ice, mast-high, came floating by,
As green as emerald.

The land of ice, and of fearful sounds, where no living thing was to be seen.

"And through the drifts the snowy clifts[6]
Did send a dismal sheen;
Nor shapes of men nor beasts we ken[7]—
The ice was all between.

"The ice was here, the ice was there,
The ice was all around;
It cracked and growled, and roared and howled,
Like noises in a swound![8]

Literary Analysis
Poetic Sound Devices and the Language of Fantasy What archaic (outdated) word-form appears in lines 37–40?

Reading Strategy
Analyzing Poetic Effects Find one line in this verse that contains the long and the short sound of the same vowel. What emphasis does this alternation create?

---

4. **over . . . noon** The ship has reached the equator.
5. **aye** ever.
6. **clifts** icebergs.
7. **ken** knew.
8. **swound** swoon.

8

Engraving by Gustave Doré for "The Rime of the Ancient Mariner" by Samuel Taylor Coleridge

9 ▲ **Critical Viewing** From the expression on the Wedding Guest's face (figure on far left), what can you infer about his reaction to the ancient Mariner? **[Infer]**

8 Background

Art

Engraving for "The Rime of the Ancient Mariner," 1875, by Gustave Doré

This engraving illustrates the stanzas of the poem in which the Mariner accosts the Wedding Guest. Like the other engravings shown with the poem, this engraving was created specifically to accompany Coleridge's poem.

French illustrator Gustave Doré was born in 1832 and began his career as a caricaturist for a weekly humor magazine in Paris. A self-taught artist, Doré refined his technique through independent study of engraving at the National Library in Paris. Doré's skillful figure drawing and composition are evident in this drawing. Use these questions for discussion:

1. What lines in the poem are reflected in the engraving's portrayal of the Mariner's eyes?
   Answer: This image suggests lines 3 and 13.
2. What does the engraving suggest about the attitudes of other wedding guests?
   Answer: They appear to be repulsed by the Mariner or afraid of him; one turns to stare with distaste or alarm; he may be fleeing the Mariner.

9 ▶Critical Viewing

Answer: Students may say that the Wedding Guest is annoyed or a bit afraid but at the same time fascinated by the Mariner.

CUSTOMIZE INSTRUCTION FOR UNIVERSAL ACCESS

For Special Needs Students	For Less Proficient Readers
Have students consider the engraving from a scene in "The Rime of the Ancient Mariner" on p. 689. Have them explain how the engraving illustrates the opening scene of the poem. For students who are still struggling with comprehension, play Side 17 of **Listening to Literature Audiocassettes,** and have students read along to support their comprehension.	Because "The Rime of the Ancient Mariner" opens with a dialogue between two somewhat mysterious characters, students may have difficulty focusing on the progress of the narrative. Encourage students to read the first few stanzas of the poem, paying special attention to who is speaking and to whom. Then have students reread "The Rime of the Ancient Mariner" silently as they listen to **Listening to Literature CDs,** CD 10. Guide students in a discussion of the way in which Coleridge incorporates dialogue into the poem.

❿ Literary Analysis

Poetic Sound Devices

- Have students read lines 67–70 to themselves. Ask them to pay attention to the sound devices that Coleridge uses in these lines.
- You may want to review some of the common sound devices that Coleridge uses in this poem.
- Then, ask students the Literary Analysis question on p. 690: Identify one sound device used in lines 67–70.
  Possible response: Students should recognize the internal rhyme between *split* and *thunder-fit* in line 69.

⓫ Reading Strategy

Analyzing Poetic Effects

- Have student volunteers offer definitions for *alliteration* and *internal rhyme.* Have a volunteer read aloud lines 91–94.
- Then, ask students the Reading Strategy question on p. 690: How does the use of alliteration and internal rhyme in lines 91–94 give a fatal feeling to the Mariner's deed?
  Answer: Alliteration and internal rhyme add emphasis and "slow down" lines of poetry. They also make the words involved seem to follow from one another, as if they were "fated," since sound as well as sense requires the use of these particular words. In this way, the alliterations *had / hellish, would / work / woe,* and *breeze / blow,* along with the internal rhyme *averred / bird,* make the stanza portentous and contribute to the fatal feeling of the Mariner's action.

Till a great sea bird, called the Albatross, came through the snow-fog, and was received with great joy and hospitality. ❿

"At length did cross an Albatross,
Thorough[9] the fog it came;
As if it had been a Christian soul,
We hailed it in God's name.

"It ate the food it ne'er had eat,[10]
And round and round it flew.
The ice did split with a thunder-fit;
The helmsman steered us through!

And lo! the Albatross proveth a bird of good omen, and followeth the ship as it returned northward through fog and floating ice.

"And a good south wind sprung up behind;
The Albatross did follow,
And every day, for food or play,
Came to the mariner's hollo!

"In mist or cloud, on mast or shroud,[11]
It perched for vespers[12] nine;
Whiles all the night, through fog-smoke white,
Glimmered the white Moonshine."

The ancient Mariner inhospitably killeth the pious bird of good omen.

"God save thee, ancient Mariner!
From the fiends, that plague thee thus!—
Why look'st thou so?"[13] "With my crossbow
I shot the Albatross."

Part II

"The Sun now rose upon the right:[14]
Out of the sea came he,
Still hid in mist, and on the left
Went down into the sea.

"And the good south wind still blew behind,
But no sweet bird did follow,
Nor any day for food or play
Came to the mariners' hollo!

His shipmates cry out against the ancient Mariner for killing the bird of good luck.

"And I had done a hellish thing,
And it would work 'em woe:
For all averred, I had killed the bird
That made the breeze to blow.

Literary Analysis
Poetic Sound Devices
Identify one sound device used in lines 67–70.

Reading Strategy
Analyzing Poetic Effects
How does the use of alliteration and internal rhyme in lines 91–94 give a fatal feeling to the Mariner's deed?

averred (ə vurd′) *v.*: stated to be true

9. **thorough** through.
10. **eat** (et) old form of *eaten.*
11. **shroud** *n.* ropes stretching from the ship's side to the masthead.
12. **vespers** evenings.
13. **God . . . so** spoken by the Wedding Guest.
14. **The Sun . . . right** The ship is now headed north.

ENRICHMENT: Science Connection

The Albatross

Several different albatross species can be found in the cold regions near Antarctica: the royal albatross (wingspan 10.5 feet); the sooty albatross (wingspan 7 feet); and the wandering albatross (wingspan 11 feet). All share the ability to glide, sometimes for hours, if there is sufficient wind. In calm, size forces albatross to rest frequently, on land or floating on the water.

Albatross breed on shore islands, bearing only one chick at a time. Young albatross mature very slowly, taking nearly a year to learn to fly and five to ten years to become independent navigators. Albatross often follow ships and feed on scraps of food tossed overboard.

12

Engraving by Gustave Doré for "The Rime of the Ancient Mariner" by Samuel Taylor Coleridge

13 ◀ **Critical Viewing** What effects does the artist, Gustave Doré, use to capture the eerie mood of the poem? **[Analyze]**

Ah wretch! said they, the bird to slay,
That made the breeze to blow!

But when the fog cleared off, they justify the same, and thus make themselves accomplices in the crime.

"Nor dim nor red, like God's own head,
The glorious Sun uprist;[15]
Then all averred, I had killed the bird
That brought the fog and mist.
'Twas right, said they, such birds to slay,
That bring the fog and mist.

The fair breeze continues; the ship enters the Pacific Ocean, and sails northward, even till it reaches the Line. The Ship hath been suddenly becalmed.

"The fair breeze blew, the white foam flew,
The furrow[16] followed free;
We were the first that ever burst
Into that silent sea.

"Down dropped the breeze, the sails
dropped down,
'Twas sad as sad could be;

14 ✓ **Reading Check** What has the ancient Mariner done to the Albatross?

15. **uprist** arose.
16. **furrow** ship's wake.

12 Background

Art

Engraving for "The Rime of the Ancient Mariner," 1875, by Gustave Doré

Between 1855 and 1865, Doré focused heavily on illustrating literary texts. His woodcuts accompanied such well-known works as Dante's *Inferno* and Cervantes' *Don Quixote.* Doré's project of illustrating an 1865 edition of the Bible was quite ambitious; the results are considered among his most highly successful.

In this engraving, Doré's evocative portrayal of the sailors clustering together to gawk at the enormous Albatross adds an extra dimension of meaning to Coleridge's words. Use these questions for discussion:

1. What lines in the poem might have inspired this engraving?
   Answer: Lines 71–78 may have inspired it.
2. How does the engraving convey the sailors' attitude?
   Answer: Their foolish grins, amazed expressions, and arms stretched out to offer food indicate the sailors' attitude of teasing affection.

13 ▶ Critical Viewing

Possible response: Students may note that Doré uses white, not black, to outline the frost-covered sailors and the icicles, an effect that adds to the ghostliness of the scene. The sharpness of detail also drops off quickly beyond the foreground, making the background a mysterious blur.

14 ✓ Reading Check

Answer: The Ancient Mariner has shot the Albatross with his crossbow.

CUSTOMIZE INSTRUCTION FOR UNIVERSAL ACCESS

For Less Proficient Readers	For Advanced Readers
After students have completed reading Part I of "The Rime of the Ancient Mariner" with teacher guidance, have them reread sections that feature especially vivid descriptions and dramatic events. They should then produce illustrations that might come from a movie version of these scenes, incorporating details from the poem along with their own elaborations.	After students have completed reading Part I of "The Rime of the Ancient Mariner," have them reread sections that feature especially vivid descriptions and dramatic events. Working in pairs, they should then write a screenplay adaptation of this section of the poem. Their scripts should include directions for camera angles and staging.

15 Reading Strategy
Analyzing Poetic Effects

- Have students read lines 115–119 to themselves. As they read, encourage students to picture the becalmed ship, unable to move.
- Then, ask them the first Reading Strategy question on p. 692: How does the repetition of words in lines 115–119 contribute to the image of the stilled ship?
Answer: The repetition of words echoes the ship's condition of rest; like the ship, the line does not "move," since the same words keep returning.

16 Reading Strategy
Analyzing Poetic Effects

- Have students read lines 127–130 to themselves. Encourage them to focus on the sound devices in these lines.
- Ask students to identify the sound devices in these lines.
- Then, ask students the second Reading Strategy question on p. 692: What effect does the increased concentration of sound devices in lines 127–130 have?
Answer: Students should recognize that the massing together of sound devices gives these lines the dramatic effect of a chant or incantation.

And we did speak only to break
The silence of the sea!

"All in a hot and copper sky,
The bloody Sun, at noon,
Right up above the mast did stand,
No bigger than the Moon.

15

"Day after day, day after day,
We stuck, nor breath nor motion;
As idle as a painted ship
Upon a painted ocean.

And the Albatross begins to be avenged.

"Water, water, everywhere,
And all the boards did shrink;
Water, water, everywhere,
Nor any drop to drink.

"The very deep did rot: O Christ!
That ever this should be!
Yea, slimy things did crawl with legs
Upon the slimy sea.

16

"About, about, in reel and rout[17]
The death fires[18] danced at night;
The water, like a witch's oils,
Burned green, and blue and white.

A Spirit had followed them; one of the invisible inhabitants of this planet, neither departed souls nor angels. They are very numerous, and there is no climate or element without one or more.

"And some in dreams assurèd were
Of the Spirit that plagued us so;
Nine fathom deep he had followed us
From the land of mist and snow.

"And every tongue, through utter drought,
Was withered at the root;
We could not speak, no more than if
We had been choked with soot.

The shipmates, in their sore distress, would fain throw the whole guilt on the ancient Mariner: in sign whereof they hang the dead sea bird round his neck.

"Ah! well a-day! what evil looks
Had I from old and young!
Instead of the cross, the Albatross
About my neck was hung.

Reading Strategy
Analyzing Poetic Effects
How does the repetition of words in lines 115–119 contribute to the image of the stilled ship?

Reading Strategy
Analyzing Poetic Effects
What effect does the increased concentration of sound devices in lines 127–130 have?

---

17. **rout** disorderly crowd.
18. **death fires** St. Elmo's fire, a visible electrical discharge from a ship's mast, believed by sailors to be an omen of disaster.

ENRICHMENT: Cultural Connection
Birds

Throughout history, birds were believed to be divine messengers through which people could foretell the future. This idea is preserved in the words *augury* ("omen") and *auspice* ("omen"; "guidance"; "patronage"), which originally meant "bird talk" and "bird view," respectively. Before undertaking any action of consequence, some ancient peoples would observe the birds, looking for an omen. This practice is still observed in some areas of Southeast Asia and the Western Pacific.

Particular birds may mean different things in different cultures. For example, the dove was a messenger of war to the Japanese, but it is an emblem of peace in the West. The owl meant death to the ancient Egyptians but wisdom to the ancient Greeks. Traditionally, sailors have attributed a number of meanings to the albatross. Killing an albatross was held to bring bad luck, and some sailors said the birds were inhabited by the souls of dead sea captains.

Part III

The ancient Mariner beholdeth a sign in the element afar off.

"There passed a weary time. Each throat
Was parched, and glazed each eye.
A weary time! a weary time!
How glazed each weary eye,
When looking westward, I beheld
A something in the sky.

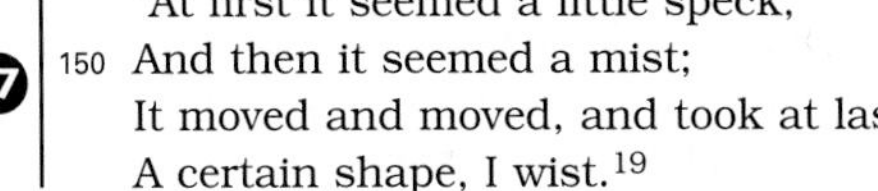

"At first it seemed a little speck,
And then it seemed a mist;
It moved and moved, and took at last
A certain shape, I wist.[19]

Reading Strategy
Analyzing Poetic Effects What poetic effect does Coleridge use in lines 149–153 to build suspense?

"A speck, a mist, a shape, I wist!
And still it neared and neared:
As if it dodged a water sprite,
It plunged and tacked and veered.

At its nearer approach, it seemeth him to be a ship; and at a dear ransom he freeth his speech from the bonds of thirst.

"With throats unslaked, with black lips baked,
We could nor laugh nor wail;
Through utter drought all dumb we stood!
I bit my arm, I sucked the blood,
And cried, A sail! a sail!

A flash of joy:

"With throats unslaked, with black lips baked,
Agape they heard me call:
Gramercy![20] for joy did grin,
And all at once their breath drew in,
As they were drinking all.

And horror follows. For can it be a ship that comes onward without wind or tide?

"See! see! (I cried) she tacks no more!
Hither to work us weal;[21]
Without a breeze, without a tide,
She steadies with upright keel!

Literary Analysis
Poetic Sound Devices and the Language of the Fantastic How does the line "Hither to work us weal" give the sense that these events are taking place in a strange, distant era?

"The western wave was all aflame.
The day was well nigh done!
Almost upon the western wave
Rested the broad bright Sun;
When that strange shape drove suddenly
Betwixt us and the Sun.

It seemeth him but the skeleton of a ship.

"And straight the Sun was flecked with bars,
(Heaven's Mother send us grace!)

Reading Check
What causes the sailors to suffer?

19. **wist** knew.
20. **Gramercy** (grə mur´ sē): great thanks.
21. **work us weal** assist us.

17 Reading Strategy
Analyzing Poetic Effects

- Have students read lines 149–153 in pairs, paying attention to the poetic effects Coleridge uses.
- Ask the Reading Strategy question on p. 693: What poetic effect does Coleridge use in lines 149–153 to build suspense?
  Answer: Coleridge uses repetition to build suspense.

18 Literary Analysis
Poetic Sound Devices and the Language of the Fantastic

- Read aloud the bracketed line. Remind students that using fantastic language and archaic vocabulary can contribute to the mood of a poem.
- Have students identify the archaic words in this line.
- Ask them the Literary Analysis question on p. 693: How does the line "Hither to work us weal," give the sense that these events are taking place in a strange, distant era?
  Answer: Words like "hither" and "weal" set this line apart from contemporary culture.

19 Reading Check
Answer: The relentless heat of the sun and the lack of potable water cause the sailors to suffer.

CUSTOMIZE INSTRUCTION FOR UNIVERSAL ACCESS

For Less Proficient Readers	For Gifted/Talented Students	For Advanced Readers
Readers may have difficulty identifying individual poetic effects in the poem. Review these devices, and then have students reread portions of the poem. To reinforce students' understanding, use the Poetic Sound Devices transparency on p. 63 of **Literary Analysis and Reading Transparencies** for support.	Have students read Part III of "The Rime of the Ancient Mariner" in small groups and devise illustrations or murals that capture a scene or episode described. Encourage students to interpret Coleridge's use of description and detail in their own illustrations.	Some students who read "The Rime of the Ancient Mariner" may be fascinated by the aspects of the journey that involve science, navigation, and survival. You may want to direct these students to p. 32 of **Beyond Literature** for a more in-depth, cross-curricular analysis to stimulate their interest.

(20) Literary Analysis

Poetic Sound Devices and the Language of the Fantastic

- After reading aloud the bracketed passage, have students reread the passage with a partner and consider any poetic sound devices or fantastic language.
- Ask students the Literary Analysis question on p. 694: In what way does the name of the woman—Life-in-Death—add to the eerie, mysterious atmosphere of the story?
  Answer: The name of the woman is like something out of an old legend or nightmare, and it adds to the mysterious feeling of the story.

(21) Reading Strategy

Analyzing Poetic Effects

- Review with students their understanding of the poetic effect of alliteration. Ask students to provide examples of alliteration from earlier passages in the poem.
- Then, ask the Reading Strategy question on p. 694: Does the alliteration in line 208 help you imagine what is being described? Explain.
  Answer: The use of alliteration in "dew did drip" adds to the slow progress of the line, which aids in visualizing the action of dew dripping.

As if through a dungeon grate he peered
With broad and burning face.

And its ribs are seen as bars on the face of the setting Sun.

"Alas! (thought I, and my heart beat loud)
How fast she nears and nears!
Are those *her* sails that glance in the Sun,
Like restless gossameres?[22]

The Specter Woman and her Death-mate, and no other on board the skeleton ship.

"Are those *her* ribs through which the Sun
Did peer, as through a grate?
And is that Woman all her crew?
Is that a Death? and are there two?
Is Death that woman's mate?

Like vessel, like crew! Death and Life-in-Death have diced for the ship's crew, and she (the latter) winneth the ancient Mariner.

(20)
"*Her* lips were red, *her* looks were free,
Her locks were yellow as gold;
Her skin was as white as leprosy,
The Nightmare Life-in-Death was she,
Who thicks man's blood with cold.

"The naked hulk alongside came,
And the twain were casting dice;
'The game is done! I've won! I've won!'
Quoth she, and whistles thrice.

No twilight within the courts of the Sun.

"The Sun's rim dips; the stars rush out:
At one stride comes the dark;
With far-heard whisper, o'er the sea,
Off shot the specter bark.

At the rising of the Moon,

"We listened and looked sideways up!
Fear at my heart, as at a cup,
My lifeblood seemed to sip!
The stars were dim, and thick the night,
The steersman's face by his lamp
gleamed white;
(21) From the sails the dew did drip—
Till clomb[23] above the eastern bar
The hornèd[24] Moon, with one bright star
Within the nether tip.

One after another,

"One after one, by the star-dogged Moon,[25]
Too quick for groan or sigh,

Literary Analysis
Poetic Sound Devices and the Language of the Fantastic In what way does the name of the woman—Life-in-Death—add to the eerie, mysterious atmosphere of the story?

Reading Strategy
Analyzing Poetic Effects Does the alliteration in line 208 help you imagine what is being described? Explain.

22. **gossameres** floating cobwebs.
23. **clomb** climbed.
24. **hornèd** crescent.
25. **star-dogged Moon** omen of impending evil to sailors.

ENRICHMENT: Cross-Curricular Connection

Science

Following the killing of the Albatross, the sailors suffer dehydration when their water supply runs out. Their suffering is realistic, since water is a necessary requirement for physical performance, as well as for life itself. Human beings can survive without food for longer than they can without water. The normal adult male requires two to three liters of water each day to replace that lost through perspiration and excretion. Without this replacement water, dehydration begins, performance diminishes, and serious health dangers soon develop.

22

Engraving by Gustave Doré for "The Rime of the Ancient Mariner" by Samuel Taylor Coleridge

23 ▲ **Critical Viewing** What reactions to the sighting of the other ship would you expect from the sailors? Can you find such reactions in the engraving? Explain. **[Connect]**

22 Background

Art

Engraving for "The Rime of the Ancient Mariner," 1875, by Gustave Doré

This illustration depicts the sailors' hopelessness and suffering while stranded at sea.

Though Doré also worked in painting and sculpture, particularly after 1870, he was never as successful in these arts as he was with book illustrating. Apparently quite obsessed with Coleridge's poem, he created in this series of illustrations some of his most eerie and disturbing images. Although the illustrated volume of Coleridge's poem was not a commercial success, it is considered an artistic triumph for Gustave Doré. Use these questions for discussion:

1. What details in the engraving convey the peril of the ship?
   Possible responses: Students may cite the sailors' agonized expressions, the calm seas around the ship, and the sailors' desperate efforts to see into the distance and perhaps signal the faraway ship.
2. What mood does this illustration evoke?
   Answer: The mood is despairing and hopeless.

23 ▶Critical Viewing

Answer: One would expect the other sailors would experience joy and relief at the sighting of another ship on the horizon. The sailors in Doré's engraving do not look joyful. Some are lost in their despair, while those who seem aware of the other ship's approach still seem grim.

CUSTOMIZE INSTRUCTION FOR UNIVERSAL ACCESS

For English Learners	For Less Proficient Readers	For Advanced Readers
Have students read portions of "The Rime of the Ancient Mariner" with teacher guidance. Whenever possible, have them summarize the content of what they have read. Students should be able to articulate the key plot elements, name the main characters, and predict what might happen next.	Have students analyze the role of the Wedding Guest. Have them reread the poem carefully, making special note of all references to and descriptions of the Wedding Guest. Then, have students write a dramatic monologue from his point of view, describing his encounter with the ancient Mariner and his reaction to the old man's story.	Ask students to consider the ways in which "The Rime of the Ancient Mariner" seems like a test of survival. Have students write brief paragraphs in which they name the hardships that befall the Mariner and his crew. Direct students to www.phschool.com for additional information on Coleridge and his work.

 **Literary Analysis**

Poetic Sound Devices and the Language of the Fantastic

- Point out the phrase "four times fifty men" to students. Ask them how many men this refers to.
- Then, ask them the Literary Analysis question on p. 696: How does Coleridge's unusual way of expressing numbers contribute to the fairy-tale atmosphere? Answer: This archaic way of enumerating makes the story seem more fanciful than real.

 **Reading Strategy**

Analyzing Poetic Effects

- Read the bracketed passage to students. Point out the repetition of "I looked upon the rotting . . ." in these lines. Ask students to describe the effect of this repetition.
- Then, ask them the Reading Strategy question on p. 696: How does repetition in lines 240–243 emphasize the starkness of the Mariner's situation—the fact that he has "no way out"? Answer: The repetition in lines 240–243 emphasizes that the Mariner has no place to turn for comfort, finding only dead men on the ship and slimy life in the ocean.

Each turned his face with a ghastly pang,
And cursed me with his eye.

His shipmates drop down dead.

"Four times fifty living men,
(And I heard nor sigh nor groan)
With heavy thump, a lifeless lump,
They dropped down one by one.

But Life-in-Death begins her work on the ancient Mariner.

"The souls did from their bodies fly—
They fled to bliss or woe!
And every soul, it passed me by,
Like the whizz of my crossbow!"

Part IV

The Wedding Guest feareth that a Spirit is talking to him;

"I fear thee, ancient Mariner!
I fear thy skinny hand!
And thou art long, and lank, and brown,
As is the ribbed sea sand.

"I fear thee and thy glittering eye,
And thy skinny hand, so brown."

But the ancient Mariner assureth him of his bodily life, and proceedeth to relate his horrible penance.

"Fear not, fear not, thou Wedding Guest!
This body dropped not down.

"Alone, alone, all, all alone,
Alone on a wide wide sea!
And never a saint took pity on
My soul in agony.

He despiseth the creatures of the calm,

"The many men, so beautiful!
And they all dead did lie:
And a thousand thousand slimy things
Lived on; and so did I.

And envieth that they should live, and so many lie dead.

"I looked upon the rotting sea,
And drew my eyes away;
I looked upon the rotting deck,
And there the dead men lay.

"I looked to heaven, and tried to pray;
But or[26] ever a prayer had gushed,
A wicked whisper came, and made
My heart as dry as dust.

"I closed my lids, and kept them close,
And the balls like pulses beat;

26. or before.

Literary Analysis
Poetic Sound Devices and the Language of the Fantastic How does Coleridge's unusual way of expressing numbers contribute to the fairy-tale atmosphere?

Reading Strategy
Analyzing Poetic Effects How does repetition in lines 240–243 emphasize the starkness of the Mariner's situation—the fact that he has "no way out"?

26 For the sky and the sea and the sea and the sky
Lay like a load on my weary eye,
And the dead were at my feet.

But the curse liveth for him in the eye of the dead men.

"The cold sweat melted from their limbs,
Nor rot nor reek did they;
The look with which they looked on me
Had never passed away.

"An orphan's curse would drag to hell
A spirit from on high;
But oh! more horrible than that
Is the curse in a dead man's eye!
Seven days, seven nights, I saw that curse,
And yet I could not die.

In his loneliness and fixedness he yearneth towards the journeying Moon, and the stars that still sojourn, yet still move onward; and everywhere the blue sky belongs to them, and is their appointed rest, and their native country and their own natural homes, which they enter unannounced, as lords that are certainly expected and yet there is a silent joy at their arrival. 27

"The moving Moon went up the sky,
And nowhere did abide:
Softly she was going up,
And a star or two beside—

"Her beams bemocked the sultry main,[27]
Like April hoarfrost spread;
But where the ship's huge shadow lay,
The charmèd water burned alway
A still and awful red.

"Beyond the shadow of the ship,
I watched the water snakes:
They moved in tracks of shining white,
And when they reared, the elfish light
Fell off in in hoary flakes.

By the light of the Moon he beholdeth God's creatures of the great calm.

"Within the shadow of the ship
I watched their rich attire:
Blue, glossy green, and velvet black,
They coiled and swam; and every track
Was a flash of golden fire.

Their beauty and their happiness.

"O happy living things! no tongue
Their beauty might declare:
A spring of love gushed from my heart,

He blesseth them in his heart.

And I blessed them unaware;
Sure my kind saint took pity on me,
And I blessed them unaware.

27. **main** open sea.

Reading Strategy
Analyzing Poetic Effects What effect is created by the repetition in line 250? How does this effect mirror the Mariner's situation?

sojourn (sō´ jʉrn) *v.* stay for a while

28 **Reading Check** What has happened to the other sailors?

26 Reading Strategy

Analyzing Poetic Effects

- Read aloud the bracketed line to students. Ask students to identify the sound devices that Coleridge uses here.
- Have students describe the image they form in their minds as they hear this line.

Monitor Progress Ask students the Reading Strategy question on p. 697: What effect is created by the repetition in line 250? How does this effect mirror the Mariner's situation?
Answer: The repetition emphasizes all that is in the Mariner's line of sight, suggesting the movement of his gaze as it travels back and forth between sky and sea, discovering no form of hope.

27 Vocabulary Development

Latin Word Roots *-journ-*

- Call students' attention in the margin notes to *sojourn*, a word that means "to stay or visit for a short while" Explain to students that *sojourn* contains the root *-journ-*, which is derived from the French and Latin words meaning "day."
- Have students suggest other words and phrases that contain this Latin root, and list them on the chalkboard.
Possible responses: *adjourn, journey, journal, journalism*
- Have students look up any unfamiliar words in a dictionary.

28 Reading Check

Answer: The other sailors have died with their eyes gaping at the Ancient Mariner.

CUSTOMIZE INSTRUCTION FOR UNIVERSAL ACCESS

For English Learners	For Less Proficient Readers
Students may find it especially difficult to detect the unusual poetic effects caused by sound devices in Coleridge's poem. Review with students the various kinds of devices in the poem. Have students read passages in which these devices are especially noticeable, and encourage students to identify them. You may want to revisit these devices by modeling for students the skill using the Poetic Effects transparency on p. 63 of **Literary Analysis and Reading Transparencies.**	Review with students the way in which sound devices are used in poetry to elicit poetic effects. Have students name and identify some of the common sound devices used by Coleridge in "The Rime of the Ancient Mariner." Then, have them practice identifying and explaining the effects of these devices. Have students practice this activity using the graphic organizer on p. 685 as a guide.

29 Literary Analysis

Poetic Sound Devices and the Language of the Fantastic

- Ask students to identify the two events described in these lines.
  Answer: As soon as the Mariner is able to pray, the Albatross falls from his neck and sinks into the sea.

  Then, encourage students to focus on the elements of fantasy in these lines.
- Ask students the first Literary Analysis question on p. 698: What does the connection of the two events in lines 288–291 add to the fairy-tale quality of the story?
  Answer: When he admires and feels love for the water snakes, the Ancient Mariner reconnects himself to nature and the forces of life, so the dead Albatross, the symbol of his rejection of nature, falls from him. The coordination of internal events (the Mariner's discovery of love) with external, symbolic events (the dropping off of the Albatross) is characteristic of fairy tales.

30 Literary Analysis

Poetic Sound Devices

- Have a volunteer provide an example of alliteration from earlier in the poem.
- Then, ask students the second Literary Analysis question on p. 698: Which repeated consonant sound in lines 303–304 creates alliteration?
  Answer: Students should note that the repeated *dr* in "drunken," "dreams," and "drank" creates alliteration.

The spell begins to break.

"The selfsame moment I could pray;
And from my neck so free
The Albatross fell off, and sank
Like lead into the sea.

Part V

"Oh sleep! it is a gentle thing,
Beloved from pole to pole!
To Mary queen the praise be given!
She sent the gentle sleep from Heaven,
That slid into my soul.

By grace of the holy Mother, the ancient Mariner is refreshed with rain.

"The silly[28] buckets on the deck.
That had so long remained,
I dreamed that they were filled with dew;
And when I awoke, it rained.

"My lips were wet, my throat was cold,
My garments all were dank;
30 Sure I had drunken in my dreams,
And still my body drank.

"I moved, and could not feel my limbs:
I was so light—almost
I thought that I had died in sleep,
And was a blessèd ghost.

He heareth sounds and seeth strange sights and commotions in the sky and the element.

"And soon I heard a roaring wind:
It did not come anear;
But with its sound it shook the sails,
That were so thin and sere.[29]

"The upper air burst into life!
And a hundred fire flags sheen,[30]
To and fro they were hurried about!
And to and fro, and in and out,
The wan stars danced between.

"And the coming wind did roar more loud,
And the sails did sigh like sedge;[31]
And the rain poured down from one
 black cloud;
The Moon was at its edge.

Literary Analysis
Poetic Sound Devices and the Language of the Fantastic What does the connection of the two events in lines 288–291 add to the fairy-tale quality of the story?

Literary Analysis
Poetic Sound Devices Which repeated consonant sound in lines 303–304 creates alliteration?

---

28. **silly** empty.
29. **sere** dried up.
30. **fire flags sheen** the aurora australis, or southern lights, shone.
31. **sedge** *n.* rushlike plant that grows in wet soil.

ENRICHMENT: Cultural Connection

Dreams

When the Mariner dreams that the buckets are filled with water, it rains upon his awakening. In some cultures, this sequence of events could be seen as confirming the prophetic powers of dreams. For example, in ancient Greece gods might visit a dreaming person to predict or order specific future actions. In another view, the Eskimo of Hudson Bay believe the dreamer's soul has actually left his or her body; it is therefore forbidden to awaken those who sleep.

Psychoanalyst Sigmund Freud's more recent perspective on dreams suggests that they reflect elements of the waking experience that are too painful or difficult to address except during sleep.

31

Engraving by Gustave Doré for "The Rime of the Ancient Mariner" by Samuel Taylor Coleridge

32 ▲ **Critical Viewing** Which details support the mood of hopelessness in this illustration? **[Support]**

31 Background

Art

Engraving for "The Rime of the Ancient Mariner," 1875, by Gustave Doré

This engraving depicts the dead crew navigating the ship as the Mariner looks on in despair. Doré has reordered the poem's events to present the Mariner still carrying the Albatross. Although the poem emphasizes the positive aspects of this bizarre scene, the artist has chosen to emphasize the night-marish aspects.

As photographic expertise grew in the 1860s, Frenchman Gustave Doré began to use sketches as his original illustrations, transferring these to the wood block photo-graphically rather than by cutting. Doré often created fantastic, dream-like images. Critics feel Doré's images succeed most in black-and-white media such as this engraving with its eerie vision of the cursed ship sailed by animated spirits. Use these questions for discussion:

1. Why might the engraver have chosen to reorganize the events for this image?
   Possible responses: The artist thought the image would be more interesting and memorable if he emphasized the horrific aspects of the scene; the artist, like the Wedding Guest, found the thought of a zombie crew frightening even if "a troop of spirits blessed" inhabited the dead bodies.
2. What elements of the engraving reflect Coleridge's description of the situation?
   Answer: As in Coleridge's descriptions, the spirit crew members' postures show them to be working hard while their faces reflect death.

32 ▶Critical Viewing

Answer: Students may say that the heaped bodies and vacant expressions, along with the Mariner's despairing posture and countenance, contribute to the mood of hopelessness.

CUSTOMIZE INSTRUCTION FOR UNIVERSAL ACCESS

For Gifted/Talented Students

Have students design a costume for a character in "The Rime of the Ancient Mariner," using details they have gleaned from their reading of the poem. Students should work in pairs, or small groups, to design an appropriate costume for the character they have chosen or been assigned. Encourage students to reread the poem to find clues about that character's appearance if they are having difficulty remembering specifics. Tell students they should use their imaginations in their designs, or they can research the clothing of the time. Refer students to Activity 5 in **Extensions Activities,** p. 32 for additional tips.

33 Literary Analysis

Poetic Sound Devices

- Read aloud the bracketed passage to students.
- Review with students the definition of assonance as the repetition of a vowel sound in stressed syllables with different consonant sounds.
- Then, ask students the first Literary Analysis question on p. 700: Find an example of assonance—the repetition of vowel sounds in unrhymed syllables—in lines 331–334.
Answer: Students should identify the assonance of the words *groaned* and *uprose* in line 331.

34 Literary Analysis

Poetic Sound Devices

- Have students read lines 350–353 to themselves.
- Review with students the definition of alliteration.
- Then, ask students the second Literary Analysis question on p. 700: Find an example of alliteration—the repetition of initial consonant sounds—in lines 350–353.
Answer: Students should cite the repetition of the *d* sound in "dawned—they dropped," in line 350 and the *s* sound in "Sweet sounds rose slowly . . ." in line 352.

Monitor Progress Have students discuss the effects that these sound devices have on the reader of the poem. Make sure they support their responses with details from the poem.
Possible response: The alliterated *s* sound unifies and emphasizes the image of the slow sweet sounds, encouraging the reader's wonder at this fantastical event.

"The thick black cloud was cleft, and still
The Moon was at its side:
Like waters shot from some high crag,
The lightning fell with never a jag,
A river steep and wide.

The bodies of the ship's crew are inspired[32] and the ship moves on;

"The loud wind never reached the ship,
Yet now the ship moved on!
Beneath the lightning and the Moon
The dead men gave a groan.

33
"They groaned, they stirred, they all uprose,
Nor spake, nor moved their eyes;
It had been strange, even in a dream,
To have seen those dead men rise.

Literary Analysis
Poetic Sound Devices Find an example of assonance—the repetition of vowel sounds in unrhymed syllables—in lines 331–334.

"The helmsman steered, the ship moved on:
Yet never a breeze up-blew;
The mariners all 'gan work the ropes,
Where they were wont[33] to do;
They raised their limbs like lifeless tools—
We were a ghastly crew.

"The body of my brother's son
Stood by me, knee to knee;
The body and I pulled at one rope,
But he said nought to me."

But not by the souls of the men, nor by demons of earth or middle air, but by a blessed troop of angelic spirits, sent down by the invocation of the guardian saint.

"I fear thee, ancient Mariner!"
"Be calm, thou Wedding Guest!
'Twas not those souls that fled in pain,
Which to their corses[34] came again,
But a troop of spirits blessed:

34
"For when it dawned—they dropped their arms,
And clustered round the mast;
Sweet sounds rose slowly through
their mouths,
And from their bodies passed.

Literary Analysis
Poetic Sound Devices Find an example of alliteration—the repetition of initial consonant sounds—in lines 350–353.

"Around, around, flew each sweet sound,
Then darted to the Sun;
Slowly the sounds came back again,
Now mixed, now one by one.

32. **inspired** inspirited.
33. **wont** accustomed.
34. **corses** corpses.

ENRICHMENT: Science Connection

The Southern Lights

The Southern Lights, or Aurora Australis, that the Mariner sees can be observed around 70° south latitude. At about 70° north latitude, a similar phenomenon called the Northern Lights, or Aurora Borealis, can be observed. Both displays of light may take many shapes, from arcs or bands to fan-shaped coronas. They originate in the upper atmosphere when auroral electrons and protons collide at high speeds with atoms, causing the atoms to glow. Because these auroral particles are linked to solar activity, changes in the sun's behavior can increase the frequency and intensity of the light displays.

"Sometimes a-dropping from the sky
I heard the skylark sing;
Sometimes all little birds that are,
How they seemed to fill the sea and air
With their sweet jargoning![35]

"And now 'twas like all instruments,
Now like a lonely flute;
And now it is an angel's song,
That makes the heavens be mute.

"It ceased; yet still the sails made on
A pleasant noise till noon,
A noise like of a hidden brook
In the leafy month of June,
That to the sleeping woods all night
Singeth a quiet tune.

"Till noon we quietly sailed on,
Yet never a breeze did breathe;
Slowly and smoothly went the ship,
Moved onward from beneath.

The lonesome Spirit from the South Pole carries on the ship as far as the Line, in obedience to the angelic troop, but still requireth vengeance.

"Under the keel nine fathom deep,
From the land of mist and snow,
The spirit slid; and it was he
That made the ship to go.
The sails at noon left off their tune,
And the ship stood still also.

"The Sun, right up above the mast,
Had fixed her to the ocean:
But in a minute she 'gan stir,
With a short uneasy motion—
Backwards and forwards half her length
With a short uneasy motion.

The Polar Spirit's fellow demons, the invisible inhabitants of the element, take part in his wrong; and two of them relate, one to the other, that penance long and heavy for the ancient Mariner hath been accorded to the Polar Spirit, who returneth southward.

"Then like a pawing horse let go,
She made a sudden bound:
It flung the blood into my head,
And I fell down in a swound.

"How long in that same fit I lay,
I have not to declare;
But ere my living life returned,

Reading Strategy
Analyzing Poetic Effects
How does the alliteration in lines 373–376 enhance the description of the boat's smooth progress?

Reading Check
What happens to the bodies of the Mariner's shipmates?

---

35. jargoning singing.

35 Reading Strategy

Analyzing Poetic Effects

- Have a student volunteer read aloud lines 373–376. Have students identify the use of alliteration in these lines.
  Answer: Alliteration occurs in the repeated *br* sound in *breeze* and *breathe* and in the repeated *s* sound in *sailed, slowly,* and *smoothly.*
- Then, ask the Reading Strategy question on p. 701: How does the alliteration in lines 373–376 enhance the description of the boat's smooth progress?
  Answer: The alliteration enables the language of these lines to flow effortlessly from one word to another, in a fashion that mimics the boat's slow and smooth progress.

36 

Answer: The bodies of the Mariner's shipmates become inhabited by angelic spirits.

CUSTOMIZE INSTRUCTION FOR UNIVERSAL ACCESS

For Less Proficient Readers	For Gifted/Talented Students
Review with students how to analyze poetic sound effects such as assonance, alliteration, consonance, and interval rhyme by using the Poetic Effects transparency in **Literary Analysis and Reading Transparencies,** p. 63. Then, guide students as they read pp. 700–701 of "The Rime of the Ancient Mariner" as a group. As students identify poetic devices, encourage them to analyze the effects of those devices using the techniques learned from the transparency.	Have students write their own poems in which they give an account of a mysterious or supernatural event—like the one in "The Rime of the Ancient Mariner" in which the dead sailors navigate the ship. Tell them that they must incorporate alliteration, assonance, consonance, and internal rhyme into their poetic creations. When students have written their poems, have them perform them for their peers in a classroom "ghost tale" storytelling.

37 Background

Art

Engraving for "The Rime of the Ancient Mariner," 1875, by Gustave Doré

This illustration, while one of the series created for Coleridge's poem, does not depict any specific event in Part VI. Rather it evokes the ship's isolation throughout the poem.

The French engraver Gustave Doré shared the exuberance of the Romantic lyric poets and illustrated many other Romantic works. Use these questions for discussion:

1. How does the light in the illustration relate to the Mariner's description of events?
   Answer: The light is only on the boat, just as the wind blows only on the Mariner and his ship.
2. What element of the composition reflects the Mariner's spiritual experience?
   Answer: The boat is isolated amidst a sea of dark and turbulent water; the Mariner is spiritually isolated amidst the dark and turbulent experiences of death and despair.

38 ▶ Critical Viewing

Possible response: Students may say that this illustration more accurately depicts events very early in the poem, when the ship is storm-tossed. In Part V, though the ship sails swiftly, the sailing is "smooth." The image is not portrayed from the Mariner's view but rather from above.

38 ◀ Critical Viewing How closely can you connect this illustration to the events in the poem? Is the image being portrayed from the Ancient Mariner's point of view? Why or why not? **[Connect]**

37

Engraving by Gustave Doré for "The Rime of the Ancient Mariner" by Samuel Taylor Coleridge

I heard and in my soul discerned
Two voices in the air.

"'Is it he?' quoth one, 'Is this the man?
By him who died on cross,
With his cruel bow he laid full low
The harmless Albatross.

"'The spirit who bideth by himself
In the land of mist and snow,

ENRICHMENT: Science Connection

The Pacific Ocean

The Pacific Ocean covers more than a third of Earth's surface, about 70 million square miles in area. It has an average depth of 12,925 feet, though at its deepest point, the Challenger Deep of the Marianas Trench, the Pacific is 36,198 feet deep. The Pacific is about 9,500 miles across at its widest running south-north, and about 12,000 miles at its widest running east-west.

Given the speed of sea travel in Coleridge's day, one can estimate the duration of the Mariner's journey—from the Equator to the Antarctic Circle and back again—at about 78 days. In the 1800s a sailing ship took approximately four weeks to sail from Liverpool to New York, a distance of approximately 3,320 miles, yielding an average speed of 118 miles a day. The Antarctic Circle, at latitude 66° south, is approximately 4,554 statute miles from the Equator (with one degree of latitude equal to about 69 statute miles).

He loved the bird that loved the man
Who shot him with his bow.'

"The other was a softer voice,
As soft as honeydew:
Quoth he, 'The man hath penance done,
And penance more will do.'

Part VI

FIRST VOICE

"'But tell me, tell me! speak again,
Thy soft response renewing—
What makes that ship drive on so fast?
What is the ocean doing?'

SECOND VOICE

"'Still as a slave before his lord,
The ocean hath no blast;
His great bright eye most silently
Up to the Moon is cast—

"'If he may know which way to go;
For she guides him smooth or grim.
See, brother, see! how graciously
She looketh down on him.'

The Mariner hath been cast into a trance; for the angelic power causeth the vessel to drive northward faster than human life could endure.

FIRST VOICE

"'But why drives on that ship so fast,
Without or wave or wind?'

SECOND VOICE

"'The air is cut away before,
And closes from behind.

"'Fly, brother, fly! more high, more high!
Or we shall be belated:
For slow and slow that ship will go,
When the Mariner's trance is abated.'

The super-natural motion is retarded; the Mariner awakes, and his penance begins anew.

"I woke, and we were sailing on
As in a gentle weather:
'Twas night, calm night, the moon was high;
The dead men stood together.

"All stood together on the deck,
For a charnel dungeon[36] fitter;

36. **charnel dungeon** vault where corpses or bones are deposited.

Literary Analysis
Poetic Sound Devices and the Language of Fantasy How do the two voices contribute to Coleridge's creation of a dream world?

Literary Analysis
Poetic Sound Devices What instance of assonance can you find in lines 414–417?

41 **✓Reading Check** What do the two voices discuss?

39 Literary Analysis

Poetic Sound Devices and the Language of Fantasy

- Have two student volunteers read aloud lines 402–409. Review with students their understanding of who says what in this passage.
- Then, ask students the first Literary Analysis question on p. 703: How do the two voices contribute to Coleridge's creation of a dream world?
  Answer: The voices that the ancient Mariner overhears are disembodied. They discuss his actions and his fate as if they had complete knowledge of him. These facts suggest that they are supernatural powers, as might be encountered in a dream world.

40 Literary Analysis

Poetic Sound Devices

- Read the bracketed passage aloud and review with students their understanding of assonance.
- Then, ask students the second Literary Analysis question on p. 703: What instance of assonance can you find in lines 414–417?
  Answer: Students should recognize assonance in words like *ocean* and *no* in line 415 and *eye* and *silently* in line 416.

41 ✓Reading Check

Answer: The two voices discuss whether or not the ancient Mariner has performed his penance for killing the Albatross, and they discuss the progress of the ship.

CUSTOMIZE INSTRUCTION FOR UNIVERSAL ACCESS

For Special Needs Students

Have students examine the illustrations throughout the text of "The Rime of the Ancient Mariner." Then, ask them to imagine that they are the publishers looking for an artist to illustrate a new edition of Coleridge's poem. Have students make a list of all the scenes they would want illustrated in a new edition. Remind students that they will probably want different scenes from the ones Doré illustrated, or they may want them done in a different manner. Students should write a list of specifications for the artist and any other ideas they have.

42 Literary Analysis

Poetic Sound Devices

- Have students read lines 460–463. Encourage them to look for examples of assonance and alliteration in these lines.
- Then, ask students the Literary Analysis question on p. 704: Find the assonance and alliteration in lines 460–463.
  Answer: Examples of alliteration include the repeated use of the letter *s* throughout lines 460–462 and the repeated use of the letter *b* in lines 462–463. Examples of assonance include the similar vowel sounds of the words "sweetly" and "breeze."

All fixed on me their stony eyes,
That in the Moon did glitter.

"The pang, the curse, with which they died,
Had never passed away;
I could not draw my eyes from theirs,
Nor turn them up to pray.

The curse is finally expiated.

"And now this spell was snapped; once more
I viewed the ocean green,
And looked far forth, yet little saw
Of what had else been seen—

expiated (ēk′ spē āt′ əd) *v.* atoned; made amends for, especially by suffering

"Like one, that on a lonesome road
Doth walk in fear and dread,
And having once turned round walks on,
And turns no more his head;
Because he knows, a frightful fiend
Doth close behind him tread.

"But soon there breathed a wind on me,
Nor sound nor motion made:
Its path was not upon the sea,
In ripple or in shade.

"It raised my hair, it fanned my cheek
Like a meadow-gale of spring—
It mingled strangely with my fears,
Yet it felt like a welcoming.

42
"Swiftly, swiftly flew the ship,
Yet she sailed softly too:
Sweetly, sweetly blew the breeze—
On me alone it blew.

Literary Analysis
Poetic Sound Devices Find the assonance and alliteration in lines 460–463.

And the ancient Mariner beholdeth his native country.

"Oh! dream of joy! is this indeed
The lighthouse top I see?
Is this the hill? is this the kirk?
Is this mine own countree?

"We drifted o'er the harbor bar,
And I with sobs did pray—
O let me be awake, my God!
Or let me sleep alway.

"The harbor bay was clear as glass,
So smoothly it was strewn![37]

---

37. **strewn** spread.

And on the bay the moonlight lay,
And the shadow of the Moon.

"The rock shone bright, the kirk no less,
That stands above the rock;
The moonlight steeped in silentness
The steady weathercock.

"And the bay was white with silent light,
Till rising from the same,
Full many shapes, that shadows were,
In crimson colors came.

The angelic spirits leave the dead bodies,

"A little distance from the prow
Those crimson shadows were:
I turned my eyes upon the deck—
Oh, Christ! what saw I there!

And appear in their own forms of light.

"Each corse lay flat, lifeless and flat,
And, by the holy rood![38]
A man all light, a seraph[39] man,
On every corse there stood.

"This seraph band, each waved his hand:
It was a heavenly sight!
They stood as signals to the land,
Each one a lovely light;

"This seraph band, each waved his hand,
No voice did they impart—
No voice; but oh! the silence sank
Like music on my heart.

"But soon I heard the dash of oars,
I heard the Pilot's cheer;
My head was turned perforce away
And I saw a boat appear.

"The Pilot and the Pilot's boy,
I heard them coming fast:

38. **rood** cross.
39. **seraph** angel.

43 ***The Tradition of Fantasy*** Coleridge's "Rime of the Ancient Mariner"—written in a dreamlike language, set in an indeterminate past, and filled with supernatural events—is part of the British tradition of fantasy literature. Writers of works of fantasy set out to create a realm distinct from the everyday world of their readers—a never-never land ruled by strange laws.

The fantasy tradition began as long ago as Sir Thomas Malory's *Morte d'Arthur,* (p. 176), which is set in a vanished past that had become a myth by Malory's own day. The idea of a vanished past fascinated writers long after Malory, reappearing in the work of Alfred, Lord Tennyson, who resorted to Arthurian and mythological elements in many poems, as in "The Lady of Shalott" (p. 821).

Fantasy writers like Coleridge use strange settings and supernatural tales to break the spell of ordinary life. By plunging us into a wild, unfamiliar world, they remind us that human imagination can always envision worlds beyond the one into which we are born—a power that enables scientific discoveries and social reforms as well as great poetry.

44 Reading Check

What place does the Mariner sail near?

43 Background

The Tradition of Fantasy

The tradition of fantasy in British literature is also echoed by Jonathan Swift in his epic, *Gulliver's Travels,* in which unusual worlds like Lilliput and Brobdingnag are inhabited by persons both like and unlike those on Earth. Later works, such as *The Adventures of Alice in Wonderland* by Lewis Carroll, Jules Verne's *20,000 Leagues Under the Sea,* and *The Lion, The Witch, and the Wardrobe* by C. S. Lewis treat imaginary worlds with great liveliness and attention to detail. Many of these works of literature are the antecedents to some of the popular contemporary fiction that incorporates many of the elements of fantasy that originated in these classics.

44 Reading Check

Answer: The Mariner sails near the church and the lighthouse of his home.

CUSTOMIZE INSTRUCTION FOR UNIVERSAL ACCESS

For Special Needs Students	For Less Proficient Readers	For Advanced Readers
Have students read smaller portions of the poem and summarize what they have read so far. To test students' retention and understanding of "The Rime of the Ancient Mariner," consider showing them **Got It! Videotapes,** Tape 3, to review material they have already read.	After students have practiced identifying poetic sound devices using transparencies, have them listen to a portion of "The Rime of the Ancient Mariner" on **Listening to Literature Audiocassettes,** Side 17. Discuss with them the effects of sound devices in the part to which they have listened.	Have students analyze the many elements of fantasy in Coleridge's account of the sailors on the ship. Students should write short essays in which they address the ways in which Coleridge makes the crew seem fantastical. Refer them to the British Tradition box on p. 705 for an overview of fantasy literature.

45 Reading Strategy

Analyzing Poetic Effects

- Have a student volunteer read aloud lines 504–513. Then, review with students their understanding of sound devices, and ask them to re-read these lines to detect any sound devices.
- Ask students the Reading Strategy question on p. 706: These lines are less crowded with sound devices than the lines describing the Mariner's nightmarish sea journey. How does this shift in language match the shift in mood?
  Answer: The language becomes less rich and surreal as the Mariner finds his way home.

46 Literary Analysis

Poetic Sound Devices and the Language of Fantasy

- Read aloud the bracketed passage to students. Remind students that Coleridge borrowed on medieval traditions in writing his poem.
- Ask students the Literary Analysis question on p. 706: Which word in lines 523–526 might Coleridge have borrowed from medieval tales of knights?
  Possible response: The word "trow" comes from the lexicon of medieval chivalry.

Dear Lord in Heaven! it was a joy
The dead men could not blast.

"I saw a third—I heard his voice:
It is the Hermit good!
He singeth loud his godly hymns
That he makes in the wood.
He'll shrieve[40] my soul, he'll
    wash away
The Albatross's blood.

Reading Strategy
Analyzing Poetic Effects
These lines are less crowded with sound devices than the lines describing the Mariner's nightmarish sea journey. How does this shift in language match the shift in mood?

Part VII

The Hermit of the Wood,

"This Hermit good lives in that wood
Which slopes down to the sea.
How loudly his sweet voice he rears!
He loves to talk with marineres
That come from a far countree.

"He kneels at morn, and noon,
    and eve—
He hath a cushion plump:
It is the moss that wholly hides
The rotted old oak-stump.

"The skiff boat neared; I heard them talk.
'Why, this is strange, I trow![41]
Where are those lights so many and fair,
That signal made but now?'

Literary Analysis
Poetic Sound Devices and the Language of Fantasy
Which word in lines 523–526 might Coleridge have borrowed from medieval tales of knights?

Approacheth the ship with wonder.

"'Strange, by my faith!' the Hermit said—
'And they answered not our cheer!
The planks looked warped! and see those sails,
How thin they are and sere!
I never saw aught like to them,
Unless perchance it were

"'Brown skeletons of leaves that lag
My forest brook along;
When the ivy tod[42] is heavy with snow,
And the owlet whoops to the wolf below,
That eats the she-wolf's young.'

"'Dear Lord! it hath a fiendish look'
(The Pilot made reply)

---

40. shrieve (shrēv) absolve from sin.
41. trow believe.
42. tod bush.

'I am a-feared'—'Push on, push on!'
Said the Hermit cheerily.

"The boat came closer to the ship,
But I nor spake nor stirred;
The boat came close beneath the ship,
And straight[43] a sound was heard.

The ship suddenly sinketh.

"Under the water it rumbled on,
Still louder and more dread:
It reached the ship, it split the bay;
The ship went down like lead.

The ancient Mariner is saved in the Pilot's boat.

"Stunned by that loud and dreadful sound,
Which sky and ocean smote,
Like one that hath been seven days drowned
My body lay afloat;
But swift as dreams, myself I found
Within the Pilot's boat.

"Upon the whirl, where sank the ship,
The boat spun round and round;
And all was still, save that the hill
Was telling of the sound.

"I moved my lips—the Pilot shrieked
And fell down in a fit;
The holy Hermit raised his eyes,
And prayed where he did sit.

"I took the oars; the Pilot's boy,
Who now doth crazy go,
Laughed loud and long, and all the while
His eyes went to and fro.
'Ha! ha!' quoth he, 'full plain I see,
The Devil knows how to row.'

"And now, all in my own countree,
I stood on the firm land!
The Hermit stepped forth from the boat,
And scarcely he could stand.

The ancient Mariner earnestly entreateth the Hermit to shrieve him; and the penance of life falls on him.

"'O shrieve me, shrieve me, holy man!'
The Hermit crossed his brow.[44]

Reading Strategy
Analyzing Poetic Effects
Which poetic effects contribute to the impact of lines 556–559?

 **Reading Check**

Who helps the Mariner when the ship sinks?

43. **straight** immediately.
44. **crossed his brow** made the sign of the cross on his forehead.

47 Reading Strategy

Analyzing Poetic Effects

- Encourage students to focus on any poetic effects in the lines. Have them identify the poetic effects they find in these lines.
- Ask students the Reading Strategy question on p. 707: What poetic effects contribute to the impact of lines 556–559?
  Answer: Students should identify the internal rhyme of *still* and *hill*, the alliteration of the words *whirl/where, sank/ship, still/save,* and the repetition in "round and round" as poetic effects that contribute to the momentum of these lines.

48  Reading Check

Answer: The Pilot helps the Mariner when the ship sinks.

CUSTOMIZE INSTRUCTION FOR UNIVERSAL ACCESS

For Less Proficient Readers	For Gifted/Talented Students	For Advanced Readers
Guide students as they read Part VII. Encourage students to pay special attention to the poetic effects used by Coleridge. If students have difficulty interpreting those effects, model these skills using the Poetic Effects transparency on p. 63 of **Literary Analysis and Reading Transparencies.**	Have students write their own marine legends, incorporating elements from "The Rime of the Ancient Mariner." When they have completed their works, have them share their "tales" with their classmates.	Have students analyze Part VII of "The Rime of the Ancient Mariner" in the context of the rest of the poem. Students should analyze the role played by the Hermit, the sinking of the ship, and the nature of the Ancient Mariner's obligation upon his return.

49 Reading Strategy

Analyzing Poetic Effects

- Read aloud the bracketed passage to students. Encourage them to focus on the alliteration in the lines.
- Ask students the Reading Strategy question on p. 708: What effect does the alliteration in line 590 featuring *tale*—a word that appears in each of the preceding two stanzas—have?
  Answer: Students should say that the alliteration related to the word *tale* emphasizes its centrality to this story—that the Mariner must tell his tale as a continued punishment for killing the Albatross.

'Say, quick,' quoth he, 'I bid thee say—
What manner of man art thou?'

"Forthwith this frame of mine was wrenched
With a woeful agony,
Which forced me to begin my tale;
And then it left me free.

And ever and anon throughout his future life an agony constraineth him to travel from land to land;

"Since then, at an uncertain hour,
That agony returns:
And till my ghastly tale is told,
This heart within me burns.

49

"I pass, like night, from land to land;
I have strange power of speech;
That moment that his face I see,
I know the man that must hear me:
To him my tale I teach.

"What loud uproar bursts from that door!
The wedding guests are there:
But in the garden bower the bride
And bridemaids singing are:
And hark the little vesper bell,
Which biddeth me to prayer!

"O Wedding Guest! this soul hath been
Alone on a wide wide sea:
So lonely 'twas, that God himself
Scarce seemèd there to be.

"O sweeter than the marriage feast,
'Tis sweeter far to me,
To walk together to the kirk
With a goodly company!—

"To walk together to the kirk,
And all together pray,
While each to his great Father bends,
Old men, and babes, and loving friends
And youths and maidens gay!

And to teach, by his own example, love and reverence to all things that God made and loveth.

"Farewell, farewell! but this I tell
To thee, thou Wedding Guest!
He prayeth well, who loveth well
Both man and bird and beast.

Reading Strategy
Analyzing Poetic Effects
What effect does the alliteration in line 590 featuring *tale*—a word that appears in each of the preceding two stanzas—have?

reverence (rēv′ ər əns) *n.* deep respect

"He prayeth best, who loveth best
All things both great and small;
For the dear God who loveth us,
He made and loveth all."

The Mariner, whose eye is bright,
Whose beard with age is hoar,
Is gone; and now the Wedding Guest
Turned from the bridegroom's door.

He went like one that hath been stunned
And is of sense forlorn:
A sadder and a wiser man,
He rose the morrow morn.

Review and Assess

Thinking About the Selection

1. **Respond:** How did your reaction to the ancient Mariner change as his story went on? Explain.
2. (a) **Recall:** On what occasion does the Mariner tell his story? (b) **Interpret:** Why do you think Coleridge chose this occasion for the poem?
3. (a) **Recall:** What contradictory connections does the crew make between the Albatross and the weather? (b) **Recall:** What does the Mariner do to the Albatross? (c) **Infer:** Why does the Mariner wear the Albatross around his neck?
4. (a) **Recall:** What happens to the Mariner's shipmates after the appearance of the Specter Woman and her Death-mate? (b) **Generalize:** What might this symbolize about the effect of guilt on an individual's perceptions of and relations with others?
5. (a) **Infer:** Why does the Albatross finally fall from the Mariner's neck? (b) **Interpret:** What do you think the Albatross symbolizes? Find evidence to support your answer.
6. (a) **Recall:** What is the Mariner's lifelong penance? (b) **Analyze:** How does his story affect his listener? (c) **Draw Conclusions:** What larger lesson about human life might his story suggest?
7. **Take a Position:** In today's world, people who have been through harrowing experiences often tell their stories in books and on talk shows, just as the Mariner tells the story of his trials. Do you think this type of response is appropriate? Explain.

CUSTOMIZE INSTRUCTION FOR UNIVERSAL ACCESS

For Gifted/Talented Students

Show Art Transparencies 10 and 11, *The Haywain* by John Constable and *Wreck of a Transport Ship* by J.W.M. Turner, in **Art Transparencies,** Vol. 2. Explain that these noted English Romantic painters, like the Romantic poets, celebrated nature. Guide students to see that, while Constable shows nature's tranquility, Turner shows a chaotic nature that threatens to overwhelm the canvas as well as the ship. Relate the paintings to the poem by exploring ways in which both faces of nature are present in the Mariner's voyage.

Answers to p. 709

Review and Assess

1. Possible responses: Students may say that at first they found him and his intensity disturbing but that as the story went on, they became more sympathetic with the ancient Mariner's plight.
2. **(a)** The Mariner tells his story on the occasion of a wedding. **(b)** Coleridge may use the occasion of a wedding for the poem because the Mariner's story is a warning about the isolation and guilt brought about by a break with nature and society, while a wedding affirms unity and community.
3. **(a)** The crew says the Albatross is responsible for the fog and then the Albatross was responsible for the wind that kept their boat moving. **(b)** The Mariner kills the Albatross with his crossbow. **(c)** The Mariner wears the Albatross around his neck as a sign of his crime in killing it.
4. **(a)** The Mariner's shipmates drop dead. **(b)** This might symbolize the ways in which guilt can cut off an individual from others.
5. **(a)** Possible response: The Albatross falls off his neck because his guilt is forgiven. **(b)** Possible responses: The Albatross is a symbol of guilt for man's break with nature or the individual's break with a community; it may also symbolize the interconnectedness of all things.
6. **(a)** The Mariner's lifelong penance is to wander the Earth telling his tale and teaching love for all things great and small. **(b)** It leaves him "sadder" and "wiser." **(c)** Possible response: Coleridge's poem might suggest that people need to respect God's creation but that they are in danger of failing to respect it.
7. Possible responses: Some students may feel that these people lack dignity; others may feel that storytelling is a natural response to trauma and may help the audience.

50 About the Selection

This poem captures the Romantic love of nature and interest in the exotic, the faraway, and the strange. The speaker imagines the sumptuous pleasure dome of Kubla Khan. By portraying that fantasy so vividly, the speaker demonstrates the extraordinary power of the imagination.

51 Background

Art

Box and Cover, first half of the 16th century

This lacquer box cover shows a Chinese palace or large estate much like the one Coleridge describes in his poem.

In sixteenth-century China, Ming artisans responded creatively to the demands of an increasingly wealthy—and consumer-oriented—merchant class. A box such as this one was typical of the precise and delicate workmanship prized by wealthy clients. Its picture is pieced together from minute slivers and petals of mother-of-pearl, shaped in myriad ways to represent buildings, natural elements, and figures. Additional details, such as the elaborate designs on the clothing, are made from individual pieces. Use these questions for discussion.

1. How might the poem's Kubla Khan feel about this box and cover?
   Answer: He might want it for his palace.
2. What elements of the box and cover reflect the sumptuousness of the poem's descriptions?
   Answer: The bright and glittering mother-of-pearl and the elaborate detail both reflect the luxuriousness of Coleridge's palace.

52 ▶Critical Viewing

Answer: Similarities include settings that feature encircling walks, a garden, an elaborate building with domes, and a river (the stylized arcs at the bottom of the box). Differences may include the scale of the palace, which is smaller on the box with respect to humans than the scale of the palace in the poem, and the lack of ice caves and a chasm in the scene on the box.

50 Kubla Khan

Samuel Taylor Coleridge

51

Box and Cover, Ming Dynasty, first half of 16th century, The Seattle Art Museum

◀**Critical Viewing** 52
How do Coleridge's poetic images compare with the details on this sixteenth-century Chinese box cover?
[Compare and Contrast]

Background

Coleridge claimed to have dreamed his poem "Kubla Khan" line for line after falling asleep while reading a passage from a work about the founder of the great Mongol dynasty. Upon awakening, he transcribed the lines as fast as he could. When he was interrupted by a visitor, however, the lines in his head disappeared, never to be remembered. As a result, Coleridge was unable to complete the poem.

ENRICHMENT: Social Studies Connection

Kubla Khan

Kubla Khan's grandfather, Genghis Khan, began the Mongols' road to conquest by uniting his own people. He then conquered China and parts of Europe in the early thirteenth century. The Mongols raised the status of merchants in China and encouraged trade with the outside world by patrolling the trade route known as the Silk Road. It was the Silk Road that brought Venetian merchant Marco Polo to China later in the thirteenth century. A special relationship arose between the ruler Kubla Khan and the merchant, who joined Khan's civil service for some twenty years.

In Xanadu[1] did Kubla Khan
A stately pleasure dome decree:
Where Alph,[2] the sacred river, ran
Through caverns measureless to man
    Down to a sunless sea.
So twice five miles of fertile ground
With walls and towers were girdled round;
And there were gardens bright with sinuous rills,[3]
Where blossomed many an incense-bearing tree;
And here were forests ancient as the hills,
Enfolding sunny spots of greenery.

But oh! that deep romantic chasm which slanted
Down the green hill athwart[4] a cedarn cover![5]
A savage place! as holy and enchanted
53 As e'er beneath a waning moon was haunted
By woman wailing for her demon lover!
And from this chasm, with ceaseless turmoil seething,
As if this earth in fast thick pants were breathing.
A mighty fountain momently was forced;
Amid whose swift half-intermitted burst
Huge fragments vaulted like rebounding hail,
Or chaffy grain beneath the thresher's flail;
And 'mid these dancing rocks at once and ever
It flung up momently the sacred river.
Five miles meandering with a mazy motion
Through wood and dale the sacred river ran,
Then reached the caverns measureless to man,
And sank in tumult to a lifeless ocean:
And 'mid this tumult Kubla heard from far
Ancestral voices prophesying war!
    54 The shadow of the dome of pleasure
    Floated midway on the waves;
    Where was heard the mingled measure
    From the fountain and the caves.
It was a miracle of rare device.[6]
A sunny pleasure dome with caves of ice!

    A damsel with a dulcimer[7]
    In a vision once I saw:

sinuous (sin′ yo͞o əs) *adj.* bending; winding

Reading Strategy
Analyzing Poetic Effects
What alliteration in lines 15–16 helps you hear the cries of the haunted woman?

tumult (to͞o′ mult′) *n.* noisy commotion

Literary Analysis
Poetic Sound Devices
Find examples of assonance and alliteration in lines 31–34.

Reading Check
What erupts continuously from the chasm?

1. **Xanadu** (zan′ ə do͞o) indefinite area in China.
2. **Alph** probably derived from the Greek river Alpheus, the waters of which, it was believed in Greek mythology, joined with a stream to form a fountain in Sicily.
3. **rills** brooks.
4. **athwart** across.
5. **cedarn cover** covering of cedar trees.
6. **device** design.
7. **dulcimer** (dul′ sə mər) *n.* stringed musical instrument played with small hammers.

53 Reading Strategy
Analyzing Poetic Effects

- Read aloud the bracketed passage to students. Review with them the definition of alliteration; then, ask them to identify any examples they find in this passage.
- Ask students the Reading Strategy question on p. 711: What alliteration in lines 15–16 helps you hear the cries of the haunted woman?
  Answer: Students should identify the repetition of the *w* sound in *waning, woman,* and *wailing*.

54 Literary Analysis
Poetic Sound Devices

- Review with students the definitions of *assonance* and *alliteration;* then ask them to reread the passage.
- Then, ask students the Literary Analysis question on p. 711: Find examples of assonance and alliteration in lines 31–34.
  Answer: Students should identify assonance in *midway/waves* and *heard/measure;* they should identify alliteration in "mingled measure."

55 Reading Check

Answer: A mighty fountain, which tosses up great fragments of rock, erupts continuously from the chasm.

CUSTOMIZE INSTRUCTION FOR UNIVERSAL ACCESS

For Less Proficient Readers	For Advanced Readers
Guide students as they read "Kubla Khan" in small groups. Explain to students that Coleridge's account of the "pleasure dome" of Kubla Khan may be based in part on his knowledge of Asia and the riches of the Mongols. To stimulate student interest in this subject, you may wish to show them "'Kubla Khan': The Silk Road" on **Interest Grabber Videos,** Tape 4.	Students may find Coleridge's account of Kubla Khan's pleasure dome mesmerizing. Encourage them to find out how much of the wealth and glory of Kubla Khan's regime was exaggerated by Coleridge, and how much was real. Direct students to resources in their school library or on the Internet that will be able to give them more information about Kubla Khan. You may want to direct students to www.phschool.com for additional resources.

ASSESS

Answers for p. 712

Review and Assess

1. **(a)** The grounds of the pleasure dome are "twice five miles" in size, and it contains gardens, creeks, incense-bearing trees, and sunny spots of greenery. **(b)** The associations with the romantic chasm are threatening and chaotic; they include a woman wailing for her demon lover and the explosive underground pressures that force the river to jet above the ground. By contrast, the dome itself is orderly and peaceful. **(c)** Beautiful elements include "gardens bright with sinuous rills," incense-bearing trees in blossom, and "sunny spots of greenery." Sinister elements include "a sunless sea," "a waning moon," a "woman wailing for her demon lover," the chasm and the emptying fountain, and the "lifeless ocean."
2. **(a)** A fountain comes from the chasm, and it bursts out of the earth and tosses up fragments of rock as it makes its way to the ocean. **(b)** Possible responses: Wild disorder of the kind present in the chasm might represent the pressures that drive artists to the ordered creation of works of art like the dome. In order to create new patterns, as artists do, it may be necessary to dissolve old patterns in chaos or to start from what is without order.
3. **(a)** The speaker would build the dome in the air if he were able to revive the maid's song. All who heard would then "see" the dome. **(b)** All who heard would cry "beware," form a circle around him, and close their eyes.
4. **(a)** The power of art is an unstable one that challenges the certainties of ordinary life. **(b)** The dread experienced by the vision of inspired art suggests that, just as the setting of the dome includes the mysterious chasm, an inspired work of art taps into deep, chaotic forces as well as presenting orderly forms.
5. Possible response: Students may say that they have felt overwhelmed by certain artworks, which supports Coleridge's view of art's great and destabilizing power.

It was an Abyssinian[8] maid,
And on her dulcimer she played,
Singing of Mount Abora.[9]
Could I revive within me
Her symphony and song,
To such a deep delight 'twould win me,
That with music loud and long,
I would build that dome in air,
That sunny dome! those caves of ice!
And all who heard should see them there,
And all should cry, Beware! Beware!
His flashing eyes, his floating hair!
Weave a circle round him thrice,
And close your eyes with holy dread,
For he on honeydew hath fed,
And drunk the milk of Paradise.

8. **Abyssinian** (ab ə sin′ ē ən) Ethiopian.
9. **Mount Abora** probably Mount Amara in Abyssinia.

Review and Assess

Thinking About the Selection

1. **(a) Recall:** Describe the pleasure dome and its setting. **(b) Compare and Contrast:** Compare the associations of the "deep romantic chasm" with those of the dome. **(c) Analyze:** What makes the pleasure dome and its setting seem beautiful? What makes them sinister?
2. **(a) Recall:** What comes from the chasm, and what are its effects? **(b) Draw Conclusions:** The pleasure dome might be thought of as a work of art. What does the existence of the chasm on the site of the dome suggest about the relation between constructive and chaotic, or "wild," forces in art?
3. **(a) Interpret:** In the last stanza, if the speaker were able to "revive" his vision, what would he do? What effect would it have on "all who heard"? **(b) Summarize:** How would "all who heard" then react to the speaker?
4. **(a) Interpret:** What does the "holy dread" experienced by "all who heard" suggest about the power of art? **(b) Connect:** What connection can you find between this "dread" and the existence of the chasm at the site of the dome?
5. **Evaluate:** Consider a work of art that has had a strong effect on you. Do you think your experience of this work supports Coleridge's views? Explain.

ASSESSMENT PRACTICE: Critical Thinking

Critical Reasoning (For more practice, see Test Preparation Workbook, p. 32.)

Many tests require students to evaluate the logic of an argument. Use the following sample item to teach students how to identify faulty logic.

'Twas right, said they, such birds to slay,
That bring the fog and mist.

The reasoning behind this statement can be described as

A faulty, because it is based entirely on coincidence.
B logical, because it is based on the sailors' years of experience.
C faulty, because albatrosses are good luck.
D logical, because it is based on facts.

Lead students to recognize that the sailors' logic is faulty because it assumes a causal relationship where none exists. The correct answer is *A*.

Review and Assess

Literary Analysis

Poetic Sound Devices

1. Find an example of the sound device **alliteration** in lines 9–12 of "The Rime of the Ancient Mariner."
2. What **sound device** does Coleridge use in the line "It cracked and growled, and roared and howled . . ." ("Rime," l. 61)?
3. What device dominates the first stanza of "Kubla Khan"? Give three examples.
4. Explain how the prevalence of sound effects in these poems creates a language suited to Coleridge's fantastic subjects.

Comparing Literary Works

5. Coleridge builds his **language of fantasy** in part from archaic words. Identify two instances of such words in the opening stanza of "The Rime of the Ancient Mariner."
6. (a) Identify four words in "Kubla Khan" that contribute to the poem's exotic atmosphere. (b) Contrast these words with the archaic words in "The Rime."
7. Using a chart like the one shown, explain how the quality of Coleridge's language suits different fantastic subjects.

Poem: ____________

Subject	Setting	Events	Language	Why Suitable?

Reading Strategy

Analyzing Poetic Effects

8. (a) What mood do lines 472–483 of "The Rime of the Ancient Mariner" create? (b) What poetic devices contribute to this mood?
9. In "Kubla Khan," how do poetic devices, including repetition, contribute to the effect of lines 45–54?

Extend Understanding

10. **Cultural Connection:** Name an example of a modern "pleasure dome," and compare it with Kubla Khan's.

Quick Review

Alliteration is the repetition of a consonant sound at the beginnings of words (*Kubla / Khan*).

Consonance is the repetition of similar final consonant sounds in stressed syllables with dissimilar vowel sounds (*fiend / behind*).

Assonance is the repetition of a vowel sound in stressed syllables ending in dissimilar consonant sounds (*wave / aflame*).

Internal rhyme is the use of rhymes within a poetic line.

In contrast to everyday language, the **language of fantasy** is used to tell of fantastic events or places.

To **analyze poetic effects,** identify the use of sound devices, images, symbols, repetition, and unusual word order, and then determine their effect on meaning or mood.

Take It to the Net

www.phschool.com

Take the interactive self-test online to check your understanding of these selections.

ENRICHMENT: Further Reading

Other Works by Coleridge

"Christabel"; *Biographia Literaria; Remorse; Aids to Reflection*

Other Works About Redemption

"God's Grandeur," Gerard Manley Hopkins

"Love (3)," George Herbert

Take It to the Net

Visit www.phschool.com for more information on Samuel Taylor Coleridge.

Answers for p. 713

Review and Assess

1. Students should identify the repeated use of the initial *h* sound in "He holds him with his skinny hand" as alliteration in lines 9–12.
2. He uses internal rhyme.
3. Coleridge uses alliteration as the dominant poetic device in the first stanza: *Kubla Khan, dome / decree,* and *sunless sea.*
4. Possible response: Students may note that the prevalence of sound effects sets the overall sound of Coleridge's language apart from everyday talk, just as his subjects are remote from everyday experience.
5. The words *stoppeth, thy, wherefore, stopp'st,* and *thou* are all archaic.
6. **(a)** Possible responses: Students may identify the following four words: *incense, Xanadu, chasm,* and *dulcimer.* **(b)** The archaic words in "The Rime of the Ancient Mariner" seem to derive from medieval poetry and the language of chivalry, whereas the exotic words in "Kubla Khan" seem to draw on an idea of life in Asia.
7. Possible response: The archaic words in "Rime" suit its setting in a generalized distant past. They are associated with legends of knights, and so suit the theme of redemption. The exotic words in "Kubla Khan" match its exotic setting, suggesting the allure of the unknown. They suit the theme of mingled danger and beauty.
8. **(a)** Coleridge gives the scene a mood of stillness and serenity. **(b)** The use of the alliterated s sound, the assonance of *smoothly / strewn,* and the internal rhyme *bay / lay* contribute to this mood.
9. The use of poetic devices make the last few lines of "Kubla Khan" more musical and hypnotic, enhancing the description of the wild-eyed visionary.
10. Possible responses: Students may name exotic destinations like resorts on far-away islands, a modern mall, or an amusement park such as Disneyland. They

continued

Answers continued

may note that such "pleasure domes" do not usually contain natural "romantic chasms," though they may contain thrills in the form of scary rides, horror movies, or views of impressive landscapes.

EXTEND

Answers for p. 714

❶ Vocabulary Development

Word Analysis

1. A sojourn is a short visit, which might be for just a day.
2. A journey is a trip that can be measured in days rather than minutes or hours.
3. Journalism is the activity or profession of recording the events of the day.
4. To adjourn a meeting or a session of a trial is to conclude it for the day.

Spelling Strategy

1. reverence
2. offense
3. reliance
4. sense

Concept Development: Antonyms

1. b	4. b
2. c	5. a
3. a	6. a

❷ Grammar and Style

1. That moment that I see his face.
2. She is red as a rose.
3. An Albatross did cross at length.
4. The merry minstrelsy goes before her, nodding their heads.
5. The white Moonshine glimmered all the night.

Writing Application

Possible response:

" 'Tis my only house," said she.
"It I'll never, ever leave."
"To the ground 'twill fall," said he.
"And no more will I ever grieve."
Thus did they part, and no more was said.
To the bus went he, and she to bed.

Integrate Language Skills

❶ Vocabulary Development Lesson

Word Analysis: Latin Root: *-journ-*

The verb *sojourn*, meaning "to visit for a while," contains the root *-journ-*, derived from French and Latin words meaning "day." Explain how the root contributes to the meaning of each of these words:

1. sojourn	3. journalism
2. journey	4. adjourn

Spelling Strategy

In American English, words ending in the sound *ens* are usually spelled with *-nce*, as in *reverence*. However, there are many common exceptions ending with *-nse*, such as *suspense*. Identify the word in each pair that is spelled correctly.

1. reverense, reverence	3. reliance, reliance
2. offense, offence	4. sense, sence

Concept Development: Antonyms

Review the words in the vocabulary list on page 685. Then, in your notebook, write the letter of the word that is the antonym of, or the word opposite in meaning to, the first word.

1. sinuous: (a) narrow, (b) straight, (c) dark
2. expiated: (a) sold, (b) atoned, (c) sinned
3. averred: (a) denied, (b) claimed, (c) wished
4. reverence: (a) respect, (b) contempt, (c) hope
5. tumult: (a) peace, (b) pleasure, (c) wealth
6. sojourn: (a) leave, (b) visit, (c) rest

❷ Grammar and Style Lesson

Inverted Word Order

To create certain effects, poets sometimes **invert word order**, or depart from the normal English pattern of subject-verb-complement (s - v - c). In these lines, to rhyme *drowned* and *found*, Coleridge inverts the standard word order:

> Like one that hath been seven days
> drowned
> My body lay afloat;
> But swift as dreams, myself (C) I (S) found (V) . . .

The inversion helps Coleridge make his rhyme and adds to the archaic sound of the poem.

Practice Rewrite these lines in standard word order.

1. That moment that his face I see, . . .
2. Red as a rose is she; . . .
3. At length did cross an Albatross, . . .
4. Nodding their heads before her goes / The merry minstrelsy.
5. Whiles all the night, . . . / Glimmered the white Moonshine.

Writing Application Write four or five poetic lines in which you invert normal word order. You may find it helpful to begin with standard word order and then invert subject, verb, and object to achieve rhyme or rhythm.

WG Prentice Hall Writing and Grammar Connection: Chapter 18, Section 2

TEACHING RESOURCES

The following resources can be used to enrich or extend the instruction for pp. 714–715.

Vocabulary

- **Selection Support:** Build Vocabulary, p. 147
- **Vocabulary and Spelling Practice Book** (Use this booklet for skills enrichment.)

Grammar

- **Selection Support:** Grammar and Style, p. 148
- **Writing and Grammar,** Diamond Level, p. 420
- **Daily Language Practice Transparencies** ■

Writing

- **Writing and Grammar,** Diamond Level, p. 317 ■
-  **Writing and Grammar iText CD-ROM**
- **Writing Models and Graphic Organizers on Transparencies,** pp. 99–102

■ **BLOCK SCHEDULING:** Resources marked with this symbol provide varied instruction during 90-minute blocks.

❸ Writing Lesson

Analysis of a Symbol

The Albatross in Coleridge's "The Rime of the Ancient Mariner" is a poetic symbol—a concrete image that stands for a cluster of ideas. Write an essay analyzing the meanings the Albatross takes on in the poem.

Prewriting Using a cluster diagram, gather details from the poem about the Albatross and about the effects on the Mariner of its death. Then, group related details under headings, such as "Guilt" and "Respect for Natural Things."

Drafting As you draft, use the headings on your prewriting lists as a guide, addressing the details you have gathered under each in turn. Link details to broader conclusions about the meaning of the Albatross.

Revising Review your draft to highlight flat, unexciting language. Replace such passages with vivid, specific descriptions or claims.

Model: Revising for Vivid, Precise Language

The sailors praise the Albatross for bringing good weather,
a deadly calm.
then blame it for bringing ~~bad weather.~~ The Polar Spirit
wreaks its vengeance through weather, including an intense drought and a supernaturally fast wind.
~~also uses weather for its vengeance.~~

Vivid words and added details keep the analysis interesting and precise.

WG Prentice Hall Writing and Grammar Connection: Chapter 14, Section 4

❹ Extension Activities

Listening and Speaking With a group, present a **dramatic reading** of a section of "The Rime of the Ancient Mariner." Assign parts and rehearse your reading, following these tips:

1. Each reader should take notes on the atmosphere of the section that he or she will read.
2. Readers should practice reading for sense, without pausing at line endings or overemphasizing rhymes.

Give your reading for the class. **[Group Activity]**

Research and Technology Wordsworth and Coleridge were collaborators and friends. Research portraits, letters, and other primary sources, and write an **evaluation** of their literary friendship. As you research, consider the kind of information each source may provide. For example, a letter might suggest the warmth of a friendship.

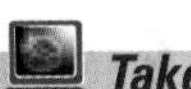
Take It to the Net www.phschool.com

Go online for an additional research activity using the Internet.

ASSESSMENT RESOURCES

The following resources can be used to assess students' knowledge and skills.

Selection Assessment

- **Formal Assessment,** pp. 155–157
- **Open Book Test,** pp. 94–96
- **Got It! Assessment Videotapes,** Tape 3
- **Test Bank Software**

Take It to the Net
Visit www.phschool.com for self-tests and additional questions on the selections.

Writing Rubric

- **Performance Assess. and Portfolio Mgmt.,** pp. 25 and 92

PRENTICE HALL ASSESSMENT SYSTEM

- **Workbook**
- **Transparencies**
- **Skill Book**
- **CD-ROM**

Lesson Support for p. 715

❸ Writing Lesson

- Explain that students will write an analysis of the poetic symbol of the Albatross in Coleridge's "The Rime of the Ancient Mariner."
- Remind students that symbols often stand for more than one thing or idea, and that it is helpful to identify as many things as possible that the Albatross might represent.
- Use the Writing Lesson to guide students in developing their analyses of a symbol.
- Suggest that in addition to or instead of the cluster diagram recommended in the Lesson, students use the Cubing organizer in **Writing Models and Graphic Organizers on Transparencies,** pp. 99–102.
- Use the Response to Literature rubric in **Performance Assessment and Portfolio Management,** p. 25, to evaluate students' essays.

❹ Listening and Speaking

- Have students work in small groups to perform a dramatic reading of a section from "The Rime of the Ancient Mariner."
- Read the Listening and Speaking Lesson with students.
- Then, encourage each group to read several times the section they will be performing and to take notes on its atmosphere.

CUSTOMIZE INSTRUCTION For Universal Access

To address different learning styles, use the activities suggested in the **Extension Activities** booklet, p. 32.

- For Visual/Spatial Learners, use Activity 5 and Activity 6.
- For Verbal/Linguistic and Intrapersonal Learners, use Activity 7.

She Walks in Beauty ✦ Apostrophe to the Ocean ✦ *from* Don Juan

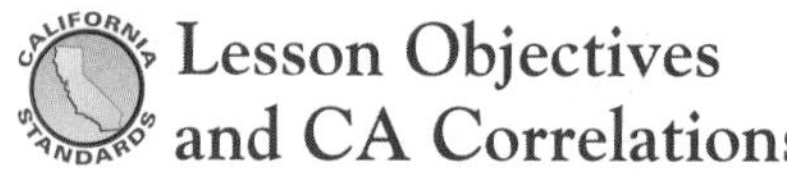

Lesson Objectives and CA Correlations

1. **To analyze and respond to literary elements**
   - Literary Analysis: Figurative Language **R 3.4**
   - Comparing Literary Works **R 3.6**
2. **To read, comprehend, analyze, and critique a poem**
   - Reading Strategy: Questioning
   - Reading Check Questions
   - Review and Assess Questions
   - Assessment Practice (ATE)
3. **To develop word analysis skills, fluency, and systematic vocabulary**
   - Vocabulary Development Lesson: Latin Suffixes: *-ous* **R 1.2**
4. **To understand and apply written and oral English language conventions**
   - Spelling Strategy **LC 1.2**
   - Grammar and Style Lesson: Subject and Verb Agreement **LC 1.1**
5. **To understand and apply appropriate writing and research strategies**
   - Writing Lesson: Monologue **W 1.3**
   - Extension Activity: Proposal for a Portrait **W 1.7**
6. **To understand and apply listening and speaking strategies**
   - Extension Activity: Eulogy **LS 1.6**

STEP-BY-STEP TEACHING GUIDE	PACING GUIDE
PRETEACH	
Motivate Students and Provide Background	
Use the Motivation activity (ATE p. 716)	5 min.
Read and discuss author and background features (SE pp. 716, 718, 724; ATE p. 716) [A]	5 min.
Introduce the Concepts	
Introduce the Literary Analysis and Reading Strategy concepts (SE/ATE p. 717) [A]	15 min.
Pronounce the vocabulary words and read their definitions (SE p. 717)	5 min.
TEACH	
Monitor Comprehension	
Informally monitor comprehension by circulating while students read independently or in groups [A]	15 min.
Monitor students' comprehension with the Reading Check notes (SE/ATE pp. 721, 725)	as students read
Develop vocabulary with Vocabulary notes (SE pp. 722, 723, 724, 725; ATE p. 725)	as students read
Develop Understanding	
Develop students' understanding of figurative language with the Literary Analysis annotations (SE/ATE pp. 719, 722, 726) [A]	5 min.
Develop students' ability to use the technique of questioning with the Reading Strategy annotations (SE/ATE pp. 720, 724)	5 min.
ASSESS	
Assess Mastery	
Assess students' mastery of the Reading Strategy and Literary Analysis concepts by having them answer the Review and Assess questions (SE/ATE p. 727)	15 min.
Use one or more of the print and media Assessment Resources (ATE p. 729) [A]	up to 45 min.
EXTEND	
Apply Understanding	
Have students complete the Vocabulary Development Lesson and the Grammar and Style Lesson (SE p. 728) [A]	20 min.
Apply students' ability to structure ideas for effect using the Writing Lesson (SE/ATE p. 729) [A]	45 min.
Apply students' understanding using one or more of the Extension Activities (SE p. 729)	20–90 min.

ACCELERATED INSTRUCTION:
Use the strategies and activities identified with an [A].

UNIVERSAL ACCESS
● = Below Level Students
▲ = On-Level Students
■ = Above Level Students

Time and Resource Manager

Reading Level: Easy, Average, Easy
Average Number of Instructional Days: 4

RESOURCES		
PRINT	**TRANSPARENCIES**	**TECHNOLOGY**
• **Beyond Literature,** Media Connection: Film Portrayal of *Don Juan,* p. 33 ▲ ■		• **Interest Grabber Videos,** Tape 4 ● ▲ ■
• **Selection Support Workbook:** ● ▲ ■ Literary Analysis, p. 154 Reading Strategy, p. 153 Build Vocabulary, p. 151	• **Literary Analysis and Reading Transparencies,** pp. 65 and 66 ● ▲ ■	
		• **Listening to Literature** ● ▲ ■ Audiocassettes, Side 17 Audio CDs, CD 10
• **Literary Analysis for Enrichment** ■	• **Fine Art Transparencies, Volume 2,** Art Transparency 11 ● ▲ ■	
• **Formal Assessment:** Selection Test, pp. 158–160 ● ▲ ■ • **Open Book Test,** pp. 97–99 ● ▲ ■ • **Performance Assessment and Portfolio Management,** pp. 15 and 37 ● ▲ ■ • PRENTICE HALL ASSESSMENT SYSTEM ● ▲ ■	• PRENTICE HALL ASSESSMENT SYSTEM ● ▲ ■ Skills Practice Answers and Explanations on Transparencies	• **Test Bank Software** ● ▲ ■ • **Got It! Assessment Videotapes,** Tape 3 ● ▲
• **Selection Support Workbook:** ● ▲ ■ Grammar and Style, p. 152 • **Writing and Grammar,** Diamond Level ● ▲ ■ • **Extension Activities,** p. 33 ● ▲ ■	• **Daily Language Practice Transparencies** ● ▲ • **Writing Models and Graphic Organizers on Transparencies,** pp. 17–24 ● ▲ ■	• **Writing and Grammar iText CD-ROM** ● ▲ ■ ***Take It to the Net*** www.phschool.com

BLOCK SCHEDULING: Use one 90-minute class period to preteach the selections and have students read them. Use a second 90-minute class period to assess students' mastery of skills and have them complete one of the Extension Activities.

PRETEACH

Step-by-Step Teaching Guide for pp. 716–717

Motivation

Call students' attention to the information on the Byronic hero on p. 716. Have students cite examples from cartoons and films of the stereotypical Romantic hero. Discuss the positive and negative aspects of this type of character—for example, he is colorful, vivacious, charismatic, moody, impatient, and melancholic. Have students look for clues to Byron's personality as they read his poems.

Interest Grabber Video

As an alternative, play "*Don Juan:* George Gordon, Lord Byron" on Tape 4 to engage student interest.

❶ Background

More About the Author

Byron's poetry was often criticized on moral grounds and frequently condemned by critics, but it remained immensely popular in England and was received even more enthusiastically abroad. In his 1822 journal, Byron noted that his sales were better in Germany, France, and America than in England. Byron was a prolific writer of letters and journals, many of which were written with an eye to publication. They offer a remarkably vivid commentary on his social milieu and his own life.

Prepare to Read

❶ She Walks in Beauty ◆ Apostrophe to the Ocean ◆ *from* Don Juan

George Gordon, Lord Byron (1788–1824)

As famous for the life he led as for the poems he wrote, George Gordon, Lord Byron, came from a long line of handsome but irresponsible aristocrats. Byron lived life in the "fast lane" and was looked on with disapproval by most of his contemporaries.

From Rags to Riches Byron was born in London to a poor but noble family. His father, a handsome ladies' man, died when Byron was just three years old. At the age of ten, while living in Aberdeen, Scotland, with his mother, Byron inherited his great-uncle's title, baron. The family moved to Nottingham, where Byron lived for a time in the ruins of the family hall. When he was seventeen, he left home to attend Trinity College at Cambridge.

A Zest for Life While at Cambridge, Byron made friends, played sports, and spent money. A dashing figure, he even kept a pet bear. He also published a volume of verse, *Hours of Idleness* (1807), that received harsh criticism in Scotland's *Edinburgh Review*. In response, he wrote his first major work, the satirical poem *English Bards and Scotch Reviewers* (1809), in which he pokes fun at the prestigious magazine that gave him a terrible review.

After graduating, Byron traveled to out-of-the-way corners of Europe and the Middle East. He returned home bearing two sections of a book-length poem entitled *Childe Harold's Pilgrimage*, which depicted a young hero not unlike himself—moody, sensitive, and reckless. The work was well received, and Byron became an overnight sensation. "I awoke one morning and found myself famous," he observed.

For a time, Byron was the darling of London society. Hostesses vied to invite him to parties, and women flocked to his side. Byron became a true celebrity, a public figure of literary genius who in turn thrilled and scandalized his contemporaries. "Mad, bad, and dangerous to know" was Lady Caroline Lamb's famous description of Lord Byron.

The Byronic Hero Although Byron could be quite charming and friendly, his admirers insisted on associating him with the dark, brooding hero, impassioned by a cause, whom he so often described. Because of this persona, or adopted personality, readers throughout the nineteenth century saw Byron as the quintessential Romantic poet.

Italy and Tragedy Byron's fame and infamy grew in equal bounds. When his marriage to Annabella Milbanke broke up, the resulting scandal drove Byron from England in 1816. He would never return to the country of his birth.

Byron continued his travels through Europe, often accompanied by the poet Percy Bysshe Shelley. The two were great friends, and their poems reveal the strong influence of their mutual devotion. Eventually, Byron settled in Italy and worked on his masterful mock epic *Don Juan* (pronounced here as jo͞o′ ən). While he was there, however, tragedy struck: One of his daughters died, and Shelley drowned in a sailing accident.

A Budding Revolutionary In 1823, Byron, a champion of liberty, joined a group of revolutionaries seeking to free Greece from Turkish rule. Soon after, while training Greek rebel troops, Byron died of a rheumatic fever. Reports at the time tell of a late, poignant gesture: Dazed with fever, Byron called out in broken English and Italian, "Forward—forward—courage! Follow my example—don't be afraid!" To this day he is revered in Greece as a national hero.

TEACHING RESOURCES

The following resources can be used to enrich or extend the instruction for pp. 716–717.

Motivation

Interest Grabber Video, Tape 4

Background

Beyond Literature, p. 33 ■

Take It to the Net

Visit www.phschool.com for Background and hotlinks for the selections.

Literary Analysis

Literary Analysis and Reading Transparencies, Figurative Language, p. 66 ■

Reading

Selection Support: Reading Strategy, p. 153; Build Vocabulary, p. 151

Literary Analysis and Reading Transparencies, Questioning, p. 65

■ **BLOCK SCHEDULING:** Resources marked with this symbol provide varied instruction during 90-minute blocks.

Preview

Connecting to the Literature

In the popular imagination, writers and other creative people are often pictured as moody and unconventional. Two centuries ago, Lord Byron set the standard for the restless, rebellious "artistic temperament."

❷ Literary Analysis

Figurative Language

Poetry usually contains **figurative language,** or language not meant to be taken literally. Figurative language includes these devices:

- **Similes**—direct comparisons of dissimilar things using *like* or *as*
- **Metaphors**—implied comparisons of dissimilar things, in which one thing is spoken of as if it were another kind of thing
- **Personifications**—attributions of human qualities to nonhuman subjects

These lines, addressed to the ocean, contain examples of each:

> These are thy toys, and, as the snowy flake,
> They melt into thy yeast of waves, . . .

Comparing Literary Works

In these poems, Byron uses figurative language to express the *sublime*—a sense of power in nature that escapes human understanding. To achieve the effect, poets express the infinite in sensory terms. For instance, Byron's sensory descriptions of the ocean convey the ocean's awesome, endless power—a power both divine and destructive. Compare the impressions that Byron creates of the infinite power of nature and human beauty.

❸ Reading Strategy

Questioning

If you **question** as you read, you can focus your understanding of poetry. Begin with *who, what, where, when,* and *why* questions. Use a chart like the one shown to note and answer your questions as you read.

Passage
She walks in beauty, like the night Of cloudless climes and starry skies; . . .
Questions
1. *Who* is she? 2. *What* is her relationship with the speaker? 3. To *what* does the speaker compare her?

Vocabulary Development

arbiter (är′ bət ər) *n.* judge; umpire (p. 722)

tempests (tem′ pists) *n.* storms (p. 723)

torrid (tôr′ id) *adj.* very hot; scorching (p. 723)

fathomless (fath′ əm lis) *adj.* too deep to be measured or understood (p. 723)

retort (ri tôrt′) *v.* respond with a clever answer or wisecrack (p. 724)

insensible (in sen′ sə bəl) *adj.* unable to feel or sense anything; numb (p. 725)

credulous (krej′ oo ləs) *adj.* willing to believe; naive (p. 725)

copious (kō′ pē əs) *adj.* abundant; plentiful (p. 725)

avarice (av′ ə ris) *n.* greed (p. 725)

❷ Literary Analysis

Figurative Language

- Tell students that in this lesson they should concentrate on figurative language, language not meant to be interpreted literally. Explain that figurative language may include similes, metaphors, and personifications.
- Read the note about figurative language together as a class. Call students' attention to the way Byron uses figurative language.
- Use the instruction for Comparing Literary Works to review with students how figurative language can also express the sublime, a sense of power in nature that surpasses understanding.
- Use the Figurative Language transparency in **Literary Analysis and Reading Transparencies,** p. 66, to show students how to identify figurative language.

❸ Reading Strategy

Questioning

- Explain to students that by questioning a text, they can better understand the work.
- Have students list the interrogatives *who, what, why, where,* and *when* on a piece of paper.
- Use the graphic organizer on p. 717 to model the skill of questioning.
- Have students practice the skill using the Questioning transparency in **Literary Analysis and Reading Transparencies,** p. 65.

Vocabulary Development

- Pronounce each vocabulary word for students, and read the definitions as a class. Have students identify any words with which they are already familiar.

CUSTOMIZE INSTRUCTION FOR UNIVERSAL ACCESS

For Less Proficient Readers	For English Learners	For Advanced Readers
To help students understand Byron's use of figurative language, review the Literary Analysis definition on p. 717 and model how to interpret similes, metaphors, and personification.	Poetic diction and syntax often create difficulties. To help students navigate Byron's poems, suggest they pay close attention to structure. By noting where lines and stanzas begin and end, and how they are punctuated, students may gain understanding of the meaning of the poem.	Paraphrasing can enable students to fully appreciate Byron's range and skill with figurative language. Urge students to compare their paraphrases with Byron's original wording.

 **E-Teach**

Visit E-Teach at www.phschool.com for teachers' essays on how to teach, with questions and answers.

TEACH

Step-by-Step Teaching Guide for pp. 718–726

CUSTOMIZE INSTRUCTION
For Visual/Spatial Learners

Urge students to access the poem's meaning through its visual imagery. As you read the poem aloud, have students mentally picture the images described. How does the exercise enhance students' comprehension and enjoyment of the poem?

❶ About the Selection

This sonnet vividly describes a woman's beauty, capturing its essential power and linking it to universal images. The poem reflects the speaker's wonder at such beauty. Byron catalogs the woman's physical charms and spiritual depths, reading her beautiful within and without.

❷ Background

Art

In the Garden, Thomas Wilmer Dewing

This painting (also known as *Spring Moonlight*) illustrates a beautiful young woman—one of three in the full painting—like the one described in Byron's sonnet.

Thomas Wilmer Dewing was born in New England, where he showed an early interest in art. He studied at the Boston Art Club and later at the Académie Julian in Paris, developing a particular knowledge of anatomical drawing. On his return to America, Dewing also taught young artists at the Art Students League in New York City. Use this question for discussion:

In what way does the painter, like Byron in his poem, mingle the qualities of the night with the qualities of his subject?
Answer: The greenish black background blends with the woman's dress and is even picked up in the tones of her skin.

❸ ▶Critical Viewing

Answer: Like Byron's cousin in the poem, the woman is beautifully dressed and has a graceful appearance; she is walking at night and seems calm.

❶ She Walks in Beauty

George Gordon, Lord Byron

❷ 

In The Garden, (detail) Thomas Wilmer Dewing, National Museum of American Art, Washington, D.C.

Background

Lord Byron became so identified with the rebellious heroes he created—brooding figures whose ironic attitude and hidden sorrow only added to their charm—that this kind of figure became known as a Byronic hero. Such heroes are a staple of Romantic literature. They survive in modern times as a Hollywood or rock-and-roll type.

The Byronic attitude may be ironic, but Byron the poet was certainly capable of direct, sincere appreciation of beauty, as this poem demonstrates. Written to be set to music, the poem was inspired by Byron's first meeting with Lady Wilmot Horton, his cousin by marriage, who was wearing a black mourning gown with spangles.

❸ **▲ Critical Viewing** How does the rendering of this woman suggest some of the qualities that Byron attributes to his cousin in the poem? **[Analyze]**

TEACHING RESOURCES

The following resources can be used to enrich or extend the instruction for pp. 718–726.

Literary Analysis

Selection Support: Literary Analysis, p. 154

Reading

Listening to Literature Audiocassettes, Side 17 ▪

Listening to Literature Audio CDs, CD 10 ▪

Extension

Fine Art Transparencies, Volume 2, Art Transparency 11 (Have students compare Byron's vision of the sublime power of the ocean in "Apostrophe to the Ocean" with that in J.M.W. Turner's *Wreck of a Transport Ship.*)

▪ **BLOCK SCHEDULING:** Resources marked with this symbol provide varied instruction during 90-minute blocks.

She walks in beauty, like the night
Of cloudless climes and starry skies;
And all that's best of dark and bright
Meet in her aspect and her eyes:
Thus mellowed to that tender light
Which heaven to gaudy day denies.

One shade the more, one ray the less,
Had half impaired the nameless grace
Which waves in every raven tress,
Or softly lightens o'er her face;
Where thoughts serenely sweet express
How pure, how dear their dwelling place.

And on that cheek, and o'er that brow,
So soft, so calm, yet eloquent,
The smiles that win, the tints that glow,
But tell of days in goodness spent,
A mind at peace with all below,
A heart whose love is innocent!

Literary Analysis
Figurative Language With what kind of poetic comparison does Byron capture the reader's imagination in the opening lines?

Review and Assess

Thinking About the Selection

1. **Respond:** Do you think the speaker idealizes the subject of "She Walks in Beauty"? Explain.
2. (a) **Recall:** To what does the speaker compare the lady's beauty? (b) **Interpret:** What might "that tender light" in line 5 be?
3. (a) **Recall:** What would have "half impaired" the lady's grace? (b) **Interpret:** What does this claim suggest about the lady's beauty?
4. (a) **Connect:** In lines 11–18, what is the woman's appearance said to reveal about her character? (b) **Compare and Contrast:** How is the focus of the last six lines different from the focus of the opening lines? (c) **Draw Conclusions:** Does Byron's portrayal emphasize the spiritual or the physical aspect of the lady? Explain.
5. (a) **Evaluate:** Do you agree that goodness is an inherent part of beauty? Explain. (b) **Relate:** Do you think people today put too much emphasis on physical beauty? Explain.

CUSTOMIZE INSTRUCTION FOR UNIVERSAL ACCESS

For Special Needs Students	For Less Proficient Readers	For Gifted/Talented Students
Have students read a section from "She Walks in Beauty" with teacher guidance. Then, ask students to visualize each line as they read the poem to themselves. Have them compare results in group discussion.	The figurative language of "She Walks in Beauty" may be an obstacle to comprehension. Have students read from the poem silently as they listen to **Listening to Literature Audio CDs,** CD 10. Then guide students in a close reading of the poem in which they paraphrase figurative language that causes them difficulty, line by line.	Invite artistically gifted students to portray Lady Horton. Have them first identify the specific physical details of her appearance in the poem and analyze each effect or meaning Byron attributes to her beauty. Then, have them draw on their analyses to create their portraits.

❹ Literary Analysis

Figurative Language

- Have students read the bracketed passage to themselves.
- Remind students that figurative language includes similes, metaphors, and personification.
- Ask the Literary Analysis question on p. 719: With what kind of poetic comparison does Byron capture the reader's imagination in the opening lines?
  Answer: Byron uses a simile that compares the woman to a cloudless, starry night sky.

Answers for p. 719

Review and Assess

1. Possible response: Some students will say that the last three lines in particular exaggerate the purity of the woman.
2. **(a)** The speaker compares her beauty to a cloudless, starry night. **(b)** The "tender light" is that of the moon or of the stars, which cannot be seen during the day.
3. **(a)** Any addition of brightness or darkness to her coloring would have "half impaired" her beauty. **(b)** This suggests that her beauty is perfect as it is and that it depends on an indefinable balance of contraries.
4. **(a)** The woman's appearance suggests sweet thoughts, virtuous activity, a peaceful mind, and innocent love. **(b)** The focus of the last six lines is on the woman's character, and the focus of the opening lines is on her physical beauty. **(c)** Byron first emphasizes the physical and then the spiritual; they receive equal space and are presented as if one blends into the other.
5. **(a)** Possible responses: Yes, a person who is evil or immoral will be unattractive, whatever his or her physical appearance; no, many vain people are handsome or beautiful. **(b)** Possible responses: Yes, the media overemphasize the importance of physical beauty; no, brains and personality get one further than physical beauty.

5 About the Selection

This poem expresses Byron's admiration and awe for the ocean. He describes its effects on him: the comfort it offers, the excitement it inspires, the humility its power elicits. Using historical references to great empires and battles, Byron celebrates the ocean's awesome power and its indifference to human political concerns. He discovers in the immeasurable depths, power, and endurance of the ocean an inspiring and reassuring revelation of something larger than humanity.

6 Reading Strategy

Questioning

- Read the bracketed passage aloud to students.
- Remind them to question aspects of the poem, using *who, what, when, where, how,* and *why* in their interrogatives.
- Then, ask the Reading Strategy question on p. 720: List three questions you might ask yourself after reading the first stanza.
  Possible responses: "What society does the speaker find when he is alone by the ocean?" "Why might someone want to 'steal/From all I may be, . . .'?" "What specific experiences drive the speaker to walk alone by the shore?"

7 ▶Critical Viewing

Possible response: Yes, the crashing waves in the painting, as well as the figure's attentive pose and the grand atmosphere created by the vivid sky help suggest the ocean's roar.

8

7 **▶Critical Viewing** Byron speaks of the sea with "music in its roar." Does this artist succeed in visually communicating the sound of the ocean? **[Assess]**

5 *from* Childe Harold's Pilgrimage Apostrophe to the Ocean

George Gordon, Lord Byron

There is a pleasure in the pathless woods,
There is a rapture on the lonely shore,
There is society, where none intrudes,
By the deep sea, and music in its roar;
6 I love not man the less, but nature more,
From these our interviews, in which I steal
From all I may be, or have been before,
To mingle with the universe, and feel
What I can ne'er express, yet cannot all conceal.

Reading Strategy
Questioning List three questions you might ask after reading the first stanza.

ENRICHMENT: Cultural Connection

The Ocean

Before space exploration was possible, the sea most clearly represented the vastness and mystery of the universe. Sea gods, sea myths, and sea sagas in various cultures date back as far as recorded history. For example, the Roman god Neptune (Poseidon to the Greeks) was believed responsible for ocean weather. Centuries later, seventeenth-century maps showed a magical and bountiful island, Atlantis, which was said to have mysteriously disappeared. Other sea sagas describe enormous fire-breathing monsters. The human relation to the sea gives it peculiar resonance. On the one hand, it is a source of life—of food or trade. On the other, it is uninhabitable—it cannot be physically claimed and cultivated as the land can be. For these reasons, the sea has often been used to symbolize the untamable power of nature and life.

Shipwreck, J.C.C. Dahl, Munich Neue Pinakothek/Kavaler

Roll on, thou deep and dark blue ocean—roll!
Ten thousand fleets sweep over thee in vain;
Man marks the earth with ruin—his control
Stops with the shore; upon the watery plain
The wrecks are all thy deed, nor doth remain
A shadow of man's ravage, save[1] his own,
When, for a moment, like a drop of rain,
He sinks into thy depths with bubbling groan,
Without a grave, unknelled, uncoffined, and unknown.

9 ✓Reading Check

According to the speaker, what impact does humanity's power have on the ocean?

1. **save** except.

8 Background

Art

Shipwreck, J.C.C. Dahl

This painting, like lines 13–18 in Byron's poem, depicts a sinking ship.

J.C.C. Dahl, a Norwegian, was interested in the naturalist approach to art—not merely mimicking nature but conveying a deeper meaning. Dahl studied and pursued his art as he traveled throughout Europe, carefully observing nature and capturing its fierce elemental forces. In *Shipwreck*, Dahl imbues the scene with a sense of immediacy and drama. Use these questions for discussion:

1. How might the artist's feelings about the ocean compare with those expressed by Byron in his poem?
   Answer: Both recognize the ocean's power and grandeur.
2. What effect might the scene depicted have had on Byron?
   Answer: He might have viewed it as confirmation of the ocean's obvious power to subdue people. He might even have reveled in that power.

9 ✓Reading Check

Answer: Humanity's power has no impact at all on the ocean.

CUSTOMIZE INSTRUCTION FOR UNIVERSAL ACCESS

For Special Needs Students	For English Learners	For Gifted/Talented Students
Some students may have difficulty with the metaphors and similes in "Apostrophe to the Ocean." Have students read the poem with teacher guidance. Model how to understand figurative language using the Figurative Language transparency on p. 66 of **Literary Analysis and Reading Transparencies.**	As students read "Apostrophe to the Ocean," have them say aloud any portions of the text containing unfamiliar words. Have them use context, footnotes, or a dictionary to define these words.	Have students design a collage to illustrate scenes from the poem. Students should organize their illustrations and collected objects into a two- or three-dimensional collage. Encourage them to provide sound effects or a spoken accompaniment to their collages.

⓾ Literary Analysis

Figurative Language

- Have student volunteers read aloud the bracketed passage.
- Remind them to interpret the language figuratively, not literally.
- Then, ask the Literary Analysis question on p. 722: Explain how the images of destructive power in lines 20–36 create a sense of forces of nature beyond human comprehension.
  Answer: The images suggest that, no matter how strong humanity may become, the ocean can still overwhelm it. This idea suggests that the ocean's power is bottomless, and so cannot be measured or comprehended.

Monitor Progress Ask students to analyze the figurative language in lines 19–21. Ask them what figure of speech is being used.
Answer: The ocean's surface is compared to the land through the metaphors "thy paths" and "thy fields" and to a person or animal in the personification or metaphor "thou dost arise / And shake him off from thee; . . .".

- Ask students in what way contradictions in these figures of speech emphasize the ungraspable power of the ocean even as they present graspable images.
  Answer: Because it is constantly shifting, the ocean has no paths, nor can it be divided into fields. If the ocean shook a person "off," the person might very well end up under the ocean. In these ways, Byron's figurative language shows by its own limitations that the ocean exceeds our ability to picture its power.

His steps are not upon thy paths—thy fields
Are not a spoil for him—thou dost arise
And shake him from thee; the vile strength he wields
For earth's destruction thou dost all despise,
Spurning him from thy bosom to the skies,
And send'st him, shivering in thy playful spray
And howling, to his gods, where haply[2] lies
His petty hope in some near port or bay,
And dashest him again to earth—there let him lay.[3]

⓾

The armaments which thunderstrike the walls
Of rock-built cities, bidding nations quake,
And monarchs tremble in their capitals,
The oak leviathans,[4] whose huge ribs make
Their clay creator[5] the vain title take
Of lord of thee, and arbiter of war—
These are thy toys, and, as the snowy flake,
They melt into thy yeast of waves, which mar
Alike the Armada's[6] pride or spoils of Trafalgar.[7]

Thy shores are empires, changed in all save thee—
Assyria, Greece, Rome, Carthage, what are they?
Thy waters washed them power while they were free,
And many a tyrant since; their shores obey
The stranger, slave, or savage: their decay
Has dried up realms to deserts—not so thou,
Unchangeable, save to thy wild waves' play.
Time writes no wrinkle on thine azure brow;
Such as creation's dawn beheld, thou rollest now.

Literary Analysis
Figurative Language Explain how the images of destructive power in lines 20–36 create a sense of forces of nature beyond human comprehension.

arbiter (är′ bət ər) *n.* judge; umpire

2. **haply** perhaps.
3. **lay** A note on Byron's proof suggests that he intentionally made this grammatical error for the sake of the rhyme.
4. **leviathans** (lə vī′ ə thənz) monstrous sea creatures, described in the Old Testament. Here the word means giant ships.
5. **clay creator** human beings.
6. **Armada's** refers to the Spanish Armada, defeated by the English in 1588.
7. **Trafalgar** battle in 1805 during which the French and Spanish fleets were defeated by the British fleet led by Lord Nelson.

Thou glorious mirror, where the Almighty's form
Glasses[8] itself in tempests: in all time,
Calm or convulsed—in breeze, or gale, or storm,
Icing the pole, or in the torrid clime
Dark-heaving—boundless, endless, and sublime;
The image of eternity, the throne
Of the Invisible; even from out thy slime
The monsters of the deep are made: each zone
Obeys thee; thou goest forth, dread, fathomless, alone.

And I have loved thee, ocean! and my joy
Of youthful sports was on thy breast to be
Borne, like thy bubbles, onward; from a boy
I wantoned with thy breakers—they to me
Were a delight: and if the freshening sea
Made them a terror—'twas a pleasing fear,
For I was as it were a child of thee,
And trusted to thy billows far and near,
And laid my hand upon thy mane—as I do here.

tempests (tem′ pists) *n.* storms

torrid (tôr′ id) *adj.* very hot; scorching

fathomless (fa*th*′ əm lis) *adj.* too deep to be measured or understood

8. **Glasses** mirrors.

Review and Assess

Thinking About the Selection

1. **Respond:** Which images from "Childe Harold's Pilgrimage" linger in your mind?
2. **(a) Recall:** What natural settings does the speaker describe in the first lines? **(b) Interpret:** What attitude toward nature do his descriptions reveal?
3. **(a) Recall:** In an apostrophe, a speaker addresses an absent person or personified quality or idea. Whom or what is the speaker addressing from line 10 on? **(b) Infer:** What is the speaker's attitude toward the subject he is addressing?
4. **(a) Recall:** How does the ocean treat such human things as cities and warships? **(b) Compare and Contrast:** What contrast between the ocean and human governments does the speaker make in lines 37–45? **(c) Draw Conclusions:** In what sense is the ocean a power that dwarfs all human endeavors?
5. **(a) Interpret:** In lines 46–54, what qualities make the ocean a reflection of "the Almighty's form"? **(b) Generalize:** What attitude toward nature do the lines encourage?
6. **Evaluate:** Is the sea still as mysterious and powerful today as it was in Byron's day? Explain.

Answers for p. 723

Review and Assess

1. Possible response: Students may cite images such as that of Byron as a boy, floating like a bubble on an ocean wave.
2. **(a)** The speaker describes the woods, the shore, and the deep sea. **(b)** He loves nature more than man.
3. **(a)** The speaker is addressing the ocean. **(b)** The speaker admires the ocean's power.
4. **(a)** The ocean sinks warships and dashes cities to the ground. **(b)** Those past empires are subject to the ravages of time, but the ocean is unchangeable. **(c)** The ocean can destroy everything in its path, including human endeavors.
5. **(a)** The ocean represents infinite extent, endurance, and power, and as such is a mirror for "the Almighty's form, since God is also infinite." **(b)** These lines encourage an attitude toward nature that is full of wonder, awe, and supreme admiration.
6. Possible response: Despite scientific advances, the ocean remains as wild and powerful as ever.

CUSTOMIZE INSTRUCTION FOR UNIVERSAL ACCESS

For Less Proficient Readers	For Advanced Readers
Display Art Transparency 11, J.W.M. Turner's *Wreck of a Transport Ship,* in **Art Transparencies, Volume 2.** Have students identify lines in the poem that the painting might illustrate. Then, have students discuss the vision of nature that both works express.	Display Art Transparency 11 in **Art Transparencies, Volume 2.** Have students discuss the representation of nature in poem and painting. Encourage them to consider why the idea of untamable nature might have been attractive at the dawn of the scientific and industrial age.

⓫ About the Selection

This excerpt from the comic epic poem recounts the speaker's thoughts on ambition, aging, and death. The narrator, or speaker, at 30 years of age, finds himself exhausted, rather disappointed in himself, and somewhat disillusioned by the world around him. He feels that since his chance for romantic passion is past and ambition is a vain idea, he will dispense advice based on his experience: Be grateful that things didn't turn out worse, read your Bible, and watch out for pickpockets! In expressing his poetic philosophy, the speaker takes humorous jabs at contemporary poets Southey and Wordsworth, the first of whom he considers not worth reading and the latter incomprehensible.

⓬ Reading Strategy

Questioning

- Have students read the bracketed passage to themselves.
- Remind them that by asking questions of the text, they may gain greater understanding.
- Then, ask the Reading Strategy question on p. 724: Ask yourself two questions about the speaker of *Don Juan*. Read on to find answers to your unanswered questions.
  Possible responses: Students may ask, "What specific experience has led to the speaker's disillusionment?" or "What will he decide to do with the rest of his life?"

from

⓫ Don Juan

George Gordon, Lord Byron

Background

Though it is unfinished, *Don Juan* (jo͞o′ ən) is regarded as Byron's finest work. A mock epic described by Shelley as "something wholly new and relative to the age," it satirizes the political and social problems of Byron's time.

Traditionally Don Juan, the poem's hero, is a wicked character driven by his obsession with beautiful women. In Byron's work, Don Juan is an innocent young man whose physical beauty, charm, and spirit prove to be alluring to ladies. As a result, he finds himself in many difficult situations.

During periodic pauses in the story, the narrator drifts away from the subject. In these digressions the narrator comments on the issues of the time and on life in general. In this excerpt the narrator sets aside the adventures of his hero to reflect on old age and death.

But now at thirty years my hair is gray
(I wonder what it will be like at forty?
I thought of a peruke[1] the other day)—
My heart is not much greener; and in short, I
Have squandered my whole summer while 'twas May,
⓬ And feel no more the spirit to retort; I
Have spent my life, both interest and principal,
And deem not, what I deemed, my soul invincible.

No more—no more—Oh! never more on me
The freshness of the heart can fall like dew,
Which out of all the lovely things we see
Extracts emotions beautiful and new,
Hived in our bosoms like the bag o' the bee:
Think'st thou the honey with those objects grew?
Alas! 'twas not in them, but in thy power
To double even the sweetness of a flower.

No more—no more—Oh! never more, my heart,
Canst thou be my sole world, my universe!

retort (ri tôrt′) *v.* respond with a clever answer or wisecrack

Reading Strategy
Questioning Ask yourself two questions about the speaker of *Don Juan*. Read on to find answers to your unanswered questions.

1. **peruke** (pə ro͞ok′) wig.

ENRICHMENT: Cultural Connection

Don Juan

The character of Don Juan is legendary and has appeared in written and musical works from several cultures over many centuries. One early version, the play *The Deceiver of Seville,* was written by Spanish author Tirso de Molina in 1634. French playwright Molière dramatized Don Juan's life in his 1665 *Don Juan.* The great eighteenth-century Austrian composer Wolfgang Amadeus Mozart wrote an opera called *Don Giovanni* about the legendary rake. Long after Byron wrote his poem, fellow Englishman George Bernard Shaw featured Don Juan in his play *Man and Superman* (1903).

Once all in all, but now a thing apart,
Thou canst not be my blessing or my curse:
The illusion's gone forever, and thou art
Insensible, I trust, but none the worse,
And in thy stead I've got a deal of judgment,
Though heaven knows how it ever found a lodgment.

My days of love are over; me no more
The charms of maid, wife, and still less of widow
Can make the fool of which they made before—
In short, I must not lead the life I did do;
13 The credulous hope of mutual minds is o'er,
The copious use of claret is forbid too,
So for a good old-gentlemanly vice,
I think I must take up with avarice.

Ambition was my idol, which was broken
Before the shrines of Sorrow and of Pleasure;
And the two last have left me many a token
O'er which reflection may be made at leisure:
Now, like Friar Bacon's brazen head, I've spoken,
"Time is, Time was, Time's past,"[2] a chymic[3] treasure
Is glittering youth, which I have spent betimes—
My heart in passion, and my head on rhymes.

What is the end of fame? 'tis but to fill
A certain portion of uncertain paper:
Some liken it to climbing up a hill,
Whose summit, like all hills, is lost in vapor;
For this men write, speak, preach, and heroes kill,
And bards burn what they call their "midnight taper,"
To have, when the original is dust,
A name, a wretched picture, and worse bust.

What are the hopes of man? Old Egypt's King
Cheops erected the first pyramid
And largest, thinking it was just the thing
To keep his memory whole, and mummy hid:
But somebody or other rummaging
Burglariously broke his coffin's lid:
Let not a monument give you or me hopes,
Since not a pinch of dust remains of Cheops.

But I, being fond of true philosophy,
Say very often to myself, "Alas!

2. **Friar Bacon . . . Time's past** In Robert Greene's comedy *Friar Bacon and Friar Burgandy* (1594), these words are spoken by a bronze bust, made by Friar Bacon.
3. **chymic** (kim′ ik) alchemic: counterfeit.

insensible (in sen′ sə bəl) *adj.* unable to feel or sense anything; numb

credulous (krej′ ōō ləs) *adj.* willing to believe; naive

copious (kō′ pē əs) *adj.* abundant; plentiful

avarice (av′ ə ris) *n.* greed

14 ▼**Critical Viewing** What traits of the poem's narrator does this famous caricature of Byron share? **[Interpret]**

Lord Byron, Shaking the Dust of England off His Shoes, from "The Poet's Corner" pub. William Heinemann, 1904 (engraving by Max Beerbohm) Central Saint Martin's College of Art and Design

15 ✔**Reading Check**
What type of experience will the speaker no longer undergo?

13 Vocabulary Development

Latin Suffix *-ous*

- Call students' attention to *credulous*, a word that means "willing to believe" or "naive." Explain that the suffix *-ous* is derived from the Latin and means "full of," and the root *-cred-* means "belief."
- Have students suggest other words and phrases that contain this suffix and list them on the chalkboard.
  Possible responses: *glamorous, porous, luscious, delicious*

14 ▶Critical Viewing

Possible response: Like the speaker of the poem, Byron as depicted in the drawing has an air of resigned boredom or world-weariness, suggested by his expression and the way he holds his head.

15 ✔Reading Check

Answer: The speaker will no longer undergo romantic experiences.

CUSTOMIZE INSTRUCTION FOR UNIVERSAL ACCESS

For Less Proficient Readers	For Gifted/Talented Students	For Advanced Readers
Remind students that they already know a bit about Byron's life from his biography on p. 716. Have them do further research on Byron's life and then write essays comparing him to the speaker of *Don Juan*. Students should address how the speaker is similar to Byron and how he is different.	Ask students to imagine that the narrator of *Don Juan* had reflected on his life when he was much younger. What might he have said? Have them write a monologue that the speaker might have delivered if he had reflected on life and death at age 20.	Byron's *Don Juan* is a satire—it makes fun of Don Juan. "She Walks in Beauty" is just the opposite—it idealizes Byron's cousin, Lady Wilmot Horton. Have students write a satirical version of "She Walks in Beauty" that pokes fun at the lady. Direct students to **Extension Activities,** p. 33, Activity 4 for more guidance.

ASSESS

16 Literary Analysis

Figurative Language

- Have students read the bracketed passage.
- Remind them that personification is one form of figurative language.
- Ask the Literary Analysis question on p. 726: How does Byron's personification of death make this abstract concept vivid?
  Answer: By personifying death, Byron makes the image of the end of life more vivid.

Answers for p. 726

Review and Assess

1. Possible responses: The narrator is amusing in his attitude and honesty; the narrator is not amusing because he should take himself more seriously.
2. **(a)** The speaker considers his age and how much of his life has passed by. **(b)** The speaker's mood seems to be wry and somewhat rueful.
3. **(a)** The speaker says his passion was the focus of his youth. **(b)** Youth is "false treasure" because it soon tarnishes and cracks as age sets in.
4. The story of Cheops suggests that no monument can truly preserve the memory of a person.
5. **(a)** The speaker's attitude toward his own epic poem is one of mocking self-deprecation. He refers to the reader as a "purchaser," as if grateful for the money, invites the reader to leave off reading if he or she is not satisfied with this sample, and notes that he deserves praise, if only because poets he does not esteem, Southey and Wordsworth, are well regarded. **(b)** This attitude is consistent with his "true philosophy," which suggests that everything born or created must die—he does not look forward to immortal fame.
6. Possible responses: Students may mention characters in advertising campaigns who are presented as having experienced everything the world has to offer (except the advertised product) or sitcom characters who remain unflappable because they have seen it all before.

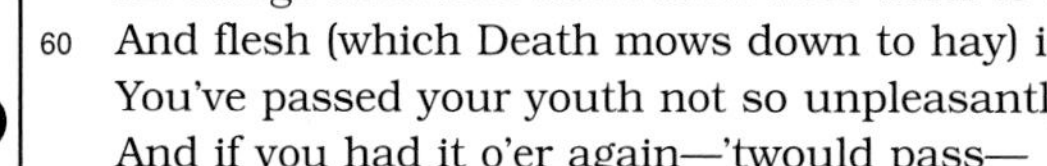

All things that have been born were born to die,
And flesh (which Death mows down to hay) is grass;
You've passed your youth not so unpleasantly,
And if you had it o'er again—'twould pass—
So thank your stars that matters are no worse,
And read your Bible, sir, and mind your purse."

But for the present, gentle reader! and
Still gentler purchaser! the bard—that's I—
Must, with permission, shake you by the hand,
And so your humble servant, and good-bye!
We meet again, if we should understand
Each other; and if not, I shall not try
Your patience further than by this short sample—
'Twere well if others followed my example.

"Go, little book, from this my solitude!
I cast thee on the waters—go thy ways!
And if, as I believe, thy vein be good,
The world will find thee after many days."[4]
When Southey's read, and Wordsworth understood,
I can't help putting in my claim to praise—
The four first rhymes are Southey's, every line:
For God's sake, reader! take them not for mine!

Literary Analysis
Figurative Language How does Byron's personification of death make this abstract concept vivid?

4. **Go . . . days** lines from the last stanza of Robert Southey's (1774–1843) Epilogue to *The Lay of the Laureate.*

Review and Assess

Thinking About the Selection

1. **Respond:** Did you find the speaker of *Don Juan* amusing? Why?
2. **(a) Recall:** What subject does the speaker consider in the opening lines? **(b) Analyze:** How would you describe the mood of the speaker's reflections?
3. **(a) Recall:** What does the speaker say was the focus of his youth? **(b) Interpret:** In lines 33–40, why does the speaker call "glittering youth" "chymic," or counterfeit, treasure?
4. **Interpret:** What point about fame does the story of King Cheops make?
5. **(a) Draw Conclusions:** What do lines 65–80 suggest about Byron's attitude toward his own epic poem? **(b) Connect:** Is this attitude consistent with his "true philosophy"? Explain.
6. **Apply:** Identify a modern character who shares the disillusioned attitude of Byron's speaker.

ASSESSMENT PRACTICE: Critical Reading

Critical Reasoning (For more practice, see Test Preparation Workbook, p. 33.)

Many tests require students to evaluate a writer's implied assumptions. Use this sample test item.

But now at thirty years my hair is gray . . .
My heart is not much greener; and in short, I
Have squandered my whole summer while
`twas May,
And feel no more the spirit to retort; I
Have spent my life . . .

Which potentially invalid assumption does the narrator make in these lines?

A He is on the brink of death.
B He has already experienced the full range of human emotions.
C Absolute power corrupts absolutely.
D He loves the summertime.

The narrator is 30; his assumption that his life is spent is probably invalid. The best choice is *B*.

Review and Assess

Literary Analysis

Figurative Language

1. Use a chart to list examples from the poems of **figurative language,** finding at least one example each of **simile, metaphor,** and **personification.** Show how each example suggests a number of different associations for what is being described.

Figurative Language	What Is Being Described	Associations Suggested

2. (a) Identify the simile in lines 10–18 of "Apostrophe to the Ocean." (b) What does the comparison suggest about the drowning man?
3. Identify and interpret the types of figurative language in the following lines: (a) "Thou glorious mirror, where the Almighty's form / Glasses itself. . . ." (b) "The freshness of the heart can fall like dew, . . ."
4. In "Apostrophe to the Ocean," what effect does the personification of the ocean have on the poem as a whole?

Comparing Literary Works

5. (a) In "She Walks in Beauty," how does Byron use imagery of the night to convey the mysterious, endless power of Lady Horton's beauty? (b) Identify three images suggesting the awesome, infinite power of nature in the "Apostrophe."
6. Compare the feelings associated with infinite power or mystery in these two poems.
7. Explain how Byron's use of such imagery expresses the Romantic faith in powers of nature that transcend reason and order.

Reading Strategy

Questioning

8. (a) List the questions you asked as you read Byron's poems and the answers you found. (b) Did **questioning** make your reading more active or focused? Explain.

Extend Understanding

9. **World Events Connection:** Describe a specific action that citizens who, like Byron, view nature with awe might advocate.

Quick Review

Figurative language is language that is not meant to be taken literally. It is used to enrich meaning by suggesting associations to the imagination.

A **simile** is a direct comparison using the word *like* or *as.*

A **metaphor** implies a comparison by speaking of one thing as if it were another kind of thing.

Personification attributes human qualities to nonhuman subjects.

To **question** a text, ask questions about *who, what, where, when,* and *why,* and answer these as you read.

 ***Take It to the Net***

www.phschool.com

Take the interactive self-test online to check your understanding of these selections.

ENRICHMENT: Further Reading

Other Works by George Gordon, Lord Byron

Hours of Idleness

The Corsair

English Bards and Scotch Reviewers

Works About the Passage of Time

"Sonnet 130," William Shakespeare

"The Last Chantey," Rudyard Kipling

"How Soon Hath Time," John Milton

 ***Take It to the Net***

Visit www.phschool.com for more information on the authors.

Answers for p. 727

Review and Assess

1. Possible response: Figurative Language: "She walks in beauty, like the night"; Associations: darkness, mystery; What Is Being Described?: a beautiful woman in mourning
2. **(a)** The speaker uses a simile to compare a man in the ocean to "a drop of rain." **(b)** The comparison suggests that the drowning man is insignificant in the larger scheme of life.
3. The figures of speech are as follows: **(a)** metaphor **(b)** simile.
4. Possible response: The personification helps to unify the poem, tying together the attributes of the ocean as if they were characteristics of a person.
5. **(a)** By comparing Lady Horton and her beauty to the night—suggesting that her beauty surrounds her like the night and that she combines light and dark as the night sky combines starlight and darkness—Byron suggests that her beauty is as endless as the night sky. **(b)** These images include the "howling" human being tossed in the "playful spray," "the wild waves' play," and the "music in its roar."
6. Both poems are concerned with the ineffable qualities of forces of nature. In "She Walks in Beauty," this focus is directed at human beauty, which is seen as reflecting inner beauty. In "Apostrophe," the infinite power of the ocean is seen as an example of the Almighty's power.
7. Byron's use of imagery that conveys the power and beauty of a woman and the ocean supports the Romantic faith in powers of nature that transcend reason and order.
8. **(a)** Answers will vary. **(b)** Possible response: Most students should say that their questioning made their reading more focused.
9. Possible response: Citizens might try to preserve nature by setting it aside as a park.

EXTEND

Answers for p. 728

❶ Vocabulary Development

Word Analysis: Latin Suffix *-ous*

1. *Glorious* means "full of glory or wonder."
2. *Spacious* means "full of space."
3. *Porous* means "full of pores or holes. "
4. *Plenteous* means "full of plenty."

Spelling Strategy

1. famous
2. piteous
3. prodigious

Concept Development: Antonyms

1. b
2. b
3. c
4. b
5. a
6. a
7. a
8. c
9. c

❷ Grammar and Style

1. joys have
2. gray is
3. charms seem
4. fame escapes
5. book goes

Writing Application

The works of Byron reflect his romantic attitudes. Each of his poems illustrates his talent for writing. His audience of enthusiastic readers also admires him for his deep sympathy for the downtrodden. Byron's commitment to political causes was, in the end, the reason for his death.

Integrate Language Skills

❶ Vocabulary Development Lesson

Word Analysis: Latin Suffix *-ous*

The suffix of the word *credulous*, *-ous*, means "full of," and its root, *-cred-*, means "belief." *Credulous* means "full of belief" or "overly willing to believe." Using the meaning of the suffix *-ous*, define each of these terms.

1. glorious
2. spacious
3. porous
4. plenteous

Spelling Strategy

When adding the suffix *-ous* to a word ending in a vowel, drop or change the vowel.

beauty + *-ous* = beauteous

adventure + *-ous* = adventurous

Add the suffix *-ous* to each word.

1. fame 2. pity 3. prodigy

Concept Development: Antonyms

For each word, choose the letter of the word that is most nearly opposite to it in meaning.

1. arbiter: (a) defendant, (b) troublemaker, (c) judge
2. tempests: (a) storms, (b) lulls, (c) fixtures
3. torrid: (a) angry, (b) obedient, (c) freezing
4. fathomless: (a) deep, (b) measurable, (c) dry
5. retort: (a) ask, (b) reply, (c) deceive
6. insensible: (a) aware, (b) silly, (c) calm
7. credulous: (a) suspicious, (b) devious, (c) notorious
8. copious: (a) anxious, (b) typed, (c) scarce
9. avarice: (a) greed, (b) sin, (c) generosity

❷ Grammar and Style Lesson

Subject and Verb Agreement

Verbs must agree with their **subjects** in number. Do not be misled when words intervene between the subject and the verb or when the subject comes after the verb.

Singular: There is (V) a pleasure (S) in the pathless woods, . . .

Plural: The monsters (S) of the deep are (V) made: . . .

Practice Identify the subject in each item. Then, choose the form of the verb that agrees with it.

1. The joys of the narrator of *Don Juan* (has, have) diminished.
2. There (is, are) much gray in his hair.
3. The charms of romance no longer (seems, seem) possible.
4. The fame of writers (escapes, escape) him.
5. Over the waters (goes, go) his book of verse.

Writing Application Rewrite this paragraph, correcting errors in agreement.

The works of Byron reflects his romantic attitudes. Each of his poems illustrate his talent for writing. His audience of enthusiastic readers also admires him for his deep sympathy for the downtrodden. Byron's commitment to political causes were, in the end, the reason for his death.

WG Prentice Hall Writing and Grammar Connection: Chapter 23, Section 1

TEACHING RESOURCES

The following resources can be used to enrich or extend the instruction for pp. 728–729.

Vocabulary

Selection Support: Build Vocabulary, p. 151

Vocabulary and Spelling Practice Book (Use this booklet for skills enrichment)

Grammar

Selection Support: Grammar and Style, p. 152

Writing and Grammar, Diamond Level, p. 586

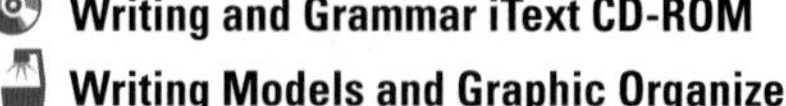

Daily Language Practice Transparencies ■

Writing

Writing and Grammar, Diamond Level, p. 84 ■

Writing and Grammar iText CD-ROM

Writing Models and Graphic Organizers on Transparencies, pp. 17–24

■ **BLOCK SCHEDULING:** Resources marked with this symbol provide varied instruction during 90-minute blocks.

❸ Writing Lesson

Monologue

The speaker in *Don Juan* reveals his innermost thoughts and emotions in a monologue—a speech by the character spoken to himself or herself. Write a monologue for a modern Byronic hero (see the Background on page 718 for a definition). Organize your ideas so that your monologue will build dramatically.

Prewriting Jot down opinions that a Byronic hero might hold today. Next, consider your hero's circumstances and his or her attitude toward them. Then, list words and phrases that convey this attitude.

Drafting Structure your monologue to lead up to your hero's strongest expression of his or her attitude. As you draft, use words and phrases that feel appropriate for your character.

Revising Review the dramatic effect of your draft. Consider rearranging words and sentences to add drama.

Model: Revising to Structure Ideas for Effect

My life has made me the actor I am. If I am great, it is because my life has been great, not perfect. The films of my long career form a celluloid parade of my flaws, *mistakes, and crimes.* ~~crimes and mistakes.~~

Rearranging *crimes* and *mistakes* creates a stronger dramatic effect—the most powerful word comes last.

Prentice Hall Writing and Grammar Connection: Chapter 5, Section 4

❹ Extension Activities

Research and Technology Work with a team to develop a **proposal for a portrait** of the woman in "She Walks in Beauty."

- Conduct research into fashions, paintings, and lifestyles of Byron's day.
- Assemble the information in a detailed description of your proposed portrait.
- Explain how the portrait will reflect both the poem and the styles and life of the day. [Group Activity]

Listening and Speaking Deliver a **eulogy,** or farewell speech, to mourn the passing of Don Juan. In your eulogy, develop his character by including details from the poem. For each detail you include, draw a conclusion about Don Juan's character.

www.phschool.com

Go online for an additional research activity using the Internet.

Lesson Support for p. 729

❸ Writing Lesson

- Review with students how *Don Juan* gives voice to the innermost thoughts of the character of Don Juan through a monologue. Tell students that in this lesson they will write monologues.
- Review students' understanding of a Byronic hero. Explain that their monologues will be for modern Byronic heroes.
- Use the Writing Lesson to guide students in developing their monologues.
- Model the process of revising a narrative using pp. 17–24 of **Writing Models and Graphic Organizers on Transparencies.**
- Use the Narration: Autobiographical Narrative rubric in **Performance Assessment and Portfolio Management,** p. 15, to evaluate students' monologues.

❹ Listening and Speaking

- Read the Listening and Speaking lesson as a class, then encourage students to gather details about Don Juan that they would include in a eulogy.
- Remind students that eulogies are celebrations of a person's life and should create a vivid portrait of the deceased.

CUSTOMIZE INSTRUCTION For Universal Access

To address different learning styles, use the activities suggested in the **Extension Activities** booklet, p. 33.

- For Visual/Spatial Learners, use Activity 5.
- For Intrapersonal Learners, use Activity 6.

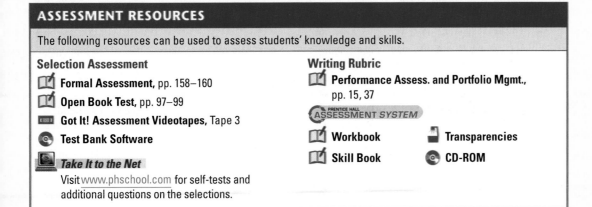

ASSESSMENT RESOURCES

The following resources can be used to assess students' knowledge and skills.

Selection Assessment

- **Formal Assessment,** pp. 158–160
- **Open Book Test,** pp. 97–99
- **Got It! Assessment Videotapes,** Tape 3
- **Test Bank Software**

Take It to the Net

Visit www.phschool.com for self-tests and additional questions on the selections.

Writing Rubric

- **Performance Assess. and Portfolio Mgmt.,** pp. 15, 37

- **Workbook**
- **Skill Book**
- **Transparencies**
- **CD-ROM**

Ozymandias ✦ Ode to the West Wind ✦ To a Skylark

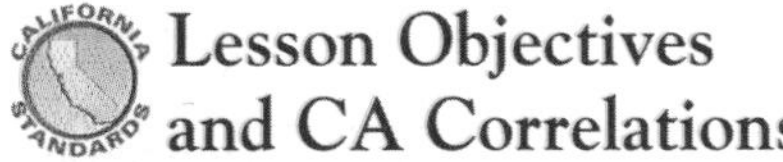

Lesson Objectives and CA Correlations

1. **To analyze and respond to literary elements**
   - Literary Analysis: Imagery **R 3.4**
   - Comparing Literary Works **R 3.7**
2. **To read, comprehend, analyze, and critique a poem**
   - Reading Strategy: Responding to Imagery **R 3.4**
   - Reading Check Questions
   - Review and Assess Questions
   - Assessment Practice (ATE)
3. **To develop word analysis skills, fluency, and systematic vocabulary**
   - Vocabulary Development Lesson: Word Analysis: Latin Root: *-puls-* **R 1.2**
4. **To understand and apply written and oral English language conventions**
   - Spelling Strategy **LC 1.2**
   - Grammar and Style Lesson: Subjunctive Mood **LC 1.1**
5. **To understand and apply appropriate writing and research strategies**
   - Writing Lesson: Introductory Background on a Poem **W 1.6**
   - Extension Activity: Cultural Report **W 1.6**
6. **To understand and apply listening and speaking strategies**
   - Extension Activity: Weather Report **LS 1.8**

STEP-BY-STEP TEACHING GUIDE	PACING GUIDE
PRETEACH	
Motivate Students and Provide Background	
Use the Motivation activity (ATE p. 730)	5 min.
Read and discuss author and background features (SE pp. 730, 733; ATE p. 730) [A]	5 min.
Introduce the Concepts	
Introduce the Literary Analysis and Reading Strategy concepts (SE/ATE p. 731) [A]	15 min.
Pronounce the vocabulary words and read their definitions (SE p. 731)	5 min.
TEACH	
Monitor Comprehension	
Informally monitor comprehension by circulating while students read independently or in groups [A]	15 min.
Monitor students' comprehension with the Reading Check notes (SE/ATE pp. 735, 737, 739)	as students read
Develop vocabulary with Vocabulary notes (SE pp. 733, 734, 735, 737, 738, 739; ATE p. 735)	as students read
Develop Understanding	
Develop students' understanding of imagery with the Literary Analysis annotations (SE/ATE pp. 734, 736, 737) [A]	5 min.
Develop students' ability to respond to imagery with the Reading Strategy annotations (SE/ATE pp. 735, 738)	5 min.
ASSESS	
Assess Mastery	
Assess students' mastery of the Reading Strategy and Literary Analysis concepts by having them answer the Review and Assess questions (SE/ATE p. 741)	15 min.
Use one or more of the print and media Assessment Resources (ATE p. 743) [A]	up to 45 min.
EXTEND	
Apply Understanding	
Have students complete the Vocabulary Development Lesson and the Grammar and Style Lesson (SE p. 742) [A]	20 min.
Apply students' ability to identify and supply necessary background for readers using the Writing Lesson (SE/ATE p. 743) [A]	45 min.
Apply students' understanding using one or more of the Extension Activities (SE p. 743)	20–90 min.

ACCELERATED INSTRUCTION:
Use the strategies and activities identified with an [A].

UNIVERSAL ACCESS
● = Below Level Students
▲ = On-Level Students
■ = Above Level Students

Time and Resource Manager

Reading Level: Average, Challenging, Easy
Average Number of Instructional Days: 4

RESOURCES		
PRINT	**TRANSPARENCIES**	**TECHNOLOGY**
• **Beyond Literature,** Career Connection: Meteorology, p. 34 ▲ ■		• **Interest Grabber Video,** Tape 4 ● ▲ ■
• **Selection Support Workbook:** ● ▲ ■ Literary Analysis, p. 158 Reading Strategy, p. 157 Build Vocabulary, p. 155	• **Literary Analysis and Reading Transparencies,** pp. 67 and 68 ● ▲ ■	
		• **Listening to Literature** ● ▲ ■ Audiocassettes, Side 18 Audio CDs, CD 10
• **Literary Analysis for Enrichment** ■		
• **Formal Assessment:** Selection Test, pp. 161–163 ● ▲ ■ • **Open Book Test,** pp. 100–102 ● ▲ ■ • **Performance Assessment and Portfolio Management,** pp. 13 and 85 ● ▲ ■ • PRENTICE HALL ASSESSMENT SYSTEM ● ▲ ■	• PRENTICE HALL ASSESSMENT SYSTEM ● ▲ ■ • **Skills Practice Answers and Explanations on Transparencies**	• **Test Bank Software** ● ▲ ■ • **Got It! Assessment Videotapes,** Tape 3 ● ▲
• **Selection Support Workbook:** ● ▲ ■ Grammar and Style, p. 156 • **Writing and Grammar,** Diamond Level ● ▲ ■ • **Extension Activities,** p. 34 ● ▲ ■	• **Daily Language Practice Transparencies** ● ▲ • **Writing Models and Graphic Organizers on Transparencies,** pp. 131–134 ● ▲ ■	• **Writing and Grammar iText CD-ROM** ● ▲ ■ ***Take It to the Net*** www.phschool.com

BLOCK SCHEDULING: Use one 90-minute class period to preteach the selections and have students read them. Use a second 90-minute class period to assess students' mastery of skills and have them complete one of the Extension Activities.

PRETEACH

Step-by-Step Teaching Guide for pp. 730–731

Motivation

Explain to students that they may already be familiar with the themes and attitudes of the second generation of English Romantics—Byron, Shelley, and Keats. Byron's bad boy image and Shelley's defiant idealism are not uncommon among modern pop and movie stars. In poems such as "Ozymandias" and "Ode to the West Wind," Shelley taps deep into the mistrust of power and the burning passion for renewal that have characterized youth culture ever since.

Interest Grabber Video

As an alternative, play "'Ozymandias': The Legacy of Ramses II" on Tape 4 to engage student interest.

1 Background

More About the Author

Shelley was encouraged to pursue writing at an early age. In his teens he privately published a series of Gothic horror novelettes and verses: *Zastrozzi* (1810), *Original Poetry by Victor and Cazire* (1810), and *St. Irvyne or The Rosicrucian* (1811).

Shelley's early years were characterized by experimental living and radical freethinking. He circulated pamphlets on vegetarianism and on the freedom of the press and tried setting up radical communes of like-minded bohemians in Devon and later in Wales.

Later in life, Shelley moved to Pisa, Italy, and was joined in 1821 by Byron and Leigh Hunt, who came to edit a monthly journal, *The Liberal*.

Prepare to Read

1 Ozymandias ◆ Ode to the West Wind ◆ To a Skylark

Percy Bysshe Shelley (1792–1822)

When he died in a boating accident at 29, Percy Bysshe (bish) Shelley was eulogized by his fellow-poet Lord Byron as "without exception the best and least selfish man I ever knew." Yet the subject of this praise was a man whose disenchantment with the world was at least as great as his appreciation of its beauties. Shelley's disenchantment, though, only led him to pursue the good more passionately. At once modest and intense, Shelley was a poet of rare gifts. He was also a passionate reformer who believed that his time had betrayed the ideal of a perfect society.

A Loner and Rebel Born into the British upper classes, Shelley was raised on a country estate in Sussex. He attended the finest schools, including the prestigious boarding school Eton, but he was never able to settle into the routine of a student. Instead, he spent most of his time wandering the countryside and performing private scientific experiments. At Oxford University, he became a friend of Thomas Jefferson Hogg, a student whose political views were as strong as his own. The friendship further fueled Shelley's rebellious nature. When, with Hogg's encouragement and support, Shelley published the radical tract *The Necessity of Atheism*, both he and Hogg were expelled from the university.

Love and Art The expulsion estranged Shelley from his father. Instead of going home, Shelley headed for London. There, he met Harriet Westbrook. An unhappy schoolgirl, Westbrook played on his sympathies with descriptions of her miserable situation at home and at school. She persuaded him to elope, and they married. The two traveled to Ireland, where Shelley tried unsuccessfully to "deliver the Irish people from tyranny."

Shelley's development as a poet was already underway. In 1813, he had completed "Queen Mab," his first important poem. The work explored ideas of social justice that Shelley had encountered in the philosopher William Godwin's *Political Justice*. The views expressed by Shelley in the poem—that government and other institutions should be reshaped to conform to the will of the people—marks much of his subsequent poetry, even his nature poems.

Turmoil, Romance, and Tragedy Shelley's marriage, meanwhile, was in trouble. Harriet felt that she could not keep up with her husband, and she had come to question his political ideals. Meanwhile, continuing his travels in radical intellectual circles, Shelley fell in love with Mary Wollstonecraft Godwin, daughter of William Godwin and the feminist Mary Wollstonecraft. After Harriet's tragic death in 1816, Shelley and his beloved Mary Godwin married.

A Poet and an Outcast His radical politics, his tract about atheism, his separation from his first wife, his elopement—all helped make Shelley an outcast from his homeland. He and Mary eventually settled in Italy, where Byron, another famous exile, also lived. The friendship nourished the literary ambitions of all three. It was during a storytelling session with Shelley, Byron, and another friend that Mary Shelley was inspired to begin work on her famous novel *Frankenstein*. Shelley himself wrote many of his finest works in Italy, including "Ode to the West Wind," "To a Skylark," and his verse drama *Prometheus Unbound* (1820), a play predicting humanity's eventual freedom from tyranny.

An Early Death Shelley never lived to see whether his dreams of social progress came true. Today, he is often referred to as the perfect poet of the Romantic Era. His intense response to life and his deep convictions about freedom justify that title.

TEACHING RESOURCES

The following resources can be used to enrich or extend the instruction for pp. 730–731.

Motivation

Interest Grabber Videos, Tape 4

Background

Beyond Literature, p. 34

Take It to the Net

Visit www.phschool.com for background and hotlinks for the selections.

Literary Analysis

Literary Analysis and Reading Transparencies, Imagery, p. 68

Reading

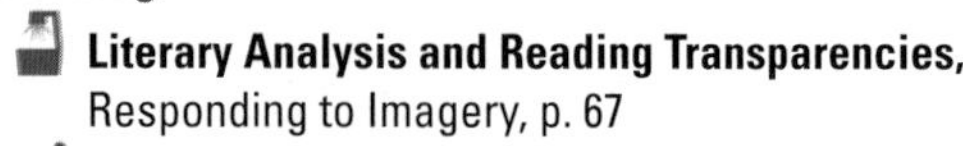

Literary Analysis and Reading Transparencies, Responding to Imagery, p. 67

Selection Support: Reading Strategy, p. 157

BLOCK SCHEDULING: Resources marked with this symbol provide varied instruction during 90-minute blocks.

Preview

Connecting to the Literature

Nature's more extravagant effects—lightning slashing through the sky or snow blowing relentlessly for hours—may leave you gasping in awe or exclaiming in exasperation. Shelley carries this direct response a step further, addressing whole poems to an aspect of nature.

❷ Literary Analysis

Imagery

Imagery is descriptive language that re-creates sensory experience. Writers may use imagery to create metaphors and other figures of speech. Poetic imagery has these characteristics:

- It appeals to any or all of the five senses.
- It often creates patterns supporting a poem's theme.

In "Ode to the West Wind," for example, Shelley uses wind images that appeal to sight, sound, and touch. As you read, think about how images and their patterns help you understand Shelley's message.

Comparing Literary Works

By gathering together powerful images of the West Wind or of a skylark, Shelley links these natural beings to the strivings of his own spirit. His images all depict concrete objects, such as leaves in the wind. Yet they also stir up longings and dreams. In the **Romantic philosophy** of the imagination, an image connects what is "outside" the mind with what is "inside," linking nature and spirit. Compare the specific ideas Shelley expresses through images. Then, judge how well his images capture both the longings of his spirit and the thing being described.

❸ Reading Strategy

Responding to Imagery

You can **respond to imagery** in a poem even before you fully understand the meaning of the work. Immerse yourself in poetic images by noticing their sensory "texture"—dark or light, rough or smooth. Then, consider the associations each evokes. Use a chart like the one shown as you read.

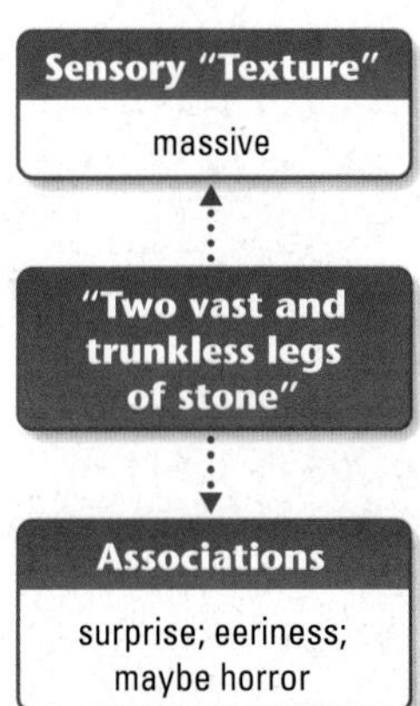

Vocabulary Development

visage (viz´ ij) *n.* face (p. 733)

verge (vurj) *n.* edge; rim (p. 734)

sepulcher (sep´ əl kər) *n.* tomb (p. 735)

impulse (im´ puls´) *n.* force driving forward (p. 735)

blithe (blīth) *adj.* cheerful (p. 737)

profuse (prō fyo͞os´) *adj.* abundant; pouring out (p. 737)

vernal (vur´ nəl) *adj.* relating to spring (p. 738)

satiety (sə tī´ ə tē) *n.* state of being filled with enough or more than enough (p. 739)

❷ Literary Analysis

Imagery

- Tell students that in this lesson they will focus on imagery, descriptive language that recreates sensory experience.
- Explain that imagery appeals to any or all of the five senses and often creates patterns that support a poem's theme.
- Read the note about imagery together as a class. Call students' attention to the way Shelley uses imagery that appeals to sound, sight, and touch.
- Use the instruction for Comparing Literary Works to review with students how Shelley's use of imagery is consistent with the Romantic philosophy of the imagination, in which an image connects the external world to the inner self.
- Use the Imagery transparency in **Literary Analysis and Reading Transparencies,** p. 68, to show students how to identify the connections between imagery and theme.

❸ Reading Strategy

Responding to Imagery

- Explain to students that they can respond to imagery in a work of literature, even before they understand the work fully.
- Use the graphic organizer on p. 731 to model the skill of responding to imagery.
- Have students practice the skill using the Respond to Imagery transparency in **Literary Analysis and Reading Transparencies,** p. 67.

Vocabulary Development

- Pronounce each vocabulary word for students and read the definitions as a class. Have students identify any words with which they are already familiar.

CUSTOMIZE INSTRUCTION FOR UNIVERSAL ACCESS

For Less Proficient Readers	For English Learners	For Advanced Readers
Review the Reading Strategy with students and encourage them to employ it as you read the poems aloud. Model the skill of responding to imagery using the graphic organizer on p. 731 or using the Respond to Imagery transparency on p. 67 of **Literary Analysis and Reading Transparencies.**	Students may stumble over Shelley's diction and poetic structure. Pair students with more advanced readers to paraphrase difficult passages. Model the skill of responding to imagery using the Respond to Imagery transparency on p. 67 of **Literary Analysis and Reading Transparencies.**	Tell students that Shelley has been called the perfect Romantic poet. As they read, challenge students to find evidence to support or refute this statement. Encourage students to base their responses on the imagery Shelley uses in his poems. Model responding to imagery using the graphic organizer on p. 731.

 ***E-Teach***

Visit E-Teach at www.phschool.com for teachers' essays on how to teach, with questions and answers.

TEACH

Step-by-Step Teaching Guide for pp. 732–740

CUSTOMIZE INSTRUCTION For Verbal/Linguistic Learners

Point out to students how the poem's structure reinforces its meaning. The first eight lines describe the statue, while the final six lines emphasize the irony in its wrecked condition. Encourage students to study the structure and the rhyme sequence for additional clues to meaning.

❶ About the Selection

This poem provides an ironic comment on human pride and ambition. In the poem, a traveler describes the ruins of an ancient statue. On its base is an arrogant inscription: "Look on my works, ye Mighty, and despair!" However, what is left of the statue stands in an empty desert; the works of Ozymandias have crumbled under the onslaught of time and nature.

❷ Background

Art

The Colossos of Memnon

According to legend, this gigantic statue emitted a musical noise at sunrise. Like the enormous statue of Ozymandias in the poem, this statue was built to represent the power and divine kingship of an Egyptian pharaoh.

The Colossos of Memnon is located in Thebes, on the banks of the Nile River. From about 4,000 years ago to about 2,700 years ago, Thebes was the capital city for many Egyptian pharaohs. Today, the city houses many examples of splendid royal monuments and tombs. Use these questions for discussion:

How can this statue help you appreciate the imagery of Shelley's poem?
Answer: This statue visually conveys the physical aspects of a decaying monument.

❸ ▶Critical Viewing

Answer: The statue in the photograph is similar because it is large, made of stone, weathered, and on a flat plain. It is different because it has a trunk, its head is still attached, and it is surrounded by grasslands.

❶ Ozymandias

Percy Bysshe Shelley

❷

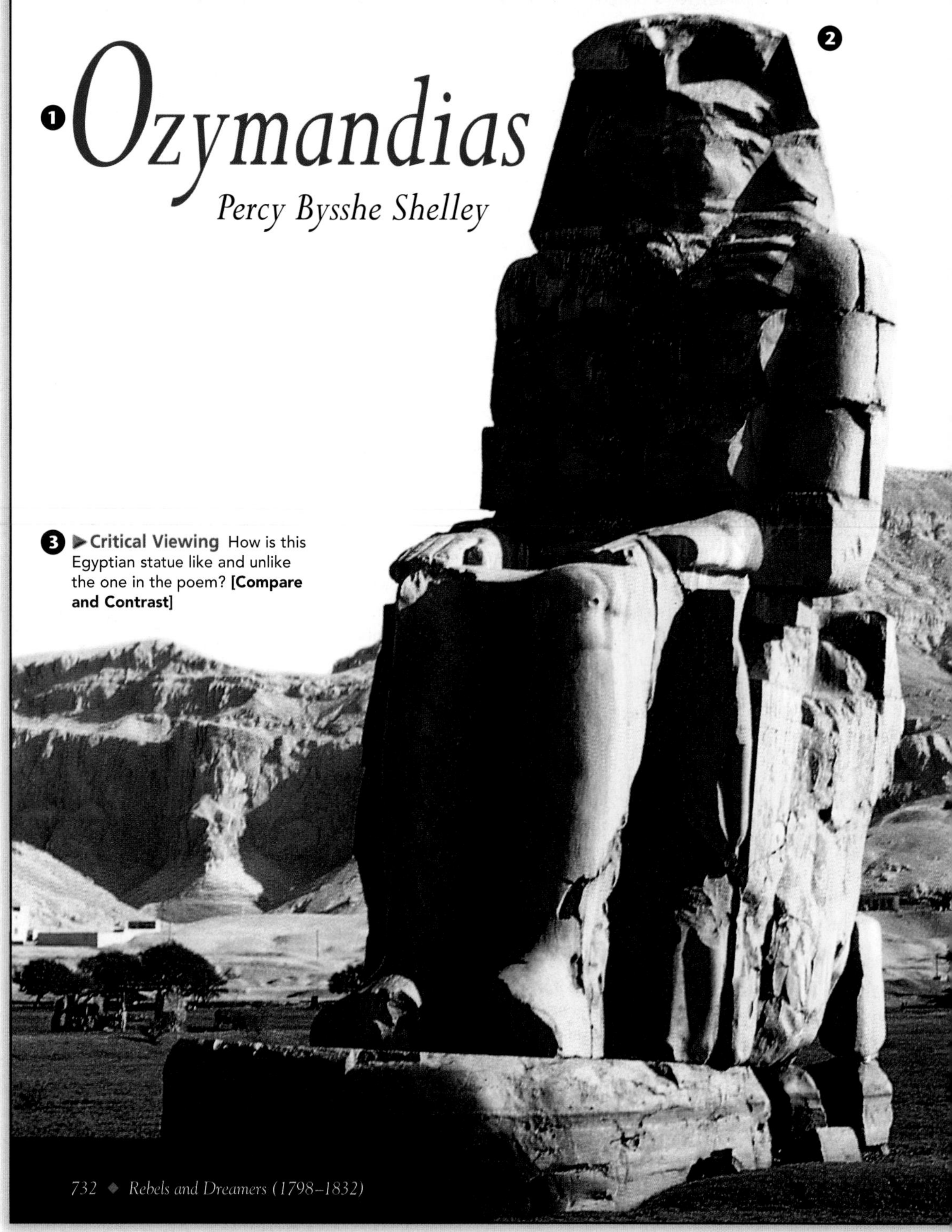

❸ ▶**Critical Viewing** How is this Egyptian statue like and unlike the one in the poem? **[Compare and Contrast]**

TEACHING RESOURCES

The following resources can be used to enrich or extend the instruction for pp. 732–740.

Literary Analysis

Selection Support: Literary Analysis, p. 158

Reading

Listening to Literature Audiocassettes, Side 18

Listening to Literature Audio CDs, CD 10

BLOCK SCHEDULING: Resources marked with this symbol provide varied instruction during 90-minute blocks.

Background

The Ozymandias of Shelley's poem is based on an actual Egyptian pharaoh, Ramses II ("Ozymandias" was his name in Greek). Ramses II ruled during the thirteenth century B.C. and figures in the biblical story of Moses. He sponsored ambitious building projects and called for huge statues of himself to be built. According to an ancient story, one of these colossal statues was inscribed with this boast about his bold deeds: "I am Ozymandias, king of kings; if anyone wishes to know what I am and where I lie, let him surpass me in some of my exploits."

I met a traveler from an antique land
Who said: Two vast and trunkless legs of stone
Stand in the desert. Near them, on the sand,
Half sunk, a shattered visage lies, whose frown,
And wrinkled lip, and sneer of cold command,
Tell that its sculptor well those passions read
Which yet survive, stamped on these lifeless things,
The hand that mocked them and the heart that fed:
And on the pedestal these words appear:
"My name is Ozymandias, king of kings:
Look on my works, ye Mighty, and despair!"
Nothing beside remains. Round the decay
Of that colossal wreck, boundless and bare,
The lone and level sands stretch far away.

visage (viz´ ij) *n.* face

Review and Assess

Thinking About the Selection

1. **Respond:** If you could speak with the statue of Ozymandias, what question would you ask?
2. **(a) Recall:** What sight does the traveler describe? **(b) Analyze:** What overall effect does this sight have?
3. **(a) Recall:** How would you describe the expression on the face of Ozymandias? **(b) Infer:** What does his expression suggest about the kind of ruler he was?
4. **(a) Interpret:** What attitude is conveyed by the words on the pedestal? **(b) Compare and Contrast:** Compare this attitude with the opening images of the poem. **(c) Analyze:** In what sense is the inscription ironic?
5. **(a) Draw Conclusions:** What is the message of this poem? **(b) Apply:** Do you think that the message is pertinent to today's world? Why or why not?

Answers for p. 733

1. Some students may say they would ask the statue of Ozymandias what happened to his empire; others may say they would ask what it had witnessed in the years it presided over the desert.
2. **(a)** He describes the crumbling remains of a statue commemorating the Egyptian pharaoh Ozymandias. **(b)** This sight creates an overall effect of ruined grandeur.
3. **(a)** The expression on the face of Ozymandias is partially obscured by its deterioration, but it includes a frown, a wrinkled lip, and a sneer. **(b)** His expression suggests he was a condescending, proud ruler.
4. **(a)** The inscription conveys an attitude of pride and arrogance. **(b)** This attitude of arrogance reflects the passions shown to belong to the king by the statue's expression, but it stands in sharp contrast with the opening images of devastation and emptiness. **(c)** It is ironic because Ozymandias, whose proud words appear on the pedestal, obviously expected his works to last forever, but the statue on the pedestal, along with his entire civilization, have long since been destroyed.
5. **(a)** Possible responses: Power is fleeting; human beings cannot escape the effects of time. **(b)** Yes, it puts accomplishments, pride, and power in perspective; no, it is rare to find people creating such self-glorifying monuments in today's world.

CUSTOMIZE INSTRUCTION FOR UNIVERSAL ACCESS

For Special Needs Students	For Less Proficient Readers	For Advanced Students
Have students read a section from "Ozymandias" with teacher guidance. Then, ask students to visualize each line as they read the rest of the poem to themselves. Play "'Ozymandias': The Legacy of Ramses II" on **Interest Grabber Videos,** Tape 4, to stimulate student interest in the poem's subject matter.	Ask students to read the poem silently as they listen to **Listening to Literature CDs,** CD 10. Guide students in a close reading of the poem in which they make associations with the images Shelley includes in the poem.	Have students choose a recent political leader. Ask students how they think the leader will be remembered after thousands of years. Have students think of an image that represents the assessment historians of the future might make of this leader, then write an extended epitaph for the leaders, using the image to represent history's assessment .

❹ About the Selection

The speaker of this poem describes the elemental force of the West Wind as it drives dead leaves, stirs up the ocean, destroys plants, and heralds winter's arrival. Awed by the wind's natural strength and disillusioned with his own spiritual barrenness, Shelley calls on the wind to lift him up, ravage him, and cleanse him. He concludes by affirming that decay will lead ultimately to the renewal of spring.

❺ Literary Analysis

Imagery

- Read the bracketed passage aloud to students.
- Remind them that imagery appeals to the five senses.
- Then, ask the Literary Analysis question on p. 734: To which sense does the image in lines 18–23 mostly appeal?
  Possible responses: Students may say that Shelley's description of the wind's "aery surge" elicits appeals to the sense of sight. Point out that the word *surge* also suggests the wind's sound and its power as it might be detected by touch.

❹ *Ode to the West Wind*

Percy Bysshe Shelley

I

O wild West Wind, thou breath of Autumn's being,
Thou, from whose unseen presence the leaves dead
Are driven, like ghosts from an enchanter fleeing,

Yellow, and black, and pale, and hectic red,
Pestilence-stricken multitudes: O thou,
Who chariotest to their dark and wintry bed

The wingèd seeds, where they lie cold and low,
Each like a corpse within its grave, until
Thine azure sister of the Spring[1] shall blow

Her clarion[2] o'er the dreaming earth, and fill
(Driving sweet buds like flocks to feed in air)
With loving hues and odors plain and hill:

Wild Spirit, which art moving everywhere;
Destroyer and preserver; hear, oh, hear!

II

Thou on whose stream, 'mid the steep sky's commotion,
Loose clouds like earth's decaying leaves are shed,
Shook from the tangled boughs of Heaven and Ocean,

❺ Angels[3] of rain and lightning: there are spread
On the blue surface of thine aery surge,
Like the bright hair uplifted from the head

Of some fierce Maenad,[4] even from the dim verge
Of the horizon to the zenith's height,
The locks of the approaching storm. Thou dirge

Literary Analysis
Imagery To which sense does the image in lines 18–23 mostly appeal?

verge (vurj) *n.* edge; rim

1. **sister of the Spring** the wind prevailing during spring.
2. **clarion** *n.* trumpet producing clear, sharp tones.
3. **angels** messengers.
4. **Maenad** (mē´ nad) a priestess of Bacchus, the Greek and Roman god of wine and revelry.

ENRICHMENT: Science Connection

The West Wind

Shelley's poem addresses the West Wind, or wind blowing from the west. That wind usually brings new weather because of Earth's rotation from west to east. At the same time, cold air from the poles moves toward the Equator while warm air moves from the Equator outward to the poles. Thus, as the North Pole gets colder with winter's approach, more frigid air reaches Earth's middle regions. That air is carried on the prevailing west wind around the globe to bring autumn. Come spring, Earth's equatorial regions warm up from proximity to the sun, and warm air is circulated by the winds to bring spring.

Of the dying year, to which this closing night
Will be the dome of a vast sepulcher,
Vaulted with all thy congregated might

Of vapors, from whose solid atmosphere
Black rain, and fire, and hail will burst: oh, hear!

III

Thou who didst waken from his summer dreams
The blue Mediterranean, where he lay,
Lulled by the coil of his crystalline streams,

6 Beside a pumice[5] isle in Baiae's bay,[6]
And saw in sleep old palaces and towers
Quivering within the wave's intenser day,

All overgrown with azure moss and flowers
So sweet, the sense faints picturing them! Thou
For whose path the Atlantic's level powers

Cleave themselves into chasms, while far below
The sea-blooms and the oozy woods which wear
The sapless foliage of the ocean, know

Thy voice, and suddenly grow gray with fear,
And tremble and despoil themselves: oh, hear!

IV

If I were a dead leaf thou mightest bear;
If I were a swift cloud to fly with thee;
A wave to pant beneath thy power, and share

7 The impulse of thy strength, only less free
Than thou, O uncontrollable! If even
I were as in my boyhood, and could be

sepulcher (sep´ əl kər) *n.* tomb

Reading Strategy
Responding to Imagery What associations do the images in lines 29–36 suggest to you?

impulse (im´ puls´) *n.* force driving forward

 8 **Reading Check**

In the first three sections, what does the speaker ask the West Wind to do?

5. **pumice** (pum´ is) *n.* volcanic rock.
6. **Baiae's** (bā´ yēz) **bay** site of the ancient Roman resort near Naples, parts of which lie submerged

6 Reading Strategy

Responding to Imagery

- Have a student volunteer read the bracketed passage aloud.
- Encourage students to make associations from images in the passage.
- Then, ask the Reading Strategy question on p. 735: What associations do the images in lines 29–36 suggest to you?
  Possible response: Associations include purity ("crystalline streams") and tranquility ("summer dreams"; the underwater ruins).

7 Vocabulary Development

Latin Root *-puls-*

- Call students' attention to *impulse,* which means "forward-driving force." Explain that the Latin root of this word is *-puls-,* which means "push or drive" and appears in many words that express force in one form or another.
- Have students suggest other words and phrases that contain this root and list them on the board.
  Possible responses: *impulsive, repulse, propulsion, compulsion*
- Have them explain how the root contributes to the meaning of each, consulting a dictionary for unfamiliar words.

8 Reading Check

Answer: The speaker asks the West Wind to listen to him.

CUSTOMIZE INSTRUCTION FOR UNIVERSAL ACCESS

For Special Needs Students	For English Learners	For Advanced Students
Have students work as a group to create a rough map of the wind's progress in the poem. They might start with a transparency of a world map and add brief descriptions of each scene Shelley describes.	Have students practice reading unfamiliar words in the poem aloud. You may want to play **Listening to Literature Audiocassettes,** Side 18, and have students listen to the sound of the poem, then go back and try to say words with which they are having difficulty.	Have students write poems in which the West Wind replies to Shelley. Have students divide their poems into five parts, like Shelley's poem, and make sure that each part is a response to the corresponding section of Shelley's work.

❾ Literary Analysis

Imagery and Romantic Philosophy

- Have students read the bracketed passage to themselves.
- Review with students their understanding of Romantic philosophy and its connection between external and internal sensibilities.
- Then, ask the Literary Analysis question on p. 736: How do the images in lines 57–63 imply a connection between the speaker and nature?
Answer: The speaker sees himself in the bittersweet autumn wind and asks the wind to enable his spirit to be one with that of the wind.

Answers for p. 736

1. **(a)** It is associated with autumn. **(b)** Shelley associates the West Wind with destruction, frenzy, decay, and fear.
2. **(a)** The speaker asks the West Wind to lift him up as a wave, leaf, or cloud and carry him. **(b)** The speaker says he is oppressed by "A heavy weight of hours."
3. **(a)** Possible response: Shelley wishes for a new era sparked by his words; he may envision a political as well as a spiritual renewal of humanity, ushering in a new era of freedom. **(b)** The West Wind is a suitable force to call on for this "new birth" because it marks the change of seasons as fall shifts to winter and the old world is destroyed, to be replaced by a new one in spring.
4. **(a)** Even the bleakest situations are followed by times of renewal and hope. **(b)** It sums up the poem's theme of hope for a new beginning.

The comrade of thy wanderings over Heaven,
As then, when to outstrip thy skyey speed
Scarce seemed a vision; I would ne'er have striven

As thus with thee in prayer in my sore need.
Oh, lift me as a wave, a leaf, a cloud!
I fall upon the thorns of life! I bleed!

A heavy weight of hours has chained and bowed
One too like thee: tameless, and swift, and proud.

V

Make me thy lyre,[7] even as the forest is:
What if my leaves are falling like its own!
The tumult of thy mighty harmonies

❾ Will take from both a deep, autumnal tone,
Sweet though in sadness. Be thou, Spirit fierce,
My spirit! Be thou me, impetuous one!

Drive my dead thought over the universe
Like withered leaves to quicken a new birth!
And, by the incantation of this verse,

Scatter, as from an unextinguished hearth
Ashes and sparks, my words among mankind!
Be through my lips to unawakened earth

The trumpet of a prophecy! O Wind,
If Winter comes, can Spring be far behind?

Literary Analysis
Imagery and Romantic Philosophy How do the images in lines 57–63 imply a connection between the speaker and nature?

7. **lyre** Aeolian (ē ō′ lē ən) lyre, or wind harp, a stringed instrument which produces musical sounds when the wind passes over it.

Review and Assess

Thinking About the Selection

1. (a) **Recall:** What season does the poet associate with the West Wind? (b) **Interpret:** What feelings does Shelley create around the West Wind in sections II and III?
2. (a) **Recall:** What does the speaker ask of the wind in section IV? (b) **Infer:** What change in his life prompts this question?
3. (a) **Interpret:** In section V, what is the "new birth" for which the speaker asks? (b) **Interpret:** Why is the West Wind a suitable force to call on for this "new birth"?
4. (a) **Interpret:** What is the meaning of the famous final line of the poem? (b) **Analyze:** How does it tie together the poem?

10 *To a Skylark*

Percy Bysshe Shelley

Hail to thee, blithe spirit!
 Bird thou never wert,
That from heaven, or near it,
 Pourest thy full heart
In profuse strains of unpremeditated art.

Higher still and higher,
 From the earth thou springest
Like a cloud of fire;
 The blue deep thou wingest,
And singing still dost soar, and soaring ever singest.

In the golden lightning
 Of the sunken sun,
O'er which clouds are brightening,
 Thou dost float and run;
Like an unbodied joy whose race is just begun.

11 The pale purple even[1]
 Melts around thy flight;
Like a star of heaven,
 In the broad daylight
Thou art unseen, but yet I hear thy shrill delight,

Keen as are the arrows
 Of that silver sphere,[2]
Whose intense lamp narrows
 In the white dawn clear,
Until we hardly see—we feel that it is there.

All the earth and air
 With thy voice is loud,
As, when night is bare,
 From one lonely cloud
The moon rains out her beams, and Heaven is overflowed.

What thou art we know not;
 What is most like thee?
From rainbow clouds there flow not
 Drops so bright to see,
As from thy presence showers a rain of melody.

blithe (blīth) *adj.* cheerful

profuse (prō fyo͞os´) *adj.* abundant; pouring out

Literary Analysis
Imagery To what three senses do lines 16–20 appeal?

12 
Reading Check
Through what sense or senses does the speaker perceive the Skylark?

1. **even** evening.
2. **silver sphere** the morning star.

10 About the Selection

This poem honors nature's glorious songs and aspires to its pure joy. Addressed to a bird, the poem captures the skylark's spiraling flight and describes its soaring music, whether in the fading evening or earliest dawn. The unending joy of the skylark's song is contrasted with human experiences of limitation and the contradictions of joy and suffering.

11 Literary Analysis

Imagery

- Read the bracketed passage aloud to students.
- Ask the Literary Analysis question on p. 737: To what three senses do lines 16–20 appeal?
  Answer: The senses are sight (including the "pale purple" of the evening), sound (the bird's "shrill delight"), and touch (the melting of the evening).

12 Reading Check

Answer: The speaker perceives the skylark through the sense of hearing (he hears the bird's song).

CUSTOMIZE INSTRUCTION FOR UNIVERSAL ACCESS

For Special Needs Students	For Less Proficient Readers	For Advanced Readers
Have each student present an image from one of the stanzas. Then, discuss what the images have in common—sense appealed to, mood, type of language—and how they differ.	For students who have difficulty interpreting Shelley's imagery, use the imagery transparency on p. 68 of **Literary Analysis and Reading Transparencies** to model how lines from Shelley's poems appeal to the senses, what emotions are evoked, and how these relate to the theme.	Have students read the final stanzas of the poem in small groups. Review with students their understanding of the Romantic philosophy and its linking of nature and spirit. Then, ask them to discuss how Shelley's speaker makes the connection between the natural world and the speaker's world in these closing stanzas.

13 Reading Strategy

Responding to Imagery

- Have students read the bracketed passage to themselves.
- Remind them that by considering imagery in a text and making associations based on the imagery, they may gain greater understanding of the poem.
- Then ask the Reading Strategy question on p. 738: What associations do the images in lines 51–55 suggest to you?
  Possible responses: Students may say the images suggest associations of a garden or of summer, of a hot day thick with the perfume with flowers, and of lush abundance and excessive indulgence.

Like a poet hidden
 In the light of thought,
Singing hymns unbidden,
 Till the world is wrought
To sympathy with hopes and fears it heeded not:

Like a highborn maiden
 In a palace tower,
Soothing her love-laden
 Soul in secret hour
With music sweet as love, which overflows her bower:

Like a glowworm golden
 In a dell of dew,
Scattering unbeholden
 Its aerial hue
Among the flowers and grass, which screen it from the view!

13
Like a rose embowered
 In its own green leaves,
By warm winds deflowered,[3]
 Till the scent it gives
Makes faint with too much sweet those heavy-wingèd thieves.[4]

Sound of vernal showers
 On the twinkling grass,
Rain-awakened flowers,
 All that ever was
Joyous, and clear, and fresh, thy music doth surpass:

Teach us, sprite or bird,
 What sweet thoughts are thine:
I have never heard
 Praise of love or wine
That panted forth a flood of rapture so divine.

Chorus Hymeneal,[5]
 Or triumphal chant,
Matched with thine would be all
 But an empty vaunt,
A thing wherein we feel there is some hidden want.

What objects are the fountains[6]
 Of thy happy strain?
What fields, or waves, or mountains?
 What shapes of sky or plain?
What love of thine own kind? what ignorance of pain?

Reading Strategy
Responding to Imagery What associations do the images in lines 51–55 suggest to you?

vernal (vurn′ əl) *adj.* relating to spring

---

3. **deflowered** fully open.
4. **thieves** the "warm winds."
5. **Chorus Hymeneal** (hī′ mə nē′ əl) marriage song, named after Hymen, the Greek god of marriage.
6. **fountains** sources, inspiration.

⓮

Cloud Study, 1821, John Constable, Yale Center for British Art

⓯ ▲ **Critical Viewing** Which lines from Shelley's poem does this painting by the Romantic painter John Constable best illustrate? **[Connect]**

With thy clear keen joyance
Languor cannot be;
Shadow of annoyance
Never came near thee;
Thou lovest—but ne'er knew love's sad satiety.

Waking or asleep,
Thou of death must deem[7]
Things more true and deep
Than we mortals dream,
Or how could thy notes flow in such a crystal stream?

We look before and after,
And pine for what is not;

satiety (sə tī´ ə tē) *n.* state of being filled with enough or more than enough

⓰ 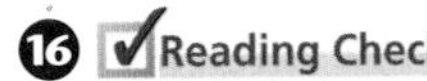

Reading Check

According to the speaker, what can the skylark's song teach us?

7. **deem** know.

⓮ Background

Art

Cloud Study, John Constable

This painting shows several birds—similar to those in the poem—in high flight against a cloudy sky.

Englishman and painter John Constable studied at the Royal Academy in London. He departed from his training in an artificial style of painting to create landscapes with truth and originality, choosing to paint outdoors rather than in a studio.

Cloud Study was one of a series of small oil sketches through which Constable studied the effects of weather, time of day, and season on the sky. Use these questions for discussion:

1. How is the painting's mood similar to that of the poem?
   Answer: Both evoke wonder at nature—the poem at the skylark's song and the painting at the birds' soaring flight.
2. What emotions might this painting evoke for Shelley?
   Answer: He would likely feel wonder and envy at the birds' seemingly limitless flight.

⓯ ▶ Critical Viewing

Answer: Any passages in lines 6–20 could be illustrated by this painting.

⓰ Reading Check

Answer: The skylark knows death more truly and deeply than humans do since its song is not marred by fear of death.

CUSTOMIZE INSTRUCTION FOR UNIVERSAL ACCESS

For Less Proficient Readers	For Gifted/Talented Students	For Advanced Readers
Have students memorize several stanzas from "To a Skylark" that they find evocative or memorable. You may want to play them a selection from the poem on **Listening to Literature Audiocassettes**, Side 18. Then, have students find musical background music and perform their renditions of the poem.	Ask students what they think would happen if Ozymandias met the skylark. Have partners develop a role-play that depicts a meeting between the two subjects. Each student should play one of the two roles and determine how Ozymandias would walk and move and what movements would be typical of the skylark.	Have students consider Shelley's comment that the world would benefit from knowing the joy of the skylark. Have students reread "To a Skylark" and note where Shelley suggests moral or ethical lessons. Have students list lessons that Shelley says humans could learn from skylarks.

ASSESS

Answers for p. 740

Review and Assess

1. **(a)** The poet claims the skylark is not a bird. **(b)** He is making the point that the bird's song sounds like something beyond the world of living things. **(c)** The images of light suggest that the bird is somehow celestial or otherworldly.
2. **(a)** The poet compares the bird to a poet, a highborn maiden, a glowworm, and a rose. **(b)** Each comparison suggests that the song can transform the world or a soul. The song is like the poet's hymns, which create new sympathies and fears; the song is like the song of a lovelorn maiden soothing herself; like the glowworm's light, the song permeates the air; like the scent of fallen roses, the song intoxicates.
3. **(a)** The speaker claims that the skylark's songs are sweeter than any human songs about love or wine, or any triumphal chants or wedding songs. **(b)** The speaker concludes that the skylark cannot know annoyance or languor, but that it understands death more truly and deeply. Unlike the bird, humans pine for what is not, and even their laughter is infected with grief.
4. The phrase suggests that the gladness of the skylark is too pure to be understood by people; translated into poetry, it would be startlingly beautiful but would not make sense.
5. Students may say that the poet's yearnings and complaints show the keen limitations of the human condition and the poet's struggle with those limitations, and that this presentation is as moving as the pure beauty of the song.

Our sincerest laughter
  With some pain is fraught;
Our sweetest songs are those that tell of saddest thought.

Yet if[8] we could scorn
  Hate, and pride, and fear;
If we were things born
  Not to shed a tear,
I know not how thy joy we ever should come near.

Better than all measures
  Of delightful sound,
Better than all treasures
  That in books are found,
Thy skill to poet were,[9] thou scorner of the ground!

Teach me half the gladness
  That thy brain must know,
Such harmonious madness
  From my lips would flow,
The world should listen then, as I am listening now.

---

8. **if** even if.
9. **were** would be.

Review and Assess

Thinking About the Selection

1. **(a) Recall:** In the first stanza, what does the poet claim the skylark is not? **(b) Interpret:** What point is he making? **(c) Analyze:** How do the images of light in lines 6–35 reinforce the point?
2. **(a) Recall:** To what four things does the speaker compare the bird in lines 36–55? **(b) Analyze:** What quality or power does each comparison suggest that the bird's song has?
3. **(a) Summarize:** What comparisons does the poet make between human song and the skylark's? **(b) Analyze:** Based on these comparisons, what does the speaker conclude about similarities and differences between the bird's life and human life?
4. **Interpret:** What does the speaker's use of the phrase "harmonious madness" (line 103) suggest about the difference between the skylark's song and human poetry?
5. **Evaluate:** Do you think the yearnings, speculations, and complaints that the skylark's song inspires in the speaker are as moving as the song itself? Explain.

ASSESSMENT PRACTICE: Critical Reading

Critical Thinking (For more practice, see Test Preparation Workbook, p. 34.)

Many tests require students to judge the relevance of facts in a writer's argument. Use this sample item.

. . . And on the pedestal these words appear:
"My name is Ozymandias, king of kings:
Look on my works, ye Mighty, and despair!"
Nothing beside remains. Round the decay
Of that colossal wreck, boundless and bare,
The lone and level sands stretch far away.

Which of these facts would support the theme of these lines from "Ozymandias"?

A The traveler was from Greece.
B The sculptor is buried in a tomb nearby.
C The writing on the pedestal is so weathered that it is scarcely legible.
D Ruins can survive for centuries in the desert.

The theme of the passage is the transitory nature of human accomplishments. This theme is supported by *C*.

Review and Assess

Literary Analysis

Imagery

1. Imagine filming the **imagery** of "Ozymandias." (a) Compare the camera placement you would use for lines 4–5, lines 9–11, and the final line. (b) Explain how each image helps convey Shelley's message.
2. (a) In "Ode to the West Wind," find three images indicating the power of the wind, and explain to which senses each appeals. (b) How do these images support Shelley's message of renewal?
3. (a) How do descriptions of sounds in "To a Skylark" suggest the bird's "unbodied joy"? (b) How does sound show the defect in human joy in lines 86–90?

Comparing Literary Works

4. Compare Shelley's images of the statue, the West Wind, and the skylark. (a) Which paints the strongest sensory picture of the object described? Explain. (b) Which provides the clearest sense of the ideas and feelings connected with the object? Explain.
5. In **Romantic philosophy,** the imagination connects nature and spirit. (a) What images in sections IV and V of "Ode to the West Wind" suggest such a connection? (b) Considering the light imagery and lines 36–40, how does "To a Skylark" make the connection?
6. Compare two instances in Shelley's poetry where an image connects the speaker and nature, using a chart like the one shown.

Image	How Vivid?	Associated Ideas

→

Link: Nature and Spirit

Reading Strategy

Responding to Imagery

7. Select a passage from each poem that contains images that you find striking or memorable. Explain your response to each.

Extend Understanding

8. **Media Connection:** What techniques are used in television films about nature to suggest poetic qualities?

Quick Review

Imagery is descriptive language re-creating sensory experience.

In **Romantic philosophy,** the poetic image provides a connection between nature and the human spirit.

To **respond to imagery,** take in the sensory experiences it suggests and examine the associations it has for you.

Take It to the Net

www.phschool.com

Take the interactive self-test online to check your understanding of these selections.

Answers for p. 741

Review and Assess

1. **(a)** Lines 4–5 and 9–11 are like close-up camera shots; the last line is a panoramic shot of the barren desert. **(b)** Each image reflects the destruction of Ozymandias' statue and the erasure of all traces of his power. In this way, each shows how pride comes to nothing.
2. **(a)** Possible responses: The scattering of leaves, the spreading of seeds to the ground, and the flutter of clouds in the sky appeal to the senses of sight and sound. **(b)** These images support Shelley's theme of renewal in that the leaves and seeds falling bring about a new season, and the clouds moving initiate new weather to bring about the season.
3. **(a)** The descriptions of sounds in "To a Skylark" suggest that the song is everywhere, heard even in heaven. **(b)** Humans' "sweetest songs" are ones that "tell of saddest thought" and show the defect in human joy compared to that of the skylark.
4. **(a)** Some students may say that the image of the statue is the strongest because of its simplicity; others may feel that the image of the wind is the richest sensory picture because of the wealth of scenes associated with it. **(b)** Possible response: The image of the statue presents the clearest sense of the ideas and feelings connected with the object because of its simplicity.
5. **(a)** Images such as "lift me as a wave, a leaf, a cloud," "Make me thy lyre," and "Be thou, Spirit fierce, / My spirit! Be thou me, impetuous one!" suggest the speaker's desire to connect nature and spirit. **(b)** "To a Skylark" makes the connection between nature and spirit by showing the power of the skylark's song to move a listener and to reveal, through contrast, the limitations and strivings of humanity.
6. Possible response for "Ode to a Skylark": Image: "Teach me half the gladness / That thy brain

continued

Answers continued

must know"; How Vivid?: fairly Associated Ideas: bird is like the poet of the animal world; Link: Nature and Spirit: speaker wishes to learn a new way of being from the bird.

7. Answers will vary.
8. Techniques such as slow-motion and blurred close-ups are used in television films about nature to suggest poetic qualities.

ENRICHMENT: Further Reading

Other Works by Percy Bysshe Shelley

Prometheus Unbound; Epipsychidion; Hellas

Works About Nature, Inspiration, and Freedom

"The Song of Nature," Ralph Waldo Emerson

"Liberty," Archibald MacLeish

"Inspiration," Henry David Thoreau

Take It to the Net

Visit www.phschool.com for more information on the authors.

EXTEND

Answers for p. 742

❶ Vocabulary Development

Word Analysis: Latin Root *-puls-*

1. c **4.** d
2. e **5.** b
3. a

Spelling Strategy

1. simplicity
2. society
3. notoriety

Concept Development: Synonyms and Antonyms

1. e **5.** b
2. h **6.** d
3. a **7.** c
4. f **8.** g

❷ Grammar and Style

1. correct
2. He wishes that he were more like the bird.
3. He thinks that if he were a skylark, he would not know pain.
4. "If I were like you," he is saying, "I would know true happiness."
5. correct

Writing Application

Possible response: If I were mayor of my town, I would eliminate traffic on Main Street. There are too many vehicles and not enough room for pedestrians. If it were my job, I would make sure there were more public walkways.

Integrate Language Skills

❶ Vocabulary Development Lesson

Word Analysis: Latin Root *-puls-*

The Latin root *-puls-* means "push or drive." It is the base of some common words that are also used for scientific concepts. Write the letter of the definition for each numbered word, using a dictionary if needed.

1. pulse
2. compulsion
3. repulse
4. impulse
5. expulsion

a. to drive back or repel
b. a forcing out
c. brief increase in voltage or current
d. change in momentum
e. irresistible inclination

Spelling Strategy

The ending *-ity* is more common than *-ety*, which is used to avoid two *i*'s in a row, as in *satiety*. In your notebook, correctly complete these words.

1. simplic__ 2. soci__ 3. notori__

Concept Development: Synonyms and Antonyms

Antonyms are words that are opposite in meaning. For each vocabulary word, write the letter of its antonym in your notebook. Then, provide a synonym—a word with nearly the same meaning—for the word. Check the meanings of the word, the antonym, and the synonym in a dictionary. Explain any differences in meaning.

1. visage
2. vernal
3. blithe
4. sepulcher
5. profuse
6. verge
7. satiety
8. impulse

a. careworn
b. scarce
c. hunger
d. center
e. back
f. cradle
g. restraint
h. wintry

❷ Grammar and Style Lesson

Subjunctive Mood

To express a wish or a condition contrary to fact, you must use a verb in the **subjunctive mood.** The past subjunctive form of *be* is *were*, used whether the subject is singular or plural.

Example: If I were a swift cloud to fly with thee; . . . (contrary to fact)

For Romantic poets like Shelley, the subjunctive was a useful tool for expressing ideals and hopes. It allows writers to imagine and describe what is not currently true, but what they hope might one day be true.

Practice Copy the following sentences, and correct any verbs that require the subjunctive mood.

1. The speaker addressed the skylark.
2. He wishes that he was more like the bird.
3. He thinks that if he was a skylark, he would not know pain.
4. "If I was like you," he is saying, "I would know true happiness."
5. He was certain that the bird was happy.

Writing Application Using the subjunctive at least twice, describe something that you would like to change.

WG *Prentice Hall Writing and Grammar Connection: Chapter 21, Section 3*

TEACHING RESOURCES

The following resources can be used to enrich or extend the instruction for pp. 742–743.

Vocabulary

Selection Support: Build Vocabulary, p. 155

Vocabulary and Spelling Practice Book (Use this booklet for skills enrichment.)

Grammar

Selection Support: Grammar and Style, p. 156

Writing and Grammar, Diamond Level, p. 548

Daily Language Practice Transparencies ■

Writing

Writing and Grammar, Diamond Level, p. 286 ■

Writing and Grammar iText CD-ROM

Writing Models and Graphic Organizers on Transparencies, pp. 131–134

■ **BLOCK SCHEDULING:** Resources marked with this symbol provide varied instruction during 90-minute blocks.

❸ Writing Lesson

Introductory Background on a Poem

Even in his lyric poetry, Shelley drew on the science and historical research of his time, as when he writes on the west wind. Write an introduction to one of his poems in which you explain the scientific or historical research that inspired him.

Prewriting Select a poem, and make a list of questions to guide your research on its background. For each specific question you generate, write two questions about related, general information. Find answers to your questions, using library or Internet sources.

Model: Generating Questions to Identify Necessary Background

Did Shelley base "Ozymandias" on actual ruins?
RELATED BACKGROUND:
1. With what ancient ruins were English people of the day acquainted?
2. How much did English historians of the time know about the ancient past? About other regions of the world?

By adding questions on background information to the first question, the writer ensures that readers will gain a good understanding of Shelley's inspiration and interests.

Drafting Begin with an overview of Shelley's poem. Then, discuss the scientific or historical research that influenced it. Conclude with your list of sources.

Revising Make sure the order of ideas in your draft is logical. Rearrange topics if necessary to ensure that readers will get necessary background information as they need it, not afterwards.

WG *Prentice Hall Writing and Grammar Connection: Chapter 13, Section 3*

❹ Extension Activities

Listening and Speaking Present a **weather report** for radio or television on the conditions in "Ode to the West Wind." Use appropriate language as follows:

1. Standard American English for clarity
2. Technical language for precision
3. Informal expressions to engage your audience

Prepare your report, including a weather map, and present it to the class.

Research and Technology With a group, present a **cultural report** on Romantic painter John Constable's work. Conduct research to find information on his art; link his work to Romantic poetry; and find reproductions of his work. Each group member should present a section of the report to the class. **[Group Activity]**

Take It to the Net www.phschool.com

Go online for an additional research activity using the Internet.

❸ Writing Lesson

- Review with students how Shelley drew on the scientific and historical research of his time in writing about the west wind. Explain that in this lesson, they will write an introductory background on a poem.
- Use the Writing Lesson to guide students in developing their introductory backgrounds.
- Suggest that they use the Context Chart in the **Writing Models and Graphic Organizers on Transparencies,** pp. 131–134, to help them identify neccessary backgrounds.
- Use the Research: Historical Investigation rubric in **Performance Assessment and Portfolio Management,** p. 13, to evaluate students' introductory backgrounds.

❹ Listening and Speaking

- Read the Listening and Speaking lesson as a class, then encourage students to review weather reports on television or the radio before they prepare their reports.
- Remind students that their weather reports should reflect the conditions in "Ode to the West Wind."
- Encourage them to use technical language for precision.

CUSTOMIZE INSTRUCTION For Universal Access

To address different learning styles, use the activities suggested in the **Extension Activities** booklet, p. 34.

- For Bodily/Kinesthetic Learners, use Activity 5.
- For Musical/Rhythmic Learners, use Activity 6.

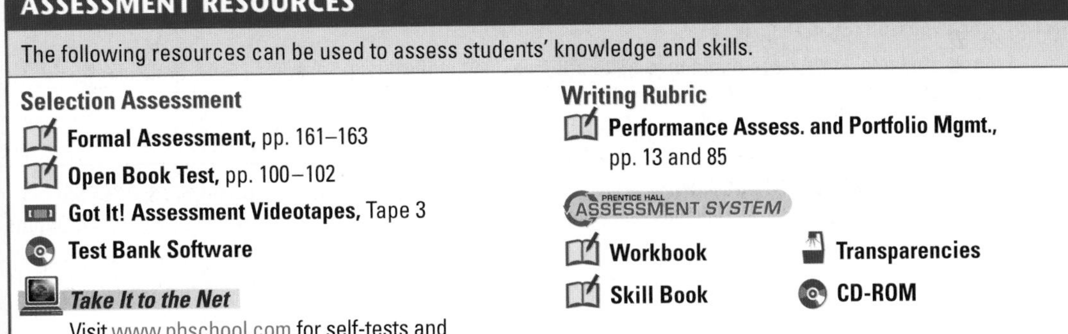

ASSESSMENT RESOURCES

The following resources can be used to assess students' knowledge and skills.

Selection Assessment

- **Formal Assessment,** pp. 161–163
- **Open Book Test,** pp. 100–102
- **Got It! Assessment Videotapes,** Tape 3
- **Test Bank Software**

Take It to the Net
Visit www.phschool.com for self-tests and additional questions on the selections.

Writing Rubric

- **Performance Assess. and Portfolio Mgmt.,** pp. 13 and 85

PRENTICE HALL ASSESSMENT SYSTEM

- **Workbook**
- **Skill Book**
- **Transparencies**
- **CD-ROM**

Poetry of John Keats

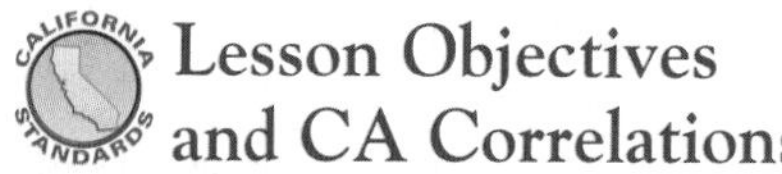

Lesson Objectives and CA Correlations

1. **To analyze and respond to literary elements**
   - Literary Analysis: The Ode **R 3.1**
   - Comparing Literary Works **R 3.2**
2. **To read, comprehend, analyze, and critique a poem**
   - Reading Strategy: Paraphrasing
   - Reading Check Questions
   - Review and Assess Questions
   - Assessment Practice (ATE)
3. **To develop word analysis skills, fluency, and systematic vocabulary**
   - Vocabulary Development Lesson: Word Analysis: Latin Suffix *-age* **R 1.1**
4. **To understand and apply written and oral English language conventions**
   - Spelling Strategy **LC 1.2**
   - Grammar and Style Lesson: Direct Address **LC 1.1**
5. **To understand and apply appropriate writing and research strategies**
   - Writing Lesson: Response to Criticism **W 2.2**
   - Extension Activity: Science Display **W 1.6**
6. **To understand and apply listening and speaking strategies**
   - Extension Activity: Oral Report

STEP-BY-STEP TEACHING GUIDE	PACING GUIDE
PRETEACH	
Motivate Students and Provide Background	
Use the Motivation activity (ATE p. 744)	5 min.
Read and discuss author and background features (SE pp. 744, 747, 750; ATE p. 744) [A]	5 min.
Introduce the Concepts	
Introduce the Literary Analysis and Reading Strategy concepts (SE/ATE p. 745) [A]	15 min.
Pronounce the vocabulary words and read their definitions (SE p. 745)	5 min.
TEACH	
Monitor Comprehension	
Informally monitor comprehension by circulating while students read independently or in groups [A]	15 min.
Monitor students' comprehension with the Reading Check notes (SE/ATE pp. 747, 751, 755)	as students read
Develop vocabulary with Vocabulary notes (SE pp. 747, 748, 750, 752; ATE p. 750)	as students read
Develop Understanding	
Develop students' understanding of the ode with the Literary Analysis annotations (SE/ATE pp. 751, 753, 755, 756) [A]	5 min.
Develop students' ability to paraphrase with the Reading Strategy annotations (SE/ATE pp. 747, 750, 752)	5 min.
ASSESS	
Assess Mastery	
Assess students' mastery of the Reading Strategy and Literary Analysis concepts by having them answer the Review and Assess questions (SE/ATE p. 757)	15 min.
Use one or more of the print and media Assessment Resources (ATE p. 759) [A]	up to 45 min.
EXTEND	
Apply Understanding	
Have students complete the Vocabulary Development Lesson and the Grammar and Style Lesson (SE p. 758) [A]	20 min.
Apply students' knowledge of responding to criticism using the Writing Lesson (SE/ATE p. 759) [A]	45 min.
Apply students' understanding using one or more of the Extension Activities (SE p. 759)	20–90 min.

ACCELERATED INSTRUCTION:
Use the strategies and activities identified with an [A].

UNIVERSAL ACCESS
● = Below-Level Students
▲ = On-Level Students
■ = Above-Level Students

Time and Resource Manager

Reading Level: Average, Average, Challenging, Challenging
Average Number of Instructional Days: 4

RESOURCES		
PRINT	**TRANSPARENCIES**	**TECHNOLOGY**
• **Beyond Literature,** Humanities Connection: Greek Art, p. 35 ▲ ■		• **Interest Grabber Videos,** Tape 4 ● ▲ ■
• **Selection Support Workbook:** ● ▲ ■ Literary Analysis, p. 162 Reading Strategy, p. 161 Build Vocabulary, p. 159	• **Literary Analysis and Reading Transparencies,** pp. 69 and 70 ● ▲ ■	
• **Adapted Reader's Companion** ● • **Reader's Companion** ● • **Authors In Depth,** The British Tradition, p. 144 ■		• **Listening to Literature** ● ▲ ■ Audiocassettes, Side 18 Audio CDs, CD 11
• **English Learner's Companion** ● ▲ • **Literary Analysis for Enrichment** ■	• **Fine Art Transparencies, Volume 1,** Art Transparency 10 ● ▲ ■	
• **Formal Assessment:** Selection Test, pp. 164–166 ● ▲ ■ • **Open Book Test,** pp. 103–105 ● ▲ ■ • **Performance Assessment and Portfolio Management** ● ▲ ■ • PRENTICE HALL ASSESSMENT SYSTEM ● ▲ ■	• PRENTICE HALL ASSESSMENT SYSTEM ● ▲ ■ • **Skills Practice Answers and Explanations on Transparencies**	• **Test Bank Software** ● ▲ ■ • **Got It! Assessment Videotapes,** Tape 3 ● ▲
• **Selection Support Workbook:** ● ▲ ■ Grammar and Style, p. 160 • **Writing and Grammar,** Diamond Level ● ▲ ■ • **Extension Activities,** p. 35 ● ▲ ■	• **Daily Language Practice Transparencies** ● ▲ • **Writing Models and Graphic Organizers on Transparencies,** pp. 123–126 ● ▲ ■	• **Writing and Grammar iText CD-ROM** ● ▲ ■ ***Take It to the Net*** www.phschool.com

BLOCK SCHEDULING: Use one 90-minute class period to preteach the selections and have students read them. Use a second 90-minute class period to assess students' mastery of skills and have them complete one of the Extension Activities.

PREETEACH

Step-by-Step Teaching Guide for pp. 744–745

Motivation

Invite students to bring in recordings of favorite songs that they believe define truth and beauty. Play selected recordings. Discuss how contemporary views of truth and beauty compare with those of a nineteenth-century poet.

Interest Grabber Video

As an alternative, play "'On First Looking Into Chapman's Homer': Reading and Student Response" on Tape 4 to engage student interest.

❶ Background

More About the Author

The grief Keats experienced at the death of his brother Tom was magnified by the early deaths of his parents. Keats's father, the manager of a livery stable in Moorfields, died when the poet was eight. His mother remarried, but died of tuberculosis when the poet was 14.

The frosty critical reception Keats's early works received may have been as much the result of class snobbery as a genuine reaction to his art. As a Londoner of humble origin, Keats was lumped with writers like William Hazlitt and Leigh Hunt in the "Cockney School of Poetry," a derisive term that emphasized the writers' ethnic background over their individual talents. Many of the attacks on Keats were published in *Blackwood's Magazine* and included a snipe at his death that he was a man who "had left a decent calling [pharmacy] for the melancholy trade of Cockney-poetry."

Prepare to Read

❶ Poetry of John Keats

John Keats (1795–1821)

Those who leave a lasting imprint on the world do not always live long. When the life of a groundbreaking figure is cut short, it leaves the world asking, What more might this person have achieved, if only he or she had lived longer? John Keats is such a figure. Although he died at age twenty-five, Keats left his indelible mark on literature, and this makes us wonder what more he might have accomplished had he lived longer.

A Defender of Worthy Causes Unlike his contemporaries Byron and Shelley, John Keats was not an aristocrat. Instead, he was born to working-class Londoners. As a child, he received attention for his striking good looks and his restless spirit. Keats developed a reputation for fighting, but always for a worthy cause. It was not until he and his schoolmaster's son, Charles Cowden Clarke, became friends that Keats developed an interest in poetry and became an avid reader.

From Medicine to Poetry In 1815, Keats began studying medicine at a London hospital. He had already begun writing poetry, but he earned his pharmacist's license before abandoning medicine for the literary world. In 1818, he published his first major work, *Endymion*, a long poem that the critics panned. Their negative reviews were due in part to Keats's association with the radical writer Leigh Hunt. The reviews also reflected the uneven quality of the verse itself. Despite the critical rejection, Keats did not swerve from his new career. Instead, he began writing the second of his long poems, *Hyperion*, a work he was never to complete.

A Year of Sorrow and Joy The year 1818 was significant for Keats in other ways as well. He lost his brother Tom to tuberculosis, but he also met the light of his life, Fanny Brawne, to whom he became engaged. The next year, 1819, was a period of feverish creativity. In just nine months, fired by grief, new-found love, and his own encroaching illness, Keats wrote the poems for which he is most famous, including "The Eve of St. Agnes," "La Belle Dame sans Merci," and his odes. Each is recognized as a masterpiece.

An Early Death Keats's engagement to Fanny and his burst of creativity might have been the prelude to a happy, productive life. Instead, Keats found his health deteriorating. Recognizing that like his brother, he had tuberculosis, Keats moved to Italy, hoping that the warmer climate would reverse the disease. Sadly, that hope proved false, and, in 1821, his battle with tuberculosis ended with his death. Keats wrote his own epitaph, which stresses the brevity of his life: "Here lies one whose name was writ in water."

A Legacy of Beauty Despite his early death and the fact that he composed his most important works in the space of just two years, John Keats remains one of the major influences in English poetry. Although he knew Percy Bysshe Shelley, he did not share Shelley's rebellious spirit, nor did he believe in using poetry for political statements. Keats worked as a pure artist who labored under the banner of beauty. He found in beauty the highest value our imperfect world could offer, and he put its pursuit at the center of his poetry. In masterful verse, he explored the beauty he found in the most ordinary circumstances.

At the same time, Keats was profoundly sensitive to the deep contradictions of life—of the sadness that every joy contains and the emptiness of every fulfillment. Although his best-remembered line is "'Beauty is truth, truth beauty,'" the poem in which it appears, "Ode on a Grecian Urn," implicitly contrasts the frozen world of a painted scene with the world of change and decay in which we live. For Keats, striving after what can never be attained was perhaps the true poetic task.

TEACHING RESOURCES

The following resources can be used to enrich or extend the instruction for pp. 744–745.

Motivation

Interest Grabber Video, Tape 4

Background

Beyond Literature, p. 35

Take It to the Net

Visit www.phschool.com for background and hotlinks for the selections.

Literary Analysis

Literary Analysis and Reading Transparencies, The Ode, p. 70

Reading

Literary Analysis and Reading Transparencies, Paraphrasing, p. 69

Selection Support: Reading Strategy, p. 161; Build Vocabulary, p. 159

BLOCK SCHEDULING: Resources marked with this symbol provide varied instruction during 90-minute blocks.

Preview

Connecting to the Literature

Fleeting moments, such as a beautiful sunset or a special smile, can linger in your memory. Keats explores such moments in his poems.

❷ Literary Analysis

The Ode

An **ode** is a lyric poem, characterized by heightened emotion, that pays respect to a person or thing, usually directly addressed by the speaker.

- The **Pindaric ode** (named for the ancient Greek poet Pindar) falls in groups of three stanzas, one of which differs in form from the other two. Pindar's odes celebrated victors at the Olympic Games.
- Roman poets later developed the **Horatian ode** (also called homostrophic), which contains only one type of stanza.
- The **irregular ode** has no set pattern.

Keats created his own form of the ode, using ten-line stanzas of iambic pentameter (lines containing ten beats with a repeated pattern of weak-strong). Often those stanzas begin with a heroic quatrain (four lines rhymed *abab*) followed by a sestet (six lines rhymed in various ways). Note the various forms of Keats's odes.

Comparing Literary Works

In his odes, Keats follows the tradition of paying respect to something. Yet his odes reveal as much about him as they do about his subjects. In "Ode to a Nightingale," for instance, Keats finds himself caught by his longing for ideal beauty—a longing he cannot fulfill in real life. As you read, compare how each work dramatizes a conflict in the speaker. Analyze how the conflict is brought on by longings for what is far away.

❸ Reading Strategy

Paraphrasing

Paraphrasing, or restating text in your own words, is a useful aid to understanding any difficult work. Using a chart like the one shown here, paraphrase difficult parts of each of Keats's poems.

Original
"When I have fears that I may cease to be . . ."
Paraphrase

Vocabulary Development

ken (ken) *n.* range of sight or knowledge (p. 747)

surmise (sər mīz′) *n.* guess; assumption (p. 747)

gleaned (glēnd) *v.* collected from bit by bit, as when gathering stray grain after a harvest (p. 748)

teeming (tēm′ iŋ) *adj.* filled to overflowing (p. 748)

vintage (vin′ tij) *n.* wine of fine quality (p. 750)

requiem (rek′ wē əm) *n.* musical composition honoring the dead (p. 752)

❷ Literary Analysis

The Ode

- Tell students that in this lesson they will focus on the ode, a lyric poem that exhibits heightened emotion, pays homage to a thing or person, and usually directly addresses that person or thing.
- Explain that the Pindaric ode was popularized by the Greek poet Pindar and consisted of groups of three stanzas. The Horatian ode, named after the Roman poet Horace, contains only one type of stanza. Irregular odes have no set pattern.
- Tell students that Keats created his own ode, using ten-line stanzas of iambic pentameter, many of which begin with a heroic quatrain and end with sestet rhymed in various ways.
- Use the Ode transparency in **Literary Analysis and Reading Transparencies,** p. 70, to help students distinguish between Pindaric, Horatian, and irregular odes.

❸ Reading Strategy

Paraphrasing

- Remind students that paraphrasing is restating a text in their own words.
- Explain that by paraphrasing they can understand difficult passages.
- Have students practice the skill of paraphrasing using the Paraphrasing transparency in **Literary Analysis and Reading Transparencies,** p. 69.

Vocabulary Development

- Pronounce each vocabulary word for students, and read the definitions as a class. Have students identify any words with which they are already familiar.

CUSTOMIZE INSTRUCTION FOR UNIVERSAL ACCESS

For Special Needs Students	For Less Proficient Readers	For English Learners
Have students read the adapted version of "Ode on a Grecian Urn" in the **Adapted Reader's Companion.** This version provides basic-level instruction in an interactive format with questions and write-on lines. Completing the adapted version will prepare students to read the selection in the Student Edition.	Have students read "Ode on a Grecian Urn" in the **Reader's Companion.** This version provides basic-level instruction in an interactive format with questions and write-on lines. After students finish the selection in the Reader's Companion, have them complete the questions and activities in the Student Edition.	Have students read the adapted version of "Ode on a Grecian Urn" in the **English Learner's Companion.** This version provides basic-level instruction in an interactive format with questions and write-on lines. Completing the adapted version will prepare students to read the selection in the Student Edition.

 ***E-Teach***

Visit E-Teach at www.phschool.com for teachers' essays on how to teach, with questions and answers.

TEACH

Step-by-Step Teaching Guide for pp. 746–756

CUSTOMIZE INSTRUCTION
For Interpersonal Learners

Review with students the lesson on Direct Address. Suggest that students read each poem as if it addressed them. How does it make them feel? What thoughts does it evoke?

❶ About the Selection

"On First Looking into Chapman's Homer" celebrates Chapman's translation of Homer's *Iliad* and *Odyssey,* which gives Keats illuminating new insights into the literature. The octave, with its formal diction and archaic words, suggests the dignified antiquity of classical poetry. The sestet, in contrast, uses simple language to convey the immediacy and excitement of discovery.

❷ Background

Art

Frontispiece, Homer's Iliad and Odyssey, William Hole

This engraving depicts the frontispiece, or page opposite the title page, of the book that inspired Keats's sonnet.

Englishman William Hole is best known for his sheet music engravings, authors' portraits, and title pages such as the one shown here. Classical allusions are the main component to the engraving, with a laurel-crowned Homer as the central image. Use this question for discussion:

What elements of this engraving reflect Keats's approach to Homer?
Answer: The formal composition is reminiscent of Keats's dignified language.

❶ ON FIRST LOOKING INTO CHAPMAN'S HOMER

John Keats

❷ 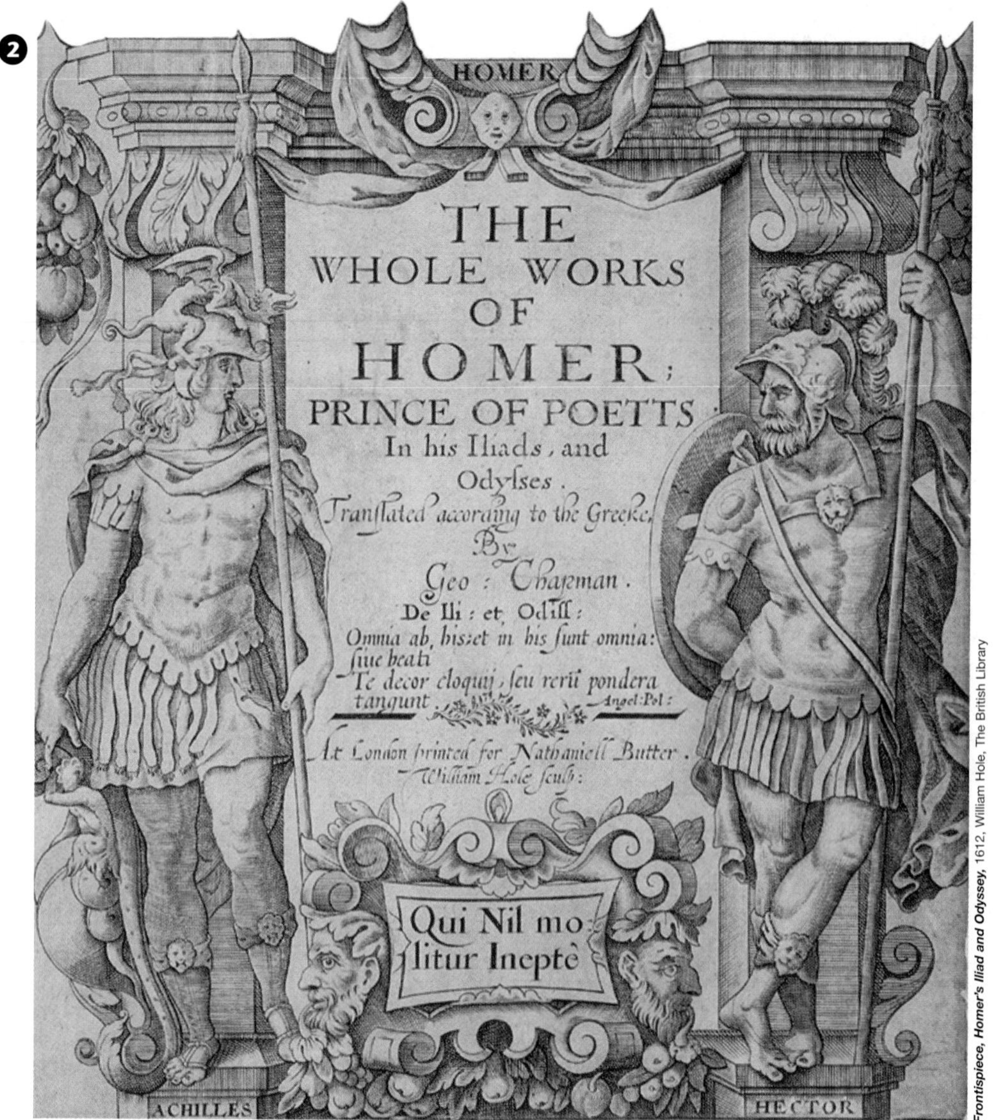

Frontispiece, Homer's Iliad and Odyssey, 1612, William Hole, The British Library

TEACHING RESOURCES

The following resources can be used to enrich or extend the instruction for pp. 746–756.

Literary Analysis

- **Selection Support:** Literary Analysis, p. 162

Reading

- **Adapted Reader's Companion**
- **Reader's Companion**
- **English Learner's Companion**
- **Listening to Literature Audiocassettes,** Side 18 ▪
- **Listening to Literature Audio CDs,** CD 11 ▪

Extension

- **Authors In Depth,** The British Tradition, p. 144 (The collection includes nine additional selections by Keats.)
- **Fine Art Transparencies, Volume 1,** Art Transparency 10 (Have students compare what "Ode to a Nightingale" and *African Jazz Series # 5* by Michael Cummings suggest about music.)

▪ **BLOCK SCHEDULING:** Resources marked with this symbol provide varied instruction during 90-minute blocks.

Background

Romantic poets such as Byron, Shelley, and Keats admired the culture of ancient Greece and derived inspiration from its art and literature. Keats's "Ode on a Grecian Urn" (p. 754), for instance, shows his tendency to associate ideas about beauty with antiquities, such as the beautifully adorned vases that ancient Greek society produced.

When Keats was twenty-one, his friend and former schoolmate, Charles Cowden Clarke, introduced him to a translation of Homer by Elizabethan poet George Chapman. The two men spent the evening reading this book, and early the next morning Keats presented this sonnet to Clarke.

Much have I traveled in the realms of gold,
    And many goodly states and kingdoms seen;
    Round many western islands have I been
Which bards in fealty to Apollo[1] hold.
Oft of one wide expanse had I been told
    That deep-browed Homer ruled as his demesne;[2]
    Yet did I never breathe its pure serene[3]
Till I heard Chapman speak out loud and bold:
Then felt I like some watcher of the skies
    When a new planet swims into his ken;
Or like stout Cortez[4] when with eagle eyes
    He stared at the Pacific—and all his men
Looked at each other with a wild surmise—
    Silent, upon a peak in Darien.[5]

Reading Strategy
Paraphrasing Paraphrase lines 5–6, paying special attention to the metaphor of a "demesne."

ken (ken) *n.* range of sight or knowledge

surmise (sər mīz′) *n.* guess; assumption

1. **Apollo** in Greek and Roman mythology, the god of music, poetry, and medicine.
2. **demesne** (di mān′) realm.
3. **serene** clear air.
4. **Cortez** Here, Keats was mistaken. The Pacific was discovered in 1513 by Balboa, not Cortez.
5. **Darien** (der′ ē ən) the Isthmus of Panama.

4 
To what kind of things does Keats compare Chapman's translation?

5 **Critical Viewing** From the design of the engraving, what would you predict about the nature of the work to which Keats is reacting? **[Predict]**

3 Reading Strategy

Paraphrasing

- Have students read the bracketed passage to themselves.
- Review with students how to paraphrase, putting phrases or ideas into their own words.
- Then, ask the Reading Strategy question on p. 747: Paraphrase lines 5–6, paying special attention to the metaphor of a "demesne." **Answer:** I'd heard a lot about Homer's works as I "traveled" through the "kingdoms" of poets (read their works), and I understood that Homer was superior to all others in his poetry.

4 Reading Check

Answer: Keats compares reading an excellent new translation to the discovery of a planet or to the discovery of a new land.

5 Critical Viewing

Answer: Students may predict that the book deals with wars and warriors in ancient times.

CUSTOMIZE INSTRUCTION FOR UNIVERSAL ACCESS

For Special Needs Students	For Less Proficient Readers	For Advanced Readers
Have students consider the frontispiece from "On First Looking into Chapman's Homer" and remind them that Keats's poem is about his reaction to reading a translation of the ancient Greek poet Homer. Play Side 18 of **Listening to Literature Audiocassettes** and have students read along silently.	Remind students that the poem was the speaker's response to a work of literature. Help students to read the poem, noting Keats's extended metaphor of discovery. Play "'On First Looking into Chapman's Homer': Reading and Student Response" on **Interest Grabber Videos,** Tape 4. Then, discuss students' reactions to the poem.	Review with students how in "On First Looking into Chapman's Homer," Keats writes a ringing tribute to a book that moved him greatly, comparing himself to the discoverer of a great new world. Have students choose books that have moved them and write tributes about the books' effects on them.

❻ About the Selection

The speaker expresses fears that he will not live to fulfill his potential. This lyric is particularly poignant because Keats died less than three years after he wrote it.

Answers for p. 748

1. **(a)** The speaker has extensively traveled the world. **(b)** These lines encourage the reader to accept the speaker's reaction to Chapman's translation of Homer, because the speaker is well-read.
2. **(a)** They convey excitement and wonder. **(b)** The comparison of reading to a journey supports these feelings, because journeys are usually full of delight at the discovery of new, unimagined worlds.
3. **(a)** The speaker fears dying before he has written a great deal. **(b)** He is concerned about missing his beloved. **(c)** The last lines do not resolve the fears, but the speaker annihilates them by thinking until they seem unimportant.
4. Keats's character is pensive and extremely intelligent.
5. Possible response: Youth today face more clear-cut responsibilities and limited opportunities than in Keats's day because of the nature of work and the economy. These facts may make them more anxious but less thrilled.

❻ When I Have Fears That I May Cease to Be

John Keats

When I have fears that I may cease to be
    Before my pen has gleaned my teeming brain,
Before high-piled books, in charactery,[1]
    Hold like rich garners[2] the full ripened grain;
When I behold, upon the night's starred face,
    Huge cloudy symbols of a high romance,
And think that I may never live to trace
    Their shadows, with the magic hand of chance;
And when I feel, fair creature of an hour,
    That I shall never look upon thee more,
Never have relish in the fairy power
    Of unreflecting love—then on the shore
Of the wide world I stand alone, and think
Till love and fame to nothingness do sink.

gleaned (glēnd) *v.* collected from bit by bit, as when gathering stray grain after a harvest

teeming (tēm′ iŋ) *adj.* filled to overflowing

1. **charactery** written or printed letters of the alphabet.
2. **garners** storehouses for grain.

Review and Assess

Thinking About the Selections

1. **(a) Recall:** In the first four lines of "Chapman's Homer," what has the speaker done? **(b) Infer:** How do these lines encourage the reader to take the speaker's experience of Homer seriously?
2. **(a) Connect:** What feelings about Chapman's translation do lines 9–14 convey? **(b) Draw Conclusions:** How does the comparison of reading to a journey support these feelings?
3. **(a) Recall:** In lines 1–4 of "When I Have Fears," what does the speaker fear he will not accomplish before he dies? **(b) Interpret:** In lines 5–12, what is he concerned about missing? **(c) Evaluate:** Do the last lines offer a convincing resolution to such fears? Explain.
4. **Draw Conclusions:** What words describe Keats's character as revealed in these two poems?
5. **Apply:** Are young people today as anxious about and thrilled by the future as Keats? Explain.

7

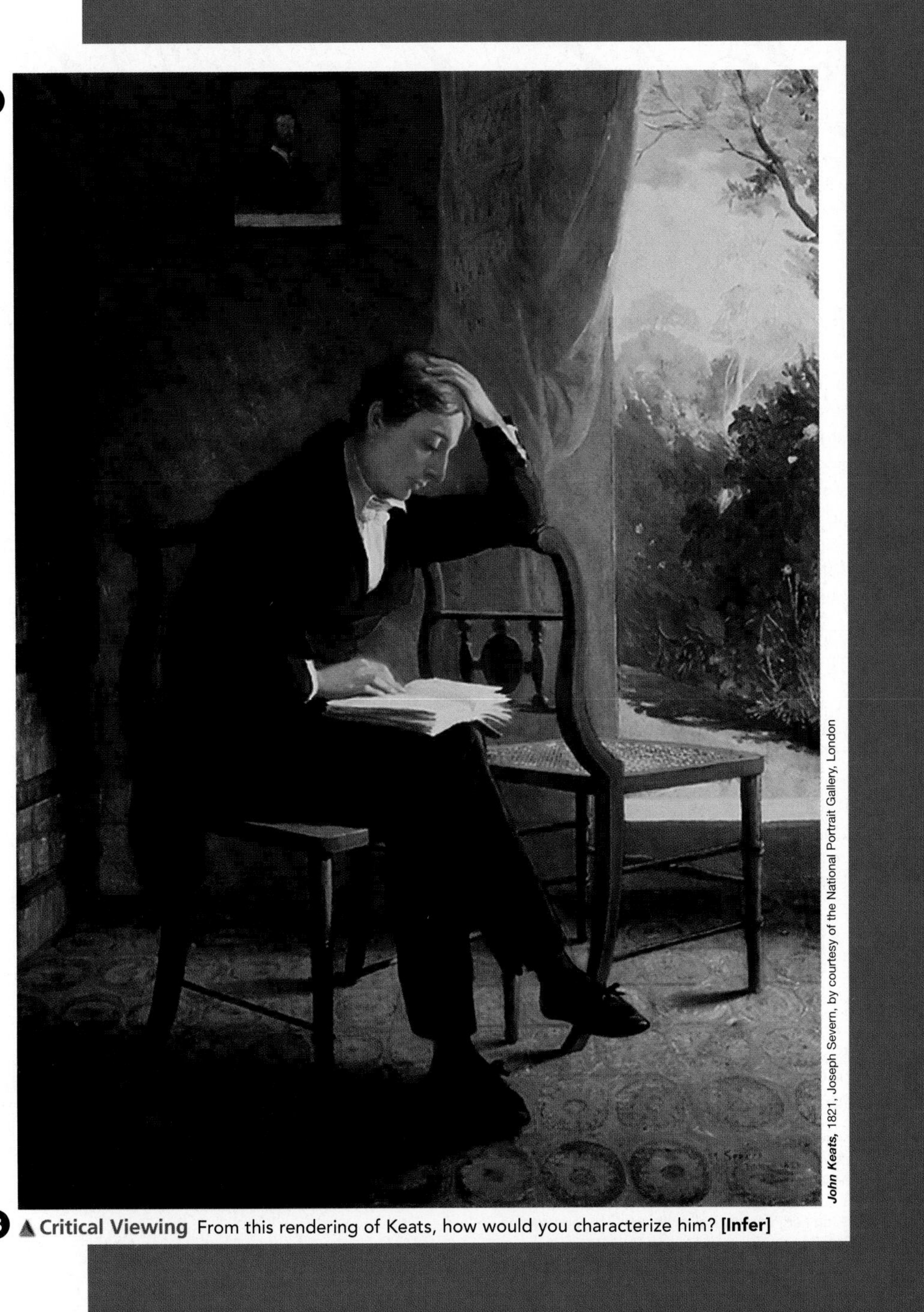

John Keats, 1821, Joseph Severn, by courtesy of the National Portrait Gallery, London

8 ▲ **Critical Viewing** From this rendering of Keats, how would you characterize him? **[Infer]**

7 Background

Art

John Keats, Joseph Severn

This painting portrays poet John Keats in a moment of sadness and perhaps doubt.

Joseph Severn, in whose arms Keats died in 1821, was born and raised in England. After apprenticing to a royal engraver and studying at the Royal Academy, Severn risked his connection to the academy to travel to Italy with the ailing Keats. He created this painting after Keats's death, basing it on a moment observed just after the writing of "Ode to a Nightingale" and using memory and masks made of Keats's face both before and after his death. Use these questions for discussion:

1. What elements of the painting suggest a mood appropriate to "When I Have Fears That I May Cease to Be"?
   Answer: Keats's despondent expression and posture and the dark and somber colors of the carpet and walls create an atmosphere of sadness and doubt.
2. How does the painting's composition reflect the themes of the poem?
   Answer: As in the poem, Keats is shown isolated with his thoughts while the bright world beckons from outside.

8 ▶Critical Viewing

Answer: Students may say that Keats is serious, contemplative, moody.

CUSTOMIZE INSTRUCTION FOR UNIVERSAL ACCESS

For Less Proficient Readers	For English Learners	For Gifted/Talented Students
Guide students as they read the poem. Remind them that the speaker in the poem is exploring his own fears of dying. Have students write letters—in the voice of Keats—in which they explain the nature of their fears. Students may want to read the author's biography on p. 744 before they begin.	Students may find the language and imagistic thoughts in the poem difficult to decode and "translate." Encourage students to paraphrase any difficult ideas and to use the footnotes for additional context. Students who have difficulty with Keats's vocabulary can use the **English Learner's Companion.**	Have students read "When I Have Fears That I May Cease to Be" aloud quietly to themselves several times, listening carefully to the rhythm and meter. Tell students that they should perform the poem as a song or spoken-word piece, using melody and/or rhythm that is sensitive to the poem's rhythms and sounds.

9 About the Selection

This poem captures what Keats termed "negative capability"—the capacity of a poet to negate himself or herself and enter fully into his or her subject so as to represent it with an especially rich and vibrant objectivity. In this case, the speaker subsumes himself into the joyous nightingale and so transcends the pain of the mortal world.

10 Vocabulary Development

Latin Suffix *-age*

- Call students' attention to *vintage,* which means "wine of a fine quality." Explain that *vintage* contains the Latin suffix *-age,* which means "state or quality of," "amount of," "cost of," "place of," or "collection of."
- Have students suggest other words and phrases that contain this Latin suffix and list them on the chalkboard.
  Possible responses: *equipage, mirage, barrage*

11 Reading Strategy

Paraphrasing

- Have students read the bracketed passage to themselves.
- Ask the Reading Strategy question on p. 750: Restate lines 11–14 in your own words.
  Answer: Oh, for a sip of wine that has been chilled over time in a cellar, tasting of flowers, the country, dance, and song, and happiness of the sun!

9 Ode to a Nightingale

John Keats

Background

Keats composed the following ode in 1819, while living in Hampstead with his friend Charles Brown. Brown wrote the following description about how the ode was composed: "In the spring of 1819 a nightingale had built her nest near my house. Keats felt a tranquil and continued joy in her song; and one morning he took his chair from the breakfast table to the grass plot under the plum tree, where he sat for two or three hours. When he came into the house, I perceived he had some scraps of paper in his hand, and these he was quietly thrusting behind the books. On inquiry, I found those scraps, four or five in number, contained his poetic feeling on the song of our nightingale."

I

My heart aches, and drowsy numbness pains
My sense, as though of hemlock[1] I had drunk,
Or emptied some dull opiate to the drains
One minute past, and Lethe-wards[2] had sunk:
'Tis not through envy of thy happy lot,
But being too happy in thine happiness,—
That thou, light-wingèd Dryad[3] of the trees,
In some melodious plot
Of beechen green, and shadows numberless,
Singest of summer in full-throated ease.

II

O, for a draft[4] of vintage! that hath been 10
Cooled a long age in the deep-delved earth,
Tasting of Flora[5] and the country green,

vintage (vin' tij) *n.* wine of fine quality

Reading Strategy
Paraphrasing Restate lines 11–14 in your own words.

1. **hemlock** poisonous herb.
2. **Lethe-wards** toward Lethe, the river of forgetfulness in Hades, the underworld, in classical mythology.
3. **Dryad** (drī' əd) in classical mythology, a wood nymph.
4. **draft** drink.
5. **Flora** in classical mythology, the goddess of flowers, or the flowers themselves.

ENRICHMENT: Cultural Connection

Birds in Song and Story

Like poets, musicians and storytellers have long been inspired by the beautiful calls of songbirds. In many cultures, bird flight and birdsong are associated with freedom from material concerns. In Japanese haiku, the nightingale is a symbol invoking spring. Some well-known examples of tunes, poems, and folktales involving songbirds are Charlie "Bird" Parker's "Ornithology," Hans Christian Andersen's "The Emperor's Nightingale," Yeats's "Sailing to Byzantium," Oscar Wilde's "The Nightingale and the Rose," Wallace Stevens's "Thirteen Ways of Looking at a Blackbird," and Robert Frost's "Never Again Would Birds' Song Be the Same."

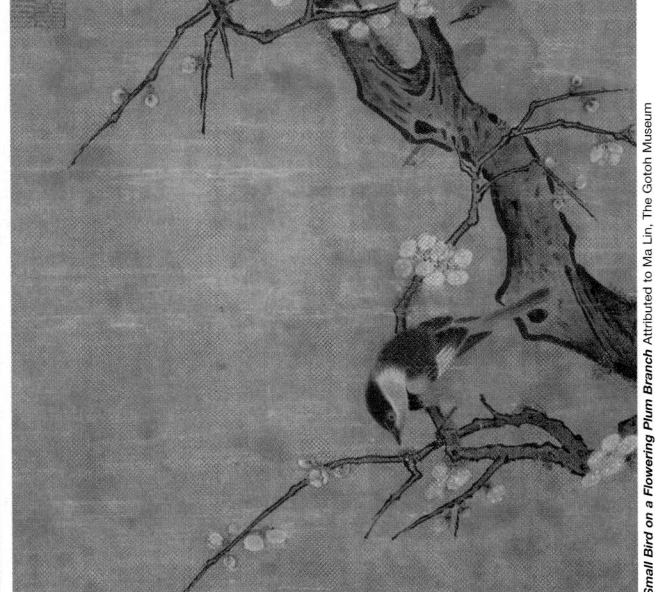

Small Bird on a Flowering Plum Branch Attributed to Ma Lin, The Gotoh Museum

Dance, and Provençal[6] song, and sunburnt mirth!
O for a beaker full of the warm South,
Full of the true, the blushful Hippocrene,[7]
With beaded bubbles winking at the brim,
And purple-stained mouth;
That I might drink, and leave the world unseen,
And with thee fade away into the forest dim:

III

Fade far away, dissolve, and quite forget
What thou among the leaves hast never known,
The weariness, the fever, and the fret
Here, where men sit and hear each other groan;
Where palsy shakes a few, sad, last gray hairs,
Where youth grows pale, and specter-thin, and dies;[8]
Where but to think is to be full of sorrow
And leaden-eyed despairs,

6. **Provencal** (prō´ vən säl´) pertaining to Provence, a region in Southern France, renowned in the late Middle Ages for its troubadours, who composed and sang love songs.
7. **Hippocrene** (hip´ ō krēn´) in classical mythology, the fountain of the Muses on Mt. Helicon. From this fountain flowed the waters of inspiration.
8. **youth . . . dies** Keats is referring to his brother, Tom, who had died from tuberculosis the previous winter.

13 ▲ **Critical Viewing**
Compare the mood of this painting with that of stanza III. **[Compare and Contrast]**

Literary Analysis
The Ode Which sentiments in stanza III are more typical of Romantic than of traditional odes?

15 ✓**Reading Check**
What does the speaker wish to do along with the nightingale?

12 Background

Art

Small Bird on a Flowering Plum Branch, attributed to Ma Lin

This painting on silk depicts a bird similar to the poem's nightingale. Like Keats's nightingale, the bird is perched on a plum tree branch.

Ma Lin was a landscape painter of China's Sung Dynasty. The bird and flower were a favored Sung motif. The serenity of the scene suggests the freedom from earthly concerns for which the speaker longs in "Ode to a Nightingale." Use these questions for discussion:

What elements of beauty might Keats admire in this painting?
Answer: He might admire the simple composition of the bird and tree, the delicacy of the blossoms, and the contrast of blank background with subject.

13 ▶Critical Viewing

Answer: Students may say that the painting conveys a sense of serenity and timeless beauty that contrasts sharply with the suffering and lack of time described in stanza III.

14 Literary Analysis

The Ode

- Have volunteers read stanza III aloud.
- Remind students of the definition of an ode: a lyric poem characterized by heightened emotion that pays homage to a person or thing.
- Then ask the Literary Analysis question on p. 751: Which sentiments in stanza III are more typical of Romantic than of traditional odes?
Answer: Keats captures the fleeting experience of the passage of time on earth and preserves it by connecting it to what the nightingale "hast never known." By linking nature with personal experience in this fashion, Keats's ode is more Romantic than the Pindaric and Horatian odes, which are more formal and less personal.

15 ✓Reading Check

Answer: The speaker wishes to fade away with the nightingale into the forest.

CUSTOMIZE INSTRUCTION FOR UNIVERSAL ACCESS

For Special Needs Students	For Less Proficient Readers	For Advanced Readers
Students who have read "Ode to a Nightingale" in its entirety and reinforced various skills such as paraphrasing may still have difficulty with comprehension. Show students **Got It! Videotape** 3 to assess what information they have retained from their reading and to determine on what material from the poem they still need to focus.	Remind students that direct address of the subject is a feature of most odes. Review how Keats uses personification—or assigning human traits to the nightingale in this poem. Have students reread the poem and find examples of personification.	Have students do research on the figure of the nightingale as it appears in European and Asian art, music, and literature. Students should present their findings in an oral report in which they compare characterizations of the bird in other works with Keats's depiction.

16 Reading Strategy

Paraphrasing

- Have students read the bracketed passage to themselves.
- Then ask the Reading Strategy question on p. 752: Paraphrase stanza V in one or two sentences. **Answer:** I can't see what flowers surround me, what smell is in the air in the darkness; standing in the dark, I guess which blossoms are out in May.

Where Beauty cannot keep her lustrous eyes,
Or new Love pine at them beyond tomorrow.

IV

Away! away! for I will fly to thee,
Not charioted by Bacchus[9] and his pards,
But on the viewless[10] wings of Poesy,[11]
Though the dull brain perplexes and retards:
Already with thee! tender is the night,
And haply[12] the Queen-Moon is on her throne,
Clustered around by all her starry Fays;[13]
But here there is no light,
Save what from heaven is with the breezes blown
Through verdurous[14] glooms and winding mossy ways.

V

I cannot see what flowers are at my feet,
Nor what soft incense hangs upon the boughs,
But, in embalmed[15] darkness, guess each sweet
Wherewith the seasonable month endows
16 The grass, the thicket, and the fruit-tree wild;
White hawthorn, and the pastoral eglantine;[16]
Fast fading violets covered up in leaves;
And mid-May's eldest child,
The coming musk-rose, full of dewy wine,
The murmurous haunt of flies on summer eves.

VI

Darkling[17] I listen; and, for many a time
I have been half in love with easeful Death,
Called him soft names in many a mused[18] rhyme,
To take into the air my quiet breath;
Now more than ever seems it rich to die,
To cease upon the midnight with no pain,
While thou art pouring forth thy soul abroad
In such an ecstasy!
Still wouldst thou sing, and I have ears in vain—
To thy high requiem become a sod.

Reading Strategy
Paraphrasing Paraphrase stanza V in one or two sentences.

requiem (rek´ wē əm) *n.* musical composition honoring the dead

---

9. **Bacchus** (bak´ əs) in classical mythology, the god of wine, who was often represented in a chariot drawn by leopards ("pards").
10. **viewless** invisible.
11. **Poesy** poetic fancy.
12. **haply** perhaps.
13. **Fays** fairies.
14. **verdurous** green-foliaged.
15. **embalmed** perfumed.
16. **eglantine** (eg´ lən tīn´) sweetbrier or honeysuckle.
17. **Darkling** in the dark.
18. **mused** meditated.

VII

17

Thou wast not born for death, immortal Bird!
No hungry generations tread thee down;
The voice I hear this passing night was heard
In ancient days by emperor and clown:
Perhaps the selfsame song that found a path
Through the sad heart of Ruth,[19] when, sick for home,
She stood in tears amid the alien corn;
The same that ofttimes hath
Charmed magic casements, opening on the foam
Of perilous seas, in fairylands forlorn.

VIII

Forlorn! the very word is like a bell
To toll me back from thee to my sole self!
Adieu! the fancy cannot cheat so well
As she is famed[20] to do, deceiving elf.
Adieu! adieu! thy plaintive anthem fades
Past the near meadows, over the still stream,
Up the hillside; and now 'tis buried deep
In the next valley-glades:
Was it a vision, or a waking dream?
Fled is that music:—Do I wake or sleep?

19. **Ruth** in the Bible (Ruth 2:1–23), a widow who left her home and went to Judah to work in the corn (wheat) fields.
20. **famed** reported.

Literary Analysis
The Ode What element of traditional odes appears in verse VII?

Review and Assess

Thinking About the Selection

1. (a) **Recall:** How does the speaker describe his emotional state in stanza I? (b) **Infer:** What appears to have brought on this state?
2. (a) **Recall:** What wish does the speaker express in lines 19–20? (b) **Compare and Contrast:** What differences does he see between the bird's life and his own that cause him to wish this?
3. (a) **Analyze:** What is the viewpoint from which the speaker describes his surroundings in stanza V? (b) **Connect:** How does this viewpoint reflect the speaker's wish in line 21?
4. (a) **Analyze:** How does stanza VII "answer" stanza VI? (b) **Synthesize:** What similarity between death and immortality does the speaker imply?
5. **Make a Judgment:** By writing a poem full of extreme feeling, is Keats just being dramatic, or is writing such a poem a way of making peace with strong feelings? Explain.

17 Literary Analysis

The Ode

- Have students read the bracketed passage.
- Review with students the definition of the ode.
- Then, ask the Literary Analysis question on p. 753: What element of traditional odes appears in verse VII?
  Answer: Keats's speaker directly addresses the nightingale, a traditional element of odes.

Answers for p. 753

1. **(a)** He describes his state as a kind of drowsy heartsickness. **(b)** The ecstasy of the songs of the nightingale has brought on this emotional state.
2. **(a)** He wishes to leave the world behind and join the nightingale. **(b)** The real world in which the speaker lives is perplexed and dull; the nightingale's world is one of permanent, dreamlike joy.
3. **(a)** The speaker cannot see his surroundings. **(b)** The speaker wishes to disappear into the darkness that engulfs him.
4. **(a)** Stanza VII suggests that the bird was not born for death, and it "answers" the speaker's musings in stanza VI that he wishes he could die. **(b)** The speaker suggests that death is a kind of immortality, since both are states in which nothing changes.
5. Some students may say that Keats is overly dramatic in his poetic musings on death; others may feel that he is coming to terms with his own mortality, a subject that deserves the extreme emotion in this poem. By expressing this emotion, he may purge himself of it.

CUSTOMIZE INSTRUCTION FOR UNIVERSAL ACCESS

For Less Proficient Readers	For English Learners	For Advanced Readers
Have students reread "Ode to a Nightingale" to themselves. Ask them to identify which kind of ode Keats has created and to note the metrical and rhythmic patterns he uses. You can use The Ode transparency on p. 70 of **Literary Analysis and Reading Transparencies** to review the elements of the ode.	Encourage students to break down longer sentences into shorter ones or to paraphrase expressions or phrases that are particularly difficult. You can model how to paraphrase using the Paraphrase transparency on p. 69 of **Literary Analysis and Reading Transparencies.**	Have students write brief essays comparing "Ode to a Nightingale" with "When I Have Fears That I May Cease to Be." Ask students to address what the themes of these poems suggest about Keats's poetic sensibility. Refer students to www.phschool.com for more information about Keats and his work.

⓲ About the Selection

In this poem, Keats comes to an understanding about the nature of truth and beauty as he gazes at an ancient Greek urn. The scenes depicted on the urn, frozen in time, eternally beautiful and unchanging, symbolize that the urn's beauty embodies the eternity of truth.

⓳ Background

Art

The Orchard Vase, Gathering Apples

This vase was made around 525 B.C. It depicts scenes from ancient Greek life that may be similar to those that inspired Keats to write his poem.

Painted vessels such as this one were usually created for utilitarian purposes. Nevertheless, they often contained highly individual scenes from mythology, legend, and everyday life. The figures and decoration on this vase reflect the red-figure style and its interest in three-dimensional space, realistic features, and natural details. Use these questions for discussion:

1. How might Keats feel about the apples shown on this vase?
   Answer: He might admire their eternal beauty and ripeness.
2. How does the existence of this vase support the feelings Keats expresses in his poem?
   Answer: Its survival over so many years symbolizes the enduring quality of beauty and, therefore, of truth.

⓴ ▶Critical Viewing

Answer: Students should come up with stories that have something to do with the women in ancient costume who are picking apples.

⓲

Ode on a Grecian Urn

John Keats

⓳

The Orchard Vase (Column Krater), Side A: Gathering Apples, The Metropolitan Museum of Art

⓴ ◀Critical Viewing
What story can you see in the picture decorating this vase? **[Speculate]**

I

Thou still unravished bride of quietness
Thou foster child of silence and slow time,
Sylvan[1] historian, who canst thus express
A flowery tale more sweetly than our rhyme:
What leaf-fringed legend haunts about thy shape
Of deities or mortals, or of both,
In Tempe[2] or the dales of Arcady?[3]
What men or gods are these? What maidens loath?[4]
What mad pursuit? What struggle to escape?
What pipes and timbrels?[5] What wild ecstasy?

II

Heard melodies are sweet, but those unheard
Are sweeter; therefore, ye soft pipes, play on;
Not to the sensual[6] ear, but, more endeared,
Pipe to the spirit ditties of no tone:
21 Fair youth, beneath the trees, thou canst not leave
Thy song, nor ever can those trees be bare;
Bold Lover, never, never canst thou kiss,
Though winning near the goal—yet, do not grieve;
She cannot fade, though thou hast not thy bliss,
Forever wilt thou love, and she be fair!

III

Ah, happy, happy boughs! that cannot shed
Your leaves, nor ever bid the Spring adieu;
And, happy melodist, unwearied,
Forever piping songs forever new;
More happy love! more happy, happy love!
Forever warm and still to be enjoyed,
Forever panting, and forever young;
All breathing human passion far above,
That leaves a heart high-sorrowful and cloyed,
A burning forehead, and a parching tongue.

IV

Who are these coming to the sacrifice?
To what green altar, O mysterious priest,
Lead'st thou that heifer lowing at the skies,

1. **Sylvan** rustic, representing the woods or forest.
2. **Tempe** (tem´ pē) beautiful valley in Greece that has become a symbol of supreme rural beauty.
3. **Arcady** (är´ kə dē) region in Greece that has come to represent supreme pastoral contentment.
4. **loath** unwilling.
5. **timbrels** tambourines.
6. **sensual** involving the physical sense of hearing.

Literary Analysis
The Ode What two figures on Keats's urn are directly addressed in stanza II?

22  **Reading Check**
Describe two scenes depicted on the urn.

21 Literary Analysis
The Ode

- Have students read the bracketed passage to themselves.
- Ask the Literary Analysis question on p. 755: What two figures on Keats's urn are directly addressed in stanza II?
  Answer: He directly addresses a youth and a lover.

22 Reading Check

Possible responses: Students may describe the scene of a pagan sacrifice of a cow or the scene of a lover pursuing a maiden.

CUSTOMIZE INSTRUCTION FOR UNIVERSAL ACCESS

For English Learners	For Gifted/Talented Students	For Advanced Readers
Have students look at the Grecian urn on p. 754, then read "Ode on a Grecian Urn." Remind them as they go to sound out any difficult words and, wherever possible, to paraphrase any complicated phrases or ideas. Direct students who are having difficulty understanding the poem to the **English Learner's Companion.**	Have students work in small groups to draw the vase described by Keats. Encourage them to pay close attention to the imagery and details of the poem. Their drawings should include two components: a picture of a vase in its entire shape as well as a single panel that shows the images and scenes in continuous form.	Explain that the ode was a favorite genre for Keats, one in which he experimented repeatedly. Refer students who wish to do more in-depth analysis of Keats and his lyric achievements to p. 147 of **Authors In Depth,** The British Tradition, for additional examples of his work. Have students compare and contrast all of Keats's odes.

ASSESS

23 Literary Analysis

The Ode

- Have students read stanza IV to themselves.
- Ask the Literary Analysis question on p. 756: What do the speaker's questions reveal about his feelings or personality?
  Possible response: The questions suggest that he is imaginative because they attempt to "fill in" what is not shown in the pictures; they also suggest that he is capable of a passionate response to art.

Answers for p. 756

Review and Assess

1. Possible responses: Students may answer yes if they find that works of art lift them out of time.
2. **(a)** The scenes on the urn depict a youth pursuing his lover against a background of trees and piping musicians, and a ritual sacrificing of an animal to the gods. **(b)** The lover in stanza II might grieve because he can never attain his beloved. **(c)** The speaker advises him not to grieve because even if he can never kiss his beloved, she will always be beautiful and he will always love her.
3. **(a)** The boughs are called happy. **(b)** They are happy because they cannot shed their leaves, or leave the springtime of the urn.
4. The speaker's comments on these scenes suggest that permanent happiness is impossible in real life.
5. **(a)** The truth represented in the scenes on the urn is the "truth" of imperishable, eternal youth, passion, and beauty. **(b)** The urn's artistic beauty is unending and true in a way that the real world can never be because the real world is transitory. **(c)** Students may say that the "truth" is only partly true—the "truth" of beauty is not the truth of suffering, aging, and death, which are part of life.
6. Keats might say that reruns on television are the equivalent of artistic time capsules, like the urn, that preserve a "present tense" that is unending.

And all her silken flanks with garlands dressed?
What little town by river or seashore,
Or mountain-built with peaceful citadel,
23 Is emptied of this folk, this pious morn?
And, little town, thy streets forevermore
Will silent be; and not a soul to tell
Why thou art desolate, can e'er return.

V

O Attic[7] shape! Fair attitude! with brede[8]
Of marble men and maidens overwrought,[9]
With forest branches and the trodden weed;
Thou, silent form, dost tease us out of thought
As doth eternity: Cold[10] Pastoral!
When old age shall this generation waste,
Thou shalt remain, in midst of other woe
Than ours, a friend to man, to whom thou say'st,
"Beauty is truth, truth beauty,"—that is all
Ye know on earth, and all ye need to know.

7. **Attic** Attica was the region of Greece in which Athens was located; the art of the region was characterized by grace and simplicity.
8. **brede** interwoven pattern.
9. **overwrought** adorned with.
10. **Cold** unchanging.

Literary Analysis
The Ode What do the speaker's questions reveal about his feelings or personality?

Review and Assess

Thinking About the Selection

1. **Respond:** Do you place the same value on art that Keats does? Explain.
2. **(a) Recall:** Describe the scenes in stanzas I and II.
   (b) Infer: Why might the lover in stanza II grieve?
   (c) Interpret: Why does the speaker advise him not to grieve?
3. **(a) Recall:** Which items are called "happy" in stanza III?
   (b) Infer: What is the reason for their happiness?
4. **Draw Conclusions:** What do the speaker's comments on these painted scenes indirectly suggest about real life?
5. **(a) Interpret:** In line 49, what is the "'truth'" represented by the scenes on the urn? **(b) Connect:** How is this truth connected to the fact that the urn will remain after "old age shall this generation waste"? **(c) Make a Judgment:** Is the truth of the urn the "whole truth"? Explain.
6. **Apply:** The images on the urn do not move. What would Keats say about reruns on television? Do they also represent a kind of eternity? Explain.

ASSESSMENT PRACTICE: Critical Reading

Critical Thinking (For more practice, see Test Preparation Workbook, p. 35.)

Many tests require students to judge the importance of points in a writer's argument. Use this sample test item.

Which of the following lines from "Ode to a Nightingale" is not an important point in Keats's argument that life is full of suffering?

A I cannot see what flowers are at my feet, / Nor what soft incense hangs upon the boughs
B The weariness, the fever, and the fret / Here, where men sit and hear each other groan
C Where but to think is to be full of sorrow / And leaden-eyed despairs
D Now more than ever seems it rich to die, / To cease upon the midnight with no pain

Choices *B, C,* and *D* support Keats's argument. Therefore, *A* is the correct answer.

Review and Assess

Literary Analysis

The Ode

1. (a) Identify the rhyme scheme of stanza I of "Ode on a Grecian Urn." (b) Is this rhyme scheme used throughout the poem? (c) Classify the **ode** as Pindaric, Horatian, or irregular.
2. What phrase does Keats use to directly address his subject in stanza I of "Ode to a Nightingale"? Identify another such phrase in the poem.
3. (a) What do Keats's two odes honor? (b) Would you say he treats his subjects with heightened emotion? Why?

Comparing Literary Works

4. (a) Compare the speaker's attitude—wonder, fear, longing—in each poem. (b) In each, an object or event represents something that the speaker desires but does not and perhaps cannot possess. Support this generalization with details from the poems.
5. Both "Ode to a Nightingale" and "Ode on a Grecian Urn" show a speaker caught between eternal beauty and the realities of life. Using a chart like the one shown, collect details to compare the relationship between the eternal and the world of time in each.

6. Explain how each poem contributes to the idea that a person's self is defined by his or her deepest conflicts.

Reading Strategy

Paraphrasing

7. **Paraphrase** lines 9–10 from "Chapman's Homer."
8. Paraphrase at least one line that you find difficult in stanza VII of "Ode to a Nightingale."

Extend Understanding

9. **Cultural Connection:** What artifacts of today would speak most about our culture to the future, as the urn speaks of ancient Greece?

Quick Review

An **ode** is a lyric poem, characterized by exalted, or heightened, emotion, that pays homage to a person or thing, often one directly addressed by the speaker.

To **paraphrase** a literary work, put lines or passages into your own words to clarify their meaning.

Take It to the Net

www.phschool.com

Take the interactive self-test online to check your understanding of the selection.

ENRICHMENT: Further Reading

Other Works by John Keats

Endymion; Hyperion; "The Eve of St. Agnes"

Other Poems About Truth and Beauty

"The History of Truth," W. H. Auden

"The Wayfarer," Stephen Crane

"Go, Lovely Rose!" Edmund Waller

Take It to the Net

Visit www.phschool.com for more information on John Keats.

Answers for p. 757

Review and Assess

1. **(a)** The rhyme scheme is *abab cdedce*. **(b)** No. Stanza II: *abab cdeced*; Stanzas III, IV: *ababcde cde*; Stanza V: same as I. **(c)** The ode is a modified Horatian because one basic type of stanza is used.
2. Keats uses the phrase "thou, light-winged Dryad of the trees" to address the nightingale. Another phrase is "immortal Bird!"
3. **(a)** The odes honor a nightingale and a Grecian urn. **(b)** Yes; he is passionate about classical and natural beauty.
4. **(a)** The speaker's wonder and longing in "Ode to a Nightingale" at the ecstasy of the bird's song is similar to the speaker's enchantment with the perpetual spring of the Grecian urn. **(b)** In "Ode to a Nightingale," the speaker longs for the complete joy of the bird as exhibited in its songs, but he feels it is not possible in this world. In "Ode on a Grecian Urn," the speaker desires the beauty possible only in art and longs for the kind of arrested present-tense enjoyed by the ceramic figures.
5. **Possible response for "Nightingale":** Longs for ecstasies experienced by a bird; Eternal World: unattainable except through death; World of Time: fever, fret, groans, grief.
6. Students may say that in "Ode to a Nightingale," the speaker's desire for contentment can be fulfilled only by death— he could never enjoy the fulfillment of desire. In "Ode on a Grecian Urn," the speaker's desire for perfect beauty and truth can be consummated only in art, which he cannot enter, except in his poem. In these ways, both associate the speaker's deepest desires with impossibility and conflict.
7. **Possible response:** I felt like an astronomer who sees a new planet in his telescope.
8. **Possible response:** (lines 61–70) Nightingale, you are not meant to die. The passage of time does not wear you down. Your voice, heard in ancient times by

continued

Answers continued

king and fool, comforted the homesick Ruth and opened the windows of the imagination.

9. Students may say our modern architecture, our highways, or our television programming will speak most about our culture to the future.

EXTEND

Answers for p. 758

❶ Vocabulary Development

Word Analysis: Latin Suffix *-age*

1. *Wattage* is the amount of watts used in generating electricity.
2. *Storage* is the place in which to store items.
3. *Patronage* is the system whereby a wealthy supporter pays someone to create a work of art or a product.
4. *Leverage* is a condition for moving an object or otherwise gaining a result against resistance.

Spelling Strategy

1. winning
2. cringing
3. gleaning

Fluency: Sentence Completion

1. requiem
2. gleaned
3. surmise
4. ken
5. teeming
6. vintage

❷ Grammar and Style

1. light winged Dryad of the trees
2. immortal Bird
3. Fair youth
4. happy, happy boughs
5. O mysterious priest

Writing Application

Possible response: I wandered through Athens thinking of you, my dear. Your memory burns in my mind. All others fade when you are near. Dearest, please stay true.

Integrate Language Skills

❶ Vocabulary Development Lesson

Word Analysis: Latin Suffix *-age*

The Latin suffix *-age*, used in *vintage*, often means "condition or result of, cost or amount of, place of, collection of." A *vintage* is the "wine produced in a particular place and time." Using this information, define the following words:

1. wattage
2. storage
3. patronage
4. leverage

Spelling Strategy

In one-syllable words ending with a single vowel and consonant, double the consonant when adding *-ing*: *swim* + *-ing* = *swimming*. In words ending in *e*, drop the *e*: *bathe* + *-ing* = *bathing*. Exceptions include words like *dyeing*, in which the *e* is retained to avoid confusion with *dying*. Add *-ing* correctly to these words.

1. win
2. cringe
3. glean

Fluency: Sentence Completion

Choose words from the vocabulary list on page 745 to complete the following sentences. Write your answers in your notebook. Use each word only once, and if necessary, change the form of the word.

1. At the funeral, the organist played a mournful __?__.
2. At harvest time, the birds __?__ stray grain from the reaped fields.
3. Despite the evidence, he remained convinced that his initial __?__ was correct.
4. There are many mysteries beyond our __?__.
5. The storage room was __?__ with supplies.
6. The wine collector carefully labeled each __?__.

❷ Grammar and Style Lesson

Direct Address

Terms of **direct address** are names or descriptive phrases used when speaking directly to a person or thing. Terms of direct address are set off by commas.

Example: And when I feel, fair creature of an hour,
That I shall never look upon thee more, . . .

Keats often uses terms of direct address to give poems immediacy and warmth.

Practice Identify the terms of direct address.

1. That thou, light-winged Dryad of the trees, / In some melodious plot . . .
2. Thou wast not born for death, immortal Bird!
3. Fair youth, beneath the trees, thou canst not leave / Thy song, . . .
4. Ah, happy, happy boughs! that cannot shed / Your leaves, . . .
5. To what green altar, O mysterious priest, / Lead'st thou that heifer. . . .

Writing Application Rewrite this paragraph, inserting two terms of direct address and punctuating them correctly.

I wandered through Athens thinking of you. Your memory burns in my mind. All others fade when you are near. Please stay true.

WG Prentice Hall Writing and Grammar Connection: Chapter 27, Section 2

TEACHING RESOURCES

The following resources can be used to enrich or extend the instruction for pp. 758–759.

Vocabulary

- **Selection Support:** Build Vocabulary, p. 159;
- **Vocabulary and Spelling Practice Book** (Use this booklet for skills enrichment.)

Grammar

- **Selection Support:** Grammar and Style, p. 160
- **Writing and Grammar,** Diamond Level, p. 694
- **Daily Language Practice Transparencies**

Writing

- **Writing and Grammar,** Diamond Level, p. 315
- **Writing and Grammar iText CD-ROM**
- **Writing Models and Graphic Organizers on Transparencies,** pp. 123–126 

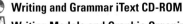

BLOCK SCHEDULING: Resources marked with this symbol provide varied instruction during 90-minute blocks.

❸ Writing Lesson

Response to Criticism

Scholar Douglas Bush writes of Keats: "The romantic elements in him remained . . . central, sane, normal—in everything but their intensity—and did not run into . . . excesses. . . ." Does this statement characterize Keats's poetry? Choose two of his poems, and compare them to decide.

Prewriting List key quotations from the two poems you have selected. Identify those that express extreme feelings or ideas. Next, check for lines in which the poet qualifies or balances these feelings or ideas. Then, draw a conclusion about Keats and excess.

Drafting Organize and draft your essay, quoting from the two poems you have selected to provide support for your points.

Revising To analyze your draft, highlight each main point. Draw a circle around sentences that connect the point to the theme of excess. Consider adding to points not accompanied by circled text.

Model: Coding to Evaluate Unified Support

While the nightingale sings, Keats says, "Now . . . seems it rich to die," but the spell is broken when the nightingale flees. His first, excessive sentiment is balanced by his return to reality: "Do I wake or sleep?"

The circled sentence adds unity by relating the author's point back to the theme of the essay—excess in Romantic poetry.

Prentice Hall Writing and Grammar Connection: Chapter 14, Section 2

❹ Extension Activities

Listening and Speaking The ancient Greek sculptures that Lord Elgin shipped to England in the 1800s had a great impact on Keats. With a group, give an **oral report** on Keats and the Elgin marbles. Divide the following tasks:

- Explaining what the Elgin marbles are
- Explaining how Keats came to know them
- Showing the influence of the experience on his poetry

Present your report to the class. **[Group Activity]**

Research and Technology Assemble a **science display** on the nightingale. Using print or Internet sources, take notes and organize them under categories such as *habitat*, *appearance*, and *behavior*. Include captioned illustrations, quotations from Keats's ode, and an annotated bibliography.

Take It to the Net www.phschool.com

Go online for an additional research activity using the Internet.

ASSESSMENT RESOURCES

The following resources can be used to assess students' knowledge and skills.

Selection Assessment

- **Formal Assessment,** pp. 164–166
- **Open Book Test,** pp. 103–105
- **Got It! Assessment Videotapes,** Tape 3
- **Test Bank Software**

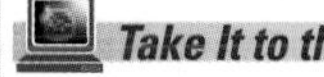

Take It to the Net
Visit www.phschool.com for self-tests and additional questions on the selections.

Writing Rubric

- **Performance Assess. and Portfolio Mgmt.,** pp. 25 and 92

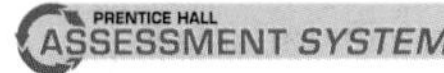

Workbook

Transparencies

Skill Book

CD-ROM

Lesson Support for p. 759

❸ Writing Lesson

- Explain that in this lesson, students will write responses to criticism of Keats.
- Remind students that one way to enhance a response to criticism is to find evidence in the text that supports or denies the critical observation to which they are responding.
- Remind students to include quotations from Keats's poetry to bolster their responses.
- Use the Writing Lesson to guide students in developing their responses to criticism.
- Encourage students to use the Outline organizer in **Writing Models and Graphic Organizers on Transparencies,** pp. 123–126, to ensure that their supporting references are thorough and well organized.
- Use the Response to Literature rubric in **Performance Assessment and Portfolio Management,** p. 25, to evaluate students' responses to criticism.

❹ Listening and Speaking

- Have students work in small groups to research how the arrival of the Elgin Marbles in England affected Keats.
- Read the Listening and Speaking Lesson with students.
- Then, encourage them to conduct research and gather evidence necessary for their oral presentations.

CUSTOMIZE INSTRUCTION For Universal Access

To address different learning styles, use the activities suggested in the **Extension Activities** booklet, p. 35.

- For Visual/Spatial Learners, use Activity 5.
- For Musical/Rhythmic Learners, use Activity 6.
- For Verbal/Linguistic Learners, use Activity 7.

Objectives

1. To understand the connection between "The Lorelei," a lyric poem of the Romantic Era, and "Haiku," the miniature poetic form of the Japanese poets
2. To broaden students' acquaintance with the varieties of lyric poetry

Connections

Lyric poetry became more than just an instrument's accompaniment in the Romantic Era. The poems became shorter but full of expression and feeling towards subjects like love and nature. In haiku, a poet writes a simple three-line poem about the complex subjects of daily life and landscape. Have students reread "The Lorelei" after they have read the haiku on pp. 762–764. What similarities and differences can students note between the two literary styles?

Lyric Poetry

- In the Romantic Era, lyric poetry was revitalized and transformed.
- Explain to students that many years prior to the Romantic Era, Japanese poets wrote three-line poems with five, seven, and five syllables in each line, respectively. These poems were carefully crafted so as not to obstruct the natural beauty being described.
- Point out to students how both lyric poetry and haiku focus on expressing a great deal of emotion with just a few lines of text. The authors of these poems used short lines to create "unclouded visions" previously hidden by excess and unnecessary words.

CONNECTIONS
Literature Around the World
Lyric Poetry

A lyric poem is a short poem expressing the thoughts or feelings of a single speaker. In ancient Greece, lyric poetry was verse recited or sung to the accompaniment of the stringed instrument called the lyre. Today, lyric poems provide their own verbal "music" as they express the personal thoughts and emotions of the poet.

The Romantic Lyric Poem Although lyric poems have been written for thousands of years, the Romantic Era put its special stamp on the form. The preference of Romantic poets for brief, expressive poems is not surprising, given their commitment to personal emotion. Wordsworth and Coleridge, writing in the Preface to *Lyrical Ballads* (1800), defined poetry itself as "the spontaneous overflow of powerful feelings." A second generation of poets—Shelley, Byron, and Keats—contributed their own melodies and perspectives to the Romantic lyric.

The World of the Lyric
One European contemporary of Byron's was the German poet Heinrich Heine (hīn′ riH hī nə). In his work, Heine seasoned the time-honored subject of love with a bittersweet flavor. His lyrics were not written for music, like those of ancient Greece, but they were later set to music by such famous composers as Robert Schumann and Franz Schubert. Writing earlier than the English Romantics, Japanese poets like Bashō (ba′ shō), Buson (bo͞o sän), and Issa (ē′ sä′) anticipated the Romantics' love of nature. These writers wrote in the miniature poetic form of the haiku, which consists of three lines of five, seven, and five syllables each. Precise and simple, haiku always contain a reference to a particular season.

ENRICHMENT: Music

Contemporary Lyric Poets

In today's world, musical artists sometimes use lyrics and music together to convey a message. Play some excerpts from contemporary songs that clearly show how lyrics and music work together to convey a message. Possibilities include Simon and Garfunkel's "Bridge Over Troubled Water," which uses hymn-like music to convey a message of comfort and reassurance.

Encourage students to look for examples of contemporary lyric poets in their musical repertoire. Students should locate a song, bring in a recording, introduce and summarize the song, and make a list of attributes that led them to believe the song is an example of lyric and music working together to convey a message.

The Lorelei[1]

Heinrich Heine
Translated by Aaron Kramer

I cannot explain the sadness
That's fallen on my breast.
An old, old fable haunts me,
And will not let me rest.

The air grows cool in the twilight,
And softly the Rhine[2] flows on;
The peak of a mountain sparkles
Beneath the setting sun.

More lovely than a vision,
A girl sits high up there;
Her golden jewelry glistens,
She combs her golden hair.

With a comb of gold she combs it,
And sings an evensong;
The wonderful melody reaches
A boat, as it sails along.

The boatman hears, with an anguish
More wild than was ever known;
He's blind to the rocks around him;
His eyes are for her alone.

—At last the waves devoured
The boat, and the boatman's cry;
And this she did with her singing,
The golden Lorelei.

1. **Lorelei** (lor′ ə lī) a legendary being, like the Siren, whose singing lured sailors to their doom.
2. **Rhine** (rīn) river in western Europe.

Heinrich Heine

(1797–1856)

The German poet Heinrich Heine was a brilliant love poet. He was also a gifted satirist and political writer whose fierce attacks on repression made him a controversial figure. Like the work of other late Romantics, his work reflects misgivings about the political and artistic promises of the early days of Romanticism.

Lady Lilith, 1868, Dante Gabriel Rosetti, Delaware Art Museum, Wilmington, DE, USA

Background

The Fable of the Lorelei

- Like so many Romantic lyric works, "The Lorelei" captures passion and pain while also linking beauty to nature. The speaker recounts his sorrow over the fable of Lorelei, whose beauty and glorious song cause boatmen to fall so madly in love with her that they are blinded to the dangers around them. His reason overwhelmed by love, a boatman caught by the Lorelei's spell is doomed to drown.
- Ask students to consider the fascination of Romantic poets with longings for the unattainable or the distant. Then, ask: Why might the fable of a fatally attractive woman inspire romantic poetry?
  Possible response: Such a woman would inspire a kind of unsatisfiable desire, since it is impossible to love her without destroying oneself. This predicament reflects the Romantic attachment to unfulfillable yearnings.

Literary Connection

- Remind students that Romantic lyric poetry is full of personal emotion.
- Point out to students the speaker's emphasis on his uncontrollable emotions.
- Ask students to name additional evidence of the genre in the first two stanzas.
  Answer: Students should note the detailed description of nature, linking the speaker with that surrounding.

Critical Thinking

Interpret

- Read lines 21–24 aloud to students.
- Then, ask them the following question: In what way are the boatman's feelings ironic?
  Answer: Students may note that love is usually thought of as a pleasant emotion; thus, the boatman's "anguish" over hearing a song of such beauty is ironic.

CUSTOMIZE INSTRUCTION FOR UNIVERSAL ACCESS

For Less Proficient Readers	For Gifted/Talented Students	For Advanced Readers
In discussion, have students elaborate on the scene in one of the haiku. List their descriptions on the chalkboard. Then, compare their descriptions with the details in the poem. Discuss how the poet has succeeded in suggesting an entire world through the selection of choice details.	In discussion, have students elaborate on the scene in one of the haiku. Then, have them illustrate the poem. Compare their illustrations with the details in the poem. Discuss how the poet has succeeded in suggesting an entire world through the selection of choice details.	In discussion, have students elaborate on the scene in one of the haiku. Then, have them discuss the mood the haiku creates and the relationship between the poet and nature that it implies. Discuss how the poet has succeeded in suggesting this mood through the selection of choice details.

Background

Haiku

- Freezing a single moment in time, these haiku can be likened to Romantic lyric poetry because of their emphasis on nature and emotion. Whether describing the connection between people and the clouds, noting a child's toy made wet by the rain, or offering a snapshot of a frog contemplating the distant horizon, these haiku demonstrate nature's constant presence in our lives.
- After students have read Bashō's haiku, use these questions for discussion:
  1. What mood predominates in these haiku?
     Possible response: The tone is quiet and meditative, with occasional flashes of wry wit, as when clouds are said to give men time to rest.
  2. What relation does Bashō indicate between humanity and nature?
     Possible response: Bashō seems to see humanity through natural objects and scenes, subordinating human concerns to their place in nature.

▶Critical Viewing

Possible response: Students may say that the painting shows the coming of the spring in the new growth on trees and hills.

Haiku

Bashō

Translated by
Harold G. Henderson (first 3)
and Geoffrey Bownas (last 3)

The sun's way:
Hollyhocks turn toward it
Through all the rain of May.

Poverty's child—
He starts to grind the rice,
And gazes at the moon.

Clouds come from time to time—
And bring to men a chance to rest
From looking at the moon.

The cuckoo—
Its call stretching
Over the water.

Seven sights were veiled
In mist—then I heard
Mii Temple's bell.[1]

Summer grasses—
All that remains
Of soldiers' visions.

▶Critical Viewing How does this painting reflect the changing of seasons in the first haiku? **[Interpret]**

Matsuo Bashō

(1644–1694)

Matsuo Bashō traveled widely through Japan, recording his observations and insights in poems and travel diaries.

1. **Mii** (mē´ ē´) **Temple's bell** The bell at Mii Temple is known for its extremely beautiful sound. The temple is located near Otsu, a city in southern Japan.

ENRICHMENT: Literature

Imagism

Though the form of the haiku was developed in seventeenth-century Japan, it exercised a decisive influence on American and English poets of the twentieth century. The American poet Ezra Pound (1885–1972), inspired in part by what haiku showed about the power of images, founded a movement called Imagism. For Pound, the true content of poetry was the image. As with haiku, Pound's Imagist works do not directly state a message. Instead, they create beautiful word-pictures in which sound, sense, and representation form a unified whole. Pound's work influenced the poet T.S. Eliot (1888–1965), who lived in England, and fellow Americans H.D. (Hilda Doolittle; 1886–1961) and William Carlos Williams (1883–1963).

Crows Taking Flight Through Spring Haze, Okada Hanko (1782–1846) Hanging scroll, Edo period, dated 1841: Foundation Toyama Memorial Museum

HAIKU

YOSA BUSON

Translated by Geoffrey Bownas

Scampering over saucers—
The sound of a rat.
Cold, cold.

———

Spring rain:
Telling a tale as they go,
Straw cape, umbrella.

———

Spring rain:
In our sedan
Your soft whispers.

———

Spring rain:
A man lives here—
Smoke through the wall.

———

Spring rain:
Soaking on the roof
A child's rag ball.

———

Fuji[1] alone
Left unburied
By young green leaves.

1. **Fuji** (fo͞o′ jē) Mount Fuji is the highest peak in Japan (12,388 ft).

Thematic Connection
What special feelings do these haiku convey through descriptions of natural scenes?

Yosa Buson

(1716–1784)

Yosa Buson presents a Romantic view of the Japanese landscape, vividly capturing the wonder and mystery of nature.

Background

Art

Crows Taking Flight Through Spring Haze, Okada Hankō

This hanging scroll depicts a spring landscape, capturing a moment in nature in much the same way as a haiku. In Japanese art, as in haiku, what is not shown or only hinted at is often as important as what is shown.

Japanese painter Okada Hankō was born in 1782 and is associated with the Edo period of Japanese art. This 250-year period of peace in Japan was centered in the city of Edo, now Tokyo. This handing scroll dates from late in the Edo period, which ended in 1868.

Use these questions for discussion:

1. Which of Issa's haiku could describe this painting?
   Answer: The third and sixth haiku both include distant views of a hilly landscape.
2. Why might the mood of this painting be appropriate to haiku?
   Answer: The delicately drawn landscape conveys a mood of simple serenity that is similar to the finely tuned language of haiku.

Thematic Connection

Answer: The first haiku captures the chill of revulsion the speaker feels when he hears a rat scampering through a cupboard. The next four reveal the stillness in a spring rain and the meditative pauses it encourages. The last suggests the triumphant, enduring strength of a mountain rising above the tumult of life's cycles.

Answers

Connecting Literature Around the World

1. **Possible response:** Students should mention that Heine's "The Lorelei" reflects a bitter-sweet attitude much like that found in Keats's odes: the speaker is torn by a desire the fulfillment of which is impossible or destructive.
2. **(a)** Bashō's first haiku and Issa's third haiku arouse images of nature's beauty and power. **Possible response:** Unlike Wordsworth's "Tintern Abbey," which also deals with the beauty of nature, these haiku focus on individual images: Bashō uses the powerful sun as the focus while Issa uses the tiny dragonfly. **(b) Possible response:** Wordsworth expects more, since he looks to nature for wisdom and moral inspiration; Bashō and Issa look simply to distill the beauty or mood of a scene.

Haiku

Kobayashi Issa

Translated by
Geoffrey Bownas

Melting snow:
And on the village
Fall the children.

Beautiful, seen through holes
Made in a paper screen:
The Milky Way.

Far-off mountain peaks
Reflected in its eyes:
The dragonfly.

A world of dew:
Yet within the dewdrops—
Quarrels.

Viewing the cherry-blossom:
Even as they walk,
Grumbling.

With bland serenity
Gazing at the far hills:
A tiny frog.

Kobayashi Issa

(1763–1828)

The poetry of Kobayashi Issa captures the essence of daily life in Japan as experienced by common people, conveying his compassion for the less fortunate.

Connecting Literature Around the World

1. Compare the speaker's troubled fascination with love in "The Lorelei" with the attitude of the speaker in another poem in this section.
2. (a) Contrast the insights into nature found in a haiku with those in another poem in this section. (b) Explain which of the poets you are comparing finds more in or expects more from nature.

ENRICHMENT: Further Reading

Other Works by the Authors

Travel Sketches, Heine
Homage to Hokuju Rosen, Buson
The Narrow Road the Deep North, Bashō
Travel Gleanings, Issa

Other Works About Nature

"Lady Moon," Christina Rossetti
"A Description of Morning," Jonathan Swift
"Mushrooms," Sylvia Plath

PART 3

The Reaction to Society's Ills

Forging the Anchor, 1831, William James Muller, City of Bristol Museum and Art Gallery

CUSTOMIZE INSTRUCTION FOR UNIVERSAL ACCESS

When assigning the selections in this part, keep in mind these factors:

"In Defense of the Lower Classes"
- Sophisticated vocabulary may prove challenging for students

"A Song: Men of England"
- A short poem that is easy to read and understand

"On the Passing of the Reform Bill"
- Short letter

"On Making an Agreeable Marriage"
- An engaging, chatty, informal letter
- Long sentences may pose difficulties for some readers

from *A Vindication of the Rights of Woman*
- Timeless appeal for fairness and gender equity touches on issues of concern to students
- Complicated sentences may challenge some readers

from *The Sense and Sensibility Screenplay and Diaries*
- High-interest connection to contemporary film

Selection Planning Guide

The selections in this section highlight the societal problems that arose during the Industrial Revolution. Byron, Shelley, and Macaulay address the need for better treatment of the working class and for political reform. Austen and Wollstonecraft comment on the foibles and unfairness in society, particularly in regard to the status of women. The excerpt from Thompson's screenplay for *Sense and Sensibility* provides a modern perspective on the early nineteenth century.

Background

Art

Forging the Anchor, 1831, by William James Muller

Although William James Muller was primarily a landscape painter, here he has dramatically re-created two of the arduous steps in the process of making a ship's anchor. At left a fire blazes, and figures who appear entirely too close to it to be either safe or comfortable wield mallets in order to shape the iron that is being forged. At right, a large number of muscular men pull in unison, like a complex human machine, in order to lift and move the weight of the iron that is suspended from a hook. The setting is dark and cavernous.

Use these questions for discussion:

1. Why do you think there is a huge chain in the foreground?
   Possible responses: The huge chain in the foreground may be symbolic of the men's enslavement to harsh labor.
2. What would be different in a photograph taken today of a factory in which ships' anchors are made?
   Possible responses: There would probably be no open fire. Workers would wear protective clothes, footwear, and goggles. Jobs such as lifting an anchor would be done with heavy equipment, driven by an operator. Today, the iron would be replaced by steel, which would be forged by machine.

Speech to Parliament: In Defense of the Lower Classes ✦ A Song: "Men of England" ✦ On the Passing of the Reform Bill

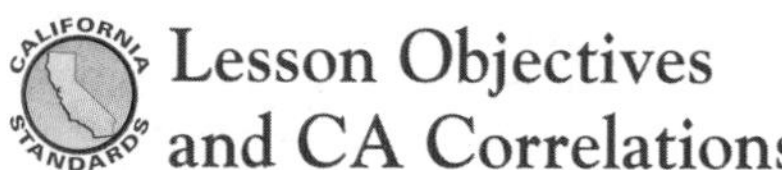

Lesson Objectives and CA Correlations

1. **To analyze and respond to literary elements**
   - Literary Analysis: Political Commentary **R 3.8**
   - Comparing Literary Works **R 2.1**
2. **To read, comprehend, analyze, and critique a speech, a poem, and nonfiction**
   - Reading Strategy: Setting a Purpose for Reading
   - Reading Check Questions
   - Review and Assess Questions
   - Assessment Practice (ATE)
3. **To develop word analysis skills, fluency, and systematic vocabulary**
   - Vocabulary Development Lesson: Word Analysis: Latin Word Root *-dec-* **R 1.2**
4. **To understand and apply written and oral language conventions**
   - Spelling Strategy **LC 1.2**
   - Grammar and Style Lesson: Correlative Conjunctions **LC 1.1**
5. **To understand and apply appropriate writing and research strategies**
   - Writing Lesson: Editorial on a Political Issue **W 1.5**
   - Extension Activity: Report on Reform **W 2.4**
6. **To understand and apply listening and speaking strategies**
   - Extension Activity: Political Speech **LS 2.5**

STEP-BY-STEP TEACHING GUIDE	PACING GUIDE
PRETEACH	
Motivate Students and Provide Background	
Use the Motivation activity (ATE p. 766)	5 min.
Read and discuss author and background features (SE pp. 766, 768; ATE p. 766) [A]	5 min.
Introduce the Concepts	
Introduce the Literary Analysis and Reading Strategy concepts (SE/ATE p. 767) [A]	15 min.
Pronounce the vocabulary words and read their definitions (SE p. 767)	5 min.
TEACH	
Monitor Comprehension	
Informally monitor comprehension by circulating while students read independently or in groups [A]	15 min.
Monitor students' comprehension with the Reading Check notes (SE/ATE pp. 769, 771, 773)	as students read
Develop vocabulary with Vocabulary notes (SE pp. 769, 770, 771, 772; ATE p. 769)	as students read
Develop Understanding	
Develop students' understanding of political commentary with the Literary Analysis annotations (SE/ATE pp. 769, 771) [A]	5 min.
Develop students' ability to set a purpose for reading with the Reading Strategy annotations (SE/ATE p. 772)	5 min.
ASSESS	
Assess Mastery	
Assess students' mastery of the Reading Strategy and Literary Analysis concepts by having them answer the Review and Assess questions (SE/ATE p. 775)	15 min.
Use one or more of the print and media Assessment Resources (ATE p. 777) [A]	up to 45 min.
EXTEND	
Apply Understanding	
Have students complete the Vocabulary Development Lesson and the Grammar and Style Lesson (SE p. 776) [A]	20 min.
Apply students' knowledge of revising for sentence variety using the Writing Lesson (SE/ATE p. 777) [A]	45 min.
Apply students' understanding using one or more of the Extension Activities (SE p. 777)	20–90 min.

ACCELERATED INSTRUCTION:
Use the strategies and activities identified with an [A].

UNIVERSAL ACCESS
● = Below-Level Students
▲ = On-Level Students
■ = Above-Level Students

Time and Resource Manager

Reading Level: Challenging, Average, Average
Average Number of Instructional Days: 4

RESOURCES		
PRINT	**TRANSPARENCIES**	**TECHNOLOGY**
• **Beyond Literature,** Community Connection: Political Commentary, p. 36 ▲ ■		• **Interest Grabber Videos,** Tape 4 ● ▲ ■
• **Selection Support Workbook:** ● ▲ ■ Literary Analysis, p. 168 Reading Strategy, p. 167 Build Vocabulary, p. 165	• **Literary Analysis and Reading Transparencies,** pp. 71 and 72 ● ▲ ■	
		• **Listening to Literature** ● ▲ ■ Audiocassettes, Sides 18, 19 Audio CDs, CD 11
• **Literary Analysis for Enrichment** ■	• **Fine Art Transparencies, Volume 1,** Transparency 13 ● ▲ ■	
• **Formal Assessment:** Selection Test, pp. 173–175 ● ▲ ■ • **Open Book Test,** pp. 106–108 ● ▲ ■ • **Performance Assessment and Portfolio Management,** pp. 10 and 32 ● ▲ ■ • PRENTICE HALL ASSESSMENT SYSTEM ● ▲ ■	• PRENTICE HALL ASSESSMENT SYSTEM ● ▲ ■ Skills Practice Answers and Explanations on Transparencies	• **Test Bank Software** ● ▲ ■ • **Got It! Assessment Videotapes,** Tape 3 ● ▲
• **Selection Support Workbook:** ● ▲ ■ Grammar and Style, p. 166 • **Writing and Grammar,** Diamond Level ● ▲ ■ • **Extension Activities,** p. 36 ● ▲ ■	• **Daily Language Practice Transparencies** ● ▲ • **Writing Models and Graphic Organizers on Transparencies,** pp. 37–44 ● ▲ ■	• **Writing and Grammar iText CD-ROM** ● ▲ ■ ***Take It to the Net*** www.phschool.com

BLOCK SCHEDULING: Use one 90-minute class period to preteach the selections and have students read them. Use a second 90-minute class period to assess students' mastery of skills and have them complete one of the Extension Activities.

PRETEACH

Step-by-Step Teaching Guide for pp. 766–767

Motivation

Write on the chalkboard the names of rock musicians who are active politically. Such a list might include Sting, Peter Gabriel, Sheryl Crow, Ben Harper, and Tracy Chapman. Introduce the subject of politically active artists such as these and ask students to add to the list. Whenever possible, ask them to describe the cause for which each musician fights. Then tell students that Byron and Shelley were like rock musicians of their time in that they were considered "wild" and "liberal," and they championed the underdog in political causes.

Interest Grabber Video

As an alternative, play "A Song: 'Men of England': The Industrial Revolution" on Tape 4 to engage student interest.

1 Background

More About the Authors

George Gordon, Lord Byron

Byron's empathy for the lower classes was perhaps sharpened by his own experiences. Born with a clubfoot, he knew something of misfortune. Although an aristocrat, he grew up in poverty until the death of an uncle brought him an inheritance.

Percy Bysshe Shelley

Shelley's political views were shaped in part by those of his father-in-law, radical philosopher William Godwin. When Shelley eloped with Godwin's daughter Mary, however, the philosopher, despite his rejection of tradition, responded with a traditional father's outrage.

Thomas Babington Macaulay

Macaulay wrote several history volumes that earned him lasting fame and recognition. His *History of England* (1849–1855) was one of the best-sellers of the nineteenth century, and it is acknowledged as including one of the most detailed factual accounts of the reign of James II.

Comparing Literary Works

Prepare to Read

1 Speech to Parliament: In Defense of the Lower Classes ◆ A Song: "Men of England" ◆ On the Passing of the Reform Bill

George Gordon, Lord Byron (1788–1824)

Although less of a firebrand than his friend Shelley, Lord Byron was in his day a far more prominent supporter of radical reform and political liberty. In Britain, his first speech in the House of Lords defended workers who had sabotaged factory equipment that had put them out of work. (You can read a portion of that speech beginning on page 768.) Overseas, he was closely associated with the Italian freedom fighters known as the Carbonari. He lost his life in the cause of independence for Greece.

Both an aristocrat and a revolutionary, Byron was a man of extremes and contradictions. The German Romantic poet Goethe once described him as "a fiery mass of living valor hurling itself on life." Despite his contradictions, Byron consistently challenged tyranny and championed freedom. (For more on Byron, see p. 716.)

Percy Bysshe Shelley (1792–1822)

Of the major Romantic poets, Percy Bysshe Shelley was probably the most politically radical. Some of his poems are rallying cries encouraging the British working classes to rebel. Living in Italy, he wrote "A Song: 'Men of England'" in 1819 as an angry response to news of the growing economic suffering and political oppression of the working classes in England. In 1820, he decided to publish a collection of his political poems. He asked a friend if he knew of "any bookseller who would like to publish a little volume of popular songs wholly political & destined to awaken & direct the imagination of the reformers." An idealist, Shelley believed in the perfectibility of the human spirit and in the power of poetry to bring about the spiritual regeneration of humanity. (For more on Shelley, see p. 730.)

Thomas Babington Macaulay (1800–1859)

Before making his lasting mark as an insightful historian and powerful politician, Thomas Babington Macaulay won fame as a literary critic with essays published in the *Edinburgh Review*. Trained as a lawyer, he entered the House of Commons, where his eloquence helped ensure passage of the Reform Bill of 1832. This measure extended the vote to shopkeepers and other middle-class men. (Previously, the right to vote had been restricted to the wealthy.)

Macaulay continued as a force for change in the House of Commons. Pressured by the prime minister's office to vote for an amendment that would weaken an antislavery bill, Macaulay refused and offered his resignation instead. Macaulay again won a majority to his side, though, and the prime minister's office backed down.

In 1834 Macaulay accepted a government position in India, where he began a national education system and drafted a code of criminal law. He returned to England in 1838 and served again in Parliament. During periods in which his party, the Whigs, were out of power, Macaulay devoted himself to writing, producing a multivolume history of England that became a best-seller and a widely respected reference book.

TEACHING RESOURCES

The following resources can be used to enrich or extend the instruction for pp. 766–767.

Motivation

Interest Grabber Videos, Tape 4

Background

Beyond Literature, p. 36

Take It to the Net

Visit www.phschool.com for Background and hotlinks for the selections.

Literary Analysis

Literary Analysis and Reading Transparencies, Political Commentary, p. 72

Reading

Literary Analysis and Reading Transparencies, Set a Purpose for Reading, p. 71

Selection Support: Reading Strategy, p. 167; Build Vocabulary, p. 165

BLOCK SCHEDULING: Resources marked with this symbol provide varied instruction during 90-minute blocks.

Preview

Connecting to the Literature

The struggle for justice through marches, editorials, and legislation continues to make news. In nineteenth-century England, Shelley, Byron, and Macaulay added their voices to the timeless struggle.

❷ Literary Analysis

Political Commentary

Political commentary offers opinions on political issues, building arguments on evidence and assumptions. Evaluate both the evidence and the assumptions that each writer uses. Shelley, for example, makes the argument shown, based on the assumption indicated:

Argument: The common people of England should rebel because those they work for oppress them.

Assumption: Duty is not a one-way street; workers and employers are bound together by mutual obligations.

Comparing Literary Works

Though each of these commentators works in a different form—speech, poem, and letter—they all seek to persuade, and each employs **persuasive devices,** including the following:

- **Rhetorical questions**—questions asked for dramatic effect, the expected answer to which is obvious
- **Balanced clauses**—two or more clauses in the same sentence that share a similar structure

Compare the types of devices each writer favors and the effectiveness of each.

❸ Reading Strategy

Setting a Purpose for Reading

You will often get more from your reading if you first **set a purpose,** or choose a reason, for reading. Assess your own knowledge of the subject and use a graphic organizer like the one shown to set a purpose for reading these selections.

Prior Knowledge/ Interest

Byron was thought of as a "bad boy," sort of like James Dean.

Reading Purpose

How serious and well informed were his political positions?

Evidence for Answer

1.
2.

Vocabulary Development

impediments (im ped′ ə mənts) *n.* hindrances; obstructions (p. 769)

decimation (des′ ə mā′ shun) *n.* destruction or killing of one in ten, or of any large part of a group (p. 769)

efficacious (ef′ i kā′ shəs) *adj.* effective (p. 770)

emancipate (ē man′ sə pāt′) *v.* to free from slavery or oppression (p. 770)

balm (bäm) *n.* a soothing ointment; anything soothing (p. 771)

inauspicious (in′ ô spish′ əs) *adj.* not promising a good outcome; unfavorable (p. 772)

CUSTOMIZE INSTRUCTION FOR UNIVERSAL ACCESS

For Less Proficient Readers	For English Learners	For Advanced Readers
Review the graphic organizer on p. 767 and explain that by reading with a purpose, or a goal, students can read strategically. Guide students as they begin reading "In Defense of the Lower Classes," prompting them to use a chart like the one shown as they read.	Use the graphic organizer on p. 767 to guide students to learn how they can use their prior knowledge of a subject to direct their reading purpose, and how evidence in the text can help them answer their questions. As students begin reading "In Defense of the Lower Classes," encourage them to use a chart like the one shown.	Before students begin reading "In Defense of the Lower Classes," prompt them to write down any prior knowledge or interest they have in the subject; then, use a chart like the one shown on p. 767 to determine whether the purpose they set for themselves was met.

❷ Literary Analysis

Political Commentary

- Tell students that in this lesson they will focus on political commentary, a kind of writing that offers opinions on political issues and builds arguments on evidence and assumptions.
- Read the note about political commentary together as a class. Call students' attention to the elements of argument and assumption they can expect to find in the selections.
- Use the instruction for Comparing Literary Works to review with students the effects of persuasive devices such as rhetorical questions and balanced clauses.
- Use the Political Commentary transparency in **Literary Analysis and Reading Transparencies,** p. 72, to demonstrate to students how to interpret features of political commentary.

❸ Reading Strategy

Setting a Purpose for Reading

- Explain to students that before they read they should establish a purpose, or goal, of what they want to gain from their reading.
- Read the note about Setting a Purpose together as a class.
- Encourage students to come up with a questions for the texts before they begin reading that they hope to answer when they have finished. (Examples: Why did the author write this work? What evidence does the author compile to illustrate her main idea?)
- Have students practice this skill using the Set a Purpose transparency on p. 71 of **Literary Analysis and Reading Transparencies.**

Vocabulary Development

- Pronounce each vocabulary word for students and read each definition as a class. Have students identify any words with which they are already familiar.

E-Teach

Visit E-Teach at www.phschool.com for teachers' essays on how to teach, with questions and answers.

TEACH

Step-by-Step Teaching Guide for pp. 768–774

CUSTOMIZE INSTRUCTION
For Musical/Rhythmic Learners

Many folk songs embody sentiments similar to the ones found in Shelley's "Men of England." Invite students to set this song to music and play it for the class.

❶ About the Selection

Byron seems to hold no insult back as he asks Parliament to reconsider the "deathbill" it is evidently about to enact in order to punish workers who have wrecked their own looms. Through a passionate series of comparisons and questions, he calls on Parliament to reconsider what it is planning to do.

❷ Background

Art

The Workshops at the Gobelins, Jean-Charles Develly

This scene shows workers in a factory, a typical occupation of the "lower classes" in England at the time of the Industrial Revolution. The factory setting is austere and unwelcoming, with workers lined up performing their separate tasks from early in the morning until late at night. In dark, uninviting rooms, with high ceilings, workers toil at looms and spinning wheels, producing textiles by, apparently, no other light than the natural light that comes from very few windows. Use these questions for discussion:

1. What do you think you would hear if you were in this setting?
   Answer: There would be a constant racket of the looms.
2. What do you think it was like to work in this factory?
   Answer: Working conditions were probably harsh in this factory. There probably wasn't enough light and/or heat. Because the tasks were repetitive, workers' backs and wrists probably ached, and they may have gotten headaches from the deafening roar and echo of the looms.

❸ ▶Critical Viewing

Answer: This painting suggests that working conditions in Byron's day were oppressive and unsafe.

❶ *Speech to Parliament:*

In Defense of the Lower Classes

George Gordon, Lord Byron

❷

The Workshops at the Gobelins, 1840, Jean-Charles Develly, Musée Carnavalet, Paris

Background

From the outbreak of the French Revolution in 1789 until Napoleon's defeat at the Battle of Waterloo in 1815, Britain focused on foreign affairs at the expense of much-needed domestic reforms. Unemployment was high, and laws such as the Corn Law of 1815 aggravated the situation by protecting the economic and political interests of wealthy landowners.

Even after Waterloo, reform was delayed by a dangerous cycle of protests and government crackdowns. In the Luddite riots from 1811 to 1817, unemployed weavers in the industrial north wrecked factory equipment that they felt had endangered their traditional livelihoods. When Parliament debated using the death penalty for these crimes, Byron spoke out in the workers' defense.

As a person in some degree connected with the suffering county, though a stranger not only to this House in general but to almost every individual whose attention I presume to solicit, I must claim some portion of your Lordships' indulgence, . . .

When we are told that these men are leagued together, not only for the destruction of their own comfort, but of their very means of subsistence, can we forget that it is the bitter policy, the destructive warfare, of the last eighteen years[1] which has destroyed their comfort, your comfort, all men's comfort—that policy which, originating with "great statesmen now no more," has survived the dead to become a curse on the living, unto the third and fourth generation! These men never destroyed their looms till they were become useless—

❸ ▲Critical Viewing What does the picture suggest about working conditions in Byron's day? **[Infer]**

1. **bitter policy . . . last eighteen years** Byron is referring to the Napoleonic Wars, which caused an economic depression.

TEACHING RESOURCES

The following resources can be used to enrich or extend the instruction for pp. 768–774.

Literary Analysis

Selection Support: Literary Analysis, p. 168

Reading

Listening to Literature Audiocassettes, Sides 18, 19

Listening to Literature Audio CDs, CD 11

BLOCK SCHEDULING: Resources marked with this symbol provide varied instruction during 90-minute blocks.

worse than useless; till they were become actual impediments to their exertions in obtaining their daily bread.

4 Can you then wonder that in times like these, when bankruptcy, convicted fraud, and imputed felony are found in a station not far beneath that of your Lordships, the lowest, though once most useful, portion of the people should forget their duty in their distresses, and become only less guilty than one of their representatives? But while the exalted[2] offender can find means to baffle the law, new capital punishments must be devised, new snares of death must be spread for the wretched mechanic who is famished[3] into guilt. These men were willing to dig, but the spade was in other hands: they were not ashamed to beg, but there was none to relieve them. Their own means of subsistence were cut off; all other employments preoccupied; and their excesses, however to be deplored or condemned, can hardly be the subject of surprise.

I have traversed the seat of war in the Peninsula;[4] I have been in some of the most oppressed provinces of Turkey; but never, under the most despotic of infidel[5] governments, did I behold such squalid wretchedness as I have seen since my return, in the very heart of a Christian country. And what are your remedies? After months of inaction, and months of action worse than inactivity, at length comes forth the grand specific, the never-failing nostrum of all state physicians from the days of Draco[6] to the present time. After feeling the pulse and shaking the head over the patient, prescribing the usual course of warm water and bleeding[7]—the warm water of your mawkish police, and the lancets of your military—these convulsions must terminate in death, the sure consummation of the prescriptions of all political Sangrados.[8] Setting aside the palpable injustice and the certain inefficiency of the bill, are there not capital punishments sufficient on your statutes? Is there not blood enough upon your penal code, that more must be poured forth to ascend to heaven and testify against you? How will you carry this bill into effect? Can you commit a whole country to their own prisons? Will you erect a 5 gibbet[9] in every field, and hang up men like scarecrows? Or will you proceed (as you must, to bring this measure into effect) by decimation; 6 place the country under martial law; depopulate and lay waste all around you, and restore Sherwood Forest as an acceptable gift to the crown in its former condition of a royal chase, and an asylum for outlaws?[10] Are these the remedies for a starving and desperate

impediments (im ped′ ə mənts) *n.* hindrances; obstructions

Literary Analysis
Political Commentary What assumption does Byron make in the argument in this paragraph?

Literary Analysis
Political Commentary and Persuasive Devices What reaction to these questions might Byron have expected from the legislators?

decimation (des′ ə mā′ shun) *n.* destruction or killing of one in ten, or of any large part of a group

7 **✓Reading Check**
What punishment does the law opposed by Byron prescribe?

---

2. **exalted** well-born; of high rank.
3. **famished** forced by hunger.
4. **the Peninsula** Iberian Peninsula (Spain and Portugal).
5. **infidel** (in′ fə del) *n.* non-Christian.
6. **Draco** (drā′ kō) ancient Greek politician famous for his very severe code of laws.
7. **bleeding** In Byron's day, doctors often bled patients as a remedy for illness.
8. **Sangrados** doctors who bled patients.
9. **gibbet** (jib′ it) device used for hanging a person.
10. **Sherwood Forest . . . outlaws** Sherwood Forest, near Nottingham, was famous as the refuge of Robin Hood and his band of outlaws.

CUSTOMIZE INSTRUCTION FOR UNIVERSAL ACCESS

For Special Needs Students	For English Learners	For Gifted/Talented Students
Encourage students who are struggling with comprehension to set a purpose before they read, making a list of questions they hope to have answered when they are done reading.	Have students read the background information to Byron's speech before they begin reading the selection with teacher guidance. Then, have students listen to this selection on **Listening to Literature CDs,** CD 11.	Tell students that when Byron made his fiery speech to Parliament in 1812, he was a worldly 24-year-old who had traveled extensively. Have students make detailed maps of the geography of Byron's life and death. Students should include captions highlighting Byron's political actions throughout the world.

4 Literary Analysis

Political Commentary

- Read the bracketed passage aloud to students.
- Explain to students that political commentary offers opinions on political issues building arguments from evidence and assumptions.
- Ask the first Literary Analysis question on p. 769: What assumption does Byron make in the argument in this paragraph?
  Answer: Byron's main argument is that the rebels were left with no alternative but crime. His main assumption is that the punishment for a crime should take social circumstances into account.

5 Literary Analysis

Political Commentary and Persuasive Devices

- Have students read the bracketed passage.
- Remind them that one feature typical of the persuasive arguments of political commentary is rhetorical questions.
- Ask the second Literary Analysis question on p. 769: What reaction to these questions might Byron have expected from the legislators?
  Answer: Byron might have expected shame or outrage.

6 Vocabulary Development

Latin Word Root *-dec-*

- Call students' attention to *decimation*, meaning literally "the killing of one in every group of ten." Explain that the root *-dec-* means "ten," and that the word *decimation* originated with the brutal punishment in the Roman army for mutiny—one in every ten soldiers was put to death.
- Have students suggest other words containing the root, and list them on the chalkboard.
  Possible responses: *decimeter, decibel, decimal*
- Have students look up unfamiliar words in the dictionary.

7 ✓Reading Check

Answer: The law opposed by Byron prescribes the death penalty for the destruction of factory equipment by unemployed weavers.

Answers for p. 770

1. Possible response: Yes, because Byron points out that the lower classes are judged unfairly.
2. **(a)** Byron says that he is "a stranger" to the house he is addressing and to every individual whose attention he hopes to gain. **(b)** Byron's tone in the opening paragraph is polite. **(c)** His tone becomes outraged, even accusatory.
3. **(a)** Byron says the looms were wrecked because they had become useless. **(b)** He says lower-class lawbreakers have no power, but upper-class lawbreakers can "baffle the law." **(c)** Byron makes the point that the lower-class lawbreakers are no worse than upper-class lawbreakers except that English society keeps them powerless.
4. **(a)** Byron compares the wretched state of the lower classes to that of a doctor's patient. **(b)** Byron hopes to make the point that the government is acting like a bad doctor towards its "patient," doing nothing and then administering a fatal remedy.
5. **(a)** Possible response: Byron opposes the proposed bill because it is more cruel than any other he has seen in despotic realms, because the wrongdoers had their only means of subsistence cut off, and because they are powerless in the social class system. **(b)** The address is an emotional appeal because it employs passionate, persuasive language and compelling comparisons; it is an appeal to reason in that it uses factual evidence and reasoning to support Byron's opinions.
6. Some students may say that Byron's status as an aristocrat makes his arguments that much more compelling. Others may feel that Byron's removal from the difficulties of the wrongdoers makes him a weaker advocate for social reform.

populace? Will the famished wretch who has braved your bayonets be appalled by your gibbets? When death is a relief, and the only relief it appears that you will afford him, will he be dragooned[11] into tranquillity? Will that which could not be effected by your grenadiers,[12] be accomplished by your executioners? If you proceed by the forms of law, where is your evidence? Those who refused to impeach their accomplices when transportation[13] only was the punishment will hardly be tempted to witness against them when death is the penalty.

With all due deference to the noble lords opposite, I think a little investigation, some previous inquiry, would induce even them to change their purpose. That most favorite state measure, so marvelously efficacious in many and recent instances, *temporizing*, would not be without its advantage in this. When a proposal is made to emancipate or relieve, you hesitate, you deliberate for years, you temporize and tamper with the minds of men; but a deathbill must be passed offhand, without a thought of the consequences.

efficacious (ef´ i kā´ shəs) *adj.* effective

emancipate (ē man´ sə pāt) *v.* to free from slavery or oppression

11. **dragooned** (drə go͞ond´) compelled by violence, especially as exerted by military troops.
12. **grenadiers** (gren´ ə dirz´) members of Britain's royal infantry.
13. **transportation** practice of sending people convicted of crimes to overseas penal colonies.

Review and Assess

Thinking About the Selection

1. **Respond:** Did you find this speech persuasive? Why or why not?
2. **(a) Recall:** In the opening paragraph of the speech, what reason does Byron give for asking their "Lordships' indulgence"? **(b) Infer:** How would you describe Byron's tone in the opening paragraph? **(c) Analyze:** How does his tone change as the speech continues?
3. **(a) Recall:** According to Byron, why did the men wreck the looms? **(b) Compare and Contrast:** What contrast does he make between lower-class lawbreakers and upper-class lawbreakers? **(c) Infer:** What point about English society does Byron make with this contrast?
4. **(a) Analyze:** In paragraph 4, what does Byron compare to a doctor's patient? **(b) Interpret:** Explain the point Byron makes with this extended comparison.
5. **(a) Summarize:** Sum up three of Byron's arguments against the proposed bill. **(b) Evaluate:** To what extent does the address appeal to emotion? To what extent to reason?
6. **Make a Judgement:** Byron is a privileged aristocrat, not a worker or the owner of a mill. Does this fact add to or detract from the power of his speech? Explain.

ENRICHMENT: History Connection

English Industrial Revolution

Between 1760 and 1830, the production of cotton textiles in England increased twelvefold. This was due in large part to the new inventions that mechanized the spinning and weaving of imported cotton. As this transition began, people who had spent their lives doing farming or working as artisans left old ways of life to become factory workers. But as one technology quickly replaced the last, their jobs were threatened.

Furthermore, the French revolutionary government declared war on England in February 1793. The result was 22 years of war. Among the effects on the economy were rapid inflation and rates of pay that lagged far behind prices.

8 A Song: "Men of England"

Percy Bysshe Shelley

Men of England, wherefore[1] plough
For the lords who lay ye low?
Wherefore weave with toil and care
The rich robes your tyrants wear?

Wherefore feed and clothe and save
From the cradle to the grave
Those ungrateful drones who would
Drain your sweat—nay, drink your blood?

Wherefore, Bees of England, forge
Many a weapon, chain, and scourge,[2]
That these stingless drones may spoil
The forced produce of your toil?

Have ye leisure, comfort, calm,
Shelter, food, love's gentle balm?
Or what is it ye buy so dear
With your pain and with your fear?

9
The seed ye sow, another reaps;
The wealth ye find, another keeps;
The robes ye weave, another wears;
The arms ye forge, another bears.

Sow seed—but let no tyrant reap:
Find wealth—let no impostor heap:
Weave robes—let not the idle wear:
Forge arms—in your defense to bear.

Shrink to your cellars, holes, and cells—
In halls ye deck another dwells.
Why shake the chains ye wrought? Ye see
The steel ye tempered[3] glance on ye.

With plough and spade and hoe and loom
Trace your grave and build your tomb
And weave your winding-sheet[4]—till fair
England be your Sepulcher.[5]

balm (bäm) *n.* a soothing ointment; anything soothing

10 

According to the speaker, who benefits from the work of the "Men of England"?

1. **wherefore** for what purpose? Why?
2. **scourge** (skurj) whip used to inflict punishment.
3. **tempered** Made hard by alternately heating and cooling.
4. **winding-sheet** sheet for wrapping a corpse; shroud.
5. **Sepulcher** (sep′ əl kər) tomb.

8 About the Selection

Shelley's song uses a series of simple questions, with implied but grim answers, followed by a series of commands, to incite the men of England to revolution. In line after line, Shelley counsels the workers to stop giving power and wealth to the powerful and rich because by doing so they are only taking away from themselves. This poem demonstrates how a poet's skill can be employed to effect social change.

9 Literary Analysis

Political Commentary and Persuasive Devices

- Have students read the bracketed passage aloud chorally.
- Remind students that persuasive language is a common element of political commentary.
- Ask the following question: What persuasive device does Shelley use in lines 17–20?
  Answer: Shelley uses parallelism of phrases and repetition to make his points memorable and persuasive in this stanza.

10 Reading Check

Answer: The lords and tyrants and ungrateful drones benefit from the work the "Men of England" do.

CUSTOMIZE INSTRUCTION FOR UNIVERSAL ACCESS

For Special Needs Students	For Less Proficient Readers	For Advanced Readers
Explain that Shelley's poem is a reaction against social conditions at the beginning of the Industrial Age. Students may be intrigued to learn about the period in which their own world was born. Show students "A Song: 'Men of England': The Industrial Revolution" on **Interest Grabber Videos,** Tape 4.	Have students read the song in small groups with teacher guidance. Ask students to identify any unusual patterns or repetitions. Use the Political Commentary transparency on p. 72 of **Literary Analysis and Reading Transparencies** to guide your instruction.	Have students read "Men of England" independently. Ask students if they think Shelley's images are effective and to whom they might be offensive. Tell students to write a dialogue between Shelley and a poetry editor in which they discuss these issues.

⓫ About the Selection

With what seems like the whole future of England riding on the vote to pass the Reform Bill, the moments of tallying are tense indeed. Thomas Babington Macaulay recounts them vividly here—and with all the pleasure of the victor (unfortunately, the bill failed to pass the House of Lords after the vote Macaulay reports in the House of Commons). This personal letter to a friend reveals an insider's view on the working of government during an exciting time in England's history.

⓬ Reading Strategy

Setting a Purpose for Reading

- Before you ask students to read the bracketed passage independently, remind them that by setting a purpose before they begin, they may get more from their reading.
- Then, ask the Reading Strategy question on p. 772: What two subjects might you learn about from this letter?
  Answer: Students may learn about what the Reform Bill sought to change, who opposed it, who supported it, and why it was of special importance to Macaulay.

⓫ On the Passing of the Reform Bill

Thomas Babington Macaulay

Background

By passing the Reform Bills of 1832–1835, the British Parliament sought to make Britain more democratic. The first Reform Bill dealt with Parliamentary representation. Some sparsely populated rural areas had a disproportionately large representation, whereas booming new industrial cities like Manchester had none. The bill passed the House of Commons three times, but the House of Lords voted it down each time. Finally, the prime minister forced King William IV to name fifty new members to the House of Lords. Liberal peers were appointed, and the bill finally passed. Macaulay's letter reports the first House of Commons vote on the bill.

Dear Ellis,

I have little news for you, except what you will learn from the papers as well as from me. It is clear that the Reform Bill must pass, either in this or in another Parliament. The majority of one does not appear to me, as it does to you, by any means inauspicious. We should perhaps have had a better plea for a dissolution if the majority had
⓬ been the other way. But surely a dissolution under such circumstances would have been a most alarming thing. If there should be a dissolution now there will not be that ferocity in the public mind which there would have been if the House of Commons had refused to entertain the Bill at all.—I confess that, till we had a majority, I was half inclined to tremble at the storm which we had raised. At present I think that we are absolutely certain of victory, and of victory without commotion.

Such a scene as the division of last Tuesday I never saw, and never expect to see again. If I should live fifty years the impression of it will be as fresh and sharp in my mind as if it had just taken place. It was like seeing Caesar stabbed in the Senate House,[1] or seeing Oliver taking the mace from the table, a sight to be seen only once and

inauspicious (in′ ô spish′ əs) *adj.* not promising a good outcome; unfavorable

Reading Strategy
Setting a Purpose for Reading What two subjects might you learn about from this letter?

1. **Caesar** (sē′ zər) **stabbed in the Senate House** Emperor Julius Caesar, assassinated in the legislative council of ancient Rome.

ENRICHMENT: History Connection

The Reform Bill

The Reform Bill was the biggest political issue in England in 1831 and 1832. When it became law in 1832, the Reform Bill resulted in a redistribution of seats in Parliament, which gave more power and voice to the growing industrial cities. It also extended the right to vote to all middle-class men and some artisans. This meant that the electorate was increased by an incredible 50 percent in both England and Wales; it grew by even more than that in Scotland and Ireland. By extending the vote to more and more "common" people, the measure weakened the power of both the monarch and the House of Lords. In short, it was a giant step toward greater democracy.

never to be forgotten. The crowd overflowed the House in every part. When the strangers were cleared out and the doors locked we had six hundred and eight members present, more by fifty five than ever were at a division before. The Ayes and Noes♦ were like two vollies of cannon from opposite sides of a field of battle. When the opposition went out into the lobby,—an operation by the by which took up twenty minutes or more,—we spread ourselves over the benches on both sides of the House. For there were many of us who had not been able to find a seat during the evening. When the doors were shut we began to speculate on our numbers. Everybody was desponding. "We have lost it. We are only two hundred and eighty at most. I do not think we are two hundred and fifty. They are three hundred. Alderman Thompson has counted them. He says they are two hundred and ninety-nine." This was the talk on our benches. I wonder that men who have been long in parliament do not acquire a better coup d'œil[2] for numbers. The House when only the Ayes were in it looked to me a very fair house,—much fuller than it generally is even on debates of considerable interest. I had no hope however of three hundred. As the tellers♦ passed along our lowest row on the left hand side the interest was insupportable,—two hundred and ninety-one:—two hundred and ninety-two:—we were all standing up and stretching forward, telling with the tellers. At three hundred there was a short cry of joy, at three hundred and two another—suppressed however in a moment. For we did not yet know what the hostile force might be. We knew however that we could not be severely beaten. The doors were thrown open and in they came. Each of them as he entered brought some different report of their numbers. It must have been impossible, as you may conceive, in the lobby, crowded as they must have been, to form any exact estimate. First we heard that they were three hundred and three—then the number rose to three hundred and ten, then went down to three hundred and seven. Alexander Baring told me that he had counted and that they were three hundred and four. We were all breathless with anxiety, when Charles Wood who stood near the door jumped on a bench and cried out, "They are only three hundred and one." We set up a shout that you might have heard to Charing Cross[3]—waving our hats—stamping against the floor and clapping our hands. The tellers scarcely got through the crowd:—for the house was thronged up to the table, and all the floor

2. **coup d'œil** (ko͞o dëy') glance.
3. **Charing Cross** London neighborhood some distance from the Houses of Parliament.

Literature in context Vocabulary Connection

13 ♦ ***Government Terms***

The following terms in the selection refer to British government:

Parliament the bicameral (two-house) legislative body of Britain

dissolution dismissal of Parliament in order to hold new elections; if major legislation fails, the prime minister resigns and Parliament is dissolved.

House of Commons the house of Parliament made up of elected members and led by the prime minister

House of Lords the house of Parliament whose membership is hereditary or by appointment

mace the symbol of the authority of the Speaker of the House of Commons. By demanding the removal of the mace in 1653, Puritan leader Oliver Cromwell (1599–1658) overrode Parliamentary authority and became virtual dictator of England.

Ayes and Noes respectively, votes in favor of and votes against a bill

tellers those appointed to count votes in Parliament

Westminster Palace, London, the home of the British Parliament

14  **Reading Check**

How close is the vote on the Bill?

13 Background

Parliament

The Parliament of England, like the American Congress, is divided into two houses: in Macaulay's day, both had to agree before a bill became a law. Since that time, the situation has changed. The House of Lords has virtually no political power in England today. Nor does the king or queen. The elected members of the House of Commons—along with the elected prime minister, who also is a member of the House of Commons—are Britain's lawmakers.

14 ✓Reading Check

Answer: The vote was 302 to 301.

CUSTOMIZE INSTRUCTION FOR UNIVERSAL ACCESS

For Special Needs Students	For Less Proficient Readers	For Advanced Readers
Have students read portions of "On the Passing of the Reform Bill" with teacher guidance. Discuss with students what Macaulay's purpose is, who his audience is, and how his letter functions as a kind of political commentary.	Remind students that "On the Passing of the Reform Bill" was a private letter intended to be read by Macaulay's friend and political ally. Encourage students to set a purpose for themselves as they read with teacher guidance, gleaning details and information pertaining to Macaulay's agenda.	Tell students that the Reform Bills were a series of laws (enacted in England in 1832, 1867, 1884, 1918, and 1928) that expanded the British voting system. Have students do research and prepare a chart that shows how voting conditions developed in these five steps from 1832 to 1928.

ASSESS

Answers for p. 774

Review and Assess

1. **(a)** The speaker asks why they work so hard to clothe the rich and make them richer, when the rich oppress them. **(b)** Are you going to continue to work yourselves into the grave for the benefit of your rich, lazy lords?
2. **(a)** He compares the workers of England to bees. **(b)** Bees are known as industrious workers, a description that also fits the laborers of England. Bees also work on behalf of a queen, a fact that parallels the system of British monarchy.
3. Shelley poses for workers the alternative of either working only for themselves or continuing to destroy themselves by laboring for the rich. The first is expressed in lines 21 to 24, where the speaker tells workers to continue working without profiting their lords: "Sow seed—but let no tyrant reap." The second alternative appears in lines 25 through 32, in which the speaker ironically encourages the workers to do nothing to change their condition. He notes that by laboring for the upper classes, they are turning England into their own tomb.
4. **(a)** First the members of the House of Commons met. Those against the Reform Bill went into the lobby while those for passage stayed and were counted as aye votes. Then those against the bill filed in, being counted as they entered. The number of members for passage of the bill was larger, so they won. **(b)** By detailing the counting of the members and the votes, Macaulay builds suspense at the outcome.
5. Macaulay's final statement links the victory to the new future it has opened up.
6. Students will probably say that Macaulay's account conveys the passion of working, day-to-day politics more successfully, while Shelley's work conveys the fiery passion of political idealism.

was fluctuating with heads like the pit of a theater. But you might have heard a pin drop as Duncannon read the numbers. Then again the shouts broke out—and many of us shed tears—I could scarcely refrain. And the jaw of Peel[4] fell; and the face of Twiss[5] was as the face of a damned soul; and Herries[6] looked like Judas taking his neck-cloth off for the last operation. We shook hands and clapped each other on the back, and went out laughing, crying, and huzzaing into the lobby. And no sooner were the outer doors opened than another shout answered that within the house. All the passages and the stairs into the waiting rooms were thronged by people who had waited till four in the morning to know the issue. We passed through a narrow lane between two thick masses of them; and all the way down they were shouting and waving their hats; till we got into the open air. I called a cabriolet—and the first thing the driver asked was, "Is the Bill carried?"—"Yes, by one." "Thank God for it, Sir." And away I rode to Grey's Inn—and so ended a scene which will probably never be equalled till the reformed Parliament wants reforming; and that I hope will not be till the days of our grandchildren—till that truly orthodox and apostolical person Dr. Francis Ellis[7] is an archbishop of eighty.

4. **Peel** Sir Robert Peel (1788–1850), a leading member of the Tory party, which opposed the bill.
5. **Twiss** Horace Twiss, another Tory who opposed the bill.
6. **Herries** J. C. Herries, another Tory who opposed the bill.
7. **Francis Ellis** six-year-old son of Thomas Ellis.

Review and Assess

Thinking About the Selections

1. **(a) Recall:** In "A Song," what questions does the speaker ask his audience in the first stanza? **(b) Connect:** In your own words, sum up all the speaker's questions in a single ironic question to the men of England.
2. **(a) Recall:** To what does the speaker compare England's workers in stanza 3? **(b) Interpret:** In your own words, explain the point of this comparison.
3. **Draw Conclusions:** Judging from the last stanzas, what alternatives is Shelley posing in the poem? Support your answer.
4. **(a) Recall:** Summarize the events of the House of Commons vote on the Reform Bill of 1832, as reported in "On the Passing of the Reform Bill." **(b) Analyze:** In what ways does Macaulay add suspense to his account?
5. **Draw Conclusions:** How does Macaulay's final statement convey the importance of the occasion?
6. **Evaluate:** Which selection conveys the passion of politics more successfully? Explain.

ASSESSMENT PRACTICE: Reading Comprehension

Critical Reasoning **(For more practice, see Test Preparation Workbook, p. 36.)**

Many tests require students to judge the relevance of facts in a writer's argument. Use this sample test item.

> . . . we had six hundred and eight members present, more by fifty-five than ever were at a division before. . . . When the opposition went out into the lobby,—an operation by the by which took up twenty minutes or more,—we spread ourselves over the benches on both sides of the House. For there were many of us who had not been able to find a seat. . . .

Which of these facts does not support the main idea of this passage?

A Fifty-five more members were present than ever before.
B Many people could not find a seat.
C It took twenty minutes for the opposition to go into the lobby.
D There were benches in the House.

A, B, and C support the main idea, concerning the unusual number of people present. The answer is *D*.

Review and Assess

Literary Analysis

Political Commentary

1. Identify one implied and one stated assumption about the causes of the workers' rebellion that Byron makes in his **political commentary** "Speech to Parliament."
2. (a) What evidence does Byron present to support his argument that the "death bill" is unjust? (b) What evidence does Byron present in his argument that it will be ineffective?
3. (a) Summarize Shelley's argument in "A Song: 'Men of England.'" (b) Evaluate his arguments, using a chart like the one shown.

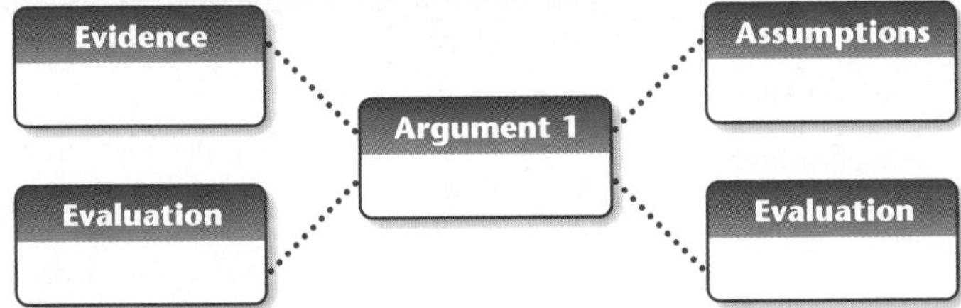

Comparing Literary Works

4. (a) Find three **rhetorical questions** in Byron's speech. (b) Find three examples of **balanced clauses** in Shelley's "A Song: 'Men of England.'" (c) Compare the effect of each device on a reader.
5. (a) Contrast Macaulay's purpose and audience with Byron's or Shelley's. (b) Explain how the drama Macaulay builds in his letter adds conviction to his claim that "the Reform Bill must pass."
6. Which of these pieces do you think was probably most effective in achieving its goal? Why?

Reading Strategy

Setting a Purpose for Reading

7. List three details on which you would focus if your purpose in reading Byron's speech was to learn more about his life.
8. Choose a section from one of the selections, and show how reading it with two different purposes uncovers different details.

Extend Understanding

9. **World Events Connection:** What new technologies today threaten the jobs of workers?

Quick Review

Political commentary is speech or writing that offers opinions on political issues.

Writers of political commentary use **persuasive devices** such as **rhetorical questions** and **balanced clauses** to make their points compelling.

Setting a purpose for reading will help you focus and find the information you want.

 ***Take It to the Net***

www.phschool.com

Take the interactive self-test online to check your understanding of these selections.

ENRICHMENT: Further Reading

Other Works by the Authors

When Man Hath No Freedom to Fight for at Home, Lord Byron

England in 1810, Percy Bysshe Shelley

The History of England, Thomas Babington Macaulay

 ***Take It to the Net***

Visit www.phschool.com for more information on the authors.

Answers for p. 775

Review and Assess

1. Byron implies that social inequalities are a cause of the workers' rebellion; he states that poverty is a cause.
2. **(a)** Byron argues that the workers were driven to crime by unbearable circumstances. **(b)** He argues that people who have faced starvation will not be deterred by the threat of death.
3. **(a)** Shelley argues that the men of England should rebel against their exploiters. **(b)** Argument: The workers should rebel because they are being exploited. Evidence: While they toil, others enjoy luxury. Assumption: Inequalities in wealth justify rebellion. Evaluation: Students may note that Shelley does not offer detailed evidence or arguments.
4. **(a)** Possible responses include: "Are these the remedies for a starving and desperate populace?" **(b)** Possible responses include: "The seed ye sow, another reaps; / The wealth ye find, another keeps; / The robes ye weave, another bears." **(c)** Students may say that Byron's repetitive hammering away at rhetorical questions is as effective as parallelism and repetition.
5. **(a)** Possible response: Macaulay's goal is to relate the actual vote on the Reform Bill; his audience is a friend. For both Byron and Shelley, the goal is to persuade; Byron's audience is Parliament; Shelley's audience is the workingmen of England. **(b)** Macaulay's account builds in suspense, creating the sense that events are rolling toward an inevitable conclusion.
6. Possible response: Byron's speech is thorough and persuasive, and it names an obtainable goal; it is the most effective.
7. Possible response: Students would focus on Byron's self-description, his account of his travels, and his infrequent attendance of Parliament.
8. Sample response: Readers who read Macaulay's second paragraph to learn more about the passage of the bill by the House will note the number of members present, the close margin of the vote, and details regarding the

continued

Answers continued

way in which the votes were counted. Readers who read to learn more about Macaulay himself will focus on the comparisons he makes, the passions he experiences, and his skill as a letter-writer.

9. Students may say that computers threaten to eliminate jobs.

EXTEND

Answers for p. 776

❶ Vocabulary Development

Word Analysis: Latin Root *-dec-*

1. d
2. a
3. e
4. c
5. b

Concept Development: Synonyms

Byron and Shelley saw the ways of the English upper class as *impediments* to the effort to *emancipate* people and give them *efficacious* control over their own lives. These poets saw poetry not as a *balm,* but as a weapon for the *decimation* of outmoded ideas. To them, the most *inauspicious* political sign was the stubbornness of the upper classes.

Spelling Strategy

1. spacious
2. simultaneous
3. beauteous

❷ Grammar and Style

1. Neither Byron nor Macaulay wrote "A Song: 'Men of England.'"
2. Both Byron and Shelley supported workers' rights.
3. Shelley not only compares English workers to bees but also compares England to a tomb.
4. Either the Tories or the Whigs would win the crucial vote.
5. Just as the Whigs celebrate the passage of the bill, so too does Macaulay.

Writing Application

Possible response: Just as the Republican Party gets much of its funding from corporate supporters, so too does the Democratic Party. Both the Democratic and the Republican Parties have faced opposition from third parties such as the Green Party in the past. Either the Democratic or the Republican Party may feel the pain of losing votes to such an outlying party.

Integrate Language Skills

❶ Vocabulary Development Lesson

Word Analysis: Latin Root *-dec-*

Byron asks whether Parliament desires the "decimation" of rebellious workers. The word *decimation* contains the Latin root *-dec-*, meaning "ten." *Decimation* originally referred to punishment for mutiny in the Roman army—killing every tenth person. Today, it means "any large-scale killing or destruction." The root *-dec-* appears in many words used in science and math.

Match each lettered word to its numbered definition.

1. animal with ten legs
2. fractions in tenths
3. unit of sound intensity
4. ten-sided figure
5. tenth of a liter

a. decimals
b. deciliter
c. decahedron
d. decapod
e. decibel

Concept Development: Synonyms

Replace each italicized word below with a synonym from the vocabulary list on page 767.

Byron and Shelley saw the ways of the English upper class as *hindrances* to the effort to *free* people and give them *effective* control over their own lives. These poets saw poetry not as a *salve*, but as a weapon for the *slaughter* of outmoded ideas. To them, the most *unfavorable* political sign was the stubbornness of the upper classes.

Spelling Strategy

Many adjectives, such as *inauspicious*, end in the suffix *-ious*. The *eous* spelling follows the consonants *n* and *t*: *spontaneous*, *courteous*. In your notebook, add *ious* or *eous* to correctly complete each word:

1. spac__ 2. simultan__ 3. beaut__

❷ Grammar and Style Lesson

Correlative Conjunctions

Correlative conjunctions work in pairs to link grammatically equal words or groups of words. Correlative conjunctions include the following: *either . . . or; not only . . . but (also); both . . . and; neither . . . nor;* and *just as . . . so (too)*.

It is clear that the Reform Bill must pass, either in this or in another Parliament.

Practice Use a pair of correlative conjunctions to combine each pair of sentences into a single sentence. Make any other changes needed.

1. (a) Byron did not write "A Song: 'Men of England.'" (b) Macaulay did not write it.
2. (a) Byron supported workers' rights. (b) Shelley supported workers' rights.
3. (a) Shelley compares English workers to bees. (b) He compares England to a tomb.
4. (a) The Tories would win the crucial vote. (b) The Whigs would win the crucial vote.
5. (a) The Whigs celebrate the passage of the bill. (b) Macaulay celebrates the passage of the bill.

Writing Application Write a short paragraph contrasting the major political parties in the United States today. Use at least three pairs of correlative conjunctions to link clauses, phrases, or words in your writing.

WG *Prentice Hall Writing and Grammar Connection: Chapter 17, Section 4*

776 ◆ *Rebels and Dreamers (1798–1832)*

TEACHING RESOURCES

The following resources can be used to enrich or extend the instruction for pp. 776–777.

Vocabulary

Selection Support: Build Vocabulary, p. 165

Vocabulary and Spelling Practice Book (Use this booklet for skills enrichment)

Grammar

Selection Support: Grammar and Style, p. 166

WG **Writing and Grammar,** Diamond Level, p. 397

Daily Language Practice Transparencies ■

Writing

WG **Writing and Grammar,** Diamond Level, p. 133 ■

Writing and Grammar iText CD-ROM

Writing Models and Graphic Organizers on Transparencies, pp. 37–44

■ **BLOCK SCHEDULING:** Resources marked with this symbol provide varied instruction during 90-minute blocks.

❸ Writing Lesson

Editorial on a Political Issue

Byron, Shelley, and Macaulay wrote persuasively on important political issues of their time. Write an editorial about a political issue of today. Report the facts clearly and concisely. Then, present your own opinion in forceful, persuasive language.

Prewriting Browse through newspapers or newsmagazines to choose a political topic. Next, take notes on the issue, answering *who, what, where, when, why,* and *how.* Then, formulate your opinion on the issue.

Drafting As you draft, use a pyramid structure: Present the most important information first, followed by details. Conclude with a forceful statement of your opinion on the issue.

Revising Review your draft, circling vague or general words and phrases. Replace these words and phrases with forceful, persuasive language.

Model: Revising for Persuasive Language

In such a tense situation, the answer "I have no comment at this time" represents more than indecisiveness. It is an *calculating cowardice.* act of ~~weakness.~~

A specific description, memorably phrased, adds persuasive force.

Prentice Hall Writing and Grammar Connection: Chapter 7, Section 4

❹ Extension Activities

Listening and Speaking Rehearse and deliver Byron's **speech** as he might have given it. Follow these tips:

1. Identify passages to emphasize for clarity or force. Alter the tone or volume of your voice, slow down, or add gestures for these parts.
2. Pay special attention to Byron's rhetorical questions, and deliver them forcefully for maximum impact.

Rehearse until you are confident, and then deliver your speech to the class.

Research and Technology Research an issue from this period of reform, such as the Luddite riots, the 1815 Corn Law, or the Peterloo Massacre. Then, write a **report** expressing an opinion on this issue. Use a variety of sources—such as encyclopedias, history books, and primary sources such as letters from the time— to research the issue. Then, decide what slant on the issue to take, and convey it in your report.

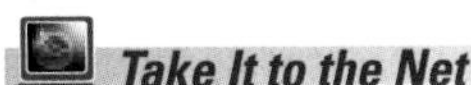

www.phschool.com

Go online for an additional research activity using the Internet.

Lesson Support for p. 777

❸ Writing Lesson

- Read with students the note for the writing lesson on p. 777, then tell students that they should develop an editorial on a political issue.
- Use the Writing Lesson to guide students in developing their thesis statements and their evidence.
- Explain to students that their editorials should report facts clearly and concisely and express their opinions in forceful language.
- Model the revision process using **Writing Models and Graphic Organizers on Transparencies,** pp. 37–44.
- Evaluate students' editorials using the rubric on p. 10 of **Performance Assessment and Portfolio Management.**

❹ Listening and Speaking

- Have students reread Byron's speech and rehearse it for delivery in front of the class.
- Read the Listening and Speaking note with students. Remind them to identify any lines that need special emphasis or inflection.
- Encourage students to practice speaking clearly and slowly, adding tone and volume where needed.
- Have students use the Delivering a Persuasive Speech Rubric, p. 32 in **Performance Assessment and Portfolio Management.**

CUSTOMIZE INSTRUCTION For Universal Access

To address different learning styles, use the activities suggested in the **Extension Activities** booklet, p. 36.

- For Visual/Spatial Learners, use Activity 5.
- For Interpersonal Learners, use Activity 6.

ASSESSMENT RESOURCES

The following resources can be used to assess students' knowledge and skills.

Selection Assessment

Formal Assessment, pp. 173–175

Open Book Test, pp. 106–108

Got It! Assessment Videotapes, Tape 3

Test Bank Software

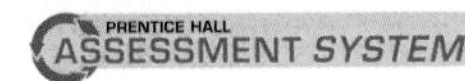

Visit www.phschool.com for self-tests and additional questions on the selections.

Listening and Speaking Rubric

Performance Assess. and Portfolio Mgmt., p. 32

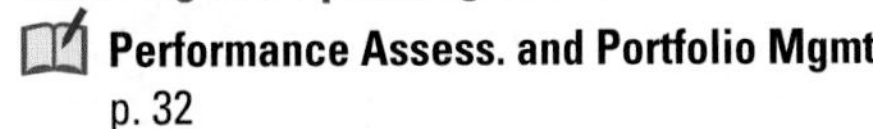

X 33422

On Making an Agreeable Marriage ✦ *from* A Vindication of the Rights of Woman

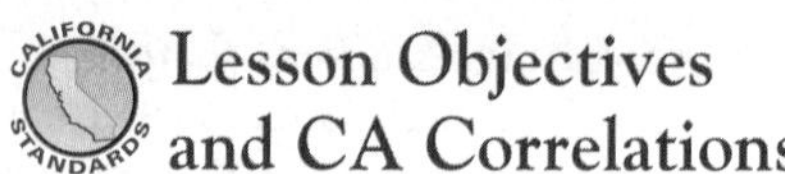

Lesson Objectives and CA Correlations

1. **To analyze and respond to literary elements**
   - Literary Analysis: Social Commentary **R 3.7**
   - Comparing Literary Works **R 2.4**
2. **To read, comprehend, analyze, and critique nonfiction**
   - Reading Strategy: Determining the Writer's Purpose **R 2.4**
   - Reading Check Questions
   - Review and Assess Questions
   - Assessment Practice (ATE)
3. **To develop word analysis skills, fluency, and systematic vocabulary**
   - Vocabulary Development Lesson: Word Analysis: Latin Root *-fort-* **R 1.1**
4. **To understand and apply written and oral English language conventions**
   - Spelling Strategy **LC 1.2**
   - Grammar and Style Lesson: Commas in a Series **LC 1.1**
5. **To understand and apply appropriate writing and research strategies**
   - Writing Lesson: Letter to an Author **W 1.9**
   - Extension Activity: Annotated Illustrated Timeline **W 1.7**
6. **To understand and apply listening and speaking strategies**
   - Extension Activity: Telephone Call Role Play **LS 1.6**

STEP-BY-STEP TEACHING GUIDE	PACING GUIDE
PRETEACH	
Motivate Students and Provide Background	
Use the Motivation activity (ATE p. 778)	5 min.
Read and discuss author and background features (SE pp. 778, 784; ATE p. 778, 785) A	5 min.
Introduce the Concepts	
Introduce the Literary Analysis and Reading Strategy concepts (SE/ATE p. 779) A	15 min.
Pronounce the vocabulary words and read their definitions (SE p. 779)	5 min.
TEACH	
Monitor Comprehension	
Informally monitor comprehension by circulating while students read independently or in groups A	15 min.
Monitor students' comprehension with the Reading Check notes (SE/ATE pp. 781, 785)	as students read
Develop vocabulary with Vocabulary notes (SE pp. 781, 782, 784, 785, 786; ATE p. 785)	as students read
Develop Understanding	
Develop students' understanding of social commentary with the Literary Analysis annotations (SE/ATE p. 782) A	5 min.
Develop students' ability to determine the writer's purpose with the Reading Strategy annotations (SE/ATE p. 781)	5 min.
ASSESS	
Assess Mastery	
Assess students' mastery of the Reading Strategy and Literary Analysis concepts by having them answer the Review and Assess questions (SE/ATE p. 787)	15 min.
Use one or more of the print and media Assessment Resources (ATE p. 789) A	up to 45 min.
EXTEND	
Apply Understanding	
Have students complete the Vocabulary Development Lesson and the Grammar and Style Lesson (SE p. 788) A	20 min.
Apply students' knowledge of appropriate language for a purpose using the Writing Lesson (SE/ATE p. 789) A	45 min.
Apply students' understanding using one or more of the Extension Activities (SE p. 789)	20–90 min.

ACCELERATED INSTRUCTION:
Use the strategies and activities identified with an A.

UNIVERSAL ACCESS
● = Below-Level Students
▲ = On-Level Students
■ = Above-Level Students

Time and Resource Manager

Reading Level: Average, Average
Average Number of Instructional Days: 4

RESOURCES		
PRINT	**TRANSPARENCIES**	**TECHNOLOGY**
• **Beyond Literature,** Cross-Curricular Connection: Social Studies, p. 37 ▲ ■		• **Interest Grabber Video,** Tape 4 ● ▲ ■
• **Selection Support Workbook:** ● ▲ ■ Literary Analysis, p. 172 Reading Strategy, p. 171 Build Vocabulary, p. 169	• **Literary Analysis and Reading Transparencies,** pp. 73 and 74 ● ▲ ■	
• **Adapted Reader's Companion** ● • **Reader's Companion** ●		• **Listening to Literature** ● ▲ ■ Audiocassettes, Side 19 Audio CDs, CD 11
• **English Learner's Companion** ● ▲ • **Literary Analysis for Enrichment** ■		
• **Formal Assessment:** Selection Test, pp. 176–178 ● ▲ ■ • **Open Book Test,** pp. 109–111 ● ▲ ■ • **Performance Assessment and Portfolio Management,** pp. 18 and 54 ● ▲ ■ • PRENTICE HALL ASSESSMENT SYSTEM ● ▲ ■	• PRENTICE HALL ASSESSMENT SYSTEM ● ▲ ■ Skills Practice Answers and Explanations on Transparencies ● ▲ ■	• **Test Bank Software** ● ▲ ■ • **Got It! Assessment Videotapes,** Tape 3 ● ▲
• **Selection Support Workbook:** ● ▲ ■ Grammar and Style, p. 170 • **Writing and Grammar,** Diamond Level ● ▲ ■ • **Extension Activities,** p. 37 ● ▲ ■	• **Daily Language Practice Transparencies** ● ▲ • **Writing Models and Graphic Organizers on Transparencies,** pp. 73–80 ● ▲ ■	• **Writing and Grammar iText CD-ROM** ● ▲ ■ ***Take It to the Net*** www.phschool.com

BLOCK SCHEDULING: Use one 90-minute class period to preteach the selections and have students read them. Use a second 90-minute class period to assess students' mastery of skills and have them complete one of the Extension Activities.

PREPARE TO READ

PRETEACH

Step-by-Step Teaching Guide for pp. 778–779

Motivation

With the class, speculate on the rights women did or did not have at the end of the eighteenth and beginning of the nineteenth-century in England. Make a three-column table with the headings *Careers, Education,* and *Marriage.* List all conjectures.

Then tell students that the selections that follow were written by two remarkable women, Jane Austen and Mary Wollstonecraft. Austen, in her novels, subtly and slyly comments on the unfair way women are treated socially and legally. In this personal letter, Austen's ideas about love and marriage are revealed to her niece. In *A Vindication,* Wollstonecraft boldly states her views on the rights women should enjoy.

Interest Grabber Video

As an alternative, play "'On Making An Agreeable Marriage': Marriage Customs Around the World" on Tape 4 to engage student interest.

1 Background

More About the Authors

Jane Austen

Jane Austen's advice to her niece is interesting in light of her own romantic life. Although she never married, she had several suitors, one of whose proposals she accepted one evening, only to withdraw her acceptance the next morning.

Mary Wollstonecraft

In 1788, after Mary Wollstonecraft returned from Ireland, where she worked as a governess to Lord Kingsborough's children, she spent some years writing reviews and translations for the radical publisher Joseph Johnson, who published her novel *Mary* (1788), *A Vindication of the Rights of Man* (1790), and *A Vindication of the Rights of Woman* (1792).

Prepare to Read

1 On Making an Agreeable Marriage ◆ *from* A Vindication of the Rights of Woman

Jane Austen (1775–1817)

Modest about her own genius, Jane Austen lived a quiet life devoted to her family. Although she never married, she nonetheless explored love, beauty, and marriage in her six novels, which include *Pride and Prejudice, Emma,* and *Sense and Sensibility.*

A Reserved Life Austen was born in Steventon, Hampshire, the daughter of a clergyman. The seventh of eight children, she was educated largely at home by her father. In her teens, Austen began writing parodies and skits to amuse her family.

An Anonymous Novelist As an adult, Austen put her gift for keen observation to work in her novels. Capturing the absurdities of social life with satirical wit, she makes brilliant observations on human nature and shows a gift for contriving dramatic situations. The opening line of *Pride and Prejudice* illustrates her satirical sense of the realities of love and marriage: "It is a truth universally acknowledged, that a single man in possession of a good fortune, must be in want of a wife." The "must be" speaks volumes about the scheming and gossiping that went on beneath the social niceties in Austen's day.

Like most women writers of the time, Austen published anonymously. As her identity became more widely known, she was honored by the Prince Regent a few years before her death. Her novel *Emma* is dedicated to him.

Hollywood Tributes Jane Austen's sharp, satirical eye and brilliant dialogue have made her enormously popular today. All of Austen's novels have been made into feature films, and Hollywood has "rediscovered" her in recent years, making new film versions of her work.

Mary Wollstonecraft (1759–1797)

Mary Wollstonecraft, the mother of writer Mary Wollstonecraft Shelley, is recognized as one of the first major feminists. She wrote revolutionary works attacking the restrictions on women's freedom and education. The movement for women's rights has been influenced by her writings ever since.

The daughter of a textile worker and sometime farmer, Mary Wollstonecraft grew up in poverty, yet she pursued an education. She worked at various times as a lady's companion and governess. With her sisters and a friend, she established a girls' school near London. In 1787, she wrote *Thoughts on the Education of Daughters,* criticizing the poor education given to most females of her day.

A Voice for Women In 1790, when the writer Edmund Burke attacked the French Revolution, Wollstonecraft defended it in *A Vindication of the Rights of Man.* Two years later, she produced her most important work, *A Vindication of the Rights of Woman,* a landmark book on women's rights.

Wollstonecraft lived for a brief time in Paris, where she witnessed the French Revolution firsthand. Returning home to England, she joined a circle of radicals that included Thomas Paine, the defender of the American Revolution, William Blake, the poet (see p. 638), William Wordsworth, the poet (see p. 662), and the radical philosopher William Godwin. In 1797, she married Godwin. Six months later, she died from complications after giving birth to their daughter, Mary. Mary was also to become an important figure in literature: She married poet Percy Bysshe Shelley and, as Mary Wollstonecraft Shelley, wrote novels, including the famous *Frankenstein* (see p. 648).

TEACHING RESOURCES

The following resources can be used to enrich or extend the instruction for pp. 778–779.

Motivation

Interest Grabber Videos, Tape 4

Background

Beyond Literature, p. 37

Take It to the Net

Visit www.phschool.com for background and hotlinks for the selections.

Literary Analysis

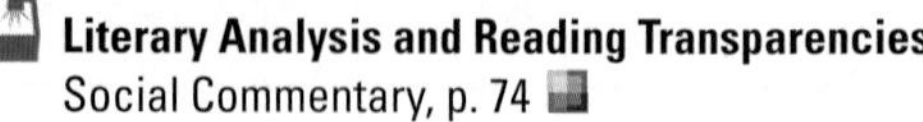

Literary Analysis and Reading Transparencies, Social Commentary, p. 74

Reading

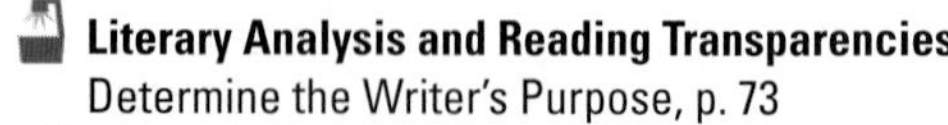

Literary Analysis and Reading Transparencies, Determine the Writer's Purpose, p. 73

Selection Support: Reading Strategy, p. 171; Build Vocabulary, p. 169

BLOCK SCHEDULING: Resources marked with this symbol provide varied instruction during 90-minute blocks.

Preview

Connecting to the Literature

"Boys will be boys. . . ." "Sugar and spice, . . . that's what little girls are made of. . . ." General assumptions like these rarely fit the facts, as these selections may suggest.

2 Literary Analysis

Social Commentary

Social commentary is writing or speech that offers insights into society. Social commentary can be *unconscious*, as when a writer points to a problem caused by social customs without explicitly challenging those customs. The commentary is *conscious* when a writer directly attributes a problem to social customs. As you read these selections, analyze the assumptions about women that they expose, consciously or unconsciously.

Comparing Literary Works

Austen and Wollstonecraft address widely different audiences for different purposes—Austen writes advice to her niece, and Wollstonecraft seeks to persuade the general reader. Both, however, use **persuasive techniques** that take the following forms:

- Appeals to logic based on sound reasoning
- Appeals to readers' sense of morality
- Appeals to emotion, addressing readers' feelings

As you read, compare the types of appeals that the writers use. Do they emphasize different ones? Evaluate the effectiveness of each.

3 Reading Strategy

Determining the Writer's Purpose

When reading, **determine the writer's purpose**—what he or she wants to accomplish—by using background knowledge and clues such as the title of the work. Use a chart like the one shown.

Background
Author supported equal rights.
Clues in Title
Vindication means "justification."
Direct Statements
Reports that she has done research on education
Writer's Tone
Reasonable, but she also expresses impatience, disbelief
↓
Writer's Purpose

Vocabulary Development

scruple (skrōō´ pəl) *n.* hesitation caused by one's principles (p. 781)

amiable (ā´ mē ə bəl) *adj.* friendly; agreeable (p. 782)

vindication (vin´ də kā´ shən) *n.* act of providing justification or support for (p. 784)

solicitude (sə lis´ ə tōōd´) *n.* care; concern (p. 784)

fastidious (fas tid´ ē əs) *adj.* particular; difficult to please (p. 785)

specious (spē´ shəs) *adj.* deceptively attractive or valid; false (p. 785)

fortitude (fôrt´ ə tōōd´) *n.* courage; strength to endure (p. 785)

preponderates (prē pän´ dər āts´) *v.* dominates; causes the arm of a balance scale to tip downward (p. 786)

gravity (grav´ i tē) *n.* weight; seriousness (p. 786)

2 Literary Analysis

Social Commentary

- Tell students that in this lesson they will focus on social commentary, writing or speech that offers insights into society.
- Read the note about social commentary together as a class. Call students' attention to the difference between unconscious and conscious social commentary.
- Use the instruction for Comparing Literary Works to review with students the effects of persuasive arguments such as appeals to logic, to morality, and to emotion.
- Use the Social Commentary transparency in **Literary Analysis and Reading Transparencies,** p. 74, to demonstrate how to interpret features of social commentary.

3 Reading Strategy

Determining the Writer's Purpose

- Explain to students that before they begin reading they should try to ascertain or determine the writer's purpose, or goal.
- Read the note about Determining the Writer's Purpose together as a class.
- Encourage students to use background knowledge and clues such as the title of a work to determine the author's purpose.
- Have students practice this skill using the Determine the Writer's Purpose transparency on p. 73 of **Literary Analysis and Reading Transparencies.**

Vocabulary Development

- Pronounce each vocabulary word for students, and read the definitions as a class. Have students identify any words with which they are already familiar.

CUSTOMIZE INSTRUCTION FOR UNIVERSAL ACCESS

For Special Needs Students	For Less Proficient Readers	For English Learners
Have students read the adapted version of "A Vindication of the Rights of Woman" in the **Adapted Reader's Companion.** This version provides basic-level instruction in an interactive format with questions and write-on lines. Completing the adapted version will prepare students to read the selection in the Student Edition.	Have students read "A Vindication of the Rights of Woman" in the **Reader's Companion.** This version provides basic-level instruction in an interactive format with questions and write-on lines. After students finish the selection in **Reader's Companion,** have them complete the questions and activities in the Student Edition.	Have students read the adapted version of "A Vindication of the Rights of Woman" in the **English Learner's Companion.** This version provides basic-level instruction in an interactive format with questions and write-on lines. Completing the adapted version will prepare students to read the selection in the Student Edition.

 ***E-Teach***

Visit E-Teach at www.phschool.com for teachers' essays on how to teach, with questions and answers.

TEACH

Step-by-Step Teaching Guide for pp. 780–786

CUSTOMIZE INSTRUCTION
For Verbal/Linguistic Learners

Invite students to focus their attention on how these social commentaries differ in style and language from commentaries they might read today. Students might comment on, for example, the length of Austen's letter, as well as the sentence structure, word choice, and even the use of the ampersand. Students might also comment on how Wollstonecraft's use of figurative language is different from any that readers might encounter today.

❶ About the Selection

Responding in a letter to her niece Fanny Knight, who has recently expressed doubts about her suitor, Austen not only advises her niece but also comments neatly on what makes a desirable marriage in Austen's social class in the early 1800s.

❷ Background

Art

Marriage à la Mode: The Marriage Contract, William Hogarth

This painting, which is the first in a series of six that Hogarth painted, shows the beginning of the marriage: the contract. At the left of the picture sit the bride- and groom-to-be. The groom is so busy looking at himself in the mirror that he does not notice the lawyer flirting with his bride-to-be. At the table, the two fathers work out the financial details of the arrangement.

Use these questions for discussion:

1. Is the scene one of social or business activity? Explain
   Answer: The fathers are discussing serious business matters. One lawyer, though, appears to be chatting or flirting with the bride, introducing a social note into this business scene.

❸ ▶Critical Viewing

Answer: Hogarth suggests that the event is a combination of a social affair and a business transaction, echoing Austen's concern with the social conventions and monetary considerations surrounding marriage.

❶ On Making an Agreeable Marriage

Jane Austen

❷ ***Marriage à la Mode: The Marriage Contract, 1743,*** William Hogarth, National Gallery of Art, London

❸ ▲**Critical Viewing** In what ways does William Hogarth's (1697–1764) satirical depiction of the signing of a wedding contract echo attitudes in Austen's letter? **[Compare and Contrast]**

TEACHING RESOURCES

The following resources can be used to enrich or extend the instruction for pp. 780–786.

Literary Analysis

- **Selection Support:** Literary Analysis, p. 172

Reading

- **Adapted Reader's Companion**
- **Reader's Companion**
- **English Learner's Companion**
- **Listening to Literature Audiocassettes,** Side 19
- **Listening to Literature Audio CDs,** CD 11

To Fanny Knight[1]
Friday 18–Sunday 20 November 1814
Chawton Nov: 18.—Friday

4 I feel quite as doubtful as you could be my dearest Fanny as to *when* my Letter may be finished, for I can command very little quiet time at present, but yet I must begin, for I know you will be glad to hear as soon as possible, & I really am impatient myself to be writing something on so very interesting a subject, though I have no hope of writing anything to the purpose.—I shall do very little more I dare say than say over again, what you have said before.—I was certainly a good deal surprised *at first*—as I had no suspicion of any change in your feelings, and I have no scruple in saying that you cannot be in Love. My dear Fanny, I am ready to laugh at the idea—and yet it is no laughing matter to have had you so mistaken as to your own feelings—And with all my heart I wish I had cautioned you on that point when first you spoke to me;—but tho' I did not think you then so *much* in love as you thought yourself, I did consider you as being attached in a degree—quite sufficiently for happiness, as I had no doubt it would increase with opportunity.—And from the time of our being in London together, I thought you really very much in love.—But you certainly are not at all—there is no concealing it.—What strange creatures we are!—It seems as if your being secure of him (as you say yourself) had made you Indifferent.—There was a little disgust I suspect, at the Races—& I do not wonder at it. His expressions then would not do for one who had rather more Acuteness, Penetration & Taste, than Love, which was your case. And yet, after all, I *am* surprised that the change in your feelings should be so great.—He is, just what he ever was, only more evidently & uniformly devoted to *you*. This is all the difference.—How shall we account for it?—My dearest Fanny, I am writing what will not be of the smallest use to you. I am feeling differently every moment, & shall not be able to suggest a single thing that can assist your Mind.—I could lament in one sentence & laugh in the next, but as to Opinion or Counsel I am sure none will [be] extracted worth having from this Letter.—I read yours through the very even[2] I received it—getting away by myself—I could not bear to leave off, when I had once begun.—I was full of curiosity & concern. Luckily Your Aunt C. dined at the other house, therefore I had not to maneuver away from *her*;—& as to anybody else, I do not care.—Poor dear Mr J. P![3]—Oh! dear Fanny, Your mistake has been one that thousands of women fall into. He was the *first* young Man who attached himself to you. That was the charm, & most powerful it is.—Among the multitudes however that make the same mistake with Yourself, there can be few indeed who have so little reason to regret it;—*his* Character & *his* attachment leave you nothing to be

scruple (skrōō′ pəl) *n.* hesitation caused by one's principles

Reading Strategy
Determining the Writer's Purpose What is Austen's purpose in claiming she has "no hope of writing anything to the purpose"?

5 
Reading Check
What news from Fanny prompts Austen's reaction?

1. **Fanny Knight** Fanny Austen Knight was the daughter of Austen's brother Edward.
2. **even** evening.
3. **Mr J. P.** Fanny's suitor.

4 Reading Strategy

Determining the Writer's Purpose

- Have students read the bracketed passage to themselves.
- Remind students that by using any prior knowledge on the subject and considering the title of a selection, they may be able to determine the writer's purpose.
- Ask the Reading Strategy question on p. 781: What is Austen's purpose in claiming she has "no hope of writing anything to the purpose"?
  Possible responses: Austen says this to offset any fear her niece may have that she will attempt to dictate her niece's actions. Indeed, Austen's letter is quite "to the purpose," giving solid advice.

5 Reading Check

Answer: Fanny's revelation that her feelings toward her suitor have changed prompts Austen's letter.

CUSTOMIZE INSTRUCTION FOR UNIVERSAL ACCESS

For Special Needs Students	For English Learners	For Advanced Readers
Encourage students who are struggling with comprehension to determine the writer's purpose before they read, making a list of questions they hope to have answered. Direct them to an abridged version of the text in the **Adapted Reader's Companion.**	Have students read the biography of Austen before they begin reading the selection with teacher guidance. Encourage students to practice repeating words or phrases that are especially difficult. Then have students listen to this selection on **Listening to Literature CDs,** CD 11.	Have students read "On Making an Agreeable Marriage" independently. Then have them imagine that they are Mr. J. P. and that Fanny has shared her aunt's letter with them. In the voice of Mr. J. P., have students write letters to Jane Austen, telling her how they feel about what she has told her niece.

6 Literary Analysis

Social Commentary

- Have students read the bracketed passage to themselves.
- Remind students that social commentary offers insights into society.
- Ask the first Literary Analysis question on p. 782: What do these details reveal about the criteria for judging a suitor in Austen's day?
  Answer: These lines suggest that Austen's society valued social status ("His situation in life"), respectability, good companionship ("His uncommonly amiable mind"), and achievement, including distinction in scholarship.

7 Literary Analysis

Social Commentary

- Read the bracketed passage aloud to students.
- Review students' understanding of the distinction between conscious and unconscious social commentary.
- Ask students in which category they would put Austen's letter to her niece.
  Answer: Students should recognize this letter as unconscious social commentary.
- Ask the second Literary Analysis question on p. 782: What assumptions about responsibility in courtship does this passage reveal?
  Answer: Austen suggests that her niece should not commit herself further unless she is prepared to marry her suitor; this advice reveals the assumption that the woman bears as much responsibility as the man in the development of a relationship.

ashamed of.—Upon the whole, what is to be done? You certainly *have* encouraged him to such a point as to make him feel almost secure of you—you have no inclination for any other person —His situation in life, family, friends, & above all his Character—his uncommonly amiable mind, strict principles, just notions, good habits—*all* that *you* know so well how to value, *All* that really is of the first importance—everything of this nature pleads his cause most strongly.—You have no doubt of his having superior Abilities—he has proved it at the University—he is I dare say such a Scholar as your agreeable, idle Brothers would ill bear a comparison with.—Oh! my dear Fanny, the more I write about him, the warmer my feelings become, the more strongly I feel the sterling worth of such a young Man & the desirableness of your growing in love with him again. I recommend this most thoroughly.—There *are* such beings in the World perhaps, one in a Thousand, as the Creature You & I should think perfection, where Grace & Spirit are united to Worth, where the Manners are equal to the Heart & Understanding, but such a person may not come in your way, or if he does, he may not be the eldest son of a Man of Fortune, the Brother of your particular friend, & belonging to your own County.—Think of all this Fanny. Mr J. P.– has advantages which do not often meet in one person. His only fault indeed seems Modesty. If he were less modest, he would be more agreeable, speak louder & look Impudenter;—and is not it a fine Character, of which Modesty is the only defect?—I have no doubt that he will get more lively & more like yourselves as he is more with you;—he will catch your ways if he belongs to you. And as to there being any objection from his *Goodness,* from the danger of his becoming even Evangelical,[4] I cannot admit *that.* I am by no means convinced that we ought not all to be Evangelicals, & am at least persuaded that they who are so from Reason & Feeling, must be happiest & safest.—Do not be frightened from the connection by your Brothers having most wit. Wisdom is better than Wit, & in the long run will certainly have the laugh on her side; & don't be frightened by the idea of his acting more strictly up to the precepts of the New Testament than others.—And now, my dear Fanny, having written so much on one side of the question, I shall turn round & entreat you not to commit yourself farther, & not to think of accepting him unless you really do like him. Anything is to be preferred or endured rather than marrying without Affection; and if his deficiencies of Manner &c &c[5] strike you more than all his good qualities, if you continue to think strongly of them, give him up at once.—Things are now in such a state, that you must resolve upon one or the other, either to allow him to go on as he has done, or whenever you are together behave with a coldness which may convince him that he has been deceiving himself.—I have no

amiable (ā′ mē ə bəl) *adj.* friendly; agreeable

Literary Analysis
Social Commentary What do these details reveal about the criteria for judging a suitor in Austen's day?

Literary Analysis
Social Commentary What assumptions about responsibility in courtship does this passage reveal?

4. **Evangelical** of or relating to a group of earnest Church of England members active in social reform movements at the time of the letter.
5. **&c &c** et cetera (the & symbol, called an ampersand, stands for *et,* Latin for "and").

ENRICHMENT: Cultural Connection

The Institution of Marriage

Although marriage is still regulated by varying laws all over the world, social and cultural regulations often prove as strong as or stronger than civil law. Endogamy, for example—the tendency of people or creatures from a group to stay within that group—often limits marriage partners to members of one's own tribe or section of a tribe, to one's own religion, or to one's own social class.

In Austen's day and among members of her class, endogamy was a key regulatory factor. The families concerned often controlled the marriage, negotiating the dowry, the living arrangements, and other crucial matters related to the union and future lives of the couple involved. The courtship period was characterized by the exchange of visits, which were chaperoned.

doubt of his suffering a good deal for a time, a great deal, when he feels that he must give you up;—but it is no creed of mine, as you must be well aware, that such sort of Disappointments kill any-body.—Your sending the Music was an admirable device,[6] it made everything easy, & I do not know how I could have accounted for the parcel otherwise; for tho' your dear Papa most conscientiously hunted about till he found me alone in the Din[g]-parlor,[7] Your Aunt C. had seen that he had a parcel to deliver.—As it was however, I do not think anything was suspected.—We have heard nothing fresh from Anna. I trust she is very comfortable in her new home. Her Letters have been very sensible & satisfactory, with no *parade* of happiness, which I liked them the better for.—I have often known young married Women write in a way I did not like, in that respect.

You will be glad to hear that the first Edit: of M.P.[8] is all sold.—Your Uncle Henry is rather wanting me to come to Town, to settle about a 2[d] Edit:—but as I could not very conveniently leave home now, I have written him my Will & pleasure, & unless he still urges it, shall not go.—I am very greedy & want to make the most of it;—but as you are much above caring about money, I shall not plague you with any particulars.—The pleasures of Vanity are more within your comprehension, & you will enter into mine, at receiving the *praise* which every now & then comes to me, through some channel or other.—

6. **device** trick; ruse; ploy.
7. **Ding-parlor** dining room.
8. **M.P.** Austen's novel *Mansfield Park*.

Review and Assess

Thinking About the Selection

1. **Respond:** How would you have reacted to this letter if you were Fanny? Explain.
2. **(a) Recall:** What is the "very interesting" subject Austen addresses in her letter? **(b) Interpret:** What change in her niece prompts Austen to comment "What strange creatures we are"? **(c) Summarize:** Summarize the problem that Austen is trying to help her niece resolve.
3. **(a) Recall:** What qualities does Austen find in Mr. J. P.? **(b) Interpret:** What does she mean when she writes that "Wisdom is better than Wit"?
4. **Summarize:** In one or two sentences, sum up Austen's advice to her niece about Mr. J. P.
5. **Make a Judgment:** Based on this letter, would you say Austen is a good judge of human nature? Why or why not?

Answers to p. 783

1. Possible responses: Fanny may have been forced by Austen's reasoning to confront what she really wanted.
2. **(a)** She addresses love and marriage. **(b)** Fanny's change in feeling toward her suitor prompts Austen's comment. **(c)** Austen is trying to help her niece resolve how she should handle her suitor if she doesn't want to commit to marrying him.
3. **(a)** Mr. J. P.'s "amiable mind," "strict principles," "just notions," and "good habits" recommend him as a suitor. **(b)** Austen implies that while Mr. J. P. may not be as much fun as others, his steady character is more important than his lack of charm.
4. Austen suggests that Mr. J. P. is a good person and a worthy husband, but if her niece cannot convince herself of this fact, she should break off their relationship immediately in order to prevent giving the wrong impression to Mr. J. P.
5. Possible response: Yes, Austen's observations about the reasons for Fanny's change in feeling—we are never satisfied with what we possess ("your being secure of him . . . has made you Indifferent")—shows real insight.

CUSTOMIZE INSTRUCTION FOR UNIVERSAL ACCESS

For Special Needs Students	For Less Proficient Readers	For Advanced Readers
Students may be intrigued to learn more about the period in which decisions about marriage were discussed with relatives and considered with special care. Show students "'On Making an Agreeable Marriage': Marriage Customs Around the World" on **Interest Grabber Videos,** Tape 4.	Explain to students that the letters of famous authors often serve as a form of autobiography. Have students write letters or e-mails to a friend, keeping in mind the assumption that their letter may turn out to be a historical document. Then, have students compare their letters to that of Jane Austen.	Ask students to discuss how Austen's letter functions as social commentary. Students should address whether the letter is unconscious or conscious social commentary. Direct students to www.phschool.com for more information on Jane Austen and her work.

8 About the Selection

Wollstonecraft sadly reflects on the fact that women's poor educational opportunities coupled with society's expectations about feminine beauty have rendered women silly and vain. In what begins as a sad voice and gradually becomes a more strident one, Wollstonecraft attacks this degradation of women.

8 *from* A Vindication of the Rights of Woman

Mary Wollstonecraft

Background

British women in the eighteenth and early nineteenth centuries had few economic or legal rights. In most cases, a woman's property was legally her father's until she married, after which the property became her husband's. Women's education focused mainly on "ladylike" accomplishments such as sewing and music. Women who showed an interest in things beyond marriage and the home were generally regarded as unfeminine. Mary Wollstonecraft focuses on the deforming effects that inadequate education had on women of her time and indicates the larger social forces holding women back.

After considering the historic page,[1] and viewing the living world with anxious solicitude, the most melancholy emotions of sorrowful indignation have depressed my spirits, and I have sighed when obliged to confess that either Nature has made a great difference between man and man,[2] or that the civilization which has hitherto taken place in the world has been very partial. I have turned over various books written on the subject of education, and patiently observed the conduct of parents and the management of schools; but what has been the result?—a profound conviction that the neglected education of my fellow creatures is the grand source of the misery I deplore, and that women, in particular, are rendered weak and

vindication (vin´ də kā´ shən) *n.* act of providing justification or support for

solicitude (sə lis´ ə tōōd) *n.* care; concern

1. **the historic page** the record of history
2. **man and man** used here in the generic sense to mean "human being and human being."

wretched by a variety of concurring causes, originating from one hasty conclusion. The conduct and manners of women, in fact, evidently prove that their minds are not in a healthy state; for, like the flowers which are planted in too rich a soil, strength and usefulness are sacrificed to beauty; and the flaunting leaves, after having pleased a fastidious eye, fade, disregarded on the stalk, long before the season when they ought to have arrived at maturity. One cause of this barren blooming I attribute to a false system of education, gathered from the books written on this subject by men who, considering females rather as women than human creatures, have been more anxious to make them alluring . . . than affectionate wives and rational mothers; and the understanding of the sex has been so bubbled by this specious homage, that the civilized women of the present century, with a few exceptions, are only anxious to inspire love, when they ought to cherish a nobler ambition, and by their abilities and virtues exact respect. . . .

The education of women has of late been more attended to than formerly; yet they are still reckoned a frivolous sex, and ridiculed or pitied by the writers who endeavor by satire or instruction to improve them. It is acknowledged that they spend many of the first years of their lives in acquiring a smattering of accomplishments; meanwhile strength of body and mind are sacrificed to libertine[3] notions of beauty, to the desire of establishing themselves—the only way women can rise in the world—by marriage. And this desire making mere animals of them, when they marry they act as such children may be expected to act—they dress, they paint, and nickname God's creatures . . . . Can they be expected to govern a family with judgment, or take care of the poor babes whom they bring into the world?

If, then, it can be fairly deduced from the present conduct of the sex, from the prevalent fondness for pleasure which takes place of ambition and those nobler passions that open and enlarge the soul, that the instruction which women have hitherto received has only tended, with the constitution of civil society, to render them insignificant objects of desire—mere propagators of fools!—if it can be proved that in aiming to accomplish them, without cultivating their understandings, they are taken out of their sphere of duties, and made ridiculous and useless when the short-lived bloom of beauty is over, I presume that *rational* men will excuse me for endeavoring to persuade them to become more masculine and respectable.

Indeed the word masculine is only a bugbear;[4] there is little
10 reason to fear that women will acquire too much courage or fortitude, for their apparent inferiority with respect to bodily strength must

3. **libertine** immoral.
4. **bugbear** frightening imaginary creature, especially one that frightens children.

The British Tradition

9 ***The Literature of Protest***

Mary Wollstonecraft writes in the tradition of protest in British literature. As early as the seventeenth century, the poet Amelia Lanier was speaking out for women's rights. By the beginning of the nineteenth century, the Romantics were urging a fair distribution of wealth and power to the working classes. Later, Charles Dickens and others would expose social problems through a newly popular form, the novel.

Twentieth-century poets, including Siegfried Sassoon, would chronicle the horrors of war. In the 1950s, the "angry young men," including Alan Sillitoe, would write grim portrayals of working-class lives. Wollstonecraft was an early voice in this tradition of protest.

fastidious (fa stid´ ē əs) *adj.* particular; difficult to please

specious (spē´ shəs) *adj.* deceptively attractive or valid; false

fortitude (fôrt´ ə to͞od) *n.* courage; strength to endure

11  **Reading Check**

According to Wollstonecraft, what does the "false system of education" train women for?

9 Background

It often takes a long time for protest literature to have a tangible result. Usually it is written on behalf of groups that have little or no power—otherwise they would not need someone else lobbying on their behalf. Also, before people change their behavior, it is necessary that they change their minds, and that is not a speedy process. There is one notable instance where protest literature led to a prompt response to a social ill. In 1906, the American writer Upton Sinclair published *The Jungle,* which told the devastating story of the meatpacking industry and the horrifying life of those who worked in it. This led to a huge public outcry—perhaps because virtually everyone eats meat—and reform of federal food inspection laws.

10 Vocabulary Development

Latin Root *-fort-*

- Call students' attention to *fortitude,* which means "strength of mind that allows one to endure pain or misfortune courageously." Explain to students that the Latin root of this word is *-fort-,* which means "strength" and appears in many words that express strength of one form or another.
- Have students suggest other words that contain this root and list them on the chalkboard.
  Possible responses: *comfort, fortify, fortress*

11 Reading Check

Answer: The false system of education trains women to be alluring rather than affectionate wives and rational mothers.

CUSTOMIZE INSTRUCTION FOR UNIVERSAL ACCESS

For Special Needs Students	For Less Proficient Readers	For Gifted/Talented Students
Have students read *A Vindication of the Rights of Woman,* with teacher guidance. Direct students who have difficulty with comprehension to reread the selection in the **Adapted Reader's Companion.** Discuss what Wollstonecraft's purpose is, who her audience is, and how her work functions as a kind of social commentary.	Have students imagine that Wollstonecraft is coming to their school to read from the work. Have students create posters or flyers that will attract people to attend the reading. Students should include key information about Wollstonecraft's message and visually reflect Wollstonecraft's ideas about women.	Remind students that social commentators sometimes create protest songs to convey their ideas. Have partners create the lyrics for a protest song that might have been written by Wollstonecraft. As they create their lyrics, students should think about the style of music that would best express their ideas.

ASSESS

Answers to p. 786

Review and Assess

1. Possible response: Yes, people need both the warmth of others' love and the dignity of their respect.
2. **(a)** Students may point to Wollstonecraft's use of *neglected education* and *misery*.
   (b) Wollstonecraft feels sad and depressed, because she believes passionately that women are treated without the respect they deserve.
3. **(a)** Wollstonecraft compares women to flowers that are planted in too rich a soil.
   (b) "Barren blooming" refers to women's being disregarded after the fading of their youthful beauty. **(c)** She attributes it to a "false system of education."
4. **(a)** "Notions of beauty" are important to women because they are socially encouraged to aspire only to marriage and reproduction. **(b)** This focus on beauty makes women neglect their intellectual and physical well-being.
5. **(a)** Wollstonecraft means that women should act as men—that is to say, rationally—and acquire courage and fortitude rather than the trappings of beauty.
   (b) Society encourages an idea of the feminine sex as more virtuous and weaker, which in turn produces an artificial weakness in women that "produces a propensity to tyrannize, and gives birth to cunning . . . which leads them to play off those contemptible infantine airs"—they become manipulative, like children.
6. Possible response: Wollstonecraft's argument is effective in that she gives many examples of how women's behavior is an outgrowth of their education. The argument could have been even more effective if she had been more scientific or specific in her examples.

render them in some degree dependent on men in the various relations of life; but why should it be increased by prejudices that give a sex to virtue, and confound simple truths with sensual reveries?

Women are, in fact, so much degraded by mistaken notions of female excellence, that I do not mean to add a paradox when I assert that this artificial weakness produces a propensity to tyrannize, and gives birth to cunning, the natural opponent of strength, which leads them to play off those contemptible infantine[5] airs that undermine esteem even whilst they excite desire. Let me become more chaste and modest, and if women do not grow wiser in the same ratio it will be clear that they have weaker understandings. It seems scarcely necessary to say that I now speak of the sex in general. Many individuals have more sense than their male relatives; and, as nothing preponderates where there is a constant struggle for an equilibrium without it has[6] naturally more gravity, some women govern their husbands without degrading themselves, because intellect will always govern.

preponderates (prē pän′ dər āts′) *v.* dominates; causes the arm of a balance scale to tip downwards

gravity (grav′ i tē) *n.* weight; seriousness

5. **infantine** infantile; childish.
6. **without it has** without having.

Review and Assess

Thinking About the Selection

1. **Respond:** Do you agree with Wollstonecraft that being respected is just as important as being loved? Explain.
2. **(a) Recall:** What emotional words does Wollstonecraft use in the first paragraph? **(b) Analyze:** Judging from the first paragraph, what is the author's attitude toward her subject?
3. **(a) Recall:** In the first paragraph, what comparison does the author use to describe the current state of women?
   (b) Interpret: What does she mean by the phrase "barren blooming"? **(c) Analyze:** To what cause does she attribute this "barren blooming"?
4. **(a) Recall:** According to the author, why are "notions of beauty" so important to women? **(b) Infer:** What effect does this focus on beauty have on women?
5. **(a) Interpret:** What does Wollstonecraft mean when she writes that women should become more "masculine"?
   (b) Summarize: According to the author, how do her society's notions of femininity encourage women to be childish and manipulative?
6. **Assess:** Which elements of Wollstonecraft's argument are effective? Which elements are not? Explain.

ASSESSMENT PRACTICE: Critical Reading

Critical Reasoning (For more practice, see Test Preparation Workbook, p. 37.)

Many tests require students to evaluate the assumptions on which a writer's argument depends. Use this sample test item.

> . . . [I have] a profound conviction that the neglected education of my fellow creatures is the grand source of misery I deplore . . . for, like the flowers which are planted in too rich a soil, strength and usefulness are sacrificed to beauty. . . .

The author's argument that women would be improved by education is based on the assumption that ___.

A nurture is an important factor in the formation of an individual
B women are less intelligent than men
C women are superior to men
D women are oppressed by their illiteracy

The author's argument is that education can fundamentally alter a person's values, judgment, and personality. The correct answer is *A*.

Review and Assess

Literary Analysis

Social Commentary

1. Judging from Austen's letter, and using a chart like the one shown, analyze the values of nineteenth-century courtship.

	Love	Compatibility	Money	Respectability
Examples				
Importance				

2. What unconscious **social commentary** does the letter offer on pressures that limited a woman's choices in the past?
3. Which social assumptions about men and women does Wollstonecraft challenge in *A Vindication of the Rights of Woman*?
4. Which assumptions about men's motives and desires does Wollstonecraft incorporate into her argument?

Comparing Literary Works

5. Compare the kinds of appeals used by Wollstonecraft and Austen in a chart like the one shown.

Logic	Ethics	Emotion

6. Compare the ways in which each writer handles an argument opposing her position.
7. How does each writer's audience affect her choice of **persuasive techniques**?
8. Explain which of the two works offer more effective commentary.

Reading Strategy

Determining the Writer's Purpose

9. Compare Wollstonecraft's and Austen's purposes in writing, explaining what clues you used to determine the purpose of each.
10. How does identifying a writer's purpose focus your reading?

Extend Understanding

11. **World Events Connection:** Is there still inequality in education for men and women? Support your opinion.

Quick Review

Social commentary is writing or speech that offers insights into a society and its customs.

Persuasive techniques are appeals to logic, ethics, and emotions used to convince readers.

To **determine a writer's purpose,** use clues such as direct statements and choice of title, details, and tone to determine what he or she wants to accomplish in a piece.

Take It to the Net

www.phschool.com

Take the interactive self-test online to check your understanding of these selections.

Answers for p. 787

Review and Assess

1. Possible response: (Top row) Love: "Anything is to be preferred or endured rather than marrying without Affection"—Importance: high. Compatibility: She cites Mr. J. P.'s amiable mind and strict principles—Importance: moderate; Money: She cites the fact that he is the eldest son of a man of fortune—Importance: moderate; Respectability: She cites his good character and good habits—Importance: high.
2. Austen's letter reflects the pressures on women to choose men who are moral and reliable whom they can rely on to support them.
3. She challenges the assumption that women should be alluring.
4. Wollstonecraft calls on male pride in male rationality; she assumes that women will remain dependent on men to some extent.
5. Possible response: Austen: Logic: He is a good prospect; Ethics: "Give him up at once" if you won't commit; Emotion: Do not marry without affection. Wollstonecraft: Logic: No "rational" man can disagree; Ethics: Men make women immoral; Emotion: Her indignation is clear.
6. Austen responds with emotion to the argument that her niece is no longer in love, saying she wishes her niece would fall back in love again; Wollstonecraft responds to male fear of independent, "masculine" women by logically pointing out the irrationality of the fear.
7. Austen can make direct appeals to her niece's emotions and ethics. Wollstonecraft's effort to reach the general public requires her to use a variety of general arguments in suggesting reform. She employs more logic and ethically persuasive language.
8. Possible response: Wollstonecraft's work is a more effective social commentary because it clearly lays out a social problem.
9. Possible response: Austen's purpose is to advise her niece, as her tactful tone makes clear.

continued

Answers continued

Wollstonecraft's purpose is to persuade by argument on a general issue, as is conveyed by her title.

10. Possible response: It helps the reader identify the main points.
11. Possible responses: Yes, males still dominate classrooms; no, males and females have equal opportunities.

ENRICHMENT: Further Reading

Other Works by Jane Austen

Pride and Prejudice; Sense and Sensibility

Other Social Commentaries by and About Women

"Ain't I a Woman?" Sojourner Truth

On the Equality of the Sexes, Judith Sargent Murray

"I Want a Wife," Judy Syfers

Take It to the Net

Visit www.phschool.com for more information on the authors.

EXTEND

Answers for p. 788

❶ Vocabulary Development

Word Analysis: Latin Root *-fort-*

1. A *fortress* is a building that is reinforced and strengthened to keep out unwanted people or attacks.
2. A *comfort* is something that makes someone feel more safe and secure.
3. To *fortify* something is to make it stronger.

Spelling Strategy

1. handle
2. double
3. marvel
4. quarrel

Concept Development: Synonym or Antonym?

1. antonyms
2. synonyms
3. synonyms
4. antonyms
5. antonyms
6. antonyms
7. synonyms
8. antonyms
9. antonyms

❷ Grammar and Style

1. Jane Austen's novel *Pride and Prejudice* is filled with grace, wit, and satire.
2. Five of its characters are Jane, Elizabeth, Mary, Kitty, and Lydia Bennet.
3. Their amusements include balls, visits, and letter writing.
4. The Bennets meet a number of people, including Mr. Darcy, Mr. Bingley, and two of Mr. Bingley's sisters, at a ball.
5. Jane falls ill at the Bingleys' home, is put to bed, and is visited by Elizabeth.

Writing Application

Possible response: Mary Wollstonecraft's tone, diction, and lucid form of address arouse my admiration for her ideas. She is intelligent, articulate, and correct in her statements that women are oppressed by society's conception of them as alluring sirens rather than as human beings.

Integrate Language Skills

❶ Vocabulary Development Lesson

Word Analysis: Latin Root *-fort-*

From the Latin word *fortis*, which means "strong," comes the English root *-fort-*, which means "strength." The word *fortitude* means "strength to endure pain or misfortune." Explain how *-fort-* contributes to the meaning of the following words:

1. fortress 2. comfort 3. fortify

Spelling Strategy

Many words, such as *scruple* and *amiable*, end in *-le*. Only a few words, such as *funnel* and *novel*, end in *-el*. When choosing between *le* and *el* to spell the *uhl* sound at the end of a word, remember that the letters *d*, *p*, and *b* are usually followed by *le*. The letters *m*, *n*, *r*, and *v* are followed by *el*. Add *-le* or *-el* in each of the following items to correctly spell an English word.

1. hand__ 2. doub__ 3. marv__ 4. quarr__

Concept Development: Synonym or Antonym?

Review the vocabulary words on page 779. Then, indicate in your notebook whether the word pairs below are synonyms—words meaning nearly the same—or antonyms—words that are opposite in meaning.

1. preponderates, dwindles
2. specious, false
3. vindication, justification
4. amiable, hostile
5. gravity, frivolity
6. solicitude, thoughtlessness
7. scruple, qualm
8. fastidious, sloppy
9. fortitude, weakness

❷ Grammar and Style Lesson

Commas in a Series

Austen and Wollstonecraft use **commas in a series**: They separate the items in a list with commas. A **coordinating conjunction** such as *and* or *or* appears before the last item in a series. (It is common to include the comma before the conjunction, but it is also acceptable to omit it.)

Example: His situation in life, family, friends, and above all his Character—

Practice Use commas to punctuate the following sentences correctly.

1. Jane Austen's novel *Pride and Prejudice* is filled with grace wit and satire.
2. Five of its characters are Jane Elizabeth Mary Kitty and Lydia Bennet.
3. Their amusements include balls visits and letter writing.
4. The Bennets meet a number of people, including Mr. Darcy Mr. Bingley and two of Mr. Bingley's sisters, at a ball.
5. Jane falls ill at the Bingleys' home is put to bed and is visited by Elizabeth.

Writing Application Write a paragraph in response to Wollstonecraft's *A Vindication of the Rights of Woman*, listing reasons you agree or disagree with her ideas. Use commas in a series to separate the reasons you list.

WG Prentice Hall Writing and Grammar Connection: Chapter 27, Section 2

788 ◆ Rebels and Dreamers (1798–1832)

TEACHING RESOURCES

The following resources can be used to enrich or extend the instruction for pp. 788–789.

Vocabulary

- **Selection Support:** Build Vocabulary, p. 169
- **Vocabulary and Spelling Practice Book** (Use this booklet for skills enrichment.)

Grammar

- **Selection Support:** Grammar and Style, p. 170
- **Writing and Grammar,** Diamond Level, p. 694

- **Daily Language Practice Transparencies** ▪

Writing

- **Writing and Grammar,** Diamond Level, p. 310 ▪
- **Writing and Grammar iText CD-ROM**
- **Writing Models and Graphic Organizers on Transparencies,** pp. 73–80

▪ **BLOCK SCHEDULING:** Resources marked with this symbol provide varied instruction during 90-minute blocks.

❸ Writing Lesson

Letter to an Author

Write a letter to either Austen or Wollstonecraft, in which you agree or disagree with her ideas. For example, you might write Austen agreeing with her views on marriage, while disagreeing with her interference in her niece's life.

Prewriting Choose an author, and jot down your reactions to the work and the author's opinions. Find specific passages within the work with which you agree or disagree.

Drafting As you draft, keep your audience and purpose in mind. To earn author's respect, use Standard English and a respectful tone. To catch her interest, choose words that convey enthusiasm about the topic.

Revising Review your word choice to make sure it sets a tone that fits your purpose and audience. Circle sentences that seem uninteresting or poorly worded, and revise them to create an appropriate, consistent tone.

Model: Revising for Audience and Purpose

Dear Ms. Austen:

~~Hey, Jane~~

was delighted to

~~I read~~ the advice you sent to Fanny regarding her choice of

wholeheartedly

a husband. I agree with your description of an ideal fiancé.

The writer's revisions show appropriate respect and enthusiasm.

WG Prentice Hall Writing and Grammar Connection: Chapter 14, Section 2

❹ Extension Activities

Listening and Speaking Update Austen's "conversation" about marriage in a role play of a **telephone call** between Austen and her niece.

- Update the language of the conversation to reflect the way an aunt and her niece might speak to each other today.
- Update Austen's logical, emotional, and ethical appeals to reflect today's values.

Rehearse and then present your phone call to the class.

Research and Technology Make an **annotated illustrated timeline** of the struggle for women's rights that began in the nineteenth century in England and in the United States. Highlight important dates, such as when women in each country won the right to hold property and when they won the right to vote.

www.phschool.com

Go online for an additional research activity using the Internet.

Lesson Support for p. 789

❸ Writing Lesson

- Read with students the note for the Writing Lesson on p. 789, then tell students that they will write a letter to either Jane Austen or Mary Wollstonecraft.
- Have students reread the selection by the author whom they will address in their letters.
- Remind students that they should jot down their reactions to the work and the author's opinions, finding specific passages with which they agree and disagree.
- You can review letter format using pp. 73–80 of **Writing Models and Graphic Organizers on Transparencies.**

❹ Listening and Speaking

- Read the Listening and Speaking note with students and have them update Austen's letter in a role play between Austen and her niece in the form of a telephone call.
- Encourage students to practice speaking clearly and slowly, rephrasing some of Austen's arguments in contemporary jargon—the way an aunt and niece might speak together today.
- Remind students to speak clearly and at an appropriate volume.
- Have students use the Persuasion: Persuasive Speech rubric on p. 18 of **Performance Assessment and Management** to evaluate one another's role-plays.

CUSTOMIZE INSTRUCTION
For Universal Access

To address different learning styles, use the activities suggested in the **Extension Activities** booklet, p. 37.

- For Visual/Spatial Learners, use Activity 5 or Activity 7.
- For Interpersonal and Musical/Rhythmic Learners, use Activity 6.

ASSESSMENT RESOURCES

The following resources can be used to assess students' knowledge and skills.

Selection Assessment

- **Formal Assessment,** Selection Test, pp. 176–178
- **Open Book Test,** pp. 109–111
- **Got It! Assessment Videotapes,** Tape 3
- **Test Bank Software**

Take It to the Net
Visit www.phschool.com for self-tests and additional questions on the selections.

Listening and Speaking Rubric

- **Performance Assess. and Portfolio Mgmt.,** pp. 18 and 54

PRENTICE HALL ASSESSMENT SYSTEM

- **Workbook**
- **Transparencies**
- **Skill Book**
- **CD-ROM**

BLOCK SCHEDULING: Resources marked with this symbol provide varied instruction during 90-minute blocks.

Objectives

1. To understand the connection between writings from the Romantic Era and culture today
2. To appreciate techniques used by filmmakers

Connections

The Romantic Era saw an influx of writers using their words to influence and educate the reading population. Whether uttered in innocence or boldly reprimanding, the political and social commentary of the times provided a catalyst for change. The issues of the Romantic Era still exist today and concern differences in the opportunities available to men and women, as well as to people of various backgrounds.

The Reactions to Society's Ills

- Bring examples of contemporary social commentary to the classroom. Include poetry as well as fiction. Encourage students to locate commentary in newspapers and magazines. Ask students if they think it is easier to find social commentary today than it was in the early nineteenth century.
- Explain that the screenplay by Emma Thompson from *Sense and Sensibility* deals with issues relevant to both Jane Austen's time and ours.

CONNECTIONS

Literature and Media

The Reaction to Society's Ills

The works in this section serve as political and social commentary on the problems of early-nineteenth-century England. Shelley and Byron champion the common worker, while Macaulay joyfully describes the passage of an important reform measure. Wollstonecraft powerfully states the need for women's rights. Austen, in her private correspondence, offers a more playful commentary on social conditions.

Social Awareness Today Much of Jane Austen's insight into social circumstances and character can still be applied today. In this excerpt from the screenplay for the movie version of Jane Austen's novel *Sense and Sensibility*, Emma Thompson follows Austen and skillfully explores issues of opportunity in what appears to be an innocent conversation between two friends.

As you read, notice how Thompson uses the directions in italics to explain the emotional atmosphere in which this revealing discussion takes place. In addition, note the CAM abbreviation that indicates camera direction. EXT stands for exterior or outside shot, and the numbers indicate the scene or shot.

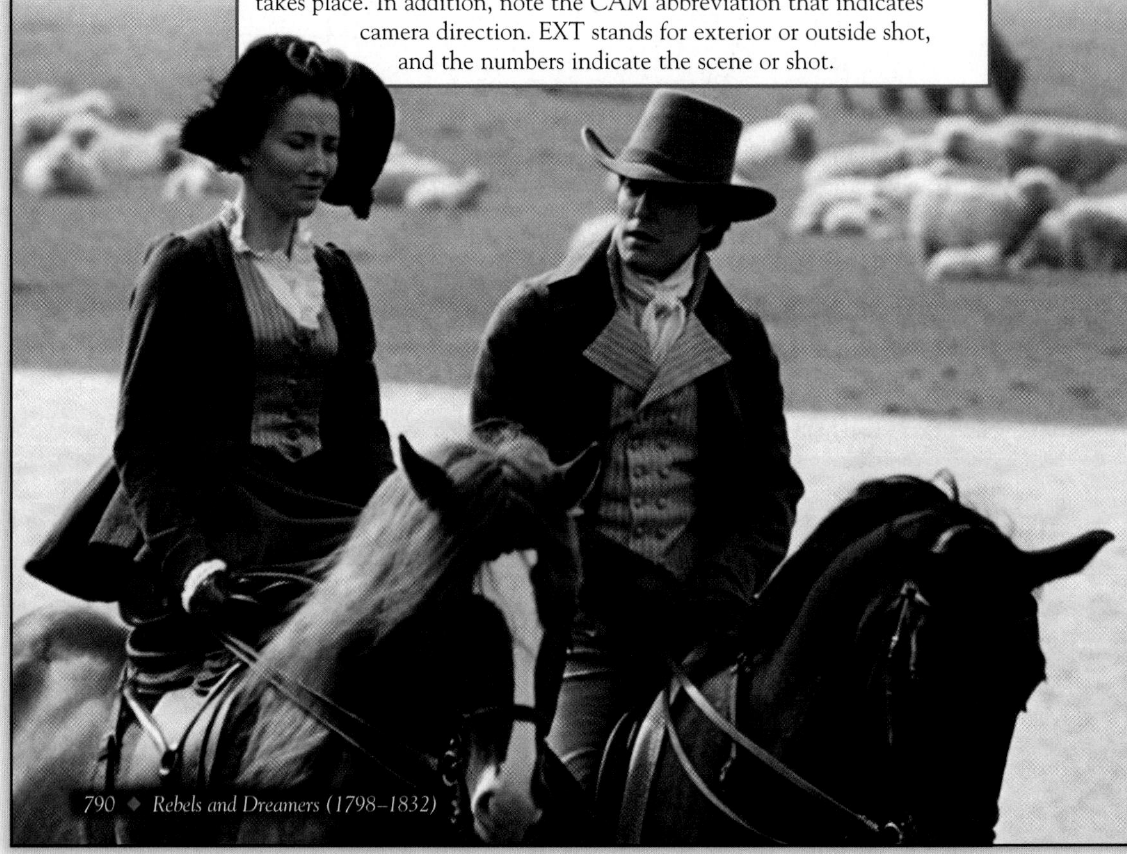

ENRICHMENT: Flim

Movie Still from *Sense and Sensibility*

This still shows a moment in the conversation between Elinor and Edward. You might point out that the still provides background information. Note the pastoral setting, with its grazing farm animals, and the kinds of clothing in which the actors are dressed.

Use these questions for discussion:

1. How does this movie still reveal the social conventions of the day?
   Answer: One can surmise from the formality of the dress that life itself was more formal. Riding sidesaddle, as Elinor does here, was probably proper for ladies.
2. In what ways does this still seem to suggest that there is some sympathy between Edward and Elinor?
   Answer: They are riding close together and slowly; they seem to be discussing something serious or taking each other quite seriously.

from Sense and Sensibility

Jane Austen, dramatized by Emma Thompson

After the recent death of Mr. Dashwood, his daughters Elinor, Marianne, and Margaret are trying to overcome their grief. Mr. Dashwood's eldest son and his wife, Fanny, have taken possession of the family home. Edward Ferrars, Fanny's brother, makes a great effort to comfort Margaret, the youngest, and in doing so begins to win the love of the eldest daughter, Elinor.

27 INT. NORLAND PARK. VELVET ROOM. ANOTHER DAY. EDWARD *comes into the doorway and sees* ELINOR *who is listening to* MARIANNE *playing a concerto.* ELINOR *stands in a graceful, rather sad attitude, her back to us. Suddenly she senses EDWARD behind her and turns. He is about to turn away, embarrassed to have been caught admiring her, when he sees she has been weeping. Hastily she tries to dry her eyes. He comes forward and offers her a handkerchief, which she takes with a grateful smile. We notice his monogram in the corner:* ECF.

ELINOR. (*apologetic*)
That was my father's favorite.

EDWARD. *nods kindly.*

ELINOR.
Thank you so much for your help with Margaret, Mr. Ferrars. She is a changed girl since your arrival.

EDWARD.
Not at all. I enjoy her company.

ELINOR.
Has she shown you her tree-house?

◀Critical Viewing What can you tell from this movie still about the type of conversation Edward and Elinor are having? **[Interpret]**

Thematic Connection
What details show the social class to which these characters belong?

Background

Social Studies

- Explain to students that a woman and man in Austen's day who were acquainted but not related by marriage or by being members of the same immediate family would have addressed each other as Miss and Mister.
- Ask students to characterize the style in which Elinor and Edward address each other.
  Answer: Elinor and Edward address each other formally.
- Ask students why this mode of interaction might seem confining.
  Possible response: The two are clearly close, even intimate, friends, so the formality may seem unnecessary.

Thematic Connection

Answer: The velvet room with the piano situated inside and the monogrammed handkerchief handed to Elinor by Edward reveal their wealth and a connection to the arts. The families in this scene are well off, probably have servants, and concentrate on the pleasures of life rather than the hardships of labor.

▶Critical Viewing

Answer: The looks on the actors' faces suggest that the conversation is a serious one. Both appear to be thoughtful, although in this particular still it seems as if Edward is posing the difficult questions and Elinor is merely contemplating them.

CUSTOMIZE INSTRUCTION FOR UNIVERSAL ACCESS

For Less Proficient Readers	For English Learners	For Advanced Readers
Explain that this screenplay selection is a conversation between Miss Elinor Dashwood and Mr. Edward Ferrars. Invite two readers to take those parts. Encourage readers to read the screenplay selection through and then re-read, stopping whenever they have questions or are unsure about what is being discussed.	There are many words throughout the text that may be unfamiliar to English Language learners, such as the words "piracy" and "swabbing." Encourage students to ask questions and assist them in making connections as they read.	Encourage students to locate a piece of current political or social commentary in a newspaper, magazine, or other piece of literature that deals with the same issues as the screenplay selection. Have students read their selections to the class and detail why the issues are similar.

Thematic Connection

Answer: Edward is saying that Margaret, who may be a young child, fancies taking him to China as her servant. The "bad" treatment he refers to is Margaret's (imagined) ordering him around to do every little thing she requires, much like the servants of the time were required.

Thematic Connections

Answer: Edward's mother seems to want to tell him what to do even though he appears to be a grown man. He is expected, because he is a man of a wealthy family, to become distinguished even if it is against his will.

- Ask students if they think this problem of parents trying to make their adult children's decisions is still common in our own times. **Possible responses:** Student may reasonably say that the problem still exists, though perhaps to a lesser extent or degree.

EDWARD.
Not yet. Would you do me the honor, Miss Dashwood? It is very fine out.

ELINOR.
With pleasure.

They start to walk out of shot, still talking.

ELINOR.
Margaret has always wanted to travel.

EDWARD.
I know. She is heading an expedition to China shortly. I am to go as her servant but only on the understanding that I will be very badly treated.

Thematic Connection What social assumptions does Edward's joke reveal?

ELINOR.
What will your duties be?

EDWARD.
Sword-fighting, administering rum and swabbing.

ELINOR.
Ah.

CAM *tilts up to find* MRS. DASHWOOD *on the middle landing of the staircase, smiling down at them.* CAM *tilts up yet further to find* FANNY *on the landing above, watching* EDWARD. *and* Elinor. *with a face like a prune.*

28 EXT. NORLAND PARK. GARDENS. DAY. EDWARD *and* ELINOR *are still talking as they walk arm in arm in the late-afternoon sun.*

EDWARD.
All I want—all I have ever wanted—is the quiet of a private life but my mother is determined to see me distinguished.

Thematic Connection What social forces shape Edward's life?

ELINOR.
As?

EDWARD.
She hardly knows. Any fine figure will suit—a great orator, a leading politician, even a barrister would serve, but only on the condition that I drive my own barouche[1] and dine in the first circles.

His tone is light but there is an underlying bitterness to it.

ELINOR.
And what do you wish for?

EDWARD.
I always preferred the church, but that is not smart enough for my mother—she prefers the army, but that is a great deal too smart for me.

1. **barouche** (be ro͞osh´) *n.* four-wheeled carriage with a collapsible hood and two seats on each side.

ELINOR.
Would you stay in London?

EDWARD.
I hate London. No peace. A country living is my ideal—a small parish where I might do some good, keep chickens and give short sermons.

30 EXT. FIELDS NEAR NORLAND. DAY. EDWARD and ELINOR *are on horseback. The atmosphere is intimate, the quality of the conversation rooted now in their affections.*

ELINOR.
You talk of feeling idle and useless—imagine how that is compounded when one has no choice and no hope whatsoever of any occupation.

EDWARD.
Nods and smiles at the irony of it.

EDWARD.
Our circumstances are therefore precisely the same.

ELINOR.
Except that you will inherit your fortune.

He looks at her slightly shocked but enjoying her boldness.

ELINOR. *(cont.)*
We cannot even earn ours.

EDWARD.
Perhaps Margaret is right.

ELINOR.
Right?

EDWARD.
Piracy is our only option.

They ride on in silence for a moment.

EDWARD. *(cont.)*
What is swabbing exactly?

Connecting Literature and Media

1. Contrast Edward's predicament with another social problem addressed in this section.
2. Do you think Edward is as oppressed by social institutions as are any of the other men and women described in this section? Explain.

Emma Thompson

(b. 1959)

London-born Emma Thompson is one of England's most talented and successful actors, both in television and in films. She received an Academy Award for her performance in *Howard's End*, along with two nominations for performances in *The Remains of the Day* and *In the Name of the Father.* Her writing career began with her script for an adaptation of Jane Austen's novel *Sense and Sensibility*, for which she won an Academy Award.

Background

Military Careers in Eighteenth-Century England

In Jane Austen's day, a career for a male in the military, presumably as a high-ranking officer, had much greater status, or was more "smart," than a career as a clergyman. Edward's present high rank in society makes it a logical choice for him to enter the armed forces rather than the church, as he would prefer.

Ask students to speculate why the army would be considered more noble than a quiet career in the cloth.
Answer: Students may say that military action at that time, especially as an officer, was considered highly difficult, requiring a high level of intelligence. The church may have been regarded as a simpler way of life, without the need for fast thinking and courage.

Answers
Connecting Literature and Media

1. Students should mention that Edward's lack of apparent choices of career are similar to that of the servant he mentioned for Margaret. Often, servants had no choice but to attend to their masters, suffering much poorer treatment than Edward.
2. Students may find Edward's problem to be trivial compared with those of the rioting weavers defended by Byron in his *Speech Before Parliament* or those of the women deformed by miseducation described by Wollstonecraft in her *Vindication of the Rights of Woman.*

ENRICHMENT: Further Reading

Other Jane Austen Novels in Film

Persuasion
Pride and Prejudice
Emma

Lesson Objectives

1. To write an evaluative essay about literary trends
2. To identify the characteristics of Romantic work
3. To understand the values of Romantic work and their place in society today
4. To use writing strategies to generate ideas and to plan, organize, evaluate, and revise writing

Prewriting

- Help students uncover Romantic values in work by first listing titles of selections in the unit. From these titles students should determine what values were presented and if these values are at all connected with modern-day values.
- If students encounter difficulty uncovering the values in their selections, have them look for specific lines in the selections that reflect Romantic values.
- When students have completed their lists, encourage them to locate examples in today's world that parallel the values from the Romantic period.

Writing About Literature

Evaluate Literary Trends

Writing about the impact of the Romantic writers, the noted critic Isaiah Berlin stated that "The world has never been the same since, and our politics and morals have been deeply transformed by them. Certainly this has been the most radical, and indeed dramatic, not to say terrifying, change in men's outlook in modern times." For some, Romanticism represented freedom and new possibilities for self-expression. For a critic like Berlin, the movement involved a frightening rejection of reason in favor of sentiment and idealistic passion.

Following the assignment outlined in the yellow box, write an essay evaluating the impact of Romanticism.

Assignment: The Legacy of Romanticism

What new values did Romantic writers celebrate? Do these values enrich our lives by emphasizing self-expression and other positive values, or do they lead to self-centered and undisciplined passion? Write an essay in which you evaluate the impact of Romantic values.

Criteria:

- Include a thesis statement that summarizes your overall evaluation of Romantic values.
- Show how two or three Romantic writers celebrate these values.
- Evaluate how these values are reflected in today's culture.
- Approximate length: 1,500 words

Prewriting

Find a focus. Review the works that you have read in this unit and think about the values celebrated by Romanticism as well as their possible impact. Use these questions and an organizing chart to help you evaluate works:

- Why is this work considered Romantic? What Romantic values does the work reflect?
- How have these values affected writers and the public? Has their impact been primarily positive or negative? Why?
- What modern values or trends can I connect with these values?

Model: Assessing Values to Focus Your Response

Work	Romantic Values	My Evaluation
". . . Tintern Abbey" Wordsworth	Nature as healer and teacher	This is a positive value that is often overlooked today.
"She Walks in Beauty" Byron	Admiration of beauty Physical beauty reflects spiritual depth	We value physical beauty too highly today.

Gather examples from literature. As you form your evaluation, look for specific lines that reflect the values of Romanticism. Concentrate on passages in which the poet celebrates or condemns an aspect of life or experience. These passages will help you formulate your thoughts and support your assessment.

Look for contemporary examples. To evaluate the full effects of Romanticism, you will also want to cite specific modern trends or events that show the impact of the values introduced by these writers. Review your notes on Romantic values, and freewrite on parallels in modern times. Then, list at least three ways that Romantic ideals influence today's world.

Read to Write

Review at least four Romantic works. You might begin with poems that you think are representative of the movement.

TEACHING RESOURCES

The following resources can be used to enrich or extend the instruction for pp. 794–795.

- **Writing and Grammar,** Diamond Level, Chapter 14, pp. 306–329
- **Performance Assessment and Portfolio Management,** pp. 25 and 92
- **Writing Models and Graphic Organizers on Transparencies,** pp. 45–56
- **Writing and Grammar iText CD-ROM** Students can use the following tools as they complete their evaluative essays:
  - Listing Tool
  - Sensory Word Bin
  - Sentence Variety Checker

Drafting

Organize. Start with a general outline. Then, fill in details and examples. As you draft, you may reconsider the structure you have chosen.

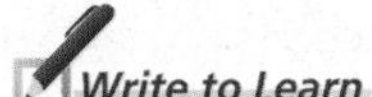

Write to Learn
If you cannot fill an outline section with two or three ideas, think about whether or not the heading is valid. You may need to rethink your evaluation to present an assessment you can support fully.

Model: Refining an Outline to Organize Ideas

Initial Outline:

II. Romanticism and Nature
- A. "Tintern Abbey"
- B. People today generally favor protecting the environment.
- C. "The Rime of the Ancient Mariner"

Reorganized, Elaborated Outline:

II. Romanticism Celebrates Connecting With Nature
- A. Examples From Romantic Writers
  - a. "Tintern Abbey": Nature as a source of wisdom
  - b. "Ancient Mariner": The mariner suffers when he violates nature
- B. Contemporary Relevance: Popular Concern With the Environment
  - a. Concern over global deforestation
  - b. Antipollution laws

Use specific examples. As you draft, include specific, relevant examples from both Romantic works and contemporary life.

Revising and Editing

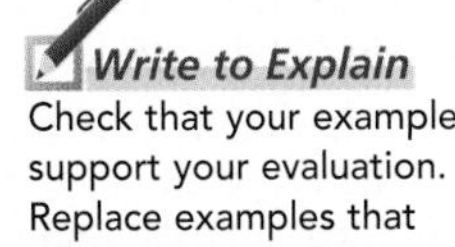

Write to Explain
Check that your examples support your evaluation. Replace examples that lead to digressions or confusion.

Review content: Begin and end powerfully. Review your opening paragraph to make sure you have introduced your evaluation clearly. Then, shape a powerful, focused conclusion.

Review style: Replace vague language. Eliminate words that are vague or imprecise. Strive for an active, vivid vocabulary.

Vague: Wordsworth *likes* nature because he can *find out lots of things* and *feel really comfortable there.*

Vivid: Wordsworth *values* nature as a *source of wisdom* and a *spiritual home.*

Publishing and Presenting

Hold a panel discussion. Find a classmate whose evaluation of Romantic values is quite different from yours. Read your essays aloud to the class, and then lead a class discussion comparing the two views.

WG *Prentice Hall Writing and Grammar Connection: Chapter 14*

CUSTOMIZE INSTRUCTION FOR UNIVERSAL ACCESS

For Less Proficient Learners	For English Language Learners	For Advanced Readers
Work with students to gather values from the Romantic Era selections by presenting specific passages where the poet speaks about life or life's experiences. Then have them work together to identify contemporary examples of these values either from literature they have read or experiences they have encountered.	Have students identify values from their own backgrounds which affect them on a day-to-day basis. Help students correlate some of these values to those of the Romantic values as presented in the literature. Encourage them to find specific lines in the passages where these values are listed.	Encourage students to look for more ideals in today's world that encounter some type of political or social commentary. Have students determine whether these ideals were reflected in the Romantic selections in the unit. If they were not, encourage students to investigate the beginnings of these values.

Drafting

- Remind students that a general outline is a way to organize the information collected during the prewriting stage. Also, it provides an opportunity to reconsider the original structure of the information.
- Have students include specific examples from their prewriting notes. These examples should be of values of both the Romantic Era and today's world and should be included in their outline.
- Tell students to elaborate on their original outlines, providing more background information to fully support their original thesis statement. In the model, the outline title was changed to incorporate an organized title and examples were grouped together to create greater impact.

Revising and Editing

- Students should check the impact of their opening and conclusion. If students find that either is weak or inconsequential, have them consider the weight of both areas. The conclusion should be as powerful as the opening. Students should rethink their thesis statement if they are not able to present their ideas in a robust manner.
- Remind students that when they remove vague wording to replace it with vivid vocabulary, they should concentrate on choosing words that engage the reader without making a dictionary search necessary. No clarity is gained by using "fancy" words.

Publishing and Presenting

- Allow students to locate individuals with differing viewpoints on the evaluation of Romantic values. Have these students meet together before presenting to discuss these different viewpoints. Have each group read among themselves and ask them to record their partners' valid points. Uncover views the writer might not have thought were present in his or her essay.
- When students have finished recording, read the essays aloud to the class. Have the partners tell the class the various viewpoints uncovered. Allow the class to add additional interpretations.

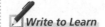

Lesson Objectives

1. To write a job portfolio
2. To use writing strategies to generate ideas and to plan, organize, evaluate, and revise the composition

Model From Literature

In the commentaries in this section the writers "sell" their ideas by supporting them with factual details. If these details were selling their qualifications to a potential employer, they would use the same basic strategies.

Prewriting

- Create an imaginary student in the classroom. Have students gather facts for this student, including the work experiences and skills that this student has. Make a list of these skills, leaving nothing uncovered. While students are at their desks, have them make the same type of list for themselves.
- Using the imaginary student's skill set, have students decide what type of position this student should apply for. Students should use their lists to determine their own job positions as well.
- If students need help deciding on the type of position they'd like to apply for, have them make two lists: one of their interests and one of their skills. They should then look over these lists and try to choose a position that relates to some of the items that appear on both.
- Students should shave down their experience and relate it to the position they are applying for. Point out to students that if they match the right information to the job, employers will be more interested in reading their résumé.
- Tell students to share their information with a partner. Partners should offer suggestions such as what items to omit from a résumé based on the job position they are trying to achieve.
- Before students draft their résumés, have them review the Rubric for Self-Assessment (p. 799) so they know what is expected.

Writing WORKSHOP

Workplace Writing: Job Portfolio

A **job portfolio** includes all of the materials you submit to an employer to introduce yourself and express interest in a job. It is centered around a **résumé,** a brief, formatted summary of your educational and work experiences. In this workshop, you will write your own résumé.

Assignment Criteria Your résumé should include the following elements:

- A list, with dates and brief descriptions, of your life and work experiences, including your education
- An emphasis on skills, interests, and experiences appropriate to the type of job you are seeking
- Precise, active language, following the résumé style
- Consistent use of a clear, easy-to-understand format

To preview the criteria on which your résumé may be assessed, see the Rubric on page 799.

Prewriting

Gather facts for the résumé. Make a list of your work experiences. Also, jot down high points from your education and real-life experiences that might mark you as a good employee. List dates for all activities. In addition, note any relevant skills you may have, such as knowledge of computer applications.

Match the information to the job. Consider the job itself and what information will most interest that employer. An ad agency may want to see creativity highlighted. A bank may be more interested in your math skills.

A résumé is often taken to represent a person's entire work history. However, you may choose to omit informal or short-term work experiences, especially if their inclusion will distract from more significant experiences. You can also use the *Objective* and the *Skills* sections of your résumé to highlight the interests or accomplishments you feel will most appeal to a particular employer.

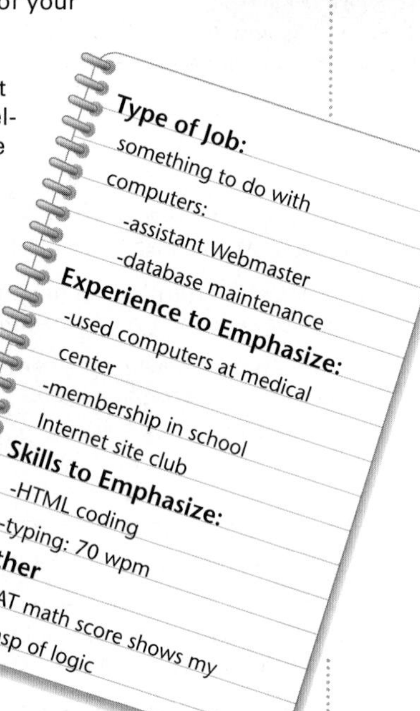

Type of Job:
something to do with computers:
-assistant Webmaster
-database maintenance
Experience to Emphasize:
-used computers at medical center
-membership in school Internet site club
Skills to Emphasize:
-HTML coding
-typing: 70 wpm
Other
-SAT math score shows my grasp of logic

TEACHING RESOURCES

The following resources can be used to enrich or extend the instruction for pp. 796–799.

- **Writing and Grammar,** Diamond Level, Chapter 16, pp. 348–363
- **Performance Assessment and Portfolio Management,** p. 12
- **Writing Models and Graphic Organizers on Transparencies,** pp. 73–80
- **Writing and Grammar iText CD-ROM** Students can use the following tools as they complete their job portfolios:
  - Cluster Diagrams
  - Descriptive Word Bins
  - Unity and Coherence Revising Tools

Student Model

Before you begin drafting your résumé, read this student model and review the characteristics of powerful résumés.

Sarah Bailey
333 Anystreet Ave.
Independence, KY 41000
(888) 555-5555
e-mail@e-mail.com

OBJECTIVE
To obtain a position in which I can utilize my computer skills and Internet knowledge.

WORK EXPERIENCE

March 2000–present — **Nutrition Assistant,** Hermes Medical Center South, 10 Hermes Drive, Anytown, KY
Monitored and implemented patient diets; consulted computer records, assembled individual patient trays, and communicated with nurses via hospital network.

May 1999–September 1999 — **Hostess,** Fine Dining, Anytown, KY,
Began as busser, promoted to hostess, July 1999; operated cash register; took responsibility for tracking receipts.

RELATED EXPERIENCE

Summer 1999 — **Web Site Developer:** Assisted in setting up a Web site for school club; devised directory structure; coded HTML

EDUCATION

Fall 1996–present — Simon Kenton High School, 11132 Madison Pike, Independence, KY 41051
Expected Graduation Date: May 2001
Special Courses: Keyboarding I; Advanced Placement Calculus; Advanced Chemistry

SKILLS

- typing: 68 wpm
- HTML coding
- knowledge of Java

SPECIAL ACHIEVEMENTS

- Perfect attendance for four years
- President of National Honor Society
- Ranked first in senior class with GPA of 4.5

References available upon request

Under headings like this one, Sarah lists her work, education, and other relevant experiences.

Sarah uses precise, active language and follows the conventions of résumé style.

Throughout, Sarah emphasizes experiences and skills related to her objective.

Bullets and boldfaced headings make Sarah's format clear and easy to follow. Headings, dates, and bulleted items are consistently aligned.

CUSTOMIZE INSTRUCTION FOR UNIVERSAL ACCESS

For Less Proficient Writers	For English Learners	For Advanced Writers
Encourage students to make a list of their experiences, including work and education, prior to beginning their job objective selection. Have them make a second list of their interests and choose a position that relates to some of the items that appear on both.	Tell students to use standard English and forceful language as they write their résumés. Concise vocabulary and brief entries will have more meaning to a potential employer.	Encourage students to view their résumé from a potential employer's perspective. Revise vocabulary that may be considered informal or "over the top" and add clear and specific details. Have students share their résumés with others to affirm these changes.

Student Model

- Ask students to name the titles of the headings in the document.
  Answer: The headings are Objective, Work Experience, Related Experience, Education, Skills, and Special Achievements.
- Discuss how Sarah uses simple and descriptive words to describe her experiences. Also point out the style in which her résumé is formatted. It follows the conventional traditions of résumé creation.
- Ask students if they notice anything about the way Sarah describes her experiences and skills in relation to her career desires.
  Possible response: Students should note that Sarah includes in her résumé work experience and skills that correlate with her desire to work with computers.
- Finally, point out to students the organization of Sarah's résumé: the typeface and structured format make the résumé easy to read.

Real-World Connection

There was a time when a smile and a handshake were enough to secure a job, but these days it takes a lot more than charisma to start a career. Employers are inundated by applicants for sought-after positions. They have to narrow their choices down before they can meet applicants in person, and their decisions are guided by applicants' relevant work experience and education. Discuss in class what types of characteristics an employer would look for in a résumé if that was the only information he or she would have to evaluate an applicant. Encourage students to think beyond the realm of experience but also point out that an organized résumé, free of grammatical and spelling errors is key to the process.

Drafting

- Explain to students that a résumé supplies the basic details that help employers determine whether one is the right person for job.
- Suggest that students begin by outlining their résumé using headings that are precise and easy for employers to understand. The best arrangement of precise headings will present the résumé builder in the most favorable light to the employer.
- Ask students to note which headings seem "the weakest" and without enough details underneath. Tell students to think about life experiences that may offer some support for these headings.
- Have students decide upon a format for their résumés based on their own personalities. A résumé should be well organized and detailed. It should be an accurate reflection of the student.
- Have students share their résumés with partners to get feedback on vocabulary, heading, and stylistic choices.

Revising

- Supply students with highlighters and have them follow the instructions in the text.
- Have students also keep an eye on the overall "look" of the résumé. While the headings may be boldfaced consistently and the information be in the right pattern, there may be too much space between certain lines. Make sure the résumé is free and clear of any formatting problems.

continued

Drafting

Outline your résumé. Begin by choosing and organizing your headings. Use clear, self-explanatory headings. *Education,* for example, is more direct than *Scholastic Preparation.* Organize headings effectively. No one résumé organization is best. You might use the order at right.

Headings	My Experiences
Education	
Work Experience	
Life Experience	
Skills	

Play to your strengths. If you, like many high-school students, do not have an extensive employment history, list life experiences you have had that in some way relate to the job, and emphasize those.

Select and follow a format. Résumés come in a variety of formats. The model on page 797 shows one. Whatever format you choose, follow it consistently. All résumé formats share these features:

- Your name, address, phone number, and any other contact information placed prominently at the top of the document
- A list of work experiences and other accomplishments beginning with the most recent
- Boldface or otherwise set-off names and addresses of employers
- Dates indicating your term of employment with each employer
- For each job listing, a brief indented description of your responsibilities

Follow résumé style. Do not use the pronoun *I,* but write as if it is understood. For example, write *Took responsibility for* or *Responsible for,* not *I took responsibility for.*

Revising

Revising for format. To check your formatting, follow these steps:

1. Scan your draft a few times without stopping to read. Check that items are correctly and consistently aligned. Mark items that are misaligned.
2. Scan the headings to confirm that you use boldfacing and capital letters consistently. Mark headings that need to be reformatted.
3. Scan the first line of your entries to ensure that, in each case, the information is ordered in the same pattern. Mark any inconsistencies.

When you have finished scanning your draft, go back and fix any problems.

March 2000–present **Nutrition Assistant,** Hermes Medical Center South

May 1999–September 1999 ^*Hostess,* The Frontier Inn, Anytown, KY, ~~Hostess~~

Boldfacing this job title and moving it to the beginning of the listing makes the format of the two listings consistent.

USING TECHNOLOGY IN WRITING

If students are using word processors to publish their résumés, they might want to consider saving a copy with minimal formatting to a disk. Many jobs can be applied for over the Internet using electronic applications. Résumés free of fancy type, italics, and underlining attach best to e-mails and paste into standard application forms with ease. Employers will also load these applications into computers for sorting, and complicated type and fancy formatting will only make the résumé less desirable. Students can also use the information on **Writing and Grammar iText CD-ROM.**

Revise for conciseness and clarity. Use brief explanations that get at the heart of things you have done. Let strong verbs carry your message.

Wordy: Made sure that surfaces were clean; disposed of fixer used in printing and other chemicals

Concise: Maintained darkroom

Compare the model and nonmodel. Why is the model more effective?

Nonmodel	Model
Looked after patients by making sure their meals were what the doctor recommended; worked with computers, looking up records and sending e-mails.	Monitored and implemented patient diets; consulted computer records, assembled individual patient trays, and communicated with nurses via hospital network.

Publishing and Presenting

Assemble a job portfolio. To complete your job portfolio, write a cover letter to a potential employer. Include the following elements:

- Brief, pertinent introductory information about yourself
- An expression of your interest in a job
- An overview of your qualifications for the job and your reasons for interest in it
- Contact information
- A sentence thanking your reader for his or her consideration

Follow standard business letter format as you draft. Proofread your work so it is error-free.

Prentice Hall Writing and Grammar Connection: Chapter 16

Rubric for Self-Assessment

Evaluate your résumé using the following criteria and rating scale:

Criteria	Rating Scale: Not very				Very
How well does the résumé convey job and life experiences?	1	2	3	4	5
How appropriate is the résumé for the type of work sought?	1	2	3	4	5
How direct and dynamic is the résumé's language?	1	2	3	4	5
How clearly is the résumé organized?	1	2	3	4	5
How consistently does the writer follow the format?	1	2	3	4	5

Revising (continued)

- Write on the board:

  Looked after people in the nursing home, fed them lunch and dinner.

  Administered daily care to nursing home residents.
- Ask students to explain the difference in the sentences.
  Answer: The second sentence is really the same activity but sounds impressive. An employer might have more confidence in an applicant that "administered daily care."
- Have students compare the Nonmodel and Model, identifying which explanations were changed. Discuss how the changes affect the impact of the Model.
  Answer: *Monitored, implemented, consulted, assembled,* and *communicated* are simple verbs that assert more power and imply more responsibility.
- Have the students go through their résumés, identifying any explanations that are wordy and replacing them with words that are concise and descriptive professionally.

Publishing and Presenting

- Ask students to think about the potential employer they had in mind when they wrote their cover letters and résumés.
- Discuss ways in which students can express interest in a position in a cover letter that highlights their qualifications while providing information that will encourage the employer to read through to the résumé.

Assessment

- Review the assessment criteria in class.
- Before students proceed with the self-assessment, have them review the criteria for assessment presented on p. 799.
- The rubric on this page, and another rubric in an alternative format, can be found on p. 12 of **Performance Assessment and Portfolio Management.**

TEST-TAKING TIP

Suggest that when students are taking a test that includes a letter-writing prompt, they use prewriting to organize information. Students should think about the audience and the purpose they are writing for and should remove any unrelated information. If students are asked to choose between two audiences, their prewriting should allow them to identify the audience better suited for their opinions or experiences.

Lesson Objectives

1. To identify the devices used by the persuasive speaker
2. To determine if the speaker's argument is invalid
3. To independently evaluate the ideas presented and respond to evidence as necessary

Analyzing Fallacious Arguments

- Remind students that often during a persuasive speech, speakers will make claims without a basis of fact to add weight to the claims. Often broad generalizations are not supported by actual data or reality. Encourage students to question any claims they feel are falsehoods, stretches of the truth, or overgeneralizations.
- After students complete the Activity on the student page, have them fill out the Feedback Form. When they finish, have them discuss their answers as a class or in small groups.

Identifying Effective Rhetorical Devices

- Ask students to give examples from advertising of repetition and parallelism.
  Answer: Students may mention copy or a visual from an advertisement that is repeated in additional commercials.
- Have students explain the value of examples, drama, and the establishment of the speaker's reliability in establishing relationships with listeners. Help them to understand that these qualities help them empathize and sympathize with the speaker and makes them feel as if the speaker really does understand them.

Listening and Speaking WORKSHOP

Critiquing Persuasive Devices

The purpose of a persuasive speech is to change listeners' minds or to incite them to action. Logical arguments are not the only tools used by speakers to reach these goals. Some speakers use invalid forms of reasoning called **fallacious arguments**. Speakers may also employ powerful **rhetorical devices,** patterns of words and images that engage an audience. When critiquing a persuasive speech, identify the speaker's use of these persuasive devices.

Analyzing Fallacious Arguments

Fallacious arguments—false forms of reasoning—are attempts to win an audience's assent without earning it. As you analyze a persuasive speech, identify any fallacies, including the following:

- **Bandwagon effect:** The speaker argues that listeners should do something simply because everyone else is doing it.
- ***Ad hominem*:** The speaker questions or attacks the character of those who hold the opposing point of view, without addressing their arguments.
- **False causality:** The speaker assumes that because one event followed another, the first is the cause of the second.
- **Overgeneralization:** The speaker makes a broad statement that is not supported by sufficient evidence.

Feedback Form for Analyzing Persuasive Devices

Rating System
+ = Excellent ✔ = average – = weak

Content
Arguments ________
Word choice, imagery ________
Drama ________
Personal relevance ________
Impression of speaker ________

Answer the following question:
Did the speaker use any fallacious arguments? If so, what type? ________

Identifying Effective Rhetorical Devices

Rhetorical devices encourage an audience to share a vision of a situation, a vision also supported by the arguments a speaker offers. As you listen to a persuasive speech, identify the use of these rhetorical devices:

- **Repetition and parallelism**—To stress an idea, the speaker may make repeated use of key words or sentence structures.
- **Use of examples relevant to the audience**—To win the audience's interest, the speaker may speak directly to members' experiences.
- **Establishment of the speaker as reliable**—The presentation of credentials, a sincere manner, and accounts of the speaker's own experiences can all bring an audience to trust the speaker.
- **Creation of drama**—A speaker may frame an issue in dramatic terms: for instance, as a battle between the "little guy" and a bloated, monstrous bureaucracy.

Activity: Listen and Analyze Analyze a persuasive speech, using the checklist shown to evaluate the speaker's use of persuasive devices.

CUSTOMIZE INSTRUCTION FOR UNIVERSAL ACCESS

For Less Proficient Readers

Correlate persuasive devices not only to speechmaking but to radio, television, and print advertisements. Break students down into groups and assign fallacies and rhetorical devices to each (e.g. to one group assign bandwagon, to another, false causality). While not all advertising is untrue, a majority of it is used to persuade consumers to try a product for various reasons.

Have these groups uncover examples of their topics in advertising today and report their findings to the class. Encourage them to bring the actual advertisements to class and determine if the advertising is persuasive or if the public would easily see beyond the devices.

Assessment WORKSHOP

Critical Reasoning

In the reading sections of some tests, you may be required to use critical reasoning skills. Use the following strategies to help you answer questions testing these skills:

- Identify a writer's implicit (unstated) assumptions, asking what else must be true for the writer's stated claims to be true.
- Read actively, making inferences based on the passage and testing those inferences against further details or your own knowledge.

Test-Taking Strategies

- Read the questions before reading the passage.
- After you have read the passage, jot down a sentence summarizing the main idea.

Sample Test Item

Directions: Read the passage, and answer the question that follows.

The serious accident at the Three Mile Island nuclear facility began with a simple mechanical error. Radiation leaked into the control room. Radioactive water discharged into the Susquehanna River. A hydrogen bubble formed in the reactor, increasing the potential of a deadly explosion. People around the world were shocked by the news. Engineers prevented the core from melting down, but the facility was damaged beyond repair. The accident caused widespread fear in the nuclear industry—a change in attitude that will prevent such accidents in the future.

1. What implicit assumption does the writer make?
   - **A** The accident began as an error.
   - **B** A hydrogen bubble can cause an explosion.
   - **C** The mechanics were incompetent.
   - **D** Fear will prevent accidents.

Answer and Explanation

The correct answer is ***D***. This assumption is implied in the writer's conclusion about the change of attitude in the industry. Answers *A* and *B* are stated directly as facts, so they are explicit, not implicit. *C* is incorrect because no details address the competence of the mechanics.

Practice

Directions: Read the passage from "The White Umbrella" by Gish Jen, and answer the question that follows.

Sisterly embarrassment seized me. Why hadn't Mona wiped her lenses when I told her to? As she resumed abuse of the piano, I stared at the umbrella. I wanted to open it, twirl it around by its slender silver handle; I wanted to dangle it from my wrist on the way to school the way the other girls did. I wondered what Miss Crosman would say if I offered to bring it to Eugenie at school tomorrow. She would be impressed with my consideration for others; Eugenie would be pleased to have it back; and I would have possession of the umbrella for an entire night. I looked at it again, toying with the idea of asking for one for Christmas. I knew, however, how my mother would react.

"Things," she would say. "What's the matter with a raincoat? All you want is things, just like an American."

1. Which of the following describes what the umbrella means to the narrator?
   - **A** It will keep her dry when she returns from the piano lesson.
   - **B** It will irritate her mother, who does not like umbrellas.
   - **C** It will make her like the other girls.
   - **D** It will be something she has stolen from Eugenie.

Lesson Objective

To use critical reasoning skills in test reading passages

Applying Reading Strategies

- Rather than simply accepting or rejecting each claim in a passage, students should connect claims with one another and with their own prior knowledge to help determine the validity of the writer's arguments.
- Explain to students that identifying words and phrases that indicate value judgments will help them assess a writer's implicit assumptions.

Applying Test-Taking Strategies

- Tell students that careful reading of test questions is vital to answering such test reading questions correctly.
- Have students read the question in the sample passages, and ask them which word alerts them to what they are to read for in order to arrive at a correct answer. Answer: The word *implicit* is important because it tells what kind of assumption the reader is to look for.

Answer

The correct answer is C. *A* is incorrect because the narrator states nowhere that she is concerned about the rain. *B* is incorrect because her mother is irritated by many things American, not specifically an umbrella. *D* is incorrect because nowhere does the narrator state her animosity toward Eugenie.

TEACHING RESOURCES

The following resources can be used to enrich or extend the instruction for p. 801.

PRENTICE HALL ASSESSMENT SYSTEM

- Workbook
- Skill Book
- Transparencies
- CD-ROM

Unit Objectives

1. To read selections from the Victorian period in English literature
2. To apply a variety of reading strategies, particularly interactive reading strategies, appropriate for reading these selections
3. To analyze literary elements
4. To use a variety of strategies to build vocabulary
5. To learn elements of grammar, usage, and style
6. To use recursive writing processes to write in a variety of forms
7. To develop listening and speaking skills
8. To present, evaluate, and critique oral presentations and performances

Meeting the Objectives

With each selection, you will find instructional materials through which students can meet these objectives. Further, you will find additional practice pages for reading strategies, literary analysis, vocabulary, and grammar in the **Selection Support: Skills Development Workbook** in your **Teaching Resources.**

Background

Art

The Railway Station
by William Powell Frith

A prominent English painter, Frith (1819–1909) was best known for depicting scenes of nineteenth-century English life. Have your students link *The Railway Station* to the focus of Unit 5, Progress and Decline, by answering the following question:

Contrast this portrait of a busy train station in 1862 with the scene you would see in such a place today. Would the contemporary scene represent progress or decline over the one painted in 1862?

Answer: On the grounds that crowds today are larger and urban public spaces are often dirtier and more chaotic, students may point to a decline.

UNIT 5 Progress and Decline (1833–1901)

The Railway Station, 1862, William Powell Frith, Royal Holloway and Bedford New College, Surrey

UNIT FEATURES

Connections	Reading Informational Material
Every unit contains features that connect literature to a related topic, such as art, science, or history. In this unit, students will explore poems by Sappho and Baudelaire, an excerpt from Leo Tolstoy's *War and Peace,* and a contemporary look at the condition of Ireland. Use the information and questions on the Connections page to help students enrich their understanding of the selections presented within the unit.	These selections will help students to analyze and evaluate informational texts, such as workplace documents, technical directions, and consumer materials. They will expose students to the organization and features unique to nonnarrative texts. In this unit, students will learn about Web sites.

The Victorian Period

"In order that people may be happy in their work, these three things are needed: They must be fit for it. They must not do too much of it. And they must have a sense of success in it."

— John Ruskin,
from *Pre-Raphaelitism*

ASSESSMENT RESOURCES

- Selection Support: Skills Development Workbook
- Formal Assessment
- Open Book Tests
- Performance Assessment and Portfolio Management
- Extension Activities

Assessing Student Progress

Listed below are tools that are available to measure the degree to which students meet the unit objectives.

Informal Assessment

The questions in the Review and Assess sections are a first-level response to the concepts and skills presented with the selections. Students' responses are a brief, informal measure of their grasp of the material. These responses can indicate where further instruction and practice are needed. Then, follow up with the practice pages in the **Selection Support: Skills Development Workbook.**

Formal Assessment

The **Formal Assessment** booklet contains Selection Tests and Unit Tests.

- Selection Tests measure comprehension and skills acquisition for each selection or group of selections.
- Each Unit Test provides students with thirty multiple-choice questions and five essay questions designed to assess students' knowledge of the literature and skills taught in the unit.

The **Open Book Tests** ask students to demonstrate their ability to synthesize and communicate information from selections or groups of selections.

To assess student writing, you will find rubrics and scoring models in the **Performance Assessment and Portfolio Management** booklet. In this booklet you will also find scoring rubrics for listening and speaking activities.

Alternative Assessment

The **Extension Activities** booklet contains writing activities, listening and speaking activities, and research and technology activities that are appropriate for students with different ability levels. You may also use these activities as an alternative measurement of students' growth.

Using the Timeline

The Timeline can serve a number of instructional purposes, as follows:

Getting an Overview

Use the Timeline to help students get a quick overview of themes and events of the period. This approach will benefit all students but may be especially helpful for visually oriented students, English language learners, and those less proficient in reading. (For strategies in using the Timeline as an overview, see the bottom of this page.)

Thinking Critically

Questions are provided on the facing page. Use these questions to have students review the events, discuss their significance, and examine the *so what* behind the *what happened.*

Connecting to Selections

Have students refer back to the Timeline when reading individual selections. By consulting the Timeline regularly, they will gain a better sense of the period's chronology. In addition, they will appreciate what was occurring in the world that gave rise to these works of literature.

Projects

Students can use the Timeline as a launching pad for projects like these:

- **Charting Responses to Change** As students read material in this unit, have them look for responses to technological and social change in literature. Using this Timeline as a framework, have them add the date of each response and the date of any specific change or development involved. (Encourage students to "stretch" to find connections: students might include, for instance, the loom in Tennyson's "The Lady of Shalott," as harking back to preindustrial technology.)
- **Report on a Scientist or Reformer** Have students scan the Timeline for an invention or scientific advance, or for a reform in society, research the people behind the advance or reform, then report on their findings to the class. Did the people concerned have any interesting literary or political connections?

Timeline 1833–1901

1833 | 1845 | 1855

British Events

- **1833** Slavery abolished in British empire.
- **1837** Victoria becomes queen. ▼
- **1839** Michael Faraday offers general theory of electricity.
- **1843 William Wordsworth** becomes poet laureate.

- **1845** Irish Potato Famine begins. ▶

- **1848** Women begin attending University of London.
- **1850 Elizabeth Barrett Browning** publishes *Sonnets from the Portuguese.*
- **1854** Britain enters Crimean War.
- **1859** Charles Darwin publishes *On the Origin of Species.*
- **1860** Florence Nightingale founds school for nurses. ▼

World Events

- **1836** United States: Ralph Waldo Emerson publishes *Nature.*
- **1841** South Pacific: New Zealand becomes a British colony.
- **1842** France: Honoré de Balzac publishes *The Human Comedy.*
- **1844** United States: Samuel F. B. Morse sends first message over a long-distance telegraph line.
- **1848** France: Revolution establishes new republic under Louis Napoleon.
- **1848** Belgium: Marx and Engels publish the *Communist Manifesto.*
- **1853** Eastern Europe: Crimean War begins.
- **1854** Japan: Trade with West reopened.
- **1854** United States: Henry David Thoreau publishes *Walden.* ▲
- **1856** France: Gustave Flaubert publishes *Madame Bovary.*
- **1857** India: Sepoy Mutiny against British.
- **1861** United States: Civil War begins.

ENRICHMENT: Getting an Overview of the Period

Introduction	Key Events
To give students an overview of the period, have them determine the amount of time covered. (Use the dates in the upper left corner). *A period of 68 years is covered.* Next, point out that the Timeline is divided into specifically British Events (on top) and World Events (on bottom). Have them practice scanning the Timeline across, looking both at the British Events and the World Events. Point out that the events charted often indicate larger trends.	Have students note events that may indicate the investment of new energy in social reform. **Possible responses:** Slavery was abolished (1833); Debtors' prisons were abolished (1869). Have students find evidence of Britain's growing role in the world. **Possible responses:** New Zealand became a British colony (1841); there were wars in Africa (1879).

British and World Events

1865 | 1875 | 1885

- **1865** London Fire Department established.
- **1865** Lewis Carroll publishes *Alice's Adventures in Wonderland.* ▲
- **1868 Robert Browning** publishes *The Ring and the Book.*
- **1869** Debtors' prisons abolished.
- **1880** Joseph Swan installs first electric lighting. ▼
- **1884** First book (*A–ant*) of *Oxford English Dictionary* published.

- **1887** First Sherlock Holmes tale published.
- **1888** English Lawn Tennis Association founded at Wimbledon. ▶
- **1891 Thomas Hardy** publishes *Tess of the d'Urbervilles.*
- **1896 A. E. Housman** publishes *A Shropshire Lad.*
- **1901** Queen Victoria dies.

- **1865** Russia: **Leo Tolstoy** publishes *War and Peace.*
- **1865** Austria: Gregor Mendel proposes laws of heredity. ▼
- **1869** Egypt: Suez Canal completed.
- **1876** United States: Alexander Graham Bell patents telephone.
- **1879** South Africa: Zulu war against British.
- **1880** Russia: Feodor Dostoevsky publishes *The Brothers Karamazov.*
- **1884** United States: Mark Twain publishes *The Adventures of Huckleberry Finn.*
- **1894** Asia: Sino–Japanese war begins.
- **1896** Greece: First modern Olympics held.
- **1897** Russia: Anton Chekhov publishes *Uncle Vanya.*
- **1898** France: Marie and Pierre Curie discover radium.
- **1900** China: Boxer Rebellion against foreign influence.

GREGORIO J. MENDEL 1884 1984

Analyzing the Timeline

1. **(a)** Name a technological improvement of the period. **(b)** What does this improvement suggest about the use to which science was being put? **[Generalize]**
   Answer: **(a)** The first electric lighting was installed (1880). **(b)** Science was being used to create convenience and comfort.
2. **(a)** What evidence can you find of women's changing status before 1855? **(b)** What does this development suggest about their economic role before this time? **[Infer]**
   Answer: **(a)** Women were admitted into University of London (1848). **(b)** They probably didn't make much money since they lacked a college education.
3. **(a)** Name a British development after 1865 that "made the day longer." **(b)** Speculate on what Britons used for this purpose previously. **(c)** Why does this development represent an improvement? **[Speculate]**
   Answer: **(a)** Electric lighting was first installed in 1880. **(b)** People may have used gas, kerosene, or oil lamps. **(c)** Electric light is constant; it does not flicker or diminish in intensity as fuel burns down, unlike lamps and candles.
4. **(a)** Name a nation that, like Britain, made technological progress at this time. Explain. **(b)** Speculate about how progress in the West affected other areas of the world. **[Speculate]**
   Answer: **(a)** The telephone was invented in the United States (1876). **(b)** Progress required raw material, which led to the colonization of other areas of the world.

▶Critical Viewing

1. From the picture (1845), what conclusions can you draw about agriculture in Ireland? **[Draw Conclusions]**
   Answer: For some Irish, farming was small scale and primitive, without draft animals or machinery.
2. What qualities does the picture of Florence Nightingale (1860) convey? Support your answer with details. **[Interpret]**
   Answer: Her solitary, perhaps nighttime vigil (she holds a candle) over the sick suggests dedication; the slope of her shoulders conveys care and humility rather than strength. The viewer is meant to be impressed with her watchful mercy.
3. **(a)** Judging from the illustration, who were *Alice in Wonderland's* intended readers? **(b)** What does this suggest about the reading public of the time? **[Draw Conclusions]**
   Answer: **(a)** Its readers included children, judging from the whimsical characters, but also perhaps adults, judging from the sophisticated drawing style. **(b)** They read for pleasure; parents bought books for children.

continued

Continued from right column

Connecting to the Literature

- For an example of Victorian optimism, see Sydney Smith's memoir, "Progress in Personal Comfort," p. 900.
- Direct students to the excerpt from Dickens's *Hard Times*, p. 858, for an example of the reforming instinct at work.
- For one response to Victorian colonialism, have students read Kipling's "Recessional," p. 886.

▶Critical Viewing

Answer: Some of the medallions that circle Victoria's head probably refer to Britain's overseas conquests: one shows an elephant; another the Southern Cross, which appears on the flag of New Zealand. They are "ornaments" to her authority.

Progress and Decline

THE VICTORIAN PERIOD (1833–1901)

Historical Background

Living in the Victorian Age During the sixty-four years of Queen Victoria's reign, from 1837 to 1901, Britain's booming economy and rapid expansion encouraged great optimism. Factory towns grew into large cities as Britain became the world leader in manufacturing. Banks, retail shops, and other businesses expanded. These changes, in turn, spurred the growth of two important classes—an industrial working class and a modern middle class—who were able to live a better life because of the low cost and large variety of mass-produced factory goods.

Economic and military power, especially naval power, helped Britain acquire new colonies in far-flung parts of the globe. In words that could convey the confidence of the Victorian Age, Robert Browning has one of his characters exclaim, "God's in his heaven— / All's right with the world!"

A Reforming Age All was not really "right with the world" of industrial England, though. Writers exposed brutal factory conditions and stinking slums, the dark underside of a manufacturing economy. Nonetheless, Victorian reformers had great faith that their efforts could indeed make everything all right in the future. Goaded by reformers and radicals of many sorts, Victorian leaders did take steps to expand democracy and better the lot of the poor.

Two key issues—trade policy and electoral reform—dominated domestic politics during the first half of the Victorian Era. The trade controversy centered on the Corn Laws, which had long placed high tariffs on "corn" (grain). These laws discouraged food imports and helped British landlords and farmers keep food prices high, which angered the poorer classes. Popular organizations sprang up to fight the Corn Laws. Reform came in 1846 when Parliament, confronting a massive famine in Ireland (1845–1849), sought to increase the food supply by suspending the Corn Laws. Over the following decade, it established a policy of free trade that was beneficial to rising British industries.

The other burning issue of the day involved strengthening democracy. In 1838, the London radical William Lovett drew up a "People's Charter" demanding, among other things, universal suffrage for all males, not just the

Plate Presented by the Ladies of Derby to Queen Victoria on Her 1887 Golden Jubilee

▲ **Critical Viewing** This plate honors Queen Victoria. Which details suggest the pride that the British took in their overseas empire? Explain. **[Infer]**

ENRICHMENT: Social Studies

The Engine of Imperialism

In existence for almost 260 years, the English East India Company was the engine powering British imperialism. The English East India Company was formed by royal charter in 1600. For much of its existence, the company had a monopoly on British trade with India, Asia, and the area bordering the Persian Gulf. The company did more than trade with foreign powers; it actually exerted political power over them. In 1757, for instance, the company acquired control of Bengal of India. For a time, British foreign policy in Asia and India and the plans and interests of the company were virtually indistinguishable. Even after Parliament intervened and asserted the government's power over political matters in India and Asia, the company still functioned as an administrative tool of policy. The English East India Company continued to rule India until the Sepoy Rebellion (or India Mutiny) of 1857, when Indian troops rebelled. After the rebellion, the British government stepped in and took direct control.

wealthy and middle classes. Renewed demands for electoral change led to the Second Reform Bill of 1867, which added 938,000 people to the number of voters by granting voting rights to numbers of urban workingmen. Two further acts, the Third Reform Act (1884–1885) and the Redistribution Act (1885), tripled the electorate and advanced the country toward universal male suffrage.

Reform affected many areas. Women were allowed to attend universities. Parliament passed laws to reduce the workday for women and children, to establish a system of free grammar schools, and to legalize trade unions. It voted to provide public sanitation and to regulate factories and housing. Agitation continued, however, for further reforms.

The Imperialist Urge Britons who supported a policy of imperialism could cite many arguments. Colonies would provide raw materials and markets for British industry. They would also offer a home for British settlers. Furthermore, Britain felt that it had no choice, because if it did not seize a territory, one of its European rivals would. Many Victorians tended to believe that Western civilization—commonly perceived as white, Christian, and progressive—was superior to all other cultures. This attitude led many Victorians to look condescendingly on non-Westerners as people in need of assistance. While such an attitude seems outrageous by today's standards, many people of the time sincerely believed it.

The Victorian years were generally peaceful. Britain fought only one major European war, the Crimean War (1853–1856). This war got its name from its location, the Crimea, a peninsula in southern Russia. Britain, France, and Ottoman Turkey teamed up to thwart Russian expansion, but the battles were largely inconclusive. Today, we remember the war mainly for the courageous efforts of Florence Nightingale, a military nurse regarded as the founder of modern nursing, and the daring but disastrous charge of Britain's Light Brigade. This charge was commemorated in a famous poem by Alfred, Lord Tennyson, some lines of which follow: "Theirs not to make reply, / Theirs not to reason why, / Theirs but to do and die, . . . "

Britain as a World Power Though the Liberals (formerly the Whigs) advocated limits to British rule, the Empire continued to grow. Britain acquired Hong Kong from China in 1842. Then, after a rebellion in

▲ **Critical Viewing** The Crystal Palace, built for a trade show in 1851, was made of iron rods and glass. Why do you think that many Victorians identified this structure with the idea of progress? **[Speculate]**

Background

Architecture

The Crystal Palace housed the Great Exhibition of 1851, organized by Prince Albert. Fourteen thousand exhibitors proudly put on view their nations' contributions to technology and agriculture. The total floor area of the Crystal Palace was perhaps 23 acres; the display tables stretched for eight miles. The offerings were varied; false teeth, chewing tobacco, the Colt pistol, articles made of rubber, and McCormick's reaper were all displayed. Over five months, from May 1 to October 11, 1851, more than 6,000,000 visitors browsed through the exhibition.

▶Critical Viewing

Answer: Glass would appear to be a modern material in contrast to the traditional materials of stone and wood.

CUSTOMIZE INSTRUCTION FOR UNIVERSAL ACCESS

For Less Proficient Readers	For English Learners	For Advanced Readers
Explain to students that during this period, some thought society had become a monster grown out of control. To others, society looked like a wise, helpful magician that could solve any problem. Ask these students to keep a chart with two columns as they read Progress and Decline.	Explain to students that during this period, some thought society had become a monster grown out of control. To others, society looked like a wise, helpful magician that could solve any problem. Ask students to write a caption for each subhead and picture in Progress and Decline.	Challenge students to trace the themes through Progress and Decline. Have them look for new modes of travel, new scientific theories, and new forms of work that would affect how people perceived or thought of time. What idea might Victorians have had of the future?

Background

Music

"When I was a Lad," from *H.M.S. Pinafore* by Gilbert and Sullivan

Some Victorian attitudes and beliefs were so patriotic and extreme that they were criticized, mocked, and parodied. W. S. Gilbert and Arthur Sullivan, who collaborated on thirteen comic operas, often parodied English life—showing it at its most absurd.

"When I Was a Lad," sung by a character named The Rt. Hon. Sir Joseph Porter, KCB (First Lord of the Admiralty), is an account of an unusual rise to high office, parodying the kind of success-through-hard-work story that Victorians loved. It is a "patter song," combining words and melody to create a "pitter-patter" effect.

Play "When I Was a Lad" on the **Listening to Music Audio-cassettes.** Ask students to raise their hands when they first hear the "patter" effect. Then, ask the following questions:

1. What is being satirized in this song?
   Answer: The song satirizes a bureaucrat's model of success.
2. Would the song be as successful without the patter effect?
   Answer: Students may answer that the effect adds humor; it gives the words a "chatty" effect.

Close-up on Society

Victorian Political and Economic Theories

We can divide into three broad groups the political and economic theories Victorians developed to account for the changed conditions of the industrial age:

• **Laissez-faire** (les´ ā fer´) **theory** This theory holds that government should avoid meddling in the affairs of business. The French term *laissez faire* means "let it be." When allowed full freedom, the theory goes, industry will use the most efficient techniques and reach the highest possible level of prosperity.

• **Reformist liberalism** Those who held this theory believed that rapid change brings problems that *laissez-faire* policies cannot solve. They argued that government intervention and regulation were sometimes necessary to protect the rights of the weak against the strong.

• **Socialism** Some thinkers and activists favored a more far-reaching policy that would end private ownership of major industries and substitute public ownership. Supporters of this socialist position also called for sweeping government measures to promote equality and to help the poor.

1857 to 1858 by sepoys (Indian troops under British command), Britain shouldered aside the British East India Company and took direct control of India.

In the last three decades of Victoria's rule, Britain expanded its influence in Africa. It gained control of the new Suez Canal in Egypt and acquired such territories as Kenya, Uganda, Nigeria, and Rhodesia (now Zimbabwe). Britain also consolidated its control over what is now South Africa, defeating Dutch settlers there in the Boer War (1899–1902).

Victorian Thought Victorian thinkers often disagreed on the crucial issues of their times, but they shared a deep confidence in humanity's ability to better itself. The changes brought about by the Industrial Revolution stirred conflicting feelings among Victorian thinkers. On the one hand, they admired the material benefits industrialization had brought. On the other, they deplored the brutality of factory life and of industrial slums. Much debate concerned whether business should be allowed free rein or whether, for the welfare of people, the government should take a strong role in the economy.

The Victorians grappled with the religious and philosophical as well as the social implications of modern life. The theory of evolution proposed by Charles Darwin (1809–1882) in *On the Origin of Species by Means of Natural Selection* (1859), for instance, stirred bitter controversy. Darwin believed that a process he called "natural selection" explained how different forms of life evolved from previous forms. His account is quite different from the Creation story found in the Bible. Some Victorian thinkers took Darwin's theory as a direct challenge to biblical truth and traditional religious faith. Others accepted both Darwin and religion, striving to reconcile scientific and religious insights.

ENRICHMENT: Social Studies Connection

Middle-Class Life

By the middle of the nineteenth century, the modern middle class had evolved its own way of life. The nuclear family lived in a large house or apartment. Even a small middle-class household was expected to have at least a cook and a maid. A strict code of etiquette dictated how to dress for every occasion, when to write letters, and how long to mourn relatives who had died. Parents strictly supervised their children, who were expected to be "seen but not heard."

When choosing a wife or husband, middle-class people considered economic reasons and their parents' wishes, yet the idea of "falling in love" was growing increasingly acceptable. Most middle-class husbands went to work in an office or a shop, and they aspired to make enough to keep their wives at home. Women spent their days raising children, directing the servants, and doing charitable work. Books, magazines, and songs celebrated the cult of domesticity that idealized women and the home.

Literature of the Period

Romanticism and Realism Romanticism continued to influence Victorian writers, but it had by now become part of the mainstream culture. When Victorian writers confronted the rapid technological and social changes amidst which they lived, a literary movement known as Realism was born. The literature of this movement focused on ordinary people facing the day-to-day problems of life, an emphasis that reflected the trend toward democracy and the growing middle-class audience for literature.

Naturalism A related movement, known as Naturalism, sought to put the spirit of scientific observation to literary use. Naturalists crammed their novels with gritty details—the sour smells of poverty, the harsh sounds of factory life—often with the aim of promoting social reform. They directly contradicted the Romantic idea that nature mirrored human feelings and instead portrayed nature as harsh and indifferent to the human suffering it caused.

Pre-Raphaelites Rather than embracing "real" life as the advocates of Realism did, the poets and painters of the Pre-Raphaelite Brotherhood, formed in 1848, rejected the ugliness of industrial life. They turned for inspiration to the spiritual intensity of medieval Italian art, the art before the time of the painter Raphael (1483–1520).

Art in the Historical Context

Changing Sensibilities in Victorian Art

The Pre-Raphaelite Brotherhood was the most important movement in the Victorian visual arts. Founded by the painter and poet Dante Gabriel Rossetti (1828–1882), the movement rejected conventional art and sought a greater purity and "truth to nature"—in part, by painting out-of-doors.

Like the Romantic writers and artists who had found inspiration in the Gothic style of the Middle Ages, the Pre-Raphaelites turned to medieval painters as models. However, the Pre-Raphaelites also showed a Victorian spirit in regarding themselves as reformers, even if, in the case of Rossetti, the reforms related more to ways of feeling and perceiving than to detailed social programs. Rosetti is especially known for his portraits of women, which emphasize color, texture, and an earthy or sadly spiritual feminine beauty.

Although the Brotherhood lasted only a few years, the works of Rossetti, John Everett Millais, and others led to the Aesthetic Movement in literature. This later movement, fostered by Walter Pater and Oscar Wilde, rejected the materialism of Victorian life and emphasized the appreciation of sensation over truth.

▶ **Critical Viewing** Could this portrait by Rossetti, entitled *Day Dream,* be regarded as a comment on the Victorian belief in progress? Why or why not? **[Interpret]**

Day Dream, 1880, Dante Gabriel Rosetti, Victoria and Albert Museum, London, UK

continued from right column

Critical Thinking

1. **(a)** Explain how landowners benefited from the Corn Laws. **(b)** Name two groups who probably opposed these laws. **[Analyze]**
   Answer: **(a)** Through high taxes on imports, these laws enabled British landowners to keep the price of their grain high. **(b)** The poor and the factory owners probably opposed them.
2. What do Tennyson's lines on the charge of the Light Brigade suggest about Victorian attitudes towards authority and war? **[Interpret]**
   Answer: The lines suggest that unquestioning obedience to authority was deemed good for its own sake and that people focused on the nobility of dutiful death rather than the irrationality of war.
3. Speculate on the type of people who served as administrators in British colonies. **[Speculate]**
   Answer: They would probably be male and middle-class, with few opportunities for advancement at home.

▶ **Critical Viewing**

Answer: This painting could be viewed as a negative commentary on the progress of the Victorian era. The painting is attempting to capture the communication and feeling in medieval art. The simplicity of the figure's face, the simple, relaxed lines of her pose and of the drapery of her robe, all suggest a clear, straightforward idea of study, grace, and repose. There are no complicating "psychological" ambiguities or tensions in her expression or manner.

Connecting to the Literature

- For a poem that may be read as a comment on the transition from Romanticism to Realism, turn to "The Lady of Shalott," p. 821.

Historical Background

Comprehension Check

1. Name two consequences of the Industrial Revolution in Britain.
   Answer: Factory towns grew into major cities; banks and other businesses expanded; a modern working class and middle class grew; cheap mass-produced goods improved life; Britain acquired more colonies.
2. **(a)** Name two key concerns of Victorian reformers. **(b)** Whom did reformers seek to help through these reforms?
   Answer: **(a)** Their concerns included repealing the Corn Laws and giving the right to vote to more people. **(b)** They sought to help the poor and, by opening free trade, industry.
3. **(a)** Name one reason Victorians gave for establishing colonies overseas. **(b)** Name one colony Britain acquired during this period.
   Answer: **(a)** To acquire raw material; to give settlers a home; to stop the expansion of other countries; to "improve" the natives. **(b)** Hong Kong, Kenya, Uganda, Nigeria, Rhodesia, and South Africa.
4. Name two issues that concerned Victorian thinkers.
   Answer: Issues of concern included the material benefits versus the human suffering caused by the Industrial Revolution, and the religious implications of new scientific theories.

continued

Connecting to the Literature

- Students will find Arnold's definitive statement of Victorian despair, "Dover Beach," on p. 884. Examples of Hardy's and Housman's naturalism appear beginning on pages 921 and 933, respectively.
- Far from the liquid elegance of Tennyson's poetry, Kipling's verse marches with common soldiers and other builders of empire, as students will find beginning on p. 886.
- Excerpts from the novels of Charles Dickens and of Charlotte Bronte appear beginning on pages 858 and 865, respectively.

Victorian Poetry The Victorian Age produced a large and diverse body of poetry. The Romantic style predominated at first, but Realism and Naturalism gained force as time went on.

Alfred, Lord Tennyson The most popular poet of the era, Alfred, Lord Tennyson (1809–1892), was influenced by earlier Romantic poets. His verse displays a keen sense of the music of language, and some of his more sentimental lyrics even reappeared in popular songs. Yet Tennyson also revealed a deeper, more thoughtful side in such powerful poems as "Ulysses" and *In Memoriam* (1850). Tennyson became poet laureate after Wordsworth died in 1850.

The Brownings Robert Browning (1812–1889) produced a body of poetry as diverse as Tennyson's, although in his lifetime he never achieved equal public acclaim. Some of Browning's poems display Romantic attitudes. Others, however, show the influence of Realism as Browning seeks to portray individuals with un-Romantic authenticity. Critics have especially admired Browning's dramatic monologues, or long speeches in which a character reveals his or her thoughts.

Elizabeth Barrett (1806–1861), Browning's wife, was the more famous poet at the time of their marriage. Today, she is remembered mostly for the beautiful love poems she wrote her husband in *Sonnets from the Portuguese* (1850).

Matthew Arnold, Thomas Hardy, and A. E. Housman One of the greatest Victorian poets to focus on "the bewildering confusion" of the Industrial Age was Matthew Arnold (1822–1888). He was haunted by

A Living Tradition

Philip Larkin Discovers Thomas Hardy

The poetry of Thomas Hardy—with its devotion to English life and landscapes, its often somber mood, and its refusal to entertain illusions—appealed greatly to the twentieth-century British poet Philip Larkin. After beginning his career under the influence of the visionary Irish poet William Butler Yeats, Larkin discovered Hardy. This account of Larkin's discovery comes from an introduction he wrote to a reprint of his first book, *The North Ship*:

> When reaction [against Yeats] came, it was undramatic, complete and permanent. In early 1946 I had some new digs [rooms] in which the bedroom faced east, so that the sun woke me inconveniently early. I used to read. One book I had at my bedside was the little blue *Chosen Poems of Thomas Hardy*: Hardy I knew as a novelist, but as regards his verse I shared Lytton Strachey's verdict that "the gloom is not even relieved by a little elegance of diction." This opinion did not last long; if I were asked to date its disappearance, I should guess it was the morning I first read "Thoughts of Phena At News of Her Death." Many years later, Vernon [the Welsh poet Vernon Watkins] surprised me by saying that Dylan Thomas had admired Hardy above all poets of this century. "He thought Yeats was the greatest by miles," he said. "But Hardy was his favorite."

ENRICHMENT: Art

The Birth of Photography

By the 1840s, a new art form, photography, was emerging. Louis Daguerre in France and William Fox Talbot in England had improved on earlier technologies to produce successful photographs. At first, many photos were stiff-posed portraits of middle-class families or prominent people. Other photographs reflected a Romantic fascination with faraway places.

In time, photographers used the camera to expose slum conditions and other social ills. Photographs provided shocking evidence to prod governments to reform.

Photography even posed a challenge to painters. Why try for realism, some artists asked, when a camera could do the same thing better? By the 1870s, instead of attempting to reproduce reality "photographically," the French painters called the Impressionists were seeking to capture fleeting impressions of the world.

▶Critical Viewing

Answer: The women's skirts and their hats, as well as the gentleman's top hat, all take up a lot of space. Crowded spaces such as this bus would encourage more practical, less showy wear. Additionally, as men and women became used to mingling in such close physical quarters, ideas of modesty may have changed.

Bayswater Omnibus, G. W. Joy, Museum of London

▲ **Critical Viewing** This picture shows a scene in the interior of a horsedrawn omnibus. How do you think that the existence of public spaces such as the inside of a bus may have influenced ways of behaving in public? Explain. **[Speculate]**

the loss of individuals' close ties to nature and with each other. Arnold was a forerunner of the more pessimistic Naturalist poets, such as Thomas Hardy (1840–1928) and A. E. Housman (1859–1936), for whom life's disappointments were a frequent subject.

Rudyard Kipling The poetry of Rudyard Kipling (1865–1936) spoke to the expansive spirit of the age, ranging across the breadth of the Empire with action-packed narrative poems like "Gunga Din" and poems written in the colorful speech of working-class soldiers in *Barrack-Room Ballads*.

Gerard Manley Hopkins While Tennyson's and Kipling's well-known lyrics turned up as popular songs, Gerard Manley Hopkins (1844–1889) remained unpublished during his own century. His innovative rhythms and deeply felt religious verse would inspire twentieth-century Modernist poets.

Victorian Drama At the beginning of the nineteenth century, playhouses were few in number. After 1843, when government restrictions were lifted, popular theater boomed. Serious dramas like Sir Arthur Wing Pinero's *The Second Mrs. Tanqueray* (1893) and satires like Oscar Wilde's *The Importance of Being Earnest* (1895) began to emerge late in the century.

Victorian Fiction If one form of literature can be seen as quintessentially Victorian, it is the novel. Members of the new middle class were avid readers, and they loved novels, especially those that reflected the major social issues of the day. Responding to the demand, weekly and monthly magazines published novels chapter by chapter in serial form. Curious readers had to continue to buy the magazine to learn what happened next. Most of the best novelists of the day wrote, at one time or another, for the magazines.

ENRICHMENT: Social Studies Connection

Victorian Progress

Technological advances abounded throughout the industrializing world in this period. Methods for mass-producing steel were invented in 1856, and steel replaced iron as a major material. By the 1890s dynamos (electric generators) powered factories. The Age of Iron and Steam was over; the Age of Steel and Electricity had begun.

Progress was not confined to industry. Paved streets; gas, then electric lighting; improved sewer systems: these were among the changes that transformed the cities of the day. Chemists produced hundreds of new products, from aspirin to new soaps to margarine to dynamite. Anesthesia was introduced in surgery. Joseph Lister, an English surgeon, discovered the importance of antiseptics in preventing infections. He was the first to insist that surgeons wash their hands. In 1870, Pasteur linked disease to germs.

Literature of the Period

Comprehension Check

1. What defined the Realist literary movement?
   Answer: The Realists chose as their subject matter the struggles of ordinary people with everyday problems.
2. What defined the Naturalist literary movement?
   Answer: The Naturalists attended to the details of life with almost scientific precision; they depicted nature as indifferent to human suffering
3. Name a group or writer who turned away from "realistic" depictions of life.
   Answer: The Pre-Raphaelites, the Aesthetes, and Oscar Wilde all turned away from Realism.
4. **(a)** Name a Victorian poet influenced by the Romantics. **(b)** Name one influenced by Realism. **(c)** Name one influenced by Naturalism.
   Answer: **(a)** Tennyson, Hopkins. **(b)** Browning, Kipling. **(c)** Arnold, Housman, Hardy.

Critical Thinking

1. **(a)** What kind of subject matter did Realists depict? **(b)** Show how the rise of Realism is connected to two social changes during this period. **[Make a Connection]**
   Answers: **(a)** Realism depicted the lives of ordinary people. **(b)** Realism reflected the concern of reformers with the lower classes, and the growth of a middle-class readership, whose lives it documented.
2. **(a)** What elements of life did the Naturalists focus on? **(b)** Is their approach more "realistic" or "natural" than other approaches to literature? Explain. **[Make a Judgment]**
   Answers: **(a)** Naturalists focused on the "grit" of modern life and on the indifference of nature to human suffering. **(b)** Yes, because it resembles a practical attitude often called "being realistic"; No, because this approach involves the imagination and selection of details as much as any other.
3. **(a)** How did readers react to the pessimism of serious late Victorian novels? **(b)** Name a similar modern trend. **[Relate]**

continued

The Brontë Sisters Romanticism heavily influenced early Victorian novelists, especially the three Brontë sisters: Emily Brontë (1818–1848), Charlotte Brontë (1816–1855), and the lesser-known Anne Brontë (1820–1849). The sisters were among six children raised by their father and aunt in the isolation of a northern English village. Bright and imaginative, these children relied on one another for entertainment and encouragement. They read great authors like Shakespeare and Byron, wrote verse and prose, and created fantasy worlds with names like Gondal and Angria.

Emily and Charlotte later drew on these vivid childhood experiences to create powerful works of fiction. Emily's classic *Wuthering Heights* (1847) tells the tale of the doomed passion of Catherine Earnshaw and Heathcliff, one of English fiction's outstanding Romantic heroes. Emily's sister Charlotte wrote *Jane Eyre* (1847), a novel recounting the adventures of a governess who falls in love with her mysterious employer, Mr. Rochester.

Charles Dickens The realistic elements of *Jane Eyre* probably owe much to the influence of Charles Dickens (1812–1870), who surpassed all other Victorian novelists in popularity and is regarded by many critics as the greatest novelist of the period. Dickens filled his novels with poignant, realistic details that dramatized the contrast between rich and poor in industrial England. To his eye for injustice he married a marvelous sense of humor. His novels abound in deliciously eccentric characters whose every peculiarity of speech and gesture affirms how individual people are. Among his greatest works are *David Copperfield* (1849–1850), *Bleak House* (1852–1853), and *Our Mutual Friend* (1864–1865).

Dickens also showed a sentimental side, often in the form of tear-provoking descriptions of innocents suffering in a cruel world. The most famous of these scenes is the death of Little Nell in *The Old Curiosity Shop* (1840–1841). A young girl fleeing the corrupt city in the company of her grandfather, Nell dies in her quest for a refuge. Dickens emphasized the sadness of her death, and his audience loved the experience of weeping for Little Nell. When a ship bringing the latest installment of *The Old Curiosity Shop* arrived in New York harbor, readers yelled out to the sailors before the ship docked, "Has Little Nell died?"

Realist Fiction Other, less sentimental Victorian Realists included Anthony Trollope (1815–1882) and Samuel Butler (1835–1902). George Meredith (1828–1909) produced careful psychological studies of his characters in novels such as *The Egoist* (1879).

Another important Realist, William Makepeace Thackeray (1811–1863), condemned hypocrisy in his novel *Vanity Fair* (1847–1848). Named for a fair that symbolizes worldly corruption in Puritan John Bunyan's allegory *Pilgrim's Progress* (1678, 1684), Thackeray's novel describes the rise of Becky Sharp from governess to woman of society. It uses her social climbing to reveal the immoral side of upper-class life.

Women Novelists As the novel came into its own, so did women novelists. In addition to the Brontë sisters, there were Elizabeth Gaskell

continued from left column

Answers: **(a)** Readers turned to escapist fiction instead. **(b)** The split between "highbrow" and "lowbrow" culture, such as between art films and Hollywood movies.

(1810–1865) and Mary Ann Evans, writing as George Eliot (1819–1880).

Charles Dickens had enormous respect for Gaskell's work in calling attention to the abuses of industrialization. Writing in his magazine *Household Words*, he commented that "there is no living English writer whose aid I would desire to enlist in preference to the authoress of *Mary Barton*." (This was the name of a novel by Gaskell that focused on life in industrial Manchester.)

Under her pen name George Eliot, Mary Ann Evans examined social issues and personal relationships in novels that fellow writer Henry James hailed as true works of art. She evoked everyday settings with careful attention to realistic specifics and focused in detail on the inner lives of her characters. *Middlemarch* (1871–1872), often considered her greatest work, describes the slow and painful maturation of its central character, Dorothea Brooke.

Edwardian London, 1901, Eugene Joseph McSwiney, Christopher Wood Gallery

▲ **Critical Viewing**
Gas lighting was introduced to London during Victoria's reign. Judging by this picture, what effects do you think this advance had on street life at night? Explain. **[Infer]**

Thomas Hardy and Late-Victorian Fiction As the century drew to a close, British novelists such as Thomas Hardy leaned more and more to Naturalism. (Later, Hardy would publish poetry in the same vein.) Late-Victorian readers shied away from Naturalism's dark outlook, though, preferring instead the adventure stories of writers like Robert Louis Stevenson (1850–1894) and Rudyard Kipling or the Sherlock Holmes mysteries of Sir Arthur Conan Doyle (1859–1930).

Prose Nonfiction All the great Victorian thinkers produced influential prose works. Matthew Arnold, for example, attacked the British class system in *Culture and Anarchy* (1869), his most famous work of social criticism. Other influential works included *Modern Painters* (1843) by John Ruskin (1819–1900), *On Liberty* (1859) by John Stuart Mill (1806–1873), *The Idea of a University* (1852) by John Henry Cardinal Newman (1801–1890), and *Studies in the History of the Renaissance* (1873) by Walter Pater (1839–1894). The greatest Victorian historians were Thomas Carlyle (1795–1881) and Thomas Babington Macaulay (1800–1859).

All in all, the Victorian Age produced a diverse body of literature that was entertaining, scholarly, humorous, and profound. Because the era is so close to our own times and because in it we see the beginnings of our own social problems, many of them still unresolved, Victorian literature has a special relevance to readers today. In addition, the Victorian writers were brilliant storytellers, and we read their works not only for literary appreciation and historical understanding but for pure pleasure.

▶**Critical Viewing**

Answer: Without lighting, people would probably not be out in such numbers, both because of the difficulties of finding one's way and the possible danger of attack. Streets were safer and businesses could consequently stay open later to admit this new wave of pedestrians.

Critical Thinking

1. **(a)** Do Lady Gough's rules suggest a secure or insecure attitude about how one comes across in public? **(b)** What connection can you make between the desire of the middle class to establish its own identity and these new standards for proper speech? **[Speculate]**
   Answer: **(a)** These standards show an insecurity about how one appears in public. **(b)** These standards may have emerged as the middle class's way of claiming moral superiority (justifying its success) and of distinguishing itself from the poor.
2. **(a)** Speculate on whether all middle-class Victorians took standards like Lady Gough's seriously. Explain your answer. **(b)** Speculate on what kind of opposing reaction such standards may have led to. **[Speculate]**
   Answer: **(a)** Some of her rules seem ludicrous, and people may have grown impatient with them. **(b)** Some people may have intentionally acted to shock others.

▶Critical Viewing

1. **(a)** What attitude toward the human body is suggested by the use of euphemisms for pregnancy? **(b)** How does the woman's clothing in the picture also express that attitude? **[Interpret]**
   Answer: **(a)** The use of such euphemisms suggests a discomfort in publicly acknowledging the body. **(b)** The woman's clothing covers all of her except face, feet, and hands.

Activities

1. Set aside time for volunteers to read their essays to the class.
2. Possible answer: Administrative assistant has replaced secretary; consultant often replaces freelance advisor.
3. Students may identify times when euphemisms would protect the feelings of people undergoing stress or grieving for losses.

THE CHANGING ENGLISH LANGUAGE

The Victorian Age

BY RICHARD LEDERER

EUPHEMISMS: THE FIG LEAVES OF LANGUAGE

Prudishness reached its golden age in the straitlaced Victorian era. Take the widely read *Lady Gough's Book of Etiquette*. Among Lady Gough's social pronouncements was that under no circumstances should books written by male authors be placed on shelves next to books written by "authoresses." Married writers, however, such as Robert and Elizabeth Barrett Browning, could be shelved together without impropriety.

So delicate were Victorian sensibilities that members of polite society would blush at the mention of anything physical. Instead of being *pregnant*, women were *in a delicate condition, in a family way*, or *expectant*. Women did not give birth; they experienced *a blessed event*. Their children were not born; rather, they were *brought by the stork*, or *came into the world*.

Such words and expressions are called *euphemisms* (from two Greek roots that mean "pleasant speech," "words of good omen"). A euphemism is a mild, indirect word or phrase used in place of one that is more direct or that may have an unpleasant connotation for some people. Using a euphemism is "calling a spade a heart" . . . or "telling it like it isn't."

In the Victorian Age, prudery extended even to animals and things. *Bull* was considered an indecent word, and the proper substitute was *he cow, male cow*, or (gasp!) *gentleman cow*. Victorian standards were so exacting that Victorians could not refer to something as vulgar as legs. They had to call them *limbs*, even when talking about the legs on a chicken or a piano. Instead of asking for a leg of chicken, they would ask for dark meat, and they went so far as to cover up piano legs with little skirts!

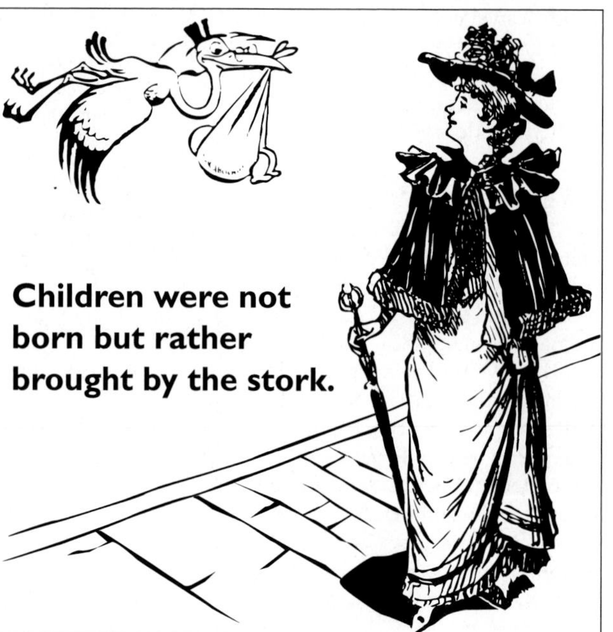

Children were not born but rather brought by the stork.

ACTIVITIES

1. Shakespeare's Juliet sighs, "What's in a name? A rose by any other name would smell as sweet." Would it? Write an essay in which you defend or rebut Juliet's opinion of the relationship between words and things.
2. Many occupations have taken on glorified, euphemistic titles. Nowadays, a garbage collector is called a sanitation engineer and a dogcatcher an animal control warden. Collect other examples and share them with classmates.
3. Are there any situations in which the use of euphemisms would be advisable? Explain your answer.

ENRICHMENT: Social Studies Connection

Domestic Sentiment

The euphemism is one way of "idealizing" life. The Victorians are also remembered for an extreme sentimentalization of the middle-class domestic scene. In paintings, songs, novels, and those famous samplers bearing the words "Home Sweet Home," motherhood, marriage, and domestic duty were glorified.

Home, though, was a "haven in a heartless world." The middle-class husband battled his way through the cruel, indifferent war zone of business, then took shelter in the warm household ordered and filled with love by his dutiful spouse.

Relationships

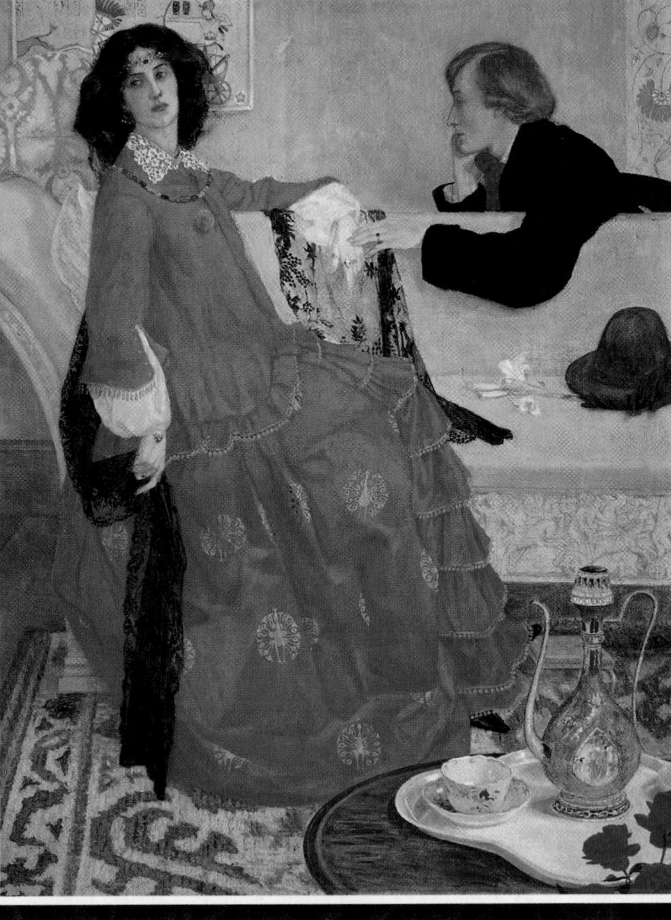

Faustine, 1904 Maxwell Armfield, Musée d'Orsay, Paris, France

Selection Planning Guide

The selections in this part are poems by Alfred, Lord Tennyson, and Robert and Elizabeth Barrett Browning that explore the theme, "Relationships." The section opens with excerpts from Tennyson's tribute to his friend, Arthur Hallam: "in Memoriam, A. H. H." Another exploration of a relationship between death and love is found in "The Lady of Shalott," a lyric narrative of a romantic heroine who chooses love and finds death. Tennyson's famous dramatic monologue, "Ulysses," provides contrasts to Browning's "My Last Ducess," and "Life in a Love," evoking multiple variations on relationships of love and life. Elizabeth Barett Browning's famous love poem "Sonnet 43" epitomizes a loving relationship between a woman and her husband.

Background

Art

Faustine,
Maxwell Armfield

This colorful painting suggests the Pre-Raphaelite movement's idealization of the vivid coloration and detail of High Renaissance art. In addition, the influence of the aesthetic Art Nouveau movement can be seen in the artist's fascination with pattern—in the border of the painting, the rug, the teapot, and the woman's gown.

Have students link the art to the focus of Part I, "Relationships," by answering the following questions:

1. What do you think is going on between the couple in this painting, and what elements of the painting lead you to this idea?
   Answer: The man is calling on the woman, indicated by his hat on the sofa. Their postures suggest that he loves her, while she is indifferent to him.
2. Choose one of the two figures in this painting and write the thoughts he or she might be having at this moment.
   Answer: He says he loves me, but I worry that he will not love me for long. I must not show him how much I love him.

E INSTRUCTION FOR UNIVERSAL ACCESS

the selections in this part, keep in mind these factors:

A. H. H."

sitive subject of
e death of a close
s young

alott"

cellent study for
nic learners of
/

"Ulysses"

- A memorable example of a dramatic monologue from *The Princess:* "Tears, Idle Tears"

"My Last Duchess"

- A psychological study of a destructive relationship

"Life in a Love"

- Students can compare the speaker in this dramatic monologue to the repellent speaker in "My Last Duchess."

"Love Among the Ruins"

- Contains challenging descriptions

from In Memoriam, A.H.H. ✦ The Lady of Shalott ✦ *from* The Princess: Tears, Idle Tears ✦ Ulysses

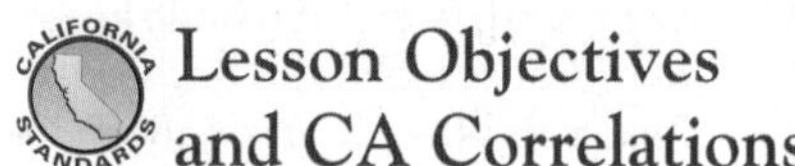

Lesson Objectives and CA Correlations

1. **To analyze and respond to literary elements**
   - Literary Analysis: The Speaker in Poetry **R 3.3**
   - Comparing Literary Works **R 3.2**
2. **To read, comprehend, analyze, and critique a poem**
   - Reading Strategy: Judging a Poet's Message **R 3.2**
   - Reading Check Questions
   - Review and Assess Questions
   - Assessment Practice (ATE)
3. **To develop word analysis skills, fluency, and systematic vocabulary**
   - Vocabulary Development Lesson: Related Words: Medieval Words **R 1.1**
4. **To understand and apply written and oral language conventions**
   - Spelling Strategy **LC 1.2**
   - Grammar and Style Lesson: Parallel Structure **LC 1.1**
5. **To understand and apply appropriate writing and research strategies**
   - Writing Lesson: Biographical Essay **W 1.6**
   - Extension Activity: Sketches of a Set **W 1.7**
6. **To understand and apply listening and speaking strategies**
   - Extension Activity: Videotaped News Report **LS 1.7**

STEP-BY-STEP TEACHING GUIDE	PACING GUIDE
PRETEACH	
Motivate Students and Provide Background	
Use the Motivation activity (ATE p. 816)	5 min.
Read and discuss author and background features (SE/ATE pp. 816, 824, 828) [A]	5 min.
Introduce the Concepts	
Introduce the Literary Analysis and Reading Strategy concepts (SE/ATE p. 817) [A]	15 min.
Pronounce the vocabulary words and read their definitions (SE p. 817)	5 min.
TEACH	
Monitor Comprehension	
Informally monitor comprehension by circulating while students read independently or in groups [A]	25 min.
Monitor students' comprehension with the Reading Check notes (SE/ATE pp. 819, 823, 825, 827, 829)	as students read
Develop vocabulary with Vocabulary notes (SE pp. 820, 823, 825, 830; ATE p. 823)	as students read
Develop Understanding	
Develop students' understanding of the speaker in poetry with the Literary Analysis annotations (SE/ATE pp. 819, 822, 823, 825, 828) [A]	5 min.
Develop students' ability to judge the poet's message with the Reading Strategy annotations (SE/ATE p. 819)	5 min.
ASSESS	
Assess Mastery	
Assess students' mastery of the Reading Strategy and Literary Analysis concepts by having them answer the Review and Assess questions (SE/ATE p. 831)	15 min.
Use one or more of the print and media Assessment Resources (ATE p. 833) [A]	up to 45 min.
EXTEND	
Apply Understanding	
Have students complete the Vocabulary Development Lesson and the Grammar and Style Lesson (SE p. 832) [A]	20 min.
Apply students' knowledge of explaining cause and effect using the Writing Lesson (SE/ATE p. 833) [A]	45 min.
Apply students' understanding using one or more of the Extension Activities (SE p. 833)	20–90 min.

[A] ACCELERATED INSTRUCTION:
Use the strategies and activities identified with an .

UNIVERSAL ACCESS
● = Below-Level Students
▲ = On-Level Students
■ = Above-Level Students

Time and Resource Manager

Reading Level: Average, Average, Average, Easy
Average Number of Instructional Days: 4

RESOURCES		
PRINT	**TRANSPARENCIES**	**TECHNOLOGY**
• **Beyond Literature,** Humanities Connection: Culture, p. 38 ▲ ■		• **Interest Grabber Video,** Tape 5 ● ▲ ■
• **Selection Support Workbook:** ● ▲ ■ Literary Analysis, p. 178 Reading Strategy, p. 177 Build Vocabulary, p. 175	• **Literary Analysis and Reading Transparencies,** pp. 75 and 76 ● ▲ ■	
• **Adapted Reader's Companion** ● • **Reader's Companion** ●		• **Listening to Literature** ● ▲ ■ Audiocassettes, Sides 19, 20 Audio CDs, CD 11
• **English Learner's Companion** ● ▲ • **Literatura en español** ● ▲ • **Literary Analysis for Enrichment** ■		
• **Formal Assessment:** Selection Test, pp. 184–186 ● ▲ ■ • **Open Book Test,** pp. 112–114 ● ▲ ■ • **Performance Assessment and Portfolio Management,** pp. 21, 69 ● ▲ ■ • PRENTICE HALL ASSESSMENT SYSTEM ● ▲ ■	• PRENTICE HALL ASSESSMENT SYSTEM ● ▲ ■ Skills Practice Answers and Explanations on Transparencies ● ▲ ■	• **Test Bank Software** ● ▲ ■ • **Got It! Assessment Videotapes,** Tape 4 ● ▲
• **Selection Support Workbook:** ● ▲ ■ Grammar and Style, p. 176 • **Writing and Grammar,** Diamond Level ● ▲ ■ • **Extension Activities,** p. 38 ● ▲ ■	• **Daily Language Practice Transparencies** ● ▲ • **Writing Models and Graphic Organizers on Transparencies,** p. 119 ● ▲ ■	• **Writing and Grammar iText CD-ROM** ● ▲ ■ ***Take It to the Net*** www.phschool.com

BLOCK SCHEDULING: Use one 90-minute class period to preteach the selections and have students read them. Use a second 90-minute class period to assess students' mastery of skills and have them complete one of the Extension Activities.

PRETEACH

Step-by-Step Teaching Guide for pp. 816–817

Motivation

Ask students to think of tributes to famous people they have heard in music or poetry. For example, some may mention Elton John's "Candle in the Wind," originally written as a tribute to Marilyn Monroe and reworked as a tribute to Diana, Princess of Wales. Tell students that the poet, Alfred, Lord Tennyson, became famous for the tribute he wrote in memory of a friend who died young—at the age of twenty-two. As they read Tennyson's tribute and other of his poems, have them consider what quality of Tennyson's poetry makes it so memorable.

Interest Grabber Video

As an alternative, play "'Ulysses': The Voyage of Odysseus" on Tape 5 to engage student interest.

❶ Background

More About the Author

Tennyson's reputation as a poet began early in his career at Cambridge University, where he received the chancellor's medal for English verse in 1829 with "Timbuctoo," the first poem in blank verse to win. Tennyson suffered poverty throughout his life until middle age because his family had been disinherited in favor of his Uncle Charles. Tennyson did not marry until he was forty, and he is believed to have tended toward emotional instability and melancholy for much of his life. The death of his friend Arthur Henry Hallam was a life-altering experience for Tennyson. In addition to the homage he paid him in his monumental *In Memoriam*, Tennyson named his son Hallam after his dead friend.

Prepare to Read

❶ *from* In Memoriam, A.H.H. ◆ The Lady of Shalott ◆ *from* The Princess: Tears, Idle Tears ◆ Ulysses

Alfred, Lord Tennyson (1809–1892)

You may think of Tennyson—or any male Victorian poet—as a bearded old man whose picture belongs in a cracked, dusty book. Think again. Here is Thomas Carlyle's description of the tall, handsome but moody young Tennyson: "One of the finest looking men in the world. A great shock of rough dusty-dark hair; bright-laughing hazel eyes . . . of sallow-brown complexion, almost Indian-looking." This is the young man who was to become in middle age the most celebrated poet of Victorian England: Alfred, Lord Tennyson.

An Unhappy Childhood Tennyson was born in the rural town of Somersby in Lincolnshire, the fourth of twelve children. He was a sensitive boy who was charmed by the magical words "far, far away." His father, a clergyman, had a large library and supervised Tennyson's early education. He predicted that his son would be "the greatest Poet of the Time." At the same time, he was extremely bitter, having been disinherited by his own father. His anger poisoned the atmosphere of the Tennyson household. As a teenager, Alfred was probably eager to escape to Cambridge University.

The Power of Friendship At first, Tennyson was disappointed by Cambridge. He wrote about his studies: "None but dry-headed, calculating, angular little gentlemen can take much delight in them." Then, he met the young man who became his closest friend, Arthur Henry Hallam. They were often together, and Hallam intended to marry Tennyson's sister Emily. In 1830, with Hallam's encouragement, Tennyson published *Poems, Chiefly Lyrical*, which was followed two years later by a volume simply entitled *Poems*.

A Stunning Tragedy In 1833, however, Hallam died suddenly, leaving a void in Tennyson's life that nearly destroyed him. The poet's grief became the inspiration for some of his greatest work. Soon after Hallam's death, Tennyson began working on a series of short poems that considered questions of death, religious faith, and immortality. This series, which grew over seventeen years into an extended elegy for his friend, was published in 1850 under the title *In Memoriam, A.H.H.*

National Honor The elegy so impressed Prince Albert that in 1850, he encouraged Queen Victoria to appoint Tennyson the poet laureate of England, replacing the recently deceased Wordsworth. For the next forty years, Tennyson published regularly. One of his most celebrated works, *Idylls of the King*, a series of poems based on the legend of King Arthur, began appearing in 1859.

In 1884, Queen Victoria made Tennyson a baron, and so added the title of Lord to his name. He was the first English writer to earn this title for his literary achievements. The honor befitted one whom most Victorians regarded as the poetic voice of their age.

Land, Literature, Long Life When royalties from *In Memoriam, A.H.H.* began to flow in, Tennyson bought a farm on the Isle of Wight. There, he and his wife Emily Sellwood raised two children. Tennyson continued to publish poems into his eighties. His poetry spoke directly to the Victorians, who found reflected in it their deepest faith and deepest doubts.

An Enduring Reputation Although early twentieth-century critics faulted Tennyson for intellectual shallowness, the value of his work endures. In clear, rich, hauntingly musical language, it expresses the aspirations that sustain the human spirit.

TEACHING RESOURCES

The following resources can be used to enrich or extend the instruction for pp. 816–817.

Motivation

Interest Grabber Video, Tape 5

Background

Beyond Literature, p. 38

Take It to the Net

Visit www.phschool.com for Background and hotlinks for the selections.

Literary Analysis

Literary Analysis and Reading Transparencies, The Speaker in Poetry, p. 76

Reading

Literary Analysis and Reading Transparencies, Judging a Poet's Message, p. 75

Selection Support: Reading Strategy, p. 177; Build Vocabulary, p. 175.

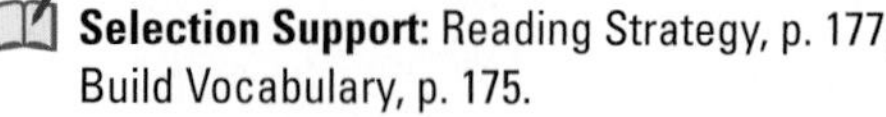

BLOCK SCHEDULING: Resources marked with this symbol provide varied instruction during 90-minute blocks.

Preview

Connecting to the Literature

When everything is going wrong, you may turn to a friend and ask: Why? When Tennyson's best friend, Arthur Hallam, died, Tennyson turned to his culture—its science, its poetry, its religion—and demanded: Tell me, why? *In Memoriam* is the result of his grief-stricken question.

❷ Literary Analysis

The Speaker in Poetry

The **speaker** in a poem—the person who "says" its words—is not necessarily the poet. Speakers fall into the following categories:

- Fictional or real
- Generalized (not described in specific detail) or with a specific identity

Even if the speaker of a poem is fictional, he or she may resemble the poem's actual author, sharing similar situations and experiences. As you read, determine the identity of each speaker and analyze the speaker's conflict and motivation.

Comparing Literary Works

Tennyson's speakers range from well-defined individuals to nonspecific narrators. Some of his speakers have histories—they have undergone a change or suffered a loss. Using such speakers as well as other characters, he dramatizes different experiences of time, including the following:

- A perpetual present, in which nothing significant changes
- A restless movement from past accomplishment into an unknown future
- The loss of the past

As you read, compare the views of time in each poem. Consider whether each poem creates its own "time"—a moment of reflection in which the speaker sums up the past, making way for the future.

❸ Reading Strategy

Judging a Poet's Message

One way to respond to a poem is to **judge the poet's message**—to decide how true and useful that message is. As you read, use a chart like the one shown to determine what the poet is saying and to evaluate the message.

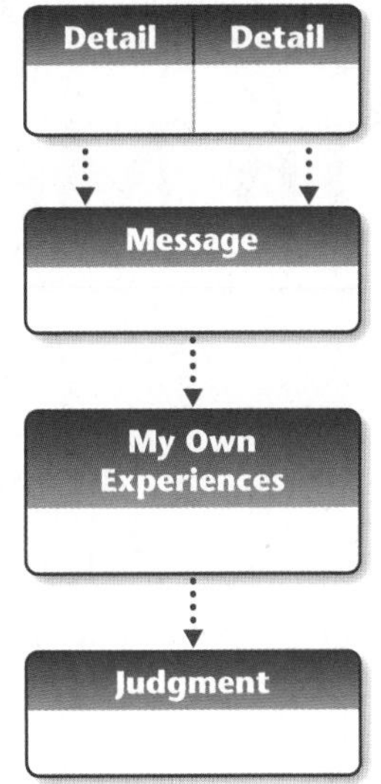

Vocabulary Development

diffusive (di fyōō′ siv) *adj.* tending to spread out (p. 820)

churls (churlz) *n.* farm laborers; peasants (p. 823)

waning (wān′ iŋ) *v.* gradually becoming dimmer or weaker (p. 825)

furrows (fur′ ōz) *n.* narrow grooves, such as those made by a plow (p. 830)

CUSTOMIZE INSTRUCTION FOR UNIVERSAL ACCESS

For Special Needs Students	For Less Proficient Readers	For English Learners
Have students read the adapted version of "The Lady of Shalott" in the **Adapted Reader's Companion.** This version provides basic-level instruction in an interactive format with questions and write-on lines. Completing the adapted version will prepare students to read the selection in the Student Edition.	Have students read "The Lady of Shalott" in the **Reader's Companion.** This version provides basic-level instruction in an interactive format with questions and write-on lines. After students finish the selection in the **Reader's Companion,** have them complete the questions and activities in the Student Edition.	Have students read the adapted version of "The Lady of Shalott" in the **English Learner's Companion.** This version provides basic-level instruction in an interactive format with questions and write-on lines. Completing the adapted version will prepare students to read the selection in the Student Edition.

❷ Literary Analysis

The Speaker in Poetry

- Tell students that in this lesson they will focus on the speaker in a poem—the person to whom the words in the poem can be attributed.
- Explain to students the distinction between the speaker and the poet.
- Read the note about the speaker together as a class. Call students' attention to the different kinds of poetic speakers—fictional vs. real, generalized or specific.
- Use the instruction for Comparing Literary Works to review with students how Tennyson's speakers have different views of time, and encourage students to consider the views of time expressed by the speaker of each poem.
- Use The Speaker in Poetry transparency in **Literary Analysis and Reading Transparencies,** p. 76, to demonstrate to students how the speakers in Tennyson's poems have different conflicts or motivations.

❸ Reading Strategy

Judging a Poet's Message

- Remind students that one way to respond to a poem is to decide how true and useful the poet's message is.
- Read the note about judging a poet's message together as a class.
- Have students practice this skill using the Judging a Poet's Message transparency on p. 75 of **Literary Analysis and Reading Transparencies.**

Vocabulary Development

- Pronounce each vocabulary word for students and read the definitions as a class. Have students identify any words with which they are already familiar.

E-Teach

Visit E-Teach at www.phschool.com for teachers' essays on how to teach, with questions and answers.

TEACH

Step-by-Step Teaching Guide for pp. 818–830.

CUSTOMIZE INSTRUCTION
For Musical/Rhythmic Learners

Tell students that a musical elegy is called a *requiem*. Have them listen to excerpts from the requiems by Verdi, Berlioz, or Fauré. Draw their attention to the slow tempo and the mournful, melancholy mood.

❶ About the Selection

In Memoriam, A.H.H., an elegy, or poem that mourns the death of an individual, was written as a tribute to Tennyson's closest friend, Arthur Henry Hallam, who died at the age of twenty-two. It took Tennyson seventeen years to complete *In Memoriam,* which, in its entirety, consists of 132 separate sections. It is a diary in poetry of Tennyson's emotional journey as he struggled to overcome despair, doubt, and anger over his friend's death.

❷ Background

Art

The Stages of Life, 1835, by Caspar David Friedrich

Friedrich (1774–1840) is considered the most important of the German Romantic painters. His landscapes are often haunting and lonely.

The painting *The Stages of Life* shows Friedrich himself with his family. It was painted shortly after he suffered a stroke, and the central figure, the artist (with the cane), is staring out to sea. The large ship is Friedrich's ship of life, and approaching night (sunset) in the painting symbolizes the artist's death. Use this question for discussion:

> How does the use of dark and light in the painting reflect the progress of *In Memoriam*?
> Answer: The poet moves through despair into hope, just as the artist looks from a dark foreground into the sunset.

❸ ▶Critical Viewing

Possible response: The speaker would reject the idea that life is like a voyage, since his friend's life did not progress toward a definite goal but was senselessly cut short.

❷

The Stages of Life, Caspar David Friedrich, Museum der Bildenden Kunst, Leipzig

❸ ▲ **Critical Viewing** This painting, *The Stages of Life,* suggests that life is like a voyage. How would the speaker in the poem react to such a comparison? Explain. **[Speculate]**

❶ *from*

In Memoriam, A. H. H.

Alfred, Lord Tennyson

1

I held it truth, with him who sings
  To one clear harp in divers[1] tones,
  That men may rise on stepping stones
Of their dead selves to higher things.

But who shall so forecast the years
  And find in loss a gain to match?

1. **divers** (dī′ vərz) *adj.* varied; having many parts.

TEACHING RESOURCES

The following resources can be used to enrich or extend the instruction for pp. 818–830.

Literary Analysis

- **Selection Support:** Literary Analysis, p. 178

Reading

- **Adapted Reader's Companion**
- **Reader's Companion**
- **English Learner's Companion**
- **Listening to Literature Audiocassettes,** Sides 19, 20 ■
- **Listening to Literature Audio CDs,** CD 11 ■

■ **BLOCK SCHEDULING:** Resources marked with this symbol provide varied instruction during 90-minute blocks.

Or reach a hand through time to catch
The far-off interest of tears?

Let Love clasp Grief lest both be drowned,
Let darkness keep her raven gloss.
Ah, sweeter to be drunk with loss,
To dance with death, to beat the ground,

Than that the victor Hours should scorn
The long result of love, and boast,
"Behold the man that loved and lost,
But all he was is overworn."

7

Dark house, by which once more I stand
Here in the long unlovely street,
Doors, where my heart was used to beat
So quickly, waiting for a hand,

❹
A hand that can be clasped no more—
Behold me, for I cannot sleep,
And like a guilty thing I creep
At earliest morning to the door.

He is not here; but far away
The noise of life begins again,
And ghastly through the drizzling rain
On the bald street breaks the blank day.

82

❺
I wage not any feud with Death
For changes wrought on form and face;
No lower life that earth's embrace
May breed with him, can fright my faith.

Eternal process moving on,
From state to state the spirit walks;
And these are but the shattered stalks,
Or ruined chrysalis of one.

Nor blame I Death, because he bare
The use of virtue out of earth;
I know transplanted human worth
Will bloom to profit, otherwhere.

For this alone on Death I wreak
The wrath that garners in my heart;
He put our lives so far apart
We cannot hear each other speak.

Literary Analysis
The Speaker in Poetry
What do you learn about the speaker in lines 21–24?

Reading Strategy
Judging a Poet's Message
In lines 29–44, what does the poet suggest about the consolations of faith and philosophy?

❻ ✓ **Reading Check**
What are two of the main feelings Tennyson conveys in these stanzas?

❹ Literary Analysis

The Speaker in Poetry

- Review with students the various kinds of speakers in poetry.
- Have a student volunteer read aloud the bracketed passage. Ask students to paraphrase the stanza.
- Then, ask the Literary Analysis question on p. 819: What do you learn about the speaker in lines 21–24?
  Answer: The speaker is grieving for a friend and suffers from insomnia.

❺ Reading Strategy

Judging a Poet's Message

- Have students read lines 29–44. As they read, have them paraphrase each stanza in order to determine the main idea or image in each, as well as the emotions that the speaker is expressing.
- For example, point out the word *chrysalis* in line 36. Ask students what the speaker implies about Hallam based on this image.
  Answer: A chrysalis is a cocoon; this image implies that death is only a transformation, as when a caterpillar turns into a butterfly.
- Then, ask students the Reading Strategy question on p. 819: In lines 29–44, what does the poet suggest about the consolations of faith and philosophy?
  Answer: They do not touch him because no explanation or theory will let him speak with his friend.

❻ ✓ Reading Check

Answer: Tennyson conveys his grief at losing his friend, and his wrath at Death for having separated them.

CUSTOMIZE INSTRUCTION FOR UNIVERSAL ACCESS

For Special Needs Students	For Less Proficient Readers	For Gifted/Talented Students
Have students read from *In Memoriam, A.H.H.* with teacher guidance. Then, ask students to visualize each line as they reread the poem to themselves.	Have students read from *In Memoriam, A.H.H.* silently as they listen to **Listening to Literature Audio CDs,** CD 11. Then, have pairs of students alternate reading stanzas from the poem to practice the rhythms and vocabulary Tennyson employs in the poem.	As students read from *In Memoriam, A.H.H.*, have them take notes as if they were preparing a performance interpretation. After they have finished reading, encourage students to cite specific points from their notes that they would interpret in performance.

Answers for p. 820

Review and Assess

1. Possible responses: Yes, the poem's use of imagery was touching; no, the poem is too full of grand imagery to be genuinely affecting.
2. **(a)** The speaker had thought men could learn from and elevate themselves through their losses.
(b) He argues that grief must be embraced to affirm the value of love.
3. **(a)** He is standing by the house where his friend had lived.
(b) The loss of his friend makes the scene bleak and empty.
4. The speaker is not angered by the thought that his friend's form or body has been destroyed or that the world has been robbed of his friend's virtues. He is angered that Death separated him from his friend.
5. **(a)** Although the friend is dead and his voice and physical presence are gone, the speaker feels close to his spirit at all times.
(b) Section 130 reconfigures the speaker's complaint that Death has put their "lives so far apart" into the idea that "Far off thou art, but ever nigh."
6. In the first two parts, the speaker is tormented by unbearable grief; in the last two, his sense of loss is softened by an awareness of the memories he carries with him.
7. Possible responses: Students may say that Tennyson's ideas and words are cold comfort to one who has just lost a dear friend; others may feel that the speaker's words are true and sincere, but that they represent the result of a long process of mourning.

130

Thy voice is on the rolling air;
I hear thee where the waters run;
Thou standest in the rising sun,
And in the setting thou art fair.

What art thou then? I cannot guess;
But though I seem in star and flower
To feel thee some diffusive power,
I do not therefore love thee less.

My love involves the love before;
My love is vaster passion now;
Though mixed with God and Nature thou,
I seem to love thee more and more.

Far off thou art, but ever nigh;
I have thee still, and I rejoice;
I prosper, circled with thy voice;
I shall not lose thee though I die.

diffusive (di fyōō′ siv) *adj.* tending to spread out

Review and Assess

Thinking About the Selection

1. **Respond:** Were you moved by Tennyson's lament for his friend? Why or why not?
2. **(a) Recall:** In section 1, what idea does the speaker say he once held as truth but now doubts? **(b) Interpret:** The speaker rejects this truth in favor of a new view of grief. Paraphrase this view.
3. **(a) Recall:** By what place is the speaker standing in section 7? **(b) Interpret:** What effect does the loss of his friend have on the scene?
4. **Compare and Contrast:** Contrast the facts that, in section 82, the speaker says do not anger him with the one fact that does.
5. **(a) Interpret:** Explain the paradox in line 57: "Far off thou art, but ever nigh." **(b) Connect:** How does section 130 answer the speaker's one reason for anger in section 82?
6. **Draw Conclusions:** How have the speaker's feelings changed from the first two sections of the poem to the last two sections?
7. **Evaluate:** Would the speaker's viewpoint in section 130 reconcile you to a grief? Explain.

7 # The Lady of Shalott

Alfred, Lord Tennyson

8

The Lady of Shalott, John Waterhouse, The Tate Gallery, London

9 ▲ **Critical Viewing** What symbols of the Lady of Shalott's occupation and eventual fate are in this painting? Explain why they are significant. **[Interpret]**

CUSTOMIZE INSTRUCTION FOR UNIVERSAL ACCESS

For Less Proficient Readers	For English Learners
Have students begin reading "The Lady of Shalott" with teacher guidance. Remind them that the speaker tells the poem from the perspective of a spectator of the Lady. Ask them to consider in an imaginary diary entry what Lancelot thought on his way to Camelot, as he stood and "mused a little space." Tell students to write as if they were Lancelot, who has been told by a peasant that the Lady set out in her boat just as they passed by.	Remind students that Tennyson sets his poem in the atmosphere of Arthurian legend, and he cloaks the Lady of Shalott with mystery. Have students begin to read the poem with teacher guidance, sounding out any words and paraphrasing any phrases that give them difficulty. Ask students to consider who the speaker of the poem is. You may want to use the The Speaker in Poetry transparency on p. 76 of **Literary Analysis and Reading Transparencies** to guide your instruction.

7 About the Selection

"The Lady of Shalott" is a poem based in Arthurian legend, but it is also about the position of the creative artist in society. The central character, the Lady of Shalott, has lived under a curse barring her from experiencing the real world—under pain of death. The Lady is locked in her tower away from the vital life of society, seeing life only through a mirror and rendering it unmoving on her tapestry. In the same way, Tennyson is suggesting that many artists are locked away from life, looking at it secondhand and not experiencing it for themselves.

8 Background

Art

The Lady of Shalott, John Waterhouse

John William Waterhouse (1849–1917) studied and exhibited at the Royal Academy in London. He is considered to be both a Classical and a Pre-Raphaelite painter of mainly romantic and poetic subjects. Much of his work was inspired by the poetry of Tennyson and Keats.

This painting, beautifully detailed and executed, was done in iridescent colors that lend a supernatural feel to it. Note the Lady's grief-stricken expression, which registers her resignation to her fate. Use these questions for discussion:

1. Does the painting appear to be true to the details of the poem?
   Possible response: In important details, the painting is true to the poem. The Lady in the painting is dressed in white, afloat on a boat that resembles the boat described in the poem. She appears beautiful, mysterious, and very much alone.
2. In what way does the mood of the painting effectively mirror that of the poem?
   Possible response: The painting is dark and sadly romantic, as is the poem's overall mood.

9 ▶ Critical Viewing

Answer: The chain in the Lady's hand may represent her bondage to fate; the flickering candle suggests the flickering flame of her life.

10 Literary Analysis

The Speaker in Poetry

- Have students read the first stanza to themselves. Ask students to explain the significance of the reference to Camelot. Have students consider why the poet would use Camelot as a setting.
- Then, ask them the Literary Analysis question on p. 822: What does setting this poem in the days of King Arthur suggest about the poet's attitude toward the past?
Answer: The poet is intrigued by the past and feels that it is a rich source of poetic material and inquiry. Perhaps he also feels that the past is a refuge from a confusing or ugly present.

Part I

On either side the river lie
Long fields of barley and of rye,
That clothe the wold[1] and meet the sky;
And through the field the road runs by
10 To many-towered Camelot,[2]
And up and down the people go,
Gazing where the lilies blow[3]
Round an island there below,
The island of Shalott.

Willows whiten, aspens quiver,
Little breezes dusk and shiver
Through the wave that runs forever
By the island in the river
Flowing down to Camelot.
Four gray walls, and four gray towers,
Overlook a space of flowers,
And the silent isle imbowers
The Lady of Shalott.

By the margin, willow-veiled,
Slide the heavy barges trailed
By slow horses; and unhailed
The shallop[4] flitteth silken-sailed
Skimming down to Camelot:
But who hath seen her wave her hand?
Or at the casement seen her stand?
Or is she known in all the land,
The Lady of Shalott?

Only reapers, reaping early
In among the bearded barley,
Hear a song that echoes cheerly,
From the river winding clearly,
Down to towered Camelot:
And by the moon the reaper weary,
Piling sheaves in uplands airy,
Listening, whispers, "'Tis the fairy
Lady of Shalott."

Literary Analysis
The Speaker in Poetry What does setting this poem in the days of King Arthur suggest about the poet's attitude toward the past?

1. **wold** rolling plains.
2. **Camelot** legendary English town where King Arthur had his court and Round Table.
3. **blow** bloom.
4. **shallop** light, open boat.

ENRICHMENT: Cultural Connection

Arthurian Legends

Explain to students that many writers have treated the legends of King Arthur and his knights of the Round Table. Tennyson himself wrote a long poem called *The Idylls of the King,* which is about Arthur's life and death. Sir Thomas Malory wrote a collection of prose romances, *Le Morte d'Arthur,* based on Arthurian legends, printed in 1485. Other well-known treatments include *Sir Gawain and the Green Knight,* a poem written in the fourteenth century; *A Connecticut Yankee in King Arthur's Court,* written by Mark Twain in 1889; and *The Once and Future King,* published in 1958 by T.H. White.

Part II

There she weaves by night and day
A magic web with colors gay.
She has heard a whisper say,
A curse is on her if she stay
To look down to Camelot.
She knows not what the curse may be,
And so she weaveth steadily,
And little other care hath she,
The Lady of Shalott.

And moving through a mirror[5] clear
That hangs before her all the year,
Shadows of the world appear.
There she sees the highway near
Winding down to Camelot:
There the river eddy whirls,
11 And there the surly village churls,
And the red cloaks of market girls,
Pass onward from Shalott.

Sometimes a troop of damsels glad,
An abbot on an ambling pad,[6]
Sometimes a curly shepherd lad,
Or long-haired page in crimson clad,
Goes by to towered Camelot;
And sometimes through the mirror blue
The knights come riding two and two:
She hath no loyal knight and true,
The Lady of Shalott.

12
But in her web she still delights
To weave the mirror's magic sights,
For often through the silent nights
A funeral, with plumes and lights
And music, went to Camelot:
Or when the moon was overhead,
Came two young lovers lately wed;
"I am half sick of shadows," said
The Lady of Shalott.

churls (churlz) *n.* farm laborers; peasants

Literary Analysis
The Speaker in Poetry
Is the speaker who tells the Lady of Shalott's story also a character in the poem? How can you tell?

13 **Reading Check**
What does the Lady of Shalott do with her time?

5. **mirror** Weavers placed mirrors in front of their looms, so that they could view the progress of their work.
6. **pad** easy-paced horse.

11 Vocabulary Development

Related Words: Medieval Words

- Point out the word *churls* to students.
- Read aloud the definition of *churls*, "farmers or peasants." Then, ask students to explain why Tennyson might have chosen a medieval word for his poem.
  Answer: Tennyson's use of the word *churls* adds atmosphere to his poem and reinforces the fact that it is set in King Arthur's court.

12 Literary Analysis

The Speaker in Poetry

- Explain to students that sometimes the speaker of a poem is a character involved in the action. In other poems, the speaker is similar to an omniscient narrator who does not participate in the action.
- Have students read lines 64–72. Ask them to pay careful attention to the speaker's relation to the action being described.
- Then, ask students the Literary Analysis question on p. 823: Is the speaker who tells the Lady of Shalott's story also a character in the poem? How can you tell?
  Answer: No, the speaker who tells her story is not a character in the poem. This is clear from the fact that the speaker is omniscient and does not participate in events.

13 Reading Check

Answer: Night and day, the Lady of Shalott weaves a tapestry showing the scenes she sees in her magic mirror.

CUSTOMIZE INSTRUCTION FOR UNIVERSAL ACCESS

For Special Needs Students	For English Learners	For Gifted/Talented Students
Students may find the elaborate description of the world of the Lady of Shalott somewhat daunting. Encourage them to read slowly, with teacher guidance, any confusing phrases or words. Ask them to paraphrase anything that gives them difficulty.	English language learners may find the descriptions of the Lady of Shalott's day-to-day activities and the Arthurian legends behind her story difficult to understand. Encourage them to question the text, to rely on the footnotes and definitions, and to paraphrase passages.	As students read from the poem, point out that in "The Lady of Shalott," Camelot is a town populated by common people going about the business of making a living, not just by legendary kings and knights. Have students make drawings of bustling Camelot, with its towers in the background, on a typical day.

14 Background

A Crisis of Faith

Charles Darwin's theory of a natural, rather than a divine, origin of species, put forth in *On the Origin of Species* (1859), was a contributing source of anxiety in the Victorian era. He believed that creatures possessing advantageous mutations survived to reproduce and pass their characteristics on to offspring; in this way, a new species could evolve from an old one. Just as Copernicus shocked the world in his *De Revolutionibus* (1543) with the theory that the planets revolved around the sun and not the Earth, so too did Darwin with his "agnostic" view of the origin of life. Darwin's work gave rise to intense opposition in his lifetime because it seemed to contradict the biblical account of creation.

15 Critical Thinking

Make Judgments

- Have students read lines 91–108 to themselves. Encourage them to focus on the description of Lancelot.
- Then, ask students to address how the Lady of Shalott feels about Sir Lancelot: What does he represent to her?
  Possible Response: She sees Lancelot as the embodiment of knightly beauty, bravery, and chivalry. He represents the life and love she has missed by staying in her tower.

Part III

A bow-shot from her bower eaves,
He rode between the barley sheaves,
The sun came dazzling through the leaves,
And flamed upon the brazen greaves[7]
  Of bold Sir Lancelot.
A red-cross knight[8] forever kneeled
To a lady in his shield,
That sparkled on the yellow field,
  Beside remote Shalott.

The gemmy[9] bridle glittered free,
Like to some branch of stars we see
Hung in the golden Galaxy.[10]
The bridle bells rang merrily
  As he rode down to Camelot:
And from his blazoned baldric[11] slung
A mighty silver bugle hung,
And as he rode his armor rung,
  Beside remote Shalott.

All in the blue unclouded weather
Thick-jeweled shone the saddle leather,
The helmet and the helmet feather
Burned like one burning flame together,
  As he rode down to Camelot.
As often through the purple night,
Below the starry clusters bright,
Some bearded meteor, trailing light,
  Moves over still Shalott.

15

His broad clear brow in sunlight glowed;
On burnish'd hooves his war horse trode;
From underneath his helmet flowed
His coal-black curls as on he rode,
  As he rode down to Camelot.
From the bank and from the river
He flashed into the crystal mirror,
"Tirra lirra," by the river
  Sang Sir Lancelot.

She left the web, she left the loom,
She made three paces through the room,

The British Tradition

14 *A Crisis of Faith*

When the grief-stricken Tennyson of *In Memoriam* pushes away the comforting philosophies of his day, or when he turns to the mythic past in "The Lady of Shalott," he reflects a broader crisis of faith that rocked Victorian society. The Industrial Revolution and its teeming urban masses had pushed aside the traditional bond between peasant and lord. The comfortable rhythms of a farming society had given way to surging spirals of economic boom and bust. Meanwhile, such intellectual developments as Charles Darwin's theory of evolution challenged religious beliefs.

In the midst of these social and intellectual changes, Victorian artists asked whether their cultural resources—religion, science, art—were still sufficient to guide their lives. After Tennyson, Matthew Arnold raises the question again in "Dover Beach" (1867; page 884), concluding that only personal relationships offer comfort in a confusing world. From Tennyson to Arnold to T. S. Eliot to Philip Larkin, the theme of a fractured culture, unable to answer its own questions, persists to this day.

7. **greaves** armor that protects the legs below the kneecaps.
8. **red-cross knight** refers to the Redcrosse Knight from *The Faerie Queene* by Edmund Spenser. The knight is a symbol of holiness.
9. **gemmy** jeweled.
10. **Galaxy** the Milky Way.
11. **blazoned baldric** decorated sash worn diagonally across the chest.

ENRICHMENT: Cultural Connection

Lancelot

In Arthurian legend, Lancelot, or Launcelot, was the most famous of the knights of the Round Table. He was first introduced in a French romance by the twelfth-century writer Chrétien de Troyes. Lancelot joins the Round Table later in the story, and as in Tennyson's poem, his arrival on the scene creates disorder. He is noble, virtuous, and extremely attractive. Many legends blame the dissolution of the Round Table on Lancelot's love for Arthur's queen, Guinevere. Lancelot's name, which may have Welsh etymological connections, refers to a legend that he was abducted at birth and raised by a lake-lady before being brought to Arthur's court by a hermit. The main elements of Lancelot's relationship with Guinevere are found in Malory's work.

She saw the waterlily bloom,
She saw the helmet and the plume,
  She looked down to Camelot.
Out flew the web and floated wide;
The mirror cracked from side to side;
"The curse is come upon me," cried
  The Lady of Shalott.

Part IV

In the stormy east wind straining,
The pale yellow woods were waning,
The broad stream in his banks complaining,
Heavily the low sky raining
  Over towered Camelot;
Down she came and found a boat
Beneath a willow left afloat,
And round about the prow she wrote
  The Lady of Shalott.

And down the river's dim expanse
Like some bold seër in a trance,
Seeing all his own mischance—
With a glassy countenance
  Did she look to Camelot.
And at the closing of the day
She loosed the chain, and down she lay;
The broad stream bore her far away,
  The Lady of Shalott.

Lying, robed in snowy white
That loosely flew to left and right—
The leaves upon her falling light—
Through the noises of the night
  She floated down to Camelot:
And as the boathead wound along
The willowy hills and fields among,
They heard her singing her last song,
  The Lady of Shalott.

Heard a carol, mournful, holy,
Chanted loudly, chanted lowly,
Till her blood was frozen slowly,
And her eyes were darkened wholly,
  Turned to towered Camelot.
For ere she reached upon the tide
The first house by the waterside,
Singing in her song she died,
  The Lady of Shalott.

Literary Analysis
The Speaker in Poetry How does the speaker create the sense that a decisive moment has arrived?

waning (wān′ iŋ) *v.* gradually becoming dimmer or weaker

Reading Check
What does the Lady of Shalott do once she sees Sir Lancelot?

16 Literary Analysis
The Speaker in Poetry

- Have students read lines 109–117 to themselves.
- Then, ask students the Literary Analysis question on p. 825: How does the speaker create the sense that a decisive moment has arrived?
  Answer: The speaker neutrally describes what the Lady sees. By not interpreting the significance of the waterlily blooming, of Lancelot's plume, or of the sight of Camelot, he lets the reader's imagination fill in the significance and so experience it more profoundly—the Lady is suddenly, decisively overwhelmed by a sense of the richness of life beyond her tower.

Monitor Progress Ask students how the scene would have been different if the Lady were the speaker.
Possible response: The Lady might have explained her thoughts, detracting from the drama.

17 Reading Check

Answer: When she sees Sir Lancelot, the Lady of Shalott looks down to Camelot and then leaves on a boat for the town.

CUSTOMIZE INSTRUCTION FOR UNIVERSAL ACCESS

For Gifted/Talented Students	For Advanced Readers
Have students write their own Arthurian legends, borrowing some of the key components used by Tennyson in "The Lady of Shalott." Students may want to use the figure of Sir Lancelot or the Lady in their legends, or the curse that hovered over the Lady's life. They may want to imagine other characters who suffer the same fate if they behold Camelot. Encourage students not only to let their imaginations loose in creating their legends but also to echo Tennyson's use of tetrameter.	Have students work in a group to cast, write, rehearse, and present a brief drama of the funeral of the Lady of Shalott. Ask students to consider what kind of service the townspeople would have given her and who would have participated. Tell students to address how Lancelot would have involved himself in the ceremony.

Answers for p. 826

Review and Assess

1. Possible responses: No, because she had no real "life" in the tower; Yes, because she knew that she would die if she left.
2. **(a)** The Lady spends her time weaving, avoiding the real world. **(b)** The Lady glimpses only "shadows of the world" because she sees the world in the reflected surface of her mirror. **(c)** Like an artist, the Lady sees life as material for her depictions, and so she is distanced from it.
3. **(a)** She abandons her weaving and sails for Camelot. **(b)** The description of Lancelot is poetic, filled with vivid imagery and giving Lancelot a legendary stature (the "Galaxy" hangs from his bridle). **(c)** The Lady leaves her room to pursue Lancelot in real life, yet the description makes him seem more like a figure on her tapestry than a real man. In this sense, what draws the Lady out into the real world is the hope that she will find her visions there.
4. **(a)** The Lady's love for Lancelot cannot be consummated because it is forbidden by the curse; her love for him, as a love for an unattainable vision, is impossible. **(b)** Possible response: We can never realize our fantasies because the allure of a fantasy is destroyed once it becomes reality.
5. Possible response: No, modern media—including "reality" shows—cut one off even more completely from reality than the Lady's curse would, since modern media offer themselves as if they were reality or a direct view of it, while the Lady knows that her visions are not real.

Under tower and balcony,
By garden wall and gallery,
A gleaming shape she floated by,
Dead-pale between the houses high,
   Silent into Camelot.
Out upon the wharfs they came,
Knight and burgher, lord and dame,
And round the prow they read her name,
   The Lady of Shalott.

Who is this? and what is here?
And in the lighted palace near
Died the sound of royal cheer;
And they crossed themselves for fear,
   All the knights at Camelot:
But Lancelot mused a little space;
He said, "She has a lovely face;
God in his mercy lend her grace,
   The Lady of Shalott."

Review and Assess

Thinking About the Selection

1. **Respond:** Do you think the Lady should not have decided to sail for Camelot? Explain.
2. **(a) Recall:** What does the Lady spend her time doing? Why? **(b) Interpret:** Why does the Lady glimpse only "shadows of the world"? **(c) Interpret:** Why might an artist share the complaint the Lady makes in lines 71–72?
3. **(a) Recall:** What does the Lady do after seeing Sir Lancelot in the mirror? **(b) Analyze:** How does the long description of Sir Lancelot make the knight seem like the real-life embodiment of a vision? **(c) Draw Conclusions:** Given this description of Lancelot, explain why the Lady might be said to leave her room in pursuit of her visions.
4. **(a) Draw Conclusions:** What does the fact that the Lady dies before meeting Lancelot suggest about her love for him? **(b) Make a Judgment:** Do you agree with Tennyson's implication that we can never realize our fantasies? Why or why not?
5. **Apply:** The poem suggests that the life of the imagination isolates one from reality. Do modern media, such as television and the Internet, suggest otherwise? Explain.

18 *from* The PRINCESS

Alfred, Lord Tennyson

The Princess (1847) is a long narrative poem that contains a number of songs. Some of these songs, including the one that follows, are considered to be among the finest of Tennyson's lyrics.

Tears, Idle Tears

Tears, idle tears, I know not what they mean,
Tears from the depth of some divine despair
Rise in the heart, and gather to the eyes,
In looking on the happy autumn fields,
And thinking of the days that are no more.

Fresh as the first beam glittering on a sail,
That brings our friends up from the underworld,
Sad as the last which reddens over one
That sinks with all we love below the verge;
So sad, so fresh, the days that are no more.

Ah, sad and strange as in dark summer dawns
The earliest pipe of half-awakened birds
To dying ears, when unto dying eyes
The casement slowly grows a glimmering square;
So sad, so strange, the days that are no more.

Dear as remembered kisses after death,
And sweet as those by hopeless fancy feigned
On lips that are for others; deep as love,
Deep as first love, and wild with all regret;
O Death in Life, the days that are no more.

19 ✓ **Reading Check**

What is the speaker's reaction to the thought of "the days that are no more"?

18 About the Selection

"Tears, Idle Tears" from *The Princess* treats a theme common in Tennyson's works: the transience, or fleeting quality, of life and the nearness of death. Tennyson said about this poem: "This song came to me on the yellowing autumn-tide at Tintern Abbey, full for me of its bygone memories. It is the sense of abiding in the transient." The poem focuses on regret for that which passes and cannot be truly possessed—love and the happy times of the past.

19 ✓ Reading Check

Answer: The speaker feels "divine despair" and weeps.

CUSTOMIZE INSTRUCTION FOR UNIVERSAL ACCESS

For Less Proficient Readers	For English Learners	For Advanced Readers
Guide students as they read the poem. Explain that Tennyson's speaker was moved to tears at a beautiful scene when his thoughts turned to "days that are no more." Help students judge the poet's message, using the Judging a Poet's Message transparency on p. 75 of **Literary Analysis and Reading Transparencies.**	Have students read "Tears, Idle Tears" from *The Princess* with teacher guidance. Encourage them to visualize the descriptions Tennyson includes in his poem as they read. If they seem to be having difficulty with the vocabulary, ask them to paraphrase what each line means as they go along.	Remind students that Tennyson wrote "Tears, Idle Tears" after a visit to Tintern Abbey, a site that also inspired William Wordsworth. After students read the poem independently, have them reread Wordsworth's "Lines Composed a Few Miles Above Tintern Abbey," p. 666, and write an essay comparing the poems.

⓴ About the Selection

"Ulysses" is based on the story of the Greek king who fought at Troy for one decade and then wandered the seas for another. The poem takes place after Ulysses' return home to Ithaca, as he is facing old age. It raises a central question about the speaker, Ulysses himself: Did Tennyson intend him to be a heroic figure, eternally questing and fighting death, or is the poet's portrayal ironic, suggesting that Ulysses is a selfish, self-justifying character who longs to cast off boredom and indulge himself by fleeing a clinging wife and unpleasant kingship?

㉑ Literary Analysis

The Speaker in Poetry

- Remind students that the speaker of the poem may be fictional or real, generalized or specific, and may or may not resemble the poem's author.
- Have students identify any details in lines 1–7 that help them determine who the speaker of the poem is.
- Then, ask students the Literary Analysis question on p. 828: Who is speaking the words of this poem? How can you tell? **Answer:** It is Ulysses himself. This fact is apparent because he uses the first-person pronoun *I* to refer to the antecedent, "an idle king."

⓴

Alfred, Lord Tennyson

Background

In this poem Tennyson extends the story of Ulysses (yoo lis´ ez´), the hero of Homer's epic the *Odyssey.* Homer's writing ends after Ulysses' triumphant return home to Ithaca. Years later, Tennyson tells us, the hero has grown restless. Although he had been away for twenty long years—ten fighting in the Trojan War and another ten making the long and adventure-filled voyage back—Ulysses finds that he is contemplating yet another journey.

It little profits that an idle king,
By this still hearth, among these barren crags,
Matched with an aged wife, I mete and dole[1]
Unequal[2] laws unto a savage race,
That hoard, and sleep, and feed, and know not me.
I cannot rest from travel; I will drink
Life to the lees.[3] All times I have enjoyed
Greatly, have suffered greatly, both with those
That loved me, and alone; on shore, and when
Through scudding drifts the rainy Hyades[4]
Vexed the dim sea. I am become a name;

Literary Analysis
The Speaker in Poetry
Who is speaking the words of this poem? How can you tell?

1. **mete and dole** measure and give out.
2. **unequal** unfair.
3. **lees** sediment.
4. **Hyades** (hī´ ə dēz´) group of stars whose rising was assumed to be followed by rain.

ENRICHMENT: Geography Connection

Tracing Odysseus's Route

The Greek king, Ulysses, whom Tennyson profiles in his poem is the hero of the *Odyssey*—known as Odysseus in Homer's epic. Odysseus' journey carries him to real places, such as Troy and Sparta, as well as to fictional places, such as Aeolia and Aeaea. In modern times, historians and explorers have tried to retrace the epic journey of Odysseus to determine the actual locations of the places with the fictional names and thus to determine Odysseus' exact route. What follows is just one of many theories about the actual route of Odysseus: From Troy in present-day Turkey, Odysseus proceeded briefly northward and then southwestward on the Aegean Sea, passing between the Greek lands of Peloponnesus and Crete. Then, sailing westward on the Mediterranean Sea, Odysseus traveled near Sicily, where he found the Cyclops and where nearby islands were homes to the Lotus Eaters, the Sirens, and Aeolus, among others. After circling Sicily clockwise, Odysseus sailed northeastward and finally reached the Ionian Islands of Greece and his home, Ithaca.

(22)

For always roaming with a hungry heart
Much have I seen and known—cities of men
And manners, climates, councils, governments,
Myself not least, but honored of them all—
And drunk delight of battle with my peers,
Far on the ringing plains of windy Troy.
I am a part of all that I have met;
Yet all experience is an arch wherethrough
Gleams that untraveled world, whose
    margin fades
Forever and forever when I move.
How dull it is to pause, to make an end,
To rust unburnished, not to shine in use!
As though to breathe were life. Life piled on life
Were all too little, and of one to me
Little remains; but every hour is saved
From that eternal silence, something more,
A bringer of new things; and vile it were
For some three suns to store and hoard myself,
And this gray spirit yearning in desire
To follow knowledge like a sinking star,
Beyond the utmost bound of human thought.
  This is my son, mine own Telemachus,
To whom I leave the scepter and the isle[5]
Well-loved of me, discerning to fulfill
This labor, by slow prudence to make mild
A rugged people, and through soft degrees
Subdue them to the useful and the good.
Most blameless is he, centered in the sphere
Of common duties, decent not to fail
In offices of tenderness, and pay
Meet[6] adoration to my household gods,
When I am gone. He works his work, I mine.
  There lies the port; the vessel puffs her sail;
There gloom the dark broad seas. My mariners,
Souls that have toiled and wrought, and thought with me—
That ever with a frolic welcome took
The thunder and the sunshine, and opposed
Free hearts, free foreheads—you and I are old;
(24) Old age hath yet his honor and his toil;
Death closes all; but something ere the end,
Some work of noble note, may yet be done,
Not unbecoming men that strove with Gods.
The lights begin to twinkle from the rocks;
The long day wanes; the slow moon climbs; the deep

Ulysses, 1827, Jean-Auguste-Dominique Ingres, National Gallery of Art, Washington, D.C.

(23) **▲ Critical Viewing** Compare the character of Ulysses conveyed by this painting with the speaker in the poem. **[Compare and Contrast]**

(25) **Reading Check** What does Ulysses feel the urge to do?

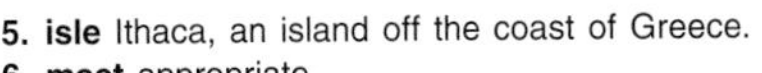
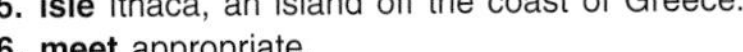

5. **isle** Ithaca, an island off the coast of Greece.
6. **meet** appropriate.

(22) Background

Art

Ulysses **by Jean-Auguste-Dominique Ingres**

Ingres (1780–1867), a French painter of historical subjects and portraits, was exposed to art by his father, a sculptor. He studied with various artists, the foremost of whom was the Neoclassicist David.

Ulysses (1827) shows Ingres's mixed commitment to Neoclassicism (the imitation of the aesthetic principles of ancient Greece and Rome). The harmonious lines and restrained colors are perhaps Neoclassical; the shadows and emotion are Romantic.

Use this question for discussion:

How does the depiction of Ulysses' gaze and hand reflect the spirit Tennyson captures?
Possible response: Ulysses' upward gaze and clenched hand make him seem expectant; the fact that his eyes are in shadow add to the sense that he is waiting. Like Tennyson's Ulysses, he looks toward the future.

(23) ▶ Critical Viewing

Answer: Accept all reasonable responses. Make sure students support their responses with details from the image and the poem.

(24) Critical Thinking

Analyze

- Have students read the bracketed passage to themselves. Ask them to concentrate on the speaker's description of growing old in Ithaca.
- Ask students why Ulysses is not satisfied with the prospect of aging in Ithaca.
  Possible response: He "strove with Gods" and feels that he still has noble work to do before he faces death.

(25) Reading Check

Answer: Ulysses feels the urge to do "some work of noble note" before he dies.

CUSTOMIZE INSTRUCTION FOR UNIVERSAL ACCESS

For Less Proficient Readers

These selections from Tennyson's poetry include references to a wide variety of historical contexts, as well as to events in the poet's own life. To help students assimilate these allusions, write on the board a fill-in graphic organizer like the one shown. Ask students to name the poem by Tennyson that goes with each entry in the chart. ("Ulysses"; "The Lady of Shalott"; *In Memoriam, A.H.H.*)

Poem	Reference
	Greek legend
	legends of King Arthur
	challenges to Victorian faith

ASSESS

Answers for p. 830

Review and Assess

1. Possible responses: Most students will feel that the upbeat conclusion of "Ulysses" makes it more optimistic than the other poem.
2. **(a)** The days are (1) fresh as the first gleam of sunrise and sad as the last ray of sunset; (2) strange as the first peep of birds at sunrise heard by dying ears and sad as fading light seen through a window by dying eyes; and (3) deep as first love and dear as kisses recalled after a loved one's death. **(b)** Each contrast involves a comparison between beginnings and endings, life and death. **(c)** The line captures the bittersweet feelings of memories of past love, which call up profound feelings precisely because its time has passed.
3. **(a)** He says he leads a dull life without adventure or risk. **(b)** This current situation is in sharp contrast to his many voyages and adventures. **(c)** Ulysses is proud of his accomplishments and past experiences.
4. **(a)** Ulysses' aim is to continue seeking challenges until he dies. **(b)** He sees aging as a process that robs him of his cherished way of life. **(c)** He sees life as empty unless it is lived in the spirit of striving and openness toward the future.
5. Possible response: Ulysses might tell the speaker of "Tears, Idle Tears" to let go of the past and "seek a newer world."
6. Possible response: Students may say that nostalgia is attractive to poets and readers because it expresses in heightened form a fact of human life—the loss of the past—and because it makes one feel larger than one's present self—one is caught between one's present and past selves.
7. Possible response: Students may name an organization like NASA, dedicated to exploration in the face of grave risks.

Moans round with many voices. Come, my friends,
'Tis not too late to seek a newer world.
Push off, and sitting well in order smite
The sounding furrows; for my purpose holds
To sail beyond the sunset, and the baths
Of all the western stars, until I die.
It may be that the gulfs will wash us down;
It may be we shall touch the Happy Isles,[7]
And see the great Achilles,[8] whom we knew.
Though much is taken, much abides; and though
We are not now that strength which in old days
Moved earth and heaven, that which we are, we are—
One equal temper of heroic hearts,
Made weak by time and fate, but strong in will
To strive, to seek, to find, and not to yield.

furrows (fʉr´ ōz) *n.* narrow grooves, such as those made by a plow

7. **Happy Isles** Elysium, or the Islands of the Blessed: in classical mythology, the place heroes went after death.
8. **Achilles** (ə kil´ ēz) Greek hero of the Trojan War.

Review and Assess

Thinking About the Selections

1. **Respond:** Which of these two poems seems more hopeful to you? Why?
2. (a) **Recall:** What three comparisons in "Tears, Idle Tears" describe "the days that are no more"? (b) **Analyze:** What contrast does each comparison involve? (c) **Interpret:** What feelings does the line "Deep as first love, and wild with all regret" capture?
3. (a) **Recall:** In "Ulysses," how does Ulysses describe his situation? (b) **Compare and Contrast:** How does this situation contrast with his previous experiences? (c) **Draw Conclusions:** What is Ulysses' attitude toward his experiences?
4. (a) **Recall:** According to lines 58–61, what is Ulysses' purpose? (b) **Draw Conclusions:** What are Ulysses' feelings about aging? (c) **Draw Conclusions:** What is his attitude toward life in general?
5. **Speculate:** What advice might Ulysses give the speaker in "Tears, Idle Tears"?
6. **Generalize:** Why is nostalgia—the intense presence of the past accompanied by the equally intense sense that it is no more—such an attractive feeling to poets and their readers?
7. **Apply:** What type of organization might take the last line of "Ulysses" as its slogan? Explain.

ASSESSMENT PRACTICE: Reading Comprehension

Paired Passages (For more practice, see Test Preparation Workbook, p. 38.)

Many tests require students to describe literary elements—sometimes by comparing two passages. Use the following sample item to demonstrate for students how to compare the tones of two passages. Have students read the last five lines of "Ulysses" and "Tears, Idle Tears," then ask them the following question.

Which of these choices best describes the tones of the passages?

A The lines from "Ulysses" are angry; the lyrics are mournful.
B Both have a nostalgic tone.
C The lines from "Ulysses" are bold; the lyrics are bittersweet.
D Both have a mournful tone.

Because the tone in the two passages is not the same, *B* and *D* are incorrect. The correct answer is *C*.

Review and Assess

Literary Analysis

The Speaker in Poetry

1. (a) Who is the **speaker** of *In Memoriam*? (b) Tennyson wrote the poem in direct response to his friend's death. How does the speaker's conflict reflect one that Tennyson might have felt?
2. (a) Who is the speaker of "The Lady of Shalott"? (b) Is the speaker fictional or real, generalized or specific? Explain.
3. Why might Tennyson have identified the situation of a poet with the Lady's situation?
4. (a) Describe the conflict faced by the speaker in "Ulysses." (b) Does Tennyson see Ulysses as heroic or as selfish and self-justifying? Support your answer by quoting from the poem.

Comparing Literary Works

5. Use a chart like the one shown to compare Ulysses' view of time with the Lady of Shalott's view.

	Past	Present	Future
Ulysses	Remembers it with satisfaction: "I am a part of all that I have met"		
The Lady of Shalott	It is identical with the present: "There she weaves by night and day"		

6. Compare the speaker's relationship with the past in "Tears, Idle Tears" and in *In Memoriam*.
7. Which did Tennyson value more—the timeless world of poetry or the perishable real world? Support your view.

Reading Strategy

Judging a Poet's Message

8. (a) Summarize the poet's message in each poem. (b) Evaluate each message, explaining the basis for your evaluations.

Extend Understanding

9. **Science Connection:** Contrast the scientific approach to time with the view in one of the poems.

Quick Review

The **speaker** in a poem is the person who "says" its words. The speaker is not necessarily the poet.

To **judge a poet's message,** relate the message to experiences that you have had or know about, to judge the truth and usefulness of the message.

Take It to the Net

www.phschool.com

Take the interactive self-test online to check your understanding of these selections.

ENRICHMENT: Further Reading

Other Works by Alfred, Lord Tennyson

The Idylls of the King

"Crossing the Bar"

Other Works About the Hero's Journey

The Odyssey, Homer; *Beowulf; Sir Gawain and the Green Knight*

Take It to the Net

Visit www.phschool.com for more information on Alfred, Lord Tennyson.

Answers continued

conflicted about that choice. "Tears, Idle Tears": Life is marked by losses. "Ulysses": It is good to courageously seek adventure. **(b)** Students should support their evaluations with details.

9. Students should note that the hard sciences do not acknowledge subjective orientation in time (the past is not "lost" in science, since its effects endure, nor does the future cause present actions).

Answers for p. 831

Review and Assess

1. (a) The speaker is Tennyson, or a character much like him. **(b)** Like Tennyson, he is grieved by the early death of a friend and struggles to reconcile himself to it.

2. (a) He is an omniscient observer. **(b)** He is generalized and fictional. He is not identified specifically and has greater knowledge than any one character.

3. Possible response: The situation of the Lady, who can safely view life through the mirror of art but who is drawn by the pull of real experience, is like that of a poet.

4. (a) He has settled down but longs for adventure. **(b)** Possible responses: Tennyson sees Ulysses as heroic (". . . strong in will / To strive, to seek, to find, and not to yield."); others may say he is selfish, since he will cast aside responsibilities to satisfy his wanderlust ("How dull it is to pause, . . .").

5. Possible response: **"Ulysses": Present:** Restless: "How dull it is to pause, to make an end." **Future:** Open: "I cannot rest from travel; I will drink / Life to the lees." **"The Lady of Shalott": Present:** Unchanging: "And so she weaveth steadily, / And little other care hath she, / the Lady of Shalott." **Future:** Doomed: "She looked down to Camelot...'The curse is upon me,' cried the Lady of Shalott."

6. In "Tears," the past is both irrecoverably lost and vividly present in the speaker's longing; in *In Memoriam*, the past is lost yet is now present in the speaker's grief, transformed into faith. The atmosphere of "Tears" is nostalgia; that of *In Memoriam*, reconciliation.

7. Possible response: Students may say that he valued the world of poetry more, given his choice of subjects—one from mythology, another from Arthurian legend, yet another the memory of his dead friend.

8. (a) Possible responses: "In Memoriam": Friendship cannot be destroyed by death. "The Lady of Shalott": The artist who hides from the world may be

continued

EXTEND

Answers for p. 832

❶ Vocabulary Development

Concept Development

1. A *knight* is one of the king's loyal servants and protectors.
2. *Reapers* are those who gather the harvest.
3. A *baldric* is a decorated sash worn across the chest.
4. A *plume* is a feather.
5. A *burgher* is a citizen, usually well-off.

Fluency: Context

From the old dirt road leading to the medieval village, the *furrows* made by the plows were clearly visible. Off in the distance, you could hear the *churls* on their journey home after a hard day's work. The *diffusive* scent of newly turned earth pervaded the air as the day was *waning*.

Spelling Strategy

1. eternal
2. whirl
3. burden

❷ Grammar and Style

1. "My love involves the love before; / My love is vaster passion now; . . ."; clauses
2. "From the bank and from the river"; phrases
3. "How dull it is to pause, to make an end, / To rust unburnished, not to shine in use!"; phrases
4. "To strive, to seek, to find, and not to yield."; phrases
5. "So sad, so fresh, the days that are no more."; words

Writing Application

Possible response for "Tears, Idle Tears":

"Dear as recalled caresses after death,
To have, to hold, to wonder all this time:
If friends long gone are fully now at rest,
Or if they feel the self-same grief and woe.
I wander through this world a ghost at best."

Integrate Language Skills

❶ Vocabulary Development Lesson

Concept Development: Medieval Words

Tennyson uses medieval English words such as *churls,* meaning "farmers" or "peasants," to add atmosphere to his poems. Many such medieval words are of Anglo-Saxon origin. Of those that are still in use, some have acquired new connotations. Today, for example, the word *churl* suggests a rude, surly person. Define the following medieval words that appear in "The Lady of Shalott," using clues to their meaning in the contexts in which they appear.

1. knight
2. reapers
3. baldric
4. plume
5. burgher

Fluency: Context

For each italicized item, write a synonym from the vocabulary list on page 817.

From the old dirt road leading to the medieval village, the *long ridges* made by the plows were clearly visible. Off in the distance, you could hear the *farm laborers* on their journey home after a hard day's work. The *spreading* scent of newly turned earth pervaded the air as the day was *growing dim*.

Spelling Strategy

In the word *churls,* the letters *ur* spell the *er* sound. In the middle of a word, this sound is also commonly spelled *er* or *ir*. In your notebook, correctly spell the words below by choosing *er*, *ir*, or *ur*.

1. et__nal 2. wh__l 3. b__den

❷ Grammar and Style Lesson

Parallel Structure

Tennyson uses **parallel structure**—similar grammatical forms for similar ideas—to give rhythm and unity to his poems. In his poem *In Memoriam,* for example, he uses three parallel infinitive phrases—phrases containing the *to* form of a verb—to stress the compelling desire to give in to grief:

> Ah, sweeter to be drunk with loss, / To dance with death, to beat the ground, . . .

Poets and speakers use parallel structure to create rhythm and drama. Tennyson achieves varied effects with this device. For instance, he uses it in "The Lady of Shalott" to create chanting, fateful feeling suited to the Lady's doom.

Practice Identify the examples of parallel structure in these passages. Then, indicate whether they involve single words, phrases, or clauses.

1. My love involves the love before; / My love is vaster passion now; . . .
2. From the bank and from the river . . .
3. How dull it is to pause, to make an end, / To rust unburnished, not to shine in use!
4. One equal temper of heroic hearts, / Made weak by time and fate, but strong in will / To strive, to seek, to find, and not to yield.
5. So sad, so fresh, the days that are no more.

Writing Application Write an additional stanza for any of Tennyson's poems. Use at least one example of parallel structure.

WG Prentice Hall Writing and Grammar Connection: Chapter 20, Section 6

TEACHING RESOURCES

The following resources can be used to enrich or extend the instruction for pp. 832–833.

Vocabulary

- **Selection Support:** Build Vocabulary, p. 175
- **Vocabulary and Spelling Practice Book** (Use this booklet for skills enrichment.)

Grammar

- **Selection Support:** Grammar and Style, p. 176
- **Writing and Grammar,** Diamond Level, p. 505

- **Daily Language Practice Transparencies** ■

Writing

- **Writing and Grammar,** Diamond Level, p. 202 ■

- **Writing and Grammar iText CD-ROM**
- **Writing Models and Graphic Organizers on Transparencies,** p. 119.

■ **BLOCK SCHEDULING:** Resources marked with this symbol provide varied instruction during 90-minute blocks.

❸ Writing Lesson

Biographical Essay

Arthur Hallam's death had a decisive influence on Tennyson's poetry. Writing *In Memoriam* gave Tennyson the money to buy his own land. Write an essay exploring the relationship between Tennyson's life and his poetry, examining cause-and-effect relations between the two.

Prewriting Research Tennyson and his work. Outline the main events and influences in his life. Then, make a chart of his major themes and literary accomplishments. Take notes on cause-and-effect relations between the two, using a diagram like the one shown.

Model: Charting Cause-and-Effect Relationships

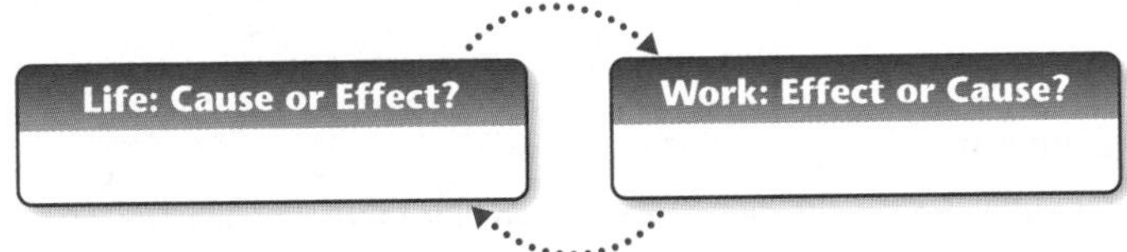

Drafting In your draft, clearly discuss the cause-and-effect relations between Tennyson's life and work. Signal such relationships with transitions such as *therefore*, *because*, *as a result*, and *due to*.

Revising Read your essay to a friend, and then ask about the connections between Tennyson's life and work. Based on your friend's response, clarify details in your essay.

WG Prentice Hall Writing and Grammar Connection: Chapter 10, Section 3

❹ Extension Activities

Listening and Speaking As a news anchor, present a **videotaped news report** on the discovery of the Lady of Shalott's body. Interview Lancelot, King Arthur, and an ordinary citizen for their eyewitness accounts.

- In a group, assign roles and rehearse.
- Create pacing by timing segments.
- Use lighting or staging to direct audience attention from one speaker to the next.

Videotape your broadcast, and play it for the class. **[Group Activity]**

Researching and Representing Make **sketches of a set** for a play based on "The Lady of Shalott." Research medieval architecture and furnishings. Consult the works of pre-Raphaelite painters, who helped create the Victorians' vision of medieval England. Accompany your sketches with an annotated bibliography.

Take It to the Net www.phschool.com

Go online for an additional research activity using the Internet.

ASSESSMENT RESOURCES

The following resources can be used to assess students' knowledge and skills.

Selection Assessment

- **Formal Assessment,** pp. 184–186
- **Open Book Test,** pp. 112–114
- **Got It! Assessment Videotapes,** Tape 4
- **Test Bank Software**

Take It to the Net
Visit www.phschool.com for self-tests and additional questions on the selections.

Writing Rubric

- **Performance Assess. and Portfolio Mgmt.,** pp. 21 and 69

PRENTICE HALL ASSESSMENT SYSTEM

- **Workbook**
- **Skill Book**
- **Transparencies**
- **CD-ROM**

Lesson Support for p. 833

❸ Writing Lesson

- Review with students the Writing Lesson on p. 833 before they begin writing their biographical essays.
- Tell students that they should research Tennyson's life and his work, and they should be extremely careful when making connections between the two, unless these seem justified by facts these find in their research.
- Encourage students to make a timeline of Tennyson's life in which they incorporate the dates of composition and publication of his major works.
- Invite them to use the Cause-and-Effect Organizer in **Writing Models and Graphic Organizers on Transparencies,** p. 119.
- Evaluate their essays using the Exposition: Cause-and-Effect Essay rubric in **Performance Assessment and Portfolio Management,** p. 21.

❹ Listening and Speaking

- Have students reread "The Lady of Shalott." Then, explain that students should imagine they are anchors for news programs who must present videotaped news reports on the discovery of the body of the Lady of Shalott.
- Review with students the instructions in the Listening and Speaking lesson, and then divide them into small groups.
- Have students assign roles and rehearse their news reports, speaking loudly and clearly and pacing their words for the camera.
- Have students videotape their reports and play them for the class.

CUSTOMIZE INSTRUCTION For Universal Access

To address different learning styles, use the activities suggested in the **Extension Activities** booklet, p. 38.

- For Visual/Spatial Learners, use Activity 5.
- For Verbal/Linguistic and Body/Kinesthetic Learners, use Activity 6.
- For Logical/Mathematical and Visual/Spatial Learners, use Activity 7.

My Last Duchess ✦ Life in a Love ✦ Love Among the Ruins ✦ Sonnet 43

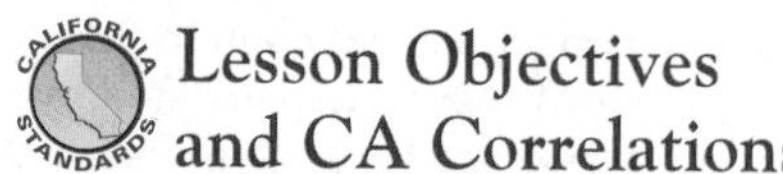

Lesson Objectives and CA Correlations

1. **To analyze and respond to literary elements**
   - Literary Analysis: Dramatic Monologue **R 3.1**
   - Comparing Literary Works **R 3.3**
2. **To read, comprehend, analyze, and critique a poem**
   - Reading Strategy: Making Inferences About the Speaker
   - Reading Check Questions
   - Review and Assess Questions
   - Assessment Practice (ATE)
3. **To develop word analysis skills, fluency, and systematic vocabulary**
   - Vocabulary Development Lesson: Word Analysis: Latin Suffix *-ence* **R 1.1, 1.2**
4. **To understand and apply written and oral language conventions**
   - Spelling Strategy **LC 1.2**
   - Grammar and Style Lesson: Usage: *like* and *as* **LC 1.1**
5. **To understand and apply appropriate writing and research strategies**
   - Writing Lesson: Written Recommendation **W 1.9**
   - Extension Activity: Guided Tour **W 1.8**
6. **To understand and apply listening and speaking strategies**
   - Extension Activity: Oral Interpretation **LS 2.5**

STEP-BY-STEP TEACHING GUIDE	PACING GUIDE
PRETEACH	
Motivate Students and Provide Background	
Use the Motivation activity (ATE p. 834)	5 min.
Read and discuss author and background features (SE/ATE pp. 834, 836, 837, 840) [A]	5 min.
Introduce the Concepts	
Introduce the Literary Analysis and Reading Strategy concepts (SE/ATE p. 835) [A]	15 min.
Pronounce the vocabulary words and read their definitions (SE p. 835)	5 min.
TEACH	
Monitor Comprehension	
Informally monitor comprehension by circulating while students read independently or in groups [A]	15 min.
Monitor students' comprehension with the Reading Check notes (SE/ATE pp. 837, 841)	as students read
Develop vocabulary with Vocabulary notes (SE pp. 837, 838, 839, 841; ATE p. 838)	as students read
Develop Understanding	
Develop students' understanding of dramatic monologue with the Literary Analysis annotations (SE p. 838; ATE pp. 837, 838) [A]	5 min.
Develop students' ability to make inferences about the speaker with the Reading Strategy annotations (SE/ATE pp. 838, 841, 843)	5 min.
ASSESS	
Assess Mastery	
Assess students' mastery of the Reading Strategy and Literary Analysis concepts by having them answer the Review and Assess questions (SE/ATE p. 845)	15 min.
Use one or more of the print and media Assessment Resources (ATE p. 847) [A]	up to 45 min.
EXTEND	
Apply Understanding	
Have students complete the Vocabulary Development Lesson and the Grammar and Style Lesson (SE p. 846) [A]	20 min.
Apply students' knowledge of cause-and-effect transitions using the Writing Lesson (SE/ATE p. 847) [A]	45 min.
Apply students' understanding using one or more of the Extension Activities (SE p. 847)	20–90 min.

ACCELERATED INSTRUCTION:
Use the strategies and activities identified with an [A].

UNIVERSAL ACCESS
● = Below-Level Students
▲ = On-Level Students
■ = Above-Level Students

Time and Resource Manager

Reading Level: Average, Average, Average, Easy
Average Number of Instructional Days: 4

RESOURCES		
PRINT	**TRANSPARENCIES**	**TECHNOLOGY**
• **Beyond Literature,** Humanities Connection: Fine Art, p. 39 ▲ ■		• **Interest Grabber Videos,** Tape 5 ● ▲ ■
• **Selection Support Workbook:** ● ▲ ■ Literary Analysis, p. 182 Reading Strategy, p. 181 Build Vocabulary, p. 179	• **Literary Analysis and Reading Transparencies,** pp. 77 and 78 ● ▲ ■	
• **Adapted Reader's Companion** ● • **Reader's Companion** ● • **Authors In Depth,** The British Tradition, p. 162 ■		• **Listening to Literature** ● ▲ ■ Audiocassettes, Side 20 Audio CDs, CD 12
• **English Learner's Companion** ● ▲ • **Literary Analysis for Enrichment** ■		
• **Formal Assessment:** Selection Test, pp. 187–189 ● ▲ ■ • **Open Book Test,** pp. 115–117 ● ▲ ■ • **Performance Assessment and Portfolio Management,** p. 10 ● ▲ ■ • Prentice Hall Assessment System ● ▲ ■	• Prentice Hall Assessment System ● ▲ ■ • **Skills Practice Answers and Explanations on Transparencies** ● ▲ ■	• **Test Bank Software** ● ▲ ■ • **Got It! Assessment Videotapes,** Tape 4 ● ▲
• **Selection Support Workbook:** ● ▲ ■ Grammar and Style, p. 180 • **Writing and Grammar,** Diamond Level ● ▲ ■ • **Extension Activities,** p. 39 ● ▲ ■	• **Daily Language Practice Transparencies** ● ▲ • **Writing Models and Graphic Organizers on Transparencies,** p. 119 ● ▲ ■	• **Writing and Grammar iText CD-ROM** ● ▲ ■ ***Take It to the Net*** www.phschool.com

BLOCK SCHEDULING: Use one 90-minute class period to preteach the selections and have students read them. Use a second 90-minute class period to assess students' mastery of skills and have them complete one of the Extension Activities.

PRETEACH

Step-by-Step Teaching Guide for pp. 834–835

Motivation

To motivate students to read the love poems in this section, have them brainstorm to list the qualities that they would look for in a loved one. Ask them as a class to rank the qualities. Then, make a list of the five most important qualities and keep them to compare and contrast with the qualities they find in these poems.

Interest Grabber Video

As an alternative, play "Sonnet 43: True Love" on Tape 5 to engage student interest.

❶ Background

More About the Authors

Robert Browning

Robert Browning was influenced most significantly in his youth by his reading of Shelley, Byron, and Keats, and by his mother's Nonconformist piety. At the age of twelve, he wrote a volume of poems, *Incondita,* that no longer survives. After the death of his wife, Elizabeth, Browning lived with his sister and formed a wide circle of acquaintances in London society. He was awarded an honorary degree by Oxford University. Browning died in Venice and is buried in Westminster Abbey.

Elizabeth Barrett Browning

Elizabeth Barrett Browning received a great deal of critical attention in her lifetime. When Wordsworth died in 1850, she was considered to be the most likely successor to the post of poet laureate. Toward the end of her life, she wrote poems that were more politically charged and less popular with her peers. In particular, *Poems Before Congress* (1860) damaged her popularity. She and Robert Browning were friends of Ruskin, Carlyle, Tennyson, Thackeray, Hawthorne, Rossetti, and scores of other literary luminaries of their day.

Prepare to Read

❶ My Last Duchess ◆ Life in a Love ◆ Love Among the Ruins ◆ Sonnet 43

Robert Browning (1812–1889)

Young Robert Browning's best teacher may not have been a person, but his father's 6,000-book library. Although he had little schooling, he eagerly devoured those books, hungry for knowledge about history, art, and literature.

Inspiration and Discouragement By the time he was a teenager, Browning had decided to make poetry his life's pursuit. He published his first book, *Pauline*, at the age of twenty-one. Success was a while coming, though. A long and highly personal poem modeled after Shelley's work, *Pauline* did not sell a single copy.

Discouraged, Browning tried his hand at something less personal, a long dramatic poem called *Paracelsus*. He also wrote a play. His work still failed to attract much public notice, and his reputation was eclipsed by that of his wife, the poet Elizabeth Barrett Browning, whom he had married in 1846.

Lasting Fame In 1869, eight years after Elizabeth's death, the publication of *The Ring and the Book* turned Browning's career around. This long poem, based on an actual trial, tells the story of a murder in a series of dramatic monologues, or speeches by characters. *The Ring and the Book* achieved wide recognition for its author. It demonstrated the unique elements that Browning contributed to nineteenth-century poetry: a more down-to-earth, less "poetic" language and a renewal of the dramatic monologue, a form ideally suited to reveal character.

Today, Browning ranks with Tennyson as one of the great Victorian poets. His shorter dramatic monologues, such as "My Last Duchess," remain favorites of many.

Elizabeth Barrett Browning (1806–1861)

Like her future husband, young Elizabeth Barrett had no formal education. However, her zest for knowledge spurred her to learn eight languages on her own. By the time she was ten, she had read plays by Shakespeare, passages of *Paradise Lost*, and histories of England, Greece, and Rome. The oldest of eleven children in an upper-middle-class family, she began writing poetry as a child. By the time she reached adulthood, she had published two volumes of verse.

Frailty and Romance Elizabeth Barrett's frail health, caused by a spinal injury, made her something of a recluse. But her poetry attracted much attention, including that of Robert Browning, who wrote her a letter of appreciation. After five months of correspondence, she and Browning met and fell in love. Her father objected to their romance, but Elizabeth and Robert married in 1846 and ran away to Florence, Italy, where they had a son they nicknamed Pen and lived in happy exile. In Italy, Elizabeth Barrett took an interest in politics and wrote denunciations of slavery in the United States. She died in Florence in 1861.

Shifting Reputations It is hard for us to believe today, when Robert Browning's reputation is so great, that Elizabeth was the more famous poet during her lifetime. Her love story in verse, *Aurora Leigh* (1857), was so popular that the income from it helped support the Brownings. Also popular was her *Sonnets from the Portuguese*, a sequence of forty-four love poems written to her husband. Sonnet 43, which comes from this collection, has appeared in countless anthologies and has assured her place in the history of English poetry.

TEACHING RESOURCES

The following resources can be used to enrich or extend the instruction for pp. 834–835.

Motivation

Interest Grabber Video, Tape 5

Background

Beyond Literature, p. 39

Take It to the Net

Visit www.phschool.com for background and hotlinks for the selections.

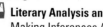

Literary Analysis

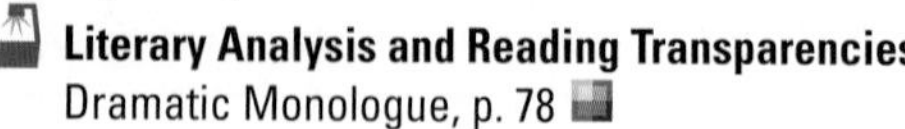

Literary Analysis and Reading Transparencies, Dramatic Monologue, p. 78

Reading

Literary Analysis and Reading Transparencies, Making Inferences About the Speaker, p. 77

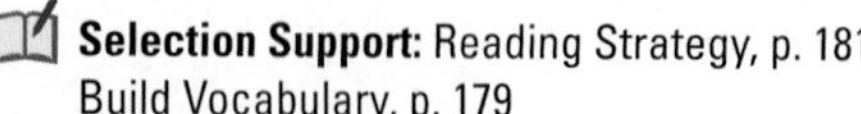

Selection Support: Reading Strategy, p. 181; Build Vocabulary, p. 179

BLOCK SCHEDULING: Resources marked with this symbol provide varied instruction during 90-minute blocks.

Preview

Connecting to the Literature

True love is hard to define: How does it differ from selfish possessiveness? True love may also be hard to find: Is it work, destiny, or sheer luck? The Brownings, very much in love, wrote many poems on these subjects.

❷ Literary Analysis

Dramatic Monologue

Chaucer and Shakespeare gave us versions of the **dramatic monologue,** in which a single character delivers a speech. Robert Browning perfected the form and made it his own. His monologues contain these elements:

- A speaker who indirectly reveals his or her situation and character
- A silent listener, addressed by the speaker and implied in what the speaker says

As you read "My Last Duchess," note the skillful use of these elements.

Comparing Literary Works

The Brownings create a wide range of tones, from the dignified to the chatty. For instance, Robert Browning's monologues capture the rhythms of everyday speech through his expert use of **run-on lines**—lines ending where the flow of words forces you to read on without pause.

But to myself they turned (since none puts by
The curtain I have drawn for you, but I)

He and Elizabeth Barrett also use **end-stopped lines,** which end just where a speaker would pause, for a sing-song effect. Compare the poets' use of these devices.

❸ Reading Strategy

Making Inferences About the Speaker

You make **inferences,** or educated guesses, about people every day. Similarly, you can infer the thoughts or feelings of a poem's speaker from his or her words and actions. Use a chart like the one shown to make inferences about the speakers of these poems.

Words / Action of Speaker
"That's my last Duchess painted on the wall, . . ."
Overt Meaning
There on the wall is a painting of my last wife.
Inferences
The duke seems indifferent about his last wife, who is probably dead.

Vocabulary Development

countenance (koun′ tə nəns) *n.* face (p. 837)

officious (ə fish′ əs) *adj.* meddlesome (p. 838)

munificence (myo͞o nif′ ə səns) *n.* lavish generosity (p. 838)

dowry (dou′ rē) *n.* property brought by a woman's family to her husband upon their marriage (p. 838)

eludes (ē lo͞odz′) *v.* avoids or escapes (p. 839)

vestige (ves′ tij) *n.* trace; remaining bit (p. 841)

sublime (sə blīm′) *adj.* inspiring awe through beauty or grandeur (p. 841)

minions (min′ yənz) *n.* attendants or agents (p. 841)

CUSTOMIZE INSTRUCTION FOR UNIVERSAL ACCESS

For Special Needs Students	For Less Proficient Readers	For English Learners
Have students read the adapted version of "My Last Duchess" in the **Adapted Reader's Companion.** This version provides basic-level instruction in an interactive format with questions and write-on lines. Completing the adapted version will prepare students to read the selection in the Student Edition.	Have students read "My Last Duchess" in the **Reader's Companion.** This version provides basic-level instruction in an interactive format with questions and write-on lines. After students finish the selection in the **Reader's Companion,** have them complete the questions and activities in the Student Edition.	Have students read the adapted version of "My Last Duchess" in the **English Learner's Companion.** This version provides basic-level instruction in an interactive format with questions and write-on lines. Completing the adapted version will prepare students to read the selection in the Student Edition.

❷ Literary Analysis

Dramatic Monologue

- Explain to students that in this lesson they will focus on dramatic monologues, or speeches uttered by single characters—a technique mastered by the poet Robert Browning.
- Explain that Browning's dramatic monologues usually reveal something indirectly about their speaker, and often they contain a silent listener.
- Use the instruction for Comparing Literary Works to review with students how dramatic monologues are especially well suited to capture the rhythms of everyday speech through the use of run-on lines.
- Use the Dramatic Monologue transparency in **Literary Analysis and Reading Transparencies,** p. 78, to show students how to identify traditional elements of dramatic monologues.

❸ Reading Strategy

Making Inferences About the Speaker

- Explain to students that just as they can infer, or guess at, what people in their lives think or mean, they can also make inferences about the speakers of poems they read.
- Use the graphic organizer on p. 835 to model the skill of making inferences about the speaker with students.
- Have students practice the skill using the Making Inferences About the Speaker transparency in **Literary Analysis and Reading Transparencies,** p. 77.

Vocabulary Development

- Pronounce each vocabulary word for students, and read the definitions as a class. Have students identify any words with which they are already familiar.

 ***E-Teach***

Visit E-Teach at www.phschool.com for teachers' essays on how to teach, with questions and answers.

TEACH

Step-by-Step Teaching Guide for pp. 836–844

CUSTOMIZE INSTRUCTION
For Visual/Spatial Learners

Encourage these students to infer character traits of the woman in the portrait and to compare them with those of the Duchess in the poem.

❶ About the Selection

In "My Last Duchess," Browning skillfully uses the dramatic monologue to provide a brilliant portrait of a jealous, possessive, arrogant man who gave orders to kill his first wife ("I gave commands; / Then all smiles stopped together") because she displeased him. The Duke describes at length his dead wife's supposed faults (she appeared to like other men as well as she liked him: "she liked whate'er / She looked on, and her looks went everywhere"). As the Duke talks, he reveals to the reader—and to his unheard listener in the poem—his chilling personality.

❷ Background

Art

Antea (Portrait of a Lady)
by Parmigianino

In this painting, also called *La Bella,* Parmigianino's expert draftsmanship is apparent. The lady's wealth and refinement are obvious through the artist's depiction of her rich clothing and graceful posture. The artist has sacrificed emphasis on her femininity in favor of portraying elegance.

Parmigianino (1503–1540) was the last true northern Italian High Renaissance painter. He painted with mannered, or formal, realism.

Use this question for discussion:

How would you describe the subject's posture and facial expression?
Answer: She is formally posed and appears young, vulnerable, serious, and (judging from her intense, direct look and the presence of the weasel-like fur) perhaps capable of malice.

❸ ▶Critical Viewing

Answer: The woman portrayed by the artist seems serious and unsentimental, not warm and lighthearted like the duchess.

②

Antea (Portrait of a Lady), Parmigianino. Museo Nazionale di Capodimonte, Naples

③ ▲**Critical Viewing** Compare the character of this woman as conveyed by the painting with the character of the duchess as described by the duke. **[Compare and Contrast]**

TEACHING RESOURCES

The following resources can be used to enrich or extend the instruction for pp. 836–844.

Literary Analysis

- **Selection Support:** Literary Analysis, p. 182

Reading

- **Adapted Reader's Companion**
- **Reader's Companion**
- **English Learner's Companion**
- **Listening to Literature Audiocassettes,** Side 20 ▪
- **Listening to Literature Audio CDs,** CD 12 ▪

Extension

- **Authors In Depth,** The British Tradition, p. 162 (The collection includes nine additional selections by Elizabeth Barrett Browning for extended reading.)

▪ **BLOCK SCHEDULING:** Resources marked with this symbol provide varied instruction during 90-minute blocks.

1

Robert Browning

Background

This poem, set in the sixteenth century in a castle in northern Italy, is based on events from the life of the duke of Ferrara, a nobleman whose first wife died after just three years of marriage. Following his wife's death, the duke began making arrangements to remarry. In Browning's poem, the duke is showing a painting of his first wife to an agent who represents the father of the woman he hopes to marry.

4

That's my last Duchess painted on the wall,
Looking as if she were alive. I call
That piece a wonder, now: Frà Pandolf's[1] hands
Worked busily a day, and there she stands.
Will't please you sit and look at her? I said
"Frà Pandolf" by design, for never read
Strangers like you that pictured countenance,
The depth and passion of its earnest glance,
But to myself they turned (since none puts by
The curtain I have drawn for you, but I)
And seemed as they would ask me, if they durst,[2]
How such a glance came there; so, not the first
Are you to turn and ask thus. Sir, 'twas not
Her husband's presence only, called that spot

countenance (koun´ tə nəns) *n.* face

5 **Reading Check**

What are the duke and his listener viewing?

1. **Frà Pandolf's** work of Brother Pandolf, an imaginary painter.
2. **durst** dared.

4 Literary Analysis

Dramatic Monologue

- Remind students that a dramatic monologue is the speech of a single speaker. It contains no stage directions or omniscient narration. Yet poets can deftly set a scene in a monologue through implication.
- Have a volunteer read lines 1–4 aloud. Ask students: In front of what object is the speaker standing in these lines?
  Answer: He is standing in front of the portrait of his former wife.

Monitor Progress Ask students: What technique does Browning use to convey this information within the form of a dramatic monologue?
Answer: The opening "That's" immediately suggests that the speaker is indicating something. The rest of the line explains what it is he is indicating and implies that he is speaking to a visitor unfamiliar with the painting. The information is conveyed in the speech of the poem's speaker, without outside narration, so it remains within the form of the monologue.

- Explain to students that one danger of the form is the risk of making speakers sound unnatural as they fill in information that readers need. Point out that this potential flaw is similar to one found in badly written science fiction, in which the writer has characters spend time explaining gadgets to each other because the reader needs the information, not because the other characters do.
- Ask students whether Browning's setting of the scene in these lines seems forced or contrived, or whether the speech seems natural to the speaker.
  Possible response: It would be natural for the duke to utter such a speech while walking with a visitor past a painting in his home: The effect is natural, not contrived.

5 Reading Check

Answer: The duke and his listener are looking at a portrait of the duke's deceased wife.

CUSTOMIZE INSTRUCTION FOR UNIVERSAL ACCESS

For Special Needs Students	For Gifted/Talented Students
Have students read a section from "My Last Duchess" with teacher guidance. Remind students that they are reading a dramatic monologue, or a speech by a single speaker. Ask students what, if any, indications there are in the poem that the speaker is talking to someone else.	Have students read "My Last Duchess" in pairs. Then, with their partners, have students write a brief scene of an exchange between the duke and the agent who listens to his monologue. Have students create dialogue that might have happened before or after the scene in the poem. Students may want to incorporate lines from the poem in their scene. Have them practice and enact their scene for their classmates.

6 Literary Analysis

Dramatic Monologue

- Remind students that dramatic monologues often indirectly reveal the situation and character of their speaker.
- Have students read lines 15–31, paying careful attention to the details about the duke indirectly revealed by his words.
- Then, ask them the Literary Analysis question on p. 838: How does the duke indirectly suggest his own deeply jealous nature?
Answer: The duke shows that he could not tolerate the ordinary pleasures his wife took in simple things, since he felt that this pleasure equaled the pleasure she took in his gifts, an equivalence his pride could not accept.

7 Reading Strategy

Making Inferences About the Speaker

- Review with students how they can make inferences about the speaker of a poem from his or her words and actions.
- Have a student volunteer read aloud lines 43–47. Encourage students to identify any details they can use to make inferences about the speaker here.
- Then, ask the Reading Strategy question on p. 838: How rational is the speaker being? How irrational are his underlying feelings?
Possible Response: Students should recognize that the duke's seeming rationality in thinking is belied by his completely irrational emotional reactions—insanely jealous of his wife's attention to anything besides himself and his rank.

8 Vocabulary Development

Latin Suffix *-ence*

- Draw students' attention to the word *munificence,* line 49.
- Explain that the Latin suffix *-ence* means "quality of being": *munificence* means "the quality of being generous."
- Ask students to list other words containing the suffix *-ence.*
Possible responses: *Benevolence, indulgence,* and *excellence.*

Of joy into the Duchess' cheek: perhaps
Frà Pandolf chanced to say "Her mantle laps
Over my lady's wrist too much," or "Paint
Must never hope to reproduce the faint
Half-flush that dies along her throat"; such stuff
Was courtesy, she thought, and cause enough
For calling up that spot of joy. She had
A heart—how shall I say?—too soon made glad,
6 Too easily impressed; she liked whate'er
She looked on, and her looks went everywhere.
Sir, 'twas all one! My favor at her breast,
The dropping of the daylight in the West,
The bough of cherries some officious fool
Broke in the orchard for her, the white mule
She rode with round the terrace—all and each
Would draw from her alike the approving speech,
Or blush, at least. She thanked men—good! but
thanked
Somehow—I know not how—as if she ranked
My gift of a nine-hundred-years-old name
With anybody's gift. Who'd stoop to blame
This sort of trifling? Even had you skill
In speech—(which I have not)—to make your will
Quite clear to such an one, and say, "Just this
Or that in you disgusts me; here you miss,
Or there exceed the mark"—and if she let
Herself be lessoned so, nor plainly set
Her wits to yours, forsooth,[3] and made excuse,
—E'en then would be some stooping; and I choose
Never to stoop. Oh sir, she smiled, no doubt,
Whene'er I passed her; but who passed without
7 Much the same smile? This grew; I gave commands;
Then all smiles stopped together. There she stands
As if alive. Will 't please you rise? We'll meet
The company below, then. I repeat,
The Count your master's known munificence 8
Is ample warrant that no one just pretense
Of mine for dowry will be disallowed;
Though his fair daughter's self, as I avowed
At starting, is my object. Nay, we'll go
Together down, sir! Notice Neptune,[4] though,
Taming a sea horse, thought a rarity,
Which Claus of Innsbruck[5] cast in bronze for me!

Literary Analysis
Dramatic Monologue How does the duke indirectly suggest his own deeply jealous nature?

officious (ə fish′ əs) *adj.* meddlesome

Reading Strategy
Making Inferences About the Speaker How rational is the speaker being? How irrational are his underlying feelings?

munificence (myo͞o nif′ ə səns) *n.* lavish generosity

dowry (dou′ rē) *n.* property brought by a woman's family to her husband upon their marriage

3. **forsooth** in truth.
4. **Neptune** in Roman mythology, the god of the sea.
5. **Claus of Innsbruck** imaginary Austrian sculptor.

ENRICHMENT: Cultural Connection

Love and Marriage

Share with the class that the relationship we call "love" has been interpreted in widely different ways in various eras and in diverse cultures. In many cultures, arranged marriages are more common than marriages in which the individuals marry the ones they love. In ancient Greece and Rome, as well as in medieval and Renaissance Europe, political marriages among individuals of the upper classes were common. Help students to recognize that the Brownings' romantic courtship was decidedly unconventional by the standards of nineteenth-century England. In many parts of the world today, such a relationship—in defiance of a parent's wishes—would still be regarded with disapproval.

❾ # *Life in a Love*

Robert Browning

Escape me?
Never—
Beloved!
While I am I, and you are you,
So long as the world contains us both,
Me the loving and you the loth,
While the one eludes, must the other pursue.
My life is a fault at last, I fear:
It seems too much like a fate, indeed!
Though I do my best I shall scarce succeed.
But what if I fail of my purpose here?
It is but to keep the nerves at strain,
To dry one's eyes and laugh at a fall,
And, baffled, get up and begin again,—
So the chase takes up one's life, that's all.
While, look but once from your farthest bound
At me so deep in the dust and dark,
No sooner the old hope goes to ground
Than a new one, straight to the self-same mark,
I shape me—
Ever
Removed!

❿ **▲ Critical Viewing** What conventional ideas of courtship does the illustration suggest? Explain. **[Infer]**

eludes (ē lo͞odz′) *v.* avoids or escapes

Review and Assess

Thinking About the Selections

1. **(a) Recall:** What complaint does the speaker make about his first wife in lines 13–24 of "My Last Duchess"? **(b) Infer:** How did he respond to her behavior? **(c) Support:** Explain what has happened to the duchess, indicating where in the poem this is revealed.
2. **(a) Recall:** To what new subject does the speaker turn in his last remark? **(b) Draw Conclusions:** What does this change of subject reveal about his character?
3. **(a) Recall:** What does the speaker of "Life in a Love" do as his beloved eludes him? **(b) Interpret:** What causes his behavior?
4. **Evaluate:** Is the speaker's "love" truly love? Explain.
5. **Apply:** Do you think irrational passions such as those in the poems still occur in modern times? Explain.

❾ About the Selection

In this dramatic monologue, the male speaker describes his persistence in pursuing a reluctant woman. Students' attitudes toward this speaker may vary widely. Some may be charmed and amused by his persistence, while others may find it sad or scary.

❿ ▶Critical Viewing

Answer: The conventional ideas of courtship, such as a man importuning a woman for her attentions, are echoed in this illustration.

Answers for p. 839

Review and Assess

1. **(a)** The speaker complains that his first wife was too free with her appreciation for things.
   (b) He responded to her behavior by having her killed. **(c)** This murder is revealed in lines 45–46: "This grew: I gave commands; / Then all smiles stopped together."
2. **(a)** The speaker turns to the subject of a bronze sculpture that he notices as they descend the stairs. **(b)** The speaker has the same attitude toward the sculpture, the portrait, and the duchess—pride of possession. He equates love with ownership.
3. **(a)** He keeps pursuing his goal and looking for a sign of encouragement. **(b)** His behavior is caused by his unrequited love.
4. Possible responses: Students may say that the speaker is in love with the "game" of love, rather than with the woman. Others may feel that the speaker really is in love to subject himself to such constant agony.
5. Possible response: Students should recognize that irrational passions such as those described in these poems still occur in modern times.

CUSTOMIZE INSTRUCTION FOR UNIVERSAL ACCESS

For Special Needs Students	For Less Proficient Readers	For Advanced Students
Have students read the poem "Life in a Love" with teacher guidance, using the Dramatic Monologue transparency on p. 78 of **Literary Analysis and Reading Transparencies**.	Have students read "Life in a Love" with teacher guidance. Then, have them paraphrase this poem in one or two paragraphs. Remind them that when they paraphrase, they take Browning's words and restate them in their own words.	Have students write a parody of Browning's "Life in a Love," in which they take his dramatic monologue of obsessive love to an extreme. Students may want to exploit some of the ideas in Browning's poem for comic effect, or they may choose to manipulate the genre of the obsequious lover in hot pursuit of his beloved.

⓫ About the Selection

In this poem, the speaker (a shepherd) describes the private joys of the rural retreat, among the ruins of an old city, which he shares with his beloved. He contrasts the pastoral scene with the public monuments, chariot racetrack, and battles that existed on the same site in ancient times when it was a great city and capital of an empire. The speaker expresses sadness over the lives wasted in the empty pursuit of imperial glory and greed ("folly, noise and sin"), asserting that "love is best" and endures, whereas other pursuits crumble in ruin.

⓬ Background

Art

Italian Ruins by John Claude Nattes

This undated watercolor was probably painted in the years between 1781 and 1784. It is done in the sepia style Nattes preferred, with details tinted in shades of brown. The ruined temple or building rises out of an Italian urban scene. A tree grows in the center, showing the degrees of decay to which the ruin has succumbed. The descriptive scene has a romantic air and a poetic charm.

The English watercolor artist John Claude Nattes (1765–1822) was born of Irish parents. His work is among that of the early English topographical painters—descriptive painters of towns, parishes, ruins, tracts of land, estates, and buildings. He published books describing Scotland, England, France, and Italy, which he illustrated with his watercolor paintings. Use these questions for discussion:

1. How well does this picture of ancient ruins reflect the spirit of Browning's poem?
   Possible response: The painting illustrates the quiet colors and the ruins that Browning describes.
2. Why might ruins like these inspire poetry?
   Possible response: Because ruins are remains of bygone civilizations, they prompt viewers to reflect on the nature of time and mortality, inspiring poetry.

⓭ ▶Critical Viewing

Answer: The phrase "quiet-colored" from line 1 of the poem could be used to describe the painting.

⓫ Love Among the Ruins

Robert Browning

⓬

Italian Ruins, John Claude Nattes, Victoria and Albert Museum

Where the quiet-colored end of evening smiles,
    Miles and miles
On the solitary pastures where our sheep
    Half asleep
Tinkle homeward through the twilight, stray or stop
    As they crop—
Was the site once of a city great and gay
    (So they say),
Of our country's very capital, its prince
    Ages since
Held his court in, gathered councils, wielding far
    Peace or war.

⓭ ▲ **Critical Viewing**
Which phrase in the first line of Browning's poem could describe this painting? Explain. **[Support]**

ENRICHMENT: Architecture Connection

Architecture and Engineering in Ancient Rome

The unnamed civilization in Browning's poem "Love Among the Ruins" resembles ancient Rome, famous for its magnificent temples, statues, monuments, forums, palaces, and public baths. Roman engineers planned wide, straight streets and great aqueducts to bring water into cities. Even private homes were carefully designed and built with painstaking precision. The ruins of the ancient city of Pompeii, preserved in volcanic ash, demonstrate the relative luxury of public and private architecture in the time of the Roman Empire, a standard that would not be reached again for several centuries.

Now—the country does not even boast a tree,
As you see,
To distinguish slopes of verdure,[1] certain rills
From the hills
Intersect and give a name to (else they run
Into one),
Where the domed and daring palace shot its spires
Up like fires
O'er the hundred-gated circuit of a wall
Bounding all,
Made of marble, men might march on nor be pressed,
Twelve abreast.

14 And such plenty and perfection, see, of grass
Never was!
Such a carpet as, this summertime, o'erspreads
And embeds
Every vestige of the city, guessed alone,
Stock or stone—
Where a multitude of men breathed joy and woe
Long ago;
Lust of glory pricked their hearts up, dread of shame
Struck them tame;
And that glory and that shame alike, the gold
Bought and sold.

Now—the single little turret that remains
On the plains,
By the caper[2] overrooted, by the gourd
Overscored,
While the patching houseleek's head of blossom winks
Through the chinks—
Marks the basement whence a tower in ancient time
Sprang sublime,
And a burning ring, all round, the chariots traced
As they raced,
And the monarch and his minions and his dames
Viewed the games.

And I know, while thus the quiet-colored eve
Smiles to leave
To their folding, all our many-tinkling fleece
In such peace,
And the slopes and rills, in undistinguished gray
Melt away—

1. **verdure** (vur´ jər) *n.* green plants.
2. **caper** prickly, trailing Mediterranean bush.

Reading Strategy
Making Inferences About the Speaker
What do the words in line 25 suggest about the speaker's feelings about the current state of the land?

vestige (ves´ tij) *n.* trace; remaining bit

sublime (sə blīm´) *adj.* inspiring awe through beauty or grandeur

minions (min´ yənz) *n.* attendants or agents

15 **Reading Check**
Which aspects of the natural landscape does the speaker praise?

14 Reading Strategy
Making Inferences About the Speaker

- Remind students that by paying attention to the speaker's words and tone, they may be able to infer additional facts about him.
- Point out the words *plenty* and *perfection.* Ask students to discuss the connotations of these words.
- Then, ask students the Reading Strategy question on p. 841: What do the words in line 25 suggest about the speaker's feelings about the current state of the land?
  Possible response: These descriptive words reveal the speaker's love for the land as it is now and his preference for the glories of nature over the glories of past empires.

15 Reading Check

Answer: The speaker praises the grasses, plants, and weeds that overgrow the ruin of the castle.

CUSTOMIZE INSTRUCTION FOR UNIVERSAL ACCESS

For Special Needs Students	For Less Proficient Readers
Students may have difficulty reading "Love Among the Ruins" because it uses difficult vocabulary and juxtaposes images of the present and the past. Have students read from the poem silently as they listen to **Listening to Literature Audiocassettes,** Side 20. Then, guide students in a close reading of the poem in which they read each line carefully and put it in their own words.	Have students read the poem "Love Among the Ruins" with teacher guidance. Then, tell them that they will assume the voice of the speaker of the poem and write a journal entry based on the information they have inferred about the speaker from his words in the poem. For example, they may wish to describe their feelings at seeing the lost civilization or their plans for meeting the girl in the ruins.

16 Critical Thinking

Analyze

- Point out to students that Browning is working in an unusual form in the poem: He alternates long lines having six stressed syllables with short lines having only two stresses.
- Have a volunteer read lines 55–60 aloud.
- Ask students to describe the effect the alternating long and short lines have on the feeling of the poem.
  Possible response: Students may note that the rhyme-word at the end of the shorter lines seems to arrive quickly, giving the short lines emphasis and the effect of an echo, an afterthought, or a conclusion.
- Read aloud lines 59–60. Ask students: Which seems emphasized by the structure of the lines, the presence of the king in the past or the arrival of the speaker in the present?
  Possible response: "Till I come," emphasized by the fact that only two syllables separate the rhyme-words *dumb* and *come,* sounds final and definitive. The speaker's arrival in the present is thus emphasized over the king's presence in the past.

17 ▶Critical Viewing

Possible response: Students may say that this scene would evoke a reflective mood in the speaker as he contrasted the present and past conditions of the structure.

16

That a girl with eager eyes and yellow hair
    Waits me there
In the turret whence the charioteers caught soul
    For the goal,
When the king looked, where she looks now, breathless, dumb
    Till I come.

But he looked upon the city, every side,
    Far and wide,
All the mountains topped with temples, all the glades'
    Colonnades,[3]

3. **Colonnades** (käl′ ə nādz′) *n.* series of columns set at regular intervals; here, groups of trees surrounding an open area.

17 ▼ **Critical Viewing** What emotions might a scene like this one evoke in the speaker? Explain. **[Connect]**

ENRICHMENT: Media Connection

The Barretts of Wimpole Street

The romance between Robert Browning and Elizabeth Barrett was brought to the stage by English playwright Rudolf Besier in 1930. The following year, *The Barretts of Wimpole Street* opened on Broadway, starring Katherine Cornell, considered by many to be the greatest actress of American theater. The play ran for a year and toured all over the United States, and Elizabeth Barrett Browning became Cornell's most popular role. In 1934, though, Katherine Cornell turned down an offer to play the role in a movie production. The part of Elizabeth went to Norma Shearer, and it catapulted her from mere popularity to icon status. The success of the 1934 film version helped its director, Sidney Franklin, become a producer. When he made a return to directing in 1957, his first project was a remake of *The Barretts of Wimpole Street,* starring Jennifer Jones.

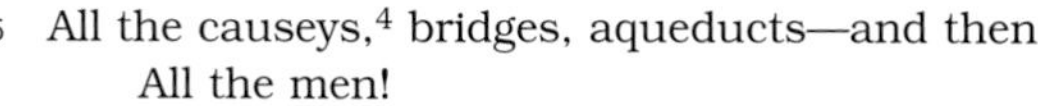

All the causeys,[4] bridges, aqueducts—and then,
    All the men!
When I do come, she will speak not, she will stand,
    Either hand
On my shoulder, give her eyes the first embrace
    Of my face,
Ere we rush, ere we extinguish sight and speech
    Each on each.

In one year they sent a million fighters forth
    South and North,
And they built their gods a brazen pillar[5] high
    As the sky,
Yet reserved a thousand chariots in full force—
    Gold, of course.
Oh heart! oh blood that freezes, blood that burns!
    Earth's returns
For whole centuries of folly, noise and sin!
    Shut them in,
With their triumphs and their glories and the rest!
    Love is best.

4. **causeys** causeways or raised roads.
5. **brazen pillar** built from the brass of captured chariots.

Reading Strategy
Making Inferences About the Speaker How does the speaker feel about the girl?

Review and Assess

Thinking About the Selection

1. **(a) Respond:** How impressed were you by the speaker's descriptions of the ancient city? Explain.
2. **(a) Recall:** What once stood where the speaker's sheep now head homeward? **(b) Compare and Contrast:** Compare the past and the present appearance of the setting.
3. **(a) Support:** In what way is the whole poem based on a contrast between past and present? **(b) Analyze:** How does Browning use the "echo" created by alternating long and short lines to emphasize both the deadness of the past and the passion of the present?
4. **(a) Analyze:** Explain how the person waiting for the speaker "replaces" the past. **(b) Interpret:** What conclusion does the speaker reach about the past and the present?
5. **Assess:** Is "Love Among the Ruins" a good title for this poem? Explain your answer.
6. **Make a Judgment:** Do you agree with the speaker's conclusion that present love is worth more than past glories? Explain.

CUSTOMIZE INSTRUCTION FOR UNIVERSAL ACCESS

For Advanced Readers

Have students analyze the poems they have read in this lesson, and write an essay in which they analyze the different kinds of love expressed in each work. Students should quote directly from each work to provide evidence of their opinions. For students who are interested in reading more of the work of Elizabeth Barrett Browning before they complete their essays, refer them to p. 165 of **Authors In Depth.**

18 Reading Strategy

Making Inferences About the Speaker

- Have students read lines 65–72 to themselves. As students read, have them list the details that would help them infer how the speaker feels about the girl.
- Then, ask them the Reading Strategy question on p. 843: How does the speaker feel about the girl?
  Answer: The speaker is in love with the girl.

Answers for p. 843

Review and Assess

1. Possible responses: Students may find the speaker's description of the ancient city powerful because of the extensive details.
2. **(a)** A great city once stood there. **(b)** The city was full of imposing buildings and home to many people; the only remaining structure is a turret, surrounded by meadows and brooks.
3. **(a)** The poem shifts between images of the epic past and intimate images of a simple, appealing present. **(b)** Possible response: The echo helps him mock the heroic pictures of the past, creating a mechanical or sardonic effect, and reinforce the images of the present.
4. **(a)** The speaker's beloved, who waits for him, has replaced the past by representing all that is now valuable or important in the scene; in addition, she stands where past kings stood. **(b)** Possible response: Even the most ambitious expressions of human vanity eventually crumble into the past, but present love is worth far more.
5. Possible response: Yes, this is a good title for the poem, because it describes the theme of the poem and emphasizes love over ruins as the speaker does.
6. Possible response: Present love is worth everything to an individual, but past glories have value to a culture as a whole.

ASSESS

19 About the Selection

To describe her love for her husband, Elizabeth Barrett Browning proposes the question "How do I love thee?" and then provides eight answers, all beginning with the words "I love thee." Browning's famous sonnet has become a universal tribute to love, admired by generations of readers.

20 Reading Strategy

Making Inferences About the Speaker

- Have students read the entire sonnet. Then, read aloud the bracketed passage to them.
- Ask students to clarify the meaning of "old griefs" and "my childhood's faith."
  Possible response: "Old griefs" suggests passionate memories of past losses; "My childhood's faith" suggests an early innocence that the speaker still remembers.
- Then, ask them the Reading Strategy question on p. 844: What do the references to childhood and old griefs suggest about the speaker?
  Answer: They suggest the speaker has a sensitive, vulnerable heart.

Answers for p. 844

Review and Assess

1. Students' responses should note the scope of the comparisons that the poet uses to describe the extent of her love.
2. **(a)** The speaker asks: In how many ways do I love you?
   (b) Possible response: She loves her beloved to the limits that her soul can reach; her love is always sufficient to the demands of each particular day; she loves with all the passion she has ever been capable of feeling.
3. **(a)** She loves him with all the force of past disappointments, suggesting that he makes up for past losses. **(b)** The images she uses mark the full range of life, from the spiritual to daily life, from grief to childhood innocence, from past to present to beyond death.
4. Possible responses: Students should cite songs that express various aspects of romantic love.

19 Sonnet 43

Elizabeth Barrett Browning

How do I love thee? Let me count the ways.
I love thee to the depth and breadth and height
My soul can reach, when feeling out of sight
For the ends of Being and ideal Grace.
I love thee to the level of every day's
Most quiet need, by sun and candlelight.
I love thee freely, as men strive for Right;
I love thee purely, as they turn from Praise.
20 I love thee with the passion put to use
In my old griefs, and with my childhood's faith.
I love thee with a love I seemed to lose
With my lost saints—I love thee with the breath,
Smiles, tears, of all my life!—and, if God choose,
I shall but love thee better after death.

Reading Strategy
Making Inferences About the Speaker What do the references to childhood and old griefs suggest about the speaker?

Review and Assess

Thinking About the Selection

1. **Respond:** Do you find the speaker's description of the depth of her love moving? Explain.
2. **(a) Recall:** In Sonnet 43, what question does the speaker ask?
   (b) Paraphrase: Briefly summarize the speaker's answers to her own question.
3. **(a) Interpret:** In lines 9–10, what does the speaker mean by ". . . with the passion put to use / In my old griefs, . . ."?
   (b) Draw Conclusions: In what way does the kind of love expressed by the speaker in Sonnet 43 draw on all parts of her life and being?
4. **Relate:** Cite a popular song that praises love, and compare its language, attitude, and images with those of Sonnet 43.

ASSESSMENT PRACTICE: Reading Comprehension

Paired Passages (For more practice, see Test Preparation Workbook, p. 39.)

Many tests require students to compare and identify literary elements in two passages. Use the following sample item to teach students how to compare the speakers of two passages. Have students read "Life in a Love" and "Sonnet 43" before answering this question.

Which of these characteristics do the speakers in the two poems share?

A devotion
B desperation
C strong religious feelings
D confusion

Suggest that students first list adjectives that describe *each* of the speakers. Then, have them compare their lists. Students should recognize that the only characteristic the speakers share is devotion. Thus, the correct answer is *A*.

Review and Assess

Literary Analysis

Dramatic Monologue

1. (a) Who is the speaker in "My Last Duchess," and who is the listener? (b) How can you tell when the listener interacts with the speaker? Give an example.
2. (a) Cite two lines in which the speaker reveals something negative about himself. (b) Do you think the speaker's next marriage will be successful? Explain.
3. (a) Who are the speaker and the listener in "Life in a Love"? (b) Is there interaction between them? Explain.

Comparing Literary Works

4. (a) Use a chart like the one shown to analyze the places at which a speaker would naturally pause in lines 14–22 of "My Last Duchess."

Line 14:	Her hus-	-band's pre-	-sence on-	-ly, called	that spot
Natural Pauses	no pause	no pause	no pause	**pause**	no pause

(b) How does the use of **run-on lines** and pauses within lines create a conversational rhythm?

5. Use a similar chart to analyze the rhythms of Elizabeth Barrett Browning's Sonnet 43.
6. (a) Compare the rhythms of speech in the two poems. (b) Which rhythm do you find more dramatic? Explain. (c) Which better captures general feelings in a memorable manner?

Reading Strategy

Making Inferences About the Speaker

7. Explaining the clues you use, **make inferences about the speaker's character** in (a) lines 31–43 of "My Last Duchess" and (b) lines 18–20 of "Life in a Love."
8. In "Love Among the Ruins," what can you infer about the speaker's attitude toward the ancient past? Identify the clues you use.

Extend Understanding

9. **Cultural Connection:** How important do you think it is to preserve monuments from the past, such as those Browning describes?

Quick Review

A **dramatic monologue** is a poem in which an imaginary character speaks to a silent listener.

A **run-on line** of poetry is a line that does not contain a stop or pause at the end. An **end-stopped line** ends where a speaker would pause.

To **make inferences about the speaker** of a poem, make informed guesses based on the speaker's words and actions.

Take It to the Net

www.phschool.com

Take the interactive self-test online to check your understanding of these selections.

ENRICHMENT: Further Reading

More Works by the Brownings

If Thou Must Love Me, Let It Be for Naught, Elizabeth Barrett Browning

Andrea del Sarto, Robert Browning

Ah, Love, But a Day, Robert Browning

Take It to the Net

Visit www.phschool.com for more information on the authors.

Answers for p. 845

Review and Assess

1. **(a)** The duke is the speaker and the listener is a messenger from the count whose daughter the duke wants to marry. **(b)** The listener and the speaker interact when the speaker asks the listener a question (line 5) or addresses him as "you" or "Sir."
2. **(a)** Possible responses: Students may cite lines 42–43: "I choose / Never to stoop. . ." or lines 45–46 "I gave commands; / Then all smiles stopped together." **(b)** Possible response: Given the speaker's treatment of his first wife, it seems unlikely that he will have a successful second marriage.
3. **(a)** The speaker addresses his beloved, but only in his own mind. **(b)** There is no interaction between them as the speaker speaks, though he describes his pursuit and her rejection.
4. **(a)** Each one of lines 14–22 is run-on; students may find natural internal pauses in every line except line 18. **(b)** The use of run-on lines and pauses within lines is closer to the natural rhythms of conversation.
5. Students should note that lines 1, 4, 6–8, and 10 are end-stopped lines.
6. **(a)** "My Last Duchess" uses many more conversational rhythms than Sonnet 43. **(b)** Possible response: Students may say that "My Last Duchess" is more dramatic because it makes the speaker and his personality vividly present. **(c)** Possible response: Students may say that the end-stopped lines of Sonnet 43 are better at capturing general feelings in a memorable manner; they are "punchy" and quotable.
7. **(a)** In "My Last Duchess," the speaker reveals his jealousy at his wife's gratitude and amiability in lines 33–34. He also suggests his inflexibility in his refusal "to stoop" in line 43. **(b)** In "Life in a Love," we can infer that the speaker is very persistent in his pursuit of the object of his attentions.

continued

Answers continued

8. In "Love Among the Ruins," the shepherd expresses sadness for the lives lost in the pursuit of glory and contempt for the pride and greed of the "monarch and his minions" of long ago.
9. Possible response: Students may say that it is essential to preserve monuments from the past because they help us understand ancient civilizations and teach us about our own culture.

EXTEND

Answers for p. 846

❶ Vocabulary Development

Word Analysis

1. *Innocence* means the quality of being guileless or pure.
2. *Prominence* means the state of being noteworthy.
3. *Permanence* means the quality of being permanent or lasting.

Spelling Strategy

1. intelligence
2. relevance
3. importance
4. obedience

Concept Development: Analogies

1. eludes
2. munificence
3. countenance
4. dowry
5. minions
6. sublime
7. vestige
8. officious

❷ Grammar and Style

1. like
2. as
3. as
4. like
5. as

Writing Application

Answers will vary. Make sure students use *like* and *as* correctly in their responses.

Integrate Language Skills

❶ Vocabulary Development Lesson

Word Analysis: Latin Suffix *-ence*

The Latin suffix *-ence* means "quality of, or state of being." The adjective *munificent,* for example, means "very generous." Drop the suffix *-ent* and add *-ence* to form the noun *munificence,* meaning "the state of being very generous." Write the noun forms of the following words, and write the definition of each new word.

1. innocent 2. prominent 3. permanent

Spelling Strategy

To form a noun from an adjective that ends with the suffix *-ent,* use the suffix *-ence: munificent* becomes *munificence*. Use the suffix *-ance* for adjectives ending in *-ant: elegant* becomes *elegance*. Complete each word below using *-ence* or *-ance*.

1. intellig____
2. relev____
3. import____
4. obedi____

Concept Development: Analogies

Complete the following analogies, using the words from the vocabulary list on page 835. Use each word only once.

1. *Chases* is to *pursuer* as ___?___ is to *escapee*.
2. *Cruelty* is to *tormentor* as ___?___ is to *benefactor*.
3. *Window* is to *curtain* as ___?___ is to *veil*.
4. *Salary* is to *employee* as ___?___ is to *husband*.
5. *Soldiers* are to *general* as ___?___ is to *king*.
6. *Plain* is to *stick figure* as ___?___ is to *masterpiece*.
7. *Totality* is to *whole* as ___?___ is to *part*.
8. *Generous* is to *philanthropist* as ___?___ is to *busybody*.

❷ Grammar and Style Lesson

Usage: *like* and *as*

The words *like* and *as,* used to make comparisons, are not interchangeable. The word ***like*** is a preposition meaning "similar to." It is used to compare nouns or pronouns. The word ***as,*** a subordinating conjunction, is used to compare actions. It introduces a clause with a noun and verb. In some cases, the verb may be understood rather than stated.

Like: Strangers like you . . . (prepositional phrase)

As: Elizabeth did not live to the same age as Robert [did]. (subordinate clause; *did* is understood)

Practice Copy these sentences, replacing the blanks with either *like* or *as*.

1. No interpretation of Browning's *The Ring and the Book* is exactly ___?___ another.
2. The duke depicted his last duchess ___?___ he chose.
3. Before the two married, his poems were not as famous ___?___ hers.
4. Are Elizabeth Barrett Browning's sonnets ___?___ contemporary love songs?
5. "My Last Duchess" has as much conflict ___?___ a one-act play does.

Writing Application Write a paragraph comparing Sonnet 43 to "Life in a Love," using *like* and *as*.

WG Prentice Hall Writing and Grammar Connection: Chapter 25, Section 2

TEACHING RESOURCES

The following resources can be used to enrich or extend the instruction for pp. 846–847.

Vocabulary

- **Selection Support:** Build Vocabulary, p. 179
- **Vocabulary and Spelling Practice Book** (Use this booklet for skills enrichment)

Grammar

- **Selection Support:** Grammar and Style, p. 180
- **Writing and Grammar,** Diamond Level, p. 646
- **Daily Language Practice Transparencies** ■

Writing

- **Writing and Grammar,** Diamond Level, p. 230 ■
- **Writing Models and Graphic Organizers on Transparencies,** p. 119
- **Writing and Grammar iText CD-ROM**

■ **BLOCK SCHEDULING:** Resources marked with this symbol provide varied instruction during 90-minute blocks.

❸ Writing Lesson

Written Recommendation About the Duke's Proposal

After listening to the duke in "My Last Duchess," how would you advise the father of the lady the duke hopes to marry? Give your advice in a written recommendation, clearly connecting your observations to your recommendations.

Prewriting Review the poem, noting what it reveals about the duke's character and first marriage. Gather details that will help you reach your recommendation.

Drafting Start by presenting your position. Then, explain the reasons for your recommendation. Include cause-and-effect transitions such as *as a result*, *because*, and *therefore* to link ideas.

Revising Review your draft, drawing arrows between observations and the conclusions they support. Where appropriate, add missing cause-and-effect transitions between sections connected by arrows.

Model: Revising to Indicate Cause-and-Effect Transitions

As a result of my observations,
^ I have concluded that the duke is a cruel and dangerous
. *Therefore,*
man, ~~and~~ I advise you to cancel your daughter's wedding
plans immediately.

Cause-and-effect transitions clarify the link between the writer's ideas.

WG *Prentice Hall Writing and Grammar Connection: Chapter 11, Section 4*

❹ Extension Activities

Listening and Speaking Present an **oral interpretation** of "My Last Duchess." Make decisions about your reading by marking up a copy of the poem. Consider these tips:

- Mark words that you want to emphasize.
- Note places where you should pause or change your tone.
- Indicate points at which to add gestures for dramatic effect.

Present your oral interpretation to the class.

Research and Technology With a group, prepare a **guided tour** of nineteenth-century Italy such as the Brownings might have given. Research the areas where the Brownings lived, note tourist attractions, and prepare a map showing the tour route. Incorporate your visual materials into your final word-processed document. **[Group Activity]**

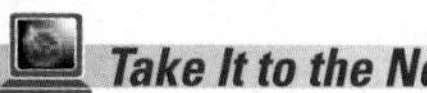

www.phschool.com

Go online for an additional research activity using the Internet.

ASSESSMENT RESOURCES

The following resources can be used to assess students' knowledge and skills.

Selection Assessment

- **Formal Assessment,** pp. 187–189
- **Open Book Test,** pp. 115–117
- **Got It! Assessment Videotapes,** Tape 4
- **Test Bank Software**

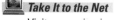

Take It to the Net

Visit www.phschool.com for self-tests and additional questions on the selections.

Writing Rubric

- **Performance Assess. and Portfolio Mgmt.,** p. 10

PRENTICE HALL ASSESSMENT SYSTEM

- **Workbook**
- **Transparencies**
- **Skill Book**
- **CD-ROM**

❸ Writing Lesson

- Tell students that in this lesson they will offer a written recommendation to the father of the lady the duke intends to marry in "My Last Duchess."
- Read the Writing Lesson with students and use it to guide them in developing their advice and formulating it into a recommendation.
- Encourage them to use the Cause-and-Effect Organizer in **Writing Models and Graphic Organizer on Transparencies,** p. 119, to help connect ideas.
- Evaluate their recommendations using the Persuasion: Persuasive Composition rubric in **Performance Assessment and Portfolio Management,** p. 10.

❹ Listening and Speaking

- Read the Listening and Speaking lesson as a class, and then encourage students to reread the poem "My Last Duchess" before they proceed.
- Remind students that oral interpretations require careful planning; they should mark up a copy of the poem from which they will read, noting places where they should pause or emphasize inflection or tone.

CUSTOMIZE INSTRUCTION For Universal Access

To address different learning styles, use the activities suggested in the **Extension Activities** booklet, p. 39.

- For Bodily/Kinesthetic and Interpersonal Learners, use Activity 5
- For Visual/Spatial and Verbal/Linguistic Learners, use Activity 6
- For Musical/Rhythmic and Intrapersonal Learners, use Activity 7.

Lesson Objectives

1. To understand the connection between the poems of love and friendship of the nineteenth century and those of ancient Greece
2. To understand how a writer's choice of style helps to extend the meaning of the text

Connections

Like the poems students encounter in this unit, the intense love poems of nineteenth-century France are often dedicated to and inspired by friends and lovers. In addition, the poems of ancient Greece are often expressions of devotion to gods and goddesses of the time, much like poems written to lovers. Have students reread Sappho's work on p. 849 after they have read the poem by Baudelaire. What similarities and differences can students note between the two poems?

Relationships

- Explain to students that the poets in this section were separated by centuries of time, yet their poetry maintains visions of romance that are remarkably similar.
- Tell students that Sappho grew up in an aristocratic family, married a rich man, and became a mother. Many of her poems were written for wedding celebrations or women's festivals. Her poems describe a woman's life from girlhood to marriage. Ask students to point out evidence of her upbringing and experience in her poem.
- Tell students that Charles Baudelaire explored the warring impulses of the self in his poetry. He showed how his own mind was torn between idealism and despair, tenderness and cruelty, the spirit and the body. His bold psychological analysis makes him one of the first truly modern poets.
- Point out that both poems are invitations to discover and uncover the history behind not only the poems but also the poets themselves. The common elements in each allow us to connect themes across cultures, continents, and centuries.

CONNECTIONS
Literature Around the World
Relationships

Silence and Words The deepest poem in the world may be the words *I love you*. These words can transform and liberate, distress and bind. Yet these deep words are surrounded by silence just as deep. Lovers discover this silence when they rush to speak to the beloved, only to find that words fail them utterly.

Love and Poetry Lovers may write love poems to fill this silence. Poets may write love poems to rediscover it. Even the most boisterous poem requires a kind of quiet, a hush in which words can finally be heard for themselves. By writing on love, a poet invokes the silence and the poverty in which all speech is based—the need to be heard and to be loved. From out of this silence rushes the intoxicating whirl of images and thoughts that make up poetry—or love.

A Lover's Devotion Most of the poems in this section grew out of intense experiences of love or friendship. For example, Alfred, Lord Tennyson's *In Memoriam* expresses grief at the death of his good friend Arthur Henry Hallam. Elizabeth Barrett Browning begins to count the uncountable ways in which she loves her husband in Sonnet 43, a poem that could sum up every lover's devotion.

The poems of Sappho (saf ō) of ancient Greece and those of Charles Baudelaire (shärl bōd ler′) of nineteenth-century France also express wholehearted devotion to a loved one. For Sappho, the loved one is Aphrodite herself, the Greek goddess of love. For Baudelaire, the beloved is a mortal woman.

Invitations to Love Both Sappho and Baudelaire wrote their poems in the form of invitations. Sappho offers a rich, alluring picture of her island to persuade Aphrodite to come from Crete and take up residence there.

Baudelaire paints for his beloved the image of a magical world of "Richness, quietness, and pleasure" where they can "live together" at peace.

ENRICHMENT: Connection

Sappho

Sappho's wealth allowed her to live her life as she chose, and she chose to spend it studying the arts on the isle of Lesbos.

In the seventh century B.C., Lesbos was a cultural center. Sappho spent most her time on the island, though she also traveled widely throughout Greece and spent time in Sicily. By this time she was admired as a poet, and the residents of Syracuse, a Greek city in Sicily, were so honored by her visit that they erected a statue to her.

Sappho was called a lyrist because she wrote her poems to be performed with the accompaniment of a lyre. Sappho composed her own music and refined the prevailing lyric meter to a point that it is now known as *sapphic* meter. Her lyric poetry was innovative in both technique and style. She was one of the first poets to write from the first person, describing love and loss as they affected her personally.

You Know the Place: Then

Sappho Translated by Mary Barnard

You know the place: then

Leave Crete and come to us
waiting where the grove is
pleasantest, by precincts

sacred to you; incense
smokes on the altar, cold
streams murmur through the

apple branches, a young
rose thicket shades the ground
and quivering leaves pour

down deep sleep; in meadows
where horses have grown sleek
among spring flowers, dill

scents the air. Queen! Cyprian![1]
Fill our gold cups with love
stirred into clear nectar.

1. **Cyprian** (siʹ prē ən) *n.* a reference to the goddess Aphrodite, who was associated with the isle of Cyprus.

Sappho

(c. 610–c. 580 B.C.)

Sappho was a lyricist from ancient Greece whose works are known for their memorable expressions of love and loss. Sappho was one of the first poets to write in the first person rather than from the viewpoint of gods and Muses. Although Sappho wrote nearly five hundred poems, only a small fraction of these survive, either intact or in fragments.

Background

Mythology

Sappho was an innovative poet, writing her poetry to the gods and goddesses rather than acting as their voice. In "You Know the Place: Then," Aphrodite is the main target of the writer's words.

Aphrodite, the goddess of love, was long the center of attention for many Greek worshipers. The goddess's name came from the Greek for sea foam (*aphors*), because she was said to have been born from the sea.

The cult of Aphrodite was centered on the islands of Crete and Cyprus. Sappho mentions these islands in her poem to Aphrodite. In line 2, she asks the goddess to "Leave Crete"; in line 14, she refers to her as "Cyprian."

CUSTOMIZE INSTRUCTION FOR UNIVERSAL ACCESS

For Less Proficient Readers	For Gifted/Talented Students	For Advanced Readers
Suggest to these students that they think of the poem as a postcard with a picture of Sappho's island on the front. Have them read the poem, and then, in a group discussion, have them list details of the scene, note the feeling created by each, and determine whether this poetic "postcard" makes them want to visit Sappho's home.	Suggest to these students that they think of the poem as a postcard with a picture of Sappho's island on the front. Have them read the poem and do additional research on Sappho, Aphrodite, and the art of ancient Greece. Then, have them produce such a postcard.	Suggest to these students that they think of the poem as a postcard with a picture of Sappho's island on the front. Have them read the poem, and then ask them to do research to determine what the temple pictured on the card would look like and what rites would be practiced there. Have them write up their results and present them to class.

Background

"Invitation to the Voyage"

In this famous lyrical poem, the speaker (Baudelaire) invites his love to escape to an idealized, dreamlike, "sumptuous" world of "Richness, quietness, and pleasure." There, he believes, love can flourish in a "kind land" and a "glowing chamber."

Thematic Connection

Answer: Browning's poem is about the way in which love changes the meaning of a setting. Baudelaire's poem is about an ideal setting in which to fall in love.

Critical Thinking

Ask students what "mystery" (line 9) in nature creates a link to his beloved in the speaker's mind.
Answer: The image of the sunset glimmering through clouds is a mystery of nature that is linked in the speaker's mind with the image of his beloved's eyes shining at him through her tears.

▶Critical Viewing

Answer: They might be sailing to a sunset-bathed town of "Richness, quietness, and pleasure."

Charles Baudelaire

TRANSLATED BY RICHARD WILBUR

My child, my sister, dream
How sweet all things would seem
Were we in that kind land to live together
And there love slow and long,
There love and die among
Those scenes that image you, that sumptuous[1] weather.
Drowned suns that glimmer there
Through cloud-disheveled[2] air
Move me with such a mystery as appears
Within those other skies
Of your treacherous eyes
When I behold them shining through their tears.

Thematic Connection
Compare the landscapes described by Baudelaire's speaker with those described by Browning in "Love Among Ruins."

▶Critical Viewing
Where, according to the speaker in this poem, might these "drowsy ships" be sailing? **[Interpret]**

---

1. **sumptuous** (sump´ cho͞o əs) *adj.* magnificent or splendid.
2. **disheveled** (di shev´ əld) *adj.* disarranged and untidy.

ENRICHMENT: Literature Connection

The Decadents and Aestheticism

Baudelaire has been grouped with others under the uncomplimentary-sounding name of the Decadents. The Decadents claimed that art was superior to nature, and they were fascinated with death and the decay of the spirit. Other Decadents include the French poets Arthur Rimbaud (1854–1891) and Paul Verlaine (1844–1896) as well as the English artists they influenced, including poet Ernest Dowson (1867–1900), playwright Oscar Wilde (1854–1900), and illustrator Aubrey Beardsley (1872–1898). The English movement is known as Aestheticism.

It was easy for some readers to view the Decadents as immoral, and, indeed, Baudelaire was prosecuted for his best-known collection, *Flowers of Evil (Les Fleurs du Mal,* 1857). Yet, in a sense, the Decadent impulse was a religious one: Baudelaire rejected mundane, conventional existence because it was inferior to man's highest spiritual aspirations.

There, there is nothing else but grace and measure,
Richness, quietness, and pleasure.

Furniture that wears
The luster of the years
Softly would glow within our glowing chamber,
Flowers of rarest bloom
Proffering their perfume
Mixed with the vague fragrances of amber;
Gold ceilings would there be,
Mirrors deep as the sea,

✔Reading Check

What does the speaker imagine doing?

Marine. Marcel Mouillot, Galleria d' arte Moderna, Nancy

✔Reading Check

The speaker imagines escaping with his love to an ideal, dreamlike world.

Background

Art

Marine by Marcel Mouillot

Although the sails of the boats and ships in this painting appear puffed with wind, the darkness of the scene and the smoothness of the water make the boats themselves seem static and unreal, like a dream scene.

Use the following questions for discussion:

1. In what ways is the mood of the painting similar to the mood of the poem?
   Answer: Both suggest slowness, quietness, and peacefulness. Both create a feeling of unreality.
2. Which lines of the poem might the painting illustrate?
   Answer: Students should suggest lines 29 ("See, Sheltered from the swells") through 34 ("Hither through all the waters of the earth").
3. What makes the ships in the painting like "Those drowsy ships that dream of sailing forth"?
   Answer: The darkness of the painting and the smoothness of the water make the ships look "drowsy," as though they may only "dream of setting forth."

CUSTOMIZE INSTRUCTION FOR UNIVERSAL ACCESS

For Less Proficient Readers	For Gifted/Talented Students	For Advanced Readers
Explain to students that the poem creates a feast for the senses. Have them read the poem, and then, in a group discussion, have them list details of the scenes the poet describes, including scents and colors, noting the feeling created by each. Then, have them reach a conclusion about the overall mood of the poem.	Explain to students that the poem creates a feast for the senses. Have them read the poem, and then, in a group discussion, have them list details of the scenes the poet describes, including scents and colors, noting the feeling created by each. Then, have them create exhibits using visuals, sounds, scents, and textures to recreate this mood.	Explain to students that the poem creates a feast for the senses. After they have read the poem, ask them to find and read Baudelaire's "Correspondences" and do research on his theory of correspondences. Have them give a group presentation analyzing "Invitation to the Voyage" in terms of Baudelaire's doctrine.

Thematic Connection

Answer: Baudelaire's descriptions of love concentrate on the intimacy and beauty of love. There is no room in his description for the realities of everyday life.

Answers

Connecting Literature Around the World

1. Place enables the poems of Sappho and Baudelaire to create a meaningful and symbolic starting point for love and friendship to blossom without boundaries. Tennyson is sorrowful at the dead friend's house but finds solace at the shore, "hearing" the friend "where the water runs." Browning contrasts the pastoral scenes of ruins to the events of ancient times to assert that "love is best." For all the poems, the settings allow the poets to connect with friends and loved ones in a deeper way.
2. The speakers in both poems will feel empty but forever searching for a way to attain love. This concept is much like Browning's "Life in a Love": returning to the quest of obtaining an unrequited love.
3. Possible responses: Students may choose Sappho's poem. The setting is full of beauty and images drawn from reality, though carefully arranged. Baudelaire's images belong to a world of dream and fantasy of which lovers often wish to be a part.

The walls all in an Eastern splendor hung—
  Nothing but should address
  The soul's loneliness,
Speaking her sweet and secret native tongue.

There, there is nothing else but grace and measure,
Richness, quietness, and pleasure.

  See, sheltered from the swells
  There in the still canals
Those drowsy ships that dream of sailing forth;
  It is to satisfy
  Your least desire, they ply
Hither through all the waters of the earth.
  The sun at close of day
  Clothes the fields of hay,
Then the canals, at last the town entire
  In hyacinth and gold:
  Slowly the land is rolled
Sleepward under a sea of gentle fire.

There, there is nothing else but grace and measure,
Richness, quietness, and pleasure.

Thematic Connection
What aspect of love do Baudelaire's descriptions emphasize?

Charles Baudelaire

(1821–1867)

Known as much for his unconventional lifestyle as he was for his poetry, Baudelaire was one of the most startling and innovative poets of the nineteenth century. Attempting to break away from the earlier Romantic tradition, Baudelaire created poems that are objective rather than sentimental and that celebrate the city and the artificial rather than nature. His work, however, still exhibits many of the imaginative and mystical qualities associated with Romanticism.

Connecting Literature Around the World

1. According to poets, how important is place in a friendship or love relationship? Support your answers with examples from Tennyson's *In Memoriam* and Browning's "Love Among Ruins" as well as from the poems by Sappho and Baudelaire.
2. How will the speakers in Sappho's and Baudelaire's poems feel after love has gone? Draw on a poem by Tennyson or the Brownings to support your answer.
3. Which poem in this section would you recommend for a lover to send his or her beloved? Explain your choice.

ENRICHMENT: Cultural Connection

Baudelaire

Baudelaire was known for his highly controversial and often dark poetry, as well as his translation of the tales of Edgar Allan Poe. Baudelaire's life was filled with drama and strife, from financial disaster to being prosecuted for obscenity and blasphemy. Many still look upon his work as representing depravity and vice; others see him as being the poet of modern civilization, seeming to speak directly to the twentieth century.

PART 2

Focus on Literary Forms: The Novel

Music and Literature, 1878, William M. Harnett, Albright-Knox Art Gallery Buffalo, New York

In an era before mass media, the new middle class looked to the novel for entertainment, ideas, and a fictional world they could share and discuss. Dickens, the premier British novelist, pioneered the publication of novels in magazines, episode by episode.

Selection Planning Guide

The selections in this section reveal how nineteenth-century novelists expressed their views about society and its problems in their works of fiction. In *Hard Times,* Dickens shows how the education system stifled individuality and imagination. The unfairness and meager living conditions in Jane Eyre's school reflect Brontë's opinions about educational institutions for poor girls. In *War and Peace,* Tolstoy criticizes the way society uses appearance rather than substance to form opinions of people.

Background

Art

Music and Literature, 1878, by William M. Harnett

William Michael Harnett (1848–1892) was born in Ireland but came to the United States as a child. He grew up in Philadelphia and studied at the Pennsylvania Academy of Fine Arts. He spent some of his professional life in Europe, where he painted his best-known work. Harnett had a few favorite subjects—firearms, books, and musical instruments—and created a number of still-life paintings of these subjects.

Encourage students to examine carefully the lovingly rendered details of the painting. Call attention to the stamped yellow envelope and the "handwritten" letter near it.

Have students link the art to Part 2 by answering the following question:

- What do you think is the painter's attitude toward music and literature, and how can you tell from the painting?
  Possible response: Judging from his care in reproducing the books, sheet music, and musical instruments here, as well as his frequency in painting these subjects, it appears that Harnett loved music and literature.

CUSTOMIZE INSTRUCTION FOR UNIVERSAL ACCESS

When assigning the selections in this part, keep in mind these factors:

from *Hard Times*
- The names of the characters, which often reflect their personalities, will appeal to most students' senses of humor.
- Students will respond to the basic conflict between conformity and individuality.

from *Jane Eyre*
- English learners and less proficient readers may have difficulty with archaic vocabulary.
- Students can relate the characters' conversation to their own conversations with friends.

from *War and Peace*
- Russian names may intimidate students.
- English learners may need help with vocabulary.

from Hard Times ✦ *from* Jane Eyre

Lesson Objectives and CA Correlations

1. **To analyze and respond to literary elements**
   - Literary Analysis: The Novel and Social Criticism **R 3.1**
   - Comparing Literary Works **R 3.7**
2. **To read, comprehend, analyze, and critique fiction**
   - Reading Strategy: Recognizing the Writer's Purpose **R 3.2**
   - Reading Check Questions
   - Review and Assess Questions
   - Assessment Practice (ATE)
3. **To develop word analysis skills, fluency, and systematic vocabulary**
   - Vocabulary Development Lesson: Greek Prefix *mono-* **R 1.2**
4. **To understand and apply written and oral English language conventions**
   - Spelling Strategy **LC 1.2**
   - Grammar and Style Lesson: Punctuation of Dialogue **LC 1.1**
5. **To understand and apply appropriate writing and research strategies**
   - Writing Lesson: Annotated Bibliography on Victorian Education **LC 1.3**
   - Extension Activity: Biography of Charles Dickens's Childhood **W 1.8**
6. **To understand and apply listening and speaking strategies**
   - Extension Activity: Debate **LS 1.5**

STEP-BY-STEP TEACHING GUIDE	PACING GUIDE
PRETEACH	
Motivate Students and Provide Background	
Use the Motivation activity (ATE p. 854)	5 min.
Read and discuss author and background features (SE pp. 854, 858; ATE pp. 854, 856, 857) [A]	5 min.
Introduce the Concepts	
Introduce the Literary Analysis and Reading Strategy (SE/ATE p. 855) [A]	15 min.
Pronounce the vocabulary words and read their definitions (SE p. 855)	5 min.
TEACH	
Monitor Comprehension	
Informally monitor comprehension by circulating while students read independently or in groups [A]	35 min.
Monitor students' comprehension with the Reading Check notes (SE/ATE pp. 859, 861, 863, 865, 867, 869, 871)	as students read
Develop vocabulary with Vocabulary notes (SE pp. 858, 859, 862, 866; ATE p. 858)	as students read
Develop Understanding	
Develop students' understanding of the novel and social criticism with the Literary Analysis annotations (SE pp. 859, 863, 866, 868, 871; ATE pp. 859, 861, 863, 865, 866, 868, 871) [A]	5 min.
Develop students' ability to recognize the writer's purpose with the Reading Strategy annotations (SE/ATE pp. 862, 869)	5 min.
ASSESS	
Assess Mastery	
Assess students' mastery of the Reading Strategy and Literary Analysis by having them answer the Review and Assess questions (SE/ATE p. 873)	15 min.
Use one or more of the print and media Assessment Resources (ATE p. 875) [A]	up to 45 min.
EXTEND	
Apply Understanding	
Have students complete the Vocabulary Development Lesson and the Grammar and Style Lesson (SE p. 874) [A]	20 min.
Apply students' knowledge of primary and secondary sources using the Writing Lesson (SE/ATE p. 875) [A]	45 min.
Apply students' understanding using one or more of the Extension Activities (SE p. 875)	20–90 min.

ACCELERATED INSTRUCTION:
Use the strategies and activities identified with an [A].

UNIVERSAL ACCESS
● = Below-Level Students
▲ = On-Level Students
■ = Above-Level Students

Time and Resource Manager

Reading Level: Average, Easy
Average Number of Instructional Days: 4

RESOURCES		
PRINT	**TRANSPARENCIES**	**TECHNOLOGY**
• **Beyond Literature,** Humanities Connection: Philosophy, p. 40 ▲ ■		• **Interest Grabber Videos,** Tape 5 ● ▲ ■
• **Selection Support Workbook:** ● ▲ ■ Literary Analysis, p. 188 Reading Strategy, p. 187 Build Vocabulary, p. 185	• **Literary Analysis and Reading Transparencies,** pp. 79 and 80 ● ▲ ■	
• **Adapted Reader's Companion** ● • **Reader's Companion** ● • **Authors In Depth,** The British Tradition, p. 182 ■		• **Listening to Literature** ● ▲ ■ Audiocassettes, Side 20 Audio CDs, CD 12
• **English Learner's Companion** ● ▲ • **Literary Analysis for Enrichment** ■	• **Fine Art Transparencies, Volume 1,** Art Transparency 19 ● ▲ ■	
• **Formal Assessment:** Selection Test, pp. 195–197 ● ▲ ■ • **Open Book Test,** pp. 118–119 ● ▲ ■ • **Performance Assessment and Portfolio Management,** p. 13 ● ▲ ■ • PRENTICE HALL ASSESSMENT SYSTEM ● ▲ ■	• PRENTICE HALL ASSESSMENT SYSTEM ● ▲ ■ Skills Practice Answers and Explanations on Transparencies ● ▲ ■	• **Test Bank Software** ● ▲ ■ • **Got It! Assessment Videotapes,** Tape 4 ● ▲
• **Selection Support Workbook:** ● ▲ ■ Grammar and Style, p. 186 • **Writing and Grammar,** Diamond Level ● ▲ ■ • **Extension Activities,** p. 40 ● ▲ ■	• **Daily Language Practice Transparencies** ● ▲ • **Writing Models and Graphic Organizers on Transparencies,** pp. 57–62 ● ▲ ■	• **Writing and Grammar iText CD-ROM** ● ▲ ■ *Take It to the Net* www.phschool.com

BLOCK SCHEDULING: Use one 90-minute class period to preteach the selections and have students read them. Use a second 90-minute class period to assess students' mastery of skills and have them complete one of the Extension Activities.

PRETEACH

Step-by-Step Teaching Guide for pp. 854–855

Motivation

Tell students that their school will be the site for filming a new television series on teenagers. Have them create the pilot show. Remind them that they can use the show to dramatize problems faced by teenagers. After they have sketched out an episode, explain that in the nineteenth century, novels were as popular as television series are today. Novelists like Dickens and Brontë used their works to call attention to society's ills.

Interest Grabber Video

As an alternative, play *"Hard Times: Schools Today"* on Tape 5 to engage student interest.

❶ Background

More About the Authors

Charles Dickens

Charles Dickens experienced tremendous commercial success with the 1843 publication of *A Christmas Carol.* This work, the first in a series of Christmas books that included *The Chimes, The Cricket on the Hearth, The Battle of Life,* and *The Haunted Man,* was described by Dickens as "a whimsical sort of masque intended to awaken loving and forebearing thoughts."

Dickens wrote many of his novels as serializations in magazines, in which a chapter or portion of the novel would appear each week. Readers would wait breathlessly for the next issue to come off the press to learn what would happen to their favorite characters.

Charlotte Brontë

The loneliness caused by the deaths of Charlotte Brontë's siblings in her later years was abated by her friendship with Mrs. Gaskell, who would later be her celebrated biographer. Even after her identity was known, Brontë continued to use her pseudonym in her publications. Charlotte was the most admired of the three sisters, although she also received the most criticism for what Matthew Arnold called the "hunger, rebellion, and rage" of her mind.

Prepare to Read

❶ *from* Hard Times ◆ *from* Jane Eyre

Charles Dickens (1812–1870)

No writer since Shakespeare has occupied as important a place in popular culture as Charles Dickens. His novels have held a special appeal for critics and the public alike. They have also been dramatized time and again in plays and films.

A Childhood of Hardship Born in Portsmouth on England's southern coast, Dickens had a generally unhappy childhood. His father was sent to debtors' prison, and the boy was sent to a "prison" of his own—a factory in which he worked long hours pasting labels. Similar experiences, dramatizing the ills of the newly industrialized society, were to figure prominently in Dickens's novels.

The Birth of a Writer As a young man, Dickens held jobs as a stenographer in the courts and as a reporter for London newspapers. At twenty-one, he began to apply his keen powers of observation to producing humorous literary sketches of everyday life in London. A collection of these, *Sketches by Boz* (1836), earned him a small following, but his first novel, *The Pickwick Papers* (1837), made him the most popular writer of his day. Closely following were *Oliver Twist* (1839) and *Nicholas Nickleby* (1839).

A Serious Novelist The young Dickens reveled in the variety and peculiarity of the human character. Memorable characters like the charming Mr. Pickwick and the evil Fagin abound in his early work, but they are perhaps more like cartoons or natural forces than full-blooded characters. Dickens shows his growing mastery of characterization in *Dombey and Son* (1848) and *David Copperfield* (1850), novels of greater psychological depth. Throughout his work, Dickens offers his distinctive brand of social criticism, which is especially prominent in his late masterpiece *Hard Times* (1854).

Charlotte Brontë (1816–1855)

Charlotte Brontë was part of a renowned literary family: Her sisters Anne and Emily were also writers. Their father, an Anglican clergyman, moved his family to the moors in Yorkshire in 1820, and the children were educated largely at home. Raised without their mother, who had died in 1821, the sisters, together with their brother Branwell, led a rich fantasy life that nurtured their artistic development.

Early Failure With three of her sisters, Charlotte briefly attended a boarding-school. Her experiences there provided material for the critical descriptions of boarding-school life at Lowood in *Jane Eyre*. Charlotte spent several years as a teacher, first of her own siblings and then at another school that she herself had briefly attended. She found this job difficult and unappealing, and in 1844 attempted to open her own school near her family home. The school's failure was quick and definite: No pupils enrolled.

Success In 1846, the three sisters published a volume of poems under the pseudonyms Currer, Ellis, and Acton Bell, but the book had little success. Charlotte had also written a novel, *The Professor,* but the book failed to find a publisher. Charlotte persevered, however, and when *Jane Eyre* was published in 1847 it met with immediate popular success.

Personal Struggle The final years of Charlotte Brontë's life were clouded by tragedy. Her brother died in 1848, and Emily and Anne died soon after. Despite her loneliness, Charlotte found the strength to complete the novels *Shirley* (1849) and *Villette* (1853). She married Arthur Bell Nicholls, her father's curate, a few months before she died.

TEACHING RESOURCES

The following resources can be used to enrich or extend the instruction for pp. 854–855.

Motivation

Interest Grabber Videos, Tape 5

Background

Beyond Literature, p. 40

Take It to the Net

Visit www.phschool.com for background and hotlinks for the selections.

Literary Analysis

Literary Analysis and Reading Transparencies, The Novel and Social Criticism, p. 80

Reading

Literary Analysis and Reading Transparencies, Recognizing the Writer's Purpose, p. 79

Selection Support: Reading Strategy, p. 187; Build Vocabulary, p. 185.

BLOCK SCHEDULING: Resources marked with this symbol provide varied instruction during 90-minute blocks.

Preview

Connecting to the Literature

You do not need to march on City Hall to make a difference. Dickens and Brontë were crusaders with their pens: Writing about the downtrodden, they won readers' sympathy for reform.

❷ Literary Analysis

The Novel and Social Criticism

A **novel** is a long work of fiction, usually containing these elements:

- A complex plot, often including subplots and spanning a few settings
- Major and minor characters
- A significant overall theme

The novel became popular in the nineteenth century, a period of disturbing social and economic changes. Many novelists of the time included **social criticism** in their works, calling attention to society's ills. As you read, notice how each author turns particular incidents into dramatizations—and criticisms—of social trends and forces.

Comparing Literary Works

In these excerpts, both Dickens and Brontë take on a social problem—misguided educational practices. Both build their critiques using techniques of fiction. As you will see, Dickens favors comic exaggeration, and Brontë applies character analysis. Compare the techniques the writers use to make their points. Then, judge whether their effort to get a message across detracts from or adds to the literary impact of their work.

❸ Reading Strategy

Recognizing the Writer's Purpose

Recognizing a writer's purpose can help you interpret specific incidents in a novel. A writer may write to entertain, to satirize, or to reveal a truth about life. Clues to a writer's purpose include details such as dialogue, events, and the writer's attitude toward characters. As you read, complete a chart like the one shown to help you identify each writer's purpose.

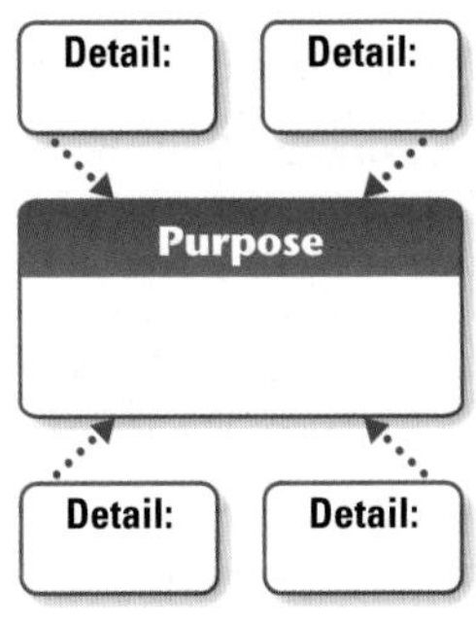

Vocabulary Development

monotonous (mə nät′ ən əs) *adj.* without variation (p. 858)

obstinate (äb′ stə nət) *adj.* stubborn; dogged (p. 859)

adversary (ad′vər ser′ ē) *n.* opponent; enemy (p. 862)

indignant (in dig′ nənt) *adj.* outraged; filled with righteous anger (p. 862)

approbation (ap′ rə bā shən) *n.* official approval or sanction (p. 862)

obscure (əb skyoor′) *adj.* not easily seen; not generally known (p. 866)

comprised (kəm prīzd′) *v.* consisted of; included (p. 866)

sundry (sun′ drē) *adj.* various; miscellaneous (p. 866)

CUSTOMIZE INSTRUCTION FOR UNIVERSAL ACCESS

For Special Needs Students	For Less Proficient Readers	For English Learners
Have students read the adapted version of the excerpt from *Hard Times* in the **Adapted Reader's Companion.** This version provides basic-level instruction in an interactive format with questions and write-on lines. Completing the adapted version will prepare students to read the selection in the Student Edition.	Have students read the excerpt from *Hard Times* in the **Reader's Companion.** This version provides basic-level instruction in an interactive format with questions and write-on lines. After students finish the selection in the **Reader's Companion,** have them complete the questions and activities in the Student Edition.	Have students read the adapted version of the excerpt from *Hard Times* in the **English Learner's Companion.** This version provides basic-level instruction in an interactive format with questions and write-on lines. Completing the adapted version will prepare students to read the selection in the Student Edition.

❷ Literary Analysis

The Novel and Social Criticism

- Tell students that novels originally appealed to a new audience of readers: educated enough and with sufficient leisure to read. Novelists could rely on their readers to take an interest in the social developments of the day, and many nineteenth-century novelists incorporated criticism of their society's ills in their works.
- Read the note about the novel and social criticism together as a class.
- Use the instruction for Comparing Literary Works to review with students how both Dickens and Brontë take on the social problem of misguided educational practices in the excerpts in this lesson, and consider how these authors address this problem in different ways.
- Use The Novel and Social Criticism transparency in **Literary Analysis and Reading Transparencies,** p. 80, to demonstrate to students how these authors incorporate social criticism into their work.

❸ Reading Strategy

Recognizing the Writer's Purpose

- Remind students that one way to respond to a work of literature is to recognize a writer's purpose. Identifying the writer's purpose for writing can help students focus their attention as they read.
- Then, use the graphic organizer on p. 855 to practice recognizing a writer's purpose.
- Have students practice this skill using the Recognizing the Writer's Purpose transparency on p. 79 in **Literary Analysis and Reading Transparencies.**

Vocabulary Development

- Pronounce each vocabulary word for students, and read the definitions as a class. Have students identify any words with which they are already familiar.

E-Teach

Visit E-Teach at www.phschool.com for teachers' essays on how to teach, with questions and answers.

Background

The Serialized Novel

The novel in Dickens's day was still in the process of defining itself, as his career testifies. Novels in Victorian England were often published in illustrated monthly installments in popular magazines. (They could also appear as more expensive "triple-deckers," in three volumes, commissioned by lending libraries.) After this initial serial publication, a novel would appear as a bound book.

The publishing venture that launched Dickens's career, *The Pickwick Papers,* was commissioned by serial publishers in 1836: Dickens was to write text to accompany the sketches of a popular artist. When the artist died, Dickens took over the project. The text, a comical ramble across England by the members of the Pickwick Club and Mr. Pickwick's servant Sam Weller, took precedence over the illustrations. The work was published in twenty monthly installments over nineteen months. Dickens had not written the full work in advance of its publication; he composed chapters to meet the monthly deadline. The work bears the mark of this origin: Episodes often end at a suspenseful moment, to make sure the readers return for more, and there is little overall direction to the story in the early parts.

As Dickens's artistry evolved, he produced well-structured novels such as *Dombey and Son* and *A Tale of Two Cities.* Yet while some Victorian novelists wrote their works before its monthly publication, Dickens preferred to start with only an outline and work month to month. This format allowed the market to drive some of his artistic decisions: When sales of *Martin Chuzzlewit* began falling off, Dickens promptly packed his hero off to America, hoping to renew British interest in the work.

A Closer Look

The Curious Workshop of Charles Dickens: Making Myths

Even if you have never read a novel by Charles Dickens, you have encountered his work. Characters such as the miser Ebenezer Scrooge and the orphan Oliver Twist stepped out from Dicken's books long ago to take up a life as old friends in musicals and cartoons. The very word *Dickensian* names a special region of the imagination, a region criss-crossed by obscure city streets, each inhabited by leering villains, honest clerks, wide-eyed innocents, and a host of knotty eccentrics, a-glee with their own special knacks and nervous twitches.

Defining Dickens This generalized picture of Dickens and his works is based on his 15 novels (one incomplete) and his Christmas stories, most published in serial form in magazines. Dicken's popularity in his own lifetime was enormous. With his first major effort, *The Pickwick Papers* (1836–1837), and for decades after, he held Victorian England spellbound, raptly awaiting the publication of the next chapter of *Oliver Twist* (1837–1839) or *Great Expectations* (1860–1861). When his character Little Nell of *The Old Curiosity Shop* (1840–1841) died, England was torn by grief.

Reformer and Myth-Maker Dickens took his popularity as a responsibility, an opportunity to use influence for social improvement. In his day, the Industrial Revolution had washed over England, leaving sprawling slums overcrowded with the new working class, riddled with epidemic fatal diseases. Dickens's stories of hard times and injured innocents challenged the forces that smothered compassion and nursed vice in the new society.

A Curious Workshop Yet Dickens does more than tell moral stories about social injustice. The most distinctive characteristic of his work might be called its mythical or fairy-tale like quality. In the shadow of the harsh, gray factories choking London with smoke and slums, Dickens set up his own workshop of the imagination. There, he cobbled together ingenious new myths of crime and redemption. The trademark of his work is stamped most clearly on his characters.

"A Perpetual Summer of Being Themselves" There are no John Smiths or Jane Joneses among Dickens's characters. From Samuel Pickwick to Wilkins Micawber to Uriah Heep, each character's name is a distinctive concoction of syllables, a two-word poem. The quirkiness of character names only reflects the quirkiness of the characters themselves. From the Rumplestiltskin-like Daniel Quilp of *The Old Curiosity Shop* to the hopelessly optimistic Mr. Micawber of *David Copperfield* (1849–1850), Dickens compounded characters of peculiar turns of speech and singular mannerisms, some endearing, some frightening. As essayist G. K. Chesterton notes, these characters are so much themselves,

ENRICHMENT: Visual Arts Connection

Magazine Illustration

Dickens's works were illustrated by artists whose styles have become inextricably associated with his work, including George Cruikshank (1792–1878), who signed his work "Boz," and John Leech (1817–1864). Hablot K. Browne (1815–1882), who signed himself "Phiz," illustrated the majority of Dickens's novels. (Phiz's portrayal of Newman Noggs for *Nicholas Nickelby* appears on the student page, p. 856.)

Magazine illustrators of the Victorian era would draw illustrations on a block of wood in pen and ink, using pencil for finer details. An engraver would then engrave the drawing on the block, from which the illustration would then be printed. Copper- or steel-plate etchings were also used: An artist would supply a drawing on paper, and an engraver would trace the drawing onto a plate and etch each line into the plate using needles and an acid bath.

it seems they will exist for ever, passing from one adventure to another like Paul Bunyan or Anansi in folklore. They live, Chesterton writes, "in a perpetual summer of being themselves."

Wicked Woods, Safe Havens Under Dickens's fairy-tale pen, the economic and social challenges of Victorian times reappear as a grotesque landscape, the literary equivalent of the woods in which the witch lives. Here is the description of landscape surrounding a new railroad:

> Everywhere were bridges that led nowhere; thoroughfares that were wholly impassable; Babel towers of chimneys, wanting half their height; temporary wooden houses and enclosures, in the most unlikely situations; carcasses of ragged tenements, and fragments of unfinished walls and arches, and piles of scaffolding, and wildernesses of bricks, and giant forms of cranes, and tripods straddling above nothing. There were a hundred thousand shapes and substances of incompleteness. . . .

Yet Dickens also creates islands of safety and refuge, such as the permanently beached boat in which David Copperfield finds happiness with the Peggoty family. In settings such as these, both Dickens's social criticism and his childlike attunement to the fairy-tale dimension of life have a place.

Dickens and Victorian England
Dickens ruled over the imagination of Victorian England as a kind of father-figure, by turns jolly and stern. He amuses his readers even while reprimanding their faults, and is never far from a childlike enjoyment of his own antics. Though there is much that is simply sentimental in Dickens, there are also depths of psychological realism, an unflagging faith in redemption, and the eternal exuberance in human variety. Modern readers can still warm themselves at the cheerful glow of his work.

Selected Characters of Dickens

Type	Sketch
Hero	**David Copperfield, *David Copperfield.*** A runaway, young David must make his way through the world to discover whether or not he is "the hero of my own life."
Villain	**Daniel Quilp, *The Old Curiosity Shop.*** A malevolent dwarf, charmed by his own ugliness and its power to frighten others, Quilp schemes for the sheer pleasure of mischief.
Morally Challenged	**Paul Dombey, *Dombey and Son.*** The egocentric businessman Dombey is wounded by the death of his son, through whom he thought to perpetuate his own self-image.
True-Hearted Grotesque	**Newman Noggs, *Nicholas Nickelby.*** "Goggle-eyed," by turns wooden and twitchy, Noggs rarely speaks but expresses emotion by explosively cracking his knuckles. He finds his courage when it is necessary to save Nicholas Nickelby.

Background

Dickens's Own Character

The compound of energy, caricature, and sentiment in Dickens's work is reflected in his own life. Dickens was a terrific mimic. Early in his career, he hoped to become an actor, attending the theater every night and memorizing numerous theatrical parts. His theatrical bent is evident in the characterizations in his novels, which share with the art of the mime the art of isolating and exaggerating a mannerism.

When Dickens was a child, his father entered debtors prison and young Charles took a job in a factory. He never gave up his bitterness at the abandonment he felt. Later, he was scarred by an ill-fated infatuation and by the death of his young sister-in-law. In each case, Dickens was haunted by the loss, as if he mourned for a part of himself that he could never recover. One can perhaps detect Dickens's nostalgia for an unbroken childhood in the cheery fireside scenes and the tragic deaths of innocents in the novels.

Critical Thinking

1. Dickens's novels were extremely popular. What effect might his descriptions of the oppression of the poor and the young have had on his society?
   Possible response: They may have encouraged legislation reforming schools and the workplace.
2. Explain how Dickens's technique of characterization enabled him to produce both endearing individuals and caricatures of social types.
   Possible response: By creating characters from exaggerated mannerisms, Dickens produced charming eccentrics. An exaggerated mannerism can also reflect the characteristics of a social role and so form the basis of a caricature of a social type.

CUSTOMIZE INSTRUCTION FOR UNIVERSAL ACCESS

For Less Proficient Readers	For Gifted/Talented Students	For Advanced Readers
Have students read A Closer Look. Then, have them read the excerpt from *Hard Times,* p. 858. Have them identify passages in which Dickens's distinctive technique of characterization is evident. Then, have them discuss the effectiveness of these passages.	Have students read A Closer Look. Then, have them read the excerpt from *Hard Times,* p. 858. Have them identify passages in which Dickens's distinctive technique of characterization is evident. Then, have them draw or perform a pantomime impression of one of the characters.	Have students read A Closer Look. Then, have them read the excerpt from *Hard Times,* p. 858, and two to three early chapters from a novel of their choice by Dickens. Have them write an essay comparing a character from each of the works, noting the various techniques Dickens uses to create a portrait of each.

TEACH

Step-by-Step Teaching Guide for pp. 858–872

CUSTOMIZE INSTRUCTION
For Visual/Spatial Learners

Students may enjoy creating their own illustration of Gradgrind's classroom. They might draw or paint the scene or create a collage out of magazine pictures.

❶ About the Selection

In this episode, from the beginning of *Hard Times,* Thomas Gradgrind questions children in his model school. Then, he turns the proceedings over to the schoolmaster M'Choakumchild. Dickens uses the occasion to satirize the deadening utilitarian philosophy of these "educators," with its devotion to facts at the expense of living knowledge. A student named Sissy Jupe, for example, is the daughter of a man who makes his living from horses. However, her inability to define a horse according to the dictionary is regarded as a deficiency. Dickens uses names—Gradgrind speaks volumes—as well as descriptions and dialogue to score more satiric points.

❷ Vocabulary Development

Greek Prefix: *mono-*

- Call students' attention to *monotonous,* a word that means "having a single 'tone' and therefore dull and unvarying."
- Explain to students that *monotonous* contains the Greek prefix *mono-,* which means "single" or "alone."
- Have students suggest other words and phrases that contain this Greek prefix, and list them on the chalkboard.
  Possible responses: *Monogamous, monopoly,* and *monomaniacal.*

❶ *from* HARD TIMES

Charles Dickens

Background

Of the many beliefs in his society with which Dickens took issue, the Utilitarianism of philosopher Jeremy Bentham (1748–1832) particularly irritated him. Bentham believed that statistics and logic could be applied to all human affairs, and he viewed human beings as essentially interested only in their own happiness. He saw the purpose of society as "the greatest happiness for the greatest number," with happiness calculated in terms of individual pleasures and pains. Dickens believed Utilitarianism discounted or even sought to negate virtues like imagination and sympathy. In *Hard Times,* Dickens used his character Mr. Gradgrind to poke fun at this philosophy.

Chapter 1
The One Thing Needful

"Now, what I want is, Facts. Teach these boys and girls nothing but Facts. Facts alone are wanted in life. Plant nothing else, and root out everything else. You can only form the minds of reasoning animals upon Facts: nothing else will ever be of any service to them. This is the principle on which I bring up my own children, and this is the principle on which I bring up these children. Stick to Facts, sir!"

The scene was a plain, bare, monotonous vault of a schoolroom, ❷ and the speaker's square forefinger emphasized his observations by underscoring every sentence with a line on the schoolmaster's sleeve. The emphasis was helped by the speaker's square wall of a forehead, which had his eyebrows for its base, while his eyes found commodious cellarage in two dark caves, overshadowed by the wall. The emphasis was helped by the speaker's mouth, which was wide, thin, and hard set. The emphasis was helped by the speaker's voice, which was inflexible, dry, and dictatorial. The emphasis was helped by the speaker's hair, which bristled on the skirts of his bald head, a plantation of firs to keep the wind from its shining surface, all covered with knobs, like

monotonous (mə nätʹ ən əs) *adj.* without variation

TEACHING RESOURCES

The following resources can be used to enrich or extend the instruction for pp. 858–872.

Literary Analysis
Selection Support: Literary Analysis, p. 188

Reading
Adapted Reader's Companion
Reader's Companion
English Learner's Companion
Listening to Literature Audiocassettes, Side 20

Listening to Literature Audio CDs, CD 12 

Extension
Fine Art Transparencies, Volume 1, Transparency 19 (Introduce the selections by displaying Art Transparency 19, *El pueblo a la universidad, la universidad al pueblo.* Invite students to comment about the work's implications about education.)

BLOCK SCHEDULING: Resources marked with this symbol provide varied instruction during 90-minute blocks.

3 the crust of a plum pie, as if the head had scarcely warehouse-room for the hard facts stored inside. The speaker's obstinate carriage, square coat, square legs, square shoulders—nay, his very neckcloth, trained to take him by the throat with an unaccommodating grasp, like a stubborn fact, as it was—all helped the emphasis.

"In this life, we want nothing but Facts, sir; nothing but Facts!"

The speaker, and the schoolmaster, and the third grown person present, all backed a little, and swept with their eyes the inclined plane of little vessels, then and there arranged in order, ready to have imperial gallons of facts poured into them until they were full to the brim.

obstinate (äb´ stə nət) *adj.* stubborn; dogged

Chapter 2
Murdering the Innocents

Thomas Gradgrind, sir. A man of realities. A man of fact and calculations. A man who proceeds upon the principle that two and two are four, and nothing over, and who is not to be talked into allowing for anything over. Thomas Gradgrind, sir—peremptorily Thomas—Thomas Gradgrind. With a rule and a pair of scales, and the multiplication table always in his pocket, sir, ready to weigh and measure any parcel of human nature, and tell you exactly what it comes to. It is a mere question of figures, a case of simple arithmetic. You might hope to get some other nonsensical belief into the head of George Gradgrind, or Augustus Gradgrind, or John Gradgrind, or Joseph Gradgrind (all suppositious, non-existent persons), but into the head of Thomas Gradgrind—no, sir!

In such terms Mr. Gradgrind always mentally introduced himself, whether to his private circle of acquaintance, or to the public in general. In such terms, no doubt, substituting the words "boys and girls," for "sir," Thomas Gradgrind now presented Thomas Gradgrind to the little pitchers before him, who were to be filled so full of facts.

Indeed, as he eagerly sparkled at them from the cellarage before mentioned, he seemed a kind of cannon loaded to the muzzle with facts, and prepared to blow them clean out of the regions of childhood at one discharge. He seemed a galvanizing apparatus, too, charged with a grim mechanical substitute for the tender young imaginations that were to be stormed away.

"Girl number twenty," said Mr. Gradgrind, squarely pointing with his square forefinger, "I don't know that girl. Who is that girl?"

"Sissy Jupe, sir," explained number twenty, blushing, standing up, and curtseying.

"Sissy is not a name," said Mr. Gradgrind. "Don't call yourself
4 Sissy. Call yourself Cecilia."

"It's father as calls me Sissy, sir," returned the young girl in a trembling voice, and with another curtsey.

"Then he has no business to do it," said Mr. Gradgrind. "Tell him he mustn't. Cecilia Jupe. Let me see. What is your father?"

"He belongs to the horse-riding, if you please, sir."

Mr. Gradgrind frowned, and waved off the objectionable calling with his hand.

Literary Analysis
The Novel and Social Criticism What outlook is Dickens criticizing through Gradgrind's identification of Sissy Jupe by a number?

5 ✓**Reading Check**
What does Gradgrind aim to do for students?

3 Critical Thinking
Make Judgments

- Have a student volunteer read aloud the second paragraph. Ask students to consider the distinction between Dickens's speaker's message and Dickens's description of the speaker.
- Then, ask students: What is the relationship between Dickens's description of the speaker and the speaker's message?
  Possible response: Student responses should reflect the utter lack of warmth or softness in the speaker. His geometrical angularity underscores his rigidity of character and viewpoint.

4 Literary Analysis
The Novel and Social Criticism

- Review with students the various ways in which Gradgrind reveals something about himself in this passage.
- Then, ask the Literary Analysis question on p. 859: What outlook is Dickens criticizing through Gradgrind's identification of Sissy Jupe by a number?
  Answer: Students may recognize that using numbers rather than names to refer to people is a way to dehumanize them and strip away their individuality.

5 ✓Reading Check

Answer: Gradgrind aims to fill the students full of facts.

CUSTOMIZE INSTRUCTION FOR UNIVERSAL ACCESS

For Special Needs Students	For Less Proficient Readers	For Gifted/Talented Students
Have students read from *Hard Times* with teacher guidance. Then, ask students to visualize each line as they reread sections from the novel to themselves. For students who are struggling with comprehension, pair them with more proficient readers.	Students may have difficulty getting engaged in the atmosphere of the excerpt from *Hard Times* because it describes an era that is foreign to them. Consider showing students *"Hard Times:* Schools Today" on **Interest Grabber Videos,** Tape 5, to stimulate their interest in the conditions in Mr. Gradgrind's classroom.	Have students read from *Hard Times* in pairs. Then, have them imagine that they are in charge of teaching Gradgrind's class for one day. Have students develop a lesson plan that focuses on subjects that are important to them. Tell them to consider using related music, stories, and visual aids.

❻ Background

Art

London School for Orphan Boys, 1870

This illustration, which shows a classroom in an orphanage, was created through the technique of wood engraving, which involves incising designs into a block of wood. This block is then inked and pressed onto paper, leaving a black-and-white image. It is an exacting art that requires strength and precision. The details in this engraving display a wide variety of textures and shading. Use these questions for discussion:

1. Does the use of only one color in this picture enhance the mood of the excerpt it illustrates? Explain.
   Possible response: The use of only one color underscores the monotony and coldness of the schoolroom portrayed in the excerpt.
2. Would the teachers and students shown in the engraving meet with the approval of Gradgrind? Why or why not?
   Answer: Gradgrind might well find the school shown to be sufficiently like a factory to meet with his approval. The teacher in the foreground, however, has a look that Gradgrind might find unacceptably caring and relaxed.

❼ ▶Critical Viewing

Answer: Students may observe that there are two adult instructors, the class contains boys only, there are no desks, and a student appears to be leading the rest of the class in a reading lesson. Students may conclude from this that classes were single-gender with a confusing mix of simultaneous activities, that taking notes was not encouraged or not allowed, and that students received little individualized attention.

❻

"We don't want to know anything about that, here. You mustn't tell us about that, here. Your father breaks horses, don't he?"

"If you please, sir, when they can get any to break, they do break horses in the ring, sir."

"You mustn't tell us about the ring, here. Very well, then. Describe your father as a horsebreaker. He doctors sick horses, I dare say?"

"Oh yes, sir."

"Very well, then. He is a veterinary surgeon, a farrier and horsebreaker. Give me your definition of a horse."

(Sissy Jupe thrown into the greatest alarm by this demand.)

"Girl number twenty unable to define a horse!" said Mr. Gradgrind, for the general behoof of all the little pitchers. "Girl number twenty possessed of no facts, in reference to one of the commonest of animals! Some boy's definition of a horse. Bitzer, yours."

The square finger, moving here and there, lighted suddenly on Bitzer, perhaps because he chanced to sit in the same ray of sunlight which, darting in at one of the bare windows of the intensely whitewashed room, irradiated Sissy. For, the boys and girls sat on the face of the inclined plane in two compact bodies, divided up the center by a narrow interval; and Sissy, being at the corner of a row on the sunny side, came in for the beginning of a sunbeam, of which Bitzer, being at the corner of a row on the other side, a few rows in advance, caught the end. But, whereas the girl was so dark-eyed and dark-haired, that she seemed to receive a deeper and more lustrous color from the sun when it shone upon her, the boy was so light-eyed and light-haired that the self-same rays appeared to draw out of him what little color he ever possessed. His cold eyes would hardly have been eyes, but for the short ends of lashes which, by bringing them into immediate contrast with something paler than themselves, expressed their form. His short-cropped hair might have been a mere continuation of the sandy freckles on his forehead and face. His skin was so unwholesomely deficient in the natural tinge, that he looked as though, if he were cut, he would bleed white.

"Bitzer," said Thomas Gradgrind. "Your definition of a horse."

"Quadruped. Graminivorous. Forty teeth, namely twenty-four grinders, four eye-teeth, and twelve incisive. Sheds coat in the spring; in marshy countries, sheds hoofs, too. Hoofs hard, but requiring to be shod with iron. Age known by marks in mouth." Thus (and much more) Bitzer.

❼ **▲ Critical Viewing** Judging from the details in this engraving, what was school like in London during Victorian times? **[Speculate]**

ENRICHMENT: Cultural Connection

Schools and Conformity

Point out that the setting of both the excerpt from Dickens's *Hard Times* and the excerpt from Brontë's *Jane Eyre* is a school. Both authors explore the theme of conformity and individuality. For young people in many cultures throughout the world, the pressures to conform to the group produce some of the most powerful conflicts of adolescence. This theme has been developed by many contemporary English and American authors in works such as J.D. Salinger's *Catcher in the Rye* and John Fowles's *A Separate Peace,* in which school scenes are used to play out these young adult conflicts.

London School for Orphan Boys, Wood engraving, 1870

"Now girl number twenty," said Mr. Gradgrind. "You know what a horse is."

8 She curtseyed again, and would have blushed deeper, if she could have blushed deeper than she had blushed all this time. Bitzer, after rapidly blinking at Thomas Gradgrind with both eyes at once, and so catching the light upon his quivering ends of lashes that they looked like the antennae of busy insects, put his knuckles to his freckled forehead, and sat down again.

The third gentleman now stepped forth. A mighty man at cutting and drying, he was; a government officer; in his way (and in most other

9 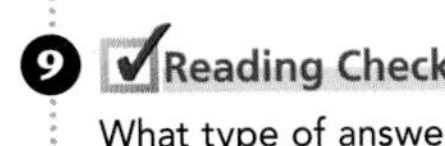

What type of answer to his question does Gradgrind accept?

CUSTOMIZE INSTRUCTION FOR UNIVERSAL ACCESS

For Less Proficient Readers	For English Learners
As students read the excerpt from *Hard Times* with teacher guidance, ask them to pay special attention to the way in which the classroom and its instructors are portrayed. Remind them that Dickens may have included materials or details that offered social criticism of his era. As students reread the selection in search of evidence of social criticism, consider reviewing this skill of identifying social criticism in the novel using The Novel and Social Criticism transparency on p. 80 of **Literary Analysis and Reading Transparencies.**	Have students read from *Hard Times* with teacher guidance. If students seem to struggle with vocabulary or the progress of the conversation between Mr. Gradgrind and his students, have them sound out words and paraphrase any concepts that they do not understand. Then, have students reread from the selection independently and listen to the selection on **Listening to Literature Audiocassettes,** Side 20.

8 Literary Analysis

The Novel and Social Criticism

- Remind students that novels can perform many jobs at the same time, such as creating characters and offering a critique of social institutions.
- Have a volunteer read aloud the paragraph beginning "She curtseyed again, . . . ".
- Ask students: What is the most immediate effect of the description of Sissy and Bitzer?
  Answer: The description clearly conveys Sissy's shyness and her embarrassment at her failure. Dickens also underscores Bitzer's "unnaturalness," from his rapid blinking to his antennae-like eyelashes. The immediate effect is to reinforce the reader's sympathy for Sissy and mild distaste for Bitzer, as well as to put the final comic touch on the scene.
- Then, ask students: How does this effect contribute to Dickens's goal of social criticism?
  Answer: The contrast between Sissy and Bitzer helps Dickens criticize the Gradgrind philosophy of education. Since Sissy does not fare well under this philosophy even though she is a likeable, "normal" child, and since the student who does do well is odd and unsympathetic, the reader's emotional sympathies are enlisted against the Gradgrind philosophy.
- Finally, ask students: Does the fact that these descriptions are clearly there to help make Dickens's larger point take away from your enjoyment of the scene?
  Possible responses: Yes, Dickens has "stacked the deck" by making Sissy likeable and Bitzer insect-like and so the scene seems false or contrived. No, although the point he is making is clear, his characters are interesting and comical in themselves. The characters are not merely stand-ins for ideas—they have individuality. Sissy is likeable, but also inarticulate, and Bitzer's oddness is interesting in itself.

9 Reading Check

Answer: Gradgrind accepts an extremely clinical and scientific definition of a horse.

10 Reading Strategy

Recognizing the Writer's Purpose

- Have students read the bracketed passage to themselves. Remind them to keep in mind the writer's purpose for including the information he does in this scene.
- Ask them the Reading Strategy question on p. 862: What does the reaction of the class hint about Dickens's purpose in this scene?
  Answer: Dickens's purpose is to poke fun at theories of education. He shows the ridiculousness of these theories in practice—because the gentleman is more interested in his own ideas than in the true education of students, he is oblivious to the fact that they simply tell him what he wants to hear.

people's too), a professed pugilist; always in training, always with a system to force down the general throat like a bolus,[1] always to be heard of at the bar of his little Public-office, ready to fight all England. To continue in fistic phraseology, he had a genius for coming up to the scratch, wherever and whatever it was, and proving himself an ugly customer. He would go in and damage any subject whatever with his right, follow up with his left, stop, exchange, counter, bore his opponent (he always fought All England[2]) to the ropes, and fall upon him neatly. He was certain to knock the wind out of common sense, and render that unlucky adversary deaf to the call of time. And he had it in charge from high authority to bring about the great public-office Millennium, when Commissioners should reign upon earth.

adversary (ad′ vər ser′ ē) *n.* opponent; enemy

"Very well," said this gentleman, briskly smiling, and folding his arms. "That's a horse. Now, let me ask you girls and boys, Would you paper a room with representations of horses?"

Reading Strategy
Recognizing the Writer's Purpose What does the reaction of the class hint about Dickens's purpose in this scene?

After a pause, one half of the children cried in chorus, "Yes, sir!" Upon which the other half, seeing in the gentleman's face that Yes was wrong, cried out in chorus, "No, sir!"—as the custom is, in these examinations.

"Of course, No. Why wouldn't you?"

A pause. One corpulent slow boy, with a wheezy manner of breathing, ventured the answer, Because he wouldn't paper a room at all, 10 but would paint it.

"You *must* paper it," said Thomas Gradgrind, "whether you like it or not. Don't tell *us* you wouldn't paper it. What do you mean, boy?"

"I'll explain to you, then," said the gentleman, after another and a dismal pause, "why you wouldn't paper a room with representations of horses. Do you ever see horses walking up and down the sides of rooms in reality—in fact? Do you?"

"Yes, sir!" from one half. "No, sir!" from the other.

"Of course no," said the gentleman, with an indignant look at the wrong half. "Why, then, you are not to see anywhere, what you don't see in fact; you are not to have anywhere, what you don't have in fact. What is called Taste, is only another name for Fact."

indignant (in dig′ nənt) *adj.* outraged; filled with righteous anger

Thomas Gradgrind nodded his approbation.

approbation (ap′ rə bā′ shən) *n.* official approval or sanction

"This is a new principle, a discovery, a great discovery," said the gentleman. "Now, I'll try you again. Suppose you were going to carpet a room. Would you use a carpet having a representation of flowers upon it?"

There being a general conviction by this time that "No, sir!" was always the right answer to this gentleman, the chorus of No was very strong. Only a few feeble stragglers said Yes; among them Sissy Jupe.

"Girl number twenty," said the gentleman, smiling in the calm strength of knowledge.

Sissy blushed, and stood up.

1. **bolus** a large pill.
2. **fought All England** fought according to the official rules of boxing.

ENRICHMENT: Art Connection

Victorian Decoration

Dickens could exaggerate to make a point, but sometimes he did not have to go far. In 1852, a Department of Practical Arts was established in Britain to study designs of textiles and other products. Henry Cole, the General Superintendent, decried portrayals of inappropriate subjects. One of his attacks, in fact, was aimed at wallpaper showing representations of horses and at carpets with floral designs.

The Department argued against the more vulgar stylistic excesses of Victorians. They would cram their homes with furnishings and decorative pieces of all sorts in a confusion of dark wood, lacquer, gilt, and mother-of-pearl. Velvet and lace covered all available surfaces; glass miniatures, shells, porcelain statuettes, bronze sculptures, and Berlin-work pillows were scattered everywhere. The walls were covered with elaborately patterned wallpaper and hung with huge paintings. Perhaps the urge to show some restraint was not so ill-advised.

"So you would carpet your room—or your husband's room, if you were a grown woman, and had a husband—with representations of flowers, would you," said the gentleman. "Why would you?"

"If you please, sir, I am very fond of flowers," returned the girl.

"And is that why you would put tables and chairs upon them, and have people walking over them with heavy boots?"

"It wouldn't hurt them, sir. They wouldn't crush and wither if you please, sir. They would be the pictures of what was very pretty and pleasant, and I would fancy—"

11 "Ay, ay, ay! but you mustn't fancy," cried the gentleman, quite elated by coming so happily to his point. "That's it! You are never to fancy."

"You are not, Cecilia Jupe," Thomas Gradgrind solemnly repeated, "to do anything of that kind."

"Fact, fact, fact!" said the gentleman. And "Fact, fact, fact!" repeated Thomas Gradgrind.

"You are to be in all things regulated and governed," said the gentleman, "by fact. We hope to have, before long, a board of fact, composed of commissioners of fact, who will force the people to be a people of fact, and of nothing but fact. You must discard the word Fancy altogether. You have nothing to do with it. You are not to have, in any object of use or ornament, what would be a contradiction in fact. You don't walk upon flowers in fact; you cannot be allowed to walk upon flowers in carpets. You don't find that foreign birds and butterflies come and perch upon your crockery. You never meet with quadrupeds going up and down walls; you must not have quadrupeds represented upon walls. You must use," said the gentleman, "for all these purposes, combinations and modifications (in primary colors) of mathematical figures which are susceptible of proof and demonstration. This is the new discovery. This is fact. This is taste."

The girl curtseyed, and sat down. She was very young, and she looked as if she were frightened by the matter of fact prospect the world afforded.

"Now, if Mr. M'Choakumchild," said the gentleman, "will proceed to give his first lesson here, Mr. Gradgrind, I shall be happy, at your request, to observe his mode of procedure."

Mr. Gradgrind was much obliged. "Mr. M'Choakumchild, we only wait for you."

So, Mr. M'Choakumchild began in his best manner. He and some one hundred and forty other schoolmasters, had been lately turned at the same time, in the same factory, on the same principles, like so many pianoforte legs. He had been put through an immense variety of paces, and had answered volumes of head-breaking questions. Orthography, etymology, syntax, and prosody, biography, astronomy, geography, and general cosmography, the sciences of compound proportion, algebra, land-surveying and leveling, vocal music, and drawing from models, were all at the ends of his ten chilled fingers. He had worked his stony way into Her Majesty's most Honorable

Literary Analysis
The Novel and Social Criticism How does Dickens exaggerate his characters' reaction to make a point about social trends?

12 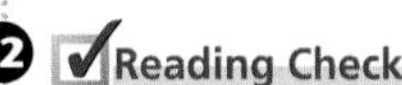

Why does the third gentleman object to horses on wallpaper and flowers on rugs?

11 Literary Analysis
The Novel and Social Criticism

- Read the bracketed passage aloud to students, and remind them as they read along in the text to pay attention to the ways in which Dickens's novel comments on social trends and situations.
- Then, ask them the Literary Analysis question on p. 863: How does Dickens exaggerate his characters' reactions to make a point about social trends?
  Answer: Dickens uses exaggeration in the gentleman's and Mr. Gradgrind's reactions to Sissy Jupe's admissions to criticize the insistence of the educational system on eliminating imagination —"fancy"— from the world.

12 Reading Check

Answer: He objects to these things because they are not what happens "in fact" in the real world.

CUSTOMIZE INSTRUCTION FOR UNIVERSAL ACCESS

For Special Needs Students	For English Learners	For Gifted/Talented Students
Students may have difficulty engaging with the excerpt from *Hard Times* because it describes an era that is foreign to them. Consider showing students "*Hard Times:* Schools Today" on **Interest Grabber Videos,** Tape 5, to stimulate their interest in the conditions experienced by the students in Mr. Gradgrind's classroom.	Students may find the exchange between Sissy Jupe and Mr. Gradgrind incomprehensible because they may not understand the attitudes Dickens is satirizing. Encourage students to ask questions of the text, to rely on the footnotes and definitions, and to paraphrase any words or expressions they find unfamiliar.	Have students work in small groups to complete a reading from *Hard Times.* When they have finished, tell them that they must adapt the chapter "Murdering the Innocents" from the novel, turning it into a scene they can perform.

Answers for p. 864

Review and Assess

1. Possible responses: Most students will express a dislike of Mr. Gradgrind's theory of education.
2. **(a)** He sees "facts" as the important element in learning. **(b)** He discourages the use of imagination or imprecise but common-sense reasoning in his class. **(c)** He sees students as passive, empty vessels to be filled with facts rather than as full people with hearts and imaginations as well as intellects.
3. **(a)** The "third gentleman" is a government officer. **(b)** He views "imagination" as completely unnecessary and "Fact" as supremely important and is in fact unable to distinguish between the two, since he will not allow representations of things to appear where the things themselves do not.
4. **(a)** Sissy's performance is weak, stumbling, and meandering; Blitzer's performance is a model of the "factual" response: he offers a formal dictionary definition in short, unrelated phrases. **(b)** Dickens expects the reader to sympathize with Sissy, whose response is more like what most readers would give.
5. **(a)** All the adults are tyrants, blinded by their theories. **(b)** Dickens thinks that this type of education will produce more automatons like Blitzer, or terrify children like Sissy.
6. Possible responses: Educational systems are extremely important in shaping the people students become as adults; some students may say that family and friends are more influential than educational systems in dictating personality traits.

Privy Council's Schedule B, and had taken the bloom off the higher branches of mathematics and physical science, French, German, Latin, and Greek. He knew all about all the Water Sheds of all the world (whatever they are), and all the histories of all the peoples, and all the names of all the rivers and mountains, and all the productions, manners, and customs of all the countries, and all their boundaries and bearings on the two-and-thirty points of the compass. Ah, rather overdone, M'Choakumchild. If he had only learnt a little less, how infinitely better he might have taught much more!

He went to work in this preparatory lesson, not unlike Morgiana in the Forty Thieves:[3] looking into all the vessels ranged before him, one after another, to see what they contained. Say, good M'Choakumchild. When from thy boiling store, thou shalt fill each jar brim full by and by, dost thou think that thou wilt always kill outright the robber Fancy lurking within—or sometimes only maim him and distort him!

3. **Morgiana in the Forty Thieves** In the tale "Ali Baba and the Forty Thieves," Ali Baba's clever servant, Morgiana, saves him from the thieves who are hiding in large jars.

Review and Assess

Thinking About the Selection

1. **Respond:** How did you feel about Mr. Gradgrind's theory of education?
2. **(a) Recall:** What does Mr. Gradgrind believe is the key to all learning? **(b) Connect:** In what ways does he put this belief into practice? **(c) Interpret:** What attitude does the description of the children as "little pitchers" reflect?
3. **(a) Recall:** What is the profession of the "third gentleman" who is visiting the classroom? **(b) Summarize:** What is his view of "Fact" and imagination?
4. **(a) Compare and Contrast:** Compare and contrast Sissy's and Bitzer's performances in the classroom. **(b) Analyze:** With whom does Dickens's expect the reader to sympathize? Why?
5. **(a) Draw Conclusions:** What conclusion does Dickens want the reader to draw about the three adults in the classroom? Explain. **(b) Draw Conclusions:** What conclusion does Dickens want the reader to draw about the kind of children this type of education will produce? Explain.
6. **Make a Judgment:** How much responsibility does a system of education have for the type of adults children become? Explain.

ENRICHMENT: History Connection

Brontë's Schooling

Lowood School is modeled after the Cowan Bridge School, which Charlotte Brontë actually attended. That school was opened in 1824, with the purpose of educating the daughters of poor clergy. She may have exaggerated some of the bad points of the real school in creating Lowood, but she did encounter harsh policies at Cowan.

13 from

Jane Eyre

Charlotte Brontë

Chapter 6

The next day commenced as before, getting up and dressing by rushlight; but this morning we were obliged to dispense with the ceremony of washing: the water in the pitchers was frozen. A change had taken place in the weather the preceding evening, and a keen northeast wind, whistling through the crevices of our bedroom windows all night long, had made us shiver in our beds, and turned the contents of the ewers to ice.

Before the long hour and a half of prayers and Bible reading was over, I felt ready to perish with cold. Breakfast time came at last, and this morning the porridge was not burnt; the quality was eatable, the quantity small; how small my portion seemed! I wished it had been doubled.

14 In the course of the day I was enrolled a member of the fourth class, and regular tasks and occupations were assigned to me: hitherto, I had only been a spectator of the proceedings at Lowood, I was now to become an actor therein. At first, being little accustomed to learn by heart, the lessons appeared to me both long and difficult: the frequent change from task to task, too, bewildered me; and I was glad, when, about three o'clock in the afternoon, Miss Smith put into my hands a border of muslin two yards long, together with needle, thimble, etc., and sent me to sit in a quiet corner of the school room, with directions to hem the same. At that hour most of the others were sewing likewise; but one class still stood round Miss Scatcherd's chair reading, and as all was quiet, the subject of their lessons could be heard, together with the manner in which each girl acquitted herself, and the animadversions or commendations of Miss Scatcherd on the performance. It was English history; among the readers, I observed my

15 ✓Reading Check

How has the narrator's role at Lowood changed?

CUSTOMIZE INSTRUCTION FOR UNIVERSAL ACCESS

For Special Needs Students	For Gifted/Talented Students	For Advanced Readers
Have students read the first three paragraphs from *Jane Eyre* with teacher guidance. Then, ask students to visualize each line as they reread this section from the novel to themselves. Ask them to consider what these descriptions suggest about the conditions of the school Jane attends.	Have students read independently from *Jane Eyre.* Remind students that both *Hard Times* and *Jane Eyre* address social issues. Have students think about a community or world issue they would like to address in a letter to their local newspaper. Then, have them write letters that will capture the attention of their readers.	Before students begin reading from *Jane Eyre,* encourage them to read more about Charlotte Brontë to understand why she might have chosen to tell the story of a young English orphan. Direct them to the biographical material on p. 854, and encourage them to do additional background reading about Brontë's talented family.

13 About the Selection

In this episode from Charlotte Brontë's *Jane Eyre,* Jane is at a boarding school named Lowood. Jane describes the harsh physical conditions, the lack of sufficient food for the girls, and the cruel way in which one of the teachers treats a girl named Helen Burns. Later, Jane has the opportunity to speak with Helen in private and is surprised by Helen's meek acceptance of the wrongs done to her. Brontë's may not editorialize quite the way Dickens does, but many of her descriptions and dialogues represent criticisms of the conditions suffered by disadvantaged girls like Jane and Helen.

14 Literary Analysis

The Novel and Social Criticism

- Remind students that novels are not essays: When a novel offers social criticism, it must create believable and engaging fiction, not just preach. To do so, novelists create situations that clearly and naturally highlight the issues they wish to address.
- Have a volunteer read aloud the first few sentences of the paragraph beginning "In the course of the day . . . ".
- Ask students: What is Jane's position in the class?
  Answer: She is a newcomer; she is just beginning to learn the routine of the school.
- Ask students: What kind of descriptions and commentary might the reader expect from Jane, given this fact?
  Possible response: Because Jane is a newcomer, the reader will expect her to describe and comment on details with fresh eyes. If she were an habituated student, she might simply accept as routine the life of the school.
- Then, ask students: Why is the fact that Jane is a newcomer a useful device for motivating social criticism?
  Possible responses: It naturally prepares for her criticism or questioning of what goes on at the school; it also gives a reason for others to explain the school and its principles to her.

15 ✓Reading Check

Answer: The narrator now participates in the schoolday as a student, no longer as a spectator.

16 Literary Analysis

The Novel and Social Criticism

- Remind students to read the passage for evidence of social commentary or criticism. Have students focus their attention on the details provided about Miss Scatcherd and Burns.
- Then, ask students the Literary Analysis question on p. 866: What does the strange relationship between Miss Scatcherd and Burns suggest about how teachers "ruled" their classrooms in Victorian times?
  Answer: Teachers had total control over their students in Victorian times, as is evident by Miss Scatcherd's ability to punish Helen Burns with impunity.

acquaintance of the verandah; at the commencement of the lesson, her place had been at the top of the class, but for some error of pronunciation or some inattention to stops, she was suddenly sent to the very bottom. Even in that obscure position, Miss Scatcherd continued to make her an object of constant notice: she was continually addressing to her such phrases as the following:—

obscure (əb skyoor′) *adj.* not easily seen; not generally known

"Burns" (such it seems was her name: the girls here, were all called by their surnames, as boys are elsewhere), "Burns, you are standing on the side of your shoe, turn your toes out immediately." "Burns, you poke your chin most unpleasantly, draw it in." "Burns, I insist on your holding your head up: I will not have you before me in that attitude," etc. etc.

A chapter having been read through twice, the books were closed and the girls examined. The lesson had comprised part of the reign of Charles I, and there were sundry questions about tonnage and poundage, and ship-money, which most of them appeared unable 16 to answer; still, every little difficulty was solved instantly when it reached Burns: her memory seemed to have retained the substance of the whole lesson, and she was ready with answers on every point. I kept expecting that Miss Scatcherd would praise her attention; but, instead of that, she suddenly cried out:—

comprised (kəm prīz′ d) *v.* consisted of; included

sundry (sun′ drē) *adj.* various, miscellaneous

Literary Analysis
The Novel and Social Criticism What does the strange relationship between Miss Scatcherd and Burns suggest about how teachers "ruled" their classrooms in Victorian times?

"You dirty, disagreeable girl! you have never cleaned your nails this morning!"

Burns made no answer: I wondered at her silence.

"Why," thought I, "does she not explain that she could neither clean her nails nor wash her face, as the water was frozen?"

My attention was now called off by Miss Smith, desiring me to hold a skein of thread: while she was winding it, she talked to me from time to time, asking whether I had ever been at school before, whether I could mark, stitch, knit, etc.; till she dismissed me, I could not pursue my observations on Miss Scatcherd's movements. When I returned to my seat, that lady was just delivering an order, of which I did not catch the import; but Burns immediately left the class, and going into the small inner room where the books were kept, returned in half a minute, carrying in her hand a bundle of twigs tied together at one end. This ominous tool she presented to Miss Scatcherd with a respectful courtesy; then she quietly, and without being told, unloosed her pinafore, and the teacher instantly and sharply inflicted on her neck a dozen strokes with the bunch of twigs. Not a tear rose to Burns's eye; and, while I paused from my sewing, because my fingers quivered at this spectacle with a sentiment of unavailing and impotent anger, not a feature of her pensive face altered its ordinary expression.

"Hardened girl!" exclaimed Miss Scatcherd, "nothing can correct you of your slatternly habits: carry the rod away."

Burns obeyed: I looked at her narrowly as she emerged from the book closet; she was just putting back her handkerchief into her pocket, and the trace of a tear glistened on her thin cheek.

ENRICHMENT: Media Connection

Productions of *Jane Eyre*

Filmmakers have found *Jane Eyre* to be an inspiring story. Charlotte Brontë's novel is the basis for four silent movies (*Jane Eyre,* 1914, which ran about 40 minutes; *The Castle of Thornfield,* 1915; *Woman and Wife,* 1918; and *Jane Eyre,* 1921), three sound era movies (1934, 1944, and 1996) at least three made-for-television versions (including a miniseries in 1983), and a Broadway musical in 2001.

The movie still shown on p. 867 is from the film released in 1944 in which a young Elizabeth Taylor (on the right) played Helen.

The most recent film adaptation, from 1996, was directed by Franco Zeffirelli. The BBC filmed the most recent television version in 1997, with Samantha Morton in the title role. The musical, *Jane Eyre,* was nominated for several Tony awards in 2001.

17 ▶Critical Viewing

Answer: Students may say that the actresses match their vision of Burns and Jane; the two girls appear to be close friends.

18 Reading Check

Answer: The narrator thinks it is surprising that Burns does not explain to Miss Scatcherd that the water for washing froze during the night.

The play-hour in the evening I thought the pleasantest fraction of the day at Lowood: the bit of bread, the draught of coffee swallowed at five o'clock had revived vitality, if it had not satisfied hunger; the long restraint of the day was slackened; the school room felt warmer than in the morning: its fires being allowed to burn a little more brightly to supply, in some measure, the place of candles, not yet introduced; the ruddy gloaming,[1] the licensed uproar, the confusion of many voices gave one a welcome sense of liberty.

On the evening of the day on which I had seen Miss Scatcherd flog her pupil, Burns, I wandered as usual among the forms and tables

17 ▲ **Critical Viewing** How well does this still from a movie version of *Jane Eyre* match your vision of Jane and Burns? Explain. **[Evaluate]**

18 **Reading Check** What does the narrator think is unusual about Burns's reaction to the charge of uncleanliness?

1. **ruddy gloaming** glowing twilight; the sunset.

CUSTOMIZE INSTRUCTION FOR UNIVERSAL ACCESS

For Less Proficient Readers	For English Learners	For Advanced Readers
Have students read from *Jane Eyre* with teacher guidance. As students read, ask them to picture what the words describe. If students seem to be having difficulty decoding the meaning of the words, consider playing **Listening to Literature Audiocassettes,** Side 20, and asking them to read along with the selection.	Help students as they read from *Jane Eyre* to identify the ways in which Brontë incorporates criticism of her society. You may want to refer students to The Novel and Social Criticism transparency on p. 80 of **Literary Analysis and Reading Transparencies.**	Remind students that both *Hard Times* and *Jane Eyre* examine institutions and attitudes of their day. Have students write short stories that examine social issues or problems in contemporary society. Encourage students to share their stories with their classmates.

19 Literary Analysis

The Novel and Social Criticism

- Have two student volunteers read aloud the bracketed dialogue. Then, have students summarize the exchange.
- Point out Helen's comment at the end of the bracketed passage: "it is weak and silly to say you *cannot bear* what it is your fate to be required to bear." Have students clarify the meaning of her comment. What do students think Brontë is saying here?
Possible response: Helen means that, if you are faced with something that you must bear, saying you cannot bear it is simply refusing to face what you cannot avoid.

Monitor Progress Ask students the Literary Analysis question on p. 868: How does Brontë address both individual ethics and social problems in this dialogue?
Answer: Brontë's description criticizes the cruelty and hypocrisy of schools in her day, and she shows how Helen's patient, forgiving attitude embodies the ideals of charity and mercy more than does the behavior of the instructors of the school.

and laughing groups without a companion, yet not feeling lonely: when I passed the windows, I now and then lifted a blind and looked out; it snowed fast, a drift was already forming against the lower panes; putting my ear close to the window, I could distinguish from the gleeful tumult within, the disconsolate moan of the wind outside.

Probably, if I had lately left a good home and kind parents, this would have been the hour when I should most keenly have regretted the separation: that wind would then have saddened my heart; this obscure chaos would have disturbed my peace: as it was I derived from both a strange excitement, and reckless and feverish, I wished the wind to howl more wildly, the gloom to deepen to darkness, and the confusion to rise to clamor.

Jumping over forms, and creeping under tables, I made my way to one of the fire-places: there, kneeling by the high wire fender, I found Burns, absorbed, silent, abstracted from all round her by the companionship of a book, which she read by the dim glare of the embers.

"Is it still 'Rasselas'?"[2] I asked, coming behind her.

"Yes," she said, "and I have just finished it."

And in five minutes more she shut it up. I was glad of this.

"Now," thought I, "I can perhaps get her to talk." I sat down by her on the floor.

"What is your name besides Burns?"

"Helen."

"Do you come a long way from here?"

"I come from a place further north; quite on the borders of Scotland."

"Will you ever go back?"

"I hope so; but nobody can be sure of the future."

"You must wish to leave Lowood?"

"No: why should I? I was sent to Lowood to get an education; and it would be of no use going away until I have attained that object."

"But that teacher, Miss Scatcherd, is so cruel to you?"

"Cruel? Not at all! She is severe: she dislikes my faults."

"And if I were in your place I should dislike her: I should resist her; if she struck me with that rod, I should get it from her hand; I should break it under her nose."

"Probably you would do nothing of the sort: but if you did, Mr. Brocklehurst would expel you from the school; that would be a great grief to your relations. It is far better to endure patiently a smart which nobody feels but yourself, than to commit a hasty action whose
19 evil consequences will extend to all connected with you—and, besides, the Bible bids us return good for evil."

"But then it seems disgraceful to be flogged, and to be sent to stand in the middle of a room full of people; and you are such a great girl: I am far younger than you, and I could not bear it."

Literary Analysis
The Novel and Social Criticism How does Brontë address both individual ethics and social problems in this dialogue?

2. **Rasselas** *The History of Rasselas, Prince of Abyssinia,* a moralizing novel by Samuel Johnson.

ENRICHMENT: Film Connection

Film Review of Zeffirelli's *Jane Eyre*

When Franco Zeffirelli's 1996 production of *Jane Eyre* was released, it was met with the following criticism in *Movie Magazine International:*

> When we want to see *Jane Eyre,* we can buy the 1934 version or we can rent the 1944 all-star classic, or we can watch the 1970 telefeature that turns up every so often . . . or we can plough through all six hours of the 1983 miniseries. Clearly, there is no shortage of Jane Eyres and Edward Rochesters in this century. Does this 1847 saga by Charlotte Brontë have anything new to say to audiences? Director Franco Zeffirelli clearly thinks so and his latest movie is a fairly faithful adaptation marred by some serious miscasting.

Students may want to view either this adaptation or some of the earlier versions of Brontë's classic.

"Yet it would be your duty to bear it, if you could not avoid it: it is weak and silly to say you *cannot bear* what it is your fate to be required to bear."

I heard her with wonder: I could not comprehend this doctrine of endurance; and still less could I understand or sympathize with the forbearance she expressed for her chastiser. Still I felt that Helen Burns considered things by a light invisible to my eyes. I suspected she might be right and I wrong; but I would not ponder the matter deeply: like Felix,[3] I put it off to a more convenient season.

"You say you have faults, Helen: what are they? To me you seem very good."

"Then learn from me, not to judge by appearances: I am, as Miss Scatcherd said, slatternly; I seldom put, and never keep, things in order; I am careless; I forget rules; I read when I should learn my lessons; I have no method; and sometimes I say, like you, I cannot *bear* to be subjected to systematic arrangements. This is all very provoking to Miss Scatcherd, who is naturally neat, punctual, and particular."

"And cross and cruel," I added; but Helen Burns would not admit my addition: she kept silence.

"Is Miss Temple as severe to you as Miss Scatcherd?"

At the utterance of Miss Temple's name, a soft smile flitted over her grave face.

"Miss Temple is full of goodness; it pains her to be severe to any-one, even the worst in the school: she sees my errors, and tells me of them gently; and, if I do anything worthy of praise, she gives me my meed liberally. One strong proof of my wretchedly defective nature is that even her expostulations, so mild, so rational, have not influence to cure me of my faults; and even her praise, though I value it most highly, cannot stimulate me to continued care and foresight."

"That is curious," said I: "it is so easy to be careful."

20 "For *you* I have no doubt it is. I observed you in your class this morning, and saw you were closely attentive: your thoughts never seemed to wander while Miss Miller explained the lesson and questioned you. Now, mine continually rove away: when I should be listening to Miss Scatcherd, and collecting all she says with assiduity,[4] often I lose the very sound of her voice; I fall into a sort of dream. Sometimes I think I am in Northumberland, and that the noises I hear round me are the bubbling of a little brook which runs through Deepden, near our house;—then, when it comes to my turn to reply, I have to be wakened; and, having heard nothing of what was read for listening to the visionary brook, I have no answer ready."

"Yet how well you replied this afternoon."

"It was mere chance: the subject on which we had been reading had interested me. This afternoon, instead of dreaming of Deepden,

Reading Strategy
Recognizing the Writer's Purpose What opinion does Brontë want you to form of Helen in this paragraph?

21  **Reading Check**
What faults does Helen Burns attribute to herself?

3. **Felix** in the Bible, governor of Judea who released Paul from prison and deferred his trial until a more "convenient season" (Acts 24:25).
4. **assiduity** (as´ ə dyo͞o´ ə tē) *n.* constant care and attention; diligence.

20 Reading Strategy
Recognizing the Writer's Purpose

- Have students read the bracketed passage to themselves.
- Remind them to consider what the author's purpose is in including this information.
- Then, ask them the Reading Strategy question on p. 869: What opinion does Brontë want you to form of Helen in this paragraph? **Possible response:** Students should see that Brontë paints a picture of a dreamy, wistful girl who suffers from homesickness. She is also extremely self-deprecating and virtuous.

21 

Answer: Helen Burns claims she is slatternly, disordered, careless, forgetful, and not methodical.

CUSTOMIZE INSTRUCTION FOR UNIVERSAL ACCESS

For Less Proficient Readers	For Advanced Readers
After students have read the scene between Jane and Helen in which the two discuss the differences between Miss Scatcherd and Miss Temple, have them write a diary entry from the point of view of Miss Scatcherd. In the entry, students should describe a typical day in the life of Scatcherd and should include information about how the instructor views her life, as well as her view on her students.	Have students write essays in which they compare the techniques of Miss Scatcherd in *Jane Eyre* with those of Mr. Gradgrind in *Hard Times*. Students should also examine in their essays how Brontë and Dickens might have created their characters as illustrations of some of the social ills of their era. Encourage students to brainstorm how these characters might have been received when these books were published. For more information on either selection, refer students to www.phschool.com.

㉒ Background

Art

Rochester and Jane Eyre **by** Frederick Walker

British engraver and painter Frederick Walker (1840–1875) was noted for his magazine illustrations, including illustrations of a serialized novel by William Makepeace Thackeray. Walker often based his paintings on such engravings. He is remembered for his leadership in the school of Social Realism, exposing the general public to the plight of the lower classes through his paintings.

This watercolor depicts a scene from *Jane Eyre* in which Jane converses with Mr. Rochester, a widower who has employed her as a governess for his daughter. Jane eventually marries Mr. Rochester. Walker suggests the emotional depth of their relationship through the relaxed, meditative poses and absorbed gazes of the two. Use this question for discussion:

> How does the artist use color and setting to create a sense of happiness and security?
> Possible response: The wall encloses the scene, blocking out other influences; the lively greens, oranges, pinks, and yellows give the scene a lightness and freshness suggesting contentment.

㉓ ▶Critical Viewing

Possible response: Though Jane appears happy in the watercolor, the novel shows that she is quick to act and to hold a grudge; she may defy Mr. Rochester's ideas about his daughter's education or criticize the way in which he runs his affairs.

㉒

Rochester and Jane Eyre, Frederick Walker, Private Collection

I was wondering how a man who wished to do right could act so unjustly and unwisely as Charles the First sometimes did; and I thought what a pity it was that, with his integrity and conscientiousness, he could see no farther than the prerogatives of the crown. If he had but been able to look to a distance, and see how what they call the spirit of the age was tending! Still, I like Charles— I respect him— I pity him, poor murdered king! Yes, his enemies were the worst: they shed blood they had no right to shed. How dared they kill him!"

Helen was talking to herself now: she had forgotten I could not very well understand her— that I was ignorant, or nearly so, of the subject she discussed. I recalled her to my level.

"And when Miss Temple teaches you, do your thoughts wander then?"

"No, certainly, not often; because Miss Temple has generally something to say which is newer to me than my own reflections: her language is singularly agreeable to me, and the information she communicates is often just what I wished to gain."

㉓ ▲ **Critical Viewing**

Judging from the excerpt from the novel, what problems do you think might lie in wait for Jane and her future employer Mr. Rochester, pictured here? **[Speculate]**

ENRICHMENT: Career Connection

The Art of Graphic Design

Each installment of a novel by Dickens or Brontë was illustrated by engaging engravings. Illustrations in magazines have largely been replaced by photographs, but the skill of manipulating images—arranging them, choosing special effects for them, as well as providing other graphics, such as borders, charts, and illustrations—is much in demand in modern publishing. Graphic designers must

- have extensive knowledge of the computer applications used to create page layouts.
- have a trained eye for balanced, effective design.
- be sensitive to the overall look and tone of a work.

"Well, then, with Miss Temple you are good?"

"Yes, in a passive way: I make no effort; I follow as inclination guides me. There is no merit in such goodness."

"A great deal: you are good to those who are good to you. It is all I ever desire to be. If people were always kind and obedient to those who are cruel and unjust, the wicked people would have it all their own way: they would never feel afraid, and so they would never alter, but would grow worse and worse. When we are struck at without a reason, we should strike back again very hard; I am sure we should—so hard as to teach the person who struck us never to do it again."

"You will change your mind, I hope, when you grow older: as yet you are but a little untaught girl."

"But I feel this, Helen: I must dislike those who, whatever I do to please them, persist in disliking me; I must resist those who punish me unjustly. It is as natural as that I should love those who show me affection, or submit to punishment when I feel it is deserved."

". . . Love your enemies; bless them that curse you; do good to them that hate you and despitefully use you."

"Then I should love Mrs. Reed, which I cannot do; I should bless her son John, which is impossible."

(24) In her turn, Helen Burns asked me to explain; and I proceeded forthwith to pour out, in my way, the tale of my sufferings and resentments. Bitter and truculent when excited, I spoke as I felt, without reserve or softening.

Helen heard me patiently to the end: I expected she would then make a remark, but she said nothing.

"Well," I asked impatiently, "is not Mrs. Reed a hard-hearted, bad woman?"

"She has been unkind to you, no doubt; because, you see, she dislikes your cast of character, as Miss Scatcherd does mine: but how minutely you remember all she has done and said to you! What a singularly deep impression her injustice seems to have made on your heart! No ill usage so brands its record on my feelings. Would you not be happier if you tried to forget her severity, together with the passionate emotions it excited? Life appears to me too short to be spent in nursing animosity or registering wrongs. We are, and must be, one and all, burdened with faults in this world: but the time will soon come when, I trust, we shall put them off in putting off our corruptible bodies; when debasement and sin will fall from us with this cumbrous frame of flesh, and only the spark of the spirit will remain,—the impalpable principle of life and thought, pure as when it left the Creator to inspire the creature: whence[5] it came it will return; perhaps again to be communicated to some being higher than man—perhaps to pass through gradations of glory, from the pale human soul to brighten to the seraph![6] Surely it will never,

Literary Analysis
The Novel and Social Criticism What characteristic of the novel is reflected in this reference to events earlier in the story?

(25)  **Reading Check**

What reason does Helen Burns give to encourage Jane to forgive Mrs. Reed?

5. **whence** the place from which.
6. **seraph** angel of the highest order.

(24) Literary Analysis

The Novel and Social Criticism

- Read aloud the bracketed passage, asking students to pay attention to the way in which Jane refers to events from earlier in the story.
- Then, ask students the Literary Analysis question on p. 871: What characteristic of the novel is reflected in this reference to events earlier in the story?
  Answer: The novel's inclusion of a complex plot with many settings is reflected in this reference to earlier events in the story. The novel's use of character analysis is exemplified in Jane's account of summarizing her past to her friend; while the content of her descriptions is not included in the text, she reveals her own feelings: "Bitter and truculent when excited, I spoke as I felt . . ."

(25) Reading Check

Answer: Helen encourages Jane to forgive Mrs. Reed because it is easier to live without grudges, and forgiveness also ensures her salvation at Judgment Day.

CUSTOMIZE INSTRUCTION FOR UNIVERSAL ACCESS

For Less Proficient Readers

Students who have trouble recognizing the writer's purpose may benefit from completing the following chart. Tell students that a writer's choice of character names often furnishes a clue to his or her purpose. Ask students to fill in the chart with two adjectives that describe each character. Then, discuss whether the name of the character did or did not help the writer achieve a purpose of showing the character in a certain light.

Name	Characteristics	Purpose
Gradgrind		
Scatcherd		

ASSESS

Answers for p. 872

Review and Assess

1. Possible responses: Most students will identify with the more feisty Jane; a few may identify with the more philosophical Helen.
2. **(a)** She punishes Helen for untidiness. **(b)** Helen would think crying self-indulgent; she feels she must bear ill treatment without complaint.
3. **(a)** Helen particularly likes Miss Temple. **(b)** Helen says that it is easy to be good in Miss Temple's class, and for that reason, it is not a test of one's virtues.
4. **(a)** Jane is independent, has tendencies to be insubordinate, and is intelligent and observant. **(b)** Jane is angry and finds storms and darkness a good background for her emotions. **(c)** Helen says that Jane should stop holding a grudge against Mrs. Reed because life is short, the grudge merely makes her unhappy, and everyone deserves forgiveness.
5. **(a)** Jane feels that she "must resist those who punish [her] unjustly." Helen says that people should love their enemies and return good for evil. **(b)** Possible responses: Most students will say that each should borrow from the other's point of view to avoid being overly naïve or overly resentful.
6. **(a)** Jane might represent the author's passion and Helen, her idealism. **(b)** A writer needs to experience and understand passions like Jane's to create believable characters; a writer needs a tolerant understanding of others like Helen's to present characters objectively.
7. Possible response: The end of corporal punishment would improve life at Lowood, as would standards that keep schools warm, require that food served be plentiful and healthy, and require teachers to have proper training and certification before instructing students.

on the contrary, be suffered to degenerate from man to fiend? No; I cannot believe that: I hold another creed; which no one ever taught me, and which I seldom mention; but in which I delight, and to which I cling: for it extends hope to all: it makes Eternity a rest—a mighty home, not a terror and abyss. Besides, with this creed, I can so clearly distinguish between the criminal and his crime; I can so sincerely forgive the first while I abhor the last: with this creed revenge never worries my heart, degradation never too deeply disgusts me, injustice never crushes me too low: I live in calm, looking to the end."

Helen's head, always drooping, sank a little lower as she finished this sentence. I saw by her look she wished no longer to talk to me, but rather to converse with her own thoughts. She was not allowed much time for meditation: a monitor, a great rough girl, presently came up, exclaiming in a strong Cumberland accent—

"Helen Burns, if you don't go and put your drawer in order, and fold up your work this minute, I'll tell Miss Scatcherd to come and look at it!"

Helen sighed as her reverie fled, and getting up, obeyed the monitor without reply as without delay.

Review and Assess

Thinking About the Selection

1. **Respond:** Do you relate more to Helen's or to Jane's attitude toward life? Explain.
2. **(a) Recall:** For what offense does Miss Scatcherd punish Helen Burns? **(b) Infer:** When punished, why does Helen make every effort to hold back tears?
3. **(a) Recall:** Which teacher does Helen particularly like? **(b) Analyze:** Why does Helen find that there is "no merit" in being good in this teacher's class?
4. **(a) Summarize:** Describe Jane's personality in a few sentences. **(b) Interpret:** Why might she wish "the wind to howl more wildly, the gloom to deepen to darkness"? **(c) Analyze:** What is Helen's criticism of Jane's reaction to Mrs. Reed?
5. **(a) Compare and Contrast:** Compare Jane's and Helen's reactions to mistreatment. **(b) Make a Judgment:** Do you think each has something to teach the other? Explain.
6. **(a) Draw Conclusions:** Helen and Jane might be seen as two sides of the author's personality. Explain. **(b) Evaluate:** Why might a novelist need both "sides" to write successfully?
7. **Apply:** What features of modern schools could improve life at Lowood? Explain your choices.

872 ◆ *Progress and Decline (1833–1901)*

ASSESSMENT PRACTICE: Reading Comprehension

Paired Passages **(For more practice, see Test Preparation Workbook, p. 40.)**

Many tests require students to compare and identify literary elements in two passages. The following sample item can teach students how to identify the tones of two passages. Have students reread Chapter 1 from *Hard Times,* pp. 858–859, and the first eight paragraphs of *Jane Eyre,* pp. 865–866.

Which of the following statements best describes the tones of the two passages?

A Both passages are sad yet hopeful.
B *Hard Times* is humorous; *Jane Eyre* is somber.
C Both passages are gloomy.
D *Hard Times* is satiric; *Jane Eyre* is dramatic.

Help students analyze the tones of the two works. Choices *A* and *C* could describe *Jane Eyre,* but not *Hard Times. Hard Times* is satiric, but *Jane Eyre* is not particularly dramatic, so students should eliminate choice *D.* The correct answer is *B.*

Review and Assess

Literary Analysis

The Novel and Social Criticism

1. (a) In the selection from the **novel** *Hard Times*, which details make the setting vivid? (b) How do they contribute to a **criticism of society**?
2. Summarize the viewpoint that Dickens criticizes.
3. (a) What does Jane and Helen's discussion in *Jane Eyre* reveal about the character of each? (b) What does it reveal about the school?
4. (a) If Helen and Jane were writers, which would write social criticism? Which one might not? Explain. (b) What does your answer suggest about Brontë's pupose in including both characters?

Comparing Literary Works

5. (a) Identify three examples in which Dickens uses comic exaggeration to criticize Gradgrind and his fellows. (b) Explain how Brontë develops interest in Helen Burns, showing her first from a distance, then in conversation.
6. Use a chart like the one shown to compare these techniques.

Passage	Intended Effect on Reader	Intended Message	Enjoyment Value

(a) Which selection held your interest better? (b) Did either seem motivated solely by the writer's desire to convey a message?

Reading Strategy

Recognizing the Writer's Purpose

7. Choose an example of each of the following elements that help clarify the writer's purpose, explaining your choice: (a) the name of a character in *Hard Times*, (b) a character's statement or dialogue in *Jane Eyre*, (c) a description of a place in either work.

Extend Understanding

8. **World Events Connection:** Dickens hints at some elements of education that Gradgrind neglects. Do modern schools address these elements? Explain.

Quick Review

A **novel** is a long work of fiction containing a complex plot and a significant overall theme. Some novels include **social criticism,** which is direct or indirect commentary on problems in society.

To **recognize a writer's purpose,** look at details in a work and determine the writer's reason for including them.

 ***Take It to the Net***

www.phschool.com

Take the interactive self-test online to check your understanding of these selections.

Answers for p. 873

Review and Assess

1. **(a)** Vivid details include the description of the "plain, bare, monotonous vault of a schoolroom" and the sole ray of sun crossing the room. **(b)** The setting suggests that society has made education inhuman.
2. Dickens is critical of ideas of education that suppress imagination and enthusiasm in favor of acquiring facts.
3. **(a)** Jane is feisty and independent; Helen philosophically endures injustice. **(b)** The school does not ensure that students are happy or treated justly.
4. **(a)** Possible response: Jane's outrage would fuel social criticism; Helen's ethics make her reluctant to criticize others. **(b)** Possible response: Brontë might be suggesting that ethical considerations should balance outrage at society.
5. **(a)** Gradgrind refuses to call Sissy by name; the third gentleman does not notice that the class simply says what he wants to hear; he argues that flowered carpets are wrong because flowers do not belong on carpets. **(b)** Possible response: Brontë shows Helen Burns submitting to mistreatment in an unusual way as Jane watches from afar; later, she has Jane question Helen.
6. Possible response for *Hard Times:* Passage: Gradgrind calls Sissy "Girl 20"; Effect: Gradgrind's stubborn applications of theory makes him ridiculous; Message: His theories are foolish; Enjoyment Value: Very comic. **(a)** Possible response: Students may respond more readily to the comedy in Dickens than to the characterization in Brontë. **(b)** Possible response: Students may say that Dickens's exaggeration is largely motivated by his desire to drum his message home.
7. **(a)** Possible response: The name *M'Choakumchild* suggests that the instructor will "choke" rather than teach, implying that Dickens wishes to show the danger of his ideas. **(b)** Possible response: Brontë uses Helen's

continued

ENRICHMENT: Further Reading

Other Works by the Authors

Oliver Twist, Charles Dickens

Bleak House, Charles Dickens

Shirley, Charlotte Brontë

Other Works With the Theme of Institutions and Relationships

The Mill on the Floss, George Eliot

A Little Princess, Frances Hodges Burnett

Answers continued

ethical ideals to suggest an alternative to Jane's impetuousness and habit of forming grudges. **(c)** Possible response: Details about Lowood, such as the small amount of porridge, suggest Brontë's intent to criticize such schools.

8. Possible response: Modern schools encourage capacities suppressed by Gradgrind, such as creativity and debate.

EXTEND

Answers for p. 874

❶ Vocabulary Development

Word Analysis

1. A *monologue* is a speech by one speaker, either to him- or herself or to another, where the other's responses are omitted.
2. A *monorail* is a short-distance train that rides on a single rail.
3. A *monopoly* is a business interest controlled by one person or institution.
4. A *monofilament* is a single filament of synthetic fiber.
5. A *monotreme* is any egg-laying mammal of the order Monotremata, meaning "one-holed" organism.

Spelling Strategy

1. designer
2. foreign
3. campaign
4. maligned

Concept Development: Antonyms

1. c
2. b
3. a
4. b
5. b
6. a
7. c
8. c

❷ Grammar and Style

1. "Sissy is not a name," said Mr. Gradgrind.
2. "Girl number twenty unable to define a horse!" said Mr. Gradgrind, . . .
3. "Bitzer," said Thomas Gradgrind. "Your definition of a horse."
4. "Yes," she said, "I have just finished it."
5. "Well," I asked impatiently, "is not Mrs. Reed a hard-hearted, bad woman?"

Writing Application

Possible response: "But I don't see how you can be so good!" exclaimed Jane. "After all, Miss Scatcherd treats you with such unkindness."

"Jane," interrupted Helen, "I don't think that I am very good."

Integrate Language Skills

❶ Vocabulary Development Lesson

Word Analysis: Greek Prefix *mono-*

The Greek prefix *mono-* means "single" or "alone." It is used to form some words in common use as well as many scientific and technical words. Explain how the prefix *mono-* contributes to the meaning of each of the following words, using a dictionary if needed.

1. monologue
2. monorail
3. monopoly
4. monofilament
5. monotreme

Spelling Strategy

In words like *indignant*, the *g* and *n* each stand for a separate sound. Sometimes, however, *gn* stands for only the *n* sound, as in *sign*. In these cases, it usually follows the letters *ai*, *ei*, or *i*. In your notebook, correctly complete the spelling of these *gn* words.

1. des__gner
2. for__gn
3. camp__gn
4. mal__gned

Concept Development: Antonyms

Write the letter of the word that is opposite in meaning to the first word.

1. monotonous: (a) lengthy, (b) loud, (c) varied
2. obstinate: (a) still, (b) cooperative, (c) taciturn
3. adversary: (a) friend, (b) turncoat, (c) enemy
4. indignant: (a) worthy, (b) pleased, (c) angry
5. approbation: (a) freedom, (b) disapproval, (c) sin
6. obscure: (a) prominent, (b) sad, (c) realistic
7. comprised: (a) noted, (b) agreed, (c) excluded
8. sundry: (a) mixed, (b) tedious, (c) homogeneous

❷ Grammar and Style Lesson

Punctuation of Dialogue

To **punctuate dialogue** correctly, enclose in quotation marks the exact words said by the characters. Commas and periods always fall within the final quotation mark. Question marks and exclamation marks also fall within the quotation marks when they are part of the quotation. Otherwise, question marks and exclamation marks go outside the quotation marks.

Examples: "Sissy Jupe, give me the Facts!"

Did the gentleman say, "I will try you again"?

"Hardened girl!" exclaimed Miss Scatcherd, "nothing can correct you. . . ."

Practice Copy these passages, correctly punctuating the dialogue.

1. Sissy is not a name, said Mr. Gradgrind.
2. Girl number twenty unable to define a horse! said Mr. Gradgrind, . . .
3. Bitzer, said Thomas Gradgrind. Your definition of a horse.
4. Yes, she said, I have just finished it.
5. Well, I asked impatiently, is not Mrs. Reed a hard-hearted, bad woman?

Writing Application Write a brief dialogue between Jane and Helen. Be sure to punctuate each speaker's words correctly.

WG Prentice Hall Writing and Grammar Connection: Chapter 27, Section 4

TEACHING RESOURCES

The following resources can be used to enrich or extend the instruction for pp. 874–875.

Vocabulary

- **Selection Support:** Build Vocabulary, p. 187
- **Vocabulary and Spelling Practice Book** (Use this booklet for skills enrichment.)

Grammar

- **Selection Support:** Grammar and Style, p. 186
- **Writing and Grammar,** Diamond Level, p. 722
- **Daily Language Practice Transparencies**

Writing

- **Writing and Grammar,** Diamond Level, p. 850
- **Writing Models and Graphic Organizers on Transparencies,** pp. 57–72
- **Writing and Grammar iText CD-ROM**

❸ # Writing Lesson

Annotated Bibliography on Victorian Education

The excerpts from Dickens and Brontë present vivid pictures of education in the Victorian Age. Compile an annotated bibliography—a bibliography with descriptions and evaluations of sources—on the topic. Include both primary sources, or sources from the times, and secondary sources.

Prewriting Use both print materials and the Internet to develop your bibliography. Find primary sources—letters and journals by students and teachers—and secondary ones, or materials written by historians. Consult style guides, and select a style for your bibliography, such as the MLA style.

Drafting Prepare your bibliography, writing annotations that show why each source is unique and valuable. Follow your chosen style.

Model: Drafting Annotations for Primary Sources

McPhail, Ellie. Letter to her mother. 1888. Collection of Teacher's School, Anytown University, Anytown. Ellie's letter, describing an incident in which the class helped one girl get away with cheating, shows how in some cases students would go against their own basic values to protect one another.

The writer's annotation shows the unique insight provided by this source.

Revising Review your bibliography, using an appropriate style guide, to make sure you have correctly presented the information about each source.

WG *Prentice Hall Writing and Grammar Connection: Chapter 31, Section 2*

❹ # Extension Activities

Listening and Speaking In a **debate,** use the ideas of these selections to inspire a discussion of the basic values of today's educational system. Prepare arguments of the following kinds:

- Inductive—arguments that lead from representative examples to generalizations
- Deductive—arguments that apply principles to specific cases

Help teammates rehearse their arguments. Then, hold your debate before the class. **[Group Activity]**

Research and Technology Devise three research questions and use them to research and write a **biography of Charles Dickens's childhood.** Note parallels between events in his early life with events in his fiction. In your word-processed report, include a graphic timeline outlining important events in Dickens's early life.

Take It to the Net www.phschool.com

Go online for an additional research activity using the Internet.

ASSESSMENT RESOURCES

The following resources can be used to assess students' knowledge and skills.

Selection Assessment

- **Formal Assessment,** pp. 195–197
- **Open Book Test,** pp. 118–119
- **Got It! Assessment Videotapes,** Tape 4
- **Test Bank Software**

Writing Rubric

- **Performance Assess. and Portfolio Mgmt.,** p. 13

Lesson Support for p. 875

❸ Writing Lesson

- Review with students the Writing Lesson on p. 875 before they begin writing their annotated bibliography on Victorian education.
- Tell students that they should research the topic of education in the Victorian age and compile annotated bibliographies—bibliographies with descriptions of the sources they have found on the topic.
- Encourage students to keep careful notes on any sources they discover in their research.
- Remind students not to limit themselves to secondary sources, but to seek out letters, journals, diaries, and other primary materials where possible.
- Model the way in which a good research report uses sources with pp. 57–72 of **Writing Models and Graphic Organizers on Transparencies.**
- Use the Historical Investigations rubric on p. 13 of **Performance Assessment and Portfolio Management** to evaluate students' work.

❹ Listening and Speaking

- Review with students the instructions in the Listening and Speaking lesson, and then divide them into small groups.
- Have students discuss the state of today's educational system in their small groups. Then, assign each group to defend a "side" in the debate.
- Encourage students to support their positions with inductive and deductive arguments.
- Have student groups debate each other in front of the class.

CUSTOMIZE INSTRUCTION For Universal Access

To address different learning styles, use the activities suggested in the **Extension Activities** booklet, p. 42.

- For Verbal/Linguistic Learners, use Activity 5.
- For Verbal/Linguistic and Visual/Spatial Learners, use Activity 6.
- For Verbal/Linguistic and Bodily/Kinesthetic Learners, use Activity 7.

Lesson Objectives

1. To understand the characteristics of novels
2. To understand how a writer's choices with regard to setting, theme, and characters help to extend the meaning and relevance of the text

Connections

The novels of the nineteenth century gained popularity not only because of the skyrocketing literacy rate throughout the world but also because of their daring plot twists and uncommon themes dealing with the daily lives of very common people. This insatiable desire to read novels enabled exposure to the works of artists of other cultures. Tolstoy's *War and Peace* enthralled readers as it explored historical, political, and psychological issues. Have students read the excerpt and uncover some of these issues presented. Why might people of the nineteenth century and today be interested in these issues?

The Novel

- Explain to students that novels sometimes explore the concerns that define a national identity. Tolstoy used his words to create a picture of Russian life for all cultures to see.
- If possible, provide pictures and paintings representative of nineteenth-century Russian life. Have students make connections from the artwork to literary elements in the story excerpt. Have them concentrate on setting, character description, and theme. Ask them to compare their original perceptions to the artwork and to note the similarities and differences.
- Point out to students that the novel's popularity spread well beyond the cultural borders and into France and the United States. Ask students to speculate what aspects of Tolstoy's novel weave a common thread through all of these cultures.

CONNECTIONS
Literature Around the World
The Novel

Charles Dickens's *Hard Times* and Charlotte Brontë's *Jane Eyre* were triumphs in their own day. Their success was an example of the huge popularity of the novel during the nineteenth century. A novel is a long work of fiction with a relatively complicated plot, many major and minor characters, a significant theme, and various settings. Nineteenth-century novelists explored the full scope of human experience, from love to war, from riches to poverty. This approach, along with the growing literacy rate, guaranteed the popularity of the form. The novel was an international success, thriving in France, the United States, and Russia as well as England.

The Russian Novel

The Russian novelist Leo Tolstoy was considered the greatest of the nineteenth-century Russian writers. In 1869, he published *War and Peace,* his masterful historical novel about Napoleon's 1812 invasion of Russia. In this novel, Tolstoy weaves together numerous plots and settings with more than 500 characters. The novel was immediately recognized as a masterpiece for its graphic depiction of war, its insights into Russian life, and its exploration of the meaning of existence.

In the following excerpt from *War and Peace,* Tolstoy defends Mikhail Kutuzov, a military general, when his tactics are criticized. Tolstoy presents the general as noble and true to himself and his people—a contrast with the glory-hungry Napolean, leader of Russia's enemy, France. As you read, note the ways in which Tolstoy brings Kutuzov to life as a character.

The Return of the Troops from the Crimera, Boulevard des Italiens, in front of the Hanover Pavillon, December, 1855. c. 19th century / Emmanuel Masses / Musée Carnavalet, Paris, France, Roger-Viollet Paris

ENRICHMENT: Literary Connection

Literary Criticism

Share with students the following comments by literary critic Paul Debreczeny on Tolstoy's outlook toward Napoleon and Kutuzov:

> Tolstoy claims that Napoleon, genius, strategy, tactics, and all, had less to do with the outcome of the military confrontation than his simplest soldier. This much is consistent enough with Tolstoy's general theory; but the question arises: How did it happen that Kutuzov managed to influence the course of events? Tolstoy's answer is that Kutuzov "with his whole Russian being" (rather than with his mere intellect) perceived the inevitable drifting of events in a particular direction, and instead of trying to influence the course of history, he harnessed it. But is an ability to harness history not a mark of genius? . . . It is obvious that Tolstoy longed to glorify Kutuzov and condemn Napoleon.

from WAR AND *Peace*

LEO TOLSTOY

CHAPTER V

In 1812 and 1813[1] Kutuzov[2] was openly accused of blunders. The Tsar[3] was dissatisfied with him. And in a recent history inspired by promptings from the highest quarters, Kutuzov is spoken of as a designing, intriguing schemer, who was panic-stricken at the name of Napoleon, and guilty through his blunders at Krasnoe and Berezina of robbing the Russian army of the glory of complete victory over the French. Such is the lot of men not recognized by Russian intelligence as "great men," *grands hommes;* such is the destiny of those rare and always solitary men who divining the will of Providence submit their personal will to it. The hatred and contempt of the crowd is the punishment of such men for their comprehension of higher laws.

Strange and terrible to say, Napoleon, the most insignificant tool of history, who never even in exile displayed one trait of human dignity, is the subject of the admiration and enthusiasm of the Russian historians; in their eyes he is a *grand homme.*

Kutuzov, the man who from the beginning to the end of his command in 1812, from Borodino to Vilna, was

1. **In 1812 and 1813** In June 1812, Napoleon and his troops invaded Russia. Their retreat from Russia began in October 1812.
2. **Kutuzov** Mikhail Illarionovich Kutuzov (1745–1813); commander in chief of all Russian forces during Napoleon's invasion.
3. **Tsar** Czar Alexander I, emperor of Russia, 1801–1825.

Reading Check

How do the majority of Russians view Kutuzov?

Background

War and Peace

One of the main themes of *War and Peace* is "There is no greatness where there is no simplicity, goodness, and truth." For Tolstoy, the man who led the Russian forces during Napoleon's invasion of Russia, Kutuzov, embodies those qualities. In praising Kutuzov, Tolstoy criticizes Russian society, which Tolstoy feels is too swayed by popular opinion to understand "higher laws" or to appreciate a true hero.

The Novel

- Remind students that the popular novels of the nineteenth century made social problems a subject of literature.
- Ask students the following question: What aspect of society is Tolstoy criticizing in this passage? Answer: Tolstoy deplores the fact that mass opinion cannot respect or take into account the superior vision of the truly exceptional individual.

Reading Check

Answer: The Russians see Kutuzov as an embarrassment to their culture and to their country. Instead they view Napoleon as a grand hero with a magnificent vision that their own countryman is lacking.

CUSTOMIZE INSTRUCTION FOR UNIVERSAL ACCESS

For Less Proficient Readers	For English Learners	For Advanced Readers
Go over the names of people and places before students begin reading. Stress that they should not "skip over" names as they read. If students still find the Russian names too difficult to manage, have them prepare a glossary that gives the name in the excerpt, such as "Kutuzov," and a simpler substitute, such as "General K."	Have students look over the excerpt and make a list of the words they do not know. Then, help students define or find simpler substitutes for the unfamiliar words. Students can then use this annotated list while reading the excerpt.	Have students make a list of the places mentioned in the story. Use the names: Krasnoe, Berezina, Borodino, Vilna, Moscow, Tarutino, Vyazma, and Austerlitz. Have students create a map to detail these locations. Ask students to share this map with the class.

Thematic Connection

Answer: Tolstoy sees Kutuzov as a man who did his duty for his country, while historians would paint him as a failure. His "lack of vision" in society's eyes pales in comparison to that of Napoleon. But Tolstoy regards Napoleon as a boastful, unworthy man.

▶Critical Viewing

Answer: Napoleon's armies were operating at a great distance from France and its allied nations. The deeper into Russia they went, the more difficult their supply problem became.

never in one word or deed false to himself, presents an example exceptional in history of self-sacrifice and recognition in the present of the relative value of events in the future. Kutuzov is conceived of by historians as a nondescript, pitiful sort of creature, and whenever they speak of him in the year 1812, they seem a little ashamed of him.

And yet it is difficult to conceive of an historical character whose energy could be more invariably directed to the same unchanging aim. It is difficult to imagine an aim more noble and more in harmony with the will of a whole people. Still more difficult would it be to find an example in history where the aim of any historical personage has been so completely attained as the aim towards which all Kutuzov's efforts were devoted in 1812.

Kutuzov never talked of "forty centuries looking down from the Pyramids," of the sacrifices he was making for the fatherland, of what he meant to do or had done.[4] He did not as a rule talk about himself, played no sort of part, always seemed the plainest and most ordinary man, and said the plainest and most ordinary things. He wrote letters to his daughters and to Madame de Staël,[5] read novels, liked the company of pretty women, made jokes with the generals, the officers, and the soldiers, and never contradicted the people, who tried to prove anything to him. When Count Rastoptchin galloped up to him at Yautsky bridge, and reproached him personally with being responsible for the loss of Moscow, and said: "Didn't you promise not to abandon Moscow without a battle?" Kutuzov answered: "And I am not abandoning Moscow without a battle," although Moscow was in fact already abandoned. When Araktcheev came to him from the Tsar to say that Yermolov was to be appointed to the command of the artillery, Kutuzov said: "Yes, I was just saying so myself," though he had said just the opposite a moment before. What had he, the one man who grasped at the time all the vast issues of events, to do in the midst of that dull-witted crowd? What did he care whether Count

Thematic Connection
What social criticism is Tolstoy offering here?

▼ Critical Viewing
Using the map, determine why Napoleon's armies might have had trouble getting supplies when they invaded Russia. **[Hypothesize]**

Napoleon's Invasion of Russia, 1812

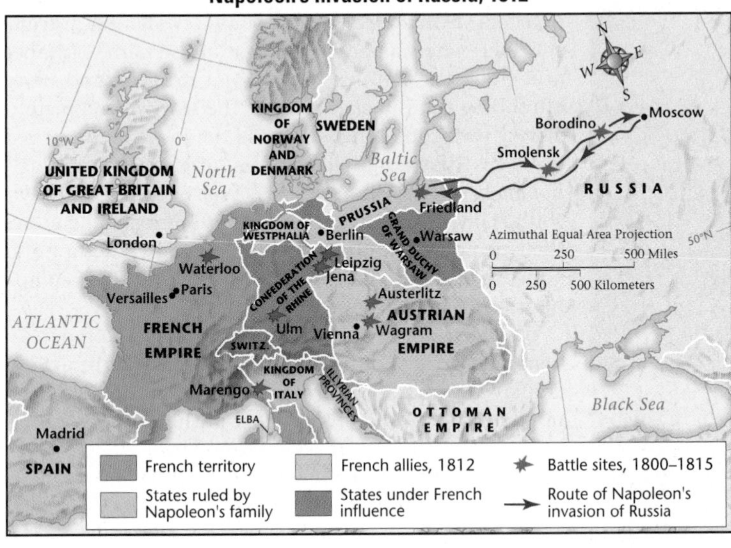

4. **"forty centuries . . ." . . . had done** references to Napoleon's reflections on his own place in history.
5. **Madame de Staël** Anne-Louise-Germaine de Staël (1766–1817) French-Swiss woman of letters; regarded as personal enemy of Napoleon and banished from Paris.

ENRICHMENT: History Connection

The Napoleonic Wars

In 1792, Europe responded to the new revolutionary government of France by provoking war. The French officer Louis Napoleon Bonaparte distinguished himself in the ensuing conflict. Returning to France as a hero from his conquest of Egypt in 1799, Napoleon took over the government as First Consul. In 1804, he was elected emperor. After defeating Britain and Austria, Napoleon set about expanding French territory in Europe and the New World.

When Russia challenged his ban on British trade, Napoleon invaded in 1812. Though the Russians withdrew farther and farther, abandoning Moscow when he arrived there, Napoleon was finally forced to retreat because of his problem supplying his troops: The distances involved were too great. Napoleon lost nearly his entire army on the campaign and the long retreat. Starvation and the bitter cold were their main enemies. Of 600,000 troops, 500,000 perished, deserted, or were captured. Three years later, the other European powers finally defeated Napoleon at Waterloo in 1815.

Rastoptchin put down the disasters of the capital to him or to himself? Still less could he be concerned by the question which man was appointed to the command of the artillery.

This old man, who through experience of life had reached the conviction that the thoughts and words that serve as its expression are never the motive force of men, frequently uttered words, which were quite meaningless—the first words that occurred to his mind.

But heedless as he was of his words, he never once throughout all his career uttered a single word which was inconsistent with the sole aim for the attainment of which he was working all through the war. With obvious unwillingness, with bitter conviction that he would not be understood, he more than once, under the most difficult circumstances, gave expression to his real thought. His first differed from all about him after the battle of Borodino,[6] which he alone persisted in calling a victory, and this view he continued to assert verbally and in reports and to his dying day. He alone said that *the loss of Moscow is not the loss of Russia.* In answer to the overtures for peace, his reply to Lauriston was: *There can be no peace, for such is the people's will.* He alone during the retreat of the French said that *all our maneuvers are unnecessary; that everything is being done of itself better than we could desire; that we must give the enemy a "golden bridge"; that the battles of Tarutino, of Vyazma, and of Krasnoe, were none of them necessary; that we must keep some men to reach the frontier with; that he wouldn't give one Russian for ten Frenchmen.* And he, this intriguing courtier, as we are told, who lied to Araktcheev to propitiate[7] the Tsar, he alone dared to face the Tsar's displeasure by telling him at Vilna that *to carry the war beyond the frontier would be mischievous and useless.*

But words alone would be no proof that he grasped the significance of events at the time. His actions—all without the slightest deviation—

Portrait of Kutuzov, Prince of Smolensk, George Dawe, Hermitage, St. Petersburg, Russia

▲ Critical Viewing
Compare and contrast this rendering of Kutuzov with the description of him in the story.
[Compare and Contrast]

Reading Check
According to Tolstoy, how did Kutuzov treat words?

6. **battle of Borodino** Kutuzov was pressured into fighting this battle against his better judgment. Although the outcome was inconclusive, Kutuzov lost half his troops.
7. **propitiate** (prō pish´ ē āt´) *v.* to cause to become favorably inclined.

Background

Art

Portrait of Kutuzov, Prince of Smolensk by George Dawe

George Dawe (1781–1829), born in England, lived for years at the Russian imperial court in St. Petersburg, where he painted portraits of many prominent men, including Tsar Alexander I. This portrait shows General Kutuzov in a traditional formal pose.

Have students list and discuss the elements of this portrait that have been included because they are traditional, as well as those that may reveal something of the individual being portrayed. Invite them to explain ways in which the portrait resembles or differs from how they thought Kutuzov would look.
Answers: Students might include the following as traditional: the medals, the hand holding the cape, the formal stance, the pointing hand, the stylized setting with weapons in the foreground. Students may see self-confidence in the stance and expression. The pointing hand and Kutuzov's being placed on a high elevation might be taken as signs of Kutuzov's vision and grasp of the broad strategic picture.

▶ Critical Viewing

Answer: Students may say that Kutuzov appears confident and capable in this portrait, which is consistent with the story. The portrait, however, does not show his conflict with those who valued appearance over substance or his determination to be true to his ideals.

Reading Check

Answer: Kutuzov was sometimes "heedless" in his use of words, saying the first thing that came to mind.

Answers

Connecting Literature Around the World

1. Brontë tends to use indirect characterization, Dickens uses a mixture of indirect and direct characterization, and Tolstoy tends to use direct characterization. Some students may prefer Tolstoy because he makes it clear what the reader should think of Kutuzov. Other students may prefer Brontë, because requiring readers to draw their own conclusions about the characters is more meaningful.
2. Students should explain which of the selections most intrigued them and why (they might mention characters, setting, and style). They may also mention other criteria that they use to evaluate a novel. These criteria may include the following: author's reputation; experience with other works by the author; and recommendations from friends, teachers, or book reviewers.

were directed toward the one threefold aim: first, to concentrate all his forces to strike a blow at the French; secondly, to defeat them; and thirdly, to drive them out of Russia, alleviating as far as was possible the sufferings of the people and the soldiers in doing so.

He, the lingerer Kutuzov, whose motto was always "Time and Patience," the sworn opponent of precipitate action, he fought the battle of Borodino, and made all his preparations for it with unwonted solemnity. Before the battle of Austerlitz he foretold that it would be lost, but at Borodino, in spite of the conviction of the generals that the battle was a defeat, in spite of the fact, unprecedented in history, of his army being forced to retreat after the victory, he alone declared in opposition to all that it was a victory, and persisted in that opinion to his dying day. He was alone during the whole latter part of the campaign in insisting that there was no need of fighting now, that it was a mistake to cross the Russian frontier and to begin a new war. It is easy enough now that all the events with their consequences lie before us to grasp their significance, if only we refrain from attributing to the multitude the aims that only existed in the brains of some dozen or so of men.

But how came that old man, alone in opposition to the opinion of all, to gauge so truly the importance of events from the national standard, so that he never once was false to the best interests of his country?

The source of this extraordinary intuition into the significance of contemporary events lay in the purity and fervor of patriotic feeling in his heart.

It was their recognition of this feeling in him that led the people in such a strange manner to pick him out, an old man out of favor, as the chosen leader of the national war, against the will of the Tsar. And this feeling alone it was to which he owed his exalted position, and there he exerted all his powers as commander-in-chief not to kill and maim men, but to save them and have mercy on them.

This simple, modest, and therefore truly great figure, could not be cast into the false mold of the European hero, the supposed leader of men, that history has invented.

To the flunky no man can be great, because the flunky has his own flunky conception of greatness.

Leo Tolstoy

(1828–1910)

Leo Tolstoy was a nineteenth-century Russian writer whose shattering spiritual crisis late in life led him to radical religious and political beliefs. After briefly attending law school, Tolstoy joined the army in 1851. While serving as an artillery officer, Tolstoy spent most of his free time writing, and by 1852 Tolstoy had published his first novel, *A History of My Childhood*. His novels *War and Peace* (1869) and *Anna Karenina* (1876), a portrait of the lives of the Russian upper classes, are among the most popular of his works. After his crisis of faith, he devoted himself to moral tales and pamphlets. His last novel, finished when he was 71, is entitled *Resurrection*.

Connecting Literature Around the World

1. Compare and contrast the methods by which Dickens, Brontë, and Tolstoy develop their main characters. Which author's characterization do you think is the most effective? Explain.
2. Which of the three novels represented in this section would you prefer to read? Explain.

PART 3

The Empire and Its Discontents

Miniature photographic portraits commemorating the 1897 Jubilee Victoria: (adult and child) Alexandra and George V

Selection Planning Guide

The selections in this section reveal the opposing forces of the Victorian Era. "Progress in Personal Comfort" shows the joyful face of progress. The poems "Dover Beach," "Recessional," "The Widow at Windsor," and the journalistic essay "Condition of Ireland" reveal the uncertainty and social problems that existed at the height of the British Empire. The speech "Opening Statement for the Inaugural Session of the Forum for Peace and Reconciliation" touches on one troubling legacy of the Empire—a divided Ireland.

Background

Art

Miniature Photographic Portraits, 1897

These photographic miniatures commemorate the sixtieth anniversary of Queen Victoria's reign. The portraits on the top are of Queen Victoria at the age of 78 (to left) and as a child (top right). Victoria became queen in 1837, at the age of eighteen, and ruled for more than sixty-three years. The portrait at the bottom right is Victoria's grandson, George Frederick, who became King George V in 1910. He is the grandfather of Queen Elizabeth II. The remaining portrait is of Princess Alexandra. A Danish princess, Alexandra married Victoria's oldest son, Albert Edward, who became King Edward VII when Victoria died in 1901.

Ask students the following questions:

1. What attitude toward monarchs do these photographs suggest?
   Possible response: They suggest great respect. The framing ribbons and flowers suggest reverence.
2. How do you think this attitude might have contributed to progress and the building of the Empire?
   Possible response: The reverence for royalty was an extension of people's feelings for their country. Much was accomplished because of an optimistic faith in the country and its rulers.

CUSTOMIZE INSTRUCTION FOR UNIVERSAL ACCESS

When assigning the selections in this part, keep in mind these factors:

"Dover Beach"
- Evocative lyric poem
- Less proficient readers may need guidance.

"Recessional"
- Historical context will make the poem's meaning more apparent.

"The Widow at Windsor"
- Students may have difficulty with the poem's Cockney dialect.

"Condition of Ireland"
- Vocabulary and sentence structure may prove daunting to less proficient readers.

"Progress in Personal Comfort"
- Entertaining look at technological advances

Dover Beach ✦ Recessional ✦ The Widow at Windsor

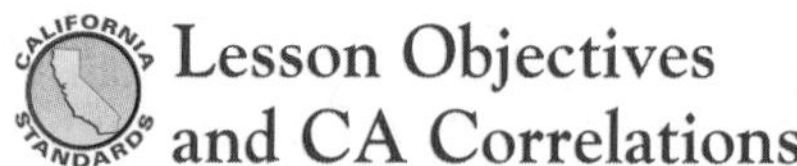

Lesson Objectives and CA Correlations

1. **To analyze and respond to literary elements**
   - Literary Analysis: Mood as a Key to Theme **R 3.2**
   - Comparing Literary Works **R 3.7**
2. **To read, comprehend, analyze, and critique a poem**
   - Reading Strategy: Drawing Conclusions
   - Reading Check Questions
   - Review and Assess Questions
   - Assessment Practice (ATE)
3. **To develop word analysis skills, fluency, and systematic vocabulary**
   - Vocabulary Development Lesson: Latin Root *-domi-* **R 1.1, 1.2**
4. **To understand and apply written and oral language conventions**
   - Spelling Strategy **LC 1.2**
   - Grammar and Style Lesson: Present Tense **LC 1.1**
5. **To understand and apply appropriate writing and research strategies**
   - Writing Lesson: Response to Criticism **W 2.2**
   - Extension Activity: Film Review **LS 1.1**
6. **To understand and apply listening and speaking strategies**
   - Extension Activity: Oral Interpretation **LS 1.10**

STEP-BY-STEP TEACHING GUIDE	PACING GUIDE
PRETEACH	
Motivate Students and Provide Background	
Use the Motivation activity (ATE p. 882)	5 min.
Read and discuss author and background features (SE/ATE pp. 882, 887) [A]	5 min.
Introduce the Concepts	
Introduce the Literary Analysis and Reading Strategy (SE/ATE p. 883) [A]	15 min.
Pronounce the vocabulary words and read their definitions (SE p. 883)	5 min.
TEACH	
Monitor Comprehension	
Informally monitor comprehension by circulating while students read independently or in groups [A]	15 min.
Monitor students' comprehension with the Reading Check notes (SE/ATE p. 889)	as students read
Develop vocabulary with Vocabulary notes (SE pp. 884, 885, 887; ATE p. 887)	as students read
Develop Understanding	
Develop students' understanding of mood as a key to theme with the Literary Analysis annotations (SE pp. 885, 890; ATE pp. 884, 885, 889, 890) [A]	5 min.
Develop students' ability to draw conclusions with the Reading Strategy annotations (SE/ATE p. 888)	5 min.
ASSESS	
Assess Mastery	
Assess students' mastery of the Reading Strategy and Literary Analysis concepts by having them answer the Review and Assess questions (SE/ATE p. 891)	15 min.
Use one or more of the print and media Assessment Resources (ATE p. 893) [A]	up to 45 min.
EXTEND	
Apply Understanding	
Have students complete the Vocabulary Development Lesson and the Grammar and Style Lesson (SE p. 892) [A]	20 min.
Apply students' knowledge of statistics as a form of support using the Writing Lesson (SE/ATE p. 893) [A]	45 min.
Apply students' understanding using one or more of the Extension Activities (SE p. 893)	20–90 min.

ACCELERATED INSTRUCTION:
Use the strategies and activities identified with an [A].

UNIVERSAL ACCESS
● = Below-Level Students
▲ = On-Level Students
■ = Above-Level Students

Time and Resource Manager

Reading Level: Average, Average, Challenging
Average Number of Instructional Days: 4

RESOURCES		
PRINT	**TRANSPARENCIES**	**TECHNOLOGY**
• **Beyond Literature,** Cross-Curricular Connection: Science, p. 41 ▲ ■		• **Interest Grabber Video,** Tape 5 ● ▲ ■
• **Selection Support Workbook:** ● ▲ ■ Literary Analysis, p. 194 Reading Strategy, p. 193 Build Vocabulary, p. 191	• **Literary Analysis and Reading Transparencies,** pp. 81 and 82 ● ▲ ■	
		• **Listening to Literature** ● ▲ ■ Audiocassettes, Sides 20 and 21 Audio CDs, CD 12
• **Literary Analysis for Enrichment** ■		
• **Formal Assessment:** Selection Test, pp. 203–205 ● ▲ ■ • **Open Book Test,** pp. 120–122 ● ▲ ■ • **Performance Assessment and Portfolio Management,** pp. 25 and 92 ● ▲ ■ • PRENTICE HALL ASSESSMENT SYSTEM ● ▲ ■	• PRENTICE HALL ASSESSMENT SYSTEM ● ▲ ■ Skills Practice Answers and Explanations on Transparencies ● ▲ ■	• **Test Bank Software** ● ▲ ■ • **Got It! Assessment Videotapes,** Tape 4 ● ▲
• **Selection Support Workbook:** ● ▲ ■ Grammar and Style, p. 192 • **Writing and Grammar,** Diamond Level ● ▲ ■ • **Extension Activities,** p. 41 ● ▲ ■	• **Daily Language Practice Transparencies** ● ▲ • **Writing Models and Graphic Organizers on Transparencies,** pp. 45–56 ● ▲ ■	• **Writing and Grammar iText CD-ROM** ● ▲ ■ ***Take It to the Net*** www.phschool.com

BLOCK SCHEDULING: Use one 90-minute class period to preteach the selections and have students read them. Use a second 90-minute class period to assess students' mastery of skills and have them complete one of the Extension Activities.

PRETEACH

Step-by-Step Teaching Guide for pp. 882–883

Motivation

Write on the chalkboard: "Our country, right or wrong." Have students discuss the meaning of the phrase. Ask students if they believe this is an appropriate attitude. Encourage students to think about the phrase as they read the poems that follow and to consider whether Matthew Arnold and Rudyard Kipling would agree or disagree with the statement.

Interest Grabber Video

As an alternative, play "'Dover Beach': White Cliffs of Dover" on Tape 5 to engage student interest.

❶ Background

More About the Authors

Matthew Arnold

Although "Dover Beach" seems to throw in the towel in the fight to find meaning in life, Matthew Arnold is famous for his faith in what he called culture. In *Culture and Anarchy* (1869), he defines culture as "the study of perfection," or the effort to critically assess and expand the spirit of a society.

Arnold abandoned poetry in favor of prose in midlife. Still pursuing questions of faith, he wrote extensively on religion toward the end of his life.

Rudyard Kipling

Traces of Kipling's life experiences can be found throughout his work. When his parents placed him with relatives back home in England, the young Kipling struggled with lack of affection and dramatically deteriorating eyesight. He documents such an experience in his novel *The Light That Failed.* Even the experiences of Mowgli in *The Jungle Books* reflect Kipling's life. A British citizen born in India, middle class but a friend of lower-class soldiers, Kipling crossed into many other worlds and learned to speak many tongues, just as Mowgli learns the language of the beasts.

Prepare to Read

❶ Dover Beach ◆ Recessional ◆ The Widow at Windsor

Matthew Arnold (1822–1888)

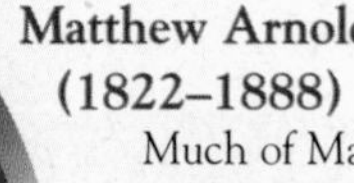

Much of Matthew Arnold's poetry concerns a theme as relevant today as it was in the nineteenth century: the isolation of individuals from one another and from society. In fact, in the 1960s, the American novelist Norman Mailer used a modified quotation from Arnold's poem "Dover Beach" for the title of his book about a Vietnam War protest, *Armies of the Night.*

A Social Conscience While attending Oxford University, Arnold developed the social conscience that was to guide his career as a public servant, poet, and literary critic. In 1851, he became Inspector of Schools, and in performing this job he did much to improve education throughout Great Britain. All the while, he remained a poet at heart, although his first two collections, published in 1849 and 1852, met with little success.

Literary Achievement Arnold's literary fortunes changed in 1853 when he published *Poems*, with its long preface that established him as a major critic. *New Poems*, published in 1867, contained Arnold's celebrated "Dover Beach."

A Return to Culture After completing this collection, Arnold believed that he had said everything he could in poetry. From that point on he wrote prose, such as the social criticism of the essays in *Culture and Anarchy* (1869). In this book, he attacks Victorian complacency and materialism, arguing that culture should open our minds to what is true and valuable. Arnold's idea of culture still influences critics today.

Rudyard Kipling (1865–1936)

Rudyard Kipling's works are known for their celebration of the British Empire, yet they also warn of the costs of world dominion. While praising the benefits of imperialism, he emphasizes the responsibility of the British to bring their "civilized" ways to other parts of the world.

Early Success Kipling was born to British parents in India, one of Britain's largest colonies. At the age of six, he was placed by his parents in a foster home in England, and later, at a chaotic boarding school. One critic speculates that the theme of self-preservation in Kipling's work was inspired by experiences at the boarding school that tested his courage. Kipling would later immortalize his school days in a collection of stories called *Stalky and Co.* (1899). In 1882, Kipling returned to India to work as a journalist. During the next seven years, he published a number of witty poems and stories, and by the time he returned to England in 1889, he was a celebrity.

Kipling's Achievements Kipling is known as a Victorian author because he produced his best work before the death of Queen Victoria in 1901. In its great variety, that work includes poetry, short stories, and novels. Some of his books have become children's classics, such as *The Jungle Books* (1894, 1895), *Captains Courageous* (1897), and *Kim* (1901).

For years, Kipling was the most popular English poet, and in 1907 he became the first English writer to receive the Nobel Prize for Literature.

TEACHING RESOURCES

The following resources can be used to enrich or extend the instruction for pp. 882–883.

Motivation

Interest Grabber Video, Tape 5 ▪

Background

Beyond Literature, p. 41

Take It to the Net

Visit www.phschool.com for background and hotlinks for the selections.

Literary Analysis

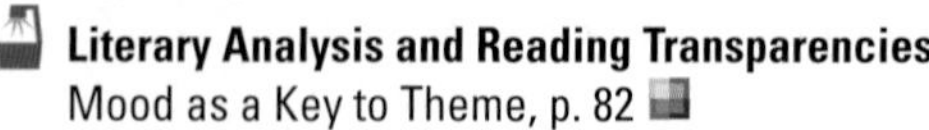

Literary Analysis and Reading Transparencies, Mood as a Key to Theme, p. 82 ▪

Reading

Selection Support: Reading Strategy, p. 193; Build Vocabulary, p. 191

Literary Analysis and Reading Transparencies, Drawing Conclusions, p. 81 ▪

▪ **BLOCK SCHEDULING:** Resources marked with this symbol provide varied instruction during 90-minute blocks.

Preview

Connecting to the Literature

Some Victorians proclaimed that the British Empire and the Victorian Era were perfect. Matthew Arnold's "Dover Beach" and Rudyard Kipling's "Recessional" both show the truth behind this boasting assertion.

❷ Literary Analysis

Mood as a Key to Theme

Poems contain emotional thoughts and thoughtful emotions. With thought and emotion so closely linked, the **mood,** or feeling, that a poem calls up is bound to be related to its central idea, or **theme**. Read poetry with your feelings—responding to emotionally charged words and images—and you will find your way to its ideas.

In "Dover Beach," for example, the crash of waves brings "The eternal note of sadness in." This mood of sadness leads you to the theme of the poem, which concerns a world with "neither joy, nor love, nor light."

Comparing Literary Works

The moods in these poems relate to a characteristic dilemma of the Victorian Period. The era was marked by increasing scientific progress, material prosperity, and British domination of the globe, yet each of these successes brought with it fresh anxieties:

- Scientific progress brought a greater questioning of religious faith.
- Material prosperity for some brought greater poverty for others.
- Expansion of the Empire brought heavy responsibilities.

Compare the ways in which these poems present and address such issues.

❸ Reading Strategy

Drawing Conclusions

By **drawing conclusions** about what you read—making generalizations based on evidence—you can link elements that seem unrelated. In "The Widow at Windsor," for example, it may be unclear at first why a "widow" has a "gold crown" and "ships on the foam." However, the later reference to "Missis Victorier's sons" leads to the conclusion that the widow is Queen Victoria. Use a graphic organizer like this one to draw further conclusions about the poems.

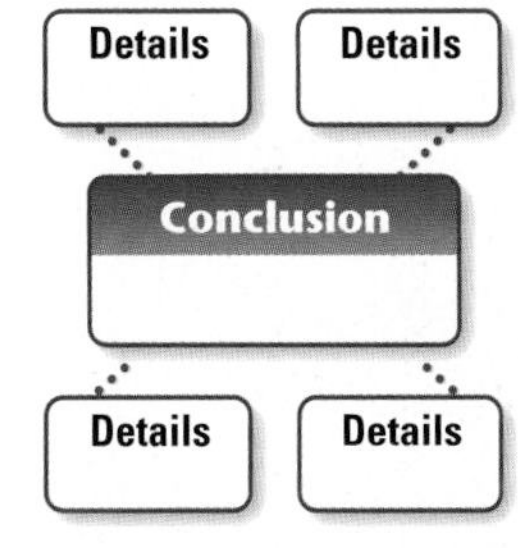

Vocabulary Development

tranquil (traŋ´ kwil) *adj.* calm; serene; peaceful (p. 884)

cadence (kād´ əns) *n.* measured movement (p. 884)

turbid (tur´ bid) *adj.* muddy or cloudy; stirred up and confused (p. 885)

dominion (də min´ yən) *n.* rule; control (p. 887)

contrite (kən trīt´) *adj.* willing to repent or atone (p. 887)

CUSTOMIZE INSTRUCTION FOR UNIVERSAL ACCESS

For Less Proficient Readers	For English Learners	For Advanced Readers
Have students follow along in their texts as they listen to the poems on the **Listening to Literature Audiocassettes.** Then, have students work in pairs, taking turns reading each poem aloud and taking notes on the feelings each poem evokes. Finally, students should compare their notes.	Find pictures to help students understand words that communicate appearance in "Dover Beach," such as *gleam, glimmer, vast,* and *calm.*	After students have read each poem, have them reread and write down the mood and rhyme scheme of each. Have them determine how the rhyme affects both the mood and the basic meaning of the poem.

❷ Literary Analysis

Mood as a Key to Theme

- Tell students that in these readings they will be focusing on the relationship of mood and theme.
- Explain that poems contain emotional thoughts and thoughtful emotions. The mood of the poem is the general feeling or set of feelings created by the images and associations they call up, as well as by the poet's word choices, rhythms, and the speaker's attitude. Tell students that by responding to emotionally charged words and images as they read, they will find their way to the poem's ideas.
- For example, in "Dover Beach" the mood of sadness will lead students to the poem's theme: a culture's loss of faith.
- Explain that the moods in these poems relate to a characteristic dilemma of the Victorian Period, when scientific progress, material prosperity, and British domination of the globe each brought anxieties as well as comforts.

❸ Reading Strategy

Drawing Conclusions

- Explain to students that by drawing conclusions—making generalizations from evidence—they can link elements that seem unrelated.
- Drawing conclusions is essential to understanding a poet's meaning, especially when the speaker of the poem is a character who may not explain relevant background. For example, the soldier-speaker in "The Widow at Windsor" does not explain whom he means by the "widow." However, the later reference to "Missis Victorier's sons" shows that the widow is Queen Victoria.
- Encourage students to record details in a graphic organizer like the one shown as they read to help them draw conclusions.

Vocabulary Development

- Pronounce each vocabulary word for students, and read the definitions as a class. Have students identify any words with which they are already familiar.

E-Teach

Visit E-Teach at www.phschool.com for teachers' essays on how to teach, with questions and answers.

TEACH

Step-by-Step Teaching Guide for pp. 884–890

CUSTOMIZE INSTRUCTION For Verbal/Linguistic Learners

Propose that students prepare an oral interpretation of a poem. Explain that an oral interpretation is an oral reading of a work of literature in which the reader conveys his or her understanding of the work through the way he or she speaks the words. In this activity, students will convey the tone of "Dover Beach." To be effective, the reader must know the work well, both on a literal and on an emotional level.

1 About the Selection

Looking out a window from the white chalk cliffs of Dover, the speaker describes a moonlit sea, which he takes as an image of the loss of certainty, faith, and peace in the world.

2 Critical Thinking

Interpret

- Point out that the speaker states that "the cliffs of England stand, / Glimmering and vast."
- Ask students with what they associate the word "cliffs."
  Answer: Students may associate the word *cliffs* with something tall, immovable, and dangerous.

3 Literary Analysis

Mood as a Key to Theme

- Have students read lines 9–11. Then, point out that imagery helps establish mood.
- Ask students if the mood in lines 9–11 seems positive or negative. Have them explain their answers.
  Possible response: Students may respond that the mood seems negative because the words "grating roar" evoke an unpleasant sound and the words "draw back and fling" evoke rejection.

4 ▶Critical Viewing

Answer: Yes, the photograph captures the "eternal note of sadness." The scene is deserted, the sea is dark, and the cliffs look black. The sun is setting, which implies an ending and adds to the sadness.

1 Dover Beach

Matthew Arnold

The sea is calm tonight.
The tide is full, the moon lies fair
Upon the straits;[1] on the French coast the light
2 Gleams and is gone; the cliffs of England stand,
Glimmering and vast, out in the tranquil bay.
Come to the window, sweet is the night air!

Only, from the long line of spray
Where the sea meets the moon-blanched land,
3 Listen! you hear the grating roar
Of pebbles which the waves draw back, and fling,
At their return, up the high strand,[2]
Begin, and cease, and then again begin,
With tremulous cadence slow, and bring
The eternal note of sadness in.

1. **straits** Straits of Dover, between England and France.
2. **strand** shore.

tranquil (traŋ′ kwəl) *adj.* calm; serene; peaceful

cadence (kād′ əns) *n.* measured movement

4 ▼**Critical Viewing** Does this photograph capture the "eternal note of sadness" Arnold describes? Explain. **[Support]**

TEACHING RESOURCES

The following resources can be used to enrich or extend the instruction for pp. 884–890.

Literary Analysis

Selection Support: Literary Analysis, p. 194 ■

Reading

Listening to Literature Audiocassettes, Sides 20 and 21 ■

Listening to Literature Audio CDs, CD 12 ■

■ **BLOCK SCHEDULING:** Resources marked with this symbol provide varied instruction during 90-minute blocks.

Sophocles[3] long ago
Heard it on the Aegaean,[4] and it brought
Into his mind the turbid ebb and flow
Of human misery; we
Find also in the sound a thought,
Hearing it by this distant northern sea.

5 The Sea of Faith
Was once, too, at the full, and round earth's shore
Lay like the folds of a bright girdle furled.
But now I only hear
Its melancholy, long, withdrawing roar,
Retreating, to the breath
Of the night wind, down the vast edges drear
And naked shingles[5] of the world.

6 Ah, love, let us be true
To one another! for the world, which seems
To lie before us like a land of dreams,
So various, so beautiful, so new,
Hath really neither joy, nor love, nor light,
Nor certitude, nor peace, nor help for pain;
And we are here as on a darkling[6] plain
Swept with confused alarms of struggle and flight,
Where ignorant armies clash by night.

turbid (tur´ bid) *adj.* muddy or cloudy; stirred up and confused

Literary Analysis
Mood as a Key to Theme How do the feelings that the final stanza evokes relate to its message in lines 29–30?

3. **Sophocles** (säf´ ə klēz´) Greek tragic dramatist (496?–406 B.C.).
4. **Aegean** (ē jē´ ən) arm of the Mediterranean Sea between Greece and Turkey.
5. **shingles** *n.* beaches covered with large, coarse, waterworn gravel.
6. **darkling** *adj.* in the dark.

Review and Assess

Thinking About the Selection

1. **(a) Recall:** Where are the speaker and his "love," and what do they hear and see? **(b) Interpret:** Why do you think the scene suggests to the speaker "the eternal note of sadness"?
2. **(a) Recall:** What does the speaker say has happened to "The Sea of Faith"? **(b) Interpret:** What does he mean by this remark?
3. **(a) Recall:** In the last stanza, what does the speaker say that he and his "love" should do? **(b) Draw Conclusions:** What problem does the speaker believe that they can alleviate if they follow his urging?
4. **Take a Position:** Is Arnold's message in the final stanza a satisfactory response to "human misery" today? Why or why not?

CUSTOMIZE INSTRUCTION FOR UNIVERSAL ACCESS

For English Learners	For Advanced Readers
Point out to students that in "Dover Beach," Matthew Arnold uses present tense verbs like *lies* and *gleams* to convey both the immediacy of an experience and the truth revealed by that experience: Experience: "...the light / Gleams and is gone..." Truth: "And we are here as on a darkling plain / Swept with confused alarms of struggle and flight, / Where ignorant armies clash by night."	Have students write a brief analysis of Arnold's poetic devices—varied line length and irregular rhythm—and how these devices relate to the overall theme of the poem.

5 Background

Culture

The "Sea of Faith" refers to religious faith. For a number of Victorians, changing times had brought traditional religious faith into question. Scholarly criticism of ancient writings had put scriptural writings in a new perspective, as had Darwin's theory of evolution. Arnold, along with many other Victorians, felt that faith was no longer a clear and certain comfort.

6 Literary Analysis

Mood as a Key to Theme

- Remind students that they should be focusing on the relationship between mood and theme as they read the poem.
- Read aloud the final stanza of the poem. Then, ask the Literary Analysis question on p. 885: How do the feelings that the final stanza evokes relate to its message in lines 29–30?
  Answer: The references to the indifference of the world to the fate of human beings creates a sense of isolation. Arnold's response in lines 29–30 to this sense of isolation is that we must fulfill our human emotional needs through romantic love.

Answers for p. 885

Review and Assess

1. **(a)** They are looking out a window from the white chalk cliffs of Dover over to France, listening to the sea. **(b)** Possible response: The sea brings in the note of sadness because its ebb and flow call to mind the meaningless repetitions and cycles of human life, which all end in death.
2. **(a)** The speaker thinks that the Sea of Faith is retreating. **(b)** He means that faith is on the decline; traditional explanations of humanity's place in the world are no longer convincing.
3. **(a)** The speaker says he and his love should "be true / To one another..." **(b)** He believes they can alleviate, for themselves, the joylessness of the world.
4. Some students may respond that love is the only way to navigate a difficult world. Others may argue that we should be proactive and face up to conflicts as they arise.

❼ About the Selection

As a recessional signals the end of a religious service, this poem heralds the end of the British Empire. Although Rudyard Kipling was a staunch supporter of British imperialism, he recognized the dangers of complacency and overblown pride.

❽ Vocabulary Development

The Latin Root *-domi-*

- Have students read lines 3–4 and ask them if they can determine what *dominion* might mean from the context.
- Point out that Kipling uses the word *dominion* when referring to the power of the British Empire.
- Explain to students that this word contains the Latin root *-domi-*, which means "lord" or "master."
- Have students look for other words in their readings that contain this root and use a dictionary to find the meanings of each. **Possible responses:** Words with this root include *dominate, domineer, dominant, predominant,* and *domain.*

❼

RECESSIONAL[1]

Rudyard Kipling

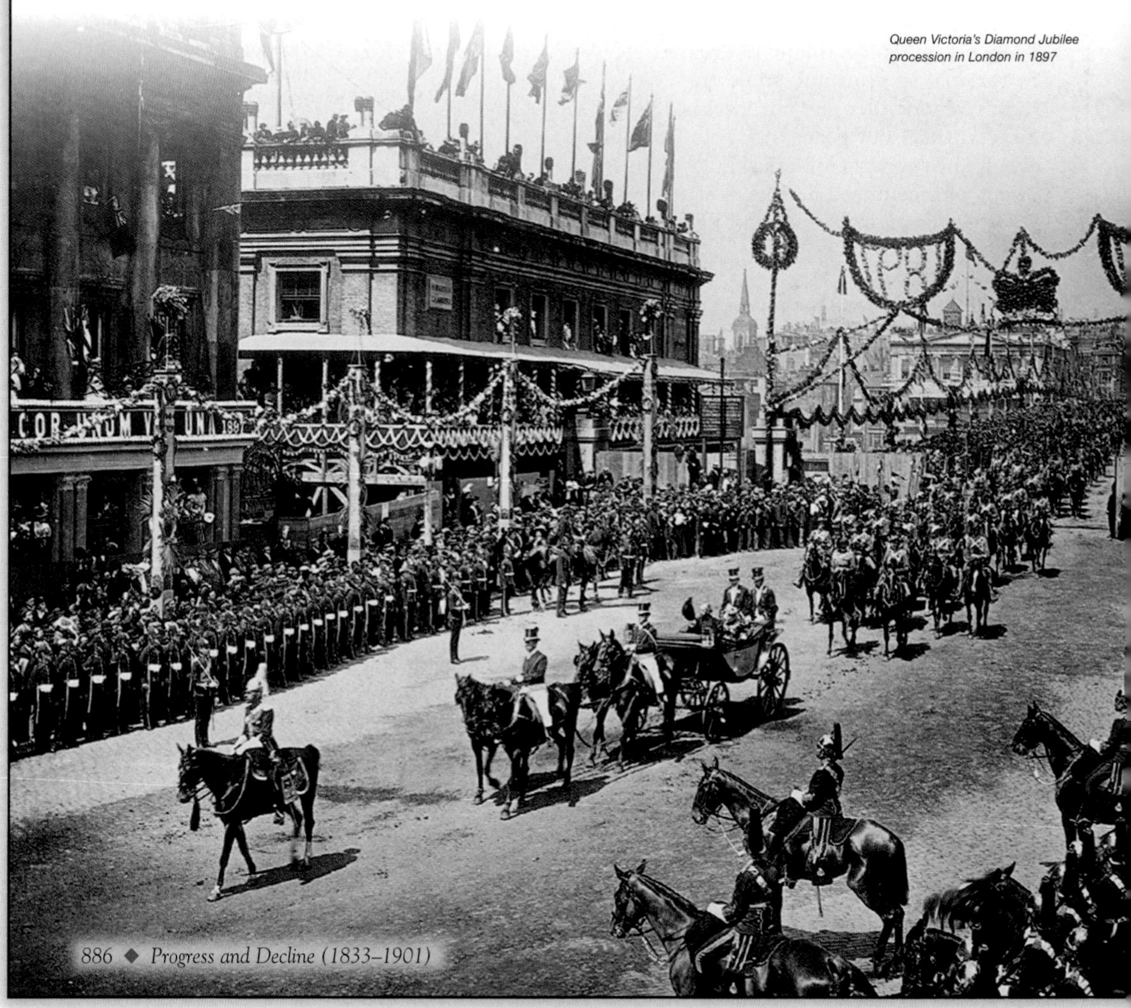

Queen Victoria's Diamond Jubilee procession in London in 1897

ENRICHMENT: Career Connection

Events Coordinator

"Recessional" was written for the national celebration of Queen Victoria's Diamond Jubilee. One can only imagine the amount of planning that went into staging the event. If a similar event were held today, an events coordinator would be hired to oversee the proceedings. Ask students what they know about events coordinators. You might share the following information and suggest that interested students find out more by contacting an events coordinator.

- Events coordinators have outgoing personalities.
- They have a "can-do" attitude and thrive on challenges.
- They know how to hire (and fire) people.
- They have outstanding organizational skills.
- Events coordinators often have degrees in Public Relations or Marketing.

Background

In 1897, a national celebration called the "Diamond Jubilee" was held in honor of the sixtieth anniversary of Queen Victoria's reign. The occasion prompted a great deal of boasting about the strength and greatness of the empire. Kipling responded to the celebration by writing this poem, reminding the people of England that the British empire might not last forever.

God of our fathers, known of old—
    Lord of our far-flung battle-line—
8 Beneath whose awful Hand we hold 9
    Dominion over palm and pine—
Lord God of Hosts, be with us yet
Lest we forget—lest we forget!

The tumult and the shouting dies—
    The Captains and the Kings depart—
Still stands Thine ancient Sacrifice,
    An humble and a contrite heart.[2]
Lord God of Hosts, be with us yet,
Lest we forget—lest we forget!

Far-called, our navies melt away—
    On dune and headland sinks the fire[3]—
Lo, all our pomp of yesterday
10 Is one with Nineveh[4] and Tyre![5]
Judge of the Nations, spare us yet,
Lest we forget—lest we forget!

dominion (də min′ yən) *n.* rule; control

contrite (kən trīt′) *adj.* willing to repent or atone

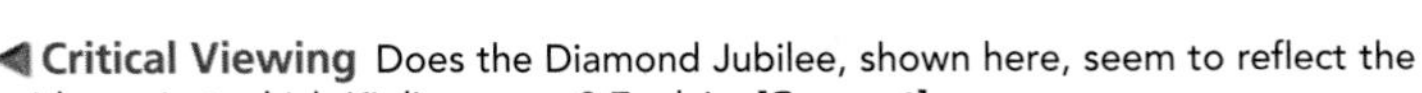

1. **Recessional** *n.* hymn sung at the end of a religious service.
2. **An . . . heart** allusion to the Bible (Psalms 51:17) "The sacrifices of God are a broken spirit: a broken and contrite heart, O God, thou wilt not despise."
3. **On . . . fire** Bonfires were lit on high ground all over Britain as part of the opening ceremonies of the Jubilee celebration.
4. **Nineveh** (nin′ ə və) ancient capital of the Assyrian Empire, the ruins of which were discovered buried in desert sands in the 1850s.
5. **Tyre** (tīr) once a great port and the center of ancient Phoenician culture, now a small town in Lebanon.

11 ◀ **Critical Viewing** Does the Diamond Jubilee, shown here, seem to reflect the pride against which Kipling warns? Explain. **[Connect]**

9 Critical Thinking

Infer

- Read aloud lines 3–4 and focus students' attention on the phrase "over palm and pine."
- Have students draw upon their knowledge of biomes from science class. Ask: What does this phrase say about the extent of the boundaries of the Empire?
  Answer: It implies that the Empire extends from subpolar forests characterized by pines to tropical desert regions where palms are the dominant trees.

10 Background

History

Remind students that an allusion is a reference to a well-known person, place, event, literary work, or work of art. Note that Kipling alludes to the ancient cities of Nineveh and Tyre. No longer glorious, these cities were once the capitals of mighty empires. Kipling's allusion, therefore, reminds Britons that their Empire may decline as all previous empires have. Encourage students to find other allusions in the poems of Kipling and Arnold and explain the references.

11 ▶ Critical Viewing

Answer: The highly formal attire, the military formations, the ornamentations—the entire pomp and circumstance of the Diamond Jubilee do indeed reflect the pride of the British Empire.

⓬ Reading Strategy

Drawing Conclusions

- Remind students to base conclusions on details from the text.
- Ask students the Reading Strategy question on p. 888: What do the final two stanzas suggest about the behavior that prompted Kipling to write this poem? Answer: They suggest that the British have grown boastful and arrogant.

Answers for p. 888

Review and Assess

1. Students may cite overconfidence in the economy or in the health of the environment as reasons to apply the lesson.
2. **(a)** The poem is addressed to God. **(b)** The poem is meant for the people of England.
3. **(a)** A recessional is a hymn at the end of a service. **(b)** The poem concludes the Jubilee and speaks of the receding power of the British Empire. **(c)** This ambiguity is appropriate because the poem is both a warning and a celebration.
4. **(a)** God, who preserves our Empire, save us from growing arrogant. **(b)** God permits the British to hold the Empire, ruling over them with his "awful Hand."
5. **(a)** The pomp has disappeared like empires of old. **(b)** The speaker condemns pride, lust for power, and lack of humility before God. **(c)** The theme is the importance of humility over pride.
6. Possible response: Yes, the actual failure of the Empire shows that excessive pride in it was inappropriate.
7. Possible response: Kipling nowhere in the poem questions Britain's right to rule, only the attitude with which it rules.
8. Possible response: Yes, it is suitable because leaders of powerful nations should be cautious and humble in their use of their power.

If, drunk with sight of power, we loose
Wild tongues that have not Thee in awe—
Such boasting as the Gentiles use
Or lesser breeds without the Law—[6]
Lord God of Hosts, be with us yet,
Lest we forget—lest we forget!

⓬

For heathen heart that puts her trust
In reeking tube[7] and iron shard[8]—
All valiant dust that builds on dust,
And guarding calls not Thee to guard—
For frantic boast and foolish word,
Thy mercy on Thy People, Lord!

Reading Strategy
Drawing Conclusions
What do the final two stanzas suggest about the behavior that may have prompted Kipling to write this poem?

6. **Such boasting . . . Law** allusion to the Bible (Romans 2:14) "For when the Gentiles, which have not the law, do by nature the things contained in the law, these, having not the law, are a law unto themselves."
7. **tube** barrel of a gun.
8. **shard** fragment of a bombshell.

Review and Assess

Thinking About the Selection

1. **Respond:** Do you think "Recessional" is relevant to contemporary society? Explain.
2. **(a) Recall:** To whom is this poem addressed? **(b) Interpret:** For whom is the message of the poem really meant?
3. **(a) Recall:** What is the literal meaning of the title of the poem? **(b) Interpret:** What double meaning is contained in the title? **(c) Analyze:** How is this ambiguity appropriate to the mood of the poem?
4. **(a) Recall:** Paraphrase the first stanza of the poem. **(b) Analyze:** According to this stanza, what is the relationship between God and empire? Explain.
5. **(a) Recall:** In lines 15 and 16, what happens to "our pomp of yesterday"? **(b) Infer:** What qualities and actions does the speaker condemn? **(c) Draw Conclusions:** What is the theme of the poem?
6. **Apply:** Britain is no longer an empire. Does this fact bear out Kipling's warning? Explain.
7. **Make a Judgment:** Is Kipling condemning the very existence of the British empire, or is he advocating a more humble approach to the responsibilities of empire? Explain.
8. **Connect:** Would this poem, or one like it, be suitable to present at a presidential inauguration? Why or why not?

ENRICHMENT: History Connection

The British Empire

In 1857, Britain took direct control of all India, and in the 1880s and 1890s, seized the African colonies of Kenya and the Sudan. Even as the British Empire expanded, however, writers expressed doubts about life in the world's most powerful nation.

In "Dover Beach," for example, Matthew Arnold laments the decline of religious faith and depicts the world as a place where "ignorant armies clash by night."

Even Kipling, who supported British imperialism, uses "Recessional" to warn against the perils of pride. Written for the sixtieth anniversary of Queen Victoria's reign, the poem was a warning to those who boasted of Britain's world domination.

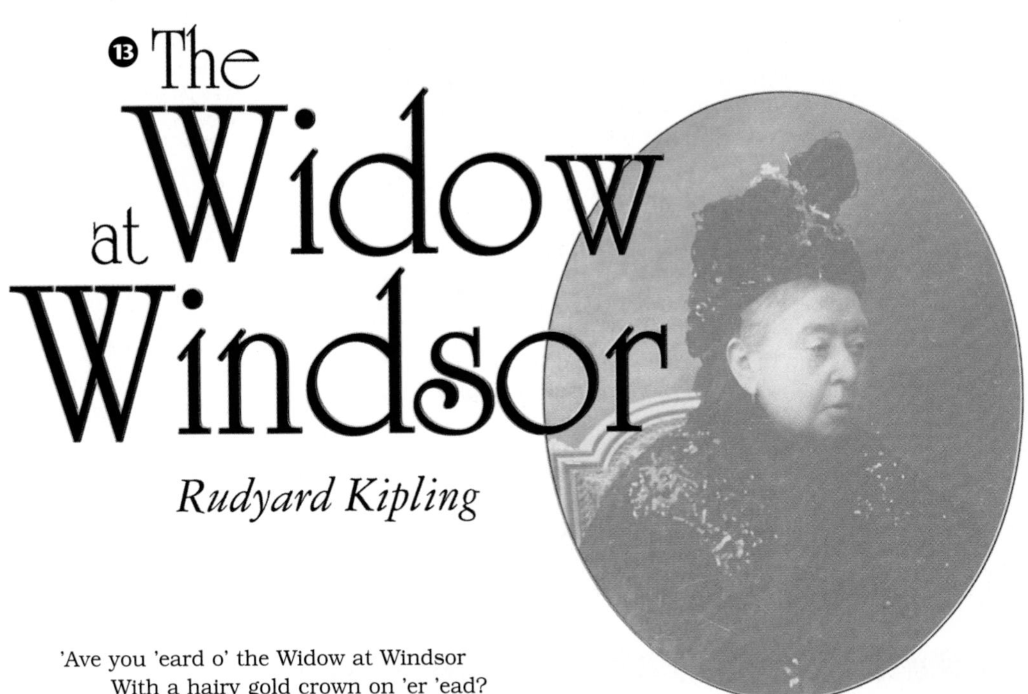

(13) The Widow at Windsor

Rudyard Kipling

'Ave you 'eard o' the Widow at Windsor
With a hairy gold crown on 'er 'ead?
She 'as ships on the foam—she 'as millions at 'ome,
An' she pays us poor beggars in red.
(Ow, poor beggars in red!)
(14) There's 'er nick on the cavalry 'orses,
There's 'er mark on the medical stores—
An' 'er troops you'll find with a fair wind be'ind
That takes us to various wars.
(Poor beggars!—barbarious wars!)
Then 'ere's to the Widow at Windsor,
(15) An' 'ere's to the stores an' the guns,
The men an' the 'orses what makes up the forces
O' Missis Victorier's sons.
(Poor beggars! Victorier's sons!)

Walk wide o' the Widow at Windsor,
For 'alf o' Creation she owns:
We'ave bought 'er the same with the sword an' the flame,
An' we've salted it down with our bones.
(Poor beggars!—it's blue with our bones!)
Hands off o' the sons o' the widow,
Hands off o' the goods in 'er shop.
For the kings must come down an' the emperors frown

(16) ▲ **Critical Viewing**
What elements of this portrait of Queen Victoria do you think the speaker of the poem might point out? Explain. **[Connect]**

(17) ✔ **Reading Check**
Where does the speaker say the Widow leaves her mark?

(13) About the Selection

During the sixty-three-year reign of Queen Victoria, Great Britain reached the height of its power. By the last decade of the nineteenth century, however, cracks in the strength of the British Empire were beginning to show. In "The Widow at Windsor," the speaker is a common soldier who reminds Britons that one country's domination always comes at a price.

(14) Background

Victoria's "Nick"

"[H]er nick on the cavalry 'orses" refers to the V.R.I. mark that shows that the horses belong to the queen. The letters stand for "Victoria, Regina Imperatrix," meaning "Victoria, Queen and Empress."

(15) Literary Analysis

Mood as a Key to Theme

- Have students read lines 11–14. Then, ask students to analyze the mood created in these lines.
  Possible response: Students may respond that the mood is cheerful on the surface, but there is an undercurrent of bitterness; when taken literally, lines 11–14 seem to be a toast to the queen. However, the repetition of "poor beggars" in line 15 is ironic and angry.
- Ask students what the mood reveals about the theme of the poem.
  Answer: The mood shows that the theme is not a happy one and will probably deal with the reasons the soldiers are bitter.

(16) ▶ Critical Viewing

Possible response: The speaker might refer to the fact that she appears to be wearing mourning or that she has a look of authority.

(17) ✔ Reading Check

Answer: The widow leaves her mark on the medical stores.

CUSTOMIZE INSTRUCTION FOR UNIVERSAL ACCESS

For Special Needs Students	For English Learners	For Gifted/Talented Students
Have students read along with the **Listening to Literature Audiocassettes,** Side 21 or CD 12, in order that they may appreciate the ironic humor and bitterness of the poem. Students will often find it easier to comprehend the dialect when they hear the words spoken.	Explain to students that the speaker in this poem is a common soldier who speaks in Cockney dialect. The initial *h* is omitted from words along with the final *f* in *of,* the *d* in *and,* and the *g* in *morning.*	Have students perform a comedy skit with a speaker reading the poem and others acting out farcical interpretations of its content.

ASSESS

18 Literary Analysis

Mood as a Key to Theme

- Have students finish reading the poem. Draw their attention to the remarks in parentheses.
- Then, ask the Literary Analysis question on p. 890: What do the remarks in parentheses suggest about the speaker's attitude toward the empire?
  Answer: The parentheses act as asides—that is, they contain short refrains that the speaker is, so to speak, uttering under his breath. They communicate an ironic and bitter attitude toward the Empire.

Answers for p. 890

Review and Assess

1. Possible response: The earth "salted down" with the soldiers' bones is a striking image.
2. **(a)** The "Widow" is Queen Victoria. **(b)** It is both fondly familiar and disrespectful.
3. **(a)** The speaker is a common soldier. **(b)** Students may respond that the tone is disrespectful, but not disloyal. The speaker resents that soldiers are sent off to die for Victoria, but he also takes pride in her power.
4. **(a)** All the "Poor beggars" lines are in parentheses. **(b)** Students may respond that the poem would lose much of its mocking, bitter tone if the remarks in parentheses were removed. Other students may point out that without the "interior monologue" of the parentheticals, the poem's meaning and intent would lose clarity.
5. **(a)** The soldiers will die far from home. **(b)** Students may respond that this device makes the reader aware of the unsung heroes that made the Empire possible.
6. Possible responses: Songwriters and poets today use dialect to sound authentic or experienced in the ways of the world, to ingratiate themselves with a particular audience, or to create a portrait of a particular lifestyle.

When the Widow at Windsor says "Stop!"
(Poor beggars!—we're sent to say "Stop!")
Then 'ere's to the Lodge o' the Widow,
From the Pole to the Tropics it runs—
To the Lodge that we tile with the rank an' the file,
An' open in form with the guns.
(Poor beggars!—it's always they guns!)

We 'ave 'eard o' the Widow at Windsor,
It's safest to leave 'er alone:
For 'er sentries we stand by the sea an' the land
18 Wherever the bugles are blown.
(Poor beggars!—an' don't we get blown!)
Take 'old o' the Wings o' the Mornin',
An' flop round the earth till you're dead;
But you won't get away from the tune that they play
To the bloomin' old rag over'ead.
(Poor beggars!—it's 'ot over'ead!)
Then 'ere's to the sons o' the Widow,
Wherever, 'owever they roam.
'Ere's all they desire, an' if they require
A speedy return to their 'ome.
(Poor beggars!—they'll never see 'ome!)

Literary Analysis
Mood as a Key to Theme What do the remarks in parentheses suggest about the speaker's attitude toward the empire?

Review and Assess

Thinking About the Selection

1. **Respond:** What images, ideas, or lines in this poem do you find most striking? Explain.
2. (a) **Recall:** Who is the Widow at Windsor?
   (b) **Infer:** What is surprising about the speaker's decision to describe this woman in this way?
3. (a) **Recall:** Who is the speaker of this poem?
   (b) **Analyze:** Would you describe the speaker's tone as disloyal or disrespectful? Explain.
4. (a) **Recall:** What various remarks of the speaker's appear in parentheses? (b) **Make a Judgment:** How would the poem be different if the remarks in parentheses were deleted? Why?
5. (a) **Recall:** According to the last line of the poem, what fate awaits the soldiers? (b) **Draw Conclusions:** Why does Kipling describe the Empire from the perspective of a common soldier?
6. **Hypothesize:** In what circumstances, if any, would poets or songwriters of today choose to have a speaker use dialect, as Kipling does? Explain.

ASSESSMENT PRACTICE: Reading Comprehension

Paired Passages (For more practice, see Test Preparation Workbook, p. 40.)

Many tests require students to compare and identify literary elements in two passages. Use the following sample item to show students how to compare the themes of two passages. Have students read "Dover Beach" and "Recessional" before completing this exercise.

Which of these themes do the two poems share?

A People have become too proud.
B War is a terrible evil.
C History repeats itself.
D In this world, nothing can be certain.

Remind students that a theme is the central idea or ideas in a poem. Choices *A* and *C* are themes in "Recessional," but they do not appear in "Dover Beach." Choice *B* is too peripheral to the poems' central ideas to be called a theme. Students should determine that the correct answer is *D*.

Review and Assess

Literary Analysis

Mood as a Key to Theme

1. Fill in a chart like the one shown here by describing the **mood** evoked by images from "Dover Beach." Then, using what you have written as a clue, state the **theme** of the poem.

Image	Where It Appears	Mood It Evokes

2. Explain how the mood of sternness and solemnity in "Recessional" relates to the theme of the poem.
3. Use the mood in "The Widow at Windsor" to explain which of these sentences best describes the theme of the poem: (a) Maintaining the Empire seems ridiculous to the soldiers who must do it. (b) Maintaining the Empire is a deadly serious game, played at the expense of the common soldier.

Comparing Literary Works

4. Compare and contrast the ways in which these poems treat the anxieties brought on by advances in science, prosperity, and empire.
5. How do both "Recessional" and "The Widow at Windsor" reflect different perspectives on the responsibilities and dangers that come with empire?

Reading Strategy

Drawing Conclusions

6. Use Arnold's descriptions of the night throughout "Dover Beach" and his use of the word "night" in line 37 to **draw conclusions** about whether he is pessimistic or optimistic.
7. Basing your answer on the concluding two lines of each stanza in "Recessional," what conclusion can you draw about Kipling's message?
8. Draw a conclusion about Kipling's reason for including the parenthetical remarks in "The Widow at Windsor."

Extend Understanding

9. **Social Studies Connection:** Could any of these poems be applied to the social conditions of today? Explain.

Quick Review

The **mood** of a work of literature is the feeling it generates.

The **theme** is the central message or insight into life it presents or an important question it explores.

To **draw conclusions** about what you read, make generalizations based on evidence in the text.

Take It to the Net

www.phschool.com

Take the interactive self-test online to check your understanding of these selections.

ENRICHMENT: Further Reading

Other Works by the Authors

Other Works by Matthew Arnold

"To Marguerite—Continued"; "Growing Old"

Other Works by Rudyard Kipling

"Tommy"; "The Song of the Sons"; "The Song of the Cities"; "England's Answer"

Take It to the Net

Visit www.phschool.com for more information on these selections.

Answers for p. 891

Review and Assess

1. Possible responses: Image: "ignorant armies clash by night"; Where It Appears: line 37; Mood: dark, foreboding, violent. The theme of the poem is that the human race is driven by conflicts it does not understand.
2. The theme is a warning against pride, taken as an offense against God's majesty, so a solemn, stern mood is appropriate.
3. The mood, which combines a pride in a soldier's trade with a sarcastic acknowledgment of the indifference of the Empire to his fate, supports (b).
4. Possible response: In response to the anxieties of the Victorian Age, "Dover Beach" finds that the culture fails to give life meaning, so the poem affirms personal love instead of faith; "Recessional" calls on the traditional religious value of humility; "Widow at Windsor" calls on the comfort and honesty of irony.
5. "Recessional" reflects both the responsibility to God and the danger that arrogance will be the downfall of the Empire. "The Widow at Windsor" reflects both the responsibility of Empire toward those who maintain it and the danger that it will simply exploit them.
6. As the poem advances, so does Arnold's pessimism. The opening images of night ("sweet is the night air!") suggest the beauties of night. By line 37, *night* has come to mean Victorian culture's failure of understanding—its inability to give meaning to human existence.
7. Kipling is pleading with God to bear with human frailty, and pleading with the people of England to relinquish their "frantic boast and foolish word."
8. Kipling's parentheticals make clear the ironic attitude soldiers need in order to cope with the fact that they both maintain the Empire and are its victims.
9. Possible response: Students may respond that the United States, like the former British Empire, has a privileged place in the world but should not be arrogant about it.

EXTEND

Answers for p. 892

❶ Vocabulary Development

Word Analysis

1. Domain - A territory over which rule or control is exercised.
2. Dominant - Exercising the most influence or control.
3. Domineer - To rule over or control arbitrarily or arrogantly; tyrannize.

Spelling Strategy

1. combine
2. delight

Concept Development: Antonyms

1. c
2. e
3. d
4. a
5. b

❷ Grammar and Style

1. Present tense verb: "is"; occurring now
2. Present tense verb: "hear"; occurring now
3. Present tense verb: "are"; generalization
4. Present tense verb: "dies"; occuring now
5. Present tense verb: "is"; generalization

Writing Application

1. The winning of empires requires great sacrifices.
2. The ebb and flow of the tide represents the cycles of life.

Integrate Language Skills

❶ Vocabulary Development Lesson

Word Analysis: Latin Root *-domi-*

Kipling uses *dominion,* or "rule," to refer to the power of the British Empire. This word contains the Latin root *-domi-*, which means "lord" or "master." Use your knowledge of this root to define these *-domi-* words.

1. domain **2.** dominant **3.** domineer

Spelling Strategy

Words ending in a long vowel sound followed by a single consonant sound often have a silent *e*, as in *contrite*. However, there are other ways to spell such words. Choose the correctly spelled word from each pair.

1. combein, combine **2.** delight, delite

Concept Development: Antonyms

Review the words in the vocabulary list on page 883, and study the vocabulary words in the context of the selections. Then, in your notebook, match each word in the first column with its antonym, or the word opposite in meaning, in the second column.

1. tranquil	**a.** clear
2. cadence	**b.** unrepentant
3. dominion	**c.** agitated
4. turbid	**d.** powerlessness
5. contrite	**e.** turmoil

❷ Grammar and Style Lesson

Present Tense

The **present tense** of a verb often expresses an action or a state of being that is occurring now. It can also express a general idea that is true at all times. Both Arnold and Kipling use the present tense effectively in expressing a generalization.

Occurring Now: . . . the light / Gleams and is gone . . .
Generalization: . . . the world . . . Hath really neither joy, nor love, . . .

Through the use of present tense, poets can make stirring or alarming statements about life in general. They can also skillfully weave together images of a present moment with general truths or symbolic images, as Arnold does in "Dover Beach."

Practice On your paper, identify the present tense verb in each of these passages from the poems. Tell whether each expresses a truth or an action or state of being occurring now.

1. The sea is calm tonight.
2. . . . you hear the grating roar / Of pebbles . . .
3. . . . we are here as on a darkling plain . . .
4. The tumult and the shouting dies— . . .
5. It's safest to leave 'er alone: . . .

Writing Application Change each statement into a generalization by using a present tense verb and, if necessary, adding or deleting words.

1. The winning of empires required great sacrifices.
2. For me, the ebb and flow of the tide represented the cycles of life.

WG Prentice Hall Writing and Grammar Connection: Chapter 21, Section 1

TEACHING RESOURCES

The following resources can be used to enrich or extend the instruction for pp. 892–893.

Vocabulary

Selection Support: Build Vocabulary p. 191

Vocabulary and Spelling Practice Book (Use this booklet for skills enrichment.)

Grammar

Selection Support: Grammar and Style, p. 192

WG **Writing and Grammar,** Diamond Level, p. 520

Daily Language Practice Transparencies ■

Writing

WG **Writing and Grammar,** Diamond Level, p. 310

Writing and Grammar iText CD-ROM ■

Writing Models and Graphic Organizers on Transparencies, pp. 45–56

■ **BLOCK SCHEDULING:** Resources marked with this symbol provide varied instruction during 90-minute blocks.

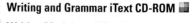

❸ Writing Lesson

Response to Criticism

Critic Walter E. Houghton writes that the Victorian Age was characterized by "widespread doubt about the nature of man, society, and the universe." Using evidence from the poems by Arnold and Kipling, support or refute this assertion.

Prewriting Review the poems, using a chart like this one to gather evidence about Victorian doubt or Victorian self-confidence.

Model: Gathering Details

Poem:			
	Images	Mood(s)	Theme(s)
Doubt			
Self-confidence			

Drafting Referring to your chart, formulate a thesis statement agreeing or disagreeing with Houghton. Then, support your thesis with the evidence you have gathered from these poems. Consider organizing your response by devoting a paragraph to each selection.

Revising Be sure that, as support, you have referred to images, moods, and themes. To make your points more effectively, quote specific phrases and lines.

WG *Prentice Hall Writing and Grammar Connection: Chapter 14, Section 2*

❹ Extension Activities

Listening and Speaking With partners, prepare an **oral interpretation** of "Recessional" for the class.

- Pause only when the punctuation dictates.
- Use a tone of voice that evokes the proper mood.
- Consider using music, paintings, photographs, and maps to enhance the reading. However, do not overuse media.

Rehearse your presentation until you are comfortable. Pay special attention to the handling of any media. Then present your interpretation to the class. **[Group Activity]**

Research and Technology View a film based on Kipling's works, such as *Captains Courageous* (1937) or *Kim* (1950). Read the work as well to get a feeling for Kipling's prose style. Then, write a **film review,** evaluating both the effectiveness of the film and its faithfulness to the book. In discussing changes to the story in the film version, remember that visual and verbal storytelling have different demands and requirements.

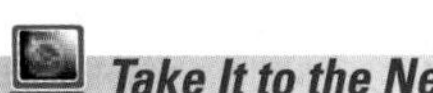

Take It to the Net www.phschool.com

Go online for an additional research activity using the Internet.

ASSESSMENT RESOURCES

The following resources can be used to assess students' knowledge and skills.

Selection Assessment

- **Formal Assessment,** pp. 203–205
- **Open Book Test,** pp. 120–122
- **Test Bank Software**
- **Got It! Assessment Videotapes,** Tape 4

Take It to the Net

Visit www.phschool.com for self-tests and additional questions on the selections.

Writing Rubric

- **Performance Assess. and Portfolio Mgmt.,** pp. 25 and 92

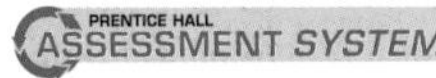

- **Workbook**
- **Skill Book**
- **Transparencies**
- **CD-ROM**

❸ Writing Lesson

- Tell students that a response to criticism is a piece of nonfiction writing that presents a reaction to an analysis or evaluation of a literary work. An effective response to criticism usually does the following: identifies the work or works being discussed; states the critical point being addressed and identifies its source; supports the writer's interpretations with precise examples, citations, or quotations; uses a clear and effective organization; and offers an evaluation of the critical point based on a close scrutiny of specific elements in the literary work.
- Model a thesis statement for the students based on one of the poems.
- Model the revision process using pp. 45–56 of the **Writing Models and Graphic Organizers on Transparencies.**
- Evaluate students' responses using the Response to Literature rubric, p. 25 in **Performance Assessment and Portfolio Management.**

❹ Listening and Speaking

- Divide the class into two groups. Tell the first group to get visuals to illustrate the poem. Tell the second group to find a recording of "Recessional" or to perform it themselves.
- Tell the students to rehearse before presenting to the rest of the class.

CUSTOMIZE INSTRUCTION For Universal Access

To address different learning styles, use the following activities suggested in the **Extension Activities** booklet, p. 40.

- For Visual/Spatial and Logical/Mathematical Learners, use Activity 5.
- For Interpersonal and Verbal/Linguistic Learners, use Activity 6.
- For Visual/Spatial Learners, use Activity 7.

Condition of Ireland ✦ Progress in Personal Comfort

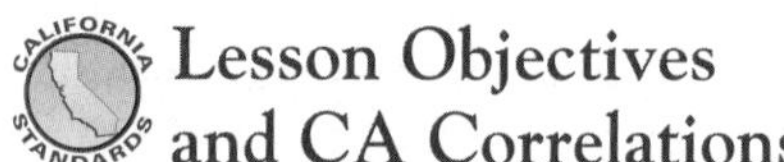

Lesson Objectives and CA Correlations

1. **To analyze and respond to literary elements**
   - Literary Analysis: Journalistic Essay **R 3.1**
   - Comparing Literary Works **R 3.3**
2. **To read, comprehend, analyze, and critique nonfiction**
   - Reading Strategy: Distinguishing Emotive and Informative Language **R 2.6**
   - Reading Check Questions
   - Review and Assess Questions
   - Assessment Practice (ATE)
3. **To develop word analysis skills, fluency, and systematic vocabulary**
   - Vocabulary Development Lesson: Humor Words
4. **To understand and apply written and oral language conventions**
   - Spelling Strategy **LC 1.2**
   - Grammar and Style Lesson: Coordinating Conjunctions **LC 1.1**
5. **To understand and apply appropriate writing and research strategies**
   - Writing Lesson: Comparison and Contrast of Viewpoints **W 2.2**
   - Extension Activity: Report **W 2.4**
6. **To understand and apply listening and speaking strategies**
   - Extension Activity: Comic Monologue **LS 2.1**

STEP-BY-STEP TEACHING GUIDE	PACING GUIDE
PRETEACH	
Motivate Students and Provide Background	
Use the Motivation activity (ATE p. 894)	5 min.
Read and discuss author and background features (SE/ATE pp. 894, 897, 898) [A]	5 min.
Introduce the Concepts	
Introduce the Literary Analysis and Reading Strategy (SE/ATE p. 895) [A]	15 min.
Pronounce the vocabulary words and read their definitions (SE p. 895)	5 min.
TEACH	
Monitor Comprehension	
Informally monitor comprehension by circulating while students read independently or in groups [A]	15 min.
Monitor students' comprehension with the Reading Check notes (SE/ATE pp. 897, 901)	as students read
Develop vocabulary with Vocabulary notes (SE pp. 897–900; ATE p. 898)	as students read
Develop Understanding	
Develop students' understanding of journalistic essay with the Literary Analysis annotations (SE pp. 897, 902; ATE pp. 897, 901, 902) [A]	5 min.
Develop students' ability to distinguish emotive and informative language with the Reading Strategy annotations (SE pp. 899, 901; ATE pp. 897, 899, 900, 901)	5 min.
ASSESS	
Assess Mastery	
Assess students' mastery of the Reading Strategy and Literary Analysis by having them answer the Review and Assess questions (SE/ATE p. 903)	15 min.
Use one or more of the print and media Assessment Resources (ATE p. 905) [A]	up to 45 min.
EXTEND	
Apply Understanding	
Have students complete the Vocabulary Development Lesson and the Grammar and Style Lesson (SE p. 904) [A]	20 min.
Apply students' knowledge of comparing viewpoints using the Writing Lesson (SE/ATE p. 905) [A]	45 min.
Apply students' understanding using one or more of the Extension Activities (SE p. 905)	20–90 min.

ACCELERATED INSTRUCTION:
Use the strategies and activities identified with an [A].

UNIVERSAL ACCESS
● = Below-Level Students
▲ = On-Level Students
■ = Above-Level Students

Time and Resource Manager

Reading Level: Average, Easy
Average Number of Instructional Days: 4

RESOURCES		
PRINT	**TRANSPARENCIES**	**TECHNOLOGY**
• **Beyond Literature,** Workplace Skills: Information Management, p. 42 ▲ ■		• **Interest Grabber Video,** Tape 5 ● ▲ ■
• **Selection Support Workbook:** ● ▲ ■ Literary Analysis, p. 198 Reading Strategy, p. 197 Build Vocabulary, p. 195	• **Literary Analysis and Reading Transparencies,** pp. 83 and 84 ● ▲ ■	
		• **Listening to Literature** ● ▲ ■ Audiocassettes, Side 21 Audio CDs, CD 12
• **Literatura en español** ● ▲ • **Literary Analysis for Enrichment** ■		
• **Formal Assessment:** Selection Test, pp. 206–208 ● ▲ ■ • **Open Book Test,** pp. 123–125 ● ▲ ■ • **Performance Assessment and Portfolio Management,** p. 20 ● ▲ ■ • PRENTICE HALL ASSESSMENT SYSTEM ● ▲ ■	• PRENTICE HALL ASSESSMENT SYSTEM ● ▲ ■ Skills Practice Answers and Explanations on Transparencies ● ▲ ■	• **Test Bank Software** ● ▲ ■ • **Got It! Assessment Videotapes,** Tape 4 ● ▲
• **Selection Support Workbook:** ● ▲ ■ Grammar and Style, p. 196 • **Writing and Grammar,** Diamond Level ● ▲ ■ • **Extension Activities,** p. 42 ● ▲ ■	• **Daily Language Practice Transparencies** ● ▲ • **Writing Models and Graphic Organizers on Transparencies,** pp. 85–92 ● ▲ ■	• **Writing and Grammar iText CD-ROM** ● ▲ ■ *Take It to the Net* www.phschool.com

BLOCK SCHEDULING: Use one 90-minute class period to preteach the selections and have students read them. Use a second 90-minute class period to assess students' mastery of skills and have them complete one of the Extension Activities.

PRETEACH

Step-by-Step Teaching Guide for pp. 894–895

Motivation

Bring to class a facsimile of a newspaper article reporting a famous historical event (the sinking of the *Titanic*, the assassination of President Kennedy, the 1929 stock market crash). Discuss the informative and emotive language found in the article. Alternatively, you may bring in a recent copy of your local daily newspaper. Compare and contrast the informational facts found on the news pages with the opinions expressed in the editorials and letters to the editor.

Interest Grabber Video

As an alternative, play "'Condition of Ireland': Irish Potato Famine" on Tape 5 to engage student interest.

❶ Background

Progress and Potatoes

At the center of the scenes of suffering and despair painted by the essay "Condition of Ireland" is the lowly Irish potato. The potato was the product of progress—of the improved navigational technology used by early European explorers to reach the New World. In the sixteenth century, Spanish explorers brought potatoes back to Europe from Peru.

By the mid-nineteenth century, the potato had become woven into the fabric of Irish life—one third of the Irish ate potatoes almost exclusively. When disease ruined the potato crop of 1845, the Irish began to starve. More than a million people died of starvation and disease from 1846 to 1851. More than a million and a half emigrated, many to the United States.

Prepare to Read

❶ Condition of Ireland ◆ Progress in Personal Comfort

Newspapers and Progress

The British Empire in the nineteenth century measured itself with a yardstick called *progress*. People wondered whether things were better in the present than they had been in the past and whether present trends would lead to a more reasonable future. These two articles from Victorian newspapers give two very different answers to these questions—one a cry of outrage and the other an exclamation of pride.

The Newspaper as Evaluator of Progress The idea of progress was perhaps born with the modern newspaper. To even ask whether progress has been made, the mind must view the world as a collection of measurable facts—the number of people fed, of miles traveled, of dieases cured. By bringing together news from near and far, Victorian newspapers assembled an image of such a world.

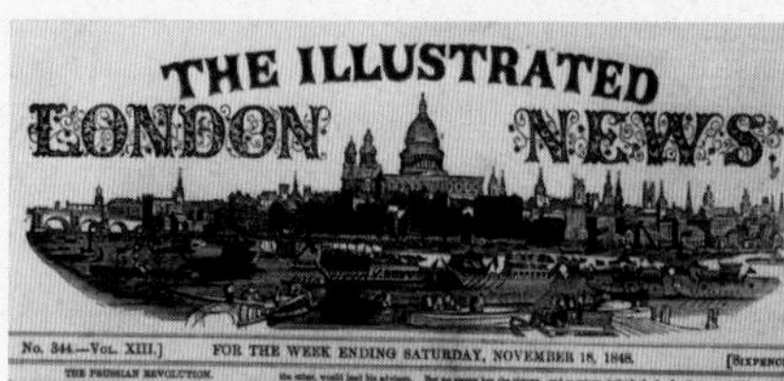

The most important British newspaper was *The Times* of London. From the beginning of the nineteenth century, this paper established a reputation for independent, objective reporting. Its circulation increased from 5,000 in 1815 to 40,000 in 1850.

Other newspapers also entered the market. Less expensive than *The Times, The Daily Telegraph* (founded in 1855) covered the news and offered thoughtful editorials. *The Illustrated London News*, in which "The Condition of Ireland" appeared, was founded as a weekly in 1842, breaking new ground in its use of graphics. It featured thirty-two woodcuts in its first edition and was also the first British periodical to use photographs.

Public Opinion These papers brought opinions as well as news to a vast public, appealing to it as witness, critic, and even judge of events. It is this era that gave meaning to a concept that is still important today: public opinion. The period also provided the overall standard by which the public could judge events, personalities, and policies: Were social conditions fairer or more efficient than they had been, and would they be even more so in the future?

Progress and Reform The author of the essay "Condition of Ireland" uses this standard of progress in criticizing English policies toward the Irish. Even though these policies were based on up-to-date economic ideas, apparent progress in economic theory spelled actual disaster in Ireland. The author judges this situation and the seemingly progressive theories that caused it by applying an ideal of progress based on common sense: the efficient and reasonable use of resources.

Progress and "Conveniences" Other Victorians used the yardstick of progress with more cheering results. Sydney Smith (1771–1845), ordained in the Church of England, was a prolific writer and preacher of his time. He was a co-founder in 1802 of *The Edinburgh Review*, a periodical to which he also contributed. In his articles, he often expressed progressive viewpoints on such serious matters as parliamentary reform, prisons, slavery, and religious freedom.

Smith was also famous for his witty essays and conversation, and his wit is evident in the essay included here. He celebrates the progress made in the area of personal comfort—innovations, large and small, that seem to have come out of nowhere but that now feel indispensable: streetlighting, railways, umbrellas.

TEACHING RESOURCES

The following resources can be used to enrich or extend the instruction for pp. 894–895.

Motivation

Interest Grabber Video, Tape 5

Background

Beyond Literature, p. 42

Take It to the Net

Visit www.phschool.com for background and hotlinks for the selections.

Literary Analysis

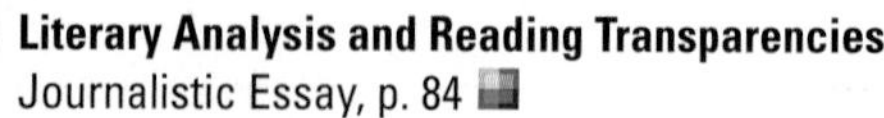

Literary Analysis and Reading Transparencies, Journalistic Essay, p. 84

Reading

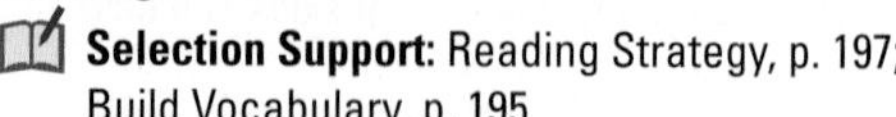

Selection Support: Reading Strategy, p. 197; Build Vocabulary, p. 195

Literary Analysis and Reading Transparencies, Distinguishing Emotive and Informative Language, p. 83

BLOCK SCHEDULING: Resources marked with this symbol provide varied instruction during 90-minute blocks.

Preview

Connecting to the Literature

In your lifetime, you have witnessed remarkable examples of technological progress. Whether you have witnessed social progress is a subject open to debate. These two essays of Victorian Britain gauge social and technological progress, respectively.

❷ Literary Analysis

Journalistic Essay

Journalistic essays are short prose pieces that provide perspectives on current events or trends. Unlike essayists who explore the world to learn about themselves, journalistic essayists construct serious or trivial stories out of the day's jumble of news. They may take one of these approaches:

- They may use the voice of an all-knowing witness or judge, as in "Condition of Ireland,"
- They may offer individual opinions about common concerns, as in "Progress in Personal Comfort."

Look for these different approaches in the two essays.

Comparing Literary Works

Writers use deliberate approaches in keeping with their subject and audience. "Condition of Ireland," an essay on a major public issue, addresses readers as concerned citizens. It takes a serious attitude toward its subject and suggests a dramatic struggle between right and wrong. By contrast, "Progress in Personal Comfort" focuses on convenience and addresses readers as amused observers of their own individual lives and habits. It uses humor and exaggeration to make its points. Compare and contrast the effectiveness of these different approaches in achieving distinct goals.

❸ Reading Strategy

Distinguishing Emotive and Informative Language

Emotive language uses words, phrases, and examples for emotional effect. **Informative language** conveys facts.

As an aid to understanding these authors' biases and opinions, use a chart like this one to distinguish between emotive and informative language.

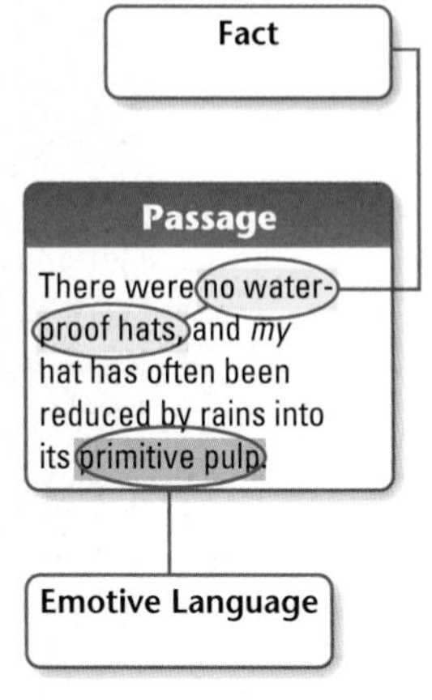

Vocabulary Development

requisites (rek′ wə zits) *n.* things necessary for a given purpose (p. 897)

sanction (saŋk′ shən) *n.* authorized approval or permission (p. 898)

exonerate (eg zän′ ər āt′) *v.* free from a charge of guilt; declare or prove blameless (p. 898)

melancholy (mel′ ən käl′ ē) *adj.* sad; depressing (p. 899)

indolence (in′ də ləns) *n.* idleness; laziness (p. 899)

depredation (dep′ rə dā′ shən) *n.* act or instance of robbing, plundering, or laying waste (p. 900)

CUSTOMIZE INSTRUCTION FOR UNIVERSAL ACCESS

For Less Proficient Readers	For English Learners	For Advanced Readers
Students may have difficulty with some of the longer, complex sentences in these selections. Encourage students to work in small groups to break down these sentences to find the basic meaning of each.	Students may need assistance with the long sentences and higher-level vocabulary in these selections. Assist students in finding synonyms for words like *hesitation, ignorant,* and *calamity,* and in breaking down long or complicated sentences.	Have students take notes as they read the selections. Then, challenge them to use these notes to write a poem or poems that capture the essence, meaning, and mood of the journalistic essays.

❷ Literary Analysis

Journalistic Essay

- Tell students that in these readings they will be learning about journalistic essays. Journalistic essays are short prose pieces that provide perspectives on current events or trends.
- Explain to students that journalistic essayists may choose from a variety of different approaches to responding to the news of their day. For example, they may write in the voice of an all-knowing witness or judge, as in "Condition of Ireland," or they may offer individual opinions about common concerns, as in "Progress in Personal Comfort."
- Show the Journalistic Essay transparency, **Literary Analysis and Reading Transparencies,** p. 84.
- Explain to students that the particular approach an essayist chooses to take to his or her subject depends upon the topic to be addressed. Have students compare these essays with regard to their tone and approach.

❸ Reading Strategy

Distinguishing Emotive and Informative Language

- Explain to students the difference between emotive and informative language. Emotive language uses words, phrases, and examples for emotional effect. Informative language conveys factual information. While few utterances are entirely free of either emotion or information, students need to distinguish the two types of language to better evaluate an author's support for his or her claims.
- Tell students that they need to evaluate the biases and opinions of the authors of these essays, and then explain how they may use a chart to distinguish between emotive and informative language.

Vocabulary Development

- Pronounce each vocabulary word for students, and read the definitions as a class. Have students identify any words with which they are already familiar.

E-Teach

Visit E-Teach at www.phschool.com for teachers' essays on how to teach, with questions and answers.

TEACH

Step-by-Step Teaching Guide for pp. 896–902

CUSTOMIZE INSTRUCTION
For Intrapersonal Learners

Have students divide a sheet of paper into two columns. The first column should be headed "Taking Notes"; the second, "Making Meaning." Encourage students to take notes in the first column and to comment on these notes in the second column.

❶ About the Selection

This journalistic essay from *The Illustrated London News* of the mid-1800s points out the injustices being done to the Irish people as a result of rigid adherence to economic policies. The author argues that these policies do not make sense during a natural disaster—in this case, when potato blight has destroyed most of the food supply.

❷ ▶Critical Viewing

Answer: Students may say that the picture aptly illustrates the starvation of the Irish people as described in the article. One difference between the picture and the article, however, is that the picture focuses on a mother and child, whereas the article focuses on the men who were put out of work and could not grow or afford food for their families.

❸ Background

Art

Woman Begging at Clonakilty by James Mahony

This illustration for *The Illustrated London News* depicts a woman begging for alms as she clutches her baby to herself. Use the following question for discussion:

If you did not know the title of this image, how could you tell that this woman is distressed and in need of assistance?

Answer: Her facial expression and outstretched arm indicate that she is in need of help.

❶ 

Illustrations of the New Poor-Law

The Illustrated London News, December 15, 1849

❷ ▶**Critical Viewing** Compare the portrayal of the Irish in this picture with the portrayal of the Irish in the article. **[Compare and Contrast]**

❸

Woman Begging at Clonakilty, James Mahony, The Illustrated London News, 1847

TEACHING RESOURCES

The following resources can be used to enrich or extend the instruction for pp. 896–902.

Literary Analysis

Selection Support: Literary Analysis, p. 198 ■

Reading

Listening to Literature Audiocassettes, Side 21 ■

Listening to Literature Audio CDs, CD 12 ■

■ **BLOCK SCHEDULING:** Resources marked with this symbol provide varied instruction during 90-minute blocks.

Background

By the early 1840s, the potato had become a staple of the Irish diet. Nearly one half of the Irish relied almost completely on potatoes for sustenance. Then, disease ruined several potato crops, leading to the Irish potato famine of 1845–1849. Because the Irish people had become so dependent on potatoes, the impact was devastating. British economic policies only worsened the situation.

More than a million Irish people died of starvation and starvation-related diseases by 1851. More than a million and a half emigrated, many to the United States and Canada. However, despite these terrible losses and a continuing population decline, the Irish rallied to preserve their heritage.

This article was one of a series in which *The Illustrated London News* presented, in words and pictures, the plight of the Irish in the midst of the famine. The *News* took a clear stand against British policies and proposed other solutions.

4 The present condition of the Irish, we have no hesitation in saying, has been mainly brought on by ignorant and vicious legislation. 5 The destruction of the potato for one season, though a great calamity, would not have doomed them, fed as they were by the taxes of the state and the charity of the world, to immediate decay; but a false theory, assuming the name of political economy,[1] with which it has no more to do than with the slaughter of the Hungarians by General Haynau,[2] led the landlords and the legislature to believe that it was a favorable opportunity for changing the occupation of the land and the cultivation of the soil from potatoes to corn.[3] When more food, more cultivation, more employment, were the requisites for maintaining the Irish in existence, the Legislature and the landlords went about introducing a species of cultivation that could only be successful by requiring fewer hands, and turning potato gardens, that nourished the maximum of human beings, into

Literary Analysis
Journalistic Essay What is the role of the pronoun "we" in a journalistic essay?

requisites (rek′ wə zits) *n.* things necessary for a given purpose

6 **Reading Check**
According to this article, what caused the "present condition of the Irish"?

1. **political economy** theory of economics and society.
2. **General Haynau** Julius Jacob; an Austrian general notorious for the brutality with which he suppressed uprisings by the Hungarians and other peoples who revolted against the Austrian empire in the 1840's. When Haynau visited London in 1850, he was attacked by outraged mobs.
3. **corn** (Brit.) grain.

CUSTOMIZE INSTRUCTION FOR UNIVERSAL ACCESS

For Less Proficient Readers	For English Learners	For Advanced Readers
Tell students to find editorials in two different newspapers that both comment on a specific event or issue in the news. Then, have them write an essay comparing the opinions that are presented.	Have students focus on the use of coordinating conjunctions in this essay. A coordinating conjunction links two sentence parts of the same grammatical kind. There are seven coordinating conjunctions: *and, but, or, nor, yet, so,* and *for.*	Have students write a journalistic essay on an event in the news. They should research the facts and then connect the facts with a dramatic theme—for instance, success, courage, or neglect.

4 Literary Analysis

Journalistic Essay

- Remind students that in their analysis of this journalistic essay, they need to be on the lookout for indications of the author's perspective and possible biases.
- Have students read the opening sentence, and then ask the Literary Analysis question on p. 897: What is the role of the pronoun "we" in a journalistic essay?
  Answer: The "we" in a journalistic essay is an all-knowing witness to the events of the times. Students need to be aware that this device is often used to draw the reader into the argument as if they, too, as a member of this "we," are in agreement with the argument being advanced.

5 Reading Strategy

Distinguishing Emotive and Informative Language

- Have students read the indicated passage. Then, ask them if this passage is largely an example of emotive or informative language. Why?
  Possible response: Students may respond that it is an example of emotive language because it expresses the author's feelings and is meant to sway the readers with phrases such as "great calamity" and "doomed them."
- Then, ask students to rewrite the passage, using less emotive language.
  Possible response: Although the loss of the potato crop for one season was a setback, the Irish people could have overcome it.

6 Reading Check

Answer: The essay argues that the then-present condition of the Irish was brought about by "ignorant and vicious legislation" that substituted the cultivation of grain for that of potatoes.

7 Background

The Irish Famine

Note that despite what may have been at times the good intentions of the British, several governmental policies actually led to a worsening of the famine. The promotion by the British government of large farms drove small farms out of business. The Corn Law of 1846, making wheat available at a lower price, did not help the Irish. Moreover, the Poor Law offered only a prison-like form of employment.

8 Critical Thinking

Infer

- Point out to students that the article lists a series of questions.
- Ask students if they think the writer intends for the reader to answer the questions. Why or why not?
  Answer: No; The questions are rhetorical and are intended to make the reader think.

9 Vocabulary Development

"Humor" Words (p. 899)

- Explain to students that the *London News* article uses the word *melancholy,* meaning "sad," to describe the plight of the Irish.
- The word originally meant "black bile," one of the four humors, or liquids, that people from ancient Greece to the Renaissance believed governed human health and personality. We still use words from this theory, such as *choleric* (from the humor *choler*), meaning "ill-tempered," to describe people.

pasture grounds for bullocks,[4] that nourished only the minimum. The Poor-Law, said to be for the relief of the people and the means of their salvation, was the instrument of their destruction. In their terrible distress, from that temporary calamity with which they were visited, they were to have no relief unless they gave up their holdings.[5] That law, too, laid down a form for evicting the people, and thus gave the sanction and encouragement of legislation to exterminate them. Calmly and quietly, but very ignorantly—though we cheerfully exonerate the parties from any malevolence; they only committed a great mistake, a terrible blunder, which in legislation is worse than a crime—but calmly and quietly from Westminster itself, which is the center of civilization, did the decree go forth which has made the temporary but terrible visitation[6] of a potato rot the means of exterminating, through the slow process of disease and houseless starvation, nearly the half of the Irish.

The land is still there, in all its natural beauty and fertility. The sparkling Shannon, teeming with fish, still flows by their doors, and might bear to them, as the Hudson and Thames bear to the people of New York and of London, fleets of ships laden with wealth. The low grounds or *Corcasses* of Clare are celebrated for their productiveness. The country abounds in limestone: coal, iron, and lead have been found. It has an area of 827,994 acres, 372,237 of which are uncultivated, or occupied by woods or water. It is estimated that there are 296,000 acres of unoccupied land; and that of these 160,000 are capable of cultivation and improvement. 8 Why are they not cultivated and improved, as the wilds of America are cultivated and improved by the brethren of the Irish? Why are these starving people not allowed and encouraged to plant their potato-gardens on the wastes? Why are they not married to the unoccupied soil, as a humane politician proposes to provide for the starving needlewomen of the metropolis by marrying them to the *Currency Lads* of New South Wales?[7]

Literature in context — Economics Connection

7 *The Irish Famine*

British economic policies, which are attacked in this essay, worsened the famine:

- The British government had promoted large farms that hired workers and exported cash crops, driving small family farms out of business. The Poor Law actually required that anyone farming a quarter acre or less give up his land before he could receive government aid. Without land, poor families could not raise crops during the famine.
- The Corn (grain) Law (1846), made wheat available at a cheaper price, but did not help Irish peasants, who had no money to buy it.
- The Poor Law provided no relief for the able-bodied unemployed except employment—and residence— in prisonlike workhouses.

4. **bullocks** oxen.
5. **The Poor-Law . . . gave up their holdings** The Poor-Law determined how aid was to be given to the poor. During the famine, farmers with small farms ("holdings") were required to give them up before they would be given aid.
6. **visitation** divine punishment or reward.
7. **needlewomen . . . New South Wales** Probably referring to a scheme encouraging emigration to Australia. The "New Currency Lads" are native-born Australians.

sanction (saŋk′ shən) *n.* authorized approval or permission

exonerate (eg zän′ ər āt′) *v.* free from a charge of guilt; declare or prove blameless

ENRICHMENT: Career Connection

Farming

Since people cannot live without food, one would think that there are many career opportunities in farming, but that is not the case. Because of the increased industrialization of farms, fewer farmers are needed. By contrast, in the mid-nineteenth century, most Americans lived on farms. Each farm produced enough food for four people. Currently, less than three percent of the population lives on farms, yet these farms often produce a surplus of food. Discuss with students some of the problems a farmer of today faces, such as pest control, unusual weather patterns, and crop surpluses.

9 A more important question cannot be asked. There is about Kilrush, and in Clare, and throughout Ireland, the doubly melancholy spectacle of a strong man asking for work as the means of getting food; and of the fertile earth wooing his labors, in order to yield up to him its rich but latent[8] stores: yet it lies idle and unfruitful. Why is not this doubly melancholy spectacle destroyed by their union, and converted into life and happiness, as oxygen and hydrogen, each in itself destructive, become, when united as water, the pabulum[9] of existence? We shall fully consider that question before we quit the subject, but we shall now only say that the whole of this land, cultivated and uncultivated, is owned by a few proprietors—that many of them are absentees[10] —that almost all are in embarrassed circumstances—and that, from ignorance, or false theory, or indolence, they prefer seeing the land covered with such misery as we have described, to either bringing the land under cultivation themselves, or allowing the people to cultivate it. Their greatest ambition, apparently, is to get rid of the people.

melancholy (mel′ ən käl′ ē) *adj.* sad; depressing

Reading Strategy
Distinguishing Emotive and Informative Language 10 What, if any, is the emotional effect of the scientific analogy regarding oxygen and hydrogen?

indolence (in′ də lens) *n.* idleness; laziness

8. **latent** potential; not yet actual.
9. **pabulum** nourishing substance.
10. **absentees** Many landowners who rented to small Irish farmers lived in England and were thought to lack sufficient motivation to make the best use of their lands.

Review and Assess

Thinking About the Selection

1. **Respond:** Does this article move you to outrage on behalf of the Irish, or does it leave you cold? Explain.
2. (a) **Recall:** What does the article say is the "current condition" of the Irish? (b) **Interpret:** What measures, according to the article, would have kept the famine from becoming a crisis?
3. (a) **Recall:** According to the article, what British measures were mainly responsible for the condition of the Irish? (b) **Infer:** What do you think were the ultimate objectives of these measures? Why?
4. (a) **Recall:** Summarize what the article says about Ireland's natural resources. (b) **Analyze:** Considering the overall purpose of this article, why do you think the author included the passage on Ireland's natural resources?
5. (a) **Recall:** What does the article say is the obvious solution to Ireland's difficulties? (b) **Analyze:** The article poses a solution as a series of questions. Why is this more effective and persuasive than making a simple statement?
6. (a) **Connect:** In what regions of the world today is famine still a threat? (b) **Draw Conclusions:** What are the best ways of overcoming this threat? Explain.

10 Reading Strategy

Distinguishing Emotive and Informative Language

- Have students read the concluding paragraph of the essay. Have students identify the scientific analogy that is drawn here.
- Then, ask them the Reading Strategy question on p. 899: What, if any, is the emotional effect of the scientific analogy regarding oxygen and hydrogen?
Possible response: Students may respond that since science is objective, the analogy to scientific facts adds the sound of authority to the proposal. The analogy makes the reader feel that putting a man and the land together is a scientific, natural solution.

Answers for p. 899

Review and Assess

1. Some students may respond that the article inflamed them. Other students may respond that they would feel more comfortable waiting until they heard or read the opposing point of view before making a judgment.
2. **(a)** They are starving. **(b)** Economic aid from the state and from charities could have averted the crisis in the short term, and maintenance of small-scale farming would have prevented future impoverishment.
3. **(a)** Economic policies encouraging the growing of grain and discouraging small farms were mainly responsible for the condition of the Irish. **(b)** Britain's objectives were to change the basis of Ireland's economy from small, independently owned farms to large, efficient farms that would hire wage-laborers and sell crops for trade. The economists thought such measures would lead to a stronger economy for Ireland.
4. **(a)** Ireland has fertile lands, with 160,000 acres capable of cultivation and improvement, the Shannon River teeming with fish, and natural resources, such as coal, iron, and lead. **(b)** The author is pointing out that with better government policies, Ireland could thrive.

continued

Answers continued

5. **(a)** The article says the obvious solution is to allow the people to cultivate small farms and make use of their natural resources. **(b)** Rhetorical questions draw the reader into the author's argument, stimulating them to participate in formulating the conclusions the author wishes to advance.
6. **(a)** Many nations of the world have widespread or pocketed famine, including many African nations, China, India, and the United States. **(b)** Students may respond that the solution will vary from country to country and from region to region, but that in general, policies that encourage self-sufficiency are most likely to effectively combat famine.

⓫ About the Selection

In this article from the mid-nineteenth century, Sydney Smith reflects on the scientific and technological advances that have taken place, noting that he can name at least eighteen improvements that have occurred in his lifetime. Important changes for the nineteenth century were gas street lamps, the steamboat, railroads, savings banks, and the postal service.

⓬ Reading Strategy

Distinguishing Emotive and Informative Language

- Have students read the first two paragraphs. Ask them to pay careful attention to the language that the writer uses.
- Then, ask them to name two facts presented in this paragraph and to find two phrases that add emotional effect.
  Possible response: Two facts are that gas was unknown and light came from an oil lamp. Some phrases that add emotional effect are "I groped about," "the utter darkness," and "exposed to every species of depredation and insult."

⓭ Critical Thinking

Analyze

- Have students read the indicated passage; point out that Smith specifically indicates how long his various travels took. Ask students what the reader needs to know in order to be impressed by this information.
  Answer: The reader needs to know the distance from Taunton to Bath (about 60 miles) and from Taunton to London (about 180 miles).
- Then, ask if it is likely that Smith's readers were knowledgeable about these distances. Why or why not?
  Answer: Yes, it is likely that Smith's readers knew the distances because Smith was writing for a local newspaper.

⓫ Progress in Personal Comfort

Sydney Smith

It is of some importance at what period a man is born. A young man, alive at this period, hardly knows to what improvements of human life he has been introduced; and I would bring before his notice the following eighteen changes which have taken place in England since I first began to breathe in it the breath of life—a period amounting now to nearly seventy-three years.

⓬ Gas[1] was unknown: I groped about the streets of London in all but the utter darkness of a twinkling oil lamp, under the protection of watchmen in their grand climacteric,[2] and exposed to every species of depredation and insult.

⓭ I have been nine hours in sailing from Dover to Calais before the invention of steam. It took me nine hours to go from Taunton to

depredation (dep′ rə dā′ shən) *n.* act or instance of robbing, plundering or laying waste

1. **gas** coal gas, piped under the streets of London and used in street lamps after 1814.
2. **climacteric** old age; a period of great change associated in some theories with the age of 63.

14 Bath, before the invention of railroads, and I now go in six hours from Taunton to London! In going from Taunton to Bath, I suffered between 10,000 and 12,000 severe contusions,[3] before stone-breaking Macadam[4] was born.

I paid £15 in a single year for repairs of carriage-springs on the pavement of London; and I now glide without noise or fracture, on wooden pavements.

I can walk, by the assistance of the police, from one end of London to the other, without molestation; or, if tired, get into a cheap and active cab, instead of those cottages on wheels, which the hackney coaches[5] were at the beginning of my life.

I had no umbrella! They were little used, and very dear. There were no waterproof hats, and *my* hat has often been reduced by rains into its primitive pulp.

3. **contusions** bruises.
4. **Macadam** (mə kad′ əm) road-surfacing made of small stones bound with adhesive.
5. **cheap and active cab . . . hackney coaches** Hackney coaches were used four-wheeled carriages for hire. The faster two-wheeled hansom cabs appeared in London in the 1830s.

Reading Strategy
Distinguishing Emotive and Informative Language Identify two examples each of emotive and informative language in the essay's third paragraph.

15  **Reading Check**

What are three examples of progress that Smith cites?

16 ◀ **Critical Viewing** Would Mr. Smith have described this locomotive as old-fashioned or up-to-date? Explain. **[Analyze]**

CUSTOMIZE INSTRUCTION FOR UNIVERSAL ACCESS

For Less Proficient Readers	For Special Needs Students	For Gifted/Talented Students
Have students research technological advances of the nineteenth century and make an oral presentation to the class.	As they read, have students keep a list of the eighteen improvements Smith lists as having happened during his lifetime. Then, have them mark those that they feel are significant.	Have students write a satirical essay poking fun at the novel inventions of our day.

14 Reading Strategy
Distinguishing Emotive and Informative Language

- Have students read the third paragraph. Review with students the difference between emotive and informative language.
- Then, ask them the Reading Strategy question on p. 901: Identify two examples each of emotive and informative language in the third paragraph.
  Answer: The exclamation point at the end of the second sentence indicates the author's emotional response to the great reduction in travel times, and his exaggerated reference to having "suffered between 10,000 to 12,000 severe contusions" is intended to affect the reader emotionally. The references to the travel times between Dover and Calais, and those between Taunton and Bath, and Taunton and London, are examples of informative language.

15 Reading Check

Answer: Smith mentions the invention of steam power, railroads, and Macadam.

16 ▶ Critical Viewing

Answer: Students may say that his locomotive appears to be old-fashioned because modern trains are streamlined and have no smokestacks. Smith would probably have been quite impressed with the modernity of this locomotive.

17 Literary Analysis
Journalistic Essay (p. 902)

- Have students complete their reading of the essay. Have students summarize the content of the article and then identify the writer's purpose for writing it.
- Then, ask the Literary Analysis question on p. 902: Why do you think Smith does not relate the detailed history of the inventions he cites?
  Possible response: Students may respond that by just citing these inventions, almost as if they had appeared out of thin air, Smith manages to express a greater sense of wonder at these technological marvels.

ASSESS

Answers for p. 902

Review and Assess

1. **(a)** The changes took place over a period of nearly seventy-three years, starting with Smith's birth in the late eighteenth century. **(b)** The changes took place before the "young man" was born, or during his childhood and young adulthood, and were interwoven into his daily life.
2. **(a)** Two changes in public safety were gas street lamps and a more robust police force. Two changes in public transportation were the invention of steamboats and railroads. **(b)** Students may mention the discomforts of unlit streets; slower, less comfortable transportation; more crime; no umbrellas; no suspenders; fewer available medications; filthy coffee houses; and no postal service.
3. **(a)** It apparently did not occur to Smith that progress would continue and his "luxurious" lifestyle would later be looked upon as out-of-date and uncomfortable. **(b)** Possible response: Values such as "progress" and "discomfort" are relative to a person's habits and expectations. Smith cannot "see" the discomfort in his own surroundings because he has not had the experience of twentieth-century conveniences.
4. **(a)** Students would be likely to mention the advances in computing and telecommunications—cell phones, the Internet, Internet telephone, GPS systems—at the tops of their lists since these technologies are the current "buzz." **(b)** Students may respond with the list above and add advances in medicine.

I could not keep my smallclothes in their proper place, for braces were unknown.[6] If I had the gout, there was no colchicum. If I was bilious, there was no calomel. If I was attacked by ague, there was no quinine.[7] There were filthy coffee houses instead of elegant clubs. Game could not be bought. Quarrels about uncommuted tithes[8] were endless. The corruption of Parliament, before Reform, infamous.[9] There were no banks to receive the savings of the poor. The Poor Laws were gradually sapping the vitals of the country; and whatever miseries I suffered, I had no post to whisk my complaints for a single penny[10] to the remotest corners of the empire; and yet, in spite of all these privations, I lived on quietly, and am now ashamed that I was not more discontented, and utterly surprised that all these changes and inventions did not occur two centuries ago.

17

I forgot to add, that as the basket of stage coaches, in which luggage was then carried, had no springs, your clothes were rubbed all to pieces. . . .

Literary Analysis
Journalistic Essay Why do you think Smith does not relate the detailed history of the inventions he cites?

6. **smallclothes . . . braces** There were no suspenders to support his trousers.
7. **If I had the gout . . . there was no quinine** Gout, bilious conditions, and ague are afflictions. Colchicum, calomel, and quinine are remedies.
8. **uncommuted tithes** taxes paid to the Church in the form of produce, "commuted" (changed to) an equivalent payment in money in 1840.
9. **The corruption of Parliament . . . infamous** Before the reforms of the 1800s, the House of Commons was dominated by a few corrupt, wealthy landowners.
10. **I had no post . . . single penny** Penny postage, in the form of an adhesive stamp, was first introduced in England in 1840.

Review and Assess

Thinking About the Selection

1. **(a) Recall:** Over what period of time did the changes that Smith reports take place? **(b) Infer:** What lack of knowledge does Smith suggest is the reason for a "young man" to take these changes for granted?
2. **(a) Recall:** What are two improvements in public safety and two in public transportation that Smith reports?
   (b) Infer: Judging from Smith's account, how uncomfortable was life before these improvements? Explain.
3. **(a) Recall:** Does Smith consider the possibility that people in the future might find his world uncomfortable?
   (b) Infer: What reason can you give for his including or not including such a consideration? Explain.
4. **(a) Generalize:** In your opinion, what advances other than those in personal comfort are also a sign of progress? Explain.
   (b) Make a Judgment: Which types of advances do you consider the most essential to progress? Why?

ASSESSMENT PRACTICE: Reading Comprehension

Paired Passages (For more practice, see Test Preparation Workbook, p. 41.)

Many tests require students to answer questions about literary elements in two passages. Use the following sample item to show students how to identify and relate the authors' purposes. Have students read pp. 896–902 before they respond to this question.

Which of these best expresses the authors' purposes in the two selections?

A Both authors wrote to persuade.
B The reporter wrote to inform; Smith wrote to entertain.
C Both authors wrote to persuade and to entertain.
D The reporter wrote to inform and persuade; Smith wrote to inform and entertain.

Lead students to recognize that an author may have more than one purpose in writing. By considering the goals of the reporter and of Smith, students should determine that *D* is the correct answer.

Review and Assess

Literary Analysis

Journalistic Essay

1. In the **journalistic essay** "Condition of Ireland," the author writes as a judge, saying "we . . . exonerate the parties. . . ." Find another passage in which the author writes as a judge, and explain your choice.
2. Look at the picture on page 896. What, if anything, does it add to the attack on the government's legislation in "Condition of Ireland"?
3. Is Sidney Smith's subject, "personal comfort," better treated humorously or seriously? Why?
4. Is Smith's focus in "Progress in Comfort" compatible with his progressive viewpoints on matters like parliamentary reform? Why or why not?

Comparing Literary Works

5. Fill in a chart like this one with examples indicating the writer's approach in each essay.

Exaggeration	Humor	Moral Drama: Good vs. Evil

6. Which essay is more persuasive? Explain your choice, using examples from each essay.

Reading Strategy

Distinguishing Emotive and Informative Language

7. **Distinguish emotive and informative language** in the sentence beginning, "In their terrible distress, . . ." in the first paragraph of "Condition of Ireland."
8. In these passages, identify examples of emotive and informative language: (a) The description of natural resources in "Condition of Ireland," and (b) Smith's description of the penny post.

Extend Understanding

9. **Science Connection:** Using a specific example, demonstrate how quickly technology changes today.

Quick Review

Journalistic essays are short prose pieces that provide a perspective on current events or trends.

Emotive language uses words, phrases, and examples for emotional effect.

Informative language conveys facts.

Take It to the Net

www.phschool.com

Take the interactive self-test online to check your understanding of these selections.

Answers for p. 903

Review and Assess

1. In the last paragraph, the writer acts as judge and condemns absentee proprietors.
2. Students may respond that the connotative value of the picture, depicting a starving mother and child, is devastating, especially in the light of the traditional role of women at the time of the famine in Ireland.
3. Students may respond that the subject is better treated humorously, since a serious treatment would seem silly.
4. Students may respond that his almost smug contentment with the present state of things seems inconsistent in spirit with progressive viewpoints.
5. "Condition of Ireland": **Exaggeration:** ". . . though a great calamity, would not have doomed them"; **Humor:** ". . . but a false theory, assuming the name of political economy, with which it has no more to do than with the slaughter of the Hungarians by General Haynau"; **Moral Drama:** "The present condition of the Irish . . . has been mainly brought abut by ignorant and vicious legislation." "Progress in Comfort": **Exaggeration:** ". . . exposed to every species of depredation and insult"; **Humor:** "I could not keep my smallclothes in their proper place . . . "; **Moral Drama:** "The Poor Laws were gradually sapping the vitals of the country."
6. Some students may respond the "Condition of Ireland" article is the more persuasive, as it wrestles with a serious problem in a comprehensive and sober manner.
7. **Emotive language:** "In their terrible distress, from that temporary calamity . . ."; **Informative language:** ". . . they were to have no relief unless they gave up their holdings."
8. **(a) Emotive:** "The sparkling Shannon, teeming with fish, still flows by their doors and might bear to them, . . . fleets of ships laden with wealth."; **Informative:** ". . . coal, iron

continued

Answers continued

and lead have been found." **(b) Emotive:** "I had no post to whisk my complaints . . . "; **Informative:** " . . . for a single penny."

9. Students may respond that new generations of computers, cell phones, Internet connections, and a multitude of GPS instruments are announced almost monthly.

EXTEND

Answers for p. 904

❶ Vocabulary Development

Concept Development

1. sanguine: cheerfully confident; optimistic
2. bilious: bad-tempered
3. phlegmatic: having or suggesting a calm, sluggish temperament; unemotional
4. choleric: easily angered; bad-tempered
5. bile: bitterness of temper; ill humor; irascibility

Synonyms

1. e
2. c
3. b
4. d
5. f
6. a

Spelling Strategy

1. sanctions
2. depredations
3. famines
4. coaches
5. potatoes
6. essays

❷ Grammar and Style

1. for
2. or
3. but
4. or
5. so

Writing Application

Have students exchange letters with a partner to check for the proper use of coordinating conjunctions.

Integrate Language Skills

❶ Vocabulary Development Lesson

Concept Development: "Humor" Words

In "Condition of Ireland," the author describes the plight of the Irish as *melancholy*, meaning "sad" or "depressing." *Melancholy* originally meant "black bile," one of the four humors, or liquids, that people once believed governed health and personality. The other three were *blood, yellow bile* or *choler*, and *phlegm*. Use sentence context to write a definition for each "humor" word italicized below. Then, check a dictionary to confirm your definitions.

1. Despite the setbacks, she remained *sanguine*.
2. Some people are sunny throughout the day, but he always seems to be *bilious* first thing in the morning.
3. Yelling "fire" just might get him going, but he is a pretty *phlegmatic* fellow.
4. She is so *choleric* that she will snap at you for the slightest thing.
5. It fills me with *bile* to see him get away with so much.

Concept Development: Synonyms

Match each word in the first column with the word in the second column that is most similar in meaning.

1. requisites	a. destruction
2. sanction	b. absolve
3. exonerate	c. approval
4. melancholy	d. sad
5. indolence	e. necessities
6. depredation	f. idleness

Spelling Strategy

To form the plural of many nouns, add *-s* or *-es*. For example, *requisite* becomes *requisites*. In your notebook, write the plural form of each of the following nouns.

1. sanction	4. coach
2. depredation	5. potato
3. famine	6. essay

❷ Grammar and Style Lesson

Coordinating Conjunctions

A **coordinating conjunction** links two sentence parts of the same grammatical kind. There are seven coordinating conjunctions: *and, but, or, nor, yet, so,* and *for*. Such conjunctions appear in both these essays, as this example demonstrates.

Example: They were little used, **and** very dear.

Practice In your notebook, complete each sentence by filling in the blank with a suitable coordinating conjunction.

1. He could not keep his smallclothes in their proper place, __?__ braces were unknown.
2. He now glides without noise __?__ fracture.
3. Calmly and quietly, __?__ very ignorantly, did the decree go forth.
4. He could walk without being bothered, __?__ he could take a cab.
5. Their greatest ambition was to get rid of the people, __?__ they would not allow the people to cultivate the land.

Writing Application In a letter to a modern newspaper, comment on advances in comfort. Use three coordinating conjunctions.

WG Prentice Hall Writing and Grammar Connection: Chapter 17, Section 4

TEACHING RESOURCES

The following resources can be used to enrich or extend the instruction for pp. 904–905.

Grammar

- **Selection Support:** Grammar and Style, p. 196
- **Writing and Grammar,** Diamond Level, p. 397
- **Daily Language Practice Transparencies** ■

Vocabulary

- **Selection Support Workbook:** Build Vocabulary, p. 195

Writing

- **Writing Models and Graphic Organizers on Transparencies,** pp. 85–92
- **Writing and Grammar,** Diamond Level, p. 174
- **Writing and Grammar iText CD-ROM**

■ **BLOCK SCHEDULING:** Resources marked with this symbol provide varied instruction during 90-minute blocks.

❸ # Writing Lesson

Comparison and Contrast of Viewpoints

One of these essays reveals a crisis in the Empire, and the other suggests that things are getting better. Compare and contrast the essays, focusing on the viewpoints of the era that they express.

Prewriting Use a chart like this one to record the viewpoints expressed in the essays and the support for each. Then, draw a conclusion about the similarities and differences between the viewpoints.

Model: Comparing Viewpoints

Viewpoints on Empire	Support for Viewpoints	Conclusions on Similarities/Differences
"Condition . . ."		
"Progress . . ."		

Drafting Incorporate your conclusion into a thesis statement. Support your thesis by comparing the viewpoints expressed in the essays, using transition words such as *similarly*, *in contrast*, and *by comparison*.

Revising Review your paper to be sure that you have supported your thesis statement and that you have indicated in your conclusion which viewpoint is more convincing. If your thesis needs further support, scan your chart for evidence that you might not have included.

WG *Prentice Hall Writing and Grammar Connection: Chapter 9, Section 2*

❹ # Extension Activities

Listening and Speaking Prepare a **comic monologue** about how inconvenient a "convenience" like a computer can be.

- Start with rhetorical questions: "What is it about my computer that is so *personal?*"
- Use parallel structure to help the audience follow your thoughts: "My *TV set* is not personal. My *microwave* is not personal."

As you continue to plan, provide a humorous perspective on computer problems. Then, deliver your monologue to an audience, using gestures to enhance the humor.

Research and Technology Write a **report** on a Victorian newspaper. Include a graphic, such as a newspaper illustration. One source might be books or Web sites on *The Illustrated London News*. Include a statistical table on newspaper circulation. For figures, scan articles on the history of newspapers or of British newspapers in encyclopedias.

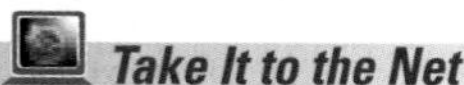

www.phschool.com

Go online for an additional research activity using the Internet.

Lesson Support for p. 905

❸ Writing Lesson

- Work as a class to identify one supporting detail and one conclusion for each selection.
- Then, have students work individually to complete their comparison charts.
- You may wish to use the Comparison-and-Contrast Essay transparencies in **Writing Models and Graphic Organizers on Transparencies,** pp. 85–92, to provide a model for students.
- Use the Comparison-and-Contrast Essay rubric in **Performance Assessment and Portfolio Management,** p. 20, to evaluate students' work.

❹ Listening and Speaking

- Divide the class into three groups. Tell the first group to prepare a monologue about personal computers. Tell the second group to prepare a monologue about microwave ovens. Tell the third group to prepare a monologue about cell phones.
- Tell each group to select a presenter. Have the class rebut each monologue after it is delivered.

CUSTOMIZE INSTRUCTION
For Universal Access

To address different learning styles, use the following activities suggested in the **Extension Activities** booklet, p. 41.

- For Verbal/Linguistic and Interpersonal Learners, use Activity 5.
- For Verbal/Linguistic and Visual/Spatial Learners, use Activity 6.
- For Visual/Spatial Learners, use Activity 7.

ASSESSMENT RESOURCES

The following resources can be used to assess students' knowledge and skills.

Selection Assessment

- **Formal Assessment,** pp. 206–208
- **Open Book Test,** pp. 123–125
- **Got It! Assessment Videotapes,** Tape 4
- **Test Bank Software**

Take It to the Net

Visit www.phschool.com for self-tests and additional questions on the selections.

Writing Rubric

- **Performance Assess. and Portfolio Mgmt.,** p. 20

PRENTICE HALL ASSESSMENT SYSTEM

- **Workbook**
- **Skill Book**
- **Transparencies**
- **CD-ROM**

Lesson Objectives

1. To evaluate the credibility of sources on the World Wide Web
2. To understand how the Web can be used as a research tool
3. To learn about the different components of a Web site

About Web Sites

- Have students read "About Web Sites." Discuss with students the kinds of Web sites with which they are familiar.
- Ask students why they think the Internet is so well suited as a tool for research.
  Possible responses: What makes the Internet such a good tool for research is the amount of information one can find on it. It puts a vast amount of information at one's fingertips.

Reading Strategy

Evaluating Credibility of Sources

- Have students read the Reading Strategy.
- Remind students that, when they conduct research on the Internet, they will come in contact with a great deal of information. It is their responsibility to determine the accuracy and validity of the information they come across. Ask students why they think they need to evaluate the credibility of the sources they find on the Internet.
  Possible responses: No one has to review information before it is put on the Internet. Different kinds of information, such as educational, entertainment, and business, are mixed in ways that aren't always apparent. This means the information may not necessarily be reliable.
- Review the graphic organizer with students and have them use it to evaluate the Web pages and links on pp. 907 and 908.

READING INFORMATIONAL MATERIALS

Web Sites

About Web Sites

The **Internet,** an electronic communications network that connects computers around the world, allows users unlimited access to a great variety of information. The World Wide Web, the most commonly accessed part of the Internet, is made up of a vast collection of **Web sites** put up by individuals and organizations around the world. A Web site typically consists of a **home page** linked to several other pages on the site. Each page consists of the set of graphics, text, sound, and video that is presented in a browser window.

The Web has become a valuable tool for conducting research. As with any tool, you must be familiar with its nature in order to use it well.

Reading Strategy

Evaluating Credibility of Sources

To use the Web properly, always evaluate the credibility of a site before using the information it presents. First, ask what the authors' or sponsors' motives are. If those responsible for the site support a particular viewpoint, the site may focus on certain details at the expense of others. Are the authors experts in their field? If so, they will be careful with facts—if only to protect their reputations. If not, they may be careless in their presentation of facts.

You can find out about the authors of "The Victorian Web" by clicking on the button labeled "Who Created the Victorian Web?" This information will help you evaluate the credibility of information on the site. For instance, the author providing information on Victorian public health is a history professor, so you can probably trust his claims. You might want to double-check claims found in the work of students, especially if the claims seem extraordinary or inconsistent.

Using a graphic organizer like the one shown, list each link on the site, as shown on pages 907 and 908, and evaluate the information you find there.

Link	Credibility	My Reasoning
Victorianism	Mixed	The link probably discusses historical issues, but the site is created largely by people studying literature and the other arts—not history.
Gender Matters		
Social Context		

The Victorian Web

With the spread of Web technology, sites sponsored by scholars and institutions of learning, like this site, have proliferated. They enable users to conveniently find the latest research on a topic. Not all sites, however, are carefully fact-checked and updated. To check credentials of those who created this site, turn to page 908.

The Victorian Web

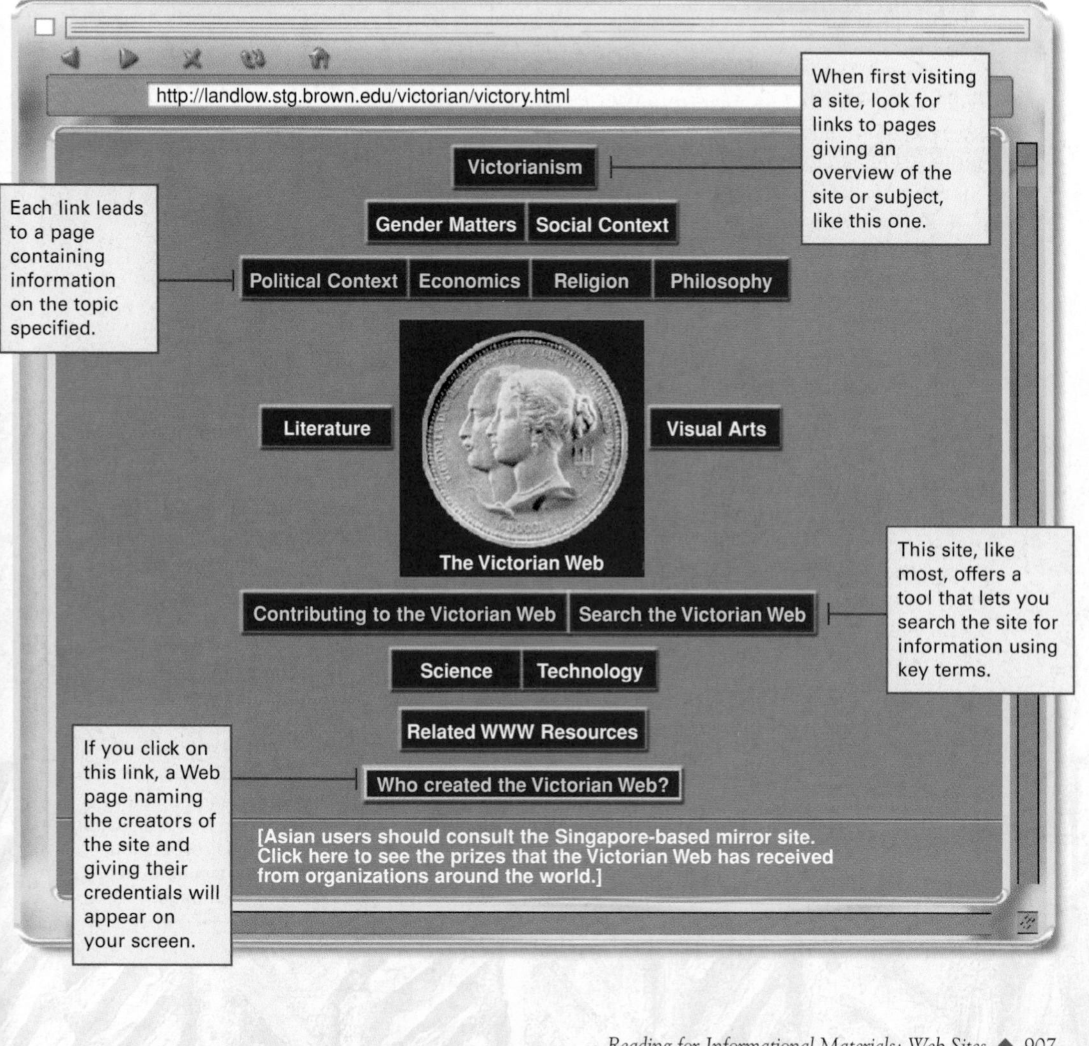

http://landlow.stg.brown.edu/victorian/victory.html
When first visiting a site, look for links to pages giving an overview of the site or subject, like this one.
Victorianism
Each link leads to a page containing information on the topic specified.
Gender Matters
Social Context
Political Context
Economics
Religion
Philosophy
Literature
Visual Arts
The Victorian Web
This site, like most, offers a tool that lets you search the site for information using key terms.
Contributing to the Victorian Web
Search the Victorian Web
Science
Technology
Related WWW Resources
If you click on this link, a Web page naming the creators of the site and giving their credentials will appear on your screen.
Who created the Victorian Web?
[Asian users should consult the Singapore-based mirror site. Click here to see the prizes that the Victorian Web has received from organizations around the world.]

The Victorian Web

- Explain to students that, though Web pages will all have different designs, they have many elements in common. This page shows an example of the kind of sites they will encounter as they use the Web for research.
- Encourage students to familiarize themselves with the different components of a typical Web page. Have them read the information on the Web page, as well as the notes that identify the different page elements. Discuss pages students have seen and elicit comments about how they are different from and similar to this example.
- Tell students that one of the most important elements to look for on a Web page is the organization or individual responsible for the information contained on the page. Students will need to evaluate the credentials of these authors in order to determine the accuracy and validity of the information.
- Explain that students do not necessarily have to ignore information from someone writing outside of their field, because some people are careful in their research, but they should always check another source to confirm the facts.

CUSTOMIZE INSTRUCTION FOR UNIVERSAL ACCESS

For Less Proficient Readers	For English Learners
Have students work in small groups to review the elements of the Web page shown on this page. Discuss the elements with students, to ensure that they understand the concepts. Then, ask students to find another example of an academic Web page and identify the major information listed in the notes for the pages they chose.	To ensure that students understand the major elements of a Web page and the significance of each element, pair them with English speakers. Have each pair work together on the Internet to further clarify the element descriptions by actually finding their counterparts on several other pages.

Internal Page

- Explain to students that not every Web page they encounter will have as much information about the author(s) of the Web page as they see here.
- Ask students why they think George P. Landow's credentials can be called "respectable."
  Answer: He is a professor of English and art history, so he is very knowledgeable about the topic.
- Encourage students to ask the following questions as they encounter Web pages during their research in order to help them evaluate the credibility of sources: What person or organization posted the information on the Web site? Are they qualified to provide information about this topic? How can you tell?

Internal Page

Shown here is the page linked to the button labeled "Who created the Victorian Web?" on the site's home page (see page 907).

The respectable credentials of the main author of the site are presented here.

This passage explains the original purpose and motive for compiling the information on the site: to aid students taking particular courses at a university.

http://landlow.stg.brown.edu/victorian/misc/credits.html

Credits: Who Created the Victorian Web?

George P. Landow, Professor of English and Art History, Brown University

The Victorian Web

The Victorian Web and *Context32*

The Victorian Web is the WWW translation of Brown University's **Context 61,** which serves as a resource for courses in Victorian literature. These materials ultimately derive from **Context 32,** the Intermedia web that provided contextual information for English 32, "Survey of English Literature From 1700 to the Present." **Context 32** was begun in Spring 1985 as part of Brown University's Institute for Research in Information and Scholarship (IRIS) Intermedia project, which IBM, Apple Computers, the Annenberg/CPB Project, and other sources funded.

George P. Landow designed and edited the entire web, made many of the links, and is responsible for most of the materials on the individual authors and works as well as those on Biblical typology. He authored multiple lexias throughout the web and selected both the external criticism cited and most of the visual images. All captions for images are his. Under his direction David Cody wrote many of the general materials and chose many of the original digitized images, and Glenn Everett wrote some of the basic materials on Romantic and Victorian poets including timelines. The following year Kathryn Stockton created many of the documents on feminism and literary theory.

Anthony S. Wohl, Professor of History at Vassar College, generously contributed much of the material on Victorian public health, race and class issues, and anti-Catholic prejudice in Victorian England. This work draws upon both his published and unpublished writings.

Specific information on other contributors and the information for which each is responsible allows users to evaluate the credibility of each page.

Check Your Comprehension

1. (a)Who created this Web site? (b)What are his credentials? (c) Explain the responsibility he has for the information on the site.
2. Who wrote materials on Romantic and Victorian poets?

Apply the Reading Strategy

Evaluating the Credibility of Sources

To evaluate the quality, possible bias, and credibility of research material you locate online, check the source of the information. Use the following questions to help you evaluate the sources of "The Victorian Web":

1. Explain whether you would give higher credibility to materials written by Professor Landow than to materials by his students.
2. Name two links on the home page that you would be inclined to trust. Name two links you would consider more cautiously. Explain your reasoning.

Activity

Designing a Web Site

Use a chart like the one shown to sketch the design of a Web site on a topic in British literature.

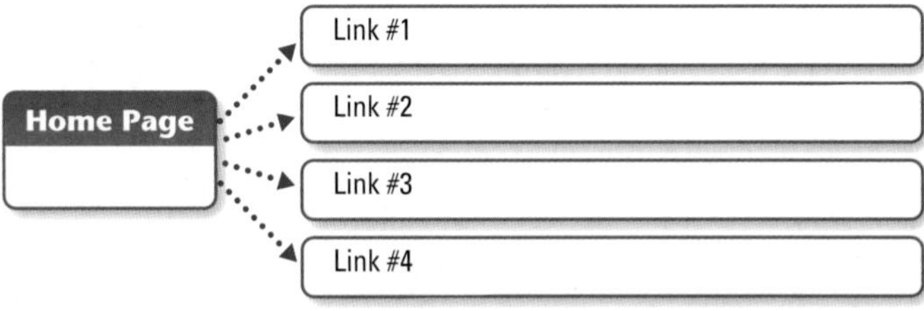

Answer to the following questions when creating your design:

1. Which page should you design first for your Web site?
2. Is there a hierarchy of topics—for example, from general to specific—that should guide your organization?

Comparing Informational Materials

Comparing Credits Pages

Find a Web site on a topic that interests you. Examine the credits for this Web site to determine whether you can trust the information presented. Compare the credits for this site with the credits for the Victorian Web. Explain which site you would rate as more credible.

Answers for p. 909

Check Your Comprehension

1. **(a)** The main author of the Web site is George P. Landow. **(b)** He is Professor of English and Art History at Brown University. **(c)** He is responsible for the accuracy of the information on authors, works, and captions.
2. Glenn Everett wrote the materials on Romantic and Victorian poets.

Apply the Reading Strategy

1. Landow is a professor of English and he would be more knowledgeable about the subject of Victorianism than his students, so he would be more credible.
2. Students may say that they would trust the links to Literature and Visual Arts because Landow teaches English and art history. They might be wary of the links to Economics and Religion because these are subject areas in which Landow is not necessarily an expert.

Activity

Encourage students to choose a topic that can be adequately covered in a Web site. Remind them that they should not attempt to cover too large a topic.

Comparing Informational Materials

Students should support their evaluations with information from both Web sites. In order to make the comparison easier and more rewarding, you may want to have students choose a Web site related to the topic of British literature or history.

Lesson Objectives

1. To understand the connection between the critiques of the British Empire during the Victorian Era and the present state of affairs in Northern Ireland
2. To use a variety of reading strategies to understand a speech

Connections

When students read Arnold's "Dover Beach" and Kipling's "Recessional," they may think of them as part of a vanished historical era. The British Empire, which they comment on indirectly or directly, ceased to exist after World War II. However, conflict between Protestants and Catholics in Northern Ireland still continues, an unwelcome legacy of the empire. Have students read the speech by Judge McGuinness and discuss her steps to create an atmosphere of peace.

The Empire and Its Discontents

- Explain to students that for residents of Northern Ireland, conflict has left deep marks. Whether it be a remembrance of past wrongs or a nationalist pride, discontent is still common in this last vestige of the British Empire.
- If possible, provide examples of conflict involving both religious and nonreligious groups throughout the world. Ask students to look for recommendations for resolution of these conflicts as they read McGuinness's speech.

CONNECTIONS

Literature Past and Present

The Empire and Its Discontents

The Two Sides of Success During the Victorian Era, Great Britain made great conquests in science and technology and exercised imperial power around the globe. The writers in this section show that British success had two sides. Sydney Smith, for example, notes the progress in personal comfort that made life easier—at least for the privileged. In sharp contrast, the article from *The Illustrated London News* reveals the harsh "aid" given the Irish by the British during the potato famine. Surveying the spirit of the times, Matthew Arnold tries to rescue meaning from a world of sadness, disillusionment, and alienation.

Discontents that Survive In "Recessional," Kipling warns that the Empire might not last forever. History has proved him right. Countries once under England's rule, such as India, are now independent. In Northern Ireland, though, still under British rule, the discontents have outlived the Empire. There, Protestants loyal to England battle with Catholics who want union with the Republic of Ireland to the south.

A New Ideal of Progress Many people of goodwill, such as Judge Catherine McGuinness, are trying to assuage the conflict. This selection is a speech by Judge McGuinness to the Forum for Peace and Reconciliation (1995), which attempted to bring together Protestants and Catholics in Northern Ireland. Her speech shows that, through the Empire is gone, ideals of progress still thrive.

ENRICHMENT: Career Connection

Judiciary Careers

Catherine McGuinness is a judge, an officer of the government who presides over a court of law. In both Great Britain and the United States, the judges of high courts are referred to as justices.

Judges very often come from the ranks of lawyers, who generally attend a four-year college and then a two-year law school.

Good verbal skills are necessary for anyone considering a career in law. Have interested students research careers in law, such as paralegal, legal secretary, bailiff, attorney, clerk, law professor, court reporter, and judge. Students may also be interested in finding out about various legal specialties, such as environmental law, taxation, or family law.

Thematic Connection

Answer: McGuinness would embrace the idea that progress lies in the achievement of peace and reconciliation.

✓ Reading Check

Answer: The ultimate aim of the Forum is to consult on solutions as well as to maintain the status of an advisory board. The Forum has no real authority.

Opening Statement for the Inaugural Session of the Forum for Peace and Reconciliation

Judge Catherine McGuinness

I am happy to welcome all who are here today in Dublin Castle, participants in the Forum, observers and distinguished guests.

The Forum for Peace and Reconciliation has been established by the Government in accordance with the intentions expressed in the Joint Declaration, to consult on, and examine, ways in which lasting peace, stability and reconciliation can be established by agreement among all the people of Ireland, and on the steps required to remove barriers of distrust, on the basis of promoting respect for the equal rights and validity of both traditions and identities. In accordance with its terms of reference it will also explore ways in which new approaches can be developed to serve economic interests common to both parts of Ireland.

It will be a fundamental principle of the Forum that all differences in relation to the exercise of the right to self-determination of the people of Ireland, and to all other matters, will be resolved exclusively by peaceful and democratic means. The purpose of the Forum will be to provide an opportunity to both major traditions, as well as to others, to assist in

Thematic Connection
What idea of progress would McGuinness embrace?

✓ Reading Check
What is the ultimate aim of the Forum?

CUSTOMIZE INSTRUCTION FOR UNIVERSAL ACCESS

For Less Proficient Readers	For Gifted/Talented Students	For Advanced Readers
Have these students divide McGuinness's speech. Have students read the speech. Then, have students work in pairs to summarize each of the paragraphs assigned to them. Then, have the class combine their summaries. Hold a discussion of McGuinness's main ideas.	Have these students read and outline McGuinness's speech. Then, have them produce a series of illustrated posters promoting McGuinness's ideas. They may use photographs from magazines or produce original illustrations.	Have these students read and outline McGuinness's speech. Then, have them present speeches of their own answering McGuinness's ideas and her call for action. Encourage them to do necessary background research.

Background

History

Tell students that James Connolly (1868–1916) was an Irish Labour leader and rebel. He joined the British Army at fourteen but deserted to marry. In 1896, he founded the Irish Socialist Republican party. He was an organizer of a massive transport strike in Ireland in 1913. Connolly was seriously wounded in the Easter rebellion in 1916, after which he was arrested and executed.

Thematic Connection

Answer: Her ideals are in direct contrast with those of the Victorian period. At that time, a person's future was established almost at birth by class, religion, and nationality. McGuinness believes that "people's rights and freedoms" should have nothing to do with religious affiliation or whether the government to which he or she owes allegiance is in Dublin or London.

identifying and clarifying issues which could most contribute to creating a new era of trust and cooperation. Participation in the Forum will be entirely without prejudice to the position on constitutional issues held by any Party.

It is clear that major negotiations regarding Ireland's future, North and South, are now taking place and will continue to take place elsewhere. This Forum is a consultative and advisory body, which I hope will create a background of mutual understanding against which those other negotiations may more readily move forward.

The Forum is inclusive in its nature; already it contains members from all of the island of Ireland. I very much hope that in the future other Parties and other individuals will feel able to join in our deliberations. The forum does not represent a threat to any section of the people of Ireland. As I have already said, participation in it is entirely without prejudice to the position on constitutional issues held by any Party. The only entry test is a commitment to "peaceful and democratic means."

This Forum is about people rather than about territory. It is about people's right to live peacefully on this island "which we love and for whose welfare we pray," as that courageous Presbyterian minister, James Armour of Ballymoney, once said. All who live in Ireland must be made to feel that their right to be here is unquestioned and that they and their traditions are valued, whether they arrived here a few years ago or whether their ancestors came here four thousand years or four hundred years ago. People's rights and freedoms should not be affected by their religion, by their political or social outlook, by their economic standing, by their race, or by the country of origin of their ancestors. "Ireland, as distinct from her people, is nothing to me" said James Connolly, in a ringing denunciation of mindless so-called patriotism. James Connolly, who established Ireland's first republican and socialist party, and who was executed following the 1916 Rising, was born in Scotland of Ulster parents, and first arrived in Ireland as a British soldier in the Royal Scots Regiment.

The people of this country have many origins; these strands are woven together to make us what we are. My own personal background is, perhaps, an illustration. My great great grandfather, William Ellis, was twice Lord Mayor of York in England in 1799 and 1807. My great grandfather arrived in this country as a soldier in the 93rd Sutherland Highlanders regiment in 1803. He married a Clare woman whose mother's name was Morony. Their son settled in Spanish Point in County Clare, my own father's place of origin. My mother, whose family had both Irish and Scottish ancestors, came from Tullamore in County Offaly. My parents spent virtually all their adult life in Dunmurry, near Belfast. I was born into the Belfast Protestant community, a "Child of the Rectory," and spent my childhood there. I in my turn have spent my adult life in Dublin. My love for Ulster is deep-rooted and my Protestant background is strong, but I am nonetheless proud to be a citizen of Ireland.

Thematic Connection
Contrast McGuinness's ideals with the ideals of the British Empire in Victorian times.

▶Critical Viewing
What elements in this photograph of McGuinness as she delivers her speech point to the solemnity of the occasion? **[Deduce]**

ENRICHMENT: History Connection

The Colonization of Ireland

In historical times, the earliest invasion of Ireland was that of the Celts, a people originally from Europe. When the Normans of France invaded England in 1066, some Normans took territory in Ireland. Concerned to control their power, England created earldoms in Ireland and appointed noblemen loyal to England to rule them. By the fourteenth century, Ireland was divided between those areas controlled by the Anglo-Irish and the Gaelic Irish who lived outside "the Pale" (as the area ruled by the Anglo-Irish was known).

Strong Catholicism among the Irish brought the country into conflict with Protestant England in the sixteenth century. To secure its rule of the island, England parceled out Irish lands to Scots and English landowners, an act called a plantation. The most successful such plantation, in the region of Ulster, formed the basis for present-day Northern Ireland.

▶**Critical Viewing**

Answer: Students may cite the conservative attire, the microphones, the reading lamp, the notes, and the attentive, serious expression of the person in the background.

CUSTOMIZE INSTRUCTION FOR UNIVERSAL ACCESS

For Special Needs Students	For Advanced Readers
Explain to students that the island of Ireland is divided between the country of Ireland and British-ruled Northern Ireland. Have students mark up a copy of McGuinness's speech, highlighting references to places. Then, have them consult an atlas to determine for each reference whether the place is in Northern Ireland or in Ireland. Hold a discussion analyzing the way in which McGuinness balances her references to both Ireland and Northern Ireland.	Have these students analyze the references in McGuinness's speech, doing any additional research necessary. Have them create charts or write essays in which they explain how McGuinness uses references to her own ancestry, to various places, and to various historical figures to weave an idea of a unified, nonpartisan Irish identity. Then, have them evaluate the persuasive power of this device.

Answers

Connecting Literature Past and Present

1. Major issues dividing Ireland are "barriers of distrust" and "the armed conflict of the past twenty-five years." Students may notice that McGuinness emphasizes the challenges ahead, such as poverty and unemployment, the struggle against which may unify people, and glosses over the divisive issues: "Protestant and Catholic . . . government in Dublin or in London."
2. "Recessional" and "The Widow at Windsor" allude to the military force needed to keep people in the empire against their will. The issues of poverty and injustice toward the poor are addressed in "The Widow at Windsor" and "Conditions of Ireland."

To say that this country faces many problems is to understate the position. In each jurisdiction the level of unemployment and under-employment is far too high; some of those in paid work or working in the home are exploited. There is poverty and deprivation in Dublin and in Belfast, in Leitrim and in Tyrone. Poverty and hardship dominate the lives of far too many people in Ireland, Protestant and Catholic, whether their government is in Dublin or in London. Of this we must not lose sight; it is part and parcel of the Irish situation and cannot be ignored. The economic aspects of the work of this Forum are vitally important.

We cannot pretend that the armed conflict of the past twenty-five years did not happen; nor can we say that it left no legacy. We mourn all those who died; we think of all who were wounded, some of whom will suffer from their injuries all their lives; we grieve for bereaved and broken families; we are conscious of homes where there are empty chairs; we know that all wars are cruel, bloody, harsh and merciless. We rejoice at the ending of violence. We salute all those who have worked for peace and who ultimately brought about the silence of the guns. Some of those are now members of this Forum; others are unsung, and wish to remain so; they each have earned the thanks and respect of us all.

This Forum is described as a Forum for Peace and Reconciliation. I would almost rather reverse the wording of the title and call it a forum for reconciliation and peace. At present we have a cessation of violence and the continuing peace process, but reconciliation is truly a prerequisite for a real and lasting peace. If we are to be reconciled we must be able to admit the errors and mistakes of the past; we must be able to express regret for past wrongs. Yet each of us must be able to retain pride and confidence in our history and in our traditions. Reconciliation can grow where there is both honesty and confidence, and where the old fears of each other are put behind us.

Unionist, socialist, republican, nationalist, liberal, conservative, feminist and all other views have legitimate rights and should be heard. There is no political test here; there is no censorship; there is openness. No party or group or tradition has a monopoly of wisdom. We hope to help banish hatred, incitement to hatred and intolerance from the politics of Ireland, and to lead through reconciliation to a true and lasting peace.

Catherine McGuinness

(b. 1934)

Judge Catherine McGuinness is the chairperson of the Forum for Peace and Reconciliation and judge of the High Court of Ireland. The conflict in Northern Ireland divides Catholics, who largely favor union with Ireland, and Protestants, who largely prefer the existing union with Britain. Combining a strong Protestant background with fierce pride in her Irish citizenship, McGuiness thus enjoys a unique perspective on the conflict in Northern Ireland. She has dedicated her career to seeking a lasting peace and an improved quality of life for all of the Irish.

Connecting Literature Past and Present

1. According to McGuinness's speech, what are the major issues dividing Northern Ireland?
2. Explain how two of the other selections in this section relate to these issues.

PART 4

Gloom and Glory

Past and Present (no. 2), Augustus Leopold Egg, Tate Gallery, London

CUSTOMIZE INSTRUCTION FOR UNIVERSAL ACCESS

When assigning the selections in this part, keep in mind these factors:

"Remembrance"
- Short, easy-to-read poem on the nature of love and life

"The Darkling Thrush"
- Exploration of despair and hope

"Ah, Are You Digging. . .?"
- Darkly humorous poem

"God's Grandeur"
- Many references to Christianity

"Spring and Fall"
- Short poem reflects on mortality

"To an Athlete Dying Young"
- Message about achievement that students will understand

"When I Was One-and-Twenty"
- Humorous, self-mocking poem about youth and wisdom

Selection Planning Guide

The selections in this part all deal with the theme of gloom and glory. Emily Brontë's "Remembrance" and Thomas Hardy's "Ah, Are You Digging on My Grave?" comment on death and love, and Hardy's "The Darkling Thrush" explores how hope can exist even in the midst of loneliness and despair.

In Gerard Manley Hopkins's poem "God's Grandeur," the speaker marvels at the presence of God in nature. In Hopkins's "Spring and Fall," the speaker conjectures that a young girl's sorrow is caused by her sense of mortality. A. E. Housman, too, examines subjects of gloom and glory in his poetry. The speaker in "To an Athlete Dying Young" tells how a young runner has died at the peak of his talent. Yet in the same poem, the speaker suggests that the runner died in his glory. Housman's "When I Was One-and-Twenty" also examines the theme of gloom and glory, but in a much lighter vein.

In Arthur Rimbaud's "Eternity," the speaker anticipates the glories of Eternity.

Background

Art

Past and Present (no. 2) by Augustus Leopold Egg

Augustus Leopold Egg (1816–1863) was both a painter and an actor. A friend of Charles Dickens, he performed in Dickens's acting company. He also painted "genre paintings," which referred to works of novelists such as William Thackeray and Sir Walter Scott.

Have students link this art to the theme of Part 4 by answering the following question:

- Describe the atmosphere in this painting, and point out elements that contribute most to its atmosphere.
  Possible response: The painting has a melancholy atmosphere, created by the weeping child, the darkness of the room, and the mother's thoughtful gaze directed toward the moon.

Remembrance ✦ The Darkling Thrush ✦ Ah, Are You Digging on My Grave?

Lesson Objectives and CA Correlations

1. **To analyze and respond to literary elements**
   - Literary Analysis: Stanza Structure and Irony **R 3.3**
   - Comparing Literary Works **R 3.2**
2. **To read, comprehend, analyze, and critique a poem**
   - Reading Strategy: Read Stanzas as Units of Meaning **R 3.1**
   - Reading Check Questions
   - Review and Assess Questions
   - Assessment Practice (ATE)
3. **To develop word analysis skills, fluency, and systematic vocabulary**
   - Vocabulary Development Lesson: Latin Root *-terr(a)-* **R 1.2**
4. **To understand and apply written and oral language conventions**
   - Spelling Strategy **LC 1.2**
   - Grammar and Style Lesson: Pronoun Case Following *than* or *as* **LC 1.1**
5. **To understand and apply appropriate writing and research strategies**
   - Writing Lesson: Comparative Analysis of Literary Sources **W 2.2**
   - Extension Activity: Biography
6. **To understand and apply listening and speaking strategies**
   - Extension Activity: Dramatic Reading **LS 2.5**

STEP-BY-STEP TEACHING GUIDE	PACING GUIDE
PRETEACH	
Motivate Students and Provide Background	
Use the Motivation activity (ATE p. 916)	5 min.
Read and discuss author and background features (SE pp. 916, 919, 924; ATE pp. 916, 924) A	5 min.
Introduce the Concepts	
Introduce the Literary Analysis and Reading Strategy (SE/ATE p. 917) A	15 min.
Pronounce the vocabulary words and read their definitions (SE p. 917)	5 min.
TEACH	
Monitor Comprehension	
Informally monitor comprehension by circulating while students read independently or in groups A	10 min.
Monitor students' comprehension with the Reading Check notes (SE/ATE pp. 919, 921, 923)	as students read
Develop vocabulary with Vocabulary notes (SE pp. 920, 922; ATE p. 922)	as students read
Develop Understanding	
Develop students' ability to read stanzas as units of meaning with the Reading Strategy annotations (SE/ATE p. 920)	5 min.
ASSESS	
Assess Mastery	
Assess students' mastery of the Reading Strategy and Literary Analysis by having them answer the Review and Assess questions (SE/ATE p. 925)	15 min.
Use one or more of the print and media Assessment Resources (ATE p. 927) A	up to 45 min.
EXTEND	
Apply Understanding	
Have students complete the Vocabulary Development Lesson and the Grammar and Style Lesson (SE p. 926) A	20 min.
Apply students' knowledge of motives for memory using the Writing Lesson (SE/ATE p. 927) A	45 min.
Apply students' understanding using one or more of the Extension Activities (SE p. 927)	20–90 min.

ACCELERATED INSTRUCTION:
Use the strategies and activities identified with an A.

UNIVERSAL ACCESS
● = Below-Level Students
▲ = On-Level Students
■ = Above-Level Students

Time and Resource Manager

Reading Level: Average, Easy, Easy
Average Number of Instructional Days: 4

RESOURCES		
PRINT	**TRANSPARENCIES**	**TECHNOLOGY**
• **Beyond Literature,** Humanities Connection: Naturalism, p. 43 ▲ ■		• **Interest Grabber Video,** Tape 5 ● ▲ ■
• **Selection Support Workbook:** ● ▲ ■ Literary Analysis, p. 204 Reading Strategy, p. 203 Build Vocabulary, p. 201	• **Literary Analysis and Reading Transparencies,** pp. 85 and 86 ● ▲ ■	
• **Authors In Depth,** The British Tradition, p. 193 ■		• **Listening to Literature** ● ▲ ■ Audiocassettes, Side 21 Audio CDs, CD 12
• **Literatura en español** ● ▲ • **Literary Analysis for Enrichment** ■	• **Fine Art Transparencies, Volume 1,** Transparency 14 ● ▲ ■	
• **Formal Assessment:** Selection Test, pp. 214–216 ● ▲ ■ • **Open Book Test,** pp. 126–128 ● ▲ ■ • **Performance Assessment and Portfolio Management,** pp. 20 and 63 ● ▲ ■ • PRENTICE HALL ASSESSMENT SYSTEM ● ▲ ■	• PRENTICE HALL ASSESSMENT SYSTEM ● ▲ ■ Skills Practice Answers and Explanations on Transparencies ● ▲ ■	• **Test Bank Software** ● ▲ ■ • **Got It! Assessment Videotapes,** Tape 4 ● ▲
• **Selection Support Workbook:** ● ▲ ■ Grammar and Style, p. 202 • **Writing and Grammar,** Diamond Level ● ▲ ■ • **Extension Activities,** p. 43 ● ▲ ■	• **Daily Language Practice Transparencies** ● ▲	• **Writing and Grammar iText CD-ROM** ● ▲ ■ ***Take It to the Net*** www.phschool.com

BLOCK SCHEDULING: Use one 90-minute class period to preteach the selections and have students read them. Use a second 90-minute class period to assess students' mastery of skills and have them complete one of the Extension Activities.

PRETEACH

Step-by-Step Teaching Guide for pp. 916–917

Motivation

To spark interest in this group of poems, display Art Transparency 14, Volume 1: *Frosty Morning* on an overhead projector. Elicit from students whether the painting conveys a hopeful mood or a sad one, or some combination of these emotions. Tell students that the poems that follow are an unusual blend of hope and despair. Encourage students to identify each speaker's outlook as they read the poem.

Interest Grabber Video

As an alternative, play "'The Darkling Thrush': Reading and Student Response" on Tape 5 to engage student interest.

❶ Background

More About the Authors

Emily Brontë

Emily Brontë's reputation rests largely on *Wuthering Heights,* her masterful novel, and the poems that she published with her sisters, Jane and Anne. In her poems, Emily Brontë created the imaginary world of Gondal, which was the setting for many of her finest poems, including "Remembrance." Emily was deeply attached to the landscape of Yorkshire—more than either of her sisters—and she is remembered as a poet of the moors of England for their repeating appearance in *Wuthering Heights.*

Thomas Hardy

A theme central to much of Thomas Hardy's work—both poetry and prose—is the struggle of man against the indifferent force that governs the world and inflicts on him the sufferings and ironies of life and love. Hardy considered taking Holy Orders but lost his religious faith and lived the life of an architect's apprentice until he found his calling as a writer. In 1885, he moved with his first wife, Emma Gifford, into a house he designed and built himself, Max Gate, near Dorchester. Hardy lived at the house until his own death in 1928.

Prepare to Read

❶ Remembrance ◆ The Darkling Thrush ◆ "Ah, Are You Digging on My Grave?"

Emily Brontë (1818–1848)

Although some literary critics of the time attacked Emily Brontë for the violent passions expressed in her novel *Wuthering Heights* (1847), her dark Romanticism is now regarded as the essence of her genius.

A Writer's Beginnings Brontë grew up in the Yorkshire moorlands, a barren wasteland in the north of England, where her father was a clergyman. When Emily was just three, her mother died. Emily and her sisters, Charlotte and Anne, were educated at home for the most part and were often on their own.

Homesickness In 1835, Charlotte became a teacher at a school some distance from her home. Emily accompanied her as a pupil, but she quickly returned home. Three years later, she took a teaching position herself but resigned after six months.

Several years later, Charlotte and Emily devised another plan to support themselves as teachers. They would establish and run a school for girls in their own town of Haworth. To learn the skills they needed for this enterprise, they traveled to Brussels, Belgium. There, many people they met admired Emily for her Romantic temperament. However, Emily became homesick again and, after learning of her aunt's death, went home for good.

A Career Cut Short As adults, the three sisters published a book of poetry. The twenty-one poems that Emily contributed are considered the best of the collection. Emily's first and only novel, *Wuthering Heights*, was published in 1847. It tells the story of a tragic love affair played out against the mysterious landscape of the Yorkshire moors. The book is now considered a classic.

Wuthering Heights is the culminating expression of Emily's fiery imagination. A year after the book was published she died of tuberculosis.

Thomas Hardy (1840–1928)

Thomas Hardy, who was unusual in being both a great novelist and a great poet, was born in Dorset, a region of southwest England. He used this region as the basis for the imaginary county of Wessex that is the setting of many of his novels.

Early Life The son of a stonemason, Hardy grew up in a rural cottage near a tract of wasteland. He received a fine education at a local school, although he never went on to study at a university. As a teenager, he began working for a local architect, and he eventually became a draftsman for an architect who specialized in churches.

While on a business trip to Cornwall, at the southwestern tip of England, Hardy met the woman who later became his first wife. She encouraged him in his literary activities, and soon he committed himself entirely to writing.

The Novelist Hardy used his writing to elaborate his own pessimistic view of life. In tragic novels like *Tess of the D'Urbervilles* (1891) and *Jude the Obscure* (1895), he showed the difficulty people experience when trying to rise above their circumstances.

The Poet The bleakness of Hardy's fiction disturbed readers, and the response to *Jude the Obscure* was so hostile that Hardy abandoned fiction and returned to writing poetry, a form of writing he had pursued in the 1860s.

A Poetic Legacy Hardy's poetry marks a transition from Victorian verse to the Modernist movement of the twentieth century. In his use of strict meter and stanza structure, Hardy was unmistakably Victorian. However, his nonpoetic language and odd rhymes, his devotion to English characters and the English countryside, and his fatalistic outlook inspired twentieth-century poets like Philip Larkin.

TEACHING RESOURCES

The following resources can be used to enrich or extend the instruction for pp. 916–917.

Motivation

Interest Grabber Video, Tape 5

Background

Beyond Literature, p. 43

Take It to the Net

Visit www.phschool.com for background and hotlinks for the selections.

Literary Analysis

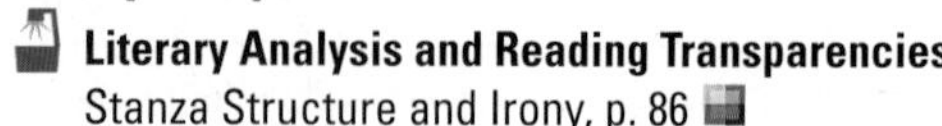

Literary Analysis and Reading Transparencies, Stanza Structure and Irony, p. 86

Reading

Literary Analysis and Reading Transparencies, Reading Stanzas as Units of Meaning, p. 85

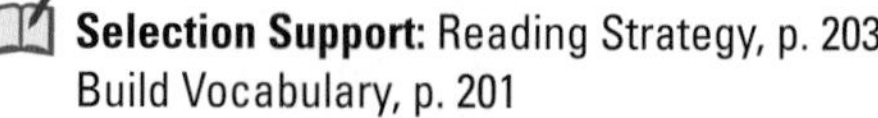

Selection Support: Reading Strategy, p. 203; Build Vocabulary, p. 201

BLOCK SCHEDULING: Resources marked with this symbol provide varied instruction during 90-minute blocks.

Preview

Connecting to the Literature

Loss of some kind—of love, of friends, of youth—enters everyone's life. Responses to loss can vary widely, from anger to intense sorrow. Both Brontë's "Remembrance" and Hardy's "Ah, Are You Digging on My Grave?" address loss through death, but in very different ways.

❷ Literary Analysis

Stanza Structure and Irony

Poets have a number of ways of addressing a reader's expectations. **Stanzas,** for instance, are repeated groupings of two or more verse lines with a definite pattern of line length, rhythm, and, frequently, rhyme. Stanzas are often units of meaning comparable to paragraphs in prose, and the **stanza structure** of a poem is the pattern of stanzas from which it is built. While stanza structure creates an expectation of a regular pattern, **irony** challenges expectations by creating a contradiction between reality and appearance or between what is said and what is meant.

Both stanza structure and irony relate to the expectations that a poem sets up and then fulfills or does not fulfill. In reading these poems, for example, notice these patterns:

- The arrangement of the first stanza leads you to expect a similar arrangement in the others.
- Irony surprises you by not fulfilling expectations.

Comparing Literary Works

Brontë's and Hardy's poems deal in different ways with the theme of absence—the sense of something missing, whether it is a loved one, a sign of hope, or the knowledge that people remember the speaker. Compare the ways in which the speakers in these poems feel about an absence and succeed or fail in handling it.

❸ Reading Strategy

Reading Stanzas as Units of Meaning

Many poetic stanzas express a single main idea, as paragraphs do in prose. By **reading stanzas as units of meaning,** noticing how each stanza builds on the preceding one, you can often get a better understanding of what the writer is saying. Use a chart like this one to understand the logical progression of stanzas in each poem.

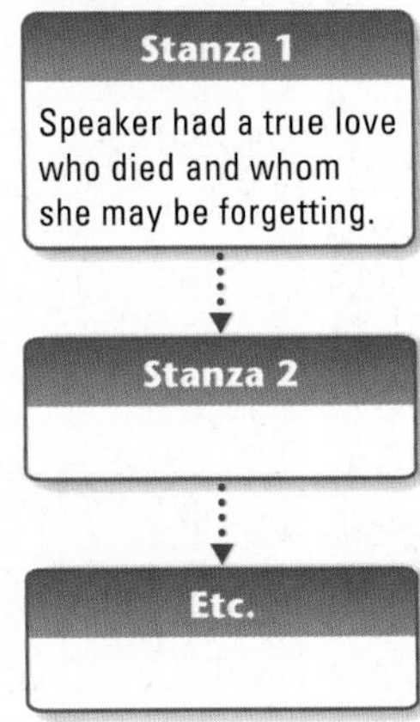
"Remembrance"
Stanza 1
Speaker had a true love who died and whom she may be forgetting.
Stanza 2
Etc.

Vocabulary Development

languish (laŋ´ gwish) *v.* become weak; suffer from longing (p. 920)

rapturous (rap´ chər əs) *adj.* filled with joy and love; ecstatic (p. 920)

gaunt (gônt) *adj.* thin and bony, as from great hunger or age (p. 922)

terrestrial (tə res´ trē əl) *adj.* relating to the earth or to this world (p. 922)

❷ Literary Analysis

Stanza Structure and Irony

- Tell students that in this lesson, they will focus on stanza structure and irony. Explain that *stanzas* are repeated groupings of two or more verse lines with a definite pattern of line length, rhythm, and rhyme. *Irony* is a contradiction between appearance and reality, or between what is said and what is meant.
- Read the note about stanza structure and irony as a class. Call students' attention to the way in which stanza structure can set up an expectation for the reader, and how both stanza structure and irony can upset that expectation.
- Use the Stanza Structure and Irony transparency in **Literary Analysis and Reading Transparencies,** p. 86, to illustrate to students how stanza structure can contribute to an ironic effect.

❸ Reading Strategy

Reading Stanzas as Units of Meaning

- Explain to students that many poetic stanzas express a single idea.
- Tell students that they should read stanzas as units of meaning.
- Read the note about Reading Stanzas as Units of Meaning, and then use the graphic organizer on p. 917 to practice this skill.
- Have students practice this skill using the Reading Stanzas as Units of Meaning transparency on p. 85 of **Literary Analysis and Reading Transparencies.**

Vocabulary Development

- Pronounce each vocabulary word for students, and read the definitions as a class. Have students identify any words with which they are already familiar.

CUSTOMIZE INSTRUCTION FOR UNIVERSAL ACCESS

For Less Proficient Readers	For English Learners	For Advanced Readers
Students may have difficulty grasping how to interpret stanza structure and its potential for irony. Remind students that stanzas function as units of meaning—that each stanza contributes to a reader's expectation, and that stanzas that break the pattern can sometimes have a dramatic effect.	English learners may find identifying patterns in literary works, or disrupted patterns, unusually difficult. Remind students that stanzas often contain complete thoughts that are connected in some way to the stanzas before and after. Encourage students to pay attention to the way in which stanzas can upset the direct line of thought.	Students should not have difficulty recognizing the way in which stanza structure and irony can act to upset a reader's expectations. For students who need practice, use the Stanza Structure and Irony transparency on p. 86 of **Literary Analysis and Reading Transparencies.**

E-Teach

Visit E-Teach at www.phschool.com for teachers' essays on how to teach, with questions and answers.

TEACH

Step-by-Step Teaching Guide for pp. 918–924

CUSTOMIZE INSTRUCTION
For Intrapersonal Learners

These students are skillful in observing and analyzing their own thoughts, feelings, and moods. Encourage them to recognize the speakers' responses to loss and to express those responses in writing, artwork, song, or dance.

❶ About the Selection

The speaker in Emily Brontë's poem addresses her only love, a man who had died fifteen years earlier. She asks him to forgive her for not indulging in "Memory's rapturous pain." To do so would not allow her to live in a world that is admittedly "empty" without his presence.

The speaker of this poem expresses an interesting blend of pragmatic and romantic thought. She is pragmatic in that she recognizes that her life is one to be lived and cherished, even without "the aid of joy." The speaker, however, even while denying that love is necessary for existence, achingly expresses her passionate longing for her long-dead lover.

❷ Background

Art

My Sweet Rose by John William Waterhouse

John William Waterhouse (1849–1917) was an English painter who studied at the Royal Academy in London. He is considered to be both a Classical and a Pre-Raphaelite painter of mainly romantic and poetic subjects. Much of his work was inspired by the work of poets.

Use this question for discussion:

What is your interpretation of the painting's title, "My Sweet Rose"?

Possible responses: Some students may say that the rose represents the beloved of the woman shown in the painting. Others may say that the title refers to the woman herself—that is, the painting depicts the artist's beloved.

②

My Sweet Rose, John William Waterhouse, Roy Miles Gallery, London

TEACHING RESOURCES

The following resources can be used to enrich or extend the instruction for pp. 918–924.

Literary Analysis

Selection Support: Literary Analysis, p. 204

Reading

Listening to Literature Audiocassettes, Side 21

Listening to Literature Audio CDs, CD 12

Extension

Authors In Depth, The British Tradition, p. 193 (The collection includes four additional selections by Emily Brontë for extended reading.)

BLOCK SCHEDULING: Resources marked with this symbol provide varied instruction during 90-minute blocks.

Possible response: Like the speaker in the poem, the woman in the painting is sad and reflective; she looks as if she were thinking of someone or something far away or far in the past.

❹ ✓Reading Check

Answer: The poem's speaker is troubled by the thought of her dead lover buried in the ground.

❶ Remembrance

Emily Brontë

Background

Victorian poets wrote in many voices and many styles. Some writers, like Emily Brontë, are classified as Romantic because they explore and celebrate the human soul, the wildness of nature, and the powers of the imagination. Thomas Hardy, however, embraced Naturalism, which focused on the victimization of ordinary people by social and natural forces.

The poems that follow call to mind both Romanticism and Naturalism. Although Brontë wrote before the start of the Naturalist movement, her poem contains an attitude that is usually exhibited by Naturalist poets, and Hardy's poems contain instances of Romanticism, which is Brontë's specialty.

Cold in the earth, and the deep snow piled above thee!
Far, far removed, cold in the dreary grave!
Have I forgot, my Only Love, to love thee,
Severed at last by Time's all-wearing wave?

Now, when alone, do my thoughts no longer hover
Over the mountains, on that northern shore;
Resting their wings where heath and fern-leaves cover
Thy noble heart for ever, ever more?

Cold in the earth, and fifteen wild Decembers
From those brown hills have melted into spring—
Faithful indeed is the spirit that remembers
After such years of change and suffering!

❹ ✓Reading Check
What is troubling the poem's speaker?

❸ ◀Critical Viewing In what ways might the woman in this painting represent the poem's speaker? **[Analyze]**

CUSTOMIZE INSTRUCTION FOR UNIVERSAL ACCESS

For Special Needs Students	For English Learners	For Gifted/Talented Students
Encourage students to read aloud from the text with teacher guidance. Tell them to pronounce each word as they go, and to visualize the scene as they read. Remind them that by focusing on each stanza at a time, and taking each as a unit of meaning, they may be able to understand the poem more clearly.	English learners may have difficulty understanding the speaker's use of irony to describe the pain she experiences remembering her beloved. Ask students if they've ever felt an impulse to do the opposite of what they were told to do. Explain that irony is sometimes similar.	Have students create a landscape painting of the scenery in "Remembrance." Tell students to convey the mood of the poem in their use of color and style.

❺ Reading Strategy

Reading Stanzas as Units of Meaning

- Remind students that as they read, they should make connections between stanzas, noticing how each successive stanza builds on the preceding one.
- Ask them the Reading Strategy question on p. 920: How do lines 25–28 elaborate on the idea in lines 21–24?
  Answer: Lines 25–28 suggest that it was only when the speaker resigned herself to the death of her beloved did she stop yearning after him. These lines elaborate on the idea expressed in lines 21–24 that the speaker had to teach herself to live without joy.

Answers for p. 920

1. Possible responses: Students may say that the speaker's refusal to indulge herself and think on her dead beloved is actually selfish; other students may find the speaker's decision to stop contemplating her beloved is the smart thing to do.
2. **(a)** The speaker's love died fifteen years ago. **(b)** The speaker means that she has not fallen in love with anyone else.
3. **(a)** The speaker plans to "forget" her lost love and move on with her life. **(b)** She is afraid that her old feelings will take over and prevent her from proceeding with her life.
4. **(a)** The basic conflict is between living in a joyless present and giving oneself up to painful memories of a joyous past.
   (b) The speaker handles this conflict by deciding not to dwell too long on her memories.
5. Possible response: Students will probably conclude that it is not usually desirable to lead an existence without joy, but that sometimes mourning requires it.
6. Possible responses: Students should defend their views.

Sweet Love of youth, forgive if I forget thee
While the World's tide is bearing me along:
Other desires and other hopes beset me,
Hopes which obscure but cannot do thee wrong.

No later light has lightened up my heaven,
No second morn has ever shone for me:
All my life's bliss from thy dear life was given—
All my life's bliss is in the grave with thee.

But when the days of golden dreams had perished
And even Despair was powerless to destroy,
Then did I learn how existence could be cherished,
Strengthened and fed without the aid of joy;

❺

Then did I check the tears of useless passion,
Weaned my young soul from yearning after thine;
Sternly denied its burning wish to hasten
Down to that tomb already more than mine!

And even yet, I dare not let it languish,
Dare not indulge in Memory's rapturous pain;
Once drinking deep of that divinest anguish,
How could I seek the empty world again?

Review and Assess

Thinking About the Selection

1. **Respond:** Were you disappointed by the speaker's final decision about his or her beloved? Why or why not?
2. **(a) Recall:** How long ago did the speaker's love die?
   (b) Interpret: What does the speaker mean by, "No later light has lightened up my heaven"?
3. **(a) Recall:** What does the speaker plan to do? **(b) Interpret:** Why is the speaker afraid to give in to his or her old feelings?
4. **(a) Draw Conclusions:** In your own words, express the basic conflict of the poem's speaker. **(b) Analyze:** How does the speaker handle this conflict?
5. **Evaluate:** Can it be desirable in some circumstances to lead an existence "without . . . joy"? Explain.
6. **Make a Judgment:** In ancient times lyric poems like this one were accompanied by music. Which of these types of music would make the best accompaniment for this poem: country, jazz, folk, rock, or hip-hop? Explain your choice.

Reading Strategy
Reading Stanzas as Units of Meaning How do lines 25–28 elaborate on the idea in lines 21–24?

languish (laŋ´ gwish) *v.* become weak; suffer from longing

rapturous (rap chər us) *adj.* filled with joy and love; ecstatic

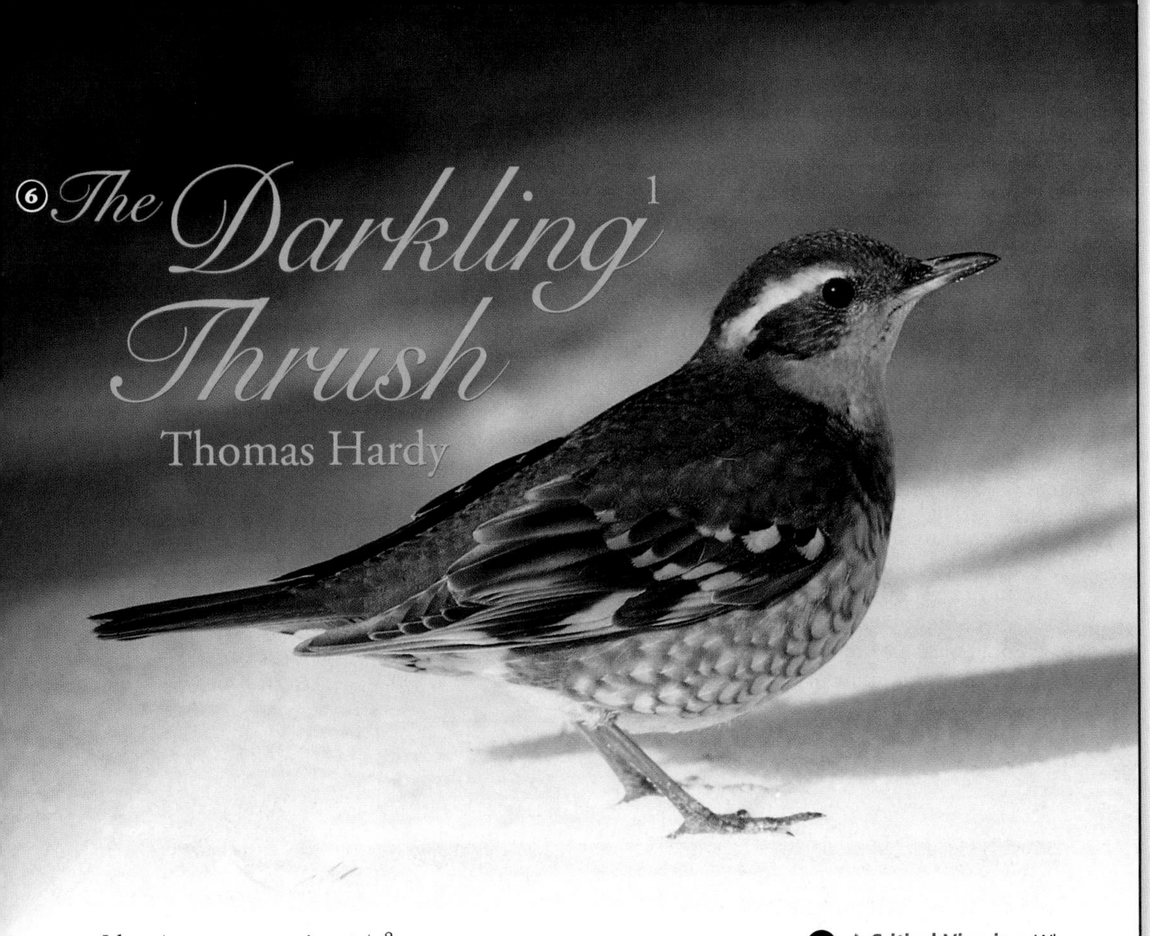

⑥ The Darkling Thrush[1]

Thomas Hardy

I leant upon a coppice gate[2]
When Frost was specter-gray,
And Winter's dregs made desolate
The weakening eye of day.
The tangled bine-stems[3] scored the sky
Like strings of broken lyres,
And all mankind that haunted nigh
Had sought their household fires.

The land's sharp features seemed to be
The Century's corpse[4] outleant,
His crypt the cloudy canopy,
The wind his death-lament.

1. **darkling** *adj.* in the dark.
2. **coppice** (kop′ is) **gate** gate leading to a thicket, or small wood.
3. **bine-stems** twining stems.
4. **Century's corpse** This poem was written on December 31, 1900, the last day of the nineteenth century.

7 ▲ Critical Viewing Why might Hardy have chosen a thrush like the one pictured to symbolize hope? **[Speculate]**

8 

Reading Check

Where is the speaker standing?

6 About the Selection

Hardy's bleak reflections—and tentative expression of hope—on the eve of the twentieth century are especially poignant as he looks back on both the tragedies and progress of the past.

7 ▶ Critical Viewing

Answer: The thrush seems small and vulnerable to the cold. It must deal with a harsh climate, but it keeps singing anyway.

8 Reading Check

Answer: The speaker is standing against a gate leading to a thicket in winter at dusk.

CUSTOMIZE INSTRUCTION FOR UNIVERSAL ACCESS

For Less Proficient Readers	For Gifted/Talented Students	For Advanced Readers
Pair students up in groups of two. Then, with their partners, have students use a clapping rhythm to find the rhythm of the poems. As one student reads the poem aloud, the other should clap on the stressed syllables. Have students repeat the reading and clapping until they successfully identify the rhythm.	The speaker of "The Darkling Thrush" refers to the "Century's corpse," an allusion to the poem's date—December 31, 1900. In a few paragraphs, explain how millennia are calculated and why the last day of 1900, rather than the last day of 1899, is the end of the century.	Tell students that both Brontë and Hardy use nature to symbolize ideas and emotions. Have them write an analysis of the symbols in "Remembrance" and "The Darkling Thrush." Ask students to identify the symbols in the poems and analyze their meaning.

9 Vocabulary Development

The Latin Root *-terr(a)-*

- Call students' attention to *terrestrial,* a word that means "relating to the earth or to this world."
- Tell students that the word is derived from the Latin word for "land."
- Have students suggest other words and phrases that use the same root.
  Possible responses: *subterranean; extraterrestrial; terrain; territory*
- Have students look up any unfamiliar words in a dictionary.

Answers for p. 922

1. Possible responses: Students may be surprised by the hopeful note.
2. **(a)** It is wintertime, toward the close of the day and the year. **(b)** The poet uses the images of "Frost," "Winter's dregs," "desolate," "weakening," and "broken lyres" to suggest a mood of gloom.
3. **(a)** The speaker hears a thrush singing. **(b)** The mood in the third stanza differs from that of the first two because it includes the joyful singing of the thrush and lifts the gloom of the preceding stanzas.
4. **(a)** The speaker thinks that if the thrush sings with such joy at such an otherwise gloomy time, there must be some hope in the air. **(b)** Possible responses: Students may note that the speaker calls the Hope signified by the thrush "blessed"—he desires such hope—but also says that he is "unaware" of any reason for such hope.
5. Possible response: In their responses, students should indicate what signs of hope or invitations to pessimism appeared at the end of the twentieth century.

The ancient pulse of germ[5] and birth
Was shrunken hard and dry,
And every spirit upon earth
Seemed fervorless as I.

At once a voice arose among
The bleak twigs overhead
In a full-hearted evensong
Of joy illimited;
An aged thrush, frail, gaunt, and small,
In blast-beruffled plume,
Had chosen thus to fling his soul
Upon the growing gloom.

So little cause for carolings
Of such ecstatic sound
Was written on terrestrial things
Afar or nigh around,
That I could think there trembled through
His happy good-night air
Some blessed Hope, whereof he knew
And I was unaware.

gaunt (gônt) *adj.* thin and bony, as from great hunger or age

terrestrial (tə res´ trē əl) *adj.* relating to the earth or to this world

5. **germ** seed or bud.

Review and Assess

Thinking About the Selection

1. **Respond:** Does the ending of this poem surprise you? Why or why not?
2. **(a) Recall:** In which season and time of year is this poem set? **(b) Classify:** In the first two stanzas, what details and images does Hardy use to convey the mood of the setting?
3. **(a) Recall:** What does the speaker suddenly hear and see in the third stanza? **(b) Compare and Contrast:** How does the mood in the third stanza differ from that in the first two?
4. **(a) Recall:** Summarize what the speaker says in the final stanza. **(b) Draw Conclusions:** Do you agree with critics who assert that Hardy longs to believe there is reason for hope but does not really think so? Why or why not?
5. **Speculate:** If Hardy had seen the end of the twentieth century, do you think he would he have felt the same way that he did at the end of the nineteenth? Explain.

ENRICHMENT: Cultural Connection

Naturalism

The Naturalist element in Thomas Hardy's novels and verse had important literary counterparts in both France and the United States. In France, the novelist Émile Zola (1840–1902) and the short-story writer Guy de Maupassant (1850–1893) espoused Naturalism. These writers believed that human behavior is rigorously determined by hereditary and environmental factors. In American literature, the chief Naturalist writers included Jack London (1876–1916) and Theodore Dreiser (1871–1945). In Dreiser's work, particularly, the boundaries between the novel and social history became blurred.

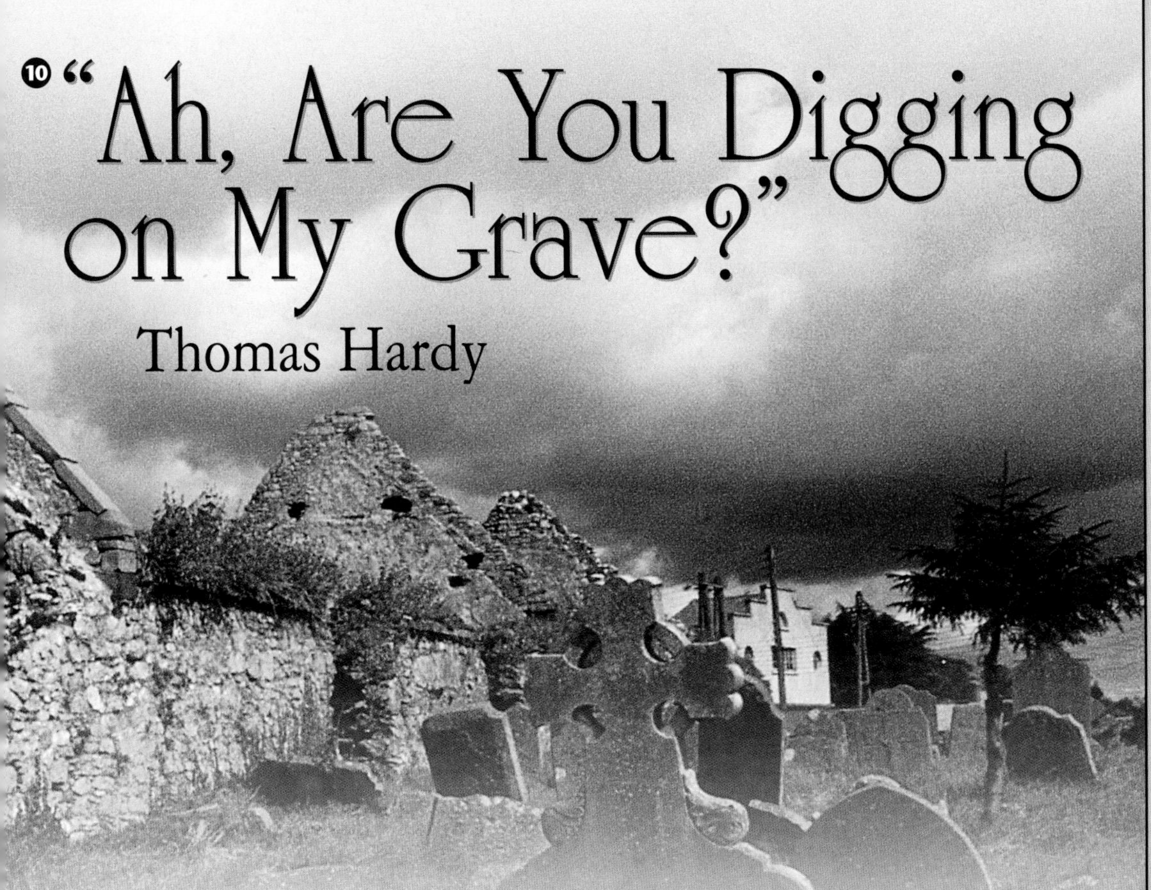

⑩ "Ah, Are You Digging on My Grave?"

Thomas Hardy

"Ah, are you digging on my grave
My loved one?—planting rue?"
—"No: yesterday he went to wed
One of the brightest wealth has bred.
'It cannot hurt her now,' he said,
'That I should not be true.'"

"Then who is digging on my grave?
My nearest dearest kin?"
—"Ah, no: they sit and think, 'What use!
What good will planting flowers produce?
No tendance of her mound can loose
Her spirit from Death's gin.'"[1]

⑪ **Reading Check**

Who is the speaker of this poem?

1. **gin** *n.* trap.

⑩ About the Selection

In Hardy's bitterly humorous and ironic poem, a dead woman keeps asking who is digging on her grave—assuming that someone who once loved or hated her still has feelings for her. An unidentified voice answers her questions. The voice is finally revealed to be that of her dog. The woman is relieved to find that her dog still remembers her, but—in the poem's final irony—the dog claims he was just burying a bone and had forgotten his mistress was buried there.

⑪ Reading Check

Answer: The speaker of the poem is a dead woman.

CUSTOMIZE INSTRUCTION FOR UNIVERSAL ACCESS

For Special Needs Students	For Less Proficient Readers	For Advanced Readers
Have students read "Ah, Are You Digging on My Grave?" with teacher guidance. Encourage them to pay attention to the dialogue in the poem, and to note who is speaking and when. You may wish to play **Got It! Videotape 4** to enable them to determine their retention of key facts from Hardy's poem.	Have students write an epitaph, or inscription for a tombstone. Tell them they might write one for the speaker in "Ah, Are You Digging on My Grave?" Encourage them to use clues from the poem to capture the essence of the person being memorialized. Students may want to include a detail about the woman's dog.	Have students write brief essays in which they compare and contrast the two interpretations of "Ah, Are You Digging on My Grave?" Have them explore how the poem might be interpreted as merely humorous or deeply pessimistic.

ASSESS

12 Critical Thinking

Interpret

- Have students read the bracketed passage.
- Then, ask students what Hardy intended by this dramatic disclosure.

Answer: Students may note that Hardy makes the disclosure to set up a false hope, which he deflates with the dark humor of the ironic comment on human vanity in the last stanza.

13 Background

The Literature of Pessimism

Challenge interested students to read poems by Philip Larkin, Matthew Arnold, and Alfred, Lord Tennyson in their textbook in search of attitudes, moods, or themes that could be considered "pessimistic" literature. In what way are these writers like Hardy in their view of the world? How do they differ?

Answers for p. 924

Review and Assess

1. Possible responses: Yes, the woman is pitiable and deserving of remembrance; no, the woman must not have been too lovable.
2. **(a)** The speaker believes in turn that it is her widower, her relatives, and her enemy digging in the three stanzas. **(b)** The responses indicate that those people seldom think about the dead woman.
3. **(a)** The woman's dog is digging on her grave. **(b)** By withholding information, Hardy achieves suspense and creates humor.
4. **(a)** The dog was burying a bone and forgot that this was his mistress's grave. **(b)** We are never as important to others as we think we are.
5. Possible responses: Students will probably find this poem more humorous than pessimistic. Encourage them to defend their views with evidence.

"But some one digs upon my grave?
My enemy?—prodding sly?"
—"Nay: when she heard you had passed the Gate
That shuts on all flesh soon or late,
She thought you no more worth her hate,
And cares not where you lie."

"Then, who is digging on my grave?
Say—since I have not guessed!"
12 —"O it is I, my mistress dear,
Your little dog, who still lives near,
And much I hope my movements here
Have not disturbed your rest?"

"Ah, yes! *You* dig upon my grave . . .
Why flashed it not on me
That one true heart was left behind!
What feeling do we ever find
To equal among human kind
A dog's fidelity!"

"Mistress, I dug upon your grave
To bury a bone, in case
I should be hungry near this spot
When passing on my daily trot.
I am sorry, but I quite forgot
It was your resting-place."

The British Tradition

13 *The Literature of Pessimism*

The final stanza of the poem suggests a pessimistic view of life. Hardy is famous for the pessimism of his novels and poems—specifically, his belief that the world is in the hands of blind fate and that a person cannot easily escape the social and economic situation into which he or she is born. Hardy passed on this strain of pessimism to the twentieth-century poet Philip Larkin. However, Hardy was not unique among Victorian poets in his pessimism. In poems like "Dover Beach" (page 884), Matthew Arnold writes about people's isolation in a confused and frightening world. Tennyson, however, was more optimistic. He concludes his elegy *In Memoriam, A.H.H.* (page 818) with a reaffirmation of his faith in God.

Review and Assess

Thinking About the Selection

1 **Respond:** Do you feel sorrow for the speaker in this poem? Why or why not?

2. **(a) Recall:** In each of the first three stanzas, who does the speaker think is digging? **(b) Infer:** What do the responses tell you about the people thought to be digging?
3. **(a) Recall:** Who is actually digging on the grave? **(b) Analyze:** What effect does Hardy achieve by withholding this information?
4. **(a) Recall:** What reason does the digger give for digging? **(b) Draw Conclusions:** What point about human vanity and self-esteem is Hardy making in this poem?
5. **Assess:** Do you think the message of this poem is overly pessimistic? Why or why not?

ASSESSMENT PRACTICE: Reading Comprehension

Paired Passages (For more practice, see Test Preparation Workbook, p. 43.)

Many tests require students to compare and identify literary elements in two passages. Use the following sample item to teach students how to identify the themes of two passages. Have students read "Remembrance" and "Ah, Are You Digging on My Grave?"

Which of these expresses a shared theme of the two poems?

A Life calls the living away from grief.
B Young people are melodramatic.
C Prolonged grief is a sign of weakness.
D The living quickly forget about the dead.

Lead students to eliminate *B* and *C* because neither is a theme of either poem. Choice *D* is a theme of Hardy's poem but not of "Remembrance." The correct answer is *A*. Both poems are about how the business of life draws a mourner's attention away from a dead loved one.

Review and Assess

Literary Analysis

Stanza Structure and Irony

1. Complete a chart like the one shown to determine whether each poem uses a consistent **stanza structure.**

Stanza	Number of lines	Rhyme scheme	Meter
1			
2			
3			

2. What is ironic about the phrases "rapturous pain" and "divinest anguish" in the final stanza of "Remembrance"?
3. (a) How do lines 25–30 of "Ah, Are You Digging on My Grave?" disappoint a reader's expectations for an established stanza structure? (b) How does the last stanza use **irony** to disappoint a character's expectations in a drastic way?

Comparing Literary Works

4. Compare and contrast the types of absence that these poems address.
5. Which of the three speakers seems to experience the sorrow of loss most keenly? Why?
6. Which speaker seems best able to handle the absence of a sign of remembrance or hope? Explain.

Reading Strategy

Reading Stanzas as Units of Meaning

7. **Read stanzas as units of meaning** in "Remembrance" to show how the speaker gradually works out an answer to the question in the first stanza.
8. (a) In "The Darkling Thrush," which stanza introduces a shift in meaning? Explain. (b) In "Ah, Are You Digging on My Grave?" what important shift in meaning occurs between the last two stanzas?

Extend Understanding

9. **Science Connection:** Do you think that recent advances in science and technology show that Hardy's ironic pessimism is outdated? Explain.

Quick Review

Stanzas are repeated groupings of two or more verse lines with a pattern of line lengths, rhythms, and, frequently, rhymes.

Stanza structure refers to the way in which poems are built from a progression of stanzas.

Irony is a contradiction between reality and appearance or between what is said and what is meant.

Read stanzas as units of meaning to notice how each stanza builds on the preceding one.

 ***Take It to the Net***

www.phschool.com

Take the interactive self-test online to check your understanding of these selections.

Answers for p. 925

Review and Assess

1. The stanzas in "Remembrance" contain four lines with a rhyme scheme of *abab*. The meter varies. The stanzas in "The Darkling Thrush" contain eight lines with a rhyme scheme of *abababab*. The meter is ballad meter (stresses: 4-3-4-3). The stanzas in "Ah, Are You Digging on My Grave?" contain six lines with a rhyme scheme of *abcccb*. The meter is 4-3-4-4-4-3.
2. The phrases "rapturous pain" and "divinest anguish" are ironic because they involve contradictions: The speaker is attached to her pain.
3. **(a)** Lines 25–30 disappoint a reader's expectations for an established stanza structure because in this stanza, the woman expresses her thoughts directly; it deviates from the consistent form of the first four stanzas, in which two speakers engaged in a dialogue. **(b)** The last stanza uses irony—the dog's digging is related to its own search for a bone rather than its mourning its mistress—to upset the dead woman's hopes that she is greatly mourned.
4. "Remembrance" treats the absence of a loved one as a gaping hole in one's life. "The Darkling Thrush" concerns the absence of hope. "Ah, Are You Digging on My Grave?" concerns the absence of the speaker's memory from the hearts of others.
5. Possible response: The speaker of "Remembrance" seems to experience the sorrow of loss most keenly, because in fifteen years, she has not been able to overcome her anguish at losing her loved one.
6. Possible response: The speaker of "Remembrance" seems best prepared to handle the absence of hope—she has reflected on her grief for years.
7. The speaker asks if she has forgotten to love her dead beloved. Each stanza builds toward her realization that even now, her feelings for the past are a danger for her.
8. **(a)** Stanza three introduces a shift in meaning. The voice of the thrush disturbs the speaker's

continued

Answers continued

gloomy reverie. **(b)** In "Ah, Are You Digging on My Grave?" the shift in meaning between the last two stanzas suggests that the seeming "remembrance" of the woman's dog is actually forgetfulness—he has forgotten where she is buried.

9. Possible response: Students may note that these advances have introduced anxiety as well as hope. They should support their answer with examples.

ENRICHMENT: Further Reading

Other Poems by the Authors

Poems by Emily Brontë

"Wild Nights"

"Last Lines"

Poems by Thomas Hardy

"The Man He Killed"

"The Reminder"

EXTEND

Answers for p. 926

❶ Vocabulary Development

Word Analysis

1. *Terrain* is another word for the surface area or ground.
2. *Terrestrial* means "of the earth" or "of this world."
3. *Subterranean* means "below the earth."

Spelling Strategy

1. nervous
2. advantageous

Fluency: Word Choice

Although Emily Brontë's hero in *Wuthering Heights* is a terrestrial being, he has an almost supernatural aura and a fateful destiny. When parted from his beloved Cathy, he begins to languish and becomes gaunt. After his reunion with Cathy, Heathcliff is rapturous.

❷ Grammar and Style

1. [it pleased] him
2. she [was]
3. he [did]
4. I [was]
5. [I like] him

Writing Application

Possible response: The bird in "The Darkling Thrush" is more a harbinger of hope than the dog in "Ah, Are You Digging on My Grave?" The dead woman had been forgotten by her friends. In the end, the dog was as callous as they.

Integrate Language Skills

❶ Vocabulary Development Lesson

Word Analysis: Latin Root *-terr(a)-*

The Latin root *-terr(a)-* comes from the Latin word for "earth." *Terrestrial,* which contains this root, means "of the earth or of this world." Explain how each of these *-terr(a)-* words relates to the meaning of the root.

1. terrain 2. terrestrial 3. subterranean

Spelling Strategy

Words ending in silent *e* drop the *e* before adding suffixes starting with vowels: rapture + -ous = rapturous. Words ending in *-ge* do not drop the *e*: outrage + -ous = outrageous. In your notebook, complete these spellings:

1. nerve + -ous 2. advantage + -ous

Fluency: Word Choice

Review the vocabulary words listed on page 917 and study their use in the context of the selections. Then, in your notebook, replace the underlined word or phrase with the correct vocabulary word.

Although Emily Brontë's hero in *Wuthering Heights* is an earthly being, he has an almost supernatural aura and a fateful destiny. When parted from his beloved Cathy, he begins to weaken and becomes very thin. After his reunion with Cathy, Heathcliff is extremely happy.

❷ Grammar and Style Lesson

Pronoun Case Following *than* or *as*

Than and *as* are conjunctions when they introduce clauses, or sentence parts containing a subject and a verb. When a pronoun follows *than* or *as*, it may function as the subject or object of the verb in the clause. The **case,** or form, of a pronoun varies depending on whether the pronoun is used as a subject or an as object. Use the nominative case for pronouns used as subjects and the objective case for pronouns used as objects. The **case of a pronoun following *than* or *as*** must be correct even if words are missing in the comparison.

> And every spirit upon earth
> Seemed fervorless as I [was].

I is the subject of the incomplete comparison *I was*. Mentally fill in missing words to determine the correct pronoun in such cases.

Practice On your paper, write the correct pronoun for each incomplete construction, and identify the missing words that complete the comparison.

1. Charlotte Brontë's *Jane Eyre* pleased me more than (he, him).
2. Charlotte's sister Emily was as talented as (she, her).
3. In Hardy's poem, the bird had more hope than (he, him).
4. The dog was as forgetful as (I, me).
5. Considering Brontë and Hardy as writers, I like her more than (he, him).

Writing Application Write a paragraph comparing the bird and the dog as messengers in Hardy's two poems. Use at least one incomplete construction involving a pronoun.

Prentice Hall Writing and Grammar Connection: Chapter 22, Section 1

TEACHING RESOURCES

The following resources can be used to enrich or extend the instruction for pp. 926–927.

Vocabulary

Selection Support Workbook: Build Vocabulary, p. 201

Vocabulary and Spelling Practice Book (Use this booklet for skills enrichment.)

Grammar

Selection Support Workbook: Grammar and Style, p. 202

Writing and Grammar, Diamond Level, p. 564

Daily Language Practice Transparencies ■

Writing

Writing and Grammar, Diamond Level, p. 850 ■

Writing and Grammar iText CD-ROM

■ **BLOCK SCHEDULING:** Resources marked with this symbol provide varied instruction during 90-minute blocks.

❸ Writing Lesson

Comparative Analysis of Literary Sources

Poets like Thomas Hardy and Emily Brontë are often subjects of biography, literary analysis, or critical review. In an essay, analyze the credibility or possible bias of two sources of information about one of these writers.

Prewriting Decide which poet or work you would like to use as the subject for your research. Then, use a chart like the one shown to identify sources and analyze their reliability. To aid your analysis, imagine you are writing a paper using these sources.

Model: Analyzing Sources

Source	Contents	Analysis
Online review	Praise; personal response	Writer is not an expert
Encyclopedia	Facts about Hardy's life	No real analysis of work
Scholarly article	Discussion of a specific theme in Hardy's poetry	Well-supported; quotes lines from poetry

Drafting Choose two distinctly different sources. Briefly describe the contents of each. Then, compare and contrast their value to a student of literature.

Revising Review your essay to make sure you have clearly shown the relative value of each source. Consider adding quotations from the sources to support the points you make about their tone, content, and bias or lack of bias.

WG *Prentice Hall Writing and Grammar Connection: Chapter 31, Section 2*

❹ Extension Activities

Research and Technology With several classmates, learn more about the remarkably creative Brontë family, and write a brief **biography** of their lives and accomplishments.

- Consult biographies, encyclopedias, and Web sites.
- Enhance your narrative with graphics, such as a Brontë family tree or a map of Yorkshire.

Make your biography available to classmates. **[Group Activity]**

Listening and Speaking With a partner, give a **dramatic reading** of "Ah, Are You Digging on My Grave?" for the class. Review the poem to determine how your characters' motives and personalities should influence the tones and gestures you use.

Take It to the Net www.phschool.com

Go online for an additional research activity using the Internet.

ASSESSMENT RESOURCES

The following resources can be used to assess students' knowledge and skills.

Selection Assessment

- **Formal Assessment:** pp. 214–216
- **Open Book Test,** pp. 126–128
- **Got It! Assessment Videotapes,** Tape 4
- **Test Bank Software**

Take It to the Net

Visit www.phschool.com for self-tests and additional questions on the selections.

Writing Rubric

- **Performance Assess. and Portfolio Mgmt.,** pp. 20 and 63.

PRENTICE HALL ASSESSMENT SYSTEM

Workbook

Transparencies

Skill Book

CD-ROM

Lesson Support for p. 927

❸ Writing Lesson

- Read with students the note for the writing lesson on p. 927, and then tell students that they will write a comparative analysis of two literary sources of information about either Brontë or Hardy.
- Have students decide which poet they will study, and then have them search for source materials on their subject to analyze and compare.
- Encourage students to formulate their comparative analyses using a chart like the one on p. 927.
- Review with students their understanding of bias and credibility.
- Remind students to choose two distinctly different sources that will enable them to make clear comparisons in their analyses.
- Evaluate students' essays using the Exposition: Comparison-and-Contrast rubric in **Performance Assessment and Portfolio Management,** p. 20.

❹ Research and Technology

- Read the Research and Technology note with students, and have them write a brief biography of the Brontë family's lives and accomplishments.
- Encourage students to use encyclopedias and Web sites to determine as much as possble about the family.
- Remind students that they should be discriminating in their research.
- Students may want to enhance their biographies with photographs of the Brontës or with maps of their location.

CUSTOMIZE INSTRUCTION For Universal Access

To address different learning styles, use the activities suggested in the **Extension Activities** booklet, p. 43.

- For Bodily/Kinesthetic and Musical/Rhythmic Learners, use Activity 5.
- For Visual/Spatial and Intrapersonal Learners, use Activity 6.
- For Logical/Mathematical and Verbal/Linguistic Learners, use Activity 7.

God's Grandeur ✦ Spring and Fall: To a Young Child ✦ To an Athlete Dying Young ✦ When I was One-and-Twenty

Lesson Objectives and CA Correlations

1. **To analyze and respond to literary elements**
   - Literary Analysis: Rhythm and Meter **R 3.3**
   - Comparing Literary Works **R 3.2, 3.6**
2. **To read, comprehend, analyze, and critique a poem**
   - Reading Strategy: Applying Biography **R 3.7**
   - Review and Assess Questions
   - Assessment Practice (ATE)
3. **To develop word analysis skills, fluency, and systematic vocabulary**
   - Vocabulary Development Lesson: Coined Words
4. **To understand and apply written and oral language conventions**
   - Spelling Strategy **LC 1.2**
   - Grammar and Style Lesson: Capitalization of Compass Points **LC 1.1**
5. **To understand and apply appropriate writing and research strategies**
   - Writing Lesson: Analytical Essay **W 2.2**
   - Extension Activity: Multimedia Presentation **W 2.6**
6. **To understand and apply listening and speaking strategies**
   - Extension Activity: Victorian Poetry Contest **LS 1.9**

STEP-BY-STEP TEACHING GUIDE	PACING GUIDE
PRETEACH	
Motivate Students and Provide Background	
Use the Motivation activity (ATE p. 928)	5 min.
Read and discuss author and background features (SE pp. 928, 931; ATE p. 928) A	5 min.
Introduce the Concepts	
Introduce the Literary Analysis and Reading Strategy (SE/ATE p. 929) A	15 min.
Pronounce the vocabulary words and read their definitions (SE p. 929)	5 min.
TEACH	
Monitor Comprehension	
Informally monitor comprehension by circulating while students read independently or in groups A	10 min.
Develop vocabulary with Vocabulary notes (SE pp. 931, 932, 934; ATE p. 932)	as students read
Develop Understanding	
Develop students' understanding of rhythm and meter with the Literary Analysis annotations (SE p. 932; ATE pp. 932, 933) A	5 min.
ASSESS	
Assess Mastery	
Assess students' mastery of the Reading Strategy and Literary Analysis by having them answer the Review and Assess questions (SE/ATE p. 935)	15 min.
Use one or more of the print and media Assessment Resources (ATE p. 937) A	up to 45 min.
EXTEND	
Apply Understanding	
Have students complete the Vocabulary Development Lesson and the Grammar and Style Lesson (SE p. 936) A	20 min.
Apply students' knowledge of supporting a thesis using the Writing Lesson (SE/ATE p. 937) A	45 min.
Apply students' understanding using one or more of the Extension Activities (SE p. 937)	20–90 min.

ACCELERATED INSTRUCTION:
Use the strategies and activities identified with an A.

UNIVERSAL ACCESS
● = Below-Level Students
▲ = On-Level Students
■ = Above-Level Students

Time and Resource Manager

Reading Level: Average, Average, Easy, Easy
Average Number of Instructional Days: 4

RESOURCES		
PRINT	**TRANSPARENCIES**	**TECHNOLOGY**
• **Beyond Literature,** Cross-Curricular Connection: Social Studies, p. 44 ▲ ■		• **Interest Grabber Video,** Tape 5 ● ▲ ■
• **Selection Support Workbook:** ● ▲ ■ Literary Analysis, p. 208 Reading Strategy, p. 207 Build Vocabulary, p. 215	• **Literary Analysis and Reading Transparencies,** pp. 87 and 88 ● ▲ ■	
		• **Listening to Literature** ● ▲ ■ Audiocassettes, Sides 21 and 22 Audio CDs, CD 12
• **Literatura en español** ● ▲ • **Literary Analysis for Enrichment** ■	• **Fine Art Transparencies, Volume 1,** Transparency 7 ● ▲ ■	
• **Formal Assessment:** Selection Test, pp. 217–219 ● ▲ ■ • **Open Book Test,** pp. 129–131 ● ▲ ■ • PRENTICE HALL ASSESSMENT SYSTEM ● ▲ ■	• PRENTICE HALL ASSESSMENT SYSTEM ● ▲ ■ Skills Practice Answers and Explanations on Transparencies ● ▲ ■	• **Test Bank Software** ● ▲ ■ • **Got It! Assessment Videotapes,** Tape 4 ● ▲
• **Selection Support Workbook:** ● ▲ ■ Grammar and Style, p. 206 • **Writing and Grammar,** Diamond Level ● ▲ ■ • **Extension Activities,** p. 44 ● ▲ ■	• **Daily Language Practice Transparencies** ● ▲	• **Writing and Grammar iText CD-ROM** ● ▲ ■ ***Take It to the Net*** www.phschool.com

BLOCK SCHEDULING: Use one 90-minute class period to preteach the selections and have students read them. Use a second 90-minute class period to assess students' mastery of skills and have them complete one of the Extension Activities.

PRETEACH

Step-by-Step Teaching Guide for pp. 928–929

Motivation

To build students' awareness of rhythm and meter, bring in a recording of rap music and encourage them to analyze the pattern of beats in the music. Inform them that Gerard Manley Hopkins was a pioneer in inventing poetic rhythms, much as rap revolutionized the music industry with its compelling and insistent rhythms.

Interest Grabber Video

As an alternative, play "'To an Athlete Dying Young': Athletes Hit by Hardship" on Tape 5 to engage student interest.

❶ Background

More About the Authors

Gerard Manley Hopkins

One of Gerard Manley Hopkins's most creative periods was ushered in by a disaster. The 1875 sinking of the *Deutschland*, a ship that had been carrying five Franciscan nuns exiled for their faith, led to a period of poetic inspiration for Hopkins, who wrote "The Wreck of the *Deutschland*," one of his longest poems. Although the poem was rejected as too difficult by the Jesuit journal to which Hopkins submitted it for publication, the renaissance of his creative powers seems to have been the spur for Hopkins to write other works, including "The Windhover" and "Pied Beauty."

A. E. Housman

A. E. Housman's *A Shropshire Lad* was published in 1896. Housman was better known as an academic at the time of its publication, which he paid for himself. The collection's sixty-three poems were mostly nostalgic, set in a partly imaginary Shropshire, and treated issues of childhood and war. Housman's book met with little success initially but became enormously popular during World War I, when Housman was appointed a professor of Latin at Cambridge University in 1911.

Prepare to Read

❶ God's Grandeur ◆ Spring and Fall: To a Young Child ◆ To an Athlete Dying Young ◆ When I Was One-and-Twenty

Gerard Manley Hopkins (1844–1889)

Although he was the most innovative poet of the Victorian period, Hopkins never published a collection of his work during his lifetime. It was not until 1918 that his work was published and a generation of poets could read and be influenced by his startling poetry.

Devotion to God and Nature This quietly rebellious poet was born just outside London, the oldest of nine children in a prosperous middle-class family. Although physically slight, he would perch fearlessly at the top of a tree and sway in the wind while observing the landscape. He began to write poetry in grammar school, a practice he continued at Oxford University, where he studied the classics.

During his third year at Oxford, Hopkins decided to become a Catholic priest in the Jesuit order—a decision that dismayed his parents, who were devout Anglicans. The discipline of Hopkins's religious vocation was sometimes at odds with his writing of verse. He temporarily gave up poetry but continued to keep detailed notebooks that recorded his fascination with words and his love of nature.

Inscape In the mid-1870s, while studying theology in Wales, he began to write poetry again, stimulated by the Welsh language and encouraged by his religious mentor. Somewhat earlier, Hopkins had found in the medieval theologian Duns Scotus a verification of his own ideas about the individuality of all things. Hopkins called this precious individuality *inscape*, and he tried to capture it in highly original poems like "God's Grandeur." He also experimented with new rhythms in his verse.

From early 1884 on, he taught at a Jesuit college in Dublin. There, he died of typhoid fever just before his forty-fifth birthday.

A. E. Housman (1859–1936)

A man of solitary habits and harsh self-discipline, Housman was also capable of creating delicately crafted poems, full of gentle regret.

Challenges of Youth Housman grew up in Worcestershire, a region northwest of London. His childhood came to an end on his twelfth birthday, when his mother died. Later, at Oxford University, his despair over an unrequited love darkened his life still further. Perhaps because of this double grief, his poetry has bitter undertones.

Upon leaving Oxford, where he had studied classical literature and philosophy, Housman went to work in the Patent Office. Determined to prove himself in the classics, he studied Greek and Latin at night and wrote scholarly articles. In 1892, his hard work paid off when he was appointed to a position as professor of Latin at University College in London.

Literary Success Although Housman spent most of his life engaged in teaching and in scholarly pursuits, he is most remembered for three slender volumes of poetry that are as romantic and melancholy as any ever written. His first and most famous collection of verse, *A Shropshire Lad* (1896), has as its central character a young man named Terence. In later years, Housman claimed, ironically, that he had "never spent much time" in Shropshire.

Housman's image is that of an emotionless intellectual, but his poems display deep feelings. In his view, the goal of poetry is to "transfuse emotion," not to transmit thought. A well-written poem, he maintained, should affect the reader like a shiver down the spine or a punch in the stomach.

TEACHING RESOURCES

The following resources can be used to enrich or extend the instruction for pp. 928–929.

Motivation

Interest Grabber Videotapes, Tape 5

Background

Beyond Literature, p. 44

Take It to the Net

Visit www.phschool.com for background and hotlinks for the selections.

Literary Analysis

Literary Analysis and Reading Transparencies, Rhythm and Meter, p. 88

Reading

Literary Analysis and Reading Transparencies, Applying Biology, p. 87

Selection Support: Reading Strategy, p. 207; Build Vocabulary, p. 205

BLOCK SCHEDULING: Resources marked with this symbol provide varied instruction during 90-minute blocks.

Preview

Connecting to the Literature

As you grow, your ideas change. Several of these poems, examine how the passing of time colors emotions and changes priorities.

❷ Literary Analysis

Rhythm and Meter

Poetry with a regular **rhythm,** or movement, is **metrical verse,** which is divided into combinations of syllables called **feet.** The following are various feet and the pattern of stressed and unstressed syllables they contain:

- **Iambic:** unstressed, stressed, as in *thĕ tíme*
- **Trochaic:** stressed, unstressed, as in *gránděur*
- **Anapestic:** unstressed, unstressed, stressed, as in *tŏ thĕ lów*

Lines with three, four, and five feet are **trimeter, tetrameter,** and **pentameter,** respectively. Iambic pentameter is a five-foot line with iambic feet, and trochaic tetrameter is a four-foot line with trochaic feet. Housman uses regular meters like iambic and trochaic tetrameter, but Hopkins invents rhythms like these:

- **counterpoint rhythm**—two opposing rhythms appear together, for example, two trochaic feet in an iambic line:
  Thĕ wórld iš chárged wĭth thĕ grándeŭr ŏf Gód.
- **sprung rhythm**—all feet begin with a stressed syllable (sometimes marked with an accent) and contain a varying number of unstressed syllables. Sprung rhythm is complex, but its result is clear: densely stressed lines with many echoing consonant and vowel sounds.

Comparing Literary Works

Beauty, or the loveliness of the world, and mortality, or the certainty of death, are two connected themes that these poets explore. Look for the ways in which they express their own unique perspectives on these traditional themes.

❸ Reading Strategy

Applying Biography

By **applying biography,** or what you know about poets' lives, to their work, you can gain a better insight into their poetry. Review the information on page 928, and use a chart like this one to apply biography to these selections.

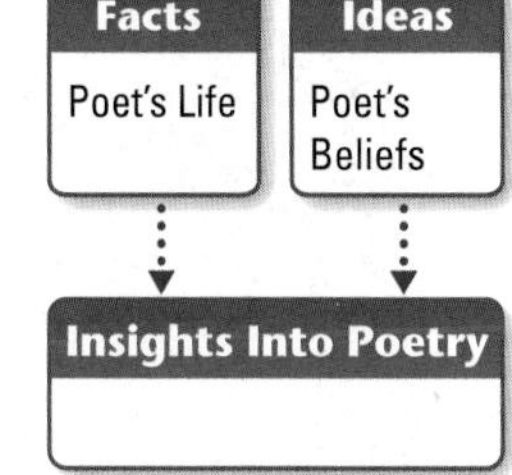

Vocabulary Development

grandeur (gran′ jər) *n.* splendor; magnificence (p. 931)

blight (blīt) *n.* condition of withering (p. 932)

rue (ro͞o) *n.* sorrow; regret (p. 934)

CUSTOMIZE INSTRUCTION FOR UNIVERSAL ACCESS

For Less Proficient Readers	For English Learners	For Advanced Readers
Ask students if they've ever read a biography of a famous figure in history. Tell them that often biographers make connections between a person's life and his or her work. Tell students that they can use some biographical clues about authors to make connections with themes in their work.	English learners may be so challenged by the text of a poem that they do not recognize that it reflects the prejudices, vision, and biography of the author. Help students to identify some elements in "God's Grandeur" that seem especially relevant to Hopkins's life, based on what they have read.	Remind students not to impose too much of a writer's biography on Hopkins's poetry, since many poets write on subjects through the mediation of a fictional speaker. Encourage students to read "God's Grandeur" and make some connections between Hopkins's subject matter as a poet and his preoccupations as a person.

❷ Literary Analysis

Rhythm and Meter

- Students should be familiar with the concept of rhythm. Explain that they will consider rhythm in poems with regular movement, or *metrical verse,* divided into combinations of syllables called *feet.*
- Review with students the definition of iambic, trochaic, and anapestic rhythms, encouraging them to give examples of each.
- Read the note on meter, and review the difference between trimeter, tetrameter, and pentameter.
- Call students' attention to the way in which counterpoint and sprung rhythm are used by Hopkins in his poetry.
- Use the Rhythm and Meter transparency in **Literary Analysis and Reading Transparencies,** p. 88, to illustrate to students how to interpret rhythm and meter in poetry.

❸ Reading Strategy

Applying Biography

- Review with students that biography is the study of a person's life.
- Ask students to consider how knowing something about an author's life might illuminate his or her poetry.
- Point out that not all poets write from their personal perspectives—some use speakers with entirely different perspectives to give voice to ideas.
- Read the note about applying biography, then use the graphic organizer on p. 929 to practice this skill.
- Have students practice applying biography using the transparency on p. 87 of **Literary Analysis and Reading Transparencies.**

Vocabulary Development

Pronounce each vocabulary word for students, and read the definitions as a class. Have students identify any words with which they are already familiar.

E-Teach

Visit E-Teach at www.phschool.com for teachers' essays on how to teach, with questions and answers.

TEACH

Step-by-Step Teaching Guide for pp. 930–934

CUSTOMIZE INSTRUCTION For Musical/Rhythmic Learners

These students will be most attuned to the rhythms and meter of the poems. Encourage them to meet in small groups and read the poems aloud, focusing on the rhythm and other sound effects used by the poets and perhaps adding sound effects or music of their own. These students may also enjoy participating in the Victorian Poetry Contest, the Listening and Speaking Extension Activity on p. 937.

❶ About the Selections

In "God's Grandeur," Hopkins marvels at how the glory of God shines out through all of nature. In "Spring and Fall," Hopkins reflects on how a young girl is intuitively responding to a sense of her own mortality as she mourns the falling leaves in autumn.

❷ Background

Art

Bird's Nest by Ros. W. Jenkins.

Ros. W. Jenkins was a British watercolorist of the Victorian era. Jenkins builds up layers of color and then creates details by stippling (applying dots of color) and cross-hatching (using a grid of intersecting lines to create texture). Use these questions for discussion:

1. How does this artist seem to regard nature?
   Answer: The artist seems delighted by the smallest details of natural life and wants to record them as closely as possible so that other people can share them.
2. Which passage in "God's Grandeur" most closely matches the content of this painting?
   Answer: The closest match is in lines 13 and 14: "Because the Holy Ghost over the bent / World broods with warm breast and with ah! Bright wings."

❷

Bird's Nest, Ros. W. Jenkins, Warrington Museum and Art Gallery

❸ ▲**Critical Viewing** How does this painting reflect Hopkins's ideas in "God's Grandeur"? **[Apply]**

TEACHING RESOURCES

The following resources can be used to enrich or extend the instruction for pp. 930–934.

Literary Analysis

Selection Support: Literary Analysis, p. 208

Reading

Listening to Literature Audiocassettes, Sides 21, 22 ■

Listening to Literature Audio CDs, CD 12 ■

Extension

Fine Art Transparencies, Volume 1, Art Transparency 7 (Use a discussion of the image of athletic glory in *The Team from Cardiff,* Robert Delaunay, to introduce Housman's "To an Athlete Dying Young.")

■ **BLOCK SCHEDULING:** Resources marked with this symbol provide varied instruction during 90-minute blocks.

❶

God's Grandeur

Gerard Manley Hopkins

Background

Surprisingly, when Gerard Manley Hopkins died, none of his obituaries mentioned that he was a poet and only a few friends were aware of this fact. One of these friends was Robert Bridges, an Oxford classmate and later the British poet laureate. Bridges had corresponded with Hopkins and took an interest in his experiments with rhythm. It was through Bridges's efforts that a volume of Hopkins's poetry was published for the first time in 1918. Today, Bridges is little known, but his once-obscure friend Gerard Manley Hopkins is a famous Victorian poet.

❹ The world is charged with the grandeur of God.
It will flame out, like shining from shook foil;[1]
It gathers to a greatness, like the ooze of oil
Crushed.[2] Why do men then now not reck his rod?[3]
Generations have trod, have trod, have trod;
And all is seared with trade; bleared, smeared with toil;
And wears man's smudge and shares man's smell: the soil
Is bare now, nor can foot feel, being shod.

And for all this, nature is never spent;
There lives the dearest freshness deep down things;
And though the last lights off the black West went
Oh, morning, at the brown brink eastward, springs—
Because the Holy Ghost over the bent
World broods with warm breast and with ah! bright wings.

grandeur (gran′ jər) *n.* splendor, magnificence

1. **foil** *n.* tinsel.
2. **crushed** squeezed from olives.
3. **reck his rod** heed God's authority.

❸ ▶Critical Viewing

Answer: The painting reflects Hopkins's ideas because it focuses on small details of nature in an intense way. The painting reveals the "freshness" of natural glory in the world, a freshness that is never "spent," despite the intrusions of humanity.

❹ Critical Thinking

Analyze

- Ask students with what force of nature the verb *charge* is usually associated. Then, ask them what effect the word has as used here.
  Answer: The verb *charge* is usually associated with electricity. By using the word here, Hopkins invests God with an electric, dynamic presence.
- You may find it necessary to explain that in Christian theology, the Holy Ghost, or Holy Spirit, is believed to be one aspect of God. The Holy Ghost is often symbolized by a dove, and that may be why Hopkins uses bird imagery to describe its presence in the world.

CUSTOMIZE INSTRUCTION FOR UNIVERSAL ACCESS

For Special Needs Students	For English Learners	For Gifted/Talented Students
Encourage these students to read aloud from "God's Grandeur" with teacher guidance. After students have become confident with the poem's subject matter, tell them to focus on the rhythm of the poem. Review with them how to identify meter, and then ask them to name the meter used.	English learners may have unusual difficulty recognizing the way in which meter and rhythm function in poetry because they are often focused on the language and the meaning of the words. Review with students the way in which meter and rhythm affect poetry and can alter its meaning.	According to Gerard Manley Hopkins, the world is bursting with God's grandeur, which is uncontainable. Tell students to create a collage of the most beautiful natural images they can find in magazines and newspapers. They may also incorporate natural objects such as leaves, flowers, and shells.

❺ Literary Analysis

Rhythm and Meter

- Remind students that in sprung rhythm, all feet begin with a stressed syllable and contain a varying number of unstressed syllables.
- Then, read the Literary Analysis directive on p. 932: Identify a visual clue that proves that this poem is written in sprung rhythm. Answer: Several of the first lines are marked with an accent, indicating that the feet begin with stressed syllables.

❻ Vocabulary Development

Coined Words

- Explain to students that Hopkins sometimes combined old words to make new ones. Point out the words *wanwood* and *leafmeal.*
- Tell them that *wanwood* means "pale trees" and *leafmeal* means "ground-up, mealy leaves."
- Encourage students to coin some of their own words.

Answers to p. 932

1. **(a)** People have tainted nature with trade and toil.
   (b) Lines 1–8 present an opposition between God's grandeur in nature and the power of humans to obscure it.
   (c) He asserts that no matter what people do, they can never obliterate God's grandeur in nature.
2. **(a)** She is unhappy because the leaves are falling off the trees.
   (b) Margaret will always be sad, but as she grows older, she will be sad for herself.
3. **(a)** As she grows older, Margaret will mourn for her own mortality.
   (b) The speaker teaches Margaret that death is a part of the human condition.
4. Yes; because he takes the beauty and integrity of nature as a sign of God's grandeur, it seems likely that Hopkins would support any movement to preserve nature.

❶ Spring and Fall: to a Young Child

Gerard Manley Hopkins

❺ Márgarét, áre you grieving
Over Goldengrove unleaving?
Leáves, like the things of man, you
With your fresh thoughts care for, can you?
Áh! ás the heart grows older
It will come to such sights colder
By and by, nor spare a sigh
❻ Though worlds of wanwood[1] leafmeal[2] lie;
And yet you will weep and know why.
Now no matter, child, the name:
Sórrow's springs áre the same.
Nor mouth had, no nor mind, expressed
What heart heard of, ghost[3] guessed:
It is the blight man was born for,
It is Margaret you mourn for.

Literary Analysis
Rhythm and Meter
Identify a visual clue that proves that this poem is written in sprung rhythm.

blight (blīt) *n.* condition of withering

1. **wanwood** (wän′ wood) pale wood.
2. **leafmeal** ground-up decomposed leaves.
3. **ghost** spirit.

Review and Assess

Thinking About the Selections

1. **(a) Recall:** According to Hopkins in "God's Grandeur," what has been the impact on nature of humanity's behavior? **(b) Analyze:** What opposition or conflict does he explore in lines 1–8 of "God's Grandeur"? **(c) Draw Conclusions:** How does Hopkins resolve that opposition?
2. **(a) Recall:** What makes Margaret unhappy in "Spring and Fall"? **(b) Interpret:** Explain how the poem's speaker suggests that Margaret will both outgrow and not outgrow this sadness.
3. **(a) Recall:** According to the speaker, how will Margaret change as she grows older? **(b) Draw Conclusions:** What lesson does the speaker offer to Margaret in this poem?
4. **Speculate:** Judging by "God's Grandeur," would Hopkins support the ecology movement if he were alive today? Explain.

❼ # To an Athlete Dying Young

A. E. Housman

The time you won your town the race
We chaired you through the marketplace;
Man and boy stood cheering by,
And home we brought you shoulder-high.

Today, the road all runners come,
Shoulder-high we bring you home,
And set you at your threshold down,
Townsman of a stiller town.

Smart lad, to slip betimes away
From fields where glory does not stay
And early though the laurel[1] grows
It withers quicker than the rose.

Eyes the shady night has shut
Cannot see the record cut,
And silence sounds no worse than cheers
After earth has stopped the ears:

❾ Now you will not swell the rout
Of lads that wore their honors out,
Runners whom renown outran
And the name died before the man.

So set, before its echoes fade,
The fleet foot on the sill of shade,
And hold to the low lintel up
The still-defended challenge cup.

And round that early-laureled head
Will flock to gaze the strengthless dead,
And find unwithered on its curls
The garland briefer than a girl's.

1. **laurel** symbol of victory.

❽ **▲Critical Viewing** Judging by his poem, would Housman believe that a moment of victory like this one could continue to be savored into old age? Explain. **[Connect]**

❼ About the Selections

In two of his most famous poems, "To an Athlete Dying Young" and "When I Was One-and-Twenty," A. E. Housman reflects on the fleeting glories of youth and the inevitable disillusionment that comes with age and experience. However, he gives the theme of disillusionment an ironic, humorous twist by having a young man voice it in a world-weary tone ("When I Was One-and-Twenty").

❽ Critical Viewing

Answer: Students should cite the lines "fields where glory does not stay" and "lads that wore their honors out, / Runners whom renown outran / And the name died before the man" as suggestive that Housman does not believe that the glory or moment of victory can be savored in old age.

❾ Literary Analysis

Rhythm and Meter

- Explain that small departures from a metrical scheme can add meaning.

Monitor Progress Ask what the metrical scheme of the poem is.
Answer: The meter is iambic tetrameter.

- Then, ask which lines in the fifth stanza do not begin with iambs.
Answer: Lines 17 and 19 begin with trochees; line 20 begins with an anapest.
- What effects do these departures have on meaning?
Possible responses: The trochee in line 17 stresses "Now," emphasizing the change that has occurred. The trochee in line 19 adds "speed" to the word *runners,* since the stress comes earlier than expected.

CUSTOMIZE INSTRUCTION FOR UNIVERSAL ACCESS

For Special Needs Students	For Less Proficient Readers	For Advanced Readers
Students may find Housman's poem "To an Athlete Dying Young" difficult subject matter to relate to. Ask them to read the poem with teacher guidance, focusing on the ways in which Housman juxtaposes the athlete's former glory with his present state.	Have students work in a small groups to gather photographs and news articles depicting a moment of glory in sports. Have them write a few sentences explaining the feelings they associate with each. Then, have them write a paragraph, quoting from Housman's poem, to explain why it might be enviable for an athlete to die after such a moment.	A. E. Housman considered himself more of a classical scholar than a poet. It is only natural that he would include classical allusions in his poetry. In "To an Athlete Dying Young," Housman refers to the athlete's "early-laureled head." Ask students why an athlete would have a laurel on his head.

ASSESS

Answers for p. 934

Review and Assess

1. **(a)** The visual image of the athlete being carried "shoulder high" appears. **(b)** The meaning is different in the second stanza because now the athlete is dead.
2. **(a)** Three advantages of dying young are getting away from a place where glory "does not stay"; not having to be like other athletes, who live on while their former glory disappears; and not having to face lack of recognition ("silence") after the "cheers." **(b)** No, the speaker does not believe that the runner was "smart" to die. He is merely trying to console himself.
3. **(a)** He was told not to fall in love. He ignored the advice. **(b)** The line "And I am two-and-twenty" shows that the speaker takes his new wisdom a bit too seriously.
4. Possible responses: Student answers will vary; encourage them to support their answers with evidence from the poems.

7 When I Was One-and-Twenty

A. E. Housman

When I was one-and-twenty
    I heard a wise man say,
"Give crowns and pounds and guineas[1]
    But not your heart away;
Give pearls away and rubies
    But keep your fancy free."
But I was one-and-twenty,
    No use to talk to me.

When I was one-and-twenty
    I heard him say again,
"The heart out of the bosom
    Was never given in vain;
'Tis paid with sighs a plenty
    And sold for endless rue."
And I am two-and-twenty,
    And oh, 'tis true, 'tis true.

rue (ro͞o) *n.* sorrow; regret

1. **crowns . . . guineas** denominations of money.

Review and Assess

Thinking About the Selections

1. **(a) Recall:** What visual image appears in each of the first two stanzas of "To an Athlete"? **(b) Contrast:** How do the meanings of the two images differ?
2. **(a) Recall:** In "To an Athlete," what are three advantages of dying young, according to the speaker? **(b) Interpret:** Does the speaker entirely mean what he says about these advantages? Explain.
3. **(a) Recall:** In "When I Was One-and-Twenty," what advice does the speaker receive, and how does he react? **(b) Interpret:** What clues are there in the poem that Housman is mocking his speaker?
4. **Make a Judgment:** Which poem conveys the most compassionate view of human mortality— "Spring and Fall," "To an Athlete," or "When I Was One-and-Twenty"? Explain.

ASSESSMENT PRACTICE: Reading Comprehension

Paired Passages (For more practice, see Test Preparation Workbook, p. 44.)

Many tests require students to identify and compare literary elements in two passages. Use the following sample item to teach students how to compare the speakers of the two poems. Have students read pp. 933–934 before they answer the item.

Which of these best describes the speakers in the two poems?

A The first speaker is suicidal; the second is brokenhearted.
B Both speakers like to laugh at themselves.
C The first speaker is sad; the second is regretful.
D Both speakers are serious and loyal.

Students should eliminate *A* and *B* because nothing in "To an Athlete Dying Young" suggests that the speaker is suicidal or self-mocking. Choice *D* is not supported by "When I Was One-and-Twenty." The correct answer is *C*.

Review and Assess

Literary Analysis

Rhythm and Meter

1. (a) Use scansion symbols (˘ ´) to identify the **feet** in line 5 of "God's Grandeur." (b) Explain how your scan demonstrates that the line uses **counterpoint rhythm.**

   Generations have trod, have trod, have trod; . . .

2. "Spring and Fall" is written with **sprung rhythm**. Using the stresses in line 11, indicate how many feet that line has.
3. (a) How does the counterpoint rhythm in line 5 of "God's Grandeur" support the meaning of the line? (b) In "Spring and Fall," how do the three stresses in line 11 reinforce the meaning of the line?
4. (a) Show that in lines 1–8 of "To an Athlete," the **meter** includes five **iambic tetrameter** lines and three **trochaic tetrameter** lines. (b) How do the trochaic lines reinforce the idea of a "stiller town"?

Comparing Literary Works

5. (a) In "God's Grandeur," does Hopkins think the beauty of nature is enduring? Explain. (b) In "Spring and Fall," does he express the same perspective on the endurance of nature's beauty as he does in "God's Grandeur"? Why or why not?
6. Would the speakers in "Spring and Fall" and "To an Athlete" agree that deep sorrow is the right response to the realization that life and earthly beauty are fleeting? Explain.

Reading Strategy

Applying Biography

7. **Apply biography** by finding a passage in "God's Grandeur" that reflects Hopkins's love of nature. Then, explain your choice.
8. Find a passage in "To an Athlete" that reflects Housman's underlying sadness. Explain your choice.

Extend Understanding

9. **Physical Education Connection:** Do you agree with Housman in "To an Athlete" that aging can bring only sadness to an athlete? Why or why not?

Quick Review

The regular **rhythms,** or movements, of **metrical verse** are measured in units called **feet,** which combine stressed (´) and unstressed (˘) syllables.

Examples of feet are **iambic** (˘ ´), **trochaic** (´ ˘), and **anapestic** (˘ ˘ ´).

Examples of metrical lines are **trimeter** (three feet), **tetrameter** (four feet), and **pentameter** (five feet).

In a **counterpoint rhythm,** two opposing rhythms appear together.

In **sprung rhythm,** all feet begin with a stressed syllable and contain a varying number of unstressed syllables.

Applying biography, or facts about a poet's life, to a poem, can help you understand it better.

 ***Take It to the Net***

www.phschool.com

Take the interactive self-test online to check your understanding of these selections.

Answers for p. 935

Review and Assess

1. **(a)** Génĕrátiŏns hăve tród, hăve tród, hăve tród. **(b)** The line uses two trochees and three iambs, and counterpoint rhythm occurs when two opposing rhythms appear together.
2. The line has four feet.
3. **(a)** The two initial trochees capture the heaviness of the generations treading, while the three iambs and the repeated words, "have trod, have trod, have trod" capture the mechanical quality of the treading. **(b)** The bunching of stressed syllables at the beginning of the line emphasizes the point that certain sorrows are inevitable and universal. The stress on the word *are* is strongly emphatic.
4. **(a)** In "To an Athlete," lines 3, 6, and 8 are trochaic tetrameter and lines 1, 2, 4, 5, and 7 are iambic tetrameter. **(b)** The trochaic lines interrupt the regular rhythm, introducing a kind of silence where the expected stresses are missing.
5. **(a)** The phrase "dearest freshness deep down things" reflects Hopkins's belief that nature's freshness is not only beautiful but also enduring; man cannot destroy nature's eternal self-renewal. **(b)** Possible response: In "Spring and Fall," Hopkins meditates on the passing of the seasons rather than on their endurance; students may say that "God's Grandeur" captures nature's endurance more completely.
6. Possible response: Some students may think that the speakers of these poems would agree that deep sorrow is the right response to the fleeting qualities of life and beauty—both express this idea. Others may note that both speakers attempt to find wisdom or perspective, not just sorrow, in this realization.
7. Possible response: "And, for all this, nature is never spent" (line 9) suggests Hopkins's faith in nature's abiding beauty.
8. Possible response: Students may say the line "Townsman of a stiller town" suggests Housman's sadness. It denotes the athlete's new place as a member of the community of the dead.

continued

ENRICHMENT: Further Reading

Other Works by the Authors

Works by Gerald Manley Hopkins

"Pied Beauty"

"The Wreck of the *Deutschland*"

"The Windhover"

Works by A. E. Housman

"Loveliest of Trees"

"Reveille"

Answers continued

9. Possible responses: Students may respond with examples of "washed-up" athletes (may be used to support Housman), athletes who enjoy unusually long careers (may be used to refute Housman), or older athletes who find successful new careers (may be used to refute Housman).

EXTEND

Answers for p. 936

❶ Vocabulary Development

Concept Development

Possible responses: Students' coined words will vary considerably. The following are some suggestions:

1. summersend
2. chillmorns
3. snow-lawns
4. tallbare trees

Concept Development: Analogies

1. blight
2. grandeur
3. rue

Spelling Strategy

1. kite
2. night
3. fright
4. bright

❷ Grammar and Style

1. northwest
2. southeast
3. northwest
4. West
5. west

Writing Application

Possible response: To get from London to Oxford, go northwest.

Integrate Language Skills

❶ Vocabulary Development Lesson

Concept Development: Coined Words

Hopkins's fascination with language can be seen in the way he coins, or invents, words. For example, he combines *wan*, meaning "pale," and *wood* to make *wanwood*, a new word to describe pale autumn trees. Similarly, he coins *leafmeal* to describe fallen dead leaves ground into a kind of meal. Imitate Hopkins, and replace each phrase with a lively new combination word that others will understand.

1. the very end of summer
2. chilly mornings right after dawn
3. snow-covered lawns
4. tall, bare trees

Concept Development: Analogies

On your paper, complete the following analogies with words from the vocabulary list on page 929.

1. *accomplishment* : *pride* :: ___?___: *mourning*
2. *shabbiness* : *shack* :: ___?___: *palace*
3. *broadness* : *wideness* :: *remorse*: ___?___

Spelling Strategy

Words that contain a long *i* sound followed by a *t* are often spelled with the letter combination *ight*, as in the word *blight*. Choose the correctly spelled word from each pair.

1. kight, kite
2. night, nite
3. fright, frite
4. brite, bright

❷ Grammar and Style Lesson

Capitalization of Compass Points

Compass points referring to places are capitalized, like proper nouns, but those indicating direction are not. For example, in the second stanza of "God's Grandeur," *West* is capitalized because it refers to a specific region, but *eastward* is not because it merely points in a direction.

> And for all this, nature is never spent;
> There lives the dearest freshness deep
> down things;
> And though the last lights off the black
> West went **[place]**
> Oh, morning, at the brown brink
> eastward springs . . . **[direction]**

Practice In your notebook, choose a capital or lowercase letter for each compass point.

1. Housman's Shropshire is located n/Northwest of London.
2. The Shropshire lad would have traveled s/Southeast to get to London.
3. Hopkins traveled n/Northwest from London to attend Oxford University.
4. Worcestershire, Housman's birthplace, is in the w/West of England.
5. Ireland, where Hopkins served as a priest, is an island w/West of England.

Writing Application Using compass points, write instructions for a tourist traveling from London to Oxford, the alma mater of both these poets.

WG *Prentice Hall Writing and Grammar Connection: Chapter 26*

TEACHING RESOURCES

The following resources can be used to enrich or extend the instruction for pp. 936–937.

Vocabulary

Selection Support, Build Vocabulary, p. 205

Vocabulary and Spelling Practice Book (Use this booklet for skills enrichment.)

Grammar

Selection Support, Grammar and Style, p. 206

Writing and Grammar, Diamond Level, p. 670

Daily Language Practice Transparencies

Writing

Writing and Grammar, Diamond Level, p. 317

Writing and Grammar iText CD-ROM

BLOCK SCHEDULING: Resources marked with this symbol provide varied instruction during 90-minute blocks.

❸ Writing Lesson

Analytical Essay

Choose one of the four poems in this group, and write an analytical essay about it that presents and supports a thesis, or central idea, about its meaning.

Prewriting Review the poem, jotting down answers to questions like these: Who is the poem's speaker? What new perspectives does the speaker offer on a traditional theme, like beauty or mortality?

Drafting Use your notes to write a thesis statement that summarizes the poem's central insight into life. Then, develop your thesis in a series of paragraphs, citing details from the poem for support.

Revising To improve your draft, look for points at which you can support your ideas with examples.

Model: Revising to Strengthen Support

The surprises in the rhythms of "God's Grandeur" contribute to the theme that nature is not worn out. *For example, the sentence beginning in line 2 slips over the brink into line 3 and ends, surprisingly, with the first word of line 4—"Crushed."*

A specific example from the poem provides support for a general statement.

Prentice Hall Writing and Grammar Connection: Chapter 14, Section 4

❹ Extension Activities

Research and Technology Both Hopkins and Housman attended Oxford University. Use readings, photographs, recordings, film clips, and artifacts to give a **multimedia presentation** on Oxford and its importance to British poetry.

- Devise three questions to guide your research, focusing on famous poets who attended Oxford.
- Develop strategies for recording and organizing your findings.

Then, write a script that shows how and when you will use the items you have gathered, and follow it in giving your presentation.

Listening and Speaking With several classmates, give oral interpretations of the Hopkins and Housman poems as part of a **Victorian Poetry Contest.** Each reader should review his or her poem's meter and meaning, work out difficult pronunciations, and develop appropriate gestures. Have members of the audience vote on the best presentation. **[Group Activity]**

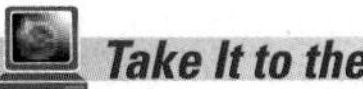
Take It to the Net www.phschool.com

Go online for an additional research activity using the Internet.

Lesson Support for p. 937

❸ Writing Lesson

- Read with students the note for the Writing Lesson on p. 937, and then tell students that they will write an essay supporting the central idea about the meaning of one of the four poems in this group.
- Encourage students to reread the poem they have chosen, focusing on a theme or perspective offered in the poem.
- Tell students that they should formulate a thesis that summarizes the poem's insights and develop it into an essay of several paragraphs.
- Review with students how to support their writing with details from the poem.

❹ Listening and Speaking

- Read the Listening and Speaking note with students, and have them prepare oral interpretations of poems by Hopkins or Housman.
- Have students determine the meter and meaning of each work and develop a presentation on the poems.
- Remind students that they should emphasize certain words and use their voices for appropriate inflections to convey tone.

CUSTOMIZE INSTRUCTION
For Universal Access

To address different learning styles, use the activities suggested in the **Extension Activities** booklet, p. 44.

- For Logical/Mathematical Learners, use Activity 5.
- For Visual/Spatial Learners, use Activity 6.
- For Interpersonal and Verbal/Linguistic Learners, use Activity 7.

ASSESSMENT RESOURCES

The following resources can be used to assess students' knowledge and skills.

Selection Assessment

- **Formal Assessment,** pp. 217–219
- **Open Book Test,** pp. 129–131
- **Got It! Assessment Videotapes,** Tape 4
- **Test Bank Software**

Take It to the Net

Visit www.phschool.com for self-tests and additional questions on the selections.

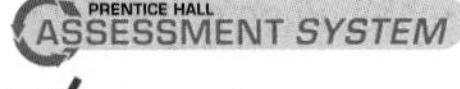

Workbook

Transparencies

Skill Book

CD-ROM

Objectives

1. To compare works of literature on the theme of life's cycles
2. To understand how an artist's choice of style, elements, and theme help to enhance the meaning of a text

Connections

Some of the writers of this period explored the two contradictory parts of life. Birth and death, the passing moment and eternity, man and nature, gloom and glory are common themes in the literature as these writers observe the cycles of life and its passing.

Gloom and Glory

- Explain to students that for writers of the nineteenth century, there was a bittersweet attitude toward progress. Tell the students that writers of this era concentrated on the idea that the "glory" of progress will always be met by the "gloom" of decline.
- Point out to students that Rimbaud does not put forward a simple image of eternity in his poem. Instead, he uses complex images, abstract ideas, and suggestive words to indicate a complex truth.

CONNECTIONS

Literature Around the World

Gloom and Glory

Cycles The Victorian Era marks a time of glorious progress for the British Empire. It also marks the beginning of its decline. The poems in this section reflect on the passing of glory as part of a cyclical process. For example, in Gerard Manley Hopkins's poem "Spring and Fall: To a Young Child," the poet provides a contrast between the innocence of childhood and the experiences of loss that disrupt and eventually bring that innocence to an end. Thomas Hardy and A. E. Housman juxtapose the glory of life with the gloom of death. In "Ah, Are You Digging on My Grave?" Hardy uses the cycle of life and death to question our natural belief in our own importance.

Eternity Like the other poets in this section, their contemporary Arthur Rimbaud (är tür′ ram bō′) focuses on the cycles of life. His affirmation of these cycles in "Eternity" is at once stark and joyous, as he voices the possibility that the only thing that is eternal is the cycle of change itself. As you read "Eternity," note what is temporary and what is truly eternal.

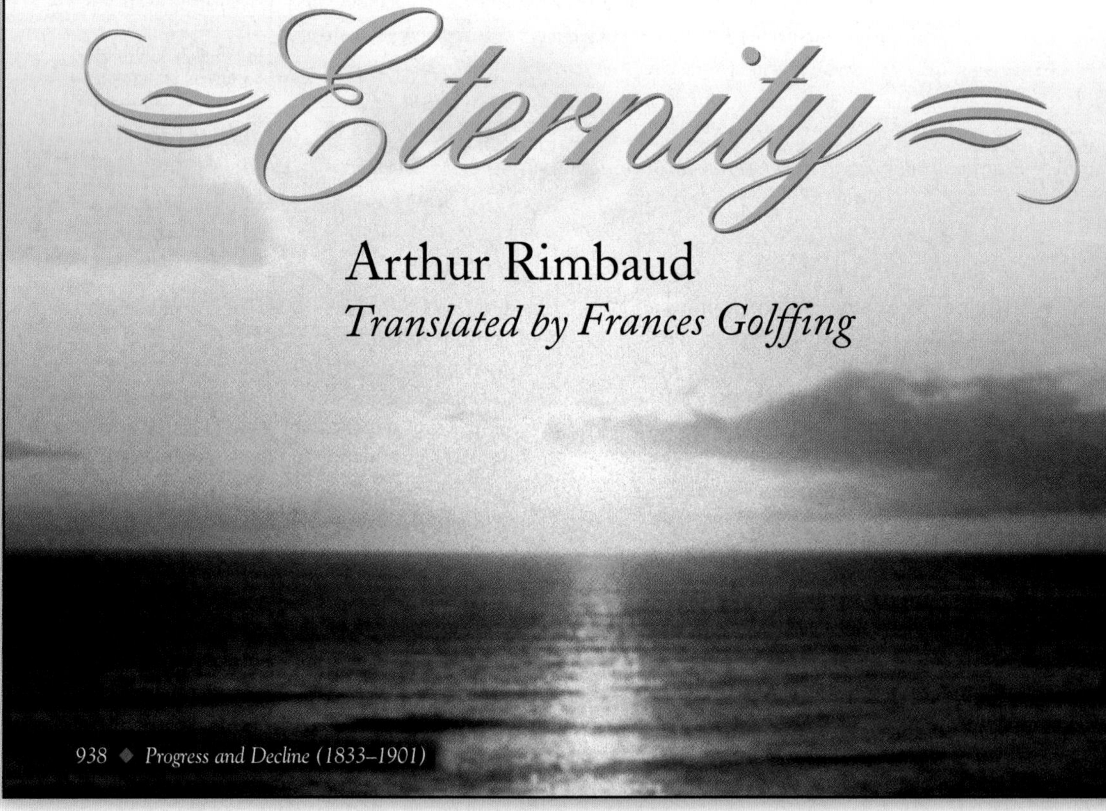

Eternity

Arthur Rimbaud

Translated by Frances Golffing

ENRICHMENT: Social Studies

Taoism

Rimbaud's concept of eternity as the union of the dark sea and the bright sun is related to Taoist ideas of the yin and the yang. According to this ancient Chinese religion, which is related to Buddhism, the ultimate source of eternal truth is based on a union of opposites: the yin and the yang. Yin represents the dark, passive, "feminine" aspects of life, while yang symbolizes the light, active, "masculine" aspects. Only by combining the two aspects can a person follow the true path, or Tao, to the ultimate source of truth. The poetic, mystical ideas of Taoism have been a source of inspiration to poets, both in the ancient world and in modern times.

I have recovered it.
What? Eternity.
It is the sea
Matched with the sun.

My sentinel soul,
Let us murmur the vow
Of the night so void
And of the fiery day.

Of human sanctions,
Of common transports,
You free yourself:
You soar according . . .

From your ardor[1] alone,
Embers of satin,
Duty exhales,
Without anyone saying: at last.

Never a hope;
No genesis.
Skill with patience . . .
Anguish is certain.

I have recovered it.
What? Eternity.
It is the sea
Matched with the sun.

1. **ardor** (är′ dər) *n.* emotional warmth; passion

Thematic Connections
How does the image of the sun and the sea express the idea of a cycle?

Arthur Rimbaud

(1854–1891)

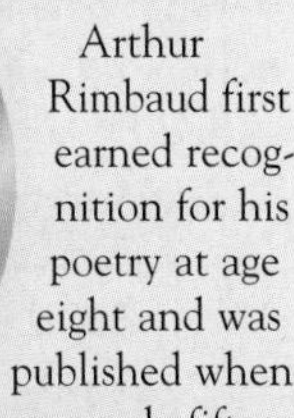

Arthur Rimbaud first earned recognition for his poetry at age eight and was published when he was only fifteen. His abrupt decision at the age of nineteen to stop writing poetry and embark on a life of adventure has made him a touchstone figure of the passion and peril of the artistic life, inspiring scores of writers, musicians, and other artists down to the present.

Rimbaud spent the remainder of his life traveling throughout Africa and the Middle East. By the time of his death, the poetry of his youth had begun to influence other writers.

Connecting Literature Around the World

1. (a) Take a position on the following statement: If we do not experience both happiness and sadness, we would not truly be able to experience either—emotions are defined by their contrast with one another. Explain why you agree or disagree. (b) Explain how your answer affects your appreciation of "Eternity."
2. In this section, which poet's view of the gloom and glory of life do you think is most realistic? Which is the most fulfilling? Explain.

Background

"Eternity"

This poem describes the speaker's quest to escape the normal bounds of consciousness and, by combining images and abstract ideas, offers a vision of eternity.

Thematic Connections

Answer: The sun rises and sets in the sea, suggesting the cycle of a day.

Answers

Connecting Literature Around the World

1. **(a)** Many students will agree with the statement, citing the happiness that comes with relief from a burden and the unhappiness that comes when a hope is disappointed. Some students, however, may point out that humans do not need to experience an emotion personally to understand it. **(b)** Students may say that such a belief helps one understand why Rimbaud finds "eternity" only when he sees how opposite feelings belong together, like the "sea/Matched with the sun" or "duty" and "ardor." Students who disagree may note that they associate eternity with one permanent feeling such as happiness and that they find it difficult to identify with the speaker's rapture.
2. Possible responses: "To an Athlete Dying Young" is the most realistic because it responds to an actual tragic occurrence; "Eternity" is realistic because it accepts both the achievement and the loss of transcendent vision.

Lesson Objectives

1. To analyze literary periods
2. To identify a key change in British society and trace its impact on Victorian literature
3. To explore the causal relationships between historical events and their impacts on literature
4. To use writing strategies to generate ideas, plan, organize, evaluate, and revise writing

Prewriting

- Help students choose a topic by reviewing some of the major historical events listed in the timeline in the unit introduction.
- Remind students that the events they choose should have a demonstrable effect on the literature of this period.
- Once students have selected a possible key event, have them review the questions as well as the graphic organizer to help assess the appropriateness of their choices.
- Explain to students that their thesis statements will be the foundation for their analyses. Students should work carefully to come up with a statement that best captures the focus of their analysis in order to help guide their attention as they work to gather details in the prewriting phase.

Writing About Literature

Analyze Literary Periods

The industrial progress of the Victorian Age transformed the world. With the development of a modern middle class and the rapid growth of industrial cities, this era brought the days of aristocrats and peasants in Europe to a close and ushered in a life closer to the one people live today. Victorian authors frequently served as insightful commentators on progress, judging the positive or negative effects—the glories and the miseries—of these dramatic changes. In the spirit of these Victorian authors, use the assignment in the yellow box to write an essay in which you analyze the impact of a specific social change on Victorian literature.

Assignment: The Effect of Social Change on Literature

Identify a key change in British society or economy, and trace its impact on Victorian literature.

Criteria:

- Include a thesis statement that identifies the social change you will analyze and introduces your view of its impact on Victorian literature.
- Discuss at least three Victorian works from this unit, demonstrating how they reflect the change that you have identified.
- Approximate length: 1,500 words

Prewriting

Find a focus. Begin by reviewing the major changes of the Victorian Age. You can find an overview of the era in the unit introduction on pages 804–813. Then, identify a specific change that had a significant impact on the literature of the period. Fill out a chart like the one shown, using these questions to guide you:

- What changes made the greatest difference to Victorian life?
- What new ideas contributed to social changes?
- How did writers respond to these changes? In what literary forms did they respond?

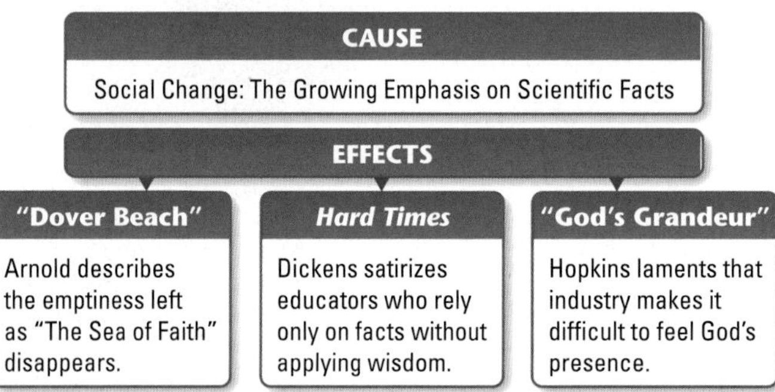

CAUSE
Social Change: The Growing Emphasis on Scientific Facts
EFFECTS
"Dover Beach"
Arnold describes the emptiness left as "The Sea of Faith" disappears.
Hard Times
Dickens satirizes educators who rely only on facts without applying wisdom.
"God's Grandeur"
Hopkins laments that industry makes it difficult to feel God's presence.

Gather details. Look for works that describe specific social, political, or economic circumstances. Also, review works that may indirectly express a more general reaction to the upheavals of the day. When you find a work that applies to your analysis, conduct a thorough rereading. Look for details of word choice or images that will add depth to your analysis.

Write a working thesis. Your thesis statement can guide your prewriting analysis. As your thoughts on the subject change, adjust your thesis statement to reflect your revised analysis.

Read to Write

Consider yourself a detective as you review the texts you have read. Look for clues concerning a particular motive for writing—an author's response to social changes.

TEACHING RESOURCES

The following resources can be used to enrich or extend the instruction for pp. 940–941.

- **Writing and Grammar,** Diamond Level, Chapter 10, pp. 194–209
- **Performance Assessment and Portfolio Management,** pp. 21 and 69
- **Writing Models and Graphic Organizers on Transparencies,** pp. 119–122

Writing and Grammar iText CD-ROM
Students can use the following tools as they complete their analyses:

- Customizable Outliner
- Transition
- Science Opener Variety

Drafting

Clarify your thesis statement. As you begin to draft, take time to make sure that your thesis statement clearly states what you want to express in your essay. This statement will guide your entire draft, so slow down and focus your thesis effectively.

Model: Focusing a Thesis

Unfocused: Science replaced faith, so Victorian authors had to warn their readers about what was happening.

Focused: As the scientific outlook replaced faith in the Victorian mind, authors of the era often warned readers about the values being lost in the race to progress.

Organize. Consider the relative strength of each of your examples when deciding the order in which you will discuss them. To leave your reader with a strong impression, you might choose to save your most effective or emphatic example for last.

Revising and Editing

Review content: Check your connections. Make sure that you introduce and explain each example you present so that your readers understand its relevance. Add transitions where necessary.

Review style: Use a variety of sentences. Include a mix of simple, compound, complex, and compound-complex sentences to create flowing prose. Identify passages lacking variety, and combine or break apart sentences in them.

Repeated sentence types: Hopkins says that humans have lost respect for the natural world. He charges that we have crushed the truest evidence of God's presence. The poem suggests that God's presence has been obscured by industrial development.

Varied sentences: Hopkins criticizes humans for losing respect for the natural world and, as a result, crushing the truest evidence of God's presence. In his view, God's presence has been obscured by industrial development.

Publishing and Presenting

Develop an oral presentation. Develop a brief talk for your class in which you present your analysis. After your presentation, ask for questions and comments from your audience.

WG Prentice Hall Writing and Grammar Connection: Chapter 14

Write to Learn
If you have trouble writing a clear thesis statement, you might need to change your essay's focus. Do not feel tied to your original idea—your second or third attempts might generate better results.

Write to Explain
You can use phrases such as "more significantly" or "most importantly" to share your evaluations with readers. These transitional phrases can clarify your position and highlight the key insights within your analysis.

Drafting

- Have students review their thesis statement. Make sure they assess the effectiveness of their statements, clarifying any parts of the statement as necessary.
- Remind them that this statement will provide a blueprint for their drafts, guiding the information they will include in their analyses and the depth into which they will go when analyzing how their chosen key event affected the literature of the period.

Revising and Editing

- Remind students that providing elaboration in the form of examples should add meaning and substance to their analyses. Help them distinguish the difference between relevant and irrelevant details.
- Have students carefully review their drafts to look for places that would benefit from sentence variety. Students may want to exchange their drafts with partners so that each partner can highlight places that lack variety.

Publishing and Presenting

- Suggest that students prepare for their oral presentations by practicing reading aloud their papers.
- Encourage students to make notes on their papers to indicate places they should vary their reading styles to help emphasize important points.

CUSTOMIZE INSTRUCTION FOR UNIVERSAL ACCESS

For Less Proficient Writers	For Advanced Writers
Have students create a list of different sentence types they can use when revising their drafts. Encourage students to refer to these lists as they revise to make sure they use as wide a variety of sentences as possible in their analyses.	Have students choose a paragraph from their analyses to rewrite in sentences that contain the same structure. Ask them to compare the two versions and discuss which one is more interesting to read.

Lesson Objectives

1. To write a research report using primary and secondary sources
2. To use writing strategies to plan, organize, write, and revise a research report

Model From Literature

Point out that Sydney Smith, who wrote "Progress in Personal Comfort" in this unit, had to conduct research to collect the facts on which he based his opinions.

Prewriting

- Ask students to identify some of the questions they hope to answer in their research papers and to list these questions in a chart. Students can identify possible sources to find answers to these questions in the other column of these charts.
- Point out to students the sample source information on this page, mentioning each aspect of information included there. Have students create note cards that serve the same purpose as they gather sources of information for their research reports.

Writing WORKSHOP

Research: Research Paper

A **research paper** is a work in which a writer explains or narrates a particular set of facts or group of events, documenting his or her claims by citing credible sources such as reference works and experiments. In this workshop, you will perform a historical investigation and write a research report analyzing the similarities and differences in the sources you examine.

Assignment Criteria Your research paper should include the following elements:

- A clear thesis statement explaining your purpose and conclusions
- A presentation of the details of the event, drawing on several primary and secondary sources
- A comparison of the sources and an analysis of any differences in the information they present
- Conclusions about the event, taking into account your evaluation of the validity and reliability of source information
- Complete and accurate citations with a formal Works-Cited list

To preview the criteria on which your report may be assessed, see the Rubric on page 947.

Prewriting

Choose a topic. For this type of report, the best topic is a historical event about which there are differing opinions and for which a variety of primary and secondary sources are available. Because primary sources—items like letters, diaries, and interviews—are often harder to find than secondary ones, use a library catalog and the Internet to make sure that such sources are available for a topic before making your final selection.

Difficult topic:	Daily life of medieval peasants (few primary sources available)
Workable topic:	Working conditions in early industrial England

Do the research. Use a library for secondary sources such as books and encyclopedias. Use the Internet for secondary sources such as online newspapers and magazines and for many primary sources. List and briefly summarize all sources.

Choose varied documents. Make sure that your sources represent varied viewpoints. Settle on at least two primary and two secondary sources.

TOPIC: Battle of New Orleans

CATALOG SCAN:

Many Secondary Sources

Horsman, R. *The War of 1812.* London: Eyre & Spottiswoode, 1969.

Some Primary Sources On-Line

Jackson, A. Address to His Troops. 8 January 1815. 4 April 2000 <http://www.hillsdale.edu/dept/History/Documents/War/America/1812/South/1815-Jackson.htm>.

TEACHING RESOURCES

The following resources can be used to enrich or extend the instruction for pp. 942–947.

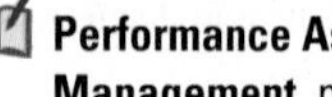

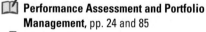

Writing and Grammar, Diamond Level, Chapter 13, pp. 274–296

Performance Assessment and Portfolio Management, pp. 24 and 85

Writing Models and Graphic Organizers on Transparencies, pp. 57–72

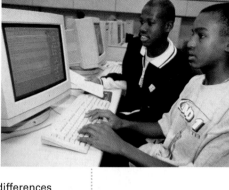

Writing and Grammar iText CD-ROM
Students can use the following tools as they complete their responses to literature:

- Note Cards
- KWL Chart
- Customizable Outliner

Student Model

Before you begin drafting your report, read this student model and review the characteristics of a powerful research paper.

Eric Southard
Lawrence, KS

A "Blessing" or a Blunder: British Defeat in the Battle of New Orleans

One of the most stirring battles of the War of 1812, the Battle of New Orleans, was actually fought weeks after the war was officially over. The battle concluded with the rousing defeat of the British by American troops under Andrew Jackson. At the time, Jackson attributed his victory to "the blessing of heaven" (Jackson, Address to His Troops). Yet it is fairly clear that misjudgments by the leaders of the British had as much to do with Jackson's victory as good fortune.

Eric identifies his thesis in his opening paragraph.

In early 1814, what would later be called the War of 1812 had already been fought for almost two years. Having finally won the war against France, the British were stepping up their efforts on the American front. (Carter 6).

Next, Eric provides readers with general background on his subject.

The city of New Orleans, holding a total of $15 million in stored merchandise, enticed the British military with the promise of prize money (Carter 91). Because of its situation at the mouth of the Mississippi, the capture of New Orleans would cut off resources from several states, including Kentucky, Tennessee, and Ohio, which were active in the attacks on Canada (Mahon 340).

Word of the British intentions reached William Claiborn, the Governor of Louisiana, through the pirate chieftain Jean Lafitte, who had been approached for assistance by the British. After several urgent requests from the governor, Major General Andrew Jackson arrived in New Orleans on December 1st, 1814 (Horsman 237).

Jackson established fortifications and reinforced forts in the region of New Orleans. Gunboats were placed in Lake Borgne and Lake Pontchartrain to the north, two of the most likely routes of attack (Carter 114). On December 12th, only 11 days after Jackson had arrived in New Orleans, the small boats of the British fleet, under the command of Admiral Alexander Cochrane, entered Lake Borgne. The British had completely destroyed all five American boats by December 14th. On the 23rd, after they had finished their lengthy disembarkation, the British forces captured the plantation of Jacques Villere on the Mississippi and encamped there, less than seven miles away from New Orleans (Horsman 240).

Eric gives a detailed account of events leading up to the battle, drawing on a variety of sources.

Jackson quickly attacked the British but with equivalent casualties on either side (Hickey, *Forgotten Conflict* 209), and on December 24, he retreated two miles to take up position behind a small canal (Horsman 240). The canal was widened and deepened and a large earthwork, or rampart, was placed on the upper bank, where the American forces would make their stand. Slaves, militia, regulars, and even Jean Laffite's pirates labored

Student Model

- Explain that the Student Model is a sample and that students' research papers may be longer.
- Point out that Eric identifies his thesis in the opening paragraph. Ask students to identify what this thesis is.
  Answer: Eric will show that the defeat of the British was caused in part by the misjudgments of British leaders.
- Draw students' attention to the fact that Eric provides background information for the reader in order to provide a historical context for his topic.
- For an additional model of a research report, see pp. 57–72 of **Writing Models and Graphic Organizers on Transparencies.**

CUSTOMIZE INSTRUCTION FOR UNIVERSAL ACCESS

For Special Needs Students	For English Learners
Encourage students to choose a fairly narrow topic for their research reports so they don't become overwhelmed with facts to include.	Have these students work in pairs to read through the Student Model, noting any words or phrases they need to look up for better understanding.

Student Model

- Point out the citations Eric uses in his report. Remind students to refer to their note cards when making citations in their papers.
- Explain that Eric addresses different points of view of the same event, revealing the importance of using primary sources in research papers.

side by side with shovel and pick to form these ramparts, which were to prove vital to the American side in the coming battle (Carter 188).

In the meantime, the British received reinforcements from Jamaica led by Major-General Edward Pakenham (Carter 192). After bringing up a quantity of artillery and then watching it destroyed by American fire, Pakenham decided to wait until further reinforcements arrived to try again (Lord 330–31). Until the troops of General Lambert, 1,700 in all, arrived on January 6, the British were mostly idle (Carter 239). Jackson used the time to shore up the rampart, which was by this time about five to eight feet tall and 20 feet thick (Tallant 145). A smaller, unfinished line, manned by fewer than one thousand troops, was established across the river (Carter 237).

Eric cites sources on his Works-Cited list properly, following MLA style.

The Battle of New Orleans was decided on January 8, 1815. Events unfolded on both sides of the river. Early in the morning, Colonel Thornton of the British took about 450 troops across the Mississippi River (Carter 245). The poorly armed American troops were surprised and took flight from the unfinished line into the swamps. In an address later that day to the troops on that side of the river, Jackson said, "no words can express the mortification I felt, at witnessing the scene on the opposite bank" (Jackson, Address).

The significance of the abandoned position may be disputed. Some historians describe it as poorly placed. Jackson saw things in a different light. Writing to Madison on the day of the battle, Jackson noted that "This unfortunate rout had totally changed the aspect of affairs." Once the British occupied the other side of the river, he said, "they occupied a position from which they might annoy us without hazard, and by means of which they might have been able to defeat, in great measure, the effects of our success on this side of the river." Jackson reported that he immediately began to prepare to dislodge the British from the new position. Fortunately, the British simply withdrew from the position during a cease-fire. "I need not tell you with how much eagerness I immediately regained possession of the position he had thus hastily quitted" (Jackson, Letter 9 January 1815). While Jackson's perspective may have been distorted by the rush of events, he clearly assigned great value to the position.

Eric contrasts different views of the same event, noting why a primary source—Jackson's letter—might give an evaluation different from that of later commentators

The main conflict, in any case, was on the other side of the river. There, the British strategy was to advance three columns of soldiers to the American line. Sent ahead of the other troops, the 44th Regiment was put in charge of carrying the ladders and equipment for climbing the rampart. Half of the regiment would put them in place, while the other half would provide covering fire. It was not an easy plan to execute, as events would soon show (Carter 242).

At daybreak, a single rocket was fired: the call to attack. The three columns, under Generals Gibbs, Keane, and Rennie, began to advance on the American line. The main column under Gibbs halted because the men of the 44th had not yet managed to get the heavy ladders in place. Suddenly,

Although his main concern is accuracy, Eric also adds drama to his narrative.

the fog lifted, leaving the troops in plain view of the American line. The Americans began to fire, and the British lines began to falter (Lord 336).

Rennie, in charge of the column nearest to the river, moved toward the far right end of Jackson's line. Decimated by American fire, they pressed on nonetheless, taking cover 50 feet from the main line (Carter 255). Keane, in the center column, was supposed to support whichever of the other columns needed help. He regrettably chose to move toward Gibb's column, which was in dire straits indeed. Had he moved toward Rennie's column, they probably would have broken through the line. The British pressed valiantly on, but most fell before they even came close to the American line (Carter 258 and Lord 336). The British fled the field. The Americans launched no counter-attack, content to let the defeated foe withdraw unopposed.

Using a variety of sources, Eric reconstructs the details of the battle.

Though Andrew Jackson steeled himself for another attack (Jackson, Letter, 9 January 1815), it never came. General Lambert, now in command of the entire British force, decided not to bring the reserves up from the rear. Thornton returned to headquarters, excited by his capture of the American position on the other side of the river, but Lambert decided not to push on the opposite bank. Supplies were running low and Lambert, despite Admiral Cochrane's suggestion of another attack, decided to retreat permanently. The British left Louisiana on February 4 and never returned.

In the heat of battle, Jackson's estimate of the importance of the position captured by Thornton may have been exaggerated. If his estimate was correct, however, then Lambert may have made a major error in withdrawing.

While General Jackson sincerely felt that the victory was a "blessing from heaven," it was as much due to the ineptitude of the British commanders, four of whom—Rennie, Gibbs, Keane, Pakenham—paid for their strategic mistakes with their lives (Mahon 366–369). If there could be any blessing from such a tragedy, perhaps it lay in the future, for this was to be the last time that Americans and English would ever fire on each other as enemies.

Eric clearly states his conclusions in his final paragraph.

Works-Cited List

Carter, Samuel. *Blaze of Glory: The Fight for New Orleans.* New York: St. Martin's Press, 1971.

Hickey, Donald R. *The War of 1812: Forgotten Conflict.* Chicago: University of Illinois Press, 1989.

Horsman, Reginald. *The War of 1812.* London: Eyre & Spottiswoode, 1969.

Jackson, A. Address to His Troops. 8 January 1815. 4 April 2000 <http://www.hillsdale.edu/dept/History/Documents/War/America/1812/South/1815-Jackson.htm>.

Letter to the Secretary of War. 9 January 1815. 4 April 2000 <http://www.hillsdale.edu/dept/History/Documents/War/America/1812/South/1815.01.09-Jackson.htm>.

Lord, Walter. *The Dawn's Early Light.* New York: W.W. Norton & Co., 1972.

Mahon, John K. *The War of 1812.* Gainesville: University of Florida Press, 1972.

Tallant, Robert. *The Pirate Lafitte and the Battle of New Orleans.* New York: Random House, 1951.

Eric provides a complete, detailed, and properly formatted list of all the works he has cited in his report.

Eric follows MLA style, a standard citation style, in citing his primary sources.

Student Model

- Point out how Eric uses his summary to offer a conclusion based on his research.
- Remind students of the importance of obtaining complete information on their note cards as they do research, so they can easily construct a bibliography at the end of their reports.

Real-World Connection

Explain that students will use the skill of writing research reports in college. They may be surprised to know that many careers also require research reports, including those of attorney, business manager, Web site writer, and graphic designer.

Drafting

- Remind students that a thesis statement clearly states the main idea or purpose of an essay. Their opening paragraphs should clearly identify this thesis and provide an introduction to the topic so that readers clearly understand the topic.
- Review the Effective Organizations chart with students. Have them determine which type of organization would best suit the topic of their research papers.
- Remind students to refer to their research note cards to note sources appropriately, as needed.

Revising

- Students may have difficulty deciding when and if they need to cite a source.
- Have students work in pairs to help evaluate when documentation is needed.

Drafting

Establish your organizational plan. Decide whether you will present conclusions about your sources as part of your introduction or build toward them throughout the paper. Use one of the plans in this chart.

Write an effective introduction. Use the opening paragraph to set the stage and establish the overall direction. Introduce the issue, and clarify background details such as time, place, and relevant political and social conditions.

Use sources well. As you draft, use a mix of paraphrases and direct quotations. Do not string quotes together without interpretation.

Analyze sources. When discussing different versions of an event or when introducing special evidence, describe your sources. Explain the differences among them or their unique perspective by analyzing the writers' circumstances and motives.

Document your information. As you draft, underline sentences for which you will need to cite sources. Include notes identifying the sources you will credit. After you finish drafting, format citations according to a standard format, such as MLA style.

Effective Organizations

Introduction	Introduction
present historical context give thesis statement DRAW CONCLUSION	present historical context establish issue in thesis statement
Body	**Body**
PROVE CONCLUSION present/analyze/compare sources	present/analyze/compare sources LEAD TO CONCLUSION
Closing	**Closing**
summarize	DRAW CONCLUSION

Revising

Revise to give proper credit. Commonly known facts need not be credited within the body of the paper, but lesser-known facts, as well as quotations and writers' opinions, should be.

1. Have a partner read your draft and mark any statements that must be documented with the source of the information.
2. Add additional credits as needed.
3. Reread your draft. Combine and condense information as needed to avoid excessive or repetitious references.

Model: Marking for Complete Citations

Jackson quickly attacked the British but with equivalent (Hickey, *Forgotten Conflict* 209), casualties on either side, and on December 24, he retreated (Horsman 240). two miles to take up position behind a small canal.

These specific factual claims, which are not common knowledge, require a cited source.

USING TECHNOLOGY IN WRITING

Point out that if students collect their research information electronically, they can use the cut-and-paste feature of their word-processing software to quickly create in-text documentation as well as their works-cited lists. Students can also use spell check and other revision tools on the **Writing and Grammar iText CD-ROM.**

Revise to establish validity and reliability of sources. Make sure that you give enough information in your text about each source to establish its credibility and relevance and to show the perspective it represents.

Vague: Joseph Hebergram testified about child labor practices.

Stronger: *Sixteen-year-old* Joseph Hebergram testified *before the Sadler Committee about his own experiences as a child worker.*

Publishing and Presenting

Prepare your Works-Cited list. Your paper is ready for presentation only after you add your Works-Cited list, an alphabetical list of all of the sources cited in your paper, properly formatted. Follow MLA or another widely accepted style to assemble the list. (See pages R30—R31 for more guidance.) The list should appear at the end of your paper. Note that some teachers prefer a bibliography in which you list all the sources you consulted during your research.

Present your report orally. Use your report as the basis of an oral presentation. Follow these suggestions:

- Review your paper beforehand so that your delivery is smooth.
- Pace your speech. Speak slowly enough to give listeners a chance to understand and follow your points, without dragging.
- As you present, project your confidence in the potential interest of your topic to listeners.
- Vary your voice and tone when presenting primary sources, giving expression to the feelings the source may show.
- Share photos and other graphics by enlarging them or circulating them to the class.

WG *Prentice Hall Writing and Grammar Connection: Chapter 13*

Rubric for Self-Assessment

Evaluate your research paper using the following criteria and rating scale:

Criteria	Rating Scale: Not very 1	2	3	4	Very 5
How clear and accurate a summary is the thesis statement?	1	2	3	4	5
How clear and well-documented is the presentation of the event?	1	2	3	4	5
How effectively are source materials analyzed and compared?	1	2	3	4	5
How strong are the conclusions about the event?	1	2	3	4	5
How complete and accurate are the citations and Works-Cited list?	1	2	3	4	5

Publishing and Presenting

- Before students present their reports orally, have them practice reading their work aloud.
- Review with students the suggestions they should keep in mind as they practice delivering their reports.

Assessment

- Review with students the assessment criteria.
- Have students evaluate the Student Model on the basis of the five criteria listed on this page.
- Then, have students complete the self-assessment after they give their presentations.
- The rubric on this page, and another rubric in an alternative format, can be found on pp. 24 and 85 of **Performance Assessment and Portfolio Management.**

TEST-TAKING TIP

On tests, students may be asked to evaluate a text to make judgments about the writer's bias. Remind students to look for loaded words, opposing points not considered, and facts not considered.

Lesson Objectives

1. To deliver a persuasive speech
2. To identify persuasive goals and choose appropriate persuasive techniques
3. To use appropriate oratory techniques, including tone of voice and body language, when delivering the speech

Preparing Your Argument

- Review the chart with students to help them focus their attention on persuasive goals and the techniques they can use to achieve these goals.
- Point out the persuasive techniques that students can use to achieve their goals. Remind students that the techniques they use will depend on their stated goals. Some techniques are more appropriate for certain goals than others.

Delivering Your Speech

- Explain to students that the degree to which a speech is persuasive will depend a great deal on its delivery. Even the most persuasive of words can fall flat if they are not delivered persuasively.
- Review the bulleted suggestions with students. If possible, provide examples for each by reading from a persuasive speech from this unit, such as Judge Catherine McGuinness's speech on p. 911.

Listening and Speaking WORKSHOP

Delivering a Persuasive Speech

A **persuasive speech** is one intended to alter listeners' views and to persuade them to take action. Use the strategies presented in this workshop and the chart below to prepare and deliver a persuasive speech.

Preparing Your Argument

To begin, identify the goals of your speech and the techniques you will use to accomplish them.

Identify your persuasive goals. To bring listeners to take a specific action, you may need to persuade them about facts, encourage them to accept a certain judgment, or bring them to feel a certain way about the issue. Use a chart like the one shown to identify the goals you need to accomplish in your speech.

Choose the appropriate persuasive techniques. In order to achieve each of your persuasive goals, you must choose an effective technique. Persuasive techniques include these:

- **Inductive reasoning**—Forming generalizations based on a selection of representative cases
- **Deductive reasoning**—Applying a general principal to a specific case to draw a conclusion
- **Parallelism**—Repeating sentence patterns or grammatical structure to build persuasive force
- **Imagery**—Using descriptive language to paint a scene, set a tone, or suggest an emotion
- **Irony**—Using words or contrasts in a situation to bring an audience to recognize surprising or amusing contradictions

Persuasive Goals and Techniques

- **What facts do you need your audience to recognize?**

Techniques to Accomplish Goal:

- **What judgments or opinions do you want them to share?**

Techniques to Accomplish Goal:

- **What emotional reactions do you want to encourage in them?**

Techniques to Accomplish Goal:

- **What action do you want them to take?**

Techniques to Accomplish Goal:

Delivering Your Speech

One of the most important persuasive tools you can use is yourself—your manner of engaging with the audience and presenting yourself. When you are giving your speech, remember to do the following:

- Establish eye contact with the audience to convey sincerity and hold audience members' attention.
- Use a confident but courteous manner. Speaking shyly or too aggressively will draw attention away from your point and place it on you.
- Speak slowly for emphasis of a serious point.

***Activity:* Prepare and Deliver** Choose a topic for a persuasive speech. Gather support, and draft your speech, using at least three of the techniques listed above. Deliver your speech to the class.

Assessment WORKSHOP

Paired Passages

In some tests, you are asked to read paired passages and answer questions comparing them. Use these strategies for such questions:

- Note the similarities and differences between the two passages.
- Write a one-sentence summary of each.

Test-Taking Strategy

Remember to review the information presented in *both* passages before answering a question.

Sample Test Item

Directions: Read the passages, and then answer the question that follows.

Passage 1

Some argue that hunters interfere with nature. On the contrary, hunters are not disruptive; they help keep animal populations healthy. Wild animals become too numerous when they lack natural predators. Hunting is a humane practice that quickly kills animals that would otherwise die of starvation.

Passage 2

The number of game hunters has declined. About 20 percent of the hunters who stopped hunting quit because they believe it is wrong. Some object to the killing of animals for decorative purposes. Other ex-hunters are repelled by the prevalence of guns and violence in society.

1. What is the relationship between the main ideas of the two passages?

A They offer opposing moral views.

B They address different aspects of hunting.

C They discuss people's positions on hunting.

D They contrast the motives of hunters and ex-hunters.

Answer and Explanation

The correct answer is ***C***. Answer *A* is incorrect because Passage 2 does not take a moral position on hunting. *B* is too general. *D* is incorrect because Passage 1 does not discuss hunters' motives.

Practice

Directions: Read the passages. (The first is from "The Way to Rainy Mountain" by N. Scott Momaday. The second is from Elie Wiesel's acceptance speech for the Nobel Peace Prize.) Then, choose the letter of the best answer to the question that follows.

Passage 1

I returned to Rainy Mountain in July. My grandmother had died in the spring, and I wanted to be at her grave. She had lived to be very old and at last infirm. Her only living daughter was with her when she died, and I was told that in death her face was that of a child.

Passage 2

I remember: it happened yesterday or eternities ago. A young Jewish boy discovered the kingdom of night. I remember his bewilderment, I remember his anguish. It all happened so fast. The ghetto. The deportation. The sealed cattle car. The fiery altar upon which the history of our people and the future of mankind were meant to be sacrificed.

1. These passages are similar because

A both involve death.

B both involve injustices done to others.

C both authors feel a need to remember.

D (*A* and *C*)

Lesson Objective

To read and compare paired passages

Applying Reading Strategies

Explain to students that they can read ahead to make note of the test question. This will help focus their attention and set a purpose for reading before they read the paired passages.

Applying Test-Taking Strategies

- Have students read the sample test item. Begin by having them read the question and identify what it is they are being asked to do.
- Have students read the passages and then identify the main idea of each. Students can then determine how these two main ideas are related.

Answer

The correct answer is *D*. Both authors are writing about their memories, which happen to involve death. Answer *B* is incorrect because only the second passage involves injustices done to others. The first passage is simply about the death of an elderly relative.

TEACHING RESOURCES

The following resources can be used to enrich or extend the instruction for p. 949.

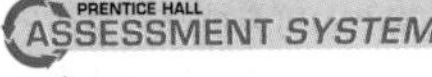

Workbook — Transparencies

Skill Book — CD-ROM

Unit Objectives

1. To read selections from English literature of the twentieth century
2. To apply a variety of reading strategies, particularly reading strategies for reading fiction, appropriate for reading these selections
3. To analyze literary elements
4. To use a variety of strategies to build vocabulary
5. To learn elements of grammar, usage, and style
6. To use recursive writing processes to write in a variety of forms
7. To develop listening and speaking skills
8. To express and support responses to various types of texts
9. To prepare, organize, and present literary interpretations

Meeting the Objectives

With each selection, you will find instructional materials through which students can meet these objectives. Further, you will find additional practice pages for reading strategies, literary analysis, vocabulary, and grammar in the **Selection Support: Skills Development Workbook** in your **Teaching Resources**.

Background

Art

The City Rises, Umberto Boccioni

The Italian painter and sculptor Umberto Boccioni (1882–1916) became a leading light of Futurism, an early twentieth-century literary and artistic movement that rejoiced in technology.

Link the art to the focus of Unit 6, "A Time of Rapid Change," by asking the following question:

- What might this turbulent, nonrepresentational cityscape suggest about literature from the twentieth century?
  Answer: The art and literature of the twentieth century is turbulent and seeks the meaning of modern experience in forces that cannot be pictured directly.

UNIT 6 A Time of Rapid Change (1901–Present)

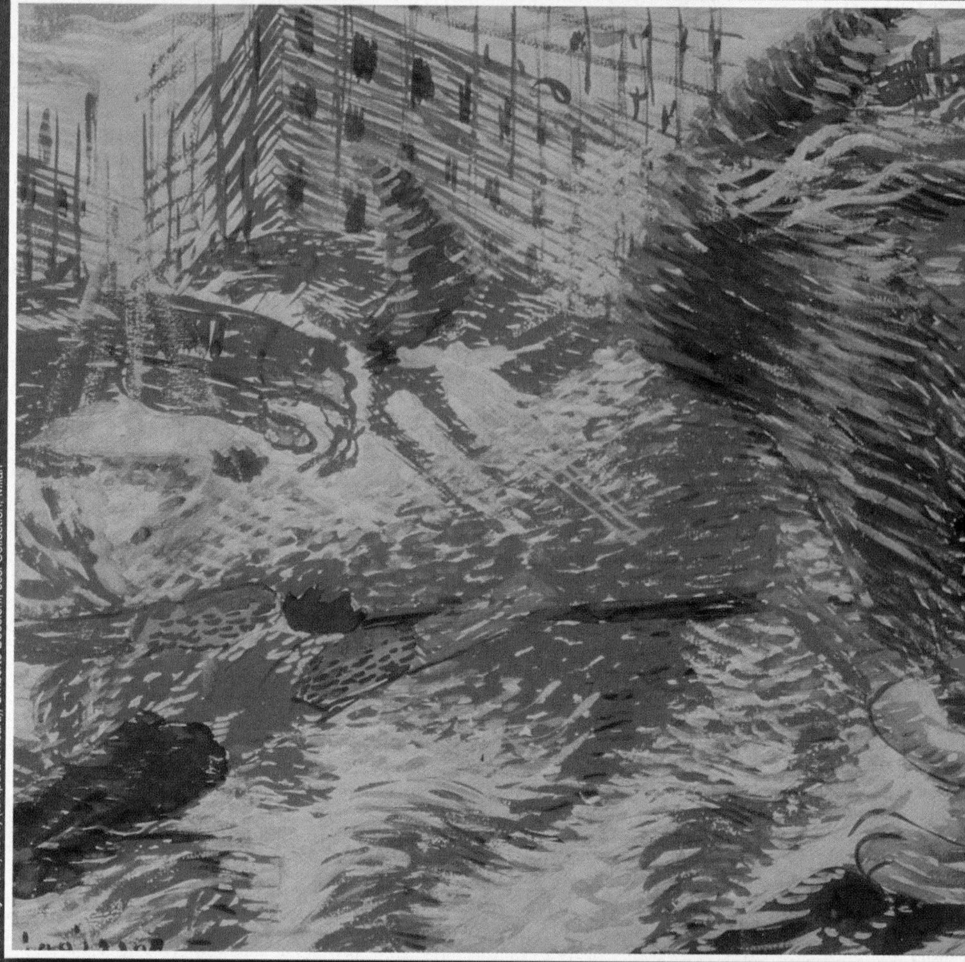

The City Rises, 1911, (tempura on card), Umberto Boccioni, Jesi Collection, Milan

UNIT FEATURES: CONNECTIONS	
Connections	**Reading Informational Material**
Every unit contains features that connect literature to a related topic, such as art, science or history. In this unit, Yehyda Amichai's poem "The Diameter of the Bomb," Tony Blair's speech "The Rights We Enjoy, The Duties We Owe," and Jorge Luis Borges's story "The Book of Sand" each contributes a perspective on modern times. Use the information and questions on the Connections page to help students enrich their understanding of the selections presented within the unit.	These selections will help students to analyze and evaluate informational texts, such as workplace documents, technical directions, and consumer materials. They will expose students to the organization and features unique to non-narrative texts. In this unit, students learn how to read and analyze a mission statement.

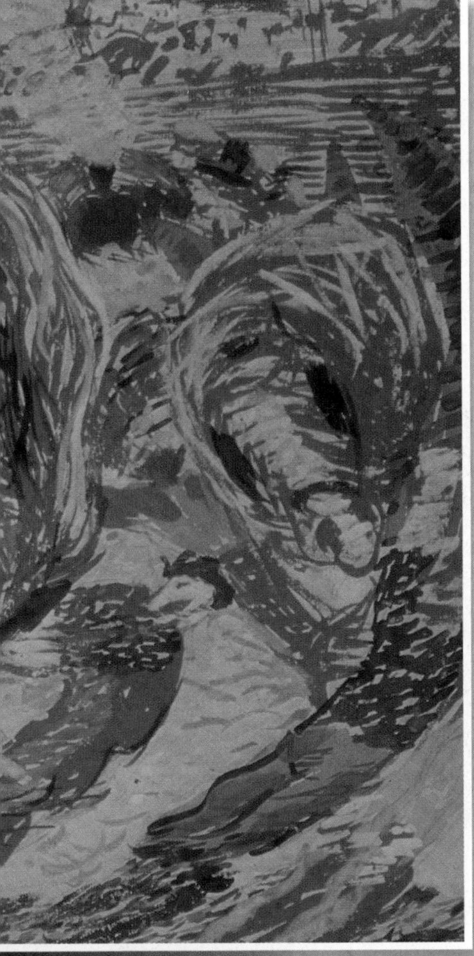

"We are living at one of the great turning points of history. . . . Yesterday, we split the atom. We assaulted that colossal citadel of power, the tiny unit of the substance of the universe. And because of this, the great dream and the great nightmare of centuries of human thought have taken flesh and walk beside us all, day and night."

— Doris Lessing, *from* "The Small, Personal Voice"

ASSESSMENT RESOURCES

The following resources can be used to assess students' knowledge and skills.

- **Selection Support:** Skills Development Workbook
- **Formal Assessment**
- **Open Book Tests**
- **Performance Assessment and Portfolio Management**
- **Extension Activities**

Assessing Student Progress

Listed below are the tools that are available to measure the degree to which students meet the unit objectives.

Informal Assessment

The questions in the Review and Assess sections are a first-level response to the concepts and skills presented with the selections. Students' responses are a brief, informal measure of their grasp of the material. These responses can indicate where further instruction and practice are needed. Then, follow up with the practice pages in the **Selection Support: Skills Development Workbook.**

Formal Assessment

The **Formal Assessment** booklet contains Selection Tests and Unit Tests.

- Selection Tests measure comprehension and skills acquisition for each selection or group of selections.
- Each Unit Test provides students with thirty multiple-choice questions and five essay questions designed to assess students' knowledge of the literature and skills taught in the unit.

The **Open Book Tests** ask students to demonstrate their ability to synthesize and communicate information from selections or groups of selections.

To assess student writing, you will find rubrics and scoring models in the **Performance Assessment and Portfolio Management** booklet. In this booklet you will also find scoring rubrics for listening and speaking activities.

Alternative Assessment

The **Extension Activities** booklet contains writing activities, listening and speaking activities, and research and technology activities that are appropriate for students with different ability levels. You may also use these activities as an alternative measurement of students' growth.

Using the Timeline

The Timeline can serve a number of instructional purposes, as follows:

Getting an Overview

Use the Timeline to help students get a quick overview of themes and events of the period. This approach will benefit all students but may be especially helpful for visually oriented students, English language learners, and those less proficient in reading. (For strategies in using the Timeline as an overview, see the bottom of this page.)

Thinking Critically

Questions are provided on the facing page. Use these questions to have students review the events, discuss their significance, and examine the *so what* behind the *what happened*.

Connecting to Selections

Have students refer back to the Timeline when reading individual selections. By consulting the Timeline regularly, they will gain a better sense of the period's chronology. In addition, they will appreciate what was occurring in the world that gave rise to these works of literature.

Projects

Students can use the Timeline as a launching pad for projects like these:

- **Building Context** For each selection students read in this unit, have them check the Timeline for possible background events. To what events is a poet or fiction writer responding directly? Does the writer's experiments with form have anything to do with major, contemporary upheavals in life and perception? To what events does the writer not seem to respond? Students can develop Cluster Diagrams in which each selection is surrounded by relevant events.
- **Report on a Movement or Trend** Have students scan the Timeline for a political movement or social trend, research the people behind it, then report on their findings to the class. What role, if any, did literary figures play in this movement or trend?

Timeline 1901–Present

1901 — 1920 — 1945

British Events

- **1901** Edward VII becomes king.
- **1902 Joseph Conrad** publishes *Heart of Darkness.*
- **1914** Britain enters World War I. ▼

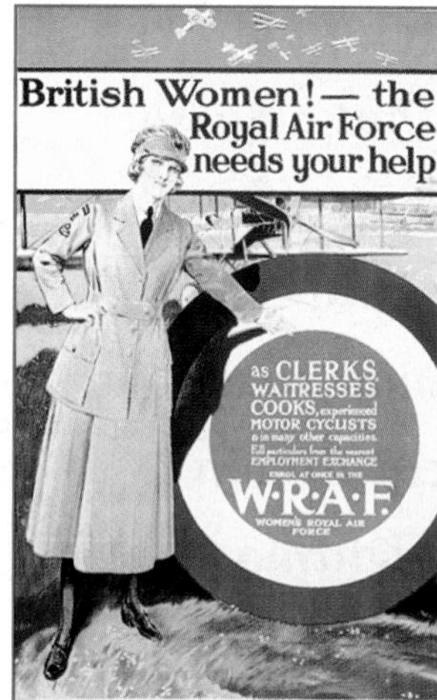

- **1918** Women over thirty achieve right to vote.
- **1922** Irish Free State formed.
- **1922 T. S. Eliot** publishes *The Waste Land.*
- **1922 James Joyce** publishes *Ulysses.*
- **1939** Britain enters World War II. ▼
- **1940 Winston Churchill** becomes prime minister.

- **1945 George Orwell** publishes *Animal Farm.*
- **1947** India and Pakistan gain independence.
- **1949** Irish Free State becomes Republic of Ireland. ▲
- **1952** Elizabeth II becomes queen.
- **1954** Roger Bannister breaks four-minute mile. ▶

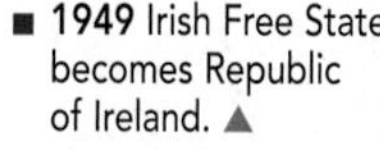

World Events

- **1903** Orville and Wilbur Wright build first successful airplane.
- **1905** Germany: Albert Einstein proposes theory of relativity.
- **1917** Austria: Sigmund Freud publishes *Introduction to Psychoanalysis.*
- **1917** Russia: Czar overthrown; Bolsheviks seize power.
- **1920** India: **Mohandas Gandhi** leads nonviolent protests.
- **1927** United States: Charles Lindbergh flies solo to Paris.
- **1939** Europe: Hitler invades Poland; World War II begins.
- **1941** United States: Japan bombs Pearl Harbor; United States enters World War II.
- **1945** Japan: World War II ends as Japan surrenders.
- **1948** Middle East: Israel established.
- **1949** China: Mao Zedong establishes People's Republic.
- **1955** United States: Martin Luther King, Jr., leads civil rights bus boycott.
- **1957** Russia: Sputnik I, first satellite launched.

ENRICHMENT: Getting an Overview of the Period

Introduction	Key Events
To give students an overview of the period, have them determine how far back the Timeline starts (use the date in the upper left-hand corner). Next, point out that the Timeline is divided into specifically British Events (on top) and World Events (on bottom). Have them practice scanning the Timeline across, looking both at the British Events and the World Events. Point out that global events often involve Britain.	Have students note world events that had an impact on Britain. **Possible responses:** Britain fought in World War I (1914) and World War II (1939). Have students note British events indicating Britain's changing place in the world. **Possible responses:** Britain went to war (1939); gave up colonies (1947).

British and World Events

1960 | 1975 | 1990 | Present

- **1962 Doris Lessing** publishes *The Golden Notebook.*
- **1965** Miniskirt becomes fashionable.
- **1967** The Beatles release *Sgt. Pepper's Lonely Hearts Club Band.*
- **1972** Britain imposes direct rule on Northern Ireland.

- **1975** North Sea oil production begins. ▼

- **1979** Margaret Thatcher becomes first woman prime minister. ▶
- **1979 V. S. Naipaul** publishes *A Bend in the River.*
- **1989** Parliament privatizes national electric and water companies.

- **1991 Nadine Gordimer** wins Nobel Prize for Literature.
- **1997 Tony Blair** elected Prime Minister.
- **1997** Scotland and Wales gain right to form separate parliaments.
- **1997** Hong Kong reverts from British to Chinese rule.
- **2000** Celebration of New Year's Eve in the Millennium Dome.

- **1960** Germany: Berlin Wall built.
- **1963** United States: President John F. Kennedy assassinated.
- **1964** Vietnam: American troops join fighting.
- **1969** United States: Apollo 11 lands on moon. ▲

- **1977** Africa: Djibouti, last remaining European colony, granted independence.
- **1979** Iran: Ayatollah Khomeini overthrows Shah.
- **1980** United States: Ronald Reagan elected president.
- **1989** Germany: Berlin Wall torn down; reunification of East and West Germany follows.

- **1991** Eastern Europe: Soviet Union dissolved.
- **1994** South Africa: Nelson Mandela elected president.
- **2001** Serbia: Slobodan Milosevic arrested.
- **2001** United States: Hijacked planes crash into the World Trade Center in New York and the Pentagon in Washington, D.C., on the same day. Thousands of lives are lost.

Analyzing the Timeline

1. **(a)** Name one sign of social change before 1960. **(b)** Note the larger implications of the change. **[Deduce]**
   Answer: **(a)** Women get the vote (1918). **(b)** By obtaining the vote, women paved the way to assuming more power and independence, changing the structure of the family.
2. **(a)** Name two signs of social change after 1960. **(b)** Note the larger implications of each change. **[Deduce]**
   Answer: **(a)** The miniskirt becomes fashionable (1965); national utilities companies are privatized (1989). **(b)** The rise of the miniskirt suggests that women are exploring new roles; the privatization of national companies suggests that government is less involved in regulating the economy.
3. **(a)** What evidence can you find of Britain's declining power during this period? **(b)** What role might Britain have in world affairs today? **[Speculate]**
   Answer: **(a)** India and Pakistan gain independence (1947); part of Ireland becomes independent (1949); Hong Kong is given back to China (1997). **(b)** While no longer a "superpower," Britain may still be a key player in international affairs.
4. The twentieth century is the "Age of the Masses"—a time of mass political movements, mass entertainment, and so on. **(a)** Find three events that support this description of the period. **(b)** Explain how one idea of "the masses" leads to movements for social justice, while another leads to mass entertainment. **[Support]**
   Answer: **(a)** Women's struggle for the vote (1918); workers' revolution in Russia (1917); Gandhi's protest in India (1920); miniskirt fad (1965). **(b)** In movements for social justice, masses means "people without social privileges." For the purposes of mass entertainment, masses means "the average person," or even "the complacent side of all people."

continued

Continued from right column

▶Critical Viewing

1. Contrast the spirit of the war suggested by the recruiting poster (1914) with that suggested by the tank (1939). **[Compare and Contrast]**
   Answer: The poster suggests that war is a matter of community effort, of individuals "pitching in"; the tank suggests anonymous, wide-scale destruction.
2. **(a)** What does the presence of the man on the moon (1969) suggest about progress? **(b)** What might the fact that we cannot see his face suggest about the price of progress? **[Interpret]**
   Answer: **(a)** Human beings can transcend their physical environment through technology. **(b)** The price of progress may be dehumanization.

Connections to Literature

- To give students a sense of life in the trenches of the First World War, and of the effect of war's barbarity on refined sensibilities, have them read the War Poets, Brooke, Sassoon, and Owen, beginning on p. 1050.
- The sufferings of war were widespread during the first half of the twentieth century. W. H. Auden provides a thought-provoking meditation on the place of suffering in art and the world in "Musée des Beaux Arts," p. 1002.
- For a taste of early twentieth century "quiet despair," students should walk through the brown city smog with T. S. Eliot in the "Preludes," p. 982.
- Like a ghost returned from the grave, the Second World War repeated the traumas of the First—as if nothing had been learned in the meantime. Elizabeth Bowen mirrors the "haunting" of the twentieth century by war in her tale of a woman haunted by her past, "The Demon Lover," p. 1032.

▶Critical Viewing

Art in the Historical Context

(a) Possible response: The painting shows parts of the subject from different angles; it does not look like the subject, while more conventional pictures resemble their subjects.
(b) Possible response: Developments such as high-speed travel, aviation, and photography gave people new perspectives on space and time; the questioning of traditional values led to questions about whether any one perspective was more important than any other.

A Time of Rapid Change

The Modern and Postmodern Periods (1901–Present)

Historical Background

The twentieth century dawned bright with promise. Progress in science and technology was helping to make life easier and the world more comprehensible. Yet, while steady advances in communications and transportation drew the world closer together, the scourge of modern warfare soon wrenched it apart. In World War I (1914–1918) about 8.5 million soldiers died from wounds or diseases, and estimates of the total dead, civilian and military, as a result of World War II (1939–1945) vary from 35 to 60 million.

The Edwardian Age The rigid class distinctions and moral certainties of Victorian times lingered on into the Edwardian Age (1901–1910), named for Victoria's son and successor, Edward VII. However, rapid changes were beginning to undermine the customs and assumptions of the Victorian Age, changes that ranged from the widespread use of electricity to protests aimed at gaining women the vote. By the time George V was crowned in 1910, the nineteenth-century way of life was fading into memory.

Art in the Historical Context

Pablo Picasso and Modern Art

While Edwardian England was experiencing the Indian summer of the nineteenth century, men and women unknown at the time were reinventing the arts for a new era. One of the greatest of these "unknowns" was the Spanish painter Pablo Picasso.

In 1900, Picasso arrived in Paris, a center of artistic activity. There, about six years later, he devised a type of painting that critics named Cubism. It fragmented the canvas into what the art historian H. W. Janson describes as "chunks of solidified space," which seemed to resemble cubes.

▶**Critical Viewing** (a) In your own words, tell in detail how this painting differs from a more conventional picture of the subject it portrays. (b) Explain how Picasso's Cubism might reflect changes in the pace and texture of life that were occurring at the beginning of the twentieth century. **[Connect]**

Head of a Woman, Pablo Picasso, Prado, Madrid, Spain

ENRICHMENT: Science

The Atomic Age

In 1938, scientists split the atom. By firing a neutron (a subatomic particle identified by British physicist James Chadwick in 1932) at a uranium atom, they produced enormous amounts of energy. A worldwide vision of horror and hope, of world destruction or of miraculous plentiful power, was unleashed. The two atomic bombs dropped by the United States on the Japanese cities of Hiroshima and Nagasaki in 1945 used this process, known as nuclear fission. The later hydrogen bomb used a process called nuclear fusion.

Merely by existing, these deadly weapons have military value. Nations possessing nuclear weapons are thought unlikely to risk direct war with each other, for fear of the destruction that would result. Scientists postulate that a major nuclear war would kill half a billion people initially. Four billion more would die later, though, as the intense heat from the bombs set off fires, blocking the sun with smoke and causing a "nuclear winter."

World War I In 1914, long-standing tensions among the nations of Europe exploded, ignited by the assassination of Austria-Hungary's archduke Francis Ferdinand. When Germany invaded neutral Belgium, Britain joined with France to stop the aggression. The people of Great Britain went to war optimistically, expecting an easy victory. Soon, however, Britons and others recoiled in horror as the realities of poison gas, massive artillery barrages, and the terrible futility of trench warfare became evident.

In 1917, in the midst of war, revolution broke out in Russia, resulting in the overthrow of the czar and the establishment of the world's first communist state, the Soviet Union. By the time the armistice was signed on November 11, 1918, other empires and monarchies had also been swept away, including imperial Germany and the Austro-Hungarian Empire. An uneasy peace followed, its harsh terms spelled out in the Treaty of Versailles.

Between the Wars The disillusioned youth of postwar Europe were known as the "lost generation." Some young people masked their lack of purpose with the pursuit of pleasure—fast cars, wild jazz, and giddy fads. Not all was disenchantment or frivolity, of course. British women age thirty and over won the right to vote in 1918, and in 1928, the voting age for all women became twenty-one, the same as that for men.

The future, however, was being determined by political developments in Europe, exhausted and desperate after the Great War. Adolf Hitler began aggressively to expand Germany's borders. However, only when Germany invaded Poland on September 1, 1939, did Britain admit that Hitler could not be stopped without violent intervention.

World War II The second of the global wars was even more destructive than World War I. Hitler's attempt to eradicate the Jewish people brought death to about 6 million Jews. The German invasion of Russia in 1941 killed soldiers and civilians by the millions. Fighting raged from Europe to North Africa, from the mountains of Burma and China to the Hawaiian Islands. Massive bombing raids turned London, Dresden, and Tokyo into infernos.

The darkest days for Britain came in 1940, when France had fallen and Britain alone bore the brunt of German air attacks. Inspired by Prime Minister Winston Churchill, Britain fought on and was joined in 1941 by two powerful allies, the United States and the Soviet Union.

Finally, in August of 1945, American atomic bombs blasted into cinder and ash two Japanese cities, Hiroshima and Nagasaki, bringing the war to a brutal and abrupt end. The death toll by then had mounted to at least four times that of World War I.

The End of an Empire In 1922, the Irish Free State, consisting of 26 of Ireland's 32 counties, had won independence from Britain. After World War II, the British Empire suffered further dramatic losses. In Asia and Africa, nationalist leaders challenged colonial rule and gained freedom for their people. Unfortunately, ethnic, racial, and border conflicts led to bloodshed in many of the newly independent former colonies. On the

Gas Mask

▲ **Critical Viewing** Gas masks such as this one were a standard part of a soldier's equipment during World War I. What does the look of this mask suggest about the war? **[Draw Conclusions]**

Background

World War I in Art

British Painter Christopher R. W. Nevinson (1889–1946) studied art in France, where he met the Italian Futurists. Nevinson was greatly influenced by these artists and became one of the first British Futurist painters. The art produced by this group glorified modern machinery and the beauty of speed. During World War I, Nevinson served in France as an Official War Artist. Show the students Nevinson's *Troops Resting* in **Fine Art Transparencies, Volume I,** Art Transparency 20. Note that its strong diagonals and the reduction of men to geometric shapes are typical of the Futurist style. Then, ask the following questions:

1. What mood does Nevinson create through color?
   Answer: The ashen shade of the faces and the blue of the helmet suggest fatigue and cold.
2. **(a)** Is Nevinson using Futurist techniques for Futurist reasons? **(b)** Why does it make sense that Futurism ended after World War I?
   Answer: **(a)** No; rather than celebrating technology, he shows human suffering. **(b)** It was hard to remain enthusiastic about technology after the war had demonstrated its destructive power.

▶Critical Viewing

Answer: The mask suggests that the war was bitterly fought using deadly ways of slaughtering the unprotected in masses.

CUSTOMIZE INSTRUCTION FOR UNIVERSAL ACCESS

For Less Proficient Readers	For English Learners	For Advanced Readers
Explain to students that during this period, huge wars swept the planet. Instruct them to preview the subheads and the pictures in the Historical Background before reading the selection.	For each subhead and picture in the Historical Background, have the students write a caption as to whether it concerns war or peacetime, or whether they cannot be sure. Then, have them read the sections, filling in their notes with the name of the war or of an important peacetime event that each section concerns.	Challenge students to trace the themes of memory and recognition through the Historical Background. What events involve a "forgetting" of the past? What events should be remembered as a warning to the future? What trends attempt to create the utterly new?

Background

Literature and Popular Culture

"Memory," from *Cats*, Andrew Lloyd Webber

The musical *Cats* had its inspiration in T. S. Eliot's *Old Possum's Book of Practical Cats.* Eliot's widow, Valerie Eliot, encouraged Andrew Lloyd Webber to develop these poems into a full-scale musical with director Trevor Nunn. *Cats* opened on Broadway in 1982 and enjoyed huge success.

The plot is rather simple: A number of cats that live in a garbage dump attend the "Jellicle Ball." On stage, the personalities and dreams of the cats take on near mythic proportions. The song "Memory" is sung by Grizabella, the Glamour Cat, who is given a second chance at life.

Play students "Memory" on the **Listening to Music Audiocassettes.** Then, ask the following questions:

1. How does the fact that the character singing is a cat affect your experience of the song?
   Possible responses: The song is less "sentimental" than if it were spoken by a person.
2. Why do you think contemporary adult audiences find the characters in *Cats* so compelling?
   Possible responses: Animal characters "get by" people's sophistication and so let people experience strong emotion.

▶Critical Viewing

Answer: The woman's clothing shows off her arms from wrist to shoulder, and her legs above the knee. The dance looks "wild" or "disorderly," suggesting unregulated passion—and also risking further exposure of her limbs.

Continent, British power declined sharply, and an "iron curtain" divided Eastern and Western Europe. The United States and the Soviet Union now dominated the world.

However, by the 1960s, Britons had apparently put many of their troubles behind them. From rock music to "mod" clothing, Britain influenced fashions around the world. However, basic industries—textiles, steelmaking, shipbuilding—that had been vital to Britain were no longer competing successfully. Factories were forced to close their gates.

British society was also changing rapidly in a number of ways. In the 1950s and 1960s, London's black population increased significantly as immigrants from Britain's former colonies arrived in the city. Many black Londoners settled in Brixton, an area south of the Thames River. The discrimination that they encountered triggered the Brixton riots of April 1981. Today, London's multiracial population includes Caribbean islanders, Indians, Bangladeshis, Pakistanis, and Africans.

Flapper Dancing the Charleston

▲ **Critical Viewing** This couple is dancing the Charleston, a popular dance in the 1920s. Why might this woman's clothing and movements have shocked ladies of her mother's generation? **[Speculate]**

Contemporary Britain Margaret Thatcher, a member of the Conservative Party and the first female prime minister, came to power in 1979 and took a fairly hands-off approach to the economy. Prosperity resulted for some, but many Britons did not benefit from "Thatcherism." She resigned her office in 1990, to be replaced by her own handpicked Conservative party successor, John Major. In 1997, however, Major was defeated by Tony Blair, the Labor candidate.

Many problems and challenges remain as Britain adjusts to a rapidly changing world. Its participation in the European Community—a trading bloc of several hundred million people—should be a benefit, but it is still in the early stages. In Northern Ireland, the Good Friday Agreement, approved in May 1998, provides for the participation of all political parties in local government. As a result, the prospects for peace have improved, but there is still the threat of sectarian violence. Wales and Scotland voted in 1997 to set up their own parliaments, and the entire nation ponders the monarchy's role in the twenty-first century.

Tradition has always been strong in Great Britain. As in previous times of trial, Britons can turn to the past as a source of pride and comfort while moving forward into the swirl and bustle of contemporary life.

ENRICHMENT: Social Studies

The Cold War

During World War II, the Soviet Union and the nations of the West, including Britain, had cooperated to defeat Nazi Germany. By 1945, however, the wartime alliance was crumbling. Conflicting ideologies and mutual distrust soon led to the conflict known as the Cold War. (Part of this distrust was created in 1918 when, in response to the Russian Revolution, the United States and Britain sent troops into Russia.) The Cold War was a state of tension and hostility among nations without armed conflict between the major rivals.

By 1946, the Cold War was underway. By that time, Josef Stalin (1879–1953), the Soviet leader, had succeeded in installing pro-Soviet communist governments throughout Eastern Europe, creating a buffer zone against Germany. Soon, the United States and its allies were engaged in an arms race with the Soviet Union, each side stockpiling greater quantities of increasingly destructive weapons.

Literature of the Period

Modernism and Postmodernism Modernism, with its commitment to creating new forms, was perhaps the most important artistic movement of the twentieth century. Many Modernists used images as symbols, leading to indirect, evocative work. They often presented experiences in fragments, rather than as a coherent whole.

The Postmodernist period in English literature refers to the time from 1965 to the present. It has been characterized by what critics William Harmon and C. Hugh Holman call "continuance and completion." However, dramatists like Harold Pinter and Tom Stoppard have experimented significantly with dialogue, sequencing, and the relationships between literature and reality. Pinter's repetitious, enigmatic dialogue, for example, creates a strangely mixed aura of absurdity and menace. In his play *Betrayal,* he reverses the usual plot sequence by tracing a relationship from its end to its beginning.

Modernism and Poetry Modernism in poetry developed with the Imagist movement, founded about 1912 by Americans Ezra Pound and Hilda Doolittle (H.D.) in collaboration with Britons Richard Aldington and F. S. Flint. Imagists stressed the use of precise visual images and unadorned, concise language.

Under the influence of Ezra Pound, William Butler Yeats (1865–1939) adopted the clearer language advocated by the Imagists. Yeats, whose work spans several literary eras, was perhaps the greatest twentieth-century poet. During the heyday of Modernism, he achieved the directness and drama that inform his powerful, visionary works. However, the preeminent Modernist poet was T. S. Eliot (1888–1965), an American who went to live in Britain. Eliot's poem *The Waste Land* (1922) not only reflects the despair of the period after World War I, but also makes daring use of a collage of "voices" to link the present with the past. This experimental technique was, in a way, similar to the Cubist collages that Picasso and others assembled and painted after 1910.

Georgian Poets and War Poets The Georgian poets—who included Robert Graves (1895–1985), Edmund Blunden (1896–1974), and Walter de la Mare (1873–1956)—named themselves for George V, the reigning British monarch at the time the group was formed (1911). The Georgians rebelled against what

▼ **Critical Viewing** During "the Blitz," which lasted from September, 1940, to May, 1941, German planes dropped bombs on London almost every night. Name two reasons why people would have taken shelter in subways during air raids. **[Infer]**

Scenes from the Blitz: Londoners Sheltering in Underground Station

▶ **Critical Viewing**

Possible responses: Subways were underground and so protected from the worst effects of bombing; people may have sought comfort by sheltering with others in a public place.

Historical Background

Comprehension Check

1. Name two worldwide, traumatic events affecting Britain in this period.
   Answer: Britain fought in both World Wars.
2. What effect did World War I have on British attitudes?
   Answer: People were disillusioned and eager for frivolity.
3. What new power emerged at the end of World War I?
   Answer: The Soviet Union emerged in 1917.
4. In what distinctive way did Britain suffer during World War II?
   Answer: Britain faced German air power alone until new allies joined the war.
5. After World War II, the British created a modern welfare state. What happened to this system in the 1980s?
   Answer: Britain's welfare state was partially dismantled by Margaret Thatcher.

Critical Thinking

1. **(a)** How did the British attitude change through World War I? **(b)** How might this shift have affected the literature of the time? **[Analyze]**
   Answer: **(a)** The British began the war confidently; grim reality disillusioned them. **(b)** Literature shifted from flag-waving to attempts to show the reality of war.
2. How might Britain's experience in World War II explain the sudden rise to power of the Labour Party after the war? **[Connect]**
   Answer: The people turned to leaders who offered domestic reform to ensure that peace would be comfortable for all.
3. What links Britain's industrial failure to its artistic success in the 1960s? **[Speculate]**
   Answer: People turned to the arts when kept from using their energy in industry.

POINT/COUNTERPOINT

Remind students that World War I traumatized and inspired a generation of aspiring poets. Then, ask the following questions.

1. Why are there both adamant supporters of the War Poets and those that find these poets without influence?
   Answer: The two critics disagree on the forward direction of poetry after the war. Silkin feels the War Poets added to the revolution while Hope feels they filled a place during the war but did nothing to make changes.
2. Is it possible that both Hope and Silkin are correct in their statements?
   Answer: Answers should include the idea that it is possible that the War Poets were not the best at their craft but that they do add a valuable piece to the historical and accurate representations of war.
3. Is there a plateau a poet must reach to be considered significant? How would the critics respond?
   Possible responses: Silkin might say that all poets are part of the forward movement of poetry, especially if they bring insight and an unseen vision into the craft. Hope may say that experiences alone may not be enough to develop a poet. Time and study of literature are what make a successful poet.

Point /Counterpoint

World War I Poets: "Not the Best" or a Valuable Resource?

Two critics debate whether the poets who experienced and wrote about the horrors of World War I were simply "not the best . . . of their time" or continue to be a valuable resource for literature.

"Not the Best" ". . . the poets involved in the First World War were not the best, perhaps, of their time, though it is always possible that, had they survived, Owen and even Sorley might have been. But as it is, the map read differently. What Pound and Eliot and Yeats had begun before the war they continued after it: a revolution in English poetry that leaves both unreformed and reformed Georgians in the loop of a by-pass. Owen and Jones and Graves are of sufficient stature to endure, but it could hardly be claimed that they influenced many successors. . . . In general they have had admirers rather than imitators. . . . In a not altogether rhetorical sense, all poetry written since 1918 is war poetry; and Yeats and Eliot and Auden have contributed more to it than Rosenberg or Blunden, or even than Owen and David Jones."

—Francis Hope, "Tommy's Tunes," ***The Review*, No. 15 (April 1965)**

A Valuable Resource "It is true that Eliot and Pound (and in a different way, Yeats) leave the war poets 'in the loop of a by-pass,' if the Eliot-Pound direction is regarded as the only desirable way forward for English poetry; but only someone totally committed to such a direction would see the poets as trapped in a disused by-pass. Francis Hope would seem to believe that not only did the war poets have few 'followers' but that, apart from the three he mentions, they are not of 'sufficient stature' (the cliché suggests the dead weight of the evaluating attitude) 'to endure.' Yet easy and obvious connections can be made between Rosenberg and Keith Douglas, between Edward Thomas and Alun Lewis. . . . Francis Hope's mild fanaticism would . . . disregard [the war poets] . . . at a time when we are in need of as much vitality . . . as we can find."

—John Silkin, *Out of Battle: The Poetry of the Great War*

they regarded as the self-consciously knowing air of Victorian poetry. They published several anthologies in the years before Eliot's *Waste Land* appeared, but as a result of Eliot's Modernist triumph, the work of these poets fell into neglect. Some critics have argued, however, that such notable war poets as Wilfred Owen (1893–1918) and Edward Thomas (1878–1917) were Georgians.

In addition to Owen and Thomas, poets who wrote about and died in World War I include Rupert Brooke (1887–1915), Isaac Rosenberg (1890–1918), and Charles Hamilton Sorley (1895–1915). Poets who survived the conflict are Robert Graves (1895–1985), David Jones (1895–1974), and Siegfried Sassoon (1886–1967).

ENRICHMENT: Social Studies

The Welfare State

World War II left Britain physically battered and economically drained. In 1945, voters put the Labour party in power. The war had helped change old attitudes toward the working class. A Labour official noted that if a working-class boy "can save us in a Spitfire [a warplane], the same brain can be turned to produce a new world."

In that new world, government nationalized major industries and expanded social welfare benefits such as unemployment insurance and old-age pensions. The government built housing for the poor and opened new state-funded universities. A national health service extended free, low-cost medical care to all citizens. Other programs gave aid to the poor and created an economic cushion to help people through hard times. To pay for all these benefits, taxes rose a great deal.

Auden and Others In the 1930s and 1940s, such poets as W. H. Auden (1907–1973), Louis MacNeice (1907–1963), and Stephen Spender (1909–1995) showed an increasing concern with political and social issues, though they did not abandon subtle symbolism and imagery. By contrast, Romanticism flared into wild brilliance in the poetry of Dylan Thomas (1914–1953).

During the 1950s and 1960s, British poets of "the Movement"—such as Philip Larkin (1922–1985), Donald Davie (1922–1995), and Thom Gunn (b. 1929)—rebelled against the type of Romanticism that Thomas expressed. They tried to capture everyday experiences in colloquial, yet tightly wrought, language.

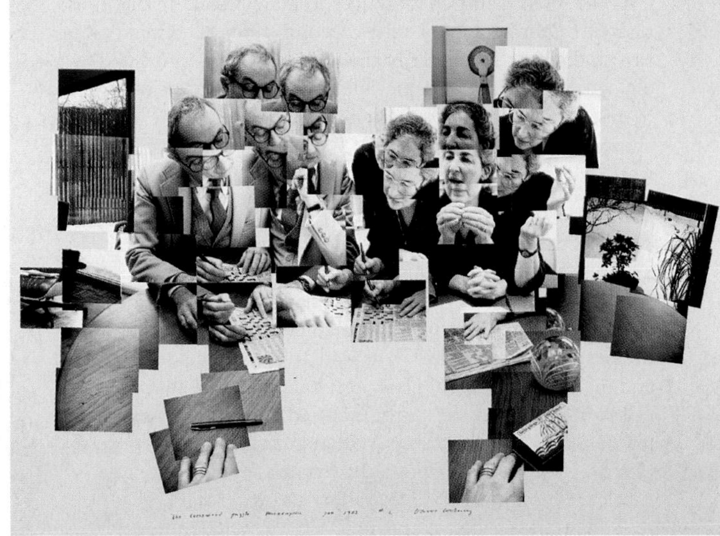

The Crossword Puzzle David Hockney

▲ **Critical Viewing** British-born David Hockney's paintings and art works are groundbreaking and influential. (a) How does Hockney's use of photographs in this piece "break up" images? (b) What does this "breaking up" suggest about the relation between still images and time? (c) Why did he match this technique with a crossword puzzle as his subject? **[Speculate]**

Although she was born at about the same time as poets of the Auden generation and published her *Selected Poems* in 1962, Stevie Smith does not fit into any group. Called an "acrobat of simplicity" by Muriel Rukeyser, Smith gave her shrewdly childlike poems the feel of popular songs and nursery rhymes.

Noteworthy British poets of recent years, such as Ted Hughes (1930–1998), Peter Redgrove (b. 1932), and the Irish-born Seamus Heaney (b. 1939) display a visionary intensity. Penelope Shuttle (b. 1947) has written poetry that spins "fairytalelike" fantasies or looks attentively at the smallest events in nature. Two remarkable poets from former British colonies in the West Indies are James Berry (b. 1925), a Jamaican, and Nobel Prize-winner Derek Walcott (b. 1930), from the island of St. Lucia.

Twentieth-Century Drama George Bernard Shaw (1856–1950) dominated late Victorian, Edwardian, and early modern drama. His witty plays manage to evoke laughter while examining social issues. Influenced by the Irish Literary Revival, John Millington Synge (1871–1909) vividly captures Irish rural life in plays like *The Playboy of the Western World* (1907). In the depression years of the 1930s, Noel Coward (1899–1973) won attention with a series of smartly sophisticated dramas and musicals.

Angry Young Men and Absurdists In the 1950s and 1960s, a group of dramatists known as Britain's "angry young men," which included John

▶Critical Viewing

Interpret

Answer: **(a)** *Each photograph shows a different part of the same scene, or the same part from a slightly different angle or at a slightly different time. They overlap, but not seamlessly: Photographs of the man's head and of the woman's head are separated from each other, suggesting that the two are sitting side by side, but we see both of them in a few poses, and there are roughly two displaced images of each pose or aspect.* **(b)** *The "breaking up" insists that still images cannot capture time, or it attempts to introduce the passage of time into the still image.* **(c)** *The relation of subject and technique is a pun: each photograph is like a filled-in square in a crossword puzzle; read the photos in relation to each other and, like the letters in a crossword, they make sense in two directions (time and space).*

▶Critical Viewing

Possible response: London is often symbolized by monuments like Buckingham Palace, Big Ben, or Westminster Abbey, monuments that date to earlier periods and that reflect traditional values and use an architecture based on stone. By contrast, this skyscraper represents the break with traditional values and the rise of corporations. It is built of steel and glass, not stone, and looks similar to skyscrapers that can be found throughout the world.

Osborne, used realistic techniques in plays attacking the injustices of Britain's class system. A second strain of contemporary British drama, the theater of the absurd, uses disconnected dialogue and action to depict life itself as a pointless series of misfortunes. Dublin-born Samuel Beckett (1906–1989), author of *Waiting for Godot* (1952), pioneered this type of work, which has also influenced Harold Pinter (b. 1930) and Tom Stoppard (b. 1937).

Canada Tower, London,Corbis

▲ **Critical Viewing** This glass-and-steel office building has left its mark on contemporary London. Compare and contrast it with more traditional images of the city. **[Compare and Contrast]**

Twentieth-Century Fiction The Edwardian Age produced a number of brilliant writers of realist and naturalist fiction. Joseph Conrad, one of the pioneers of psychological realism, examines internal conflicts and themes of courage and loyalty in tales like *Lord Jim* (1900), as well as issues of colonialism and injustice in *Heart of Darkness* (1902). D. H. Lawrence (1885–1930) unleashes a savage hatred of conventional British manners and morals in his novels, among them *Sons and Lovers* (1913). E. M. Forster opposes the hypocrisies of society in a gentler fashion in such novels as *A Passage to India* (1924).

Perhaps the greatest pioneer of Modernist fiction was the Irish writer James Joyce (1882–1941). Joyce revolutionized the form and structure of both the short story and the novel. His brilliant novel *Ulysses* (1922) contains a great variety of innovative techniques, including stream of consciousness—the technique of immersing readers in the associational, disjointed flow of one or more characters' thoughts—and the use of myth to structure everyday occurrences. The novelist Virginia Woolf (1882–1941) also uses stream of consciousness, in novels like *To the Lighthouse* (1927).

Political and social issues gained attention among novelists like Aldous Huxley (1894–1963) and George Orwell (1903–1950) in the 1930s and 1940s. Huxley's *Brave New World* (1932) and Orwell's *1984* (1949) paint frightening pictures of the future based on the present. Two of Britain's most popular novelists are Graham Greene (1904–1991), author of *The Power and the Glory* (1940), and P. G. Wodehouse (1881–1975), a brilliant humorist. More recent British novelists include William Golding (1911–1993), who won the Nobel Prize for Literature in 1983; Anthony Burgess (1917–1993); Kingsley Amis (1922–1995); John Fowles (b. 1926); and Alan Sillitoe (b. 1928).

In literature, as in other aspects of British life, women have been highly visible and productive in recent decades. Irish-born Iris Murdoch (1919–1999) is known for her intricate novels exploring human relationships, among them *The Message to the Planet* (1989). Doris Lessing (b. 1919) grew up in Rhodesia (now Zimbabwe) and has gained fame for a series of novels set in Africa, including *The Four-Gated City* (1969). Nobel Prize-winner Nadine Gordimer (b. 1923) writes novels and short stories that examine the moral and political dilemmas of racially divided South Africa, where she lives.

From Former Colonies In more recent years, a number of talented writers from what used to be the far-flung British Empire have enriched English literature. Among these are Frank Sargeson (1903–1982) of New Zealand; Patrick White (1912–1990), the Nobel Prize-winner from Australia; Wilson Harris (b. 1921) of Guyana; Chinua Achebe (b. 1930) and Nobel Prize-winner Wole Soyinka (b. 1934), both of Nigeria. V. S. Naipaul (b. 1932), a writer from the island of Trinidad, has achieved success with both fiction and nonfiction. The award-winning novel *In a Free State* (1971) is one of his finest works.

These ex-colonial writers are busy making classics for a new age. Borrowing a famous line from Shakespeare's *The Tempest*, we can say that they are transforming English literature "into something rich and strange."

A Living Tradition

Seamus Heaney Summons Joyce's Ghost

To serve the future, writers draw from the past, studying the works of their predecessors. However, writers can also summon the ghosts of their dead colleagues—not with a séance, but with words. That is exactly what contemporary Irish poet Seamus Heaney does when he wants advice from his great Modernist forbear James Joyce. At the end of "Station Island," a long poem that is "a sequence of dream encounters with familiar ghosts," Heaney gets some emphatic wisdom about writing from Joyce's apparition.

from "Station Island," XII

His voice eddying with the vowels of all rivers
came back to me, though he did not speak yet,
a voice like a prosecutor's or a singer's,

cunning, narcotic, mimic, definite
as a steel nib's° downstroke, quick and clean, °pen point's
and suddenly he hit a litter basket

with his stick, saying, "Your obligation
is not discharged by any common rite.° °ritual
What you must do must be done on your own

so get back in harness. The main thing is to write
for the joy of it. . . .

let others wear the sackcloth and the ashes.° °symbols of repentance
Let go, let fly, forget.
You've listened long enough. Now strike your note."

Literature of the Period

Comprehension Check

1. Name two features characterizing Modernist literature.
   Answer: Modernists use symbolic images; they present experience in fragmentary form; and they use colloquial language.
2. Name three focuses of British poetry after Modernism, and name a poet associated with each.
   Answer: Political and social issues (W. H. Auden); a rekindled Romanticism (Dylan Thomas); everyday experience (Philip Larkin).
3. What part of Great Britain was associated with a renewal of the drama?
   Answer: Ireland was central in the renewal of the drama.
4. **(a)** What kind of plays did the Angry Young Men write? **(b)** What kind of plays did the Absurdists write?
   Answer: **(a)** They wrote realistic attacks on social injustice. **(b)** They wrote plays depicting life's pointlessness, filled with disconnected dialogue and action.
5. How did the novel evolve in this time?
   Answer: Novelists such as Joyce and Woolf began to use innovative techniques such as stream-of-consciousness.

Critical Thinking

1. The Modernists show reality in fragments of images and speech. Name two modern realities that have a fragmentary quality. **[Make a Connection]**
   Possible answers: Television, with its commercial interruptions and leaps from one scene to another, fragments reality; the division between public life, at work or in school, and private life at home fragments experience.
2. Modern writers have experimented with the basics of storytelling, often making their work difficult for audiences. **(a)** Why might these artists reject ordinary storytelling? **(b)** Explain whether their experimentation is or is not justified. **[Make a Judgment]**
   Possible answers: **(a)** Old forms of storytelling may seem dishonest about the complexity or

continued

continued from right column

meaninglessness of modern experience. **(b)** They are justified in showing the truth as they see it; they are not justified in shutting out an audience.

3. Important writers have emerged from Britain's former colonies. What special issues might they face in their work? **[Hypothesize]**
   Answers: The English tradition is not entirely "theirs"—they may have spoken another language at home or have suffered from the same colonization that brought that tradition to them.

Critical Thinking

1. **(a)** Name a television program produced in Britain that is shown on American television. **(b)** Is the dialogue difficult to follow? Explain where difficulties arise. **[Analyze]**
   Answer: **(a)** Students may name *Masterpiece Theater, The Benny Hill Show*, or *The Young Ones*. **(b)** Students may note that accent and cultural references present as much of a problem for understanding as differing word usage, but that the universal humor or drama of these shows makes understanding easy.
2. Are there splits in the language of the United States that are similar to the split between British and American English? Explain. **[Speculate]**
   Answer: There are distinctive differences in usage between the American Southeast, the Northeast, and Midwest (e.g., *stoop* versus *porch*).
3. **(a)** How is the split between British and American English changing? **(b)** Is this development good or bad? Explain. **[Make a Judgment]**
   Answer: **(a)** Similarity between the two is increasing. **(b)** Possible response: Greater similarity suggests the prospect of a boring, homogenized world.

▶Critical Viewing

1. Find a British word in the chart for which you would easily guess the American equivalent.
   Answer: *Hair grip* for *bobby pin*.
2. Do the differing usages charted have to do with a few specialized areas of life? Explain.
   Answer: No, they range from the calendar to food.

Activities

1. Other examples include *bonnet* (British for *hood*), *boot* (for *trunk*), *tracks* (for *treads*), *gearbox* (for *transmission*), *windscreen* (for *windshield*), *silencer* (for *muffler*), *wing* (for *fender*).
2. *Biscuit* means *cookie*; *braces, suspenders*; *chemist, drugstore*; *chips, French fries*; *crisp, potato chip*; *lift, elevator*; *plaster, bandaid*; *pudding, sausage*; *spectacles, eyeglasses*; *tin, can*; *torch, flashlight*.

THE CHANGING ENGLISH LANGUAGE

Britspeak, A to ZED

BY RICHARD LEDERER

At the end of World War II, Winston Churchill tells us, the Allied leaders nearly came to blows over a single word during their negotiations when some diplomats suggested that it was time to "table" an important motion. For the British, table meant that the motion should be put on the table for discussion. For the Americans it meant just the opposite—that it should be put on the shelf and dismissed from discussion.

This confusion serves to illustrate the truth of George Bernard Shaw's pronouncement that "England and America are two countries divided by a common language." Or, as Oscar Wilde put it, "We have really everything in common with America nowadays, except, of course, language." Wilde made this comment when he heard that audiences in New York weren't queuing up to see his plays. Instead, they were waiting in line.

British	American
gangway	aisle
hair grip	bobby pin
ironmonger	hardware store
serviette	napkin
fortnight	two weeks
zed	the letter Z [pronounced-zē]
prawn	shrimp

SEPARATED BY THE SAME LANGUAGE

Many of the most beguiling misunderstandings can arise where identical words have different meanings in the two cultures and lingoes. When an American exclaims, "I'm mad about my flat," he is upset about his tire. When a Brit exclaims, "I'm mad about my flat," she is not bemoaning the "puncture" of her "tyre"; she is delighted with her apartment. When a Brit points out that you have "a ladder in your hose," the situation is not as bizarre as you might at first think. Quite simply, you have a run in your stocking.

Our buses are their coaches. When a hotel in the British Isles posts a large sign proclaiming, "No football coaches allowed," the message is not directed at the Don Shulas and Joe Paternos of the world. *No football coaches allowed* means "No soccer buses permitted."

With the increasing influence of film, radio, television, and international travel, the two main streams of the English language are rapidly converging like the streets of a circus (British for "traffic circle"). Nonetheless, there are scores of words, phrases, and spellings about which Brits and Yanks still do not agree.

ACTIVITIES

1. If you choose to rent an automobile in the UK, with it will come a whole new vocabulary. Be sure to fill it with petrol, not gas. Investigate other differences between the words that Brits and Americans have for vehicles and roadways.
2. Define these words in American English first, then British English: biscuit, braces, chemist, chips, crisp, lift, plaster, pudding, spectacles, tin, torch.

ENRICHMENT: Social Studies

Other Englishes

The divisions in English do not stop with the distance between Britain and the United States. Various regions of Britain still have their own distinctive accents, vocabulary, and idiom, as do regions of the United States. Additionally, English, like other languages, has developed numerous vernaculars and slangs—words and expressions that are used by people practicing the same profession or leading similar lifestyles. These pockets for new vocabulary can shift and fade over time. Some words may become fashionable with a group wider than the one that introduced them. Some may even become part of the larger, "official" English language.

Waking From the Dream

The Children Enter the Palace of Luxury Frederick Cayley Robinson. The Fine Art Society, London

ZE INSTRUCTION FOR UNIVERSAL ACCESS

ning the selections in this part, keep in mind these factors:

n, Eliot, MacNeice, Spender

rk is highly allusive, marked by com- expression and abstract ideas. For the ficult poems, readers should work as a roposing and testing interpretations.

Lover"

e less proficient readers to the setting ation; they can enjoy the story as a simple ghost tale.

"Shooting an Elephant"

- Orwell's direct style and dramatic situation will keep readers' interest.

Amichai, Akhmatova, Dao

- Though the language is clear and simple, less proficient readers should paraphrase to grasp the theme.

Selection Planning Guide

The selections in this section present the great writers of the twentieth century confronting disillusionment —and the renewal of perception to which disillusionment sometimes leads. Yeats charts the dreams of love, age, and art, as well as the nightmare of history. Disenchantment with modern life finds its own voice in T. S. Eliot's poems. While Auden, MacNeice, and Spender question the task of poetry, Orwell tells of adventure and political disillusionment. In "The Demon Lover," the return of a ghostly past shatters a woman's illusion of normal life.

Background

Art

The Children Enter the Palace of Luxury, Frederick Cayley Robinson

This painting shows two children outside a classical archway beneath the night sky, gazing intently on what lies within.

British painter, mural decorator, and book illustrator Frederick Cayley Robinson studied art at the Royal Academy and at Paris's Academie Julian. *The Children Enter the Palace of Luxury* probably appeared as an illustration in Maurice Maeterlinck's play *The Bluebird,* which expressed his belief in a reality deeper than ordinary, waking life.

Use these questions for discussion:

1. In what way does the painting resemble a scene from a dream? **[Analyze]**
   Answer: There are a few specific details characterizing the place; those presented (the statue, the stars) are striking.
2. **(a)** What is the difference between a person dreaming and a person remembering a dream? **(b)** In what way is becoming an adult like awakening from a dream? **[Interpret]**
   Answer: **(a)** The person remembering distinguishes dreams and reality, the dreamer does not. **(b)** An adult distinguishes a time when he or she saw things differently (childhood).

Poetry of William Butler Yeats

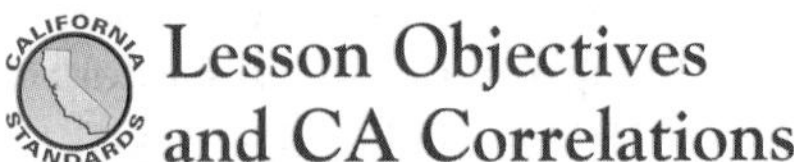

Lesson Objectives and CA Correlations

1. **To analyze and respond to literary elements**
   - Literary Analysis: Symbolism **R 3.3**
   - Comparing Literary Works **R 3.4**
2. **To read, comprehend, analyze, and critique a poem**
   - Reading Strategy: Applying Literary Background **R 3.2, 3.7**
   - Reading Check Questions
   - Review and Assess Questions
3. **To develop word analysis skills, fluency, and systematic vocabulary**
   - Vocabulary Development Lesson: Latin Root *-ques-* **R 1.1, 1.2**
4. **To understand and apply written and oral language conventions**
   - Spelling Strategy **LC 1.2**
   - Grammar and Style Lesson: Noun Clauses **LC 1.1**
5. **To understand and apply appropriate writing and research strategies**
   - Writing Lesson: Response to Criticism
   - Extension Activity: Visual Display **W 1.1, 1.9, 2.2**
   - Assessment Practice (ATE) **W 1.4, 1.6**
6. **To understand and apply listening and speaking strategies**
   - Extension Activity: Oral Interpretation **LS 2.5**

STEP-BY-STEP TEACHING GUIDE	PACING GUIDE
PRETEACH	
Motivate Students and Provide Background	
Use the Motivation activity (ATE p. 964)	5 min.
Read and discuss author and background features (SE/ATE pp. 964, 971) A	5 min.
Introduce the Concepts	
Introduce the Literary Analysis and Reading Strategy (SE/ATE p. 965) A	15 min.
Pronounce the vocabulary words and read their definitions (SE p. 965)	5 min.
TEACH	
Monitor Comprehension	
Informally monitor comprehension by circulating while students read independently or in groups A	10 min.
Monitor students' comprehension with the Reading Check notes (SE/ATE pp. 969, 973)	as students read
Develop vocabulary with Vocabulary notes (SE pp. 969, 970, 971, 973, 974; ATE p. 970)	as students read
Develop Understanding	
Develop students' understanding of symbolism with the Literary Analysis annotation (ATE pp. 969, 971) A	5 min.
Develop students' ability to apply literary background with the Reading Strategy annotations (ATE p. 967)	5 min.
ASSESS	
Assess Mastery	
Assess students' mastery of the Reading Strategy and Literary Analysis by having them answer the Review and Assess questions (SE/ATE p. 975)	20 min.
Use one or more of the print and media Assessment Resources (ATE p. 977) A	up to 45 min.
EXTEND	
Apply Understanding	
Have students complete the Vocabulary Development Lesson and the Grammar and Style Lesson (SE p. 976) A	20 min.
Apply students' understanding of knowledge level of readers using the Writing Lesson (SE/ATE p. 977) A	45 min.
Apply students' understanding using one or more of the Extension Activities (SE p. 977)	20–90 min.

ACCELERATED INSTRUCTION: Use the strategies and activities identified with an A.

UNIVERSAL ACCESS
- ● = Below-Level Students
- ▲ = On-Level Students
- ■ = Above-Level Students

Time and Resource Manager

Reading Level: Easy, Easy, Easy, Average, Challenging
Average Number of Instructional Days: 4

RESOURCES		
PRINT	**TRANSPARENCIES**	**TECHNOLOGY**
• **Beyond Literature,** Humanities Connection: Philosophy, p. 45 ▲ ■		• **Interest Grabber Video,** Tape 6 ● ▲ ■
• **Selection Support Workbook:** ● ▲ ■ Literary Analysis, p. 214 Reading Strategy, p. 213 Build Vocabulary, p. 211	• **Literary Analysis and Reading Transparencies,** pp. 89 and 90 ● ▲ ■	
• **Authors In Depth,** The British Tradition, p. 206 ■		• **Listening to Literature** ● ▲ ■ Audiocassettes, Side 22 Audio CDs, CD 12
• **Literatura en español** ● ▲ • **Literary Analysis for Enrichment** ■		
• **Formal Assessment:** Selection Test, pp. 225–227 ● ▲ ■ • **Open Book Test,** pp. 132–134 ● ▲ ■ • PRENTICE HALL ASSESSMENT SYSTEM ● ▲ ■	• PRENTICE HALL ASSESSMENT SYSTEM ● ▲ ■ Skills Practice Answers and Explanations on Transparencies ● ▲ ■	• **Test Bank Software** ● ▲ ■ • **Got It! Assessment Videotapes,** Tape 5 ● ▲
• **Selection Support Workbook:** ● ▲ ■ Grammar and Style, p. 212 • **Writing and Grammar,** Diamond Level ● ▲ ■ • **Extension Activities,** p. 45 ● ▲ ■	• **Daily Language Practice Transparencies** ● ▲	• **Writing and Grammar iText CD-ROM** ● ▲ ■ *Take It to the Net* www.phschool.com

BLOCK SCHEDULING: Use one 90-minute class period to preteach the selections and have students read them. Use a second 90-minute class period to assess students' mastery of skills and have them complete one of the Extension Activities.

PRETEACH

Step-by-Step Teaching Guide for pp. 964–965

Motivation

Write this description on the chalkboard and have students begin to improvise a horror movie based on it: "Somewhere in the sands of the desert is a shape with the body of a lion and the head of a man. The creature, its gaze blank and pitiless, is just beginning to move." After students have launched into their "movies," tell them that the image comes from Yeats's poem "The Second Coming" and invite them to compare their scenarios with his.

Interest Grabber Video

As an alternative, play "The Second Coming" on Tape 6 to engage student interest.

❶ Background

More About the Author

Yeats had a lifelong involvement with the occult. He joined a branch of the Hermetic Order of the Golden Dawn, which hoped to prove that occult phenomena were possible. The Golden Dawn incorporated traditional magic and astronomy. Yeats adopted as his personal motto within the club "Demon est Deus Inversus" (the Devil is God inverted) and rose through the ranks to become a major officer. Maud Gonne was also a member, adopting the motto, "Per Ignum, Ad Astra" (Through the Fire, to the Light). Elements of Yeats's fascination with magic and the supernatural are evident in his poems.

Prepare to Read

❶ Poetry of William Butler Yeats

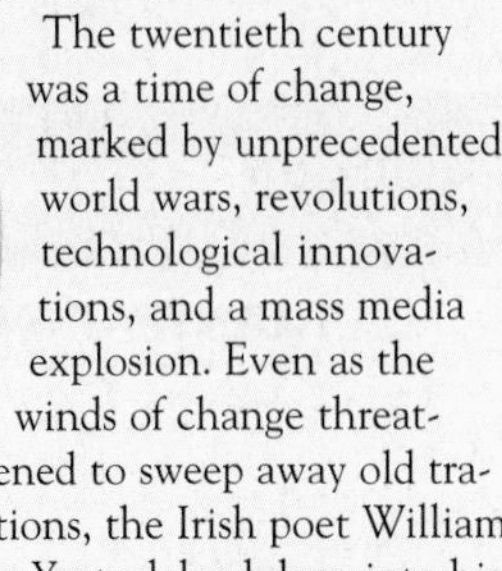

William Butler Yeats (1865–1939)

The twentieth century was a time of change, marked by unprecedented world wars, revolutions, technological innovations, and a mass media explosion. Even as the winds of change threatened to sweep away old traditions, the Irish poet William Butler Yeats delved deep into his nation's mythological past for insight. Winner of the Nobel Prize for Literature in 1923, Yeats is generally regarded as one of the finest poets of the century. His return to the past helped earn him an abiding place in the future.

Born in Dublin, Ireland, Yeats was educated there and in London. His heart lay to the west, though, in County Sligo, where he spent childhood vacations with his grandparents. In the shadow of Sligo's barren mountains, the young Yeats was immersed in the mythology and legends of Ireland. This experience led to a lifelong enthusiasm for the roots of Irish culture.

Philosophical Influences After three years of studying painting in Dublin, Yeats moved to London to pursue a literary career. He became a friend of the poet Arthur Symons, who awakened his interest in the symbolic, visionary poetry of William Blake and the delicate, musical verse of the French Symbolists. Yeats's early poems show Symbolist influences as well as an affinity with the Pre-Raphaelites, a group of nineteenth-century British painters and writers who turned to medieval art as they strove for simplicity and beauty. Symbolism, Pre-Raphaelite elements, and Irish myths combined in Yeats's first important collection of verse, *The Wanderings of Oisin*, published in 1889.

Political and Personal Influences In the 1890s, Yeats led the Irish Literary Revival, helping to establish the Irish Literary Society based in London and the Irish National Literary Society based in Dublin. He also became involved in politics and supported the movement for Irish independence from England.

Perhaps some of Yeats's political activity was spurred by his love for a beautiful Irish actress and revolutionary named Maud Gonne. This attraction lasted his entire life, but it was never reciprocated. To his sorrow—after many refusals of his marriage proposals—Gonne chose to marry a soldier. It was only many years later that Yeats himself married.

From Poetry to Plays to Poetry As the century turned, Yeats became interested in drama. He joined with his friend Lady Augusta Gregory in founding the Irish National Theatre Society. In 1892, Yeats had written *The Countess Cathleen*, a play that was to become one of his most popular dramatic works. With the acquisition and opening of the Abbey Theatre in Dublin, Yeats turned increasingly to writing plays, producing such works as *On Baile's Strand* (1904) and *Deirdre* (1907). When Yeats returned to poetry, it was with a new voice, subtler and more powerful than the one he had used before. The poems in *The Tower* (1928) show Yeats at the height of his abilities. "Sailing to Byzantium" dates from this period of his work.

Ireland's Hero In 1922, Yeats was appointed a senator of the new Irish Free State. On his seventieth birthday, he was hailed by his nation as the greatest living Irishman. Though his quarrels with the tastes and politics of middle-class Ireland were often fierce, no one could deny his stature. He continued to write up until a day or two before his death in France. One of his last poems contains his famous epitaph: "Cast a cold eye / On life, on death. / Horseman, pass by!"

TEACHING RESOURCES

The following resources can be used to enrich or extend the instruction for pp. 964–965.

Motivation

Interest Grabber Video, Tape 6

Background

Beyond Literature, p. 45

Take It to the Net

Visit www.phschool.com for background and hotlinks for more about William Butler Yeats.

Literary Analysis

Literary Analysis and Reading Transparencies, Symbolism, p. 90

Selection Support: Literary Analysis, p. 214

Reading

Literary Analysis and Reading Transparencies, Apply Literary Background, p. 89

Preview

Connecting to the Literature

Life turns in cycles—holidays and seasons repeat. Yeats believed that civilizations also had cycles, each lasting two thousand years.

2 Literary Analysis

Symbolism

In literature, a **symbol** is an image, character, object, or action that fulfills these functions:

- It stands for something beyond itself, such as a general idea.
- It gives rise to a number of associations.
- It intensifies feelings and adds complexity to meaning by concentrating these associations together.

The swans in "The Wild Swans at Coole" combine associations of beauty (they are graceful and attractive), purity (they are white), freedom (they are wild), and the eternal (they return year after year). Like other strong symbols, the swans support multiple meanings: They symbolize both the cycle of nature and the speaker's lost youth. As you read, explore the meanings of Yeats's symbols.

Comparing Literary Works

In "The Wild Swans at Coole," Yeats builds multiple meanings by contrasting two encounters with the swans, one past and one present. He weaves his symbol from personal experiences. In other poems, though, he builds multiple meanings by turning to traditional symbols, such as the mythological Sphinx in "The Second Coming." As you read, compare the types of symbols Yeats uses and consider the different effect of each.

3 Reading Strategy

Applying Literary Background

No poem is written in a vacuum. A writer's experiences, beliefs, and knowledge shape his or her works. As you read, **apply literary background**—information about history, literature, and the writer's life—to aid your understanding. Use a chart like the one shown.

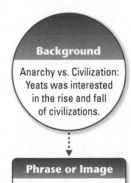

Background

Anarchy vs. Civilization: Yeats was interested in the rise and fall of civilizations.

Phrase or Image

"Mere anarchy is loosed upon the world, . . . "

Vocabulary Development

clamorous (klam′ ər əs) *adj.* loud and confused; noisy (p. 969)

conquest (käŋ′ kwest′) *n.* the winning of the submission or affection of (p. 970)

anarchy (an′ ər kē) *n.* absence of government; disorder (p. 971)

conviction (kən′ vik′ shən) *n.* belief; faith (p. 971)

paltry (pôl′ trē) *adj.* practically worthless; insignificant (p. 973)

artifice (ärt′ ə fis) *n.* skill; the product of skill, especially a skillfull deception (p. 974)

CUSTOMIZE INSTRUCTION FOR UNIVERSAL ACCESS

For Less Proficient Readers	For English Learners	For Advanced Readers
These students may take Yeats's words literally and may miss the symbolism they contain. Review with students the symbolism in each poem, then have them reread the selection, keeping the symbolic meaning in mind. If necessary, photocopy the poem and have them write notes between the lines.	For English learners, symbolism may be difficult when the symbols are directly tied to Western or British culture. What is common knowledge for other students may be lacking or attached to completely different meanings. Pair these students with English speakers who can help them understand the symbolism.	Advanced readers may like to find other poems that incorporate a high degree of symbolism. Have them look through books of poetry to find such poems, especially those that echo the symbols used by Yeats—swans, Byzantium, the Sphinx.

2 Literary Analysis

Symbolism

- Help students understand what symbolism is—the use of an image, character, object, or action that stands for something else or that gives rise to certain feelings.
- Discuss how symbols may be understood: through background knowledge, through common knowledge, and through careful reading. If students come across an object that seems misplaced or unusual, have them think of whether this object could be a symbol for something else.
- Yeats used many symbols in his poetry. Some symbols were obvious and within common knowledge, such as the swans at Innisfree. Others, such as the Sphinx, are more esoteric and more difficult to interpret.
- As they read, have students make a list of objects that are possibly symbols. These can be discussed later and edited as a class.
- Use the Symbolism transparency in **Literary Analysis and Reading Transparencies,** p. 90, to demonstrate for students how to decipher some symbols.

3 Reading Strategy

Applying Literary Background

- Literary background consists of knowledge of the author, his life and works, and the era in which he lived.
- Before reading any work, students should learn at least a little about the author. Encourage them to read biographical notes before reading the selection.
- Knowing a little about Yeats promotes understanding. Knowing that he had an unrequited love for Maud Gonne, for example, will lead to a more intimate interpretation of "When You Are Old."

Vocabulary Development

- Pronounce each vocabulary word for students and read the definitions as a class. Have students identify any words with which they are already familiar.

E-Teach

Visit E-Teach at www.phschool.com for teachers' essays on how to teach, with questions and answers.

Step-by-Step Teaching Guide for pp. 966–974

CUSTOMIZE INSTRUCTION For Visual/Spatial Learners

Invite these learners to use the illustrations on pp. 966, 969, and 973, as well as Yeats's highly vivid sensory language, to "see" the poems' images.

❶ About the Selection

All five poems are attempts to overcome the disappointments of mortal life. The first poem, "When You Are Old," offers a softer-edged, more "poetic" strategy to solve this problem. Here, the speaker takes gentle revenge on the lover who spurned him by imagining her regret in old age.

❷ Background

Art

Her Signal by Norman Garstin

Irishman Norman Garstin was both a painter and a writer. He studied art in Antwerp, Paris, and finally in Venice, where he was influenced by a group of painters later known as the Newlyn school. *Her Signal* was one of the many portraits or large anecdotal scenes Garstin produced mainly for financial motives.

Use the following question for discussion:

> How might the woman in the painting view her past loves?
> Possible responses: She might view them calmly, with the distance of old age; she might view them with deep regret, since they are probably irrecoverable at her time in life.

❸ ▶Critical Viewing

Answer: Students may note that the soft light and the woman's serene expression are sweet; her isolation, however, may suggest bitterness.

❷

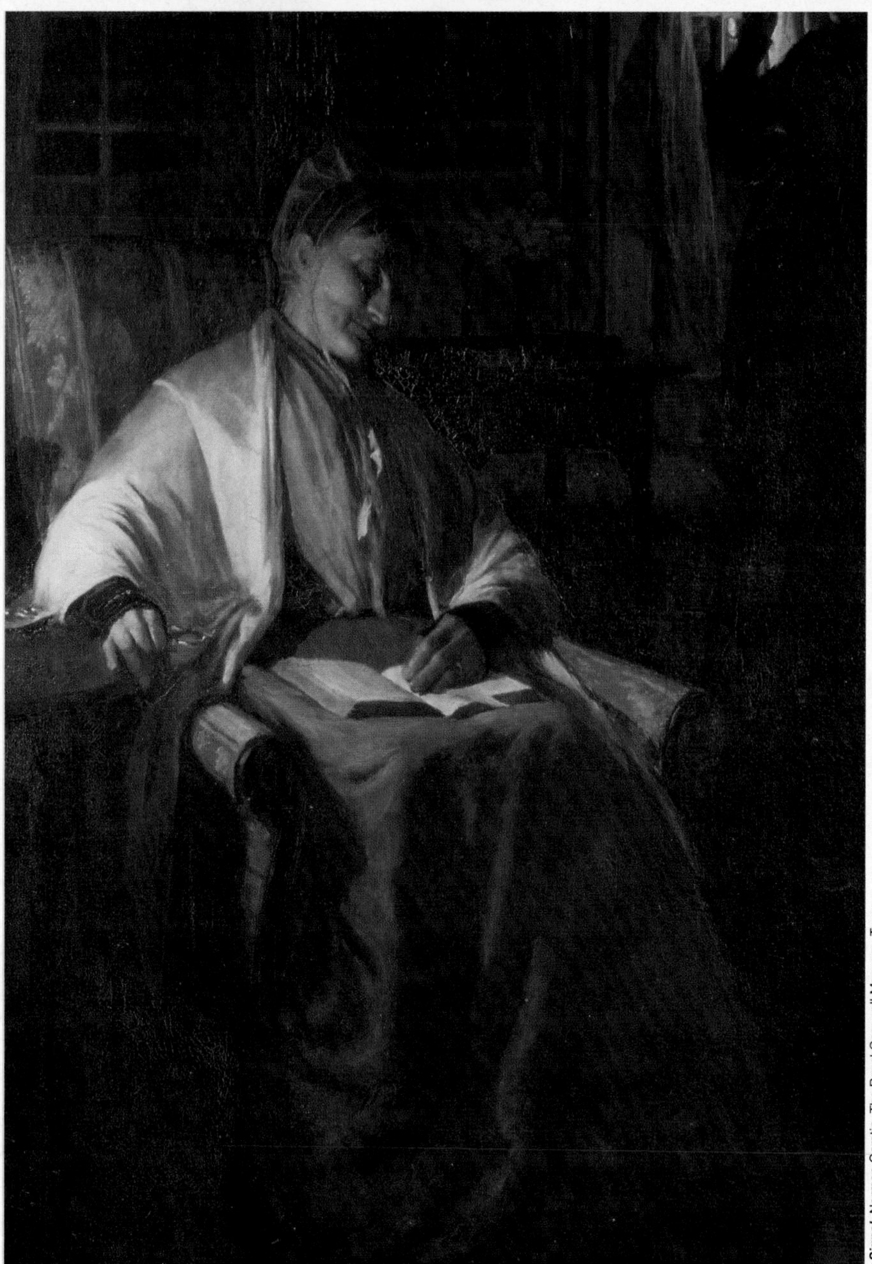

Her Signal, Norman Garstin, The Royal Cornwall Museum, Truro

❸ ▲ **Critical Viewing** The mood in "When You Are Old" is gentle and bittersweet. What elements in this painting mirror that mood? **[Classify]**

TEACHING RESOURCES

The following resources can be used to enrich or extend the instruction for pp. 966–974.

Literary Analysis

Literary Analysis and Reading Transparencies, p. 90

Reading Strategy

Selection Support: Reading Strategy, p. 213; Build Vocabulary, p. 211

Adapted Reader's Companion

Listening to Literature Audiocassettes, Side 22

Listening to Literature Audio CDs, CD 12

Extension

Authors In Depth, The British Tradition, p. 206 (This collection includes 10 additional selectio by W.B. Yeats for extended reading.)

❶

When You Are Old

William Butler Yeats

When you are old and gray and full of sleep,
And nodding by the fire, take down this book,
And slowly read, and dream of the soft look
Your eyes had once, and of their shadows deep;

How many loved your moments of glad grace,
And loved your beauty with love false or true,
But one man loved the pilgrim soul in you,
And loved the sorrows of your changing face;

❹

And bending down beside the glowing bars,
Murmur, a little sadly, how Love fled
And paced upon the mountains overhead
And hid his face amid a crowd of stars.

Review and Assess

Thinking About the Selection

1. **(a) Recall:** What does the speaker request of the person to whom the poem is addressed? **(b) Infer:** Who is this person?
2. **(a) Recall:** In line 7, what does the speaker claim distinguishes his love from that of others? **(b) Interpret:** Does the speaker intend this claim to inspire regret? Explain.
3. **Interpret:** What do lines 10–12 suggest about what the speaker wants his beloved to acknowledge?
4. **Draw Conclusions:** What does the speaker gain by imagining the words the person addressed will "murmur"?
5. **Make a Judgment:** Do you think this poem is comforting? Why or why not?

❹ Reading Strategy

Applying Literary Background

- Discuss with students what they know about Yeats's background that might help them interpret this poem.
- Remind them of Yeats's long, but unrequited, love for Maud Gonne, who was loved by "many." Yeats could be saying he's the "one man" who loved her truly.
- Discuss how this knowledge helps students read the poem in a different light.

Answers for p. 967

Review and Assess

1. **(a)** The speaker asks that the addressee take a moment to think about their relationship. **(b)** This person may have been a former lover.
2. **(a)** He claims to have loved her "pilgrim" soul. **(b)** Yes, the writer expects to inspire regret. He probably hopes this argument will cause her to regret her rejection of him.
3. He wants his beloved to acknowledge that his love for her was better than that of others.
4. The imagined words of regret are the writer's form of revenge against the lover who refused him.
5. Possible response: The poem might be comforting to the writer, as it allows him revenge without doing any real deed. Imagining her feeling regretful consoles him for the fact that she did not return or ceased to return his love.

CUSTOMIZE INSTRUCTION FOR UNIVERSAL ACCESS

For Special Needs Students	For Gifted/Talented Students
Have students listen to a reading of the poem from the **Listening to Literature Audiocassettes.** Then, have them read the poem themselves, paying attention to the rhythm of the poem and the beats in each line. Have them underline the stressed beats on a photocopy and determine if these are the most important words in the poem.	Those students with musical ability might enjoy the challenge of setting this poem to music. Discuss what kind of music would be most appropriate for the poem, and what instruments would best carry the ideas expressed in the poem across to the audience. Also discuss tempo of the music, and whether playing in a minor key would emphasize the melancholy of the piece.

❺ About the Selections

In "The Lake Isle of Innisfree," the softer image is once again presented. The writer imagines a Walden-like retreat to which he can flee from "the pavements gray." Yeats himself said, "I had still the ambition, formed in Sligo in my teens, of living in imitation of Thoreau on Innisfree, a little island on Lough Gill. . . ."

"The Wild Swans at Coole" exchanges the softness of the previous two poems for a tougher, more impersonal solution to the problems of mortality. This poem is set in Coole Park, the estate of Lady Gregory. She was Yeats's patron as well as his collaborator in establishing the Irish National Theatre Society. Yeats spent a great deal of time at Coole Park, a large estate with ponds, forest paths, and orchards.

Answers for p. 968

Review and Assess

1. Students may say that they would like to visit Innisfree because it sounds like a quiet, peaceful place.
2. **(a)** Peace comes dropping slow. **(b)** Innisfree is probably less hurried and calmer than his current life.
3. **(a)** The image of peace dropping unites "the veils of morning" to the evening ("where the cricket sings;"); images of light ("glimmer" and "purple glow") unite midnight and noon. **(b)** The places are united by the fact that the speaker hears the lapping water in each place mentioned. **(c)** The imagery inspires a peaceful, calm feeling.
4. The tone of the poem is itself peaceful. The long lines also have a soothing, rhythmical feel, much like the lapping water.
5. Possible response: "When You Are Old" acts out a subtle, imaginary revenge; "Lake Isle" creates a desired tranquil mood. In this way, both poems satisfy an unsatisfied or disappointed desire.

❺ The Lake Isle of Innisfree

William Butler Yeats

I will arise and go now, and go to Innisfree,
And a small cabin build there, of clay and wattles[1] made:
Nine bean-rows will I have there, a hive for the honeybee,
And live alone in the bee-loud glade.

And I shall have some peace there, for peace comes dropping slow,
Dropping from the veils of the morning to where the cricket sings;
There midnight's all a glimmer, and noon a purple glow,
And evening full of the linnet's wings.[2]

I will arise and go now, for always night and day
I hear lake water lapping with low sounds by the shore:
While I stand on the roadway, or on the pavements gray,
I hear it in the deep heart's core.

1. **wattles** stakes interwoven with twigs or branches.
2. **linnet's wings** wings of a European singing bird.

Review and Assess

Thinking About the Selection

1. **Respond:** Based on the speaker's descriptions, would you like to visit Innisfree? Why or why not?
2. (a) **Recall:** What "comes dropping slow" at Innisfree? (b) **Infer:** How does life at Innisfree contrast with the speaker's current surroundings?
3. (a) **Analyze:** What imagery in the second stanza unites the various times of day? (b) **Analyze:** What images in the last stanza unite the various places? (c) **Interpret:** What mood does this unity inspire?
4. **Draw Conclusions:** In what way does the poem itself create the feeling the speaker hopes to find in Innisfree?
5. **Compare and Contrast:** Do you think that this poem and "When You Are Old" suggest that writing poetry is a way of compensating for disappointments? Why or why not?

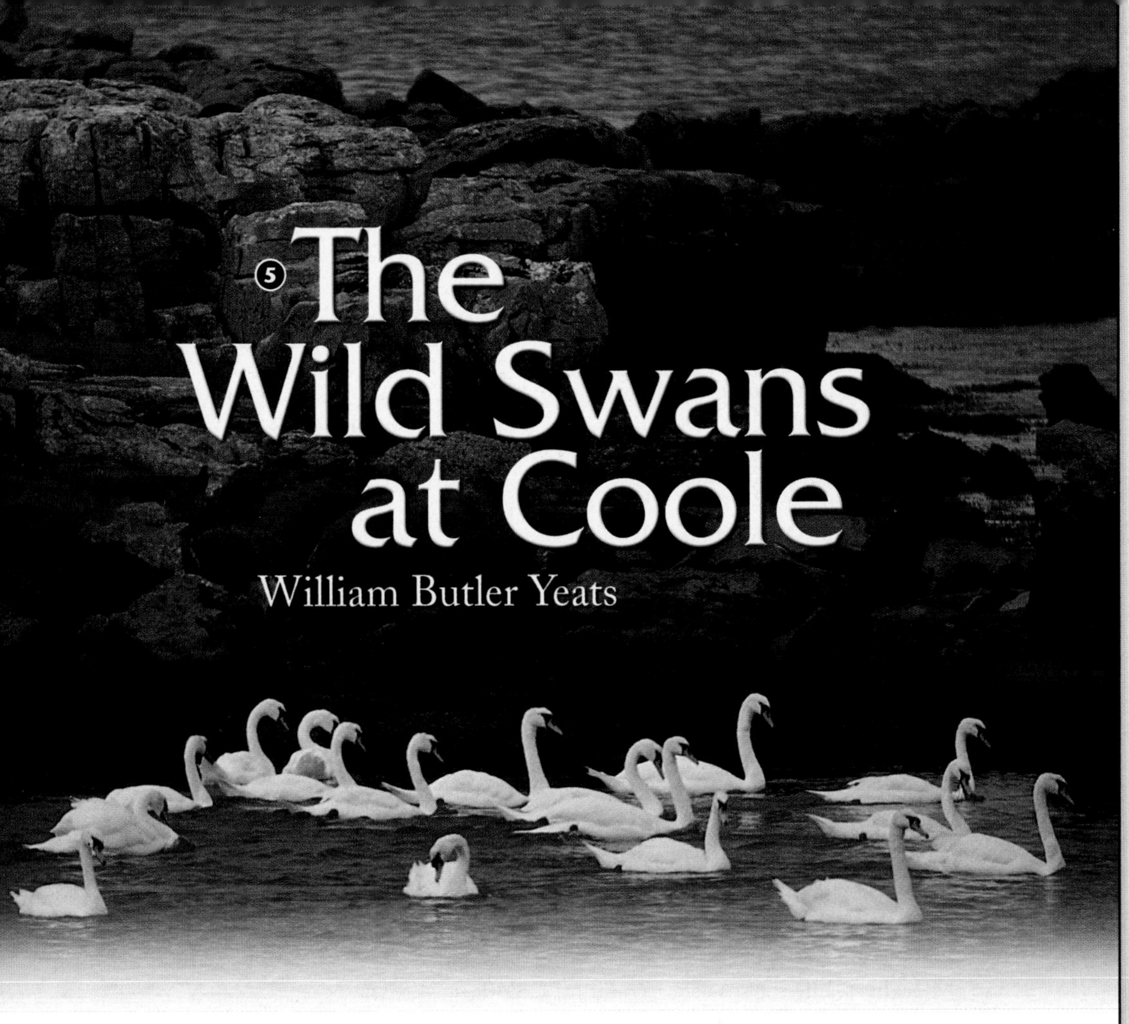

⑤ The Wild Swans at Coole

William Butler Yeats

The trees are in their autumn beauty,
The woodland paths are dry,
Under the October twilight the water
Mirrors a still sky;
Upon the brimming water among the stones
Are nine-and-fifty swans.

The nineteenth autumn has come upon me
Since I first made my count;
I saw, before I had well finished,
All suddenly mount
And scatter wheeling in great broken rings
Upon their clamorous wings. ⑦

⑥ **Critical Viewing** Why might Yeats describe drifting swans such as these as "mysterious" and "beautiful"? **[Infer]**

clamorous (klam´ər əs) *adj.* loud and confused; noisy

⑧ **Reading Check** How much time has passed since the speaker last saw the swans?

CUSTOMIZE INSTRUCTION FOR UNIVERSAL ACCESS

For Less Proficient Readers	For English Learners	For Advanced Readers
Help students understand "The Wild Swans at Coole" by having them make two lists. Title one "Things That Have Changed," and the other "Things That Have Not Changed." Help them decide what objects in the poem belong in each category, then discuss the results.	Encourage students to use signal words such as *since, before,* and *will* to track past, present, and future in "The Wild Swans at Coole." Then, have them list the poem's events in chronological order.	Encourage students to extend the meaning of "The Wild Swans at Coole" by analyzing the depictions of swans in other cultures. Direct them to architectural decorations, book illustrations, fairy tales, fiction, and poetry as possible sources.

⑥ Critical Viewing

Answer: Students may respond that the curve of the swans' backs and the bend in their necks give them a mysteriously balanced beauty.

⑦ Literary Analysis

Symbolism

- Explain to students that the thoughts and events linked to an image in a poem contribute to its symbolic value.
- Ask students what the passage of time since the speaker first counted the swans indicates about their symbolic meaning.
  Possible response: The swans are connected with youth; they are connected with what stays the same despite the passage of time.

⑧ Reading Check

Answer: Nineteen years have passed.

⑨ Critical Thinking (p. 970)

Infer

- Have students read lines 13–24 to themselves. Have them briefly restate the meaning of these lines.
- Ask students to identify what has changed for the speaker over the nineteen years of watching the swans.
  Answer: Students should recognize that the poet has aged and no longer experiences "passion or conquest"; he laments the losses that aging brings.

⑩ Vocabulary Development

Latin Root *-ques-*

- Point out the word *conquest* in line 23. Explain to students that the Latin root *-ques-* means "to seek or acquire."
- Explain that a *conquest* is an acquisition of another's affection or submission. It carries the association of victory and of a struggle between two powers.
- Have students identify other words formed from the root *-ques-*. Possible responses: Words formed from *-ques-* include *inquest, request, question, query,* and *bequest.*
- Have students use the dictionary to check the meaning of any unfamiliar words.

Answers for p. 970

Review and Assess

1. Students may say they were moved by the sight of an animal seen in the wild.
2. **(a)** The setting of the poem is a lake at Coole, inhabited by swans. **(b)** Autumn is a common symbol of old age and approaching death. **(c)** The passing of time is suggested by the swans' flight.
3. **(a)** The swans suddenly take flight. **(b)** The speaker realizes how much has changed since he last saw the swans.
4. **(a)** The speaker is now older, and perhaps more tired and less lighthearted than at first sighting, when he "Trod with a lighter tread." **(b)** The swans are still youthful and unwearied; they do not change, while the speaker does.
5. **(a)** The flight may represent the loss of his youth, love, and passion; it may represent his death. **(b)** It suggests that their beauty is only a passing experience, though it suggests the abiding or eternal: The swans will fly away (or the speaker will die).
6. **(a)** The speaker measures the passage of time between his first and his present count of them. **(b)** Possible response: Both photographs and the swans evoke memories of past times by virtue of the fact that they do not change.

I have looked upon those brilliant creatures,
And now my heart is sore.
All's changed since I, hearing at twilight,
The first time on this shore,
The bell-beat of their wings above my head,
Trod with a lighter tread.

⑨

Unwearied still, lover by lover,
They paddle in the cold
Companionable streams or climb the air;
Their hearts have not grown old;
Passion or conquest, wander where they will, | ⑩
Attend upon them still.

But now they drift on the still water,
Mysterious, beautiful;
Among what rushes will they build,
By what lake's edge or pool
Delight men's eyes when I awake some day
To find they have flown away?

conquest (käŋ′ kwest′) *n.* the winning of the submission or affection of

Review and Assess

Thinking About the Selection

1. **Respond:** Have you ever been moved by the sight of an animal, as the swans move the speaker? Explain.
2. **(a) Recall:** Where is the poem set? **(b) Interpret:** How does the time of year reflect the speaker's place in life? **(c) Analyze:** Which details suggest the passing of time?
3. **(a) Recall:** While the speaker is counting the swans, what do they suddenly do? **(b) Interpret:** What reflection does their action prompt in the speakers?
4. **(a) Infer:** What has changed in the speaker since he first heard the swans? **(b) Compare and Contrast:** How does the swans' condition contrast with that of the speaker?
5. **(a) Interpret:** The speaker says he will "awake some day / To find they have flown away. . . ." What event might this flight represent for him? **(b) Draw Conclusions:** How does this imagined absence increase the poignancy of the sight of the swans?
6. **(a) Interpret:** In what way does the sight of the swans help the speaker measure the passage of time? **(b) Apply:** Compare this experience with another way in which people measure the passage of time, such as viewing family photographs or videos.

ENRICHMENT: Science Connection

A Scientist's View of Swans

There are seven or eight different species of swans, but all share some of the characteristics Yeats describes. Though some swans weigh as much as 50 pounds, they are graceful in flight, with their long, outstretched necks and steady wingstrokes.

Swans mate for life, producing about 6 babies (called *cygnets*) each breeding season. The cygnets are gray or brown; most gradually become white, but a few species have other colorations. Although the male swan, or *cob,* will defend his family against outsiders, these families do merge with others to migrate in a large group. Flying at high altitudes, in either diagonal or V-formations, swans travel southward in fall and northward in spring.

Have students observe swans in your community, at a zoo, on the Internet, or in books. Ask students to compare and contrast a scientist's view of swans with Yeats's.

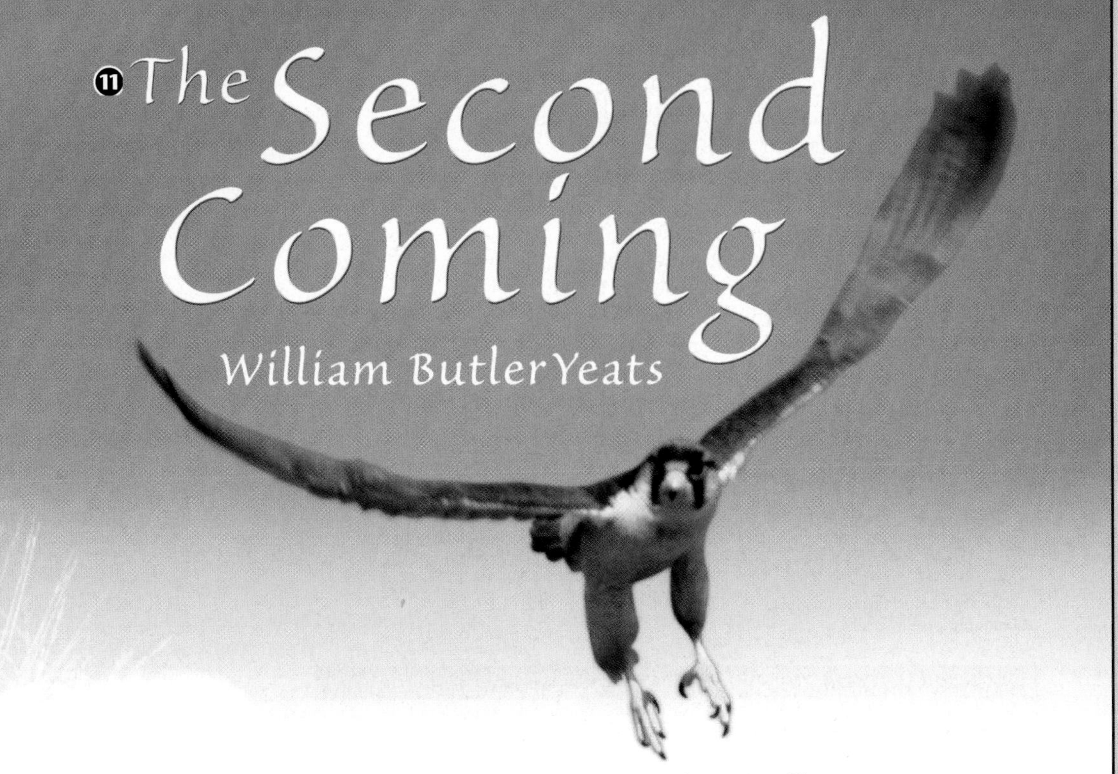

Background

In 1925, Yeats published *A Vision*, a work that explained the mythology, symbolism, and philosophy that he strove to express in his poetry. Yeats believed that history occurs in two-thousand-year cycles, during which a particular civilization is born, grows, and decays. Each civilization then gives way to a new one that is the direct opposite of it. Yeats believed that the society of the early twentieth century was decaying and would lead to another sort of rebirth, very different from the birth of Christ. These ideas are vividly expressed in the poem "The Second Coming."

12 ▲ Critical Viewing
Judging from this image, what associations might Yeats be emphasizing by using a falcon as a symbol? **[Connect]**

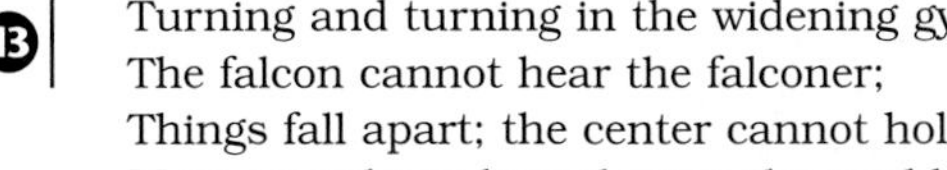

13
Turning and turning in the widening gyre
The falcon cannot hear the falconer;
Things fall apart; the center cannot hold;
Mere <u>anarchy</u> is loosed upon the world,
The blood-dimmed tide is loosed, and everywhere
The ceremony of innocence is drowned;
The best lack all <u>conviction</u>, while the worst
Are full of passionate intensity.[1]

anarchy (an´ ər kē) *n.* absence of government; disorder

conviction (kən´ vik´ shən) *n.* belief; faith

1. **Mere . . . intensity** refers to the Russian Revolution of 1917.

11 About the Selection

The fierce and disturbing images in "The Second Coming" represent Yeats's vision of the great cycles of history. Yeats wrote this poem in January, 1919, just after World War I came to a close, shortly after the Russian Revolution, and just as war in Ireland was breaking out between the English forces and the Irish patriots. The "blood-dimmed tide" of the poem is therefore an image of the violence that seemed to be filling the world.

12 ▶Critical Viewing

Answer: The falcon might represent something that is free, since the falcon is soaring on the wind. It may also represent something that is deadly, for falcons have been trained to kill.

13 Literary Analysis

Symbolism

- Remind students that symbols may be traditional or may reflect the poet's experience.
- Read lines 1–2, and ask where they think the symbols of the gyre and falcon derive from.
  Possible response: The gyre, or spiral, is probably an obscure traditional symbol that Yeats adapted to his theory of history. Falcons have traditional associations of nobility, obedience, and fierceness.

CUSTOMIZE INSTRUCTION FOR UNIVERSAL ACCESS

For Less Proficient Readers	For Gifted/Talented Students	For Advanced Readers
To help those students understand the symbolism in this poem, explain the historical background and write on the chalkboard the phrase "things fall apart." Have these students come up with their own images and symbols to convey this idea. Then have them compare these symbols to Yeats's.	Students with an interest in art may be familiar with several paintings that depict chaos similar to that predicted by Yeats. Have them assemble a portfolio of paintings, including their own original works, that represent the turmoil and anxiety about civilization expressed in the poem.	Have students respond to critic Richard Ellmann's appraisal of this poem: ". . .an awareness of [Yeats's mythological] system was more useful for writing than it is for reading the poem. . . . It is more necessary that we be familiar with the ancient, traditional myth of a second coming . . . than that we understand [Yeats's system].

Answers for p. 972

Review and Assess

1. Possible response: Yes, I think things are falling apart because people are becoming more violent in our society.
2. **(a)** The falcon cannot hear its master's voice. **(b)** The falcon is now out of control and the "order" of authority, falconer over falcon, has broken down; the falcon's disobedience is innocent, though, since it cannot hear the falconer's command.
3. **(a)** The speaker believes that "some revelation is at hand." **(b)** The lines may represent the age before the birth of Christ, since the Sphinx is a figure in the mythology of ancient Greece and Egypt. **(c)** The birth of Christ began a new religion, and the gods of ancient times were abandoned.
4. **(a)** A "rough beast" is about to be born." **(b)** In the traditional version, it is Christ who returns at the Second Coming; often symbolized as a lamb, the merciful figure of Christ contrasts with Yeats's ominous "rough beast."
5. Possible response: Yeats's images are so strong and vibrant that even though they are unpleasant, one can appreciate the craftsmanship the poem exhibits.
6. Possible response: Yes, his vision is manifest today in the violence that is occurring around the world.

Surely some revelation is at hand;
Surely the Second Coming is at hand.
The Second Coming! Hardly are those words out
When a vast image out of *Spiritus Mundi*[2]
Troubles my sight: somewhere in sands of the desert
A shape with lion body and the head of a man,[3]
A gaze blank and pitiless as the sun,
Is moving its slow thighs, while all about it
Reel shadows of the indignant desert birds.
The darkness drops again; but now I know
That twenty centuries[4] of stony sleep
Were vexed to nightmare by a rocking cradle,[5]
And what rough beast, its hour come round at last,
Slouches towards Bethlehem to be born?

---

2. ***Spiritus Mundi*** (spir′ i təs mo͞on′dē) Universal Spirit or Soul, in which the memories of the entire human race are forever preserved.
3. **A . . . man** the Sphinx, a monster in Greek mythology that posed a riddle to passing travelers and destroyed those who could not answer it. The answer to the riddle was "man."
4. **twenty centuries** historical cycle preceding the birth of Christ.
5. **rocking cradle** cradle of Jesus Christ.

Review and Assess

Thinking About the Selection

1. **Respond:** Do you agree that in the modern world "Things fall apart"? Explain.
2. **(a) Recall:** In the first two lines of the poem, why does the falcon not return to the falconer, as it ordinarily would? **(b) Analyze:** Why is the image of the falcon an effective introduction to Yeats's ideas about order and innocence?
3. **(a) Recall:** At the beginning of the second stanza, what does the speaker believe is at hand? **(b) Interpret:** What era of history might the vision in lines 11–17 represent? Explain. **(c) Interpret:** In what sense did a past birth in Bethlehem bring this era to an end?
4. **(a) Analyze:** What birth does the speaker predict will end the modern era? **(b) Draw Conclusions:** How does the traditional idea of the Second Coming differ from what the speaker is envisioning?
5. **Evaluate:** Yeats draws on his own theories of history for the theme and imagery of this poem. Why might the poem be appreciated even by readers who do not share his beliefs?
6. **Apply:** In your opinion, do any contemporary events bear out Yeats's vision of history? Explain.

ENRICHMENT: History Connection

Falconry

Students will not appreciate this opening image, and its symbolism, unless they understand something about falconry. This sport involved the use of trained falcons to hunt small birds and animals. After killing their prey, but otherwise leaving it untouched, falcons return to the trainer's wrist. (They cannot be trained to retrieve prey.) Falconry was practiced by the ancient Chinese and was popular among the nobility in Europe during the Middle Ages and the Renaissance. In Yeats's poem, the falcon, flying in wider and wider circles, "cannot hear the falconer" and is therefore out of control.

Ravenna: City and Port of Classis. Mosaic, late 6th century, from Basilicia of St. Apollinare Nuovo

SAILING TO BYZANTIUM

William Butler Yeats

I

That is no country for old men. The young
In one another's arms, birds in the trees
—Those dying generations—at their song,
The salmon-falls, the mackerel-crowded seas,
Fish, flesh, or fowl, commend all summer long
Whatever is begotten, born, and dies.
Caught in that sensual music all neglect
Monuments of unaging intellect.

II

An aged man is but a paltry thing,
A tattered coat upon a stick, unless
Soul clap its hands and sing, and louder sing
For every tatter in its mortal dress,
Nor is there singing school but studying
Monuments of its own magnificence;
And therefore I have sailed the seas and come
To the holy city of Byzantium.[1]

1. **Byzantium** (bi zan′ shē əm) ancient capital of the Eastern Roman (or Byzantine) Empire and the seat of the Greek Orthodox Church; today, Istanbul, Turkey. For Yeats, Byzantium symbolized the world of art as opposed to the world of time and nature.

16 ▲ **Critical Viewing** In what way do the colors and textures of this Byzantine mosaic convey the idea that the ships have arrived at a wondrous place? **[Interpret]**

paltry (pôl′ trē) *adj.* practically worthless; insignificant

17  **Reading Check**

What does his age motivate the speaker to do?

14 About the Selection

"Sailing to Byzantium" is another impersonal poem. It represents attempts to imagine a pattern of existence beyond the individual—the immortality of art.

15 Background

Art

Ravenna: City and Port of Classis

This mosaic illustrates the city of Ravenna and its nearby port of Classis, both in what is now Italy. Ravenna was an important city during both the latter years of the Western Roman Empire and the Byzantine effort to recapture Italy from the Goths. This mosaic—and the basilica of St. Appolinare Nuovo in which it resides—was created during the reign of Ostrogothic Emperor Theodoric (493–526). Theodoric's palace appears at the far right of the picture. The mosaic is one of the earliest in the West to reflect the features of Byzantine art—for example, the gold background and the continuous path around the church walls. Use these questions for discussion:

1. What language from the poem could be used to describe this mosaic?
   Answer: Apt phrases include: "holy city of Byzantium" and "gold mosaic of a wall."
2. What elements of the mosaic suggest the comparison Yeats makes between the worlds of art and nature?
   Answer: The port (left) could stand for the world of nature, while the palace (right) can stand for the world of art.

16 ▶Critical Viewing

Answer: The glowing earth-colors and the tops of the buildings seen over the wall convey a sense of magical luxury.

17 Reading Check

Answer: The speaker's age motivates him to sail to Byzantium in an attempt to escape his mortality.

CUSTOMIZE INSTRUCTION FOR UNIVERSAL ACCESS

For Gifted/Talented Students	For English Learners	For Advanced Readers
Have students research Byzantium and Byzantine art in the library or on the Internet. Have them pool their findings and list several adjectives that describe the place and the culture. Remind students that Yeats thought of Byzantium as the ideal place, and discuss what attributes may have influenced his thinking.	Help students read through the poem. Then, using a photocopy of the poem, have them underline words and phrases that apply to the natural world. Using another color, they can underline words that apply to the ideal world Yeats longed for. Work with students to help them understand the difference between the two worlds.	Have students discuss what the golden bird might symbolize for Yeats. Discuss the paradoxical nature of this symbol: on one hand the bird symbolizes the artist who has transcended the natural world through his art, but the bird sings about that natural world.

ASSESS

Answers for p. 974

Review and Assess

1. **(a)** They commend "Whatever is begotten, born, or dies." They neglect "Monuments of unaging intellect." **(b)** Yeats means the world of nature and time, not a specific country.
2. **(a)** An aged man is "a paltry thing, / A tattered coat upon a stick." **(b)** The aged are not caught up in the tumult of nature—their passions may have diminished, and they may have already "begotten" young—and therefore have little or no place in nature.
3. **(a)** The speaker is urging his soul to clap hands as a symbol for creating beauty and order (song) to compensate for the frailties, wounds, and imperfections of bodily, mortal existence ("for every tatter in its mortal dress"). **(b)** It suggests that people create works of art to provide themselves with some form of immortality and that they are motivated to do so by the frustrations and disappointments inherent in life.
4. **(a)** He asks the sages to consume his heart and gather him "Into the artifice of eternity"—to change his mortal being into something immortal. **(b)** The request reveals that the speaker believes that works of art provide entry into a world beyond nature and change.
5. The speaker hopes to escape nature by leaving behind a work of art that will immortalize him.
6. Possible responses: Byzantium is the dream, because we only really exist in the world of change; the world of nature is a dream, because everything in it passes away like a dream.

III

O sages standing in God's holy fire
As in the gold mosaic of a wall,[2]
Come from the holy fire, perne in a gyre,[3]
And be the singing-masters of my soul.
Consume my heart away; sick with desire
And fastened to a dying animal
It knows not what it is; and gather me
Into the <u>artifice</u> of eternity.

artifice (ärt′ə fis) *n.* skill; the product of skill; especially a skillful deception

IV

Once out of nature I shall never take
My bodily form from any natural thing,
But such a form as Grecian goldsmiths make
Of hammered gold and gold enameling
To keep a drowsy Emperor awake;
Or set upon a golden bough to sing[4]
To lords and ladies of Byzantium
Of what is past, or passing, or to come.

---

2. **sages . . . wall** wise men portrayed in mosaic on the walls of Byzantine churches.
3. **perne . . . gyre** spin in a spiraling motion.
4. **To . . . sing** Yeats wrote, "I have read somewhere that in the Emperor's palace at Byzantium was a tree made of gold and silver, and artificial birds that sang."

Review and Assess

Thinking About the Selection

1. **(a) Recall:** What do the people and things of the country referred to in the first stanza "commend"? What do they "neglect"? **(b) Interpret:** What "country" is Yeats describing in the first stanza?
2. **(a) Recall:** What is an "aged man," according to the second stanza? **(b) Interpret:** Why might the aged not belong to the "country" of the first stanza?
3. **(a) Interpret:** Why must the soul "clap its hands and sing" in line 11? **(b) Draw Conclusions:** What does the second stanza suggest about the reason people create works of art?
4. **(a) Interpret:** In the third stanza, what does the speaker ask the sages to change in him? **(b) Draw Conclusions:** What does this request reveal about the speaker's faith in artistic production?
5. **Interpret:** In the last stanza, how does the speaker hope to escape nature?
6. **Make a Judgment:** In your view, which is a "dream"—Byzantium or the world of what "is begotten, born, and dies"?

ASSESSMENT PRACTICE: Writing Skills

Style **(For more practice, see Test Preparation Workbook, p. 46.)**

Many tests require students to recognize effective stylistic devices and language. Use the following sample test item to teach students how to recognize parallel structure.

How many loved your moments of glad grace,
And loved your beauty with love false or true,
But one man loved the pilgrim soul in you,
And loved the sorrows of your changing face.

Which of the following appears in these lines?

A allusion
B metaphor
C parallel structure
D dangling modifier

Knowing that parallel structure is the repetition of a basic grammatical pattern leads to the correct answer, *C*.

Review and Assess

Literary Analysis

Symbolism

1. (a) What associations does the speaker in "The Lake Isle of Innisfree" build around the **symbol** of Innisfree? (b) Explain two things Innisfree might symbolize.
2. Explain what the dry "woodland paths," "October twilight," and the "still sky" symbolize in "The Wild Swans at Coole."
3. (a) In "The Second Coming," what symbol does Yeats use for the era of civilization preceding Christ? (b) What multiple meanings is he able to create by not naming it directly?
4. (a) In "Sailing to Byzantium," what do the monuments in lines 8 and 14 symbolize? (b) Find two examples in this poem of Yeats's use of Byzantine art to symbolize perfection.

Comparing Literary Works

5. Using a chart like the one shown, compare the effect and meaning of the swans in "The Wild Swans at Coole" with those of the Sphinx in "The Second Coming."

Symbol:____________________

Personal / Traditional	Vivid / Flat	Rich / Poor in Associations	Easy / Hard to Interpret

6. Based on Yeats's poems, do you think symbols based on personal associations, such as Innisfree, are more compelling than traditional symbols such as the Sphinx? Explain.

Reading Strategy

Applying Literary Background

7. Review the information on page 964. (a) What events in Yeats's life might have inspired "When You Are Old"? (b) What experiences might have inspired "Sailing to Byzantium"?
8. How does knowing the historical era in which Yeats wrote "The Second Coming" help you interpret the first stanza?

Extend Understanding

9. **Science Connection:** Compare Yeats's idea of historical cycles with the scientific view of time.

Quick Review

A **symbol** is an image, character, object, or action that stands for something beyond itself.

To **apply literary background,** use your knowledge of a writer's beliefs and experiences, as well as preceding literature and historical events, to help you interpret the text.

Take It to the Net

www.phschool.com

Take the interactive self-test online to check your understanding of these selections.

ENRICHMENT: Further Reading

Other Works by William Butler Yeats

The Autobiography of William Butler Yeats; The Shadowy Waters; The Tower

Take It to the Net

Visit www.phschool.com for more information on William Butler Yeats.

Answers for p. 975

Review and Assess

1. **(a)** The speaker builds the associations of youth and peace around Innisfree. **(b)** Innisfree might symbolize the speaker's youth, which he regrets not having any more, or it may symbolize the peace that does not exist in his city life.
2. The phrases symbolize the speaker's advanced age. October is near the end of the year, and the speaker is near the end of his life. Twilight is the end of the day; dry paths suggest an end of growth; the "still sky" suggests an end of change.
3. **(a)** He uses the symbol of the Sphinx. **(b)** Yeats is able to create a mystery about the era and leave it open for personal interpretation. By not directly naming the Sphinx, he lets the images with which he describes it add additional meanings of horror (the "pitiless" gaze) and perhaps decay (the birds suggest carrion nearby).
4. **(a)** The monuments symbolize cultural achievements of lasting value, such as works of art. **(b)** Possible response: The gold mosaic and the artificial bird symbolize the unchanging perfection of art.
5. Possible response: Swans **Personal/Traditional:** both traditional and personal; **Vivid/Flat:** vivid; **Rich/Poor:** rich; **Easy/Hard:** easy
   Possible response: Sphinx **Personal/Traditional:** traditional; **Vivid/Flat:** flat; **Rich/Poor:** rich; **Easy/Hard:** hard
6. Students may say that the personal symbols are more compelling, because they can more directly convey a speaker's passions and experiences. The use of traditional symbols involves pre-set associations and pre-set responses, so they can easily seem flat or stale.
7. **(a)** His lifelong unrequited love for Maud Gonne may have inspired it. **(b)** Yeats's advancing age at the time helps you to understand why he wrote the poem.

continued

Answers continued

8. It enables readers to recognize the "anarchy" mentioned as a reference to World War I or the Russian Revolution.
9. Yeats believed that history makes sudden, drastic changes in moral climate every 2,000 years. Scientists mark periods of history as progressive, rather than repetitious or marked by cataclysmic reversals.

EXTEND

Answers for p. 976

❶ Vocabulary Development

Word Analysis: Latin Root *-ques-*

1. A search; the purpose of a search is to find and possibly to acquire something.
2. An examination before a jury; the goal of an inquest is to seek information.
3. A stated wish for something; the goal of a request is to communicate the search for something.
4. A stated desire to learn information; a question seeks information.

Spelling Strategy

1. righteous
2. clamorous
3. beauteous

Concept Development: Synonyms

1. (c)
2. (a)
3. (c)
4. (a)
5. (b)
6. (c)

❷ Grammar and Style

1. how Love fled; direct object
2. where the cricket sings; object of a preposition
3. That twenty centuries of stony sleep / Were vexed to nightmare; direct object
4. what it is; direct object
5. how many loved your moments of glad grace; direct object

Writing Application

Sample responses:

1. What the Irish National Movement sought was independence.
2. Yeats believed that the twentieth century was a time of decay.

Integrate Language Skills

❶ Vocabulary Development Lesson

Word Analysis: Latin Root *-ques-*

The root *-ques-* means "to seek or acquire." It appears in the word *conquest*, referring to "an acquisition by force." Write a definition for each word, showing how the root affects its meaning:

1. quest
2. inquest
3. request
4. question

Spelling Strategy

To form an adjective with the suffix *-ous*, the ending of the word base may be altered and the suffix may be spelled *-eous*: *instant* becomes *instantaneous* and *miscellany* becomes *miscellaneous*. Use *-ous* to form adjectives from the following:

1. right 2. clamor 3. beauty

Concept Development: Synonyms

In your notebook, write the letter of the word below whose meaning is closest to that of the word from the vocabulary list on page 965.

1. clamorous: (a) angry, (b) peaceful, (c) loud
2. conquest: (a) victory, (b) failure, (c) riches
3. anarchy: (a) peace, (b) systematicity, (c) disorder
4. conviction: (a) belief, (b) system, (c) violence
5. paltry: (a) magnificent, (b) trivial, (c) lying
6. artifice: (a) acquisitiveness, (b) beauty, (c) ingenuity

❷ Grammar and Style Lesson

Noun Clauses

In his poetry, Yeats often uses **noun clauses** to connect one image or complex thought to another. A noun clause contains a subject and a verb. Noun clauses frequently begin with *how, that, who, whom, which, what, whatever, whether, whoever,* or *whomever.* A noun clause can function as subject, direct object, or object of a preposition.

Direct Object: Fish, flesh, or fowl, commend all summer long / Whatever is begotten, born, and dies.

Object of Preposition: . . . to sing . . . / . . . Of what is past, or passing, or to come.

Many noun clauses, like the ones in the examples, create a "blank" that the reader's imagination must fill in.

Practice Identify the noun clause and its function in each of the following passages.

1. Murmur, a little sadly, how Love fled. . . .
2. Dropping from the veils of the morning to where the cricket sings; . . . /
3. . . . now I know / That twenty centuries of stony sleep / Were vexed to nightmare . . .
4. It knows not what it is; . . .
5. . . . . and dream . . . / . . . / How many loved your moments of glad grace, . . .

Writing Application Write a sentence using the clause given in the function indicated.

1. What the Irish National Movement sought . . . (subject)
2. . . . that the twentieth century was a time of decay. (direct object)

WG Prentice Hall Writing and Grammar Connection: Chapter 19, Section 3

TEACHING RESOURCES

The following resources can be used to enrich or extend the instructions for pp. 976–977.

Vocabulary

- **Selection Support:** Build Vocabulary, p. 211
- **Vocabulary and Spelling Practice Book** (Use this booklet for skills enrichment.)

Grammar

- **Selection Support,** Grammar and Style, p. 212
- **Writing and Grammar,** Diamond Level, p. 458
- **Daily Language Practice Transparencies**

Writing

- **Writing and Grammar,** Diamond Level, p. 317
- **Writing and Grammar iText CD-ROM**

❸ Writing Lesson

Response to Criticism

Scholar Reuben A. Brower wrote that Yeats succeeded "by letting his dreamlike symbols materialize to express and connect conflict he could never resolve outside his poetry." Write an essay expressing your agreement or disagreement. Supply any background information readers may need.

Prewriting Divide Brower's statement into parts—for instance, "dreamlike symbols" or "symbols expressing conflict." Under each, list examples from Yeats's poems. Then, review your notes and write your opinion of Brower's statement.

Drafting As you draft, support your evaluation with examples from the poems. Keep your audience in mind. Explain any details with which they may not be familiar.

Revising Review your essay, marking off difficult ideas or references. For each, ask yourself whether the reader needs more background. Supply any missing information.

Model: Revising to Address Knowledge Level of Readers

Yeats uses the Sphinx, a mythological figure with the body of a lion and the head of a person, to symbolize the era before Christ.

When Yeats describes the Sphinx, he creates a dreamlike image.

The writer realizes that readers need more background on the Sphinx and so adds this sentence.

WG Prentice Hall Writing and Grammar Connection: Chapter 14, Section 4

❹ Extension Activities

Listening and Speaking Deliver an **oral interpretation** of one poem from each of the following Irish poets: Yeats, J. M. Synge, George Russell ("A.E."), and James Stephens.

- Focus on pacing and volume, speaking slowly and loudly enough for listeners.
- Read with the meaning of the poem in mind, finding and emphasizing words that carry the weight of each image or idea.
- Read expressively, but do not let expression overwhelm the music or sense of the verse.

Research and Technology Referring to "Sailing to Byzantium," develop three specific research questions about Byzantine society and art. Carry out your research, and develop a **visual display** presenting some of Byzantium's treasures, showing their connection to Yeats's poem and the aspects of Byzantine culture they illustrate.

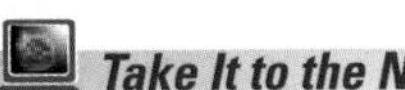

www.phschool.com

Go online for an additional research activity using the Internet.

ASSESSMENT RESOURCES

The following resources can be used to assess students' knowledge and skills.

Selection Assessment

- **Formal Assessment,** pp. 225–227
- **Open Book Test,** pp. 132–134
- **Test Bank Software**
- **Got It! Assessment Videotapes,** Tape 5

Visit www.phschool.com for self-tests and additional questions on the selections.

PRENTICE HALL ASSESSMENT SYSTEM

CD-ROM

Lesson Support for p. 977

❸ Writing Lesson

- Before students begin their writing project, ask them to read the criticism through once to form a general impression of the critic's intent.
- Caution students not to look for details that support the critic's claim or details that refute the claim. Ask students to form their own opinion after they have gathered all the facts.
- During the drafting portion of the activity, remind students to place references in logical order, such as those from one poem together, followed by those from another poem.

❹ Listening and Speaking

- Play readings of Yeats's poems on the **Listening to Literature Audiocassette.** Have students analyze the readings by focusing on pace, volume, and emphasis.
- Point out that the readers pause according to the punctuation of the poem, not automatically at the end of every line.
- Encourage students to select a poem that has personal meaning or that provokes a strong personal response.
- Allow students to rehearse the poem and mark up a photocopy of it to indicate pauses and stresses.
- Have students briefly introduce their chosen poet to listeners; then have them present their readings.

CUSTOMIZE INSTRUCTION For Universal Access

To address different learning styles, use the following activities suggested in the **Extension Activities** booklet, p. 45.

- For Bodily/Kinesthetic and Musical/Rhythmic Learners, use Activity 5.
- For Verbal/Linguistic and Visual/Spatial Learners, use Activity 6.
- For Visual/Spatial Learners, use Activity 7.

Preludes ✦ Journey of the Magi ✦ The Hollow Men

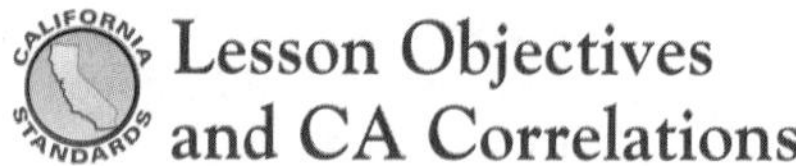

Lesson Objectives and CA Correlations

1. **To analyze and respond to literary elements**
   - Literary Analysis: Modernism **R 3.7**
   - Comparing Literary Works **R 3.4**
2. **To read, comprehend, analyze, and critique a poem**
   - Reading Strategy: Interpreting
   - Reading Check Questions
   - Review and Assess Questions
3. **To develop word analysis skills, fluency, and systematic vocabulary**
   - Vocabulary Development Lesson: Latin Root *-fract-* **R 1.1, 1.2**
4. **To understand and apply written and oral language conventions**
   - Spelling Strategy **LC 1.2**
   - Grammar and Style Lesson: Adjectival Modifiers **LC 1.1**
5. **To understand and apply appropriate writing and research strategies**
   - Writing Lesson: Response to Criticism **W 1.1, 1.9, 2.2**
   - Extension Activity: Cultural Report **W 1.8**
   - Assessment Practice (ATE)
6. **To understand and apply listening and speaking strategies**
   - Extension Activity: Debate on Modernism **LS 1.5**

STEP-BY-STEP TEACHING GUIDE	PACING GUIDE
PRETEACH	
Motivate Students and Provide Background	
Use the Motivation activity (ATE p. 978)	5 min.
Read and discuss author and background features (SE pp. 978, 980, 981, 984, 986–988, 989, 991; ATE pp. 978, 980, 981, 986, 987, 988, 989, 991) A	5 min.
Introduce the Concepts	
Introduce the Literary Analysis and Reading Strategy (SE/ATE p. 979) A	15 min.
Pronounce the vocabulary words and read their definitions (SE p. 979)	5 min.
TEACH	
Monitor Comprehension	
Informally monitor comprehension by circulating while students read independently or in groups A	25 min.
Monitor students' comprehension with the Reading Check notes (SE/ATE pp. 989, 991)	as students read
Develop vocabulary with Vocabulary notes (SE pp. 984, 985, 990, 991; ATE p. 984)	as students read
Develop Understanding	
Develop students' understanding of Modernism with the Literary Analysis annotations (SE p. 982; ATE pp. 982, 991) A	5 min.
Develop students' ability to interpret with the Reading Strategy annotations (SE/ATE pp. 985, 990)	5 min.
ASSESS	
Assess Mastery	
Assess students' mastery of the Reading Strategy and Literary Analysis by having them answer the Review and Assess questions (SE/ATE p. 993)	20 min.
Use one or more of the print and media Assessment Resources (ATE p. 995) A	up to 45 min.
EXTEND	
Apply Understanding	
Have students complete the Vocabulary Development Lesson and the Grammar and Style Lesson (SE p. 994) A	20 min.
Apply students' ability to use details as support using the Writing Lesson (SE/ATE p. 995) A	45 min.
Apply students' understanding using one or more of the Extension Activities (SE p. 995)	20–90 min.

A **ACCELERATED INSTRUCTION:** Use the strategies and activities identified with an .

UNIVERSAL ACCESS
● = Below-Level Students
▲ = On-Level Students
■ = Above-Level Students

Time and Resource Manager

Reading Level: Average, Easy, Challenging
Average Number of Instructional Days: 4

RESOURCES		
PRINT	**TRANSPARENCIES**	**TECHNOLOGY**
• **Beyond Literature,** Cross-Curricular Connection: Music, p. 46 ▲ ■		• **Interest Grabber Video,** Tape 6 ● ▲ ■
• **Selection Support Workbook:** ● ▲ ■ Literary Analysis, p. 218 Reading Strategy, p. 217 Build Vocabulary, p. 215	• **Literary Analysis and Reading Transparencies,** pp. 91 and 92 ● ▲ ■	
• **Adapted Reader's Companion** ● • **Reader's Companion** ●		
• **English Learner's Companion** ● ▲ • **Literatura en español** ● ▲ • **Literary Analysis for Enrichment** ■		
• **Formal Assessment:** Selection Test, pp. 228–230 ● ▲ ■ • **Open Book Test,** pp. 135–137 ● ▲ ■ • PRENTICE HALL ASSESSMENT SYSTEM ● ▲ ■	• PRENTICE HALL ASSESSMENT SYSTEM ● ▲ ■ Skills Practice Answers and Explanations on Transparencies ● ▲ ■	• **Test Bank Software** ● ▲ ■ • **Got It! Assessment Videotapes,** Tape 5 ● ▲
• **Selection Support Workbook:** ● ▲ ■ Grammar and Style, p. 216 • **Writing and Grammar,** Diamond Level ● ▲ ■ • **Extension Activities,** p. 46 ● ▲ ■	• **Daily Language Practice Transparencies** ● ▲	• **Writing and Grammar iText CD-ROM** ● ▲ ■ ***Take It to the Net*** www.phschool.com

BLOCK SCHEDULING: Use one 90-minute class period to preteach the selections and have students read them. Use a second 90-minute class period to assess students' mastery of skills and have them complete one of the Extension Activities.

PRETEACH

Step-by-Step Teaching Guide for pp. 978–979

Motivation

People who punch the clock every day and wonder what they do it for. People who can't encounter something new without asking, "I don't know, what do *you* think?" For Eliot, this kind of uncertainty and despair characterizes life in modern times. Point out to students that Eliot's diagnosis of modern ills might be confirmed by the number of "answers" available today. Have students bring in examples (from advertisements, books, film, or their own lives) of modern responses to despair. Discuss what these alternatives—psychiatry, crystals, yoga, exercise, religious reawakening, health food—have in common and how they seek to calm the despair in modern life.

Interest Grabber Video

As an alternative, play "'Preludes': T. S. Eliot" on Tape 6 to engage student interest.

❶ Background

More About the Author

Eliot had a definite affinity for both the metaphysical poets of the seventeenth century (primarily John Donne) and the nineteenth-century French symbolists (including Baudelaire and Laforgue). He combined these influences with the post–World War I generation, whose values and conventions were born of the Victorian era but changed by the harsh realities of war. The later influence of orthodox Christianity turned him more toward social and religious conservatism.

Prepare to Read

❶ Preludes ◆ Journey of the Magi ◆ The Hollow Men

T. S. Eliot (1888–1965)

T. S. Eliot was the most famous English poet of his time. He was also the most influential. His distinctive style and novel ideas affected not only poets, but also critics, fiction writers, playwrights, and even philosophers. From the 1920s on, he was a leader of the artistic movement called Modernism. Eliot and fellow Modernist Ezra Pound transformed English-language poetry, grounding their work in the power of images rather than in individual sentiment.

Eliot's poetry is sometimes difficult to understand because it is filled with subtle, even obscure allusions to myth, history, religion, and other literature. His themes, however, are universal. In his poems, plays, and essays, he raises fundamental questions about human aspirations and the nature of civilized society.

Crossing the Atlantic Born Thomas Stearns Eliot in St. Louis, Missouri, he was educated at prestigious Harvard University. He went on to study at Oxford University in England and at the Sorbonne in Paris. The outbreak of World War I in 1914 found Eliot in England, where he lived for most of his adult life, eventually becoming a citizen of Britain.

In 1915, Eliot married the sensitive, intelligent, and witty Vivien Haigh-Wood. While writing poetry and critical reviews, Eliot taught school, worked for the banking firm of Lloyd's, and in 1925 took an editorial position with the publishing company that became Faber and Faber.

Early Work Because of its unconventional style, Eliot's earliest work was greeted with less than universal acclaim, although the American poet Ezra Pound, who was also living in England during this period, was a vocal supporter from the beginning. Pound saw that Eliot spoke in an authentic new voice and offered an original, if bleak, vision. From *Prufrock and Other Observations* (1917) through *The Waste Land* (1922) and "The Hollow Men" (1925), Eliot portrayed the modern world as one of fragmented experiences and despair. Eliot may have been responding to World War I, an event that damaged the faith of many. At the same time, the war may have prompted readers to catch up with Eliot, who had written works such as "Preludes" and "The Love Song of J. Alfred Prufrock" before the war.

A Spiritual Rebirth Eventually, Eliot found an answer to despair in religion. In 1927, he joined the Church of England and became a devout Anglican. His new faith shaped the writing of "Journey of the Magi" (1927), *Ash Wednesday* (1930), and the *Four Quartets* (1935–1943), which he completed during World War II.

As he grew older, Eliot turned his attention increasingly to poetic drama and literary criticism. Although the verse plays *Murder in the Cathedral* (1935) and *The Cocktail Party* (1950) are often performed, none of his plays have gained the critical admiration accorded his poetry. As a literary critic, though, Eliot had a profound influence on his contemporaries. His re-evaluations of past poetry shaped the tastes of a generation. In 1948, the same year in which his philosophical work *Notes Toward the Definition of Culture* appeared, Eliot received the Nobel Prize for Literature.

Poet's Corner In 1967, on the second anniversary of Eliot's death, a memorial to the poet was unveiled in the Poet's Corner of Westminster Abbey in London. In this gesture, Eliot's status as one of the most significant voices in twentieth-century English literature was confirmed in stone.

TEACHING RESOURCES

The following resources can be used to enrich or extend the instruction for pp. 978–979.

Motivation

Interest Grabber Video, Tape 6

Background

Beyond Literature, p. 46

Take It to the Net
Visit www.phschool.com for background and hotlinks for more about T. S. Eliot.

Literary Analysis

Literary Analysis and Reading Transparencies, Modernism, p. 92

Selection Support: Literary Analysis, p. 218

Reading

Literary Analysis and Reading Transparencies, Interpret, p. 91

Selection Support: Reading Strategy, p. 217

BLOCK SCHEDULING: Resources marked with this symbol provide varied instruction during 90-minute blocks.

Preview

Connecting to the Literature

Long before special effects and music videos, Modernist poets were cutting rapidly from one image to another, creating dreamlike sequences rich with implied meaning. Eliot's poems are masterpieces of this technique.

❷ Literary Analysis

Modernism

Modernism was an early twentieth-century movement in the arts, responding to the fragmented world created by mass society and industrialism. The work of Modernists is characterized by the following features:

- A new objectivity or impersonality, in which a work is built from images and allusions, not direct statements of thoughts and feelings
- A rejection of realistic depictions of life in favor of the use of images for artistic effect
- Critical attention to the spiritual troubles of modern life

In "Preludes," for example, the image "The showers beat / On broken blinds . . ." indirectly expresses the sadness of a world deprived of spiritual life. As you read, notice the Modernist characteristics of these poems.

Comparing Literary Works

Eliot applies the spirit and techniques of Modernism in various ways.

- "Preludes" juxtaposes snapshots of modern city life to convey a sense of its futility and spiritual exhaustion.
- "Journey of the Magi" takes the conventional form of a dramatic speech, yet it is also imagistic and addresses spiritual homelessness.
- "The Hollow Men" juxtaposes snapshots, not from life, but from literature. It indicts the modern lack of passion and vision.

As you read, compare what each poem shows about Modernism.

❸ Reading Strategy

Interpreting

Modernist works may suggest themes without stating them directly. Readers must **interpret** these themes by linking different passages in a work and drawing conclusions from the patterns they find. Use a chart like the one shown to analyze patterns in the poems.

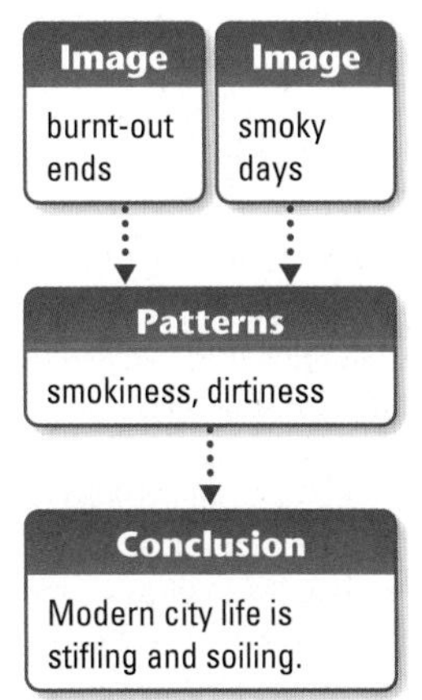

Vocabulary Development

galled (gôld) *adj.* injured or made sore by rubbing or chafing (p. 984)

refractory (ri frak′ tər ē) *adj.* hard to manage; stubborn (p. 984)

dispensation (dis′ pən sā′ shən) *n.* religious system or belief (p. 985)

supplication (sup′ lə kā′ shən) *n.* act of praying or pleading (p. 990)

tumid (to͞o′ mid) *adj.* swollen (p. 991)

CUSTOMIZE INSTRUCTION FOR UNIVERSAL ACCESS

For Special Needs Students	For Less Proficient Readers	For English Learners
Have students read the adapted version of "Journey of the Magi" in the **Adapted Reader's Companion.** This version provides basic-level instruction in an interactive format with questions and write-on lines. Completing the adapted version will prepare students to read the selection in the Student Edition.	Have students read "Journey of the Magi" in the **Reader's Companion.** This version provides basic-level instruction in an interactive format with questions and write-on lines. After students finish the selection in Reader's Companion, have them complete the questions and activities in the Student Edition.	Have students read the adapted version of "Journey of the Magi" in the **English Learner's Companion.** This version provides basic-level instruction in an interactive format with questions and write-on lines. Completing the adapted version will prepare students to read the selection in the Student Edition.

❷ Literary Analysis

Modernism

- Have students read the definition of modernism on p. 979 and discuss the features of the genre: objectivity and impersonality, rejection of realistic impressions, and attention to the spiritual.
- Remind students that objectivity denotes the lack of personal involvement: emotions should not play any role.
- Discuss how industrialism could be interpreted to have fragmented and depressed the general populace. Point out that assembly-line jobs were mundane, repetitious, and monotonous. Workers were often at the mercy of the employer in terms of low wages and long hours.
- Ask students to find examples of each modernistic trait as they read through the selections.

❸ Reading Strategy

Interpreting

- Help students understand that interpreting literary works is much like reading between the lines. They are looking for something that is not overtly stated in the work, but rather implied.
- Point out that while there is some leeway for differing opinions about the correct interpretation, students should look for clues that will help them determine the general theme and meaning of each selection.
- Demonstrate how patterns in a poem can lead to an interpretation of the poet's intent by following the example shown in the graphic organizer. Encourage students to make other similar charts to help them interpret each poem.

Vocabulary Development

- Pronounce each vocabulary word for students and read the definitions as a class. Have students identify any words with which they are already familiar.

E-Teach

Visit E-Teach at www.phschool.com for teachers' essays on how to teach, with questions and answers.

TEACH

Background

World War I and Culture

- Explain to students that World War I challenged public preconceptions about war.
- The war introduced new technologies, such as poison gas and barbed wire, and tactics, such as trench warfare. War could no longer be seen as heroic combat between individuals. Death came as mass slaughter; glory was replaced by waiting and suffering in the muddy trenches.
- By undermining heroic ideas of war, World War I shone an unflattering light on public life. The specter of the anonymous individual, a mere number in the state's calculations, was born.

  Use this question for discussion:

  Traditional speakers in literature spoke with authority about their lives or culture. Why might World War I have moved writers to experiment with forms that replaced the traditional speaker?
  Possible response: The anonymity of the war implied that the significance individuals saw in life was illusory. Writers turned to forms that registered this crisis in meaning.

Background

Subject and Object in Art

- Write the following chart on the chalkboard:

  Conrad: *stories about a person telling a story*

  Woolf: *stories about a person's train of thought*

  Eliot: *poems composed from "anonymous" images*

  Joyce: *stories in which an individual is disillusioned*

Use the following question for discussion:

Explain how each writer discovered a new subjectivity or a new objectivity in literature.
Possible response: Conrad: focused on the subjectivity of storytelling; Woolf: based stories in subjective experience; Eliot: eliminated subjectivity by treating words as objects (allusions and images); Joyce: dramatized the destruction of subjective illusion by an indifferent objective world.

A Closer Look

Modernism and Beyond

At the beginning of the twentieth century, the world woke up and discovered that it had changed. Electricity, engines, telephones, radios—the globe sizzled and crackled with new energy. Airplanes, machine guns, chemical warfare—human beings were now equipped to destroy each other with horrendous efficiency. The First World War (1914–1918) claimed ten million lives. The Russian Revolution foreshadowed deep international political changes. Disillusionment with established standards in politics and society was common.

In this climate of change and uncertainty, artists broke with the past and began to pursue new ideals and visions. They began to see themselves not just as preservers of culture but as creators of culture; they did not simply follow traditions, but participated in the creation of new ones.

The dramatic trends in the arts in the early twentieth century are collectively known as Modernism (1890–1945). For a basic grasp of Modernism, you might start with one simple modern development: the photograph.

Photographs and Images A photograph is a window into the past. When you take a photograph, you record what is happening now. Years later, the photograph will still tell you exactly what the world looked like at that moment.

Modernism could be thought of as a complex response to what photographs imply. On the one hand, Modernists such as the American poet Ezra Pound (1885–1972) and the British poet T. S. Eliot wrote poetry as if they were taking snapshots of the world and then cutting and pasting them into collages. Eliot celebrated what he called objectivity in poetry. Eliminating the outpourings of sentiment or the dramatic speeches of past poetry, he relied on images, well-chosen and artfully rendered, to encapsulate a feeling or perspective.

On the other hand, the British Modernist novelist Virginia Woolf perfected techniques for conveying an individual's moment-by-moment experience. For Woolf, the mind is like a camera filming continuously. Unlike a camera, though, her writing does not record the moment—it records what the moment looks like to an individual. In a way, her idea is the exact opposite of a photograph. A photograph shows us exactly what the world looks like; Woolf suggests that what the world looks like depends on who is looking.

Visual Arts Photography makes a good analogy for Modernist literary developments. It had a clear impact on painting. Photography now had the job of recording literal appearances, so artists were freed from the necessity of directly imitating the look of things. The revolutionary French painter Paul Cézanne (1839–1906) began to emphasize the canvas as a two-dimensional arrangement of form and color. His work led to the innovations of Modernists such as Pablo Picasso (1881–1973). In 1907, Picasso created a stir by unveiling *Les Desmoiselles d'Avignon*, the first Cubist painting—a picture in which multiple perspectives on the subject are depicted simultaneously.

ENRICHMENT: Visual Arts Connection

Photography

The first successful technologies for photography were introduced by Louis-Jacques-Mandé Daguerre (1789–1851) in 1839. Daguerrotypes, images created using his process, introduced a broad public to the possibilities of recording the moment. In addition to its personal use, such as providing families with portraits, photography quickly took on a public dimension. Pioneers such as Mathew Brady (1823–1896) used the camera as a tool to record contemporary events. The Photo-Secession group, led by Alfred Stieglitz (1864–1946), brought photography to the status of a fine art. In their footsteps, Paul Strand (1890–1976) and others explored the potential of the medium for abstract composition. By contrast, Henri Cartier-Bresson (b.1908) celebrated the "discoveries"—the humor or beauty of a moment— made by squeezing the shutter at the right time in the right place.

Past and Present Time is a central theme of Modernism. The word *modern* comes from the Latin word modus, meaning "just now." The "Modern" period, then, includes any event that has recently passed. A photographer is quite "modern": He or she captures whatever has happened just now. Every moment is equal to every other, another present to be captured. Yet Eliot was deeply preoccupied with the thought that the past and present are quite unequal. In a poem like "Journey of the Magi" (p. 984), Eliot portrays the present as a time of despair, an emptiness left behind when the past has disappeared.

Modernism	Postmodernism
• Viewed the massive casualties of World War I as undercutting pretensions to rationality and civilization	• Viewed World War II, with the Holocaust and the dropping of the A-bomb, as undercutting assumptions of life's meaning
• Influenced by Freud's studies of the unconscious and a new interest in the art of primitive peoples	• Influenced by studies of media and language and by the explosive growth of information technology
• Confidence that the work of art is a unique and powerful creation with its own individual aura	• Conviction that culture endlessly duplicates and copies itself
• Belief that "high" culture and "low" culture are separated by a meaningful dividing line and that a work of fine art is inherently superior to a cartoon	• Loss of belief in the meaningful dividing line between "high" culture and "low" culture, so that in Pop Art, the subject matter of fine art can be a cartoon

Making the New At the same time that Eliot seemed to mourn the past, Modernism also turned toward the future. Modernist fiction writers broke with traditional narrative methods. Describing how characters saw their lives became more important than constructing a traditional plot, and endings were sometimes unresolved. Joseph Conrad (1857–1924), for example, a precursor to Modernist novelists, used abrupt shifts of time and space and multiple points of view, echoing Woolf's concern with the power of individual perspective to shape reality. Modernist poets, too, favored experimentation over traditional forms and rhyme schemes. Their poems draw images from a variety of sources such as history, everyday life, and other texts and cultures.

Music Around the year 1900, important changes were also taking place in music. Like Modernist literature and art, much of this music, by composers such as Arnold Schoenberg (1874–1951) and Igor Stravinsky (1882–1971), breaks with traditional ideas and prescribes its own methods for composition. In music, the power of the artist to create as well as implement rules is especially clear.

Beyond Modernism The Modernist literary movement climaxed in 1922, when both James Joyce's *Ulysses* and T. S. Eliot's *The Waste Land* were published. In ensuing decades, the arts took another turn in the developments known as Postmodernism (see chart), a movement that replaced the hopes Modernism placed on innovative artistic breakthroughs with a sometimes cynical questioning of the nature of art and perception. The Modernist legacy lives on, though, in the continuing drive for the new.

▲ **Critical Viewing**
Which themes listed on the chart are reflected in contemporary television programs? Explain your choices. **[Connect]**

CUSTOMIZE INSTRUCTION FOR UNIVERSAL ACCESS

For Less Proficient Readers	For Gifted / Talented Students	For Advanced Readers
Have students read Modernism and Beyond. As they read the "Preludes" on p. 982, have them identify images that suggest photographs or collages of photographs. In a group discussion, have students share passages and discuss the impact of these anonymous snapshots of life.	Have students read Modernism and Beyond. After they have read the "Preludes" on p. 982, have them create collages of photographs reflecting the spirit of Eliot's city. In a group discussion, have students explain which passages in the poem are reflected in their collages.	Have students read Modernism and Beyond. Then, have them read the "Preludes" on p. 982, Arnold's "Dover Beach" on p. 884, and "Progress in Personal Comfort," p. 900. Have them present comparisons of the speaker and theme of each work, taking into account historical context. Hold a class discussion of the presentations.

Background

Postmodernism

- Explain to students that, while Modernists created new forms, Postmodernists throw the concept of form into question.
- Key Postmodernist devices include quotation and context-shift. Roy Lichtenstein (1923–1997), for instance, quotes from popular culture by painting comic strip panels, raising the question: Is this a painting of a scene or a painting of a comic book drawing? Marcel Duchamp (1887–1968) lined a spoon and bowl with fur. By rendering these objects useless and exhibiting them, he changed their context from the dinner table to the museum.
- Postmodernism might be interpreted as persistent irony in response to meaninglessness. Alternatively, it might be seen as the isolation of the moment at which an object is born as art.

Critical Thinking

1. Compare Picasso's work and Woolf's narrative technique.
   Possible responses: Both underscore the fact that experience is always filtered through a perspective.
2. Why is Modernist art more suited to modern life than an epic that tells of a culture's hero?
   Possible response: An epic assumes clear ideas of the significance of action. In the modern era, the significance of action is often unclear.
3. Does every era consider itself "modern"? Explain.
   Possible response: Yes, every era contrasts itself with a lost past and a hopeful future; no, our era is more preoccupied with novelty than any other era.

▶Critical Viewing

Possible response: Postmodern television includes self-conscious reflections on the medium (as when the host throws a pencil at the camera) or blurrings of the line between reality and script (as on "reality" shows, where it is unclear which actions are spontaneous and which are motivated by the camera's presence).

TEACH

Step-by-Step Teaching Guide for pp. 982–992

CUSTOMIZE INSTRUCTION
For Visual/Spatial Learners

Have these students draw pictures of, or represent in some other media, the images presented in the selections. They may need to interpret the emotions and feelings, if any, of the people in each poem.

❶ About the Selection

This poem presents a bleak and despairing vision of the world—a world in which suffering, grime, and dreariness are the main features. Yet, Eliot may not just have been reveling in despair: He may have seen it as a necessary "prelude" to spiritual awakening. Each segment, or prelude, describes a different urban scene: a cold, smoky winter evening in a run-down neighborhood; the morning routine of facing yet another hopeless day; a dream-filled night spent in misery. In Prelude IV, though a new note is sounded—that of something "infinitely gentle/ Infinitely suffering."

❷ Literary Analysis

Modernism

- Remind students that modernism is frequently based on the despair of the people. Have them point out words that Eliot uses to create this feeling.
- Discuss how this stanza demonstrates the modernistic trait of objectivity. Have students note that none of the people mentioned are mentioned by name or as individuals.
- Ask students the Literary Analysis question on p. 982: What fragmented images of a city scene appear in this stanza?
  Answer: The images include stale smells, muddy streets, people buying coffee at a vendor's stand, and poor people raising the blinds to look out at the day.

❶ PRELUDES

T. S. Eliot

I

The winter evening settles down
With smell of steaks[1] in passageways.
Six o'clock.
The burnt-out ends of smoky days.
And now a gusty shower wraps
The grimy scraps
Of withered leaves about your feet
And newspapers from vacant lots;
The showers beat
On broken blinds and chimney-pots,
And at the corner of the street
A lonely cab-horse steams and stamps.
And then the lighting of the lamps.

II

❷ The morning comes to consciousness
Of faint stale smells of beer
From the sawdust-trampled street
With all its muddy feet that press
To early coffee-stands.
With the other masquerades
That time resumes,
One thinks of all the hands
That are raising dingy shades
In a thousand furnished rooms.

Literary Analysis
Modernism What fragmented images of a city scene appear in this stanza?

III

You tossed a blanket from the bed,
You lay upon your back, and waited;
You dozed, and watched the night revealing
The thousand sordid images
Of which your soul was constituted;
They flickered against the ceiling.
And when all the world came back

1. **steaks** In 1910, when this poem was composed, steaks were inexpensive and were commonly eaten by members of the lower class.

TEACHING RESOURCES

The following resources can be used to enrich or extend the instruction for pp. 982–992.

Literary Analysis
- **Selection Support:** Literary Analysis, p. 218
- **Literary Analysis for Enrichment,** p. 46

Reading
- **Adapted Reader's Companion**
- **Reader's Companion**
- **English Learner's Companion**

And the light crept up between the shutters
And you heard the sparrows in the gutters,
You had such a vision of the street
As the street hardly understands;
Sitting along the bed's edge, where
You curled the papers from your hair,
Or clasped the yellow soles of feet
In the palms of both soiled hands.

IV

His soul stretched tight across the skies
That fade behind a city block,
Or trampled by insistent feet
At four and five and six o'clock;
And short square fingers stuffing pipes,
And evening newspapers, and eyes
Assured of certain certainties,
The conscience of a blackened street
Impatient to assume the world.

I am moved by fancies that are curled
Around these images, and cling:
The notion of some infinitely gentle
Infinitely suffering thing.

Wipe your hands across your mouth, and laugh;
The worlds revolve like ancient women
Gathering fuel in vacant lots.

Review and Assess

Thinking About the Selection

1. **Respond:** Does the poem make beauty from ugliness? Explain.
2. **(a) Recall:** In Prelude I, what is the time of year and the time of day? **(b) Interpret:** What cycle of time takes place from Prelude I to Prelude IV? **(c) Support:** What effect does the poet achieve by representing this complete cycle?
3. **(a) Draw Conclusions:** What is the character of modern life as Eliot depicts it? **(b) Compare and Contrast:** Contrast this character with "The notion of some infinitely gentle / Infinitely suffering thing" (lines 50–51)? **(c) Speculate:** Based on this contrast, what do you think the "thing" might be?
4. **Apply:** Think of a sight in a modern city that conveys joy. How might Eliot react to that image?

Answers for p. 983

Review and Assess

1. Possible response: No, the poem does not create beauty from ugliness, but the last stanza does offer some hope that the cycle of despair and hopelessness can be broken.
2. **(a)** It is winter, at 6 P.M. **(b)** The cycle of time is one day, from evening through the night to morning and back to evening. **(c)** The poet implies that life is a never-ending cycle and, by doing so, reinforces the mood of despair.
3. **(a)** The general character of modern life is monotony, lack of individualism, and lack of spiritual hope. **(b)** The lines paint a different picture by introducing the idea of compassion and gentleness, creating a small amount of hope that the cycle will be broken. **(c)** Possible responses: The "thing" might be Christ; it might be humanity taken in its totality.
4. Sample response: A fountain in a park might inspire joy. Eliot might convert it, though, into an image of despair by noting the litter floating in it (for example).

CUSTOMIZE INSTRUCTION FOR UNIVERSAL ACCESS

For Less Proficient Readers	For English Learners	For Advanced Readers
Help these students access Eliot's poem by directing them to focus on his mood, rather than on literal meaning. Explain that, like a musical prelude to a longer work, each of these preludes establishes a mood. Give students some signposts to that mood by pointing out words such as "withered," "soiled," and "vacant."	English learners may have difficulty reading beyond the literal translation of the words. Help them select a few words in each line and find each meaning. Then, have them think about what kind of picture they would describe using these words. Finally, ask them to think about the mood of each line, according to the pictures in their minds.	Tell these students that about the time Eliot was writing these poems in the United States, Ezra Pound was helping to create the Imagist movement in England. That movement favored briefer poems, concrete descriptions, deletion of unnecessary words, and the use of free verse rather than the traditional meters.

❸ About the Selection

The speaker, one of the three biblical wise men who honor the baby Jesus, recounts the practical challenges and physical discomforts of the long journey to Bethlehem. By affiliating those discomforts with the religious awakening of Christianity, the speaker acknowledges the difficulties of spiritual growth and change.

❹ Vocabulary Development

Latin Root *-fract-*

- Point out the word *refractory* in line 6. Tell students that the word means "to break."
- Have students suggest other words that contain the root *-fract-*. Possible responses: Such words include *fracture, fraction,* and *fractious.*
- Then, encourage students to use a dictionary to find out how the meaning of this root contributes to the specific meaning of each word.

Background

In his work, Eliot often uses *allusions*—indirect references to people, places, events, or works of literature. "Journey of the Magi," for instance, is a dramatic monologue spoken by one of the three wise men ("magi") who, according to the Bible, visited the infant Jesus. In the poem, the speaker uses modern conversational language to describe events, making vividly present the spiritual agony of a man who lived long ago.

"A cold coming we had of it,
Just the worst time of the year
For a journey, and such a long journey:
The ways deep and the weather sharp,
The very dead of winter."[1]
❹ And the camels galled, sore-footed, refractory,
Lying down in the melting snow.
There were times we regretted
The summer palaces on slopes, the terraces,
And the silken girls bringing sherbet.
Then the camel men cursing and grumbling
And running away, and wanting their liquor and women,
And the night-fires going out, and the lack of shelters,
And the cities hostile and the towns unfriendly
And the villages dirty and charging high prices:
A hard time we had of it.
At the end we preferred to travel all night,
Sleeping in snatches,
With the voices singing in our ears, saying
That this was all folly.

galled (gôld) *adj.* injured or made sore by rubbing or chafing

refractory (ri frak′ tər ē) *adj.* hard to manage; stubborn

1. **"A . . . winter"** Adapted from a part of a sermon delivered by 17th-century Bishop Lancelot Andrewes: "A cold coming they had of it at this time of year, just the worst time of the year to take a journey, and specially a long journey in. The ways deep, the weather sharp, the days short, the sun farthest off . . . the very dead of winter."

ENRICHMENT: Cultural Connection

The Magi

In many Christian churches, the Magi who visited the baby Jesus on his twelfth day of life are honored almost as much as Jesus himself. The commemoration of their visit, called Epiphany, is celebrated on January 6 with feasting, bright lights, religious services, and gift-giving. In Cataluna, in eastern Spain, children spend the day banging on drums and blowing tin whistles to make sure the gift-giving kings don't pass their own town over. Throughout the Spanish-speaking world, *El Día de los Reyes,* "The Day of Kings," is celebrated with a parade in which stand-ins for the three kings ride camels through the streets. In the United States, such a parade can be seen in Latino communities such as those in New York City.

Tell students that people of many religions undertake pilgrimages. Have students share their knowledge of such journeys gleaned from their own knowledge and encyclopedia research. What common features exist among the many pilgrimages discussed?

❺ Then at dawn we came down to a temperate valley,
Wet, below the snow line, smelling of vegetation;
With a running stream and a water-mill beating the darkness,
And three trees on the low sky,
And an old white horse galloped away in the meadow.
Then we came to a tavern with vine-leaves over the lintel,
Six hands at an open door dicing for pieces of silver,
And feet kicking the empty wine-skins.
But there was no information, and so we continued
And arrived at evening, not a moment too soon
Finding the place; it was (you may say) satisfactory.

All this was a long time ago, I remember,
And I would do it again, but set down
This set down
This: were we led all that way for
Birth or Death? There was a Birth, certainly,
We had evidence and no doubt. I had seen birth and death,
But had thought they were different; this Birth was
Hard and bitter agony for us, like Death, our death.
We returned to our places, these Kingdoms,
But no longer at ease here, in the old dispensation,
With an alien people clutching their gods.
I should be glad of another death.

Reading Strategy
Interpreting Why might Eliot use a pattern of specific, ordinary details in a description of this important event?

dispensation (dis′ pən sā′ shən) *n.* religious system or belief

Review and Assess

Thinking About the Selection

1. **Respond:** Do you feel sympathy for the speaker? Explain.
2. **(a) Recall:** What event has the speaker in "Journey of the Magi" gone to witness? **(b) Compare and Contrast:** How do the descriptions of the journey compare to that of the descriptions of the event? **(c) Interpret:** Why might the speaker say so little about one and so much about the other?
3. **(a) Interpret:** How has the event changed the speaker's relation to his own people? **(b) Draw Conclusions:** Consider the speaker's own religious traditions. What does he mean when he says "this Birth was/ . . . like Death, our death." (lines 38–39)?
4. **(a) Compare and Contrast:** In what way is Eliot's choice of details similar in the first stanzas of "Preludes" and "Journey of the Magi"? **(b) Draw Conclusions:** What do you think Eliot was trying to achieve in each case?
5. **(a) Apply:** Do you think that modern society would make poets like Eliot feel as the speaker in the poem does? Explain.

CUSTOMIZE INSTRUCTION FOR UNIVERSAL ACCESS

For Special Needs Students	For Gifted/Talented Students	For Advanced Readers
Be sure that students understand that the Magi are the three wise men from Christian stories. Have students relate what they may know about the three wise men, from pictures, from song, or through religious teachings. Prepare them for the difference between the conventional picture of the Magi and the picture Eliot presents.	Those students with an interest in drama and theater might like the chance to perform this poem. Have students write a monologue from the point of view of one of the Magi that tells, in common modern language, of the journey undertaken. Some students may like to match Eliot's view, while others may wish to present a different view.	Eliot makes no mention of the traditional gifts the Magi bore for Jesus: gold, frankincense, and myrrh. Have students research these substances and determine whether they would have supported Eliot's view of the events in the poem.

❺ Reading Strategy

Interpreting

- Have students read the first stanza, and ask what "this" the speaker is referring to in the last line (line 20). Help them interpret the meaning as the long, difficult journey of the Magi and the promise of witnessing the birth of a savior.
- Then, ask the Reading Strategy question on p. 985: Why might Eliot use a pattern of specific, ordinary details in a description of this important event?
  Answer: He might use ordinary details to make the event more human and more within reach for the common person.

Answers for p. 985

Review and Assess

1. Students may say that they feel some sympathy because the trip was obviously a difficult one.
2. **(a)** They had made the journey to witness a birth. **(b)** The journey shows many different places, each different, and each in detail. The birth is rather glossed over. **(c)** Possible responses: The speaker has yet to be able to evaluate the significance of the birth; the birth is too momentous to be readily put into words.
3. **(a)** The speaker is no longer at ease in his old surroundings because he does not share the beliefs of those around him. **(b)** The birth of the Magi's new spiritual consciousness requires the death of the Magi's existing religious beliefs.
4. **(a)** In both poems, he masses together fragmented details of scenes that he indicates are repeated. **(b)** Possible response: In "Preludes," these details suggest the meaninglessness of modern life; in "Magi," they create a sense of passing time and of expectancy: The jumbled events of the journey appear insignificant besides the journey's goal.
5. Possible response: The speaker does not share the beliefs of his fellows; a poet like Eliot would not fit in with people who are optimistic about or indifferent to spiritual questions.

Background

Religious Themes in "The Hollow Men"

- Explain to students that when Eliot wrote "The Hollow Men," he had already secured international renown with the publication of *The Waste Land* in 1922.
- In 1927, the year he published the volume containing "The Hollow Men," he also became an English citizen and entered the Anglican Church. The poetry he wrote after this point had a decidedly religious cast.
- One can already detect his religious interests, though, in "The Hollow Men," which is set in Hell and describes the damnation of those without sufficient spirit to commit evil.
- Eliot states some of the views implied in the poem in his critical writing. Read the class the following quotation, written by Eliot about Baudelaire:

  > It is better, in a paradoxical way, to do evil, than to do nothing: at least we exist. . . . The worst that can be said of most of our malefactors, from statesmen to thieves, is that they are not man enough to be damned.

  Use the following questions for discussion:

1. What might it mean to be a "malefactor" (wrongdoer) who is "not man enough to be damned"?
   Possible response: A malefactor who is not man enough to be damned might be one who does wrong hypocritically or with excuses, pretending that he or she has not really chosen to do evil.
2. Why might Eliot view those who choose evil (the "lost violent souls" of "The Hollow Men") more highly?
   Possible response: By acting as people who have made a choice, even if it is a choice for evil, these people affirm their own freedom, for good or evil.

A Closer Look

Critical Commentary on "The Hollow Men"

How It Was Written

T.S. Eliot had written a long poem called *The Waste Land*. He used sections that had been edited out of *The Waste Land* as the basis for "The Hollow Men." He often worked this way, building a poem from pieces that had been written independently and using discarded fragments of one poem to create the next.

He explained this process of working in a craft interview with Donald Hall (*The Paris Review*, No. 21). Hall begins this part of the interview by pointing out that two minor poems of Eliot's, probably "Eyes that last I saw in tears" and "The wind sprang up at four o'clock," sound to him like "The Hollow Men":

Interviewer. Are any of your minor poems actually sections cut out of longer works? There are two that sound like "The Hollow Men."

Eliot. Oh, those were the preliminary sketches. Those things were earlier. Others I published in periodicals but not in my collected poems . . .

Interviewer. You seem often to have written poems in sections. Did they begin as separate poems? I am thinking of "Ash Wednesday," in particular.

Eliot. Yes, like "The Hollow Men," it originated out of separate poems. As I recall, one or two early drafts of parts of "Ash Wednesday" appeared in *Commerce* [a magazine] and elsewhere. Then gradually I came to see it as a sequence. That's one way in which my mind does seem to have worked throughout the years poetically—doing things separately and then seeing the possibility of fusing them together, altering them, and making a kind of whole of them.

The Theme of "The Hollow Men"

It makes sense to assume that "The Hollow Men," which uses fragments discarded from *The Waste Land*, is thematically related to this earlier, longer poem. *The Waste Land*, as the word "waste" in its title suggests, deals with a

ENRICHMENT: Literature Connection

Dante's *Divine Comedy*

An important source of references in "The Hollow Men" is the *Divine Comedy,* a poem in three books by the thirteenth-century poet Dante Alighieri (1265–1321).

At the opening of the poem, Dante finds himself physically and spiritually "lost in the woods." He embarks on a quest for righteousness that takes him through Hell, Purgatory (where the dead may work off their sins), and Heaven. The Roman poet Virgil guides him through Hell. In Heaven, he meets his beloved, Beatrice.

Each book in the work, the *Inferno,* the *Purgatorio,* and the *Paradiso,* corresponds to a stage in Dante's journey and to a division of the afterlife in medieval Christianity. In the *Inferno,* Dante meets and speaks with a number of the damned, whose tortures he describes.

sense of emotional and spiritual barrenness after the destruction wrought by World War I. (Eliot began the poem in 1921, three years after the end of the war.) Throughout the poem, however, Eliot uses allusions to past works of literature in order to compare the present with other historical moments. "The Hollow Men," published in 1925, also deals with a barren and empty (hollow) existence. Although it is quieter than *The Waste Land* and less rhythmically varied, it resembles the earlier poem in its use of literary allusions to convey this theme of barrenness and to compare the present with other historical eras.

Using Allusions to Interpret the Poem

Critics have identified four key allusions in the poem:

- Joseph Conrad's story "Heart of Darkness"
- A historical reference to the Gunpowder Plot of 1605, in which Guy Fawkes and other Catholics seeking revenge for the anti-Catholic laws under James I plotted to blow up the king and Parliament
- Shakespeare's *Julius Caesar,* with its account of the assassination of Caesar
- Dante's *Divine Comedy,* a medieval Italian poem which describes the three realms of the afterlife according to Roman Catholic belief: inferno, purgatory, and paradise

More details about these allusions appear in specific footnotes to the poem. The following information explains how to use the allusions to build meaning from this difficult work.

Joseph Conrad's "Heart of Darkness" Kurtz, referred to in a line introducing the poem, is a mysterious character in Conrad's "Heart of Darkness." He travels to the Belgian Congo on a mission to uplift and educate the Congolese people. However, he develops his own little kingdom in which he exercises absolute power over the people he intended to save. It is only when he is dying that he sees the "horror" of what he has done and how he has been, in Conrad's words, a "hollow sham," or fake. Yet Kurtz is in some ways the best of the white men that Conrad's narrator encounters. His tragic downfall, therefore, exposes the hollowness of his noble ideals and of the whole colonial enterprise. That enterprise is supported by a host of administrators and clerks who seem like ghosts wandering in a twilight world. It is these men who are most like the

Background

Allusions in "The Hollow Men"

In 1935, after many had inquired, Eliot revealed the sources for the title, "The Hollow Men." He said that the title represents a combination of the titles of two poems by well-known British authors: "The Hollow Land" by William Morris (1834–1896) and "The Broken Man" by Rudyard Kipling (1865–1936).

B.C. Southam, in *A Guide to the Selected Poems of T.S. Eliot,* points out other possible sources for the title in two works that clearly influenced the poem:

- Shakespeare's *Julius Caesar* (IV.ii):

  But hollow men, like horses
  hot at hand,
  Make gallant show and promise
  of their mettle;
  But when they should endure
  the bloody spur;
  They fail their crests, and, like
  deceitful jades,
  Sink in the trial.

- Joseph Conrad's *Heart of Darkness:* As is mentioned in the student edition, Kurtz is called a "hollow sham" in Conrad's work.

CUSTOMIZE INSTRUCTION FOR UNIVERSAL ACCESS

For Less Proficient Readers	For Gifted/Talented Students	For Advanced Readers
Have students read Critical Commentary on "The Hollow Men." As they read "The Hollow Men," p. 989, have them enter allusions in the poem in a chart. Then, have them discuss the differences in reading the poem before and after charting these allusions.	Have students read Critical Commentary on "The Hollow Men" and "The Hollow Men," p. 989. Have them devise storyboards for a video based on the poem. Have them present their plans to the class, addressing the connection between Eliot's use of allusions and the use of rapid cuts between charged images in film.	Have students read Critical Commentary on "The Hollow Men" and "The Hollow Men," p. 989. Then, have them read one of the sources cited in the Commentary and give a presentation analyzing its tie with Eliot's poem. They should evaluate whether Eliot's allusions to the work add depth or obscurity to his own poem.

Background

Eliot's "Tradition and the Individual Talent"

- Explain that Eliot's essay "Tradition and the Individual Talent" has helped shaping modern perspectives on and tastes in literature.
- In the essay, Eliot discounts the idea that poetry expresses the poet's sentiments or personality.
- The essay suggests that it is by "concentrating" together ordinary experiences and emotions not ordinarily associated that art achieves its effects. Eliot concludes that "Poetry is not a turning loose of emotion, but an escape from emotion. . . ." and that "The emotion of art is impersonal."
- Eliot also argues that poetry is only ever understood by comparing and contrasting it with the body of significant works that precede it—a tradition.
- At the same time, while all works in a tradition form "a simultaneous order" among themselves, a significant new work alters that order. The arrival of Arthur Miller changes Shakespeare, if only because we can then appreciate the specific ways in which Shakespeare is not Miller.

Use the following question for discussion:

What connection can you see between Eliot's critical theory and his poetic practice in "The Hollow Men"?
Possible answer: By constructing the poem out of allusions, Eliot both celebrates the tradition he is drawing on and effaces his own personality, since the "speaker" of the poem barely exists.

Critical Thinking

1. What do Brutus and Fawkes have in common?
Possible response: Both are traitors who assassinate or attempt to assassinate a ruler.
2. Why are they a suitable contrast with the "hollow men"?
Possible response: They acted out of principles, however misguided. The "hollow men" drift through life without principle.

speakers in Eliot's poem, a chorus of paralyzed nonentities: "We are the hollow men. . . ." Eliot may also be suggesting that this chorus includes his readers.

The Gunpowder Plot The hollow men are also like the effigies of Guy Fawkes burned to commemorate the uncovering of the Gunpowder Plot. Fawkes himself was tortured until he revealed the names of his co-conspirators. His dream of a powerful explosion that would destroy the government of England was therefore not realized. As Eliot writes at the end of the poem, "This is the way the world ends / Not with a bang but a whimper." Just as Fawkes is now only a straw figure to be burned, so the speakers of Eliot's poem are as helpless and ineffective as straw dummies: "Leaning together / Headpiece filled with straw. Alas!"

Shakespeare's *Julius Caesar* This play deals with another conspiracy to betray a leader. Brutus, a high-minded Roman, is lured by flattery into a plot to assassinate the Roman ruler Julius Caesar. Section V of "The Hollow Men" quotes lines from Shakespeare's play in which Brutus experiences the nightmarelike emptiness of the time before the deed. Like Kurtz in Conrad's story, Brutus is a tragic figure, a self-deluded man who commits murder in the name of high ideals. In this sense, he too is a form of hollow man.

Dante's *Divine Comedy* Brutus is one of the betrayers that Dante punishes in the lowest circle of his inferno. The speakers in Eliot's poem are also being punished for their spiritual emptiness in a kind of inferno: a "dead land" (line 39); a "cactus land" (line 40); a "valley of dying stars" (line 54). It does not appear that these speakers will gain salvation, but Eliot uses images drawn from Dante's description of paradise to suggest the existence of higher realms: ". . . the perpetual star / Multifoliate rose . . ." (lines 63–64). "The Hollow Men" is therefore a poem about spiritual despair that contains only the slightest hints that such despair can be overcome. In terms of Dante's work, it is like an inferno (a realm of punishment) that is almost without the promise of a purgatory or a paradise.

Eliot's Theory of Tradition

Eliot's allusions create a distinctive, dreamlike world for a reader to explore. They also reflect his theory of poetry. In an essay, Eliot compares the poet to a catalyst in a chemical reaction. A catalyst adds nothing of itself, but without it, the reaction will not take place. The poet's mind is the catalyst that causes images and feelings to combine in a poem, but the poem does not necessarily reflect the poet's own life. For Eliot, a tradition of past literature was a key source of ingredients for the reaction. Eliot's allusions reflect both of these values: impersonality and tradition.

CUSTOMIZE INSTRUCTION FOR UNIVERSAL ACCESS

For Advanced Readers

Have these students read Eliot's essay "Tradition and the Individual Talent." Then, have them write their own essays summarizing Eliot's points and giving their own evaluation. Encourage them to consult commentaries that may help them understand the essay and its impact on later critics.

6 

T.S. Eliot

7 Background

As in "Journey of the Magi," Eliot uses allusions at the beginning of "The Hollow Men" to help him contrast the past with the present. For example, "A penny for the Old Guy" is a traditional cry of children on Guy Fawkes Day. Fawkes was executed for attempting to blow up the king and Parliament on November 5, 1605. He is one of the "lost / Violent souls" of the past who contrast with the "hollow men" of today.

Mistah Kurtz[1]*—he dead.*

A penny for the Old Guy[2]

I

We are the hollow men
We are the stuffed men
Leaning together
Headpiece filled with straw. Alas!
Our dried voices, when
We whisper together
Are quiet and meaningless
As wind in dry grass
Or rats' feet over broken glass
In our dry cellar

Shape without form, shade without color,
Paralyzed force, gesture without motion;

1. **Mistah Kurtz** character in Joseph Conrad's "Heart of Darkness" who hopes to improve the lives of native Africans, but who finds instead that he is corrupted by his power over them.
2. **A . . . Guy** traditional cry used by children on Guy Fawkes Day (November 5), celebrating the execution of a famous English traitor of the same name. The "Old Guy" refers to stuffed dummies representing Fawkes.

8  **Reading Check**

How does the speaker characterize the sounds made by the hollow men?

6 About the Selection

Perhaps the bleakest of the Eliot poems presented here, "The Hollow Men" describes a world in which people have no faith, no courage, no spirit, and no awareness. Spoken by the hollow men themselves, the poem is a self-portrait of the typical modern person.

7 Background

Eliot's Personal Trauma

In addition to the social and political changes of the modern post-World War I experience, Eliot had faced personal despair in caring for his deeply troubled first wife, Vivien Haigh-Wood. Haigh-Wood was ultimately unable to function in the world and spent her latter years in a psychiatric hospital.

8 Reading Check

Answer: The voices are characterized as quiet and meaningless.

CUSTOMIZE INSTRUCTION FOR UNIVERSAL ACCESS

For Less Proficient Readers	For Advanced Readers
To help less proficient readers navigate this difficult poem, suggest contemporary images of "hollow men": slackers, couch potatoes. Urge these students to identify the poem's speakers. As students read on, direct them to continually analyze the speakers' attitudes.	Point out the apparent contradictions in lines 11–12 of the poem. Have students think about the meaning of the contradictions and how each could be possible, if at all. Is it possible to have "shape without form"? If not, what is the meaning behind these images?

❾ Reading Strategy
Interpreting

- Direct students' attention to the footnote for line 14 at the bottom of the page. Students need not be familiar with *Paradiso* to understand the image Eliot wishes to convey.
- Discuss the speakers' reaction to those with "direct eyes."
- Have students determine how the hollow men wish to be remembered by those with "direct eyes." Help students understand that hollow men are not necessarily evil; they have simply not found the religious spirit that will make them complete.
- Then, ask students the Reading Strategy question on p. 990: What pattern of images does Eliot create in lines 13–21?
  Answer: The pattern of images involves speakers who are afraid of meeting the eyes of the blessed.

Those who have crossed
With direct eyes, to death's other Kingdom[3]
Remember us—if at all—not as lost
Violent souls, but only
As the hollow men
❾ The stuffed men.

II

Eyes I dare not meet in dreams
In death's dream kingdom
These do not appear:
There, the eyes are
Sunlight on a broken column
There, is a tree swinging
And voices are
In the wind's singing
More distant and more solemn
Than a fading star.
Let me be no nearer
In death's dream kingdom
Let me also wear
Such deliberate disguises
Rat's coat, crowskin, crossed staves
In a field[4]
Behaving as the wind behaves
No nearer—

Not that final meeting
In the twilight kingdom

III

This is the dead land
This is cactus land
Here the stone images
Are raised, here they receive
The supplication of a dead man's hand
Under the twinkle of a fading star.

Is it like this
In death's other kingdom
Waking alone
At the hour when we are
Trembling with tenderness
Lips that would kiss
Form prayers to broken stone.

Reading Strategy
Interpreting What pattern of images does Eliot create in lines 13–21?

supplication (sup′ lə kā′ shən) *n.* act of praying or pleading

3. **Those . . . kingdom** allusion to Dante's *Paradiso,* in which those "with direct eyes" are blessed by God in Heaven.
4. **crossed . . . field** scarecrows.

ENRICHMENT: Cultural Connection
Religious Imagery

The religious images in this poem are almost exclusively Christian. Christianity is a monotheistic religion, focused around the belief of one god. Judaism and Islam are both monotheistic as well, while Hinduism recognizes one supreme god amongst many lesser gods. Buddhists focus on human behavior rather than a god.

Despite differences amongst religions, they share many characteristics. Prayers, such as the Lord's Prayer alluded to by Eliot, are Judeo-Christian in origin; however, most religions include some form of prayer. This may include reciting words from a sacred book such as Islam's Koran or silent meditation. Many religions have important symbols as well, just as the star and rose are Christian symbols.

Have willing students share examples of prayer and symbols from religions they know. Discuss how these could be interchanged with Eliot's without losing the poet's central theme about the value of religion in human existence.

IV

The eyes are not here
There are no eyes here
In this valley of dying stars
In this hollow valley
This broken jaw of our lost kingdoms

In this last of meeting places
We grope together
And avoid speech
Gathered on this beach of the tumid river[5]

Sightless, unless
The eyes reappear
As the perpetual star[6]
Multifoliate rose[7]
Of death's twilight kingdom
The hope only
Of empty men.

V

11 *Here we go round the prickly pear*
Prickly pear prickly pear
Here we go round the prickly pear
At five o'clock in the morning.[8]

Between the idea
And the reality
Between the motion
And the act[9]
Falls the Shadow

For Thine is the Kingdom[10]

Between the conception
And the creation
Between the emotion
And the response
Falls the Shadow

5. **river** from Dante's *Inferno,* the river Acheron, which the dead cross on the way to Hell.
6. **star** traditional symbol for Christ.
7. **Multifoliate rose** rose with many leaves. Dante describes paradise as such a rose in his *Paradiso.* The rose is a traditional symbol for the Virgin Mary.
8. **Here . . . morning** adaptation of a common nursery rhyme. A prickly pear is a cactus.
9. **Between . . . act** reference to *Julius Caesar,* Act II, Scene i, 63–65: "Between the acting of a dreadful thing / And the first motion, all the interim is / Like a phantasma or hideous dream."
10. **For . . . Kingdom** from the ending of the Lord's Prayer.

The British Tradition

10 *The Literary Magazine*

No institution played a more important role in the development of Modernism than the literary magazine. These modest periodicals were published on both sides of the Atlantic. In England, Eliot founded *The Criterion* (later called *The New Criterion*) in 1922. The first issue featured Eliot's celebrated poem *The Waste Land.* In the United States, the premier literary magazine was *The Dial.* During the 1920s, it published the work of Eliot, W. B. Yeats, Ezra Pound, and D. H. Lawrence. Another important journal, *The Egoist,* serialized *A Portrait of the Artist as a Young Man,* James Joyce's first major work, in 1914 to 1915.

These literary magazines were grandchildren of eighteenth-century periodicals such as Joseph Addison's *The Spectator.* Instead of focusing on manners and social observations, however, Modernist periodicals dedicated themselves to promoting new trends in art. The profound impact of Eliot's work would perhaps not have been as great if it had not found a home in such journals.

tumid (to͞o′ mid) *adj.* swollen

12 **Reading Check**

To what kingdom does the speaker refer?

10 Background

The Literary Magazine

Many regions, areas, colleges, and local groups publish literary magazines. Some nationwide literary magazines students may be familiar with are *The New Yorker, Harper's,* and *The Atlantic Monthly.* Eliot's journal, though, like the small literary quarterlies published today, did not try to appeal to a broad public but instead gave a home to new developments in the arts. This aim was particularly important in fostering Modernism, since much Modernist art was difficult and could not hope to achieve immediate, broad public recognition. Eliot's journal helped the movement thrive among a limited but appreciative audience.

11 Literary Analysis

Modernism

- Explain that the Modernist tactic of fragmenting experience extended to language as well as images.
- Ask students: What effect does Eliot achieve through the abrupt shift to a fragment of a nursery rhyme in lines 68–71?
  Possible response: Out of context as it is here, the words seem meaningless, their repetition mechanical. The nightmarish effect reflects the meaninglessness of the hollow men's lives.

12 Reading Check

Answer: The kingdom referred to is the Kingdom of Heaven.

CUSTOMIZE INSTRUCTION FOR UNIVERSAL ACCESS

For Less Proficient Readers	For English Learners	For Gifted/Talented Students
Less proficient readers are unlikely to be familiar with the referenced texts, Dante's *Inferno* or Shakespeare's *Julius Caesar.* Invite students familiar with these works to summarize them briefly or do so yourself.	Remind these students that one feature of Modernist poetry is dreamlike jumps from one topic to another. Urge English language learners to regard Eliot's use of italics as signals of such jumps.	Have dramatically inclined students prepare, rehearse, and perform a reading of the poem. Have them mark which passages should be read by the chorus (the hollow men) and which would be read by a narrator or a solo speaker for the hollow men. Allow students time to rehearse, then ask them to perform for the others in the class.

ASSESS

Answers for p. 992

Review and Assess

1. Students may say they would use the images of the scarecrow ("Headpiece filled with straw") and the one of the dead man's hand because they have immediate vivid impact.
2. **(a)** Descriptive words include *hollow, stuffed,* and *leaning together.* **(b)** Students may infer that what the hollow men say is as meaningless as the noise of the wind; that what they say is produced by outside forces (they say "what everybody is saying"); that their lives have as little substance as and leave as little trace as the wind.
3. **(a)** The Shadow repeatedly falls. **(b)** The Shadow can be interpreted as fear. It falls between the idea and the achievement, preventing the hollow men from accomplishing anything.
4. **(a)** Eliot is alluding to Conrad's "Heart of Darkness" and to Guy Fawkes's conspiracy to blow up Parliament. **(b)** These individuals had a direction to their lives and were not afraid of dying.
5. Eliot's use of the nursery rhyme effectively depicts the speakers as lost children chanting words that have lost their meaning.
6. **(a)** The world has lost its sense of purpose, and people have no spirituality.
   (b) Possible response: Eliot is perhaps right in pointing out that many people lose themselves by "going along with the crowd," but he judges this natural tendency of people harshly, with little charity.

Life is very long[11]

Between the desire
And the spasm
Between the potency
And the existence
Between the essence
And the descent
Falls the Shadow

For Thine is the Kingdom

For Thine is
Life is
For Thine is the

This is the way the world ends
This is the way the world ends
This is the way the world ends
Not with a bang but a whimper.

---

11. **Life . . . long** Quotation from Joseph Conrad's *An Outcast of the Islands.*

Review and Assess

Thinking About the Selection

1. **Respond:** If you wanted to make a music video of this poem, which images from it would you use? Why?
2. **(a) Recall:** Which words are used to describe the hollow men in the first ten lines? **(b) Infer:** What do the images of wind in Parts I and II suggest about the hollow men?
3. **(a) Recall:** In Part V, what repeatedly "falls"?
   (b) Interpret: How is this action related to the poem's theme?
4. **(a) Analyze:** To what literary work and to which historical event does Eliot allude in the quotations at the beginning of the poem? **(b) Interpret:** In what way are Kurtz, a "hollow sham," and Guy Fawkes, a traitor, superior to the hollow men?
5. **Evaluate:** Do you think the nursery rhymes and other fragmented allusions that Eliot uses in Part V are effective in conveying the speakers' plight? Explain.
6. **(a) Draw Conclusions:** What overall point about the modern spiritual condition is Eliot making in the poem?
   (b) Make a Judgment: Do you think Eliot's point is fair, or do you think he is too harsh? Support your judgment.

ASSESSMENT PRACTICE: Writing Skills

Style **(For more practice, see Test Preparation Workbook, p. 47.)**

Many tests require students to recognize effective style. Use the following sample test item to teach students how to recognize the mood of a passage.

The winter evening settles down
With smells of steaks in passageways.
Six o'clock.
The burnt-out ends of smoky days.
And now a gusty shower wraps
The grimy scraps
Of withered leaves about your feet

Which of these words *best* describes the mood of the passage?

A isolation
B suspense
C obscurity
D hopefulness

Knowing that mood describes a piece's prevailing emotional effect, students should eliminate *C* because it cannot describe a mood. *B* and *D* do not describe the mood of these lines. The correct answer is *A*.

Review and Assess

Literary Analysis

Modernism

1. Identify three images in the "Preludes" that suggest the **Modernist** view that modern life is empty. Explain your choices.
2. What Modernist qualities characterize "The Hollow Men"? Use a chart like the one shown to help you in answering.

Passage	Fragmented Images vs. Realistic Pictures	Critical of Modern Life?

3. (a) What escape from modern despair does "Journey of the Magi" suggest? (b) What despair appears in the poem?

Comparing Literary Works

4. (a) Quoting passages in support, identify two aspects of Modernism illustrated by the "Preludes." (b) Does "Journey of the Magi" also illustrate these aspects? Explain, quoting from the poem.
5. Compare the use of allusion—brief references to literature—in "The Hollow Men" with the use of images in the "Preludes." How are they similar?
6. Which poem is easiest to relate to? Explain.
7. Why might Eliot have found it necessary to turn to past literature to make a point about what is missing in the present?

Reading Strategy

Interpreting

8. (a) Find two patterns of images in the "Preludes." (b) What theme does each pattern reflect?
9. (a) In "Journey of the Magi," what pattern of images appears in the first stanza? (b) How does this pattern reinforce the idea that the journey has changed the Magi?
10. (a) Find four references to eyes in "The Hollow Men." (b) What does this pattern of images suggest about the hollow men?

Extend Understanding

11. **Cultural Connection:** To what extent does Eliot's criticism of the hollow men apply to people today? Explain.

Quick Review

Modernism is a movement in the arts emphasizing images over self-expression, the juxtaposition of images over realism, and a concern with the spiritual ills of modern life.

To **interpret** a sophisticated work, identify its patterns, and then draw conclusions about what these patterns reveal about the meaning of the work.

Take It to the Net

www.phschool.com

Take the interactive self-test online to check your understanding of these selections.

Answers for p. 993

1. Images include: "The burnt-out ends of smoky days"; "Of withered leaves about your feet / And newspapers from vacant lots"; and "With the other masquerades / That time resumes." All three images depict waste, decay, or futility.
2. Possible response: **Passage:** "And voices are / In the wind's singing / More distant and more solemn / Than a fading star"; **Fragmented Images vs. Realistic Pictures:** Fragmented; **Critical of Modern Life?:** Yes
3. **(a)** Spirituality offers an escape from despair. **(b)** The speaker despairs at being caught between old traditions and new beliefs.
4. **(a)** Possible response: The passage "The showers beat / On broken blinds and chimney-pots" uses an image to convey a feeling of dreariness and hopelessness. The passage "all the hands / That are raising dingy shades" uses a fragmented image. **(b)** An image that conveys dreariness and hopelessness is "A cold coming we had of it, / Just the worst time of the year. . . . " The fragmented details from the journey resemble the fragmented images in "Preludes."
5. In both cases, an abbreviated part of a thing—a name from a book or a glimpse of a scene—is used to suggest a world of meaning.
6. The literary allusions in "The Hollow Men" are not as easy to understand as the commonplace scenes in "Preludes."
7. Past literature might contain expressions of values that have disappeared from modern life.
8. **(a)** Possible response: Images of feet appear in each of the Preludes. **(b)** This pattern suggests that the modern world has cut off people's bodies from their hearts and minds.
9. **(a)** The images show that the journey was a difficult one. **(b)** This reinforces the idea that the spiritual change they underwent was difficult.
10. **(a)** (i) "Those who have crossed / With direct eyes, to death's other Kingdom" (ii) "Eyes I dare not meet in dreams" (iii) "In death's

continued

ENRICHMENT: Further Reading

Other Works by T. S. Eliot

"The Love Song of J. Alfred Prufrock"

The Waste Land

Four Quartets

Take It to the Net

Visit www.phschool.com for more information about T. S. Eliot.

Answers continued

dream kingdom / These do not appear:" (iv) "There, the eyes are / Sunlight on a broken column"
(b) It suggests the shame and anonymity of the hollow men, who will not meet the eyes of others.

11. Answers should respond to Eliot's idea that modern people do not act on principle or in their own name, but dodge responsibility.

EXTEND

Answers for p. 994

1 Vocabulary Development

Word Analysis

1. An infraction of the law is an act of breaking the law.
2. The path of refracted light is broken from that of a straight ray.
3. A fractal is made of an infinity of "broken" parts, none of which is complete.
4. A fractious boy is likely to have broken some rules.
5. Fracto-stratus clouds appear to be broken into pieces.

Concept Development: Analogies

1. galled
2. dispensation
3. supplication
4. tumid
5. refractory

Spelling Strategy

Sample responses:

1. hardship
2. contentment
3. aligning
4. swarmed
5. delighted
6. risking

2 Grammar and Style

1. "of faint stale smells" modifies *consciousness;* "beer" modifies *smells;* "with all its muddy feet" modifies *street;* "that press / To early coffee-stands" modifies *feet.* The effect is to imply a whole set of activities and events.
2. "Of which your soul was constituted" modifies *images.* The effect is to produce an effective image of the soul.
3. "bringing sherbet" modifies *silken girls,* "cursing and grumbling," "running away" and "wanting their liquor and women" modify *camel men.* The effect is to suggest the chaos and comforts of the trip.
4. "when we are trembling with tenderness" modifies *hour;* "trembling with tenderness" modifies *we;* "that would kiss" modifies *lips;* "to broken stone" modifies *prayers.* The modifiers add poignancy.
5. "Gathered on this beach of a tumid river" modifies *we;* "of a tumid river" modifies *beach.* The modifier adds sensory details to an abstract scene.

Integrate Language Skills

1 Vocabulary Development Lesson

Word Analysis: Latin Root *-fract-*

The Latin root *-fract-* means "to break." A refractory animal is one that "breaks away." The root *-fract-* appears in some scientific and mathematical terms, such as *fraction.* A fraction is a part "broken away" from a larger whole. Explain how the root *-fract-* contributes to the meaning of each italicized word.

1. Although her motives were good, she was guilty of an *infraction* of the law.
2. When white light is *refracted,* it produces a spectrum.
3. A *fractal* is an irregular shape made up of an infinity of irregular parts.
4. The *fractious* boys caused a good deal of trouble at school.
5. The *fracto-stratus* clouds were ragged and appeared in long, threadlike layers.

Concept Development: Analogies

Choose the word from the vocabulary list on page 979 that best completes each analogy.

1. burning : charred :: chafing : __?__
2. category : group :: system : __?__
3. contempt : insult :: humility : __?__
4. knife : dull :: river : __?__
5. prudent : thoughtless :: obedient : __?__

Spelling Strategy

When adding a suffix to words ending in two consonants, keep both consonants. For example, adding the suffix *-ed* to the word *gall* forms the word *galled.* Choose from the suffixes *-ed, -ment, -ship,* and *-ing* to generate another English word from each of the following words.

1. hard
2. content
3. align
4. swarm
5. delight
6. risk

2 Grammar and Style Lesson

Adjectival Modifiers

Using a variety of phrases and clauses as modifiers, Eliot links diverse images. Among the structures that Eliot uses as **adjectival modifiers** are the following:

Prepositional Phrase: The burnt-out ends of smoky days. . . . (Phrase modifies *ends.*)

Participial Phrase: Headpiece filled with straw. . . . (Phrase modifies *headpiece.*)

Adjective Clause: . . . hands / That are raising dingy shades . . . (Clause modifies *hands.*)

Practice Identify the adjectival modifiers in these lines, and explain their effect:

1. "Preludes," lines 14–18
2. "Preludes," lines 26–28
3. "Journey of the Magi," lines 10–12
4. "The Hollow Men," lines 47–51
5. "The Hollow Men," lines 58–60

Writing Application Write a brief profile of the speaker in "Journey of the Magi," using a series of adjectival modifiers to describe your subject, as Eliot does. Identify the grammatical structure of each modifier.

WG *Prentice Hall Writing and Grammar Connection: Chapter 19, Sections 1–3*

TEACHING RESOURCES

The following resources can be used to enrich or extend the instruction for pp. 994–995.

Vocabulary

- **Selection Support:** Build Vocabulary, p. 215
- **Vocabulary and Spelling Practice Book,** (Use this booklet for skills enrichment.)

Grammar

- **Selection Support:** Grammar and Style, p. 216
- WG **Writing and Grammar,** Diamond Level, p. 440
- **Daily Language Practice Transparencies** ■

Writing

- WG **Writing and Grammar,** Diamond Level, p. 317 ■
- WG **Writing and Grammar iText CD-ROM**

■ **BLOCK SCHEDULING:** Resources marked with this symbol provide varied instruction during 90-minute blocks.

❸ Writing Lesson

Response to Criticism

In an essay, respond to the following comparison: "'Preludes' suggests humanity is trapped in a dreary, meaningless cycle of time. In 'Journey of the Magi,' Eliot's symbolic world has a new center: the Incarnation. Nevertheless, the poem's speaker is profoundly displaced. Like 'Preludes,' the poem invokes what is of highest value by showing how far from it we are."

Prewriting Gather details from the poems concerning time and the condition of displacement or not belonging. Then, jot down a few conclusions about Eliot's attitude towards these themes.

Drafting Begin with a general statement of your response to the quotation. As you draft, support your response with details from the poems.

Revising Jot down a few details about each of your main points on a self-sticking note. Attach the notes to your draft, and compare each note to the paragraph it concerns. In cases where a detail appears in a note but not in the draft, consider adding it.

Model: Revising for Elaboration

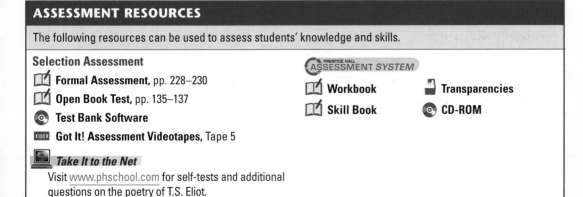

"Preludes"— coarseness despair, but also an "infinitely gentle thing"

In the "Preludes," the speaker has "The notion of some infinitely gentle / Infinitely suffering thing." Similarly,
~~Just like in "Preludes,"~~ the speaker in "Journey of the Magi" has an idea of spiritual truth, but there is nothing and no one in his homeland who also recognizes this truth.

Replacing a vague assertion of similarity with a specific detail strengthens the main point.

Prentice Hall Writing and Grammar Connection: Chapter 14, Section 4

❹ Extension Activities

Listening and Speaking Is Eliot's view of modern life valid or distorted? Form teams and hold a **debate on Modernism**. Prepare arguments using

- Analogy—a comparison that explains the relationship between two things
- Induction—the derivation of a general conclusion from a sampling of specific cases

Help teammates strengthen their arguments, and then hold your debate before the class. **[Group Activity]**

Research and Technology Write a **cultural report** on Modernism in the visual arts. Compare Eliot's subject matter and his techniques to such Modernist developments as collage and Cubism. Incorporate reproductions of art-works in your word-processed report.

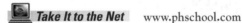

www.phschool.com

Go online for an additional research activity using the Internet.

❸ Writing Lesson

- Before students begin their writing project, ask them to read the critical quotation through once to form a general impression of the critic's intent.
- Caution students not to look for details that support the critic's claim or details that refute the claim. Ask students to form their own opinion after they have gathered all the facts.
- During the drafting portion of the activity, remind students to place references in logical order, such as those from one poem together, followed by those from another poem.

❹ Listening and Speaking

- Before students begin their debate, urge them to incorporate the following strategies:
  - Choose one side of the proposition to debate. Focus first on the emotional response, then try to support it intellectually.
  - Use research and discussion to identify supporting reasons, facts, and examples.
  - Structure arguments in a logical manner, beginning or ending with the most effective points.

CUSTOMIZE INSTRUCTION For Universal Access

To address different learning styles, use the activities suggested in the **Extension Activities** booklet, p. 46.

- For Verbal/Linguistic Learners, use Activity 5.
- For Verbal/Linguistic and Logical/Mathematical Learners, use Activity 6.
- For Visual/Spatial Learners, use Activity 7.

ASSESSMENT RESOURCES

The following resources can be used to assess students' knowledge and skills.

Selection Assessment

- **Formal Assessment,** pp. 228–230
- **Open Book Test,** pp. 135–137
- **Test Bank Software**
- **Got It! Assessment Videotapes,** Tape 5

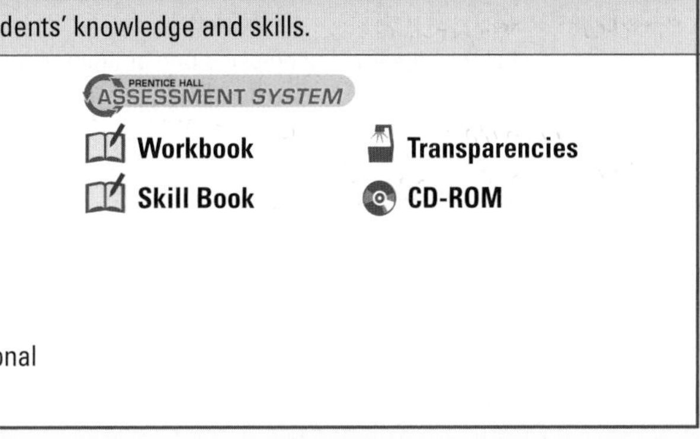

PRENTICE HALL
ASSESSMENT SYSTEM
Workbook
Skill Book
Transparencies
CD-ROM

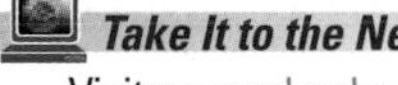

Visit www.phschool.com for self-tests and additional questions on the poetry of T.S. Eliot.

In Memory of W. B. Yeats ✦ Musée des Beaux Arts ✦ Carrick Revisited ✦ Not Palaces

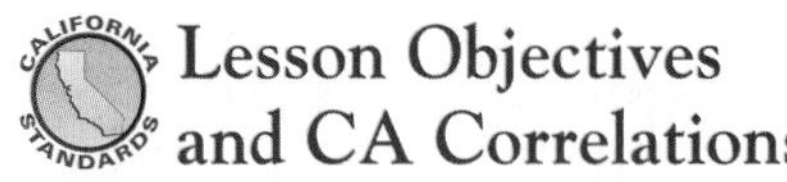

Lesson Objectives and CA Correlations

1. **To analyze and respond to literary elements**
   - Literary Analysis: Theme **R 3.2**
   - Comparing Literary Works **R 3.7**
2. **To read, comprehend, analyze, and critique a poem**
   - Reading Strategy: Paraphrasing
   - Reading Check Questions
   - Review and Assess Questions
3. **To develop word analysis skills, fluency, and systematic vocabulary**
   - Vocabulary Development Lesson: Greek Root *-top-* **R 1.2**
4. **To understand and apply written and oral language conventions**
   - Spelling Strategy **LC 1.2**
   - Grammar and Style Lesson: Parallel Structure **LC 1.1**
5. **To understand and apply appropriate writing and research strategies**
   - Writing Lesson: Poem About an Artwork **W 1.1, 1.5, 1.9**
   - Extension Activity: Art Exhibition **W 1.7**
   - Assessment Practice (ATE)
6. **To understand and apply listening and speaking strategies**
   - Extension Activity: Group Reading **LS 2.5**

STEP-BY-STEP TEACHING GUIDE	PACING GUIDE
PRETEACH	
Motivate Students and Provide Background	
Use the Motivation activity (ATE p. 996)	5 min.
Read and discuss author and background features (SE pp. 996, 999; ATE p. 999) A	5 min.
Introduce the Concepts	
Introduce the Literary Analysis and Reading Strategy (SE/ATE p. 997) A	15 min.
Pronounce the vocabulary words and read their definitions (SE p. 997)	5 min.
TEACH	
Monitor Comprehension	
Informally monitor comprehension by circulating while students read independently or in groups A	15 min.
Monitor students' comprehension with the Reading Check notes (SE/ATE p. 999)	as students read
Develop vocabulary with Vocabulary notes (SE pp. 1001, 1005, 1006, 1007; ATE p. 1005)	as students read
Develop Understanding	
Develop students' understanding of theme with the Literary Analysis annotations (SE pp. 999, 1000; ATE pp. 999, 1000, 1003, 1007) A	5 min.
Develop students' ability to paraphrase with the Reading Strategy annotations (SE/ATE p. 1000)	5 min.
ASSESS	
Assess Mastery	
Assess students' mastery of the Reading Strategy and Literary Analysis by having them answer the Review and Assess questions (SE/ATE p. 1009)	20 min.
Use one or more of the print and media Assessment Resources (ATE p. 1011) A	up to 45 min.
EXTEND	
Apply Understanding	
Have students complete the Vocabulary Development Lesson and the Grammar and Style Lesson (SE p. 1010) A	20 min.
Apply students' knowledge of conveying a main impression using the Writing Lesson (SE/ATE p. 1011) A	45 min.
Apply students' understanding using one or more of the Extension Activities (SE p. 1011)	20–90 min.

ACCELERATED INSTRUCTION:
Use the strategies and activities identified with an A.

UNIVERSAL ACCESS
● = Below-Level Students
▲ = On-Level Students
■ = Above-Level Students

Time and Resource Manager

Reading Level: Average, Average, Challenging, Challenging
Average Number of Instructional Days: 4

RESOURCES		
PRINT	**TRANSPARENCIES**	**TECHNOLOGY**
• **Beyond Literature,** Cross-Curricular Connection: Social Studies, p. 47 ▲ ■		• **Interest Grabber Video,** Tape 6 ● ▲ ■
• **Selection Support Workbook:** ● ▲ ■ Literary Analysis, p. 222 Reading Strategy, p. 221 Build Vocabulary, p. 219	• **Literary Analysis and Reading Transparencies,** pp. 93 and 94 ● ▲ ■	
		• **Listening to Literature** ● ▲ ■ Audiocassettes, Side 23 Audio CDs, CD 13
• **Literatura en español** ● ▲ • **Literary Analysis for Enrichment** ■		
• **Formal Assessment:** Selection Test, pp. 231–233 ● ▲ ■ • **Open Book Test,** pp. 138–140 ● ▲ ■ • PRENTICE HALL ASSESSMENT SYSTEM ● ▲ ■	• PRENTICE HALL ASSESSMENT SYSTEM ● ▲ ■ Skills Practice Answers and Explanations on Transparencies ● ▲ ■	• **Test Bank Software** ● ▲ ■ • **Got It! Assessment Videotapes,** Tape 5 ● ▲
• **Selection Support Workbook:** ● ▲ ■ Grammar and Style, p. 220 • **Writing and Grammar,** Diamond Level ● ▲ ■ • **Extension Activities,** p. 47 ● ▲ ■	• **Daily Language Practice Transparencies** ● ▲	• **Writing and Grammar iText CD-ROM** ● ▲ ■ ***Take It to the Net*** www.phschool.com

BLOCK SCHEDULING: Use one 90-minute class period to preteach the selections and have students read them. Use a second 90-minute class period to assess students' mastery of skills and have them complete one of the Extension Activities.

PRETEACH

Step-by-Step Teaching Guide for pp. 996–997

Motivation

Hold up this textbook, or ask students to examine their own copies. Ask students to consider for a moment the art—poetry, fiction, drama, paintings—the book contains. Ask: What is the purpose of art? What does it do? Out of what impulses do people create it? In three very different ways, each of the poets in this section asks and perhaps answers these questions.

Interest Grabber Video

As an alternative, play "'Musée des Beaux Arts': Icarus" on Tape 6 to engage student interest.

❶ Background

More About the Authors

W.H. Auden

One of Auden's strengths was being able to mimic almost any style of poetry, from the classic poets to the Modernists. His poetry frequently tells, literally or metaphysically, of journeys or quests, backed by his own extensive travels. His early works reflect a Socialist bend, and he supported Freudian psychoanalysis. Later, he became an advocate of modern Protestant theology.

Louis MacNeice

MacNeice taught Greek at Bedford College in London and later became a skilled translator of the Greek classics. He also wrote and produced radio plays for the BBC. His characteristic mood was that of the slightly detached, wry observant, ironic, and witty commentator.

Stephen Spender

Sir Stephen Harold Spender was influenced by the German poet Rainer Maria Rilke and the Spanish poet Federico Garcia Lorca. His poems were self-critical and compassionate and had a personal, almost autobiographical nature. He was the first non-American to serve as poetry consultant to the Library of Congress. He was knighted in 1983.

Prepare to Read

❶ In Memory of W. B. Yeats ◆ Musée des Beaux Arts ◆ Carrick Revisited ◆ Not Palaces

W. H. Auden (1907–1973)

Much as T. S. Eliot became established as the poetic voice of the 1920s, so Wystan Hugh Auden emerged as the voice of the 1930s. As a young poet, Auden was greatly influenced by Eliot's work, particularly *The Waste Land*. He soon developed his own poetic style, however, characterized by versatility, wit, and dazzling technique.

Born in York, England, Auden had early dreams of becoming an engineer but gravitated to poetry instead. His commitment to social justice and his opposition to fascism made him a poetic spokesperson for the political left. In 1939, Auden left England for the United States, where he taught at a number of universities. He became an American citizen in 1946. From 1956 to 1960, he taught at Oxford as Professor of Poetry.

Achievements in Poetry Auden's early poems, along with works by his friends Louis MacNeice and Stephen Spender, appeared in *Oxford Poetry*, a series of annual collections of verse by the university's undergraduates. Auden's first published collection, entitled *Poems*, appeared in 1930. Full of cryptic images and references, Auden's verse struck some readers of the day as impenetrable. His more straightfoward second collection, *On This Island* (1937), generated greater enthusiasm. In 1948, Auden won a Pulitzer Prize for the collection *The Age of Anxiety*.

A Versatile Poet Auden wrote equally well in the idiom of the street or in the archaic measures of *Beowulf*. His voice is original, achieving a kind of personable intimacy even as he makes polished pronouncements on the general human condition. With Yeats and Eliot, he is among the most highly regarded British poets of the twentieth century.

Louis MacNeice (1907–1963)

Louis MacNeice was the son of a Protestant clergyman in Belfast, Northern Ireland. A gifted youth, he began to write poetry at age seven. His first collection, *Blind Fireworks*, appeared in 1929, followed six years later by *Poems*, the volume that established his reputation. During the 1930s, MacNeice taught classical literature. In 1941, he joined the British Broadcasting Corporation, writing radio plays in verse.

Today, many consider MacNeice second only to Auden among the poets of their generation. His poetry is restrained and precise, with overtones of melancholy. It is the poetry of a man who, as the poet Edwin Muir put it, "is never swept off his feet."

Stephen Spender (1909–1995)

No poet of the 1930s provided a more honest picture of the era between the wars than did Stephen Spender. Much of his early poetry deals with the world of the thirties, the "low dishonest decade" that saw the world lurch from depression to fascism to war. Yet Spender, never a pessimist, celebrates technology at the same time as he confronts the problems of industrial progress.

Born in London and educated at Oxford, Spender's first important book, *Poems* (1933), was published while he was living in Germany. A political activist, Spender promoted antifascist propaganda in Spain during its Civil War (1936–1939). He later coedited the literary magazine *Horizon* and the political, cultural, and literary review *Encounter*.

TEACHING RESOURCES

The following resources can be used to enrich or extend the instruction for pp. 996–997.

Motivation

Interest Grabber Video, Tape 6

Background

Beyond Literature, p. 47

Take It to the Net

Visit www.phschool.com for background and hotlinks for the selections.

Literary Analysis

Literary Analysis and Reading Transparencies, Theme, p. 94

Reading

Literary Analysis and Reading Transparencies, Paraphrasing, p. 93

Selection Support, Reading Strategy, p. 221

BLOCK SCHEDULING: Resources marked with this symbol provide varied instruction during 90-minute blocks.

Preview

Connecting to the Literature

You just spent three hours finishing up your short story. You are tired, you are elated—but what exactly did you do? You put words on a page and moved them around until they rang true—but has all that work changed anything? These poets address similar questions about art generally.

2 Literary Analysis

Theme

The **theme** of a literary work is its central concern or purpose, or the central question that it raises. A poet may approach theme from these angles:

- Making direct statements expressing a theme
- Indicating a theme through word choice and imagery

In the poem "In Memory of W. B. Yeats," for example, Auden explores the link between poetry and life. Statements like "poetry makes nothing happen" (line 36) speak directly to this theme. The imagery of the "dark cold day" of Yeats's death is an indirect clue to the theme.

Comparing Literary Works

A central theme in poetry is the nature of poetry itself. Renaissance poets, for instance, wrote poems claiming that their verse immortalized their subjects. Modern poets offer a range of ideas on poetry.

- "In Memory of W. B. Yeats" suggests that poetry cannot change reality. However, by "singing" our limitations—failure, death—poetry affirms life and so causes joy.
- "Not Palaces" suggests that poems can change reality by inspiring and fueling social change.

As you read, compare the questions the poems raise about poetry.

3 Reading Strategy

Paraphrasing

To understand poetry, it is often helpful to **paraphrase** dense or difficult lines by restating the writer's words in your own words. This chart shows how you might paraphrase two lines from "In Memory of W. B. Yeats." Use a similar chart to paraphrase complex passages as you read.

Lines

"And snow disfigured the public statues; / The mercury sank in the mouth of the dying day."

Paraphrase

Snow fell all over town. The temperature fell as the day ended.

Vocabulary Development

sequestered (si kwes′ tərd) *adj.* kept apart from others (p. 1001)

topographical (täp′ ə graf′ i kəl) *adj.* representing the surface features of a region (p. 1005)

affinities (ə fin′ i tēz) *n.* family connections; sympathies (p. 1006)

prenatal (prē nāt′ əl) *adj.* existing or taking place before birth (p. 1006)

intrigues (in trēgz′) *v.* plots or schemes (p. 1007)

CUSTOMIZE INSTRUCTION FOR UNIVERSAL ACCESS

For Less Proficient Readers	For English Learners	For Advanced Readers
To help less proficient readers unravel the subtleties of these poems, urge them to read slowly. Tell them to pause at the end of each stanza and paraphrase for comprehension, rereading the stanza if necessary. Urge students to check their comprehension with a partner.	Guide English language learners to use the punctuation in the poetry to help them read in sentences for meaning.	More advanced students can enhance their response to these poets by comparing the stylistic choices each poet makes. Urge students to look at tone, diction, and theme in their comparisons.

2 Literary Analysis

Theme

- Remind students that the theme of a work is its central concern or purpose, or the main question it raises. Tell students that they should be able to express the theme of any work in one word or a short phrase.
- Have students name the theme of several earlier-read works. For example, the theme of Yeats's poem "When You Are Old" could be summed up as "revenge" or as "remembering a lost love."
- As students read the selections, have them think about the theme of each piece. What basic idea is the poet trying to convey to readers?
- Caution students that a theme should reflect the whole of the work, not just the prevalent idea of one stanza or a portion of the piece.

3 Reading Strategy

Paraphrasing

- Elicit from students that paraphrasing is retelling the actions and thoughts of a work in their own words. The words are parallel to the author's but differ in phrasing or form.
- Help students practice paraphrasing by having them paraphrase the information about the authors on page 996.
- Students should understand that by paraphrasing lines of a poem, they can give themselves a clearer idea of the actions and thoughts portrayed in sometimes obscure ways.

Vocabulary Development

- Pronounce each vocabulary word for students and read the definitions as a class. Have students identify any words with which they are already familiar.

 ***E-Teach***

Visit E-Teach at www.phschool.com for teachers' essays on how to teach, with questions and answers.

TEACH

Step-by-Step Teaching Guide for pp. 998–1008

CUSTOMIZE INSTRUCTION
For Visual/Spatial Learners

Encourage these learners to use the selection illustrations as aids to comprehension. Have them preview the images on page 998, 1002, 1004, and 1007 and list emotions and ideas evoked by each image.

1 About the Selection

This poem celebrates and honors the life of poet W. B. Yeats. Structured as an elegy, "In Memory . . ." sums up Yeats's lifetime accomplishments and crafts a vivid picture of the man. Part 1 describes his all-too-human death and the gap it will leave behind. In Part 2, Auden addresses Yeats directly to reassure him of poetry's enduring qualities. Part 3, addressed both to the Earth and to a generic poet, focuses on the nature of poetry. As a whole, the poem celebrates the power of poetry. Although it "makes nothing happen," poetry teaches joy in the human condition.

2 ▶Critical Viewing

Answer: Encourage students to keep this question in mind while reading. After further reading, students may find the photograph shows both aspects of Yeats, the old and frail man described in Part 1 and the writer—surrounded by books and papers—of Part 3.

1 *In Memory of* W. B. Yeats

—W. H. Auden—

2 ▲ **Critical Viewing** Does this photograph of Yeats present him as the mortal man described in parts 1 and 2 of Auden's poem or as the great writer eulogized in part 3? **[Interpret]**

TEACHING RESOURCES

The following resources can be used to enrich or extend the instruction for pp. 998–1008.

Literary Analysis

Selection Support: Literary Analysis, p. 222

Literary Analysis and Reading Transparencies, Theme, p. 94

Reading

Listening to Literature Audiocassettes, Side 23

Listening to Literature Audio CDs, CD 13

BLOCK SCHEDULING: Resources marked with this symbol provide varied instruction during 90-minute blocks.

Background

The 1930s was a decade poised between a worldwide economic depression and the impending devastation of World War II. The complex concerns of the period are reflected in the poems of the Auden circle, which included Auden himself, Spender, MacNeice, and C. Day Lewis. The political urgencies of the times—the opposition to fascism and the movement for social justice for the working classes—shaped much of the poetry the Auden circle wrote then. Yet along with their social concerns, each of these poets shared a deep sense of a specifically poetic vocation—to make something happen in language.

1

He disappeared in the dead of winter:
The brooks were frozen, the airports almost deserted,
And snow disfigured the public statues;
The mercury sank in the mouth of the dying day.
O all the instruments agree
The day of his death was a dark cold day.

Far from his illness
The wolves ran on through the evergreen forests,
The peasant river was untempted by fashionable quays;[1]
By mourning tongues
The death of the poet was kept from his poems.

But for him it was his last afternoon as himself,
An afternoon of nurses and rumors;
The provinces of his body revolted,
The squares of his mind were empty,
Silence invaded the suburbs,
The current of his feeling failed: he became his admirers.

Now he is scattered among a hundred cities
And wholly given over to unfamiliar affections;
To find his happiness in another kind of wood
And be punished by another code of conscience.
3 The words of a dead man
Are modified in the guts of the living.

But in the importance and noise of tomorrow
When the brokers are roaring like beasts on the floor
of the Bourse,[2]

1. **quays** (kēz) wharfs with facilities for loading or unloading ships.
2. **Bourse** (bo͝ors) Paris Stock Exchange.

Literary Analysis
Theme How does the image in lines 22–23 relate to the theme of the relationship between poetry and life?

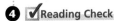

4 

According to the speaker, where is Yeats now?

3 Literary Analysis

Theme

- Have students read the entire poem through first for mood and tone. Then, have them reread the first stanza.
- Ask: What is being described in this stanza? Have students paraphrase Auden's lines in brief sentences.
- Tell students that the subject of the poem is the death of Yeats. How does this differ from the theme of the poem?
- Ask students the Literary Analysis question on p. 999: How does the image in lines 22–23 relate to the theme of the relationship between poetry and life?
  Answer: The image of a dead writer's poem affecting the living fits exactly into Auden's theme of the endurance of art.

4 Reading Check

Answer: According to Auden, Yeats may be found in a hundred different cities—in the libraries of those cities and in the minds of the readers all around the world.

CUSTOMIZE INSTRUCTION FOR UNIVERSAL ACCESS

For Special Needs Students	For Gifted/Talented Students	For Advanced Readers
Help students find images in the poem that reinforce the topic of Yeats's death: frozen brooks, deserted airports, dying day. Help students see that these are all images meant to parallel the death of the poet. Help students summarize and paraphrase each sentence within the poem to promote understanding.	Ask students who are interested in art to create an art piece that reflects the tone of the poem. Is the author sad at Yeats's death? How does he reassure himself and readers? Discuss what colors might be appropriate for the sorrow and the hopefulness expressed in the poem. Post the art so other students may comment or relate them to the poem.	Auden in his youth was a supporter of Socialism, but in his later years he embraced modern Protestant theology. Have advanced students analyze this poem to determine if one or the other—or both—of these beliefs were greatly influencing Auden when he wrote this, or if the poem's subject is neutral and not subjected to personal dogma.

❺ Reading Strategy

Paraphrasing

- Remind students that to paraphrase lines from a poem is to repeat the lines in one's own words. Students may think of this as translating from a foreign language ("poetry") to their language (vernacular English).
- Stress that paraphrasing should not change the order of the ideas.
- Have students read lines 36–41 and then paraphrase each complete sentence or thought in these lines separately.
- Then, ask students the Reading Strategy question on p. 1000: Use your own words to paraphrase Auden's ideas in lines 36–41.
  Possible response: You didn't change Ireland, poetry does nothing; it is not the concern of those in power. Poetry is born of isolation and grief; it flows beyond them and survives in its own right.

❻ Literary Analysis

Theme

- Some students may have difficulty separating the theme from the topic, or subject of the poem. Remind students that the theme of a poem is the overall message the poet wishes to convey to readers.
- Review the theme as being directly stated or stated through word choice and imagery.
- Have students identify the topic of the poem. Then discuss the theme of the poem. Was the theme stated directly, or by word choice and imagery?
  Possible response: The topic of the poem is, first, the death of Yeats; second, the survival of his poetry after him; and, third, the nature of poetry. The theme is stated directly as well as in images.
- Finally, ask students the Literary Analysis question on p. 1000: What idea about the power of poetry over time appears in these lines?
  Answer: The lines offer the idea that poetry will endure long past the death of the poet.

And the poor have the sufferings to which they are
fairly accustomed,
And each in the cell of himself is almost convinced of
his freedom;
A few thousand will think of this day
As one thinks of a day when one did something
slightly unusual.

O all the instruments agree
The day of his death was a dark cold day.

2

You were silly like us: your gift survived it all;
The parish of rich women, physical decay,
Yourself; mad Ireland hurt you into poetry.
Now Ireland has her madness and her weather still,
❺ For poetry makes nothing happen: it survives
In the valley of its saying where executives
Would never want to tamper; it flows south
From ranches of isolation and the busy griefs,
Raw towns that we believe and die in; it survives,
A way of happening, a mouth.

3

Earth, receive an honored guest;
William Yeats is laid to rest:
Let the Irish vessel lie
Emptied of its poetry.

Time that is intolerant
Of the brave and innocent,
And indifferent in a week
To a beautiful physique,

❻ Worships language and forgives
Everyone by whom it lives;
Pardons cowardice, conceit
Lays its honors at their feet.

Time that with this strange excuse
Pardoned Kipling and his views,[3]
And will pardon Paul Claudel,[4]
Pardons him for writing well.

Reading Strategy
Paraphrasing Use your own words to paraphrase Auden's ideas in lines 36–41.

Literary Analysis
Theme What idea about the power of poetry over time appears in these lines?

3. **Kipling . . . views** English writer Rudyard Kipling (1865–1936) was a supporter of imperialism.
4. **pardon Paul Claudel** (klō del′) French poet, dramatist, and diplomat. Paul Claudel (1868–1955) had antidemocratic political views, which Yeats at times shared.

ENRICHMENT: Science Connection

Meteorology

In this poem, both Auden's observations and "the instruments" agree that the weather is very cold. In Auden's time, these instruments would have been much simpler than those used today to evaluate and predict weather.

Meteorologists now use computer modeling, satellite photographs, and sophisticated monitoring equipment. Have interested students learn more about these methods and share their findings with the class.

Discuss how modern methods compare with human observations—such as Auden's—in measuring and predicting weather.

In the nightmare of the dark
All the dogs of Europe bark,
And the living nations wait,
Each sequestered in its hate;

Intellectual disgrace
Stares from every human face,
And the seas of pity lie
Locked and frozen in each eye.

Follow, poet, follow right
To the bottom of the night,
With your unconstraining voice
Still persuade us to rejoice;

With the farming of a verse
Make a vineyard of the curse,
Sing of human unsuccess
In a rapture of distress;

In the deserts of the heart
Let the healing fountain start,
In the prison of his days
Teach the free man how to praise.

sequestered (si kwes′ tərd) *adj.* kept apart from others

Review and Assess

Thinking About the Selection

1. **(a) Recall:** What kept "The death of the poet" from his poems? **(b) Interpret:** What does the speaker mean by saying Yeats "became his admirers"?
2. **Interpret:** What does the second section suggest about the sources and effects of poetry?
3. **(a) Interpret:** Considering the kind of fame great past poets enjoy, why does the speaker say that time "Worships language and forgives / Everyone by whom it lives"? **(b) Interpret:** What kind of poetry might poets produce who "Sing of human unsuccess / In a rapture of distress; . . ."?
4. **Summarize:** Summarize the view of poetry presented in the poem.
5. **Analyze:** In phrases such as "ranches of isolation," Auden combines the abstract and the specific. Identify three other images that combine abstract ideas and concrete details.
6. **Evaluate:** Is Auden's style suited to an elegy, a poem of mourning? Explain.

Answers for p. 1001

Review and Assess

1. **(a)** His mourners kept his poems alive, even after his death. **(b)** Though Yeats the man has died, Yeats the poet, a voice and a source of pleasure, lives on in his readers' enjoyment of his poems.
2. It suggests that the source of poetry is a "gift," perhaps associated with private griefs. It also suggests that poetry has no effect in the sense of things it makes happen. Instead, it is "a way of happening."
3. **(a)** The speaker believes that language will last eternally and that people will forgive any sins committed by the poet. **(b)** The poetry may very well be in the Modernist style, with topics of human despair but signs of hopefulness.
4. Poetry has little to do with the personal lives or political beliefs of poets; good poetry is immortal; it is the essence of poetry to "Sing of human unsuccess," affirming the human condition in all its limitations.
5. Students may cite "all the instruments agree"; "Now Ireland has her madness"; "the farming of a verse."
6. Possible responses: Yes, the style suits the elegy, as it praises Yeats and acknowledges his public stature. No, Auden's style is too public and philosophical to express personal grief.

CUSTOMIZE INSTRUCTION FOR UNIVERSAL ACCESS

For Special Needs Students	For English Learners	For Advanced Readers
Have students read along to the recorded version of "In Memory of W. B. Yeats" on the **Listening to Literature Audiocassettes.** Pause after every stanza to discuss what the speaker is talking about. Have a volunteer recount the ideas in the poem up to that point each time you stop for discussion.	Help English language learners read the poem by having them pay attention to the punctuation of the lines. Helping them to construct reasonable sentences, which may or may not end at the end of a line or stanza, will contribute to their understanding of the poem.	The poem mentions that Kipling will be forgiven for "his views," and Claudel will be forgiven for "writing well." For what must Yeats be forgiven? Have students research his life in depth to determine what Auden is referring to in this veiled indication that Yeats was something less than a saint.

7 About the Selection

This poem gives depth to the truism that "People suffer, yet the world moves on." Focusing on a painting by Pieter Brueghel, Auden points out how Brueghel's figures placidly ignore Icarus' tragic fall. The world of the painting is innocently indifferent to suffering, and Auden seems convinced that this indifference holds a profound truth. This indifference may show that there is something deeply private, even religious, about an individual's suffering that cannot be shared with others or directly depicted in art. Whatever the case, Brueghel's painting is not "wrong" about Icarus' suffering, precisely because it shows us what suffering is *not.*

8 Background

Art

The Fall of Icarus, by Pieter Brueghel

This painting illustrates the last scene in the myth of Icarus, in which he falls into the sea. It is a visual depiction of the ideas Auden expresses in the poem.

Flemish painter Pieter Brueghel the Elder (he had a son Pieter Brueghel the Younger) served an artistic apprenticeship with Belgian artist Pieter Coecke van Aelst. As he developed his own style, Brueghel often roamed the countryside, making candid drawings of the landscape and its inhabitants for later use in his paintings. *The Fall of Icarus* could be one such painting, in which the everyday people are captured in exquisite detail. Use these questions for discussion:

1. What specific elements from the painting does Auden describe? *He describes the ploughman, the sun shining, the white legs disappearing into the water, and the delicate ship sailing on.*
2. How do the attitudes of poet and painter toward human indifference compare? *Both draw a lesson about the nature of suffering.*

9 ▶Critical Viewing

Answer: Nobody in the picture is paying any attention to Icarus' plunge to Earth. In this way, the painting reflects Auden's idea that suffering belongs only to the sufferer and is not part of everyday life.

8

The Fall of Icarus, Pieter Brueghel, Musée Royaux des Beaux-Arts de Belgique, Bruxelles

9 ▲ **Critical Viewing** In this painting by Brueghel, the drowning Icarus appears in the lower right. What is Brueghel implying about the place of suffering in life? **[Interpret]**

7 Musée des Beaux Arts[1]

W. H. AUDEN

10

About suffering they were never wrong,
The Old Masters: how well they understood
Its human position; how it takes place
While someone else is eating or opening a window or just
    walking dully along;
How, when the aged are reverently, passionately waiting

1. **Musée des Beaux Arts** Museum of Fine Arts in Brussels, Belgium, which contains Brueghel's *Icarus.*

ENRICHMENT: Social Studies Connection

Icarus

Daedalus, Icarus' father, designed the labyrinth in which King Minos of Crete imprisoned the Minotaur (a monster half-man, half-bull). Daedalus revealed the labyrinth's secret, enabling the hero Theseus to slay the Minotaur and escape with Minos' daughter Ariadne. When King Minos then imprisoned Daedalus and Icarus, Daedalus fashioned wings of wax and feathers and he and Icarus flew off. Icarus flew too close to the sun; the wax on his wings melted and he plummeted to his death.

For the miraculous birth, there always must be
Children who did not specially want it to happen, skating
On a pond at the edge of the wood:
They never forgot
That even the dreadful martyrdom must run its course
Anyhow in a corner, some untidy spot
Where the dogs go on with their doggy life and the
 torturer's horse
Scratches its innocent behind on a tree.

In Brueghel's *Icarus*,[2] for instance: how everything turns away
Quite leisurely from the disaster; the ploughman may
Have heard the splash, the forsaken cry,
But for him it was not an important failure; the sun shone
As it had to on the white legs disappearing into the green
Water; and the expensive delicate ship that must have seen
Something amazing, a boy falling out of the sky,
Had somewhere to get to and sailed calmly on.

---

2. **Brueghel's** (brü′ gəlz) ***Icarus*** (ik′ ə rəs) *The Fall of Icarus,* a painting by Flemish painter Pieter Brueghel (1525?–1569). In Greek mythology, Icarus flies too close to the sun. The wax of his artificial wings melts, and he falls into the sea.

Review and Assess

Thinking About the Selection

1. **(a) Recall:** Who are the "Old Masters"? **(b) Interpret:** What general device used by the Old Masters does the speaker discuss?
2. **(a) Recall:** What disaster do the "ploughman" and the "ship" witness? **(b) Compare and Contrast:** How do their responses contrast with the gravity of the event?
3. **(a) Infer:** What is the relation of the children to the important events near them? **(b) Connect:** Is the attitude of the ploughman to Icarus' fall similar? Explain.
4. **(a) Analyze:** Look at Brueghel's *The Fall of Icarus* (p. 1002). What does the artist imply by showing only Icarus' legs in the right corner of the picture? **(b) Infer:** What does Brueghel, an Old Master, realize about the place of suffering in the world?
5. **Support:** Which of these statements best captures the sense of the poem? (a) A person's suffering belongs to him or her in a way that not even pity can change. (b) Suffering gives meaning to innocent everyday life and vice versa. Support your choice.
6. **(a) Apply:** Identify two examples of indifference to suffering today. **(b) Relate:** What might Auden say about them?

CUSTOMIZE INSTRUCTION FOR UNIVERSAL ACCESS

For Less Proficient Readers	For English Learners	For Advanced Readers
Have less proficient readers examine the painting and write down what each person or thing is doing. Discuss whether Icarus' death will change their lives in any way, or make anything different. Help students understand the theme of the world's indifference to personal suffering as told in the poem and in the painting.	English learners may not be familiar with the full story of Icarus. Find, or have them find, the story of Icarus and Daedalus in the library. Help them read the story to provide the background necessary for them to interpret the picture and the poem.	Have advanced students research more about the painter Pieter Brueghel the Elder. The story of Icarus dates from the Greek era. Was there a relationship between Brueghel and the classical myths? Did he paint more scenes such as this?

10 Literary Analysis

Theme

- Read aloud lines 1–4 to students. Have students paraphrase the main idea of these lines.
- Then, ask students how Auden communicates his theme in these first few lines.
  Answer: Auden attributes the theme to the works of the Old Masters. Auden states the theme almost directly: It is the nature of things and of suffering that the world goes on, even while individuals suffer.

Answers for p. 1003

Review and Assess

1. **(a)** The Old Masters are Belgian, Italian, and Dutch painters of the thirteenth to the sixteenth centuries; the speaker is viewing their paintings. **(b)** They depict momentous events surrounded by indifferent figures pursuing ordinary activities.
2. **(a)** They witness the fall of Icarus. **(b)** Although the event is both wondrous and tragic—a winged boy falls to his death—they continue their routine activities.
3. **(a)** The children have no reaction; they continue playing in ignorance of what is happening. **(b)** Yes, both are disassociated from the important events nearby.
4. **(a)** The artist implies that Icarus' event is, at least from the outside, only one event among others. **(b)** Brueghel realizes that suffering takes place against a background of daily life.
5. Students should provide reasons for their choice. In support of (a), they should note that Auden emphasizes but does not criticize the isolation of the sufferer from others. In support of (b), they should note that, in both painting and poem, the contrast between details of everyday life and extraordinary events emphasizes the significance of both.
6. **(a)** Students should supply instances of indifference to suffering. Answers will vary. **(b)** Auden might note that, even in cases where people are wrong not to notice others' suffering, they cannot share another's suffering or abandon their own concerns entirely.

⓫ About the Selection

This poem takes readers on a journey back to the poet's birthplace in an effort to understand and define the influences on an artist's identity. The speaker—presumably MacNeice—describes Carrickfergus, with its castle and green hills, its familiar sights and sounds. As he tours the natural and human landscape, recalling the Carrick of his childhood, the poet acknowledges the irrefutable influence of Northern Ireland—a chance "Particular," neither the pure Irish of the west nor the pure English across the water—on his character.

⓬ ▶Critical Viewing

Answer: Students may note the isolation, physical beauty, distance from urban noise and crowds, and the rural surroundings. Students may see each of these factors as an advantage or disadvantage.

⓫ Carrick Revisited

Louis MacNeice

⓬ ▼**Critical Viewing** In "Carrick Revisited," MacNeice explores the relationship between a person's childhood home and his or her identity. What memories might a person have growing up in the setting shown in this photograph? **[Speculate]**

ENRICHMENT: History Connection

Feudal Ireland

Carrickfergus Castle, mentioned by MacNeice, was built by an Anglo-Norman lord, John de Courci, sometime after he conquered the area in 1177. The Normans, a people who conquered England in 1066, also conquered parts of Ireland. Soon, though, the kings of England became wary of the independence of the Anglo-Norman lords of Ireland and took steps to limit their power. Thus began the enduring conflict between England and Ireland.

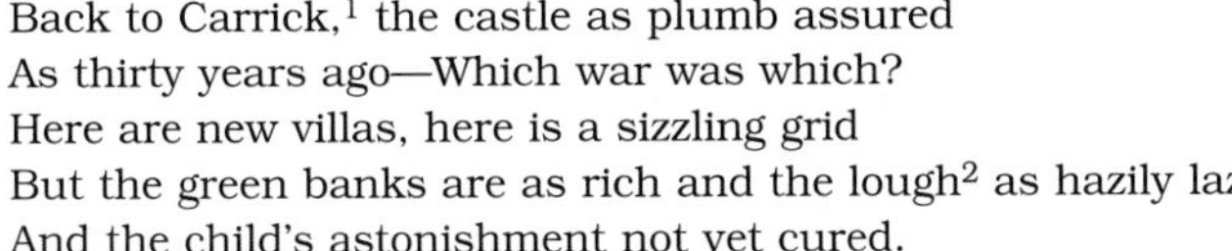

Back to Carrick,[1] the castle as plumb assured
As thirty years ago—Which war was which?
13 Here are new villas, here is a sizzling grid
But the green banks are as rich and the lough[2] as hazily lazy
And the child's astonishment not yet cured.

Who was—and am—dumbfounded to find myself
14 In a topographical frame—here, not there—
The channels of my dreams determined largely
By random chemistry of soil and air;
Memories I had shelved peer at me from the shelf.

Fog-horn, mill-horn, corncrake and church bell
Half-heard through boarded time as a child in bed
Glimpses a brangle of talk from the floor below
But cannot catch the words. Our past we know
But not its meaning—whether it meant well.

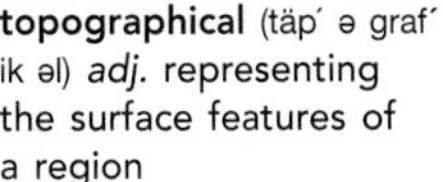

topographical (täp′ ə graf′ ik əl) *adj.* representing the surface features of a region

1. **Carrick** shortened form of Carrickfergus, a town in Northern Ireland.
2. **lough** (läkh) lake, specifically Belfast Lough. Carrickfergus is situated on the northern shore of Belfast Lough.

13 Critical Thinking

Speculate

- Have students speculate about whether MacNeice would have the same reaction to his childhood home if he returned in the twenty-first century, more than 60 years from the date of the poem. What may have changed in his absence? Take into account the history of the world and that of Ireland.
  Possible reponses: Population growth and tourism may have led to the building up of the area. Roads may have been modernized and enlarged.
- Then, ask students to consider whether these changes would have inspired a different reaction in the speaker from the reaction expressed in the poem.
  Possible response: The speaker's reaction would be different insofar as he might be reminded of childhood scenes by the absence of familiar details. At the same time, he might still be moved to reflect on how those scenes shaped his identity.

14 Vocabulary Development

Greek Root *-top-*

- Point out to students the word *topographical* in line 7. Explain that the root word *-top-* means "place."
- Have students identify other words that contain this Greek root.
  Possible response: Such words include *topic, topical,* and *topology.*
- Then, encourage students to use a dictionary to find out how this root word contributes to the meaning of each word.

CUSTOMIZE INSTRUCTION FOR UNIVERSAL ACCESS

For Less Proficient Readers	For Gifted/Talented Students
Have less proficient readers read each stanza of the poem in a choral reading. Remind students to pay attention to the punctuation of the lines, and point out that the end of a line does not always mean the end of a sentence. If you think it would be helpful, provide copies of the poem and ask students to draw a red or blue slash to indicate the end of each sentence.	Gifted or talented students might enjoy creating for the class a rendition of their childhood memories. This may be accomplished in art, drama, music, or dance. Encourage students to plan some discussion time after a performance or showing so that other students can determine whether they interpreted the art and its meaning correctly.

Answers for p. 1006

Review and Assess

1. Possible response: Yes, one may easily be surprised by the strength of memories when returning to a place known in childhood.
2. **(a)** He finds himself back at Carrickfergus, where he spent some childhood years. **(b)** The castle, green hills, and lake are the same, while new houses show change.
3. **(a)** He is dumbfounded to find himself in territory more familiar than expected. **(b)** His personal history affects the way he imagines things, yet his imagination lets him discern the arbitrariness of the particulars of his past.
4. **(a)** The specifics reinforce and add details to his imagination, such as the sounds of "Foghorn, mill-horn, corncrake and church bell . . . ." **(b)** We cannot choose our own past, and the past defines who we are. **(c)** He might expect poetry to record and interpret the past.
5. **(a)** It is an interlude between his ancestry in the western part of Ireland and his schooling in the south of England. **(b)** He is influenced by both the Irish and English portions of his life, but he feels as though he does not belong to either totally.
6. Many people today are of mixed ethnic lineage or have relocated to new countries.

Time and place—our bridgeheads into reality
But also its concealment! Out of the sea
We land on the Particular and lose
All other possible bird's-eye views, the Truth
That is of Itself for Itself—but not for me.

Torn before birth from where my fathers dwelt,
Schooled from the age of ten to a foreign voice,
Yet neither western Ireland nor southern England
Cancels this interlude; what chance misspelt
May never now be righted by my choice.

Whatever then my inherited or acquired
Affinities, such remains my childhood's frame
Like a belated rock in the red Antrim[3] clay
That cannot at this era change its pitch or name—
And the prenatal mountain is far away.

affinities (ə fin′ i tēz) *n.* family connections; sympathies

prenatal (prē nāt′ əl) *adj.* existing or taking place before birth

3. **Antrim** county in Northern Ireland in which Carrickfergus is located.

Review and Assess

Thinking About the Selection

1. **Respond:** Do you empathize with the poet's "astonishment" on returning to his birthplace? Explain.
2. **(a) Recall:** Where does the speaker find himself at the beginning of the poem?
   (b) Compare and Contrast: According to the first stanza, what has changed and what has remained the same?
3. **(a) Recall:** What discovery dumbfounds the poet?
   (b) Interpret: What relationship does the speaker discover between the imagination—which enables us to picture ourselves in any circumstances—and the facts of his personal history?
4. **(a) Interpret:** What effect do the specifics of the place have on the speaker's imagination? **(b) Interpret:** What does the speaker mean in saying "Our past we know / But not its meaning. . . ." **(c) Speculate:** What task concerning the past might MacNeice assign to poetry?
5. **(a) Interpret:** Why does the speaker call his childhood in Carrick an "interlude"? **(b) Draw Conclusions:** How is MacNeice's identity, as described in this poem, influenced by two cultures but separate from both?
6. **Extend:** Name two ways in which issues of identity are even more complex today than when MacNeice was writing.

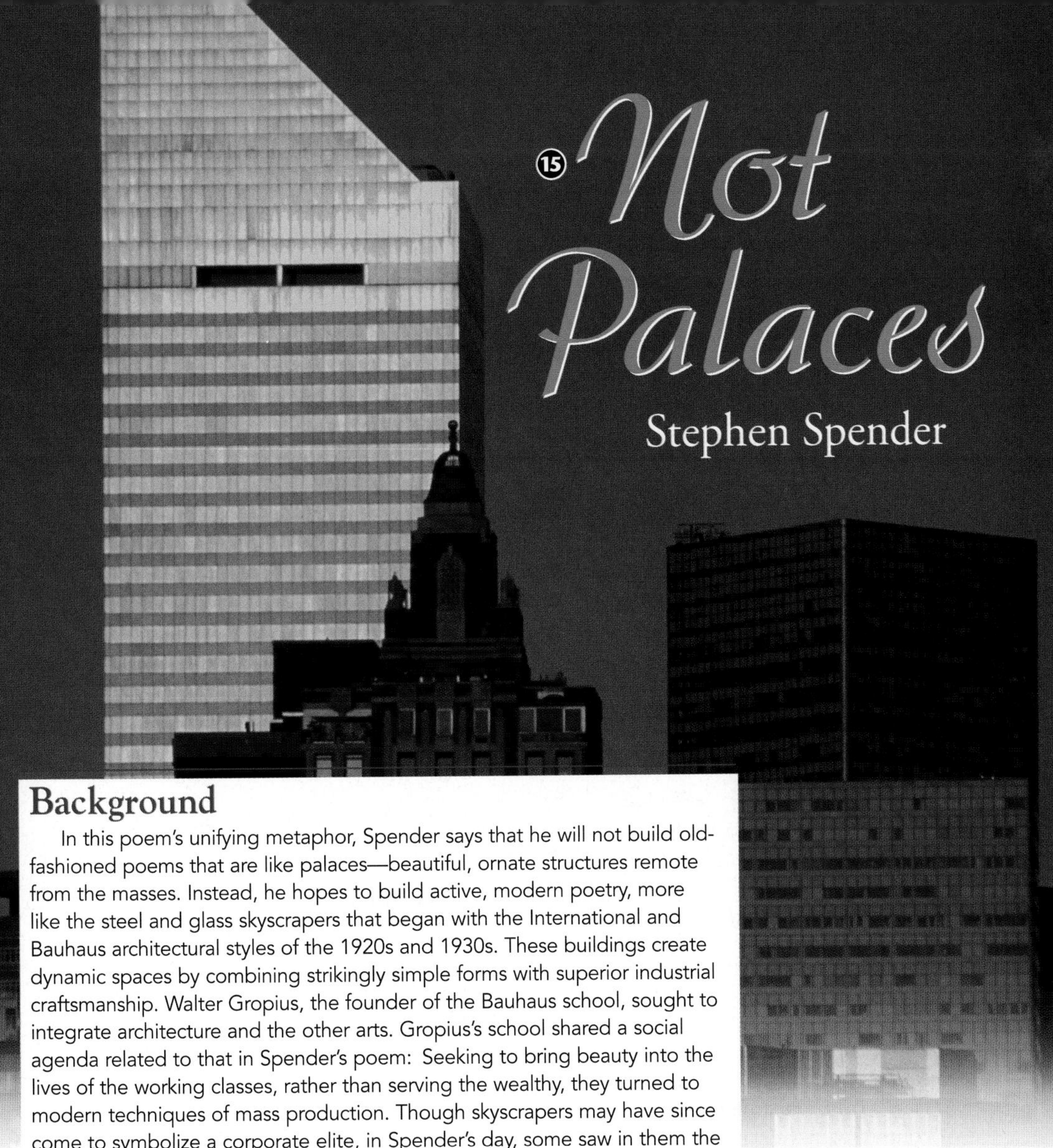

(15) Not Palaces

Stephen Spender

Background

In this poem's unifying metaphor, Spender says that he will not build old-fashioned poems that are like palaces—beautiful, ornate structures remote from the masses. Instead, he hopes to build active, modern poetry, more like the steel and glass skyscrapers that began with the International and Bauhaus architectural styles of the 1920s and 1930s. These buildings create dynamic spaces by combining strikingly simple forms with superior industrial craftsmanship. Walter Gropius, the founder of the Bauhaus school, sought to integrate architecture and the other arts. Gropius's school shared a social agenda related to that in Spender's poem: Seeking to bring beauty into the lives of the working classes, rather than serving the wealthy, they turned to modern techniques of mass production. Though skyscrapers may have since come to symbolize a corporate elite, in Spender's day, some saw in them the promise of true social equality.

(16)

Not palaces, an era's crown
Where the mind dwells, intrigues, rests:
Architectural gold-leaved flower
From people ordered like a single mind,
I build: this only what I tell:

intrigues (in trēgz′) *v.* plots or schemes

(15) About the Selection

This poem contrasts the aesthetic values of art with its potential for social change. The poet discusses and rejects the idea that art should be merely a "palace"—a beautiful home for the imagination, remote from society. He calls emphatically instead for commitment to social action, asking artists to inspire change.

(16) Literary Analysis

Theme

- Have a volunteer read aloud lines 1–5. Ask students to restate the meaning of these lines in their own words.
- Then, ask students to identify the clues that Spender offers about his theme in these lines. **Answer:** Spender refers to what he will not build—a palace. Associated with the idea of a palace are certain ideas of history and society and of the uses of art.

CUSTOMIZE INSTRUCTION FOR UNIVERSAL ACCESS

For Less Proficient Readers	For Advanced Readers
Less proficient readers may need help navigating Spender's poetic structure. Direct them to break down the sentences in the poem and read them, at first, according to punctuation only. Note that often semicolons take the place of periods, and sections may be deemed to be whole sentences for this purpose.	Advanced students may enjoy researching to determine to what extent the era of palaces involved a society of "people ordered like a single mind." Have some students investigate society, architecture, painting, and music during the reign of the famous palace builder, Louis XIV. Have them put their research together to write essays evaluating Spender's assumption.

ASSESS

Answers for p. 1008

Review and Assess

1. Students may say that they prefer "palaces," as they have more respect for the detail and workmanship needed to erect them than for the casual or even chaotic appearance of some modern art.
2. **(a)** He is rejecting the importance of building great and elaborate monuments or collecting rare objects from the past. **(b)** He is rejecting the vision of art as merely recording reality.
3. **(a)** Times have changed; it is too late. **(b)** He wants to use poetry to inspire and motivate others toward social action.
4. **(a)** The images of flashing glass may refer to modern skyscrapers. **(b)** These buildings are plainer, more modern, and more functional than the "palaces" of yesteryear.
5. **(a)** He urges them to leave gardens, feasts, and dreams of an afterlife. **(b)** The senses should attend to "images of flashing glass" that strike the will.
6. **(a)** Poetry used to be written for the pleasure of those with the leisure to appreciate its elaborate beauty and wit. **(b)** He thinks it should now be used to communicate views about society.
7. Possible response: Auden's view would not coincide with Spender's view of poetry in the present: it can be used to affect social change.

It is too late for rare accumulation,
For family pride, for beauty's filtered dusts;
I say, stamping the words with emphasis,
Drink from here energy and only energy
To will this time's change.
Eye, gazelle, delicate wanderer,
Drinker of horizon's fluid line;
Ear that suspends on a chord
The spirit drinking timelessness;
Touch, love, all senses;
Leave your gardens, your singing feasts,
Your dreams of suns circling before our sun,
Of heaven after our world.
Instead, watch images of flashing glass
That strike the outward sense, the polished will,
Flag of our purpose which the wind engraves.
No spirit seek here rest. But this: No one
Shall hunger: Man shall spend equally;
Our goal which we compel: Man shall be man.

Review and Assess

Thinking About the Selection

1. **Respond:** Do you prefer "palaces"—ornate, traditional artworks—to modern art? Why or why not?
2. (a) **Recall:** In lines 1–7, what does the speaker say he will not do? (b) **Interpret:** What vision of art is he rejecting?
3. (a) **Recall:** What reason does the poet give for rejecting the "accumulation" of rarities? (b) **Interpret:** What connection does the speaker make between his poem and social progress in lines 9–10?
4. (a) **Interpret:** What might the poet mean by "images of flashing glass"? (b) **Compare and Contrast:** How does this image contrast with the palaces described in the poem's opening?
5. (a) **Infer:** What does the speaker tell the senses to leave in lines 16–18? (b) **Interpret:** What should the senses attend to instead?
6. (a) **Analyze:** What does Spender think the job of poetry once was? (b) **Analyze:** What does he think it should be now?
7. **Relate:** In "In Memory of W. B. Yeats," Auden writes that although "poetry makes nothing happen," it teaches us a kind of joy in what is. Would Spender agree with Auden's ideas? Explain your answer.

ASSESSMENT PRACTICE: Writing Skills

Style **(For more practice, see Test Preparation Workbook, p. 48.)**

Many tests require students to recognize effective stylistic devices and language. Use the following sample test item to teach students how to recognize the tone of a passage.

He disappeared in the dead of winter:
The brooks were frozen, the airports
almost deserted,
And snow disfigured the public statues;
The mercury sank in the mouth of the dying day.

Which of these *best* describes the tone of the passage?

A whimsical
B controversial
C melodramatic
D solemn

Guide students to see that words like *dead, frozen, deserted,* and *dying* lead to a tone best described as *D, solemn.*

Review and Assess

Literary Analysis

Theme

1. What details of the ploughman's response to the disaster in "Musée des Beaux Arts" help convey the poem's **theme**?
2. The theme of "Carrick Revisited" may be summed up in the question "What creates an artist's identity?" (a) What clue to the theme does the setting provide? (b) Identify two passages that express the theme directly. (c) Does MacNeice fully answer this question? Explain.
3. In "Not Palaces," Spender advocates rejecting old artistic attitudes. In what way does his architectural imagery express this theme?

Comparing Literary Works

4. Use a chart like the one shown to compare the ideas in these poems about the nature of art.

Poem	Central Issues	Supporting Passages	Interpretation
"In Memory of W. B. Yeats"	What difference does art make?	"Teach the free man how to praise."	

5. Both "In Memory of W. B. Yeats" and "Carrick Revisited" question the connection between the particulars of an artist's life and his or her work. Compare their answers.
6. (a) Which of these poets believe that art in some sense rises above life? (b) Which do not? Explain, using examples. (c) With which poet's view of art do you agree? Why?

Reading Strategy

Paraphrasing

7. (a) **Paraphrase** lines 32–41 of "In Memory of W. B. Yeats." (b) Paraphrase a section of a poem of your choice.
8. (a) How did paraphrasing help you understand these lines? (b) What is lost in the translation?

Extend Understanding

9. **Science Connection:** MacNeice analyzes his identity. Using ideas of heredity and environment, how might a scientist respond?

Quick Review

The **theme** of a literary work is its central concern or purpose, or the main question it raises.

To **paraphrase,** restate a writer's words in your own words.

Take It to the Net

www.phschool.com

Take the interactive self-test online to check your understanding of these selections.

Answers for p. 1009

Review and Assess

1. The ploughman's indifference to the disaster offers an example of the world's indifference to individual suffering.
2. **(a)** The setting—the poet's birthplace—points to an interest in his history. **(b)** (i) "Our past we know / But not its meaning" (ii) "Whatever then my inherited or acquired / Affinities, such remains my childhood's frame" **(c)** Possible response: MacNeice gives us only part of the equation (history) of what makes an artist's identity.
3. Spender rejects the ornate buildings of the past in favor of the modern skyscraper, thus reinforcing the theme.
4. **Poem:** "Carrick Revisited": **Central Issues:** What creates an artist's identity? **Supporting Passages:** "Whatever then my inherited or acquired / Affinities, such remains my childhood's frame" **Interpretation:** A poet's art derives in part from the accidents of his or her history.
5. Auden seems to think that the beauty of Yeats's poetry has little to do with his experiences. MacNeice seems to think that past experiences are part of what makes an artist and is present within the poetry.
6. **(a)** Auden believed that art rises above life, in that art will remain when mortal man is gone. **(b)** Spender and MacNeice focus on art's involvement in life, either looking back at the past or forward to the future. **(c)** Answers will vary. Students should support their answers with reasons or examples.
7. **(a)** Possible response: You were human but your poetry survives your flaws and those of your homeland. Poetry survives in itself, not by changing the world. **(b)** From "Carrick Revisited," lines 26–30: Regardless of family traditions or the choices I have made, my childhood experiences remain the same and exert a strong influence on who I am.

continued

ENRICHMENT: Further Reading

Other Works by the Poets

Other Works by W. H. Auden
On This Island

Other Works by Louis MacNeice
Letters from Iceland

Other Works by Stephen Spender
World Within a World

Answers continued

8. **(a)** Paraphrasing aids comprehension of literal meaning. **(b)** The vivid, suggestive images and the rhythm of the words are lost.
9. A scientist might argue that genetics make more of a contribution to a person's identity than Spender indicates.

EXTEND

Answers for p. 1010

Review and Assess

❶ Vocabulary Development

Word Analysis

1. the mathematics of surfaces
2. study or mapping of places
3. intended for surface application, as an ointment

Spelling Strategy

1. achiever
2. communicator
3. dissenter

Concept Development: Synonyms

1. (b)
2. (a)
3. (c)
4. (c)
5. (a)

❷ Grammar and Style

1. Time worships language and *pardons* cowardice.
2. Suffering takes place while someone is eating or *opening* a window.
3. This is no time for collecting objects or *admiring* beautiful artifacts in museums.
4. I am not interested in building palaces or in *creating* rare objects.
5. MacNeice tried his hand at various genres, including poetry, drama, and *translations of verse.*

Writing Application

Possible response: Brueghel was noted for his ability to understand country folk and to paint details of their life. Roaming the countryside, Brueghel learned about the life of peasants and the look of nature. *The Fall of Icarus* shows that he mastered the play of light as well as the details of life.

Integrate Language Skills

❶ Vocabulary Development Lesson

Word Analysis: Greek Root *-top-*

The Greek root *-top-* means "place" or "surface." The word *topographical*, used by MacNeice, means "relating to a map of the surface features of a place." Explain how the root *-top-* contributes to the meanings of these words from science and mathematics:

1. topology 2. topography 3. topical

Spelling Strategy

In words that end in a vowel and *r*, *-er* is the most common spelling. Nouns formed from verbs that end in *-ate*, *-ess*, or *-ct* use *-or:* as in *generate, generator; profess, professor; act, actor.* Choose the correctly spelled word from each pair below.

1. achiever, achievor
2. communicater, communicator
3. dissenter, dissentor

Concept Development: Synonyms

Review the vocabulary list on page 997. For each numbered word below, write the letter of its synonym, the word or phrase that has the meaning closest to it.

1. sequestered: (a) convicted, (b) kept apart, (c) silent
2. intrigues: (a) schemes, (b) fails, (c) deceives
3. topographical: (a) reflecting a person's life, (b) atypical, (c) representing a place
4. affinities: (a) immensities, (b) ends, (c) attractions
5. prenatal: (a) before birth, (b) naive, (c) not natural

❷ Grammar and Style Lesson

Parallel Structure

Poets often use **parallel structure**—repeated use of the same grammatical form or pattern—to make their writing memorable and effective. These lines from "Not Palaces" contain parallel prepositional phrases.

Example: It is too late for rare accumulation, For family pride, for beauty's filtered dusts; . . .

Practice Rewrite each underscored item to make the sentence structure parallel.

1. Time worships language and is pardoning cowardice.
2. Suffering takes place while someone is eating or opens a window.
3. This is no time for collecting objects or to admire beautiful artifacts in museums.
4. I am not interested in building palaces or the creation of rare objects.
5. MacNeice tried his hand at various genres, including poetry, drama, and translating in verse.

Writing Application Write three sentences on art that use parallel structure to produce an effective rhythm. Your sentences might connect gerunds such as *writing* and *creating* or infinitive phrases such as *to inspire* and *to create*.

WG *Prentice Hall Writing and Grammar Connection: Chapter 20, Section 6*

TEACHING RESOURCES

The following resources can be used to enrich or extend the instruction for pp. 1010–1011.

Vocabulary

- **Selection Support:** Build Vocabulary, p. 219
- **Vocabulary and Spelling Practice Book,** (Use this booklet for skills enrichment.)

Grammar

- **Selection Support:** Grammar and Style, p. 220
- **Writing and Grammar,** Diamond Level, p. 505
- **Daily Language Practice Transparencies**

Writing

- **Writing and Grammar,** Diamond Level, p. 108
- **Writing and Grammar iText CD-ROM**

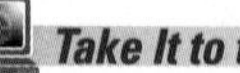

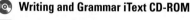

Take It to the Net

Visit www.phschool.com for self-tests and additional questions on the selections.

BLOCK SCHEDULING: Resources marked with this symbol provide varied instruction during 90-minute blocks.

❸ Writing Lesson

Poem About an Artwork

Auden's poem "Musée des Beaux Arts" was inspired by a Brueghel painting. Choose another painting or a photograph, and respond to it in a poem of your own. To convey one main impression, establish and maintain a strong, consistent tone.

Prewriting For five minutes, write down whatever comes to mind about the artwork you have chosen. Review your notes, and circle the most interesting details. Use these notes as the basis for your draft.

Drafting Choose a logical organization. You might begin with a physical description and then describe your emotional response. As you draft, concentrate on choosing words that will result in a strong, consistent tone—whether it be wonder, amusement, or disappointment.

Revising Ask a partner to summarize the main impression of your poem. Make adjustments if your partner's response does not match your intentions.

Model: Revising to Strengthen a Main Impression

bold
A ^ blue stripe splits the canvas in two,
Mocking, laughing—
~~Challenging the viewer,~~ ^ "On which side are you?"

Flatly descriptive language is revised to suggest the self-confident energy of the painting.

WG Prentice Hall Writing and Grammar Connection: Chapter 6, Section 4

❹ Extension Activities

Listening and Speaking Present a **group reading** of "In Memory of W.B. Yeats." To prepare, follow these tips:

- Analyze the various moods and tones of each section.
- Identify the most appropriate tone, volume, and pace for each.
- Assign each section as a separate part, and rehearse your reading.

When you have rehearsed sufficiently, present your reading to the class.

Research and Technology With a group, install an **art exhibition** of works in the spirit of "Not Palaces." Determine which twentieth-century artists pursue the same ideals as Spender. Then, collect copies of artworks for display. Devise strategies for highlighting the features you want to address. Produce your exhibition. **[Group Activity]**

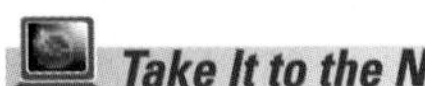

www.phschool.com

Go online for an additional research activity using the Internet.

ASSESSMENT RESOURCES

The following resources can be used to assess students' knowledge and skills.

Selection Assessment

- **Formal Assessment,** pp. 231–233
- **Open Book Test,** pp. 138–140
- **Test Bank Software**
- **Got It! Assessment Videotapes,** Tape 5

Take It to the Net
Visit www.phschool.com for self-tests and additional questions on the selections.

PRENTICE HALL ASSESSMENT SYSTEM

- **Workbook**
- **Skill Book**
- **Transparencies**
- **CD-ROM**

Lesson Support for p. 1011

❸ Writing Lesson

- Be sure that you approve students' choices of art or photo before allowing them to continue.
- During the Prewriting phase, ask students to also review their notes to see if they can find a theme within their ideas. This may focus the poem more easily.
- Students who have another idea for organization should be encouraged to arrange their poem in a different sequence.
- Students may work in pairs to ascertain first impressions and for help with revisions.
- If you ask students to read their poems aloud before the class, be sure they can also display the painting or photograph so others can evaluate the poem in better perspective.

❹ Listening and Speaking

- If possible, assign an equal number of boys and girls to each group. Then, discuss how students might determine which portions are more suited for a male voice, and which are better suited for a female voice.
- Inform students that some dramas, notably the ancient Greek dramas, make use of a chorus. In a chorus, several people speak at once, usually to give narrative or exposition. Discuss whether this might have a place in their reading.
- Monitor students' discussions and rehearsals to be sure every student is given an opportunity to read.

CUSTOMIZE INSTRUCTION For Universal Access

To address different learning styles, use the following activities suggested in the **Extension Activities** booklet, p. 47.

- For Logical/Mathematical and Visual/Spatial Learners, use Activity 5.
- For Bodily/Kinesthetic and Interpersonal Learners, use Activity 6.
- For Musical/Rhythmical Learners, use Activity 7.

Lesson Objectives

1. To read mission statements to learn information about a group's objectives
2. To identify and assess the organization of a mission statement

About Mission Statements

- Have students read "About Mission Statements."
- Then, ask them what information a mission statement gives to interested readers.
  Answer: It describes the guiding purpose, specific objectives, and daily activities of the organization.
- Next, discuss the various organizations that use mission statements. Then, ask students to list student organizations that have mission statements.
  Possible response: Groups include the Boy Scouts or Girl Scouts of America.

Reading Strategy

Interpreting the Organization of a Mission Statement

- Have students read the Reading Strategy, and ask what the most important goal of a mission statement is in terms of its organization.
  Answer: The most important goal is making the information it gives easily accessible.
- Ask students what allows readers to easily follow the main ideas of a mission statement.
  Answer: Short focused paragraphs and groups of bulleted items make them easy to follow.
- Ask students what other kinds of materials use bulleted items and boldface subheadings to convey information to readers.
  Possible response: Most students will mention their textbooks. Some may mention various types of consumer guides.
- Have students refer to the boxed annotations as they read the National Gallery's mission statement.

READING INFORMATIONAL MATERIALS

Mission Statements

About Mission Statements

Suppose that you want to volunteer your spare time working for a charitable organization. To learn the group's objectives, it may help to read its mission statement. A **mission statement** is a document provided by a company, a charitable organization, or another group to identify itself and describe its guiding purpose, specific objectives, and daily activities. Mission statements help introduce the organization to the general public. They can also help nonprofit organizations obtain government grants.

Reading Strategy

Interpreting the Organization of a Mission Statement

The organization of a mission statement is imperative to its success. To engage casual browsers, the statement must make basic information easy to find. At the same time, the statement must contain enough facts to satisfy those who desire specific information. The following organizational strategies are commonly used in mission statements and other documents that give a brief, businesslike overview of a subject:

- Short and concise boldfaced subheads to allow readers to quickly take in the main points covered
- Short, focused paragraphs and groups of bulleted items to allow readers the opportunity to follow ideas easily
- The organization of points in order of importance to focus readers' attention
- The organization of details in chronological order to allow readers to follow the order in which steps are taken to accomplish objectives.

The National Gallery, located in London, was established in 1824 with Parliament's purchase of a private collection of art. Its mission statement appears on the following pages. Use a chart like the one shown to help you determine whether it uses organizational strategies successfully.

Organizational Strategy	Purpose	Effectiveness

The National Gallery

Role and Objectives

Large heads clearly divide the mission statement into sections.

Role

The National Gallery houses the national Collection of Western European paintings from around 1250 to 1900.

The Gallery's aim is to care for, enhance and study its Collection, so as to offer the fullest access to the pictures for the education and enjoyment of the widest possible public now and in the future. It aims for the highest international standards in all its activities.

The Collection belongs to the people of the United Kingdom. It is open, free of charge, to all.

An important introductory statement is set off in boldface.

The Gallery serves a very wide and diverse public, which includes:

- those who visit the Gallery of London—both those who visit frequently and those who visit only occasionally;
- those who see its pictures while they are on loan elsewhere, both inside and outside the UK, and those who know the Collection through publications, multimedia and TV;
- those who live nearby as well as those who live further away in the United Kingdom and overseas;
- every age group—from children to pensioners;
- the socially excluded and the privileged; the uninformed and the specialist; and those with special needs;
- the worldwide community of museums and galleries;
- and, most importantly, future generations.

Objectives

The Gallery aims to:

Care for the Collection

Objectives are listed in order of importance, with the most important appearing first.

- keep the pictures in the nation's Collection safe for future generations by maintaining a secure and appropriate environment for them, monitoring their condition regularly, and undertaking suitable restoration or conservation;
- do everything possible to secure the pictures from fire, theft and other hazards;
- do everything possible to ensure that pictures loaned out are in sound enough condition to travel safely.

The National Gallery: Roles and Objectives

- Point out the various headings, subheadings, and bulleted information, and ask students what separates the bulleted group under the heading *Role* from the rest of the section.
  Answer: The bulleted group gives information on the services that the Gallery provides for the public.
- Ask students what group is the most important one that the museum serves.
  Answer: The statement identifies future generations as its most important beneficiary.
- Ask students what is the least important objective concerning care for the collection, and what heading(s) can it be found under.
  Answer: Ensuring "that pictures loaned out are in sound enough condition to travel safely," which is under the subheading Care for the Collection, is perhaps the least important.

continued on p. 1014

continued from p. 1013

- Point out the first call-out box to students and ask if there might be another reason behind the red boldfaced heads.
  Answer: Some students may remark that added color enhances the overall design of the mission statement, which may resemble a brochure.
- Ask students if the subheadings are placed in any discernible order.
  Possible response: Some students may say that it moves from object to groups of people, and geographically from national to international.
- Ask students what subheading scholars fall under, and why they are not listed under the subheading concerning access.
  Possible response: They fall under Study of the Collection. Scholars may warrant their own special heading because they are doing the research on the collection, research that will educate the layperson, inform other experts, and validate claims about the authorship, subject, or dates of paintings.

Boldfaced red heads call out general topics clearly for the reader who is skimming.

Enhance the Collection

- acquire great pictures across the whole range of European painting to enhance the Collection now and for future generations.

Study the Collection

- encourage all aspects of scholarship on the Collection, researching and documenting the pictures to the highest international standards, and ensuring that this work is disseminated.

Provide Access to the Collection for the Education and Enjoyment of the Widest Possible Public

In this section the mission statement breaks out specific objectives the Gallery has set itself for meeting its general purpose.

- encourage the public to use the Collection as their own by maintaining free admission, during the most convenient possible hours, to as much as possible of the permanent Collection;
- display the pictures well;
- promote knowledge of the Collection and encourage the public to visit it;
- help the widest possible public both in the Gallery and beyond to understand and enjoy the paintings, taking advantage of the opportunities created by modern technology;
- offer the highest possible standards in services for our visitors.

Stand as a National and International leader in All Its Activities

- work with other regional museums and galleries in the United Kingdom.
- enhance the national and international standing of the Gallery.

CUSTOMIZE INSTRUCTION FOR UNIVERSAL ACCESS

For Gifted/Talented Students

Encourage these students to research the collection at the National Gallery. Much information on the collection is available on the Web. They may even obtain a CD-ROM at their local library. Students may wish to break into pairs and divide up the research, concentrating on the important aspects of the collection, famous paintings, and the layout of the museum itself. Have these students construct a multimedia presentation on the Gallery, helping them to obtain any equipment necessary. Then, have them present their work to the rest of the class.

Check Your Comprehension

1. Who owns the National Gallery's Collection?
2. How is the National Gallery going to enhance its Collection in the future?
3. What steps does the National Gallery take to ensure that its Collection receives proper care?
4. What is the National Gallery's general purpose?

Applying the Reading Strategy

Organizing a Mission Statement

After reading the National Gallery's mission statement, use the information within it to answer the following questions:

5. Briefly scan the subheads within the mission statement. (a) Write a summary based on your scan of the points covered. (b) Read the brochure. Does it cover everything predicted by your summary? Explain.
6. (a) Are the details within the mission statement organized in the order of their importance or in chronological order? (b) Is this organization strategy effective?
7. How does grouping related details help provide a more clearly defined mission statement?
8. Does the organization of this mission statement help you understand the National Gallery's goals and objectives? Explain.

Activity

Writing a Mission Statement

Many high schools have a number of clubs and societies. Before a student decides to join a particular organization, he or she might want to read a mission statement to ensure that he or she agrees with the group's goals and objectives. Choose an organization in your school, research it, and write a mission statement for it. Use the Web shown to help you devise the subheads for your mission statement.

Comparing Informational Materials

Evaluating Mission Statements

Most organizations and businesses have mission statements that are easily obtained by the general public. Read and compare a mission statement from a business or museum in your area with the mission statement from the National Gallery. Which mission statement is more effective in the presentation of its message? Explain your evaluation.

Answers for p. 1015

Check Your Comprehension

1. The people of the United Kingdom own the Collection.
2. It will "acquire great pictures across the whole range of European painting."
3. The Gallery monitors the condition of pieces and provides for restoration; it attends to their security; it ensures that the items it loans out can travel safely.
4. The Gallery's general purpose is to enhance, care for, and study its collection so as to offer free, full access to the paintings, and education and enjoyment to the widest possible public.

Applying the Reading Strategy

5. Make sure students cover all the bulleted points following the subheads, and clearly explain whether their predictions are or are not met.
6. **(a)** They are organized in order of importance. **(b)** Most students will say that this organization strategy is effective because it distills quite a bit of information and allows readers to focus on important points.
7. Grouping related details helps to clarify the ideas within the mission statement and allows the reader to follow the ideas easily.
8. Make sure students support their answers.

Activity

Make sure students choose an organization about which information is easily accessible through the local library, Web sites, or printed matter available through the club or organization. Tell them to use the graphic organizer shown to organize the information for their mission statement.

Comparing Informational Materials

- Tell students to stick to organizations and businesses that are somewhat known in their community.
- Remind students that mission statements can often be obtained from Web sites of businesses and organizations.
- Tell students to provide a copy of the mission statement when turning in their assignment.

Shooting an Elephant

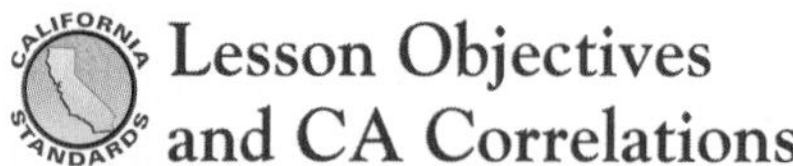

Lesson Objectives and CA Correlations

1. **To analyze and respond to literary elements**
   - Literary Analysis: Irony **R 3.3**
   - Connecting Literary Elements: Tone **R 3.2**
2. **To read, comprehend, analyze, and critique nonfiction**
   - Reading Strategy: Recognizing the Writer's Attitudes **R 2.5**
   - Reading Check Questions
   - Review and Assess Questions
3. **To develop word analysis skills, fluency, and systematic vocabulary**
   - Vocabulary Development Lesson: Words About Politics **R 1.1**
4. **To understand and apply written and oral language conventions**
   - Spelling Strategy **LC 1.2**
   - Grammar and Style Lesson: Participial Phrases: Restrictive and Nonrestrictive **LC 1.1**
5. **To understand and apply appropriate writing and research strategies**
   - Writing Lesson: Essay in Orwell's Style **W 1.2**
   - Extension Activity: Biography **W 2.4**
   - Assessment Practice (ATE)
6. **To understand and apply listening and speaking strategies**
   - Extension Activity: Audiovisual Presentation **LS 2.4**

STEP-BY-STEP TEACHING GUIDE	PACING GUIDE
PRETEACH	
Motivate Students and Provide Background	
Use the Motivation activity (ATE p. 1016)	5 min.
Read and discuss author and background features (SE/ATE pp. 1016, 1019, 1021) [A]	10 min.
Introduce the Concepts	
Introduce the Literary Analysis and Reading Strategy (SE/ATE p. 1017) [A]	15 min.
Pronounce the vocabulary words and read their definitions (SE p. 1017)	5 min.
TEACH	
Monitor Comprehension	
Informally monitor comprehension by circulating while students read independently or in groups [A]	25 min.
Monitor students' comprehension with the Reading Check notes (SE/ATE pp. 1019, 1021, 1023, 1025)	as students read
Develop vocabulary with Vocabulary notes (SE pp. 1020, 1022, 1025; ATE p. 1020)	as students read
Develop Understanding	
Develop students' understanding of irony with the Literary Analysis annotations (SE/ATE p. 1022) [A]	5 min.
Develop students' ability to recognize the writer's attitudes with the Reading Strategy annotations (SE/ATE pp. 1019, 1023, 1025)	5 min.
ASSESS	
Assess Mastery	
Assess students' mastery of the Reading Strategy and Literary Analysis by having them answer the Review and Assess questions (SE/ATE p. 1027)	15 min.
Use one or more of the print and media Assessment Resources (ATE p. 1029) [A]	up to 45 min.
EXTEND	
Apply Understanding	
Have students complete the Vocabulary Development Lesson and the Grammar and Style Lesson (SE p. 1028) [A]	20 min.
Apply students' ablility to use consistent style using the Writing Lesson (SE/ATE p. 1029) [A]	45 min.
Apply students' understanding using one or more of the Extension Activities (SE p. 1029)	20–90 min.

ACCELERATED INSTRUCTION:
Use the strategies and activities identified with an [A].

UNIVERSAL ACCESS
● = Below-Level Students
▲ = On-Level Students
■ = Above-Level Students

Time and Resource Manager

Reading Level: Average
Average Number of Instructional Days: 4

RESOURCES		
PRINT	**TRANSPARENCIES**	**TECHNOLOGY**
• **Beyond Literature,** Cross-Curricular Connection: Social Studies, p. 48 ▲ ■		• **Interest Grabber Video,** Tape 6 ● ▲ ■
• **Selection Support Workbook:** ● ▲ ■ Literary Analysis, p. 226 Reading Strategy, p. 225 Build Vocabulary, p. 223	• **Literary Analysis and Reading Transparencies,** pp. 95 and 96 ● ▲ ■	
• **Adapted Reader's Companion** ● • **Reader's Companion** ●		• **Listening to Literature** ● ▲ ■ Audiocassettes, Side 23 Audio CDs, CD 13
• **English Learner's Companion** ● ▲ • **Literatura en español** ● ▲ • **Literary Analysis for Enrichment** ■		
• **Formal Assessment:** Selection Test, pp. 234–236 ● ▲ ■ • **Open Book Test,** pp. 141–143 ● ▲ ■ • PRENTICE HALL ASSESSMENT SYSTEM ● ▲ ■	• PRENTICE HALL ASSESSMENT SYSTEM ● ▲ ■ Skills Practice Answers and Explanations on Transparencies ● ▲ ■	• **Test Bank Software** ● ▲ ■ • **Got It! Assessment Videotapes,** Tape 5 ● ▲
• **Selection Support Workbook:** ● ▲ ■ Grammar and Style, p. 224 • **Writing and Grammar,** Diamond Level ● ▲ ■ • **Extension Activities,** p. 48 ● ▲ ■	• **Daily Language Practice Transparencies** ● ▲	• **Writing and Grammar iText CD-ROM** ● ▲ ■ ***Take It to the Net*** www.phschool.com

BLOCK SCHEDULING: Use one 90-minute class period to preteach the selection and have students read it. Use a second 90-minute class period to assess students' mastery of skills and have them complete one of the Extension Activities.

PRETEACH

Step-by-Step Teaching Guide for pp. 1016–1017

Motivation

Have students imagine themselves in a tense situation in which they must make a quick decision. They want to act one way, but they're expected to act in another. Now have them imagine that their decision involves a potentially dangerous situation. What would go through their minds? What kinds of feelings would they have? Tell students that this is the situation in which the narrator of this essay finds himself.

Interest Grabber Video

As an alternative, play "'Shooting an Elephant': Saving an Elephant" on Tape 6 to engage student interest.

1 Background

More About the Author

Orwell adopted his nom de plume from the beautiful River Orwell in East Anglia. In time, this name became so attached to him that few people other than close relatives ever knew him as Eric Arthur Blair.

Many phrases and words he used in his books have become catch-phrases and buzzwords today. Orwell is responsible for such bons mots as "All animals are equal, but some animals are more equal than others," "Big Brother is watching you," "newspeak," and "doublethink."

Prepare to Read

1 Shooting an Elephant

George Orwell (1903–1950)

Many television reports today are on-the-scene newscasts or in-depth documentaries, showing people in the middle of an event. These reports, like best-selling "nonfiction novels," give us not just facts but a close-up, personal perspective on events. George Orwell pioneered this first-person style of reporting. Whether writing on the Spanish Civil War or life among the downtrodden, he penetrated prejudice and dishonest politics to expose the truth in a simple act—telling what he had seen, what he knew. He still stands as a figure of political and literary honesty, challenging us to tell the truth simply and directly.

Becoming an Officer Orwell was born Eric Blair in colonial India, was educated in England, and then joined the Imperial Police in Burma. His experiences there were typical of the small group of young Englishmen recruited as police officers for the British Empire. These men had no experience of police work and no knowledge of the country they would police. Their training in Burma consisted of memorizing laws and procedures and learning the native languages. They lived apart from the Burmese, who resented British rule.

Orwell was keenly aware of the inequities of imperialism. As an officer of the Burmese police, he headed a native-born police force of 13,000. Among the 90 officers, Englishmen held almost all the top ranks—a few white men governing 13 million Asians.

Disillusioned In 1928, after five years of service as an imperial police officer, the disillusioned Orwell resigned. His first novel, *Burmese Days* (1934), describes these bitter years. "Shooting an Elephant," one of his most famous essays, is based on a defining experience from this period.

Becoming George Orwell Orwell seemed to have a talent for immersing himself in difficult situations and then writing about them with extraordinary insight. Every book that emerged from an Orwell experience was a one-of-a-kind classic. In *Down and Out in Paris and London* (1933), for example, Orwell describes what it is like to be poor in two big cities.

In a strange way, his experience of life's shabbiness gave him a stronger sense of identity. After his journeys on the seamier side of things, he published and lived under a new name: George Orwell.

Adventuring During the 1930s, Orwell gave himself to political causes. In *The Road to Wigan Pier* (1937), he wrote about the English coal miners with whom he had lived. Then, during the Spanish Civil War (1936–1939), he fought for democracy with anarchists and socialist Republicans. He witnessed the infighting among the groups defending the Spanish government, infighting that enabled the Fascists to win. In his book on that crisis, *Homage to Catalonia* (1938), Orwell blamed the interference of the Soviet Union for undermining the Republican cause—a charge that made him unpopular with his fellow leftists. The book is a gripping adventure story, one in which the narrator's cool presence of mind allows him to recall in precise detail his experience of being wounded.

A Political Prophet During World War II, Orwell wrote political and literary journalism. In 1945, he published *Animal Farm*, a satirical fable attacking both fascism and communism. In 1949, he shared a dark vision of the future in his novel *1984*, in which a dictator rules by controlling all thought and language. The year 1984 has passed, but George Orwell's lifelong commitment to political freedom and to the honest use of language is as relevant as ever.

TEACHING RESOURCES

The following resources can be used to enrich or extend the instruction for pp. 1016–1017.

Motivation

Interest Grabber Video, Tape 6

Background

Beyond Literature, p. 48

Take It to the Net

Visit www.phschool.com for background and hotlinks for more about George Orwell.

Literary Analysis

Literary Analysis and Reading Transparencies, Irony, p. 96

Selection Support: Literary Analysis, p. 226

Reading

Literary Analysis and Reading Transparencies, Recognizing the Writer's Attitudes, p. 95

BLOCK SCHEDULING: Resources marked with this symbol provide varied instruction during 90-minute blocks.

Preview

Connecting to the Literature

It is time to give your speech. You reach the front of the room, only to realize that you have lost your notes, your topic still confuses you, and your hands are clammy with sweat. If you have had an experience like this one, you know a little about how Orwell feels in this memoir.

2 Literary Analysis

Irony

Orwell uses irony to underscore the no-win situation he faced in Burma. **Irony** is a device that brings out a contradiction between appearance and reality. It can take a few forms, including the following:

- **Verbal irony**—an intentional clash between the words chosen to talk about a thing and its reality; for example, calling a tall person "Shorty"
- **Irony of situation**—an opposition between the pattern of events and expectations or hopes; for example, on the day you are kicked off the team, someone you admire tells you she is eager to see you play.

As you read, notice how Orwell uses both kinds of irony.

Connecting Literary Elements

Tone is a writer's attitude toward the reader and the subject, as expressed in word choice, sentence structure, and other elements of style. Orwell's direct, matter-of-fact sentences achieve a conversational tone. In addition, his simple observations create a tone of ironic detachment—as when he sums up the complex Burmese situation with, "All this was perplexing and upsetting." As you read, notice the way Orwell develops his tone.

3 Reading Strategy

Recognizing the Writer's Attitudes

To understand the full meaning of a text, move beyond the words on the page to **recognize the writer's attitudes** toward his or her subject. To analyze Orwell's attitudes, use a chart like the one shown.

Attitude Toward Imperialism

". . . imperialism was an evil thing . . ."

Attitude Toward Burmese

". . . my rage against the evil-spirited little beasts who tried to make my life impossible."

Vocabulary Development

prostrate (präs′ trāt) *adj.* overcome; lying face downward (p. 1020)

imperialism (im pir′ ē əl iz′ əm) *n.* policy of forming an empire and securing economic power by conquest and colonization (p. 1020)

despotic (des pät′ ik) *adj.* tyrannical (p. 1020)

squalid (skwäl′ id) *adj.* miserably poor; wretched (p. 1020)

dominion (də min′ yən) *n.* rule or power over a territory (p. 1022)

senility (si nil′ ə tē) *n.* mental deterioration due to old age (p. 1025)

CUSTOMIZE INSTRUCTION FOR UNIVERSAL ACCESS

For Special Needs Students	For Less Proficient Readers	For English Learners
Have students read the adapted version of "Shooting an Elephant" in the **Adapted Reader's Companion.** This version provides basic-level instruction in an interactive format with questions and write-on lines. Completing the adapted version will prepare students to read the selection in the Student Edition.	Have students read "Shooting an Elephant" in the **Reader's Companion.** This version provides basic-level instruction in an interactive format with questions and write-on lines. After students finish the selection in Reader's Companion, have them complete the questions and activities in the Student Edition.	Have students read the adapted version of "Shooting an Elephant" in the **English Learner's Companion.** This version provides basic-level instruction in an interactive format with questions and write-on lines. Completing the adapted version will prepare students to read the selection in the Student Edition.

2 Literary Analysis

Irony

- Define irony for students as "a device that brings out a contradiction between appearance and reality."
- Offer as an example the first sentence of the essay, in which Orwell ironically equates being hated by many with being "important."
- Point out that many comedians of today use irony in their routines. Have students think of examples of comedians they have seen or examples from comedic shows on TV where irony was found to be humorous.
- Have students categorize their examples as *verbal irony* or *situational irony.*
- Help students understand that irony often involves the unexpected. Adjectives applied to an object with which they are not generally used and people or objects that do not behave as expected may be instances of irony.

3 Reading Strategy

Recognizing the Writer's Attitudes

- Point out to students that the attitude of the writer can color a piece without the direct intention of the writer.
- Remind students that personal beliefs can create an attitude. As a reader, one must accept the attitude of the writer.
- Help students find phrases and sentences in the first few paragraphs that are indicative of the writer's attitude.
- As students read the remainder of the essay, have them use self-sticking notes to keep track of sentences that strongly show Orwell's attitude at the time.

Vocabulary Development

- Pronounce each vocabulary word for students, and read the definitions as a class. Have students identify any words with which they are already familiar.

TEACH

Step-by-Step Teaching Guide for pp. 1018–1026

CUSTOMIZE INSTRUCTION
For Bodily/Kinesthetic Learners

Have these students look at the photograph on p. 1018. Ask them to mime the actions by which a human being might attempt to control an animal of the elephant's size.

❶ About the Selection

This essay reveals the ambivalence a person may feel in a position of power. On the one hand, young George Orwell (then Eric Blair) sympathizes with the Burmese people, who he feels are oppressed by the British colonists. On the other hand, Orwell, as a police officer, is committed to continuing and even defending that oppression. When an elephant goes wild in a Burmese marketplace, Orwell must act, making decisions more from his confused feelings than from common sense, and in the process demonstrating the intense human desire to avoid embarrassment.

❶ Shooting an Elephant

George Orwell

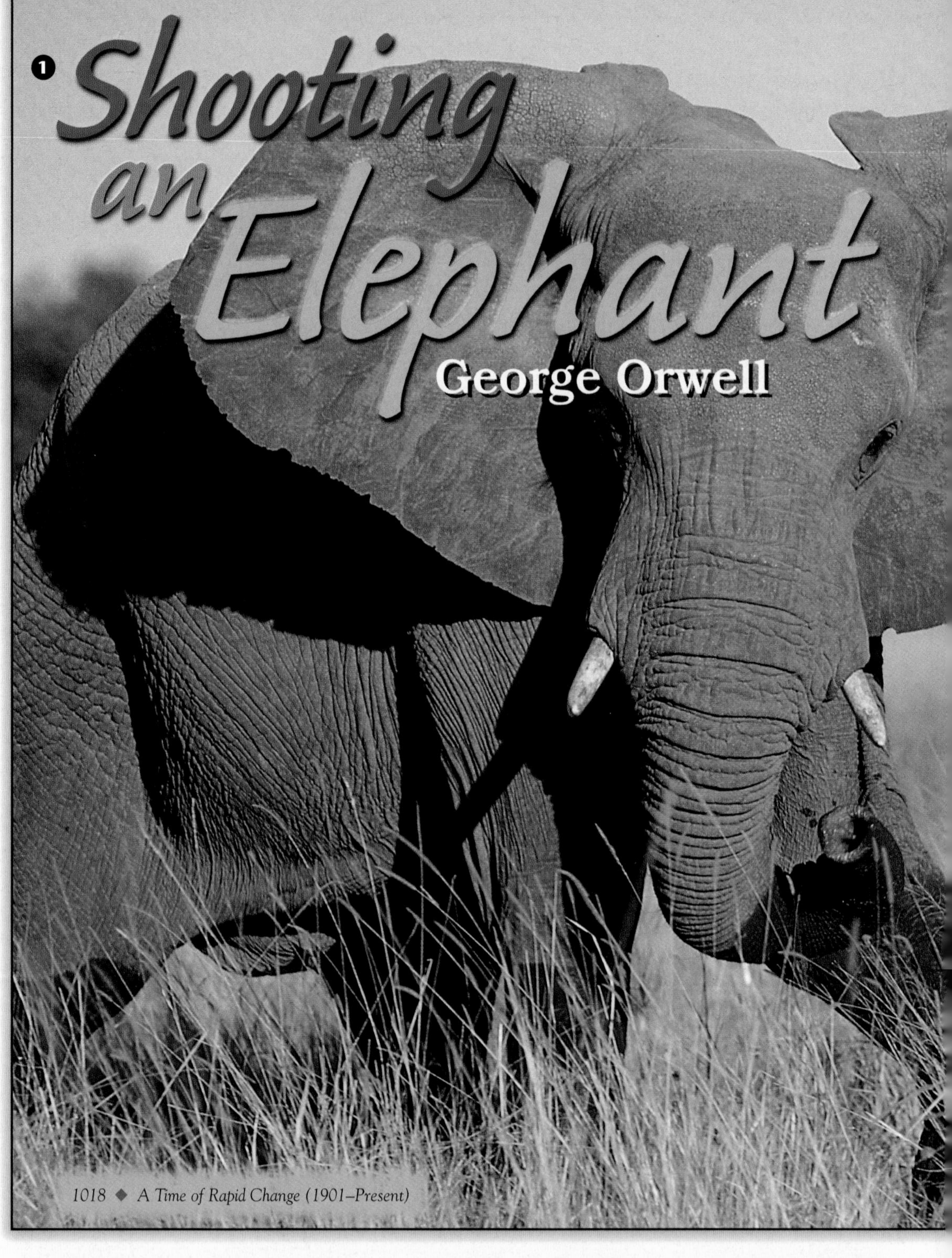

TEACHING RESOURCES

The following resources can be used to enrich or extend the instruction for pp. 1018–1026.

Literary Analysis

- **Literary Analysis and Reading Transparencies,** Irony, p. 96

Reading Strategy

- **Selection Support:** Reading Strategy, p. 225; Build Vocabulary, p. 223
- **Adapted Reader's Companion**
- **English Learner's Companion**

- **Listening to Literature Audiocassettes,** Side 23
- **Listening to Literature Audio CDs,** CD 13

BLOCK SCHEDULING: Resources marked with this symbol provide varied instruction during 90-minute blocks.

Background

Hoping to secure a better trade route with China, Great Britain fought several wars against Burma during the 1800s, finally conquering the country in 1885. Although the desired "golden path" to China did not prosper, Burma provided Britain with other economic opportunities, such as the export of Burmese rice. Many Burmese, however, were unwilling to accept British rule. Opponents of the British formed the Anti-Fascist People's Freedom League, led by Aung San. The group was instrumental in winning Burma's independence from Britain in 1948. In this essay, Orwell writes of the days of English rule in Burma.

In Moulmein, in lower Burma, I was hated by large numbers of people—the only time in my life that I have been important enough for this to happen to me. I was subdivisional police officer of the town, and in an aimless, petty kind of way anti-European feeling was very bitter. No one had the guts to raise a riot, but if a European woman went through the bazaars alone somebody would probably spit betel juice over her dress. As a police officer I was an obvious target and was baited whenever it seemed safe to do so. When a nimble Burman tripped me up on the football field and the referee (another Burman) looked the other way, the crowd yelled with hideous laughter. This happened
2 more than once. In the end the sneering yellow faces of young men that met me everywhere, the insults hooted after me when I was at a safe distance, got badly on my nerves. The young Buddhist priests were the worst of all. There were several thousands of them in the town and none of them seemed to have anything to do except stand on street corners and jeer at Europeans.

All this was perplexing and upsetting. For at that time I had already made up my mind that imperialism was an evil thing and the sooner I chucked up my job and got out of it the better. Theoretically—and secretly, of course—I was all for the Burmese and all against their oppressors, the British. As for the job I was doing, I hated it more bitterly than I can perhaps make clear. In a job like that you see the dirty work of Empire at close quarters. The wretched prisoners huddling in the stinking cages of the lockups, the gray, cowed faces of the long-term convicts, the

3 ◀ **Critical Viewing** Does this photograph depict a useful beast or a dangerous menace? Explain. **[Make a Judgment]**

Reading Strategy
Recognizing the Writer's Attitudes Identify Orwell's conflicting attitudes in these opening paragraphs.

4 

According to Orwell, how do the Burmese view the English?

2 Reading Strategy

Recognizing the Writer's Attitudes

- Ask students how Orwell felt about the Burmese, his job as a police officer, the treatment of Europeans in Burma, the Burmese priests, and British rule in general. Have students point out the sentence in which each attitude is revealed.
- Keep a running list of his attitudes on the board, separated under the headings of "Like" and "Dislike."
- Ask students the Reading Strategy question on p. 1019: Identify Orwell's conflicting attitudes in these opening paragraphs.
  Answer: Students should identify Orwell's sympathy for the Burmese, his dislike of imperialism, and his desire to leave his job. All these attitudes conflict with his role as police officer, and his bad treatment by the Burmese.

3 ▶ Critical Viewing

Answer: Students should recognize that the elephant has the potential to be either useful or dangerous, depending on the situation.

4 

Answer: The Burmese hated the English and most Europeans.

CUSTOMIZE INSTRUCTION FOR UNIVERSAL ACCESS

For Special Needs Students	For English Learners	For Advanced Readers
Help these students by having them read along to the recording of "Shooting an Elephant" on **Listening to Literature Audiocassettes.** Pause the recording frequently to discuss what has happened in the story. Write the main events, as suggested by students, on the board as they occur for future reference.	Have English learners take turns reading aloud from the essay. Help students with correct pronunciation. If students encounter an unfamiliar word, stop and allow them time to look it up in the dictionary and share with other students.	Ask advanced readers to recognize the almost conversational style in which Orwell has written this essay. Have them identify several devices that create an intimate atmosphere. Then, have students recall other material, or find new material, that creates this same tone.

5 Critical Thinking

Connect

- Remind students that Orwell was a young man of 19 when he went to serve in the Indian Imperial Police in Burma. Ask students to think about how this fact may have affected his ambivalent feelings toward the Burmese.
- Discuss whether Orwell would, at this age, have had fixed, ready ways of responding to the world. Would he have felt differently about his job and the British rule if he had been older?
- Have students brainstorm ideas about why Orwell did not speak up about the abuses he witnessed in Burma.

6 Vocabulary Development

Words About Politics

- Have students keep a running list of political and military titles in Orwell's essay, such as *subinspector* and *orderly*.
- Ask students to research other political and military titles, then list the ones from the story into a hierarchy, from the most powerful to the least powerful. Separate lists should be kept for the political and military titles.

scarred buttocks of the men who had been flogged with bamboos—all these oppressed me with an intolerable sense of guilt. But I could get nothing into perspective. I was young and ill educated and I had had to think out my problems in the utter silence that is imposed on every Englishman in the East. I did not even know that the British Empire is dying, still less did I know that it is a great deal better than the younger empires that are going to supplant it. All I knew was that 5 I was stuck between my hatred of the empire I served and my rage against the evil-spirited little beasts who tried to make my job impossible. With one part of my mind I thought of the British Raj[1] as an unbreakable tyranny, as something clamped down, *in saecula saeculorum*,[2] upon the will of prostrate peoples; with another part I thought that the greatest joy in the world would be to drive a bayonet into a Buddhist priest's guts. Feelings like these are the normal byproducts of imperialism; ask any Anglo-Indian official, if you can catch him off duty.

One day something happened which in a roundabout way was enlightening. It was a tiny incident in itself, but it gave me a better glimpse than I had had before of the real nature of imperialism—the real motives for which despotic governments act. Early one morning the subinspector at a police station the other end of the town rang me up on the phone and said that an elephant was ravaging the bazaar. Would I please come and do something about it? I did not know what I could do, but I wanted to see what was happening and I got onto a pony and started out. I took my rifle, an old .44 Winchester and much too small to kill an elephant, but I thought the noise might be useful *in terrorem*.[3] Various Burmans stopped me on the way and told me about the elephant's doings. It was not, of course, a wild elephant, but a tame one which had gone "must."[4] It had been chained up, as tame elephants always are when their attack of "must" is due, but on the previous night it had broken its chain and escaped. Its mahout,[5] the only person who could manage it when it was in that state, had set out in pursuit, but had taken the wrong direction and was now twelve hours' journey away, and in the morning the elephant had suddenly reappeared in the town. The Burmese population had no weapons and were quite helpless against it. It had already destroyed somebody's bamboo hut, killed a cow and raided some fruit stalls and devoured the stock; also it had met the municipal rubbish van and, when the driver jumped out and took to his heels, had turned the van over and inflicted violences upon it.

6 The Burmese subinspector and some Indian constables were waiting for me in the quarter where the elephant had been seen. It was a very poor quarter, a labyrinth of squalid bamboo huts, thatched with

prostrate (präs´ trāt) *adj.* overcome; lying face downward

imperialism (im pir´ ē əl iz´əm) *n.* policy of forming an empire and securing economic power by conquest and colonization

despotic (de spät´ ik) *adj.* tyrannical

squalid (skwäl´ id) *adj.* miserably poor; wretched

1. **Raj** (räj) rule.
2. ***in saecula saeculorum*** (in sē´ ko͞o lə sē´ ko͞o lôr´ əm) Latin for "forever and ever."
3. ***in terrorem*** Latin for "for terror."
4. **must** into a dangerous, frenzied state.
5. **mahout** (mə ho͞ot´) elephant keeper and rider.

ENRICHMENT: History Connection

British Imperialism in Burma

Orwell resented his position as an officer of the British Empire whose responsibility it was to enforce a system of imperialism that he disliked, but the Burmese had even greater cause to resent the British for failing to recognize and respect the peculiarities of Burma's culture. The Burmese were profoundly insulted that, for the sake of administrative efficiency, the British treated Burma as a province of India. Not only was Burma different from India in language, race, religious traditions, and customs, but India had fought with the British in the wars that subjugated Burma to Britain's empire.

The British were especially inept in accommodating Burmese religious traditions. Great Britain had an imperial policy of strict neutrality in religious matters, yet instead of establishing government schools, it allowed Christian missionaries to develop mission schools that were staffed by teachers who were often ignorant of or hostile to Burma's Buddhist traditions and culture.

palm leaf, winding all over a steep hillside. I remember that it was a cloudy, stuffy morning at the beginning of the rains. We began questioning the people as to where the elephant had gone and, as usual, failed to get any definite information. That is invariably the case in the East; a story always sounds clear enough at a distance, but the nearer you get to the scene of events the vaguer it becomes. Some of the people said that the elephant had gone in one direction, some said that he had gone in another, some professed not even to have heard of any elephant. I had almost made up my mind that the whole story was a pack of lies, when we heard yells a little distance away. There was a loud scandalized cry of "Go away, child! Go away this instant!" and an old woman with a switch in her hand came round the corner of a hut, violently shooing away a crowd of naked children. Some more women followed, clicking their tongues and exclaiming; evidently there was something that the children ought not to have seen. I rounded the hut and saw a man's dead body sprawling in the mud. He was an Indian, a black Dravidian[6] coolie,[7] almost naked, and he could not have been dead many minutes. The people said that the elephant had come suddenly upon him round the corner of the hut, caught him with its trunk, put its foot on his back and ground him into the earth. This was the rainy season and the ground was soft, and his face had scored a trench a foot deep and a couple of yards long. He was lying on his belly with arms crucified and head sharply twisted to one side. His face was coated with mud, the eyes wide open, the teeth bared and grinning with an expression of unendurable agony. (Never tell me, by the way, that the dead look peaceful. Most of the corpses I have seen looked devilish.) The friction of the great beast's foot had stripped the skin from his back as neatly as one skins a rabbit. As soon as I saw the dead man I sent an orderly to a friend's house nearby to borrow an elephant rifle. I had already sent back the pony, not wanting it to go mad with fright and throw me if it smelled the elephant.

The orderly came back in a few minutes with a rifle and five cartridges, and meanwhile some Burmans had arrived and told us that the elephant was in the paddy fields[8] below, only a few hundred yards away. As I started forward practically the whole population of the quarter flocked out of the houses and followed me. They had seen the rifle and were all shouting excitedly that I was going to shoot the elephant. They had not shown much interest in the elephant when he

6. **Dravidian** (drə vid′ ē ən) belonging to the race of people inhabiting southern India.
7. **coolie** laborer.
8. **paddy fields** rice fields.

Literature in context Vocabulary Connection

7 ***Vocabulary of Empire***

The key terms in Orwell's political vocabulary often have Latin origins:

- *Imperialism* comes from a Latin word for "command" or "empire."
- *Dominion* comes from a Latin word meaning "lord" or "master."

Supporters of British imperialism may have chosen Latinate words to describe the British Empire as a way of suggesting a comparison with the glory of the Roman Empire. However, critics like Orwell seized the word *imperialism*, and it gained strongly negative connotations.

Some meanings reflect history inaccurately. In an irony that Orwell would have appreciated, the word *despot* is derived from a Greek term for "ruler." Even though our ideas of democracy come from ancient Greece, where some rulers strove for democratic goals, the term has come to describe the opposite of a democratic leader—an oppressive tyrant.

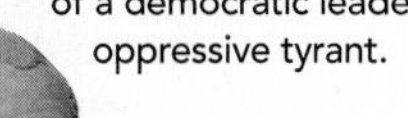

8  **Reading Check**

What has the elephant done that shows how dangerous it is?

7 Background

Vocabulary of Empire

Other important political words are derived from Greek. For example, the Greek word *kratos*, meaning "strength" or "power," forms the basis of many words describing different forms of government, including *democracy, monarchy, technocracy,* and *oligarchy.*

8 Reading Check

Answer: The elephant has destroyed a bamboo hut, killed a cow, raided some fruit stalls, overturned a van, and finally killed a man.

CUSTOMIZE INSTRUCTION FOR UNIVERSAL ACCESS

For Less Proficient Readers	For Gifted/Talented Students	For Advanced Readers
Have students use flowcharts to track the decisions Orwell must make during this essay. Students can use a different color pen or pencil to show the flow of events that actually occurred, through each decision Orwell made.	Those students with a flair for the dramatic might enjoy acting out the rampage of the elephant. Suggest that they mime, rather than make elephant noises. Have students rehearse their presentation, then ask them to perform before others in the class.	Have advanced students research other British colonies that underwent similar difficulties under imperialism. Were these difficulties confined to British colonies, or did other nations have troubles as well? Students can log on to www.phschool.com for links to appropriate research sites.

9 Literary Analysis

Irony

- Review both verbal and situational irony with students, asking that they give an example of each.
- Discuss with students any experiences they might have had facing a large crowd. Did the crowd make them feel safe or insecure? How did the crowd treat the student?
- Then, ask students the first Literary Analysis question on p. 1022: How does Orwell's description of the crowd's reaction create situational irony?
  Answer: Orwell claims that the crowd seemed indifferent about the threat of the elephant to their homes, reacting only to the prospect of seeing him shot. The contradiction in the situation is between the expected interests of homeowners (keen interest in preserving their homes) and the actual behavior of the crowd.

10 Literary Analysis

Irony

- Have students skim the passage. Then, ask them to make a list of what Orwell thinks his relation to the crowd *should* be. Make another list of what his position really *is.*
- Have students compare the two lists. Do the lists have anything in common?
- Ask students the second Literary Analysis question on p. 1022: What ironic observation does Orwell share here?
  Answer: Orwell has discovered that to rule the natives is actually to be ruled by them, since his conduct is guided at every moment by the need to impress them.

9 was merely ravaging their homes, but it was different now that he was going to be shot. It was a bit of fun to them, as it would be to an English crowd; besides they wanted the meat. It made me vaguely uneasy. I had no intention of shooting the elephant—I had merely sent for the rifle to defend myself if necessary—and it is always unnerving to have a crowd following you. I marched down the hill, looking and feeling a fool, with the rifle over my shoulder and an ever-growing army of people jostling at my heels. At the bottom, when you got away from the huts, there was a metaled road[9] and beyond that a miry waste of paddy fields a thousand yards across, not yet plowed but soggy from the first rains and dotted with coarse grass. The elephant was standing eight yards from the road, his left side toward us. He took not the slightest notice of the crowd's approach. He was tearing up bunches of grass, beating them against his knees to clean them, and stuffing them into his mouth.

Literary Analysis
Irony How does Orwell's description of the crowd's reaction create situational irony?

I had halted on the road. As soon as I saw the elephant I knew with perfect certainty that I ought not to shoot him. It is a serious matter to shoot a working elephant—it is comparable to destroying a huge and costly piece of machinery—and obviously one ought not to do it if it can possibly be avoided. And at that distance, peacefully eating, the elephant looked no more dangerous than a cow. I thought then and I think now that his attack of "must" was already passing off; in which case he would merely wander harmlessly about until the mahout came back and caught him. Moreover, I did not in the least want to shoot him. I decided that I would watch him for a little while to make sure that he did not turn savage again, and then go home.

But at that moment I glanced round at the crowd that had followed me. It was an immense crowd, two thousand at the least and growing every minute. It blocked the road for a long distance on either side. I looked at the sea of yellow faces above the garish clothes—faces all happy and excited over this bit of fun, all certain that the elephant was going to be shot. They were watching me as they would watch a conjurer about to perform a trick. They did not like me, but with the magical rifle in my hands I was momentarily worth watching. And suddenly I realized that I should have to shoot the elephant after all. The people expected it of me and I had got to do it; I could feel their two thousand wills pressing me forward, irresistibly. And it was at this moment, as I stood there with the rifle in my hands, that I first grasped the hollowness, the futility of the white man's dominion in the East. Here was I, the white man with his gun, standing in front of the unarmed native
10 crowd—seemingly the leading actor of the piece; but in reality I was only an absurd puppet pushed to and fro by the will of those yellow faces behind. I perceived in this moment that when the white man turns tyrant it is his own freedom that he destroys. He becomes a sort of hollow, posing dummy, the conventionalized figure of a sahib.[10] For

dominion (də min´ yən) *n.* rule or power over a territory

Literary Analysis
Irony What ironic observation does Orwell share here?

9. **metaled road** road in which the pavement is reinforced with metal strips.
10. **sahib** (sä´ ib) Indian word for European gentleman.

it is the condition of his rule that he shall spend his life in trying to impress the "natives," and so in every crisis he has got to do what the "natives" expect of him. He wears a mask, and his face grows to fit it. I had got to shoot the elephant. I had committed myself to doing it when I sent for the rifle. A sahib has got to act like a sahib; he has got to appear resolute, to know his own mind and do definite things. To come all that way, rifle in hand, with two thousand people marching at my heels, and then to trail feebly away, having done nothing—no, that was impossible. The crowd would laugh at me. And my whole life, every white man's life in the East, was one long struggle not to be laughed at.

But I did not want to shoot the elephant. I watched him beating his bunch of grass against his knees with that preoccupied grandmotherly air that elephants have. It seemed to me that it would be murder to shoot him. At that age I was not squeamish about killing animals, but I had never shot an elephant and never wanted to. (Somehow it always seems worse to kill a *large* animal.) Besides, there was the beast's
11 owner to be considered. Alive, the elephant was worth at least a hundred pounds, dead, he would only be worth the value of his tusks, five pounds, possibly. But I had got to act quickly. I turned to some experienced-looking Burmans who had been there when we arrived, and asked them how the elephant had been behaving. They all said the same thing: he took no notice of you if you left him alone, but he might charge if you went too close to him.

Reading Strategy
Recognizing the Writer's Attitudes What attitude toward the elephant does Orwell communicate here?

It was perfectly clear to me what I ought to do. I ought to walk up to within, say, twenty-five yards of the elephant and test his behavior. If he charged, I could shoot; if he took no notice of me, it would be safe to leave him until the mahout came back. But also I knew that I was going to do no such thing. I was a poor shot with a rifle and the ground was soft mud into which one would sink at every step. If the elephant charged and I missed him, I should have about as much chance as a toad under a steamroller. But even then I was not thinking particularly of my own skin, only of the watchful yellow faces behind. For at that moment, with the crowd watching me, I was not afraid in the ordinary sense, as I would have been if I had been alone. A white man mustn't be frightened in front of "natives"; and so, in general, he isn't frightened. The sole thought in my mind was that if anything went wrong those two thousand Burmans would see me pursued, caught, trampled on, and reduced to a grinning corpse like that Indian up the hill. And if that happened it was quite probable that some of them would laugh. That would never do. There was only one alternative. I shoved the cartridges into the magazine and lay down on the road to get a better aim.

The crowd grew very still, and a deep, low, happy sigh, as of people who see the theater curtain go up at last, breathed from innumerable throats. They were going to have their bit of fun, after all. The rifle was a beautiful German thing with cross-hair sights. I did not then know that in shooting an elephant one would shoot to cut an imaginary bar running from ear hole to ear hole. I ought, therefore, as the elephant was sideways on, to have aimed straight at his ear-hole;

12 **✓Reading Check**
What is the main reason Orwell gives for deciding to shoot the elephant?

11 Reading Strategy

Recognizing the Writer's Attitudes

- Have students identify the reasons that Orwell gives for not shooting the elephant. What reasons does he give for having to shoot the elephant?
- Then, ask students the Reading Strategy question on p. 1023: What attitude toward the elephant does Orwell communicate here?
 Answer: Orwell sees the animal as a piece of property as well as a creature with which to sympathize.

12 ✓Reading Check

Answer: Orwell decides to shoot the elephant because the crowd expects him to do so.

CUSTOMIZE INSTRUCTION FOR UNIVERSAL ACCESS

For Less Proficient Readers	For English Learners	For Advanced Readers
Help readers understand the complexity of the situation in which Orwell found himself. Have students refer to the condensed version of the essay in the **Adapted Reader's Companion.** Discuss with them the forces that affected Orwell at this point in the narrative.	For these students, idiomatic expressions and informal asides or pauses in the story might pose a challenge. Have them indicate phrases that do not seem to translate well in the literal sense. Students can use an on-line dictionary to find the idiomatic meanings of these words.	Challenge advanced students to write about a time when they knew what they should do from a moral standpoint but were forced to accept another course of action through peer pressure. Have them relate their experiences to that of Orwell.

13 ▶Critical Viewing

Possible response: The officers' formal dress, pith helmets, long coats, Sam Browne belts, and high boots would have been a stark contrast to the informal, loose clothing of the Burmese.

actually I aimed several inches in front of this, thinking the brain would be further forward.

When I pulled the trigger I did not hear the bang or feel the kick—one never does when a shot goes home—but I heard the devilish roar of glee that went up from the crowd. In that instant, in too short a time, one would have thought, even for the bullet to get there, a mysterious, terrible change had come over the elephant. He neither stirred nor fell, but every line of his body had altered. He looked suddenly stricken, shrunken, immensely old, as though the frightful impact of the bullet had paralyzed him without knocking him down. At last, after what seemed a long time—it might have been five seconds,

13 ▲Critical Viewing Judging from the details in this photograph, what made Orwell (third from left in back row) and his fellow officers conspicuous and therefore possible targets for ridicule? **[Analyze]**

ENRICHMENT: Career Connection

Police Officer

The speaker in this essay is a police officer attempting to defuse a tense situation.

Police officers face duties ranging from monitoring political unrest to directing traffic around road construction. Depending on the area for which an officer is responsible, he or she may walk, ride a bicycle or horse, or drive a car. Have interested students inquire at a local police station about the types of police work done by that precinct and the related training officers receive in undertaking those duties. After reviewing those findings as a class, discuss the physical and emotional challenges police officers face in these various types of duties.

I dare say—he sagged flabbily to his knees. His mouth slobbered. An enormous senility seemed to have settled upon him. One could have imagined him thousands of years old. I fired again into the same spot. At the second shot he did not collapse but climbed with desperate slowness to his feet and stood weakly upright, with legs sagging and head drooping. I fired a third time. That was the shot that did for him. You could see the agony of it jolt his whole body and knock the last remnant of strength from his legs. But in falling he seemed for a moment to rise, for as his hind legs collapsed beneath him he seemed to tower upward like a huge rock toppling, his trunk reaching skyward like a tree. He trumpeted, for the first and only time. And then down he came, his belly toward me, with a crash that seemed to shake the ground even where I lay. 

I got up. The Burmans were already racing past me across the mud. It was obvious that the elephant would never rise again, but he was not dead. He was breathing very rhythmically with long rattling gasps, his great mound of a side painfully rising and falling. His mouth was wide open—I could see far down into caverns of pale pink throat. I waited a long time for him to die, but his breathing did not weaken. Finally I fired my two remaining shots into the spot where I thought his heart must be. The thick blood welled out of him like red velvet, but still he did not die. His body did not even jerk when the shots hit him, the tortured breathing continued without a pause. He was dying, very slowly and in great agony, but in some world remote from me where not even a bullet could damage him further. I felt that I had got to put an end to that dreadful noise. It seemed dreadful to see the great beast lying there, powerless to move and yet powerless to die, and not even to be able to finish him. I sent back for my small rifle and poured shot after shot into his heart and down his throat. They seemed to make no impression. The tortured gasps continued as steadily as the ticking of a clock.

senility (si nil′ ə tē) *n.* mental deterioration due to old age

Reading Strategy
Recognizing the Writer's Attitudes What does Orwell's detailed description of the elephant's collapse suggest about his attitude toward the grim side of life?

Reading Check 15
What happens to the elephant after Orwell's first shot?

14 Reading Strategy
Recognizing the Writer's Attitudes

- Ask students to read the passage in which Orwell describes the death of the elephant.
- Ask students how Orwell treats the scene. Does he make it attractive or repulsive to the reader?
- Then, ask students the Reading Strategy question on p. 1025: What does Orwell's detailed description of the elephant's collapse suggest about his attitude toward the grim side of life?
  Answer: The detailed description shows that Orwell's attitude towards the grim side of life was to remain unflinching and coolheaded.

15 
Reading Check

Answer: The elephant seems to age and become senile.

CUSTOMIZE INSTRUCTION FOR UNIVERSAL ACCESS

For Less Proficient Readers

To help students better understand the concept of irony, work with students to complete a chart like the one shown here. Have students identify different ironic situations and then explain the clash or opposition that creates the irony in the situation.

Subject	Expected	Actual
I. Orwell's attitude toward British Empire	As an officer—loyalty, patriotism	Hates job. Disapproves of Empire. Sides with Burmese.

ASSESS

Answers for p. 1026

Review and Assess

1. **Possible responses:** Yes, quitting the job would provide an escape from its difficult choices. No, staying on would enable one to change the situation.
2. **(a)** Orwell was hated because he was European and a representative of British-Indian rule. **(b)** On one hand, he sympathized with the Burmese, but on the other hand, they bullied him constantly. **(c)** He is complex enough to have ambivalent feelings and honest enough to admit to them.
3. **(a)** The elephant is a costly working machine; it seems like murder, especially to shoot such a large animal; it is probably unnecessary for safety; the owner will lose a valuable animal. **(b)** He shoots the elephant mostly to avoid looking foolish. **(c)** It shows that he was basically a moral, considerate person, but that he was weak enough in such a situation to be influenced by expectations of others.
4. **(a)** Orwell feels he has no choice but to shoot the elephant; thus his own freedom has been limited by the role he must play as "ruler." **(b)** Yes, not shooting the elephant would have emphasized Orwell's freedom to do as he saw fit. It would have suggested that British policy could be changed by individual actions.
5. **(a)** In his description, he calmly describes gory details with clinical accuracy, yet he reports that, at the time, he could not stand watching as the animal slowly died. **(b)** **Possible response:** It suggests that writing enables a writer to attain distance from his or her own experience.
6. **(a)** **Possible response:** By admitting something of which he is not proud, Orwell is honest about his motives and feelings at the time, but most people would make more excuses for their own actions—in this sense, Orwell is harsh on himself. **(b)** **Possible response:** Orwell comes across as a man of admirable qualities, but one who lacks the inner strength to stand up for what he believes.

In the end I could not stand it any longer and went away. I heard later that it took him half an hour to die. Burmans were bringing dahs[11] and baskets even before I left, and I was told they had stripped his body almost to the bones by the afternoon.

Afterward, of course, there were endless discussions about the shooting of the elephant. The owner was furious, but he was only an Indian and could do nothing. Besides, legally I had done the right thing, for a mad elephant has to be killed, like a mad dog, if its owner fails to control it. Among the Europeans opinion was divided. The older men said I was right, the younger men said it was a shame to shoot an elephant for killing a coolie, because an elephant was worth more than any Coringhee[12] coolie. And afterward I was very glad that the coolie had been killed; it put me legally in the right and it gave me a sufficient pretext for shooting the elephant. I often wondered whether any of the others grasped that I had done it solely to avoid looking a fool.

11. **dahs** (däz) knives.
12. **Coringhee** (cor in´ gē) Southern Indian.

Review and Assess

Thinking About the Selection

1. **Respond:** If you were in the narrator's position, would you give up your job? Why or why not?
2. (a) **Recall:** Why did the Burmese hate George Orwell? (b) **Analyze:** Why does this hatred cause conflict in him? (c) **Interpret:** What does this conflict show about Orwell?
3. (a) **Recall:** Why does Orwell think that the elephant need not be killed? (b) **Analyze Cause and Effect:** What is the primary factor influencing Orwell's decision to shoot the elephant? (c) **Interpret:** What does this decision, and his honesty about it, suggest about his character?
4. (a) **Draw Conclusions:** How does Orwell's ultimate decision show that "when the white man turns tyrant it is his own freedom that he destroys"? (b) **Modify:** If Orwell had not shot the elephant, would that have changed the meaning of the essay? Why or why not?
5. (a) **Compare and Contrast:** Compare Orwell's calm, detailed description of the dying elephant with his reactions to it at the time. (b) **Draw Conclusions:** What relationship between life and the act of writing does this contrast suggest?
6. (a) **Evaluate:** How fairly does Orwell evaluate his own actions? (b) **Make a Judgment:** Do you think that Orwell comes across as an admirable man in this selection? Explain.

ASSESSMENT PRACTICE: Writing Skills

Strategy (For more practice, see Test Preparation Workbook, p. 49.)

Many tests require students to apply revision strategies to given passages. Use the following sample item to give students practice with this skill.

As soon as I saw the elephant I knew with certainty that I ought not to shoot him. It is a serious matter to shoot a working elephant—comparable to destroying a huge, costly piece of machinery—and obviously one should not do it if it can be avoided.

To add more information, which of the following sentences would be most suitable?

A This was clearly a working elephant: I had to figure out a way to avoid shooting it.
B I wished I had brought more ammunition.
C Elephants must reproduce.
D The elephant flapped its ears slowly.

Lead students to see that the correct answer is *A*.

Review and Assess

Literary Analysis

Irony

1. What **irony** lies in Orwell's fantasy of attacking a Buddhist priest?
2. What type of irony—verbal or situational—lies in Orwell's comment about the crowd following him: "They were going to have their bit of fun, after all." Explain your categorization.
3. Use a chart like the one shown to analyze Orwell's use of irony. Then, choose the two most effective examples.

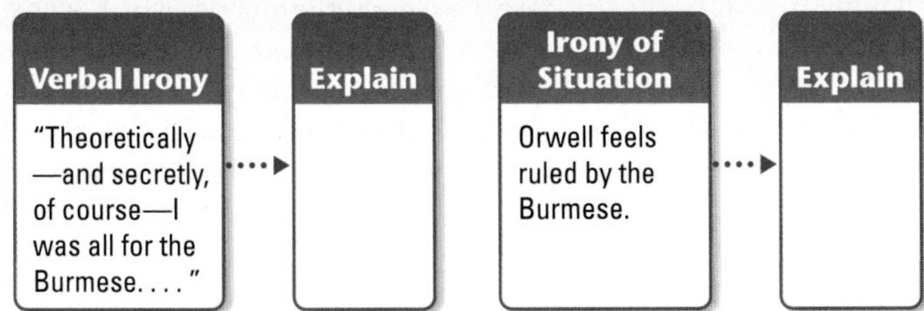

4. Do you think that Orwell's sense of irony reflects his privileged position in Burma? Explain.

Connecting Literary Elements

5. (a) Find examples of Orwell's use of dashes and of phrases such as "sort of." (b) What do such elements add to his **tone**?
6. (a) Identify and analyze three passages in which style, sentence length, or word choice create a distinctive tone. (b) Based on these passages, what would you say is the tone of the essay?
7. (a) Describe another tone that Orwell might have chosen for his essay. (b) Explain whether or not it would have been more effective.

Reading Strategy

Recognizing the Writer's Attitude

8. Describe Orwell's conflicting attitudes in the paragraph beginning "It was perfectly clear to me what I ought to do."
9. What does this conflict reveal about his views of imperialism?

Extend Understanding

10. **Career Connection:** What do you think would be the best training for a journalist like Orwell? Why?

Quick Review

Irony is the recognition of a contradiction between appearance and reality.

Verbal irony is used to reveal the contrast between words and reality.

Irony of situation shows the contradiction between expectation and the pattern of events.

Tone is an author's attitude toward the reader and the subject, as expressed in word choice, sentence structure, choice of details, and other elements of style.

To **recognize the writer's attitude,** look for details or assumptions that reveal the writer's thoughts or feelings.

 ***Take It to the Net***

www.phschool.com

Take the interactive self-test online to check your understanding of the selection.

Answers for p. 1027

Review and Assess

1. The irony lies in the fact that, although he hates the British Empire and sees the Burmese as oppressed, he still thinks about killing the priest.
2. It is verbal irony: one would expect people to be saddened at the death of an elephant, but Orwell describes it in terms of "fun."
3. Possible response: **Situational Irony:** "We began questioning the people as to where the elephant had gone, and, as usual, failed to get any definite information." **Explain:** One would expect that the police would give up questioning people if it usually yielded no information. **Verbal Irony:** ". . . with the magical rifle in my hands I was momentarily worth watching." **Explain:** The rifle is not "magical" but deadly.
4. Possible response: Yes, in the sense that, without the privilege of easily leaving the country, he might not have had such a sense of humor about events there.
5. **(a)** "I was hated by large numbers of people—the only time . . ."; "Theoretically—and in secret, or course—I was . . ."; "Moreover, . . ." **(b)** Such phrases make the essay seem more intimate and personal, as if directed at the individual reader.
6. **(a)** Students should identify each passage and tell how the style, sentence length, and word choice create a tone, and give examples. **(b)** The tone of the essay is wry and conversational, with touches of embarrassment or defensiveness.
7. **(a)** Possible response: Orwell might have chosen a more aggressive, defensive tone. **(b)** This tone would not have been more effective. It would have made him seem a violent and unlikable person.
8. He quite reasonably wants to spare the elephant unless killing it is necessary for safety. Conversely, he doesn't want to be ridiculed for this position.

continued

ENRICHMENT: Further Reading

Other Works by George Orwell

Animal Farm

1984

Down and Out in Paris and London

 ***Take It to the Net***

Visit www.phschool.com for more information on George Orwell.

Answers continued

9. Imperialism creates a complex relationship between ruler and ruled in which each side "rules" and resents the other.
10. Possible response: Firsthand experience of a variety of challenging situations would be the best training because it would sharpen his or her ability to observe under stress.

EXTEND

Answers for p. 1028

❶ Vocabulary Development

Concept Development

1. Policy and practice of forming and maintaining an empire by the conquest of other countries and the establishment of colonies to control raw materials and world markets
2. Rule or power to rule; a governed territory
3. tyrannical

Spelling Strategy

1. colonialism
2. diplomatic
3. regrettable
4. questioner

Fluency: Context

As a veteran of summer camps from Maine to Wyoming, I can tell you about some of the *squalid* conditions under which many *despotic* counselors force one to live. Under their *dominion*, the camp is run like a colony under *imperialism*, which leaves some campers totally *prostrate* with fear instead of overwhelmed with the joy of the outdoors. Only *senility* could lead me to forget my traumatic summer experiences.

❷ Grammar and Style

1. thatched with palm leaf; nonrestrictive; modifies "huts"
2. sprawling in the mud; restrictive; modifies "body"
3. looking and feeling a fool; nonrestrictive; modifies "I"
4. peacefully eating, nonrestrictive; modifies "elephant"
5. pushed to and fro; restrictive; modifies "puppet"

Writing Application

Possible response:

Nonrestrictive: Orwell, *acting out of a sense of family duty,* became a policeman in Burma. *Living among the Burmese,* he learned the worst about imperialism.

Restrictive: The elephant *calmly eating grasses in the paddy* hardly resembled the maddened creature reported to the police. A crowd *clamoring for blood* was more a danger to Orwell.

Integrate Language Skills

❶ Vocabulary Development Lesson

Concept Development: Words About Politics

Use your knowledge of the political words in this essay to define these words:

1. imperialism 2. dominion 3. despotic

Spelling Strategy

When adding a suffix beginning with a vowel to a multisyllable word, double the final consonant of the word only if the last syllable is stressed: *begin* + *-er* = *beginner*. Otherwise, do not double it: *imperial* + *-ism* = *imperialism*. Add the suffix indicated to these words:

1. colonial (*-ism*)
2. diplomat (*-ic*)
3. regret (*-able*)
4. question (*-er*)

Fluency: Context

Copy the following paragraph into your notebook. Using context clues in the paragraph, replace each italicized word or phrase with a word from the vocabulary list on page 1017.

As a veteran of summer camps from Maine to Wyoming, I can tell you about some of the *wretched* conditions under which many *tyrannical* counselors force one to live. Under their *rule*, the camp is run like a colony under *a policy of political and economic control*, which leaves some campers totally *overcome* with fear instead of overwhelmed with the joy of the outdoors. Only *mental decay* could lead me to forget my traumatic summer experiences.

❷ Grammar and Style Lesson

Participial Phrases: Restrictive and Nonrestrictive

Participial phrases—participles with their modifiers or complements—modify nouns and pronouns. Restrictive participial phrases are essential to the meaning of the words they modify and are not set off by commas. Nonrestrictive phrases are not essential and are set off by commas.

Restrictive: The wretched prisoners huddling in the stinking cages of the lockups, . . . (tells which prisoners)

Nonrestrictive: Some more women followed, clicking their tongues and exclaiming; . . . (does not tell which women)

Participial phases allow writers to fill in details of a scene even as they narrate a main action.

Practice Write each participial phrase and the word it modifies. Identify the phrase as restrictive or nonrestrictive.

1. It was . . . a labyrinth of squalid bamboo huts, thatched with palm leaf, . . .
2. I . . . saw a man's dead body sprawling in the mud.
3. I marched down the hill, looking and feeling a fool, . . .
4. . . . peacefully eating, the elephant looked no more dangerous than a cow.
5. . . . in reality I was only an absurd puppet pushed to and fro. . . .

Writing Application Write about Orwell's experiences, using two restrictive and two nonrestrictive participial phrases.

WG Prentice Hall Writing and Grammar Connection: Chapter 19, Section 2

TEACHING RESOURCES

The following resources can be used to enrich or extend the instruction for pp. 1028–1029.

Vocabulary

- **Selection Support:** Build Vocabulary, p. 223
- **Vocabulary and Spelling Practice Book** (Use this booklet for skills enrichment.)

Grammar

- **Selection Support:** Grammar and Style, p. 224
- **Writing and Grammar,** Diamond Level, p. 446
- **Daily Language Practice Transparencies**

Writing

- **Writing and Grammar,** Diamond Level, p. 60
- **Writing and Grammar iText CD-ROM**

BLOCK SCHEDULING: Resources marked with this symbol provide varied instruction during 90-minute blocks.

❸ Writing Lesson

Essay in Orwell's Style

Orwell's style is plainspoken, but it is nonetheless distinctive. Write an essay in his style on a problem you once encountered.

Prewriting Reread Orwell's essay, jotting down notes on his style. Then, choose an experience on which to write and outline the details.

Drafting Begin, as Orwell does, with a general account of your response to your experience. Then, present events in clear order, relating each detail to your general response. As you draft, "listen" to what you write to make sure it sounds like Orwell.

Revising Review Orwell's essay, and then review your draft. Highlight any parts that are inconsistent with his style. For instance, look for long, elaborate sentences or vague, flowery descriptions. Rewrite or eliminate such passages to create a consistent style.

Model: Revising for Consistent Style

I had only gone along with the others for fear of being laughed at. ~~When those rotten cowards Johnny and Rafael ran away, leaving me all alone to face our parents, I thought, "This really stinks!"—I mean, can you believe what they did?~~ *When Johnny and Rafael ran away, I now had a different fear to face: being the only one blamed.*

Eliminating a long, impassioned sentence makes the style more consistent with Orwell's. The new sentence adds irony like Orwell's.

WG Prentice Hall Writing and Grammar Connection: Chapter 4, Section 4

❹ Extension Activities

Listening and Speaking Burma became independent after World War II. With a group, prepare and deliver an **audiovisual presentation** about Burmese independence. Your presentation should link historical facts to Orwell's essay. Use these materials:

- Historic timeline
- Photographs for overhead projection
- Recordings of Burmese music

Discuss which audiovisual aids will be practical and effective. Have each group member direct one section of the presentation. **[Group Activity]**

Research and Technology In 1991, a Burmese freedom fighter, Aung San Suu Kyi, won the Nobel Peace Prize. Write a brief **biography** comparing her political positions and practices to Orwell's. Consult primary sources such as San's essays, speeches, and letters. Confirm facts by locating information in more than one source.

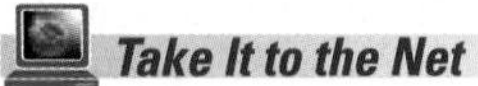

www.phschool.com

Go online for an additional research activity using the Internet.

Lesson Support for p. 1029

❸ Writing Lesson

- Before students begin the Prewriting activities, have them draw up a list of adjectives that describe Orwell's style in this essay. Leave the list on the board during the complete writing exercise so students can refer to it.
- Encourage students to select a topic that includes and explains personal conflict. Doing this will make it easier to follow Orwell's style of writing.
- Students can trade drafts to check for events that are unclear or seem to be out of order, then revise their drafts accordingly.

❹ Research and Technology

- Remind student that there are two kinds of sources for research: *primary sources* (actual words of people present at historical events or essential documents related to that event) and *secondary sources* (the ideas and thoughts about historical events developed by those who were not present).
- Have students use the library catalogs and Internet resources to find as many primary resources as they can about Aung San Suu Kyi. Whenever possible, suggest they print copies of findings in addition to taking notes.
- Evaluate the variety of sources students used to look for primary sources and the results of their searches.

CUSTOMIZE INSTRUCTION For Universal Access

To address different learning styles, use the activities suggested in the **Extension Activities** booklet, page 48.

- For Logical/Mathematical and Visual/Spatial Learners, use Activity 5.
- For Intrapersonal Learners, use Activity 6.
- For Visual/Spatial Learners, use Activity 7.

ASSESSMENT RESOURCES

The following resources can be used to access students' knowledge and skills.

Selection Assessment

- **Formal Assessment,** pp. 234–236
- **Open Book Test,** pp. 141–143
- **Got It! Assessment Videotapes,** Tape 5
- **Test Bank Software**

PRENTICE HALL ASSESSMENT SYSTEM

- **Workbook**
- **Skill Book**
- **Transparencies**
- **CD-ROM**

Take It to the Net

Visit www.phschool.com for self-tests and additional questions on the essays and writings of George Orwell.

The Demon Lover

Lesson Objectives and CA Correlations

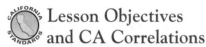

1. **To analyze and respond to literary elements**
   - Literary Analysis: The Ghost Story **R 3.1**
   - Connecting Literary Elements: Ambiguity **R 3.4**
2. **To read, comprehend, analyze, and critique a short story**
   - Reading Strategy: Responding to the Story **R 3.3**
   - Reading Check Questions
   - Review and Assess Questions
3. **To develop word analysis skills, fluency, and systematic vocabulary**
   - Vocabulary Development Lesson: Latin Root *-loc-* **R 1.1, 1.2**
4. **To understand and apply written and oral language conventions**
   - Spelling Strategy
   - Grammar and Style Lesson: Sentence Beginnings: Participial Phrases **LC 1.1, 1.2, 1.3**
5. **To understand and apply appropriate writing and research strategies**
   - Writing Lesson: Sequel **W 1.1, 1.9, 2.1**
   - Extension Activity: History Report **W 2.4**
   - Assessment Practice (ATE)
6. **To understand and apply listening and speaking strategies**
   - Extension Activity: Story Reading **LS 1.10**

STEP-BY-STEP TEACHING GUIDE	PACING GUIDE
PRETEACH	
Motivate Students and Provide Background	
Use the Motivation activity (ATE p. 1030)	5 min.
Read and discuss author and background features (SE/ATE pp. 1030, 1032, 1034) [A]	5 min.
Introduce the Concepts	
Introduce the Literary Analysis and Reading Strategy (SE/ATE p. 1031) [A]	15 min.
Pronounce the vocabulary words and read their definitions (SE p. 1031)	5 min.
TEACH	
Monitor Comprehension	
Informally monitor comprehension by circulating while students read independently or in groups [A]	25 min.
Monitor students' comprehension with the Reading Check notes (SE/ATE pp. 1033, 1035, 1037)	as students read
Develop vocabulary with Vocabulary notes (SE pp. 1034, 1035, 1038; ATE p. 1035)	as students read
Develop Understanding	
Develop students' understanding of the ghost story with the Literary Analysis annotations (SE pp. 1033, 1035, 1036; ATE pp. 1033, 1034, 1035, 1036) [A]	5 min.
ASSESS	
Assess Mastery	
Assess students' mastery of the Reading Strategy and Literary Analysis by having them answer the Review and Assess questions (SE/ATE p. 1039)	15 min.
Use one or more of the print and media Assessment Resources (ATE p. 1041) [A]	up to 45 min.
EXTEND	
Apply Understanding	
Have students complete the Vocabulary Development Lesson and the Grammar and Style Lesson (SE p. 1040) [A]	20 min.
Apply students' knowledge of clear and logical organization using the Writing Lesson (SE/ATE p. 1041) [A]	45 min.
Apply students' understanding using one or more of the Extension Activities (SE p. 1041)	20–90 min.

ACCELERATED INSTRUCTION:
Use the strategies and activities identified with an [A].

UNIVERSAL ACCESS
● = Below-Level Students
▲ = On-Level Students
■ = Above-Level Students

Time and Resource Manager

Reading Level: Average
Average Number of Instructional Days: 4

RESOURCES		
PRINT	**TRANSPARENCIES**	**TECHNOLOGY**
• **Beyond Literature,** Cross-Curricular Connection: Social Studies, p. 49 ▲ ■		• **Interest Grabber Video,** Tape 6 ● ▲ ■
• **Selection Support Workbook:** ● ▲ ■ Literary Analysis, p. 230 Reading Strategy, p. 229 Build Vocabulary, p. 227	• **Literary Analysis and Reading Transparencies,** pp. 97 and 98 ● ▲ ■	
		• **Listening to Literature** ● ▲ ■ Audiocassettes, Side 24 Audio CDs, CD 13
• **Literatura en español** ● ▲ • **Literary Analysis for Enrichment** ■		
• **Formal Assessment:** Selection Test, pp. 237–239 ● ▲ ■ • **Open Book Test,** pp. 144–146 ● ▲ ■ • PRENTICE HALL ASSESSMENT SYSTEM ● ▲ ■	• PRENTICE HALL ASSESSMENT SYSTEM ● ▲ ■ Skills Practice Answers and Explanations on Transparencies ● ▲ ■	• **Test Bank Software** ● ▲ ■ • **Got It! Assessment Videotapes,** Tape 5 ● ▲
• **Selection Support Workbook:** ● ▲ ■ Grammar and Style, p. 228 • **Writing and Grammar,** Diamond Level ● ▲ ■ • **Extension Activities,** p. 49 ● ▲ ■	• **Daily Language Practice Transparencies** ● ▲	• **Writing and Grammar iText CD-ROM** ● ▲ ■ ***Take It to the Net*** www.phschool.com

BLOCK SCHEDULING: Use one 90-minute class period to preteach the selection and have students read it. Use a second 90-minute class period to assess students' mastery of skills and have them complete one of the Extension Activities.

PRETEACH

Step-by-Step Teaching Guide for pp. 1030–1031

Motivation

Have students imagine they are living in London during the Blitz (the place and time of this story). Have students describe daily life with nightly bombings under these conditions. They can better appreciate the eerie atmosphere of the story—especially its scanty references to the violence that was all around.

Interest Grabber Video

As an alternative, play "'The Demon Lover': The Blitz" on Tape 6 to engage student interest.

❶ Background

More About the Author

Elizabeth Dorothea Cole Bowen had a difficult childhood, but the inherited wealth allowed her to pursue her career as a writer. She was able to live independently in London and to winter in Italy before the war. She later inherited the family house at Kildorrery, County Cork. The history of the house is told in *Bowen's Court* (1942) and serves as the scene of her novel *The Last September* (1929).

Prepare to Read

❶ The Demon Lover

Elizabeth Bowen (1899–1973)

The fiction of Elizabeth Bowen is distinguished by her subtle observation of landscape, by her innovative and believable use of the supernatural, and by her haunting portrayal of England during one of the darkest eras of the country's history—World War II, which lasted from 1939 to 1945.

A Troubled Childhood Bowen was born into comfortable circumstances. Her parents were wealthy, and she grew up in Dublin and on their country estate in County Cork, Ireland. Early in life, though, she suffered serious losses. Her father had a breakdown when she was seven years old, and he was confined to an institution. She and her mother moved to England, where, Bowen later said, she and her mother waged a "campaign of not noticing" her father's absence. When Bowen was thirteen, her mother died of cancer. Bowen was not allowed to attend the funeral.

From Life Into Art As an adult, Bowen was to write about such experiences of the denial of emotion and about the helplessness of the heart to understand itself or others in the absence of love. In her characters' insecure lives, in the damage that is done them when their feelings are not acknowledged, one can still trace the marks left by Bowen's own early abandonment.

A Writer's Life After her mother's death, Bowen lived with her relatives and then attended boarding school until she was seventeen, when she moved to London. Her one ambition was to write, and her family's money was enough to support her as she wrote her first short stories.

Her first collection of short stories, published in 1923, received little attention. Through the 1930s, while living with her husband in Oxford, she perfected her craft, publishing regularly. In 1938, she completed *The Death of the Heart*, one of her best-known works. The novel is about the disillusionment of an innocent teenage girl, taken in by uncaring relatives after her mother's death.

The War and After During the war, Bowen observed England's hardships keenly and with compassion. She incorporated the brutal realities of the war—air raids, blackouts, betrayal—into some of her best stories. By using a wartime setting and playing on the heightened emotions and perceptions people have at such times, Bowen was able to expose the innermost workings of her characters' minds.

After the war, Bowen widened her literary activities to include literary criticism and book reviews. She wrote for such journals as the *Tatler* and contributed scripts to the British Broadcasting Company, which programmed all British radio and television broadcasts at the time. In 1948, she was honored by the prestigious award Commander, Order of the British Empire (C.B.E.). In 1949, she published *The Heat of the Day*, a much acclaimed novel. Set in wartime London, the novel movingly juxtaposes a tragic love affair with the larger crisis of the nation.

After the death of her husband in 1952, Bowen returned to Ireland. Her later novels—including, *A World of Love* (1955), *The Little Girls* (1964), and *Eva Trout* (1969)—exhibit a more symbolic, more poetic style than her earlier works. All of her work, however, testifies to her sensitivity to finer shades of emotion and her eye for telling details.

Bowen defined the novel as the "non-poetic statement of poetic truth." Guided by the hardships she had undergone, working in a deceptively simple style, she achieved this goal admirably.

TEACHING RESOURCES

The following resources can be used to enrich or extend the instruction for pp. 1030–1031.

Motivation

Interest Grabber Video, Tape 6

Background

Beyond Literature, p. 49

Take It to the Net

Visit www.phschool.com for background and hotlinks about Elizabeth Bowen.

Literary Analysis

Literary Analysis and Reading Transparencies, The Ghost Story, p. 98

Reading

Literary Analysis and Reading Transparencies, Responding to the Story, p. 97

BLOCK SCHEDULING: Resources marked with this symbol provide varied instruction during 90-minute blocks.

Preview

Connecting to the Literature

Becoming a "ghost" is easy; it's just a trick of time and place. Walk by your old elementary school . . . linger in your old home just before moving. . . . All it takes to become a ghost—or perhaps to see one—is a sideways step out of familiar routines, as "The Demon Lover" suggests.

❷ Literary Analysis

The Ghost Story

A **ghost story** is a tale in which part of the past—typically, a dead person—seems to make a supernatural appearance in the present. Many good ghost stories are characterized by these elements:

- An eerie or mysterious atmosphere
- The suggestion that supernatural forces are at work
- An open possibility that the eerie events they recount have a "natural" explanation

By suggesting—not directly asserting—the activity of supernatural forces and by causing the reader to hesitate between "natural" and "supernatural" interpretations of events, a ghost story eerily blurs the line between the familiar and the unfamiliar. As you read "The Demon Lover," analyze these elements of a ghost story, using a chart like the one shown.

Past ···▸ Present

Familiar ···▸ Unfamiliar

Natural ···▸ Supernatural

Connecting Literary Elements

Some of the best ghost stories contain **ambiguity**—they support two or more divergent interpretations. In literature, words may be used in intentionally ambiguous ways to add layers of meaning. As you read, notice how Bowen adds to the mysterious quality of her tale through ambiguity, making readers wonder whether the "ghost" in the story is a dead man or a hallucination brought on by unresolved feelings about the past.

❸ Reading Strategy

Responding to the Story

The first step in understanding literature is also the most basic—**responding to the story** as you read, whether with puzzlement or terror. Your next step is to judge how the writer evoked that response. As you read, note your reactions and look for what the writer has done to elicit them.

Vocabulary Development

spectral (spek´ trəl) *adj.* ghostly (p. 1034)

dislocation (dis´ lō kā´ shən) *n.* condition of being out of place (p. 1035)

arboreal (är bôr´ ē´ əl) *adj.* of, near, or among trees (p. 1035)

circumscribed (sur´ kəm skrībd´) *adj.* limited; having a definite boundary (p. 1035)

aperture (ap´ ər chər´) *n.* opening (p. 1038)

CUSTOMIZE INSTRUCTION FOR UNIVERSAL ACCESS

For Less Proficient Readers	For English Learners	For Advanced Readers
Some of Elizabeth Bowen's long sentences or list-like descriptions may prove confusing for less proficient readers. Encourage these students to read slowly, translating the complicated sentences into a simple list of events and actions.	For these students, try annotating the margins of a copy of the story with simple descriptions of the actions and events. Then, have them follow along as they listen to the story on the **Listening to Literature Audiocassette.**	Urge students to focus on Bowen's masterful ability to create a particular mood. Challenge students to identify descriptive and sensory language that contributes to the mood.

❷ Literary Analysis

The Ghost Story

- Have students read the description of a ghost story and look over the listed characteristics.
- Have students name some books, stories, TV shows, or films they have seen that have at least two of these characteristics. Discuss how each characteristic was demonstrated and what it added to the effect of the piece.
- As they read the selection, ask students to use self-stick notes to mark places in the story that show one or more of the ghost story characteristics. They can return to that place in the story later to review the marked passages.
- Use the Literary Focus: Ghost Story in the **Literary Analysis and Reading Transparencies,** p. 98, to help students understand the type of story they are about to encounter.

❸ Reading Strategy

Responding to the Story

- Inform students that an important step in understanding a text is identifying your own reaction to that text. You may then judge whether your response was intended by the author, and how this response was evoked.
- Discuss other stories or books students have read that have elicited strong reactions. Have them identify the reaction and tell what caused it: the plot, the characters, the circumstances of the tale, or something else.
- Caution students to be aware of their reactions as they read. They can briefly list the events in the story that caused some reaction, then reread those passages and think about how the reaction was created by the author.

Vocabulary Development

- Pronounce each vocabulary word for students, and read the definitions as a class. Have students identify any words with which they are already familiar.

 ***E-Teach***

Visit E-Teach at www.phschool.com for teachers' essays on how to teach, with questions and answers.

TEACH

Step-by-Step Teaching Guide for pp. 1032–1038

CUSTOMIZE INSTRUCTION
For Bodily/Kinesthetic Learners

Ask these students to act out Mrs. Drover's physical movements as the story progresses. Have them speculate about how her changing movements create and convey the story's mood.

❶ About the Selection

This chilling ghost story poses the question: Are there supernatural elements at work here, or is the inexplicable a product of the human imagination? When the story's main character, Mrs. Drover, returns to her deserted London home during a pause in World War II bombing, she discovers a letter that appears to be from a long-ago, and presumably dead, fiancé, calling for an assignation on that very day. Her responses to the letter demonstrate the vulnerability of the human psyche, especially during wartime. They also leave readers wondering: Is there really a ghost or is Mrs. Drover hallucinating? Even more profoundly, the story suggests a larger social meaning: A world that can go to war a second time is perhaps, like Mrs. Drover, in love with a demon.

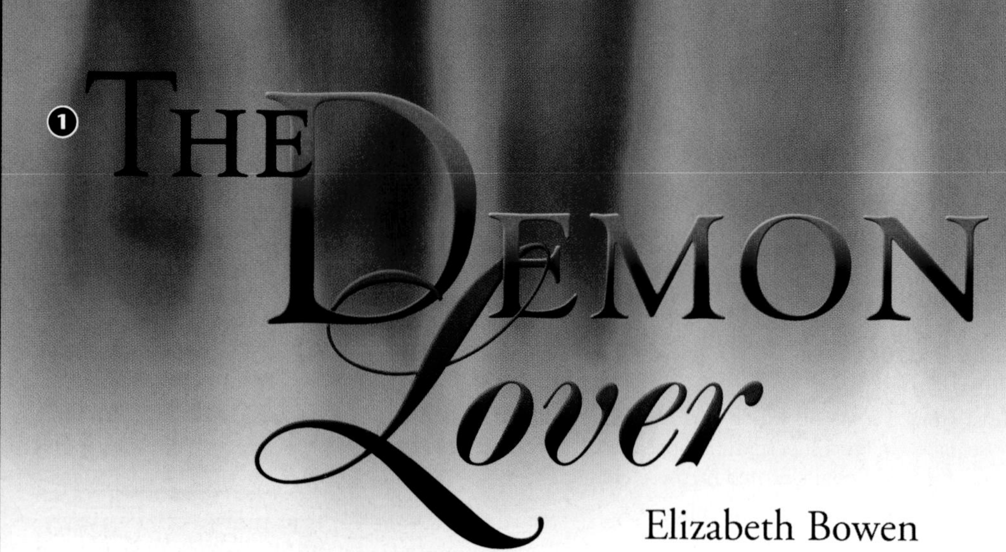

❶ The Demon Lover

Elizabeth Bowen

Background

World War II was a fact of daily life in the London of the 1940s. After decisive victories in Europe, Germany determined to break Britain with a steady bombardment focused on London. During "the Blitz," from September 1940 to May 1941, German planes dropped bombs on the city almost every night. Whole communities were evacuated periodically, leaving street after street of deserted buildings. Elizabeth Bowen lived in London during this time, and the eerie quality of "The Demon Lover" stems from her experience of a time when war's horrors had become all too "ordinary."

Toward the end of her day in London Mrs. Drover went round to her shut-up house to look for several things she wanted to take away. Some belonged to herself, some to her family, who were by now used to their country life. It was late August; it had been a steamy, showery day: at the moment the trees down the pavement glittered in an escape of humid yellow afternoon sun. Against the next batch of clouds, already piling up ink-dark, broken chimneys and parapets stood out. In her once familiar street, as in any unused channel, an unfamiliar queerness had silted up; a cat wove itself in and out of railings, but no human eye watched Mrs. Drover's return. Shifting some parcels under her arm, she slowly forced round her latchkey in an unwilling lock, then gave the door, which had warped, a push with her knee. Dead air came out to meet her as she went in.

TEACHING RESOURCES

The following resources can be used to enrich or extend the instruction for pp. 1032–1038.

Literary Analysis

Selection Support: Literary Analysis, p. 230

Reading

Selection Support: Reading Strategy, p. 229; Build Vocabulary, p. 227

Listening to Literature Audiocassettes, Side 24

Listening to Literature Audio CDs, CD 13

BLOCK SCHEDULING: Resources marked with this symbol provide varied instruction during 90-minute blocks.

2 The staircase window having been boarded up, no light came down into the hall. But one door, she could just see, stood ajar, so she went quickly through into the room and unshuttered the big window in there. Now the prosaic woman, looking about her, was more perplexed than she knew by everything that she saw, by traces of her long former habit of life—the yellow smoke stain up the white marble mantel-piece, the ring left by a vase on the top of the escritoire,[1] the bruise in the wallpaper where, on the door being thrown open widely, the china handle had always hit the wall. The piano, having gone away to be stored, had left what looked like claw marks on its part of the parquet.[2] Though not much dust had seeped in, each object wore a film of another kind; and, the only ventilation being the chimney, the whole drawing room smelled of the cold hearth. Mrs. Drover put down her parcels on the escritoire and left the room to proceed upstairs; the things she wanted were in a bedroom chest.

She had been anxious to see how the house was—the part-time caretaker she shared with some neighbors was away this week on his holiday, known to be not yet back. At the best of times he did not look in often, and she was never sure that she trusted him. There were some cracks in the structure, left by the last bombing, on which she was anxious to keep an eye. Not that one could do anything—

A shaft of refracted daylight now lay across the hall. She stopped dead and stared at the hall table—on this lay a letter addressed to her.

She thought first—then the caretaker *must* be back. All the same, who, seeing the house shuttered, would have dropped a letter in at the box? It was not a circular, it was not a bill. And the post office redirected, to the address in the country, everything for her that came through the post. The caretaker (even if he *were* back) did not know she was due in London today—her call here had been planned to be a surprise—so his negligence in the manner of this letter, leaving it to wait in the dusk and the dust, annoyed her. Annoyed, she picked up the letter, which bore no stamp. But it cannot be important, or they would know . . . She took the letter rapidly upstairs with her, without a stop to look at the writing till she reached what had been her bedroom, where she let in light. The room looked over the garden and other gardens: the sun had gone in; as the clouds sharpened and lowered, the trees and rank lawns seemed already to smoke with dark. Her reluctance to look again at the letter came from the fact that she felt intruded upon—and by someone contemptuous of her ways. However, in the tenseness preceding the fall of rain she read it: it was a few lines.

DEAR KATHLEEN,

You will not have forgotten that today is our anniversary, and the day we said. The years have gone by at once slowly and fast. In view of the fact that nothing has changed, I shall rely upon you to

1. **escritoire** (es′ krə twär′) *n.* a writing desk or table.
2. **parquet** (pär kā′) *n.* flooring of inlaid woodwork in geometric forms.

Literary Analysis
The Ghost Story How does Bowen prepare the reader for the suggestion that there is something supernatural about the letter?

3 

What does Mrs. Drover unexpectedly discover in her vacant house?

2 Literary Analysis
The Ghost Story

- Have students read the first five paragraphs of the story, then pause to identify their reaction to the setting and opening exposition.
- Discuss what the author did to create this reaction.
- Review with students the three given traits of a ghost story, and have students identify which are evident in this passage. Have students identify specific passages, words, or phrases.
- Then, ask students the Literary Analysis question on p. 1033: How does Bowen prepare the reader for the suggestion that there is something supernatural about the letter?
  Answer: The author hints at inexplicable aspects of the letter's arrival with clues such as the caretaker's absence and the lack of a stamp on the letter.

3 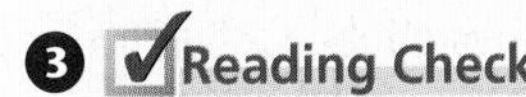

Answer: Mrs. Drover unexpectedly discovers a letter addressed to her.

CUSTOMIZE INSTRUCTION FOR UNIVERSAL ACCESS

For Special Needs Students	For Gifted/Talented Students	For Advanced Readers
Help these students decipher the exposition and setting of the story. Have them make a list of the objects on the street, and a list of the objects in the house, including any descriptive adjectives. Review with students the background of the Blitz, and talk about what life might have been like at that time.	Those students with a talent for drawing might be encouraged to draw or paint a scene such as that described in the opening of the story. Discuss what medium might be most appropriate, and what colors would elicit the same reaction in onlookers as students felt as they read. Post completed drawings for all to see.	Ask students to find elements of symbolism within the exposition of the story. For instance, how might the image of the cat watching Mrs. Drover be interpreted? Have students find as many symbols as possible and have them determine the origin and contribution of each.

keep your promise. I was sorry to see you leave London, but was satisfied that you would be back in time. You may expect me, therefore, at the hour arranged.
Until then . . . K.

Mrs. Drover looked for the date: it was today's. She dropped the letter onto the bedsprings, then picked it up to see the writing again—her lips, beneath the remains of lipstick, beginning to go white. She felt so much the change in her own face that she went to the mirror, polished a clear patch in it and looked at once urgently and stealthily in. She was confronted by a woman of forty-four, with eyes starting out under a hatbrim that had been rather carelessly pulled down. She had not put on any more powder since she left the shop where she ate her solitary tea. The pearls her husband had given her on their marriage hung loose round her now rather thinner throat, slipping into the V of the pink wool jumper her sister knitted last autumn as they sat round the fire. Mrs. Drover's most normal expression was one of controlled worry, but of assent. Since the birth of the third of her little boys, attended by a quite serious illness, she had had an intermittent muscular flicker to the left of her mouth, but in spite of this she could always sustain a manner that was at once energetic and calm.

Turning from her own face as precipitately as she had gone to meet it, she went to the chest where the things were, unlocked it, threw up the lid and knelt to search. But as rain began to come crashing down she could not keep from looking over her shoulder at the stripped bed on which the letter lay. Behind the blanket of rain the clock of the church that still stood struck six—with rapidly heightening apprehension she counted each of the slow strokes. "The hour arranged . . . My God," she said, "*What hour?* How should I . . . ? After twenty-five years. . . ."

❺ The young girl talking to the soldier in the garden had not ever completely seen his face. It was dark; they were saying goodbye under a tree. Now and then—for it felt, from not seeing him at this intense moment, as though she had never seen him at all—she verified his presence for these few moments longer by putting out a hand, which he each time pressed, without very much kindness, and painfully, on to one of the breast buttons of his uniform. That cut of the button on the palm of her hand was, principally, what she was to carry away. This was so near the end of a leave from France that she could only wish him already gone. It was August 1916. Being not kissed, being drawn away from and looked at intimidated Kathleen till she imagined spectral glitters in the place of his eyes. Turning away and looking back up the lawn she saw, through branches of trees, the drawing-room window alight; she caught a breath for the

spectral (spek´ trəl) *adj.* ghostly

The British Tradition

❹ In "The Demon Lover," Bowen hardly mentions World War II—the war appears only as the implied explanation for the Drovers' flight from their home. Bowen's story, though, captures the oppressive atmosphere of the Blitz, a time when familiar routines were routinely shattered by blackouts, air-raid sirens, and explosions. The menace Mrs. Drover confronts is not a bombing raid, but like the Blitz itself, it is a menace that lurks behind the most ordinary scenes.

Literary writers frequently engage with events of their time using the imagination to fashion a meaning from history. In *Gulliver's Travels,* Jonathan Swift criticized the political and social absurdities of his day. In poetry, Matthew Arnold lamented the spirit of the Victorian Age, while later poets such as Wilfred Owen condemned the horrors of World War I.

Such literary works may satisfy a reader's need to find sense in the jumble of historical events. At the same time, these works may challenge events, refusing to assent to the values they represent. In her portrait of Mrs. Drover, who lives a life cracked by war, Bowen may be suggesting that our world is haunted by madness, a madness that spawned two world wars less than thirty years apart.

❹ Background

The Literature of History

"The Blitz" is derived from the German word *blitzkrieg,* meaning "lightning war." During the Blitz in World War II, the Germans conducted a number of surprise bombing attacks on heavily populated areas in England, especially London.

❺ Literary Analysis

The Ghost Story and Ambiguity

- Have two volunteers act out the meeting between Kathleen and her fiancé. Remind these students to read the description of the meeting carefully so the interpretation is Bowen's, and not their own.
- Discuss as a class how the scene could be interpreted. Keep a list of opinions on the board, as well as any supporting facts students mention.
- Then, ask students the Literary Analysis question on p. 1035: In what two ways might Kathleen's fiancé's remarks be interpreted? **Answer:** The fiancé's promises might mean just what they seem to—that the fiancé will not be that far away (France is close to Britain), and that he plans to return after the war ends. The remarks may also be interpreted to mean that he shall return to haunt her.

ENRICHMENT: History Connection

World War I

World War I began in 1914, sparked by the assassination of Austro-Hungarian Archduke Francis Ferdinand. At first, Germany advanced quickly through Belgium and France. After a certain point, the war became primarily defensive. Soldiers from England and France dug themselves into a maze of trenches to fight off German attack. Three horrible and disillusioning years followed, in which neither side gained much ground but both sides suffered great losses. This was warfare of a type Europeans had never seen before—poison gas, mud, and a shockingly high number of casualties. Among the millions of war dead, a generation of young Englishmen was decimated.

Have students discuss how the memory of World War I horrors might contribute to Mrs. Drover's state of mind.

moment when she could go running back there into the safe arms of her mother and sister, and cry: "What shall I do, what shall I do? He has gone."

Hearing her catch her breath, her fiancé said, without feeling: "Cold?"

5 "You're going away such a long way."

"Not so far as you think."

"I don't understand?"

"You don't have to," he said. "You will. You know what we said."

"But that was—suppose you—I mean, suppose."

"I shall be with you," he said, "sooner or later. You won't forget that. You need do nothing but wait."

Only a little more than a minute later she was free to run up the silent lawn. Looking in through the window at her mother and sister, who did not for the moment perceive her, she already felt that unnatural promise drive down between her and the rest of all humankind. No other way of having given herself could have made her feel so apart, lost and foresworn. She could not have plighted a more sinister troth.

Kathleen behaved well when, some months later, her fiancé was reported missing, presumed killed. Her family not only supported her but were able to praise her courage without stint because they could not regret, as a husband for her, the man they knew almost nothing about. They hoped she would, in a year or two, console herself—and had it been only a question of consolation things might have gone
6 much straighter ahead. But her trouble, behind just a little grief, was a complete dislocation from everything. She did not reject other lovers, for these failed to appear: for years she failed to attract men—and with the approach of her thirties she became natural enough to share her family's anxiousness on this score. She began to put herself out, to wonder; and at thirty-two she was very greatly relieved to find herself being courted by William Drover. She married him, and the two of them settled down in this quiet, arboreal part of Kensington; in this house the years piled up, her children were born and they all lived till they were driven out by the bombs of the next war. Her movements as Mrs. Drover were circumscribed, and she dismissed any idea that they were still watched.

As things were—dead or living the letter writer sent her only a threat. Unable, for some minutes, to go on kneeling with her back exposed to the empty room, Mrs. Drover rose from the chest to sit on an upright chair whose back was firmly against the wall. The desuetude[3] of her former bedroom, her married London home's whole air of being a cracked cup from which memory, with its reassuring power, had either evaporated or leaked away, made a crisis—and at just this crisis the letter writer had, knowledgeably, struck. The hollowness of the house this evening canceled years on years of voices, habits and steps. Through the shut windows she only heard rain fall

3. **desuetude** (des´ wi to͞od´) *adj.* condition of not being used any more.

Literary Analysis
The Ghost Story and Ambiguity In what two ways might Kathleen's fiancé's remarks be interpreted?

dislocation (dis´ lō kā´ shən) *n.* condition of being out of place

arboreal (är bôr´ ē əl) *adj.* of, near, or among trees

circumscribed (sʉr´ kəm skrībd´) *adj.* limited; having a definite boundary

7 **Reading Check**
What happens to Kathleen's fiancé after he returns to war?

6 Vocabulary Development

Latin Root *-loc-*

- Bowen writes that, before her marriage, Kathleen experiences "a complete *dislocation* from everything." Have students read the meaning of the word in the margin.
- Inform students that a second meaning of dislocation is "disruption of an established order."
- Tell students that the word dislocation is built on the Latin root *-loc-*, meaning "place." Have them brainstorm for other words they know that might be built on the same root.
  Possible answers: Such words include *local, relocate, locus,* and *allocate.*
- Have them check their suggestions in the dictionary to determine what the root contributes to the meaning of each word.

7 

Answer: He was reported missing and presumed killed.

CUSTOMIZE INSTRUCTION FOR UNIVERSAL ACCESS

For Less Proficient Readers	For English Learners	For Advanced Readers
Clarify the jumps in time taking place in the story. Mrs. Drover's flashback begins, "The young girl . . . " (p. 1034). Explain that the leap from present to past occurs quickly while the transition from past to present is gradual. Have students list events in their proper order.	Students might at first interpret the section of the story about Kathleen as being about a different person. Explain the device of the flashback, and point out that early in the passage we learn that it is 1916. Help readers trace "Kathleen" through the years until she becomes "Mrs. Drover" and the connection can be made.	Have students write a brief essay answering this question: Would it have been more effective, as effective, or less effective to have the story told in strict chronological order? Students with strong opinions might be invited to debate this point before the class.

8 Literary Analysis

The Ghost Story

- Have students find details in the story that show Mrs. Drover's practical nature, and those that support the feeling of the supernatural.
  Answer: She considers her alternatives in a practical manner, deciding to collect the objects she has come to fetch and to make her train; she plans to get a taxi and tries to calm herself. These details show her practicality. At the same time, the rush of her thoughts and the indications of her rapid breath and fumbling sustain the feelings of uncertainty and fear the letter has created. They suggest the possibility that something supernatural is about to happen.
- Point out that these details are mingled together, not separated by sentence or paragraph.
- Then, ask students the Literary Analysis question on p. 1036: In this paragraph, how do Mrs. Drover's fear of the supernatural and her attention to practical details blur the lines between the familiar world and the unknown?
  Answer: Her attention to practical details is motivated by her fear of the supernatural. In this way, ordinary reasoning is mixed up with fear of the unknown.

9 Critical Thinking

Connect

- Encourage students to recognize the link between young Kathleen's inability to see her fiancé's face during the leave-taking and the mature Mrs. Drover's inability to recall that face.
- Have students discuss whether the two represent related symptoms. Has Mrs. Drover built her practical personality around her refusal to look her demon "in the face"?
  Possible response: Her references to not being herself after her fiancé left and the unexplained emphasis on the idea that "*under no conditions* could she remember his face" show that she did not successfully deal with their traumatic parting. The fact that this ultimate, dread-inspiring prohibition against remembering has become part of her being suggests that the rest of her personality is a defense against or a shell around the past trauma.

on the roofs around. To rally herself, she said she was in a mood—and, for two or three seconds shutting her eyes, told herself that she imagined the letter. But she opened them—there it lay on the bed.

On the supernatural side of the letter's entrance she was not permitting her mind to dwell. Who, in London, knew she meant to call at the house today? Evidently, however, this had been known. The caretaker, *had* he come back, had had no cause to expect her: he would have taken the letter in his pocket, to forward it, at his own time, through the post. There was no other sign that the caretaker had been in—but, if not? Letters dropped in at doors of deserted houses do not fly or walk to tables in halls. They do not sit on the dust of empty tables with the air of certainty that they will be found. There is needed some human hand—but nobody but the caretaker had a key. Under circumstances she did not care to consider, a house can be entered without a key. It was possible that she was not alone now. She might be being waited for, downstairs. Waited for—until when? Until "the hour arranged." At least that was not six o'clock; six has struck.

She rose from the chair and went over and locked the door.

The thing was, to get out. To fly? No, not that: she had to catch her train. As a woman whose utter dependability was the keystone of her family life she was not willing to return to the country, to her husband, her little boys and her sister, without the objects she had come up to fetch. Resuming work at the chest she set about making up a
8 number of parcels in a rapid, fumbling-decisive way. These, with her shopping parcels, would be too much to carry; these meant a taxi—at the thought of the taxi her heart went up and her normal breathing resumed. I will ring up the taxi now; the taxi cannot come too soon; I shall hear the taxi out there running its engine, till I walk calmly down to it through the hall. I'll ring up—But no: the telephone is cut off . . . She tugged at a knot she had tied wrong.

The idea of flight . . . He was never kind to me, not really. I don't remember him kind at all. Mother said he never considered me. He was set on me, that was what it was—not love. Not love, not meaning a person well. What did he do, to make me promise like that? I can't remember—But she found that she could.

She remembered with such dreadful acuteness that the twenty-five
9 years since then dissolved like smoke and she instinctively looked for the weal[4] left by the button on the palm of her hand. She remembered not only all that he said and did but the complete suspension of *her* existence during that August week. I was not myself—they all told me so at the time. She remembered—but with one white burning blank as where acid has dropped on a photograph: *under no conditions* could she remember his face.

So wherever he may be waiting, I shall not know him. You have no time to run from a face you do not expect.

Literary Analysis
The Ghost Story In this paragraph, how do Mrs. Drover's fear of the supernatural and her attention to practical details blur the lines between the familiar world and the unknown?

4. **weal** *n.* raised mark, line, or ridge on the skin caused by an injury.

ENRICHMENT: Literature Connection

More About Bowen

It has been said that Elizabeth Bowen had an extraordinary ability to get inside the mind of children. This was most likely a result of her own troubled childhood. She was interested in the psychological and emotional dynamics found in families, and in particular in parent-child relationships. Bowen often returned to this theme, creating works in which children were orphaned, abandoned, misunderstood, and frequently sacrificed by an uncaring and selfish adult world.

Bowen also wrote a number of nonfiction works, including *Bowen's Court* (1942), on her ancestral home; *The Shelbourne Hotel* (1951); and *Afterthought* (1962), a collection of childhood memories and literary studies. *Pictures and Conversations* (1975) is a collection of miscellaneous writings, including portions of a novel and autobiography left unfinished at the time of her death.

Ox House, Shaftsbury, 1932, John R. Biggs

11 ◀ Critical Viewing
Compare the suggestion of "life" this engraving gives to material objects with the role of objects in the story. Are they a threat, a consolation, or indifferent? **[Compare and Contrast]**

The thing was to get to the taxi before any clock struck what could be the hour. She would slip down the street and round the side of the square to where the square gave on the main road. She would return in the taxi, safe, to her own door, and bring the driver into the house with her to pick up the parcels from room to room. The idea of the taxi driver made her decisive, bold; she unlocked her door, went to the top of the staircase and listened down.

She heard nothing—but while she was hearing nothing the passé[5] air of the staircase was disturbed by a draft that traveled up to her face. It emanated from the basement: down there a door or window was being opened by someone who chose this moment to leave the house.

The rain had stopped; the pavements steamily shone as Mrs. Drover let herself out by inches from her own front door into the empty street. The unoccupied houses opposite continued to meet her look with their damaged stare. Making toward the thoroughfare and the taxi, she tried not to keep looking behind. Indeed, the silence was so intense—one of those creeks of London silence exaggerated this summer by the damage of war—that no tread could have gained on hers unheard. Where her street debouched on the square where people went on living, she grew conscious of, and checked, her unnatural pace. Across the open end of

12 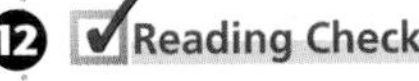
What does Mrs. Drover struggle to avoid?

5. **passé** (pa sā´) *adj.* stale.

10 Background

Art

Ox House, Shaftsbury
by John R. Biggs

This scene offers a partial glimpse from one room into another. Like Mrs. Drover or the ghost in the story, the viewer might be either hesitantly or stealthily moving through a home.

John R. Biggs created this black-and-white wood block print. Once a flourishing means of reproducing pictorial images, wood block printing was less common by 1932. The process—in which lines are incised into wooden blocks, which are then inked and pressed onto paper—enabled Biggs to create a striking but hauntingly quiet scene. Use the questions for discussion:

1. If this were a room in Mrs. Drover's house, what might happen next?
   Answer: Allow students to speculate freely. Some may say that the ghost might be hiding in the room beyond or that Mrs. Drover might walk fearfully but with determination into the room beyond to complete her tasks.
2. What elements in the image evoke the mysterious mood of the story?
   Answer: The contrast of darkness and light lends an eerie feeling of a mysterious presence.

11 ▶ Critical Viewing

Answer: Students may say that some objects in the story—the letter, for example—are definitely threatening. The objects in the engraving may seem similarly threatening to students, either because they are partly in shadow or because the light mysteriously suggests that the chair itself is watching through the doorway.

12 ✓Reading Check

Answer: She tries her best not to remember her fiancé or the times she had after his disappearance.

CUSTOMIZE INSTRUCTION FOR UNIVERSAL ACCESS

For Less Proficient Readers	For Gifted/Talented Students	For Advanced Readers
Have students each take a portion of the story to illustrate in a comic book manner—that is, with pictures and dialogue in speech balloons. Help them think of the story and how it could be scary, and urge them to illustrate the events in that manner. Post the entire "comic book" for all to see.	Have students work together to make a "silent movie" of the story, using either a video camera, computer video, or a stage presentation without dialogue. Students can add music that enhances the dramatics. Discuss what moments would be emphasized by the music, and in what manner.	Encourage students to write their own short ghost story. Review the emotions and reactions they experienced while reading "The Demon Lover" and how the author elicited that reaction. Remind them of the basic characteristics of a ghost story. Students can read their original ghost stories to the class for review and comment.

ASSESS

Answers for p. 1038

Review and Assess

1. Students may say that they sympathize with Mrs. Drover. She was simply scared and, given the fact that they were at war, one cannot blame her for being scared.
2. **(a)** The letter is unexpected because the Post Office has been diverting their mail to the country house. **(b)** She is upset because it appears to be from her old fiancé, whom she thought dead; the letter contains an eerie reminder of a past promise.
3. **(a)** The fiancé had promised her that he would be with her, sooner or later. **(b)** She feels watched after the disappearance of her fiancé, when she is searching through the chest, and when she feels the draft from the staircase. Each passage heightens the story's tension or links the present tension to an eerie past. **(c)** The feeling that she is watched might be a disguised expression of the fact that her conscience "watches" her. It suggests that she felt guilty about not loving him as others thought she did, and not feeling tremendous sorrow when he was presumably killed.
4. **(a)** Traces include a smoke stain, a bruise in the wallpaper, a ring left by a vase, claw marks from the piano on the floor, and the mark on Kathleen's palm from the button. **(b)** Ghosts and memories, like scars and stains, are a present indication of the past, of something or someone that is now absent. **(c)** The accumulated references to traces all suggest the ways in which an absence can make its presence felt. This pattern echoes the story's theme: The past, though absent, haunts those who have not made peace with it.
5. Mrs. Drover is surrounded by signs of an interrupted routine—her family has had to leave the house she is in. Her attempts to calm herself and to escape the ghost all involve efforts to return to routine tasks or familiar places. Her fate suggests that, without familiar routines, human beings are extremely vulnerable.

the square two buses impassively passed each other; women, a perambulator,[6] cyclists, a man wheeling a barrow signalized, once again, the ordinary flow of life. At the square's most populous corner should be—and was—the short taxi rank. This evening, only one taxi—but this, although it presented its blank rump, appeared already to be alertly waiting for her. Indeed, without looking round the driver started his engine as she panted up from behind and put her hand on the door. As she did so, the clock struck seven. The taxi faced the main road. To make the trip back to her house it would have to turn—she had settled back on the seat and the taxi *had* turned before she, surprised by its knowing movement, recollected that she had not "said where." She leaned forward to scratch at the glass panel that divided the driver's head from her own.

The driver braked to what was almost a stop, turned round and slid the glass panel back. The jolt of this flung Mrs. Drover forward till her face was almost into the glass. Through the aperture driver and passenger, not six inches between them, remained for an eternity eye to eye. Mrs. Drover's mouth hung open for some seconds before she could issue her first scream. After that she continued to scream freely and to beat with her gloved hands on the glass all round as the taxi, accelerating without mercy, made off with her into the hinterland of deserted streets.

aperture (ap′ ər chər′) *n.* opening

6. **perambulator** *n.* baby carriage.

Review and Assess

Thinking About the Selection

1. **Respond:** Do you feel sympathetic toward Mrs. Drover? Why or why not?
2. **(a) Recall:** Why is the appearance of the letter in Mrs. Drover's house unexpected? **(b) Infer:** Why is she so upset by it?
3. **(a) Recall:** Before returning to the war, what had Mrs. Drover's fiancé promised her? **(b) Analyze:** Identify three points at which she feels that she is being watched, and describe what each moment adds to the story. **(c) Draw Conclusions:** What does this feeling suggest about her guilt toward her fiancé?
4. **(a) Analyze:** Identify three references in the story to "traces," marks left behind by objects or actions. **(b) Interpret:** In what sense are ghosts and memories also traces? **(c) Draw Conclusions:** How do the references to traces suggest and support the story's theme?
5. **Draw Conclusions:** What does Mrs. Drover's fate suggest about the importance of habit and the familiar in human life?

ASSESSMENT PRACTICE: Writing Skills

Strategy (For more practice, see Test Preparation Workbook, p. 45.)

Many tests require students to apply revision strategies to a given passage. Use the following sample test item to practice that skill.

> Only a little more than a minute later she was free to run up the silent lawn. Looking in through the window at her mother and sister, who did not for the moment perceive her, she felt that unnatural promise drive down between her and the rest of all humankind.

Which of these sentences would best fit after the first sentence of the paragraph?

A Her palm was still bleeding.
B It was time for her favorite radio program.
C She ran quickly, eager to feel safe again.
D Her father had already gone to bad.

Lead students to recognize *C* is the best answer because it fits with the tone of the passage.

Review and Assess

Literary Analysis

The Ghost Story

1. Find examples in the tale of each of these characteristics of a **ghost story:** (a) the intrusion of the past and, (b) the suggestion of supernatural explanations for events.
2. (a) Identify two details hinting at supernatural influences in Kathleen's last meeting with her fiancé. Explain your choice. (b) Name two details that make the parting seem psychologically realistic and not supernatural. Explain your choice.
3. (a) Find two passages that contrast the familiar with the eerie. In each, what allows the strange to "leak into" the familiar? (b) What do these passages suggest about Bowen's view of the fragility of life?

Connecting Literary Elements

4. (a) Identify two examples of **ambiguity** in phrases in the story's opening paragraph. (b) Explain how they hint at the eerie events to come.
5. (a) In what two ways might events in the story be interpreted? (b) Does the evidence favor one over the other? Explain.
6. Either Mrs. Drover or her fiancé might be the "demon lover" of the title. Explain, showing how this ambiguity sheds light on the story.

Reading Strategy

Responding to the Story

7. What was your **response** to the atmosphere at the beginning of the story? Explain.
8. Use an organizer like the one shown to analyze your responses to events in the story and the devices Bowen uses to elicit them.

Detail
Sight of letter on table
My Response
It feels a little creepy.
Technique
Appearance announced with sudden break in Mrs. Drover's thoughts.

Extend Understanding

9. **Psychology Connection:** Mrs. Drover is haunted by an unresolved problem from the past. According to psychologists, how may a person be "haunted" by the past?

Quick Review

A **ghost story** is a tale in which part of the past—typically, a dead person—seems to make a supernatural appearance in the present.

Ambiguity is the quality by which a single word, phrase, description, or narrative conveys two or more divergent meanings.

To **respond** to literature, identify your own reaction and then determine how the author evoked it.

Take It to the Net

www.phschool.com

Take the interactive self-test online to check your understanding of the selection.

Answers for p. 1039

Review and Assess

1. **(a)** The letter and the memory of the fiancé are intrusions from the past. **(b)** That the letter arrived from a person thought to be dead, and without the help of the Post Office, brings a supernatural feel to the story.
2. **(a)** The fact that she had never completely seen his face and the spectral glitters in place of his eyes are both supernatural details. **(b)** She continually touches her fiancé for reassurance, and she plans to cry from loneliness and sadness when he is gone; both of these are expected reactions to the situation.
3. **(a)** Possible response: Passages include the opening of the story, in which the emptiness of the scene contrasts with Mrs. Drover's ordinary-seeming actions, and the passage in which Mrs. Drover applies practical reasoning because she fears the supernatural. **(b)** The passages suggest that Bowen thinks our identity becomes fragile when we are stripped of our habits and when familiar surroundings become foreign.
4. **(a)** Ambiguous passages include "no human eye watched" and "Dead air came out to meet her . . . ." **(b)** The passages subtly hint at the watchful presence of the dead fiancé.
5. **(a)** The events might be simply a figment of her imagination, or they might show a supernatural power at work. **(b)** Possible response: The evidence, coupled with the knowledge of the time in which the story is set, would suggest that the events are in her mind.
6. If "the demon lover" of the title is the fiancé, it supports the idea that Mrs. Drover actually encounters a ghost (a demon lover). If Mrs. Drover is "the demon lover," that is, a lover of demons, then the title suggests that her unresolved past love causes her to hallucinate an encounter with a ghost.
7. Students may say that they felt uneasy about the deserted house and neighborhood, and how a lone woman might fare.

continued

ENRICHMENT: Further Reading

Other Works by Elizabeth Bowen

The Hotel

The Heat of the Day

The Last September

Take It to the Net

Visit www.phschool.com for more information about Elizabeth Bowen.

Answers continued

8. Possible response: **Detail:** Kathleen can't see the face of her fiancé, sees glitter in his eye; **My Response:** frightened by the fiancé, how cold he seems; **Technique:** she describes an absence of what usually makes people seem most present (face, eyes)
9. Possible response: Psychoanalysts hold that past traumas can unconsciously influence a person's present actions and outlook.

EXTEND

Answers for p. 1040

❶ Vocabulary Development

Word Analysis

1. getting from one place to another
2. a specific and defined place
3. move from one place to another

Spelling Strategy

1. note
2. equate
3. inflate

Fluency: Words in Context

1. correct
2. incorrect
3. incorrect
4. correct
5. incorrect

❷ Grammar and Style

1. having been sent away; piano
2. left by the last bombing; cracks
3. entering the lighted room; soldier
4. halting the conversation; girl
5. Pulling away from the stand; taxi

Writing Application

Possible response: The taxi, being a familiar and safe sight, was a stroke of genius. Entering the vehicle, she had no idea I was waiting for her. And her family, having no idea that I even exist, will wonder for years what happened to her.

Integrate Language Skills

❶ Vocabulary Development Lesson

Word Analysis: Latin Root *-loc-*

The word *dislocation,* formed from the Latin root *-loc-*, meaning "place," means "the condition of being out of place." Using your knowledge of the root, define the following words:

1. locomotion
2. local
3. relocating

Spelling Strategy

When adding the suffix *-tion* to a verb that ends in *-te*, first drop these letters. Then, add the suffix *-tion*: *dislocate*, *dislocation*. For each of these words ending in *-tion*, give the related verb.

1. notation
2. equation
3. inflation

Fluency: Words in Context

Review the vocabulary list on page 1031. Then, in your notebook, explain whether the italicized word in each of the sentences below is used correctly. Let the context created by the sentence guide you.

1. I was relieved when I touched not a *spectral* presence, but solid flesh.
2. Given the pollution in the world's waterways, I am surprised that more *arboreal* species are not endangered.
3. Take whatever you wish; my generosity is strictly *circumscribed*.
4. The letter fit through the *aperture*.
5. The doctor has caused a permanent *dislocation* of your shoulder; you should feel fine in a day or two.

❷ Grammar and Style Lesson

Sentence Beginnings: Participial Phrases

Bowen begins some sentences with participial phrases. A **participle** is a verb form usually ending in *-ed* or *-ing*. A **participial phrase** is a participle, together with its modifiers and complements. The whole phrase acts as an adjective.

Participial Phrase: Shifting some parcels under her arm, she slowly forced round her latchkey . . . (modifies *she*)

Participle: Shocked, she stopped to catch her breath. (modifies *she*)

When a sentence begins with a participial phrase, it seems to start "in the middle" of an action that is already underway—an effect that draws readers in. For clarity, a participial phrase should be placed next to the word it modifies.

Practice Identify the participial phrases and the words they modify.

1. The piano, having been sent away, had left claw marks on the floor.
2. The cracks, left by the last bombing, ran down the wall.
3. The soldier, entering the lighted room, pulled his hat down to cover his face.
4. The young girl, halting the conversation, ran away from the soldier.
5. Pulling away from the stand, the taxi sped down the street.

Writing Application Write a brief paragraph about the story from the perspective of the demon lover. Use three participial phrases.

WG Prentice Hall Writing and Grammar Connection: Chapter 19 Section 2

TEACHING RESOURCES

The following resources can be used to enrich or extend the instruction for pp. 1040–1041.

Vocabulary

- **Selection Support:** Build Vocabulary, p. 227
- **Vocabulary and Spelling Practice Book** (Use this booklet for skills enrichment.) ■

Grammar

- **Selection Support:** Grammar and Style, p. 228
- **Writing and Grammar,** Diamond Level, p. 446
- **Daily Language Practice Transparencies**

Writing

- **Writing and Grammar,** Diamond Level, p. 82 ■
- **Writing and Grammar iText CD-ROM**

■ **BLOCK SCHEDULING:** Resources marked with this symbol provide varied instruction during 90-minute blocks.

❸ Writing Lesson

Sequel

Write a sequel to "The Demon Lover," answering the question, What happened next? To ensure that your sequel is well-connected with the original, use clear and logical organization.

Prewriting Jot down questions that "The Demon Lover" leaves unanswered. Then, suggest answers to these questions. Select a few of these answers as a starting point.

Drafting Outline the events in your story in a logical way. As you draft, give only enough information to prepare readers for what happens next. Choose logical places to fill in background from the original story.

Revising Number the main events in your story in chronological order. Review out-of-sequence passages. For each, consider whether your order will confuse readers or whether it creates a desirable effect. Reorganize your draft as necessary.

Model: Revising to Create Clear and Logical Organization

(3) Shaking off his surprise, he stepped through the now open door. (2) Someone had prepared the way for him, almost as if he were expected. (1) The day before, the door had been rusted shut.

Placing the description of event 2 after event 3 heightens the tension. Event 1 should be narrated earlier in the story.

WG Prentice Hall Writing and Grammar Connection: Chapter 5, Section 3

❹ Extension Activities

Listening and Speaking Choose a ghost story that you find especially effective for a spooky **story reading.** Prepare, using these strategies:

- Read the text through several times.
- Note passages where a hushed tone will give a chill or where a raised voice and rapid speech will build suspense.
- Incorporate and practice using visual or sound effects to enhance your retelling.

Dim the lights, and present your reading to the class.

Research and Technology With a group, present a **history report** on life in London during the Blitz, linking your research to Bowen's story. Each group member should cover an aspect of the topic, such as historical background or daily life. Consult varied sources, including photographs and other primary sources.

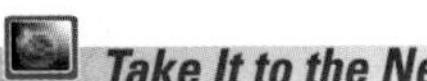

www.phschool.com

Go online for an additional research activity using the Internet.

ASSESSMENT RESOURCES

The following resources can be used to assess students' knowledge and skills.

Selection Assessment

- **Formal Assessment,** pp. 237–239
- **Open Book Test,** pp. 144–146
- **Got It! Assessment Videotapes,** Tape 5
- **Test Bank Software**

Visit www.phschool.com for self-tests and additional questions on the writings of Elizabeth Bowen.

- **Workbook**
- **Skill Book**
- **Transparencies**
- **CD-ROM**

Lesson Support for p. 1041

❸ Writing Lesson

- During Prewriting, have students check with each other to be sure the "unanswered questions" have logical answers that grow out of the original story.
- Students may want to first write the events of the original story in chronological order to determine where gaps in knowledge occur. They can then work toward filling in the gaps in their sequel.
- For the students intending to narrate events out of order for dramatic effect, point out Bowen's use of line spaces to separate the narrative in the past from the narrative in the present in her story. This is one method to use to indicate a shift in focus.

❹ Listening and Speaking

- Have students share examples of favorite ghost stories from books, film, or storytelling sessions. Discuss what makes these so effective, reviewing both content and presentation. Point out that "The Demon Lover" has no violence or bloodshed in it, yet it is very frightening.
- Before students present their stories, encourage them to review and discuss how tone of voice and gestures can lend dramatic effects to readings.
- Have students work together to create a versatile backdrop for the readings, perhaps draped black cloth behind a single chair. Allow them to rehearse their readings and plan effective changes in tone and appropriate gestures. Point out that overacting may undercut the suspense they want to create.

CUSTOMIZE INSTRUCTION
For Universal Access

To address different learning styles, use the activities suggested in the **Extension Activities** booklet, p. 49.

- For Visual/Spatial and Verbal/Linguistic Learners, use Activity 5.
- For Verbal/Linguistic Learners, use Activity 6.
- For Interpersonal and Verbal/Linguistic Learners, use Activity 7.

Lesson Objectives

1. To understand the connection between the realities of the twentieth century across cultural lines
2. To understand how a poet's choice of style and elements in the text connect to make a dramatic thematic representation

Connections

The violence of the twentieth century represents a change in popular attitude as well as accessibility to insight on a shrinking planet. Have students read the poetry on pp. 1043–1046. What similarities and differences in the poetry can students make to the writings of Eliot, Bowen, Yeats, and Orwell?

Waking From the Dream

- Explain to students that for the artists in the twentieth century, responding to the violent changes in our world enables them to carry their message across borders and into other cultures.
- Point out to students that the changes these poets respond to in their work are only some of the many political, social, and economic upheavals in the world during the twentieth century.
- Encourage students to consider how the themes of these works might apply to late twentieth-century events in the former Soviet Union, China, and Germany.

▶Critical Viewing

Possible response: Students may link the oval above with the bomb and the splattered black paint with the explosion.

CONNECTIONS

Literature Around the World

Waking From the Dream

Awakenings The writers in this section respond to the disconcerting, often violent, changes of the twentieth century. These upheavals mark their work with imagery of dreams and disillusion. Bowen in "The Demon Lover" and Yeats in "The Second Coming" stress the nightmarish aspects of war and of historical cycles. In "Preludes," T. S. Eliot portrays an awakening of the soul to a confused and fragmented world. In "Shooting an Elephant," Orwell shows how, as a young imperial police officer, he first awakened to the detrimental effects of colonialism.

"From Starry Bullet-holes" Yehuda Amichai (yə hōō´ də ä´ mi khī), Anna Akhmatova (ak mä´ tō və) and Bei Dao (bā dou) also record awakenings to the century's grim realities. Akhmatova, writing just after a bitter civil war in Russia (1918–1920), describes both the "misery" she sees around her and the "miraculous" that she senses. Amichai, a veteran of Israel's wars, shows the devastating and far-reaching effects of an act of terrorism. Bei Dao writes the "Testament" of a prisoner about to be executed by the Chinese government. Although soon to die, this man holds out the possibility that his death will be a source of renewal: "From starry bullet-holes / the blood-red dawn will flow."

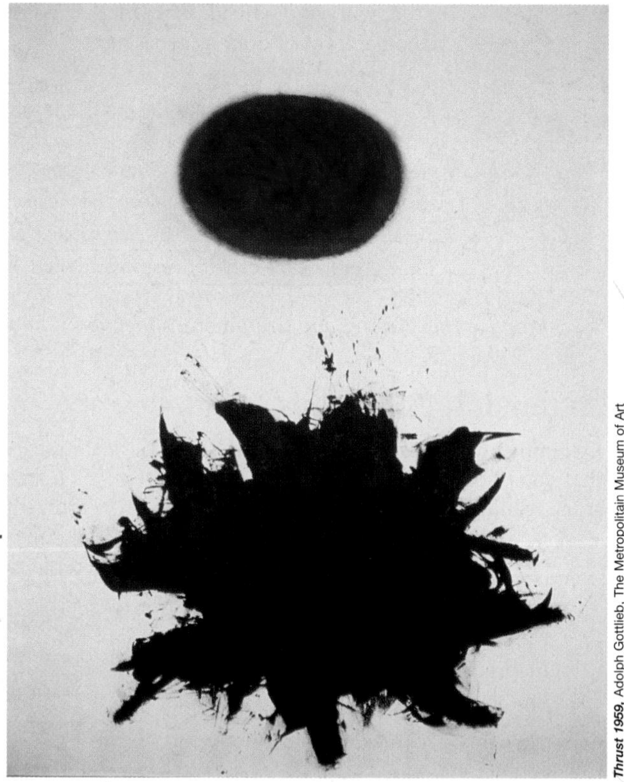

Thrust 1959, Adolph Gottlieb, The Metropolitain Museum of Art

▶Critical Viewing In what ways does this image illustrate Amichai's poem? **[Connect]**

The Diameter of the Bomb

Yehuda Amichai
Translated by Chana Bloch

The diameter of the bomb was thirty centimeters
and the diameter of its effective range about seven meters,
with four dead and eleven wounded.
And around these, in a larger circle
of pain and time, two hospitals are scattered
and one graveyard. But the young woman
who was buried in the city she came from,
at a distance of more than a hundred kilometers,
enlarges the circle considerably,
and the solitary man mourning her death
at the distant shores of a country far across the sea
includes the entire world in the circle.
And I won't even mention the crying of orphans
that reaches up to the throne of God and
beyond, making
a circle with no end and no God.

Yehuda Amichai

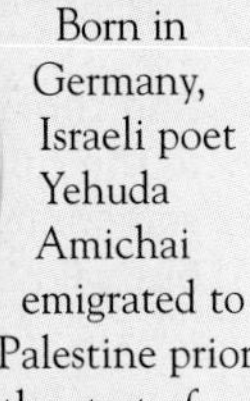

(1924–2000)

Born in Germany, Israeli poet Yehuda Amichai emigrated to Palestine prior to the start of World War II. He then fought in nearly all of Israel's wars and wrote poetry that expresses the thoughts and feelings of a whole generation of Israelis. In his poems, written in Hebrew, he skillfully combines biblical phrases and down-to-earth, everyday language.

Connecting Literature Around the World

1. Auden's "In Memory of W. B. Yeats" and Orwell's "Shooting an Elephant" both deal with the impact of historical events on individual lives. Compare one of these selections with Amichai's poem.
2. Compare the effect that war has on the speaker's vision of the world in this poem with the effect of war on Bowen's Mrs. Drover.
3. How would Auden's speaker in "Musée des Beaux Arts" respond to the vision of suffering in "The Diameter of the Bomb"? Why?

Background

About the Selection

This poem vividly evokes the ripple effects of a single hostile action—of the devastation terrorism can wreak upon the world. The speaker traces that action, the detonation of a bomb, in enlarging concentric circles, from the diameter of the bomb itself, to the area of its damage, to the wounded and dead, to the grief of survivors, to the children orphaned or unborn because of death. By tracing the furthest consequences of this action, the poet is able to question the nature of a world that permits such suffering.

Answers

Connecting Literature Around the World

1. **Possible reponse:** Students may choose to compare Orwell's work to Amichai; while both deal with a singular event, the bomb has more immediate devastation and the impact is felt by much fewer than the population in "Shooting an Elephant."
2. For Mrs. Drover, the war has canceled her ordinary life and caused her to "dissolve" as a person. Yet, she is not conscious of the damage or of any injustice to herself. Amichai's speaker deals explicitly with the personal ramifications of war.
3. **Possible response:** Auden's speaker would respond with a sigh to "The Diameter of the Bomb." The speaker feels that while these tragedies happen, the world will go on, even while individuals suffer.

ENRICHMENT: Art

***Thrust*, Adolph Gottlieb**

This painting of a red oval and black splatter captures the images of a bomb and its explosion described in Amichai's poem. American painter Adolph Gottlieb was born in New York City and studied there at the Art Students' League. He later studied at the Academie de la Grande Chaumière in Paris. Abstract Expressionist works such as *Thrust* are among Gottlieb's best-known works.

Use these questions for discussion:

1. How do the colors of the painting reflect the content of Amichai's poem?
   Possible response: The red reflects the fire of a bomb while the black suggests its destructive force.
2. How does the painting's composition contrast with Amichai's theme of cause and effect?
   Possible response: The white background suggests an isolated event; the poem stresses links between events.

Background

About the Selections

Both the poems on pages 1044–1046 refer to the oppression that may follow in the wake of revolution. In "Everything Is Plundered," Anna Akhmatova answers despair with the mystery of nature and human resiliency. "Testament," which follows, honors its speaker's desire to be free even when condemned, and to die with grace. These poems demonstrate the strength of human spirit against despair.

Everything Is Plundered

Anna Akhmatova
Translated by Stanley Kunitz

Everything is plundered, betrayed, sold,
Death's great black wing scrapes the air,
Misery gnaws to the bone.
Why then do we not despair?

By day, from the surrounding woods,
cherries blow summer into town;
at night the deep transparent skies
glitter with new galaxies.

And the miraculous comes so close
to the ruined, dirty houses—
something not known to anyone at all,
but wild in our breast for centuries.

Connecting Literature Around the World

1. How would the speaker in Eliot's "Preludes" respond to Akhmatova's poem? Explain.
2. How would the speaker in Yeats's "The Wild Swans at Coole" respond to the poem? Explain.
3. Akhmatova refers to the miraculous—the survival of the beautiful amid the upheavals of life—as "something not known to anyone at all, / but wild in our breast for centuries." Does this "something" only make its presence felt through poetry? Explain.

Anna Akhmatova

(1889–1966)

Russian poet Anna Akhmatova began writing poems at age eleven. During her long life, she experienced and wrote about a host of devastating events, from the Russian Revolution to the oppression of Stalin's dictatorship. Stalin banned her work for a time, but in 1940, the ban was lifted. She continued to write and publish until her death.

▲ **Critical Viewing** Does the Anna Akhmatova depicted in the portrait seem as if she could have written this poem? Why or why not? **[Compare and Contrast]**

▶Critical Viewing

Answer: The woman depicted may seem too young and healthy to have suffered much; yet her relaxed, poised pose suggests Akhmatova's receptiveness to mystery.

Answers

Connecting Literature Around the World

1. Possible response: The speaker in Eliot's "Preludes" might sympathize with the images in the first stanza suggesting that meaning has been "plundered" from the world. He might reject the drama of the images since that drama does not represent the monotony of existence that he discovers. He might also sympathize with the idea of "the miraculous" in the third stanza, which is reminiscent of his "fancy" of an "infinitely gentle, infinitely suffering thing" ("Preludes," lines 50–51). He would probably not find hope in this presence outside of the ordinary as Akhmatova finds hope in the miraculous.
2. Possible response: The speaker in "The Wild Swans at Coole" would sympathize with the experience of living in a world in which much has been lost, since he is feeling the loss of his youth. Like Akhmatova, who finds "the miraculous" in cherries and the night sky, he finds an enduring power in natural beauty (the swans). Where Akhmatova suggests that this power counteracts despair, Yeats finds the truth of his own death in the vision of the swans: Their beauty will endure when he is no longer present.
3. Possible responses: No: Akhmatova is suggesting that "the miraculous" is the reason that people do not despair in a plundered world. In this sense, the miraculous is practically present in life, not just in poetry. Yes: Akhmatova discovers a mystery in natural beauty and the endurance of the human spirit. While this mystery is part of life, only the connections made by a poet draw our attention to it.

Answers

Connecting Literature Around the World

1. Eliot's "hollow men" live a life that is like a death—an unreal dream. Bei Dao envisions death as a morning, an awakening. This vision keeps him from the nightmare of despair.
2. **(a)** Possible response: Yes, in "Testament," the event of the speaker's death does seem justified; in Amichai's "The Diameter of the Bomb," the suffering caused by violence cannot be justified or explained even by God; in Eliot's "Preludes" the routine of ordinary existence appears senseless; in Auden's "Musée des Beaux Arts" suffering appears to be without a meaning that can appear in the ordinary world. **(b)** Possible response: Yes, even the most despairing of these poems creates a meaning out of senselessness. Bei Dao creates a fierce assertion of freedom from the vision of his own death; Amichai creates a kind of memorial to the dead and testifies to the injustice of events; by reflecting on the emptiness of routine existence Eliot creates a marker for what is missing; Auden's wisdom about indifference to suffering shows how this indifference actually contributes to the beauty of ordinary, routine life.

Testament[1]

Bei Dao

Translated by Donald Finkel and Xueliang Chen

Perhaps the time has come.
I haven't left a will,
just one pen, for my mother.

I'm no hero, you understand.
This isn't the year for heroes.
I'd just like to be a man.

The horizon still divides
the living from the dead,
but the sky's all I need.

I won't kneel on the earth—
the firing squad might block
the last free breaths of air.

From starry bullet-holes
the blood-red dawn will flow.

1. **Testament** (Tes´ tə ment) *n.* will; also, a statement of one's beliefs.

Bei Dao

(b. 1949)

Bei Dao is a Chinese poet whose work is—in the words of one of his translators, Bonnie S. McDougall—a "complex reaction to the pressures of a brutalized and corrupt society." He was traveling abroad during the Tiananmen Square massacre (June 4, 1989), in which the Chinese government violently ended pro-democracy rallies. Since that time, Bei has lived in exile from China.

Connecting Literature Around the World

1. Eliot criticizes modern people for a lack of self-definition and decisiveness. How would the speaker in this poem answer his criticism?
2. (a) In this poem and in other poems in this section, do events in the modern world appear senseless? (b) Can poetry make meaning out of senseless events? Explain, using two works for support.

 **ENRICHMENT: Further Reading**

Other Works by the Poets

Amen, Travels, Yehuda Amichai
Rosary, Plantain, Anna Akhmatova
Forms of Distance, Old Snow, Bei Dao

PART 2

Conflicts Abroad and at Home

A Balloon Site, Coventry, 1940, Dame Laura Knight, Imperial War Museum

Selection Planning Guide

The violence of two World Wars, as well as simmering conflicts at home and in British colonies abroad, left their mark on modern literature. In the work of the War Poets (Brooke, Sassoon, and Owen), students can get a sense of life in the trenches of World War I and witness the transformation of a generation's vigorous patriotism as it is dragged through mud and suffering. Courage in the face of conflict resounds in Churchill's and Gandhi's speeches—one calling on a nation's courage in an hour of common danger, the other displaying an individual's courage in standing up for his principles. Conflicts within a community raise questions of identity—for the working class, in Sillitoe's "The Fiddle," and for Ireland, in the work of Trevor, Heaney, and Boland. In the end, Lessing discovers, conflict has many levels, as cultural conflict creates personal conflict in British-colonized Africa.

Background

Art

***A Balloon Site, Coventry*, 1940,** by Dame Laura Knight

This painting illustrates a group of female war workers launching a World War II barrage balloon. It captures women's crucial participation in England's war effort at home.

Use the following questions for discussion:

1. What elements in the painting suggest the challenges England faced?
   Answer: The women's presence in the scene and the evidence of war damage suggest the turmoil of war and the resulting changes in Britain's social structure and economy.
2. How do the details in the painting suggest a contrast between nineteenth- and twentieth-century Britain?
   Answer: The women's clothing and physical activity are in stark contrast to the dress and activities that Victorian women were permitted.

CUSTOMIZE INSTRUCTION FOR UNIVERSAL ACCESS

When assigning the selections in this part, keep in mind these factors:

Brooke, Owen, and Sassoon
- Should be read as a group, to emphasize their contrasting responses to war

Churchill and Gandhi
- The speeches are formal, but the situation in which each was delivered was truly dramatic. Have less proficient readers paraphrase as they read.

Sillitoe
- Students may identify with the working class character's decision to improve his life—with a sacrifice.

Heaney and Boland
- Students may require context on the conflict in Ireland before reading the poems.

Lessing
- This story reveals a cultural chasm between a British family and African servants.

The Soldier ✦ Wirers ✦ Anthem for Doomed Youth ✦ Birds on the Western Front

Lesson Objectives and CA Correlations

1. **To analyze and respond to literary elements**
   - Literary Analysis: Tone **R 3.3**
   - Comparing Literary Works **R 3.7**
2. **To read, comprehend, analyze, and critique poems and nonfiction**
   - Reading Strategy: Making Inferences
   - Reading Check Questions
   - Review and Assess Questions
3. **To develop word analysis skills, fluency, and systematic vocabulary**
   - Vocabulary Development Lesson: Latin Root *-laud-*
4. **To understand and apply written and oral language conventions**
   - Spelling Strategy **LC 1.2**
   - Grammar and Style Lesson: Adjective Clauses with *Who* and *Whom* **LC 1.1**
5. **To understand and apply appropriate writing and research strategies**
   - Writing Lesson: Critical Response **W 2.2**
   - Extension Activity: Report **W 1.1, 1.6, 1.9**
   - Assessment Practice (ATE)
6. **To understand and apply listening and speaking strategies**
   - Extension Activity: Debate **LS 1.5**

STEP-BY-STEP TEACHING GUIDE	PACING GUIDE
PRETEACH	
Motivate Students and Provide Background	
Use the Motivation activity (ATE p. 1048)	5 min.
Read and discuss author and background features (SE/ATE pp. 1048, 1051) A	5 min.
Introduce the Concepts	
Introduce the Literary Analysis and Reading Strategy (SE/ATE p. 1049) A	15 min.
Pronounce the vocabulary words and read their definitions (SE p. 1049)	5 min.
TEACH	
Monitor Comprehension	
Informally monitor comprehension by circulating while students read independently or in groups A	15 min.
Monitor students' comprehension with the Reading Check notes (SE/ATE pp. 1055, 1057)	as students read
Develop vocabulary with Vocabulary notes (SE pp. 1052, 1053, 1054, 1055)	as students read
Develop Understanding	
Develop students' understanding of tone with the Literary Analysis annotations (SE pp. 1051, 1055; ATE pp. 1051, 1052, 1054, 1055, 1056) A	5 min.
Develop students' ability to make inferences with the Reading Strategy annotations (SE p. 1057; ATE pp. 1055, 1057)	5 min.
ASSESS	
Assess Mastery	
Assess students' mastery of the Reading Strategy and Literary Analysis by having them answer the Review and Assess questions (SE/ATE p. 1059)	15 min.
Use one or more of the print and media Assessment Resources (ATE p. 1061) A	up to 45 min.
EXTEND	
Apply Understanding	
Have students complete the Vocabulary Development Lesson and the Grammar and Style Lesson (SE p. 1060) A	20 min.
Apply students' ability to support a thesis using the Writing Lesson (SE/ATE p. 1061) A	45 min.
Apply students' understanding using one or more of the Extension Activities (SE p. 1061)	20–90 min.

ACCELERATED INSTRUCTION:
Use the strategies and activities identified with an A.

UNIVERSAL ACCESS
● = Below-Level Students
▲ = On-Level Students
■ = Above-Level Students

Time and Resource Manager

Reading Level: Easy, Easy, Average, Average
Average Number of Instructional Days: 4

RESOURCES		
PRINT	**TRANSPARENCIES**	**TECHNOLOGY**
• **Beyond Literature,** Cross-Curricular Connection: Social Studies, p. 50 ▲ ■		• **Interest Grabber Video,** Tape 6 ● ▲ ■
• **Selection Support Workbook:** ● ▲ ■ Literary Analysis, p. 236 Reading Strategy, p. 235 Build Vocabulary, p. 233	• **Literary Analysis and Reading Transparencies,** pp. 99 and 100 ● ▲ ■	
		• **Listening to Literature** ● ▲ ■ Audiocassettes, Side 24 Audio CDs, CD 13
• **Literatura en español** ● ▲ • **Literary Analysis for Enrichment** ■	• **Fine Art Transparencies, Volume 1,** Transparency 20 ● ▲ ■	
• **Formal Assessment:** Selection Test, pp. 246–248 ● ▲ ■ • **Open Book Test,** pp. 147–149 ● ▲ ■ • **Performance Assessment and Portfolio Management,** p. 13 ● ▲ ■ • PRENTICE HALL ASSESSMENT SYSTEM ● ▲ ■	• PRENTICE HALL ASSESSMENT SYSTEM ● ▲ ■ Skills Practice Answers and Explanations on Transparencies ● ▲ ■	• **Test Bank Software** ● ▲ ■ • **Got It! Assessment Videotapes,** Tape 5 ● ▲
• **Selection Support Workbook:** ● ▲ ■ Grammar and Style, p. 234 • **Writing and Grammar,** Diamond Level ● ▲ ■ • **Extension Activities,** p. 50 ● ▲ ■	• **Daily Language Practice Transparencies** ● ▲ • **Writing Models and Graphic Organizers on Transparencies,** pp. 103–106 ● ▲ ■	• **Writing and Grammar iText CD-ROM** ● ▲ ■ ***Take It to the Net*** www.phschool.com

BLOCK SCHEDULING: Use one 90-minute class period to preteach the selections and have students read them. Use a second 90-minute class period to assess students' mastery of skills and have them complete one of the Extension Activities.

PREТEACH

Step-by-Step Teaching Guide for pp. 1048–1049

Motivation

Though students may see modern war in grisly detail on television, few will have heard firsthand accounts of war's battles, destruction, and horror. To prepare students for this selection's writings, discuss students' feelings about recent wars. Explain that the writers in this section, while perhaps against the war or affected by its horrors, took very seriously their patriotic duty to fight.

Interest Grabber Video

As an alternative, you may wish to play "'The Soldier': A Vietnam Veteran Remembers" on Tape 6 to engage student interest.

❶ More About the Authors

Rupert Brooke

Handsome, intelligent, and a good athlete, Brooke was also a popular young man who counted among his friends E.M. Forster, Virginia Woolf, Maynard Keynes, and Edward Thomas.

Wilfred Owen

Owen was teaching on the Continent in September 1915 when he visited a hospital for the wounded, which spurred him to return to England and enlist. In October 1918 he said, "I came out in order to help these boys—directly by leading them as well as an officer can; indirectly, by watching their sufferings that I may speak of them as well as a pleader can. I have done the first."

Siegfried Sassoon

The British poet fought in France and Palestine during World War I, earning a Military Cross. However, he was so horrified by the brutalities and bloodshed of war, he threw his Military Cross into the river.

Saki

Hector Hugh Munro ("Saki" was his pen name) is considered to be one of the most inventive and wittiest satirists of early twentieth-century England. He worked as a foreign correspondent in Russia and then in France for *The Morning Post* before returning to London in 1908 to write full-time.

Prepare to Read

❶ The Soldier ◆ Wirers ◆ Anthem for Doomed Youth ◆ Birds on the Western Front

Rupert Brooke (1887–1915)

Rupert Brooke had striking good looks, personal charm, and high intelligence. Before World War I began, Brooke had already established himself as a serious poet. He traveled a great deal, writing essays as well as poetry. When war broke out in 1914, he joined the Royal Navy. Tragically, he died from blood poisoning while on a mission to defeat the Turks.

Brooke's war sonnets, traditional and idealistic, were among the last from the soldier-poets of World War I to express wholehearted patriotism. The prolonged, inhuman slaughter of trench warfare extinguished the idealism of many of them.

Siegfried Sassoon (1886–1967)

Born into a wealthy family in Kent, England, Siegfried Sassoon published poetry while still in his twenties. In 1914, he joined the army and showed such reckless courage in battle that he earned the nickname "Mad Jack," along with a medal for gallantry.

By 1916 or 1917, though, Sassoon's attitude toward war had changed. He began to write starkly realistic "trench poems" about war's agonies. He was wounded early in 1917 and, while recovering, wrote a statement condemning the war. Partly to defuse his criticism and partly to protect him from its consequences, he was placed in a hospital for victims of shell shock.

Sassoon survived the war and lived almost fifty years longer, but he wrote little to match his wartime verses.

Wilfred Owen (1893–1918)

Always interested in literature, Wilfred Owen studied at London University, later worked as a tutor, and joined the army in 1915. A respected officer, he was wounded three times in 1917 and won a medal for outstanding bravery in 1918. Owen's work, at first an imitation of Keats's, became grittier and angrier under the influence of Siegfried Sassoon, whom he had met at a military hospital in 1917. It was a terrible loss to English poetry when Owen was killed in battle just one week before the end of the war.

Having published only five poems during his lifetime, Owen was unknown as a poet until Sassoon published a collection of his work, *Poems*, in 1920. Today, Owen is regarded as one of the greatest war poets in the English language. In the Preface to his poems, he is quoted as writing, "My subject is War, and the pity of War. The Poetry is in the pity. . . ."

Saki (H. H. Munro) (1870–1916)

Brought up from an early age by strict and unsympathetic aunts, Saki endured an unhappy childhood. However, he went on to become the author of many witty and humorous short stories. He also took revenge on his aunts by mocking bossy aunts in a number of the short stories he wrote. Dry, sometimes malice-tinged, his mockery is directed at those who lack imagination.

When the Great War broke out, Saki refused a commission as an officer, preferring instead to serve as an enlisted man. He was killed in the Battle of the Somme two years after volunteering.

TEACHING RESOURCES

The following resources can be used to enrich or extend the instruction for pp. 1048–1049.

Motivation

Interest Grabber Video, Tape 6

Background

Beyond Literature, p. 50

Take It to the Net

Visit www.phschool.com for background and hotlinks for the selections.

Literary Analysis

Literary Analysis and Reading Transparencies, Tone, p. 100

Reading

Literary Analysis and Reading Transparencies, Making Inferences, p. 99

BLOCK SCHEDULING: Resources marked with this symbol provide varied instruction during 90-minute blocks.

Preview

Connecting to the Literature

World War I, the first example of mechanized warfare on an international scale, brought untold suffering and devastation. It also inspired millions of words—patriotic, indignant, or disillusioned. These authors were among the firsthand witnesses who suffered from and wrote about this cataclysmic event.

❷ Literary Analysis

Tone

The **tone** of a literary work is the writer's attitude toward the readers and toward the subject. A writer's choice of words and details conveys the tone of a work. For example, in these lines from Rupert Brooke's "The Soldier," the underlined words and phrases communicate a tone of patriotic devotion and wistful memory:

Her sights and sounds; dreams happy as her day;
And laughter, learnt of friends; and gentleness,
In hearts at peace, under an English heaven.

Be alert to the way phrases and details in these poems convey various tones.

Comparing Literary Works

In a way, these selections are like letters sent home by soldiers during World War I. These "letters" each contain a message about the war for those who are back in England, removed from the fighting. In figuring out these messages, use tone as a clue—identify words and phrases that reveal each writer's attitude toward the war and toward civilian readers. Then, compare and contrast the messages about the war that these writers convey.

❸ Reading Strategy

Making Inferences

Because writers often suggest rather than state elements like tone, theme, and speaker, readers must **make inferences,** or educated guesses, about them based on clues in the text. Use a chart like the one shown to make inferences about tone and other elements in these works.

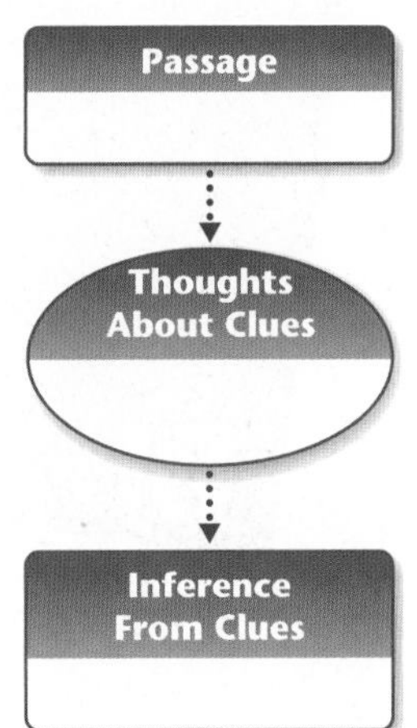

Vocabulary Development

stealthy (stelʹ thē) *adj.* secretive; furtive (p. 1052)

desolate (desʹ ə lit) *adj.* deserted; forlorn (p. 1052)

mockeries (mäkʹ ər ēz) *n.* futile or disappointing efforts; ridicule (p. 1053)

pallor (palʹ ər) *n.* lack of color; paleness (p. 1053)

laudable (lôdʹ ə bəl) *adj.* worthy of praise (p. 1054)

requisitioned (rekʹ wə zishʹ ənd) *v.* requested or applied for with a formal written order (p. 1055)

disconcerted (disʹ kən sʉrtʹ əd) *adj.* embarrassed or confused (p. 1057)

❷ Literary Analysis

Tone

- Remind students that tone refers to the writer's attitude toward his or her audience and characters.
- Tell them that writers carefully choose words and phrases to create the tone they want.
- Read the instruction about tone together as a class. Call students' attention to the excerpt from one of the poems.
- Use the Tone transparency in **Literary Analysis and Reading Transparencies,** p. 100, to demonstrate for students how to determine tone by examining the details, word choice, and voice of a piece.

❸ Reading Strategy

Making Inferences

- Tell students when they make an inference, they are drawing a conclusion using information found in the text.
- Read aloud the instruction about making inferences.
- Encourage students to use an inference chart like the one shown on p. 1049 to record their inferences as they read the selections.

Vocabulary Development

- Pronounce each vocabulary word for students, and read the definitions as a class. Have students identify any words with which they are already familiar.

CUSTOMIZE INSTRUCTION FOR UNIVERSAL ACCESS

For Less Proficient Readers	For English Learners	For Advanced Readers
Tone can be difficult to recognize for some students. To assist students, review with them the Literary Analysis: Tone on p. 1049, and model some examples from the selections. Encourage students to think about how they feel about each piece as they read. Tell them to use that feeling as a clue when they are trying to figure out tone.	These students may have difficulty figuring out tone if they find the vocabulary unfamiliar. Instruct students to look up the meanings of unfamiliar words and to discuss in groups the connotations of those words. Remind them that the author's word choice can be used to determine the tone.	Have students analyze one selection to find key words and phrases that indicate the tone of that piece. Then, using a thesaurus or their own knowledge, instruct them to choose synonyms for those words and phrases. Have the students rewrite the selection with the synonyms replacing the original words.

 ***E-Teach***

Visit E-Teach at www.phschool.com for teachers' essays on how to teach, with questions and answers.

TEACH

Step-by-Step Teaching Guide for pp. 1050–1058

CUSTOMIZE INSTRUCTION
For Intrapersonal Learners

Have students write in a response log as they read, recording their thoughts and emotions. Also ask them to note examples of their own personal experiences or knowledge of war.

❶ About the Selection

"The Soldier" records a soldier's love for his country and his wish to preserve all that he associates with that country. The speaker catalogs the features of his beloved England that he will never see again should he die in battle. His portrait of the Englishness he embodies—the sights, sounds, and very air that have shaped him—poignantly demonstrates the strong bond that can exist between the individual and society.

❷ ▶Critical Viewing

Answer: Students may say that the poster and poem express sentiments of patriotism and a longing to be home.

❶ The Soldier

Rupert Brooke

"If ye break faith —
we shall not sleep"
BUY VICTORY BONDS

❷ ▲**Critical Viewing** How does the sentiment expressed in this poster relate to that in "The Soldier"? **[Connect]**

TEACHING RESOURCES

The following resources can be used to enrich or extend the instruction for pp. 1050–1058.

Literary Analysis

Selection Support: Literary Analysis, p. 236 ■

Reading

Selection Support: Reading Strategy, p. 235; Build Vocabulary, p. 233

Listening to Literature Audiocassettes, Side 24 ■

Listening to Literature Audio CDs, CD 13 ■

Extension

Fine Art Transparencies, Volume 1, Fine Art Transparency 20
Display this transparency, *Troops Resting,* and have students speculate about the conditions of trench warfare. ■

■ **BLOCK SCHEDULING:** Resources marked with this symbol provide varied instruction during 90-minute blocks.

Background

World War I (1914–1918) pitted Great Britain, France, Russia, Japan, Italy, and later the United States (the Allies) against Germany, Austria-Hungary, and Turkey (the Central Powers). The war was fought not only in Europe but also in regions like the Middle East and Asia Minor. Typical of this conflict, especially in Western Europe, was trench warfare. Armies faced each other in defensive trenches protected by barbed wire. Periodically, one army would attack another in the face of machine-gun and artillery fire. Such warfare and the illnesses resulting from life in filthy trenches led to a total loss of about 8.5 million soldiers.

If I should die, think only this of me:
    That there's some corner of a foreign field
That is forever England. There shall be
    In that rich earth a richer dust concealed;
A dust whom England bore, shaped, made aware,
    Gave, once, her flowers to love, her ways to roam,
A body of England's, breathing English air,
Washed by the rivers, blest by suns of home. ❸

And think, this heart, all evil shed away,
    A pulse in the eternal mind, no less
        Gives somewhere back the thoughts by England given;
Her sights and sounds; dreams happy as her day;
    And laughter, learnt of friends; and gentleness,
        In hearts at peace, under an English heaven.

Literary Analysis
Tone What are three adjectives that describe the tone of this poem? Explain.

Review and Assess

Thinking About the Selection

1. **(a) Recall:** How does the speaker ask his readers to remember him, should he die? **(b) Infer:** Why would the speaker go off to war, knowing he could be killed?
2. **(a) Recall:** Name some of the things England has given the speaker. **(b) Interpret:** What is the "richer dust" to which the speaker refers?
3. **(a) Recall:** In lines 9 and 10, what does the speaker say his "heart" will become? **(b) Interpret:** What does the speaker mean by this statement?
4. **Take a Position:** Brooke's attitude has been called a "ridiculous anachronism"—something outdated—in the face of modern warfare. Do you agree or disagree? Why?

❸ Literary Analysis

Tone

- Read aloud the poem.
- Ask students what "...the corner of a foreign field/That is forever England" is.
  Answer: The speaker is referring to his grave on foreign soil.
- Then, ask students the Literary Analysis question on p. 1051: What are three adjectives that describe the tone of this poem? Explain.
  Possible response: Three adjectives that describe this poem would be *patriotic*—it deals with one's duty to country, *wistful*—it is written by a young man who may not return home to his beloved country, *sentimental*—because it is filled with warm, positive feeling.

Answers for p. 1051

Review and Assess

1. **(a)** The speaker asks the reader to think of him as being forever a part of England. **(b)** He believed that it was his duty and that England was worth defending.
2. **(a)** England gave the speaker flowers to appreciate, paths to roam, air, water, sun, and the laughter of friends. **(b)** The "richer dust" is the dust of the speaker's body, incorporating his English experiences.
3. **(a)** He says his heart will become "a pulse in the eternal mind." **(b)** The speaker's spirit will join other heavenly spirits.
4. Possible responses: Some students will agree, saying that today's governments do not deserve such loyalty. Others will disagree, saying that patriotism is never outdated.

CUSTOMIZE INSTRUCTION FOR UNIVERSAL ACCESS

For Special Needs Students	For Advanced Readers
Some students will have difficulty understanding the poem because of Brooke's usage of figurative language. Guide students through the poem line by line, asking students to paraphrase what Brooke wrote and what they think he means. Clarify with students that Brooke is speaking metaphorically by describing himself as part of England.	Encourage students to appreciate Brooke's ability to evoke such powerful images with so few words. Point out the repetition of words such as *dust* and *England.* Ask students to discuss how these repetitions contribute to the overall effect. Have students find other examples of musical devices and figurative language used by Brooke.

❹ About the Selection

Both "Wirers" and "Anthem for Doomed Youth" focus on illustrating war's horrors. "Wirers" transports readers immediately into the experience of waiting out a battlefield night, watching with bated breath as the fence-menders risk almost-certain death. "Anthem for Doomed Youth" captures the sad despair of battlefield death that undergoes no loving rituals of peacetime mourning. Together these poems convey the cynicism war often elicits.

❺ ▶Critical Viewing

Answer: Details in the painting that support Sassoon's depiction of war include the wire fence, the wounded or dead soldiers lying in the grass, the soldiers moving toward the wire fence, perhaps to mend it, and the darkness-into-dawn feel of the colors.

❻ Literary Analysis

Tone

- Read aloud the bracketed passage.
- Ask students what words characterize the actions of the wirers in the first stanza.
  Answer: Some words are "unraveling; twisting;" and "hammering" with "stealthy haste" and "anger in their blood."
- Then, ask students how these words set the tone in the poem.
  Possible answer: The quick, tangled, and jarring action is analogous to the chaos, hatred, and broken bodies that are indicative of war.

▶ **Monitor Progress** Ask students to describe the tone of the poem's final lines.
Answer: Students should recognize that the tone is ironic. Sassoon creates the irony by trivializing the serious injury suffered by one of the wirers.

❹ Wirers[1]

Siegfried Sassoon

Drawing of Tanks, World War I

❻
"Pass it along, the wiring party's going out"—
And yawning sentries mumble, "Wirers going out."
Unraveling; twisting; hammering stakes with muffled thud,
They toil with stealthy haste and anger in their blood.

The Boche[2] sends up a flare. Black forms stand rigid there,
Stock-still like posts; then darkness, and the clumsy ghosts
Stride hither and thither, whispering, tripped by clutching
    snare
Of snags and tangles.
        Ghastly dawn with vaporous coasts
Gleams desolate along the sky, night's misery ended.

Young Hughes was badly hit; I heard him carried away,
Moaning at every lurch; no doubt he'll die today.
But *we* can say the front-line wire's been safely mended.

❺ ▲Critical Viewing Which details in this painting support Sassoon's depiction of warfare? Explain. **[Connect]**

stealthy (stel´ thē) *adj.* secretive; furtive

desolate (des´ ə lit) *adj.* deserted; forlorn

1. **wirers** soldiers who were responsible for repairing the barbed-wire fences that protected the trenches in World War I.
2. **Boche** (bōsh) French slang for a German soldier.

ENRICHMENT: Art Connection

Art of the War

When a country goes to war, artists and writers don soldiers' uniforms along with other civilians and professional soldiers. The drawing on p. 1052 is the work of one such soldier-artist, an unknown World War I soldier, and it depicts a battlefield like the one described in Sassoon's poem, showing the haggard troops as they follow the ominous shapes of the tanks. This brief and honest sketch is the work of someone who has experienced the horrors of war and paused to record that reality.

Use these questions for discussion:

1. What elements of this illustration capture the immediacy of Sassoon's poem?
   Possible response: Its sketchy, hurried nature suggests that the artist, like Sassoon, paused briefly from battle to record his impressions.
2. What emotions do both the poem and the drawing suggest?
   Possible response: The poem and the drawing suggest despair, sadness, and fear.

4 Anthem *for* Doomed Youth

Wilfred Owen

What passing-bells for these who die as cattle?
Only the monstrous anger of the guns.
Only the stuttering rifles' rapid rattle
Can patter out their hasty orisons.[1]
No mockeries for them from prayers or bells,
Nor any voice of mourning save the choirs—
The shrill, demented choirs of wailing shells;
And bugles calling for them from sad shires.[2]

What candles may be held to speed them all?
Not in the hands of boys, but in their eyes
Shall shine the holy glimmers of good-byes.
The pallor of girls' brows shall be their pall;
Their flowers the tenderness of patient minds,
And each slow dusk a drawing-down of blinds.

---

1. **orisons** (ôr´ i zənz) *n.* prayers.
2. **shires** (shīrz) *n.* any of the counties of England.

7 **▲ Critical Viewing** Does the compassion Owen shows in the poem come through in this photograph of him? Explain. **[Analyze]**

mockeries (mäk´ ər ēz) *n.* futile or disappointing efforts; ridicule

pallor (pal´ ər) *n.* lack of color; paleness

Review and Assess

Thinking About the Selections

1. **Respond:** Which of these two poems conveys the horrors of war more effectively for you? Explain.
2. **(a) Recall:** What are the men getting ready to do at the beginning of "Wirers"? **(b) Infer:** How do the men feel about the job they have to do?
3. **(a) Recall:** In "Wirers," what happens in the course of the mission? **(b) Draw Conclusions:** What is the speaker's attitude toward the mission and toward the war? Explain.
4. **(a) Recall:** In lines 9–14 of "Anthem for Doomed Youth," what conventional signs of mourning are mentioned? **(b) Analyze:** What do Owen's suggested replacements for these signs have in common?
5. **Make a Judgment:** Which of these poems better captures the horrors of mechanized warfare? Why?

7 **▶ Critical Viewing**

Answer: Most students will say that Owen's face seems serious and caring.

Answers for p. 1053

Review and Assess

1. Possible response: "Wirers" vividly conveys war's horrors through a soldier's view. "Anthem for Doomed Youth" conveys war's horrors by focusing on the unceremonial deaths of the soldiers.
2. **(a)** The wirers are getting ready to mend barbed wire on the front line. **(b)** They probably loathe their job and are afraid they will be killed.
3. **(a)** The enemy sends a flare up to light the area and the soldiers stand rigid to avoid being seen and shot. **(b)** The speaker is angry and hates the mission and war.
4. **(a)** Signs include passing-bells, candles, drawn blinds, pall, flowers, and the drawing down of blinds. **(b)** The replacements are less ceremonial and more human.
5. Possible response: "Wirers" better captures the horrors of the war because it describes in vivid, sensory detail typical experiences from the war.

CUSTOMIZE INSTRUCTION FOR UNIVERSAL ACCESS

For Less Proficient Readers	For Advanced Readers
Students may understand the selections better if they have a sense of the historical setting in which these selections were written. You may want to show "'The Soldier': A Vietnam Veteran Remembers" on **Interest Grabber Video,** Tape 6, to give students more background on what a soldier faces during combat. After viewing the segment, discuss with students their knowledge or experiences with war.	Encourage students to use their knowledge of the historical background to expand their understanding of the selections. As students make inferences while reading, challenge them to incorporate contextual information into the explanation. Ask for volunteers to run a class discussion on one of the texts, sharing their knowledge of history in an explanation of the inferences they made.

8 About the Selection

"Birds on the Western Front" throws the absurdity of war into sharp relief with a bitingly ironic tone. The narrator describes how battle has—and has not—affected the birds of the combat region. He catalogs the sturdy efforts of barn owls to withstand war's impact, the apparent immunity rooks and other birds have acquired to war's noises and destruction, and the surprising commitment the birds have to their surroundings. Using the birds as a possible metaphor for people, Saki suggests the stubborn determination of the human race to keep building as it is simultaneously destroying.

9 ▶Critical Viewing

Answer: The owls have come to the front line of the war because that is where the mice are and most people are not.

10 Literary Analysis

Tone

- Call on a volunteer to read aloud the bracketed passage.
- Have students use the details in the passage to identify the tone of this piece.
  Possible response: By using verbs associated with war to describe the actions of bird life, Saki gives the essay a humorous, satirical tone.

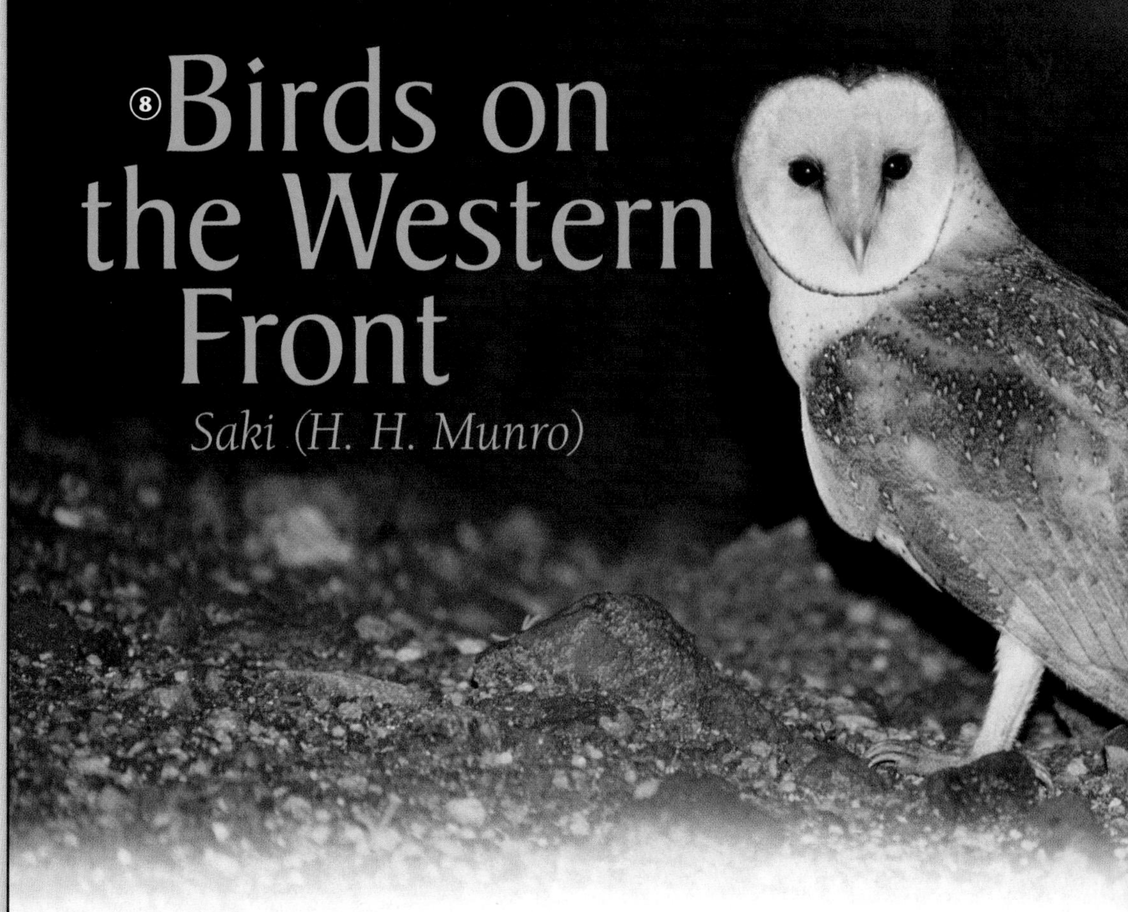

8 Birds on the Western Front

Saki (H. H. Munro)

Considering the enormous economic dislocation which the war operations have caused in the regions where the campaign[1] is raging, there seems to be very little corresponding disturbance in the bird life of the same districts. Rats and mice have mobilized and swarmed into the fighting line, and there has been a partial
10 mobilization of owls, particularly barn owls, following in the wake of the mice, and making <u>laudable</u> efforts to thin out their numbers. What success attends their hunting one cannot estimate; there are always sufficient mice left over to populate one's dug-out and make a parade-ground and race-course of one's face at night. In the matter of nesting accommodation the barn owls are well provided for; most of

9 ▲ **Critical Viewing** According to Saki, how is the war affecting owls like this one? **[Connect]**

laudable (lôd′ ə bəl) *adj.* worthy of praise

1. **campaign** battles being fought against the Germans during World War I.

ENRICHMENT: Art Connection

War Memorials

War memorials throughout the world honor those who fought for their countries. The Vietnam Memorial in Washington, D.C., was designed by a young college student named Maya Lin. She submitted her idea as part of a national design competition held in 1980–1981. Lin's memorial is a large V-shaped sculpture built within the landscape of Constitution Gardens. Lin says the idea "just popped into my head...while I was visiting the site." From a clay model, Lin envisioned the final polished granite structure. Today, visitors gather daily in front of the memorial to search the inscribed names for a loved one or to honor all those listed.

Have students identify and visit a war memorial in their own communities. What emotions do these stir? How do any words included in the memorials support their artistic intent?

the still intact barns in the war zone are requisitioned for billeting[2] purposes, but there is a wealth of ruined houses, whole streets and clusters of them, such as can hardly have been available at any previous moment of the world's history since Nineveh and Babylon[3] became humanly desolate. Without human occupation and cultivation there can have been no corn, no refuse, and consequently very few mice, and the owls of Nineveh cannot have enjoyed very good hunting; here in Northern France the owls have desolation and mice at their disposal in unlimited quantities, and as these birds breed in winter as well as in summer, there should be a goodly output of war owlets to cope with the swarming generations of war mice.

Apart from the owls one cannot notice that the campaign is making any marked difference in the bird life of the country-side. The vast flocks of crows and ravens that one expected to find in the neighborhood of the fighting line are nonexistent, which is perhaps rather a pity. The obvious explanation is that the roar and crash and fumes of high explosives have driven the crow tribe in panic from the fighting area; like many obvious explanations, it is not a correct one. The crows of the locality are not attracted to the battlefield, but they certainly are not scared away from it. The rook is normally so gun-shy and nervous where noise is concerned that the sharp banging of a barn door or the report of a toy pistol will sometimes set an entire rookery in commotion; out here I have seen him sedately busy among the refuse heaps of a battered village, with shells bursting at no great distance, and the impatient-sounding, snapping rattle of machine-guns going on all round him; for all the notice that he took he might have been in some peaceful English meadow on a sleepy Sunday afternoon. Whatever else German frightfulness may have done it has not frightened the rook of North-Eastern France; it has made his nerves steadier than they have ever been before, and future generations of small boys, employed in scaring rooks away from the sown crops in this region, will have to invent something in the way of super-frightfulness to achieve their purpose. Crows and magpies are nesting well within the shell-swept area, and over a small beech-copse I once saw a pair of crows engaged in hot combat with a pair of sparrow-hawks, while considerably higher in the sky, but almost

2. **billeting** (bil′ it iŋ) *adj.* designated for sleeping by written order as soldiers' quarters.
3. **Nineveh** (nin′ ə və) **and Babylon** (bab′ ə lən) two great and prosperous ancient civilizations that fell to ruin and desolation.

requisitioned (rek′ wə zish′ ənd) *v.* requested or applied for with a formal written order

Literary Analysis
Tone What tone does Saki use in this description of the rook?

✓ Reading Check
Apart from its effect on owls, is the war having a strong influence on bird life? Why or why not?

11 Reading Strategy

Making Inferences

- Call on a volunteer to read aloud the bracketed passage.

Monitor Progress Ask students: What can you infer about the narrator and his situation?
Answer: You can infer that the narrator is a soldier or at least a firsthand observer in Northern France and that the situation in that region is bleak.

12 Literary Analysis

Tone

- Read aloud the bracketed passage.
- Then, ask students the Literary Analysis question on p. 1055: What tone does Saki use in this description of the rook?
  Answer: Students may say Saki's tone is humorous as he notes that the rooks have become inured to war's effects.

13 ✓ Reading Check

Answer: No, the war does not appear to have much influence on bird life since the birds are still around, regardless of the noise and commotion of combat.

CUSTOMIZE INSTRUCTION FOR UNIVERSAL ACCESS

For Gifted/Talented Students	For Advanced Readers
Have students formulate a hypothesis about the effects of an environmental change on a bird population in a given area and describe the method they might use to test the hypothesis. Tell students they may be able to find ideas by researching on the Internet or contacting local bird watching groups.	Lead students in a discussion about why people go to see war movies or read stories about war. Elicit from students that through seeing movies or reading literature, they can understand the experiences of others—experiences they may not wish to personally endure. After students have read the poems and the essay by Saki, encourage them to verbalize how the selections have helped them see war from several perspectives.

14 Literary Analysis

Tone

- Call on a volunteer to read aloud the bracketed passage.
- Then, ask students: What is the tone of this passage?
  Possible response: Students will probably say that the tone is satirical and bitter.
- Ask students: What words or phrases give you clues to the tone?
  Possible response: Students will most likely point out the phrase in the first sentence, *the magpies have had their choice of building sites considerably restricted.* Some students may also point to the phrases *blown to bits, dreary-looking rows, shattered and splintered,* and *affection for a particular tree.*

15 ▶Critical Viewing

Possible response: The scene in the photograph corresponds to the description on p. 1056 of the trees having been "blown to bits, leaving nothing but dreary-looking rows of shattered and splintered trunks."

directly above them, two Allied battle-planes were engaging an equal number of enemy aircraft.

14 Unlike the barn owls, the magpies have had their choice of building sites considerably restricted by the ravages of war; the whole avenues of poplars, where they were accustomed to construct their nests, have been blown to bits, leaving nothing but dreary-looking rows of shattered and splintered trunks to show where once they stood. Affection for a particular tree has in one case induced a pair of magpies to build their bulky, domed nest in the battered remnants[4] of a poplar of which so little remained standing that the nest looked almost

15 ▲Critical Viewing Does the scene in this photograph correspond to any of Saki's descriptions? Explain. **[Connect]**

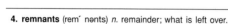

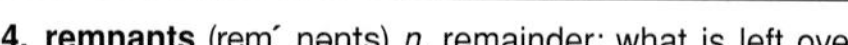

4. remnants (remʹ nənts) *n.* remainder; what is left over.

bigger than the tree; the effect rather suggested an archiepiscopal enthronement[5] taking place in the ruined remains of Melrose Abbey. 16 The magpie, wary and suspicious in his wild state, must be rather intrigued at the change that has come over the erst-while[6] fearsome not-to-be-avoided human, stalking everywhere over the earth as its possessor, who now creeps about in screened and sheltered ways, as chary of showing himself in the open as the shyest of wild creatures.

The buzzard, that earnest seeker after mice, does not seem to be taking any war risks, at least I have never seen one out here, but kestrels[7] hover about all day in the hottest parts of the line, not in the least disconcerted, apparently, when a promising mouse-area suddenly rises in the air in a cascade of black or yellow earth. Sparrow-hawks are fairly numerous, and a mile or two back from the firing line I saw a pair of hawks that I took to be red-legged falcons, circling over the top of an oak-copse. According to investigations made by Russian naturalists, the effect of the war on bird life on the Eastern front has been more marked than it has been over here. "During the first year of the war rooks disappeared, larks no longer sang in the fields, the wild pigeon disappeared also." The skylark in this region has stuck tenaciously to the meadows and crop-lands that have been seamed and bisected with trenches and honeycombed with shell-holes. In the chill, misty hour of gloom that precedes a rainy dawn, when nothing seemed alive except a few wary waterlogged sentries[8] and many scuttling rats, the lark would suddenly dash skyward and pour forth a song of ecstatic jubilation that sounded horribly forced and insincere. It seemed scarcely possible that the bird could carry its insouciance[9] to the length of attempting to rear a brood in that desolate wreckage of shattered clods and gaping shell-holes, but once, having occasion to throw myself down with some abruptness on my face, I found myself nearly on the top of a brood of young larks. Two of them had already been hit by something, and were in rather a battered condition, but the survivors seemed as tranquil and comfortable as the average nestling.

At the corner of a stricken wood (which has had a name made for it in history, but shall be nameless here), at a moment when lyddite and shrapnel[10] and machine-gun fire swept and raked and bespattered that devoted spot as though the artillery of an entire Division had suddenly concentrated on it, a wee hen-chaffinch flitted wistfully to and fro, amid splintered and falling branches that had never a green bough left on them. The wounded lying there, if any of them noticed the small bird, may well have wondered why anything having

168th Infantry French and American Raiding Party, Badonviller, France, March 1918

Reading Strategy
Making Inferences
What can you infer about Saki's feelings toward nature and war from his description of humans as now resembling "the shyest of wild creatures"?

disconcerted (dis´ kən sʉrt´ əd) *adj.* embarassed or confused

---

5. **archiepiscopal** (är´ kē ə pis´ kə pəl) **enthronement** ceremony during which the rank and duties of archbishop are conferred.
6. **erst-while** (ʉrst´ hwīl´) *adv.* formerly.
7. **kestrels** (kes´ trəlz) *n.* small reddish-gray European falcons.
8. **sentries** (sen´ trēz) *n.* men of military guard that are posted to warn others of danger.
9. **insouciance** (in so͞o´ sē əns) *n.* the state of being calm and untroubled.
10. **lyddite** (lid´ it) **and shrapnel** (shrap´ nəl) *n.* Lyddite is a powerful explosive, and shrapnel is a collection of fragments scattered by an exploding shell or bomb.

17 

What has been the effect of the war on bird life in the region of the Eastern front?

16 Reading Strategy

Making Inferences

- Call on a volunteer to read aloud the bracketed passage.
- Have students answer the Reading Strategy question on p. 1057: What can you infer about Saki's feelings toward nature and war from his description of humans as now resembling "the shyest of wild creatures"?

  Possible response: From his description, you can tell Saki thinks it is humorous and ironic the way war changes the "erst-while fearsome" human into "the shyest of wild creatures" and that the war has the opposite effect on birds. You can also tell that he admires nature's endurance and resilience in the face of war.

17 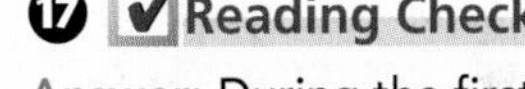

Answer: During the first year on the Eastern front, rooks and the wild pigeon disappeared and larks did not sing in the fields anymore.

CUSTOMIZE INSTRUCTION FOR UNIVERSAL ACCESS

For English Learners	For Gifted/Talented Students
The long and complex sentences of this essay may pose difficulty for English learners. Direct students to use punctuation to identify meaningful sentence parts, to paraphrase each of these, and then to construct an overall paraphrase of the entire sentence or passage. You may wish to pair up students with other English learners or with native speakers for this activity.	Challenge students to create a television nature report, with Saki as the reporter, using information and text from "Birds on the Western Front." Students can work in groups to create a script for the report, as well as find more visuals to go along with it. Have students decide who will be Saki, the reporter; who will write the script on large poster-size cards for the reporter to read during the "broadcast"; and who will hold up the visuals that complement the report.

ASSESS

Answers for p. 1058

Review and Assess

1. Students may have initially found his slant surprising because he addresses a relatively trivial aspect of war, as if he simply took the human suffering in stride.
2. **(a)** Barn owls followed the mice to the front line, the larks did not leave their homes, but most of the chaffinches did leave the area. **(b)** Students may say the lark's reaction was most surprising because it did not seem to be at all affected by the war—it stayed where it was, continued to sing, and raise babies.
3. **(a)** Humans are now fearful, hiding out in trenches rather than assuming ownership of nature. **(b)** Humanity has the ability to destroy itself.
4. Saki wants to share his ideas about human behavior and destructiveness by contrasting human actions and suffering with an aspect of the natural world.
5. Possible response: If nuclear bombs were used in a full-scale modern war, it is highly unlikely that any wildlife in the war zone would survive.

wings and no pressing reason for remaining should have chosen to stay in such a place. There was a battered orchard alongside the stricken wood, and the probable explanation of the bird's presence was that it had a nest of young ones whom it was too scared to feed, too loyal to desert. Later on, a small flock of chaffinches blundered into the wood, which they were doubtless in the habit of using as a highway to their feeding-grounds; unlike the solitary hen-bird, they made no secret of their desire to get away as fast as their dazed wits would let them. The only other bird I ever saw there was a magpie, flying low over the wreckage of fallen tree-limbs; "one for sorrow," says the old superstition. There was sorrow enough in that wood.

The English gamekeeper, whose knowledge of wild life usually runs on limited and perverted lines, has evolved a sort of religion as to the nervous debility[11] of even the hardiest game birds; according to his beliefs a terrier trotting across a field in which a partridge is nesting, or a mouse-hawking kestrel hovering over the hedge, is sufficient cause to drive the distracted bird off its eggs and send it whirring into the next county.

The partridge of the war zone shows no signs of such sensitive nerves. The rattle and rumble of transport, the constant coming and going of bodies of troops, the incessant rattle of musketry and deafening explosions of artillery, the night-long flare and flicker of star-shells, have not sufficed to scare the local birds away from their chosen feeding grounds, and to all appearances they have not been deterred from raising their broods. Gamekeepers who are serving with the colors might seize the opportunity to indulge in a little useful nature study.

11. **debility** (də bil´ ə tē) *n.* weakness or feebleness of body.

Review and Assess

Thinking About the Selection

1. **Respond:** Did you find Saki's slant on war surprising? Explain your reaction.
2. **(a) Recall:** Briefly describe the reactions to the war of barn owls, larks, and chaffinches. **(b) Evaluate:** Which bird's reaction seems most surprising? Explain.
3. **(a) Recall:** Describe the change in human behavior witnessed by the magpie (page 1057, top). **(b) Infer:** What does this change suggest about the state of humanity?
4. **Draw Conclusions:** What do you think is Saki's purpose in writing this description of wildlife in a war zone? Explain.
5. **Take a Position:** Do you think any wildlife would survive in a full-scale modern war? Why or why not?

ASSESSMENT PRACTICE: Writing Skills

Style **(For more practice, see Test Preparation Workbook, p. 50.)**

Many standardized tests require students to evaluate the appropriateness of a piece of writing for a particular audience. Use the following sample item to teach students how to recognize a text's intended audience.

Considering the enormous economic dislocation which the war operations have caused in the regions where the campaign is raging, there seems to be very little corresponding disturbance in the bird life of the same districts.

The language of this passage suggests it is written for an audience of—

A elementary school students
B a group of close friends
C bankers and brokers
D scientists who study the environment

Although the selection mentions economics briefly, it seems to introduce a discussion of birds, most appropriate for *D*.

Review and Assess

Literary Analysis

Tone

1. Using a chart like this one, briefly describe the **tone** in two or three key passages from each work.

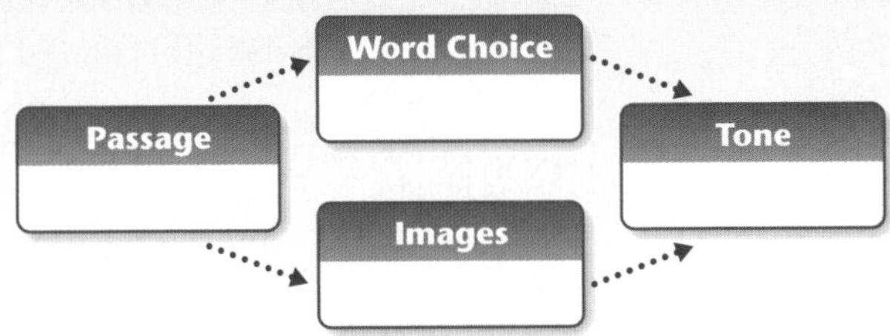

2. (a) Of the four selections, which is the least angry in tone? Explain. (b) Which is the most sarcastic? Explain.
3. (a) Which of the selections has the most surprising tone or mixture of tones? Why? (b) What is less surprising about the tone or tones of the other selections?

Comparing Literary Works

4. For English civilians of the time, which of these selections probably conveyed the most positive message about the conflict? Explain.
5. (a) Which selections are most concerned with war's destruction? Why? (b) Which criticize how the war is being run? Explain.
6. Compare the attitudes that these writers seem to have toward civilian readers.

Reading Strategy

Making Inferences

7. (a) **Make inferences** about the speaker's role in the action of "Wirers." For example, can you figure out whether he goes on this mission? (b) What details led you to your conclusions? Explain.
8. Make inferences about Owen's purpose in altering funeral rituals in lines 9–14 of "Anthem for Doomed Youth." Explain your reasoning.

Extend Understanding

9. **Science Connection:** What advances in military technology do these selections describe or hint at?

Quick Review

Tone is the writer's attitude toward the readers or toward the subject of a work.

Making inferences means using clues in a work to make educated guesses about the writer's intended meaning.

 ***Take It to the Net***

www.phschool.com

Take the interactive self-test online to check your understanding of these selections.

ENRICHMENT: Further Reading

Other Works by the Authors

Works by Saki (H.H. Munro)

The Chronicles of Clovis

Reginald in Russia

"The Open Window"

Works by Wilfred Owen

"Dulce et decorum est"

Answers for p. 1059

Review and Assess

1. **Possible response:** "The Soldier": **Passage:** lines 1–14; **Word Choice:** *gentleness, peace, heaven;* **Images:** field, England, rich earth, flowers, rivers, sun; **Tone:** patriotic, touching, sentimental.
2. **(a) Possible response:** "The Soldier" is least angry in tone—it is very sentimental. **(b) Possible response:** "Birds on the Western Front" is the most sarcastic because Saki uses verbs associated with war to describe the actions of birds, while showing the destruction humans cause.
3. **(a) Possible response:** Students may say "Birds on the Western Front" has the most surprising tone because Saki focuses on the effects of war on birds but in reality is showing the horror and destructiveness of war. **(b) Possible response:** The other selections are less surprising because their focus is on the effects of the war on humans.
4. **Possible response:** "The Soldier" probably conveyed the most positive message because it is steeped in patriotism.
5. **(a)** "Wirers," "Anthem for Doomed Youth," and "Birds on the Western Front" are more concerned with war's destruction—they each describe the horrors of war. **(b)** "The Wirers" seems to criticize how the war is being run because it trivializes the fatally wounded soldier who tried to help mend the fence.
6. Brooke's attitude is one of conveying his sense of patriotism and duty to readers. The others all seem to be trying to convey to civilian readers the horrors, senselessness, and destruction of war.
7. **(a)** It is not clear that the speaker went on this mission, but you can infer that he has been on similar missions. **(b)** His knowledge of every step of the mission and procedure indicates he has been on similar missions; moreover, the last sentence uses the word *we*.

continued

Answers continued

8. He alters the conventional funeral rituals to show the emotional effect of the death of these soldiers and to underscore the fact that no public acknowledgment is equal to the true loss their death represents.
9. The selections describe the use of bombs, machine guns, and fighter planes, which all combined to make World War I so destructive.

EXTEND

Answers for p. 1060

❶ Vocabulary Development

Word Analysis

1. expressing praise
2. to praise

Spelling Strategy

1. lazily
2. enemies

Fluency: Synonyms

1. b
2. a
3. a
4. b
5. a
6. c
7. b

❷ Grammar and Style

1. who
2. who
3. whom
4. who
5. whom

Writing Application

Sample paragraph:

Soldiers, for whom these poems were written, should be treated as heroes who fought for their country. Soldiers who died in battle should always be remembered.

Integrate Language Skills

❶ Vocabulary Development Lesson

Word Analysis: The Latin Root *-laud-*

The word *laudable* means "worthy of praise." Knowing that the root *-laud-* means "praise," define the italicized words.

1. *laudatory* reviews
2. to *laud* a performance

Spelling Strategy

In words that end in *-y* preceded by a consonant, change the *y* to *i* before adding an ending, except when adding *-ing*: *stealthy* + *-ily* = *stealthily*, but *carry* + *-ing* = *carrying*.

Spell the word that results from each change:

1. *lazy* as an adverb
2. the plural of *enemy*

Concept Development: Synonyms

In your notebook, choose the letter of the word that is the closest in meaning to the first word.

1. stealthy: (a) smart, (b) furtive, (c) honest
2. desolate: (a) forlorn, (b) crowded, (c) happy
3. mockeries: (a) ridicule, (b) bravery, (c) praise
4. pallor: (a) care, (b) paleness, (c) friends
5. laudable: (a) praiseworthy, (b) low, (c) awesome
6. requisitioned: (a) wasted, (b) needed, (c) ordered
7. disconcerted: (a) untuned, (b) confused, (c) aided

❷ Grammar and Style Lesson

Adjective Clauses With *Who* and *Whom*

When *who* and *whom* are used in **adjective clauses,** which modify nouns, the correct form is determined by the use of the word in the clause. ***Who*** is used for subjects and subject complements. ***Whom*** is used for objects of verbs or prepositions.

Subject in Clause: What passing-bells for these who die as cattle?

Direct Object in Clause: A dust whom England bore, . . .

Practice In your notebook, correctly complete each sentence with *who* or *whom*. Then, identify the pronoun's function in the clause.

1. Brooke, (whom, who) wrote "The Soldier," died before seeing battle.
2. The talented and intelligent Brooke, (who, whom) was born in 1887, was the son of a school official.
3. Owen, (who, whom) Sassoon befriended and encouraged, was wounded several times in battle.
4. Owen, (who, whom) was killed a week before the war ended, once wrote about "the pity of war."
5. Sassoon, without (who, whom) Owen would be unknown, wrote his best poems during the war.

Writing Application Write a short paragraph about young soldiers who die in wartime, incorporating details that you encountered in these selections. Include adjective clauses that use *who* and *whom*.

WG Prentice Hall Writing and Grammar Connection: Chapter 22, Section 2

TEACHING RESOURCES

The following resources can be used to enrich or extend the instruction for pp. 1060–1061.

Vocabulary

- **Selection Support:** Build Vocabulary, p. 233
- **Vocabulary and Spelling Practice Book** (Use this booklet for skills enrichment.)

Grammar

- **Selection Support:** Grammar and Style, p. 234
- **Writing and Grammar,** Diamond Level, p. 574
- **Daily Language Practice Transparencies**

Writing

- **Writing and Grammar,** Diamond Level, p. 315
- **Writing Models and Graphic Organizers on Transparencies,** pp. 103–106
- **Writing and Grammar iText CD-ROM**

BLOCK SCHEDULING: Resources marked with this symbol provide varied instruction during 90-minute blocks.

❸ Writing Lesson

Critical Response

Charles Sorley said of Brooke's patriotism, "He has clothed his attitude in fine words; but he has taken the sentimental attitude." In a critical response, agree or disagree with this observation, comparing "The Soldier" with Sassoon's "Wirers."

Prewriting Review "The Soldier" and "Wirers," jotting down details that are sentimental—that show an optimistic overemphasis of noble and positive emotions—or unsentimental.

Drafting Write a thesis statement reflecting your opinion of Sorley's observation. To structure the body of your essay, consider using an organization similar to the one shown here.

Model: Organizing a Critical Response

Paragraph 1	Paragraph 2	Paragraph 3	Paragraph 4	Paragraph 5
Thesis mentioning Sorley's observation	Definition of *sentimental*	Analysis of "The Soldier" in terms of definition	Comparison of "The Soldier" with "Wirers"	Conclusion

Revising Be sure that your definition of *sentimental* matches the arguments you make in the rest of your essay. Confirm that you have supported your response with details from both poems.

WG *Prentice Hall Writing and Grammar Connection: Chapter 14, Section 3*

❹ Extension Activities

Listening and Speaking With classmates, hold a **debate** on this resolution: "There are occasions when war is necessary." Consider these issues:

- The costs of war, such as suffering and loss of life and resources
- The possible benefits of war, such as self-defense and overcoming oppression

Use statistics and accounts in histories and primary sources as support. Help teammates strengthen their arguments. Then, present your debate in class. **[Group Activity]**

Research and Technology Write a **report** on trench warfare in World War I. Begin with a specific research focus, such as the daily routines of soldiers in the trenches. Look for information in various sources, including works like Paul Fussell's *The Great War in Modern Memory*, documentary videos, and Web sites with oral histories.

www.phschool.com

Go online for an additional research activity using the Internet.

Lesson Support for p. 1061

❸ Writing Lesson

- Prepare a model critical response ahead of time and have photocopies available to pass out to students.
- Remind students to use details from the poems to support their position.
- You may want to use the Argument Organizer in **Writing Models and Graphic Organizers on Transparencies,** pp. 103–106, as an alternative way to help students organize the information for their writings.

❹ Research and Technology

- Explain to students that not all sources have equally useful information about a topic. Tell students they will need to evaluate their sources before using them.
- Give students some criteria for evaluating a source: Do I need background material or detailed analysis? Objective facts or personal reactions? Current information or historical information? Which of these does this source provide?
- Have students use the Historical Investigation rubric in **Performance Assessment and Portfolio Management,** p. 13.

CUSTOMIZE INSTRUCTION
For Universal Access

To address different learning styles, use the following activities suggested in the **Extension Activities** booklet, p. 50.

- For Visual/Spatial Learners, use Activity 5.
- For Interpersonal and Bodily/Kinesthetic Learners, use Activity 6.
- For Musical/Rhythmic Learners, use Activity 7.

ASSESSMENT RESOURCES

The following resources can be used to assess students' knowledge and skills.

Selection Assessment

- **Formal Assessment,** pp. 246–248
- **Open Book Test,** pp. 147–149
- **Test Bank Software**
- **Got It! Assessment Videotapes,** Tape 5

Take It to the Net

Visit www.phschool.com for self-tests and additional questions on the selections.

Writing Rubric

- **Performance Assess. and Portfolio Mgmt.,** p. 13

PRENTICE HALL ASSESSMENT SYSTEM

- **Workbook**
- **Skill Book**
- **Transparencies**
- **CD-ROM**

Wartime Speech ✦ Defending Nonviolent Resistance

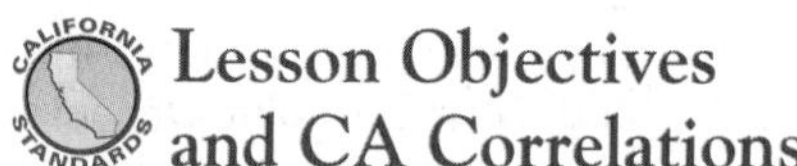

Lesson Objectives and CA Correlations

1. **To analyze and respond to literary elements**
   - Literary Analysis: Speech **R 2.1**
   - Comparing Literary Works **R 3.3**
2. **To read, comprehend, analyze, and critique a speech**
   - Reading Strategy: Identifying Main Points and Support **R 2.2**
   - Reading Check Questions
   - Review and Assess Questions
3. **To develop word analysis skills, fluency, and systematic vocabulary**
   - Vocabulary Development Lesson: Latin Root *-dur-* **R 1.2**
4. **To understand and apply written and oral language conventions**
   - Spelling Strategy **LC 1.2**
   - Grammar and Style Lesson: Parallel Structure **LC 1.1**
5. **To understand and apply appropriate writing and research strategies**
   - Writing Lesson: Persuasive Speech **W 1.1, 1.3, 1.9**
   - Extension Activity: Critique **W 1.6**
6. **To understand and apply listening and speaking strategies**
   - Extension Activity: Panel Discussion **LS 1.6**

STEP-BY-STEP TEACHING GUIDE	PACING GUIDE
PRETEACH	
Motivate Students and Provide Background	
Use the Motivation activity (ATE p. 1062)	5 min.
Read and discuss author and background features (SE/ATE pp. 1062, 1064) [A]	10 min.
Introduce the Concepts	
Introduce the Literary Analysis and Reading Strategy (SE/ATE p. 1063) [A]	15 min.
Pronounce the vocabulary words and read their definitions (SE p. 1063)	5 min.
TEACH	
Monitor Comprehension	
Informally monitor comprehension by circulating while students read independently or in groups [A]	25 min.
Monitor students' comprehension with the Reading Check notes (SE/ATE pp. 1065, 1069, 1071)	as students read
Develop vocabulary with Vocabulary notes (SE pp. 1065, 1066, 1068, 1069; ATE p. 1065)	as students read
Develop Understanding	
Develop students' understanding of speeches with the Literary Analysis annotations (SE/ATE pp. 1066, 1069, 1071, 1072) [A]	5 min.
Develop students' ability to identify main points and support with the Reading Strategy annotations (SE pp. 1067, 1068; ATE pp. 1067, 1068, 1070)	5 min.
ASSESS	
Assess Mastery	
Assess students' mastery of the Reading Strategy and Literary Analysis by having them answer the Review and Assess questions (SE/ATE p. 1073)	15 min.
Use one or more of the print and media Assessment Resources (ATE p. 1075) [A]	up to 45 min.
EXTEND	
Apply Understanding	
Have students complete the Vocabulary Development Lesson and the Grammar and Style Lesson (SE p. 1074) [A]	20 min.
Apply students' knowledge of anticipating questions using the Writing Lesson (SE/ATE p. 1075) [A]	45 min.
Apply students' understanding using one or more of the Extension Activities (SE p. 1075)	20–90 min.

ACCELERATED INSTRUCTION:
Use the strategies and activities identified with an [A].

UNIVERSAL ACCESS
● = Below-Level Students
▲ = On-Level Students
■ = Above-Level Students

Time and Resource Manager

Reading Level: Challenging, Average
Average Number of Instructional Days: 4

RESOURCES		
PRINT	**TRANSPARENCIES**	**TECHNOLOGY**
• **Beyond Literature,** Community Connection: Community Action, p. 51 ▲ ■		• **Interest Grabber Video,** Tape 6 ● ▲ ■
• **Selection Support Workbook:** ● ▲ ■ Literary Analysis, p. 240 Reading Strategy, p. 239 Build Vocabulary, p. 237	• **Literary Analysis and Reading Transparencies,** pp. 101 and 102 ● ▲ ■	
		• **Listening to Literature** ● ▲ ■ Audiocassettes, Sides 24 and 25 Audio CDs, CD 14
• **Literatura en español** ● ▲ • **Literary Analysis for Enrichment** ■		
• **Formal Assessment:** Selection Test, pp. 249–251 ● ▲ ■ • **Open Book Test,** pp. 150–152 ● ▲ ■ • **Performance Assessment and Portfolio Management,** p. 18 ● ▲ ■ • PRENTICE HALL ASSESSMENT SYSTEM ● ▲ ■	• PRENTICE HALL ASSESSMENT SYSTEM ● ▲ ■ Skills Practice Answers and Explanations on Transparencies ● ▲ ■	• **Test Bank Software** ● ▲ ■ • **Got It! Assessment Videotapes,** Tape 5 ● ▲
• **Selection Support Workbook:** ● ▲ ■ Grammar and Style, p. 238 • **Writing and Grammar,** Diamond Level ● ▲ ■ • **Extension Activities,** p. 51 ● ▲ ■	• **Daily Language Practice Transparencies** ● ▲	• **Writing and Grammar iText CD-ROM** ● ▲ ■ ***Take It to the Net*** www.phschool.com

BLOCK SCHEDULING: Use one 90-minute class period to preteach the selections and have students read them. Use a second 90-minute class period to assess students' mastery of skills and have them complete one of the Extensions Activities.

PRETEACH

Step-by-Step Teaching Guide for pp. 1062–1063

Motivation

Present either or both of these scenarios to students:

(a) You're a leader of a country that's been at war for two years. There have been many casualties, and the war is turning against you. Your people's optimism is fading fast, yet you need to persuade the people to fight on—to boost their morale. What do you say?

(b) You're facing a long prison sentence for protesting the mistreatment of your people. You are guilty, but you want to make sure that people understand your cause. You also hope to inspire your people to continue to fight while you're imprisoned. What do you say?

Point out to students that both Churchill and Gandhi were impassioned, effective speakers. As they read, have students look for evidence of oratorical skills.

Interest Grabber Video

As an alternative, you may wish to play "'Wartime Speech': Blitzkrieg" on Tape 6 to engage student interest.

❶ More About the Authors

Sir Winston Churchill

Churchill was a correspondent for *The Morning Post* in South Africa during the Boer War in 1899. During one battle, Churchill was captured and imprisoned by Louis Botha. He, as well as other captured officers, was kept in a school building in Pretoria. Churchill boldly escaped and made his way back to British lines—300 miles away!

Mohandas K. Gandhi

Gandhi, known to millions of Hindus as *Mahatma,* which means "great soul," dedicated himself to social and political progress through peace and brotherhood. Imprisoned multiple times for leading his people in acts of civil disobedience, Gandhi ended British rule in India without striking a single blow.

Prepare to Read

❶ Wartime Speech ◆ Defending Nonviolent Resistance

Sir Winston Churchill (1874–1965)

At times during World War II, it might have seemed as if the fate of freedom depended on the gruff voice of Winston Churchill, prime minister of England. Broadcast worldwide, even to Nazi-occupied Europe, this voice spoke with memorable eloquence, as in this tribute to the Royal Air Force: "Never in the field of human conflict was so much owed by so many to so few."

Truly, it might be said of Churchill himself: Never in the field of human conflict was so much owed by so many to just one!

Churchill the Warrior Directly descended from the dukes of Marlborough, Churchill was educated at Harrow and the Royal Military College at Sandhurst. After serving as a soldier and a journalist in Cuba, India, and South Africa, he was first elected to Parliament in 1900 and went on to play an important role in the government during World War I.

In the 1930s, Churchill vigorously criticized government policies, warning against the ominous ambitions of Nazi Germany. He became prime minister in May 1940, after World War II had broken out, and went on to play a key role in the victory of the Allies.

Churchill the Writer Amazingly, Churchill found time to write, despite a busy public career. During the 1930s, he produced a four-volume historical work on his ancestor, the first Duke of Marlborough. His monumental six-volume history entitled *The Second World War* (1948–1954) is now regarded as a classic. Following this work, Churchill wrote *A History of the English-Speaking Peoples,* completed in 1958. He was awarded the Nobel Prize for Literature in 1953.

Mohandas K. Gandhi (1869–1948)

Mohandas K. Gandhi held no political office in his native India, yet few leaders have had such a decisive impact on their country's destiny. He was never a military officer, yet he waged three great wars of supreme importance to world history—battling colonialism, racism, and violence.

Finding a Mission Born in the northwestern Indian state of Gujarat, Gandhi went to London to study law when he was eighteen. From 1893 to 1914, he worked for an Indian law firm in South Africa. His experiences there as a victim of racial discrimination led him to join and lead protest campaigns on behalf of the Indian community in that British-ruled colony. When he returned to India, he became the leader of the Indian National Congress and led the fight for independence from Britain.

Passive Resistance Working fearlessly for independence, Gandhi gradually developed the principles of his philosophy of *satyagraha,* "devotion to truth," or nonviolent resistance, which was to have worldwide influence, notably on the American civil rights leader Martin Luther King, Jr. Using this technique, Gandhi led thousands in acts of peaceful civil disobedience that clogged the jails and confounded the British.

Gandhi also devoted himself to improving the lot of India's lowest castes—social groups defined by ancestry and occupation—and he worked for harmony between the country's two major religions, Hinduism and Islam. India gained independence in August 1947, but to Gandhi's distress, Pakistan was established as a separate dominion. A little more than five months afterward, Gandhi was assassinated by a Hindu fanatic.

TEACHING RESOURCES

The following resources can be used to enrich or extend the instruction for pp. 1062–1063.

Motivation

Interest Grabber Video, Tape 6

Background

Beyond Literature, p. 51

Take It to the Net

Visit www.phschool.com for background and hotlinks for the selections.

Literary Analysis

Literary Analysis and Reading Transparencies, Speech, p. 102

Reading

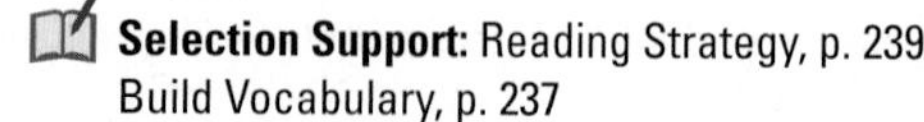

Selection Support: Reading Strategy, p. 239; Build Vocabulary, p. 237

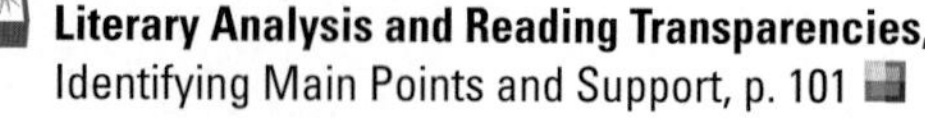

Literary Analysis and Reading Transparencies, Identifying Main Points and Support, p. 101

BLOCK SCHEDULING: Resources marked with this symbol provide varied instruction during 90-minute blocks.

Preview

Connecting to the Literature

The speeches included here demonstrate that Winston Churchill and Mohandas K. Gandhi took great risks to assert their beliefs.

❷ Literary Analysis

Speech

A **speech** is an oral presentation on an important issue. Three elements of a speech are its *purpose*, the reason for its presentation; its *occasion*, the event that inspires it; and its *audience*, those who hear it at the time or who hear or read it later.

In historically significant speeches, the speaker often transforms the occasion and the audience. Gandhi does this when, speaking at his own trial, he redefines his "crime" as a legitimate act of protest—a "duty."

Comparing Literary Works

Both Churchill and Gandhi use the following **rhetorical devices**—special patterns of language—to make their ideas memorable and to stir emotions:

- **Repetition,** the repeating of key words and concepts
- **Parallelism,** similar ideas expressed in similar grammatical forms
- **Allusions,** references to well-known people, places, and events
- **Dramatic alternatives,** the posing of sharply contrasting alternatives

However, the writers do not use these devices in the same ways. For example, as befits a radio address, Churchill's uses of parallelism are briefer and punchier than Gandhi's. Compare these speakers' use of other devices.

❸ Reading Strategy

Identifying Main Points and Support

The **main points** in a speech are the key ideas that the speaker wishes to convey. The **support** consists of the facts, examples, or reasons that explain or justify these ideas. Use a chart like this one to identify main points and support as you read these speeches.

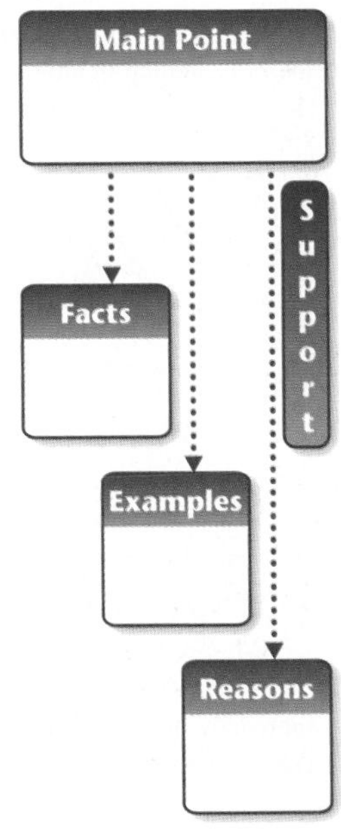

Vocabulary Development

intimidated (in tim′ ə dāt′ əd) *v.* made afraid; frightened (p. 1065)

endurance (en door′ əns) *n.* ability to last or continue (p. 1065)

formidable (fôr′ mə də bəl) *adj.* hard to overcome (p. 1065)

invincible (in vin′ sə bəl) *adj.* unconquerable (p. 1065)

retaliate (ri tal′ ē āt′) *v.* pay back an injury or wrong (p. 1066)

disaffection (dis′ ə fek′ shən) *n.* discontent; disillusionment (p. 1068)

diabolical (dī′ ə bäl′ i kəl) *adj.* evil (p. 1068)

extenuating (ek sten′ yoo āt′ iŋ) *adj.* lessening the seriousness of; excusing (p. 1069)

excrescence (eks kres′ əns) *n.* abnormal or disfiguring outgrowth (p. 1069)

❷ Literary Analysis

Speech

- Tell students that any time they speak to a group of people, they are in effect giving a speech.
- Read the instruction about speech together as a class.
- Use the instruction for Comparing Literary Works to introduce to students different devices used in effective speaking.
- Use the Speech transparency in **Literary Analysis and Reading Transparencies,** p. 102, to show students the characteristics of an effective speech.

❸ Reading Strategy

Identifying Main Points and Support

- Remind students that the main point of a speech is the same as its topic sentence or main idea, while support is any information or details that further show that the main idea is true.
- Tell students that effective speeches include main points and support.
- Encourage students to create a chart like the one shown on p. 1063 to record the main idea and support of each speech as they read.

Vocabulary Development

- Pronounce each vocabulary word for students, and read the definitions as a class. Have students identify any words with which they are already familiar.

CUSTOMIZE INSTRUCTION FOR UNIVERSAL ACCESS

For Less Proficient Readers	For English Learners	For Advanced Readers
Some students may find the dense language and contextual references of these speeches difficult. Urge these students to decrease their reading pace as they read the material and to restate paragraphs in their own words for clarity.	Students may find the language and historical references of the speeches somewhat difficult. You may need to guide students through the speeches, pausing to explain unfamiliar vocabulary or give some historical background. Students may benefit from working in groups to paraphrase passages as they work their way through the speeches.	Have students listen to and analyze the selections on **Listening to Literature** Audiocassettes, Sides 24 and 25, or **Listening to Literature** Audio CDs, CD 14. Have students analyze ways in which variations in emphasis, tone, and cadence contribute to each speech's overall impact.

E-Teach

Visit E-Teach at www.phschool.com for teachers' essays on how to teach, with questions and answers.

TEACH

Step-by-Step Teaching Guide for pp. 1064–1072

CUSTOMIZE INSTRUCTION
For Visual/Spatial Learners

Show students a map of Allied and Axis battlefield movements during 1940. Have them use the map to understand the status of Allied forces at the time of Churchill's speech. Encourage them to share their findings with the rest of the class.

1 About the Selection

This speech will captivate students with its dramatic call to bravery and unity. Delivered in May of 1940, when the Germans were rapidly advancing across France, Churchill's speech desperately sought to reassure and inspire the British armed services and general population. He cites his confidence in the skill and courage of both French and British services and his expectation of loyalty and sacrifice by citizens at home. By linking his belief in the possibility of success with the difficulty of the challenges ahead, Churchill demonstrates his extraordinary power of confident leadership.

2 ▶Critical Viewing

Answer: Students should note that a radio speech makes no allowance for gestures or body language nor gives the speaker any emotional feedback from the audience.

2 ▲ **Critical Viewing** Sir Winston Churchill is shown here making a radio broadcast. In what ways does the presentation of a radio speech differ from a speech given in person? **[Compare and Contrast]**

1 WARTIME SPEECH

Sir Winston Churchill

BBC, London, 19 May 1940

Background

When Churchill gave this speech, his first radio address as prime minister, France was Britain's only ally in opposing German aggression. Germany had already overrun several other countries. Soon after this speech was delivered, France surrendered.

TEACHING RESOURCES

The following resources can be used to enrich or extend the instruction for pp. 1064–1072.

Literary Analysis

Selection Support: Literary Analysis, p. 240

Reading

Listening to Literature Audiocassettes, Sides 24 and 25

Listening to Literature Audio CDs, CD 14

BLOCK SCHEDULING: Resources marked with this symbol provide varied instruction during 90-minute blocks.

I speak to you for the first time as Prime Minister in a solemn hour for the life of our country, of our Empire, of our Allies, and, above all, of the cause of Freedom. A tremendous battle is raging in France and Flanders.[1] The Germans, by a remarkable combination of air bombing and heavily armored tanks, have broken through the French defenses north of the Maginot Line,[2] and strong columns of their armored vehicles are ravaging the open country, which for the first day or two was without defenders. They have penetrated deeply and spread alarm and confusion in their track. Behind them there are now appearing infantry in lorries,[3] and behind them, again, the large masses are moving forward. The regroupment of the French armies to make head against, and also to strike at, this intruding wedge has been proceeding for several days, largely assisted by the magnificent efforts of the Royal Air Force.

We must not allow ourselves to be intimidated by the presence of these armored vehicles in unexpected places behind our lines. If they are behind our Front, the French are also at many points fighting actively behind theirs. Both sides are therefore in an extremely dangerous position. And if the French Army, and our own Army, are well handled, as I believe they will be; if the French retain that genius for recovery and counter-attack for which they have so long been famous;
3 | and if the British Army shows the dogged endurance and solid fighting power of which there have been so many examples in the past—then a sudden transformation of the scene might spring into being.

It would be foolish, however, to disguise the gravity of the hour. It would be still more foolish to lose heart and courage or to suppose that well-trained, well-equipped armies numbering three or four millions of men can be overcome in the space of a few weeks, or even months, by a scoop, or raid of mechanized vehicles, however formidable. We may look with confidence to the stabilization of the Front in France, and to the general engagement of the masses, which will enable the qualities of the French and British soldiers to be matched squarely against those of their adversaries. For myself, I have invincible confidence in the French Army and its leaders. Only a very small part of that splendid army has yet been heavily engaged; and only a very small part of France has yet been invaded. There is good evidence to show that practically the whole of the specialized and mechanized forces of the enemy have been already thrown into the battle; and we know that very heavy losses have been inflicted upon them. No officer or man, no brigade or division, which grapples at close quarters with the enemy, wherever encountered, can fail to make a worthy contribution to the general result. The Armies must cast away the idea of resisting behind concrete lines or natural obstacles, and must realize that mastery can only be

1. **Flanders** (flan´ dərz) region in Northwest Europe, on the North Sea, that includes Northwest France and the provinces of East Flanders and West Flanders in Belgium.
2. **Maginot** (mazh´ ə nō´) **Line** heavy fortifications built before World War II on the Eastern frontier of France; they did not prevent invasion during World War II.
3. **lorries** (lôr´ ēz) *n.* British for "trucks."

intimidated (in tim´ ə dāt´ əd) *v.* made afraid; frightened

endurance (en dʊ̅o̅r´ əns) *n.* ability to last or continue

formidable (fôr´ mə də bəl) *adj.* hard to overcome

invincible (in vin´ sə bəl) *adj.* unconquerable

4  **Reading Check**

According to Churchill, what military victories have the Germans won?

3 Vocabulary Development

Latin Root *-dur-*

- Call students' attention to the word *endurance* and its definition. Tell them that the Latin word root *-dur-* means "hard" or "lasting."
- Have students suggest words that contain this root and list them on the chalkboard.
  Possible answers: Words with this root include *duration, durable,* and *endurable.*
- Next, have students look up the meanings of these words in a dictionary.
- Have students write sentences in which they use each of the listed words correctly.

4 Reading Check

Answer: The Germans have penetrated the Maginot Line and have advanced deeply into French territory.

CUSTOMIZE INSTRUCTION FOR UNIVERSAL ACCESS

For Special Needs Students	For Advanced Readers
Students may have difficulty understanding the speeches because of the difficult language, historical context, and Briticisms. You may wish to group these students with more advanced students to discuss what they know of the time period in which the speech was given.	Encourage interested students to find out what was happening at the time of Churchill's speech. Have them research in the library or on the Internet to find out where different countries' front lines were and then locate those places on a map. Also, have them research the new military tactics and weaponry that were being used during WWII. Students can present to the class the information they found, including a map of sites of engagement.

❺ Literary Analysis

Speech

- Read aloud the bracketed passage.
- Remind students that a topic sentence states the main point of the paragraph. Have students find the topic sentence.
  Answer: "My confidence in our ability to fight it out to the finish with the German Air Force has been strengthened by the fierce encounters which have taken place and are taking place."

Monitor Progress Then, ask the Literary Analysis question on p. 1066: What do you think is the purpose of this paragraph?
Possible Response: Students may say that the purpose of this paragraph is to boost morale—Churchill is telling of continued successes against the German Air Force and is, therefore, giving people reason to hope.

❻ Literary Analysis

Speech

- Call on a volunteer to read aloud the bracketed passage.
- Discuss with students Churchill's goal of inspiring popular support for the war and its necessary sacrifices.
- Ask students how this passage serves that purpose.
  Possible Response: Students should note that Churchill points out that many people will suffer hardship during the war, but that it is up to everyone to help in the war effort. He appeals to national pride and identifies for listeners specific ways that they can help, making them feel part of the team.

regained by furious and unrelenting assault. And this spirit must not only animate the High Command, but must inspire every fighting man.

In the air—often at serious odds—often at odds hitherto[4] thought overwhelming—we have been clawing down three or four to one of our enemies; and the relative balance of the British and German Air Forces is now considerably more favorable to us than at the beginning of the battle. In cutting down the German bombers, we are fighting our own battle as well as that of France. 5 My confidence in our ability to fight it out to the finish with the German Air Force has been strengthened by the fierce encounters which have taken place and are taking place. At the same time, our heavy bombers are striking nightly at the taproot of German mechanized power, and have already inflicted serious damage upon the oil refineries on which the Nazi effort to dominate the world directly depends.

We must expect that as soon as stability is reached on the Western Front, the bulk of that hideous apparatus of aggression which gashed Holland into ruin and slavery in a few days, will be turned upon us. I am sure I speak for all when I say we are ready to face it; to endure it; and to retaliate against it—to any extent that the unwritten laws of war permit. There will be many men, and many women, in this island who when the ordeal comes upon them, as come it will, will feel comfort, and even a pride—that they are sharing the perils of our lads at the Front—soldiers, sailors and airmen, God bless them—and are drawing away from them a part at least of the onslaught they have to bear. Is not this the appointed time for all to make the utmost exertions in their 6 power? If the battle is to be won, we must provide our men with ever-increasing quantities of the weapons and ammunition they need. We must have, and have quickly, more airplanes, more tanks, more shells, more guns. There is imperious need for these vital munitions. They increase our strength against the powerfully armed enemy. They replace the wastage of the obstinate struggle; and the knowledge that wastage will speedily be replaced enables us to draw more readily upon our reserves and throw them in now that everything counts so much.

Our task is not only to win the battle—but to win the War. After this battle in France abates[5] its force, there will come the battle for our island—for all that Britain is, and all that Britain means. That will be the struggle. In that supreme emergency we shall not hesitate to take every step, even the most drastic, to call forth from our people the last ounce and the last inch of effort of which they are capable. The interests of property, the hours of labor, are nothing compared with the struggle for life and honor, for right and freedom, to which we have vowed ourselves.

I have received from the Chiefs of the French Republic, and in particular from its indomitable Prime Minister, M. Reynaud, the most sacred pledges that whatever happens they will fight to the

Literary Analysis
Speech What do you think is the purpose of the paragraph beginning, "In the air . . ."? Explain.

retaliate (ri tal′ ē āt′) *v.* pay back an injury or wrong

4. **hitherto** (hith′ ər to͞o) *adv.* until this time.
5. **abates** (ə bāts′) *v.* makes less in amount.

ENRICHMENT: Media Connection

Wartime Communication

When Winston Churchill gave his wartime speech, listeners saw no accompanying graphic images of war and destruction. There was no fax, e-mail, or live television broadcast to speed news instantly around the globe. As a result, a speaker could craft a particular description of the situation designed to serve his or her purpose. In Churchill's case, public knowledge of just how bad the Allied situation was would not have helped him reassure the public or inspire its dedication to the war cause.

Have interested students debate the issue of whether the media should report all facts during wartime or withhold information that may damage public morale.

end, be it bitter or be it glorious. Nay, if we fight to the end, it can only be glorious.

7 Having received His Majesty's commission, I have found an administration of men and women of every party and of almost every point of view. We have differed and quarreled in the past; but now one bond unites us all—to wage war until victory is won, and never to surrender ourselves to servitude and shame, whatever the cost and the agony may be. This is one of the most awe-striking periods in the long history of France and Britain. It is also beyond doubt the most sublime. Side by side, unaided except by their kith and kin in the great Dominions and by the wide Empires which rest beneath their shield—side by side, the British and French peoples have advanced to rescue not only Europe but mankind from the foulest and most soul-destroying tyranny which has ever darkened and stained the pages of history. Behind them—behind us—behind the armies and fleets of Britain and France—gather a group of shattered States and bludgeoned races: the Czechs, the Poles, the Norwegians, the Danes, the Dutch, the Belgians—upon all of whom the long night of barbarism will descend, unbroken even by a star of hope, unless we conquer, as conquer we must; as conquer we shall.

Today is Trinity Sunday. Centuries ago words were written to be a call and a spur to the faithful servants of Truth and Justice; "Arm yourselves, and be ye men of valor, and be in readiness for the conflict; for it is better for us to perish in battle than to look upon the outrage of our nation and our altar. As the Will of God is in Heaven, even so let it be."

Reading Strategy
Identifying Main Points and Support What do you think is the main point of the paragraph beginning, "Having received . . ."?

Review and Assess

Thinking About the Selection

1. **Respond:** Do Churchill's words still have the power to stir a listener? Explain.
2. **(a) Recall:** What new development in the war does Churchill report at the beginning of his speech? **(b) Analyze:** What answers does Churchill provide to any concerns that this development might cause?
3. **(a) Recall:** For what future crisis does Churchill prepare his listeners? **(b) Analyze:** With what double mission does he try to inspire his listeners so that they will meet the crisis?
4. **(a) Analyze:** Describe the tone of this speech, providing examples in support. **(b) Draw Conclusions:** Judging by his tone, how confident is Churchill of his public support? Explain your reasoning.
5. **Connect:** Does any politician today speak with the same force and urgency as Churchill does in this speech? Explain.

CUSTOMIZE INSTRUCTION FOR UNIVERSAL ACCESS

For Special Needs Students	For Proficient Readers
Some students will have difficulty understanding the speeches because of the formal style. Guide students through the difficult passages. Students may also benefit from listening to segments of the speech and then working together to paraphrase what they heard.	Students may benefit from listening to these speeches read aloud. Instruct students to read along as they listen to the **Listening to Literature** Audiocassettes, Sides 24 and 25, or **Listening to Literature** Audio CDs, CD 14. Pause the recording periodically to check for understanding.

7 Reading Strategy

Identifying Main Points and Support

- Read aloud the bracketed passage, and have students paraphrase its contents.

Monitor Progress Ask students the Reading Strategy question on p. 1067: What do you think is the main point of this passage?
Possible response: The main point is to affirm British unity and to inspire the British to heroic efforts by noting the international and historic significance of the war.

Answers for p. 1067

Review and Assess

1. Yes, his words exude confidence and stir listeners by including them in a common agenda. No, the language is too complex for a modern listener to follow.
2. **(a)** The Germans have broken through France's Maginot Line and are advancing. **(b)** Churchill mentions France's ability to recover and counterattack, the quality of their leaders, and the contributions of each soldier.
3. **(a)** Churchill prepares them for Germany's attack on Great Britain. **(b)** Churchill tells his listeners that should Germany attack them, they will be in effect drawing away some of the onslaught on their soldiers. He also tells them that their soldiers need more weapons and munitions if they are to defeat Germany and win the war.
4. **(a)** The tone is urgent and dramatic, but composed: "We must expect that . . . the bulk of that hideous apparatus of aggression which gashed Holland into ruin and slavery in a few days, will be turned upon us." **(b)** His urgent tone indicates that he is not taking for granted his people's support.
5. Some students may note political figures who speak with similar force. Other students may say that since we do not face the same type of threat as Churchill did—a hostile power that had already taken over several countries—no one speaks with the same force and urgency today.

8 About the Selection

This courtroom statement very calmly but effectively lays out the origin of Gandhi's beliefs and positions. He explains his journey from British supporter and public servant to prime motivator of Indian protest against the colonial presence. He credits experiences such as his time in South Africa, where he was categorized as socially inferior for his Indian race, and events such as the massacre at Jallianwala Bagh for revolutionizing his views. Gandhi is proud to seek independence for his people, despite the need to break laws he had previously upheld, and thus shows his passionate love for his country.

9 Reading Strategy

Identifying Main Points and Support

- Read aloud the bracketed passage.
- Have students answer the Reading Strategy question on p. 1068: What is the main point of this passage?
  Answer: I admit I have broken the law, but I did so knowingly to pursue just goals.

8 Defending Nonviolent Resistance

Mohandas K. Gandhi

The following speech was given by Mohandas Gandhi before he was sentenced to six years in prison for stirring up rebellion. Gandhi, India's spiritual leader, worked to achieve political goals through nonviolent resistance. Through boycotts and passive refusal, he helped India gain freedom from British rule.

Before I read this statement, I would like to state that I entirely endorse the learned advocate general's remarks in connection with my humble self. I think that he was entirely fair to me in all the statements that he has made, because it is very true, and I have no desire whatsoever to conceal from this court the fact that to preach disaffection toward the existing system of government has become almost a passion with me; and the learned advocate general is also entirely in the right when he says that my preaching of disaffection did not commence with my connection with *Young India*, but that it commenced much earlier; and in the statement that I am about to read, it will be my painful duty to admit before this court that it commenced much earlier than the period stated by the advocate general. 9 It is the most painful duty with me, but I have to discharge that duty knowing the responsibility that rests upon my shoulders, and I wish to endorse all the blame that the learned advocate general has thrown on my shoulders, in connection with the Bombay occurrences, Madras occurrences, and the Chauri Chaura occurrences.[1] Thinking over these deeply and sleeping over them night after night, it is impossible for me to dissociate myself from the diabolical crimes of Chauri Chaura or the mad outrages of Bombay. He is quite right when he says that as a man of responsibility, a man having received a fair share of education, having had a fair share of experience of this world, I should have known the consequences of every one of my acts. I know that I was playing with fire. I ran the risk, and if I was set free, I would still do the same. I have felt it this morning that I would have failed in my duty, if I did not say what I said here just now.

I wanted to avoid violence, I want to avoid violence. Nonviolence is the first article of my faith. It is also the last article of my creed. But I

Reading Strategy
Identifying Main Points and Support What is the main point in the first paragraph of the speech?

disaffection (dis´ ə fek´ shən) *n.* discontent; disillusionment

diabolical (dī´ ə bäl´ ik əl) *adj.* evil

1. **Bombay . . . Chauri Chaura occurrences** outbreaks of violence in Indian cities and villages.

ENRICHMENT: Social Studies Connection

Unrest in India

The "occurrences" Gandhi mentions—Bombay, Madras, and Chauri Chaura—were only a few examples of the political unrest India experienced in 1918 and 1919. Under Gandhi's leadership, Indians were boycotting British products as well as institutions such as courts, offices, and schools. Thousands of Indians were willingly arrested as they pursued Gandhi's strategy of nonviolent resistance. Chauri Chaura, where violence did break out, persuaded Gandhi to end the mass protests. He was arrested soon thereafter.

Have students discuss the responsibility leaders have for the effects of protest strategies. How does that responsibility affect Gandhi as he negotiates the penalties he will pay personally?

had to make my choice. I had either to submit to a system which I considered had done an irreparable harm to my country, or incur the risk of the mad fury of my people bursting forth, when they understood the truth from my lips. I know that my people have sometimes gone mad. I am deeply sorry for it, and I am therefore here to submit not to a light penalty but to the highest penalty. I do not ask for mercy. I do not plead any extenuating act. I am here, therefore, to invite and
10 cheerfully submit to the highest penalty that can be inflicted upon me for what in law is a deliberate crime and what appears to me to be the highest duty of a citizen. The only course open to you, the judge, is, as I am just going to say in my statement, either to resign your post or inflict on me the severest penalty, if you believe that the system and law you are assisting to administer are good for the people. I do not expect that kind of conversation, but by the time I have finished with my statement, you will perhaps have a glimpse of what is raging within my breast to run this maddest risk which a sane man can run.

I owe it perhaps to the Indian public and to the public in England to placate[2] which this prosecution is mainly taken up that I should explain why from a staunch loyalist and cooperator I have become an uncompromising disaffectionist and non-cooperator. To the court too I should say why I plead guilty to the charge of promoting disaffection toward the government established by law in India.

My public life began in 1893 in South Africa in troubled weather. My first contact with British authority in that country was not of a happy character. I discovered that as a man and as an Indian I had no rights. More correctly, I discovered that I had no rights as a man because I was an Indian.

But I was not baffled. I thought that this treatment of Indians was an excrescence upon a system that was intrinsically and mainly good. I gave the government my voluntary and hearty cooperation, criticizing it freely where I felt it was faulty but never wishing its destruction.

Consequently, when the existence of the empire was threatened in 1899 by the Boer challenge,[3] I offered my services to it, raised a volunteer ambulance corps, and served at several actions that took place for the relief of Ladysmith. Similarly in 1906, at the time of the Zulu revolt, I raised a stretcher-bearer party and served till the end of the "rebellion." On both these occasions I received medals and was even mentioned in dispatches. For my work in South Africa I was given by Lord Hardinge a Kaiser-i-Hind Gold Medal. When the war broke out in 1914 between England and Germany,[4] I raised a volunteer ambulance corps in London consisting of the then resident Indians in London, chiefly students. Its work was acknowledged by the authorities to be valuable. Lastly, in India, when a special appeal was made at the War Conference in Delhi in 1918 by

2. **placate** (plā′ kāt′) *v.* to stop from being angry.
3. **Boer challenge** rebellion in South Africa against British rule; the British suppressed the rebellion in 1902 after resorting to guerrilla warfare.
4. **the war . . . between England and Germany** World War I.

Literary Analysis
Speech With what words does Gandhi redefine the situation by shifting the guilt from himself to the British? Explain.

extenuating (ek sten′ yo͞o āt′ iŋ) *adj.* lessening the seriousness of; excusing

excrescence (eks kres′ əns) *n.* abnormal or disfiguring outgrowth

11  **Reading Check**
What choice does Gandhi offer the judge?

10 Literary Analysis
Speech

- Call on a volunteer to read aloud the bracketed passage.
- Ask students why Gandhi begins this paragraph by repeating his position.
  Answer: The repetition and restatement of the idea in the first three lines are persuasive tactics which help drive home his position on violence—nonviolence; it contrasts his viewpoint with the British system.
- Then, ask students the Literary Analysis question on p. 1069: With what words does Gandhi redefine the situation by shifting the guilt from himself to the British?
  Answer: "I had either to submit to a system which I considered had done an irreparable harm to my country . . ."; " . . . for what in law is a deliberate crime and what appears to me to be the highest duty of a citizen."; and " . . . if you believe that the system and law you are assisting to administer are good for the people."

11 Reading Check
Answer: Gandhi offers the choice of either resigning his position or charging Gandhi with the severest penalty.

CUSTOMIZE INSTRUCTION FOR UNIVERSAL ACCESS	
For Less Proficient Readers	**For Gifted/Talented Students**
Clarify with students that while Gandhi is accepting, even inviting, a heavy penalty for breaking the law, he believes his actions were correct and justifiable. He isn't expressing contrition; rather, he is accepting responsibility for his protests. Discuss how Gandhi's tone—of polite resignation—supports this position.	Have students envision Gandhi in a courtroom making his statement to the judge. Using the rendering on p. 1070 as a stimulus, challenge students to describe Gandhi's demeanor, tone of voice, and body language, as well as the overall mood he conveys. Encourage students to speak aloud to the class a part of his speech, using what they think was his demeanor, tone, and body language.

12 Reading Strategy

Identifying Main Points and Support

- Call on a volunteer to read the bracketed passage aloud.
- Then, ask students to note some of the details Gandhi uses to support his main point.
  Answer: Students should mention any of the services Gandhi undertakes for the British government, either in South Africa, London, or India.

13 Background

Social Studies

The Rowlatt Act (1919) enabled the British to imprison without a trial any Indians suspected of encouraging rebellion. Gandhi urged Indians not to obey such "unjust, subversive laws." Protest against this law led to the Amritsar massacre, in which British troops fired on an unarmed crowd, killing 400 Indians. This and a later violent outbreak in the village of Chauri Chaura caused Gandhi to give up temporarily his campaign of nonviolent resistance. Then, on March 10, 1922, the British arrested him for stirring up rebellion. This was the speech he gave to that court.

14 ▶Critical Viewing

Answer: Students may note that Gandhi's expression is one of peaceful resignation. Also he is wearing white, a traditional color of peace.

12 Lord Chelmsford[5] for recruits, I struggled at the cost of my health to raise a corps in Kheda, and the response was being made when the hostilities ceased and orders were received that no more recruits were wanted. In all these efforts at service I was actuated by the belief that it was possible by such services to gain a status of full equality in the empire for my countrymen.

13 The first shock came in the shape of the Rowlatt Act,[6] a law designed to rob the people of all real freedom. I felt called upon to lead an intensive agitation against it. Then followed the Punjab horrors beginning with the massacre at Jallianwala Bagh[7] and culminating in crawling orders, public floggings, and other indescribable humiliations. I discovered too that the plighted word of the prime minister to the Mussulmans of India regarding the integrity of Turkey and the holy places of Islam was not likely to be fulfilled. But in spite of the forebodings and the grave warnings of friends, at the Amritsar Congress in 1919, I fought for cooperation and working with the Montagu-Chelmsford reforms,[8] hoping that the prime minister would redeem his promise to the Indian Mussulmans, that the Punjab wound would be healed, and that the reforms, inadequate and unsatisfactory though they were, marked a new era of hope in the life of India.

But all that hope was shattered. The Khilafat promise was not to be redeemed. The Punjab crime was whitewashed, and most culprits went not only unpunished but remained in service and in some cases continued to draw pensions from the Indian revenue, and in some cases were even rewarded. I saw too that not only did the reforms not mark a change of heart, but they were only a method of further draining India of her wealth and of prolonging her servitude.

I came reluctantly to the conclusion that the British connection had made India more helpless than she ever was before, politically and economically. A disarmed India has no power of resistance against any aggressor if she wanted to engage in an armed conflict with him. So much is this the case that some of our best men consider that India must take generations before she can achieve the dominion status. She has become so poor that she has little power of resisting famines. Before the British advent, India spun and wove in her millions of cottages just the supplement she needed for adding to her meager agricultural resources. This cottage industry, so vital for India's existence, has been ruined by incredibly heartless and inhuman processes as described by English witnesses. Little do town dwellers know how the semistarved masses of India are slowly sinking to lifelessness. Little do they know that their miserable comfort represents the brokerage they

▼ **Critical Viewing** How does this depiction of Gandhi reflect his beliefs about violence? **[Draw Conclusions]**

5. **Lord Chelmsford** viceroy or governor as representative of Edwin Montagu, Secretary of State.
6. **Rowlatt Act** series of repressive acts that limited the powers of the Indian people.
7. **the massacre at Jallianwala Bagh** Under orders of General R. H. Dyer, fifty British soldiers opened fire on a crowd of peaceful Indians, firing 1,650 rounds of ammunition. The general was dismissed from his duties.
8. **Montagu-Chelmsford reforms** formally known as The Government of India Act of 1919; an attempt to slowly place power in Indian hands.

ENRICHMENT: Film Connection

Movie Review

In 1982, the movie *Gandhi* won Academy Awards for Best Picture, Best Director (Richard Attenborough), and Best Actor (Ben Kingsley). Nonetheless, Dave Kehr, a reviewer for the *Chicago Reader,* had some criticism.

> . . . the film has no flavor but that of the standard Hollywood . . . in which the hero is rhetorically elevated to sainthood by systematically stripping him of all his psychology and inner life. Luckily, Ben Kingsley is charismatic enough in his title role to command some warmth and interest.

Have students look for evidence in "Defending Nonviolent Resistance" of Gandhi's humanity that Kehr might have liked to see shown in the movie. Students can compare Kehr's review to their own film responses after completing the Research and Technology activity on p. 1075.

get for the work they do for the foreign exploiter, that the profits and the brokerage are sucked from the masses. Little do they realize that the government established by law in British India is carried on for this
15 exploitation of the masses. No sophistry,[9] no jugglery in figures can explain away the evidence that the skeletons in many villages present to the naked eye. I have no doubt whatsoever that both England and the town dwellers of India will have to answer, if there is a God above, for this crime against humanity which is perhaps unequaled in history. The law itself in this country has been used to serve the foreign exploiter. My unbiased examination of the Punjab Martial Law cases has led me to believe that at least 95 percent of convictions were wholly bad. My experience of political cases in India leads me to the conclusion that in nine out of every ten the condemned men were totally innocent. Their crime consisted in the love of their country. In ninety-nine cases out of a hundred justice has been denied to Indians as against Europeans in the courts of India. This is not an exaggerated picture. It is the experience of almost every Indian who has had anything to do with such cases. In my opinion, the administration of the law is thus prostituted consciously or unconsciously for the benefit of the exploiter.

The greatest misfortune is that Englishmen and their Indian associates in the administration of the country do not know that they are engaged in the crime I have attempted to describe. I am satisfied that many Englishmen and Indian officials honestly believe that they are administering one of the best systems devised in the world and that India is making steady though slow progress. They do not know that a subtle but effective system of terrorism and an organized display of force, on the one hand, and the deprivation of all powers of retaliation or self-defense, on the other, have emasculated the people and induced in them the habit of simulation. This awful habit has added to the ignorance and the self-deception of the administrators. Section 124-A, under which I am happily charged, is perhaps the prince among the political sections of the Indian Penal Code[10] designed to suppress the liberty of the citizen. Affection cannot be manufactured or regulated by law. If one has an affection for a person or system, one should be free to give the fullest expression to his disaffection, so long as he does not contemplate, promote, or incite to violence. But the section under which Mr. Banker [a colleague in nonviolence] and I are charged is one under which mere promotion of disaffection is a crime. I have studied some of the cases tried under it, and I know that some of the most loved of India's patriots have been convicted under it. I consider it a privilege, therefore, to be charged under that section. I have endeavored to give in their briefest outline the reasons for my disaffection. I have no personal ill will against any single administrator, much less can I have any disaffection toward the king's person. But I hold it to be a virtue

9. **sophistry** (säf′ is trē) *n.* unsound or misleading arguments.
10. **Section 124-A . . . Penal Code** Gandhi was charged with sedition, inciting people to riot against British rule.

Literary Analysis
Speech and Rhetorical Devices What is an example of parallelism in this paragraph?

According to Gandhi, what harm has Britain done to India?

15 Literary Analysis

Speech and Rhetorical Devices

- Call on a volunteer to read aloud the bracketed passage.
- Then, ask students the Literary Analysis question on p. 1071: What is an example of parallelism in this passage?
  Answer: Students should identify the sentences starting with "Little . . .": "Little do town dwellers know . . ."; "Little do they know . . ."; and "Little do they realize . . .", as well as "No sophistry, no jugglery . . . ."
- Ask students how this parallelism might increase the impact of Gandhi's words.
  Answer: Parallel structure makes the text more memorable and therefore more effective.

16 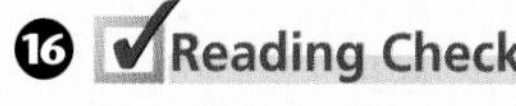

Answer: Britain has made India into a desperately poor, helpless, and emasculated country.

CUSTOMIZE INSTRUCTION FOR UNIVERSAL ACCESS

For Gifted/Talented Students	For Advanced Readers
Have students create a poster of the principles of Gandhi's philosophy. Encourage them to use words as well as graphics. Display the poster, and engage the class in a discussion about ways they could apply these principles in their own lives.	To enable students to appreciate the nature of Gandhi's concern about his fellow Indians, link his analysis to other world situations in which a people has become so accustomed to authoritarian rule that its members lose the ability to lead themselves. For example, point out the frequency with which colonial rule has been replaced by harsh native rule, whether military or civil. Invite students to research some examples from the continents of Africa or South America.

ASSESS

17 Literary Analysis

Speech

- Read aloud the bracketed passage.
- Then, ask students the Literary Analysis question on p. 1072: In what way is Gandhi judging the judge in this passage?
  Possible response: Gandhi is saying, in essence, that the judge's decision in his case will represent the judge's judgment on the system whose evils Gandhi opposes. If the judge fulfills his job, Gandhi will judge him guilty in assenting to this evil system.

Answers for p. 1072

Review and Assess

1. **(a)** Gandhi pleads guilty. **(b)** He wants to keep the focus on the injustice of the laws, rather than on whether he is guilty.
2. **(a)** He helped the British in South Africa, in London, and in India. **(b)** He describes them to show that he has previously supported the British government and been a loyal citizen.
3. **(a)** British support of South African racial policies, British actions against Indian civilians at Punjab, and British exploitation of Indian workers and resources all explain Gandhi's disaffection. **(b)** "Promotion of disaffection" is a charge that men he considers great patriots have been guilty of, so he considers it a privilege to be counted among them.
4. Gandhi's *satyagraha* probably would not have worked against the Nazis because they had no conscience, as evidenced by the inhumane treatment and atrocities they committed against millions of people.

to be disaffected toward a government which in its totality has done more harm to India than any previous system. India is less manly under the British rule than she ever was before. Holding such a belief, I consider it to be a sin to have affection for the system. And it has been a precious privilege for me to be able to write what I have in the various articles, tendered in evidence against me.

In fact, I believe that I have rendered a service to India and England by showing in non-cooperation the way out of the unnatural state in which both are living. In my humble opinion, non-cooperation with evil is as much a duty as is cooperation with good. But in the past, non-cooperation has been deliberately expressed in violence to the evildoer. I am endeavoring to show to my countrymen that violent non-cooperation only multiplies evil and that as evil can only be sustained by violence, withdrawal of support of evil requires complete abstention from violence. Nonviolence implies voluntary submission
17 to the penalty for non-cooperation with evil. I am here, therefore, to invite and submit cheerfully to the highest penalty that can be inflicted upon me for what in law is a deliberate crime and what appears to me to be the highest duty of a citizen. The only course open to you, the judge, is either to resign your post, and thus dissociate yourself from evil if you feel that the law you are called upon to administer is an evil and that in reality I am innocent, or to inflict on me the severest penalty if you believe that the system and the law you are assisting to administer are good for the people of this country and that my activity is therefore injurious to the public weal.[11]

Literary Analysis
Speech In what way is Gandhi judging the judge in the final paragraph of the speech?

11. **weal** (wēl) *n.* well-being; welfare.

Review and Assess

Thinking About the Selection

1. (a) **Recall:** How does Gandhi plead to the charges against him? (b) **Infer:** Why do you think he resists the strategy of claiming to be innocent?
2. (a) **Recall:** What are three missions Gandhi has undertaken to help the British? (b) **Infer:** Why do you think he describes these missions here?
3. (a) **Recall:** Identify three reasons for Gandhi's "disaffection" toward the British system of rule. (b) **Draw Conclusions:** Why does Gandhi consider it a privilege to be charged with "promoting disaffection"?
4. **Take a Position:** Some claim that Gandhi's policy of *satyagraha*, nonviolent resistance, was ideal for use against the British, who had a conscience, but that it would not have worked against the Nazis. Explain why you agree or disagree.

ASSESSMENT PRACTICE: Writing Skills

Organization (For more practice, see Test Preparation Workbook, p. 51)

Many standardized tests ask students to analyze a text's organization. Use the following sample test item to teach students how to recognize patterns of organization:

During the 1930s Churchill produced a four-volume historical work on his ancestor, the first Duke of Marlborough. His monumental history entitled *The Second World War* (1948–1954) is now regarded as a classic. In 1953 he was awarded the Nobel Prize in literature.

According to the organization of the paragraph, a reference to Churchill's death in 1965 should be placed

A before sentence 1
B after sentence 1
C after sentence 2
D after sentence 3

Because the paragraph is arranged in chronological order, the correct answer is *D*.

Review and Assess

Literary Analysis

Speech

1. Use a chart like the one shown to identify the elements in each speech.

Speaker	Purpose	Audience	Occasion

2. (a) How does Churchill's purpose motivate him to redefine a frightening occasion as an inspiring opportunity? (b) Which words transform his listeners from scattered individuals to a committed group? Explain.
3. (a) How does Gandhi attempt to redefine the role of the judge, his primary audience? (b) What larger audience might Gandhi be addressing? Explain. (c) How does Gandhi's purpose motivate him to transform a narrowly defined occasion into one with greater meaning?

Comparing Literary Works

4. Identify examples of these **rhetorical devices** in both speeches: (a) repetition, (b) parallelism, (c) allusion, (d) dramatic alternatives.
5. Choose one of these devices. Comparing and contrasting its use in the two speeches, decide which speaker employs it more effectively.
6. Although Gandhi did not deliver his speech on the radio, would it have been as effective a radio address as Churchill's? Explain.

Reading Strategy

Identifying Main Points and Support

7. (a) What is the **main point** of Gandhi's ninth paragraph ("I came reluctantly . . .")? (b) Which details provide **support** for it?
8. (a) What are two main points in Churchill's speech? (b) List several details he uses to support each point.

Extend Understanding

9. **Media Connection:** What different speechmaking skills do radio, television, and a public appearance require? Explain.

Quick Review

A **speech** is an oral presentation in which a speaker addresses an important issue. Three elements of a speech are its *purpose,* the reason for its presentation; its *occasion,* the event that gives rise to it; and its *audience,* those who hear it immediately or view, hear, or read it later.

Rhetorical devices, or uses of language designed to persuade, include repetition, parallelism, dramatic alternatives, and allusions.

To **identify main points and support,** find the most important ideas in a work and the examples, facts, and reasons that strengthen them.

Take It to the Net

www.phschool.com

Take the interactive self-test online to check your understanding of these selections.

ENRICHMENT: Further Reading

Other Works by the Authors

Works by Mohandas K. Gandhi

The Story of My Experiments With Truth

The Collected Works of Mahatma Gandhi

"Satyagraha in South Africa"

Works by Winston Churchill

"Blood, Sweat, and Tears"

Answers for p. 1073

Review and Assess

1. Sample response: **Speaker:** Winston Churchill; **Purpose:** to boost morale; **Occasion:** when Germans were advancing across France; **Audience:** British armed service and the general population.
2. **(a)** Churchill needed to inspire people to keep fighting. **(b)** He uses *we* throughout the speech and calls on the pride and sense of historical mission of the British.
3. **(a)** Gandhi shows that if the judge finds him guilty, then the judge is guilty of supporting an evil social system. **(b)** Gandhi's real audience is his fellow Indians and the rest of the world. **(c)** He is using the situation of his prominent arrest to gain attention for his cause.
4. **(a)** Repetition in Gandhi's speech: At the beginning and end of his speech, he states that the judge has two choices, resign from his post or support the evil laws. **(b)** Parallelism in Gandhi's speech: The sentences that start with "Little . . ." at the bottom of p. 1070. **(c)** Allusion in Churchill's speech: he ends his speech with a religious quote. **(d)** Dramatic alternatives in Gandhi's speech: his statement to the judge of two choices: resign or charge him with the highest penalty.
5. Possible response: Gandhi uses parallelism more effectively.
6. Possible response: Yes, it would have been just as effective a radio address as Churchill's because it was written for the world to hear.
7. **(a)** Gandhi believes British rule is sapping India's strength. **(b)** Supporting examples include: using the nation's resources solely for British gain; enforcing a skewed legal system; allowing poverty to continue.
8. **(a)** The situation is grave; the British and French armies can win. **(b)** Support for the first includes his points that French defensive lines have been infiltrated and that Allied armies are outnumbered. Support for the second includes his point that French soldiers have made gains behind German lines; his point

continued

Answers continued

that they have a genius for recovery and counterattack; and his claim that the British have endurance and determination.

9. A radio speech requires vocal skills; television requires vocal skills and stage presence; a public appearance requires vocal skills, stage presence, and ability to speak well in front of a live audience.

EXTEND

Answers for p. 1074

❶ Vocabulary Development

Word Analysis

1. durable: something which is tough enough to last a long time
2. duress: subject to hard or tough pressure
3. endure: the ability to withstand difficult conditions
4. duration: the time during which something lasts

Spelling Strategy

1. disappoint
2. intolerable
3. reeducate
4. misstatement

Fluency: Words in Context

Answers in order are as follows: intimidated; endurance; formidable; invincible; retaliate; disaffection; diabolical; excrescence; extenuating.

❷ Grammar and Style

1. Either to disguise the gravity of the hour or to surrender prematurely to despair would be a great mistake.
2. The British were ready to face Hitler's aggression, to endure it, and to retaliate against it.
3. Churchill's administration included every party and represented a complete spectrum of opinion.
4. Gandhi's choice was submitting to a harmful system or running the risk of stirring up anger.
5. Gandhi said affection cannot be either manufactured or regulated by law.

Writing Application

Sample response:

As a judge, my job is not only to follow the law but to uphold the law, regardless of how I feel about how good it is for the people. I would not be a good judge if I did otherwise.

Integrate Language Skills

❶ Vocabulary Development Lesson

Word Analysis: Latin Root *-dur-*

The Latin root *-dur-* means "hard" or "lasting," and *endurance* means "the toughness to withstand pain, exhaustion, or wear." Use this knowledge to write definitions of the following words. Then, verify your definitions in a dictionary.

1. durable
2. duress
3. endure
4. duration

Spelling Strategy

Adding a prefix to a word never changes the spelling of the base word. For example, adding the prefix *dis-* to *affection* yields the word *disaffection*. Spell the words that result from the following combinations of prefixes and base words.

1. *dis-* + appoint
2. in- + tolerable
3. *re-* + educate
4. *mis-* + statement

Fluency: Words in Context

In your notebook, replace each italicized word or phrase with a word from the vocabulary list on page 1063. Your choices should be guided by the context created by the paragraph.

Churchill was not *frightened* by the Nazi offensive. He counted on the *toughness* of the British people and their ability to resist a foe, no matter how *fearsome* or apparently *unconquerable*. He knew that the British would *revenge themselves* against the Nazis and not give way to *discontent* as a result of Hitler's victories and *evil* plans. For Churchill, the Nazis were an *abnormal outgrowth* that had to be eliminated. No *excusing* circumstances could justify surrender to the Germans.

❷ Grammar and Style Lesson

Parallel Structure

Parallel structure is the use of the same grammatical form to express similar ideas.

Infinitive Phrases: Our task is not only to win the battle—but to win the War.

Writers use parallel structure to create a rhythm of ideas. This rhythm creates the sense that each idea "belongs" or is necessary, adding to its persuasive force.

Practice On your paper, rewrite each sentence below, correcting errors of faulty parallelism.

1. Either to disguise the gravity of the hour or surrendering prematurely to despair would be a great mistake.
2. The British were ready to face Hitler's aggression, enduring it, and to retaliate against it.
3. Churchill's administration included every party and representing a complete spectrum of opinion.
4. Gandhi's choice was submitting to a harmful system or to run the risk of stirring up anger.
5. Gandhi said affection cannot be either manufactured or regulating it by law.

Writing Application As the judge to whom Gandhi appeals, write a response to his speech. In an effort to match Gandhi's persuasive skill, include two examples of parallel structure.

WG Prentice Hall Writing and Grammar Connection: Chapter 20, Section 6

TEACHING RESOURCES

The following resources can be used to enrich or extend the instruction for pp. 1074–1075.

Vocabulary

- **Selection Support:** Build Vocabulary, p. 237
- **Vocabulary and Spelling Practice Book** (Use this booklet for skills enrichment.) ■

Grammar

- **Selection Support:** Grammar and Style, p. 238
- **Writing and Grammar,** Diamond Level, p. 505
- **Daily Language Practice Transparencies** ■

Writing

- **Writing and Grammar,** Diamond Level, p. 133
- **Writing and Grammar iText CD-ROM** ■

■ **BLOCK SCHEDULING:** Resources marked with this symbol provide varied instruction during 90-minute blocks.

❸ Writing Lesson

Persuasive Speech

Churchill's and Gandhi's speeches were persuasive because each communicated viewpoints in a strong, effective style. Follow their lead by writing an effective persuasive speech on an issue important to you.

Prewriting Choose an issue and an audience. Then, list your main points and the facts, reasons, and examples you will use to support them. Also, note any questions that your audience might have, and write answers to them.

Drafting Include support for your main points, and reinforce them with rhetorical devices such as repetition and parallel structure. Strengthen support by using allusions and presenting dramatic alternatives.

Revising Read your draft aloud to a classmate. If he or she has questions you did not anticipate, revise your speech to deal with them. If sentences expressing your main points sound flat, add rhetorical devices to dramatize them.

Model: Adding Rhetorical Devices

neither frivolous nor fanciful.
Creating a new park is ~~important.~~ It may be the most important action the town council takes this year.

By using parallelism of adjectives, the writer states the main point more forcefully.

WG Prentice Hall Writing and Grammar Connection: Chapter 7, Section 4

❹ Extension Activities

Listening and Speaking Conduct a **panel discussion** to consider how Gandhi might have responded to the Nazis if he had been in Churchill's place. Discuss Gandhi's possible actions and the types of arguments he would have made, including appeals to

- Logic, with clear arguments
- Emotions, with specific, charged examples
- Ethics, with references to his core values

To conclude, decide which appeals Gandhi might have favored. **[Group Activity]**

Research and Technology View a film on Gandhi's or Churchill's life. (A possible choice is *Gandhi,* directed by Richard Attenborough.) Devise a strategy for taking notes on the film. Then, compare the information in the film with information from a print source, such as a biography of Gandhi or of Churchill. Use your notes to write a **critique** of the film.

 ***Take It to the Net*** www.phschool.com

Go online for an additional research activity using the Internet.

ASSESSMENT RESOURCES

The following resources can be used to assess students' knowledge and skills.

Selection Assessment

- **Formal Assessment,** pp. 249–251
- **Open Book Test,** pp. 150–152
- **Got It! Assessment Videotapes,** Tape 5
- **Test Bank Software**

Take It to the Net

Visit www.phschool.com for self-tests and additional questions on the selections.

Writing Rubric

- **Performance Assess. and Portfolio Mgmt.,** p. 18

PRENTICE HALL ASSESSMENT SYSTEM

- **Workbook**
- **Skill Book**
- **Transparencies**
- **CD-ROM**

❸ Writing Lesson

- Discuss with students the features of an effective speech, inviting them to cite recent examples from television or radio.
- Point out that effective speeches use persuasive techniques such as vivid language, parallel structure, clearly stated main ideas, and support that bolsters those ideas.
- Remind students that pacing and emphasis should derive from the speech text, using the main points as a structural outline. Main points should be supported with evidence.
- Tell students that effective speakers articulate clearly and audibly without shouting.
- Use the Persuasive Speech rubric in **Performance Assessment and Portfolio Management,** p. 18, to evaluate students' speeches.

❹ Research and Technology

- You may want to view *Gandhi* together as a class.
- Discuss with students how they should take notes while viewing the film.
- After viewing the film, encourage students to find a biography of Gandhi with which to compare their film notes. Discuss with them how representative they felt the film was of Gandhi's life.

CUSTOMIZE INSTRUCTION
For Universal Access

To address different learning styles, use the following activities suggested in the **Extension Activities** booklet, p. 51.

- For Visual/Spatial Learners, use Activity 5.
- For Verbal/Linguistic and Logical/Mathematical Learners, use Activity 6.
- For Musical/Rhythmic Learners, use Activity 7.

The Fiddle

Lesson Objectives and CA Correlations

1. **To analyze and respond to literary elements**
   - Literary Analysis: Setting and Atmosphere **R 3.3**
   - Connecting Literary Elements: Style **R 3.4**
2. **To read, comprehend, analyze, and critique a short story**
   - Reading Strategy: Predicting the Effect of a Setting
   - Reading Check Questions
   - Review and Assess Questions
3. **To develop word analysis skills, fluency, and systematic vocabulary**
   - Vocabulary Development Lesson: Latin Word Origins: *Sublime* **R 1.1, 1.2**
4. **To understand and apply written and oral language conventions**
   - Spelling Strategy **LC 1.2**
   - Grammar and Style Lesson: Vary Sentence Beginnings **LC 1.1**
5. **To understand and apply appropriate writing and research strategies**
   - Writing Lesson: Description of a Setting **W 1.1, 1.9, 2.1**
   - Extension Activity: Multimedia **W 2.6**
   - Assessment Practice (ATE)
6. **To understand and apply listening and speaking strategies**
   - Extension Activity: Debate **LS 1.6**

STEP-BY-STEP TEACHING GUIDE	PACING GUIDE
PRETEACH	
Motivate Students and Provide Background	
Use the Motivation activity (ATE p. 1076)	5 min.
Read and discuss author and background features (SE/ATE pp. 1076, 1078) [A]	5 min.
Introduce the Concepts	
Introduce the Literary Analysis and Reading Strategy (SE/ATE p. 1077) [A]	15 min.
Pronounce the vocabulary words and read their definitions (SE p. 1077)	5 min.
TEACH	
Monitor Comprehension	
Informally monitor comprehension by circulating while students read independently or in groups [A]	20 min.
Monitor students' comprehension with the Reading Check notes (SE/ATE pp. 1079, 1081, 1083)	as students read
Develop vocabulary with Vocabulary notes (SE pp. 1079, 1080, 1081, 1082; ATE p. 1081)	as students read
Develop Understanding	
Develop students' understanding of setting and atmosphere with the Literary Analysis annotations (SE pp. 1079, 1081, 1083; ATE pp. 1079, 1080, 1081, 1083) [A]	5 min.
Develop students' ability to predict effect of a setting with the Reading Strategy annotations (SE/ATE p. 1082)	5 min.
ASSESS	
Assess Mastery	
Assess students' mastery of the Reading Strategy and Literary Analysis by having them answer the Review and Assess questions (SE/ATE p. 1085)	20 min.
Use one or more of the print and media Assessment Resources (ATE p. 1087) [A]	up to 45 min.
EXTEND	
Apply Understanding	
Have students complete the Vocabulary Development Lesson and the Grammar and Style Lesson (SE p. 1086) [A]	20 min.
Apply students' ability to convey an impression using the Writing Lesson (SE/ATE p. 1087) [A]	45 min.
Apply students' understanding using one or more of the Extension Activities (SE p. 1087)	20–90 min.

ACCELERATED INSTRUCTION:
Use the strategies and activities identified with an [A].

UNIVERSAL ACCESS
● = Below-Level Students
▲ = On-Level Students
■ = Above-Level Students

Time and Resource Manager

Reading Level: Average
Average Number of Instructional Days: 4

RESOURCES		
PRINT	**TRANSPARENCIES**	**TECHNOLOGY**
• **Beyond Literature,** Cross-Curricular Connection: Science, p. 52 ▲ ■		• **Interest Grabber Video,** Tape 6 ● ▲ ■
• **Selection Support Workbook:** ● ▲ ■ Literary Analysis, p. 244 Reading Strategy, p. 243 Build Vocabulary, p. 241	• **Literary Analysis and Reading Transparencies,** pp. 103 and 104 ● ▲ ■	
		• **Listening to Literature** ● ▲ ■ Audiocassettes, Side 25 Audio CDs, CD 14
• **Literatura en español** ● ▲ • **Literary Analysis for Enrichment** ■		
• **Formal Assessment:** Selection Test, pp. 252–254 ● ▲ ■ • **Open Book Test,** pp. 153–155 ● ▲ ■ • **Performance Assessment and Portfolio Management,** p. 17 ● ▲ ■ • PRENTICE HALL ASSESSMENT SYSTEM ● ▲ ■	• PRENTICE HALL ASSESSMENT SYSTEM ● ▲ ■ Skills Practice Answers and Explanations on Transparencies ● ▲ ■	• **Test Bank Software** ● ▲ ■ • **Got It! Assessment Videotapes,** Tape 5 ● ▲
• **Selection Support Workbook:** ● ▲ ■ Grammar and Style, p. 242 • **Writing and Grammar,** Diamond Level ● ▲ ■ • **Extension Activities,** p. 52 ● ▲ ■	• **Daily Language Practice Transparencies** ● ▲ • **Writing Models and Graphic Organizers on Transparencies,** pp. 13–16 ● ▲ ■	• **Writing and Grammar iText CD-ROM** ● ▲ ■ ***Take It to the Net*** www.phschool.com

BLOCK SCHEDULING: Use one 90-minute class period to preteach the selection and have students read it. Use a second 90-minute class period to assess students' mastery of skills and have them complete one of the Extension Activities.

PRETEACH

Step-by-Step Teaching Guide for pp. 1076–1077

Motivation

Tell students that some authors, Sillitoe among them, use setting as if it were a character in their stories. Ask them to consider their own environment—the region, the neighborhood, the school, their home—and think about its effect on a story they might write. Have students write ten sentences about the local environment to show the impact its features would have on their piece. Invite students to share their ideas.

Interest Grabber Video

As an alternative, you may wish to play "'The Fiddle': Symbolism" on Tape 6 to engage student interest.

❶ More About the Author

In 1950, Sillitoe met Ruth Fainlight, an American poet. They lived together in France, Italy, and Spain from 1952 to 1958, getting by mostly on Sillitoe's military pension. They were married in 1959, had a son together, and adopted a daughter.

Prepare to Read

❶ The Fiddle

Alan Sillitoe (b. 1928)

Growing up in poverty left a permanent impression on Alan Sillitoe. Much of his writing revolves around the struggles of the working poor, those whose hard labor results in a hand-to-mouth existence—the experience of never having enough money to get ahead of the immediate needs of self and family.

A Short Military Career The son of an often unemployed tannery worker, Sillitoe grew up in Nottingham, an industrial city northwest of London. He left school at the age of fourteen and worked in a bicycle plant and a plywood mill. At the same time, he enrolled in the Air Training Corps. In 1946, he joined the Royal Air Force and, for a time, was a radio operator in Malaya. There, he contracted the tuberculosis that eventually led to his discharge. His illness entitled him to a pension, which he collected for thirteen years, until he was pronounced cured.

A Focused Writer Sillitoe had begun to write while in Malaya, and his small pension enabled him to survive without having to get a job. In his 1995 autobiography, *Life Without Armour,* he refers to this period of his life: "Such an extended period of cosseting merely for doing my duty turned into a much appreciated case of patronage." Sillitoe spent six years in France and Spain, writing and rewriting several books. He ended up scrapping the manuscripts of nine completed novels, finally publishing *Saturday Night and Sunday Morning*. This novel, which describes the numbing effects of working-class life on a tough young man, met with instant success. It won the Author's Club Prize for the best English novel of 1958 and was later made into a movie starring Albert Finney. Of Sillitoe's work, one critic remarked, "For the first time, English working-class life is treated . . . as a normal subject matter for a writer."

"Angry Young Men" In 1959, Sillitoe published a short story collection entitled *The Loneliness of the Long Distance Runner*, perhaps his most famous work. The title story, later made into a film starring Tom Courtenay and Michael Redgrave, tells of a young juvenile delinquent in an English reform school. The boy runs in order to escape his oppressive surroundings and gain a sense of freedom.

These early works earned Sillitoe a place among a group of writers—known as the "Angry Young Men"—who believed that British social and political traditions had become outmoded.

Like the other "Angry Young Men," Sillitoe explored the theme of rebellion. His heroes, firmly rooted in the working classes, sought self-discovery by opposing much of organized society.

The scope of Sillitoe's subject matter has broadened to some extent in his later works, although he has remained primarily a chronicler of working-class people who must scratch out a living as best they can. He is one of the more prolific British writers of our time, having published more than forty books, including novels, short story collections, plays, essays, children's stories, and an autobiography.

The Story Behind the Story During his childhood, Alan Sillitoe lived for a time in a tiny cottage in Nottingham, England, near the River Leen. After a week of rain, the Sillitoes' cottage was flooded and had to be abandoned. The River Leen and the cottages on its banks are the setting of "The Fiddle." Perhaps Sillitoe's former neighbors served as inspiration for the story's characters.

TEACHING RESOURCES

The following resources can be used to enrich or extend the instruction for pp. 1076–1077.

Motivation

Interest Grabber Video, Tape 6

Background

Beyond Literature, p. 52

Take It to the Net

Visit www.phschool.com for background and hotlinks for "The Fiddle."

Literary Analysis

Literary Analysis and Reading Transparencies, Setting and Atmosphere, p. 104

Reading

Literary Analysis and Reading Transparencies, Predicting the Effect of Setting, p. 103

BLOCK SCHEDULING: Resources marked with this symbol provide varied instruction during 90-minute blocks.

Preview

Connecting to the Literature

You may feel carefree on a sunny day or gloomy when you walk down a dark street. Just as your environment affects your mood, the time and place of a story affects the outlook of each character. This is especially true in "The Fiddle," set in a mining town.

❷ Literary Analysis

Setting and Atmosphere

A story's **setting** is the time and place in which the characters live. The general setting of "The Fiddle" is an English coal-mining town in the 1930s, but the setting also includes the characters' customs and beliefs. Various details of the setting contribute to the **atmosphere,** the overall feeling, or mood, of the work. In the following passage from "The Fiddle," the underlined words describe the physical setting and the word *ruinous* suggests an atmosphere of bleak poverty.

> On the banks of the sinewy River Leen, where it flowed through Radford, stood a group of cottages called Harrison's Row. There must have been six to eight of them, all in a ruinous condition, but lived in nevertheless.

As you read, look for key words and phrases that establish the setting and suggest the atmosphere of the selection.

Connecting Literary Elements

An author brings a setting to life through his or her **style,** or approach to writing. Style includes such elements as word choice, images, and rhythm. In "The Fiddle," Sillitoe uses simple words, clear images, and informal speech. As a result, the narrator seems like one of the neighbors. In reading, notice how the informal style invites you to feel like a part of the neighborhood circle.

❸ Reading Strategy

Predicting the Effect of Setting

A story's setting can shape the characters' personalities and actions. As you read, make educated guesses about the outcome of the story by using a chart like this one to **predict the effects of the setting** on the characters' lives.

Vocabulary Development

persistent (pər sist′ ənt) *adj.* continuing without letup (p. 1079)

obliterate (ə blit′ ər āt′) *v.* destroy utterly (p. 1080)

sublimity (sə blim′ ə tē) *n.* quality of being majestic or noble (p. 1081)

harried (har′ ēd) *v.* harassed; worried by repeated requests (p. 1082)

❷ Literary Analysis

Setting and Atmosphere

- Tell students that as they read "The Fiddle," they will focus on setting, the time and place in which the action occurs, and atmosphere, the overall mood of the work.
- Read the instruction about setting and atmosphere together as a class. Call students' attention to the excerpt from the story.
- Use the instruction for Connecting Literary Elements to connect the setting and atmosphere of the story to the author's style.
- Use the Setting and Atmosphere transparency in **Literary Analysis and Reading Transparencies,** p. 104, to demonstrate for students how setting informs the atmosphere.

❸ Reading Strategy

Predicting the Effect of Setting

- Tell students that the setting can affect the outcome of a story.
- Then, tell students they can therefore make predictions, or educated guesses, about what will happen to the characters based on the setting.
- Encourage students to use a chart like the one on p. 1077 in which to record their predictions as they read.

Vocabulary Development

- Pronounce each vocabulary word for students and read the definitions as a class. Have students identify any words with which they are already familiar.

CUSTOMIZE INSTRUCTION FOR UNIVERSAL ACCESS

For Less Proficient Readers	For English Learners	For Advanced Readers
Model for students how to predict the effect of the setting on characters' lives. Use the Predicting the Effect of Setting transparency in **Literary Analysis and Reading Transparencies,** p. 103, to demonstrate for students how to base predictions on the setting. Guide students through the story as a group.	Encourage students to use a chart like the one on p. 1077 in which to record their predictions as they read. You may need to help some students with the Briticisms that appear throughout. Encourage students to note any unfamiliar words and to try to use context clues to figure out the meanings.	Discuss with students how a change in setting might affect the characters' lives. Ask them to think of a different setting and place these same characters there. How would their lives be different? How might the characters themselves be different?

 ***E-Teach***

Visit E-Teach at www.phschool.com for teachers' essays on how to teach, with questions and answers.

TEACH

Step-by-Step Teaching Guide for pp. 1078–1084

CUSTOMIZE INSTRUCTION
For Visual/Spatial Learners

Have students imagine the setting in and around Harrison's Row. They can picture the sameness of the drab row houses and dirty coal-blackened workers trudging back from the unsightly coal mines. Help them imagine the commanding presence of huge and grim factories for coal processing, with their smoke-stacks and railroad sidings.

❶ About the Selection

In "The Fiddle," Alan Sillitoe describes the bleak physical setting of Harrison's Row in the coal-mining town of Radford, the views of its inhabitants, and the activities that take place there. In particular, he describes the sacrifice one man makes to successfully escape the misery of the miner's life, and the impact of his decision on his neighbors.

❷ ▶Critical Viewing

Answer: Students may suggest that the sameness and closeness of the flats could cause the inhabitants to know each other's business and to develop a sameness in outlook and lifestyle. Either neighbors would have a unique camaraderie as a result of the cramped quarters and a lack of privacy, or the bleak, claustrophobic setting might cause residents to feel trapped and despairing.

❶ The Fiddle

Alan Sillitoe

Background

This story is set during the 1930s in a town dependent on coal mining. The coal industry has been crucial to the British economy for generations, but the conditions in which miners work have often been brutal. Until the mid-1600s, miners were often serfs or paroled convicts whose safety was of little concern to mine operators. By the twentieth century, both working conditions and wages had improved. Yet the miners and their families still led difficult lives, especially during the economic depression of the 1930s.

On the banks of the sinewy River Leen, where it flowed through Radford, stood a group of cottages called Harrison's Row. There must have been six to eight of them, all in a ruinous condition, but lived in nevertheless.

They had been put up for stockingers[1] during the Industrial Revolution a hundred years before, so that by now the usual small red English housebricks had become weatherstained and, in some places, almost black.

Harrison's Row had a character all of its own, both because of its situation, and the people who lived there. Each house had a space of

❷ ▼ **Critical Viewing** What effect do you think this setting would have on residents? **[Analyze Cause and Effect]**

1. **stockingers** *n.* stocking weavers.

TEACHING RESOURCES

The following resources can be used to enrich or extend the instruction for pp. 1078–1084.

Literary Analysis

Selection Support: Literary Analysis, p. 244

Reading

Selection Support: Reading Strategy, p. 243; Build Vocabulary, p. 241

Listening to Literature Audiocassettes, Side 25 ■

Listening to Literature Audio CDs, CD 14 ■

■ **BLOCK SCHEDULING:** Resources marked with this symbol provide varied instruction during 90-minute blocks.

3 pebbly soil rising in front, and a strip of richer garden sloping away from the kitchen door down to the diminutive River Leen at the back. The front gardens had almost merged into one piece of common ground, while those behind had in most cases retained their separate plots.

As for the name of the isolated row of cottages, nobody knew who Harrison had been, and no one was ever curious about it. Neither did they know where the Leen came from, though some had a general idea as to where it finished up.

A rent man walked down cobblestoned Leen Place every week to collect what money he could. This wasn't much, even at the best of times which, in the "thirties," were not too good—though no one in their conversation was able to hark back to times when they had been any better.

From the slight rise on which the houses stood, the back doors and windows looked across the stream into green fields, out towards the towers and pinnacles of Wollaton Hall in one direction, and the woods of Aspley Manor in the other.

After a warm summer without much rain the children were able to wade to the fields on the other side. Sometimes they could almost paddle. But after a three-day downpour when the air was still heavy with undropped water, and colored a menacing gun-metal blue, it was best not to go anywhere near the river, for one false slip and you would get sucked in, and be dragged by the powerful current along to the Trent some miles away. In that case there was no telling where you'd end up. The water seemed to flow into the River Amazon[2] itself, indicated by the fact that Frankie Buller swore blind how one day he had seen a crocodile snapping left and right downstream with a newborn baby in its mouth. You had to be careful—and that was a fact. During the persistent rain of one autumn water came up over the gardens and almost in at the back doors.

Harrison's Row was a cut-off place in that not many people knew about it unless they were familiar with the district. You went to it along St. Peter's Street, and down Leen Place. But it was delightful for the kids who lived there because out of the back gardens they could go straight into the stream of the Leen. In summer an old tin hip bath would come from one of the houses. Using it for a boat, and stripped to their white skins, the children were happy while sun and weather lasted.

The youths and older kids would eschew this fun and set out in a gang, going far beyond, to a bend of the canal near Wollaton Pit where the water was warm—almost hot—due to some outlet from the mine itself. This place was known as "'otties," and they'd stay all day with a bottle of lemonade and a piece of bread, coming back late in the evening looking pink and tired as if out of a prolonged dipping in the ritual bath. But a swim in 'otties was only for the older ones, because a boy of four had once been drowned there.

Harrison's Row was the last of Nottingham where it met the countryside. Its houses were at the very edge of the city, in the days

2. **River Amazon** largest, most powerful river in South America.

Literary Analysis
Setting What do you learn about the setting from the first four paragraphs of the story?

persistent (pər sis′ tənt) *adj.* continuing without letup

4 **Reading Check**
What do the children and older kids of Harrison's Row do for fun?

Hillside in Wales, (detail), L. S. Lowry, The Tate Gallery, London

3 Literary Analysis

Setting and Atmosphere

- Call on volunteers to read aloud the bracketed passage.
- Have students answer the Literary Analysis question on p. 1079: What do you learn about the setting from the first four paragraphs of the story?
  Answer: The setting is dreary—an isolated row of ruinous cottages made of almost black-stained bricks, shared backyards, and a lack of inspiration or curiosity amongst the people who lived there.

4 Reading Check

Answer: The young children would use bathtubs as boats in the stream of the Leen for fun. Older kids would go swimming in 'otties, a warm spot in the stream farther away.

CUSTOMIZE INSTRUCTION FOR UNIVERSAL ACCESS

For Special Needs Students	For Advanced Readers
Students may find the language of the story challenging. Help students clarify the meanings of the several Briticisms Sillitoe uses that are not already defined in footnotes. Words include *brilliantined, wash-copper, wireless, quid, slice of bluff, collier,* and *queue.* Encourage students to find words with which they are unfamiliar and work as a group to define them using either context clues or a dictionary.	Guide students to look for the symbolic meaning of things and places in this story. They can notice, for example, that the fiddle symbolizes beauty and that the River Leen represents freedom, a link to the unknown outside world.

5 Literary Analysis

Setting and Atmosphere

- Call on a volunteer to read aloud the bracketed passage, and ask students what words Sillitoe uses to describe the figure in this passage.
  Answer: He describes the figure in phrases such as "unemployed husband"; "his cap on but wearing no shirt."
- Ask students: What is the figure doing?
  Answer: He is staring out from his "bit of suburb" at the farmers and their machines, which are working the land.

Monitor Progress Then, ask students: What mood or atmosphere is created through these setting details?
Answer: Students may say that the details create a mood of resignation, hopelessness, depression, and stagnation.

before those numerous housing estates had been built beyond. The line of dwellings called Harrison's Row made a sort of outpost bastion before the country began.

Yet the houses in the city didn't immediately start behind, due to gardens and a piece of wasteground, which gave to Harrison's Row a feeling of isolation. It stood somewhat on its own, as if the city intended one day to leapfrog over it and obliterate the country beyond.

obliterate (ə blit′ ə rāt) *v.* destroy utterly

On the other hand, any foreign army attacking from the west, over the green fields that glistened in front, would first have to flatten Harrison's Row before getting into the innumerable streets of houses behind.

Across the Leen, horses were sometimes to be seen in the fields and, in other fields beyond, the noise of combine harvesters could be heard at work in the summer. Children living there, and adults as well, had the advantage of both town and country. On a fine evening late in August one of the unemployed husbands might be seen looking across at the noise of some machinery working in a field, his cap on but wearing no shirt, as if wondering why he was here and not over there, and why in **5** fact he had ever left those same fields in times gone by to be forced into this bit of a suburb where he now had neither work nor purpose in life. He was not bitter, and not much puzzled perhaps, yet he couldn't help being envious of those still out there in the sunshine.

In my visions of leaving Nottingham for good—and they were frequent in those days—I never reckoned on doing so by the high road or railway. Instead I saw myself wading or swimming the Leen from Harrison's Row, and setting off west once I was on the other side.

A tale remembered with a laugh at that time told about how young Ted Griffin, who had just started work, saw two policemen one day walking down Leen Place towards Harrison's Row. Convinced they had come to arrest him for meter-breaking, he ran through the house and garden, went over the fence, jumped into the Leen—happily not much swollen—waded across to the field, then four-legged it over the railway, and made his way to Robins Wood a mile or so beyond. A perfect escape route. He stayed two days in hiding, and then crept home at night, famished and soaked, only to find that the police had not come for him, but to question Blonk next door, who was suspected of poaching. When they did get Ted Griffin he was pulled out of bed one morning even before he'd had time to open his eyes and think about a spectacular escape across the Leen.

Jeff Bignal was a young unmarried man of twenty-four. His father had been killed in the Great War,[3] and he lived with his mother at Number Six Harrison's Row, and worked down nearby Radford Pit. He was short in height, and plump, his white skin scarred back and front with livid blue patches where he had been knocked with coal at the mine face. When he went out on Saturday night he brilliantined his hair.

3. **Great War** World War I.

 **ENRICHMENT: Media Connection**

An Alan Sillitoe Film Festival

Two of Alan Sillitoe's angry works about working-class life in twentieth-century Great Britain were made into powerful films. The adaptation of his novel *Saturday Night and Sunday Morning* (1958) appeared in 1960, directed by Karel Reisz and starring Albert Finney. Sillitoe himself wrote the screenplay. He also wrote the screenplay for the film of *The Loneliness of the Long Distance Runner* (story: 1959; film: 1962). Tom Courtenay and Michael Redgrave starred in this highly acclaimed film, directed by Tony Richardson.

Invite students to view either or both of these films; each movie is available on video. Use the following question for discussion:

How would you describe the view of life each film expresses?

Possible response: Students should focus on the dreary, grim, demoralized lives of the working classes.

After tea in summer while it was still light and warm he would sit in his back garden playing the fiddle, and when he did everybody else came out to listen. Or they opened the doors and windows so that the sound of his music drifted in, while the woman stayed at the sink or wash-copper, or the man at his odd jobs. Anyone with a wireless would turn it down or off.

6 Even tall dark sallow-faced elderly Mrs. Deaffy (a kid sneaked into her kitchen one day and thieved her last penny-packet of cocoa and she went crying to tell Mrs. Atkin who, when her youngest came in, hit him so hard with her elbow that one of his teeth shot out and the blood washed away most of the cocoa-stains around his mouth)—old Mrs. Deaffy stood by her back door as if she weren't stone deaf any more and could follow each note of Jeffrey Bignal's exquisite violin. She smiled at seeing everyone occupied, fixed or entranced, and therefore no torment to herself, which was music enough to her whether she could hear it or not.

Literary Analysis

Setting, Atmosphere, and Style Which elements of style in this paragraph help bring the setting to life?

And Blonk, in the secretive dimness of the kitchen, went on mending his poaching nets before setting out with Arthur Bede next door on that night's expedition to Gunthorpe by the banks of the Trent, where the green escarpment between there and Kneeton was riddled with warrens and where, so it was said, if you stood sufficiently still the rabbits ran over your feet, and it was only necessary to make a quick grab to get one.

Jeff sat on a chair, oblivious to everybody, fed up with his day's work at the pit and only wanting to lose himself in his own music. The kids stopped splashing and shouting in the water, because if they didn't they might get hauled in and clouted with just the right amount of viciousness to suit the crime and the occasion. It had happened before, though Jeff had always been too far off to notice.

His face was long, yet generally cheerful—contrary to what one would expect—a smile settling on it whenever he met and passed anybody on the street, or on his way to the group of shared lavatories at the end of the Row. But his face was almost down and lost to the world as he sat on his chair and brought forth his first sweet notes of a summer's evening.

It was said that a neighbor in the last place they had lived had taught him to play like that. Others maintained it was an uncle who had shown him how. But nobody knew for sure because when someone asked directly he said that if he had any gift at all it must have come from God above. It was known that on some Sundays of the year, if the sun was out, he went to the Methodist chapel on St. Peter's Street.

He could play anything from "Greensleeves" to "Mademoiselle from Armentières." He could do a beautiful heart-pulling version of Handel's *Largo*, and throw in bits from *The Messiah* as well. He would go from one piece to another with no rhyme or reason, from ridiculousness to
7 sublimity, with almost shocking abruptness, but as the hour or so went by it all appeared easy and natural, part of a long piece coming from Jeff Bignal's fiddle while the ball of the sun went down behind his back.

sublimity (sə blim′ ə tē) *n.* quality of being majestic or noble

8 **Reading Check**

Who is Jeff Bignal?

6 Literary Analysis

Setting, Atmosphere, and Style

- Read aloud the bracketed passage.
- Have students answer the Literary Analysis question on p. 1081: Which elements of style in this passage help bring the setting to life?
  Answer: The use of a parenthetical anecdote that reveals a casual, matter-of-fact attitude the characters have toward violence makes the setting seem even more bleak. Also, the image of the deaf woman enjoying the violin music because it keeps people from tormenting her suggests the cruelty of people in the community.

7 Vocabulary Development

Latin Word Origins: *Sublime*

- Call students' attention to the word *sublimity* and its definition. Tell students that the word contains the Latin prefix *sub-*, which means "up to," and the Latin root *-limen-*, which means "lintel, the horizontal crosspiece over a door."
- Have students suggest words that contain either the prefix or the root, and list them on the chalkboard.
  Possible response: Examples include *subliminal, eliminate,* and *subordinate*.
- Next, have students look up the meanings of these words in the dictionary.
- Then, have students write sentences in which they use each of the listed words correctly.

8 Reading Check

Answer: Jeff Bignal is a young unmarried man who plays the violin on warm summer nights.

CUSTOMIZE INSTRUCTION FOR UNIVERSAL ACCESS

For English Learners	For Gifted/Talented Students
Clarify the meanings of the unfamiliar regional or unusual terms in paragraph 6 on p. 1080, beginning "A tale remembered. . . ." Explain that Ted Griffin probably broke the gas, water, or electric meter in his house to avoid paying his bills. When he sees the policemen, he speeds from the scene of the crime as fast as he can. Explain that *poaching* is trespassing and illegal hunting, and here it probably refers to the theft of fish, game, or eggs.	Have students collect samples of fiddle music for a class presentation. Students should classify different styles of fiddle music and explain each category to the class. Then, have students speculate which of their samples is most like the music played by Jeff Bignal in the story. Encourage the rest of the class to voice their speculations, too.

❾ Reading Strategy

Predicting the Effect of Setting

- Read aloud the bracketed passage.

Monitor Progress Then, ask students the Reading Strategy question on p. 1082: What do you think Jeff might do to escape the mines?

Possible response: Students may say that Jeff would have to leave Harrison's Row because his options are limited there. They might guess that he would leave the region and become a professional musician.

To a child it seemed as if the songs lived in the hard collier's muscle at the top of his energetic arm, and that they queued one by one to get out. Once free, they rushed along his flesh from which the shirtsleeves had been rolled up, and split into his fingertips, where they were played out with ease into the warm evening air.

The grass in the fields across the stream was livid and lush, almost blue, and a piebald horse stood with bent head, eating oats out of a large old pram whose wheels had long since gone. The breeze wafted across from places farther out, from Robins Wood and the Cherry Orchard, Wollaton Roughs and Bramcote Hills and even, on a day that was not too hot, from the tops of the Pennines in Derbyshire.

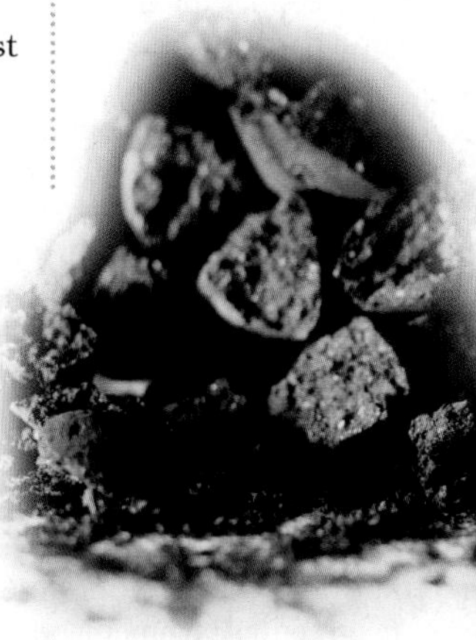

Jeff played for himself, for the breeze against his arm, for the soft hiss of the flowing Leen at the end of the garden, and maybe also for the horse in the field, which took no notice of anything and which, having grown tired of its oats in the pram, bent its head over the actual grass and began to roam in search of succulent pastures.

In the middle of the winter Jeff's fiddling was forgotten. He went into the coal mine before it was light, and came up only after it had got dark. Walking down Leen Place, he complained to Blonk that it was hard on a man not to see daylight for weeks at a time.

"That's why I wain't go anywhere near the bleddy pit," Blonk said vehemently, though he had worked there from time to time, and would do so again when harried by his wife and children. "You'd do better to come out on a bit o' poaching with me and Arthur," he suggested.

harried (har´ ēd) *v.* harassed; worried by repeated requests

It was virtually true that Jeff saw no daylight, because even on
❾ Sunday he stayed in bed most of the day, and if it happened to be dull there was little enough sky to be seen through his front bedroom window, which looked away from the Leen and up the hill.

The upshot of his complaint was that he would do anything to change such a situation. A man was less than an animal for putting up with it.

Reading Strategy
Predicting the Effect of Setting What do you think Jeff might do to escape the mines?

"I'd do anything," he repeated to his mother over his tea in the single room downstairs.

"But what, though?" she asked. "What can you do, Jeff?"

"Well, how do I know?" he almost snapped at her. "But I'll do summat,[4] you can be sure of that."

He didn't do anything till the weather got better and life turned a bit sweeter. Maybe this improvement finally got him going, because it's hard to help yourself towards better things when you're too far down in the dumps.

On a fine blowy day with both sun and cloud in the sky Jeff went out in the morning, walking up Leen Place with his fiddle under his arm. The case had been wiped and polished.

In the afternoon he came back without it.

"Where's your fiddle?" Ma Jones asked.

He put an awkward smile on to his pale face, and told her: "I sold it."

"Well I never! How much for?"

---

4. **summat** something.

ENRICHMENT: Social Studies Connection

Mining Towns

"The Fiddle" presents a vivid look at what life is like for people living and working in a coal-mining town. Students can appreciate the way things stayed the same for the inhabitants of Harrison's Row despite progress and the passage of time. They may assume that life in Harrison's Row is indicative of life in other coal-mining towns throughout Great Britain. Is it indicative of life in mining towns in the United States? Have students find out.

Ask students to form groups. Each group should choose a mining town from a different part of the United States. They can, for example, find coal-mining towns in Pennsylvania, copper-mining towns in Arizona, silver-mining towns in Colorado and Nevada, and gold-mining towns in California and Alaska. Each group should research life in a mining town, now or in the past, comparing and contrasting it with life in Harrison's Row.

He was too shocked at her brazen question not to tell the truth: "Four quid."

"That ain't much."

"It'll be enough," he said roughly.

"Enough for what, Jeff?"

He didn't say, but the fact that he had sold his fiddle for four quid rattled up and down the line of cottages till everybody knew of it. Others swore he'd got ten pounds for it, because something that made such music must be worth more than a paltry four, and in any case Jeff would never say how much he'd really got for it, for fear that someone would go in and rob him.

They wondered why he'd done it, but had to wait for the answer, as one usually does. But there was nothing secretive about Jeff Bignal, and if he'd sold his music for a mess of pottage he saw no point in not letting them know why. They'd find out sooner or later, anyway.

All he'd had to do was make up his mind, and he'd done that lying on his side at the pit face while ripping coal out with his pick and shovel. Decisions made like that can't be undone, he knew. He'd brooded on it all winter, till the fact of having settled it seemed to have altered the permanent expression of his face, and given it a new look which caused people to wonder whether he would ever be able to play the fiddle again anyway—at least with his old spirit and dash.

10 With the four quid he paid the first week's rent on a butcher's shop on Denman Street, and bought a knife, a chopper, and a bit of sharpening stone, as well as a wooden block. Maybe he had a quid or two more knocking around, though if he had it couldn't have been much, but with four quid and a slice of bluff he got enough credit from a wholesaler at the meat market downtown to stock his shop with mutton and beef, and in a couple of days he was in trade. The people of Harrison's Row were amazed at how easy it was, though nobody had ever thought of doing it themselves.

Literary Analysis
Setting, Atmosphere, and Style Which words and phrases in this paragraph are examples of Sillitoe's informal style?

Like a serious young man of business Mr. Bignal—as he was now known—parted his hair down the middle, so that he didn't look so young any more, but everyone agreed that it was better than being at Radford Pit. They'd seen how he had got fed up with selling the sweat of his brow.

No one could say that he prospered, but they couldn't deny that he made a living. And he didn't have to suffer the fact of not seeing daylight for almost the whole of the winter.

Six months after opening the shop he got married. The reception was held at the chapel on St. Peter's Street, which seemed to be a sort of halfway house between Harrison's Row on the banks of the Leen and the butcher's shop on Denman Street farther up.

Everybody from Harrison's Row was invited for a drink and something to eat; but he knew them too well to let any have either chops or chitterlings (or even black puddings) on tick[5] when they came into his shop.

11 
What does Jeff finally do with his fiddle?

5. **tick** credit.

10 Literary Analysis

Setting, Atmosphere, and Style

- Call on a volunteer to read aloud the bracketed passage.
- Have students answer the Literary Analysis question on p. 1083: Which words and phrases in this passage are examples of Sillitoe's informal style?
  Answer: Words and phrases that are examples of his informal style include *quid, chopper, a quid or two more knocking around,* and *a slice of bluff.*

11 

Answer: Jeff sells his fiddle to have enough money to open his own butcher shop.

CUSTOMIZE INSTRUCTION FOR UNIVERSAL ACCESS

For English Learners	For Gifted/Talented Students
In paragraph 5 on p. 1082, read the first sentence aloud so that students can hear the accent as written in the dialogue: "That's why I wain't go anywhere near the bleddy pit." Explain that *bleddy* is how "bloody" sounds in dialect. Point out that *bloody* is a vulgar British term that means "cursed" or "damned."	Encourage interested students to learn to speak with a British dialect and then speak the dialogue on pp. 1082–1083 for the class. Students may learn the dialect from listening to British speakers or watching movies that are set in Great Britain. When students are comfortable with the dialect, have them read aloud the dialogue from the story. Discuss with the class whether it was easier to understand what the words meant when they heard it read aloud.

ASSESS

12 Literary Analysis

Setting and Atmosphere

- Read aloud the bracketed passage.
- Then, ask students how the description of the demolition affects the atmosphere. Possible response: The demolition of the old run-down houses does not change the atmosphere of the story, but rather reinforces its depressing mood. There is still no hope for the people who lived there, and they have just moved on to live in poverty and hopelessness elsewhere.

Answers for p. 1084

Review and Assess

1. **(a)** He plays his violin. **(b)** Jeff's fiddle playing makes him an integral part of the small community and earns him the respect and admiration of his neighbors.
2. **(a)** Blonk says he should come poaching with him rather than work in the mines. **(b)** Jeff detests the coal mines like all the other workers, but only he is willing and determined to do something to change his life.
3. **(a)** He sells his fiddle. **(b)** The fiddle symbolizes the manifestation of beauty in an otherwise dreary environment. **(c)** It emphasizes the sacrifice that the protagonist makes to make a living.
4. Possible response: No, people should be able to earn a living while still having beauty in their lives—they should not be exclusive.

The people of Harrison's Row missed the sound of his fiddle on long summer evenings, though the children could splash and shout with their tin bathtub undisturbed, floundering through shallows and scrambling up to grass on the other bank, and wondering what place they'd reach if they walked without stopping till it got dark.

Two years later the Second World War began, and not long afterwards meat as well as nearly everything else was put on the ration. Apart from which, Jeff was only twenty-six, so got called up into the army. He never had much chance to make a proper start in life, though people said that he came out all right in the end.

The houses of Harrison's Row were condemned as unfit to live in, and a bus depot stands on the site.

The packed mass of houses on the hill behind—forty years after Jeff Bignal sold his violin—is also vanishing, and high-rise hencoops (as the people call them) are put in their place. The demolition crew knock down ten houses a day—though the foreman told me there was still work for another two years.

12 Some of the houses would easily have lasted a few more decades, for the bricks were perfect, but as the foreman went on: "You can't let them stand in the way of progress"—whatever that means.

The people have known each other for generations but, when they are moved to their new estates and blocks of flats,[6] they will know each other for generations more, because as I listen to them talking, they speak a language which, in spite of everything and everyone, never alters.

---

6. **flats** apartments.

Review and Assess

Thinking About the Selection

1. **(a) Recall:** What does Jeff Bignal do in the summer when he comes home from the coal mines? **(b) Connect:** What is the connection between Jeff's fiddle and his status in the town?
2. **(a) Recall:** When Jeff complains to his friend Blonk about working in the mines, what does Blonk say in response? **(b) Compare and Contrast:** How is Jeff's attitude toward the coal mines different from his friend's?
3. **(a) Recall:** What does Jeff finally do with his fiddle? **(b) Interpret:** What does the fiddle symbolize? Explain. **(c) Draw Conclusions:** What theme does this symbol reveal?
4. **Generalize:** Do you think that the necessities of earning a living should take precedence over the pursuit of beauty? Why or why not?

ASSESSMENT PRACTICE: Writing Skills

Organization (For more practice, see Test Preparation Workbook, p. 52.)

Many standardized tests ask students about a text's organization. Use the following sample item to show how to note patterns of organization.

Even Mrs. Deaffy (a kid sneaked into her kitchen one day and thieved her last penny-packet of cocoa and she went crying to tell Mrs. Atkin who, when her youngest came in, hit him so hard with her elbow that one of his teeth shot out and the blood washed away most of the cocoa-stains around his mouth)—old Mrs. Deaffy stood by her back door . . .

Which of the following *best* describes the organization of this passage?

A stream-of-consciousness
B chronological
C comparison-contrast
D foreshadow

The author's return to the first idea after a parenthetical interruption supports the correct answer, *A*.

Review and Assess

Literary Analysis

Setting and Atmosphere

1. Fill in a chart like this one to explain how details of the **setting** create an ominous **atmosphere** in "The Fiddle."

Description of Setting	Ominous Atmosphere
Passage From Story	Which Details? Why?

2. Using examples from the story as support, explain the effects that descriptions of the River Leen have on the atmosphere of this story.
3. Describe the effects of the fiddle, an element of setting, on the story's atmosphere.

Connecting Literary Elements

4. Using examples from the story, illustrate these aspects of the author's **style:** (a) conversational language, (b) clear images, (c) a sense that the narrator is part of the neighborhood.
5. (a) Referring to one passage, explain how the author's style brings the setting to life. (b) Describe the author's attitude towards the setting in the passage—is he amused, concerned, detached, accepting, or angry?
6. How might the style and the setting have changed if the narrator had been a social worker? Explain.

Reading Strategy

Predicting the Effect of Setting

7. What effect did the fiddle, an important detail of the setting, have on the outcome of events?
8. (a) Speculate about the effects that World War II had on Jeff's life. (b) Why do you think the author was not more specific about them?
9. Which elements of the setting pointed most strongly to a particular outcome in the story? Why?

Extend Understanding

10. **Science Connection:** How do Jeff's feelings about the mine in winter illustrate what scientists have learned about the link between sunlight and mood?

Quick Review

The **setting** of a story is the time and place in which the events occur. A story's setting contributes to its **atmosphere,** its overall feeling or mood.

A writer's **style,** or typical way of writing, can help bring a story's setting to life. Style may include such elements as word choice, images, and rhythm.

To **predict the effects of a setting,** make educated guesses about how the details of the setting will influence characters' decisions and actions.

 **Take It to the Net**

www.phschool.com

Take the interactive self-test online to check your understanding of the selection.

ENRICHMENT: Further Reading

Other Works by Alan Sillitoe

Saturday Night and Sunday Morning

The Loneliness of the Long Distance Runner

The Ragman's Daughter

 **Take It to the Net**

Visit www.phschool.com for more information on Alan Sillitoe.

Answers for p. 1085

Review and Assess

1. Possible response: **Passage:** "But after a three-day downpour when the air was still heavy with undropped water and colored a menacing gun-metal blue, it was best not to go anywhere near the river, for one false step and you would get sucked in . . ." **Details:** Sillitoe's choice of words, such as the adjectives *heavy, undropped,* and *menacing,* creates the ominous atmosphere.
2. Students may say that the fact that no one knew or cared where the Leen came from suggests that people are at the mercy of their environment. They may say that the river contributes to a feeling of hopelessness, as it represents a barrier to opportunities.
3. The fiddle is a symbol of beauty in an otherwise dreary setting. When Jeff plays, the music gives his neighbors a moment of pleasure.
4. Possible responses: **(a) Conversational language:** ". . . but with four quid and a slice of bluff he got enough credit from a wholesaler . . ." **(b) Clear images:** "To a child it seemed as if the songs lived in the hard collier's muscle at the top of his energetic arm . . ." **(c) Narrator's participation:** "In my visions of leaving Nottingham for good—and they were frequent in those days . . ."
5. **(a)** On p. 1080, the author creates a clear image of the man looking across the river, which brings the setting to life. **(b)** The author observes the scene with detachment.
6. If the narrator had been a social worker, the language would have reflected more shock and outrage at the conditions under which the people lived.
7. By selling the fiddle, Jeff was able to escape working in the mines; at the same time, the community was deprived of one of its few experiences of beauty.
8. **(a)** World War II did not have much effect on Jeff—he went back to his butcher shop when it was over. **(b)** Possible response: The author wanted to maintain focus on the community.

continued

Answers continued

9. Possible response: Students may say that the isolation of Harrison's Row and the bleak outlook of the people leading dreary lives there were the strongest contributors to the continuation of hopelessness.
10. Jeff would become depressed in winter because he would never see daylight, and scientists have found that lack of sunlight during winter months can lead to depression.

EXTEND

Answers for p. 1086

❶ Vocabulary Development

Latin Word Origins

1. To purify or refine something is to make it better or "nobler" by lifting it up from a baser substance.
2. Changing something from a solid to the vapor state is to lift it up or elevate it from a baser state.
3. *To sublimate* means to take a base or primitive thought or emotion and convert or lift it into a more refined and thus higher cultural or ethical realm.

Concept Development: Analogies

1. persistent
2. obliterate
3. sublimity
4. harried

Spelling Strategy

1. intensity
2. agility
3. anxiety

❷ Grammar and Style

1. subject
2. introductory phrase
3. introductory adverb
4. introductory clause
5. introductory adverb

Writing Application

Sample sentences:

1. Born to working-class parents, Alan Sillitoe grew up in Nottingham, England. [phrase]
2. Eventually, by the age of fourteen, he was earning enough to help his family. [adverb]
3. After he passed the necessary tests, he joined the Royal Air Force. [clause]
4. He knew at age twenty-one that he wanted to be a writer. [subject]
5. He became famous as one of England's "Angry Young Men." [subject]

Integrate Language Skills

❶ Vocabulary Development Lesson

Latin Word Origins: *Sublime*

The word *sublimity* contains the Latin prefix *sub-*, meaning "up to," and the root *-limen-*, meaning "lintel, the horizontal crosspiece over a door." *Sublimity* is therefore "the quality of being uplifted or noble."

Explain how the origin of *sublime* influences the meaning of these scientific words:

1. To *sublimate* is to purify or refine a substance. (chemistry)
2. To *sublime* a substance is to change it directly from a solid to a gaseous state. (chemistry)
3. To *sublimate* is to express unacceptable impulses in constructive forms. (psychology)

Concept Development: Analogies

Using the vocabulary words on page 1077, complete each analogy by forming a new word pair with the same relationship as the first pair.

1. organized : neat :: persevering : __?__
2. believe : disprove :: create : __?__
3. boring : routine :: awe-inspiring : __?__
4. ideas : inspired :: responsibilities : __?__

Spelling Strategy

Sometimes the suffix *-ity* is spelled *-ety* to avoid a double *i* when the base word part already ends in *i*, as in *society*. In your notebook, add *-ity* or *-ety* to complete these words:

1. intens___ 2. agil___ 3. anxi___

❷ Grammar and Style Lesson

Vary Sentence Beginnings

If every sentence in a story began with the word *the*, the resulting monotonous rhythm would catch your attention, maybe even annoy you. By **varying sentence beginnings**—starting sentences with different parts of speech or sentence elements—a writer avoids monotomy. The right introductory word, phrase, or clause can propel you from one event to the next. To see how good writers vary sentence beginnings, note examples from the story:

Introductory Adverb: Sometimes they could almost paddle.

Introductory Phrase: In that case there was no telling where you'd end up.

Introductory Clause: When they did get Ted Griffin, he was pulled out of bed. . . .

Practice In your notebook, identify each of the italicized sentence beginnings as subject, adverb, phrase, or clause.

1. *Allan Sillitoe* grew up in Nottingham, England.
2. *By age fourteen*, he was earning enough to help his family.
3. *Fortunately*, he passed the necessary tests to join the Royal Air Force.
4. *When he was twenty-one*, he knew that he wanted to be a writer.
5. *Eventually*, he became famous as one of England's "Angry Young Men."

Writing Application In your notebook, rewrite sentences 1–5 above. Have each begin with one of the following sentence parts: subject, adverb, clause, or phrase.

WG *Prentice Hall Writing and Grammar Connection: Chapter 20, Section 3*

TEACHING RESOURCES

The following resources can be used to enrich or extend the instruction for pp. 1086–1087.

Vocabulary

- **Selection Support:** Build Vocabulary, p. 241
- **Vocabulary and Spelling Practice Book** (Use this booklet for skills enrichment.) ■

Grammar

- **Selection Support:** Grammar and Style, p. 242
- **Writing and Grammar,** Diamond Level, p. 488
- **Daily Language Practice Transparencies** ■

Writing

- **Writing and Grammar,** Diamond Level, p. 108
- **Writing and Grammar iText CD-ROM** ■
- **Writing Models and Graphic Organizers on Transparencies,** pp. 13–16

■ **BLOCK SCHEDULING:** Resources marked with this symbol provide varied instruction during 90-minute blocks.

❸ Writing Lesson

Description of a Setting

Sillitoe describes Harrison's Row with phrases like "small red English housebricks . . . weatherstained . . . almost black" to support an overall impression of neglect. Choose a place that you know, and describe it just as vividly.

Prewriting Gather details that express the feeling you want to convey. Consider all five senses.

Drafting Convey an overall impression, as Sillitoe does in his opening paragraphs. Then, support that impression by including sensory descriptions arranged in a logical way, such as spatial order.

Revising Be sure that your descriptions support the overall impression. If your organizing principle seems too mechanical, use a more interesting one. For example, you might use accounts of children's play to describe a place, as Sillitoe does.

Model: Revising to Clarify Organization

As you approach the basketball court, you
~~You~~ hear the sound of sneakers squeaking and the broken rhythm of the bouncing ball. Suddenly, voices rise out of the noise as players call excitedly to teammates.

The additional text helps organize the spatial description.

WG *Prentice Hall Writing and Grammar Connection: Chapter 6, Section 4*

❹ Extension Activities

Research and Technology Research and present a **multimedia report** on Britain's "Angry Young Men": Alan Sillitoe, John Osborne, and Arnold Wesker, among others. Include items like these:

- Charts illustrating the British class system, against which these writers rebelled
- Readings from the works of these writers
- Clips from films based on their works: *The Loneliness of the Long-Distance Runner* (1962) and *Look Back in Anger* (1959)

After gathering materials, write a script to guide your presentation. Rehearse presenting your materials, and give your report for the class.

Listening and Speaking With several classmates, stage a **debate** on this resolution: Old neighborhoods like Harrison's Row should be torn down and replaced by new housing. Use arguments that appeal to logic with cause-and-effect relationships, to ethics with statements of values, and to emotions with charged language. Also, consider general issues, such as when, if ever, progress justifies disruption of traditional ways. **[Group Activity]**

Take It to the Net www.phschool.com

Go online for an additional research activity using the Internet.

ASSESSMENT RESOURCES

The following resources can be used to assess students' knowledge and skills.

Selection Assessment

- **Formal Assessment,** pp. 252–254
- **Open Book Test,** pp. 153–155
- **Test Bank Software**
- **Got It! Assessment Videotapes,** Tape 5

Take It to the Net
Visit www.phschool.com for self-tests and additional questions on "The Fiddle."

Writing Rubric

- **Performance Assess. and Portfolio Mgmt.,** p. 17

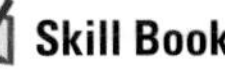

Lesson Support for p. 1087

❸ Writing Lesson

- Tell students that the setting they choose could be a place they see every day, one they remember, or just a place they admire.
- Inform students that they will need to gather vivid details to capture how their setting looks, smells, sounds, tastes, and feels.
- To evoke these sensations, tell them to choose exact nouns, use vivid verbs (those that suggest as closely as possible the action being described), and use strong, precise modifiers to help their readers envision the scene.
- You may want to use the Descriptive and Observational Writing transparencies from **Writing Models and Graphic Organizers on Transparencies,** pp. 13–16, to help students create vivid settings.
- Use the Description rubric in **Performance Assessment and Portfolio Management,** p. 17, to evaluate students' work.

❹ Listening and Speaking

- Write the resolution on the chalkboard.
- Guide students to identify and discuss the pertinent issues.
- Point out that teams should be prepared to argue either side of the issue.
- Remind students to rely on logic to build and present their points.

CUSTOMIZE INSTRUCTION For Universal Access

To address different learning styles, use the following activities suggested in the **Extension Activities** booklet, p. 52.

- For Logical/Mathematical and Visual/Spatial Learners, use Activity 5.
- For Intrapersonal and Verbal/Linguistic Learners, use Activity 6.
- For Verbal/Linguistic Learners, use Activity 7.

The Distant Past

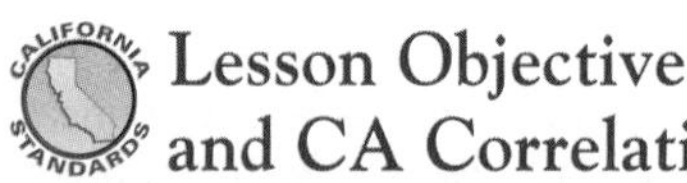

Lesson Objectives and CA Correlations

1. **To analyze and respond to literary elements**
    - Literary Analysis: Social Conflict **R 3.2**
    - Connecting Literary Elements: Motives **R 3.9**
2. **To read, comprehend, analyze, and critique a short story**
    - Reading Strategy: Questioning Causes and Effects
    - Reading Check Questions
    - Review and Assess Questions
3. **To develop word analysis skills, fluency, and systematic vocabulary**
    - Vocabulary Development Lesson: Latin Suffix *-ity (-ty)* **R 1.1, 1.2**
4. **To understand and apply written and oral language conventions**
    - Spelling Strategy **LC 1.2**
    - Grammar and Style Lesson: Restrictive and Nonrestrictive Adjective Clauses **LC 1.1**
5. **To understand and apply appropriate writing and research strategies**
    - Writing Lesson: Persuasive Poster **W 1.1**
    - Extension Activity: Celebration of Irish Culture **LS 2.4**
    - Assessment Practice (ATE)
6. **To understand and apply listening and speaking strategies**
    - Extension Activity: Eulogy **LS 1.6**

STEP-BY-STEP TEACHING GUIDE	PACING GUIDE
PRETEACH	
Motivate Students and Provide Background	
Use the Motivation activity (ATE p. 1088)	5 min.
Read and discuss author and background features (SE/ATE pp. 1088, 1090) A	5 min.
Introduce the Concepts	
Introduce the Literary Analysis and Reading Strategy (SE/ATE p. 1089) A	15 min.
Pronounce the vocabulary words and read their definitions (SE p. 1089)	5 min.
TEACH	
Monitor Comprehension	
Informally monitor comprehension by circulating while students read independently or in groups A	20 min.
Monitor students' comprehension with the Reading Check notes (SE/ATE pp. 1091, 1093, 1095, 1097)	as students read
Develop vocabulary with Vocabulary notes (SE pp. 1090, 1091, 1092, 1093, 1096; ATE p. 1091)	as students read
Develop Understanding	
Develop students' understanding of social conflict with the Literary Analysis annotations (SE pp. 1092, 1094, 1097; ATE pp. 1092, 1094, 1096, 1097) A	5 min.
Develop students' understanding of cause and effect with the Reading Strategy annotations (SE/ATE p. 1093)	5 min.
ASSESS	
Assess Mastery	
Assess students' mastery of the Reading Strategy and Literary Analysis by having them answer the Review and Assess questions (SE/ATE p. 1099)	15 min.
Use one or more of the print and media Assessment Resources (ATE p. 1101) A	up to 45 min.
EXTEND	
Apply Understanding	
Have students complete the Vocabulary Development Lesson and the Grammar and Style Lesson (SE p. 1100) A	20 min.
Apply students' knowledge of brevity and clarity using the Writing Lesson (SE/ATE p. 1101) A	45 min.
Apply students' understanding using one or more of the Extension Activities (SE p. 1101)	20–90 min.

ACCELERATED INSTRUCTION:
Use the strategies and activities identified with an A.

UNIVERSAL ACCESS
● = Below-Level Students
▲ = On-Level Students
■ = Above-Level Students

Time and Resource Manager

Reading Level: Average
Average Number of Instructional Days: 4

RESOURCES		
PRINT	**TRANSPARENCIES**	**TECHNOLOGY**
• **Beyond Literature,** Career Connection: Screenwriter, p. 53 ▲ ■		• **Interest Grabber Video,** Tape 6 ● ▲ ■
• **Selection Support Workbook:** ● ▲ ■ Literary Analysis, p. 248 Reading Strategy, p. 247 Build Vocabulary, p. 245	• **Literary Analysis and Reading Transparencies,** pp. 105 and 106 ● ▲ ■	
		• **Listening to Literature** ● ▲ ■ Audiocassettes, Side 25 Audio CDs, CD 14
• **Literatura en español** ● ▲ • **Literary Analysis for Enrichment** ■		
• **Formal Assessment:** Selection Test, pp. 255–257 ● ▲ ■ • **Open Book Test,** pp. 156–158 ● ▲ ■ • PRENTICE HALL ASSESSMENT SYSTEM ● ▲ ■	• PRENTICE HALL ASSESSMENT SYSTEM ● ▲ ■ Skills Practice Answers and Explanations on Transparencies ● ▲ ■	• **Test Bank Software** ● ▲ ■ • **Got It! Assessment Videotapes,** Tape 5 ● ▲
• **Selection Support Workbook:** ● ▲ ■ Grammar and Style, p. 246 • **Writing and Grammar,** Diamond Level ● ▲ ■ • **Extension Activities,** p. 53 ● ▲ ■	• **Daily Language Practice Transparencies** ● ▲	• **Writing and Grammar iText CD-ROM** ● ▲ ■ ***Take It to the Net*** www.phschool.com

BLOCK SCHEDULING: Use one 90-minute class period to preteach the selection and have students read it. Use a second 90-minute class period to assess students' mastery of skills and have them complete one of the Extension Activities.

PRETEACH

Step-by-Step Teaching Guide for pp. 1088–1089

Motivation

Invite a popular teacher or student to your classroom to pitch an *unpopular* idea. Then ask that person to leave. Have students debate the point of view. Then ask them if their view of the person who made the pitch has changed because of his or her opinion. At the conclusion, clarify that the visit was an act. Tell students that in "The Distant Past" people's unpopular political opinions led to conflict.

Interest Grabber Video

As an alternative, you may wish to play "'The Distant Past': Northern Ireland" on Tape 6 to engage student interest.

❶ More About the Author

William Trevor writes his stories very quickly and then puts them away for a year or two, to come back to them later to see if he likes them. When he rewrites stories, he works them over completely from start to finish. He says that he writes out of curiosity, that he is still bewildered by the world. He also says that writing has changed the way he sees the world and that he has learned much more than he would have learned had he not become a writer.

Prepare to Read

❶ The Distant Past

William Trevor (b. 1928)

Like his protagonists in "The Distant Past," William Trevor was born into a Protestant family in the largely Catholic Republic of Ireland. This experience of being outside the dominant culture gave him a sympathy for the outsiders about whom he writes in his short stories and novels. Trevor himself has said, "I think the feeling of not belonging is very strong in me. In order to write about people, you have got actually to stand back quite a distance."

An Unusual Education The son of a bank manager who moved around a great deal, Trevor attended thirteen different schools. For long periods, however, he was left simply to roam the countryside, occasionally being tutored by neighboring farmers or clergymen. Still, he completed his formal education, graduating from Trinity College in Dublin in 1950. His unusual education probably helped develop his ability as a fiction writer to present clear insights about many different kinds of people and circumstances.

Finding His Art After college, Trevor taught school to support his wife and young family while devoting his creative energies to sculpture. Eventually, his sculpture became too abstract to interest him. "There weren't any people in it anymore, and I didn't like it," he says.

After abandoning sculpture, he took up fiction writing, he says, to express a humanity that he could not find in the visual arts. His art background helps him describe the craft of writing: "A short story is like an impressionist painting. You cut down everything enormously and you get the effects from one big splash or explosion. You have to cut to the very edge. What excites me is to go as far as I can."

A Pessimistic View Trevor earned a living as an advertising copywriter in London. He also achieved immediate success in his new art, publishing short stories in magazines as fast as he could write them. His stories and novels explore a wide variety of subjects and themes. He displays a deep understanding of human nature, often portraying the pointless misunderstandings that develop between individuals or groups of people. Trevor admits that his view of life is pessimistic. The "villain" in his stories is usually circumstance. People's lives are troubled—and sometimes crushed—by historical events that are beyond their control. "I'm very interested in the sadness of fate, the things that just happen to people," Trevor remarks.

Acclaim for Stories Today, William Trevor is recognized as one of the greatest living writers of short stories in the English language. In fact, critics have compared his stories to those of Anton Chekhov, Muriel Spark, and James Joyce. He has been praised for the "gritty detail" of his stories, his lack of sentimentality, and the subtle sense of humor that infuses his work.

Novelist and Playwright Having lived in both Ireland and England, Trevor is comfortable setting his fiction in either place. He has received awards from literary societies in both countries. In addition to his accomplishments as a short-story writer, Trevor is an acclaimed novelist. His works of full-length fiction include *The Old Boys* (1964) and *The Silence in the Garden* (1988). He has also written dozens of plays, many for television and many based on his own stories or those of other writers, such as Charles Dickens, Thomas Hardy, Graham Greene, and Elizabeth Bowen.

TEACHING RESOURCES

The following resources can be used to enrich or extend the instruction for pp. 1088–1089.

Motivation

Interest Grabber Video, Tape 6

Background

Beyond Literature, p. 53

Take It to the Net

Visit www.phschool.com for background and hotlinks for "The Distant Past."

Literary Analysis

Literary Analysis and Reading Transparencies, Social Conflict, p. 106

Reading

Literary Analysis and Reading Transparencies, Questioning Causes and Effects, p. 105

BLOCK SCHEDULING: Resources marked with this symbol provide varied instruction during 90-minute blocks.

Preview

Connecting to the Literature

Joining a group means uniting with others. However, it can also mean separating from those who belong to different groups. In "The Distant Past," a brother and sister support a viewpoint and share a loyalty that is unpopular in their town. This story suggests that some differences can never really be overcome.

2 Literary Analysis

Social Conflict

Conflict, a struggle between opposing forces, is at the heart of most stories. Some conflicts are individual and personal; others are communal or universal. **Social conflict** refers to a struggle between those with opposing loyalties, interests, and views about the society in which they live. The underlined words in the following passage indicate a conflict about large social issues.

> They attended on Sundays St. Patrick's Protestant Church, a place that matched their mood, for prayers were still said there for the King whose sovereignty their country had denied.

In reading, notice how social conflict separates the two main characters from everyone else.

Connecting Literary Elements

Trevor explores the way social conflict in Ireland affects his characters' **motives,** the reasons and explanations for their actions. He seems to ask readers to consider this question: What role do social conflicts play in shaping people's motives and everyday behavior? As you read, figure out how he would answer this question—and whether you agree with him.

3 Reading Strategy

Questioning Causes and Effects

In reflecting on social conflicts and motives, you must determine why certain things happen. You can do this by **questioning causes and effects,** asking yourself what actions or conditions (causes) bring about other actions or conditions (effects). Use a chart like this one to question causes and effects as you read. Remember that the effect of one event can also be the cause of a later event.

Vocabulary Development

countenance (koun′ tə nəns) *n.* face; facial features (p. 1090)

adversity (ad vur′ sə tē) *n.* misfortune (p. 1091)

sovereignty (säv′ rən tē) *n.* supreme political authority (p. 1092)

anachronism (ə nak′ rə niz′ əm) *n.* something out of its proper time in history (p. 1093)

internment (in turn′ mənt) *n.* confinement; a form of imprisonment often practiced during a war (p. 1096)

2 Literary Analysis

Social Conflict

- Remind students that the term *conflict* refers to problems or complications in a story.
- Read the instruction about social conflict together as a class. Call students' attention to the excerpt from the story.
- Use the instruction for Connecting Literary Elements to connect social conflict to the characters' motives.
- Use the Social Conflict transparency in **Literary Analysis and Reading Transparencies,** p. 106, to show students examples of social conflict they will find in the story.

3 Reading Strategy

Questioning Causes and Effects

- Remind students that a *cause* makes something happen and an *effect* is the result. Some events can be both causes and effects.
- Then, tell students that a chain of causes and effects advances the plot in a short story. To illustrate this point, discuss the cause-and-effect chart on p. 1089.
- Instruct students to create a chart like the one shown on p. 1089 to question the causes and effects of events as they read "The Distant Past."

Vocabulary Development

- Pronounce each vocabulary word for students, and read the definitions as a class. Have students identify any words with which they are already familiar.

CUSTOMIZE INSTRUCTION FOR UNIVERSAL ACCESS

For Less Proficient Readers	For English Learners	For Advanced Readers
Make sure students understand one of the important conflicts in the story: that the Middletons have very little income despite having inherited the house and the property and all the prestige that comes with those items. The Middletons are by no means rich, although they may be perceived as such because of their circumstances.	Have students find evidence of social conflict in this story. Instruct them to note details from the story that demonstrate the conflict. Also, help students make sense of any unfamiliar language Trevor uses that isn't otherwise identified and defined.	Discuss with students that social conflict has existed in every society throughout history and has always affected the way people behave and think. Tell them that characters in realistic fiction are sometimes shaped by historical events that occur during the period in which the story is set.

E-Teach

Visit E-Teach at www.phschool.com for teachers' essays on how to teach, with questions and answers.

TEACH

Step-by-Step Teaching Guide for pp. 1090–1098

CUSTOMIZE INSTRUCTION
For Musical/Rhythmic Learners

The Irish rock group U2 has recorded songs that deal with the continuing Catholic-Protestant turmoil. To introduce this short story, you may want to play the song "Sunday, Bloody Sunday" while students read the lyrics. Discuss students' reactions.

❶ About the Selection

"The Distant Past" explores the effects of historical events and social change on relationships among neighbors in a village. When economic times are good and conflict between the Irish Catholics and the British government is eased, a once-wealthy British family living in Ireland is thought odd by villagers, but accepted nonetheless. When that conflict flares up again, the villagers' reaction to the family illustrates that social and political forces can have a profound impact on personal relationships.

❷ ▶Critical Viewing

Possible response: Students may suggest that the image shows the house set apart from and inaccessible to outsiders. The Middletons, who were once set apart by their wealth and status, are now set apart by their religion and loyalty to the crown.

❶ The Distant Past

William Trevor

Background

After five years of insurrection by the Irish against the British government, beginning with the Easter Rising in 1916, Ireland was divided. In the South, the Irish Free State was created. With 26 of Ireland's 32 counties and a Catholic majority, the Free State began as a self-governing dominion of the British Commonwealth. In 1948 it left the Commonwealth to become the Republic of Ireland, a separate country. In the North, the remaining six counties, all with a Protestant majority, were given home rule under British sovereignty.

The story is set in a town in the Republic of Ireland, not far from the border with Northern Ireland.

In the town and beyond it they were regarded as harmlessly peculiar. Odd, people said, and in time this reference took on a burnish of affection.

They had always been thin, silent with one another, and similar in appearance: a brother and sister who shared a family face. It was a bony countenance, with pale blue eyes and a sharp, well-shaped nose and high cheekbones. Their father had had it too, but unlike them their father had been an irresponsible and careless man, with red flecks in his cheeks that they didn't have at all. The Middletons of Carraveagh the family had once been known as, but now the brother and sister were just the Middletons, for Carraveagh didn't count any more, except to them.

countenance (koun′ tə nəns) *n.* face; facial features

❷ ▶Critical Viewing How does the image of this house illustrate the Middletons' relationship with the townspeople? **[Apply]**

TEACHING RESOURCES

The following resources can be used to enrich or extend the instruction for pp. 1090–1098.

Literary Analysis

- **Selection Support:** Literary Analysis, p. 248

Reading

- **Selection Support:** Reading Strategy, p. 247; Build Vocabulary, p. 245
- **Listening to Literature Audiocassettes,** Side 25
- **Listening to Literature Audio CDs,** CD 14

BLOCK SCHEDULING: Resources marked with this symbol provide varied instruction during 90-minute blocks.

They owned four Herefords,[1] a number of hens, and the house itself, three miles outside the town. It was a large house, built in the reign of George II,[2] a monument that reflected in its glory and later decay the fortunes of a family. As the brother and sister aged, its roof increasingly ceased to afford protection, rust ate at its gutters, grass thrived in two thick channels all along its avenue. Their father had mortgaged his inherited estate, so local rumor claimed, in order to keep a Catholic Dublin woman in brandy and jewels. When he died, in 1924, his two children discovered that they possessed only a dozen acres. It was

3 locally said also that this adversity hardened their will and that because of it they came to love the remains of Carraveagh more than they could ever have loved a husband or a wife. They blamed for their ill-fortune the Catholic Dublin woman whom they'd never met and they blamed as well the new national regime, contriving in their eccentric way to relate the two. In the days of the union jack[3] such women would have known their place—wasn't it all part and parcel?

adversity (ad vur´ sə tē) *n.* misfortune

4  **Reading Check**

How do the townspeople regard the Middletons?

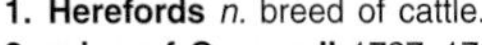

1. **Herefords** *n.* breed of cattle.
2. **reign of George II** 1727–1760.
3. **union jack** British flag; symbol of British rule.

3 Vocabulary Development

Latin Suffix *-ity (-ty)*

- Call students' attention to the word *adversity* and its definition. Tell students that the Latin suffix *-ity* (or *-ty*) means "the state or quality of."
- Have students suggest words that contain the suffix, and list them on the chalkboard.
- Next, have students look up the meanings of these words in a dictionary.
- Then direct students to reread the story, looking for places where they can replace an existing word or phrase with a word containing the Latin suffix *-ity* or *-ty.*
- Call on volunteers to read aloud their new sentences.

4 Reading Check

Answer: The townspeople find the Middletons odd but do feel affection toward them.

CUSTOMIZE INSTRUCTION FOR UNIVERSAL ACCESS

For Special Needs Students	For Advanced Readers
Students may benefit from reading along with a recorded version of the story. Use **Listening to Literature** Audiocassettes, Side 25, or **Listening to Literature** Audio CDs, CD 14. You may need to pause the recording occasionally to clarify word or phrase meaning and check for understanding.	After reading the story, ask students to explain how the decay in the fortunes of the Middletons can be seen as a metaphor for the decline in the fortunes of the British Empire. Point out that in the period following World War I, some British colonies demanded and achieved their independence.

5 Literary Analysis

Social Conflict

- Call on a volunteer to read aloud the bracketed passage.
- Ask students what institution stands in opposition to St. Patrick's Protestant Church.
  Answer: The Roman Catholic Church stands in opposition to it.

Monitor Progress Then, ask the Literary Analysis question on p. 1092: What social conflict is revealed in this passage?
Answer: Students may respond that the social conflict revealed here is that a patriotic English Protestant family still loyal to the English Crown is living among Catholics in a small Irish village.

6 Critical Viewing

Possible response: Students will probably say it would be easier to conceal a social conflict in a city because in a small town everyone tends to know everything about everyone else, including their loyalties, opinions, and beliefs.

5 Twice a week, on Fridays and Sundays, the Middletons journeyed into the town, first of all in a trap[4] and later in a Ford Anglia car. In the shops and elsewhere they made, quite gently, no secret of their continuing loyalty to the past. They attended on Sundays St. Patrick's Protestant Church, a place that matched their mood, for prayers were still said there for the King whose sovereignty their country had denied. The revolutionary regime would not last, they quietly informed the Reverend Packham—what sense was there in green-painted pillar boxes[5] and a language that nobody understood?

Literary Analysis
Social Conflict What social conflict is revealed in this paragraph?

sovereignty (säv′ rən tē) *n.* supreme political authority

On Fridays, when they took seven or eight dozen eggs to the town, they dressed in pressed tweeds and were accompanied over the years by a series of red setters, the breed there had always been at Carraveagh. They sold the eggs in Keogh's grocery and then had a drink with Mrs. Keogh in the part of her shop that was devoted to the consumption of refreshment. They enjoyed the occasion, for they liked Mrs. Keogh and were liked by her in return. Afterwards they shopped, chatting to the shopkeepers about whatever news there was, and then they went to Healy's Hotel for a few more drinks before driving home.

6 **▼ Critical Viewing** In a town this size, would it be easier to conceal a social conflict than it would be in a city? Why or why not? **[Analyze]**

. . . In spite of their loyalty to the past, they built up convivial relationships with the people of the town. Fat Driscoll, who kept the butcher's shop, used even to joke about the past when he stood with them in Healy's Hotel or stood behind his own counter cutting their slender chops or thinly slicing their liver. "Will you ever forget it, Mr. Middleton? I'd ha' run like a rabbit if you'd lifted a finger at me." Fat Driscoll would laugh then, rocking back on his heels with a glass of stout in his hand or banging their meat on to his weighing-scales. Mr. Middleton would smile. "There was alarm in your eyes, Mr. Driscoll," Miss Middleton would murmur, smiling also at the memory of the distant occasion.

Fat Driscoll, with a farmer called Maguire and another called Breen, had stood in the hall of Carraveagh, each of them in charge of a shotgun. The Middletons, children then, had been locked with their mother and father and an aunt into an upstairs room. Nothing else had happened: the expected British soldiers had not, after all, arrived and the men in the hall had eventually relaxed their vigil. "A massacre they wanted," the Middletons' father said after they'd gone. . . . "Bloody ruffians."

The Second World War took place. Two Germans, a man and his wife called Winkelmann who ran a glove factory in the town, were suspected by the Middletons of being spies for the Third Reich.[6] People laughed, for they knew the Winkelmanns well and could lend no credence to the Middletons' latest fantasy—typical of them, they explained to the Winkelmanns, who had been worried. Soon after the War the Reverend Packham died and was replaced by the Reverend Bradshaw, a younger

4. **trap** *n.* two-wheeled, horse-drawn carriage.
5. **pillar boxes** mail collection boxes.
6. **Third Reich** (rīk) German government under the Nazis (1933–1945).

ENRICHMENT: Social Studies Connection

Irish Struggle for Independence

Social conflict separated the Middletons from everyone else in their community; they were British patriots living in Ireland. Tell students that in the Irish struggle for independence in the early part of the last century, as in any highly charged sociopolitical movement, there were conflicts not only between people on opposing sides, but between people within a side. Rebellion leaders Michael Collins and Eamon de Valera became antagonists, although they fought for the same goals.

For a dynamic look at the issues in the conflict between the rebel leaders and the British government, and among the factions within the rebel movement itself, students can view the film *Michael Collins* (1996; directed by Neil Jordan).

man who laughed also and regarded the Middletons as an anachronism.
7 They protested when prayers were no longer said for the Royal Family in St. Patrick's, but the Reverend Bradshaw considered that their protests were as absurd as the prayers themselves had been. Why pray for the monarchy of a neighboring island when their own island had its chosen President now? The Middletons didn't reply to that argument. In the Reverend Bradshaw's presence they rose to their feet when the BBC played "God Save the King," and on the day of the coronation of Queen Elizabeth II they drove into the town with a small union jack propped up in the back window of their Ford Anglia.
8 "Bedad, you're a holy terror, Mr. Middleton!" Fat Driscoll laughingly exclaimed, noticing the flag as he lifted a tray of pork steaks from his display shelf. The Middletons smiled. It was a great day for the Commonwealth of Nations, they replied, a remark which further amused Fat Driscoll and which he later repeated in Phelan's public house. "Her Britannic Majesty," guffawed his friend Mr. Breen.

Situated in a valley that was noted for its beauty and with convenient access to rich rivers and bogs over which gamebirds flew, the town benefited from post-war tourism. Healy's Hotel changed its title and became, overnight, the New Ormonde. Shopkeepers had their shop-fronts painted and Mr. Healy organized an annual Salmon Festival. Even Canon Kelly, who had at first commented severely on the habits of

anachronism (ə nak′ rə niz′ əm) *n.* something out of its proper time in history

Reading Strategy
Questioning Causes and Effects What causes Fat Driscoll to react with amusement to the Middletons' loyalties, rather than with anger?

9 **Reading Check**
What did Fat Driscoll do at Carraveagh when the Middletons were children?

7 Background

History

Inform students that the changes in the church reflect the ongoing changes in society as a whole. Point out that the Irish Free State had become increasingly detached from Great Britain and in 1949 severed all ties with Britain and renamed itself the Republic of Ireland.

Also, tell students that Queen Elizabeth II was crowned in 1952, three years after Ireland officially severed ties with Great Britain. Tell them that "God Save the King (or Queen)" is the British national anthem.

8 Reading Strategy

Questioning Causes and Effects

- Call on a volunteer to read aloud the bracketed passage.

Monitor Progress Then, ask students the Reading Strategy question on p. 1093: What causes Fat Driscoll to react with amusement to the Middletons' loyalties, rather than with anger?
Possible response: Driscoll reacts with amusement because he finds it silly that the Middletons are still holding on to their British loyalties since Ireland is now a free state. Driscoll thinks the Middletons are behind the times.

9 Reading Check

Answer: Driscoll, along with other men, had temporarily held the Middletons prisoner in their own house during tense times.

CUSTOMIZE INSTRUCTION FOR UNIVERSAL ACCESS

For Gifted/Talented Students

Encourage interested students to turn the short story into a short play. Students can rewrite the text into play format. Challenge them to present all the necessary information without the use of a narrator. Tell students that they can create dialogue that does not exist within the text of the story in order to avoid using a narrator. They can recreate scenes from the past, fleshing them out with what they think people did or said. Remind them to use details from the text to support any additions they make. They should be able to base all of their newly created scenes on clues and details from the story; that is, from what they have learned about each character, they should be able to infer how a character would have acted or what the character would have said.

When students have a script they feel will work well, allow them time to memorize and practice their scenes. Have a class period set aside for the presentation of the play or plays.

10 Literary Analysis

Social Conflict and Motives

- Ask a volunteer to read aloud the bracketed passage.
- Then, ask students the Literary Analysis question on p. 1094: What motivates the Middletons to look forward to Fridays, even though they do not share the loyalties of the townspeople?
Possible response: As old age approaches and English influence in Ireland declines, the Middletons feel more and more isolated. In response, they seek out the companionship of those who are nearby. Some students may point out that the passage of time helps to smooth past difficulties.

Monitor Progress Discuss with students how prevalent they feel the social conflict is at this point in the story.
Possible response: The conflict is still there because the Middletons are still completely loyal to England and are still considered a bit of an oddity in the town, but the lines have softened and the villagers and Middletons feel a common bond.

the tourists, and in particular on the summertime dress of the women, was in the end obliged to confess that the morals of his flock remained unaffected. "God and good sense," he proclaimed, meaning God and his own teaching. In time he even derived pride from the fact that people with other values came briefly to the town and that the values esteemed by his parishioners were in no way diminished. . . .

From the windows of their convent the Loretto nuns observed the long, sleek cars with G.B. plates; English and American accents drifted on the breeze to them. Mothers cleaned up their children and sent them to the Golf Club to seek employment as caddies. Sweet shops sold holiday mementoes. The brown, soda and currant breads of Murphy-Flood's bakery were declared to be delicious. Mr. Healy doubled the number of local girls who served as waitresses in his dining room, and in the winter of 1961 he had the builders in again, working on an extension for which the Munster and Leinster Bank had lent him twenty-two thousand pounds.

But as the town increased its prosperity Carraveagh continued its decline. The Middletons were in their middle sixties now and were reconciled to a life that became more uncomfortable with every passing year. Together they roved the vast lofts of their house, placing old paint tins and flowerpot saucers beneath the drips from the roof. At night they sat over their thin chops in a dining room that had once been gracious and which in a way was gracious still, except for the faded appearance of furniture that was dry from lack of polish and of a wallpaper that time had rendered colorless. In the hall their father gazed down at them, framed in ebony and gilt, in the uniform of the Irish Guards. He had conversed with Queen Victoria, and even in their middle sixties they could still hear him saying that God and Empire and Queen formed a trinity unique in any worthy soldier's heart. In the hall hung the family crest, and on ancient Irish linen the Cross of St. George.[7]

The dog that accompanied the Middletons now was called Turloch, an animal whose death they dreaded for they felt they couldn't manage the antics of another pup. Turloch, being thirteen, moved slowly and was blind and a little deaf. He was a reminder to them of their own advancing years and of the effort it had become to tend the Herefords and collect the weekly eggs. More and more they looked forward to Fridays, to the warm companionship of Mrs. Keogh and Mr. Healy's chatter in the hotel. They stayed longer now with Mrs. Keogh and in the hotel, and idled longer in the shops, and drove
10 home more slowly. Dimly, but with no less loyalty, they still recalled the distant past and were listened to without ill-feeling when they spoke of it and of Carraveagh as it had been, and of the Queen whose company their careless father had known.

The visitors who came to the town heard about the Middletons and were impressed. It was a pleasant wonder, more than one of them

Literary Analysis
Social Conflict and Motives What motivates the Middletons to look forward to Fridays, even though they do not share the loyalties of the townspeople?

7. **St. George** patron saint of England.

remarked, that old wounds could heal so completely, that the Middletons continued in their loyalty to the past and that, in spite of it, they were respected in the town. When Miss Middleton had been ill with a form of pneumonia in 1958 Canon Kelly had driven out to Carraveagh twice a week with pullets and young ducks that his housekeeper had dressed. "An upright couple," was the Canon's public opinion of the Middletons, and he had been known to add that eccentric views would hurt you less than malice. "We can disagree without guns in this town," Mr. Healy pronounced in his cocktail room, and his visitors usually replied that as far as they could see that was the result of living in a Christian country. That the Middletons bought their meat from a man who had once locked them into an upstairs room and had then waited to shoot soldiers in their hall was a fact that amazed the seasonal visitors. You lived and learned, they remarked to Mr. Healy.

The Middletons, privately, often considered that they led a strange life. Alone in their two beds at night they now and again wondered why they hadn't just sold Carraveagh forty-eight years ago when their father had died—why had the tie been so strong and why had they in perversity encouraged it? They didn't fully know, nor did they attempt to discuss the matter in any way. Instinctively they had remained at Carraveagh, instinctively feeling that it would have been cowardly to go. Yet often it seemed to them now to be no more than a game they played, this worship of the distant past. And at other times it seemed as real and as important as the remaining acres of land, and the house itself.

"Isn't that shocking?" Mr. Healy said one day in 1967. "Did you hear about that, Mr. Middleton, blowing up them post offices in Belfast?"

Mr. Healy, red-faced and short-haired, spoke casually in his Cocktail Room, making midday conversation. He had commented in much the same way at breakfast-time, looking up from the *Irish Independent*. Everyone in the town had said it too: that the blowing up of sub-post offices in Belfast was a shocking matter.

"A bad business," Fat Driscoll remarked, wrapping the Middletons' meat. "We don't want that old stuff all over again."

"We didn't want it in the first place," Miss Middleton reminded him. He laughed, and she laughed, and so did her brother. Yes, it was a game, she thought—how could any of it be as real or as important as the afflictions and problems of the old butcher himself, his rheumatism and his reluctance to retire? Did her brother, she wondered, privately think so too?

"Come on, old Turloch," he said, stroking the flank of the red setter with the point of his shoe, and she reflected that you could never tell

in context World Events

11 ***"The Troubles" in Northern Ireland***

The "shocking" event to which Mr. Healy refers marks the start of "The Troubles," an approximately thirty-year period of strife, beginning in the 1960s, between majority Protestants and minority Catholics in Northern Ireland. During this time, about 40,000 people were wounded and 3,100 killed in shootings and bombings.

The source of the violence goes back about three hundred years to a time when Britain encouraged Scottish Protestants to emigrate to Northern Ireland and confiscate land owned by Catholics. For the next two hundred years, there was periodic violence between the two groups.

In 1922, the southern part of Ireland became the Irish Free State, which would eventually become the Republic of Ireland. The northern part, with a Protestant majority, remained part of Britain. Catholics who still lived in the North experienced discrimination, a situation that led to "The Troubles." It was not until 1996 that a cease-fire was declared and negotiations begun. The Middletons would probably have died by then.

12  **Reading Check**

What "shocking" event occurs in 1967?

11 Background

History

Inform students that the "shocking" event that started "The Troubles," the bombings of the post offices in Belfast, were at first attributed to the rebellious group known as the Irish Republican Army (IRA). Later, however, it was determined that the explosions were the work of a Protestant paramilitary group keen on removing the Prime Minister from office.

12 Reading Check

Answer: The shocking event in 1967 was the bombings of the post offices in Belfast.

CUSTOMIZE INSTRUCTION FOR UNIVERSAL ACCESS

For Advanced Readers

Tell students that Nobel Prize-winning Irish poet William Butler Yeats (1865–1939) took an active role in political movements bent on achieving Ireland's independence from England. In 1922, he was appointed a senator of the new Irish Free State. In some of his poems, Yeats celebrated the efforts of the early fighters and martyrs for Irish freedom and referred to some of the bloody historical events that paved the way for the eventual success of the rebellion.

Encourage students to look through Yeats's work for poems that reflect his political views about the struggle for Irish independence. Have them choose one poem to display on a poster with illustrations, pictures, or historical notes to accompany it. Allow time for students to read their chosen poems aloud to classmates, and then hang the posters in the classroom for the class to peruse.

13 Background

History

Inform students that Belfast is the capital of Northern Ireland and that Derry, or Londonderry, is a seaport there. Tell them that in 1969, following bloody riots in those two cities, British troops were sent into Northern Ireland. In 1972, as the violence continued, the British government took over direct control of the region.

14 Literary Analysis

Social Conflict

- Read aloud the bracketed passage.
- Then, ask students to describe how the Middletons' relationship with their neighbors is affected by the early stages of the new conflict. **Answer:** At first, it seems as if they will maintain their friendly attitudes toward each other. This is illustrated by Mr. Healy's attempt to commiserate with Mr. Middleton over the tourist situation.

15 ▶ Critical Viewing

Possible response: Some students may say that the flags symbolize the divided loyalty of the Middletons; they are loyal both to Great Britain and to their home and community in Ireland. Others might point to the conflict caused by living under one flag while remaining loyal to another.

what he was thinking. Certainly it wasn't the kind of thing you wanted to talk about.

"I've put him in a bit of mince," Fat Driscoll said, which was something he often did these days, pretending the mince would otherwise be thrown away. There'd been a red setter about the place that night when he waited in the hall for the soldiers; Breen and Maguire had pushed it down into a cellar, frightened of it.

"There's a heart of gold in you, Mr. Driscoll," Miss Middleton murmured, nodding and smiling at him. He was the same age as she was, sixty-six—he should have shut up shop years ago. He would have, he'd once told them, if there'd been a son to leave the business to. As it was, he'd have to sell it and when it came to the point he found it hard to make the necessary arrangements. "Like us and Carraveagh," she'd said, even though on the face of it it didn't seem the same at all.

13 Every evening they sat in the big old kitchen, hearing the news. It was only in Belfast and Derry, the wireless said; outside Belfast and Derry you wouldn't know anything was happening at all. On Fridays they listened to the talk in Mrs. Keogh's bar and in the hotel. "Well, thank God it has nothing to do with the South," Mr. Healy said often, usually repeating the statement.

The first British soldiers landed in the North of Ireland, and soon people didn't so often say that outside Belfast and Derry you wouldn't know anything was happening. There were incidents in Fermanagh and Armagh, in border villages and towns. One Prime Minister resigned and then another one. The troops were unpopular, the newspapers said; internment became part of the machinery of government. In the town, in St. Patrick's Protestant Church and in the Church of the Holy Assumption, prayers for peace were offered, but no peace came.

14 "We're hit, Mr. Middleton," Mr. Healy said one Friday morning. "If there's a dozen visitors this summer it'll be God's own stroke of luck for us."

"Luck?"

"Sure, who wants to come to a country with all that malarkey in it?"

"But it's only in the North."

"Tell that to your tourists, Mr. Middleton."

The town's prosperity ebbed. The border was more than sixty miles away, but over that distance had spread some wisps of the fog of war. As anger rose in the town at the loss of fortune so there rose also the

15 ▲ **Critical Viewing** What do these flags symbolize to the characters in the story? **[Analyze]**

internment (in turn′ mənt) *n.* confinement; a form of imprisonment often practiced during war

ENRICHMENT: Career Connection

Travel Agent

Times are considerably better now for tourism in Ireland than they were in the Middletons' later years. Have groups of students imagine that they are travel agents specializing in creative theme tours of the Republic of Ireland. Invite them to choose a specific theme and plan a trip accordingly, presenting their efforts in a travel brochure. For instance, one group can choose "Sights and Sounds of the Rebellion," while others may select "Irish Castles and Great Homes," "Irish Literary Landmarks," "Irish Music and Dance," "Crafts of Ireland," and so on.

To gather ideas for their brochures, groups can contact tourist offices, visit the library and bookstores, look at travel videos, browse the Internet, and talk with people who have visited or lived in Ireland. Have groups contribute their polished brochures to an Irish travel center set up by the class or to the school library.

kind of talk there had been in the distant past. There was talk of atrocities and counteratrocities, and of guns and gelignite[8] and the rights of people. There was bitterness suddenly in Mrs. Keogh's bar because of the lack of trade, and in the empty hotel there was bitterness also.

On Fridays, only sometimes at first, there was a silence when the Middletons appeared. It was as though, going back nearly twenty years, people remembered the union jack in the window of their car and saw it now in a different light. It wasn't something to laugh at any more, nor were certain words that the Middletons had gently spoken, nor were they themselves just an old, peculiar couple. Slowly the change crept about, all around them in the town, until Fat Driscoll didn't wish it to be remembered that he had ever given them mince for their dog. He had stood with a gun in the enemy's house, waiting for soldiers so that soldiers might be killed—it was better that people should remember that.

One day Canon Kelly looked the other way when he saw the Middletons' car coming and they noticed this movement of his head, although he hadn't wished them to. And on another day Mrs. O'Brien, who had always been keen to talk to them in the hotel, didn't reply when they addressed her.

The Middletons naturally didn't discuss these rebuffs but they each of them privately knew that there was no conversation they could have at this time with the people of the town. The stand they had taken and kept to for so many years no longer seemed ridiculous in the town. Had they driven with a union jack now they would, astoundingly, have been shot.

"It will never cease." He spoke disconsolately one night, standing by the dresser where the wireless was.

She washed the dishes they'd eaten from, and the cutlery. "Not in our time," she said.

"It is worse than before."

"Yes, it is worse than before."

They took from the walls of the hall the portrait of their father in the uniform of the Irish Guards because it seemed wrong to them that at this time it should hang there. They took down also the crest of their family and the Cross of St. George, and from a vase on the drawing-room mantelpiece they removed the small union jack that had been there since the coronation of Queen Elizabeth II. They did not remove these articles in fear but in mourning for the *modus vivendi*[9] that had existed for so long between them and the people of the town. They had given their custom to a butcher who had planned to shoot down soldiers in their hall and he, in turn, had given them mince for their dog. For fifty years they had experienced, after suspicion had seeped away, a tolerance that never again in the years that were left to them would they know.

8. **gelignite** *n.* explosive.
9. ***modus vivendi*** (vi ven′ dī) Latin for "manner of getting along."

Literary Analysis
Social Conflict and Motives At this point, do townspeople seem motivated more by social pressure or by their own individual judgments? Explain.

Reading Check
What happens to the town's prosperity during the troubles?

16 Literary Analysis

Social Conflict and Motives

- Read aloud the bracketed passage.
- Ask students how Fat Driscoll and Mrs. O'Brien respond to the Middletons.
  Answer: Driscoll wishes to be remembered for his violence toward the Middletons instead of his kindness to their dog; Mrs. O'Brien does not reply to the Middletons when they address her.
- Then, ask students the Literary Analysis question on p. 1097: At this point, do the townspeople seem motivated more by social pressure or by their own individual judgments?
  Possible response: The townspeople are motivated by social pressure, not their individual judgments. They are feeling the pressure of the conflict and are resentful of what the Middletons represent—Britain, which is killing their trade and tourism—not the Middletons themselves as individual people.

17 Reading Check

Answer: The town's prosperity decreases—just about comes to a halt—during "The Troubles."

CUSTOMIZE INSTRUCTION FOR UNIVERSAL ACCESS

For Less Proficient Readers	For Advanced Readers
Discuss with students the difference between the past and present. Have students consider how Driscoll's attitude has changed based on his reaction to the Middletons' dog—How did he react to the dog long ago when he went to their house with a shotgun? (He was scared of the dog then and locked it in the basement.) How did he react to the dog so many years later when the Middletons bought meat in his store? (He sent home treats to their dog—mince—for free.)	Encourage interested students to research the political happenings in Ireland in recent years and now. Have them use sources in the library, on the Internet, or from news programs or publications to gather their information. Instruct them to compare and contrast the state of affairs now to what it was in "The Distant Past." Allow time for students to present their findings to the class.

ASSESS

Answers for p. 1098

Review and Assess

1. Some students may describe the Middletons as naïve because they don't understand how outside conflicts can affect their lives and those of the people around them. Others may think they are simply stuck in the past, detached from and oblivious to change.
2. **(a)** Their father is responsible, but they blame his girlfriend and the new government. **(b)** The Middletons were running out of money and influence, and their property was deteriorating at about the same time the British Empire was dwindling through the loss of many of its colonies.
3. **(a)** For most of the story, they have a cordial relationship with the townspeople. **(b)** It is surprising because they were at political odds with the villagers, but as long as the town prospered, it did not seem to matter.
4. **(a)** As violence erupts in the North, tourism declines in the town. **(b)** As the town's prosperity decreases, the people blame Great Britain, which the Middletons represent to them. Therefore, they blame the Middletons by association. **(c)** Students may say that deeply felt loyalties never change and that old wounds never heal—they lie in wait, ready to be revived by new stress or conflict.
5. Some students will agree that they would have suffered less had they been murdered. As it was, they lived a lonely, isolated life, suffering the anger and silent aggression of their neighbors.
6. Answers will vary. Students should give examples, such as outbreaks of old conflicts or the disappearance of such conflicts, that show the power or inability of the past to influence the present.

One November night their dog died and he said to her after he had buried it that they must not be depressed by all that was happening. They would die themselves and the house would become a ruin because there was no one to inherit it, and the distant past would be set to rest. But she disagreed: the *modus vivendi* had been easy for them, she pointed out, because they hadn't really minded the dwindling of their fortunes while the town prospered. It had given them a life, and a kind of dignity: you could take a pride out of living in peace.

He did not say anything and then, because of the emotion that both of them felt over the death of their dog, he said in a rushing way that they could no longer at their age hope to make a living out of the remains of Carraveagh. They must sell the hens and the four Herefords. As he spoke, he watched her nodding, agreeing with the sense of it. Now and again, he thought, he would drive slowly into the town, to buy groceries and meat with the money they had saved, and to face the silence that would sourly thicken as their own two deaths came closer and death increased in another part of their island. She felt him thinking that and she knew that he was right. Because of the distant past they would die friendless. It was worse than being murdered in their beds.

Review and Assess

Thinking About the Selection

1. **Respond:** Would you describe the Middletons as odd, foolish, or courageous, or would you use some other adjective? Explain.
2. **(a) Recall:** Who is responsible for the Middletons' reduced economic position? Whom do they blame? **(b) Connect:** How does the decline in the Middletons' fortunes parallel the decline of the British Empire?
3. **(a) Recall:** What kind of relationship do the Middletons have with the townspeople through most of the story? **(b) Analyze:** What, if anything, is unexpected or surprising about this relationship?
4. **(a) Recall:** How is the town altered by the violence in the North? **(b) Analyze Cause and Effect:** What is the link between these changes and the changes in the town's attitudes toward the Middletons? **(c) Draw Conclusions:** What does the change in attitude toward the Middletons suggest about human nature?
5. **Evaluate:** Do you agree with Mr. Middleton that he and his sister would have been better off "murdered"? Explain.
6. **Speculate:** Do your observations and reading suggest that the "distant past" can influence events in the present? Why or why not?

ASSESSMENT PRACTICE: Writing Skills

Style **(For more practice, see Test Preparation Workbook, p. 53.)**

Many tests require students to recognize effective stylistic devices and language. Use the following sample test item to teach students how to recognize the tone of a passage.

> Their…father had been an irresponsible and careless man, with red flecks in his cheeks that they didn't have at all. The Middletons of Carraveagh the family had once been known as, but now the brother and sister were just the Middletons, for Carraveagh didn't count any more, except to them.

Which of these *best* describes the tone of the selection?

A neutral
B sad
C instructive
D lively

Lead students to recognize that the description evokes sad emotions in the reader so *A, C,* and *D* are incorrect. The correct answer is *B.*

Review and Assess

Literary Analysis

Social Conflict

1. What is the **social conflict** between the Middletons and the townspeople?
2. Using a chart like this one, show how this social conflict changes or does not change in response to various outside events.

Outside Events	Anglo–Irish War (Fat Driscoll at Carraveagh)	World War II	Period of Prosperity After World War II	Beginning of "The Troubles"
Effects on Social Conflict				

3. How do the changes in Fat Driscoll's relationship with the Middletons reflect changes in Ireland's level of conflict?
4. Explain the links among these items: the social conflict in the story, the title of the story, and the theme of the story.

Connecting Literary Elements

5. What do you think is the **motive** for the Middletons' "continuing loyalty to the past"?
6. What motivates the townspeople to think of the Middletons for many years "as harmlessly peculiar"?
7. (a) Do you think the author sees the social conflict between his characters as being motivated primarily by their independent choices or by social pressures? Explain. (b) Would Trevor say his character can escape "the distant past"? Explain.

Reading Strategy

Questioning Causes and Effects

8. Show a **cause** for each of the following events and an **effect** that results from each: (a) The Middletons drive into town with a small Union Jack. (b) Tourists stop coming to the town.

Extend Understanding

9. **History Connection:** What events of today will influence future events when our times are the "distant past"? Explain.

Quick Review

A **social conflict** is a struggle between people with opposing loyalties, interests, or views about society.

Characters' **motives** are the reasons or explanations for their actions and decisions.

To **question causes and effects,** determine how certain actions or conditions (causes) bring about other actions or conditions (effects).

 **Take It to the Net**

www.phschool.com

Take the interactive self-test online to check your understanding of the selection.

ENRICHMENT: Further Reading

Other Works by William Trevor

A Standard of Behavior

Angels at the Ritz, and Other Stories

Family Sins

 **Take It to the Net**

Visit www.phschool.com for more information on William Trevor.

Answers for p. 1099

Review and Assess

1. The social conflict is the differing loyalties of the villagers and the Middletons.
2. Sample response: **Event:** Anglo-Irish War; **Effect:** conflict intensified, Middletons endangered; **Event:** World War II; **Effect:** Middletons' suspicion of German couple elicits amusement; **Event:** Post-war prosperity; **Effect:** Middletons' declining fortunes increase their alienation; **Event:** "The Troubles"; **Effect:** conflict worsens; Middletons blamed.
3. Driscoll shuns the Middletons as the level of conflict rises.
4. The political conflict between Great Britain and Ireland creates the social conflict in the story and reflects the theme: the power of historical forces from "the distant past."
5. Students may say the Middletons continue to be loyal to their past because it is what they feel defines who they are.
6. The Middletons are nice people and are therefore considered harmless; because they hold onto their past loyalty to Great Britain, they seem a bit peculiar to the Irish villagers.
7. **(a)** Possible response: The Middletons are motivated by a definition of their role that dates from their birth. The villagers drop their natural friendliness toward and fondness of the Middletons as soon as events remind them of their (largely symbolic) differences. Both are motivated by social pressures. **(b)** Possible response: The characters cannot escape the distant past. However distant it grows, it is still ready to assign roles and shape actions in the present, when the occasion arises.
8. **(a)** The Middletons drive into town with a small Union Jack because they are ardent supporters of the British Crown; the townspeople find it funny. **(b)** As a result of the violence in the North, tourists stop coming to the town and the villagers start to blame the Middletons because of their British allegiances.

continued

Answers continued

9. Students may say that events involving military conflict, whether within our own country or abroad, will most likely affect future events.

EXTEND

Answers for p. 1100

❶ Vocabulary Development

Word Analysis

1. serenity; The music gave me a sense of serenity.
2. civility; Even though they were angry, the people maintained their civility when conversing.
3. adversity; The campers encountered one adversity after another.

Spelling Strategy

1. payment
2. enjoyment
3. improvement

Fluency: Sentence Completion

1. anachronism
2. sovereignty
3. adversity
4. countenance
5. internment

❷ Grammar and Style

1. The Middletons, who had once lived comfortably, found themselves impoverished.
2. They rode to town, where they had friendly encounters with the townspeople.
3. The dog that accompanied them was a red setter.
4. The shopkeepers with whom they did business considered them odd.
5. They made the trip back to their rundown home, which they called Carraveagh.

Writing Application

Sample sentences:

"The Distant Past," which was written by William Trevor, is about two loyal British people who live in Ireland. The main characters, who are a brother and sister, live on a rundown estate left to them by their father. The story's plot revolves around their conflict with the townsfolk, who do not share their loyalties. The old conflict between the townsfolk and these characters, which has been lain dormant, resurfaces. The story shows that the conflicts that existed in the past can still affect the present.

Integrate Language Skills

❶ Vocabulary Development Lesson

Word Analysis: Latin Suffix *-ity (-ty)*

In "The Distant Past," two characters experience *adversity* ("misfortune") because they insist on the *sovereignty* ("ruling power") of the British crown. Both words contain the suffix *-ity* (or *-ty*), meaning "the state or the quality of." In your notebook, add *-ity* to each word—deleting a final *e* if necessary—and use the new word in a sentence.

1. serene 2. civil 3. adverse

Spelling Strategy

Adding the suffix *-ment* changes certain verbs to nouns without affecting the spelling of the word root: *intern* + *-ment* = *internment*. In your notebook, add *-ment* to these verbs:

1. pay 2. enjoy 3. improve

Fluency: Sentence Completion

Review the vocabulary list on page 1089. Then, choose the word from the vocabulary list that best completes each sentence.

1. The townspeople regarded the Middletons as an __?__.
2. The Middletons did not question the __?__ of the English king.
3. Financial __?__ bore down on them after their father's death.
4. Kindly eyes sparkled from the sister's careworn __?__.
5. Townspeople shuddered, horrified, at news of the unjust __?__ of innocent citizens.

❷ Grammar and Style Lesson

Restrictive and Nonrestrictive Adjective Clauses

A subordinate clause is a group of words that contains a subject and a verb but cannot stand alone as a sentence. An **adjective clause** is a subordinate clause that modifies a noun or pronoun. A **restrictive adjective clause** contains essential information, so it is not set off by commas. In contrast, a **nonrestrictive adjective clause** contains information that is not essential, so it is set off by commas.

Restrictive: Mr. Healey doubled the number of local girls who served as waitresses in his dining room, . . . (essential: tells which *girls*)

Nonrestrictive: Fat Driscoll, who kept the butcher's shop, used even to joke about the past. . . . (nonessential: modifies *Driscoll*)

Practice In your notebook, underline each adjective clause and add commas where needed:

1. The Middletons who had once lived comfortably found themselves impoverished.
2. They rode to town where they had friendly encounters with the townspeople.
3. The dog that accompanied them was a red setter.
4. The shopkeepers with whom they did business considered them odd.
5. They made the trip back to their rundown home which they called Carraveagh.

Writing Application Write five sentences about "The Distant Past," using an adjective clause in each and inserting commas around the clause where necessary.

WG Prentice Hall Writing and Grammar Connection: Chapter 19, Section 3

TEACHING RESOURCES

The following resources can be used to enrich or extend the instruction for pp. 1100–1101.

Vocabulary

- **Selection Support,** Build Vocabulary, p. 245
- **Vocabulary and Spelling Practice Book** (Use this booklet for skills enrichment.)

Grammar

- **Selection Support,** Grammar and Style, p. 246
- **Writing and Grammar,** Diamond Level, p. 458
- **Daily Language Practice Transparencies**

Writing

- **Writing and Grammar,** Diamond Level, p. 155
- **Writing and Grammar iText CD-ROM**

BLOCK SCHEDULING: Resources marked with this symbol provide varied instruction during 90-minute blocks.

❸ Writing Lesson

Persuasive Poster

During "The Troubles," the Middletons or some townspeople might have created a persuasive poster to advocate their side of the conflict. Design a poster that one of the factions might have displayed.

Prewriting Review the historical background in the box on page 1095. Then, choose a side, and note poster ideas on a chart like this one.

Model: Planning Key Features of a Persuasive Poster

	Headline	Visual Image	Text
Tips for Feature	Brief and catchy	Communicates instantly; goes with headline	Briefly persuades viewer to think or act in a certain way
Notes			

Drafting Referring to your chart, (1) write a one-sentence headline that tells viewers what they should know or do, (2) draw or find a visual to support your headline, and (3) write a few brief sentences to inform or direct viewers.

Revising Display your poster, and have classmates role-play a group of townspeople viewing it. Ask them to evaluate whether it takes a position that one side in the conflict would have endorsed and whether it is persuasive. Make changes based on their comments.

WG Prentice Hall Writing and Grammar Connection: Chapter 8, Section 3

❹ Extension Activities

Research and Technology With classmates, stage a **celebration of Irish culture** that includes music, food, and storytelling.

- Gather information from history books and Web sites.
- Interview Irish members of the community
- Find tapes and CDs of Irish music to play
- Find recipes from which to prepare Irish foods.

Schedule and present your celebration. **[Group Activity]**

Listening and Speaking Imagine that Miss Middleton has died. As Fat Driscoll, give the **eulogy** at her funeral service. Present a vivid and honest portrait of the deceased and your relationship with her. To play the role of Fat Driscoll convincingly, review the story to determine the speech patterns and humor that suit his character.

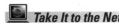

Take It to the Net www.phschool.com

Go online for an additional research activity using the Internet.

Lesson Support for p. 1101

❸ Writing Lesson

- Have students work in pairs to complete this activity—you may want to try to pair up less artistic students with an artistic partner.
- Tell students that to be effective, their posters must be visually stimulating, brief—saying only what needs to be said—and clear—stating exactly what they propose people do.
- Remind students to be as exact as possible when choosing their words, and to leave out any words or details that don't advance their arguments.
- Evaluate students' posters using the Persuasion: Advertisement rubric in **Performance Assessment and Portfolio Management,** p. 19.

❹ Listening and Speaking

- Discuss the concept of eulogies. If possible, students should read actual eulogies to get a better appreciation of their style and tone.
- Have them gather information about Miss Middleton, about Driscoll, and about their friendship, rereading parts of the story as necessary to check the details.
- Have students write and edit their eulogies and then practice their delivery prior to presenting them to the class.

CUSTOMIZE INSTRUCTION for Universal Access

To address different learning styles, use the following activities suggested in the **Extension Activities** booklet, p. 53.

- For Verbal/Linguistic Learners, use Activity 5.
- For Interpersonal and Verbal/ Linguistic Learners, use Activity 6.
- For Visual/Spatial and Bodily/ Kinesthetic Learners, use Activity 7.

ASSESSMENT RESOURCES

The following resources can be used to assess students' knowledge and skills.

Selection Assessment

Formal Assessment, pp. 255–257

Open Book Test, pp. 156–158

Test Bank Software

Got It! Assessment Videotapes, Tape 5

Take It to the Net

Visit www.phschool.com for self-tests and additional questions on the "The Distant Past."

Writing Rubric

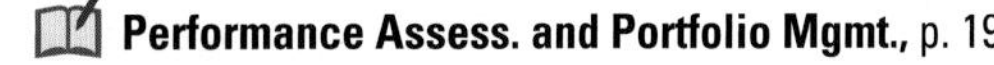
Performance Assess. and Portfolio Mgmt., p. 19

Workbook

Transparencies

Skill Book

CD-ROM

Follower ✦ Two Lorries ✦ Outside History

Lesson Objectives and CA Correlations

1. **To analyze and respond to literary elements**
   - Literary Analysis: Diction and Style **R 3.3**
   - Comparing Literary Works **R 3.4**
2. **To read, comprehend, analyze, and critique a poem**
   - Reading Strategy: Summarizing
   - Reading Check Questions
   - Review and Assess Questions
3. **To develop word analysis skills, fluency, and systematic vocabulary**
   - Vocabulary Development Lesson: Latin Root *-mort-* **R 1.1, 1.2**
4. **To understand and apply written and oral language conventions**
   - Spelling Strategy **LC 1.2**
   - Grammar and Style Lesson: Concrete and Abstract Nouns **LC 1.1**
5. **To understand and apply appropriate writing and research strategies**
   - Writing Lesson: Poem With a Strong Central Image **W 1.1, 1.2, 1.4, 1.9**
   - Extension Activity: Report **W 1.8, 2.4**
   - Assessment Practice (ATE)
6. **To understand and apply listening and speaking strategies**
   - Extension Activity: Interpretative Reading **LS 2.5**

STEP-BY-STEP TEACHING GUIDE	PACING GUIDE
PRETEACH	
Motivate Students and Provide Background	
Use the Motivation activity (ATE p. 1102)	5 min.
Read and discuss author and background features (SE/ATE pp. 1102, 1107) [A]	5 min.
Introduce the Concepts	
Introduce the Literary Analysis and Reading Strategy (SE/ATE p. 1103) [A]	15 min.
Pronounce the vocabulary words and read their definitions (SE p. 1103)	5 min.
TEACH	
Monitor Comprehension	
Informally monitor comprehension by circulating while students read independently or in groups [A]	10 min.
Monitor students' comprehension with the Reading Check notes (SE/ATE pp. 1107, 1109)	as students read
Develop vocabulary with Vocabulary notes (SE pp. 1106, 1109, 1110; ATE p. 1110)	as students read
Develop Understanding	
Develop students' understanding of diction and style with the Literary Analysis annotation (SE/ATE p. 1107) [A]	5 min.
Develop students' ability to summarize with the Reading Strategy annotations (SE/ATE p. 1107)	5 min.
ASSESS	
Assess Mastery	
Assess students' mastery of the Reading Strategy and Literary Analysis by having them answer the Review and Assess questions (SE/ATE p. 1111)	15 min.
Use one or more of the print and media Assessment Resources (ATE p. 1113) [A]	up to 45 min.
EXTEND	
Apply Understanding	
Have students complete the Vocabulary Development Lesson and the Grammar and Style Lesson (SE p. 1112) [A]	20 min.
Apply students' knowledge of choosing a strong organizing image using the Writing Lesson (SE/ATE p. 1113) [A]	45 min.
Apply students' understanding using one or more of the Extension Activities (SE p. 1113)	20–90 min.

A **ACCELERATED INSTRUCTION:**
Use the strategies and activities identified with an .

UNIVERSAL ACCESS
● = Below-Level Students
▲ = On-Level Students
■ = Above-Level Students

Time and Resource Manager

Reading Level: Easy, Average, Average
Average Number of Instructional Days: 4

RESOURCES		
PRINT	**TRANSPARENCIES**	**TECHNOLOGY**
• **Beyond Literature,** Career Connection: Contemporary Farmer, p. 54 ▲ ■		• **Interest Grabber Video,** Tape 6 ● ▲ ■
• **Selection Support Workbook:** ● ▲ ■ Literary Analysis, p. 252 Reading Strategy, p. 251 Build Vocabulary, p. 249	• **Literary Analysis and Reading Transparencies,** pp. 107 and 108 ● ▲ ■	
		• **Listening to Literature** ● ▲ ■ Audiocassettes, Side 26 Audio CDs, CD 14
• **Literatura en español** ● ▲ • **Literary Analysis for Enrichment** ■		
• **Formal Assessment:** Selection Test, pp. 258–260 ● ▲ ■ • **Open Book Test,** pp. 159–161 ● ▲ ■ • PRENTICE HALL ASSESSMENT SYSTEM ● ▲ ■	• PRENTICE HALL ASSESSMENT SYSTEM ● ▲ ■ Skills Practice Answers and Explanations on Transparencies ● ▲ ■	• **Test Bank Software** ● ▲ ■ • **Got It! Assessment Videotapes,** Tape 5 ● ▲
• **Selection Support Workbook:** ● ▲ ■ Grammar and Style, p. 250 • **Writing and Grammar,** Diamond Level ● ▲ ■ • **Extension Activities,** p. 54 ● ▲ ■	• **Daily Language Practice Transparencies** ● ▲	• **Writing and Grammar iText CD-ROM** ● ▲ ■ ***Take It to the Net*** www.phschool.com

BLOCK SCHEDULING: Use one 90-minute class period to preteach the selections and have students read them. Use a second 90-minute class period to assess students' mastery of skills and have them complete one of the Extension Activities.

PRETEACH

Step-by-Step Teaching Guide for pp. 1102–1103

Motivation

Ask the class to brainstorm for television shows, rock groups, cartoon shows, and fads that were popular when they were around eight years old. List responses on the board. Then, ask students to observe how they now view the things listed. For example, do the shows seem silly? Also, ask students what they learned from those past entertainments. Then, tell students that the poems in this section all deal with how the poets' pasts form part of their present.

Interest Grabber Video

As an alternative, play "'Outside History': Eavan Boland on Appreciating Literature," on Tape 6 to engage student interest.

1 Background

More About the Authors

Seamus Heaney

Seamus Heaney belonged to a group of poets when he was in college at the University of Belfast in Northern Ireland. He has written of these friends: "[We] used to talk poetry day after day with an intensity and prejudice that cannot but have left a mark on us all." Heaney's modern translation of *Beowulf* was met with widespread acclaim.

Eavan Boland

Eavan Boland's role in the poetic tradition in Ireland is an important one. She has secured a place for the feminine experience in the pantheon of Irish literature, traditionally a male domain. Boland's evocative poetry is often critical of the Irish political and cultural legacy.

Prepare to Read

1 Follower ◆ Two Lorries ◆ Outside History

Seamus Heaney (b. 1939)

Born in County Derry, Northern Ireland, Seamus Heaney has devoted much of his poetry to the life and history of his homeland. He is a gifted traditionalist whom the American poet Robert Lowell called "the most important Irish poet since Yeats." Heaney has earned that high praise with visionary books of poetry, like *Seeing Things* (1991) and *The Spirit Level* (1996), and with his brilliant lectures on poetry, collected in *The Redress of Poetry* (1995).

A Happy Childhood The eldest of nine children, Heaney spent a happy childhood on a farm that had been in his family for generations. He has said that his deep regard for tradition grew from his early experiences in the countryside.

Leaving Home Heaney first published as an undergraduate at Queen's University in Belfast, Northern Ireland. In 1972, having struggled with the role of the artist in Northern Ireland's troubled political climate, he left and settled in the independent Irish Republic. His departure was called an artistic necessity by some and by others a betrayal. Heaney nevertheless remains the leading Irish poet—Republican or Northern.

Popular Success Heaney's accessible and deeply felt poetry has achieved a popularity that is rare among modern poets. Readers around the world have generated a strong demand for his poems, including his best-selling translation of *Beowulf* (2000). His readings are well attended by enthusiastic fans.

Since 1984, he has been Boylston Professor of Rhetoric and Poetry at Harvard. From 1989 to 1994 he also held the chair of Professor of Poetry at Oxford. In 1995, Heaney received the Nobel Prize for Literature.

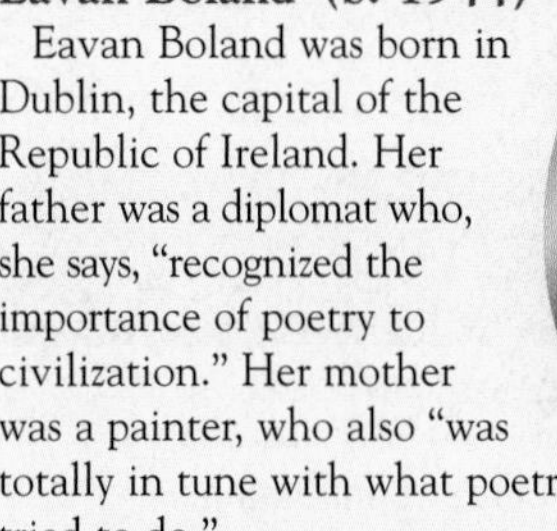

Eavan Boland (b. 1944)

Eavan Boland was born in Dublin, the capital of the Republic of Ireland. Her father was a diplomat who, she says, "recognized the importance of poetry to civilization." Her mother was a painter, who also "was totally in tune with what poetry tried to do."

Away From Ireland During much of Boland's early life, she was away from Ireland. When she was five, her father became ambassador to Great Britain and the family moved to London. Later, Boland was sent to school in New York City. There, she experienced anti-Irish hostility and felt "a great sense of isolation." Returning to Ireland when she was fifteen, Boland found "a great imaginative release."

A Personal Yet Public Poet Since 1967, she has published several acclaimed volumes of poetry, including *The War Horse* (1975), *In Her Own Image* (1980), *Night Feed* (1982), and *In a Time of Violence* (1994). Boland's poetry is notable for its intense focus on her personal experiences—she freely shares incidents from her life to uncover universal themes and insights. Her 1995 collection of essays, *Object Lessons: The Life of the Woman and Poet in Our Time*, combines her explorations of history, autobiography, and poetry. In addition to publishing poetry, she writes reviews and teaches at universities in both England and the United States.

Married to a novelist and the mother of two daughters, Boland often writes about domestic life, but she shuns the label "woman poet." She says poetry should create only statements that are "bound to be human." Unwilling to yoke poetry to a political program, she notes that "My poetry begins for me where certainty ends."

TEACHING RESOURCES

The following resources can be used to enrich or extend the instruction for pp. 1102–1103.

Motivation

Interest Grabber Video, Tape 6

Background

Beyond Literature, p. 54 

Take It to the Net

Visit www.phschool.com for background and hotlinks for the selections.

Literary Analysis

Literary Analysis and Reading Transparencies, Diction and Style, p. 108

Reading

Literary Analysis and Reading Transparencies, Summarizing, p. 107

Selection Support: Reading Strategy, p. 251; Build Vocabulary, p. 249.

BLOCK SCHEDULING: Resources marked with this symbol provide varied instruction during 90-minute blocks.

Preview

Connecting to the Literature

Take over your older brother's paper route. . . . Get a driver's license, and drive yourself to all the places your mom used to take you. . . . The past has a habit of reappearing every time you grow. In these poems, Heaney and Boland explore ways in which the past repeats itself.

2 Literary Analysis

Diction and Style

To create a literary work, a writer must make choices about diction and other elements of style.

- **Diction** refers to a writer's typical choice of words—formal or informal, homespun or intellectual.
- **Style** takes in a writer's whole manner of expression, including his or her word choice, use of forms and rhythms (traditional or otherwise), and themes and imagery.

A poem is a work in words, and style and diction—both formed from patterns of words—are as crucial to what a poem is and how it affects you as its message is. As you read, identify the characteristics of Heaney's and Boland's styles.

Comparing Literary Works

Heaney and Boland both write poems exploring their relationship to the past, but in very different styles. Heaney's style is marked by his use of traditional forms like the **sestina** ("Two Lorries"), which recycles six words to end each line. His language is precise and down to earth. Boland works in a freer form and blends the abstract and concrete in her imagery. As you read, compare the effect of each writer's style on your experience of the poem.

3 Reading Strategy

Summarizing

Summarizing a poem—restating its key points in brief—can help you focus on its central images and ideas. You might summarize an entire poem or an individual stanza. Use a chart like the one shown to summarize the poems or individual stanzas in them.

Passage

I wanted to grow up and plow,
To close one eye, stiffen my arm.
All I ever did was follow
In his broad shadow round the farm.
("Follower")

↓

Main Points

Son following his father; looking up to him; wanting to be like him.

↓

Summary

I wanted to be a farmer, like my father.

Vocabulary Development

furrow (fur´ ō) *n.* narrow groove made in the ground by a plow (p. 1106)

nuisance (no͞o´ səns) *n.* act, thing, or condition causing trouble (p. 1106)

inklings (iŋk´ liŋz) *n.* indirect suggestions; vague ideas (p. 1109)

mortal (môr´ təl) *adj.* of that which must eventually die (p. 1110)

ordeal (ôr dēl´) *n.* difficult or painful experience that tests one (p. 1110)

2 Literary Analysis

Diction and Style

- Tell students that in this lesson they will focus on diction and style, and read the Literary Analysis note with students.
- Explain that *diction* is the writer's choice of words, and that it can range from informal to formal.
- Review with students that *style* denotes the writer's manner of expression, including word choice, tone, rhythms, themes, and imagery.
- Call students' attention to the way in which diction and style can indicate whether a writer's work is concrete or abstract in nature and theme.
- Use the Diction and Style transparency in **Literary Analysis and Reading Transparencies,** p. 108, to illustrate to students how to analyze style and diction in a poem.

3 Reading Strategy

Summarizing

- Review with students that summarizing a poem is briefly restating its key points.
- Encourage students to summarize as they read, quickly explaining to themselves what has just been said.
- Read the note about Summarizing, then use the graphic organizer on p. 1103 to practice this skill.
- Have students practice summarizing using the Summarizing transparency on p. 107 of **Literary Analysis and Reading Transparencies.**

Vocabulary Development

- Pronounce each vocabulary word for students, and read the definitions as a class. Have students identify any words with which they are already familiar.

CUSTOMIZE INSTRUCTION FOR UNIVERSAL ACCESS

For Less Proficient Readers	For English Learners	For Advanced Readers
These students may have difficulty recognizing how diction, or word choice, affects the overall impression or impact of a poem. Ask students to look at "Follower" and think about what kinds of words Heaney uses, and how they function in the poem.	English learners may find that the subtleties of diction and style are especially difficult to discern. Have students practice analyzing words in "Follower" with teacher guidance. Encourage students to think about how certain words are reflective of the environment described by Heaney in the poem.	Encourage students to think about how word choice affects the overall impression of a work. Ask students to read Heaney's poem "Follower" and consider how different choices of words would alter the nature of the poem. Encourage students to "rewrite" the poem using different diction.

E-Teach

Visit E-Teach at www.phschool.com for teachers' essays on how to teach, with questions and answers.

TEACH

Step-by-Step Teaching Guide for pp. 1104–1110

CUSTOMIZE INSTRUCTION
For Musical/Rhythmic Learners

Have students listen to the selection audiotape in order to appreciate how the poem evokes elements of the traditional ballad.

1 About the Selections

Both of Seamus Heaney's poems refer to his relationship with his parents and, by extension, with his Irish homeland. "Follower" focuses on the personal interaction between a small boy and his farmer father, poignantly conveying how the roles of parent and child shift as they age. In "Two Lorries," the poet laments the threat of Irish terrorism, contrasting a terrorist's truck bomb with a flirtatious delivery-truck driver—both might have taken his mother away from him, and both involve a "cheap," unreal passion. Each poem shows the two faces of Ireland, one turned toward the past, the other turned toward the present; the strong emotions tying the Irish to their land; and the powerful ability of memories from daily life to focus those emotions.

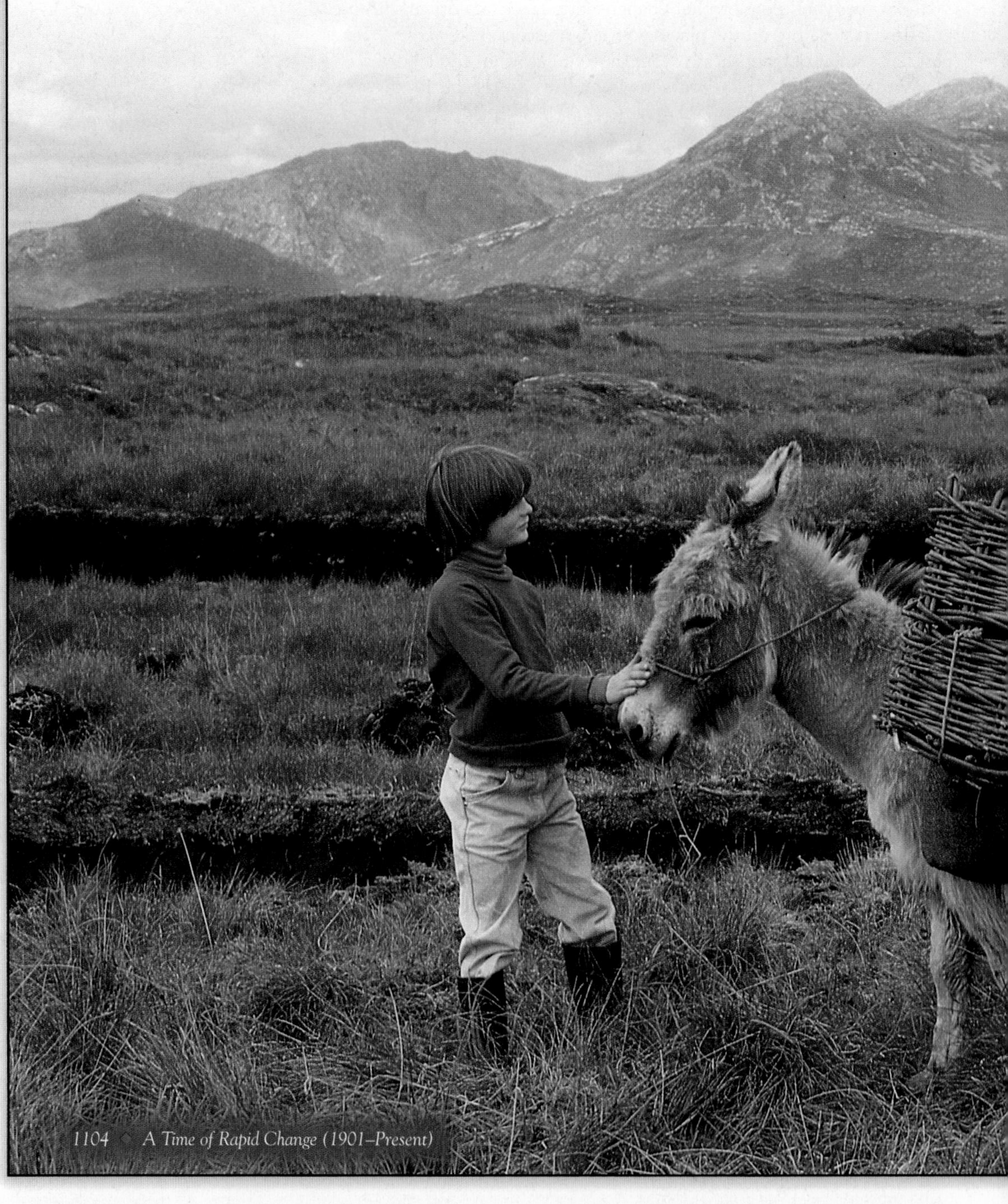

TEACHING RESOURCES

The following resources can be used to enrich or extend the instruction for pp. 1104–1110.

Literary Analysis

Selection Support: Literary Analysis, p. 252

Reading

Listening to Literature Audiocassettes, Side 26 ■

Listening to Literature Audio CDs, CD 14 ■

■ **BLOCK SCHEDULING:** Resources marked with this symbol provide varied instruction during 90-minute blocks.

Follower

Seamus Heaney

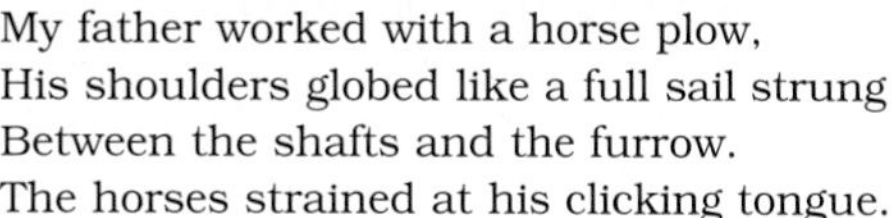

My father worked with a horse plow,
His shoulders globed like a full sail strung
Between the shafts and the furrow.
The horses strained at his clicking tongue.

An expert. He would set the wing
And fit the bright steel-pointed sock.
The sod rolled over without breaking.
At the headrig, with a single pluck

Of reins, the sweating team turned round
And back into the land. His eye

CUSTOMIZE INSTRUCTION FOR UNIVERSAL ACCESS		
For Special Needs Students	**For English Learners**	**For Gifted/Talented Students**
Encourage students to read aloud from "Follower" with teacher guidance. Tell them to pronounce each word as they go, and to summarize what they have just read to keep it clear in their thoughts. To help students practice the skill of summarizing, use p. 107 of **Literary Analysis and Reading Transparencies.**	English learners may have difficulty recognizing the role diction plays in Heaney's poem. Encourage them to note any words in "Follower" that are confusing, are unfamiliar, or seem particular to the scene described by the author. Review these words with students.	Seamus Heaney's "Follower" is full of solid, expressive, concrete images. Have students choose one of them to reproduce in a drawing or painting. Tell students to keep in mind the setting of the poem as they focus on their single image. Have them try to match the mood or tone of the image in their drawing or painting.

Answers for p. 1106

Review and Assess

1. Possible responses: Some students may recall admiring an adult, then later experiencing a role reversal.
2. **(a)** The father is plowing his farm fields. **(b)** The boy wants to imitate his father's expertise and mastery in every detail.
3. **(a)** Heaney uses such words as "shafts," "furrow," "wing," "steel-pointed sock," and "headrig."
   (b) The use of precise words echoes the boy's careful imitation of his father.
4. **(a)** Heaney has become an adult, and his father now seems dependent on him. **(b)** The speaker sees himself as a nuisance to his father when he was a boy, and his father as a kind of nuisance to him as an adult—no difference at all except his father won't go away.
5. Possible response: Parents can serve as their children's models into adulthood. Sometimes, living up to these ideals is a burden.
6. Possible responses: Students may say that even if the two had talked about the son's feelings for the father, the speaker would still feel as if his father were shadowing him; others may disagree. Have students defend their views.
7. Possible responses: Students may say that it is increasingly rare for father and son to work together, but that they still learn a great deal from one another in all of their interactions.

Narrowed and angled at the ground,
Mapping the furrow exactly.

I stumbled in his hobnailed wake,
Fell sometimes on the polished sod;
Sometimes he rode me on his back
Dipping and rising to his plod.

I wanted to grow up and plow,
To close one eye, stiffen my arm.
All I ever did was follow
In his broad shadow round the farm.

I was a nuisance, tripping, falling,
Yapping always. But today
It is my father who keeps stumbling
Behind me, and will not go away.

furrow (fur´ ō) *n.* narrow groove made in the ground by a plow

nuisance (no͞o´ səns) *n.* act, thing, or condition causing trouble

Review and Assess

Thinking About the Selection

1. **Respond:** Have you ever felt about an adult the way the speaker feels about his father in "Follower"? Explain.
2. **(a) Recall:** In "Follower," what is the father doing?
   (b) Interpret: Why does the boy want "To close one eye" and "stiffen" his "arm"?
3. **(a) Recall:** Give two examples of precise words Heaney uses to describe tools, actions, or other things associated with farming. **(b) Analyze:** How does the use of such words help convey the child's fascination with his father's life?
4. **(a) Compare and Contrast:** How does the relationship between father and son shift at the end of "Follower"?
   (b) Draw Conclusions: What difference between his childhood view of his father and his own experience of adulthood does the speaker see?
5. **Generalize:** Do people's relations with their parents always leave lasting marks or burdens? Explain.
6. **Hypothesize:** Do you think the speaker would still feel that his father was shadowing him if the two had talked about the son's feelings for his father? Explain.
7. **Apply:** Do you think that father-son relationships like the one Heaney describes have become less common in our times? Explain.

ENRICHMENT: History Connection

Ireland

The conflict in Ireland, while often polarized around religious differences, has socioeconomic causes as well. When the English aristocrats seized ownership of much of the land and instituted a feudal system, the Irish peasantry became dependent on foreign land owners.

Explain that Seamus Heaney made a significant choice about his relation to his own Irish past when he settled in the Irish Republic in 1972. His own disquiet about living away from the continued conflict in Northern Ireland (his birthplace) might be compared to the father who follows him, stumbling, in "Follower." His regret at the terrorism that besieges his homeland is evident in "Two Lorries."

❶ Two Lorries

Seamus Heaney

Background

For large parts of its history, Ireland was under English control. Since the 1920s, Ireland has been partitioned into the Irish Republic in the South and Ulster, or Northern Ireland, which remains allied with Great Britain. Northern Ireland has been a focus of conflict between Protestants and Catholics. The Ulster Protestants generally support British rule of Northern Ireland. For the most part, Northern Irish Catholics want "the British out" and Ireland united. From the late 1960s on, this conflict has produced terrorism by Catholics and Protestants. Heaney's poem refers to a bombing incident sparked by this ongoing struggle, while Boland's poem reflects on the speaker's present responsibilities to the Irish past.

It's raining on black coal and warm wet ashes.
There are tire-marks in the yard, Agnew's old lorry[1]
Has all its cribs down and Agnew the coalman
With his Belfast accent's sweet-talking my mother.
Would she ever go to a film in Magherafelt?
But it's raining and he still has half the load

❷

To deliver farther on. This time the lode
Our coal came from was silk-black, so the ashes
Will be the silkiest white. The Magherafelt
(Via Toomebridge) bus goes by. The half-stripped lorry
With its emptied, folded coal-bags moves my mother:
The tasty ways of a leather-aproned coalman!

And films no less! The conceit of a coalman . . .
She goes back in and gets out the black lead
And emery paper, this nineteen-forties mother,
All business round her stove, half-wiping ashes
With a backhand from her cheek as the bolted lorry
Gets revved and turned and heads for Magherafelt

Reading Strategy
Summarizing What happens during the first coalman's visit?

❸ **Reading Check**
What does the coalman invite the speaker's mother to do?

1. **lorry** truck.

❷ Reading Strategy

Summarizing

- Encourage students to summarize what they have read by restating the key points to themselves.
- Then, ask them the Reading Strategy question on p. 1107: What happens during the first coalman's visit?
  Answer: The coalman flirts with the speaker's mother and asks her to go and see a film in Magherafelt.

❸ Reading Check

Answer: The coalman asks the speaker's mother to go and see a film in Magherafelt.

CUSTOMIZE INSTRUCTION FOR UNIVERSAL ACCESS

For Special Needs Students	For Less Proficient Readers	For Advanced Readers
Students may find Heaney's comparison and collapse of two incidents into "Two Lorries" unusually daunting. Encourage them to break down each incident into its bare details—summarizing where necessary—to understand why he chooses to juxtapose these events.	Review with students what happens in "Two Lorries." Encourage them to give an account of the separate events in the poem by summarizing what occurs in each. If students seem to be having difficulty summarizing, use the Summarizing transparency on p. 107 of **Literary Analysis and Reading Transparencies.**	Remind students that Heaney's "Two Lorries" is a sestina—a sophisticated form that recycles the same six words at the end of each line in a stanza. Have students reread the poem to see the novel ways in which Heaney reuses each word. Encourage students to think of ending words that can be used in this fashion.

Answers for p. 1108

Review and Assess

1. In the first incident, the coal delivery man asks Heaney's mother for a date to the movies. In the second incident, a bomb-carrying truck explodes, destroying a city bus station. **(b)** The movie and the bomb both are set in Magherafelt.
2. **(a)** The coalman who "sweet-talks" Heaney's mother is a threat because he is flirting with her and could upset domestic harmony. **(b)** The threat of Heaney's mother being taken away is similar to the threat of Heaney's motherland being destroyed by terrorism.
3. **(a)** The coalman's invitation might be a kind of empty tease—like the promises and results of terrorist policies—it might not lead to anything at all, or it might lead to something very bad. **(b)** The invitation to a movie is relatively benign flirtation, whereas the act of political violence is a profound threat.
4. **(a)** Possible response: He dislikes it for threatening to take away what he loves in Ireland, just as a sweet-talking coalman tried to steal away his mother. **(b)** Possible responses: Students will probably say that Heaney's poem is a kind of political activism, because he takes a position on the evil of terrorism.

And the last delivery. Oh, Magherafelt!
Oh, dream of red plush and a city coalman
As time fastforwards and a different lorry
Groans into shot, up Broad Street, with a payload
That will blow the bus station to dust and ashes . . .
After that happened, I'd a vision of my mother,

A revenant[2] on the bench where I would meet her
In that cold-floored waiting-room in Magherafelt,
Her shopping bags full up with shoveled ashes.
Death walked out past her like a dust-faced coalman
Refolding body-bags, plying his load
Empty upon empty, in a flurry

Of motes and engine-revs, but which lorry
Was it now? Young Agnew's or that other,
Heavier, deadlier one, set to explode
In a time beyond her time in Magherafelt . . .
So tally bags and sweet-talk darkness, coalman.
Listen to the rain spit in new ashes

As you heft a load of dust that was Magherafelt,
Then reappear from your lorry as my mother's
Dreamboat coalman filmed in silk-white ashes.

---

2. **revenant** (rev′ ə nənt) *n.* one who returns; ghost.

Review and Assess

Thinking About the Selection

1. (a) **Recall:** What are the two incidents described in "Two Lorries"? (b) **Analyze:** What details connect the two?
2. (a) **Infer:** How is the coalman who "sweet-talk[s]" Heaney's mother a threat to the young Heaney? (b) **Connect:** What connection can you find between this threat and the threat of terrorism in Northern Ireland, Heaney's "motherland"?
3. (a) **Hypothesize:** In Heaney's view, what might the coalman's invitation to a movie, not meant or taken seriously, have in common with the promises and results of terrorist politics? (b) **Compare and Contrast:** What differences distinguish the two?
4. (a) **Draw Conclusions:** Judging from "Two Lorries," how would you describe Heaney's attitude toward the Irish conflicts? (b) **Evaluate:** Do you think that writing a poem like "Two Lorries" is a form of political activism? Explain.

ENRICHMENT: Science Connection

The Stars

The stars of which Boland speaks number in the billions. They range from stars as big as the Sun to giant stars that would cover the distance from the Earth to the Sun. Each emits light from the nuclear furnace at its center, in which atoms are continually fused to release intense, radiant energy. On Earth we see this light many centuries after it first leaves the star.

Stars are born, shine for a period of time, and then slowly die. Larger stars burn the brightest but more briefly; perhaps for only 10 million years. Though they appear as mere sparkles in the sky, stars have colors, ranging from white to yellow, blue, or red.

Have students locate data about the number of light years it takes light from each of ten stars to reach Earth. After making a chart with the data, ask students to calculate the Earth year in which the light reaching us today first left each star.

5 

Starry Night Over the Rhone River, Vincent van Gogh, Musée d'Orsay, Paris, France

6 ▲ **Critical Viewing** Compare the stars in the painting with those in the poem. Do both suggest the eternal, or does one suggest the explosive? **[Compare and Contrast]**

4 Outside History

Eavan Boland

There are outsiders, always. These stars—
these iron inklings of an Irish January,
whose light happened

thousands of years before
our pain did: they are, they have always been
outside history.

inklings (iŋk′ liŋz) *n.* indirect suggestions; vague ideas

7 **Reading Check**

According to the speaker, what is outside history?

4 About the Selection

This poem poses the choice between immortality—a place outside human history—and participation in the struggles of flawed life. The poet presents the stars as the symbol of immortality, a landscape impervious to history's pain. Against this image, she contrasts the many dead Irish whose memory clots the Earth's landscape. In choosing to join history, Boland engages in the fight to relieve pain and injustice, but she knows she will always be too late.

5 Background

Art

Starry Night Over the Rhone River, 1888, by Vincent van Gogh

Vincent van Gogh, though virtually unknown and often impoverished in his lifetime, is today one of the best-known Postimpressionist painters. Born in Holland, Van Gogh turned to painting in his late twenties, around 1880, studying on his own as well as with other painters. Though he experienced periods of deep unhappiness and mental instability, Van Gogh's short career was highly productive. Use these questions for discussion:

1. What parts of the painting are most intense and alive?
   Answer: The orange-yellow lights along the shore and their reflections in the water are the most intense and alive.
2. Describe the manner in which the people are painted.
   Answer: The people seem insubstantial, scraped together out of paint.
3. From these facts, speculate about how Van Gogh would respond to Boland's decision to move "inside" history.
   Possible response: He might respond that life within history is insubstantial unless a light burns through from outside.

6 ▶ Critical Viewing

Answer: Both the stars in the painting and those in Boland's poem suggest the eternal.

7 Reading Check

Answer: The stars are outside history.

CUSTOMIZE INSTRUCTION FOR UNIVERSAL ACCESS

For Special Needs Students	For Less Proficient Readers	For Gifted/Talented Students
Have students read "Outside History" with teacher guidance. Encourage them to pay attention to the way in which the speaker of the poem addresses concrete objects, like the stars, in an abstract fashion. Encourage them to isolate concrete and abstract concepts in the poem.	Students may find the abstract nature of the poem an obstacle to their appreciation. If time allows, show students an interview with the author, Eavan Boland, on **Interest Grabber Video,** Tape 6, to engage student interest. After students have seen the video, encourage them to reread "Outside History."	Tell students that Eavan Boland's poem "Outside History" is about a choice the speaker makes. Have students write poems about making choices. Encourage them to imitate Boland's style in the beginning of the poem, reflecting the uncertainty with which the making of a decision begins.

ASSESS

8 Vocabulary Development

Latin root *-mort-*

- Call students' attention to *mortal.* Explain to students that *mortal* is derived from the Latin root *-mort-,* which means "death."
- Have students suggest other words and phrases that contain this Latin root.
  Possible responses: *immortal; mortified; mortuary; mortician*

Answers for p. 1110

Review and Assess

1. Possible responses: No, we cannot "erase" past suffering; yes, we can prevent the same injustices from recurring.
2. **(a)** The speaker is viewing the stars. **(b)** She claims this sight is "outside history" because it takes thousands of years for a star's light to reach the earth.
3. **(a)** Beneath the stars lie a place where people discover they are human, and a landscape in which they know they are mortal. **(b)** The speaker must choose between them because she wants to be part of history, inside history.
4. **(a)** She uses an image of darkness to contrast with the light of the stars. **(b)** The "dead" in line 18 are those who have fallen, perhaps for a cause. **(c)** Yes, acknowledging the dead requires involvement.
5. Choosing to live in myth might mean accepting things as they are ("as the gods will"); choosing history means acknowledging responsibility to remedy the past.
6. **(a)** Boland's decision to "participate" in history is based on her own myth of the continuity of the ordeal. **(b)** Possible response: Students may point out that life is too short to engage in conflict.

They keep their distance. Under them remains
a place where you found
you were human, and

8 a landscape in which you know you are mortal.
And a time to choose between them.
I have chosen:

Out of myth into history I move to be
part of that ordeal
whose darkness is

only now reaching me from those fields,
those rivers, those roads clotted as
firmaments[1] with the dead.

How slowly they die
as we kneel beside them, whisper in their ear.
And we are too late. We are always too late.

mortal (môr′ təl) *adj.* of that which must eventually die

ordeal (ôr dēl′) *n.* difficult or painful experience that tests one

1. **firmaments** *n.* the heavens.

Review and Assess

Thinking About the Selection

1. **Respond:** Do you think Boland is too pessimistic when she writes, "We are always too late"? Explain.
2. **(a) Recall:** What is the speaker viewing at the opening of the poem? **(b) Interpret:** Why does the speaker claim this sight is "outside history"?
3. **(a) Interpret:** According to the speaker, what two things lie under the stars? **(b) Interpret:** Why must the speaker choose between them?
4. **(a) Analyze:** What image does the speaker use to contrast the "ordeal" of history with the stars? **(b) Infer:** Who are "the dead" in line 18? **(c) Interpret:** Is acknowledging the dead a way of becoming part of the "ordeal"? Explain.
5. **Hypothesize:** What might it mean to live in myth instead of in history?
6. **(a) Evaluate:** In writing this poem, does Boland become part of a larger "ordeal," or is that itself a myth? Explain. **(b) Defend:** How might you justify a person's right to stay uninvolved in a conflict?

ASSESSMENT PRACTICE: Writing Skills

Style **(For more practice, see Test Preparation Workbook, p. 54.)**

Many tests require students to recognize stylistic devices and effective language. Use the following sample item to teach students how to describe a writer's diction.

An expert. He would set the wing
And fit the bright steel-pointed sock.
The sod rolled over without breaking.
At the headrig, with a single pluck

Heaney's diction in these lines is best characterized as—

A highly academic vocabulary
B the frequent use of colloquialisms
C long alliterative phrases
D terms specific to a particular profession

Students should determine that the correct answer is *D,* because this passage contains many terms related to farming.

Review and Assess

Literary Analysis

Diction and Style

1. Explain how Heaney's **style** and **diction** in "Follower" fit the subject of the poem.
2. Complete this chart to analyze Boland's **style** in "Outside History." Then, summarize the distinctive elements of her style.

	Diction	Imagery	Rhythm/ Rhyme	Form
Examples				
Conclusion				

3. (a) What restrictions might the **sestina** form in "Two Lorries" place on Heaney? (b) What advantage might it have?

Comparing Literary Works

4. (a) Contrast Heaney's diction, as exemplified in words such as "headrig," "hobnailed," and "leather-aproned," with Boland's, as exemplified in phrases such as "iron inklings," "out of myth," and "clotted as firmaments." (b) Which poet's diction is more conversational? Which is more abstract? Explain.
5. (a) How does Heaney's diction and style help him to re-create the past? Explain, using examples. (b) How does Boland make abstract ideas of history vivid?
6. Compare the way in which both poets use their poetry to find a way into the past.

Reading Strategy

Summarizing

7. Write a **summary** of "Two Lorries," including a comparison of the two incidents the poet recalls.
8. Write a summary of "Outside History."

Extend Understanding

9. **World Events Connection:** Should Irish literature be studied as its own tradition, separate from British literature? Explain.

Quick Review

Diction refers to the type of words a writer chooses to use—abstract or concrete, formal or informal.

Style refers to a writer's whole manner of expression, including choice of words, forms, imagery, and themes.

A **sestina** is a poem made of six six-line stanzas and a three-line conclusion called an envoy. The final word of each line in the first stanza is re-used as the final word of a line in each subsequent stanza. The order of end-words is varied in each stanza.

To **summarize** a poem or part of a poem, briefly restate the key ideas and images.

Take It to the Net

www.phschool.com

Take the interactive self-test online to check your understanding of these selections.

Answers for p. 1111

Review and Assess

1. Heaney's use of homespun diction, with precise terms for the work his father does, a rueful tone, and a reflective narrative style, fits the subject of "Follower."
2. *Examples:* **Diction:** "iron inklings," "mortal," "ordeal"; **Imagery:** "a landscape," "those fields," "roads clotted"; **Rhythm/Rhyme:** irregular; **Form:** 3-line stanza. *Conclusion:* **Diction:** Philosophical/abstract diction; **Imagery:** simple, general imagery with abstract ideas; **Rhythm/ Rhyme:** conversational; **Form:** simple
3. **(a)** The sestina requires Heaney to use the same six end-words in each stanza. **(b)** The form allows him to explore a series of variations on a theme.
4. **(a)** Heaney's diction is more homespun and oriented toward tools used by a farmer; Boland's diction tends to be mythical or abstract. **(b)** Possible response: Some students may say that both poets' dictions are conversational. Boland's poem is decidedly more abstract than Heaney's in its meditations.
5. **(a)** Heaney's diction in "Two Lorries" enables him to re-create the 1940s scene in which a coalman flirts with his mother. Heaney uses "old" words that bring us back to the scene. **(b)** Boland makes abstract ideas of history vivid in such lines as "those roads clotted as / firmaments with the dead."
6. Possible response: Heaney uses concrete experiences from his past and meditates on them for insight; similarly, Boland draws on the past as a kind of source to understand the present.
7. In the first incident, the poet's mother chats with the coal deliveryman who invites her to see a film. She declines; the coalman drives off to the city. In the second incident, a terrorist-driven truck explodes, destroying the bus station in which the poet used to meet his mother. In a vision, the poet sees his mother's ghost at the bus station, attended by the coalman as a figure of death.

continued

Answers continued

8. People have a choice as to whether or not to engage in conflicts stemming from the past. In choosing to participate in Ireland's painful history, the poet accepts that her efforts cannot really undo the losses suffered in the past.
9. Answers will vary. Have students defend their answers.

ENRICHMENT: Further Reading

Other Works by the Poets

Other Works by Seamus Heaney

Door into the Dark

Other Works by Eavan Boland

"The Achill Woman"

Take It to the Net

Visit www.phschool.com for more information on the poets.

EXTEND

Answers for p. 1112

❶ Vocabulary Development

Word Analysis

1. A *mortician* is a person who prepares a deceased person's body for burial or cremation.
2. A *mortality* rate is the death rate.
3. *Immortal* means immune from death, eternal.
4. A *mortuary* is the place where dead bodies are kept before burial or cremation.

Spelling Strategy

1. excesses
2. republics
3. contexts
4. equinoxes

Fluency: Context

When as a child, Seamus Heaney followed his father around the farm, he may have made a nuisance of himself. However, young Seamus's tripping over a furrow was probably more a source of amusement than an ordeal for his father. One thing is sure, no inklings that his father was mortal had yet reached young Seamus Heaney.

❷ Grammar and Style

1. concrete
2. concrete
3. abstract
4. abstract
5. abstract

Writing Application

Possible response: I remember the day we moved away from my childhood home to Mexico. We packed up our car, and we drove away at night. How painful distance is! How lonely those long vistas and ancient memories!

Integrate Language Skills

❶ Vocabulary Development Lesson

Word Analysis: Latin Root *-mort-*

The word *mortal* means "subject to death." This word contains the Latin root *-mort-*, which means "death." Using this information, define the italicized words.

1. He studied to be a *mortician*.
2. The *mortality* rate for smokers is high.
3. Poetry made her *immortal*.
4. The *mortuary* was respectfully silent.

Spelling Strategy

When forming regular plurals, add *-es* only if the noun ends in *h, s,* or *x*. Write the plurals of these nouns:

1. excess
2. republic
3. context
4. equinox

Fluency: Context

Copy this paragraph into your notebook, and fill in each blank with the most appropriate word from the vocabulary list on page 1103. Let the context created by the paragraph guide your choices. Use each word only once.

When, as a child, Seamus Heaney followed his father around the farm, he may have made a __?__ of himself. However, young Seamus's tripping over a __?__ was probably more a source of amusement than an __?__ for his father. One thing is sure, no __?__ that his father was __?__ had yet reached young Seamus Heaney.

❷ Grammar and Style Lesson

Concrete and Abstract Nouns

Heaney and Boland use **concrete nouns,** which name things that can be sensed and counted, and **abstract nouns,** which name general aspects of things, such as a quality.

Concrete Nouns: shafts, furrow, horses, sod

Abstract Nouns: death, myth, place

Boland achieves a distinctive effect by using abstract nouns such as *myth* and *history* as if they were concrete ("Out of myth into history I move . . ."). She also uses concrete nouns such as *fields* in a symbolic way, as if they were abstract. In this way, she creates images that integrate intellectual concerns, the imagination, and the emotions.

Practice Identify which underlined nouns are concrete and which are abstract.

1. My father worked with a horse plow, . . .
2. All I ever did was follow / In his broad shadow. . . .
3. The conceit of a coalman . . .
4. . . . a landscape in which you know you are mortal.
5. . . . I move to be / part of that ordeal. . . .

Writing Application Write four sentences to describe a memory that is important to you. In two sentences, use only concrete nouns. In the other two, use only abstract nouns. Then, read the sentences aloud, and compare the impact of your sentences.

WG Prentice Hall Writing and Grammar Connection: Chapter 17, Section 1

TEACHING RESOURCES

The following resources can be used to enrich or extend the instruction for pp. 1112–1113.

Vocabulary

- **Selection Support:** Build Vocabulary, p. 249
- **Vocabulary and Spelling Practice Book** (Use this booklet for skills enrichment.)

Grammar

- **Selection Support:** Grammar and Style, p. 250
- **Writing and Grammar,** Diamond Level, p. 368
- **Daily Language Practice Transparencies**

Writing

- **Writing and Grammar,** Diamond Level, p. 117
- **Writing and Grammar iText CD-ROM**

BLOCK SCHEDULING: Resources marked with this symbol provide varied instruction during 90-minute blocks.

❸ Writing Lesson

Poem With a Strong Central Image

Heaney and Boland build their poems around strong central images, such as the lorry-driving coalman in "Two Lorries." Write a poem around such an image, carefully choosing words for meaning and sound.

Prewriting Draw on your memories or on photographs or artworks for inspiration. Choose a topic and the central image you will develop.

Drafting Decide on the form you will follow, and then begin drafting. As you draft, let ideas flow. Do not worry about formal problems, such as missing rhymes. You can fix them when you revise.

Revising Review your central image to determine whether it is effective and to confirm that it is reflected in details throughout the poem. Consider revising word choices or adding details to increase its impact.

Model: Revising to Strengthen a Central Image

The ancient elevator ~~climbs~~ wheezes up another floor,
Thin metal ~~frame,~~ skin, shuddering door.
It groans, halts, and ~~lets~~ spits us out on four.

By revising word choices to personify the elevator, the writer strengthens the central image in a description of an office building.

WG Prentice Hall Writing and Grammar Connection: Chapter 6, Connected Assignment

❹ Extension Activities

Listening and Speaking Prepare and give an **interpretive reading** of a poem by Heaney or Boland. To prepare:

- Check the pronunciation of any words of which you are unsure.
- Effectively highlight the "soundscape" of the poem—for instance, you might linger over repeated vowel sounds in the opening stanza of "Follower."

Rehearse your reading, and then present it to the class.

Research and Technology With a group, write a conflict report on the "Troubles," the ongoing strife in Northern Ireland. Relate your research to "Two Lorries" and "Outside History." Consider incorporating: photographs, population maps, timelines, and public opinion graphs. **[Group Activity]**

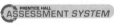

Take It to the Net www.phschool.com

Go online for an additional research activity using the Internet.

❸ Writing Lesson

- Read with students the note for the writing lesson on p. 1113, then tell students that they will write a poem around a strong central image.
- Encourage students to isolate an image from their memories, or an event that they find unforgettable; then, have them choose a topic.
- Help students to choose a form and begin drafting their poems. Remind them that their poems do not need to rhyme, but they may.
- Review with students how to make the central image effective and have them verify that details throughout the poem increase its impact.

❹ Listening and Speaking

- Read the Listening and Speaking note with students, and have them prepare interpretive readings of poems by Heaney or Boland.
- Have students practice their readings, checking pronunciation of unfamiliar words, and getting a sense of line flow.
- Remind students that they should emphasize certain words and use their voices for appropriate inflections to convey tone.

CUSTOMIZE INSTRUCTION For Universal Access

To address different learning styles, use the activities suggested in the **Extension Activities** booklet, p. 54.

- For Visual/Spatial Learners, use Activity 5.
- For Verbal/Linguistic Learners, use Activity 6.
- For Interpersonal and Verbal/ Linguistic Learners, use Activity 7.

ASSESSMENT RESOURCES

The following resources can be used to assess students' knowledge and skills.

Selection Assessment

- **Formal Assessment,** pp. 258–260
- **Open Book Test,** pp. 159–161
- **Got It! Assessment Videotapes,** Tape 5
- **Test Bank Software**

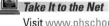

PRENTICE HALL ASSESSMENT SYSTEM

- **Workbook**
- **Skill Book**
- **Transparencies**
- **CD-ROM**

Take It to the Net

Visit www.phschool.com for self-tests and additional questions on the selections.

No Witchcraft for Sale

Lesson Objectives and CA Correlations

1. **To analyze and respond to literary elements**
   - Literary Analysis: Cultural Conflict **R 3.7**
   - Connecting Literary Elements: Point of View **R 3.3**
2. **To read, comprehend, analyze, and critique a short story**
   - Reading Strategy: Analyzing Cultural Differences **R 3.9**
   - Reading Check Questions
   - Review and Assess Questions
3. **To develop word analysis skills, fluency, and systematic vocabulary**
   - Vocabulary Lesson: Word Analysis: Forms of *skeptical* **R 1.2**
4. **To understand and apply written and oral language conventions**
   - Spelling Strategy **LC 1.2**
   - Grammar and Style Lesson: Correct Use of *like* and *as* **LC 1.1**
5. **To understand and apply appropriate writing and research strategies**
   - Writing Lesson: Problem-and-Solution Essay **W 1.1, 1.3, 1.9**
   - Extension Activity: Oral Report on Medical Botany **W 1.6**
   - Assessment Practice (ATE)
6. **To understand and apply listening and speaking strategies**
   - Extension Activity: Debate on Colonialism **LS 1.4**

STEP-BY-STEP TEACHING GUIDE	PACING GUIDE
PRETEACH	
Motivate Students and Provide Background	
Use the Motivation activity (ATE p. 1114)	5 min.
Read and discuss author and background features (SE/ATE pp. 1114, 1116) A	5 min.
Introduce the Concepts	
Introduce the Literary Analysis and Reading Strategy (SE/ATE p. 1115) A	15 min.
Pronounce the vocabulary words and read their definitions (SE p. 1115)	5 min.
TEACH	
Monitor Comprehension	
Informally monitor comprehension by circulating while students read independently or in groups A	25 min.
Monitor students' comprehension with the Reading Check notes (SE/ATE pp. 1117, 1121)	as students read
Develop vocabulary with Vocabulary notes (SE pp. 1116, 1117, 1118, 1120; ATE p. 1120)	as students read
Develop Understanding	
Develop students' understanding of cultural conflict with the Literary Analysis annotations (SE/ATE pp. 1118, 1120) A	5 min.
Develop students' ability to analyze with the Reading Strategy annotations (SE/ATE pp. 1117, 1118)	5 min.
ASSESS	
Assess Mastery	
Assess students' mastery of the Reading Strategy and Literary Analysis by having them answer the Review and Assess questions (SE/ATE p. 1123)	15 min.
Use one or more of the print and media Assessment Resources (ATE p. 1125) A	up to 45 min.
EXTEND	
Apply Understanding	
Have students complete the Vocabulary Development Lesson and the Grammar and Style Lesson (SE p. 1124) A	20 min.
Apply students' knowledge of elaboration to enhance understanding using the Writing Lesson (SE/ATE p. 1125) A	45 min.
Apply students' understanding using one or more of the Extension Activities (SE p. 1125)	20–90 min.

ACCELERATED INSTRUCTION:
Use the strategies and activities identified with an A.

UNIVERSAL ACCESS
● = Below-Level Students
▲ = On-Level Students
■ = Above-Level Students

Time and Resource Manager

Reading Level: Easy
Average Number of Instructional Days: 4

RESOURCES		
PRINT	**TRANSPARENCIES**	**TECHNOLOGY**
• **Beyond Literature,** Cross-Curricular Connection: Science, p. 55 ▲ ■		• **Interest Grabber Video,** Tape 6 ● ▲ ■
• **Selection Support Workbook:** ● ▲ ■ Literary Analysis, p. 256 Reading Strategy, p. 255 Build Vocabulary, p. 253	• **Literary Analysis and Reading Transparencies,** pp. 109 and 110 ● ▲ ■	
• **Adapted Reader's Companion** ● • **Reader's Companion** ●		
• **English Learner's Companion** ● ▲ • **Literatura en español** ● ▲ • **Literary Analysis for Enrichment** ■		
• **Formal Assessment:** Selection Test, pp. 261–263 ● ▲ ■ • **Open Book Test,** pp. 162–164 ● ▲ ■ • **Performance Assessment and Portfolio Management,** p. 22 ● ▲ ■ • PRENTICE HALL ASSESSMENT SYSTEM ● ▲ ■	• PRENTICE HALL ASSESSMENT SYSTEM ● ▲ ■ Skills Practice Answers and Explanations on Transparencies ● ▲ ■	• **Test Bank Software** ● ▲ ■ • **Got It! Assessment Videotapes,** Tape 5 ● ▲
• **Selection Support Workbook:** ● ▲ ■ Grammar and Style, p. 254 • **Writing and Grammar,** Diamond Level ● ▲ ■ • **Extension Activities,** p. 55 ● ▲ ■	• **Daily Language Practice Transparencies** ● ▲	• **Writing and Grammar iText CD-ROM** ● ▲ ■ ***Take It to the Net*** www.phschool.com

BLOCK SCHEDULING: Use one 90-minute class period to preteach the selection and have students read it. Use a second 90-minute class period to assess students' mastery of skills and have them complete one of the Extension Activities.

PREFTEACH

Step-by-Step Teaching Guide for pp. 1114–1115

Motivation

Before introducing this story, compile a list of folk remedies. Examples include currant tea for sore throats; cranberries to cure blood poisoning; raw meat to reduce swelling; crushed garlic, mud, or sour cream to soothe stings; sugar to stop hiccups; fennel to sharpen eyesight; strawberries to cure gout; papaya for indigestion; parsley for clean breath; and okra paste to ease muscle pain. Write substances in one column and ailments, in mixed order, in another. Have students try to pair a substance with what it treats or cures. As you reveal the correct matches, invite discussion of which remedies, if any, students have heard of or used. Then, tell them that in the story they will read, folk medicine plays a key role.

Interest Grabber Video

As an alternative, play "The Rights We Enjoy, the Duties We Owe," on Tape 6 to engage student interest.

❶ Background

More About the Author

In her prolific career, Doris Lessing has not only shown her seemingly inexhaustible talent, but has also demonstrated her commitment to political issues by pursuing subjects of equality and civil rights in her fiction. In her 1950 book *The Grass Is Singing,* Lessing describes the complicated relationship between a white farmer's wife and her black servant. Lessing left school when she was 15 and worked variously as a nurse, a typist, and a telephone operator. After the end of her first marriage, she became involved in radical politics and moved to England with her son. There, she continued to support herself with her writing, turning to subjects as varied as mental breakdown, social disintegration, and technological disaster.

Prepare to Read

❶ No Witchcraft for Sale

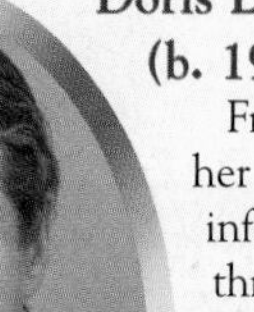

Doris Lessing (b. 1919)

Freely admitting her deep desire to influence others through her works of fiction, Doris Lessing has said that publishing a story or novel is "an attempt to impose one's personality and beliefs on other people. If a writer accepts this responsibility, he must see himself . . . as an architect of the soul."

Exposing Injustice One of the ways that Lessing fulfills this responsibility is by writing about social injustice, challenging ideas of race and women's roles. Her own experiences give her a unique perspective on the problems caused when cultures conflict. In much of her writing, Lessing explores the intricate connections between personal experience and political reality.

She was born in Persia (now Iran), the daughter of a British bank clerk. When she was five, her family moved to the British colony of Rhodesia (now the independent country of Zimbabwe) in southcentral Africa. Her memoir *Under My Skin* (1994) describes some ways that Europeans mistreated Africans, displacing them from their lands and suppressing their traditions.

Reflecting on the era of British rule in Africa, Lessing noted that many of the British immigrants honestly thought that colonization would be good for Africa. She suggests that this kind of misguided belief is enough to make us "wonder which of the idealisms that make our hearts beat faster will seem wrong-headed to people a hundred years from now."

Experience Shapes a Writer Lessing's talent for writing developed as a response to a variety of experiences, including a childhood she described as a mixture of some pleasure and much pain. Strictly disciplined by her mother at home and by teachers at school, the young Lessing sought refuge in reading and in explorations of nature with her brother.

Acknowledging that unhappy childhoods sometimes lead people to become fiction writers, Lessing adds, "Of course, I wasn't thinking in terms of being a writer then—I was just thinking about how to escape, all the time."

Her father's bitter memories of World War I were another striking influence on the developing writer's world view. Lessing absorbed them as a kind of "poison." She would later comment that "We are all of us made by war, twisted and warped by war, but we seem to forget it."

Personal and Political Themes The turbulent influences that drove Lessing to write also taught her about the relationship between individuals and society. Early works such as her first novel, *The Grass Is Singing* (1950), and *African Stories* (1964), reflect her awareness of European injustices against Africans. Martha Quest, the heroine of a five-novel series by Lessing called *Children of Violence* (1952–1969), faces private battles that reflect global conflicts. *The Golden Notebook* (1962), Lessing's best-known novel, explores social issues through one woman's persistent search for identity. The dominant theme in her works is the free woman who struggles for individuality and equality despite social assumptions and pressures.

An Artist's Responsibility Throughout her writing career, Lessing has honored her responsibility to her audience. Her works have explored the roles of women in modern society, the evils of racism, and the limits of idealism in solving problems facing society. Her vision is broad; her voice is direct and challenging.

TEACHING RESOURCES

The following resources can be used to enrich or extend the instruction for pp. 1114–1115.

Motivation

Interest Grabber Video, Tape 6

Background

Beyond Literature, p. 55 ■

Take It to the Net

Visit www.phschool.com for background and hotlinks for the selection.

Literary Analysis

Literary Analysis and Reading Transparencies, Cultural Conflict, p. 110 ■

Reading

Literary Analysis and Reading Transparencies, Analyzing Cultural Differences, p. 109

Selection Support: Reading Strategy, p. 255; Build Vocabulary, p. 253

■ **BLOCK SCHEDULING:** Resources marked with this symbol provide varied instruction during 90-minute blocks.

Preview

Connecting to the Literature

You may be a friend of the captain of the team, but when she unfairly decides to bench you during a big game, friendship suddenly seems less important than power. In this story, Lessing explores a conflict between a servant and his masters, who are also his friends.

❷ Literary Analysis

Cultural Conflict

Many British stories of the mid-twentieth century reflect the conflicts of British colonialism, the rule of other regions by Britain. These conflicts include **cultural conflicts**—disagreements arising from differences in beliefs and values. As you read, note how Lessing shows the connections among cultural, political, and personal conflicts.

Connecting Literary Elements

Every conflict has at least two sides, so the **point of view** from which a struggle is reported is significant. Different types of point of view include

- **First person point of view:** The story is told by a character involved in the action.
- **Limited third-person point of view:** The narrator is outside the action but tells the story as it was experienced by one character.
- **Omniscient third-person point of view:** The narrator is outside the action and presents more information than any one character could have, such as details about the thoughts of a number of characters.

As you read, determine the point of view Lessing uses and how her use of it—the information she gives and does not give—affects your understanding of the conflicts in the story.

❸ Reading Strategy

Analyzing Cultural Differences

To appreciate and understand a story involving conflicts between cultures, **analyze the cultural differences**—the contrast in customs, beliefs, and values—that contribute to the problems. Use a Venn diagram like the one shown to analyze cultural conflict in "No Witchcraft for Sale."

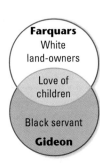

Farquars
White land-owners

Love of children

Black servant
Gideon

Vocabulary Development

reverently (rev′ ər ənt lē) *adv.* with deep respect or awe (p. 1116)

defiantly (di fī′ ənt lē) *adv.* disobediently; in open resistance (p. 1117)

efficacy (ef′ i kə sē) *n.* power to produce intended effects (p. 1118)

incredulously (in krej′ o͞o ləs lē) *adv.* in a manner expressing doubt or disbelief (p. 1120)

skeptical (skep′ ti kəl) *adj.* doubting; not easily persuaded (p. 1120)

❷ Literary Analysis

Cultural Conflict

- Tell students that in this lesson they will focus on cultural conflicts, disagreements that arise from differences in beliefs and values.
- Read the note about cultural conflict as a class. Call students' attention to the differences between cultural, political, and personal conflicts.
- Use the instruction for Connecting Literary Elements to review with students the different types of point of view, including first-person, limited third-person, and omniscient third-person points of view.
- Use the Cultural Conflict transparency in **Literary Analysis and Reading Transparencies,** p. 110, to demonstrate to students how to interpret story incidents in terms of cultural conflict.

❸ Reading Strategy

Analyzing Cultural Differences

- Explain to students that before they begin reading a story about cultural conflicts, they should analyze cultural differences—differences in customs, beliefs, and values—that exacerbate the problem.
- Read the note about Analyzing Cultural Differences together as a class.
- Have students practice this skill using the graphic organizer on p. 1115 and the Analyzing Cultural Differences transparency on p. 109 of **Literary Analysis and Reading Transparencies.**

Vocabulary Development

- Pronounce each vocabulary word for students, and read the definitions as a class. Have students identify any words with which they are already familiar.

CUSTOMIZE INSTRUCTION FOR UNIVERSAL ACCESS

For Special Needs Students	For Less Proficient Readers	For English Learners
Have students read the adapted version of "No Witchcraft for Sale" in the **Adapted Reader's Companion.** This version provides basic-level instruction in an interactive format with questions and write-on lines. Completing the adapted version will prepare students to read the selection in the Student Edition.	Have students read "No Witchcraft for Sale" in the **Reader's Companion.** This version provides basic-level instruction in an interactive format with questions and write-on lines. After students finish the selection in **Reader's Companion,** have them complete the questions and activities in the Student Edition.	Have students read the adapted version of "No Witchcraft for Sale" in the **English Learner's Companion.** This version provides basic-level instruction in an interactive format with questions and write-on lines. Completing the adapted version will prepare students to read the selection in the Student Edition.

 ***E-Teach***

Visit E-Teach at www.phschool.com for teachers' essays on how to teach, with questions and answers.

TEACH

Step-by-Step Teaching Guide for pp. 1116–1122

CUSTOMIZE INSTRUCTION
For Intrapersonal Learners

Ask students, as they read, to put themselves in Gideon's place to try to understand his feelings: his pride, his sense of betrayal, his resignation to his role as a black African man working on a white, Eurocentric homestead, and so on. Challenge students not to judge Gideon, as the Farquars do, but to grasp his point of view.

1 About the Selection

The Farquars, a white family living on a homestead in Africa, employ Gideon, a local man, as their cook. He is kind and loving toward their young son, Teddy, but never forgets his place as a servant. When a medical emergency causes Gideon to use his traditional healing skills to restore Teddy's eyesight, the family is deeply grateful. But the incident leads to a cultural clash when the Farquars misunderstand Gideon's tribal position as a healer. The stand-off between the Farquars and Gideon underscores a cultural gap that cannot be bridged.

2 ▶ Critical Viewing

Answer: Students may predict that the story will be about plants or animals used for ritual purposes.

1 No Witchcraft for Sale

DORIS LESSING

Background

By 1924, the year Lessing's family moved to Southern Rhodesia (now Zimbabwe), the country had been under British control for just two decades. Previously, the region had been ruled by a succession of black African empires. Under British and then white Rhodesian rule, the political rights of black Rhodesians were limited, and most blacks were constrained to work as low-paid servants.

The Farquars had been childless for years when little Teddy was born; and they were touched by the pleasure of their servants, who brought presents of fowls and eggs and flowers to the homestead when they came to rejoice over the baby, exclaiming with delight over his downy golden head and his blue eyes. They congratulated Mrs. Farquar as if she had achieved a very great thing, and she felt that she had—her smile for the lingering, admiring natives was warm and grateful.

Later, when Teddy had his first haircut, Gideon the cook picked up the soft gold tufts from the ground, and held them reverently in his hand. Then he smiled at the little boy and said: "Little Yellow Head." That became the native name for the child. Gideon and Teddy were great friends from the first. When Gideon had finished his work, he would lift Teddy on his shoulders to the shade of a big tree, and play with him there, forming curious little toys from twigs and leaves and grass, or shaping animals from wetted soil. When Teddy learned to walk it was often Gideon who crouched before him, clucking encouragement,

2 ▲ Critical Viewing Using this picture and the title, predict what this story will be about. **[Predict]**

reverently (rev´ ər ənt lē) *adv.* with deep respect or awe

TEACHING RESOURCES

The following resources can be used to enrich or extend the instruction for pp. 1116–1122.

Literary Analysis
Selection Support: Literary Analysis, p. 256

Reading
Adapted Reader's Companion
English Learner's Companion

BLOCK SCHEDULING: Resources marked with this symbol provide varied instruction during 90-minute blocks.

finally catching him when he fell, tossing him up in the air till they both became breathless with laughter. Mrs. Farquar was fond of the old cook because of his love for her child.

3 There was no second baby; and one day Gideon said: "Ah, missus, missus, the Lord above sent this one; Little Yellow Head is the most good thing we have in our house." Because of that "we" Mrs. Farquar felt a warm impulse toward her cook; and at the end of the month she raised his wages. He had been with her now for several years; he was one of the few natives who had his wife and children in the compound and never wanted to go home to his kraal,[1] which was some hundreds of miles away. Sometimes a small piccanin who had been born the same time as Teddy, could be seen peering from the edge of the bush, staring in awe at the little white boy with his miraculous fair hair and Northern blue eyes. The two little children would gaze at each other with a wide, interested gaze, and once Teddy put out his hand curiously to touch the black child's cheeks and hair.

Gideon, who was watching, shook his head wonderingly, and said: "Ah, missus, these are both children, and one will grow up to be a baas, and one will be a servant"; and Mrs. Farquar smiled and said sadly, "Yes, Gideon, I was thinking the same." She sighed. "It is God's will," said Gideon, who was a mission boy. The Farquars were very religious people; and this shared feeling about God bound servant and masters even closer together.

Teddy was about six years old when he was given a scooter, and discovered the intoxications of speed. All day he would fly around the homestead, in and out of flowerbeds, scattering squawking chickens and irritated dogs, finishing with a wide dizzying arc into the kitchen door. There he would cry: "Gideon, look at me!" And Gideon would laugh and say: "Very clever, Little Yellow Head." Gideon's youngest son, who was now a herdsboy, came especially up from the compound to see the scooter. He was afraid to come near it, but Teddy showed off in front of him. "Piccanin," shouted Teddy, "get out of my way!" And he raced in circles around the black child until he was frightened, and fled back to the bush.

"Why did you frighten him?" asked Gideon, gravely reproachful.[2]

Teddy said defiantly: "He's only a black boy," and laughed. Then, when Gideon turned away from him without speaking, his face fell. Very soon he slipped into the house and found an orange and brought it to Gideon, saying: "This is for you." He could not bring himself to say he was sorry; but he could not bear to lose Gideon's affection either. Gideon took the orange unwillingly and sighed. "Soon you will be going away to school, Little Yellow Head," he said wonderingly, "and then you will be grown up." He shook his head gently and said, "And that is how our lives go." He seemed to be putting a distance between himself and Teddy, not because of resentment, but in the way a person accepts

1. **kraal** (kräl) village of South African natives, usually fenced in with a stockade.
2. **reproachful** (ri prōch′ fəl) *adj.* expressing blame.

Reading Strategy
Analyzing Cultural Differences What cultural values do the Farquars and Gideon share?

defiantly (di fī′ ənt lē) *adv.* disobediently; in open resistance

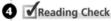

4 
Reading Check
What is Gideon's role in the Farquar household?

3 Reading Strategy
Analyzing Cultural Differences

- Remind students that by paying attention to differences in cultural background, they may be able to identify cultural differences more readily.
- Ask students the Reading Strategy question on p. 1117: What cultural values do the Farquars and Gideon share?
  Answer: Both the Farquars and Gideon believe in God and destiny; however, the white colonists believe they are born to rule, and the black servant believes he is born to serve.

4 Reading Check

Answer: Gideon's role in the Farquar household is that of cook.

CUSTOMIZE INSTRUCTION FOR UNIVERSAL ACCESS

For Special Needs Students	For English Learners	For Advanced Readers
Encourage students to read aloud from the text with teacher guidance. Tell them to pronounce each word as they go, and to visualize the scene as they read. Remind them that the story is set in Africa, and that many of the words will be unfamiliar to them. Encourage students to determine the meaning of the words from context.	Students may find some African terms such as *baas, veld,* and *kaffir* in Lessing's "No Witchcraft for Sale" especially difficult, because they are totally unfamiliar. Encourage students to concentrate on the sounds of words with which they have trouble, and to use the footnotes and margin definitions to enhance their understanding.	Have students read "No Witchcraft for Sale" independently. Remind them that as a child, Doris Lessing lived in Rhodesia, a country now known by the name Zimbabwe. Ask students to research and provide a timeline overview of the changes and turmoil the country has undergone in the past century.

❺ Literary Analysis

Cultural Conflict

- Remind students that cultural conflict is often brought about by a difference in values or beliefs.
- Ask them the Literary Analysis question on p. 1118: How do Gideon and Teddy manage the differences in their social status to protect their vulnerable emotions?
  Answer: Gideon and Teddy treat each other with formality and politeness; they do not touch each other.

❻ Reading Strategy

Analyzing Cultural Differences

- Review with students their understanding of how to analyze cultural differences and conflicts.
- Ask students the Reading Strategy question on p. 1118: When Teddy is injured by the snake, what do the reactions of Gideon and Mrs. Farquar show about their cultural differences and similarities?
  Answer: In this incident, Mrs. Farquar, the mistress of the house, is reduced to helplessness, while Gideon, the servant, is master of the situation. Both are afraid of the consequences of the snake poison, but Gideon is confident that if he finds the plant remedy soon enough, he can save Teddy's sight.

something inevitable. The baby had lain in his arms and smiled up into his face: the tiny boy had swung from his shoulders and played with him by the hour. Now Gideon would not let his flesh touch the flesh of
5 the white child. He was kind, but there was a grave formality in his voice that made Teddy pout and sulk away. Also, it made him into a man: with Gideon he was polite, and carried himself formally, and if he came into the kitchen to ask for something, it was in the way a white man uses toward a servant, expecting to be obeyed.

But on the day that Teddy came staggering into the kitchen with his fists to his eyes, shrieking with pain, Gideon dropped the pot full of hot soup that he was holding, rushed to the child, and forced aside his fingers. "A snake!" he exclaimed. Teddy had been on his scooter, and had come to a rest with his foot on the side of a big tub of plants. A tree-snake, hanging by its tail from the roof, had spat full into his eyes. Mrs. Farquar came running when she heard the commotion. "He'll go blind," she sobbed, holding Teddy close against her. "Gideon, he'll go blind!" Already the eyes, with perhaps half an hour's sight left in them, were swollen up to the size of fists: Teddy's small white face was distorted by great purple oozing protuberances.[3] Gideon said: "Wait a minute, missus, I'll get some medicine." He ran off into the bush.

Mrs. Farquar lifted the child into the house and bathed his eyes with permanganate.[4] She had scarcely heard Gideon's words; but when she saw that her remedies had no effect at all, and remembered how she had seen natives with no sight in their eyes, because of the spitting of a snake, she began to look for the return of her cook, remembering what she heard of the efficacy of native herbs. She stood by the window, holding the terrified, sobbing little boy in her arms, and peered helplessly into the bush. It was not more than a few minutes before she saw Gideon come bounding back, and in his hand he held a plant.

"Do not be afraid, missus," said Gideon, "this will cure Little Yellow Head's eyes." He stripped the leaves from the plant, leaving a small white fleshy root. Without even washing it, he put the root in his mouth,
6 chewed it vigorously, and then held the spittle there while he took the child forcibly from Mrs. Farquar. He gripped Teddy down between his knees, and pressed the balls of his thumbs into the swollen eyes, so that the child screamed and Mrs. Farquar cried out in protest: "Gideon, Gideon!" But Gideon took no notice. He knelt over the writhing child, pushing back the puffy lids till chinks of eyeball showed, and then he spat hard, again and again, into first one eye, and then the other. He finally lifted Teddy gently into his mother's arms, and said: "His eyes will get better." But Mrs. Farquar was weeping with terror, and she could hardly thank him: it was impossible to believe that Teddy could keep his sight. In a couple of hours the swellings were gone: the eyes were inflamed and tender but Teddy could see. Mr. and Mrs. Farquar went to Gideon in the kitchen and thanked him over and over again. They felt

Literary Analysis
Cultural Conflict How do Gideon and Teddy manage the differences in their social status to protect their vulnerable emotions?

efficacy (ef′ i kə sē) *n.* power to produce intended effects

Reading Strategy
Analyzing Cultural Differences When Teddy is injured by the snake, what do the reactions of Gideon and Mrs. Farquar show about their cultural differences and similarities?

3. **protuberances** (prō to͞o′ bər əns iz) *n.* bulges; swellings.
4. **permanganate** (pər maŋ′ gə nāt′) salt of permanganic acid.

ENRICHMENT: Cultural Connection

Folk Medicine

Long before people could obtain synthetic medicines and compounds from doctors or pharmacies, people all over the world relied on the natural materials of their environment to battle illness and injury. For example, an aspirin tablet contains salicylic acid, which can relieve pain and reduce fever. But for centuries, Native Americans chewed on willow bark for the same purpose. Scientists now know that willow bark contains that compound.

Some folk remedies use local plants or herbs for soothing teas or poultices. Others combine crushed minerals or animal by-products with plant substances to form compounds that cure various ailments.

helpless because of their gratitude: it seemed they could do nothing to express it. They gave Gideon presents for his wife and children, and a big increase in wages, but these things could not pay for Teddy's now completely cured eyes. Mrs. Farquar said: "Gideon, God chose you as an instrument for His goodness," and Gideon said: "Yes, missus, God is very good."

Now, when such a thing happens on a farm, it cannot be long before everyone hears of it. Mr. and Mrs. Farquar told their neighbors and the story was discussed from one end of the district to the other. The bush is full of secrets. No one can live in Africa, or at least on the veld,[5] without learning very soon that there is an ancient wisdom of leaf and soil and season—and, too, perhaps most important of all, of the darker tracts of the human mind—which is the black man's heritage. Up and down the district people were telling anecdotes, reminding each other of things that had happened to them.

"But I saw it myself, I tell you. It was a puff-adder bite. The kaffir's[6] arm was swollen to the elbow, like a great shiny black bladder. He was groggy after half a minute. He was dying. Then suddenly a kaffir walked out of the bush with his hands full of green stuff. He smeared something on the place, and next day my boy was back at work, and all you could see was two small punctures in the skin."

This was the kind of tale they told. And, as always, with a certain amount of exasperation, because while all of them knew that in the bush of Africa are waiting valuable drugs locked in bark, in simple-looking leaves, in roots, it was impossible to ever get the truth about them from the natives themselves.

The story eventually reached town; and perhaps it was at a sun-downer party, or some such function, that a doctor, who happened to be there, challenged it. "Nonsense," he said. "These things get exaggerated in the telling. We are always checking up on this kind of story, and we draw a blank every time."

Anyway, one morning there arrived a strange car at the homestead, and out stepped one of the workers from the laboratory in town, with cases full of test-tubes and chemicals.

Mr. and Mrs. Farquar were flustered and pleased and flattered. They asked the scientist to lunch, and they told the story all over again, for the hundredth time. Little Teddy was there too, his blue eyes sparkling with health, to prove the truth of it. The scientist explained how humanity might benefit if this new drug could be offered for sale; and the Farquars were even more pleased: they were kind, simple people, who liked to think of something good coming about because of them. But when the scientist began talking of the money that might result, their manner showed discomfort. Their feelings over the miracle (that was how they thought of it) were so strong and deep and religious, that

7 ▲ Critical Viewing
In what ways does the expression and appearance of this southern African illustrate the wisdom of Gideon's generation? **[Evaluate]**

5. **veld** in South Africa, open grassy country, with few bushes and almost no trees.
6. **kaffir's** belonging to a black African; in South Africa, a contemptuous term.

7 ▶ Critical Viewing

Answer: Students may say that his gray hair and weathered face suggest the experience and wisdom of age, and that his long stare can represent a concern for those around him or a wariness of strangers.

CUSTOMIZE INSTRUCTION FOR UNIVERSAL ACCESS

For Special Needs Students	For Less Proficient Readers
As students read the selection with teacher guidance, have students identify some of the details the author provides that suggest the differences between the Farquars and Gideon. To help students identify the way in which these differences are cultural conflicts, use the Cultural Conflict transparency on p. 110 of **Literary Analysis and Reading Transparencies.**	Have students read "No Witchcraft for Sale" with teacher guidance. Encourage students as they read to pay attention to the way in which the story is told. Help them to identify the point of view of the narrator as third-person limited. Then, ask them to imagine Mrs. Farquar's perspective on Gideon. Have them write three diary entries for her, one from the day of the snake bite, one from the day of the scientist's visit, and one from years later when Teddy is an adult.

8 Vocabulary Development

Forms of *skeptical*

- Call students' attention to *skeptical*, a word that means "not easily persuaded."
- Have students suggest other words and phrases that are forms of skeptical.
  Possible responses: *skeptic; skepticism; skeptically*
- Have students look up any unfamiliar words in a dictionary.

9 Literary Analysis

Cultural Conflict

- Have students read the bracketed passage to themselves. Ask them to consider any cultural conflicts in the passage.
- Then, ask them the Literary Analysis question on p. 1120: How is the Farquars' earlier reaction to the scientist's offer of money similar to Gideon's reaction to their request?
  Answer: Both the Farquars and Gideon find the idea of sharing the secret of the healing herb for profit distasteful.

it was distasteful to them to think of money. The scientist, seeing their faces, went back to his first point, which was the advancement of humanity. He was perhaps a trifle perfunctory:[7] it was not the first time he had come salting the tail of a fabulous bush secret.[8]

Eventually, when the meal was over, the Farquars called Gideon into their living room and explained to him that this baas, here, was a Big Doctor from the Big City, and he had come all that way to see Gideon. At this Gideon seemed afraid; he did not understand; and Mrs. Farquar explained quickly that it was because of the wonderful thing he had done with Teddy's eyes that the Big Baas had come.

Gideon looked from Mrs. Farquar to Mr. Farquar, and then at the little boy, who was showing great importance because of the occasion. At last he said grudgingly: "The Big Baas want to know what medicine I used?" He spoke incredulously, as if he could not believe his old friends could so betray him. Mr. Farquar began explaining how a useful medicine could be made out of the root, and how it could be put on sale, and how thousands of people, black and white, up and down the continent of Africa, could be saved by the medicine when that spitting snake filled their eyes with poison. Gideon listened, his eyes bent on the ground, the skin of his forehead puckering in discomfort. When Mr. Farquar had finished he did not reply. The scientist, who all this time had been leaning back in a big chair, sipping his coffee and
8 smiling with skeptical good humor, chipped in and explained all over again, in different words, about the making of drugs and the progress of science. Also, he offered Gideon a present.

incredulously (in krej´ oo ləs lē) *adv.* in a manner expressing doubt or disbelief

skeptical (skep´ ti kəl) *adj.* doubting; not easily persuaded

There was silence after this further explanation, and then Gideon remarked indifferently that he could not remember the root. His face was sullen and hostile, even when he looked at the Farquars, whom he usually treated like old friends. They were beginning to feel annoyed; and this feeling annulled[9] the guilt that had been sprung into life by Gideon's accusing manner. They were beginning to feel that he was unreasonable. But it was at that moment that they all realized he would never give in. The magical drug would remain where it was,
9 unknown and useless except for the tiny scattering of Africans who had the knowledge, natives who might be digging a ditch for the municipality in a ragged shirt and a pair of patched shorts, but who were still born to healing, hereditary healers, being the nephews or sons of the old witch doctors whose ugly masks and bits of bone and all the uncouth[10] properties of magic were the outward signs of real power and wisdom.

The Farquars might tread on that plant fifty times a day as they passed from house to garden, from cow kraal to mealie field, but they would never know it.

Literary Analysis
Cultural Conflict How is the Farquar's earlier reaction to the scientists offer of money similar to Gideon's reaction to their request?

7. **perfunctory** (pər fuŋk´ tə rē) *adj.* done without care or interest.
8. **salting . . . bush secret** allusion to the humororus and ironic advice given to children about how to catch a bird—by putting salt on its tail. In other words, the scientist does not really expect to capture a valuable bit of information.
9. **annulled** (ə nuld´) *v.* did away with; neutralized.
10. **uncouth** (un ko͞oth´) *adj.* uncultured; crude; strange.

ENRICHMENT: Science Connection

Ethnobotany

Most students know that *botany* is the scientific study of plants. A special area of botany that combines science with folk culture is *ethnobotany*. Ethnobotanists study the plant lore of a region or group of people and learn the ways indigenous people use plants for food, medicine, commerce, art, or any other purpose. Unlike the scientist in "No Witchcraft for Sale," ethnobotanists are trained in botany *and* in cultural anthropology, which enables them to respect the ancient lore and knowledge local people possess and to analyze their remedies scientifically.

But they went on persuading and arguing, with all the force of their exasperation; and Gideon continued to say that he could not remember, or that there was no such root, or that it was the wrong season of the year, or that it wasn't the root itself, but the spit from his mouth that had cured Teddy's eyes. He said all these things one after another, and seemed not to care they were contradictory. He was rude and stubborn. The Farquars could hardly recognize their gentle, lovable old servant in this ignorant, perversely obstinate African, standing there in front of them with lowered eyes, his hands twitching his cook's apron, repeating over and over whichever one of the stupid refusals that first entered his head.

And suddenly he appeared to give in. He lifted his head, gave a long blank angry look at the circle of whites, who seemed to him like a circle of yelping dogs pressing around him, and said: "I will show you the root."

11 They walked single file away from the homestead down a kaffir path. It was a blazing December afternoon, with the sky full of hot rain clouds. Everything was hot: the sun was like a bronze tray whirling overhead, there was a heat shimmer over the fields, the soil was scorching underfoot, the dusty wind blew gritty and thick and warm in their faces. It was a terrible day, fit only for reclining on a verandah with iced drinks, which is where they would normally have been at that hour.

From time to time, remembering that on the day of the snake it had taken ten minutes to find the root, someone asked: "Is it much further, Gideon?" And Gideon would answer over his shoulder, with angry politeness: "I'm looking for the root, baas." And indeed, he would frequently bend sideways and trail his hand among the grasses with a gesture that was insulting in its perfunctoriness. He walked them through the bush along unknown paths for two hours, in that melting destroying heat, so that the sweat trickled coldly down them and their heads ached. They were all quite silent: the Farquars because they were angry, the scientist because he was being proved right again; there was no such plant. His was a tactful silence.

At last, six miles from the house, Gideon suddenly decided they had had enough; or perhaps his anger evaporated at that moment. He picked up, without an attempt at looking anything but casual, a handful of blue flowers from the grass, flowers that had been growing plentifully all down the paths they had come.

He handed them to the scientist without looking at him, and marched off by himself on the way home, leaving them to follow him if they chose.

When they got back to the house, the scientist went to the kitchen to thank Gideon: he was being very polite, even though there was an amused look in his eyes. Gideon was not there. Throwing the flowers

10 *Colonial Rhodesia*

Starting in the 1400s, Southern Rhodesia was ruled by a series of Shona empires. British exploitation of the area began in the late 1800s, when Cecil Rhodes brought the British South Africa Company to mine gold there, crushing outbursts of violent resistance by the local peoples. White Rhodesians voted to become a British colony in 1922.

In 1965, Rhodesia declared independence from Britain, and in 1969 a new constitution was enacted to ensure that the black majority would never rule the country. It was only in the 1970s, after years of civil war and the deaths of more than 250,000 guerrilla fighters, that blacks were granted equal rights. In 1980, Rhodesia became officially independent, changing its name to Zimbabwe ("house of stone"), the name of an ancient Shona city.

Zimbabwe (Rhodesia)

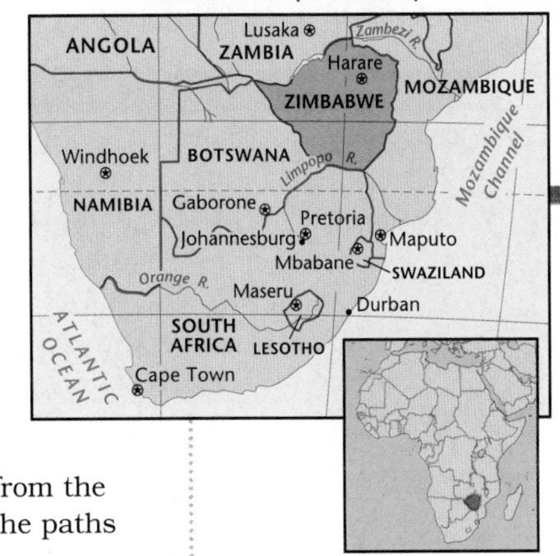

12 Reading Check

What does Gideon finally do in response to requests that he identify the plant?

10 Background

Colonial Rhodesia

Cecil Rhodes (1853–1902) studied at Oxford University and built his fortune at the diamond mines in Kimberley, South Africa, before becoming a statesman of the British colony there. He was prime minister of Cape Colony from 1890 but resigned the post after being found guilty of breach of duty for an unauthorized raid on the Transvaal, the Dutch controlled part of the region. Rhodes is famous today for the approximately ninety Rhodes scholarships he endowed at Oxford University for students of the colonies, America, and Germany. Many Rhodes scholars have gone on to important political posts, including former President Bill Clinton and former New Jersey Governor Bill Bradley.

11 Critical Thinking

Analyze

- Review with students the narrative points of view from the Connecting Literary Elements chart on p. 1115.
- Then, ask students to identify the point of view and bias of the narrator here.
  Answer: The narrator uses a third-person limited point of view with a Eurocentric bias. None of Gideon's thoughts are revealed, and the description is slanted to the colonial viewpoint. It is unlikely that Gideon would judge the day as ". . . fit only for reclining on a verandah with iced drinks."

12 Reading Check

Answer: Gideon takes the Farquars and the scientist on a six-mile walk and proceeds to hand them blue flowers from a plant they had walked past the entire route.

CUSTOMIZE INSTRUCTION FOR UNIVERSAL ACCESS

For Special Needs Students	For English Learners	For Advanced Readers
Have students read "No Witchcraft for Sale," with teacher guidance. Remind them to pay attention to the characters and their conflicts as they read, and encourage them to read multiple times any sections with which they have difficulty to help aid their comprehension.	English learners may find this story especially relevant, because they have no doubt encountered some of their own cultural conflicts as they have been learning a new language. Ask students to comment on the cultural conflicts Gideon and the Farquars experience, and to address in what way the conflicts could have been resolved.	Students may find the craze for herbal remedies an interesting topic to pursue for an extended project. Encourage students to prepare a report on herbal medicines—both traditional and experimental.

ASSESS

Answers for p. 1122

Review and Assess

1. Possible responses: Some students may feel that Gideon was right to honor his cultural traditions over the importunities of his white employers. Others may say that the opportunity to help many people should take precedence over his traditions.
2. **(a)** Gideon gives him his nickname when his hair is cut. **(b)** At first, "Little Yellow Head" is a term of affection. As Teddy grows, the term brings sadness at the loss of innocence and reinforces the fact that Gideon and Teddy have vastly different lives and positions.
3. **(a)** Gideon uses a folk remedy to save his sight. **(b)**The incident reveals to the Farquars that Gideon has knowledge that is useful to their existence and their well-being.
4. **(a)** When the scientist tries to get Gideon to reveal his secret, the Farquars do not understand Gideon's reluctance; that misunderstanding forces a wedge into their otherwise amicable relationship. **(b)** Possible response: He refuses to share his knowledge because it is part of his family's tradition, not something to be shared with strangers.
5. Gideon realizes that very soon Teddy will become a white master over other black servants.
6. Possible response: Yes, Gideon should hold his heritage in respect; no, he should pass along his knowledge to help people.

casually into the back of his car, the eminent visitor departed on his way back to his laboratory.

Gideon was back in his kitchen in time to prepare dinner, but he was sulking. He spoke to Mr. Farquar like an unwilling servant. It was days before they liked each other again.

The Farquars made inquiries about the root from their laborers. Sometimes they were answered with distrustful stares. Sometimes the natives said: "We do not know. We have never heard of the root." One, the cattle boy, who had been with them a long time, and had grown to trust them a little, said: "Ask your boy in the kitchen. Now, there's a doctor for you. He's the son of a famous medicine man who used to be in these parts, and there's nothing he cannot cure." Then he added politely: "Of course, he's not as good as the white man's doctor, we know that, but he's good for us."

After some time, when the soreness had gone from between the Farquars and Gideon, they began to joke: "When are you going to show us the snake-root, Gideon?" And he would laugh and shake his head, saying, a little uncomfortably: "But I did show you, missus, have you forgotten?"

Much later, Teddy, as a schoolboy, would come into the kitchen and say: "You old rascal, Gideon! Do you remember that time you tricked us all by making us walk miles all over the veld for nothing? It was so far my father had to carry me!"

And Gideon would double up with polite laughter. After much laughing, he would suddenly straighten himself up, wipe his old eyes, and look sadly at Teddy, who was grinning mischievously at him across the kitchen: "Ah, Little Yellow Head, how you have grown! Soon you will be grown up with a farm of your own . . ."

Review and Assess

Thinking About the Selection

1. **Respond:** Do you sympathize with Gideon's resistance? Explain.
2. **(a) Recall:** How does "Little Yellow Head" get his nickname? **(b) Infer:** How does this nickname emphasize the differences between the Farquars and their servants?
3. **(a) Recall:** How does Gideon save Teddy's sight? **(b) Interpret:** In what way does this incident reveal an aspect of Gideon previously unknown to the Farquars?
4. **(a) Analyze:** What effect does the scientist's visit have on the Farquars' relationship with Gideon? **(b) Draw Conclusions:** Why does Gideon refuse to share his knowledge?
5. **Interpret:** What do Gideon's last words to Teddy mean?
6. **Make a Judgment:** Do you think Gideon's decision to withhold information about the plant is justified? Explain.

ASSESSMENT PRACTICE: Writing Skills

Strategy **(For more practice, see Test Preparation Workbook, p. 55.)**

Many tests require students to apply revision strategies to passages. Use the following sample test item to give students practice.

Mr. and Mrs. Farquar were flustered and pleased and flattered. They asked the scientist to lunch and they told the story all over again, for the hundredth time.

Which of these sentences would *best* fit after the first sentence in the paragraph?

A The day was warm and rain was forecast.
B Mrs. Farquar blushed whenever the scientist spoke, and Mr. Farquar cleared his throat from time to time.
C Mrs. Farquar suspected that the scientist might really be a criminal.
D The scientist was tall and had curly hair.

Remind students that the Farquars were flustered by the scientist's presence. The correct answer is *B*.

Review and Assess

Literary Analysis

Cultural Conflict

1. Using a chart like the one shown, identify three incidents in the story that reflect **cultural conflict.** Explain your choices.

2. (a) Summarize the viewpoint of each side in this conflict. (b) How is the conflict political, personal, and cultural?
3. In what way does the story both resolve and leave unresolved the conflict between Gideon and the Farquars?
4. Do you think Lessing could have communicated the same message in a newspaper article? Why or why not?

Connecting Literary Elements

5. From what **point of view** is the story told? Explain.
6. (a) Does the narrator identify more closely with either cultural perspective? (b) What details help you decide?
7. How would the story be different if it had been told from Gideon's perspective?
8. (a) Does Lessing successfully use point of view to reflect the fact that, as a white Rhodesian, her knowledge of the experience of blacks is limited? Explain. (b) Does this use of point of view show respect for the experience of black Rhodesians? Explain.

Reading Strategy

Analyzing Cultural Differences

9. Identify two incidents that reflect Teddy's or his family's sense of superiority over black Africans.
10. (a) What values do the Farquars and Gideon share? Support your answer with details. (b) What values set them apart?

Extend Understanding

11. **World Events Connection:** In what other countries or times could a story with the same theme be set? Explain.

Quick Review

Cultural conflicts are disagreements arising from differences in customs, beliefs, and values.

The **point of view,** or perspective, from which a story is told determines the scope and kind of information the narrator gives readers.

Point of view is defined by the relation of the narrator to the story. In **first-person point of view,** the narrator is a character inside the story. In **third-person point of view,** the narrator is outside the story. **Limited third-person point of view** filters the story through the experience of one character.

To **analyze cultural differences,** consider the contrasts between the customs, beliefs, and values of two groups.

Take It to the Net

www.phschool.com

Take the interactive self-test online to check your understanding of the selection.

Answers for p. 1123

Review and Assess

1. Sample response: **Incident:** Teddy frightens Gideon's son; **Farquars' Values:** White people are superior; **Gideon's Values:** Acceptance of Teddy's inevitable estrangement.
2. **(a)** The Farquars do not understand Gideon's refusal to identify the root he used to save Teddy's eyesight. Gideon and other residents believe that the healing methods are sacred. **(b)** Possible response: Gideon's reasons for not sharing the healing method with the scientist are personal and cultural; the scientist's desire to learn the secret is political; the conflict between Gideon and the Farquars is cultural, personal, and political.
3. The conflict is resolved in that life eventually goes back to normal, but neither Gideon nor the Farquars ever completely understands the other's viewpoint.
4. Possible response: Students may say that a newspaper article might be too abstract to engage readers.
5. The story is told from the third-person limited point of view.
6. **(a)** Possible response: Students may say that Lessing tries for an even-handed portrayal of the conflict. **(b)** She gives evidence of Gideon's pride in his heritage and acknowledges that others praise his skills. She also presents logical arguments from the scientist that, when divorced from his arrogance, hold western appeal.
7. Possible response: If the story had been told from Gideon's perspective, it might have included his anger at being asked to reveal his culture's healing secrets.
8. **(a)** Possible response: Yes, Lessing's use of the third-person limited point of view allows her to create a narrator who knows much about the Farquars and the perspective of whites generally, but much less about what Gideon thinks and feels. In this way, Lessing, a white writer, carefully avoids claiming to "know" black experience from

continued

Answers continued

the inside. **(b)** Possible response: Yes, Lessing uses perspective to comment on the experience of black Rhodesians in a way that shows respect.

9. Possible responses: Teddy's frightening of Gideon's youngest son, coupled with the Farquars' insistence that Gideon obey their wishes, suggest the family's sense of superiority over black Africans.
10. **(a)** Both the Farquars and Gideon celebrate their children and have strong religious faith. **(b)** The Farquars see his knowledge as "witchcraft" that should be available as a commercial remedy; Gideon probably sees his folk medicine tradition as something to which only those to whom he is tied by bonds of tradition or loyalty have rights.
11. Possible response: India in the late nineteenth century is a possible alternative setting.

EXTEND

Answers for p. 1124

❶ Vocabulary Development

Word Analysis

1. The Skeptics believed that real knowledge was impossible.
2. A skeptical store owner might not be willing to accept a personal check presented by a stranger because he doubts its validity.

Spelling Strategy

1. The light entering the crystal created a kaleidoscopic pattern.
2. Kinesiologists study skeletons.

Concept Development: Synonyms

1. b
2. a
3. c
4. a
5. c

❷ Grammar and Style

1. like
2. as if
3. as if
4. like
5. as if

Writing Application

Possible response: Gideon raced into the veld *as if* his feet were on fire in search of the precious herb that would restore Teddy's sight *like* magic. Teddy cried *like* a small bush baby, but Gideon pried his eyes open *as* a vise would, and spit into his eyes *as if* he were the snake that spat its poison into Teddy's eyes in the first place.

Integrate Language Skills

❶ Vocabulary Development Lesson

Word Analysis: Forms of *skeptical*

The word *skeptical* means "inclined to doubt or question." Consider this definition as you answer each of the following questions.

1. What did the ancient philosophers called *Skeptics* believe about knowledge?
2. What might a *skeptical* store owner do when a stranger presents a personal check?

Spelling Strategy

In many scientific or philosophical words derived from Greek, the letter *k* is used to spell the *k* sound, as in *skeptical* and *kleptomania*. Use this knowledge to correct the spelling errors below.

1. The light entering the crystal created a caleidoscopic pattern.
2. Cinesiolgists study sceletons.

Concept Development: Synonyms

Synonyms are pairs of words that share nearly the same meaning. In your notebook, write the letter of the word that is the synonym of the word from the vocabulary list on page 1115.

1. reverently: (a) politely, (b) respectfully, (c) slyly
2. defiantly: (a) disobediently, (b) wryly, (c) strongly
3. efficacy: (a) stamina, (b) reliability, (c) effectiveness
4. incredulously: (a) disbelievingly, (b) sincerely, (c) vaguely
5. skeptical: (a) trusting, (b) irate, (c) suspicious

❷ Grammar and Style Lesson

Correct Use of *like* and *as*

Do not confuse ***like*** and ***as***. The subordinating conjunctions *as*, *as if*, and *as though* introduce a subordinate clause, which has its own subject and verb. The preposition *like* introduces a prepositional phrase that includes an object and modifiers.

Subordinating Conjunction: They congratulated Mrs. Farquar as if she had achieved a very great thing. . . .

Preposition: He spoke to Mr. Farquar like an unwilling servant.

Remember that the verb in a clause introduced by *as*, *as if*, or *as though* may be understood, not directly stated.

Practice In your notebook, correctly complete each comparison with the conjunction *as*, *as if*, or *as though* or with the preposition *like*.

1. Teddy's hair was colored __?__ straw.
2. At first, Gideon stared __?__ he did not understand.
3. The scientist looked __?__ he were skeptical.
4. The noon sun was __?__ a furnace.
5. Teddy laughed __?__ he had said something clever.

Writing Application Write a paragraph describing how Gideon saved Teddy from blindness, using *like* and *as* to make at least two comparisons.

WG Prentice Hall Writing and Grammar Connection: Chapter 25, Section 2

TEACHING RESOURCES

The following resources can be used to enrich or extend the instruction for pp. 1124–1125.

Vocabulary

- **Selection Support:** Build Vocabulary, p. 253
- **Vocabulary and Spelling Practice Book** (Use this booklet for skills enrichment.)

Grammar

- **Selection Support:** Grammar and Style, p. 254
- **Writing and Grammar,** Diamond Level, p. 646
- **Daily Language Practice Transparencies** ■

Writing

- **Writing and Grammar,** Diamond Level, p. 228 ■
- **Writing and Grammar iText CD-ROM**

■ **BLOCK SCHEDULING:** Resources marked with this symbol provide varied instruction during 90-minute blocks.

❸ Writing Lesson

Problem-and-Solution Essay

The Farquars and Gideon have a problem: The Farquars cannot understand Gideon's uncooperativeness, and he feels betrayed by them. In an essay, offer a solution to this problem. Make your explanations precise and complete.

Prewriting Take notes on the problem between Gideon and the Farquars. Review your notes to propose a few possible solutions.

Drafting Begin your draft by describing the problem. Then, introduce your solutions. Specify any conditions that would have to be met to implement each solution, and explain each step in logical order.

Revising As you review your draft, mark off steps that are incomplete or imprecise. Add details to answer the questions *why*, *for how long*, *what kind*, and so on.

Model: Revising to Elaborate for Precision

First, Gideon and the Farquars should talk with ~~someone else.~~ *a person, such as Lessing, who has insight into both white and black worlds.* The person can help "translate" their concerns. Then, ~~they should be exposed to each other's culture.~~ *Gideon should visit with white doctors and the Farquars should visit with black healers.*

Precise descriptions help a reader understand exactly *who* and *what* is involved in the solution.

WG *Prentice Hall Writing and Grammar Connection: Chapter 11, Section 3*

❹ Extension Activities

Listening and Speaking Form two teams and hold a **debate on colonialism.** Using details from Lessing's story, consider whether the benefits colonialism may bring outweigh the injustices it may involve. Keep the following tips in mind:

- Use details from the story to support your main points.
- Use parallelism—the expression of related ideas in similar grammatical forms—to make your arguments memorable.

Hold your debate before the class. **[Group Activity]**

Research and Technology Research the discovery of medicines derived from plants in Africa, such as the one used by Gideon in the story. Prepare an **oral report on medical botany** for your class. Consult both print and electronic sources, including books, magazines, and Web sites. Consider experts you might interview, such as doctors or the staff at plant nurseries or nature preserves.

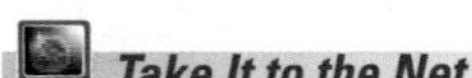

Take It to the Net www.phschool.com

Go online for an additional research activity using the Internet.

Lesson Support for p. 1125

❸ Writing Lesson

- Read with students the note for the writing lesson on p. 1125, then tell students that they will write a problem-and-solution essay in which they solve the conflict between Gideon and the Farquars.
- Have students reread "No Witchcraft for Sale," taking notes on the problem or misunderstanding between Gideon and the Farquars.
- Encourage students to formulate their ideas and possible solutions to the problem by outlining the conflict precisely.
- Use the rubric for Problem-and-Solution Essay in **Performance Assessment and Portfolio Management,** p. 22, to evaluate student work.

❹ Research and Technology

- Read the Research and Technology note with students, and have them do research on medical botany.
- Encourage students to use encyclopedias, Web sites, and medical books to determine what illnesses can be cured with herbs.
- Students may want to consult herbalists, health food shops, doctors, or medical Web sites for additional information.
- Remind students that they should be cautious and discriminating in their research.

CUSTOMIZE INSTRUCTION For Universal Access

To address different learning styles, use the activities suggested in the **Extension Activities** booklet, p. 55.

- For Musical/Rhythmic Learners, use Activity 5.
- For Interpersonal and Verbal/Linguistic Learners, use Activity 6.
- For Verbal/Linguistic Learners, use Activity 7.

ASSESSMENT RESOURCES

The following resources can be used to assess students' knowledge and skills.

Selection Assessment

- **Formal Assessment,** pp. 261–263
- **Open Book Test,** pp. 162–164
-  **Got It! Assessment Videotapes,** Tape 5
- **Test Bank Software**

Take It to the Net

Visit www.phschool.com for self-tests and additional questions on the selection.

Writng Rubric

- **Perfomance Assessment and Portfolio Mgmt.,** p. 22

-  **Workbook**
-  **Transparencies**
-  **Skill Book**
-  **CD-ROM**

Lesson Objectives

1. To understand the thematic connection between conflicts at home and abroad in Great Britain throughout history
2. To understand how a writer's choice of words and style help to extend the message of the text

Connections

Many of the poems and stories in this section deal with social and political conflicts that were resolved at great cost—or that have not yet been resolved. By contrast with the solemn, defiant, or pessimistic moods of these works, this speech by Tony Blair strikes a note of optimism. Blair seems to believe that, with rights and responsibilities in balance, Great Britain can meet the global challenges of a new century.

Conflicts at Home and Abroad

- Explain to students that the twentieth century for Great Britain represented a loss of empire and a change in traditional values. Great Britain was forced to come to grips with the conflicts of the time, and now focuses on recreating the country from the inside.
- Point out that Tony Blair moved to political prominence in the early 1980s, winning elections in part due to his ability to resolve conflicts and find a middle ground between divergent views. The changes Blair made as Labor Party leader brought his party closer to the political center and made it more acceptable to business leaders.
- Point out that the speech by Tony Blair is not equally revered by all Great Britons. If possible, have the students locate and read Britain's Conservative Party's responses to Blair's positions. Encourage students to compare and contrast Blair's speech with the responses.

CONNECTIONS

Literature Past and Present

Conflicts at Home and Abroad

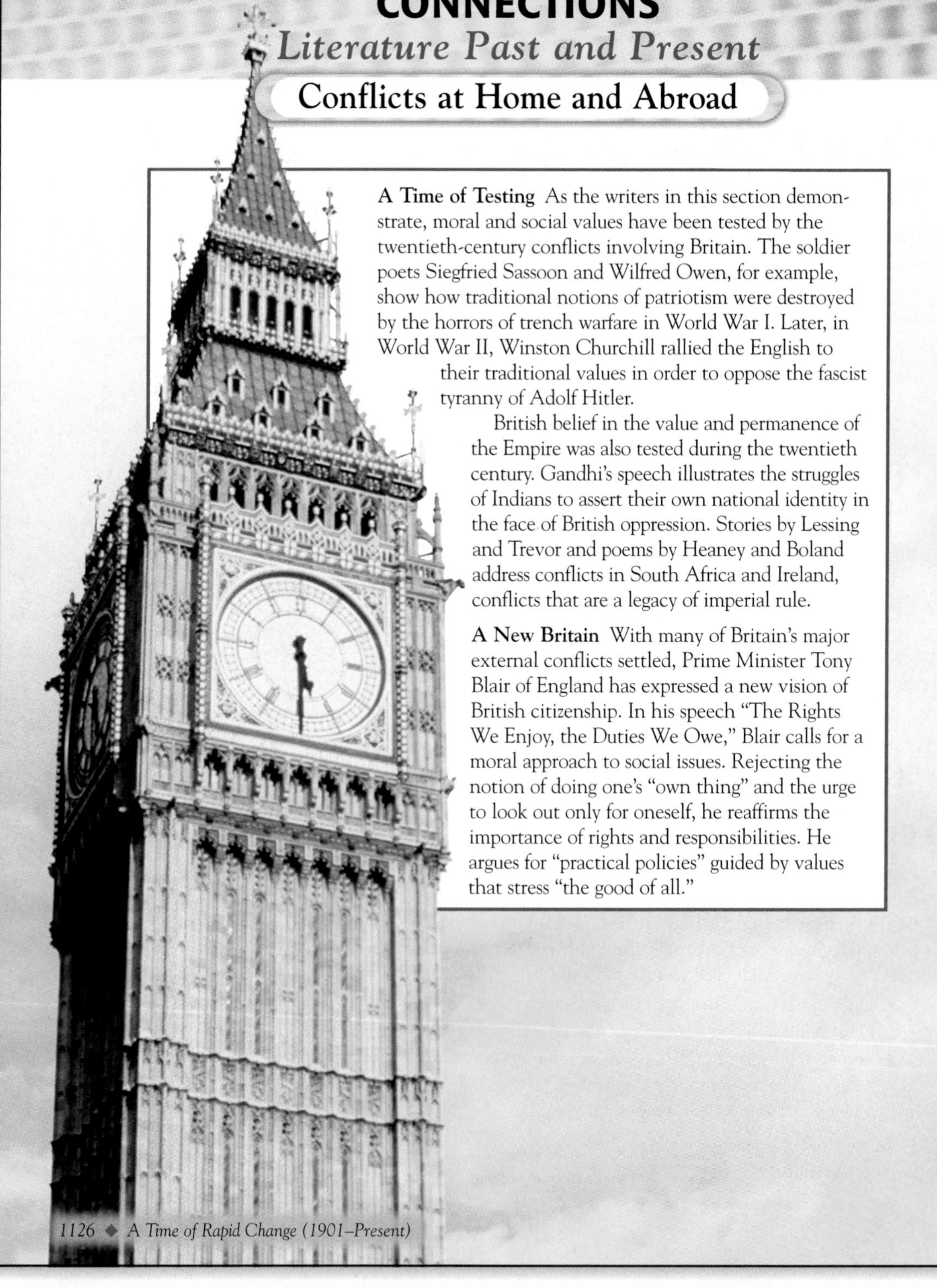

A Time of Testing As the writers in this section demonstrate, moral and social values have been tested by the twentieth-century conflicts involving Britain. The soldier poets Siegfried Sassoon and Wilfred Owen, for example, show how traditional notions of patriotism were destroyed by the horrors of trench warfare in World War I. Later, in World War II, Winston Churchill rallied the English to their traditional values in order to oppose the fascist tyranny of Adolf Hitler.

British belief in the value and permanence of the Empire was also tested during the twentieth century. Gandhi's speech illustrates the struggles of Indians to assert their own national identity in the face of British oppression. Stories by Lessing and Trevor and poems by Heaney and Boland address conflicts in South Africa and Ireland, conflicts that are a legacy of imperial rule.

A New Britain With many of Britain's major external conflicts settled, Prime Minister Tony Blair of England has expressed a new vision of British citizenship. In his speech "The Rights We Enjoy, the Duties We Owe," Blair calls for a moral approach to social issues. Rejecting the notion of doing one's "own thing" and the urge to look out only for oneself, he reaffirms the importance of rights and responsibilities. He argues for "practical policies" guided by values that stress "the good of all."

The Rights We Enjoy, The Duties We Owe

from *New Britain: My Vision of a Young Country*

Tony Blair

Individuals prosper best within a strong and cohesive society. Especially in a modern world, we are interdependent. Unless we act together to provide common services, prepare our industry and people for industrial and technological challenge, and guarantee a proper system of law and government, we will be worse off as individuals. In particular, those without the best start in life through birth are unlikely to make up for it without access to the means of achievement. Furthermore—though this may be more open to debate—a society which is fragmented and divided, where people feel no sense of shared purpose, is unlikely to produce well-adjusted and responsible citizens.

But a strong society should not be confused with a strong state, or with powerful collectivist institutions. That was the confusion of early Left[1] thinking. It was compounded by a belief that the role of the state was to grant rights, with the language of responsibility spoken far less fluently. In a further strain of thinking, connected with the libertarian Left, there was a kind of social individualism espoused,[2] where you "did your own thing." In fact this had very little to do with any forms of left-of-center philosophy recognizable to the founders of the Labor Party.[3]

The reaction of the Right,[4] after the advent of Mrs. Thatcher, was to stress the notion of the individual as against the state. Personal responsibility was extolled.[5] But then a curious thing happened. In a mirror-image of the Left's confusion, the Right started to define personal responsibility as responsibility not just for yourself but to

Thematic Connection
How does Blair redefine the idea of self-interest in this opening paragraph, as Gandhi redefines the idea of a law in his speech?

---

1. **Left** of those with liberal or socialist views.
2. **espoused** (e spouzd′) *v.* advocated.
3. **Labor Party** British political party.
4. **the Right** those with conservative or authoritarian political views.
5. **extolled** (eks tōld′) *v.* praised highly.

Background

About the Selection

Students will find this speech reasonable or reactionary, depending on their political views, but almost certainly engaging. Prime Minister Blair advocates practical morality—rules of behavior for citizens and businesses that acknowledge duty to society, individual rights, and legitimate self-interest. In examining preconceptions about his Labor Party's views, Blair constructs a new view of the "strong society" in which modern insecurity is met with definable rules and expectations, duty is viewed as healthy, and all policies are required to be both moral and practical.

Thematic Connection

Answer: Gandhi puts individual conscience outside, but not above the rules. Law and conscience are separate domains: the judge must either punish Gandhi fully (follow the rules), or resign (follow conscience). By contrast, Blair holds out for a world in which rules can always be revised to serve both society and self-interest.

ENRICHMENT: Social Studies

The Labor Party and the Fabian Society

From Lord Byron to William Morris (a friend of the Pre-Raphaelites) to George Bernard Shaw to Stephen Spender, many British writers sympathized with the plight of workers. Some advocated socialism (the use of society's wealth for the benefit of all). George Bernard Shaw, the Irish dramatist, helped lead a socialist movement called the Fabian Society, founded in 1884. Together with trade unionists, the Fabian Society was key to the founding of the Labor Party.

▶Critical Viewing

Answer: Students may say Blair dresses neatly and formally, has confident body language, and wears an assured expression.

Critical Thinking

- Point out that Blair defines community as a "recognition of interdependence, but not overweening government power" in relation to countries.
- Ask students to think about their role in the global community. Ask them if they see themselves as a member of this community. Explain. Answer: Students may respond that complex economic interdependence binds them to the global community, even while the extreme disparity between life in the United States and life elsewhere isolates them.

▲ **Critical Viewing** In what ways does this photograph present Tony Blair as a leader? **[Evaluate]**

yourself. Outside of a duty not to break the law, responsibility appeared to exclude the broader notion of duty to others. It became narrowly acquisitive[6] and rather destructive. The economic message of enterprise—of the early 1980s—became a philosophy of "Get what you can."

All over the Western world, people are searching for a new political settlement which starts with the individual but sets him or her within the wider society. People don't want an overbearing state, but they don't want to live in a social vacuum either. It is in the search for this different, reconstructed, relationship between individual and society that ideas about "community" are found. "Community" implies a recognition of interdependence, but not overweening[7] government power. It accepts that we are better equipped to meet the forces of change and insecurity through working together. It provides a basis for the elements of our character that are cooperative as well as competitive, as part of a more enlightened view of self-interest.

People know they face a greater insecurity than ever before: a new global economy; massive and rapid changes in technology; a labor market where half the workers are women; a family life that has been

6. **acquisitive** (ə kwiz´ ə tiv) *adj.* eager to acquire possessions.
7. **overweening** (ō´ vər wēn´ iŋ) *adj.* arrogant; excessively proud.

altered drastically; telecommunications and media that visit a common culture upon us and transform our expectations and behavior.

This insecurity is not just about jobs or mortgages—though of course these are serious problems. It is about a world that in less than a lifetime has compressed the historical change of epochs. It is bewildering. Even religion—once a given—is now an exception. And of course the world has the nuclear weapons to destroy itself many times over. Look at our children and the world into which they are growing. What parent would not feel insecure?

People need rules which we all stand by, fixed points of agreement which impose order on chaos. That does not mean a return to the old hierarchy of deference. That is at best nostalgia, at worst reactionary. We do not want old class structures back. We do not want women chained to the sink. We do not want birth rather than merit to become once again the basis of personal advancement. Nor does it mean bureaucracy and regulation. Bad and foolish rules are bad and foolish rules, but they do not invalidate the need to have rules.

Duty is the cornerstone of a decent society. It recognizes more than self. It defines the context in which rights are given. It is personal; but it is also owed to society. Respect for others—responsibility to them—is an essential prerequisite of a strong and active community. It is the method through which we can build a society that does not subsume our individuality but allows it to develop healthily. It accords instinct with common sense. It draws on a broader and therefore more accurate notion of human nature than one formulated on insular[8] self-interest. The rights we receive should reflect the duties we owe. With power should come responsibility.

Thematic Connection
What difficulties have twentieth-century people faced in doing their duty to society? Think of Sassoon's or Owen's view of British rule.

Duty Is a Labor Value

The assertion that each of us is our brother's keeper has motivated the Labor movement since the mid nineteenth century. It is time to reassert what it really means.

The Left has always insisted that it is not enough to argue that our only duty is not to infringe on the lives and rights of others—what might be called negative duty. A minimal community creates a society of minimal citizens. It is a broader notion of duty that gives substance to the traditional belief of the Left in solidarity. This was well understood by the early pioneers of socialism. William Morris[9] put it colorfully: "Fellowship is life, and lack of fellowship is death."

But solidarity[10] and fellowship are the start of the story, and not the end, because they will be achieved only on the basis of both social equality and personal responsibility.

The historians of *English Ethical Socialism,* Norman Dennis and A.H. Halsey, argue that William Cobbett,[11] who lived before the word

8. **insular** (in´ sə lər) *adj.* detached or isolated.
9. **William Morris** early English socialist (1834–1896).
10. **solidarity** (säl´ ə dar´ ə tē) *n.* the unity of individuals in a common cause.
11. **William Cobbett** (käb´ it) English journalist and reformer (1763–1835).

Thematic Connection

Answer: Blair stresses the possibility of balancing both rights in and duties to society. Sassoon and Owen discovered that social duty (the duty to serve in war) was counterbalanced, not by individual rights, but by the irrationality and ugliness of what society asked for—which was war. Students may conclude that Blair's view cannot apply in times of crisis.

Critical Thinking

Draw Conclusions

- Have students think about Blair's concept of duty as it applies to them and to citizens of the United States. Does the United States recognize the delicate balance between individual rights and duty to the country? In a time of crisis, would the balance exist? Cite examples.
  Answer: Students may discuss the voluntary draft for armed services or the issues arising around the detention of immigrants in the wake of the September 11 destruction of the World Trade Center. They may also bring up the social and political rights that are compromised on the basis of gender even today.

Answers

Connecting Literature Past and Present

1. Blair and Churchill would share the idea that a citizen's duty was to fight for the traditional values of Great Britain. To be divisive in these times would be detrimental to the success of the country.
2. Blair would respond that Gandhi should have done all he could not to break the law in any way. If there was a need for a law to be revised, he should have concentrated on revision. By acting against the law, he is compromising the rights of others in society. Students may note that Blair's model of mutual obligation between state and individual breaks down in a case like Gandhi's India, where the state has so compromised its obligation to individuals that drastic, illegal action is ethically warranted.
3. Blair would be apologetic but also pleased at the heroic acts of the countrymen and women who fought for Great Britain.
4. Students should select a story and explain the great cost at which happiness has been removed from society. They should mention changes in the world that contribute to a sense of insecurity.

"socialism" achieved common currency, took it for granted that people stood a better chance of having a happy life if they were not selfish. They write that "a person matching Cobbett's ideal, therefore, was one who enjoyed the rights and performed the duties of citizenship."

Early socialists like Robert Owen understood very clearly that a society which did not encourage people voluntarily to carry out their responsibilities to others would always be in danger of slipping either into the anarchy[12] of mutual indifference—and its corollary, the domination of the powerless by the powerful—or the tyranny of collective coercion, where the freedom of all is denied in the name of the good of all.

Ethical socialists have long asserted that there was and is a distinctive socialist view of both human nature and social morality. R.H. Tawney[13] put it clearly in the 1920s: "Modern society is sick through the absence of a moral ideal," he wrote. "What we have been witnessing . . . both in international affairs and in industry, is the breakdown of society on the basis of rights divorced from obligations." And G.D.H Cole said that "A socialist society that is to be true to its egalitarian principles of human brotherhood must rest on the widest possible diffusion of power and responsibility, so as to enlist the active participation of as many of its citizens in the tasks of democratic self-government."

In his book *Liberals and Social Democrats*, the historian Peter Clarke drew a distinction between "moral reformers" and "mechanical reformers." The moral reformers were the ethical socialists like Tawney and Morris. They looked around the communities in which they lived, and called for a new moral impulse to guide them. The mechanical reformers, on the other hand, concentrated on the technicalities of social and economic reform. They were severely practical in their outlook.

Values without practical policies are useless; but policies without a set of values guiding them give no sense of meaning or direction to public life.

12. **anarchy** (an´ ər kē) *n.* complete absence of government.
13. **Robert Tawney** (tô´ nē) British economic historian (1880–1962).

Tony Blair

(b. 1953)

Tony Blair, Britain's youngest prime minister in modern times, is a skillful orator and noted speech writer. Educated as an attorney, he became a member of Parliament in 1983. He went on to become leader of the Labor Party in 1994, transforming it into what became known as the "New Labor Party." In May 1997, Blair became the first prime minister elected from the Labor Party in eighteen years.

Connecting Literature Past and Present

1. What common ideas of duty might Blair and Churchill share?
2. How might Blair respond to Gandhi's claim that it was his duty to break the law?
3. How might Blair respond to Owens's anthem to those who lost their lives doing their duty in World War I?
4. Choose one of the short stories in this section. Explain how, in the story's setting, duties or rights have become disconnected from an ideal of human dignity and happiness.

ENRICHMENT: Further Reading

Other Works by Tony Blair

"The Welfare Reform Address," *Vital Speeches of the Day*, 6/2/97

"Far More Carrot Than Stick," *London Times Educational Supplement*, 1/19/96

PART 3

Focus on Literary Forms: The Short Story

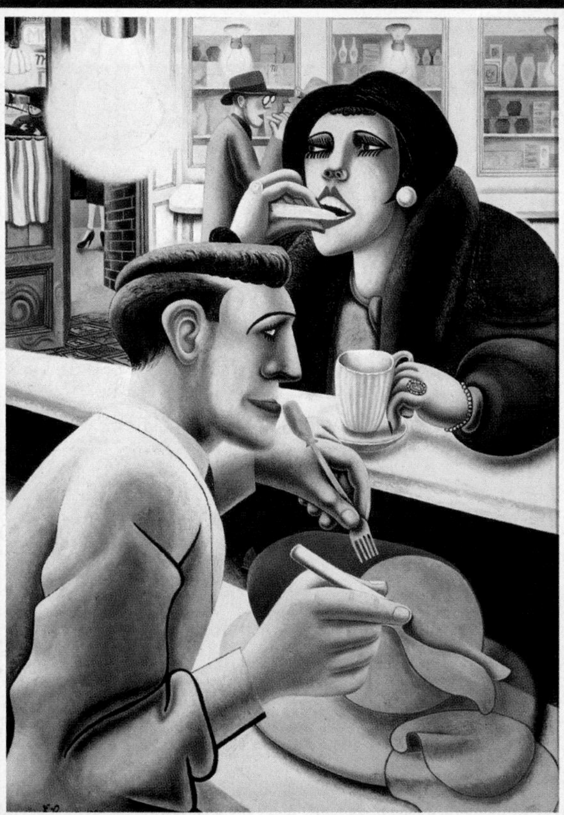

The Snack Bar, 1930, Edward Burra, Tate Gallery, London

The short story was the perfect form for a century in a hurry. It had all the elements of a novel—plot, setting, character, theme—but on a smaller scale. It could take you to the house next door, to Ireland, or to Southeast Asia, but wherever you went you got back quickly. It could also display the latest fictional techniques, sometimes taking you right into a character's mind.

Selection Planning Guide

The short stories in this section allow students to explore a variety of fictional techniques and topics. "The Lagoon" tells a story within a story, taking students to Malaysia. The main character in "Araby" stays close to home but learns so much about himself that he feels as if he has traveled far. "The Lady in the Looking Glass: A Reflection" explores the random thoughts of one character's mind. In "The First Year of My Life," Muriel Spark's narrator is a baby who is able to comment on the events of World War I. "The Rocking-Horse Winner" is the story of a family desperate to improve its financial situation. "A Shocking Accident" highlights life's absurdity. "The Book of Sand" is a fantastic story filled with symbolism.

Background

Art

The Snack Bar, by Edward Burra

British painter and theatrical designer Edward Burra (1905–1976) was deeply interested in human vitality and style. He was fascinated by life at the edge of society and delighted in the grotesque and flamboyant. His oil painting *The Snack Bar* shows how he intensifies unremarkable elements to increase their impact.

Use the following question for discussion:

- In what ways does this painting tell a story?
  Possible response: The artist causes viewers to wonder what the counterman and the woman are thinking. As a result of the artist's exaggeration of their features, they become interesting "characters."

CUSTOMIZE INSTRUCTION FOR UNIVERSAL ACCESS

When assigning the selections in this part, keep in mind these factors:

"The Lagoon" and "Araby"
- Cultural differences may make these selections difficult for some to understand.

"The Lady in the Looking Glass: A Reflection" and "The First Year of My Life"
- Some students may need help working through the unconventional techniques used in these stories.

"The Rocking-Horse Winner" and "A Shocking Accident"
- Most students will find the traditional narrative styles easy to understand.

"The Book of Sand"
- The mysterious quality of this story will capture students' interest.
- Less proficient readers may need help with vocabulary.

The Lagoon ✦ Araby

Lesson Objectives and CA Correlations

1. **To analyze and respond to literary elements**
   - Literary Analysis: Plot Devices **R 3.1**
   - Comparing Literary Works **R 3.3**
2. **To read, comprehend, analyze, and critique a short story**
   - Reading Strategy: Picturing the Action and Situation
   - Reading Check Questions
   - Review and Assess Questions
3. **To develop word analysis skills, fluency, and systematic vocabulary**
   - Vocabulary Development Lesson: Latin Root *-vinc-* **R 1.1**
4. **To understand and apply written and oral language conventions**
   - Spelling Strategy **LC 1.2**
   - Grammar and Style Lesson: Adverb Clauses **LC 1.1**
5. **To understand and apply appropriate writing and research strategies**
   - Writing Lesson: Personal Essay **W 1.1, 1.9, 2.2**
   - Extension Activity: Research Presentation **W 1.4, 1.6**
   - Assessment Practice (ATE)
6. **To understand and apply listening and speaking strategies**
   - Extension Activity: Literary Trial **LS 1.4**

STEP-BY-STEP TEACHING GUIDE	PACING GUIDE
PRETEACH	
Motivate Students and Provide Background	
Use the Motivation activity (ATE p. 1132)	5 min.
Read and discuss author and background features (SE/ATE pp. 1132, 1139) [A]	5 min.
Introduce the Concepts	
Introduce the Literary Analysis and Reading Strategy (SE/ATE p. 1133) [A]	15 min.
Pronounce the vocabulary words and read their definitions (SE p. 1133)	5 min.
TEACH	
Monitor Comprehension	
Informally monitor comprehension by circulating while students read independently or in groups [A]	50 min.
Monitor students' comprehension with the Reading Check notes (SE/ATE pp. 1135, 1137, 1139, 1141, 1143, 1145, 1147, 1149, 1151)	as students read
Develop vocabulary with Vocabulary notes (SE pp. 1135, 1136, 1138, 1139, 1147, 1148, 1150; ATE p. 1136)	as students read
Develop Understanding	
Develop students' understanding of plot devices with the Literary Analysis annotations (SE pp. 1138, 1139, 1142, 1143, 1148; ATE pp. 1138, 1139, 1142, 1143, 1148, 1151) [A]	5 min.
Develop students' ability to picture the action and situation with the Reading Strategy annotations (SE pp. 1136, 1141, 1142, 1145, 1148; ATE pp. 1135, 1136, 1137, 1141, 1142, 1145, 1148)	5 min.
ASSESS	
Assess Mastery	
Assess students' mastery of the Reading Strategy and Literary Analysis by having them answer the Review and Assess questions (SE/ATE p. 1153)	20 min.
Use one or more of the print and media Assessment Resources (ATE p. 1155) [A]	up to 45 min.
EXTEND	
Apply Understanding	
Have students complete the Vocabulary Development Lesson and the Grammar and Style Lesson (SE p. 1154) [A]	20 min.
Apply students' knowledge of elaboration to entertain using the Writing Lesson (SE/ATE p. 1155) [A]	45 min.
Apply students' understanding using one or more of the Extension Activities (SE p. 1155)	20–90 min.

ACCELERATED INSTRUCTION:
Use the strategies and activities identified with an [A].

UNIVERSAL ACCESS
● = Below-Level Students
▲ = On-Level Students
■ = Above-Level Students

Time and Resource Manager

Reading Level: Challenging, Average
Average Number of Instructional Days: 5

RESOURCES		
PRINT	**TRANSPARENCIES**	**TECHNOLOGY**
• **Beyond Literature,** Humanities Connection: Fine Art, p. 56 ▲ ■		• **Interest Grabber Videos,** Tape 6 ● ▲ ■
• **Selection Support Workbook:** ● ▲ ■ Literary Analysis, p. 262 Reading Strategy, p. 261 Build Vocabulary, p. 259	• **Literary Analysis and Reading Transparencies,** pp. 111 and 112 ● ▲ ■	
• **Adapted Reader's Companion** ● • **Reader's Companion** ● • **Authors In Depth,** The British Tradition, p. 222 ■		• **Listening to Literature** ● ▲ ■ Audiocassettes, Side 26 Audio CDs, CD 15
• **English Learner's Companion** ● ▲ • **Literatura en español** ● ▲ • **Literary Analysis for Enrichment** ■	• **Fine Art Transparencies, Volume 1,** Transparency 18	
• **Formal Assessment:** Selection Test, pp. 269–271 ● ▲ ■ • **Open Book Test,** pp. 165–167 ● ▲ ■ • PRENTICE HALL ASSESSMENT SYSTEM ● ▲ ■	• PRENTICE HALL ASSESSMENT SYSTEM ● ▲ ■ • **Skills Practice Answers and Explanations on Transparencies** ● ▲ ■	• **Test Bank Software** ● ▲ ■ • **Got It! Assessment Videotapes,** Tape 6 ● ▲
• **Selection Support Workbook:** ● ▲ ■ Grammar and Style, p. 260 • **Writing and Grammar,** Diamond Level ● ▲ ■ • **Extension Activities,** p. 56 ● ▲ ■	• **Daily Language Practice Transparencies** ● ▲	• **Writing and Grammar iText CD-ROM** ● ▲ ■ ***Take It to the Net*** www.phschool.com

BLOCK SCHEDULING: Use one 90-minute class period to preteach the selection and have students read it. Use a second 90-minute class period to assess students' mastery of skills and have them complete one of the Extension Activities.

PREETEACH

Step-by-Step Teaching Guide for pp. 1132–1133

Motivation

Before assigning "The Lagoon" or "Araby," play the Carly Simon song "Anticipation." Then, have students think back to something they eagerly anticipated, such as a vacation or a special event. Have them share their recollections about which was better: the event itself or the buildup to it. Then, tell students that in "The Lagoon" and "Araby," the main characters' sense of anticipation plays a key role in each story.

Interest Grabber Video

As an alternative, play "'The Lagoon': Joseph Conrad" on Tape 6 to engage student interest.

❶ Background

More About the Authors

Joseph Conrad

Joseph Conrad's given name was Jozef Teodor Konrad Korzeniowski. His work was generally panned by critics and the public, and he suffered financial problems for most of his adult life. The 1913 publication of his novel *Chance* brought Conrad his first popular and financial success. By the time of his death, he was considered one of the leading Modernists.

James Joyce

James Joyce came to fame relatively late in life. With the publication of *Ulysses* on his fortieth birthday, he was met with critical acclaim from Ezra Pound, T.S. Eliot, and Ernest Hemingway. His early influences included Ibsen (whom he greatly admired) Dante, and Yeats (who befriended Joyce). Many of Joyce's works were problematic—*Ulysses* was banned in the United States for a time because of its "pornographic" content; the proofs of *Dubliners* were destroyed in Dublin because the publisher feared a libel suit. Despite these and other setbacks, Joyce created some of the masterpieces of modernism in his lifetime, many of which used the stream-of-consciousness narrative form in an innovative way.

Prepare to Read

❶ The Lagoon ◆ Araby

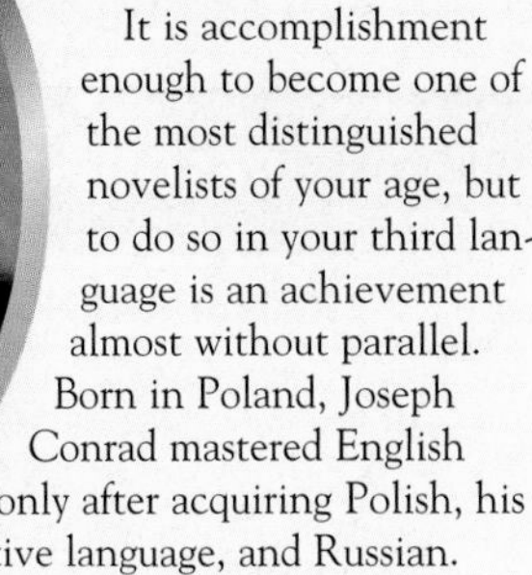

Joseph Conrad (1857–1924)

It is accomplishment enough to become one of the most distinguished novelists of your age, but to do so in your third language is an achievement almost without parallel. Born in Poland, Joseph Conrad mastered English only after acquiring Polish, his native language, and Russian.

At Sea in the World Orphaned at the age of eleven, Conrad fled his Russian-occupied homeland when he was sixteen. He landed first in France and later in England. He spent the next six years as an apprentice seaman. The voyages Conrad made to the corners of the globe—Asia, Africa, and South America—became the vivid settings of much of his fiction. In 1886, he became a master mariner and an English citizen.

A Storytelling Life Conrad published his first novel, *Almayer's Folly*, when he was in his late thirties. In 1897, *The Nigger of the "Narcissus"* appeared. Three masterpieces followed: *Lord Jim* (1900); *Youth*, a collection of shorter pieces that includes his famous "Heart of Darkness" (1902); and *Nostromo* (1904).

Although many of Conrad's works may be read as thrilling tales of the sea, the notion of "voyage" in a work by Conrad translates to a voyage of self-discovery. The question of loyalty, so crucial for the survival of a ship's crew, appears as a question of the general frailty of human relationships and the limits of self-knowledge. The menacing jungles, vast oceans, and exotic people that confront the characters become metaphors for the hidden depths of the self. Telling tales set around the globe, Conrad charts a geography of the human soul.

James Joyce (1882–1941)

The Dublin writer James Joyce's innovations in plot, character, and language make him one of the most challenging and distinguished writers of the twentieth century.

Experimentation Joyce's family and teachers wanted him to become a priest, but he pursued his own way as a writer. In 1904, he left Ireland for the continent. Ten years later, he published a landmark collection of short stories entitled *Dubliners*. These deceptively simple tales focus on the psychological conflicts of ordinary people. In the course of each story, the main character is forced to alter his or her perspective on life.

In 1916, Joyce published *A Portrait of the Artist as a Young Man*, a semiautobiographical work. Like Joyce, the novel's main character is in conflict with his Irish roots and chooses to become a writer.

Mature Fiction *A Portrait of the Artist* reveals a heightened awareness of language and an immersion in the minds of characters. Joyce carried these characteristics to a new level in *Ulysses* (1922). A stream-of-consciousness novel that roughly parallels Homer's *Odyssey*, the work presents a day in the life of three Dubliners. *Ulysses* represents a liberation of the novel from old ideas. Using a variety of styles and techniques, it places a new and thoroughly modern emphasis on the play of language.

In his final novel, *Finnegans Wake* (1939), Joyce took his fascination with words a step further. Written in what one scholar terms "a dream language of Joyce's own invention," it explores the author's view of human existence. With such radical innovations, Joyce guaranteed his place as one of the re-inventors of modern fiction.

TEACHING RESOURCES

The following resources can be used to enrich or extend the instruction for pp. 1132–1133.

Motivation

Interest Grabber Video, Tape 6

Background

Beyond Literature, p. 56

Take It to the Net

Visit www.phschool.com for background and hotlinks for the selections.

Literary Analysis

Literary Analysis and Reading Transparencies, Plot Devices, p. 112

Reading

Literary Analysis and Reading Transparencies, Picturing the Action and Situation, p. 111

Selection Support: Reading Strategy, p. 261; Build Vocabulary, p. 259

BLOCK SCHEDULING: Resources marked with this symbol provide varied instruction during 90-minute blocks.

Preview

Connecting to the Literature

Losing something important is a painful experience. Perhaps just as painful, though, is the discovery that something has lost its importance to you. Each of these stories explores a discovery of loss.

❷ Literary Analysis

Plot Devices

Both Conrad and Joyce use **plot devices** to achieve innovative effects as they relate the events of a story.

- In "The Lagoon," Conrad tells a **story within a story**—a tale told by a character within a framing fictional narrative.
- In "Araby," Joyce builds toward an **epiphany**—a character's sudden insight, which forms the climax of the story.

As you read, notice how these devices structure the stories.

Comparing Literary Works

As these selections reveal, plot devices have a close connection with the **theme,** or central concern, of a story. "The Lagoon" is told by a neutral narrator outside the story—but the story within this story is told in the first person, with passion. By juxtaposing these two points of view, Conrad announces his theme: the relation of passion and the act of storytelling. Joyce's epiphany depends on a similar contrast in point of view, the contrast between the narrator's passion at the time of the story and his later detachment. As you read, compare the implications that these plot devices have for the theme of the stories in which they are used.

❸ Reading Strategy

Picturing the Action and Situation

To better appreciate a well-crafted short story, pause occasionally to **picture the action and situation,** using your imagination to help you understand the characters' reactions to events. Use a graphic organizer like the one shown to aid you.

Story Passage

A breath of warm air touched the two men's faces and passed on with a mournful sound. . . .

↓

Action and Situation

Arsat pauses in his story. In the silence, a wind passes.

↓

Characters' Inner Responses

Both characters may be uneasy—Arsat because of his memories and the narrator because of Arsat's distress.

Vocabulary Development

portals (pôr′ təlz) *n.* doors (p. 1135)

invincible (in vin′ sə bəl) *adj.* unconquerable (p. 1136)

propitiate (prō pish′ ē āt) *v.* win the goodwill of; appease (p. 1136)

conflagration (kän′ flə grā′ shən) *n.* great fire (p. 1138)

august (ô gust′) *adj.* worthy of great respect; inspiring awe (p. 1139)

imperturbable (im′ pər tur′ bə bəl) *adj.* calm; not easily ruffled (p. 1147)

litanies (lit′ ən ēz) *n.* prayers in which a congregation repeats a fixed response; repetitive recitations (p. 1148)

garrulous (gar′ ə ləs) *adj.* talkative (p. 1150)

derided (di rīd′ id) *v.* made fun of; ridiculed (p. 1152)

❷ Literary Analysis

Plot Devices

- Tell students that in this lesson, they will focus on plot devices in the works of Conrad and Joyce.
- Read the instruction for Plot Devices with students, and help them distinguish between the techniques of a story within a story and an epiphany.
- Use the instruction for Comparing Literary Works to review with students how the use of point of view can affect the interpretation of the story.
- Use the Plot Devices transparency in **Literary Analysis and Reading Transparencies,** p. 112, to demonstrate to students how to identify plot devices from clues in the text.

❸ Reading Strategy

Picturing the Action and Situation

- Remind students that as they read, they should pause and picture the action and the situation to better understand characters' reactions to events.
- Show students how this technique works using the graphic organizer on p. 1133.
- Have students practice this skill using the Picturing the Action and Situation transparency in **Literary Analysis and Reading Transparencies,** p. 111.

Vocabulary Development

- Pronounce each vocabulary word for students, and read the definitions as a class. Have students identify any words with which they are already familiar.

CUSTOMIZE INSTRUCTION FOR UNIVERSAL ACCESS

For Special Needs Students	For Less Proficient Readers	For English Learners
Have students read the adapted version of "Araby" in the **Adapted Reader's Companion.** This version provides basic-level instruction in an interactive format with questions and write-on lines. Completing the adapted version will prepare students to read the selection in the Student Edition.	Have students read "Araby" in the **Reader's Companion.** This version provides basic-level instruction in an interactive format with questions and write-on lines. After students finish the selection in Reader's Companion, have them complete the questions and activities in the Student Edition.	Have students read the adapted version of "Araby" in the **English Learner's Companion.** This version provides basic-level instruction in an interactive format with questions and write-on lines. Completing the adapted version will prepare students to read the selection in the Student Edition.

 ***E-Teach***

Visit E-Teach at www.phschool.com for teachers' essays on how to teach, with questions and answers.

TEACH

Step-by-Step Teaching Guide for pp. 1134–1152

CUSTOMIZE INSTRUCTION
For Interpersonal and Intrapersonal Learners

Have students analyze the role of Arsat's friend as a bridge between the particular story of Arsat and the universal human truths his story represents.

❶ About the Selection

Two old comrades—a Malay and a white man—meet near a Malaysian lagoon landscape. As his beloved lies dying inside the hut, Arsat, the Malay, tells how he betrayed his own brother, impelled by passion for the woman now dying. In leaving Arsat to his misery, the white man seems to commit a betrayal as well.

❶ The Lagoon

Joseph Conrad

Background

Between 1883 and 1888, Conrad sailed the Malay Archipelago—a group of Pacific islands that includes the Philippines and Indonesia—in British merchant ships. He used the knowledge he acquired of the region—of its language, landscape, and customs—to enrich his seafaring tales. It is likely that Captain William Lingard, revered as a spellbinding storyteller among sailors of the Malay settlements, was the model for Marlowe, who appears as the narrator of several Conrad stories.

The white man, leaning with both arms over the roof of the little house in the stern of the boat, said to the steersman—

"We will pass the night in Arsat's clearing. It is late."

The Malay[1] only grunted, and went on looking fixedly at the river. The white man rested his chin on his crossed arms and gazed at the wake of the boat. At the end of the straight avenue of forests cut by the intense glitter of the river, the sun appeared unclouded and dazzling, poised low over the water that shone smoothly like a band of metal. The forests, somber and dull, stood motionless and silent on each side of the broad stream. At the foot of big, towering trees trunkless nipa palms rose from the mud of the bank, in bunches of leaves enormous and heavy, that hung unstirring over the brown swirl of eddies. In the stillness of the air every tree, every leaf, every bough, every tendril of creeper and every petal of minute blossoms seemed to have been bewitched into an immobility perfect and final. Nothing moved on the river but the eight paddles that rose flashing regularly, dipped together with a single splash; while the steersman swept right and left with a periodic and sudden flourish of his blade describing a glinting semicircle above his head. The churned-up water frothed alongside with a confused murmur. And the white man's canoe,

1. **Malay** (mā′ lā) native of the Malay peninsula in Southeast Asia.

TEACHING RESOURCES

The following resources can be used to enrich or extend the instruction for pp. 1134–1152.

Literary Analysis

- **Selection Support:** Literary Analysis, p. 262

Reading

- **Adapted Reader's Companion**
- **English Learner's Companion**

- **Listening to Literature Audiocassettes,** Side 26 ■
- **Listening to Literature Audio CDs,** CD 15 ■

Extension

- **Fine Art Transparencies, Volume1,** Art Transparency 18 (Display the transparency when discussing Conrad's impressionistic style of writing.)

■ **BLOCK SCHEDULING:** Resources marked with this symbol provide varied instruction during 90-minute blocks.

advancing up stream in the short-lived disturbance of its own making, seemed to enter the portals of a land from which the very memory of motion had forever departed.

The white man, turning his back upon the setting sun, looked along the empty and broad expanse of the sea-reach. For the last three miles of its course the wandering, hesitating river, as if enticed irresistibly by the freedom of an open horizon, flows straight into the sea, flows straight to the east—to the east that harbors both light and darkness. Astern of the boat the repeated call of some bird, a cry discordant and feeble, skipped along over the smooth water and lost itself, before it could reach the other shore, in the breathless silence of the world.

3 The steersman dug his paddle into the stream, and held hard with stiffened arms, his body thrown forward. The water gurgled aloud; and suddenly the long straight reach seemed to pivot on its center, the forests swung in a semicircle, and the slanting beams of sunset touched the broadside of the canoe with a fiery glow, throwing the slender and distorted shadows of its crew upon the streaked glitter of the river. The white man turned to look ahead. The course of the boat had been altered at right-angles to the stream, and the carved dragonhead of its prow was pointing now at a gap in the fringing

2 ▲ **Critical Viewing** Judging from this photograph, would it be difficult to escape from an enemy in jungle territory? **[Make a Judgment]**

portals (pôr təlz) *n.* doors

4 ✓ **Reading Check** What is the white man's destination?

2 ▶ **Critical Viewing**

Answer: Students may say that the thick foliage, dark shadows, and wide waterways would probably make escape possible for someone well acquainted with that region.

3 Reading Strategy

Picturing the Action and Situation

- Read aloud the bracketed passage to students. Remind them to visualize what is being described as it is read aloud to them.
- Then, ask them to describe their mental picture of what is happening in this passage.
  Answer: The boat that has calmly carried the men into this place of suspended time makes a sudden and sharp turn.

4 ✓ **Reading Check**

Answer: The man's destination is Arsat's lagoon.

CUSTOMIZE INSTRUCTION FOR UNIVERSAL ACCESS

For Special Needs Students	For Gifted/Talented Students
Have students consider the illustration on p. 1135 before they begin reading "The Lagoon" with teacher guidance. Ask students what the illustration suggests about Conrad's story. Tell students that one way of reading "The Lagoon" is to picture the action and the situation as they are described—to create, in effect, their own mental "illustrations" for the story as they read.	Have students read "The Lagoon" independently, focusing on the atmosphere in which the story is set. Tell them that in the story, Conrad paints a vivid picture of the physical surroundings. Have students reread the descriptions of the lagoon, and its "impenetrable forests." Then, have students select several pieces of music to share with the class that reflect the mood created in the story.

5 Reading Strategy

Picturing the Action and Situation

- Tell students to picture the action and the situation as they are described.
- Then, ask them the Reading Strategy question on p. 1136: As you picture the boat ride, what contrasts strike you?
  Answer: Students may mention the gloom of the harrow creek in contrast to the "pure and shining" blue of the sky, or the loud voices of the paddlers contrasting with the "somber walls of vegetation."

6 Vocabulary Development

Latin Root *-vinc-*

- Call students' attention to the margin note to *invincible*, a word that means "unconquerable." Explain to students that *invincible* contains the root *-vinc-*, which is derived from the Latin verb *vincere*, meaning "to conquer."
- Have students suggest other words and phrases that contain this Latin root, and list them on the chalkboard.
  Possible responses: Students may cite *convince* and *evince*. Have students look up any unfamiliar words in a dictionary.

bushes of the bank. It glided through, brushing the overhanging twigs, and disappeared from the river like some slim and amphibious creature leaving the water for its lair in the forests.

5 The narrow creek was like a ditch: tortuous, fabulously deep; filled with gloom under the thin strip of pure and shining blue of the heaven. Immense trees soared up, invisible behind the festooned draperies of creepers. Here and there, near the glistening blackness of the water, a twisted root of some tall tree showed amongst the tracery of small ferns, black and dull, writhing and motionless, like an arrested snake. The short words of the paddlers reverberated loudly between the thick and somber walls of vegetation. Darkness oozed out from between the trees, through the tangled maze of the creepers, from behind the great fantastic and unstirring leaves; the darkness, mysterious and invincible; 6 the darkness scented and poisonous of impenetrable forests.

The men poled in the shoaling[2] water. The creek broadened, opening out into a wide sweep of a stagnant lagoon. The forests receded from the marshy bank, leaving a level strip of bright green, reedy grass to frame the reflected blueness of the sky. A fleecy pink cloud drifted high above, trailing the delicate coloring of its image under the floating leaves and the silvery blossoms of the lotus. A little house, perched on high piles, appeared black in the distance. Near it, two tall nibong palms, that seemed to have come out of the forests in the background, leaned slightly over the ragged roof, with a suggestion of sad tenderness and care in the droop of their leafy and soaring heads.

The steersman, pointing with his paddle, said, "Arsat is there. I see his canoe fast between the piles."

The polers ran along the sides of the boat glancing over their shoulders at the end of the day's journey. They would have preferred to spend the night somewhere else than on this lagoon of weird aspect and ghostly reputation. Moreover, they disliked Arsat, first as a stranger, and also because he who repairs a ruined house, and dwells in it, proclaims that he is not afraid to live amongst the spirits that haunt the places abandoned by mankind. Such a man can disturb the course of fate by glances or words; while his familiar ghosts are not easy to propitiate by casual wayfarers upon whom they long to wreak the malice of their human master. White men care not for such things, being unbelievers and in league with the Father of Evil, who leads them unharmed through the invisible dangers of this world. To the warnings of the righteous they oppose an offensive pretense of disbelief. What is there to be done?

So they thought, throwing their weight on the end of their long poles. The big canoe glided on swiftly, noiselessly, and smoothly, toward Arsat's clearing, till, in a great rattling of poles thrown down, and the loud murmurs of "Allah[3] be praised!" it came with a gentle knock against the crooked piles below the house.

Reading Strategy
Picturing the Action and Situation As you picture the boat ride, what contrasts strike you?

invincible (in vin′ sə bəl) *adj.* unconquerable

propitiate (pro pish′ ē āt′) *v.* win the good will of; appease

2. **shoaling** shallow.
3. **Allah** (al′ ə) Muslim name for God.

ENRICHMENT: Social Studies Connection

British Empire

Write this saying on the chalkboard: "The sun never sets on the British Empire." Explain that at one time in British history, the British Empire was so large that it extended to all parts of the globe, including North, Central, and South America, the Caribbean, the Middle East, Asia, Africa, and the South Pacific.

Point out that Malaysia, where this story is set, was a British colony. Invite students to select Malaysia or another country that was once a British colony, such as India, Belize, the Bahamas, Kenya, or Guyana, to name a few. Challenge them to find out about Britain's colonization in that area, and the process by which the region gained independence. Display a world map with information about former British colonies.

7 The boatmen with uplifted faces shouted discordantly, "Arsat! O Arsat!" Nobody came. The white man began to climb the rude ladder giving access to the bamboo platform before the house. The juragan[4] of the boat said sulkily, "We will cook in the sampan,[5] and sleep on the water."

"Pass my blankets and the basket," said the white man curtly.

He knelt on the edge of the platform to receive the bundle. Then the boat shoved off, and the white man, standing up, confronted Arsat, who had come out through the low door of his hut. He was a man young, powerful, with a broad chest and muscular arms. He had nothing on but his sarong.[6] His head was bare. His big, soft eyes stared eagerly at the white man, but his voice and demeanor were composed as he asked, without any words of greeting—

"Have you medicine, Tuan?"[7]

"No," said the visitor in a startled tone. "No. Why? Is there sickness in the house?"

"Enter and see," replied Arsat, in the same calm manner, and turning short round, passed again through the small doorway. The white man, dropping his bundles, followed.

In the dim light of the dwelling he made out on a couch of bamboos a woman stretched on her back under a broad sheet of red cotton cloth. She lay still, as if dead; but her big eyes, wide open, glittered in the gloom, staring upward at the slender rafters, motionless and unseeing. She was in a high fever, and evidently unconscious. Her cheeks were sunk slightly, her lips were partly open, and on the young face there was the ominous and fixed expression—the absorbed, contemplating expression of the unconscious who are going to die. The two men stood looking down at her in silence.

"Has she been long ill?" asked the traveler.

"I have not slept for five nights," answered the Malay, in a deliberate tone. "At first she heard voices calling her from the water and struggled against me who held her. But since the sun of today rose she hears nothing—she hears not me. She sees nothing. She sees not me—me!"

He remained silent for a minute, then asked softly—

"Tuan, will she die?"

"I fear so," said the white man sorrowfully. He had known Arsat years ago, in a far country in times of trouble and danger, when no friendship is to be despised. And since his Malay friend had come unexpectedly to dwell in the hut on the lagoon with a strange woman, he had slept many times there, in his journeys up and down the river. He liked the man who knew how to keep faith in council and how to fight without fear by the side of his white friend. He liked him—not so much perhaps as a man likes his favorite dog—but still

4. **juragan** (jo͞o rä´ gän) captain or master.
5. **sampan** small flat-bottomed boat with a cabin formed by mats.
6. **sarong** long, brightly colored strip of cloth worn like a skirt.
7. **Tuan** (twan) Malayan for "sir."

8 **Reading Check**

What is wrong in Arsat's house?

7 Reading Strategy

Picturing the Action and Situation

- Have students summarize the information in the bracketed passage.
- Then, ask them to describe what is happening and how it affects the situation.
  Answer: The white man is being left at this mysterious hut where no one answers. The mental image of him climbing the ladder as the boat moves away creates a sense of isolation.

8 Reading Check

Answer: A woman in Arsat's house is feverish and may die.

CUSTOMIZE INSTRUCTION FOR UNIVERSAL ACCESS

For Special Needs Students	For Less Proficient Readers
Have students read portions of "The Lagoon" with teacher guidance. Some students may have difficulty understanding the Malay words that Conrad intersperses to heighten the realism of his tale. Remind students that many stories and legends use the language of the milieu to set the scene. Encourage them to look up any words they do not know or to refer to the footnotes.	Students may find that the exotic setting of Conrad's story "The Lagoon" is sufficiently foreign that they cannot fully enter it. For these students, consider showing them a short video clip that explains why Joseph Conrad drew much inspiration from islands and the ocean. You may want to play "'The Lagoon': Joseph Conrad" on **Interest Grabber** Tape 6 to stimulate student interest and help students focus their attention.

9 Literary Analysis

Plot Devices

- Remind students of the various kinds of plot devices Conrad uses to enhance the story.
- Then, ask students the Literary Analysis question on p. 1138: Is the narrator of the story closer in point of view to the white man or Arsat? Explain.
  Possible response: Students may say that the narrator is closer to the white man; his description of the man's affection for Arsat is likened to feelings about a favorite dog.

10 Reading Strategy

Picturing the Action and Situation

- Ask students to identify the details they used to help them picture this scene in their heads.
- Then, ask students the Reading Strategy question on p. 1138: What type of impression dominates as you picture the scene in this paragraph?
  Answer: The image of isolation dominates in this paragraph.

9 he liked him well enough to help and ask no questions, to think sometimes vaguely and hazily in the midst of his own pursuits, about the lonely man and the long-haired woman with audacious face and triumphant eyes, who lived together by the forests—alone and feared.

The white man came out of the hut in time to see the enormous conflagration of sunset put out by the swift and stealthy shadows that, rising like a black and impalpable vapor above the treetops, spread over the heaven, extinguishing the crimson glow of floating clouds and the red brilliance of departing daylight. In a few moments all the stars came out above the intense blackness of the earth, and the great lagoon gleaming suddenly with reflected lights resembled an oval patch of night sky flung down into the hopeless and abysmal night of the wilderness. The white man had some supper out of the basket, then collecting a few sticks that lay about the platform, made up a small fire, not for warmth, but for the sake of the smoke, which would keep off the mosquitos. He wrapped himself in his blankets and sat with his back against the reed wall of the house, smoking thoughtfully.

Arsat came through the doorway with noiseless steps and squatted down by the fire. The white man moved his outstretched legs a little.

"She breathes," said Arsat in a low voice, anticipating the expected question. "She breathes and burns as if with a great fire. She speaks not; she hears not—and burns!" He paused for a moment, then asked in a quiet, incurious tone—

"Tuan . . . will she die?"

The white man moved his shoulders uneasily, and muttered in a hesitating manner—

"If such is her fate."

"No, Tuan," said Arsat calmly. "If such is my fate. I hear, I see, I wait. I remember . . . Tuan, do you remember the old days? Do you remember my brother?"

"Yes," said the white man. The Malay rose suddenly and went in. The other, sitting still outside, could hear the voice in the hut. Arsat said: "Hear me! Speak!" His words were succeeded by a complete silence. "O Diamelen!" he cried suddenly. After that cry there was a deep sigh. Arsat came out and sank down again in his old place.

10 They sat in silence before the fire. There was no sound within the house, there was no sound near them; but far away on the lagoon they could hear the voices of the boatmen ringing fitful and distinct on the calm water. The fire in the bows of the sampan shone faintly in the distance with a hazy red glow. Then it died out. The voices ceased. The land and the water slept invisible, unstirring and mute. It was as though there had been nothing left in the world but the glitter of stars streaming, ceaseless and vain, through the black stillness of the night.

The white man gazed straight before him into the darkness with wide-open eyes. The fear and fascination, the inspiration and the wonder of death—of death near, unavoidable, and unseen, soothed the unrest of his race and stirred the most indistinct, the most intimate

Literary Analysis
Plot Devices Is the narrator of the story closer in point of view to the white man or Arsat? Explain.

conflagration (kän′ flə grā′ shən) *n.* great fire

Reading Strategy
Picturing the Action and Situation What type of impression dominates as you picture the scene in this paragraph?

ENRICHMENT: Art Connection

Impressionism

Conrad is sometimes termed an impressionistic writer because he seeks to capture the atmosphere and texture of reality as well as the complexity of subjective experience. Originally, the term *impressionism* was applied to the work of a group of nineteenth-century painters in Paris. These painters tried to show in their paintings impressions gained from direct observation of nature, rather than precise representations. They painted with dabs of discontinuous color, allowing the viewer's eye to recombine the colors into an image.

While it is not strictly speaking an impressionist work, Yuan Lee's *The Reflection in the Store Window Glass*, **Fine Art Transparencies,** Volume 1, Transparency 18, may provide students with a visual analogy for Conrad's impressionistic writing. Point out to students how Lee gives viewers impressionistic "slices" of a scene as it is reflected in the glass of a store window. As with Conrad, the result is an atmospheric rendering of reality, rather than a "snapshot" of it.

of his thoughts. The ever-ready suspicion of evil, the gnawing suspicion that lurks in our hearts, flowed out into the stillness round him—into the stillness profound and dumb, and made it appear untrustworthy and infamous, like the placid and impenetrable mask of an unjustifiable violence. In that fleeting and powerful disturbance of his being the earth enfolded in the starlight peace became a shadowy country of inhuman strife, a battlefield of phantoms terrible and charming, august or ignoble, struggling ardently for the possession of our helpless hearts. An unquiet and mysterious country of inextinguishable desires and fears.

august (ô gust′) *adj.* worthy of great respect; inspiring awe

A plaintive murmur rose in the night; a murmur saddening and startling, as if the great solitudes of surrounding woods had tried to whisper into his ear the wisdom of their immense and lofty indifference. Sounds hesitating and vague floated in the air round him, shaped themselves slowly into words; and at last flowed on gently in a murmuring stream of soft and monotonous sentences. He stirred like a man waking up and changed his position slightly. Arsat, motionless and shadowy, sitting with bowed head under the stars, was speaking in a low and dreamy tone—

". . . for where can we lay down the heaviness of our trouble but in a friend's heart? A man must speak of war and of love. You, Tuan, know what war is, and you have seen me in time of danger seek death as other men seek life! A writing may be lost; a lie may be written; but what the eye has seen is truth and remains in the mind!"

"I remember," said the white man quietly. Arsat went on with mournful composure—

"Therefore I shall speak to you of love. Speak in the night. Speak before both night and love are gone—and the eye of day looks upon my sorrow and my shame; upon my blackened face; upon my burnt-up heart."

A sigh, short and faint, marked an almost imperceptible pause,
11 and then his words flowed on, without a stir, without a gesture.

"After the time of trouble and war was over and you went away from my country in the pursuit of your desires, which we, men of the islands, cannot understand, I and my brother became again, as we had been before, the sword bearers of the Ruler. You know we were men of family, belonging to a ruling race, and more fit than any to carry on our right shoulder the emblem of power. And in the time of prosperity Si Dendring showed us favor, as we, in time of sorrow, had showed to him the faithfulness of our courage. It was a time of peace. A time of deer hunts and cock fights; of idle talks and foolish squabbles between men whose bellies are full and weapons are rusty. But the sower watched the young rice shoots grow up without fear, and the traders came and went, departed lean and returned fat into the river of peace. They brought news too. Brought lies and truth mixed together, so that no man knew when to rejoice and when to be sorry. We heard from them about you also. They had seen you here and had seen you there. And I was glad to hear, for I remembered the stirring

Literary Analysis
Plot Devices and Point of View What shift in point of view alerts you to the fact that a story within a story begins here?

12 ✓ **Reading Check**
What does Arsat say his story concerns?

11 Literary Analysis

Plot Devices and Point of View

- Review with students how point of view can alter the interpretation of a passage.
- Then, ask students the Literary Analysis question on p. 1139: What shift in point of view alerts you to the fact that a story within a story begins here?
  Answer: Students should recognize Arsat's lines: "Therefore I shall speak to you of love," as an indication that a story within a story is about to begin. The pause that follows his remark and precedes the story marks a shift in narration.

12 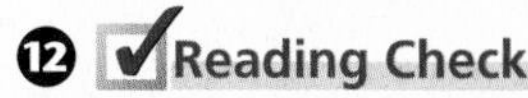

Answer: Arsat says his story concerns love.

CUSTOMIZE INSTRUCTION FOR UNIVERSAL ACCESS

For Special Needs Students	For Less Proficient Readers	For Advanced Readers
Some students may find the progress of Conrad's account difficult to follow because of its abundant use of poetic effects like alliteration, assonance, and consonance. Encourage students to read chorally in small groups to help them understand the language of the story and the poetic sound effects.	As students continue to read "The Lagoon" with teacher guidance, remind them that Conrad uses many plot devices to keep the attention of his reader. Ask students to note these plot devices as they read.	In "The Lagoon" Arsat shares his story. Ask students to recall or invent an occasion on which a friend took them into his or her confidence and shared a problem. Have students describe in several paragraphs the emotions they experienced as they listened to their friend.

13 ▶ **Critical Viewing**

Answer: Students may say that the beach shown in the photograph seems sunnier and more hospitable than Arsat's lagoon, which is a lonely, eerie place.

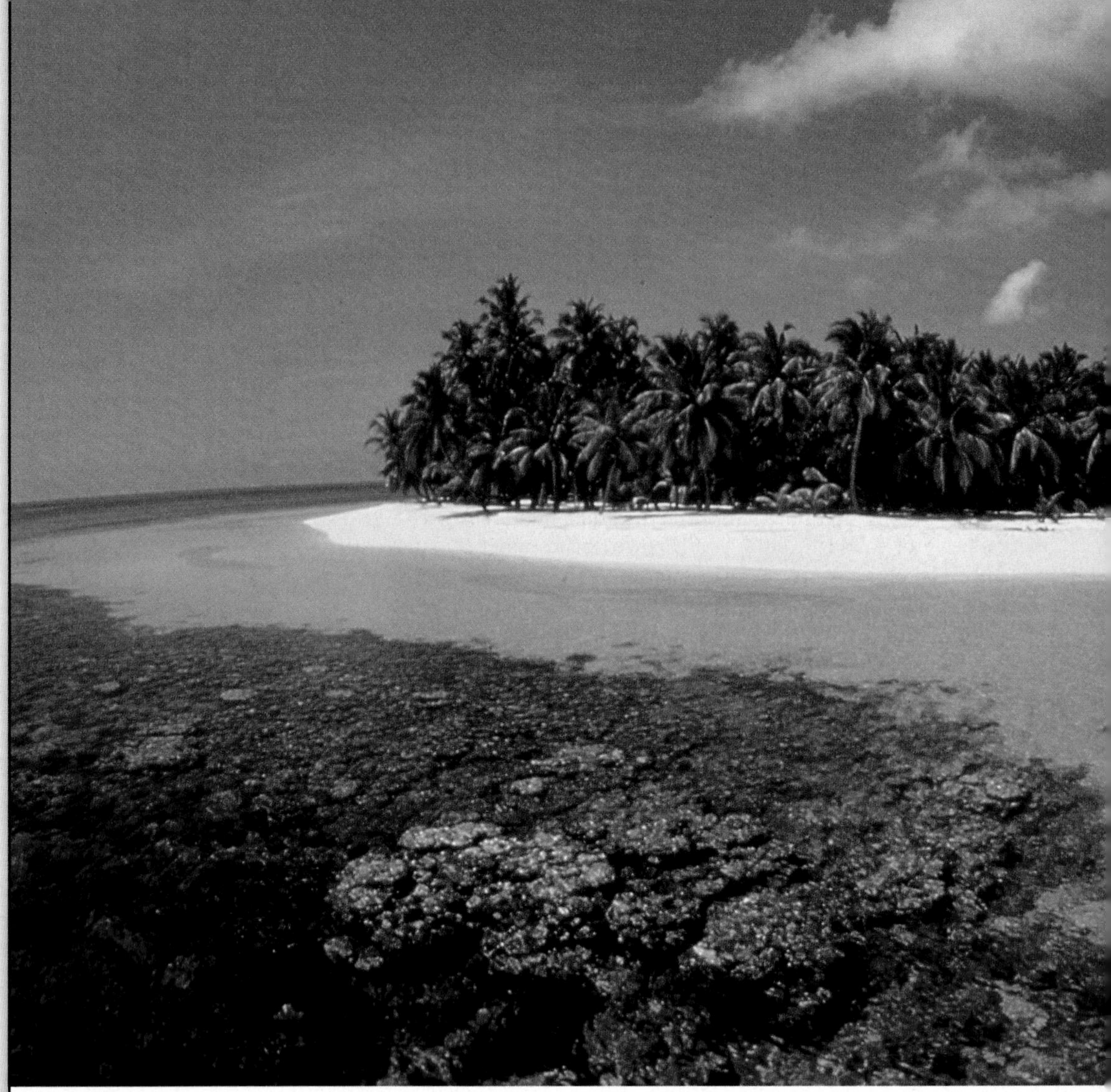

times, and I always remembered you, Tuan, till the time came when my eyes could see nothing in the past, because they had looked upon the one who is dying there—in the house."

He stopped to exclaim in an intense whisper, "O Mara bahia! O Calamity!" then went on speaking a little louder.

"There's no worse enemy and no better friend than a brother, Tuan, for one brother knows another, and in perfect knowledge is strength for good or evil. I loved my brother. I went to him and told him that I could see nothing but one face, hear nothing but one voice. He told

13 ▲ **Critical Viewing** Compare the mood of Arsat's story with the feelings you associate with a setting such as this one. **[Compare and Contrast]**

ENRICHMENT: Cultural Connection

Malay

Tuan is a Malay term of respect. The term *tuan* was probably used to describe Captain William Lingard, a local hero at the time Conrad sailed through Malaysia. According to Conrad's biographer, Frederick Karl, Lingard was also known as "Rajah Laut" or "King of the Sea" for his "…shrewdness as a trader, daring as a contender with sea pirates for routes and goods, and expertise as a handler of sailing vessels." Men like Arsat probably worked with and fought beside Lingard in a number of his daring adventures.

Conrad used facts about local people to enrich his stories. Inchi Midah was a local woman married to a chief of Perak. The princess of Perak, described as "light, spare and a little witch like," was probably the model for Conrad's Inchi Midah.

me: 'Open your heart so that she can see what is in it—and wait. Patience is wisdom. Inchi Midah may die or our Ruler may throw off his fear of a woman!'. . . I waited! . . . You remember the lady with the veiled face, Tuan, and the fear of our Ruler before her cunning and temper. And if she wanted her servant, what could I do? But I fed the hunger of my heart on short glances and stealthy words. I loitered on the path to the bath houses in the daytime, and when the sun had fallen behind the forest I crept along the jasmine hedges of the women's courtyard. Unseeing, we spoke to one another through the scent of flowers, through the veil of leaves, through the blades of long grass that stood still before our lips; so great was our prudence, so faint was the murmur of our great longing. The time passed swiftly . . . and there were whispers amongst women—and our enemies watched—my brother was gloomy, and I began to think of killing and of a fierce death. . . . We are of a people who take what they want—like you whites. There is a time when a man should forget loyalty and respect. Might and authority are given to rulers, but to all men is given love and strength and courage. My brother said, 'You shall take her from their midst. We are two who are like one.' And I answered, 'Let it be soon, for I find no warmth in sunlight that does not shine upon her.' Our time came when the Ruler and all the great people went to the mouth of the river to fish by torchlight. There were hundreds of boats, and on the white sand, between the water and the forests, dwellings of leaves were built for the households of the Rajahs.[8] The smoke of cooking fires was like a blue mist of the evening, and many voices rang in it joyfully. While they were making the boats ready to beat up the fish, my brother came to me and said, 'Tonight!'

Reading Strategy
Picturing the Action and Situation As you picture the situation among Arsat, his beloved, his ruler, and Inchi Midah, his beloved's mistress, what attitude does each convey?

14

15 **Reading Check**
What do Arsat and his brother decide to do?

8. **Rajahs** (ra´ jəz) Malayan chiefs.

14 Reading Strategy

Picturing the Action and Situation

- Have students identify and record any key details about each of the characters being described.
- Then, ask them the Reading Strategy question on p. 1141: As you picture the situation among Arsat, his beloved, his ruler, and Inchi Midah, his beloved's mistress, what attitude does each convey?
  Answer: Students may say that Arsat seems daring, his beloved seems smitten, his ruler seems hamstrung, and Inchi Midah seems cunning and malevolent.

15 Reading Check

Answer: Arsat and his brother decide to help Arsat's beloved escape during a night ceremony.

CUSTOMIZE INSTRUCTION FOR UNIVERSAL ACCESS

For Less Proficient Readers	For Advanced Readers
As students read "The Lagoon" with teacher guidance, they may want to consider the character of Arsat in greater depth. Have them write character descriptions for Arsat and describe his appearance, his personality, dreams or goals, and regrets or sorrows, based on what he recounts in the story.	Some students who read "The Lagoon" may be fascinated by aspects of the account and their visual representation. You may want to direct these students to p. 56 of **Beyond Literature** for a more in-depth, cross-curricular analysis that connects the experience of reading Conrad's story to additional humanities resources to stimulate their interest.

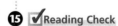

16 Reading Strategy

Picturing the Action and Situation

- Remind students to visualize the scene as it is described. You may wish to have students identify the details in this passage that help them picture the action.
- Then, ask the Reading Strategy question on p. 1142: What details in this account of elopement stand out for you?
  Answer: Students may say the excitement and danger of Diamelen's escape from the sheds stand out for them.

17 Literary Analysis

Plot Devices

- Have students consider why Arsat pauses during his story.
- Then, ask the Literary Analysis question on p. 1142: What do the pauses in Arsat's story indicate to the white man and the reader about Arsat's emotional state?
  Answer: Arsat's pauses seem to occur at parts of the story that affect his present emotions concerning Diamelen, which heightens the suspense.

I looked to my weapons, and when the time came our canoe took its place in the circle of boats carrying the torches. The lights blazed on the water, but behind the boats there was darkness. When the shouting began and the excitement made them like mad we dropped out. The water swallowed our fire, and we floated back to the shore that was dark with only here and there the glimmer of embers. We could hear the talk of slave girls amongst the sheds. Then we found a place deserted and silent. We waited there. She came. She came running along the shore, rapid and leaving no trace, like a leaf driven by the wind into the sea. My brother said gloomily, 'Go and take her; carry her into our boat.' I lifted her in my arms. She panted. Her heart was beating against my breast. I said, 'I take you from those people. You came to the cry of my heart, but my arms take you into my boat against the will of the great!' 'It is right,' said my brother. 'We are men who take what we want and can hold it against many. We should have taken her in daylight.' I said, 'Let us be off'; for since she was in my boat I began to think of our Ruler's many men. 'Yes. Let us be off,' said my brother. 'We are cast out and this boat is our country now—and the sea is our refuge.' He lingered with his foot on the shore, and I entreated him to hasten, for I remembered the strokes of her heart against my breast and thought that two men cannot withstand a hundred. We left, paddling downstream close to the bank; and as we passed by the creek where they were fishing, the great shouting had ceased, but the murmur of voices was loud like the humming of insects flying at noonday. The boats floated, clustered together, in the red light of torches, under a black roof of smoke; and men talked of their sport. Men that boasted, and praised, and jeered—men that would have been our friends in the morning, but on that night were already our enemies. We paddled swiftly past. We had no more friends in the country of our birth. She sat in the middle of the canoe with covered face; silent as she is now; unseeing as she is now—and I had no regret at what I was leaving because I could hear her breathing close to me—as I can hear her now."

He paused, listened with his ear turned to the doorway, then shook his head and went on.

"My brother wanted to shout the cry of challenge—one cry only—to let the people know we were freeborn robbers who trusted our arms and the great sea. And again I begged him in the name of our love to be silent. Could I not hear her breathing close to me? I knew the pursuit would come quick enough. My brother loved me. He dipped his paddle without a splash. He only said,'There is half a man in you now—the other half is in that woman. I can wait. When you are a whole man again, you will come back with me here to shout defiance. We are sons of the same mother.' I made no answer. All my strength and all my spirit were in my hands that held the paddle—for I longed to be with her in a safe place beyond the reach of men's anger and of women's spite. My love was so great, that I thought it could guide me to a country where death was unknown, if I could only escape from

Reading Strategy
Picturing the Action and Situation What details in this account of the elopement stand out for you?

Literary Analysis
Plot Devices What do the pauses in Arsat's story indicate to the white man and the reader about Arsat's emotional state?

ENRICHMENT: Media Connection

A Joseph Conrad Film Festival

There have been many films whose ideas come from the writings of Joseph Conrad. Some of the films are fairly literal versions of the literature.

Invite interested students to get together to view some of the available films based on Conrad's writings: *Victory* (1940), *Outcast of the Islands* (1951), *Lord Jim* (1965), *and Heart of Darkness* (1994). However, you should preview films before showing them to students.

Inchi Midah's fury and from our Ruler's sword. We paddled with haste, breathing through our teeth. The blades bit deep into the smooth water. We passed out of the river; we flew in clear channels amongst the shallows. We skirted the black coast; we skirted the sand beaches where the sea speaks in whispers to the land; and the gleam of white sand flashed back past our boat, so swiftly she ran upon the water. We spoke not. Only once I said, 'Sleep, Diamelen, for soon you may want all your strength.' I heard the sweetness of her voice, but I never turned my head. The sun rose and still we went on. Water fell from my face like rain from a cloud. We flew in the light and heat. I never looked back, but I knew that my brother's eyes, behind me, were looking steadily ahead, for the boat went as straight as a bushman's dart, when it leaves the end of the sumpitan.[9] There was no better paddler, no better steersman than my brother. Many times, together, we had won races in that canoe. But we never had put out our strength as we did then—then, when for the last time we paddled together! There was no braver or stronger man in our country than my brother. I could not spare the strength to turn my head and look at him, every moment I heard the hiss of his breath getting louder behind me. Still he did not speak. The sun was high. The heat clung to my back like a flame of fire. My ribs were ready to burst, but I could no longer get enough air into my chest. And then I felt I must cry out with my last breath. 'Let us rest!' . . . 'Good!' he answered; and his voice was firm. He was strong. He was brave. He knew not fear and no fatigue . . . My brother!"

18 A murmur powerful and gentle, a murmur vast and faint; the murmur of trembling leaves, of stirring boughs, ran through the tangled depths of the forests, ran over the starry smoothness of the lagoon, and the water between the piles lapped the slimy timber once with a sudden splash. A breath of warm air touched the two men's faces and passed on with a mournful sound—a breath loud and short like an uneasy sigh of the dreaming earth.

Literary Analysis
Plot Devices How do the descriptions of the setting in which Arsat tells his tale provide a kind of commentary on his tale?

Arsat went on in an even, low voice:

"We ran our canoe on the white beach of a little bay close to a long tongue of land that seemed to bar our road; a long wooded cape going far into the sea. My brother knew that place. Beyond the cape a river has its entrance, and through the jungle of that land there is a narrow path. We made a fire and cooked rice. Then we lay down to sleep on the soft sand in the shade of our canoe, while she watched. No sooner had I closed my eyes than I heard her cry of alarm. We leaped up. The sun was halfway down the sky already, and coming in sight in the opening of the bay we saw a prau[10] manned by many paddlers. We knew it at once; it was one of our Rajah's praus. They were watching the shore, and saw us. They beat the gong, and turned the head of the prau into the bay. I felt my heart become weak within my

19 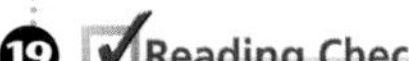
Reading Check
Have Arsat, his brother, and Diamelen escaped the Rajah? Explain.

9. **sumpitan** (sump´ ə tän) Malayan blowgun which discharges poisonous darts.
10. **prau** (prou) swift Malayan boat with a large sail.

18 Literary Analysis

Plot Devices

- Review with students how Conrad's use of a story within a story is an effective plot device.
- Then, ask students the Literary Analysis question on p. 1143: How do the descriptions of the setting in which Arsat tells his tale provide a kind of commentary on his tale?
Answer: Arsat's story takes place in the blazing heat of the day; the shift to nighttime is identifiable because Conrad describes the starry reflection in the lagoon. The return to the lagoon in the middle of Arsat's story reinforces the concept of isolation—a concept that will become increasingly important in Arsat's story.

19 Reading Check

Answer: No; the Rajah has sent a prau after them.

CUSTOMIZE INSTRUCTION FOR UNIVERSAL ACCESS

For English Learners	For Advanced Readers
Have students read portions of "The Lagoon" with teacher guidance. Whenever possible, have them summarize the content of what they have read. Students should be able to articulate the key plot elements, name the main characters, and predict what might happen next.	Ask students to assess the ways in which the story Arsat tells in "The Lagoon" seems like a tragedy. Tell students to write brief essays in which they analyze the elements of Arsat's experience, his relationship with his brother, his feelings for Diamelen, and the restrictions on his life.

20 ▶**Critical Viewing**

Possible response: The image suggests some of the isolation of Conrad's story, but it does not capture the sense of danger or fear that pervades the story.

breast. Diamelen sat on the sand and covered her face. There was no escape by sea. My brother laughed. He had the gun you had given him, Tuan, before you went away, but there was only a handful of powder. He spoke to me quickly: 'Run with her along the path. I shall keep them back, for they have no firearms, and landing in the face of a man with a gun is certain death for some. Run with her. On the other side of that wood there is a fisherman's house—and a canoe. When I have fired all the shots I will follow. I am a great runner, and before they can come up we shall be gone. I will hold out as long as I can, for she is but a woman—that can neither run nor fight, but she has your heart in her weak hands.' He dropped behind the canoe. The prau was coming. She and I ran, and as we rushed along the path I heard shots. My brother fired—once —twice—and the booming of the gong ceased. There was silence behind us. That neck of land is narrow. Before I heard my brother fire the third shot I saw the shelving shore, and I saw the water again: the mouth of a broad river. We crossed a grassy glade. We ran down to the water. I saw a low hut above the black mud, and a small canoe hauled up. I heard another shot behind me. I thought, 'That is his last charge.' We rushed down to the canoe; a man came running from the hut, but I leaped on him, and we rolled together in the mud. Then I got up, and he lay still at my feet. I don't know whether I had killed him or not. I and Diamelen pushed the canoe afloat. I heard yells behind me, and I saw my brother run across the glade. Many men were bounding after him. I took her in my arms and threw her into the boat, then leaped in myself. When I looked back I saw that my brother had fallen. He fell and was up again, but the men were closing round him. He shouted, 'I am coming!' The men were close to him. I looked. Many men. Then I looked at her. Tuan, I pushed the canoe! I pushed it into deep water. She was kneeling forward looking at me, and I said, 'Take your paddle,' while I struck the water with mine. Tuan, I heard him cry. I heard him cry my name twice; and I heard voices shouting, 'Kill! Strike!' I never turned back. I heard him calling my name again with a great shriek, as when life is going out together with the voice—and I never turned my head. My own name! . . . My brother! Three times he called—but I was not afraid of life. Was she not there in that canoe? And could I not with her find a country where death is forgotten—where death is unknown!"

The white man sat up. Arsat rose and stood, an indistinct and silent figure above the dying embers of the fire. Over the lagoon a mist drifting and low had crept, erasing slowly the glittering images of the stars. And now a great expanse of white vapor covered the land; it flowed cold and gray in the darkness, eddied in noiseless whirls round the tree-trunks and about the platform of the house, which seemed to float upon a restless and impalpable illusion of a sea. Only far away the tops of the trees stood outlined on the twinkle of heaven, like a somber and forbidding shore—a coast deceptive, pitiless and black.

20 ▲**Critical Viewing**
What aspects of Conrad's story does this photograph capture? What aspects does it fail to capture? **[Connect]**

Arsat's voice vibrated loudly in the profound peace.

"I had her there! I had her! To get her I would have faced all mankind. But I had her—and—"

21 His words went out ringing into the empty distances. He paused, and seemed to listen to them dying away very far—beyond help and beyond recall. Then he said quietly—

"Tuan, I loved my brother."

22 A breath of wind made him shiver. High above his head, high above the silent sea of mist the drooping leaves of the palms rattled together with a mournful and expiring sound. The white man stretched his legs. His chin rested on his chest, and he murmured sadly without lifting his head—

"We all love our brothers."

Arsat burst out with an intense whispering violence—

"What did I care who died? I wanted peace in my own heart."

He seemed to hear a stir in the house —listened—then stepped in noiselessly. The white man stood up. A breeze was coming in fitful puffs. The stars shone paler as if they had retreated into the frozen depths of immense space. After a chill gust of wind there were a few seconds of perfect calm and absolute silence. Then from behind the black and wavy line of the forests a column of golden light shot up into the heavens and spread over the semicircle of the eastern horizon. The sun had risen. The mist lifted, broke into drifting patches, vanished into thin flying wreaths; and the unveiled lagoon lay, polished and black, in the heavy shadows at the foot of the wall of trees. A white eagle rose over it with a slanting and ponderous flight, reached the clear sunshine and appeared dazzlingly brilliant for a moment, then soaring higher, became a dark and motionless speck before it vanished into the blue as if it had left the earth forever. The white man, standing gazing upward before the doorway, heard in the hut a confused and broken murmur of distracted words ending with a loud groan. Suddenly Arsat stumbled out with outstretched hands, shivered, and stood still for some time with fixed eyes. Then he said—

"She burns no more."

Before his face the sun showed its edge above the treetops, rising steadily. The breeze freshened; a great brilliance burst upon the lagoon, sparkled on the rippling water. The forests came out of the clear shadows of the morning, became distinct, as if they had rushed nearer—to stop short in a great stir of leaves, of nodding boughs, of swaying branches. In the merciless sunshine the whisper of unconscious life grew louder, speaking in an incomprehensible voice round the dumb darkness of that human sorrow. Arsat's eyes wandered slowly, then stared at the rising sun.

"I can see nothing," he said half aloud to himself.

"There is nothing," said the white man, moving to the edge of the platform and waving his hand to his boat. A shout came faintly over the lagoon and the sampan began to glide toward the abode of the friend of ghosts.

Reading Strategy
Picturing the Action and Situation What expression do you think is on each character's face when Arsat concludes his story within a story?

Reading Check
What happens to Arsat's brother?

21 Reading Strategy

Picturing the Action and Situation

- Tell students to visualize Conrad's descriptions as you read aloud the bracketed passage to them.
- Then, ask them the Reading Strategy question on p. 1145: What expression do you think is on each character's face when Arsat concludes his story within a story?
  Answer: Students may imagine that Arsat has a look of pain, resignation, or sorrow on his face, and that Tuan looks serious, thoughtful, and sympathetic.

22 Critical Thinking

Assess

- Have students clarify the white man's words in this passage. What do they think he is suggesting?
- Then, ask students what price Arsat has paid for his desires. Do students think this price was worth peace in his heart?
  Answer: Some students may say that the price was too high, that his guilt has followed him all his life. Others may point out that he thought he could flee death itself, yet now Diamelen is dying.

23  Reading Check

Answer: Arsat's brother is caught, and presumably killed, by the Rajah's men.

CUSTOMIZE INSTRUCTION FOR UNIVERSAL ACCESS

For English Learners

English learners may find it especially difficult to detect the plot devices used by Conrad in "The Lagoon," because they are subtly interspersed with the story within a story. Have students read passages in which these devices are especially noticeable, and encourage students to identify them on their own or with teacher guidance.

Answers for p. 1146

Review and Assess

1. **(a)** He hopes the white man can cure Diamelen. **(b)** Arsat is disturbed and anxious.
2. **(a)** He shoots at the Rajah's henchmen and tries to escape, but he is captured and killed. **(b)** Arsat is desperate to escape with Diamelen. **(c)** He might have urged Diamelen to escape and gone back to help his brother; however, both brothers might have died.
3. **(a)** To Arsat, life means nothing now that Diamelen is dead. The white man means that there are no illusions to cling to. **(b)** Conrad is saying that all human life is illusion.
4. **(a)** Possible responses: Students may point to the descriptions of the gun shots, of the brother's screams across the water, and the sound of the silence as the two men sit in front of the fire. These descriptions suggest that the act of storytelling involves representing both the silence and the noise of an episode and of the surroundings in which the episode is related. **(b)** Arsat is torn by guilt for acting out of passion and contributing to his brother's death. **(c)** If Arsat hoped to expunge his guilt for his brother's death, he has not succeeded.
5. **(a)** Conrad might say that a person must struggle to see through illusions to understand. **(b)** Possible responses: Students may agree or disagree, but should provide reasons for their opinions.

"If you want to come with me, I will wait all the morning," said the white man, looking away upon the water.

"No, Tuan," said Arsat softly. "I shall not eat or sleep in this house, but I must first see my road. Now I can see nothing—see nothing! There is no light and no peace in the world; but there is death—death for many. We were sons of the same mother—and I left him in the midst of enemies; but I am going back now."

He drew a long breath and went on in a dreamy tone:

"In a little while I shall see clear enough to strike—to strike. But she has died, and . . . now . . . darkness."

He flung his arms wide open, let them fall along his body, then stood still with unmoved face and stony eyes, staring at the sun. The white man got down into his canoe. The polers ran smartly along the sides of the boat, looking over their shoulders at the beginning of a weary journey. High in the stern, his head muffled up in white rags, the juragon sat moody, letting his paddle trail in the water. The white man, leaning with both arms over the grass roof of the little cabin, looked back at the shining ripple of the boat's wake. Before the sampan passed out of the lagoon into the creek he lifted his eyes. Arsat had not moved. He stood lonely in the searching sunshine; and he looked beyond the great light of a cloudless day into the darkness of a world of illusions.

Review and Assess

Thinking About the Selection

1. (a) **Recall:** Why does Arsat ask the white man if he has medicine? (b) **Infer:** What is Arsat's state of mind?
2. (a) **Recall:** What does Arsat's brother do while Arsat and Diamelen run to the canoe? (b) **Analyze Cause and Effect:** What motivates Arsat to leave his brother behind? (c) **Speculate:** How else could he have responded, and what might have been the results?
3. (a) **Interpret:** Following Diamelen's death, Arsat says, "I can see nothing," and the white man replies, "There is nothing." What does each statement mean? (b) **Connect:** How might this dialogue relate to the story's final line?
4. (a) **Analyze:** Find three examples of Conrad's descriptions in the story of sounds, including descriptions of silence and speech. What do these images suggest about the act of storytelling? (b) **Draw Conclusions:** What is Arsat's purpose in telling his story? (c) **Evaluate:** Does he achieve it? Explain.
5. (a) **Draw Conclusions:** What do you think Conrad would recommend to people as a way to deal with past mistakes or regrets? (b) **Make a Judgment:** Would you agree? Explain.

24 

25 North Richmond Street, being blind,[1] was a quiet street except at the hour when the Christian Brothers' School set the boys free. An uninhabited house of two stories stood at the blind end, detached from its neighbors in a square ground. The other houses of the street, conscious of decent lives within them, gazed at one another with brown imperturbable faces.

imperturbable (im′ pər tʉr′ bə bəl) *adj.* calm; not easily ruffled

The former tenant of our house, a priest, had died in the back drawing room. Air, musty from having been long enclosed, hung in all the rooms, and the waste room behind the kitchen was littered with old useless papers. Among these I found a few paper-covered books, the pages of which were curled and damp: *The Abbot*, by Walter Scott, *The Devout Communicant* and *The Memoirs of Vidocq*.[2] I liked the last best because its leaves were yellow. The wild garden behind the house contained a central apple tree and a few straggling bushes under one of which I found the late tenant's rusty bicycle pump. He had been a very charitable priest: in his will he had left all his money to institutions and the furniture of his house to his sister.

When the short days of winter came dusk fell before we had well eaten our dinners. When we met in the street the houses had grown somber. The space of sky above us was the color of ever-changing violet and toward it the lamps of the street lifted their feeble lanterns. The cold air stung us and we played till our bodies glowed. Our shouts echoed in the silent street. The career of our play brought us through the dark muddy lanes behind the houses where we ran the gantlet of the rough tribes from the cottages, to the back doors of the dark dripping gardens where odors arose from the ashpits, to the dark odorous stables where a coachman smoothed and combed the horse or shook music from the buckled harness. When we returned to the street, light from the kitchen windows had filled the areas. If my uncle was seen turning the corner we hid in the shadow until we had seen him safely housed. Or if Mangan's sister came out on the doorstep to call her brother in to his tea we watched her from our

 **Reading Check**

When and where does the story take place?

1. **blind** a dead end.
2. ***The Abbot . . . Vidocq*** a historical tale, a religious manual, and the remembrances of a French adventurer, respectively.

24 About the Selection

A boy has a deep crush on the older sister of a neighborhood friend. He watches her and dreams of their romantic future. Late one night he goes on a mission to a bazaar called "Araby" to get her a gift, only to realize that Araby is not the exotic world he had imagined. In the darkness of the closing bazaar, he has a sudden vision of himself "as a creature driven and derided by vanity." This vision, provoking "anguish and anger," seems to take in his imaginary relationship with the girl and all his illusions.

25 Critical Thinking

Analyze

- Remind students of the different types of figurative language they have encountered in their readings.
- Then, ask them to identify the figurative technique Joyce uses in this passage, and tell how it helps set the scene.
  Answer: Joyce personifies the houses as if they gaze at one another and judge the behavior of their inhabitants.

26 Reading Check

Answer: The story takes place on the dead-end North Richmond Street in the evening.

CUSTOMIZE INSTRUCTION FOR UNIVERSAL ACCESS

For Gifted/Talented Students	For Advanced Readers
Encourage students to draw an illustration of the neighborhood described by the narrator of "Araby" in the first few paragraphs of the story. Tell them to focus on specific descriptions of the community and to reproduce them with as much accuracy as possible. If students are interested, have them draw their image of the narrator into the scene they depict.	Have students read the description of the narrator's neighborhood in "Araby," independently. Then, tell them to write a proposal for a documentary film project on Dublin's poor neighborhoods. Using James Joyce's descriptions, have them briefly describe the problems that Dublin's poor residents face and suggest a topical angle for the documentary.

27 Literary Analysis

Plot Devices and Point of View

- Review with students the different kinds of narrative points of view, focusing on the level of narrative information provided by each. If possible, have students identify examples of each type of point of view from selections they have previously read.
- Then, ask students the Literary Analysis question on p. 1148: What effect does the use of first-person point of view have on your impression of Mangan's sister?
  Answer: Students should recognize that the first-person point of view makes us see Mangan's sister through the narrator's lovesick eyes.

28 Reading Strategy

Picturing the Action and Situation

- As students read the passage, have them describe the mental image they form. Make sure students can identify the details they used to help them form these images.
- Then, ask students the Reading Strategy question on p. 1148: Which vivid details in this passage help you form a mental picture of the scene?
  Answer: Students should describe the sounds of rain falling, the gleam of a lamp, and the speaker's gesture of pressing his hands together as all forming a vivid picture.

shadow peer up and down the street. We waited to see whether she would remain or go in and, if she remained, we left our shadow and walked up to Mangan's steps resignedly. She was waiting for us, her figure defined by the light from the half-opened door. Her brother always teased her before he obeyed and I stood by the railings looking at her. Her dress swung as she moved her body and the soft rope of her hair tossed from side to side.

Every morning I lay on the floor in the front parlor watching her door. The blind was pulled down to within an inch of the sash so that I could not be seen. When she came out on the doorstep my heart
27 leaped. I ran to the hall, seized my books and followed her. I kept her brown figure always in my eye and, when we came near the point at which our ways diverged, I quickened my pace and passed her. This happened morning after morning. I had never spoken to her, except for a few casual words, and yet her name was like a summons to all my foolish blood.

Her image accompanied me even in places the most hostile to romance. On Saturday evenings when my aunt went marketing I had to go to carry some of the parcels. We walked through the flaring streets, jostled by drunken men and bargaining women, amid the curses of laborers, the shrill litanies of shop-boys who stood on guard by the barrels of pigs' cheeks, the nasal chanting of street singers, who sang a *come-all-you* about O'Donovan Rossa,[3] or a ballad about the troubles in our native land. These noises converged in a single sensation of life for me: I imagined that I bore my chalice safely through a throng of foes. Her name sprang to my lips at moments in strange prayers and praises which I myself did not understand. My eyes were often full of tears (I could not tell why) and at times a flood from my heart seemed to pour itself out into my bosom. I thought little of the future. I did not know whether I would ever speak to her or not or, if I spoke to her, how I could tell her of my confused adoration. But my body was like a harp and her words and gestures were like fingers running upon the wires.

One evening I went into the back drawing room in which the priest had died. It was a dark rainy evening and there was no sound in the house. Through one of the broken panes I heard the rain impinge upon the earth, the fine incessant needles of water playing in the
28 sodden beds. Some distant lamp or lighted window gleamed below me. I was thankful that I could see so little. All my senses seemed to desire to veil themselves and, feeling that I was about to slip from them, I pressed the palms of my hands together until they trembled, murmuring: *"O love! O love!"* many times.

At last she spoke to me. When she addressed the first words to me I was so confused that I did not know what to answer. She asked me was I going to *Araby*. I forget whether I answered yes or no. It would be a splendid bazaar, she said; she would love to go.

"And why can't you?" I asked.

Literary Analysis
Plot Devices and Point of View What effect does the use of first-person point of view have on your impression of Mangan's sister?

litanies (lit´ ən ēz) *n.* prayers in which a congregation repeats a fixed response; repetitive recitations

Reading Strategy
Picturing the Action and Situation Which vivid details in this passage help you form a mental picture of the scene?

3. ***come-all-you . . . Rossa*** opening of a ballad about an Irish hero.

ENRICHMENT: Cultural Connection

Epiphany

In the works of James Joyce, an *epiphany* is a profound revelation experienced by a main character. The term was used in Greek mythology to describe an occasion when a god or goddess would suddenly reveal his or her true identity to a mortal. The word *epiphany* also has an ecclesiastical meaning. The Epiphany, or Twelfth Night, is a Christian holiday celebrated twelve days after Christmas, on January 6. It commemorates the day that the Magi arrived to visit the Christ child and the beasts in the stable were able to talk. Religious symbols and references are common in the works of Joyce.

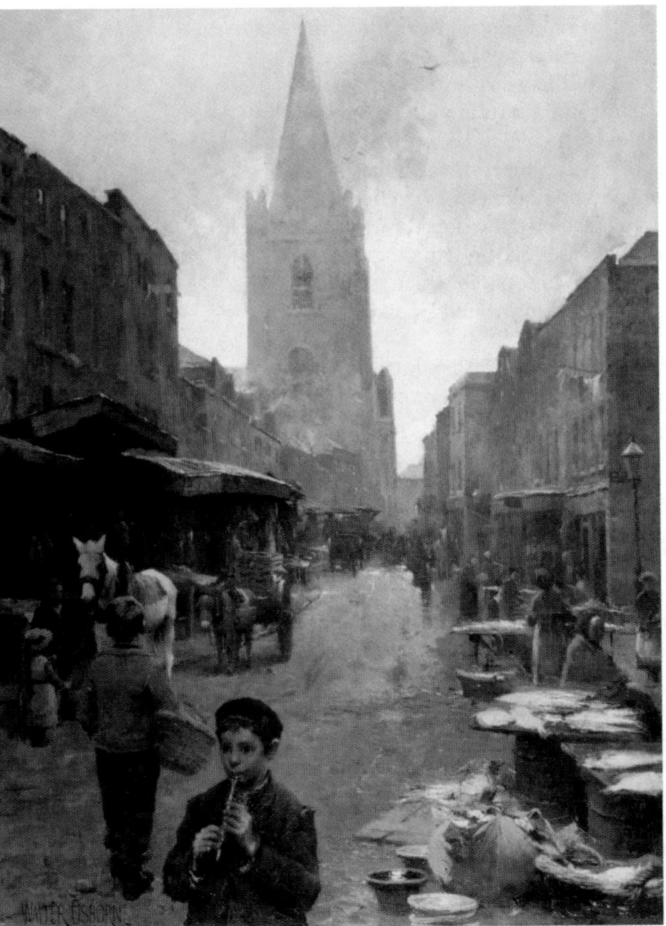

St. Patrick's Close, Walter Osborne, Courtesy of the National Gallery of Ireland

30 ◄ **Critical Viewing**
Why might the prospect of a fair or bazaar be appealing to someone who lived in a setting such as this? **[Infer]**

While she spoke she turned a silver bracelet round and round her wrist. She could not go, she said, because there would be a retreat[4] that week in her convent.[5] Her brother and two other boys were fighting for their caps and I was alone at the railings. She held one of the spikes, bowing her head towards me. The light from the lamp opposite our door caught the white curve of her neck, lit up her hair that rested there and, falling, lit up the hand upon the railing. It fell over one side of her dress and caught the white border of a petticoat, just visible as she stood at ease.

"It's well for you," she said.

"If I go," I said, "I will bring you something."

32 ↓ What innumerable follies laid waste my waking and sleeping thoughts after that evening! I wished to annihilate the tedious

Literary Analysis
Plot Devices In what way might the narrator's comments on his own past thoughts and feelings prepare for an epiphany?

31 
What does the narrator promise Mangan's sister?

4. **retreat** *n.* period of retirement or seclusion for prayer, religious study, and meditation.
5. **convent** *n.* school run by an order of nuns.

29 Background

Art

St. Patrick's Close, by Walter Osborne

Walter Frederick Osborne (1859–1903) was an Irish landscape painter who lived in Ireland and received his art training there, at the Royal Hibernian Academy. His paintings generally portray urban scenes with a special focus on children. Use these questions for discussion:

1. Is the artist observing the scene or judging it?
   Possible response: Some students might say that his realistic representation suggests that he is an observer.
2. Compare and contrast this scene with the description of North Richmond Street in Joyce's story.
   Answer: Students may say that, like Joyce's street, this street has low attached row houses with brown facades. However, this street is dominated by the cathedral.

30 ► Critical Viewing

Answer: Students may say that the allure of an exotic, romantic bazaar would be a welcome contrast to the bleak, squalid conditions of the neighborhood.

31 Reading Check

Answer: The narrator promises Mangan's sister something from the Araby bazaar.

32 Literary Analysis

Plot Devices

- Review with students their understanding of the word *epiphany.*
- Then, ask them the Literary Analysis question on p. 1149: In what way might the narrator's comments on his own past thoughts and feelings prepare for an epiphany?
  Answer: The narrator provides the background information that explains the buildup toward his epiphany.

CUSTOMIZE INSTRUCTION FOR UNIVERSAL ACCESS

For Less Proficient Readers	For English Learners	For Gifted/Talented Students
Remind students as they read that they should picture the action and situation of what is being described. As they read "Araby" with teacher guidance, tell them to visualize the scenes Joyce describes. If it helps them picture the action, encourage them to sketch pictures in a notebook to help them remember what has occurred.	Students may have difficulty with some of the more complicated vocabulary and some of the Anglicisms Joyce's narrator uses to describe his situation. Encourage them to sound out any words that give them unusual difficulty, to consult any footnotes or margin notes, and to try to put words into the context of sentences.	Have students work with partners to role-play for the class the conversation from "Araby" between the boy and Mangan's sister. In addition to delivering their lines, tell students to concentrate on conveying each character's inner reactions to the situation through facial expressions, body language, and tone of voice.

33 Reading Strategy

Picturing the Action and Situation

- As students focus on this paragraph, have them note the physical details that contribute to the narrator's mood.
- Ask the Reading Strategy question on p. 1150: As you picture the narrator daydreaming, do you also share the daydream? Explain. Possible response: Students may report that they can imagine who the narrator is dreaming of.

intervening days. I chafed against the work of school. At night in my bedroom and by day in the classroom her image came between me and the page I strove to read. The syllables of the word *Araby* were called to me through the silence in which my soul luxuriated and cast an Eastern enchantment over me. I asked for leave to go to the bazaar on Saturday night. My aunt was surprised and hoped it was not some Freemason[6] affair. I answered few questions in class. I watched my master's face pass from amiability to sternness; he hoped I was not beginning to idle. I could not call my wandering thoughts together. I had hardly any patience with the serious work of life which, now that it stood between me and my desire, seemed to me child's play, ugly monotonous child's play.

On Saturday morning I reminded my uncle that I wished to go to the bazaar in the evening. He was fussing at the hallstand, looking for the hat brush, and answered me curtly:

"Yes, boy, I know."

As he was in the hall I could not go into the front parlor and lie at the window. I left the house in bad humor and walked slowly toward the school. The air was pitilessly raw and already my heart misgave me.

When I came home to dinner my uncle had not yet been home. Still it was early. I sat staring at the clock for some time and, when its ticking began to irritate me, I left the room. I mounted the staircase and gained the upper part of the house. The high cold empty gloomy rooms liberated me and I went from room to room singing. From the front window I saw my companions playing in the street. Their cries reached me weakened and indistinct and, leaning my forehead against the cool glass, I looked over at the dark house where she lived. I may have stood there for an hour, seeing nothing but the brown-clad figure cast by my imagination, touched discreetly by the lamplight at the curved neck, at the hand upon the railings and at the border below the dress.

When I came downstairs again I found Mrs. Mercer sitting at the fire. She was an old garrulous woman, a pawnbroker's widow, who collected used stamps for some pious purpose. I had to endure the gossip of the tea table. The meal was prolonged beyond an hour and still my uncle did not come. Mrs. Mercer stood up to go: she was sorry she couldn't wait any longer, but it was after eight o'clock and she did not like to be out late, as the night air was bad for her. When she had gone I began to walk up and down the room, clenching my fists. My aunt said:

"I'm afraid you may put off your bazaar for this night of Our Lord."

At nine o'clock I heard my uncle's latchkey in the hall door. I heard him talking to himself and heard the hallstand rocking when it had received the weight of his overcoat. I could interpret these signs.

Reading Strategy
Picturing the Action and Situation As you picture the narrator daydreaming, do you also share the daydream? Explain.

garrulous (gar´ ə ləs) *adj.* talkative

6. **Freemason** Free and Accepted Masons, an international secret society.

ENRICHMENT: Social Studies Connection

Orientalism

People in the West have long had a fascination for the East. This phenomenon goes back at least to the 1200s, when the Italian trader Marco Polo returned from China and central Asia and wrote a book about his fabulous adventures. In the 1800s, *The Arabian Nights*—a collection of two hundred folk tales from Arabia, Egypt, India, and Persia—was translated into English by the explorer and scholar Richard Francis Burton. The book, which became an instant classic in the West, reinforced people's impressions of the East as an exotic land of genies and flying carpets.

When he was midway through his dinner I asked him to give me the money to go to the bazaar. He had forgotten.

"The people are in bed and after their first sleep now," he said.

I did not smile. My aunt said to him energetically:

"Can't you give him the money and let him go? You've kept him late enough as it is."

34 My uncle said he was very sorry he had forgotten. He said he believed in the old saying: *All work and no play makes Jack a dull boy.* He asked me where I was going and, when I had told him a second time he asked me did I know *The Arab's Farewell to His Steed.*[7] When I left the kitchen he was about to recite the opening lines of the piece to my aunt.

I held a florin[8] tightly in my hand as I strode down Buckingham Street toward the station. The sight of the streets thronged with buyers and glaring with gas recalled to me the purpose of my journey. I took my seat in a third-class carriage of a deserted train. After an intolerable delay the train moved out of the station slowly. It crept onward among ruinous houses and over the twinkling river. At Westland Row Station a crowd of people pressed to the carriage doors; but the porters moved them back, saying that it was a special train for the bazaar. I remained alone in the bare carriage. In a few minutes the train drew up beside an improvised wooden platform. I passed out onto the road and saw by the lighted dial of a clock that it was ten minutes to ten. In front of me was a large building which displayed the magical name.

I could not find any sixpenny entrance and, fearing that the bazaar would be closed, I passed in quickly through a turnstile, handing a shilling to a weary-looking man. I found myself in a big hall girdled at half its height by a gallery. Nearly all the stalls were closed and the greater part of the hall was in darkness. I recognized a silence like that which pervades a church after a service. I walked into the center of the bazaar timidly. A few people were gathered about the stalls which were still open. Before a curtain, over which the words *Café Chantant*[9] were written in colored lamps, two men were counting money on a salver.[10] I listened to the fall of the coins.

Remembering with difficulty why I had come I went over to one of the stalls and examined porcelain vases and flowered tea sets. At the door of the stall a young lady was talking and laughing with two young gentlemen. I remarked their English accents and listened vaguely to their conversation.

"O, I never said such a thing!"

"O, but you did!"

7. ***The Arab's . . . His Steed*** popular nineteenth-century poem.
8. **florin** two shilling coin of the time.
9. ***Café Chantant*** café with musical entertainment.
10. **salver** tray usually used for the presentation of letters or visiting cards.

The British Tradition

35 *The Irish Tradition*

Joyce's stories are a modern addition to the rich cultural legacy of Ireland. Irish literature began with an oral tradition of epics and flourished through the medieval period, when Irish monasteries guarded learned culture amid an inflowing tide of Danish and Germanic invaders. Bede's *History* is a culminating testament to the Irish preservation of learning on the islands—Irish books and Irish teaching flowing into Bede's England made the work possible.

Although the Irish cultural tradition is strong, centuries of rule by the English in Ireland and the Irish struggles against that rule have raised questions of cultural identity. When W. B. Yeats reinvigorated Irish poetry, he helped to launch the Irish Literary Revival. This literary assertion of Irish identity was also a political gesture reinforcing the movement to free Ireland. Since Yeats, writers such as Joyce, Louis MacNeice, and Seamus Heaney have made the Irish identity, as well as the splits it suffered under English rule, a theme for literary exploration.

36 Reading Check

In what way does the narrator's uncle delay the narrator's arrival at Araby?

34 Reading Strategy

Picturing the Action and Situation

- Have students identify the details in the passage that help them form a picture of the uncle.
- Then, ask students, based on the details in the paragraph, how they picture the uncle.
  Answer: Students may say that the uncle is detached, is somewhat self-absorbed, and has little appreciation of his nephew's state of mind.

35 Background

The Irish Tradition

Irish monasteries played a vital role as a cultural bridge between classical antiquity and the Middle Ages. This little-known story is brought to light in Thomas Cahill's slightly hyperbolic book *How the Irish Saved Civilization.*

36 Reading Check

Answer: The uncle's late arrival delays the narrator's trip to Araby because he must wait to get money from his uncle.

CUSTOMIZE INSTRUCTION FOR UNIVERSAL ACCESS

For Less Proficient Readers	For English Learners	For Gifted/Talented Students
Have students write a journal entry that the boy in "Araby" might have written upon returning home from the bazaar. Tell them to explain the hopes the boy had and his feelings about those hopes upon returning home.	Have students read the narrator's description of the bazaar with teacher guidance. Remind them that the narrator has been looking forward to the bazaar since his conversation with Mangan's sister. As students read, encourage them to picture the action and situation.	Tell students to create two drawings of the bazaar in "Araby." In one drawing, students should depict the bazaar as the boy imagines it before he arrives. In the other drawing, students should depict the contrasting reality of the bazaar.

ASSESS

Answers for p. 1152

Review and Assess

1. Possible responses: Most students will identify with such feelings.
2. **(a)** Mangan's sister says that she would love to go and tells the narrator how fortunate he is to be able to go. **(b)** The narrator notices that she calls in her brother from play, he sees her leave for school, and he talks to her about the bazaar. Her lack of a name makes her seem more remote; it also shows how little the narrator knows her.
3. **(a)** He overpays, he finds almost nobody there, and the people he encounters seem bored. **(b)** He expects the Araby bazaar will be exotic and the prospect of going "cast an Eastern enchantment" over him. Nothing he sees at the bazaar meets his expectations.
4. **(a)** Possible responses: Most students will say that the descriptions of the narrator's neighborhood were evocative and romantic. **(b)** No, the qualities of his descriptions do not make the ordinary world as exciting and interesting as the fabled world of Araby, because they are essentially commonplace.
5. **(a)** The narrator has lost his illusions of Araby. **(b)** He might have gained the experience and maturity that come from encountering disappointment.
6. Possible responses: Students may say that dreams of youth should be protected because they are precious and nurturing; others may say that a disillusioning experience can help ground a person in reality.

"O, but I didn't!"
"Didn't she say that?"
"Yes. I heard her."
"O, there's a . . . fib!"

Observing me the young lady came over and asked me did I wish to buy anything. The tone of her voice was not encouraging; she seemed to have spoken to me out of a sense of duty. I looked humbly at the great jars that stood like Eastern guards at either side of the dark entrance to the stall and murmured:

"No, thank you."

The young lady changed the position of one of the vases and went back to the two young men. They began to talk of the same subject. Once or twice the young lady glanced at me over her shoulder.

I lingered before her stall, though I knew my stay was useless, to make my interest in her wares seem the more real. Then I turned away slowly and walked down the middle of the bazaar. I allowed the two pennies to fall against the sixpence in my pocket. I heard a voice call from one end of the gallery that the light was out. The upper part of the hall was now completely dark.

Gazing up into the darkness I saw myself as a creature driven and derided by vanity; and my eyes burned with anguish and anger.

derided (di rīd′ id) *v.* made fun of; ridiculed

Review and Assess

Thinking About the Selection

1. **Respond:** Have you ever had doubts or ambivalent feelings about a promise like those of the narrator? Explain.
2. **(a) Recall:** What does Mangan's sister do to make a trip to the bazaar so important to the narrator? **(b) Analyze:** Describe three scenes that establish the narrator's feelings for her.
3. **(a) Recall:** Describe the narrator's experience at Araby. **(b) Analyze Causes and Effects:** What features of the Araby bazaar conflict with the narrator's expectations?
4. **(a) Evaluate:** Did you find the narrator's descriptions of his neighborhood and childhood colorful, even romantic? Explain. **(b) Connect:** Do his descriptions make the ordinary world as exciting and interesting as the world he hopes to find at the bazaar?
5. **(a) Draw Conclusions:** What has the narrator lost by the end of the story? **(b) Draw Conclusions:** What might he have gained?
6. **Apply:** Should the dreams of youth be protected, or can a disillusioning experience like the narrator's teach a valuable lesson? Explain.

ASSESSMENT PRACTICE: Writing Skills

Strategy (For more practice, see Test Preparation Workbook, p. 56.)

Many tests require students to apply revision strategies to a passage. Use the following sample item to teach students how to evaluate the appropriateness of a sentence. Write this sentence from the selection on the board:

He had known Arsat years ago, in a far country in times of trouble and danger, when no friendship is to be despised.

To add information about Tuan and Arsat's shared past, which of the following sentences would be most suitable?

A Tuan was orphaned at the age of ten.
B As a boy, Arsat most admired his uncle.
C Tuan had seen Arsat several times recently.
D Arsat had once saved Tuan's life.

Help students determine that the correct answer is *D*.

Review and Assess

Literary Analysis

Plot Devices

1. Conrad uses the **plot device** of a **story within a story** in "The Lagoon." What specific information would you lack if "The Lagoon" had been narrated entirely in the first person by Arsat?
2. Why do you think Conrad chose to have Arsat narrate his own story?
3. (a) Where in "Araby" does the **epiphany** occur? (b) What does the narrator in "Araby" suddenly realize?
4. Explain in what sense the narrator's epiphany in "Araby" is as much a loss of vision as it is a gain of insight.

Comparing Literary Works

5. Contrast the mood of the parts of "The Lagoon" narrated by Arsat with the mood of the framing story, narrated in the third-person.
6. Use a chart like the one shown to compare how each story uses plot devices to establish distance between an experience of passion and the act of telling a story about passion.

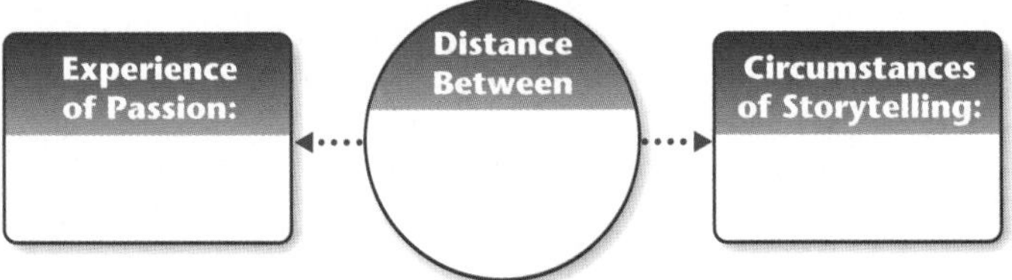

7. (a) Compare the way that each story creates an "outsider's" perspective on a narrator's obsessive, passionate concerns. (b) Explain how plot devices add to the **theme** of each story.

Reading Strategy

Picturing the Action and Situation

8. Write a paragraph describing a scene in "The Lagoon."
9. Write a paragraph describing the narrator's feelings when he experiences his epiphany in "Araby."

Extend Understanding

10. **Psychology Connection:** How important do you think storytelling is in the mourning process? Why?

Quick Review

Writers use **plot devices** to achieve innovative effects.

A **story within a story** is a tale told by a character within a fictional narrative.

An **epiphany**—a profound revelation experienced by a character—gives a story a psychological climax.

The **theme** of a work is its central concern, the question about life that it raises, or the message it sends.

To better understand the characters' actions and inner lives, pause to **picture the action and situation** in scenes of a narrative.

 ***Take It to the Net***

www.phschool.com

Take the interactive self-test online to check your understanding of these selections.

Answers for p. 1153

Review and Assess

1. You would not know the antagonism the locals felt toward him or the sense of mystery that surrounds him.
2. Arsat can dramatize his story with his own emotions.
3. **(a)** The epiphany occurs at the bazaar, when the narrator's illusions are shattered. **(b)** The narrator realizes that his "romance" with Mangan's sister is as imaginary as the romance of the Araby bazaar.
4. The narrator has lost an exotic image of romance and lost some of his self-image as well.
5. The framing story has the objective, matter-of-fact mood of daylight. Arsat's story has a lonely, anguished mood of the darkness of night.
6. ***"Lagoon"*—Experience of Passion:** Arsat's elopement with Diamelen, leading to his betrayal of his brother; **Circumstances of Storytelling:** Arsat tells his story to the white man as Diamelen is dying; **Distance Between:** The story of a man's passion is presented not as it unfolds, but as a story told to a neutral character. Further, the tale is told while the reason for the teller's passion is being taken away from him (Diamelen is dying).
***"Araby"*—Experience of Passion:** the narrator's crush on Mangan's sister, which leads to his desire to go to Araby; **Circumstances of Storytelling:** The narrator tells the story from the present, after he has been to Araby. **Distance Between:** The narrator tells of his passion after he has been robbed of the romantic illusions it created.
7. **(a) "Lagoon":** The white man has an outsider's perspective: He listens to a story in which he is not centrally involved. **"Araby":** The narrator himself has an outsider's perspective: He tells the story of a romantic illusion after he has lost it. **(b) "Lagoon":** The theme concerns doomed human attempts to rescue meaning from loss; because the story-within-a-story device gives us an outsider's view of Arsat's words, we can see their futility. **"Araby":** The theme concerns the way in which a

continued

Answers continued

poetical passion can thrive on possibility but cannot survive its embodiment in reality. The device of the epiphany moves the speaker from the first to the second aspect of passion.

8. Possible response: In "The Lagoon," when Arsat stumbles out of the hut and says "She burns no more," it sends a chill down the spine. Arsat must announce the death of his beloved to the white man. I see him with his lips tight but trembling and a sad, distant look in his teary eyes. The white man is silent, knowing that there is nothing he can say to comfort his friend, knowing that it is time to show quiet respect.
9. Possible response: The narrator feels the vacancy of the nearly closed bazaar—the mundane conversation of the stall keepers, the shoddy products being offered, and the sense that he has overpaid and expected too much from "Araby" all contribute to the sinking feeling he has in his heart.
10. Possible response: Students may say that storytelling enables the grief process to begin.

EXTEND

Answers for p. 1154

❶ Vocabulary Development

Word Analysis

1. To *convince* is to persuade someone—essentially conquering their resistance.
2. To *evince* is to show clearly or make evident—as if what is being shown overcomes any doubts about its existence or any resistance to its disclosure.
3. *Invincibility* is the inability to be conquered.

Spelling Strategy

1. galleries
2. cries
3. families

Concept Development: Synonyms

1. b
2. a
3. a
4. c
5. c
6. b
7. b
8. a
9. b

❷ Grammar and Style

1. *Before the sampan passed out of the lagoon into the creek;* lifted
2. *since his Malay friend had come unexpectedly to dwell in the hut on the lagoon with a strange woman;* slept
3. *When we met in the street;* had grown
4. *when it had received the weight of his overcoat;* heard
5. *though I knew my stay was useless;* lingered

Writing Application

Possible response: *Before the sun rose,* I crept out of the cabin on the beach. Without realizing it, I'd let the door slam behind me, waking everyone in the cabin. They poured out *after me,* and we began wandering the length of the beach. Dogs and wild horses trailed *behind us* as we began our exploration.

Integrate Language Skills

❶ Vocabulary Development Lesson

Word Analysis: Latin Root *-vinc-*

Early in Conrad's "The Lagoon," you will find the word *invincible*, which means "unconquerable." *Invincible* is formed with the root *-vinc-*, which comes from a Latin verb meaning "to conquer." Write definitions for the following words, explaining how the meaning of the root affects the meaning of the word.

1. convince 2. evince 3. invincibility

Spelling Strategy

If a noun ends in the letter *y* preceded by a consonant, form the plural by dropping the *y* and adding *-ies: litany* becomes *litanies*. Write the plural form of each of the following words:

1. gallery
2. cry
3. family

Concept Development: Synonyms

Choose the synonym for the first word in each item.

1. portals: (a) arteries, (b) doors, (c) chairs
2. invincible: (a) unconquerable, (b) warriorlike, (c) facile
3. propitiate: (a) appease, (b) refuse, (c) resign
4. conflagration: (a) battle, (b) dispute, (c) fire
5. august: (a) portly, (b) virtuous, (c) awe-inspiring
6. imperturbable: (a) indifferent, (b) calm, (c) ruthless
7. litanies: (a) lawsuits, (b) prayers, (c) cries
8. garrulous: (a) talkative, (b) coy, (c) rich
9. derided: (a) ejected, (b) ridiculed, (c) exaggerated

❷ Grammar and Style Lesson

Adverb Clauses

Conrad and Joyce both use **adverb clauses**—subordinate clauses that modify a verb, an adjective, or an adverb.

Adverb Clause: . . . the repeated call of some bird . . . skipped along over the smooth water and lost itself, before it could reach the other shore, . . . (modifies *lost* by telling when)

Practice In your notebook, identify the adverb clause in each sentence and the word(s) it modifies.

1. Before the sampan passed out of the lagoon into the creek, he lifted his eyes.
2. And since his Malay friend had come unexpectedly to dwell in the hut on the lagoon with a strange woman, he had slept many times there, ...
3. When we met in the street, the houses had grown somber.
4. I . . . heard the hallstand rocking when it had received the weight of his overcoat.
5. I lingered before her stall, though I knew my stay was useless, . . .

Writing Application Write a brief account of a journey you have taken into another "world," using at least three adverb clauses.

WG Prentice Hall Writing and Grammar Connection: Chapter 19, Section 3

TEACHING RESOURCES

The following resources can be used to enrich or extend the instruction for pp. 1154–1155.

Vocabulary

- **Selection Support:** Build Vocabulary, p. 259
- **Vocabulary and Spelling Practice Book** (Use this booklet for skills enrichment.)

Grammar

- **Selection Support:** Grammar and Style, p. 260
- **Writing and Grammar,** Diamond Level, p. 458
- **Daily Language Practice Transparencies** ■

Writing

- **Writing and Grammar,** Diamond Level, p. 317 ■
- **Writing and Grammar iText CD-ROM**

■ **BLOCK SCHEDULING:** Resources marked with this symbol provide varied instruction during 90-minute blocks.

❸ Writing Lesson

Literary Essay

Conrad's "The Lagoon" abounds with descriptions of silence and repeated uses of the word *nothing.* Write an essay tracing these images through the story, mapping them against events in Arsat's tale and in the framing narrative. Conclude with a general insight into the relationship of silence, storytelling, passion, and "nothing" in the story.

Prewriting Review the story, taking notes on images of silence and "nothing" and the narration surrounding each. Draft a few statements of what the references suggest. Consider the extent to which Arsat's storytelling is an interruption of silence.

Drafting As you draft, present your ideas in logical sequence. Relate each idea to your central insight into the story.

Revising Highlight vague passages in you draft. For each, review "The Lagoon," and jot down notes showing how the story supports your ideas. Consider incorporating your new ideas to improve vague passages.

Model: Revising to Sharpen Insight

Like the bird's cry described by Conrad, Arsat's story "loses itself" in the void. It cannot make up for his brother's or for Diamelen's death.
Arsat badly wants to tell his story. Silence, though, surrounds him. ~~His words do not make any difference in his situation.~~

A reference to Conrad's image helps focus the writer's point.

WG Prentice Hall Writing and Grammar Connection: Chapter 14, Section 4

❹ Extension Activities

Listening and Speaking With a group, hold a **literary trial** of Arsat to determine whether he is responsible for his brother's death. Divide the roles of defense team, prosecution, and judge.

- Use concrete images and evidence from Arsat's account to help you state your case.
- Use figurative language—striking comparisons and images—to present your ideas.

Present your arguments before the "jury" (the class), and have them return a verdict. **[Group Activity]**

Research and Technology Develop a **research presentation** on poster art at the turn of the twentieth century, such as might have been used to advertise Araby. Explore art books, galleries, and Web sites. Then, write a brief report on the history of such posters. Produce a poster for Araby, and present it with your report.

www.phschool.com

Go online for an additional research activity using the Internet.

Lesson Support for p. 1155

❸ Writing Lesson

- Explain that students will write an analysis of repeated descriptions of silence and uses of the word *nothing* in Conrad's "The Lagoon."
- Remind students that images often stand for more than one thing or idea and that it is helpful to identify recurring uses of images to connect them to theme.
- Use the Writing Lesson to guide students in developing their analyses of literary images and themes.

❹ Listening and Speaking

- Have students work in small groups to hold a literary trial of Arsat to determine his responsibility in his brother's death.
- Read the Listening and Speaking lesson with students, and then divide them into three teams: judge, defense, and prosecution.
- Encourage each group to reread the passage in which Arsat explains what happened to his brother.

CUSTOMIZE INSTRUCTION
For Universal Access

To address different learning styles, use the activities suggested in the **Extension Activities** booklet, p. 56.

- For Musical/Rhythmic Learners, use Activity 5.
- For Visual/Spatial Learners, use Activity 6.
- For Bodily/Kinesthetic and Interpersonal Learners, use Activity 7.

ASSESSMENT RESOURCES

The following resources can be used to assess students' knowledge and skills.

Selection Assessment

- **Formal Assessment,** pp. 269–271
- **Open Book Test,** pp. 165–167
- **Got It! Assessment Videotapes,** Tape 6
- **Test Bank Software**

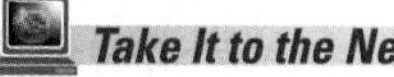

Visit www.phschool.com for self-tests and additional questions on the selections.

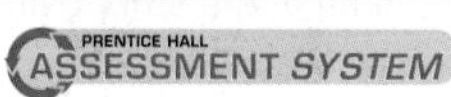

- **Workbook**
- **Skill Book**
- **Transparencies**
- **CD-ROM**

The Lady in the Looking Glass: A Reflection ✦ The First Year of My Life

Lesson Objectives and CA Correlations

1. **To analyze and respond to literary elements**
   - Literary Analysis: Point of View: Modern Experiments **R 3.7**
   - Comparing Literary Works **R 3.3**
2. **To read, comprehend, analyze, and critique a short story**
   - Reading Strategy: Questioning
   - Reading Check Questions
   - Review and Assess Questions
3. **To develop word analysis skills, fluency, and systematic vocabulary**
   - Vocabulary Development Lesson: Latin Prefix *-trans-* **R 1.2**
4. **To understand and apply written and oral language conventions**
   - Spelling Strategy **LC 1.2**
   - Grammar and Style Lesson: Subject-Verb Agreement in Inverted Sentences **LC 1.1**
5. **To understand and apply appropriate writing and research strategies**
   - Writing Lesson: Essay on a Literary Theme **W 1.1, 1.3, 2.2**
   - Extension Activity: Report on Cultural Trends **W 1.6**
   - Assessment Practice (ATE)
6. **To understand and apply listening and speaking strategies**
   - Extension Activity: Discussion Group **LS 2.3, 2.5**

STEP-BY-STEP TEACHING GUIDE	PACING GUIDE
PRETEACH	
Motivate Students and Provide Background	
Use the Motivation activity (ATE p. 1156)	5 min.
Read and discuss author and background features (SE/ATE pp. 1156, 1164) [A]	5 min.
Introduce the Concepts	
Introduce the Literary Analysis and Reading Strategy (SE/ATE p. 1157) [A]	15 min.
Pronounce the vocabulary words and read their definitions (SE p. 1157)	5 min.
TEACH	
Monitor Comprehension	
Informally monitor comprehension by circulating while students read independently or in groups [A]	30 min.
Monitor students' comprehension with the Reading Check notes (SE/ATE pp. 1159, 1161, 1165, 1167, 1169)	as students read
Develop vocabulary with Vocabulary notes (SE pp. 1158, 1159, 1160, 1162, 1164, 1165; ATE p. 1160)	as students read
Develop Understanding	
Develop students' understanding of modern experiments with point of view with the Literary Analysis annotations (SE/ATE pp. 1161, 1165, 1166, 1169) [A]	5 min.
Develop students' understanding of asking questions while reading with the Reading Strategy annotations (SE/ATE pp. 1165, 1167, 1168)	5 min.
ASSESS	
Assess Mastery	
Assess students' mastery of the Reading Strategy and Literary Analysis by having them answer the Review and Assess questions (SE/ATE p. 1171)	15 min.
Use one or more of the print and media Assessment Resources (ATE p. 1173) [A]	up to 45 min.
EXTEND	
Apply Understanding	
Have students complete the Vocabulary Development Lesson and the Grammar and Style Lesson (SE p. 1172) [A]	20 min.
Apply students' ability to contrast details using the Writing Lesson (SE/ATE p. 1173) [A]	45 min.
Apply students' understanding of the story using one or more of the Extension Activities (SE p. 1173)	20–90 min.

ACCELERATED INSTRUCTION:
Use the strategies and activities identified with an [A].

UNIVERSAL ACCESS
● = Below-Level Students
▲ = On-Level Students
■ = Above-Level Students

Time and Resource Manager

Reading Level: Challenging, Average
Average Number of Instructional Days: 4

RESOURCES		
PRINT	**TRANSPARENCIES**	**TECHNOLOGY**
• **Beyond Literature,** Cross-Curricular Connection: Science, p. 57 ▲ ■		• **Interest Grabber Video,** Tape 6 ● ▲ ■
• **Selection Support Workbook:** ● ▲ ■ Literary Analysis, p. 266 Reading Strategy, p. 265 Build Vocabulary, p. 263	• **Literary Analysis and Reading Transparencies,** pp. 113 and 114 ● ▲ ■	
		• **Listening to Literature** ● ▲ ■ Audiocassettes, Sides 26 and 27 Audio CDs, CD 5
• **Literatura en español** ● ▲ • **Literary Analysis for Enrichment** ■		
• **Formal Assessment:** Selection Test, pp. 272–274 ● ▲ ■ • **Open Book Test,** pp. 168–170 ● ▲ ■ • PRENTICE HALL ASSESSMENT SYSTEM ● ▲ ■	• PRENTICE HALL ASSESSMENT SYSTEM ● ▲ ■ Skills Practice Answers and Explanations on Transparencies ● ▲ ■	• **Test Bank Software** ● ▲ ■ • **Got It! Assessment Videotapes,** Tape 6 ● ▲
• **Selection Support Workbook:** ● ▲ ■ Grammar and Style, p. 264 • **Writing and Grammar,** Diamond Level ● ▲ ■ • **Extension Activities,** p. 57 ● ▲ ■	• **Daily Language Practice Transparencies** ● ▲	• **Writing and Grammar iText CD-ROM** ● ▲ ■ ***Take It to the Net*** www.phschool.com

BLOCK SCHEDULING: Use one 90-minute class period to preteach the selection and have students read it. Use a second 90-minute class period to assess students' mastery of skills and have them complete one of the Extension Activities.

PRETEACH

Step-by-Step Teaching Guide for pp. 1156–1157

Motivation

Before students read the story by Virginia Woolf, bring in 6–10 unrelated objects and place them together on a table in full view of students. Challenge pairs of students to do one of two things: describe the type of character to whom these things belong or contrive some connection between all these items. After students have had time to share their ideas, tell them that in "The Lady in the Looking Glass" the narrator tries to understand a character by viewing her possessions. In "The First Year of My Life" the narrator tries to understand a series of seemingly unrelated events and make sense of the connections among them.

Interest Grabber Video

As an alternative, play "'The First Year of My Life': World War I" on Tape 6 to engage student interest.

❶ Background

More About the Authors

Virginia Woolf

Virginia Woolf's involvement with the Bloomsbury Group, which began in 1905–1906, was centered in her home at 46 Gordon Square, Bloomsbury, in London. Its members were against the artistic, social, and sexual restrictions of the Victorian period, and many of them radically affected the development of the *avant-garde* in art and literature in Britain. After her marriage to Leonard Woolf, Virginia and her husband founded the Hogarth Press in 1917, a publishing firm that alleviated the repeated bouts of depression Woolf suffered by providing her with constant work and intellectual distractions.

Muriel Spark

Muriel Spark spent several years in central Africa, which is the setting for many of her works of short fiction, including *The Go-Away Bird.* Her conversion from Judaism to Roman Catholicism in 1954 plays out in much of her later fiction, as does her settling in Italy, in which her 1976 novel, *The Take Over,* is set.

Prepare to Read

❶ The Lady in the Looking Glass: A Reflection ◆ The First Year of My Life

Virginia Woolf (1882–1941)

Virginia Woolf revolutionized modern fiction as one of the pioneers of the stream-of-consciousness technique. This device allows readers to tune in directly to the flow of thoughts and images in a character's mind.

A Literary Life Woolf came from a prim and proper Victorian family, but it was one in which literature was prized. Her father, the renowned editor Leslie Stephen, made sure that his daughter grew up surrounded by books. At the age of twenty-three, Woolf began contributing reviews to *The Times* of London. Later, she and her husband, author Leonard Woolf, made their house in the Bloomsbury section of London into a meeting place for writers and intellectuals. This circle of thinkers became known as the Bloomsbury Group.

Revolutionizing Fiction Woolf's first two novels were not unusual, but *Jacob's Room* (1922) shattered the conventions of fiction by telling the story of a young man's life entirely through an examination of his room. (She also uses this device in "The Lady in the Looking Glass: A Reflection.") Woolf continued to refine her fluid, inward-looking style with three more stream-of-consciousness novels—*Mrs. Dalloway* (1925), *To the Lighthouse* (1927), and *The Waves* (1931). In her more revolutionary works, she virtually abolishes a traditional plot, preferring to concentrate on what she called "an ordinary mind on an ordinary day."

Depression and Tragedy Woolf suffered episodes of severe depression brought on by poor health and the turmoil of World War II. In 1941, she drowned. Today, she is recognized as one of the defining forces of modern fiction.

Muriel Spark (b. 1918)

The Scottish novelist Muriel Spark is best known for her novel *The Prime of Miss Jean Brodie* (1961), which has been successfully adapted for both the stage and the screen.

A Prolific Career Born and educated in Edinburgh, Scotland, Spark began her literary career as an editor and biographer. After winning a short-story competition sponsored by the *Observer,* a Sunday newspaper, she focused her writing efforts on fiction. A number of her early stories were set in central Africa, where she had spent several years of her youth. Her first collection, *The Go-Away Bird and Other Stories,* was published in 1958.

Novels and Faith In 1954, after Spark converted to Roman Catholicism, she searched for ways to apply the psychological and spiritual insights of her new faith to her fiction. Many of her novels, including *The Mandelbaum Gate* (1965), *Territorial Rights* (1979), and *The Only Problem* (1984), reveal a writer preoccupied with questions of good and evil.

Perverse Whimsy At the same time, an element of perverse whimsy enters much of her work. Spark's narratives make leaps and loops, and it is sometimes hard to tell how far her narrators can be trusted. It is as if she wishes to caution us against being deceived by the ideal of an all-knowing—or completely self-knowing—narrator. We are all limited creatures, she seems to be saying, and when we try to narrate the stories of our lives, we often deceive ourselves.

Carefully crafted, suspenseful, witty, and morally charged, Spark's novels and short stories are distinctive contributions to modern literature.

TEACHING RESOURCES

The following resources can be used to enrich or extend the instruction for pp. 1156–1157.

Motivation

Interest Grabber Video, Tape 6

Background

Beyond Literature, p. 57

Take It to the Net

Visit www.phschool.com for background and hotlinks for the selections.

Literary Analysis

Literary Analysis and Reading Transparencies, Point of View: Modern Experiments, p. 114

Reading

Literary Analysis and Reading Transparencies, Questioning, p. 113

Selection Support: Reading Strategy, p. 265; Build Vocabulary, p. 263

BLOCK SCHEDULING: Resources marked with this symbol provide varied instruction during 90-minute blocks.

Preview

Connecting to the Literature

As you sit in the dentist's office, you glance at a magazine cover featuring a model who looks like your friend who just got into college—and suddenly you wonder if you forgot to mail your application. The mind flows by such associations, as Woolf shows in her stream-of-consciousness narration.

❷ Literary Analysis

Point of View: Modern Experiments

Searching for forms suited to modern experience, writers experiment with **point of view,** the perspective from which a story is told.

- **Stream-of-consciousness** narration follows the flowing, branching currents of thought in a character's mind.
- **An omniscient narrator**—one with access to more information than any single character could have—may be used in surprising ways.

Woolf uses the stream-of-consciousness technique in "The Lady in the Looking Glass." Spark's omniscient narrator in "My First Year" is herself—as a baby who knows "everything." As you read, note the effect these experiments have on your experience of the events in the stories.

Comparing Literary Works

Both these works experiment with point of view, enabling the writers to explore the connection between appearance and reality in unique ways. Woolf sifts through the outward appearance of a character's life to reach its reality. By contrast, Spark's narrator takes in a hodgepodge of events to find ironic contrasts between reality and people's descriptions of it. Compare the ways in which these stories contrast appearance and reality.

❸ Reading Strategy

Questioning

Experimental works offer great rewards but also place great demands on readers. Find your way in the story by continually **asking questions** as you read. Use a chart such as the one shown.

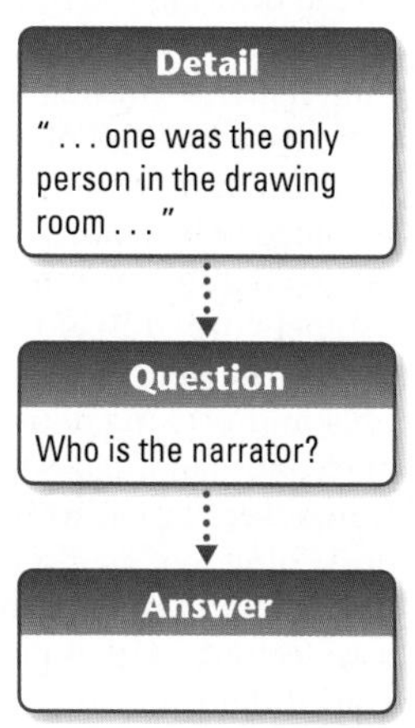

Detail
"... one was the only person in the drawing room ..."
Question
Who is the narrator?
Answer

Vocabulary Development

suffused (sə fyo͞ozd´) *v.* spread throughout; filled (p. 1158)

transient (tran´ shənt) *n.* that which passes quickly (p. 1159)

upbraidings (up brād´ iŋz) *n.* stern words of disapproval; scoldings (p. 1160)

evanescence (ev´ ə nes´ əns) *n.* vanishing or tendency to vanish (p. 1162)

reticent (ret´ ə sənt) *adj.* silent; reserved (p. 1162)

omniscient (äm nish´ ənt) *adj.* having infinite knowledge; knowing all (p. 1164)

authenticity (ô thən tis´ ə tē) *n.* reality; genuineness (p. 1165)

discerned (di surnd´) *v.* perceived clearly; recognized as separate (p. 1165)

CUSTOMIZE INSTRUCTION FOR UNIVERSAL ACCESS

For Less Proficient Readers	For English Learners	For Advanced Readers
Tell students that asking questions of a text is one of the most direct ways to interpret what they read. Ask them to name some of the interrogatives with which to begin questions *(Who, What, When, Where, How, Why)* and encourage them to keep these interrogatives in mind as they read.	Remind students that one of the most effective ways of understanding what they read is to ask questions of it. English learners may be used to asking questions of the words in their reading; tell them that they should also ask questions about what is happening in the text.	Have students read the opening paragraphs of "The Lady in the Looking Glass: A Reflection" independently. Before they begin, tell them that they should be able to ask five questions of the text as they read.

❷ Literary Analysis

Point of View: Modern Experiments

- Tell students that in this lesson, they will focus on point of view, or the perspective from which a story is told.
- Explain to students that writers like Virginia Woolf and Muriel Spark sought points of view that reflected modern experience, including stream-of-consciousness narration and omniscient narrators. Review these definitions with students.
- Use the instruction for Comparing Literary Works to review with students how Woolf and Spark play with the relationship between appearances and reality.
- Use the Point of View: Modern Experiments transparency in **Literary Analysis and Reading Transparencies,** p. 114, to demonstrate to students the difference between stream-of-consciousness and first-person omniscient narration.

❸ Reading Strategy

Questioning

- Remind students that one way to interpret experimental works of literature is to ask questions as they read.
- Read the note about questioning to the class.
- Then, use the graphic organizer on p. 1157 to practice questioning.
- Have students practice this skill using the Questioning transparency on p. 113 of **Literary Analysis and Reading Transparencies.**

Vocabulary Development

- Pronounce each vocabulary word for students, and read the definitions as a class. Have students identify any words with which they are already familiar.

E-Teach

Visit E-Teach at www.phschool.com for teachers' essays on how to teach, with questions and answers.

TEACH

Step-by-Step Teaching Guide for pp. 1158–1170

CUSTOMIZE INSTRUCTION
For Visual/Spatial Learners

Invite students to visualize, and perhaps diagram, the room, house, and garden in Woolf's story. They can also create a World War I timeline to help them track the events referred to in Spark's story.

❶ About the Selection

Isabella, a wealthy woman living alone, is in her garden. The narrator forms a concept of her by examining the objects in her home partly as they appear in a mirror and by imagining Isabella in the garden. To the narrator, Isabella's wealth and possessions are signs of happiness and success; her silence implies mystery and passion. When Isabella returns from the garden and appears in the mirror, the true loneliness and emptiness of her life are revealed. Her letters, which seemed so mysterious, turn out to be only a collection of bills.

❷ Reading Strategy

Questioning

- As they read, encourage students to ask questions of the text to help them understand what is happening. Have students record these questions and any answers they find as they read.
- Ask students the Reading Strategy question on p. 1158: What questions about the narrator does this paragraph prompt?
Answer: Students may say that they may wonder who the narrator is, why the narrator is so keenly observant, why the narrator is describing nocturnal creatures instead of the interior of the house.

❶ The Lady in the Looking Glass: A Reflection

Virginia Woolf

People should not leave looking glasses hanging in their rooms any more than they should leave open checkbooks or letters confessing some hideous crime. One could not help looking, that summer afternoon, in the long glass that hung outside in the hall. Chance had so arranged it. From the depths of the sofa in the drawing room one could see reflected in the Italian glass not only the marble-topped table opposite, but a stretch of the garden beyond. One could see a long grass path leading between banks of tall flowers until, slicing off an angle, the gold rim cut it off.

❷ The house was empty, and one felt, since one was the only person in the drawing room, like one of those naturalists who, covered with grass and leaves, lie watching the shyest animals—badgers, otters, king-fishers—moving about freely, themselves unseen. The room that afternoon was full of such shy creatures, lights and shadows, curtains blowing, petals falling—things that never happen, so it seems, if someone is looking. The quiet old country room with its rugs and stone chimney pieces, its sunken bookcases and red and gold lacquer cabinets, was full of such nocturnal creatures. They came pirouetting across the floor, stepping delicately with high-lifted feet and spread tails and pecking allusive beaks as if they had been cranes or flocks of elegant flamingoes whose pink was faded, or peacocks whose trains were veiled with silver. And there were obscure flushes and darkening too, as if a cuttlefish had suddenly suffused the air with purple; and the room had its passions and rages and envies and sorrows coming over it and clouding it, like a human being. Nothing stayed the same for two seconds together.

Reading Strategy
Questioning What questions about the narrator does this paragraph prompt?

suffused (sə fyo͞ozd′) *v.* spread throughout; filled

TEACHING RESOURCES

The following resources can be used to enrich or extend the instruction for pp. 1158–1170.

Literary Analysis

Selection Support: Literary Analysis, p. 266

Reading

Listening to Literature Audiocassettes, Sides 26 and 27

Listening to Literature Audio CDs, CD 15

BLOCK SCHEDULING: Resources marked with this symbol provide varied instruction during 90-minute blocks.

But, outside, the looking glass reflected the hall table, the sunflowers, the garden path so accurately and so fixedly that they seemed held there in their reality unescapably. It was a strange contrast—all changing here, all stillness there. One could not help looking from one to the other. Meanwhile, since all the doors and windows were open in the heat, there was a perpetual sighing and ceasing sound, 5 the voice of the transient and the perishing, it seemed, coming and going like human breath, while in the looking glass things had ceased 6 to breathe and lay still in the trance of immortality.

transient (tran′ shənt) *n.* that which passes quickly

✓**Reading Check**

Where is the narrator?

3

The Garden of Love, (detail), Walter Richard Sickert, The Fitzwilliam Museum, Cambridge

4 ▲ **Critical Viewing** This story is a stream-of-consciousness narrative, in which thoughts, dreams, and ideas blend together to reveal a story. What aspects of this painting mirror this style of writing? **[Interpret]**

3 Background

Art

The Garden of Love, by Walter Sickert

Walter Richard Sickert (1860–1942) was born in Munich, Germany, but became a British subject. Sickert's greatest contribution to British art was his willingness to experiment with, teach, and defend new ideas in art. Use the following question for discussion:

- How does the garden in the painting compare with the garden in the story?
  Answer: In the story, the garden—described as "the lower garden," —is more dense with flowers and plants than the garden in the painting; the garden in the story has a path, but no path appears in the painting.

4 ▶Critical Viewing

Possible response: Students may say that the painting has the same playful, scattered quality as a stream-of-consciousness narrative, referring to the interplay of light and shadow and the contrast between hard edges and curves. They may say that their eyes are drawn all over the canvas, even off its edge, since only some of the objects shown appear in full view.

5 Vocabulary Development

Latin Prefix: *trans-*

- Call students' attention to *transient.* Explain to students that the prefix *trans-* is derived from Latin and means "through" or "across."
- Have students suggest other words and phrases that contain this prefix, and list them on the chalkboard.
  Possible responses: *transubstantiate; transistor; transatlantic; transitory*

6 ✓Reading Check

Answer: The narrator is located in "the depths of the sofa in the drawing room."

CUSTOMIZE INSTRUCTION FOR UNIVERSAL ACCESS

For Special Needs Students	For Less Proficient Readers	For Gifted/Talented Students
Have students read from "The Lady in the Looking Glass: A Reflection" with teacher guidance. Tell students to visualize each word they read or to slow down until they have a clear image of what is being described.	Students may have difficulty reading from "The Lady in the Looking Glass: A Reflection" because the narrator's complex series of ideas and images follow her stream of consciousness and lack a clear narrative for them to follow. Review with students what stream of consciousness is, and then have students read the selection.	Have students examine with a partner the painting *The Garden of Love,* p. 1159, that accompanies "The Lady in the Looking Glass: A Reflection." Ask them to take turns detailing aloud what they see in the painting. Tell them to try to keep a continual train of thought, or stream of consciousness, including whatever associations occur to them.

7 ▸Critical Viewing

Answer: Students' responses will vary. Make sure they support their answers with details from the text and the image.

Half an hour ago the mistress of the house, Isabella Tyson, had gone down the grass path in her thin summer dress, carrying a basket, and had vanished, sliced off by the gilt rim of the looking glass. She had gone presumably into the lower garden to pick flowers; or as it seemed more natural to suppose, to pick something light and fantastic and leafy and trailing, traveler's-joy, or one of those elegant sprays of convolvulus that twine round ugly walls and burst here and there into white and violet blossoms. She suggested the fantastic and the tremulous convolvulus rather than the upright aster, the starched zinnia, or her own burning roses alight like lamps on the straight posts of their rose trees. The comparison showed how very little, after all these years, one knew about her; for it is impossible that any woman of flesh and blood of fifty-five or sixty should be really a wreath or a tendril. Such comparisons are worse than idle and superficial—they are cruel even, for they come like the convolvulus itself trembling between one's eyes and the truth. There must be truth; there must be a wall. Yet it was strange that after knowing her all these years one could not say what the truth about Isabella was; one still made up phrases like this about convolvulus and traveler's-joy. As for facts, it was a fact that she was a spinster; that she was rich; that she had bought this house and collected with her own hands—often in the most obscure corners of the world and at great risk from poisonous stings and Oriental diseases—the rugs, the chairs, the cabinets which now lived their nocturnal life before one's eyes. Sometimes it seemed as if they knew more about her than we, who sat on them, wrote at them, and trod on them so carefully, were allowed to know. In each of these cabinets were many little drawers, and each almost certainly held letters, tied with bows of ribbon, sprinkled with sticks of lavender or rose leaves. For it was another fact—if facts were what one wanted—that Isabella had known many people, had had many friends; and thus if one had the audacity to open a drawer and read her letters, one would find the traces of many agitations, of appointments to meet, of upbraidings for not having met, long letters of intimacy and affection, violent letters of jealousy and reproach, terrible final words of parting—for all those interviews and assignations had led to nothing—that is, she had never married, and yet, judging from the masklike indifference of her face, she had gone through twenty times more of passion and experience than those whose loves are trumpeted forth for all the world to hear. Under the stress of thinking about Isabella, her room became more shadowy and symbolic; the corners seemed darker, the legs of chairs and tables more spindly and hieroglyphic.

7 ▾Critical Viewing In what way does this image, like the story, suggest that mirrors show the truth? **[Connect]**

upbraidings (up brād′ iŋz) *n.* stern words of disapproval; scoldings

ENRICHMENT: Art Connection

Mirrors

For centuries mirrors were rare and expensive. The first mirrors were made of polished metal; in the Middle Ages the idea of using glass with a metal backing was introduced. Venice, known for the art of glass blowing during the fifteenth century, was also a center for making mirrors.

The use of mirrors in the main rooms at the Palace of Versailles in France is one reason that observers consider it so magnificent. Built for Louis XIV in the seventeenth century, Versailles has a famous Hall of Mirrors named for the huge mirrors that face each window.

Suddenly these reflections were ended violently and yet without a sound. A large black form loomed into the looking glass; blotted out everything, strewed the table with a packet of marble tablets veined with pink and gray, and was gone. But the picture was entirely altered. For the moment it was unrecognizable and irrational and entirely out of focus. One could not relate these tablets to any human purpose. And then by degrees some logical process set to work on
8 them and began ordering and arranging them and bringing them into the fold of common experience. One realized at last that they were merely letters. The man had brought the post.

There they lay on the marble-topped table, all dripping with light and color at first and crude and unabsorbed. And then it was strange to see how they were drawn in and arranged and composed and made part of the picture and granted that stillness and immortality which the looking glass conferred. They lay there invested with a new reality and significance and with a greater heaviness, too, as if it would have needed a chisel to dislodge them from the table. And, whether it was fancy or not, they seemed to have become not merely a handful of casual letters but to be tablets graven with eternal truth—if one could read them, one would know everything there was to be known about Isabella, yes, and about life, too. The pages inside those marble-looking envelopes must be cut deep and scored thick with meaning. Isabella would come in, and take them, one by one, very slowly, and open them, and read them carefully word by word, and then with a profound sigh of comprehension, as if she had seen to the bottom of everything, she would tear the envelopes to little bits and tie the letters together and lock the cabinet drawer in her determination to conceal what she did not wish to be known.

The thought served as a challenge. Isabella did not wish to be known—but she should no longer escape. It was absurd, it was monstrous. If she concealed so much and knew so much one must prize her open with the first tool that came to hand—the imagination. One must fix one's mind upon her at that very moment. One must fasten her down there. One must refuse to be put off any longer with sayings and doings such as the moment brought forth—with dinners and visits and polite conversations. One must put oneself in her
9 shoes. If one took the phrase literally, it was easy to see the shoes in which she stood, down in the lower garden, at this moment. They were very narrow and long and fashionable —they were made of the softest and most flexible leather. Like everything she wore, they were exquisite. And she would be standing under the high hedge in the lower part of the garden, raising the scissors that were tied to her waist to cut some dead flower, some overgrown branch. The sun would beat down on her face, into her eyes; but no, at the critical moment a veil of cloud covered the sun, making the expression of her eyes doubtful—was it mocking or tender, brilliant or dull? One could only see the indeterminate outline of her rather faded, fine face looking at the sky. She was thinking, perhaps, that she must order a new

Literary Analysis
Point of View What effect does the narrator's attention to the workings of his or her own mind have on the narration?

Literary Analysis
Point of View In what way does this paragraph illustrate the use of stream-of-consciousness narration?

10 
Reading Check
What interrupts the narrator's reflection?

8 Literary Analysis
Point of View
- Review with students how the narrator's description of this scene affects the reader's understanding of the story.
- Then, ask the first Literary Analysis question on p. 1161: What effect does the narrator's attention to the workings of his or her own mind have on the narration?
  Answer: The narrator's stream-of-consciousness description gives the narration a "you-are-there" immediacy.

9 Literary Analysis
Point of View
- Review with students their understanding of stream-of-consciousness narration.
- Then, ask the second Literary Analysis question on p. 1161: In what way does this paragraph illustrate the use of stream-of-consciousness narration?
  Answer: Guide students to notice the stream-of-consciousness style of narration here: from speaking figuratively about putting oneself in Isabella's shoes to imagining seeing those shoes and Isabella in them.

10 Reading Check
Answer: The arrival of the postman interrupts the narrator's reflections.

CUSTOMIZE INSTRUCTION FOR UNIVERSAL ACCESS

For Less Proficient Readers	For English Learners
Encourage students to summarize what they have learned of Isabella Tyson so far in "The Lady in the Looking Glass: A Reflection." Have them write a sketch of her character, describing her appearance, personality, and motivations.	Remind students that Virginia Woolf, the author of "The Lady in the Looking Glass: A Reflection," wrote during a period in literary history that was full of experimentation. Her use of stream-of-consciousness narration—or narrating whatever thoughts occur in the mind of the speaker—was considered extremely modern at the time.

11 ▶**Critical Viewing**

Answer: An unopened letter suggests communication with the outside world, but—by virtue of its being unopened—it also suggests a kind of privacy, or separateness from others.

net for the strawberries; that she must send flowers to Johnson's widow; that it was time she drove over to see the Hippesleys in their new house. Those were the things she talked about at dinner certainly. But one was tired of the things that she talked about at dinner. It was her profounder state of being that one wanted to catch and turn to words, the state that is to the mind what breathing is to the body, what one calls happiness or unhappiness. At the mention of those words it became obvious, surely, that she must be happy. She was rich; she was distinguished; she had many friends; she traveled—she bought rugs in Turkey and blue pots in Persia. Avenues of pleasure radiated this way and that from where she stood with her scissors raised to cut the trembling branches while the lacy clouds veiled her face.

Here with a quick movement of her scissors she snipped the spray of traveler's-joy and it fell to the ground. As it fell, surely some light came in too, surely one could penetrate a little farther into her being. Her mind then was filled with tenderness and regret. . . . To cut an overgrown branch saddened her because it had once lived, and life was dear to her. Yes, and at the same time the fall of the branch would suggest to her how she must die herself and all the futility and evanescence of things. And then again quickly catching this thought up, with her instant good sense, she thought life had treated her well; even if fall she must, it was to lie on the earth and molder sweetly into the roots of violets. So she stood thinking. Without making any thought precise—for she was one of those reticent people whose minds hold their thoughts enmeshed in clouds of silence—she was filled with thoughts. Her mind was like her room, in which lights advanced and retreated, came pirouetting and stepping delicately, spread their tails, pecked their way; and then her whole being was suffused, like the room again, with a cloud of some profound knowledge, some unspoken regret, and then she was full of locked drawers, stuffed with letters, like her cabinets. To talk of "prizing her open" as if she were an oyster, to use any but the finest and subtlest and most pliable tools upon her was impious and absurd. One must imagine—here was she in the looking glass. It made one start.

She was so far off at first that one could not see her clearly. She came lingering and pausing, here straightening a rose, there lifting a pink to smell it, but she never stopped; and all the time she became larger and larger in the looking glass, more and more completely the person into whose mind one had been trying to penetrate. One verified her by degrees—fitted the qualities one had discovered into this visible body. There were her gray-green dress, and her long shoes, her basket, and something sparkling at her throat. She came so

11 ▲**Critical Viewing** Make an analogy comparing an unopened letter like this one with Isabella as seen by the narrator. **[Connect]**

evanescence (ev′ ə nes′ əns) *n.* vanishing or tendency to vanish

reticent (ret′ ə sənt) *adj.* silent; reserved

gradually that she did not seem to derange the pattern in the glass, but only to bring in some new element which gently moved and altered the other objects as if asking them, courteously, to make room for her. And the letters and the table and the grass walk and the sunflowers which had been waiting in the looking glass separated and opened out so that she might be received among them. At last there she was, in the hall. She stopped dead. She stood by the table. She stood perfectly still. At once the looking glass began to pour over her a light that seemed to fix her; that seemed like some acid to bite off the unessential and superficial and to leave only the truth. It was an enthralling spectacle. Everything dropped from her—clouds, dress, basket, diamond—all that one had called the creeper and convolvulus. Here was the hard wall beneath. Here was the woman herself. She stood naked in that pitiless light. And there was nothing. Isabella was perfectly empty. She had no thoughts. She had no friends. She cared for nobody. As for her letters, they were all bills. Look, as she stood there, old and angular, veined and lined, with her high nose and her wrinkled neck, she did not even trouble to open them.

People should not leave looking glasses hanging in their rooms.

Review and Assess

Thinking About the Selection

1. **Respond:** How did you feel toward Isabella Tyson by the end of the story?
2. **(a) Recall:** Where are the narrator and Isabella, respectively, at the opening of the story? **(b) Infer:** From what perspective does the narrator observe Isabella? **(c) Speculate:** Who might the narrator be? Explain.
3. **(a) Recall:** Briefly describe the layout and furnishings of the room in the story. **(b) Summarize:** How does the looking glass "guide" the narrator to an understanding of Isabella? **(c) Interpret:** What does the last sentence of the story, repeated from the beginning, mean?
4. **(a) Draw Conclusions:** In the story, what is the relation between imagination and "the hard wall" of the truth? **(b) Make a Judgment:** Is Isabella really "perfectly empty," or has the narrator's imagination run dry? Explain.
5. **Criticize:** Does Woolf succeed in creating a vivid portrait of Isabella? Why or why not?
6. **(a) Apply:** Do you think that you can ever "fasten someone down" and know his or her true nature with certainty? Explain. **(b) Take a Position:** Is the fact that a person is easy to get to know a mark his or her integrity? Explain.

CUSTOMIZE INSTRUCTION FOR UNIVERSAL ACCESS

For Special Needs Students	For English Learners
Students may have difficulty following the story about Isabella Tyson, since it is told almost totally without her direct involvement. Review with students how the narrator describes Isabella's life and personality through what she observes in her home.	English learners may find some of the complex vocabulary in Woolf's story an obstacle to their comprehension. Encourage them to sound out any words that are difficult, and to try to grasp their meaning from context if they are unable to use the margin definitions and footnotes.

Answers for p. 1163

Review and Assess

1. Possible responses: Students may say they felt sorry for Isabella Tyson by the end of the story.
2. **(a)** Isabella is in the garden gathering flowers, and the narrator is in the drawing room. **(b)** The narrator observes Isabella from the drawing room, gazing at her reflection in the mirror. **(c)** Possible responses: Students may say that the narrator is someone well acquainted with the superficial aspects of Isabella's life, perhaps a longtime but not very close friend.
3. **(a)** The room is richly furnished and filled with Isabella's impressive possessions. **(b)** At first, the looking glass provides a view of Isabella through her possessions. When Isabella herself appears in the looking glass, the narrator sees the true emptiness of her life. **(c)** It means that the reflections in the mirror and the mental reflections they lead to can be dangerously revealing.
4. **(a)** The hard wall of reality is in conflict with the imagination's version of reality. **(b)** Possible responses: The narrator's description of Isabella as "perfectly empty" could be as accurate as her previous speculations.
5. Possible responses: Students may say that Woolf presents a vivid portrait of who Isabella appears to be. They may say that her description of who she really is is limited.
6. Possible responses: **(a)** Most students will probably recognize that it is impossible to know anyone's true nature with complete certainty. Others may feel that it is possible in very close relationships, such as those of parent and child, or siblings. **(b)** Encourage students to support their position with specific examples from their experiences.

⓬ About the Selection

Using the improbable and comical idea of an omniscient infant, Spark presents her amusing, yet perceptive and poignant, views on the state of the world as it was in 1918, the year of her birth. Like a fly on the wall, the narrator witnesses key events and eavesdrops on the conversations of politicians and writers. The effect is a devastating attack on the insanities of World War I and the leaders who supported the war.

⓬ The First Year of My Life

Muriel Spark

Background

The title of Spark's story refers to 1918, the final year of World War I. For over three years, Britain—allied with France, Italy, Russia, and the United States—had fought against Germany, Austria-Hungary, and Turkey. Spark's narrator "observes" a number of wartime events and leaders.

I was born on the first day of the second month of the last year of the First World War, a Friday. Testimony abounds that during the first year of my life I never smiled. I was known as the baby whom nothing and no one could make smile. Everyone who knew me then has told me so. They tried very hard, singing and bouncing me up and down, jumping around, pulling faces. Many times I was told this later by my family and their friends; but, anyway, I knew it at the time.

You will shortly be hearing of that new school of psychology, or maybe you have heard of it already, which after long and far-adventuring research and experiment has established that all of the young of the human species are born omniscient. Babies, in their waking hours, know everything that is going on everywhere in the world; they can tune in to any conversation they choose, switch on to any scene. We have all experienced this power. It is only after the first year that it was brainwashed out of us; for it is demanded of us by our immediate environment that we grow to be of use to it in a practical way. Gradually, our know-all brain-cells are blacked out, although traces remain in some individuals in the form of E.S.P., and in the adults of some primitive tribes.

omniscient (äm nish´ ənt) *adj.* having infinite knowledge; knowing all

It is not a new theory. Poets and philosophers, as usual, have been there first. But scientific proof is now ready and to hand. Perhaps the final touches are being put to the new manifesto[1] in some cell at Harvard University. Any day now it will be given to the world, and the world will be convinced.

1. **manifesto** (man´ ə fes´ tō) *n.* public declaration of motives and intentions.

ENRICHMENT: Social Studies Connection

World War I

In 1914, a Serbian Nationalist assassinated Archduke Francis Ferdinand of Austria-Hungary, which ruled a restless Serbia struggling for independence. Following the assassination, Austria sent Serbia an ultimatum. Serbia's refusal to comply led Austria, backed by Germany, to declare war. Although at first it seemed this would be a short-lived European war, it was actually the start of World War I. Serbia sought the aid of Russia; Germany declared war on Russia and France, which wanted to avenge its defeat in the Franco-Prussian War. When Germany violated a treaty by invading Belgium, Britain joined the conflict as well. German submarine attacks on merchant and passenger ships traveling in the Atlantic led the United States to enter the war in 1917. The human cost of this war was staggering. Approximately 10 million people died. Double that number had been wounded, many handicapped for life. (Note that Spark's figures vary somewhat.)

Let me therefore get my word in first, because I feel pretty sure, now, about the authenticity of my remembrance of things past. My autobiography, as I very well perceived at the time, started in the very worst year that the world had ever seen so far. Apart from being born bedridden and toothless, unable to raise myself on the pillow or utter anything but farmyard squawks or police-siren wails, my bladder and my bowels totally out of control, I was further depressed by the curious behavior of the two-legged mammals around me. There were those
13 black-dressed people, females of the species to which I appeared to belong, saying they had lost their sons. I slept a great deal. Let them go and find their sons. It was like the special pin for my nappies[2] which my mother or some other hoverer dedicated to my care was always losing. These careless women in black lost their husbands and their brothers. Then they came to visit my mother and clucked and crowed over my cradle. I was not amused.

"Babies never really smile till they're three months old," said my mother. "They're not *supposed* to smile till they're three months old."

My brother, aged six, marched up and down with a toy rifle over his shoulder:

> The grand old Duke of York
> He had ten thousand men;
> He marched them up to the top of the hill
> And he marched them down again.
>
> 14 And when they were up, they were up.
> And when they were down, they were down.
> And when they were neither down nor up
> They were neither up nor down.

"Just listen to him!"

"Look at him with his rifle!"

I was about ten days old when Russia stopped fighting. I tuned in to the Czar,[3] a prisoner, with the rest of his family, since evidently the country had put him off his throne and there had been a revolution not long before I was born. Everyone was talking about it. I tuned in to the Czar. "Nothing would ever induce me to sign the treaty of Brest-Litovsk,"[4] he said to his wife. Anyway, nobody had asked him to.

At this point I was sleeping twenty hours a day to get my strength up. And from what I discerned in the other four hours of the day I knew I was going to need it. The Western Front on my frequency was sheer blood, mud, dismembered bodies, blistered crashes, hectic flashes of light in the night skies, explosions, total terror. Since it was

---

authenticity (ô′ thən tis′ ə tē) *n.* reality; genuineness

Literary Analysis
Point of View Does the narrator understand everything that she "knows"? Explain.

Reading Strategy
Questioning What question might you ask about the author's purpose in including this scene with the narrator's brother? Explain.

discerned (di zʉrnd′) *v.* perceived clearly; recognized as separate

15 **Reading Check**
What does the narrator claim to have known during the first year of her life?

---

2. **nappies** (nap′ ēz) *n.* British term for diapers.
3. **Czar** Czar Nicholas II of Russia, who was removed from power during the Russian Revolution of 1917.
4. **treaty of Brest-Litovsk** treaty in which Russia's new Communist government made peace with Germany and withdrew from the war eight months before its end.

13 Literary Analysis

Point of View

- Review with students the definition of an omniscient narrator. Ask students to describe the level of narrative information provided by such a narrator.
- Then, ask students the Literary Analysis question on p. 1165: Does the narrator understand everything that she "knows"? Explain.
  Answer: Students should recognize that the baby-speaker is omniscient, but she doesn't truly understand everything. By comparing the loss of sons and husbands to the loss of a diaper pin, she reveals the limits of her understanding.

14 Reading Strategy

Questioning

- Read aloud the passage to students. Encourage them to ask questions of the text as you read.
- Ask them the Reading Strategy question on p. 1165: What question might you ask about the author's purpose in including this scene with the narrator's brother? Explain.
  Answer: Students might ask, Why are the adults seemingly pleased with the brother's soldierlike behavior?

15 Reading Check

Answer: The narrator claims to have known everything that was going on in the world—to have been omniscient.

CUSTOMIZE INSTRUCTION FOR UNIVERSAL ACCESS

For Special Needs Students	For Gifted/Talented Students	For Advanced Readers
Students may have difficulty reading "The First Year of My Life" because the narrator elaborates on historical facts that may bog them down. Encourage students to read the selection slowly, pausing to consider the footnotes that explain some of the narrator's references.	Have students read "The First Year of My Life" independently, making a list of questions about the narrator or the period she develops in her account as they go. When students have finished reading the selection, have them refer to their list of questions and write answers to the questions based on what they have learned.	Have students read "The First Year of My Life" by Muriel Spark independently. Then, ask students to address how the story creates a narrator who is a vivid character, even though the narrative is unconventional. Tell students to describe the narrator in a few paragraphs and analyze how Spark shapes the narrator's character.

16 ▶Critical Viewing

Answer: Students may suggest that the soldiers look both weary and numb. You may wish to point out that this photograph is from 1914, when the full horrors of the war were as yet unknown to many; the soldiers' exhaustion may have resulted from a long march rather than from combat.

17 Literary Analysis

Point of View

- Ask students to describe how they can tell that the narration is omniscient in this passage.
- Then, ask them the Literary Analysis question on p. 1166: How does this paragraph demonstrate Spark's unusual form of omniscient narration?
  Answer: The narrator's ability to know what was going on in Austria and Germany while she was being rocked in her cradle shows that Spark's narrator has the limited experience and understanding of a baby and yet can "eavesdrop" on history.

plain I had been born into a bad moment in the history of the world, the future bothered me, unable as I was to raise my head from the pillow and as yet only twenty inches long. "I truly wish I were a fox or a bird," D. H. Lawrence[5] was writing to somebody . . . I fell asleep.

Red sheets of flame shot across the sky. It was 21 March, the fiftieth day of my life, and the German Spring Offensive[6] had started before my morning feed. Infinite slaughter. I scowled at the scene, and made an effort to kick out. But the attempt was feeble. Furious, and impatient for some strength, I wailed for my feed. After which I stopped wailing but continued to scowl.

The grand old Duke of York
He had ten thousand men . . .

17 They rocked the cradle. I never heard a sillier song. Over in Berlin and Vienna the people were starving, freezing, striking, rioting and yelling in the streets. In London everyone was bustling to work and muttering that it was time the whole . . . business was over.

The big people around me bared their teeth; that meant a smile, it meant they were pleased or amused. They spoke of ration cards[7] for meat and sugar and butter.

16 ▲ **Critical Viewing** This story takes place in 1918, the last year of World War I. Judging by this photograph from the time, would you say the soldiers pictured were excited, weary, or numb? **[Infer]**

Literary Analysis
Point of View How does this paragraph demonstrate Spark's unusual form of omniscient narration?

5. **D. H. Lawrence** (1885–1930) English novelist and poet.
6. **German Spring Offensive** After signing the peace treaty with Russia in March of 1918, Germany began to push to win the war along the western front.
7. **ration cards** used to limit individuals' purchases of goods that were in short supply during the war.

 **ENRICHMENT: Science Connection**

Child Development

In the story, Spark uses an all-knowing yet self-absorbed infant to create clever social and political commentary. The infant's imagined mental activity is set against a backdrop of realistic developmental stages. While development does vary from individual to individual, psychologists have identified sequential stages of development and an appropriate age range at which they should occur.

"Where will it all end?"

I went to sleep. I woke and tuned into Bernard Shaw[8] who was telling someone to shut up. I switched over to Joseph Conrad[9] who,
18 strangely enough, was saying precisely the same thing. I still didn't think it worth a smile, although it was expected of me any day now. I got on to Turkey. Women draped in black huddled and chattered in their harems; yak-yak-yak. This was boring, so I came back to home base.

In and out came and went the women in British black. My mother's brother, dressed in his uniform, came coughing. He had been poison-gassed in the trenches. *"Tout le monde à la bataille!"*[10] declaimed Marshal Foch[11] the old swine. He was now Commander-in-Chief of the Allied Forces. My uncle coughed from deep within his lungs, never to recover but destined to return to the Front. His brass buttons gleamed in the firelight. I weighed twelve pounds by now; I stretched and kicked for exercise, seeing that I had a lifetime before me, coping with this crowd. I took six feeds a day and kept most of them down by the time the *Vindictive* was sunk in Ostend harbor,[12] on which day I kicked with special vigor in my bath.

In France the conscripted[13] soldiers leapfrogged over the dead on the advance and littered the fields with limbs and hands, or drowned in the mud. The strongest men on all fronts were dead before I was born. Now the sentries[14] used bodies for barricades and the fighting men were unhealthy from the start. I checked my toes and fingers, knowing I was going to need them. *The Playboy of the Western World* was playing at the Court Theatre in London, but occasionally I beamed over to the House of Commons[15] which made me drop off gently to sleep. Generally, I preferred the Western Front[16] where one got the true state of affairs. It was essential to know the worst, blood and explosions and all, for one had to be prepared, as the boy scouts said. Virginia Woolf[17] yawned and reached for her diary. Really, I preferred the Western Front.

In the fifth month of my life I could raise my head from my pillow and hold it up. I could grasp the objects that were held out to me. Some of these things rattled and squawked. I gnawed on them to get my teeth started. "She hasn't smiled yet?" said the dreary old aunties.

---

8. **Bernard Shaw** George Bernard Shaw (1856–1950), British dramatist and critic.
9. **Joseph Conrad** (1857–1924) English novelist, born in Poland.
10. ***Tout le monde à la bataille*** (tōō lə mônd′ ä lä bä tī′) The whole world into the battle!
11. **Marshal Foch** (fôsh) Ferdinand Foch, a French general who, after March 1918, became commander of all Allied forces on the Western Front.
12. ***Vindictive* was sunk in Ostend harbor** referring to a ship sunk in May 1918 by Allied forces to block the harbor of Ostend, Belgium, used by the Germans as a submarine base.
13. **conscripted** (kən skript′ əd) *adj.* enrolled for compulsory service in the armed service.
14. **sentries** (sen′ trēs) *n.* men of the military guard.
15. **House of Commons** lower house of British Parliament.
16. **Western Front** 450-mile-long battlefront starting in Belgium and moving across France. This line is where the allies and Germany engaged in trench warfare from 1914 to 1918.
17. **Virginia Woolf** (1882–1941) English novelist and critic.

Reading Strategy
Questioning What questions do the references to Conrad and Shaw suggest to you?

19  **Reading Check**

Identify two different kinds of scenes of which the narrator is aware.

18 Reading Strategy

Questioning

- Read aloud the bracketed passage to students. Ask volunteers to identify who Shaw and Conrad are.
  Answer: George Bernard Shaw (1856–1950) was a Nobel-Prize-winning playwright. Joseph Conrad (1857–1924) was a Polish-born novelist. His short story "The Lagoon" appears on p. 1134.
- Then, ask them the Reading Strategy question on p. 1167: What questions do the references to Conrad and Shaw suggest to you?
  Possible responses: These references suggest that the narrator can "tune in" to literature as well as current events. They also confirm the story's irreverent take on history (telling someone to shut up is not the most dignified action for a famous writer). They might also suggest that not even these great writers had something significant and true to say about the war or in the face of war's horrors.

19 Reading Check

Answer: The narrator is aware of scenes involving her immediate surroundings. She is also aware of scenes and persons of historic importance from around the world.

CUSTOMIZE INSTRUCTION FOR UNIVERSAL ACCESS

For Less Proficient Readers	For English Learners
Review with students how asking questions of a text can enable them to understand it more completely. Then, guide students as they continue reading "The First Year of My Life" to ask questions about the events and the famous people Spark describes and to look to context clues, footnotes, and margin notes for possible answers.	Tell students that one way to understand Muriel Spark's narrator's account of the war is to keep a list of all the dates and events she mentions in "The First Year of My Life." English learners may find it easy to identify dates and events because they are concrete and do not require additional interpretation. Encourage students to create a timeline of the world events in 1918 using the story as their guide. Tell students to begin their timelines on February 1, 1918, and to end on November 11, 1918, the day of the armistice.

20 Reading Strategy

Questioning

- Have students identify what they think the writer's purpose is in this passage.
- Then, ask them the Reading Strategy question on p. 1168: What questions might this paragraph lead you to ask about the writer's purpose?
  Possible responses: Students may ask "Why does the writer feel it is effective for the narrator to include details from politics of the era?"

21 ▶Critical Viewing

Answer: Students may say that the baby in the photograph seems focused on her birthday cake, not on world events.

My mother, on the defensive, said I was probably one of those late smilers. On my wavelength Pablo Picasso[18] was getting married and early in that month of July the Silver Wedding of King George V and Queen Mary was celebrated in joyous pomp at St. Paul's Cathedral. They drove through the streets of London with their children. Twenty-five years of domestic happiness. A lot of fuss and ceremonial handing over of swords went on at the Guildhall where the King and Queen received a check for $53,000 to dispose of for charity as they thought fit. *Tout le monde à la bataille!* Income tax in England had reached six shillings in the pound. Everyone was talking about the Silver Wedding; yak-yak-yak, and ten days later the Czar and his family, now in Siberia, were invited to descend to a little room in the basement. Crack, crack, went the guns; screams and blood all over the place, and that was the end of the Romanoffs.[19] I flexed my muscles. "A fine healthy baby," said the doctor; which gave me much satisfaction.

Reading Strategy
Questioning What questions might this paragraph lead you to ask about the writer's purpose?

20 *Tout le monde à la bataille!* That included my gassed uncle. My health had improved to the point where I was able to crawl in my playpen. Bertrand Russell[20] was still cheerily in prison for writing something seditious about pacifism. Tuning in as usual to the Front Lines it looked as if the Germans were winning all the battles yet losing the war. 21 And so it was. The upper-income people were upset about the income tax at six shillings to the pound. But all women over thirty got the vote. "It seems a long time to wait," said one of my drab old aunts, aged twenty-two. The speeches in the House of Commons always sent me to sleep which was why I missed, at the actual time, a certain oration by Mr. Asquith[21] following the armistice on 11 November.[22] Mr. Asquith was a greatly esteemed former prime minister later to be an Earl, and had been ousted by Mr. Lloyd George.[23] I clearly heard Asquith, in private, refer to Lloyd George as "that . . . Welsh goat."

▼ Critical Viewing
What does the one-year-old in this photograph seem to be thinking? Contrast her probable thoughts with those of the narrator.
[Compare and Contrast]

18. **Pablo** (pä´ blō) **Picasso** (pi kä´ sō) (1881–1973) Spanish painter and sculptor.
19. **Romanoffs** (rō mə nôfs´) ruling family of Russia from 1613 to 1917.
20. **Bertrand Russell** (1872–1970) British philosopher, mathematician, and writer.
21. **Mr. Asquith** (as´ kw*ith*) Herbert Henry Asquith (1852–1928), Prime Minister of Britain from 1908–1916.
22. **armistice on 11 November** the agreement that brought World War I to an end.
23. **Mr. Lloyd George** David Lloyd George (1863–1945), British Prime Minister from 1916 to 1922.

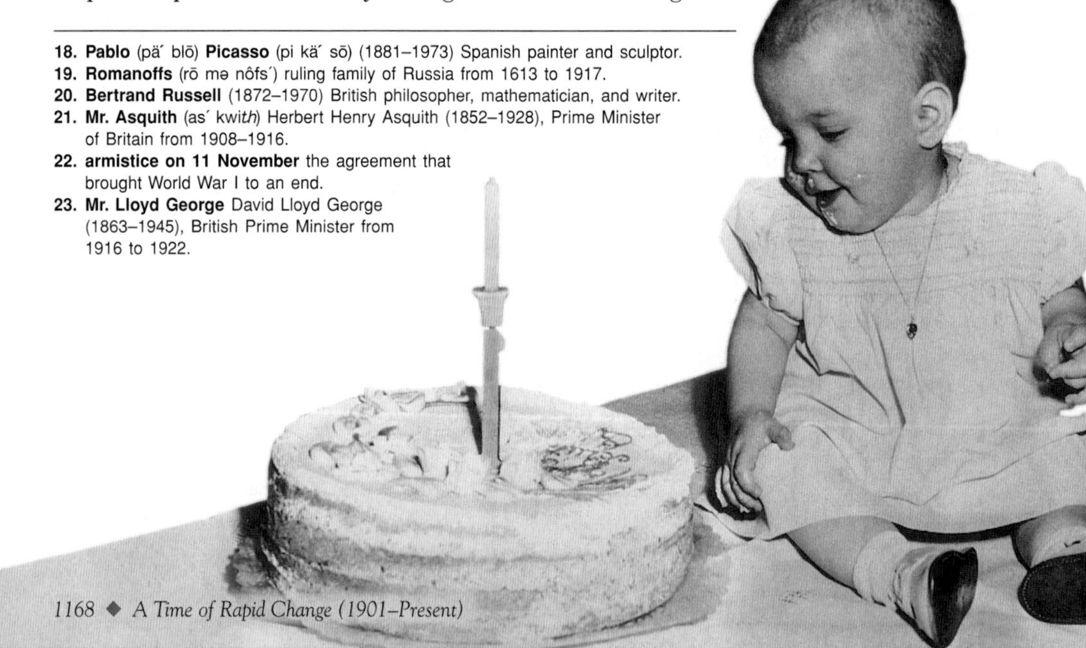

ENRICHMENT: Media Connection

War in the Movies

Novelists, poets, and painters were not the only artists who attempted to make some sense of the catastrophe of World War I. Without a single battle scene, Jean Renoir's masterpiece, *Grand Illusion,* powerfully captures the futility and demoralizing features of conflict. Other powerful films about the war include *All Quiet on the Western Front* (1930, directed by Lewis Milestone) and *Gallipoli* (1981, directed by Peter Weir). *Gallipoli,* which stars a young Mel Gibson, offers a striking feel for period detail in its depiction of one of the war's most devastating battles.

What other movies have students seen that depict war? How is war portrayed? Students may suggest films such as *Pearl Harbor, Saving Private Ryan, The Deer Hunter, Full Metal Jacket,* or *Glory.* Most of these films portray the horrors of war, but students may also suggest films that portray the glory of war or the loyalties and friendships formed during the war.

22 The armistice was signed and I was awake for that. I pulled myself on to my feet with the aid of the bars of my cot. My teeth were coming through very nicely in my opinion, and well worth all the trouble I was put to in bringing them forth. I weighed twenty pounds. On all the world's fighting fronts the men killed in action or dead of wounds numbered 8,538,315 and the warriors wounded and maimed were 21,219,452. With these figures in mind I sat up in my high chair and banged my spoon on the table. One of my mother's black-draped friends recited:

> I have a rendezvous with Death
> At some disputed barricade,
> When spring comes back with rustling shade
> And apple blossoms fill the air—
> I have a rendezvous with Death.[24]

Most of the poets, they said, had been killed. The poetry made them dab their eyes with clean white handkerchiefs.

Next February on my first birthday, there was a birthday-cake with one candle. Lots of children and their elders. The war had been over two months and twenty-one days. "Why doesn't she smile?" My brother was to blow out the candle. The elders were talking about the war and the political situation. Lloyd George and Asquith, Asquith and Lloyd George. I remembered recently having switched on to Mr. Asquith at a private party where he had been drinking a lot. He was playing cards and when he came to cut the cards he tried to cut a large box of matches by mistake. On another occasion I had seen him putting his arm around a lady's shoulder in a Daimler motor car, and generally behaving towards her in a very friendly fashion. Strangely enough she said, "If you don't stop this nonsense immediately, I'll order the chauffeur to stop and I'll get out." Mr. Asquith replied, "And pray, what reason will you give?" Well anyway it was my feeding time.

23 The guests arrived for my birthday. It was so sad, said one of the black widows, so sad about Wilfred Owen[25] who was killed so late in the war, and she quoted from a poem of his:

> What passing-bells for these who die as cattle?
> Only the monstrous anger of the guns.[26]

The children were squealing and toddling around. One was sick and another wet the floor and stood with his legs apart gaping at the puddle. All was mopped up. I banged my spoon on the table of my high chair.

> But I've a rendezvous with Death
> At midnight in some flaming town;

24. **I . . . Death** from the poem "I Have a Rendezvous with Death" by American poet Alan Seeger, killed in war.
25. **Wilfred Owen** (1893–1918) English poet.
26. **What . . . guns** from Wilfred Owen's "Anthem for Doomed Youth" (see p. 1053 for the complete poem).

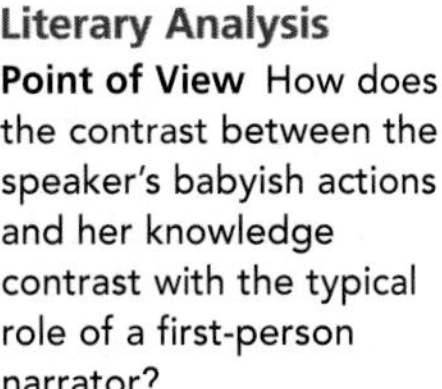

Literary Analysis
Point of View How does the contrast between the speaker's babyish actions and her knowledge contrast with the typical role of a first-person narrator?

Literary Analysis
Point of View In what way does Spark's use of point of view suggest that she has cut and pasted her story together from different points of view?

24  **Reading Check**
What occurs in the narrator's life after the armistice?

CUSTOMIZE INSTRUCTION FOR UNIVERSAL ACCESS

For Less Proficient Readers	For Gifted/Talented Students
Remind students that Muriel Spark's story is set during World War I. Ask students to relate any information they have learned about World War I based on their reading so far. If students seem interested in learning more about this terrible international conflict, you may want to show them "'The First Year of My Life': World War I" on **Interest Grabber Video,** Tape 6.	Have students write brief stories in which they tell what they remember from the first year of their lives, borrowing from Muriel Spark's inventive form of telling these events. Students may want to do research to find out what major events occurred during the year of their births. Encourage them to use the Internet, encyclopedias, or almanacs to determine what occurred in the first year of their lives. Have students read their stories aloud for their classmates.

22 Literary Analysis

Point of View

- Read aloud the bracketed passage to students. Have students identify three different points of view suggested by the information in the passage.
  Possible response: The baby's firsthand experience is suggested by her report of teething; an adult's perspective on the baby is suggested by the detail about her weight; the point of view of a historian writing after the fact is suggested by the casualty figures.
- Then, ask students the Literary Analysis question on p. 1169: How does the contrast between the speaker's babyish actions and her knowledge contrast with the typical role of a first-person narrator?
  Answer: Students should recognize that first-person narrators are, in general, intelligent commentators on events of which they have direct knowledge and in which they are directly involved. By contrast, Spark's narrator is directly involved only in the simple things of a baby's life, but her knowledge extends to world events.

23 Literary Analysis

Point of View

- Guide students to see the omniscient narration here, as the scene moves from the narrator's birthday party to distant social events attended by Mr. Asquith and back to the party.
- Then, ask the Literary Analysis question on p. 1169: In what way does Spark's use of point of view suggest that she has cut and pasted her story together from different points of view?
  Answer: Students should recognize that the swiveling point of view—from events in the speaker's midst to those elsewhere—suggest a kind of patchwork of different points of view.

24 Reading Check

Answer: After the armistice, the speaker's teeth come in.

ASSESS

Answers for p. 1170

Review and Assess

1. **(a)** The narrator can "tune in" on what is happening everywhere.
(b) From the news briefs, we learn how the war is affecting soldiers and civilians, and from the poems, we learn of the terror and inevitability of death on the battlefield.
2. She smiles at the foolishness and irony of Asquith's remarks about the armistice.
3. Students should say that the image of an infant that concerns herself with "banging her spoon on the table of her high chair" while contemplating the serious issues of the war is absurd.
4. **(a)** "Firsthand accounts" are usually given by eyewitnesses, not by a "tuned-in" baby.
(b) Possible response: Spark might be suggesting that those who tell of war without having experienced it firsthand are as qualified to tell of it as a baby.
5. Possible response: Students may say that the message of this story—that war is horrible and futile and the lack of understanding of its causes and effects dooms humanity to suffer interminably—is still very relevant today.

When spring trips north again this year,
And I to my pledged word am true,
I shall not fail that rendezvous.

More parents and children arrived. One stout man who was warming his behind at the fire, said, "I always think those words of Asquith's after the armistice were so apt. . . ."

They brought the cake close to my high chair for me to see, with the candle shining and flickering above the pink icing. "A pity she never smiles."

"She'll smile in time," my mother said, obviously upset.

"What Asquith told the House of Commons just after the war," said that stout gentleman with his backside to the fire, "—so apt, what Asquith said. He said that the war has cleansed and purged the world . . . I recall his actual words: 'All things have become new. In this great cleansing and purging it has been the privilege of our country to play her part. . . .'"

That did it. I broke into a decided smile and everyone noticed it, convinced that it was provoked by the fact that my brother had blown out the candle on the cake. "She smiled!" my mother exclaimed. And everyone was clucking away about how I was smiling. For good measure I crowed like a demented raven. "My baby's smiling," said my mother.

"It was the candle on her cake," they said.

. . . . Since that time I have grown to smile quite naturally, like any other healthy and house-trained person, but when I really mean a smile, deeply felt from the core, then to all intents and purposes it comes in response to the words uttered in the House of Commons after the First World War by the distinguished, the immaculately dressed and the late Mr. Asquith.

Review and Assess

Thinking About the Selection

1. **(a) Recall:** What special power does the narrator possess?
(b) Infer: Sum up what you learn about World War I from the narrator's "news briefs" and from the poems.
2. **Interpret:** What statement is the narrator making with her first smile?
3. **Support:** Why does Spark's attempt to combine details of her infancy with the history of the time seem absurd?
4. **(a) Compare and Contrast:** Compare Spark's idea of a "firsthand account" with the typical use of this notion.
(b) Draw Conclusions: What does Spark's version of a "firsthand account" say about our attempts to tell of war?
5. **Apply:** Is the message of the story relevant today? Explain.

ASSESSMENT PRACTICE: Writing Skills

Style **(For more practice, see Test Preparation Workbook, p. 57.)**

Many tests require students to describe recognized stylistic devices and effective language. Use the following sample item to review with students how to recognize the tone of a passage. Have students read pp. 1164–1170 before answering the question.

The tone of this selection can *best* be described as

A matter-of-fact
B whiny
C dry and academic
D sad yet hopeful

Lead students to recognize that although Spark's piece is meant to entertain, it is told objectively and includes many facts. The tone is never whiny, so *B* is incorrect. "Sad yet hopeful" also does not describe the tone, so *D* is also incorrect. Although the selection includes historical information, neither Spark's tone nor her diction is academic. The correct answer is *A*.

Review and Assess

Literary Analysis

Point of View: Modern Experiments

1. Give three examples of the use of the **stream-of-consciousness** technique in Woolf's narrative.
2. (a) How does the literal reflection of Isabella in the mirror serve as a climax for the narrator's mental reflections? (b) What does this climax reveal about Isabella?
3. (a) How does Spark explain her unusual omniscient narrator? (b) In what way is a person telling about her own infancy like a historian, reporter, or politician telling the story of a war?

Comparing Literary Works

4. Compare Spark's narrative technique to Woolf's, using a chart like the one shown.

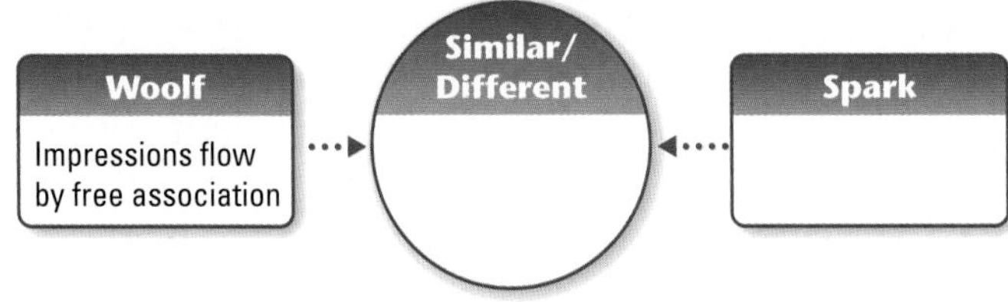

5. What does Woolf's use of the stream-of-consciousness technique show about how we construct a picture of another person?
6. What contrast between the reality and the representation of war does the narrator make in "The First Year of My Life"?
7. Which story offers more hope for our ability to penetrate appearances and discover reality? Explain.

Reading Strategy

Questioning

8. (a) In Woolf's story, what questions about the narrator might you ask? (b) What answers does the story suggest?
9. (a) What questions arise from the final paragraph of Spark's story? (b) What light do these questions shed on the theme?

Extend Understanding

10. **Science Connection:** How might a psychologist gain insight into a person through the person's free associations?

Quick Review

Point of view is the perspective from which a story is told.

Stream-of-consciousness narration presents the flow of thoughts in a character's mind.

An **omniscient narrator** knows more than any single character can.

To understand a work of fiction, ask **questions** as you read based on details in the work.

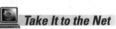

Take It to the Net

www.phschool.com

Take the interactive self-test online to check your understanding of these selections.

Answers for p. 1171

Review and Assess

1. Possible responses: Students may cite the description of the letters on the marble-topped table, the narrator's account of how she needed to "put oneself in [Isabella's] shoes," and the contrast between appearance and reality at the end of the story.
2. **(a)** The narrator's fanciful reflections on Isabella's character end suddenly as Isabella appears in the mirror. **(b)** The climax reveals that Isabella is nothing like the person the narrator has imagined her to be; she is devoid of feeling, lonely, and detached.
3. **(a)** She humorously claims that research has verified infant omniscience. **(b)** Possible response: A person recounting her infancy usually has memories of it based on what others have told her; historians, politicians, and reporters often have no direct experience of the war but ground their accounts in what others have told them.
4. **Woolf:** impressions flow by free association; **Spark:** impressions flow though omniscient narrator's consciousness; **Similar/Different:** Both narrators have many impressions, but Woolf's narrator is limited by her associations, while Spark's narrator has no limitations.
5. Woolf's use of stream of consciousness shows how the narrator constructs a reality for Isabella out of what proves to be merely an appearance.
6. The narrator makes the contrast between the reality of war as described in the poetry she quotes with its representation by politicians.
7. Possible response: Students may say that Spark's story demonstrates the possibility of seeing the truth about a horrible war.
8. **(a)** Possible responses: One might ask precisely who the narrator is, why she is in Isabella's house, and what relationship she has to Isabella. **(b)** The story suggests that she is an acquaintance, but not a close friend.
9. **(a)** Possible responses: Students might wonder what exactly the

continued

Answers continued

Prime Minister means by his remark and why it is that these comments cause the narrator to smile for the first time. **(b)** By examining Asquith's statement and the narrator's reaction to it, students can appreciate the author's message about the folly and futility of war.

10. Possible response: A psychologist might learn more about a person's unspoken, private, inner thoughts by reading or overhearing a person's free associations.

EXTEND

Answers for p. 1172

❶ Vocabulary Development

Word Analysis

1. A *transnational corporation* is a business organization that extends across international boundaries.
2. A *social transaction* is an activity or a process that occurs between individuals or groups.
3. *Transatlantic communication* is a means of communicating across the Atlantic Ocean.

Spelling Strategy

1. ancient
2. perceive
3. sufficient

Fluency: Sentence Completions

The *omniscient* baby in Spark's story knew everything. She may have been *reticent* with regard to her power, not telling the adults, but there is no doubt as to the *authenticity* of her abilities. She *discerned* events on remote battlefields, no matter how *transient* they were. The *evanescence* of human interactions, whether tender kisses or harsh *upbraidings*, did not protect these events from her knowledge. She was *suffused* with joy as she exercised her strange powers.

❷ Grammar and Style

1. were; subjects = flushes, darkening
2. was; subject = sound
3. were; subject = drawers
4. were; subject = people
5. was; subject = cake

Writing Application

Possible response:
In my bedroom, there are three cats who like to sleep and there are also a bed, a chair, and a bookshelf. The mirror reflects my curtains, my closet, and the framed photographs of my friends. There is also a bench on which I keep my pet snake's cage.

Integrate Language Skills

❶ Vocabulary Development Lesson

Word Analysis: Latin Prefix *-trans-*

The Latin prefix *-trans-*, meaning "through" or "across," appears in the word *transient*, meaning "passing through quickly." Use the meaning of the prefix to define these phrases from the social sciences.

1. transnational corporation
2. social transaction
3. transatlantic communication

Spelling Strategy

When a *c* in a word creates a *sh* or *ch* sound, it may be followed by *ie*, as in *omniscient*, but not by *ei*. On your paper, complete the following words by adding the *ie* or *ei* that is needed.

1. anc__nt 2. perc__ve 3. suffic__nt

Fluency: Sentence Completions

On your paper, fill in each blank with the most suitable word from the vocabulary list on page 1157.

The __?__ baby in Spark's story knew everything. She may have been __?__ with regard to her power, not telling the adults, but there is no doubt as to the __?__ of her abilities. She __?__ events on remote battlefields, no matter how __?__ they were. The __?__ of human interactions, whether tender kisses or harsh __?__, did not protect these events from her knowledge. She was __?__ with joy as she exercised her strange powers.

❷ Grammar and Style Lesson

Subject-Verb Agreement in Inverted Sentences

A verb must agree in number with its subject even when the verb precedes the subject in the sentence. Such sentences, called **inverted sentences,** often begin with *here* or *there*. They may also begin with prepositional phrases. In these cases, do not be misled into thinking that the subject is *here*, *there*, or any nouns or pronouns that are part of a phrase preceding the verb.

Plural Subject: There (were)[V] her gray-green <u>dress</u>[S], and her long <u>shoes</u>[S], . . .

Inverted sentences may be used by writers to throw emphasis on the words that are out of order.

Practice On your paper, identify the subject in each sentence and choose the verb that agrees.

1. And there (was, were) obscure flushes and darkening too. . . .
2. . . . there (was, were) a perpetual sighing and ceasing sound . . .
3. In each of these cabinets (was, were) many little drawers. . . .
4. There (was, were) those black-dressed people, . . .
5. Next February on my first birthday, there (was, were) a birthday cake with one candle.

Writing Application Write a paragraph describing the reflection in a mirror in a room you know. Use two sentences in inverted form.

WG Prentice Hall Writing and Grammar Connection: Chapter 20, Section 3

TEACHING RESOURCES

The following resources can be used to enrich or extend the instruction for pp. 1172–1173.

Vocabulary

- **Selection Support:** Build Vocabulary, p. 263
- **Vocabulary and Spelling Practice Book** (Use this booklet for skills enrichment.)

Grammar

- **Selection Support:** Grammar and Style, p. 264
- **Writing and Grammar,** Diamond Level, p. 490
- **Daily Language Practice Transparencies** ■

Writing

- **Writing and Grammar,** Diamond Level, p. 310 ■
- **Writing and Grammar iText CD-ROM**

■ **BLOCK SCHEDULING:** Resources marked with this symbol provide varied instruction during 90-minute blocks.

❸ Writing Lesson

Essay on a Literary Theme

Woolf's story suggests that our knowledge of others is clouded by the web of associations and assumptions we weave around them. Write an essay on our knowledge of others, considering whether Woolf's ideas are true or exaggerated.

Prewriting Review the story. Use a chart like the one shown to compare Isabella as "seen" through the mirror with the "real" Isabella. Summarize Woolf's ideas about our knowledge of others. Then, jot down your own ideas about knowing others, and make a judgment about Woolf's position.

Model: Analyzing a Theme by Contrasting Details

Inference from "Mirror" View	Evidence

Inference About "Real" Isabella	Evidence

Drafting Begin by presenting Woolf's idea of knowledge, supporting your claims with details from the story. Then, using generalizations from your own experience, explain your response to her idea.

Revising Review your draft, adding support for your ideas where necessary.

WG Prentice Hall Writing and Grammar Connection: Chapter 14, Section 2

❹ Extension Activities

Research and Technology Before Woolf wrote her stream-of-consciousness narratives, Sigmund Freud used free association as a technique in therapy. Write a **report on cultural trends** comparing Freud's method with Woolf's technique. Begin with these steps:

- Formulate a description of Woolf's technique.
- Do preliminary research on Freud's method.
- Develop a set of clear research questions and answer them through additional research.

Listening and Speaking Lead a **discussion group** on literary responses to World War I. Begin by preparing readings of poems by Alan Seeger and Wilfred Owen, mentioned by Spark. Read aloud the poems you have chosen. Then, lead a discussion comparing the tone and mood of these poems with the tone and mood of Spark's story. **[Group Activity]**

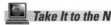

Take It to the Net www.phschool.com

Go online for an additional research activity using the Internet.

Lesson Support for p. 1173

❸ Writing Lesson

- Review with students the Writing Lesson on p. 1173 before they begin writing their essays on a literary theme.
- Tell students that they should review Woolf's story and compare the imagined Isabella with the real Isabella.
- Encourage students to brainstorm for any ideas that suggest other ways in which appearance and reality are difficult to disentangle when it comes to knowing people.
- Have students write drafts of their essays, supporting their arguments with examples from the story and any personal experiences.

❹ Research and Technology

- Have students read the Research and Technology note on p. 1173 with teacher guidance.
- Encourage students to research Sigmund Freud and free association, a technique of psychotherapy he popularized.
- As students write their cultural reports, remind them that they should compare these trends to Woolf's technique.

CUSTOMIZE INSTRUCTION
For Universal Access

To address different learning styles, use the activities suggested in the **Extension Activities** booklet, p. 57.

- For Logical/Mathematical Learners, use Activity 5.
- For Visual/Spatial Learners, use Activity 6.
- For Intrapersonal and Interpersonal Learners, use Activity 7.

ASSESSMENT RESOURCES

The following resources can be used to assess students' knowledge and skills.

Selection Assessment

- **Formal Assessment,** pp. 272–274
- **Open Book Test,** pp. 168–170
- **Got It! Assessment Videotapes,** Tape 6
- **Test Bank Software**

Take It to the Net

Visit www.phschool.com for self-tests and additional questions on the selections.

PRENTICE HALL ASSESSMENT SYSTEM

- **Workbook**
- **Skill Book**
- **Transparencies**
- **CD-ROM**

The Rocking-Horse Winner ✦ A Shocking Accident

Lesson Objectives and CA Correlations

1. **To analyze and respond to literary elements**
   - Literary Analysis: Theme and Symbol **R 3.4**
   - Comparing Literary Works **R 3.2**
2. **To read, comprehend, analyze, and critique a short story**
   - Reading Strategy: Identifying With a Character
   - Reading Check Questions
   - Review and Assess Questions
3. **To develop word analysis skills, fluency, and systematic vocabulary**
   - Vocabulary Development Lesson: Word Analysis: Latin Prefix *ob-* **R 1.1, 1.2**
4. **To understand and apply written and oral language conventions**
   - Spelling Strategy **LC 1.2**
   - Grammar and Style Lesson: Subjunctive Mood **LC 1.1**
5. **To understand and apply appropriate writing and research strategies**
   - Writing Lesson: Product Description **W 1.1, 1.4, 1.9**
   - Extension Activity: Multimedia Travelogue **W 2.6**
   - Assessment Practice (ATE)
6. **To understand and apply listening and speaking strategies**
   - Extension Activity: Soliloquy **LS 1.7, 1.9**

STEP-BY-STEP TEACHING GUIDE	PACING GUIDE
PRETEACH	
Motivate Students and Provide Background	
Use the Motivation activity (ATE p. 1174)	5 min.
Read and discuss author and background features (SE/ATE pp. 1174, 1176) [A]	5 min.
Introduce the Concepts	
Introduce the Literary Analysis and Reading Strategy (SE/ATE p. 1175) [A]	15 min.
Pronounce the vocabulary words and read their definitions (SE p. 1175)	5 min.
TEACH	
Monitor Comprehension	
Informally monitor comprehension by circulating while students read independently or in groups [A]	45 min.
Monitor students' comprehension with the Reading Check notes (SE/ATE pp.1177, 1179, 1181, 1183, 1185, 1187, 1193)	as students read
Develop vocabulary with Vocabulary notes (SE pp. 1177, 1179, 1182, 1186, 1190, 1191, 1193; ATE p. 1182)	as students read
Develop Understanding	
Develop students' understanding of theme with the Literary Analysis annotations (SE/ATE pp. 1176, 1178, 1179, 1180, 1181, 1184, 1185, 1186, 1187, 1188, 1189, 1191) [A]	5 min.
Develop students' ability to identify with a character with the Reading Strategy annotations (SE/ATE pp. 1177, 1178, 1180, 1182, 1184, 1190, 1192, 1193)	5 min.
ASSESS	
Assess Mastery	
Assess students' mastery of the Reading Strategy and Literary Analysis by having them answer the Review and Assess questions (SE/ATE p. 1195)	20 min.
Use one or more of the print and media Assessment Resources (ATE p. 1197) [A]	up to 45 min.
EXTEND	
Apply Understanding	
Have students complete the Vocabulary Development Lesson and the Grammar and Style Lesson (SE p. 1196) [A]	20 min.
Apply students' ability to use symbolism using the Writing Lesson (SE/ATE p. 1197) [A]	45 min.
Apply students' understanding using one or more of the Extension Activities (SE p. 1197)	20–90 min.

[A] **ACCELERATED INSTRUCTION:**
Use the strategies and activities identified with an .

UNIVERSAL ACCESS
● = Below-Level Students
▲ = On-Level Students
■ = Above-Level Students

Time and Resource Manager

Reading Level: Average, Average
Average Number of Instructional Days: 5

RESOURCES		
PRINT	**TRANSPARENCIES**	**TECHNOLOGY**
• **Beyond Literature,** Humanities Connection: Greek Notion of Fate, p. 58 ▲ ■		• **Interest Grabber Video,** Tape 6 ● ▲ ■
• **Selection Support Workbook:** ● ▲ ■ Literary Analysis, p. 270 Reading Strategy, p. 269 Build Vocabulary, p. 267	• **Literary Analysis and Reading Transparencies,** pp. 115 and 116 ● ▲ ■	
		• **Listening to Literature** ● ▲ ■ Audiocassettes, Sides 27 and 28 Audio CDs, CD 16
• **Literatura en español** ● ▲ • **Literary Analysis for Enrichment** ■		
• **Formal Assessment:** Selection Test, pp. 275–277 ● ▲ ■ • **Open Book Test,** pp. 171–173 ● ▲ ■ • **Performance Assessment and Portfolio Management,** p. 17 ● ▲ ■ • PRENTICE HALL ASSESSMENT SYSTEM ● ▲ ■	• PRENTICE HALL ASSESSMENT SYSTEM ● ▲ ■ Skills Practice Answers and Explanations on Transparencies ● ▲ ■	• **Test Bank Software** ● ▲ ■ • **Got It! Assessment Videotapes,** Tape 6 ● ▲
• **Selection Support Workbook:** ● ▲ ■ Grammar and Style, p. 268 • **Writing and Grammar,** Diamond Level ● ▲ ■ • **Extension Activities,** p. 58 ● ▲ ■	• **Daily Language Practice Transparencies** ● ▲	• **Writing and Grammar iText CD-ROM** ● ▲ ■ ***Take It to the Net*** www.phschool.com

BLOCK SCHEDULING: Use one 90-minute class period to preteach the selections and have students read them. Use a second 90-minute class period to assess students' mastery of skills and have them complete one of the Extension Activities.

PRETEACH

Step-by-Step Teaching Guide for pp. 1174–1175

Motivation

Before assigning the D. H. Lawrence story, write down a "secret" number between 1 and 10. Ask students to guess the number, record their guesses, and tally all responses on the chalkboard. Then, reveal the number you wrote. How many students guessed it correctly? If any did, have them tell how they made their choice: Luck? Intuition? Chance? Lead a discussion about the role of luck and chance in students' lives. Then, tell students that these elements play a very important role in these two stories.

Interest Grabber Video

As an alternative, you may wish to play "'The Rocking-Horse Winner': D. H. Lawrence" on Tape 6 to engage student interest.

❶ Background

More About the Authors

Although both writers were inveterate travelers and their destinations often became settings for their fiction, only Greene's story here uses travel as an element of the plot. Still, Lawrence continues to be best known for his characters with a British background, while Greene's most popular works often feature an African or a Latin American setting.

Prepare to Read

❶ The Rocking-Horse Winner ◆ A Shocking Accident

D. H. Lawrence (1885–1930)

During his lifetime, D. H. Lawrence's literary achievements were overshadowed by controversy. Like Percy Bysshe Shelley and Lord Byron in their day, Lawrence took unorthodox positions on politics and morality that shocked mainstream society.

Early Years Lawrence was born in Eastwood, Nottinghamshire, the son of an almost illiterate coal miner father and a more educated mother. Through her influence, he pursued a scholarship to the Nottingham High School, where he studied from 1898 to 1901. After leaving school for a job as a clerk, he contracted pneumonia and, on recovering, became a teacher.

Lawrence also began to write poems, stories, and novels, and his poetry attracted the attention of the well-known writer and editor Ford Madox Ford. In 1913, Lawrence published his first major novel, *Sons and Lovers*, a thinly disguised autobiography. Two years later, he published *The Rainbow*, which was banned in Britain.

Travels Abroad During World War I, Lawrence and his German wife, Frieda, lived in poverty in England and were unreasonably suspected of being German spies. At the end of the war, they left England and never returned. They traveled to Italy, Ceylon, Australia, Mexico, and the United States, and Lawrence used many of these locales in his fiction. In 1920, he published *Women in Love*, one of his greatest novels. A few years later, although suffering from tuberculosis, he completed *Lady Chatterley's Lover*. Shortly afterward, in the south of France, he died from that disease.

In the years since Lawrence's death, society's views of his writings have changed profoundly. Today, his fiction is widely admired for its vivid settings, fine craftsmanship, and psychological insight.

Graham Greene (1904–1991)

The search for salvation, a theme addressed by poets like T. S. Eliot, is a central concern in the fiction of novelist Graham Greene. Like Eliot, Greene was a religious convert who wrote works exploring pain, fear, despair, and alienation.

Journalism and Travel The son of a schoolmaster, Greene was born in Berkhamsted in Hertfordshire. He converted to Roman Catholicism after studying at Oxford University. Then, he began working as a copy editor in London and married. Eventually, he became a traveling freelance journalist.

Thrillers and More His journalism helped him develop the powers of observation, sensitivity to atmosphere, and simplicity of language that became hallmarks of his fiction. While traveling, he was able to scout out locations for his stories and novels.

Some of these novels, such as *Orient Express* (1932), he called "entertainments." These were an unusual type of thriller that went beyond the genre in its concern with moral issues.

Even more deeply involved with spiritual crisis, however, were such Greene classics as *Brighton Rock* (1938), *The Power and the Glory* (1940), and two novels set in Africa, *The Heart of the Matter* (1948) and *A Burnt-Out Case* (1961). In these works, Greene's concern with salvation burns with intensity.

Psychological Insight Greene's best fiction focuses on the psychology of human character rather than on plot. Many of his protagonists are people without roots or beliefs—people in pain. They may be odd, but they almost always excite the reader's curiosity and pity—and, almost always, Greene treats them with compassion as they strive to achieve salvation.

TEACHING RESOURCES

The following resources can be used to enrich or extend the instruction for pp. 1174–1175.

Motivation

Interest Grabber Video, Tape 6

Background

Beyond Literature, p. 58

Take It to the Net

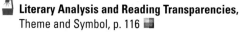

Visit www.phschool.com for background and hotlinks for the selections.

Literary Analysis

Literary Analysis and Reading Transparencies, Theme and Symbol, p. 116

Reading

Selection Support: Reading Strategy, p. 269; Build Vocabulary, p. 267

Literary Analysis and Reading Transparencies, Identify With a Character, p. 115

BLOCK SCHEDULING: Resources marked with this symbol provide varied instruction during 90-minute blocks.

Preview

Connecting to the Literature

In each of these stories, characters look for someone whom they can trust with secrets or sensitive information.

2 Literary Analysis

Theme and Symbol

Most short stories contain a **theme,** a central idea or question, that the writer explores. Writers often reveal theme through a **symbol,** a person, object, or action that suggests deeper meanings. To identify symbols, look for descriptions that carry a special emphasis. In this passage from "The Rocking-Horse Winner," the underlined words suggest that the horse is a symbol:

> . . . he would sit on his big rocking horse, charging madly into space, with a frenzy that made the little girls peer at him uneasily.

As you read, identify symbols and use the meanings they suggest to figure out the author's central idea or concern.

Comparing Literary Works

Each of these stories is told from a **third-person point of view,** meaning that the narrator does not take part in the action. As you read, compare the ways in which both authors use this point of view to reveal their themes: for example, by disclosing the thoughts of characters and by creating symbols to suggest meanings. Also ask yourself how the third-person point of view is different in each story. Consider, for instance, whether Greene's narrative has the same intensity as Lawrence's.

3 Reading Strategy

Identifying With a Character

Identifying with a character—putting yourself in that character's place in order to understand his or her feelings, needs, problems, and goals—can help you understand the theme of a work. As you read, fill in a chart like this one to help you identify with the main characters.

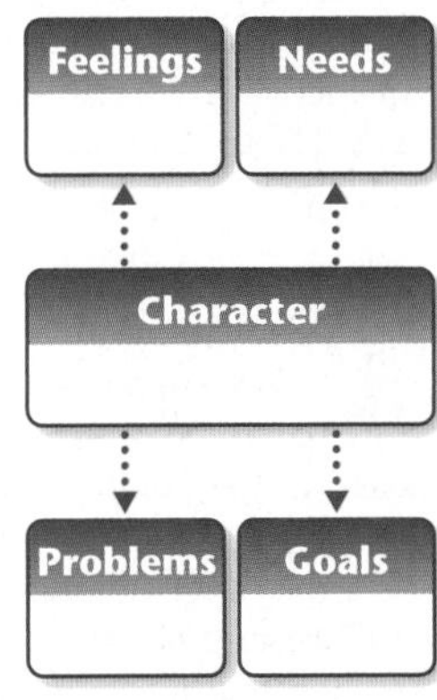

Vocabulary Development

discreet (di skrēt′) *adj.* wise; prudent (p. 1177)

brazening (brā′ zən iŋ) *v.* daring boldly or shamelessly (p. 1179)

careered (kə rird′) *v.* rushed wildly (p. 1179)

obstinately (äb′ stə nət lē) *adv.* in a determined way; stubbornly (p. 1182)

uncanny (un kan′ ē) *adj.* mysterious; hard to explain (p. 1183)

remonstrated (ri män′ strāt′ id) *v.* objected strongly (p. 1186)

apprehension (ap′ rē hen′ shən) *n.* anxious feeling of foreboding; dread (p. 1190)

embarked (em bärkt′) *v.* engaged in something, such as a conversation (p. 1191)

intrinsically (in trin′ sik lē) *adv.* at its core; inherently; innately (p. 1193)

CUSTOMIZE INSTRUCTION FOR UNIVERSAL ACCESS

For Less Proficient Readers	For English Learners	For Advanced Readers
Have students identify the part of speech of each vocabulary word, and then list the words in groups of adjectives, adverbs, and verbs. Be sure they understand that *brazening,* a participle, can be used as a verb or an adjective.	Have students use each of the vocabulary words in a sentence. To make the words more accessible, suggest that students use the words in sentences about themselves. For example, "I was *discreet* when I overheard my sister's phone call to her boyfriend."	Give students the ambitious task of using the vocabulary words in a related group of paragraphs. They may write a narrative or a scene containing dialogue.

2 Literary Analysis

Theme and Symbol

- Tell students that as they read the next two selections, they will focus on theme—the central message of a literary work—and symbols—people, objects, or actions that stand for something other than themselves.
- Read the instruction about theme and symbol as a class, and call students' attention to the example from the story.
- Use the instruction for Comparing Literary Works to connect the theme of each story with the third-person point of view.
- Use the Theme transparency in **Literary Analysis and Reading Transparencies**, p. 116, to demonstrate for students how a theme can be revealed by characters, events, and symbols.

3 Reading Strategy

Identifying With a Character

- Remind students that they often can understand a character much better if they can also identify with him or her.
- Tell students that they can identify with a character if they share the character's feelings, needs, problems, or goals, or any combination of these.
- Instruct students to create a character web like the one on the Identify With a Character transparency, p. 115 of **Literary Analysis and Reading Transparencies**.
- Have students use character webs as they read the two stories and see how closely they identify with each main character.

Vocabulary Development

- Pronounce each vocabulary word for students, and read the definitions as a class. Have students identify any words with which they are already familiar.

E-Teach

Visit E-Teach at www.phschool.com for teachers' essays on how to teach, with questions and answers.

TEACH

Step-by-Step Teaching Guide for pp. 1176–1194

CUSTOMIZE INSTRUCTION
For Logical/Mathematical Learners

To emphasize the uncanny nature of Paul's ability in "The Rocking-Horse Winner," have students calculate the odds of choosing the winning horse in a field of ten completely by chance.

❶ About the Selection

In this parable about the ill effects of greed, a family is in constant need of money; at least that is what the mother tells her impressionable son. She says that having money is a matter of being lucky. Eager to please his mother and help her obtain the wealth she desires, the boy sets out to prove that he is lucky. His ability to choose winning racehorses and the price he pays for this ability will lead students to analyze their own ideas about luck and money.

❷ Literary Analysis

Theme and Symbol

- Point out to students that this story begins much like a conventional fairy tale. Ask them what this choice of opening might symbolize.
  Possible response: Fairy tales generally have a lesson to teach or a moral to impart. Perhaps this story will do the same.
- Ask students to describe what they have learned so far about the woman in the story.
  Answer: The woman is beautiful. She does not love her husband or her children and always feels at fault for something she cannot change.
- Ask students the Literary Analysis question on p. 1176: What ideas about the story's theme does this first paragraph suggest?
  Possible response: The mother who doesn't love her children will experience some kind of setback, and she will not be the "winner" referred to in the title.

❶ The Rocking-Horse Winner

D. H. Lawrence

Background

Both these stories involve wealth and class. Britain had a rigid class structure, and its upper classes tried to live at the "right" addresses, attend the "right" schools, and have the "right" friends. In "The Rocking-Horse Winner," Paul's mother is desperate to maintain upper-class appearances despite her husband's "small income." In "A Shocking Accident," Jerome attends an "expensive preparatory school"—private schools in Britain are referred to as public schools—and must deal with classmates' reactions to a tragedy that is bizarrely improper.

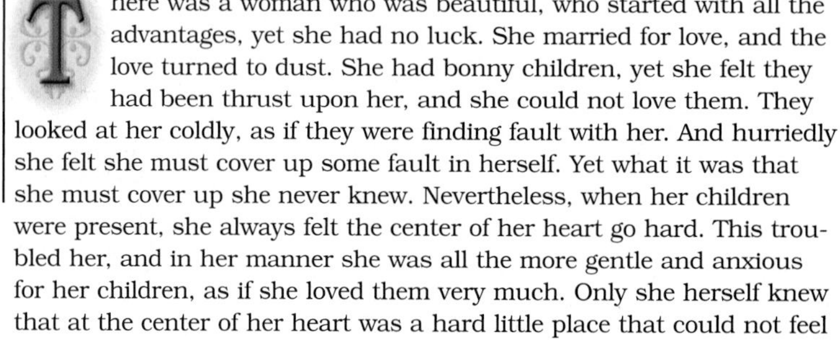

❷ There was a woman who was beautiful, who started with all the advantages, yet she had no luck. She married for love, and the love turned to dust. She had bonny children, yet she felt they had been thrust upon her, and she could not love them. They looked at her coldly, as if they were finding fault with her. And hurriedly she felt she must cover up some fault in herself. Yet what it was that she must cover up she never knew. Nevertheless, when her children were present, she always felt the center of her heart go hard. This troubled her, and in her manner she was all the more gentle and anxious for her children, as if she loved them very much. Only she herself knew that at the center of her heart was a hard little place that could not feel

Literary Analysis
Theme and Symbol What ideas about the story's theme does this first paragraph suggest?

TEACHING RESOURCES

The following resources can be used to enrich or extend the instruction for pp. 1176–1194.

Literary Analysis

Selection Support: Literary Analysis, p. 270

Reading

Listening to Literature Audiocassettes, Sides 27 and 28

Listening to Literature Audio CDs, CD 16

BLOCK SCHEDULING: Resources marked with this symbol provide varied instruction during 90-minute blocks.

3 love, no, not for anybody. Everybody else said of her: "She is such a good mother. She adores her children." Only she herself, and her children themselves, knew it was not so. They read it in each other's eyes.

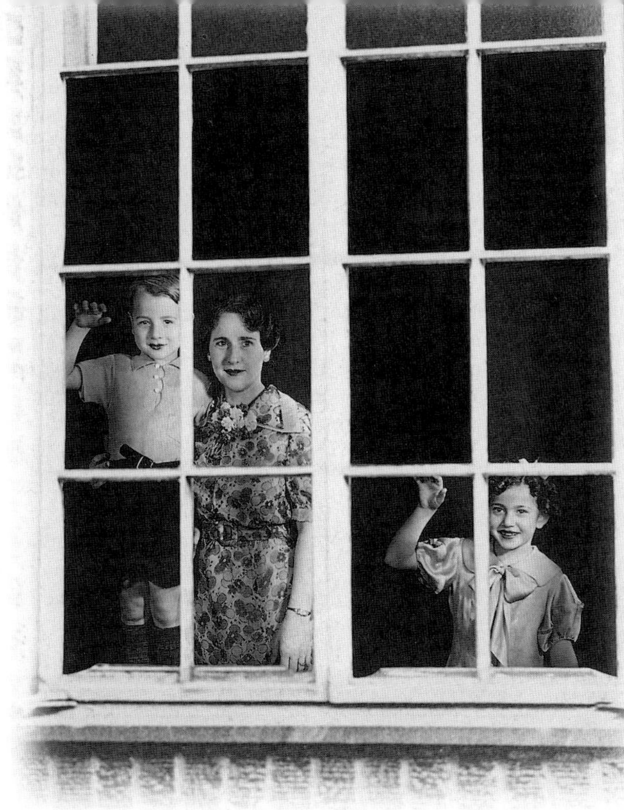

There were a boy and two little girls. They lived in a pleasant house, with a garden and they had discreet servants, and felt themselves superior to anyone in the neighborhood.

Although they lived in style, they felt always an anxiety in the house. There was never enough money. The mother had a small income and the father had a small income, but not nearly enough for the social position which they had to keep up. The father went into town to some office. But though he had good prospects, these prospects never materialized. There was always the grinding sense of the shortage of money, though the style was always kept up.

At last the mother said, "I will see if *I* can't make something." But she did not know where to begin. She racked her brains, and tried this thing and the other, but could not find anything successful. The failure made deep lines come into her face. Her children were growing up, they would have to go to school. There must be more money, there must be more money. The father, who was always very handsome and expensive in his tastes, seemed as if he never *would* be able to do anything worth doing. And the mother, who had a great belief in herself, did not succeed any better, and her tastes were just as expensive.

And so the house came to be haunted by the unspoken phrase: *There must be more money! There must be more money!* The children could hear it all the time, though nobody said it aloud. They heard it at Christmas, when the expensive and splendid toys filled the nursery. Behind the shining modern rocking horse, behind the smart doll's house, a voice would start whispering: "There *must* be more money! There *must* be more money!" And the children would stop playing, to listen for a moment. They would look into each other's eyes to see if they had all heard. And each one saw in the eyes of the other two that they too had heard. "There *must* be more money! There *must* be more money!"

It came whispering from the springs of the still-swaying rocking horse, and even the horse, bending his wooden, champing head,

4 ▲ **Critical Viewing**
Would the casual observer have seen Paul's family in the way that this family is depicted? Explain. **[Connect]**

discreet (di skrēt′) *adj.* wise; prudent

5 **Reading Check**
What does the mother feel toward her children?

3 Reading Strategy

Identifying With a Character

- Ask students what others said about the woman in the story.
  Answer: They said, "She is such a good mother. She adores her children."
- Have students identify the children's view of these statements.
  Answer: The children knew it was not true that she loved them.
- Then, ask students how the children know their mother doesn't love them.
  Answer: Children can sense when adults' feelings do not match their words. Children can also sense unspoken feelings.

4 ▶Critical Viewing

Possible response: The casual observer would have seen the family in this way because this is the way the mother wanted them to be seen. The children are clean and smiling as they wave at the camera.

5 Reading Check

Answer: The mother does not love them; her heart goes "hard" in their presence.

CUSTOMIZE INSTRUCTION FOR UNIVERSAL ACCESS

For Special Needs Students	For English Learners	For Advanced Readers
Point out that the term *rocking horse* is hyphenated in the title of the work and is not hyphenated when it is used toward the bottom of p. 1177 and elsewhere in the story. Explain that if *rocking horse* is used as a noun, as it is on p. 1177, it has no hyphen. When the term is used as an adjective, modifying the word *winner*, it needs a hyphen.	Guide students to understand that the "small income" each parent receives is an annuity, the result of being born into families of wealth. Ask students to look up the word *annuity* to find its meaning and to suggest another related word with which they are familiar (*annual*).	Use this long selection to develop students' ability to read with comprehension for a sustained period of time. Tell students to keep a reading journal of questions and observations. Follow up with a discussion in which students share their observations and explain what they have read.

6 Literary Analysis

Theme and Symbol

- Ask students if there is an actual whisper heard in the house. If not, what is it?
  Answer: No one is actually whispering, "There *must* be more money." The whisper is the message that the children discern from the behavior of the adults, particularly their mother.
- Ask students the Literary Analysis question on p. 1178: How does this secret whispering help reveal a potential theme?
  Possible response: A potential theme is that what is communicated through feelings may be more important than what is spoken.

7 Reading Strategy

Identifying With a Character

- Have students explain why Paul asks his mother if luck is the same thing as money.
  Answer: Paul has overheard his uncle use the phrase "filthy lucre" as "filthy lucker."
- After students have read the exchange between Paul and his mother, ask them the Reading Strategy question on p. 1178: If you were Paul, what impact might this exchange have on you?
  Possible response: Students may say that they would be motivated to look for ways to bring luck, or money, to their family.

heard it. The big doll, sitting so pink and smirking in her new pram,[1] could hear it quite plainly, and seemed to be smirking all the more self-consciously because of it. The foolish puppy, too, that took the place of the teddy bear, he was looking so extraordinarily foolish for **6** no other reason but that he heard the secret whisper all over the house: "There *must* be more money."

Yet nobody ever said it aloud. The whisper was everywhere, and therefore no one spoke it. Just as no one ever says: "We are breathing!" in spite of the fact that breath is coming and going all the time.

"Mother!" said the boy Paul one day. "Why don't we keep a car of our own? Why do we always use uncle's, or else a taxi?"

"Because we're the poor members of the family," said the mother.

"But why *are* we, mother?"

"Well—I suppose," she said slowly and bitterly, "it's because your father has no luck."

The boy was silent for some time.

"Is luck money, mother?" he asked, rather timidly.

"No, Paul! Not quite. It's what causes you to have money."

"Oh!" said Paul vaguely. "I thought when Uncle Oscar said *filthy lucker,* it meant money."

"*Filthy lucre* does mean money," said the mother. "But it's lucre, not luck."

"Oh!" said the boy. "Then what *is* luck, mother?"

7 "It's what causes you to have money. If you're lucky you have money. That's why it's better to be born lucky than rich. If you're rich, you may lose your money. But if you're lucky, you will always get more money."

"Oh! Will you! And is father not lucky?"

"Very unlucky, I should say," she said bitterly.

The boy watched her with unsure eyes.

"Why?" he asked.

"I don't know. Nobody ever knows why one person is lucky and another unlucky."

"Don't they? Nobody at all? Does *nobody* know?"

"Perhaps God! But He never tells."

"He ought to, then. And aren't you lucky either, mother?"

"I can't be, if I married an unlucky husband."

"But by yourself, aren't you?"

"I used to think I was, before I married. Now I think I am very unlucky indeed."

"Why?"

"Well—never mind! Perhaps I'm not really," she said.

The child looked at her, to see if she meant it. But he saw, by the lines of her mouth, that she was only trying to hide something from him.

"Well, anyhow," he said stoutly, "I'm a lucky person."

"Why?" said his mother, with a sudden laugh.

He stared at her. He didn't even know why he had said it.

1. **pram** baby carriage.

Literary Analysis
Theme and Symbol How does this secret whispering help reveal a potential theme?

Reading Strategy
Identifying With a Character If you were Paul, what impact might this exchange have on you?

ENRICHMENT: Literature Connection

Greek Tragedy

In "The Rocking-Horse Winner," tragic consequences follow when a boy tries to "beat the odds." The struggle between fate and self-determination is a major theme in ancient Greek tragedies. Tell students as they read to look for how a basically noble hero is brought down by a tragic flaw such as hubris (excessive pride) and/or the will of the gods. This theme carries through centuries of Western literature, including the works of Shakespeare. In a twist on classical tragedy, some modern writers have used absurdity to emphasize humans' helplessness in an irrational world. Students will see an example of this in Greene's "A Shocking Accident." Have students discuss how these stories and others they know illustrate the qualities of classical tragedy and the absurd.

"God told me," he asserted, brazening it out.

"I hope He did, dear!" she said, again with a laugh, but rather bitter.

"He did, mother!"

"Excellent!" said the mother, using one of her husband's exclamations.

The boy saw she did not believe him; or rather, that she paid no attention to his assertion. This angered him somewhere, and made him want to compel her attention.

brazening (brā′ zən iŋ) *v.* daring boldly or shamelessly

8 He went off by himself, vaguely, in a childish way, seeking for the clue to "luck." Absorbed, taking no heed of other people, he went about with a sort of stealth, seeking inwardly for luck. He wanted luck, he wanted it, he wanted it. When the two girls were playing dolls, in the nursery, he would sit on his big rocking horse, charging madly into space, with a frenzy that made the little girls peer at him uneasily. Wildly the horse careered, the waving dark hair of the boy tossed, his eyes had a strange glare in them. The little girls dared not speak to him.

careered (kə rird′) *v.* rushed wildly

When he had ridden to the end of his mad little journey, he climbed down and stood in front of his rocking horse, staring fixedly into its lowered face. Its red mouth was slightly open, its big eye was wide and glassy bright.

"Now!" he would silently command the snorting steed. "Now take me to where there is luck! Now take me!"

And he would slash the horse on the neck with the little whip he had asked Uncle Oscar for. He *knew* the horse could take him to where there was luck, if only he forced it. So he would mount again, and start on his furious ride, hoping at last to get there. He knew he could get there.

"You'll break your horse, Paul!" said the nurse.

"He's always riding like that! I wish he'd leave off!" said his elder sister Joan.

But he only glared down on them in silence. Nurse gave him up. She could make nothing of him. Anyhow he was growing beyond her.

One day his mother and his Uncle Oscar came in when he was on one of his furious rides. He did not speak to them.

"Hallo! you young jockey! Riding a winner?" said his uncle.

"Aren't you growing too big for a rocking horse? You're not a very little boy any longer, you know," said his mother.

But Paul only gave a blue glare from his big, rather close-set eyes. He would speak to nobody when he was in full tilt. His mother watched him with an anxious expression on her face.

At last he suddenly stopped forcing his horse into the mechanical gallop, and slid down.

"Well, I got there!" he announced fiercely, his blue eyes still flaring, and his sturdy long legs straddling apart.

"Where did you get to?" asked his mother.

"Where I wanted to go to," he flared back at her.

9 
Reading Check

What does Paul do to find "the clue to 'luck'"?

8 Reading Strategy

Identifying With a Character

- Ask students what they think Paul might be doing as he rides his horse so wildly.
  Possible responses: Paul is riding madly while looking for luck. He is working off nervousness while he thinks about how to find luck
- Ask students why they think it is so important to Paul to find luck for the family.
  Possible responses: Children often feel responsible for things that go wrong with their families and also believe that such problems are their fault. Paul hopes that if he finds luck for the family, his mother will then love him.

9 Reading Check

Answer: Paul rides his rocking horse to find the clue to luck.

CUSTOMIZE INSTRUCTION FOR UNIVERSAL ACCESS

For Special Needs Students	For Less Proficient Readers	For English Learners
Prepare students by giving them the meanings of unfamiliar words or familiar words used in unfamiliar ways. Examples are *lucre* ("money gotten through questionable means"), *mad* ("crazy") on pp. 1178 and 1179, and *go down* ("lose") and *writs* ("legal documents ordering the payment of debts") further on.	Students may need assistance with unfamiliar cultural references. In addition, you may need to guide students to understand that the whispering is not really in the house but in the children's minds.	Show students the video "'The Rocking-Horse Winner': D. H. Lawrence." Ask them to make notes of unfamiliar words in order to discuss them at the end of the film. Also, have them discuss what they learned of Lawrence's beliefs and values and to compare them with the values they find in the story.

⑩ Literary Analysis

Theme and Symbol

- Ask students what they learn, during this exchange between Paul and Uncle Oscar, about why the rocking horse is so central to Paul's life.
  Possible response: Paul has become a horse-racing fan, and the rocking horse probably represents a racehorse.
- Have students identify the source of Paul's information about horse racing.
  Answer: Paul learns about horse racing from Bassett, who is the gardener for Paul's family.
- Ask students the Literary Analysis question on p. 1180: Bassett and the small boy "live" in the racing events. What might this detail suggest about their lives?
  Answer: This detail suggests that both Bassett and Paul need an exciting and fulfilling escape from their daily lives.

⑪ Reading Strategy

Identifying With a Character

- Have students explain how Uncle Oscar finds out that Paul is betting on the horses.
  Answer: Uncle Oscar finds out from Bassett.
- Ask students what they think the phrase "honor bright" means.
  Possible responses: Students may mention "cross my heart" or "I promise."
- Ask students the Reading Strategy question on p. 1180: If you were Paul, would you feel loyal to Bassett? Why or why not?
  Possible response: Students may feel loyal because Bassett has been loyal and a good friend to him and has given him good advice on the races.

"That's right, son!" said Uncle Oscar. "Don't you stop till you get there. What's the horse's name?"

"He doesn't have a name," said the boy.

"Gets on without all right?" asked the uncle.

"Well, he has different names. He was called Sansovino last week."

"Sansovino, eh? Won the Ascot.[2] How did you know his name?"

"He always talks about horse races with Bassett," said Joan.

10 he uncle was delighted to find that his small nephew was posted with all the racing news. Bassett, the young gardener who had been wounded in the left foot in the war, and had got his present job through Oscar Cresswell, whose batman[3] he had been, was a perfect blade of the "turf."[4] He lived in the racing events, and the small boy lived with him.

Oscar Cresswell got it all from Bassett.

"Master Paul comes and asks me, so I can't do more than tell him, sir," said Bassett, his face terribly serious, as if he were speaking of religious matters.

"And does he ever put anything on a horse he fancies?"

"Well—I don't want to give him away—he's a young sport, a fine sport, sir. Would you mind asking him yourself? He sort of takes a pleasure in it, and perhaps he'd feel I was giving him away, sir, if you don't mind."

Bassett was serious as a church.

The uncle went back to his nephew, and took him off for a ride in the car.

"Say, Paul, old man, do you ever put anything on a horse?" the uncle asked.

The boy watched the handsome man closely.

"Why, do you think I oughtn't to?" he parried.

"Not a bit of it! I thought perhaps you might give me a tip for the Lincoln."[5]

The car sped on into the country, going down to Uncle Oscar's place in Hampshire.

11 "Honor bright?" said the nephew.

"Honor bright, son!" said the uncle.

"Well, then, Daffodil."

"Daffodil! I doubt it, sonny. What about Mirza?"

"I only know the winner," said the boy. "That's Daffodil!"

"Daffodil, eh?"

There was a pause. Daffodil was an obscure horse comparatively.

"Uncle!"

"Yes, son?"

"You won't let it go any further, will you? I promised Bassett."

---

2. **Ascot** major English horse race.
3. **batman** British military officer's orderly.
4. **blade . . . "turf"** horse-racing fan.
5. **Lincoln** major English horse race.

Literary Analysis
Theme and Symbol Bassett and the small boy "live" in the racing events. What might this detail suggest about their lives?

Reading Strategy
Identifying With a Character If you were Paul, would you feel loyal to Bassett? Why or why not?

ENRICHMENT: Career Connection

Financial Planning

Paul's mother and father can't seem to manage their money. Today, professional financial planners help people to invest their money wisely. Career opportunities abound as many more kinds of investments become available, as companies grow and expand here and overseas, as computers process and provide information on a global scale, and as individuals become more savvy about saving or investing money and more interested in preparing for longer lives. Trained people are needed to design tools; to record, interpret, and manage the data; to identify trends; and to develop strategies to advise and direct investors.

Have students look into opportunities in this field. Invite a professional who is knowledgeable about the field to address the class and answer their questions about what opportunities are available.

"Bassett be hanged, old man! What's he got to do with it?"

"We're partners! We've been partners from the first! Uncle, he lent me my first five shillings, which I lost. I promised him, honor bright, it was only between me and him: only you gave me that ten-shilling note I started winning with, so I thought you were lucky. You won't let it go any further, will you?"

The boy gazed at his uncle from those big, hot, blue eyes, set rather close together. The uncle stirred and laughed uneasily.

"Right you are, son! I'll keep your tip private. Daffodil, eh! How much are you putting on him?"

"All except twenty pounds," said the boy. "I keep that in reserve."

The uncle thought it a good joke.

"You keep twenty pounds in reserve, do you, you young romancer? What are you betting, then?"

"I'm betting three hundred," said the boy gravely. "But it's between you and me, Uncle Oscar! Honor bright?"

The uncle burst into a roar of laughter.

"It's between you and me all right, you young Nat Gould,"[6] he said, laughing. "But where's your three hundred?"

"Bassett keeps it for me. We're partners."

"You are, are you! And what is Bassett putting on Daffodil?"

"He won't go quite as high as I do, I expect. Perhaps he'll go a hundred and fifty."

"What, pennies?" laughed the uncle.

"Pounds," said the child, with a surprised look at his uncle. "Bassett keeps a bigger reserve than I do."

Between wonder and amusement, Uncle Oscar was silent. He pursued the matter no further, but he determined to take his nephew with him to the Lincoln races.

"Now, son," he said, "I'm putting twenty on Mirza, and I'll put five for you on any horse you fancy. What's your pick?"

"Daffodil, uncle!"

"No, not the fiver on Daffodil!"

"I should if it was my own five," said the child.

"Good! Good! Right you are! A fiver for me and a fiver for you on Daffodil."

12 The child had never been to a race meeting before, and his eyes were blue fire. He pursed his mouth tight, and watched. A Frenchman just in front had put his money on Lancelot. Wild with excitement, he flayed his arms up and down, yelling *"Lancelot! Lancelot!"* in his French accent.

Daffodil came in first, Lancelot second, Mirza third. The child, flushed and with eyes blazing, was curiously serene. His uncle brought him five five-pound notes: four to one.

"What am I to do with these?" he cried, waving them before the boy's eyes.

6. **Nat Gould** famous English sportswriter and authority on horse racing.

Literary Analysis
Theme, Symbol, and Third-Person Point of View What does the narrator suggest about Paul's need by describing his eyes as "blue fire"?

13 **Reading Check**
What kind of a partnership does Paul have with Bassett?

12 Literary Analysis

Theme, Symbol, and Third-Person Point of View

- Ask students why Paul thinks his Uncle Oscar is lucky.
  Answer: Paul started winning on the races with a ten-shilling note his Uncle Oscar gave him.
- Have students identify the fact that shocks Uncle Oscar in this exchange.
  Answer: Uncle Oscar learns that Paul has won a significant amount of money betting on the races.
- Ask students the Literary Analysis question on p. 1181: What does the narrator suggest about Paul's need by describing his eyes as "blue fire"?
  Possible response: Paul's need is great, because "blue fire" suggests something hot and intense.

13 Reading Check

Answer: Paul and Bassett have a trusting partnership. Bassett keeps track of Paul's winnings for him.

CUSTOMIZE INSTRUCTION FOR UNIVERSAL ACCESS

For English Learners	For Gifted/Talented Students
Point out that the word *obscure* on p. 1180, fourth line from the bottom, is formed by combining the prefix *ob-*, meaning "on" or "over," and the root *scuro*, meaning "to conceal or cover." By definition, something that is obscure lacks light, is dark, or is not easily perceived. Daffodil is what is known as a "dark horse," the unexpected winner of a race.	Have students draw a picture of Paul based on one of the descriptions of him on pp. 1180–1181. Encourage them to pay particular attention to his eyes as they are described in several places. They might draw Paul in conversation with his Uncle, or at the racetrack.

⓮ Reading Strategy

Identifying With a Character

- Have students describe how Bassett and Paul became friends. **Answer:** Paul asked Bassett about racing, and they found they had a common interest.
- Have students determine whether Bassett and Paul have a trusting relationship. How do students know? **Answer:** The two have a trusting relationship. They both contribute to telling the story to Uncle Oscar. Bassett keeps silent about how much Paul has won until Paul tells Uncle Oscar.
- Ask students the Reading Strategy question on p. 1182: In what way does Bassett serve as a substitute father or older brother for Paul? **Answer:** Bassett listens and talks to Paul, shares interests with him, keeps his confidence, and provides a supportive male figure for the boy.

⓯ Vocabulary Development

Latin Prefix: *ob-*

- Point out the word *obstinately* to students. Explain that the Latin prefix *ob-* can mean "before," "to," or "against."
- Using the definition provided in the margin, have students explain how the meaning of this prefix contributes to the overall meaning of the word. If students cannot explain, have them use a dictionary to find out the etymology of the word.
- Then, ask students to suggest other words that contain this prefix and to offer definitions of each word.

"I suppose we'll talk to Bassett," said the boy. "I expect I have fifteen hundred now; and twenty in reserve; and this twenty."

His uncle studied him for some moments.

"Look here, son!" he said. "You're not serious about Bassett and that fifteen hundred, are you?"

"Yes, I am. But it's between you and me, uncle! Honor bright!"

"Honor bright all right, son! But I must talk to Bassett."

"If you'd like to be a partner, uncle, with Bassett and me, we could all be partners. Only you'd have to promise, honor bright, uncle, not to let it go beyond us three. Bassett and I are lucky, and you must be

⓮ lucky, because it was your ten shillings I started winning with. . . ."

Uncle Oscar took both Bassett and Paul into Richmond Park for an afternoon, and there they talked.

"It's like this, you see, sir," Bassett said. "Master Paul would get me talking about racing events, spinning yarns, you know, sir. And he was always keen on knowing if I'd made or if I'd lost. It's about a year since, now, that I put five shillings on Blush of Dawn for him—and we lost. Then the luck turned, with that ten shillings he had from you, that we put on Singhalese. And since that time, it's been pretty steady, all things considering. What do you say, Master Paul?"

Reading Strategy
Identifying With a Character In what way does Bassett serve as a substitute father or older brother for Paul?

"We're all right when we're *sure*," said Paul. "It's when we're not quite sure that we go down."

"Oh, but we're careful then," said Bassett.

"But when are you *sure*?" smiled Uncle Oscar.

"It's Master Paul, sir," said Bassett, in a secret, religious voice. "It's as if he had it from heaven. Like Daffodil now, for the Lincoln. That was as sure as eggs."

"Did you put anything on Daffodil?" asked Oscar Cresswell.

"Yes, sir. I made my bit."

"And my nephew?"

⓯ Bassett was obstinately silent, looking at Paul.

obstinately (äb′ stə nət lē) *adv.* in a determined way; stubbornly

"I made twelve hundred, didn't I, Bassett? I told uncle I was putting three hundred on Daffodil."

"That's right," said Bassett, nodding.

"But where's the money?" asked the uncle.

"I keep it safe locked up, sir. Master Paul, he can have it any minute he likes to ask for it."

"What, fifteen hundred pounds?"

"And twenty! And *forty*, that is, with the twenty he made on the course."

"It's amazing!" said the uncle.

"If Master Paul offers you to be partners, sir, I would, if I were you; if you'll excuse me," said Bassett.

Oscar Cresswell thought about it.

"I'll see the money," he said.

They drove home again, and sure enough, Bassett came round to the garden house with fifteen hundred pounds in notes. The twenty pounds reserve was left with Joe Glee, in the Turf Commission deposit.

ENRICHMENT: Literature Connection

Uncle Oscar/Oscar Wilde

Point out that Uncle Oscar is always joking, that he supplies Paul with the whip for his rocking horse, and that he gives Paul the incentive to keep wagering. Tell students that Uncle Oscar may be an allusion to Oscar Wilde, who prefaced his Gothic novel *The Picture of Dorian Gray* with the words "there is no such thing as a moral or immoral book." The character Uncle Oscar echoes Wilde's individualism and his ideas on morality. The "changeable" name of Paul's horse suggests a reference to Wilde's pen name, Speranza. Just as Wilde firmly believed that art must stand apart from life, Uncle Oscar, like the story's omniscient narrator, stays emotionally aloof.

"You see, it's all right, uncle, when I'm *sure!* Then we go strong, for all we're worth. Don't we, Bassett?"

"We do that, Master Paul."

"And when are you sure?" said the uncle, laughing.

16 "Oh, well, sometimes I'm *absolutely* sure, like about Daffodil," said the boy, "and sometimes I have an idea; and sometimes I haven't even an idea, have I, Bassett? Then we're careful, because we mostly go down."

"You do, do you! And when you're sure, like about Daffodil, what makes you sure, sonny?"

"Oh, well, I don't know," said the boy uneasily. "I'm sure, you know, uncle; that's all."

"It's as if he had it from heaven, sir," Bassett reiterated.

"I should say so!" said the uncle.

But he became a partner. And when the Leger was coming on, Paul was "sure" about Lively Spark, which was a quite inconsiderable horse. The boy insisted on putting a thousand on the horse, Bassett went for five hundred, and Oscar Cresswell two hundred. Lively Spark came in first, and the betting had been ten to one against him. Paul had made ten thousand.

"You see," he said. "I was absolutely sure of him."

Even Oscar Cresswell had cleared two thousand.

"Look here, son," he said, "this sort of thing makes me nervous."

"It needn't, uncle! Perhaps I shan't be sure again for a long time."

"But what are you going to do with your money?" asked the uncle.

"Of course," said the boy, "I started it for mother. She said she had no luck, because father is unlucky, so I thought if *I* was lucky, it might stop whispering."

"What might stop whispering?"

"Our house! I *hate* our house for whispering."

"What does it whisper?"

"Why—why"—the boy fidgeted—"why, I don't know! But it's always short of money, you know, uncle."

"I know it, son, I know it."

"You know people send mother writs, don't you, uncle?"

"I'm afraid I do," said the uncle.

"And then the house whispers like people laughing at you behind your back. It's awful, that is! I thought if I was lucky . . ."

"You might stop it," added the uncle.

The boy watched him with big blue eyes, that had an uncanny cold fire in them, and he said never a word.

"Well then!" said the uncle. "What are we doing?"

17 ▲ **Critical Viewing**
In what way does this picture give you a perspective on Paul's furious riding of his rocking horse? Explain. **[Connect]**

uncanny (un kan´ ē) *adj.* mysterious; hard to explain

18 **Reading Check**
Why does Paul want to win money?

16 Critical Thinking

Compare and Contrast

- Ask students to describe the hierarchy of sureness that Bassett and Paul use when betting on the horses.
  Answer: When Paul is *absolutely* sure, they bet a lot of money; when Paul has an idea, they bet less; and when Paul has no idea at all, they bet very little, because they usually lose.
- Ask students to compare and contrast the beliefs of Bassett and Paul as to why Paul is able to predict the winning racers.
  Answer: Bassett thinks the answers come from God; Paul says he's just sure, but he doesn't know why.

17 ▶ Critical Viewing

Possible response: Because Paul is still a small boy, he has to ride furiously in order to make the horse move at all.

18 Reading Check

Answer: Paul wants to win money so he can give it to his mother and so the house will stop whispering.

CUSTOMIZE INSTRUCTION FOR UNIVERSAL ACCESS

For Special Needs Students	For Less Proficient Readers	For Gifted/Talented Students
Have students work in groups of three to prepare the two scenes of dialogue on pp. 1182 and 1183: the first among Bassett, Uncle Oscar, and Paul and the second between Uncle Oscar and Paul. Have them use their bodies and voices to communicate the excitement of the scenes.	Have students decide whether there are other characters besides Paul in the story with whom they might identify. Have them make a character web for Uncle Oscar and Bassett, as well as for Paul's mother.	Have students use context to determine the meaning of the British usages in phrases such as *spinning yarns*, *sure as eggs*, and *I'll see the money.*

19 Literary Analysis

Theme and Symbol

- Ask students to summarize the plan that Paul and Uncle Oscar formulate for using the money.
  Answer: Paul will give 5,000 pounds of his winnings to Uncle Oscar. Oscar will deposit it with the family lawyer, who will inform Paul's mother that she is to receive 1,000 pounds on each birthday for five years.
- Have students identify the experience Paul has as his mother's birthday approaches.
  Answer: Paul hears the house "whispering" worse than ever.
- Ask students what they think the "whispering" symbolizes in this story.
  Possible answer: The whispering symbolizes the degree of the mother's nervousness and worry, as experienced by her son.

20 Reading Strategy

Identifying With a Character

- Ask students what additional disappointment Paul's mother has had just before her birthday.
  Answer: She has been disappointed because she cannot earn more money with drawing.
- Have students describe Paul's mother's reaction to the letter she receives in the mail on her birthday.
  Answer: She reads it, gets a cold look on her face and buries the letter in a pile of others.
- Ask students the Reading Strategy question on p. 1184: How would you feel about your mother's reaction to the letter if you were Paul? Why?
  Possible response: They would be hurt or surprised, because they would have expected their mother to be excited about the extra money.

"I shouldn't like mother to know I was lucky," said the boy.

"Why not, son?"

"She'd stop me."

"I don't think she would."

"Oh!"—and the boy writhed in an odd way—"I *don't* want her to know, uncle."

"All right, son! We'll manage it without her knowing."

They managed it very easily. Paul, at the other's suggestion, handed over five thousand pounds to his uncle, who deposited it with the family lawyer, who was then to inform Paul's mother that a relative had put five thousand pounds into his hands, which sum was to be paid out a thousand pounds at a time, on the mother's birthday, for the next five years.

"So she'll have a birthday present of a thousand pounds for five successive years," said Uncle Oscar. "I hope it won't make it all the harder for her later."

19 Paul's mother had her birthday in November. The house had been "whispering" worse than ever lately, and even in spite of his luck, Paul could not bear up against it. He was very anxious to see the effect of the birthday letter, telling his mother about the thousand pounds.

When there were no visitors, Paul now took his meals with his parents, as he was beyond the nursery control. His mother went into town nearly every day. She had discovered that she had an odd knack of sketching furs and dress materials, so she worked secretly in the studio of a friend who was the chief "artist" for the leading drapers. She drew the figures of ladies in furs and ladies in silk and sequins for the newspaper advertisements. This young woman artist earned several thousand pounds a year, but Paul's mother only made several hundreds, and she was again dissatisfied. She so wanted to be first in something, and she did not succeed, even in making sketches for drapery advertisements.

20 She was down to breakfast on the morning of her birthday. Paul watched her face as she read her letters. He knew the lawyer's letter. As his mother read it, her face hardened and became more expressionless. Then a cold, determined look came on her mouth. She hid the letter under the pile of others, and said not a word about it.

"Didn't you have anything nice in the post for your birthday, mother?" said Paul.

"Quite moderately nice," she said, her voice cold and absent.

She went away to town without saying more.

But in the afternoon Uncle Oscar appeared. He said Paul's mother had had a long interview with the lawyer, asking if the whole five thousand could not be advanced at once, as she was in debt.

"What do you think, uncle?" said the boy.

"I leave it to you, son."

"Oh, let her have it, then! We can get some more with the other," said the boy.

Reading Strategy Identifying With a Character How would you feel about your mother's reaction to the letter if you were Paul? Why?

ENRICHMENT: Math Connection

Probability

When Paul picks his winners, he pays no attention to which horses are favored and which are "dark horses." For him, the choice of a winner is based on a mysterious process of intuition, not on science or mathematics. The mathematical study of probability deals with the likelihood that events will occur. This field of study can be quite complex. A simple example of probability, however, involves the tossing of a die with six faces. The probability of one face appearing is equal to the ratio of that event (1) over the number of possible outcomes (6). Therefore, the probability of throwing a die and having a particular face come up is 1/6.

However, here is a point about probability that many people do not understand. The die has no memory. You might think that having thrown a particular face four times in succession, you have a lesser chance of throwing it on the next, or fifth throw. This is wrong. The probability of throwing the same face again is still 1/6.

"A bird in the hand is worth two in the bush, laddie!" said Uncle Oscar.

"But I'm sure to *know* for the Grand National; or the Lincolnshire; or else the Derby.[7] I'm sure to know for *one* of them," said Paul.

So Uncle Oscar signed the agreement, and Paul's mother touched the whole five thousand. Then something very curious happened. The voices in the house suddenly went mad, like a chorus of frogs on a spring evening. There were certain new furnishings, and Paul had a tutor. He was *really* going to Eton,[8] his father's school, in the following autumn. There were flowers in the winter, and a blossoming of the luxury Paul's mother had been used to. And yet the voices in the house, behind the sprays of mimosa and almond blossom, and from under the piles of iridescent cushions, simply trilled and screamed in a sort of ecstasy: "There *must* be more money! Oh-h-h! There *must* be more money! Oh, now, now-w! now-w-w—there *must* be more money!—more than ever! More than ever!"

It frightened Paul terribly. He studied away at his Latin and Greek
21 with his tutors. But his intense hours were spent with Bassett. The Grand National had gone by: he had not "known," and had lost a hundred pounds. Summer was at hand. He was in agony for the Lincoln. But even for the Lincoln he didn't "know," and he lost fifty pounds. He became wild-eyed and strange, as if something were going to explode in him.

"Let it alone, son! Don't you bother about it!" urged Uncle Oscar. But it was as if the boy couldn't really hear what his uncle was saying.

"I've got to know for the Derby! I've *got* to know for the Derby!" the child reiterated, his big blue eyes blazing with a sort of madness.

His mother noticed how overwrought he was.

"You'd better go to the seaside. Wouldn't you like to go now to the seaside, instead of waiting? I think you'd better," she said, looking down at him anxiously, her heart curiously heavy because of him.

But the child lifted his uncanny blue eyes.

"I couldn't possibly go before the Derby, mother!" he said. "I couldn't possibly!"

"Why not?" she said, her voice becoming heavy when she was opposed. "Why not? You can still go from the seaside to see the Derby with your Uncle Oscar, if that's what you wish. No need for you to wait here. Besides, I think you care too much about these races. It's a bad sign. My family has been a gambling family, and you won't know till you grow up how much damage it has done. But it has done damage. I shall have to send Bassett away, and ask Uncle Oscar not to talk racing to you, unless you promise to be reasonable about it; go away to the seaside and forget it. You're all nerves!"

"I'll do what you like, mother, so long as you don't send me away till after the Derby," the boy said.

7. **Grand National . . . Derby** major English horse races.
8. **Eton** prestigious private school in England.

Literary Analysis
Theme, Symbol, and Third-Person Point of View If the story were told from Paul's point of view, would you know about the mother's "curiously heavy" feelings concerning Paul? Why or why not?

22  **Reading Check**
What present does Paul give his mother?

21 Literary Analysis
Theme, Symbol, and Third-Person Point of View

- Ask students what happens after Paul's mother gets the whole 5,000 pounds.
  Answer: She buys many new things, Paul gets a tutor, and the voices go mad.
- Have students describe what happens to Paul's predictions of winners for the horse races.
  Answer: He does not "know" about winning horses for two major races and loses money on both of them.
- Ask students what Paul's mother decides to do when she sees Paul getting so overwrought.
  Answer: She decides to send him to the seashore.
- Ask students the Literary Analysis question on p. 1185: If the story were told from Paul's point of view, would you know about the mother's "curiously heavy" feelings concerning Paul? Why or why not?
  Answer: If the story were told from Paul's point of view, readers would know only the feelings of Paul.

22  Reading Check

Answer: Paul gives his mother 5,000 pounds of his winnings at the races.

CUSTOMIZE INSTRUCTION FOR UNIVERSAL ACCESS

For Special Needs Students	For Gifted/Talented Students	For Advanced Readers
Guide students to understand that in households like this one, parents were relieved of the "burden" of messy meals with their small children. Paul is now at an age when he may dine with the grown-ups. Ask students to look for more evidence in the story that this family has a privileged place in society.	Have students design a sculpture, paint a picture, or choreograph a dance that captures the intensity of young Paul's trying to prevent his mother from sending him away before the Derby. Encourage students to consider abstract as well as representational possibilities.	Ask students to identify and explain the personification in the long paragraph at the top of p. 1185. (The atmosphere of the house is personified as a crowd of voices. The talk is always of money, more money, and the personification symbolizes the demands that an environment or emotional climate can make.)

23 Critical Thinking

Interpret

- Ask why Paul does not want to go to the seashore before the Derby.
  Answer: Paul does not want to leave the house.
- Ask students why they think Paul is desperate not to leave the house.
  Possible response: There is something about being in the house that allows Paul to be "sure" when he guesses the horse race winners.
- Have students interpret Paul's thoughts when the narrator says, "He had a secret within a secret, something he had not divulged. . . ."
  Answer: Paul has a secret about something that is a part of the other secret the reader already knows—that the money Paul's mother has received is from Paul.

24 Literary Analysis

Theme and Symbol

- Ask what Paul's mother said when he asked to have his rocking horse moved to his bedroom.
  Answer: Paul's mother said, "Surely you're too big for a rocking horse!"
- Ask students what is ironic about the mother's statement.
  Possible response: The statement is ironic because it indicates that the mother sees Paul as a child, when it is his acting like an adult that has brought her the recent 5,000 pounds.
- Ask students the Literary Analysis question on p. 1186: In the paragraph beginning, "Paul's secret . . . ," which words or phrases suggest that the rocking horse is a symbol?
  Answer: The phrase "that which had no name" suggests that the horse is a symbol for luck, for success—for that which will win him his mother's love.

"Send you away from where? Just from this house?"

"Yes," he said, gazing at her.

23 "Why, you curious child, what makes you care about this house so much, suddenly? I never knew you loved it!"

He gazed at her without speaking. He had a secret within a secret, something he had not divulged, even to Bassett or to his Uncle Oscar.

But his mother, after standing undecided and a little bit sullen for some moments, said:

"Very well, then! Don't go to the seaside till after the Derby, if you don't wish it. But promise me you won't let your nerves go to pieces! Promise you won't think so much about horse racing and *events*, as you call them!"

"Oh, no!" said the boy, casually. "I won't think much about them, mother. You needn't worry. I wouldn't worry, mother, if I were you."

"If you were me and I were you," said his mother, "I wonder what we should do!"

"But you know you needn't worry, mother, don't you?" the boy repeated.

"I should be awfully glad to know it," she said wearily.

"Oh, well, you *can*, you know. I mean you *ought* to know you needn't worry!" he insisted.

"Ought I? Then I'll see about it," she said.

24 Paul's secret of secrets was his wooden horse, that which had no name. Since he was emancipated from a nurse and a nursery governess, he had had his rocking horse removed to his own bedroom at the top of the house.

"Surely you're too big for a rocking horse!" his mother had remonstrated.

"Well, you see, mother, till I can have a *real* horse, I like to have *some* sort of animal about," had been his quaint answer.

Literary Analysis

Theme and Symbol In the paragraph beginning, "Paul's secret . . . ," which words or phrases suggest that the rocking horse is a symbol?

remonstrated (ri män′ strāt id) *v.* objected strongly

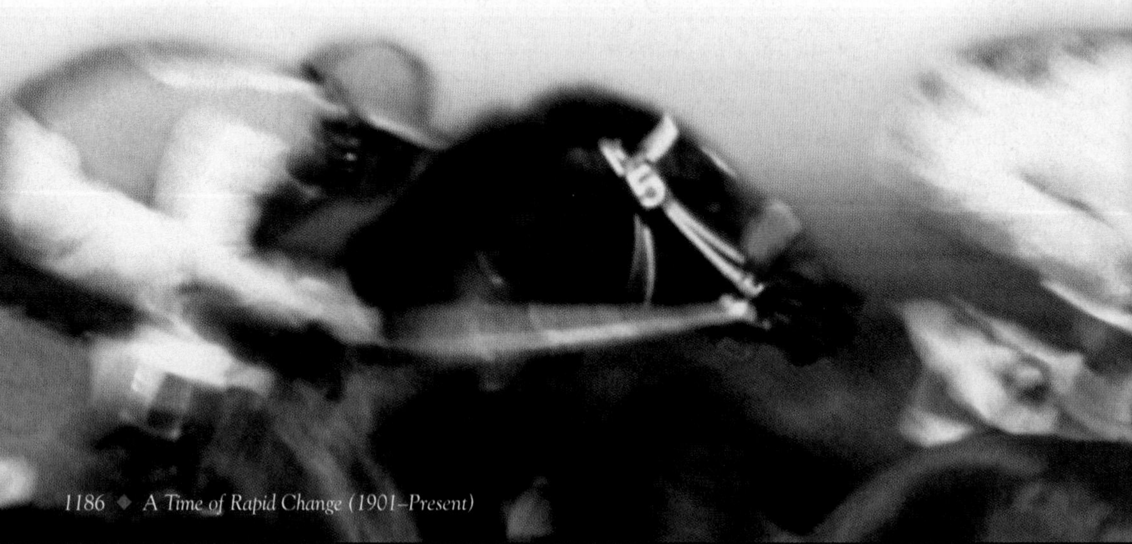

ENRICHMENT: Literature Connection

Literary Criticism

"The Rocking-Horse Winner," like much of Lawrence's work, has sparked a huge output of critical commentary. In an article entitled, "A Rocking Horse: The Symbol, the Pattern, the Way to Live," critic W. D. Snodgrass examines the names of the horses on which Paul, Bassett, and Oscar gamble. He notes that the first winner, Singhalese, and his last, Malabar, have names of former British colonial regions in India. He sees in another name, Mirza, the suggestion of a third colony, Mirzapur. Snodgrass suggests that Lawrence deliberately selected these names and that he sees a parallel between Paul's fate and the fate of the British Empire.

"Do you feel he keeps you company?" she laughed.

"Oh, yes! He's very good, he always keeps me company, when I'm there," said Paul.

So the horse, rather shabby, stood in an arrested prance in the boy's bedroom.

25 The Derby was drawing near, and the boy grew more and more tense. He hardly heard what was spoken to him, he was very frail, and his eyes were really uncanny. His mother had sudden strange seizures of uneasiness about him. Sometimes, for half an hour, she would feel a sudden anxiety about him that was almost anguish. She wanted to rush to him at once, and know he was safe.

Two nights before the Derby, she was at a big party in town, when one of her rushes of anxiety about her boy, her firstborn, gripped her heart till she could hardly speak. She fought with the feeling, might and main, for she believed in common sense. But it was too strong. She had to leave the dance and go downstairs to telephone to the country. The children's nursery governess was terribly surprised and startled at being rung up in the night.

26 "Are the children all right, Miss Wilmot?"

"Oh yes, they are quite all right."

"Master Paul? Is he all right?"

"He went to bed as right as a trivet.[9] Shall I run up and look at him?"

"No!" said Paul's mother reluctantly. "No! Don't trouble. It's all right. Don't sit up. We shall be home fairly soon." She did not want her son's privacy intruded upon.

"Very good," said the governess.

Literary Analysis
Theme, Symbol, and Third-Person Point of View Does the third-person narrator's insight into the mother's anxiety make you feel more sympathy for her? Explain.

 **Reading Check**
Why is Paul especially tense just before the Derby?

9. **right as a trivet** perfectly right.

25 Background

Conflicts Abroad and at Home

Discuss with students that Paul, by betting on the horses in tandem with Bassett and Uncle Oscar, hopes to alleviate the conflict at home between his mother's desire to have a certain lifestyle and the family's inability to pay for it. Have students link this conflict with Britain's struggle to maintain its empire.

26 Literary Analysis

Theme, Symbol, and Third-Person Point of View

- Ask students to compare the house's "whispering" to Paul with his mother's seizures of anxiety about him.
  Answer: Paul's mother's sudden seizures of anxiety are symbolic of Paul's stress over the racing losses, just as the "whispering" is symbolic of his mother's fears about money.
- Ask students the Literary Analysis question on p. 1187: Does the third-person narrator's insight into the mother's anxiety make you feel sympathy for her? Explain.
  Possible response: Knowing that she can feel anxiety and worry about Paul makes her seem less cold and more concerned. This makes her more sympathetic to the readers.

27 Reading Check

Answer: Paul has already lost money on two previous races because he hasn't "known" who the winner would be. He really wants to "know" which horse to choose for the Derby.

CUSTOMIZE INSTRUCTION FOR UNIVERSAL ACCESS

For Less Proficient Readers	For English Learners	For Gifted/Talented Students
Guide students to understand that Paul's secret is that he finds his winners by riding furiously on the rocking horse.	Explain that Paul is obsessed with finding the Derby winner. Define *obsession* as "a persistent preoccupation with an idea or emotion." Point out the word comes from the Latin *ob-* meaning "toward," "over," or "against," and *sedere,* meaning "to sit."	Ask students why they think the author left the father out of this story, except for introducing him at the beginning and having him go out to dinner with the mother toward the end. What plot reasons might Lawrence have had for making this decision? What thematic reasons might he have had?

28 Literary Analysis

Theme and Symbol

- Have students explain why the mother goes up to Paul's room when she returns from her evening out.
  Answer: She has been anxious about him all evening and she is still anxious even though she is home now.
- Ask what the mother finds when she throws open the door to Paul's bedroom.
  Answer: She finds Paul riding his rocking horse in a frenzy.
- Ask students the Literary Analysis question on p. 1188: In what way is the rocking horse connected with the whispering of the house?
  Possible response: The noise of the rocking horse and the noise of the "whispering" are symbolic and reflect the anguished feelings of people in the house.

29 Critical Thinking

Deduce

- Ask students if they think Paul is riding for enjoyment when his mother finds him. Why or why not?
  Answer: Paul screams in a powerful, strange voice, and his eyes blaze at her. This suggests that his riding is not enjoyable but obsessive.
- Ask students who Malabar is, and how they know.
  Answer: Since earlier hints suggest that the rocking horse has something to do with Paul's choices, and since Paul wants to stay in the house until the Derby, students can deduce that Malabar will be the Derby winner.

It was about one o'clock when Paul's mother and father drove up to their house. All was still. Paul's mother went to her room and slipped off her white fur cloak. She had told her maid not to wait up for her. She heard her husband downstairs, mixing a whisky-and-soda.

And then, because of the strange anxiety at her heart, she stole upstairs to her son's room. Noiselessly she went along the upper corridor. Was there a faint noise? What was it?

28 She stood, with arrested muscles, outside his door, listening. There was a strange, heavy, and yet not loud noise. Her heart stood still. It was a soundless noise, yet rushing and powerful. Something huge, in violent, hushed motion. What was it? What in God's name was it? She ought to know. She felt that she *knew* the noise. She knew what it was.

Yet she could not place it. She couldn't say what it was. And on and on it went, like madness.

Softly, frozen with anxiety and fear, she turned the door handle.

The room was dark. Yet in the space near the window, she heard and saw something plunging to and fro. She gazed in fear and amazement.

Then suddenly she switched on the light, and saw her son, in his green pajamas, madly surging on his rocking horse. The blaze of light suddenly lit him up, as he urged the wooden horse, and lit her up, as she stood, blond, in her dress of pale green and crystal, in the doorway.

"Paul!" she cried. "Whatever are you doing?"

29 "It's Malabar!" he screamed, in a powerful, strange voice. "It's Malabar!"

His eyes blazed at her for one strange and senseless second, as he ceased urging his wooden horse. Then he fell with a crash to the ground, and she, all her tormented motherhood flooding upon her, rushed to gather him up.

But he was unconscious, and unconscious he remained, with some brain fever. He talked and tossed, and his mother sat stonily by his side.

"Malabar! It's Malabar! Bassett, Bassett, I *know* it's Malabar!"

So the child cried, trying to get up and urge the rocking horse that gave him his inspiration.

"What does he mean by Malabar?" asked the heart-frozen mother.

"I don't know," said the father, stonily.

"What does he mean by Malabar?" she asked her brother Oscar.

"It's one of the horses running for the Derby," was the answer.

And, in spite of himself, Oscar Cresswell spoke to Bassett, and himself put a thousand on Malabar: at fourteen to one.

The third day of the illness was critical: they were watching for a change. The boy, with his rather long, curly hair, was tossing ceaselessly on the pillow. He neither slept nor regained consciousness, and his eyes were like blue stones. His mother sat, feeling her heart had gone, turned actually into a stone.

In the evening, Oscar Cresswell did not come, but Bassett sent a message, saying could he come up for one moment, just one moment?

Literary Analysis
Theme and Symbol In what way is the rocking horse connected with the whispering of the house?

ENRICHMENT: Film Connection

***The Rocking-Horse Winner*, 1949, directed by Anthony Pelissier**

The director wrote the screenplay for this beautifully done adaptation. Show the film and invite students to compare and contrast it with Lawrence's story. Use these questions for discussion:

1. Are the characters in the film faithful to the story? Explain.
   Answer: Students may point to the more sympathetic portrayal of the mother in the film and to the fact that the boy is portrayed as being much older than the very young child shown in the photo that accompanies this text.
2. How do the visual images in the film compare with the mental images you formed when reading the story?
   Possible response: The movie version takes place much later, perhaps in the 1930s or 1940s, and the family's home is more opulent than readers of the story might have imagined.

Paul's mother was very angry at the intrusion, but on second thoughts she agreed. The boy was the same. Perhaps Bassett might bring him to consciousness.

The gardener, a shortish fellow with a little brown moustache and sharp little brown eyes, tiptoed into the room, touched his imaginary cap to Paul's mother, and stole to the bedside, staring with glittering, smallish eyes at the tossing, dying child.

"Master Paul!" he whispered. "Master Paul! Malabar came in first all right, a clean win. I did as you told me. You've made over seventy thousand pounds, you have; you've got over eighty thousand. Malabar came in all right, Master Paul."

"Malabar! Malabar! Did I say Malabar, mother? Did I say Malabar? Do you think I'm lucky, mother? I knew Malabar, didn't I? Over eighty thousand pounds! I call that lucky, don't you, mother? Over eighty thousand pounds! I knew, didn't I know I knew? Malabar came in all right. If I ride my horse till I'm sure, then I tell you, Bassett, you can go as high as you like. Did you go for all you were worth, Bassett?"

"I went a thousand on it, Master Paul."

"I never told you, mother, that if I can ride my horse, and *get there,* then I'm absolutely sure—oh, absolutely! Mother, did I ever tell you? I *am* lucky!"

"No, you never did," said the mother.

But the boy died in the night.

30 And even as he lay dead, his mother heard her brother's voice saying to her: "My God, Hester, you're eighty-odd thousand to the good, and a poor devil of a son to the bad. But, poor devil, poor devil, he's best gone out of a life where he rides his rocking horse to find a winner."

Literary Analysis
Theme and Symbol In explaining the meaning of Paul's brief life, what would you add to his uncle's final words about him?

Review and Assess

Thinking About the Selection

1. **Respond:** Which character in this story did you find most likable? Least likable? Explain.
2. **(a) Recall:** From the point of view of Paul's mother, what is the main problem of the family? **(b) Infer:** What does the mother's statement that the father is "unlucky" suggest about her values?
3. **(a) Recall:** Over the course of the story, how does Paul react to the house's "whispers"?
   (b) Analyze Cause and Effect: Why is he affected as he is?
4. **(a) Recall:** What does Uncle Oscar say at the end of the story? **(b) Interpret:** Do you think Uncle Oscar is speaking for the author? Why or why not?
5. **Take a Position:** What, if anything, is more important than the luck and money that Paul's mother wanted so desperately?

30 Literary Analysis

Theme and Symbol

- Ask students why they think Bassett asks to see Paul.
  Answer: Bassett cares about Paul and also wants to tell him he chose the winning horse.
- Ask students the Literary Analysis question on p. 1189: In explaining the meaning of Paul's brief life, what would you add to his uncle's final words about him?
  Possible answer: He died a victim of the family's greed.

Answers for p. 1189

Review and Assess

1. Students may suggest that Bassett and Uncle Oscar were the most likable and that Paul's mother was the least likable.
2. **(a)** The family's main problem is that it is not lucky. **(b)** Her statement suggests that she believes one's life is ruled by fate, not by one's own actions.
3. **(a)** The continuing whispers fuel Paul's frenzied attempts to find luck. **(b)** He wants to help his mother so that she will love him.
4. **(a)** He says "My God, Hester, you're eighty-odd thousand to the good, and a poor devil of a son to the bad. But, poor devil, poor devil, he's best gone out of a life where he rides his rocking horse to find a winner."
   (b) Possible response: Oscar seems to be speaking for the author because his statement forms a thematic summary of the story.
5. Possible responses: Love, satisfying work, and happiness are more important.

31 About the Selection

In this story about the absurdities of life, a prep school boy learns that his father, whom he hardly knows and whom he has romanticized, has died in an abrupt, embarrassing manner: A pig fell on him. The bizarre nature of this accident haunts the young man as he grows up, making him feel isolated and odd. In a surprising twist at the end of the story, his intended bride doesn't laugh when she hears the story for the first time. Her sympathetic response shows that even in the face of absurdity, people can find comfort and a measure of stability. Ironically, the young man's sense of humiliation ends when another person appreciates the ghastliness of his father's absurd death.

32 Background

English Boarding Schools

Tell students that here the author is describing routines in one of England's private boarding schools. These preparatory schools, which are largely the domain of the wealthy, are called "public schools."

33 Reading Strategy

Identifying With a Character

- Have students read the first two sentences in the passage and explain what the writer means.
  Answer: Jerome worshiped his father as other people worship God.
- Ask what Jerome imagines his father to be, and what his father really is.
  Answer: Jerome imagines his father as a gunrunner or a member of the British Secret Service. Actually, he is a writer whose wife has died.
- Ask students the Reading Strategy question on p. 1190: If you were Jerome, what might be your reasons for romanticizing your absent father's job?
  Possible response: Jerome, a boarding school student who doesn't have a close relationship with his father, may romanticize what his father does to justify why his father is away so much and pays so little attention to him. The father's job is just too important for him to give time to Jerome.

31 A Shocking Accident

Graham Greene

1

Jerome was called into his housemaster's room in the break between the second and the third class on a Thursday morning. He had no fear of trouble, for he was a warden—the name that the proprietor and headmaster of a rather expensive preparatory school had chosen to give to approved, reliable boys in the lower forms (from a warden one became a guardian and finally before leaving, it was hoped for Marlborough or Rugby, a crusader). The housemaster, Mr. Wordsworth, sat behind his desk with an appearance of perplexity and apprehension. Jerome had the odd impression when he entered that he was a cause of fear.

apprehension (ap′ rē hen′ shən) *n.* anxious feeling of foreboding; dread

"Sit down, Jerome," Mr. Wordsworth said. "All going well with the trigonometry?"

"Yes, sir."

"I've had a telephone call, Jerome. From your aunt. I'm afraid I have bad news for you."

"Yes, sir?"

"Your father has had an accident."

"Oh."

Mr. Wordsworth looked at him with some surprise. "A serious accident."

"Yes, sir?"

Jerome worshipped his father: the verb is exact. As man re-creates God, so Jerome re-created his father—from a restless widowed author into a mysterious adventurer who traveled in far places—Nice, Beirut, Majorca, even the Canaries. The time had arrived about his eighth birthday when Jerome believed that his father either "ran guns" or was a member of the British Secret Service. Now it occurred to him that his father might have been wounded in "a hail of machine-gun bullets."

Reading Strategy Identifying With a Character If you were Jerome, what might be your reasons for romanticizing your absent father's job?

Mr. Wordsworth played with the ruler on his desk. He seemed at a loss how to continue. He said, "You knew your father was in Naples?"

"Yes, sir."

"Your aunt heard from the hospital today."

"Oh."

Mr. Wordsworth said with desperation, "It was a street accident."

"Yes, sir?" It seemed quite likely to Jerome that they would call it

ENRICHMENT: Career Connection

Travel Writer

Jerome's father was neither a Secret Service agent nor a mysterious adventurer. He did, in fact, have a job that many people would envy: He was a travel writer. Have students imagine a life that consists of exploring the world's exciting regions, acquainting oneself with the bounties of its cultures, tasting different foods, meeting all kinds of people, and staying in fine hotels and inns. Is travel writing a job students would want to have? Have the class brainstorm a list of the pros and cons of such an occupation. Students can verify their suggestions by interviewing a travel writer, or by reading travel writings.

Have interested students examine travel books at a local bookstore, at the library, or on the Internet. Ask them to suggest ways that they, as future travel writers, would distinguish themselves in the field. What aspects of travel would they focus on? What would they de-emphasize? How would their books be different from others in the field? Have students share their responses.

a street accident. The police, of course, had fired first; his father would not take human life except as a last resort.

"I'm afraid your father was very seriously hurt indeed."

"Oh."

34 "In fact, Jerome, he died yesterday. Quite without pain."

"Did they shoot him through the heart?"

"I beg your pardon. What did you say, Jerome?"

"Did they shoot him through the heart?"

"Nobody shot him, Jerome. A pig fell on him." An inexplicable convulsion took place in the nerves of Mr. Wordsworth's face; it really looked for a moment as though he were going to laugh. He closed his eyes, composed his features, and said rapidly, as though it were necessary to expel the story as rapidly as possible, "Your father was walking along a street in Naples when a pig fell on him. A shocking accident. Apparently in the poorer quarters of Naples they keep pigs on their balconies. This one was on the fifth floor. It had grown too fat. The balcony broke. The pig fell on your father."

Mr. Wordsworth left his desk rapidly and went to the window, turning his back on Jerome. He shook a little with emotion.

Jerome said, "What happened to the pig?"

Literary Analysis
Theme and Symbol Do you think that the way Jerome's father died could be symbolic? Why or why not?

embarked (em bärkt′) *v.* engaged in something, such as a conversation

35 **▼ Critical Viewing** How well does this photograph convey Jerome's reaction to his father's death? **[Evaluate]**

2

This was not callousness on the part of Jerome as it was interpreted by Mr. Wordsworth to his colleagues (he even discussed with them whether, perhaps, Jerome was not yet fitted to be a warden). Jerome was only attempting to visualize the strange scene and to get the details right. Nor was Jerome a boy who cried; he was a boy who brooded, and it never occurred to him at his preparatory school that the circumstances of his father's death were comic—they were still part of the mystery of life. It was later in his first term at his public school, when he told the story to his best friend, that he began to realize how it affected others. Naturally, after that disclosure he was known, rather unreasonably, as Pig.

Unfortunately his aunt had no sense of humor. There was an enlarged snap-shot of his father on the piano: a large sad man in an unsuitable dark suit posed in Capri with an umbrella (to guard him against sunstroke), the Faraglioni rocks forming the background. By the age of sixteen Jerome was well aware that the portrait looked more like the author of *Sunshine and Shade* and *Rambles in the Balearics* than an agent of the Secret Service. All the same, he loved the memory of his father: he still possessed an album filled with picture-postcards (the stamps had been soaked off long ago for his other collection), and it pained him when his aunt embarked with strangers on the story of his father's death.

"A shocking accident," she would begin, and the stranger would compose his or her features into the correct shape for interest and commiseration. Both reactions, of course, were false,

34 Literary Analysis

Theme and Symbol

- As students read the first eight lines of p. 1191, ask them how they think Jerome's father died.
  Possible response: Since Mr. Wordsworth says he died in a street accident, the father probably was hit by a car or a bus.
- Ask students what their first response is on hearing that Jerome's father died because a pig fell on him.
  Possible response: Students probably laughed and wondered how the accident happened. Some may have worried about the pig.
- Ask students the Literary Analysis question on p. 1191: Do you think that the way Jerome's father died could be symbolic? Why or why not?
  Possible response: The manner of death is symbolic of the absurdity and unexpectedness of life and death.

35 ▶Critical Viewing

Possible response: The boy looks thoughtful, as if he were trying to puzzle something out, which is what Jerome feels when he hears the news of his father's death.

CUSTOMIZE INSTRUCTION FOR UNIVERSAL ACCESS

For Less Proficient Readers	For English Learners	For Gifted/Talented Students
Guide students to understand the conflict here: The headmaster is trying to give Jerome the bad news, but the boy is still busy working on his fantasy.	Let students discuss the common practice of giving nicknames to friends. Some nicknames may be painful, while others might be a sign of affection. Do students think the nickname given to Jerome is meant in affection or as a joke?	Have students make a character web for Jerome based on p. 115 in **Literary Analysis and Reading Transparencies.** Have students note the specific descriptions the author gives of Jerome; for example, he was not "a boy who cried; he was a boy who brooded" and he did not think the manner of his father's death was comic.

36 Reading Strategy

Identifying With a Character

- Ask students what Jerome fears will eventually happen in connection with his father.
  Answer: Since his father was an author, Jerome fears that someone will want to write a biography of him and will focus on the absurd manner of his death.
- Have students describe how Jerome plans to counteract this possibility.
  Answer: Jerome rehearses how he will describe his father's death to any potential biographer.
- Ask students the Reading Strategy question on p. 1192: Why do you think Jerome is so desperate to reduce "the comic element" in the story of the accident?
  Answer: Jerome wants to control the way his father might be remembered in a book about his life; more deeply, the implied humiliation of his father's death causes him pain and diminishes his own self-esteem.

but it was terrible for Jerome to see how suddenly, midway in her rambling discourse, the interest would become genuine. "I can't think how such things can be allowed in a civilized country," his aunt would say. "I suppose one has to regard Italy as civilized. One is prepared for all kinds of things abroad, of course, and my brother was a great traveler. He always carried a water-filter with him. It was far less expensive, you know, than buying all those bottles of mineral water. My brother always said that his filter paid for his dinner wine. You can see from that what a careful man he was, but who could possibly have expected when he was walking along the Via Dottore Manuele Panucci on his way to the Hydrographic Museum that a pig would fall on him?" That was the moment when the interest became genuine.

Jerome's father had not been a distinguished writer, but the time always seems to come, after an author's death, when somebody thinks it worth his while to write a letter to *The Times Literary Supplement* announcing the preparation of a biography and asking to see any letters or documents or receive any anecdotes from friends of the dead man. Most of the biographies, of course, never appear—one wonders whether the whole thing may not be an obscure form of blackmail and whether many a potential writer of a biography or thesis finds the means in this way to finish his education at Kansas or Nottingham. Jerome, however, as a chartered accountant, lived far from the literary world. He did not realize how small the menace really was, nor that the danger period for someone of his father's obscurity had long passed. Sometimes he rehearsed the method of recounting his father's death so as to reduce the comic element to
36 its smallest dimensions—it would be of no use to refuse information, for in that case the biographer would undoubtedly visit his aunt, who was living to a great old age with no sign of flagging.

Reading Strategy
Identifying With a Character Why do you think Jerome is so desperate to reduce "the comic element" in the story of the accident?

It seemed to Jerome that there were two possible methods—the first led gently up to the accident, so well prepared that the death came really as an anticlimax. The chief danger of laughter in such a story was always surprise. When he rehearsed this method Jerome began boringly enough.

"You know Naples and those high tenement buildings? Somebody once told me that the Neapolitan always feels at home in New York just as the man from Turin feels at home in London because the river runs in much the same way in both cities. Where was I? Oh, yes, Naples, of course. You'd be surprised in the poorer quarters what things they keep on the balconies of those skyscraping tenements—not washing, you know, or bedding, but things like livestock, chickens or even pigs. Of course the pigs get no exercise whatever and fatten all the quicker." He could imagine how his hearer's eyes would have glazed by this time. "I've no idea, have you, how heavy a pig can be, but those old buildings are all badly in need of repair. A balcony on the fifth floor gave way under one of those pigs. It struck the third-floor balcony on its way down and sort of ricocheted into the street. My father was on the way to the Hydrographic Museum when the pig hit him. Coming from that height and that angle it broke his neck." This was really a masterly attempt to make an intrinsically interesting subject boring.

The other method Jerome rehearsed had the virtue of brevity.

"My father was killed by a pig."

"Really? In India?"

"No, in Italy."

"How interesting. I never realized there was pig-sticking in Italy. Was your father keen on polo?"

In course of time, neither too early nor too late, rather as though, in his capacity as a chartered accountant, Jerome had studied the statistics and taken the average, he became engaged to be married: to a pleasant fresh-faced girl of twenty-five whose father was a doctor in Pinner. Her name was Sally, her favorite author was still Hugh
37 Walpole, and she had adored babies ever since she had been given a doll at the age of five which moved its eyes and made water. Their relationship was contented rather than exciting, as became the love affair of a chartered accountant; it would never have done if it had interfered with the figures.

One thought worried Jerome, however. Now that within a year he might himself become a father, his love for the dead man increased; he realized what affection had gone into the picture-postcards. He felt a longing to protect his memory, and uncertain whether this quiet
38 love of his would survive if Sally were so insensitive as to laugh when she heard the story of his father's death. Inevitably she would hear it when Jerome brought her to dinner with his aunt. Several times he tried to tell her himself, as she was naturally anxious to know all she could that concerned him.

"You were very small when your father died?"

"Just nine."

"Poor little boy," she said.

"I was at school. They broke the news to me."

"Did you take it very hard?"

"I can't remember."

"You never told me how it happened."

"It was very sudden. A street accident."

"You'll never drive fast, will you, Jemmy?" (She had begun to call him "Jemmy.") It was too late then to try the second method—the one he thought of as the pig-sticking one.

They were going to marry quietly at a registry-office and have their honeymoon at Torquay. He avoided taking her to see his aunt until a week before the wedding, but then the night came, and he could not have told himself whether his apprehension was more for his father's memory or the security of his own love.

The moment came all too soon. "Is that Jemmy's father?" Sally asked, picking up the portrait of the man with the umbrella.

"Yes, dear. How did you guess?"

"He has Jemmy's eyes and brow, hasn't he?"

intrinsically (in trin′ sik lē) *adv.* at its core; inherently; innately

Reading Strategy
Identifying With a Character Why do you think Jerome feels that Sally's laughter could menace his "quiet love" for his father?

39  **Reading Check**
What two methods of narrating his father's death does Jerome rehearse?

37 Background

Hugh Walpole Tell students that Hugh Walpole (1884–1941) was a British novelist whose popular and, perhaps, old-fashioned works set a pattern for books and plays about schoolmasters. This allusion adds to the impression of Sally as a conventional woman.

38 Reading Strategy

Identifying With a Character

- Ask why Jerome's love for his dead father seems to increase as he approaches his wedding day.
  Answer: Jerome realizes that he may be a father himself in a short time.
- Ask students the Reading Strategy question on p. 1193: Why do you think Jerome feels that Sally's laughter could menace his "quiet love" for his father?
  Possible response: Since he loves Sally and will be spending his life with her, Jerome is afraid that his love for his father will be damaged if she thinks the manner of his father's death is funny.

39 Reading Check

Answer: Jerome rehearses a long and rambling account that blunts the shock of the ending, and a quick and to-the-point account.

40 Literary Analysis

Theme and Symbol

- Ask why Jerome keeps putting off telling Sally about his father's death.
  Answer: Jerome worries about a possibly insensitive response from Sally.
- Have students compare Sally's and Jerome's response to the story when they first hear it.
  Answer: Both ask what happened to the pig.
- Ask students the Literary Analysis question on p. 1194: What does the contrast between Sally's reaction and those of other characters suggest about the theme?
  Possible responses: What is considered absurd and laughable to one person is a horror story to another. Life is full of surprises, some tragic, some joyful.

CUSTOMIZE INSTRUCTION FOR UNIVERSAL ACCESS

For Special Needs Students	For English Learners	For Gifted/Talented Students
Greene's long sentences may be hard for students to understand. Have them break down a sentence, finding the meaning in the individual parts, and then put the sentence back together again. An example is the sentence beginning, "Sometimes he rehearsed the method of recounting his father's death . . . ," on p. 1192.	Point out that a Neapolitan is a person from Naples, Italy. Ask students to suggest other somewhat atypical ways that people from different cities, states, or countries are identified. For instance, a person from Denmark is a Dane and an inhabitant of Glasgow, Scotland, is a Glaswegian.	Ask students to determine what Greene intended by the following comments: "Jerome, however, as a chartered accountant, lived far from the literary world" as well as the two slyly negative comments in the first long paragraph on p. 1193. Why might Greene be making fun of people who work in accounting?

ASSESS

Answers for p. 1194

Review and Assess

1. Some students may not have expected Sally's perfect response, while others might have predicted the absurdity of the ending.
2. **(a)** Mr. Wordsworth and Jerome's aunt both use the phrase. **(b)** These two characters see the accident as just a trick of fate. Also, his aunt relishes the absurdity while Jerome is embarrassed by it. His aunt enjoys telling the story to strangers, while Jerome dreads telling it.
3. **(a)** He develops a long, anticlimactic way and a short, quick way of telling the story of his father's death. **(b)** Jerome wants to protect his father's memory and wonders whether his fiancée, Sally, will be sensitive to his feelings about his father when he tells her about the accident.
4. **(a)** Sally says the story is horrible and makes her think about how quickly life can change. **(b)** Sally's reaction tells Jerome she has a character he can trust. **(c)** Jerome's conflicts are resolved when his aunt tells Sally about the event and Sally's reaction shows her understanding, concern, and sympathy.
5. Encourage students to support their opinions with details from their reading or experience.

"Has Jerome lent you his books?"

"No."

"I will give you a set for your wedding. He wrote so tenderly about his travels. My own favorite is *Nooks and Crannies.* He would have had a great future. It made that shocking accident all the worse."

"Yes?"

How Jerome longed to leave the room and not see that loved face crinkle with irresistible amusement.

"I had so many letters from his readers after the pig fell on him." She had never been so abrupt before.

40 And then the miracle happened. Sally did not laugh. Sally sat with open eyes of horror while his aunt told her the story, and at the end, "How horrible," Sally said. "It makes you think, doesn't it? Happening like that. Out of a clear sky."

Jerome's heart sang with joy. It was as though she had appeased his fear forever. In the taxi going home he kissed her with more passion than he had ever shown, and she returned it. There were babies in her pale blue pupils, babies that rolled their eyes and made water.

"A week today," Jerome said, and she squeezed his hand. "Penny for your thoughts, my darling."

"I was wondering," Sally said, "what happened to the poor pig?"

"They almost certainly had it for dinner," Jerome said happily and kissed the dear child again.

Literary Analysis
Theme and Symbol What does the contrast between Sally's reaction and those of other characters suggest about the theme?

Review and Assess

Thinking About the Selection

1. **Respond:** Were you surprised by the way that this story ended? Why or why not?
2. **(a) Recall:** Which two characters use the phrase "a shocking accident" to describe the death of Jerome's father? **(b) Compare and Contrast:** How do the reactions of these two characters to the death compare to Jerome's reaction?
3. **(a) Recall:** How does Jerome protect himself from the embarrassing aspects of the death? **(b) Analyze:** What are some inner conflicts Jerome experiences about his father's death?
4. **(a) Recall:** How does Sally react when she hears the story? **(b) Infer:** What does Sally's reaction reveal to Jerome about her character? **(c) Draw Conclusions:** Are Jerome's conflicts about his father's death resolved at the end of the story? Why or why not?
5. **Take a Position:** One implication of the "shocking accident" might be that what happens in life is basically beyond our control. Do you agree with this idea? Why or why not?

ASSESSMENT PRACTICE: Writing Skills

Strategy **(For more practice, see Test Preparation Workbook, p. 58.)**

Many tests require students to apply revision strategies to a given passage. Use this sample item:

Your father was walking along a street in Naples when a pig fell on him.

The best place to add the words *on his way to the Hydrographic Museum* in this sentence is after ___.

A was
B walking
C Naples
D him

The first step in answering a question of this type is to use the phrase in each of the possible locations. If the phrase sounds awkward or the meaning of the sentence is changed, that choice is probably incorrect. The correct answer is *C*.

Review and Assess

Literary Analysis

Theme and Symbol

1. Using the terms *love and money,* state a central question, issue, or concern that expresses the **theme** in "The Rocking-Horse Winner."
2. Complete a chart like this with (a) passages illustrating the **symbolic** meanings of the rocking horse and (b) explanations linking these meanings to the theme.

Symbolic Meanings	Passages That Illustrate	Links to Overall Theme
• Frantic effort to satisfy an unsatisfiable need • Frightening power of desires and wishes		

3. For "A Shocking Accident," explain how the accident might symbolize either of these meanings: (a) that which makes no sense (b) that which is unacceptable according to upper-class notions.
4. Use the symbolic meanings of the accident to state the story's theme.

Comparing Literary Works

5. Show that "The Rocking-Horse Winner" and "A Shocking Accident" are similar in using the **third-person point of view.**
6. In which story does the point of view work most effectively to reveal the theme? Explain.
7. In which story is the third-person narrative more like a fairy tale and in which is it more like an anecdote? Explain.

Reading Strategy

Identifying With a Character

8. **Identify with the character** Paul in "A Rocking-Horse Winner," and express his most important goal.
9. In "A Shocking Accident," what makes Jerome most uneasy about telling the story of his father's death? Why?

Extend Understanding

10. **Psychology Connection:** How might a child psychologist try to help Paul in "A Rocking-Horse Winner"?

Quick Review

A **theme** is a central idea, issue, or question that a literary work explores.

A **symbol** is a person, place, or thing that reveals the theme by suggesting deeper meanings.

When a story is told from a **third-person point of view,** the narrator does not take part in the action and may know the thoughts of one or more characters.

To **identify with characters,** use what you know about their emotions, goals, and problems to put yourself in their place.

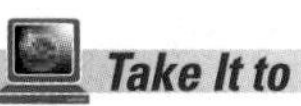
Take It to the Net

www.phschool.com

Take the interactive self-test online to check your understanding of these selections.

ENRICHMENT: Further Reading

Other Works by the Authors

Works by D. H. Lawrence

The White Peacock

The Plumed Serpent

Works by Graham Greene

The Power and the Glory

Our Man in Havana

Answers for p. 1195

Review and Assess

1. The striving for money exhausts all energy for love.
2. **Symbolic Meanings:** Frantic effort to satisfy an unsatisfiable need; **Passages That Illustrate:** Any passage in which the mother talks about needing more money or Paul talks about needing to find luck; **Links to Overall Theme:** Greed is destructive because all the frantic energy in the world is not enough to satisfy it. **Symbolic Meanings:** Frightening power of desires and wishes; **Passages That Illustrate:** Any passage that describes the whispering, Paul's rocking on his rocking horse, the mother's focus on money, or Paul's focus on picking winners of horse races; **Links to Overall Theme:** Time spent in getting money is time not spent on building a satisfying life.
3. The accident symbolizes "what makes no sense" because of its absurdity—whoever expects to be killed by a falling pig? It symbolizes "what is unacceptable to upper-class notions" because people expect death to be dignified.
4. Life is absurd, but people deeply desire to protect themselves and their ideals from the implications of this absurdity.
5. Both stories reveal, through the third-person viewpoint, the thoughts and feelings of more than one character.
6. Possible response: The third-person narrative reveals the theme more effectively in "The Rocking-Horse Winner." The reader learns much more about Paul, his mother, his uncle, and Bassett, which all help relate the events to the theme of greed.
7. The third-person narrative is more like a fairy tale in "The Rocking-Horse Winner" because the characters are somewhat like stock figures—the bad mother, the kindly uncle, and so on. The narrative is more like an anecdote in "A Shocking Accident" because everything in the story flows from a single event.
8. Paul's most important goal in the story is to bring more money into

continued

Answers continued

the house so that his mother will not be worried all the time.

9. Jerome is uneasy when he tells the story of his father's death because he fears people will laugh and that might lessen his love and his positive memory of his father.
10. A psychologist might help Paul understand his own need for love and security and to see that he cannot hold himself responsible for his mother's happiness.

EXTEND

Answers for p. 1196

❶ Vocabulary Development

Word Analysis

1. object—to speak out against
2. obligation—the action of binding oneself, legally or morally, to a course of action
3. obnoxious—offensive; putting unpleasantness "before" someone

Spelling Strategy

1. problematically
2. publicly
3. thematically

Fluency: Words in Context

1. No; *discreet* means "prudent."
2. No; *brazening* means "daring boldly."
3. Yes; *careered* means "rushed wildly"
4. Yes; Paul was stubbornly and *obstinately* determined to win money.
5. Yes: *uncanny* means "mysterious."
6. Yes; *remonstrated* means "objected strongly."
7. Yes; *apprehension* means "dread."
8. Yes; *embark* means "engage in something, such as telling a story."
9. No; *intrinsically* means "inherently."

❷ Grammar and Style

1. go
2. be
3. weren't
4. were
5. were

Integrate Language Skills

❶ Vocabulary Development Lesson

Word Analysis: Latin Prefix *ob-*

The Latin prefix *ob-* can mean "against," "opposed to," "before," or "to." *Obstinately* means "as if standing against" or "stubbornly." Speculate how the meaning of the prefix influences the definitions of the words below. Then, use a dictionary containing word origins to verify your speculations.

1. object (*verb*) 2. obligation 3. obnoxious

Spelling Strategy

To form an adverb from words of two or more syllables ending in *-c*, you usually add the ending *-ally*. For example, *instrinsic* becomes *intrinsically*. On your paper, change the adjectives below into adverbs. Use a dictionary to check your spellings.

1. problematic 2. public 3. thematic

Fluency: Words in Context

Answer each question, and explain your answer.

1. Do *discreet* people gossip?
2. Is *brazening* out a lie easy?
3. Did Paul ride until the horse *careered?*
4. Was Paul *obstinately* determined to win?
5. Were Paul's eyes *uncanny*?
6. Had Paul's mother *remonstrated* with him about riding the rocking-horse?
7. Did Jerome feel *apprehension* about describing his father's death?
8. Did Jerome's aunt *embark* on the death with strangers?
9. Was the story of Jerome's father's death *intrinsically* dull?

❷ Grammar and Style Lesson

Subjunctive Mood

The **subjunctive mood** of a verb states a wish or a condition contrary to fact. The subjunctive is also used in *that* clauses of recommendation, resolution, command, or demand. The subjunctive form appears in

- Certain forms of the verb *to be*—the present is *be* and the past is *were*
- The third-person singular of other verbs, usually used without the final *s*

Condition Contrary to Fact: If you were me and I were you . . . I wonder what we should do! (form of *to be*)

***That* Clause of Command:** Paul's mother insisted that he stop rocking. (third-person singular without *-s*)

Practice Identify the correct verb for each sentence.

1. She insisted that the child (goes, go) to a first-class boarding school.
2. Bassett and Paul thought it essential that they (are, be) sure of a winner before betting.
3. Paul wished that she (wasn't, weren't) so worried.
4. It had seemed for a moment as if the housemaster (was, were) going to laugh.
5. Jerome thought that if Sally (was, were) insensitive, their engagement might end.

Writing Application As Paul's mother, write a paragraph about what you wish for your son. Use the subjunctive mood at least twice to express your hopes, wishes, or fears.

WG Prentice Hall Writing and Grammar Connection: Chapter 21, Section 3

TEACHING RESOURCES

The following resources can be used to enrich or extend the instruction for pp. 1196–1197.

Vocabulary

- **Selection Support:** Build Vocabulary, p. 267
- **Vocabulary and Spelling Practice Book** (Use this booklet for skills enrichment.)

Grammar

- **Selection Support:** Grammar and Style, p. 268
- **Writing and Grammar,** Diamond Level, p. 548 ■
- **Daily Language Practice Transparencies**

Writing

- **Writing and Grammar,** Diamond Level, p. 151 ■
- **Writing and Grammar iText CD-ROM**

■ **BLOCK SCHEDULING:** Resources marked with this symbol provide varied instruction during 90-minute blocks.

❸ Writing Lesson

Product Description

Advertisers use the same techniques of symbolism that Lawrence does. Demonstrate this truth for yourself by writing a product description of a new toy. Sell the toy to parents and children by making it into a symbol of wonder, knowledge, or power.

Prewriting Sketch the toy, and make notes about its function, size, sounds, color, and moving parts. Jot down the quality or qualities that it will symbolize.

Drafting Describe the toy, in action. Using a word bank of vivid verbs and adverbs, like the one shown below, choose the ones that will suggest the symbolic meanings you want to convey.

Model: Consulting a Word Bank

	Knowledge	Magic	Power
Verbs	appreciate, recognize, grasp	charm, enchant, conjure	sway, control, arm, energize
Adverbs	keenly, perceptively, intelligently	hypnotically, magically, hauntingly	powerfully, strongly, irresistibly

Revising Have a partner read the description to identify the quality or qualities the toy symbolizes. If your partner fails to interpret the toy correctly, insert verbs and adverbs that will suggest the correct symbolism.

WG Prentice Hall Writing and Grammar Connection: Chapter 8, Section 2

❹ Extension Activities

Listening and Speaking Imagine that you are playing the character of Jerome in a play adapted from "A Shocking Accident." Rehearse and deliver a **soliloquy**—a speech made by a character who is alone—about other people's reactions to your father's death. In your rehearsal, pay particular attention to pacing, gestures, and staging, and keep these goals in mind:

- Expressing emotion
- Adding drama and sentence variety

Then, present your speech to the class.

Research and Technology With a group, research Graham Greene's travels, and create a **multimedia travelogue** following in the footsteps of the novelist. Each person might focus on a different country, finding suitable music, readings, and slides. However, work together to script your presentation. **[Group Activity]**

Take It to the Net www.phschool.com

Go online for an additional research activity using the Internet.

❸ Writing Lesson

- Have students write words that could be used as symbols to sell their toy.
- Use the Writing Lesson to guide students in writing a product description.
- Use the Description rubric in **Performance Assessment and Portfolio Management**, p. 17, to evaluate students' product descriptions.

❹ Listening and Speaking

- Remind students that a soliloquy is a long speech delivered by a character who is alone on stage.
- Help students recall the characteristics of Jerome to use in their soliloquy.
- Tell students that they may use hand and body language as well as words in presenting their soliloquies.

CUSTOMIZE INSTRUCTION For Universal Access

To address different learning styles, use the activities suggested in the **Extension Activities** booklet, p. 58.

- For Logical/Mathematical and Verbal/Linguistic Learners, use Activity 5.
- For Bodily/Kinesthetic and Intrapersonal Learners, use Activity 6.
- For Visual/Spatial Learners, use Activity 7.

ASSESSMENT RESOURCES

The following resources can be used to assess students' knowledge and skills.

Selection Assessment

- **Formal Assessment,** Selection Test, pp. 275–277
- **Open Book Test,** pp. 171–173
- **Got It! Assessment Videotapes,** Tape 6
- **Test Bank Software**

Take It to the Net

Visit www.phschool.com for self-tests and additional questions on the selections.

Writing Rubric

- **Performance Assess. and Portfolio Mgmt.,** p. 17

- **Workbook**
- **Skill Book**
-  **Transparencies**
- **CD-ROM**

Lesson Objectives

1. To understand the connection between the writers of the twentieth century and the evolution of the short story
2. To understand how a writer's choice of style, elements, and medium reflects character development and incident

Connections

In the twentieth century, short story writers pioneered bold fictional techniques of character development. Ask students to compare Borges's short story *The Book of Sand* to the works of Conrad and Joyce in previous sections. What elements in these works of fiction are similar and dissimilar?

The Short Story

- Explain to students that the short story cannot be defined as to its literary elements or styles due to the widely varying techniques employed by the writers. The short story tends to have a simpler plot and setting than a novel.
- Point out that though both short stories and novels desire to spark a reader's thought processes, stories tend to spend less time on character development and more time on incidents.
- Point out that in *The Book of Sand* a variety of techniques is used to generate questions in the minds of the readers. Have students watch for these techniques as they read.

CONNECTIONS

Literature Around the World

The Short Story

Defining the short story as a form is no easy task. All short stories are brief works of fiction. They generally have simpler plots than novels. In addition, a short story tends to reveal character at a crucial moment rather than developing it through many incidents. Yet, as each story in this section shows, one writer's idea of a story may be quite different from another's.

Masters of Storytelling In "The Lagoon," Conrad uses elements that appear in much of his fiction: a tale of betrayal set in an exotic, dreamlike place and a story-within-a-story narrative. In "Araby," as in many of his other stories, Joyce builds to an epiphany —a character's flash of awareness that illuminates the story's meaning. Woolf and Spark use unusual narrative devices in their stories—a stream-of-consciousness narration that mirrors the random thoughts in a character's mind and an omniscient point of view attributed to an infant. Each of these writers helped make the short story an important literary form in the twentieth century. At the same time, each redefines the form.

Argentine writer Jorge Luis Borges uses storytelling techniques as original as those of early twentieth-century English writers. His tale "The Book of Sand," for example, is a fantastic story inspired by philosophical speculations about infinity. Told by a first-person narrator, it replaces conventional action with the "adventure" of an unfolding idea. The tale may be brief, but it will cause you to think about its narrator's discovery and dilemma for a long time.

THE BOOK OF SAND

Jorge Luis Borges

Translated by Andrew Hurley

. . . thy rope of sands . . .

—George Herbert (1593–1633)[1]

The line consists of an infinite number of points; the plane, of an infinite number of lines; the volume, of an infinite number of planes; the hypervolume, of an infinite number of volumes . . . No—this, *more geometrico*,[2] is decidedly not the best way to begin my tale. To say that the story is true is by now a convention of every fantastic tale; mine, nevertheless, *is* true.

I live alone, in a fifth-floor apartment on Calle Belgrano.[3] One evening a few months ago, I heard a knock at my door. I opened it, and a stranger stepped in. He was a tall man, with blurred, vague features, or perhaps my nearsightedness made me see him that way. Everything about him spoke of honest poverty: he was dressed in gray, and carried a gray valise. I immediately sensed that he was a foreigner. At first I thought he was old; then I noticed that I had been misled by his sparse hair, which was blond, almost white, like the Scandinavians'. In the course of our conversation, which I doubt lasted more than an hour, I learned that he hailed from the Orkneys.[4]

I pointed the man to a chair. He took some time to begin talking. He gave off an air of melancholy, as I myself do now.

"I sell Bibles," he said at last.

"In this house," I replied, not without a somewhat stiff, pedantic[5] note, "there are several English Bibles, including the first one, Wyclif's.[6] I also have Cipriano de Valera's, Luther's (which is, in literary terms, the worst of the lot), and a Latin copy of the Vulgate.[7] As you see, it isn't exactly Bibles I might be needing."

After a brief silence he replied.

"It's not only Bibles I sell. I can show you a sacred book that might interest a man such as yourself. I came by it in northern India, in Bikaner."[8]

He opened his valise and brought out the book. He laid it on the table. It was a clothbound octavo[9] volume that had clearly passed through many hands. I examined it; the unusual heft of it surprised me. On the spine was printed *Holy Writ*, and then *Bombay*.[10]

1. **George Herbert** English metaphysical poet whose poem "The Collar" refers to religious principles of conduct as God's "rope of sands."
2. ***more geometrico*** (môr′ ā gā′ ō me′ tri cō) "by the method of geometry," a learned Latin phrase. The philosopher Benedict de Spinoza (1632–1677), who wrote on the infinite, described his method using this phrase.
3. **Calle Bellgrano** street in Buenos Aires, capital of Argentina.
4. **Orkneys** Orkney Islands; group of islands north of Scotland.
5. **pedantic** (pe dan′ tic) *adj.* stressing minor or trivial points of learning unnecessarily.
6. **Wyclif's** (wik′ lifs) John Wyclif (or Wycliffe; 1330–1384), English religious reformer who, in the late 1300s, made the first translation of the Bible into English from the official Latin version.
7. **Capriano de Valera's . . . Vulgate** different translations of the Bible.
8. **Bikaner** (bē kə nir′) city in northwest India.
9. **octavo** (äk tā′ vō) *n.* page size of a book, made up of printer's sheets folded into eight leaves: the usual size of each leaf is six by nine inches.
10. **Bombay** (bäm′ bā′) seaport in west India.

Thematic Connection

What connection can you see between a story about a book, such as this one, and a story that tells the story of a story, such as Conrad's "The Lagoon"?

Background

Literature

About the Selection: In this fantastical allegory about time and life, a book collector receives an unexpected visit from a stranger who wishes to sell him a rare book from India. At first, the book looks like any old volume, but the book's strange properties tempt the man. For example, a page once seen will never be seen again. He buys the book, which comes to preoccupy his thoughts. At last, he rids himself of the book to preserve his sanity. His experience suggests that no one can master the infinite mysteries of the universe.

Background

Literature

George Herbert (1593–1633) was a metaphysical poet noted for his steadfast religious devotion and his use of allegory. Borges chose to open the story with a brief quotation from Herbert's writings.

Thematic Connection

Answer: Students may note that in both cases, the power or nature of words becomes a theme of the story.

ENRICHMENT: Social Studies

Sacred Books

Almost every culture has one or more sacred books that express its teachings, beliefs, myths, legends, laws, or philosophies. One example is the *Qur'an* (Koran), the sacred Islamic scripture that Muslims accept as the infallible Word of God, revealed over a twenty-year period to the Prophet Muhammad. The *Bhagavadgita* (Sanskrit for "Song of the Lord") is one of the great Hindu scriptures. It forms Book IV of the Indian epic the *Mahabharata;* its verses consider, among other things, the nature of God and how mortals can know Him.

Invite interested students to learn about a sacred book of a culture of their choosing. It can be a book, a manuscript, something in picture writing, or any form appropriate to that culture. Have them find out when and where the work was composed, where the original is kept, and how it expresses its principal philosophical or ethical precepts.

Thematic Connection

Answer: Students may say that Borges's infinity represents time, the universe, or the power of language to comment on itself infinitely (one word leading to another without end).

Background

Infinity

Discuss the meaning of *infinite*. One mathematical definition of infinite, with respect to a set of things, is that it is unlimited in number, or unbounded in space or magnitude.

"Nineteenth century, I'd say," I observed.

"I don't know," was the reply. "Never did know."

I opened it at random. The characters were unfamiliar to me. The pages, which seemed worn and badly set, were printed in double columns, like a Bible. The text was cramped, and composed into versicles.[11] At the upper corner of each page were Arabic numerals. I was struck by an odd fact: the even-numbered page would carry the number 40,514, let us say, while the odd-numbered page that followed it would be 999. I turned the page; the next page bore an eight-digit number. It also bore a small illustration, like those one sees in dictionaries: an anchor drawn in pen and ink, as though by the unskilled hand of a child.

It was at that point that the stranger spoke again.

"Look at it well. You will never see it again."

There was a threat in the words, but not in the voice.

I took note of the page, and then closed the book. Immediately I opened it again. In vain I searched for the figure of the anchor, page after page. To hide my discomfiture, I tried another tack.

"This is a version of Scripture in some Hindu language, isn't that right?"

"No," he replied.

Then he lowered his voice, as though entrusting me with a secret.

"I came across this book in a village on the plain, and I traded a few rupees and a Bible for it. The man who owned it didn't know how to read. I suspect he saw the Book of Books as an amulet. He was of the lowest caste;[12] people could not so much as step on his shadow without being defiled. He told me his book was called the Book of Sand because neither sand nor this book has a beginning or an end."

He suggested I try to find the first page.

I took the cover in my left hand and opened the book, my thumb and forefinger almost touching. It was impossible: several pages always lay between the cover and my hand. It was as though they grew from the very book.

"Now try to find the end."

I failed there as well.

"This can't be," I stammered, my voice hardly recognizable as my own.

"It can't be, yet it *is*," the Bible peddler said, his voice little more than a whisper. "The number of pages in this book is literally infinite. No page is the first page; no page is the last. I don't know why they're numbered in this arbitrary way, but perhaps it's to give one to understand that the terms of an infinite series can be numbered any way whatever."

Then, as though thinking out loud, he went on.

"If space is infinite, we are anywhere, at any point in space. If time is infinite, we are at any point in time."

Thematic Connection
How does Borges's presentation of the idea of infinity compare and contrast with the presentation of a sequence of events in other stories?

---

11. versicles (vur′ si kəlz) *n.* short verses or verse parts from the Bible used in prayers with melodies.

12. lowest caste (kast) *n.* lowest social class in Indian society; the class of "untouchables."

His musings irritated me.

"You," I said, "are a religious man, are you not?"

"Yes, I'm Presbyterian. My conscience is clear. I am certain I didn't cheat that native when I gave him the Lord's Word in exchange for his diabolic[13] book."

I assured him he had nothing to reproach himself for, and asked whether he was just passing through the country. He replied that he planned to return to his own country within a few days. It was then that I learned he was a Scot, and that his home was in the Orkneys. I told him I had great personal fondness for Scotland because of my love for Stevenson[14] and Hume.[15]

"And Robbie Burns,"[16] he corrected.

As we talked I continued to explore the infinite book.

"Had you intended to offer this curious specimen to the British Museum then?" I asked with feigned indifference.

"No," he replied, "I am offering it to you," and he mentioned a great sum of money.

I told him, with perfect honesty, that such an amount of money was not within my ability to pay. But my mind was working; in a few moments I had devised my plan.

▲ Critical Viewing What qualities of the books in this picture convey the same atmosphere as the book in the story? **[Connect]**

"I propose a trade," I said. "You purchased the volume with a few rupees and the Holy Scripture; I will offer you the full sum of my pension, which I have just received, and Wyclif's black-letter Bible. It was left to me by my parents."

"A black-letter Wyclif!" he murmured.

I went to my bedroom and brought back the money and the book. With a bibliophile's[17] zeal he turned the pages and studied the binding.

"Done," he said.

I was astonished that he did not haggle. Only later was I to realize that he had entered my house already determined to see the book. He did not count the money, but merely put the bills into his pocket.

We chatted about India, the Orkneys, and the Norwegian jarls[18] that had once ruled those islands. Night was falling when the man left. I have never seen him since, nor do I know his name.

---

13. **diabolic** (dī´ə bäl´ik) *adj.* of the devil; evil.
14. **Stevenson** Robert Louis Stevenson, (1850–1894); noted Scottish novelist, poet, and essayist.
15. **Hume** (hyo͞om) David Hume, (1711–1776); noted Scottish philosopher and historian, prominent in the period known as the Scottish Enlightenment.
16. **Robbie Burns** Robert Burns, (1759–1796); famous Scottish poet.
17. **bibliophile's** (bib´ lē ə filz´) *n.* of a person who loves books.
18. **jarls** (yärlz) *n.* chieftains or noblemen in early Scandinavia.

▶Critical Viewing

Answer: Students may say that the books in the photograph look worn, ornate, hand-bound, thick, rare, sacred, dog-eared, or antique. The book in the story is of the same character, very rare and mysterious in presentation.

Critical Thinking

Hypothesize

- Ask students to imagine why the stranger's speculations irritated the narrator.
  Answer: Students may say that the musings about infinity were wasting the narrator's time, or that he felt that the stranger was trying to engage him in a philosophical discussion when the narrator really wanted details about the book.

Background

Literature

Remind students that *The Thousand and One Nights* is a book of tales told by the wife of a cruel king. She prevents her husband from killing her by telling him a story each night. Like her stories, the Book of Sand seems to go on and on.

Critical Thinking

Speculate

- Ask students to explain why they think the Book of Sand so consumes the narrator.
  Answer: He becomes obsessed with trying to understand the book.

Answers

Connecting Literature Around the World

1. **(a)** Answers will depend on each student's opinion on the author's effective use of symbolism. D. H. Lawrence used a child's rocking horse to sum up and criticize a whole society's materialism. Virginia Woolf used a looking glass to symbolize the skin-deep, superficial personality of a character. **(b)** Students may find the Borges story more challenging in its symbolism.
2. Student's answers should include concrete ideas of a "discovery" contrasting how they were used and the messages conveyed.

I thought of putting the Book of Sand in the space left by the Wyclif, but I chose at last to hide it behind some imperfect volumes of the *Thousand and One Nights*.

I went to bed but could not sleep. At three or four in the morning I turned on the light. I took out the impossible book and turned its pages. On one, I saw an engraving of a mask. There was a number in the corner of a page—I don't remember now what it was—raised to the ninth power.

I showed no one my treasure. To the joy of possession was added the fear that it would be stolen from me, and to that, the suspicion that it might not be truly infinite. Those two points of anxiety aggravated my already habitual misanthropy.[19] I had but few friends left, and those, I stopped seeing. A prisoner of the Book, I hardly left my house. I examined the worn binding and the covers with a magnifying glass, and rejected the possibility of some artifice. I found that the small illustrations were spaced at two-thousand-page intervals. I began noting them down in an alphabetized notebook, which was very soon filled. They never repeated themselves. At night, during the rare intervals spared me by insomnia, I dreamed of the book.

Summer was drawing to a close, and I realized that the book was monstrous. It was cold consolation to think that I, who looked upon it with my eyes and fondled it with my ten flesh-and-bone fingers, was no less monstrous than the book. I felt it was a nightmare thing, an obscene thing, and that it defiled and corrupted reality.

I considered fire, but I feared that the burning of an infinite book might be similarly infinite, and suffocate the planet in smoke.

I remembered reading once that the best place to hide a leaf is in the forest. Before my retirement I had worked in the National Library, which contained nine hundred thousand books; I knew that to the right of the lobby a curving staircase descended into the shadows of the basement, where the maps and periodicals are kept. I took advantage of the librarians' distraction to hide the Book of Sand on one of the library's damp shelves; I tried not to notice how high up, or how far from the door.

I now feel a little better, but I refuse even to walk down the street the library's on.

19. **misanthropy** (mis an´ thrə pē) *n.* hatred or distrust of people.

Jorge Luis Borges

(1899–1986)

Jorge Luis Borges (hōr´ he lo͞o ēs´ bōr´ hes) was an Argentine writer known for his inventive, fantastic short stories and poetry. The strangeness of his tales recalls the fiction of Edgar Allan Poe.

Borges stories deal with universal themes like the meaning of time and infinity and the nature of personal identity. He received the International Publisher's Prize in 1961.

Connecting Literature Around the World

1. Compare Borges's story with another story in this section. (a) What are their general similarities? (b) What are their major differences?
2. In several stories in this section, a character or narrator discovers something fundamentally disquieting about life. Compare these discoveries in two of the selections.

ENRICHMENT: Further Reading

Other Works by Jorge Luis Borges

A Universal History of Infamy

Other Inquisitions

The Book of Imaginary Beings

PART 4

From the National to the Global

Political World, Kenneth Eward

Selection Planning Guide

The selections in this part are by modern writers nurtured in the British tradition. Poets Dylan Thomas, Ted Hughes, Philip Larkin, Peter Redgrove, and Stevie Smith are modern writers redefining that tradition. Writers V. S. Naipaul, Nadine Gordimer, Derek Walcott, and Anita Desai are leading voices of cultures once dominated by the British Empire, cultures with unique world views. Science-fiction writer Arthur C. Clarke addresses the daunting prospect of conquering space.

Background

Art

Political World, by Kenneth Eward

This painting depicts a world that is dominated by political concerns. Have students link the art to the focus of Part 4 by responding to the following questions:

1. Which nations are represented by flags in this painting?
   Answer: Students may recognize, starting at the lower left, flags of the United States, Great Britain, Sweden, Japan, and Austria.
2. What countries are shown on the globe?
   Answer: Students may be able to identify eastern portions of the United States and Canada, Cuba and other Caribbean islands, the British Isles, Spain, and France.
3. What point about the struggle between national and global concerns does the artist make?
   Possible response: The artist makes flags disproportionately large, suggesting that national interests can dominate global issues.

CUSTOMIZE INSTRUCTION FOR UNIVERSAL ACCESS

When assigning the selections in this part, keep in mind these factors:

Dylan Thomas and Ted Hughes
- Short, accessible poems

Philip Larkin
- Two poems about prospects of immortality

Peter Redgrove and Stevie Smith
- Striking use of water imagery

V. S. Naipaul, Nadine Gordimer, Anita Desai
- Three stories explore cultures of modern Trinidad, South Africa, and India

Derek Walcott and James Berry
- Difficult allusions
- Dialect may be challenging for less proficient readers

Arthur C. Clarke
- High-interest essay on the future consequences of space exploration

Do Not Go Gentle Into That Good Night ✦ Fern Hill ✦ The Horses ✦ The Rain Horse

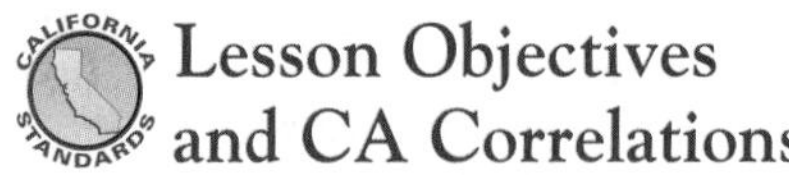

Lesson Objectives and CA Correlations

1. **To analyze and respond to literary elements**
   - Literary Analysis: Voice **R 3.3**
   - Comparing Literary Works **R 3.4**
2. **To read, comprehend, analyze, and critique poems and a short story**
   - Reading Strategy: Judging the Writer's Message
   - Reading Check Questions
   - Review and Assess Questions
3. **To develop word analysis skills, fluency, and systematic vocabulary**
   - Vocabulary Development Lesson: Latin Root *-vol-* **R 1.1, 1.2**
4. **To understand and apply written and oral language conventions**
   - Spelling Strategy **LC 1.2**
   - Grammar and Style Lesson: Sentence Beginnings: Adverb Clauses **LC 1.1**
5. **To understand and apply appropriate writing and research strategies**
   - Writing Lesson: Parody of a Poet's Voice **W 1.1, 1.2, 1.9; LS 1.9**
   - Extension Activity: Panel Presentation **LS 2.3**
   - Assessment Practice (ATE)
6. **To understand and apply listening and speaking strategies**
   - Extension Activity: Oral Interpretations **LS 1.9, 2.5**

STEP-BY-STEP TEACHING GUIDE	PACING GUIDE
PRETEACH	
Motivate Students and Provide Background	
Use the Motivation activity (ATE p. 1204)	5 min.
Read and discuss author and background features (SE/ATE pp. 1204, 1210) [A]	10 min.
Introduce the Concepts	
Introduce the Literary Analysis and Reading Strategy (SE/ATE p. 1205) [A]	15 min.
Pronounce the vocabulary words and read their definitions (SE p. 1205)	5 min.
TEACH	
Monitor Comprehension	
Informally monitor comprehension by circulating while students read independently or in groups [A]	40 min.
Monitor students' comprehension with the Reading Check notes (SE/ATE pp. 1211, 1213, 1215, 1217, 1219)	as students read
Develop vocabulary with Vocabulary notes (SE pp. 1207, 1213, 1214, 1218; ATE p. 1218)	as students read
Develop Understanding	
Develop students' understanding of voice with the Literary Analysis annotations (SE pp. 1207, 1208, 1210, 1215, 1217; ATE pp. 1207, 1208, 1210, 1214, 1215, 1216, 1217) [A]	5 min.
Develop students' ability to judge the message with the Reading Strategy annotations (SE/ATE pp. 1209, 1211, 1212, 1214, 1216, 1218, 1219, 1220)	5 min.
ASSESS	
Assess Mastery	
Assess students' mastery of the Reading Strategy and Literary Analysis by having them answer the Review and Assess questions (SE/ATE p. 1221)	20 min.
Use one or more of the print and media Assessment Resources (ATE p. 1223) [A]	up to 45 min.
EXTEND	
Apply Understanding	
Have students complete the Vocabulary Development Lesson and the Grammar and Style Lesson (SE p. 1222) [A]	20 min.
Apply students' ability to analyze voice using the Writing Lesson (SE/ATE p. 1223) [A]	45 min.
Apply students' understanding using one or more of the Extension Activities (SE p. 1223)	20–90 min.

ACCELERATED INSTRUCTION:
Use the strategies and activities identified with an [A].

UNIVERSAL ACCESS
● = Below-Level Students
▲ = On-Level Students
■ = Above-Level Students

Time and Resource Manager

Reading Level: Average, Average, Average, Easy
Average Number of Instructional Days: 5

RESOURCES		
PRINT	**TRANSPARENCIES**	**TECHNOLOGY**
• **Beyond Literature,** Community Connection: Preservation of Wilderness Lands, p. 59 ▲ ■		• **Interest Grabber Video,** Tape 6 ● ▲ ■
• **Selection Support Workbook:** ● ▲ ■ Literary Analysis, p. 276 Reading Strategy, p. 275 Build Vocabulary, p. 273	• **Literary Analysis and Reading Transparencies,** pp. 117 and 118 ● ▲ ■	
		• **Listening to Literature** ● ▲ ■ Audiocassettes, Side 28 Audio CDs, CDs 16 and 17
• **Literatura en español** ● ▲ • **Literary Analysis for Enrichment** ■	• **Fine Art Transparencies, Volume 1,** Transparency 17 ● ▲ ■	
• **Formal Assessment:** Selection Test, pp. 283–285 ● ▲ ■ • **Open Book Test,** pp. 174–176 ● ▲ ■ • PRENTICE HALL ASSESSMENT SYSTEM ● ▲ ■	• PRENTICE HALL ASSESSMENT SYSTEM ● ▲ ■ Skills Practice Answers and Explanations on Transparencies ● ▲ ■	• **Test Bank Software** ● ▲ ■ • **Got It! Assessment Videotapes,** Tape 6 ● ▲
• **Selection Support Workbook:** ● ▲ ■ Grammar and Style, p. 274 • **Writing and Grammar,** Diamond Level ● ▲ ■ • **Extension Activities,** p. 59 ● ▲ ■	• **Daily Language Practice Transparencies** ● ▲	• **Writing and Grammar iText CD-ROM** ● ▲ ■ ***Take It to the Net*** www.phschool.com

BLOCK SCHEDULING: Use one 90-minute class period to preteach the selections and have students read them. Use a second 90-minute class period to assess students' mastery of skills and have them complete one of the Extension Activities.

PRETEACH

Step-by-Step Teaching Guide for pp. 1204–1205

Motivation

On the board, write the general heading *Nature* and then create two columns headed *Creative Power* and *Destructive Power*. Invite students to brainstorm phenomena that fit each category. After discussing such contrasting entries as "plant growth" and "hurricanes," tell students that the works in this section will help them further explore both aspects of nature's awesome power.

Interest Grabber Video

As an alternative, you may wish to play "'Fern Hill': Dylan Thomas" on Tape 6 to engage student interest.

❶ More About the Authors

Dylan Thomas

Although Dylan Thomas's work appears to have flowed without stopping out of his brain and through his pen, in fact the poet was a meticulous craftsman. He was almost obsessive in reworking his poems; he wrote many of them in the flush of his youth and refined them when he became an adult. One wonders what he would have produced had he lived beyond the age of 39.

Ted Hughes

The poet Ted Hughes also wrote books for children. One of them is *The Iron Man*, which was published as *The Iron Giant*, some say to avoid buyers' confusing it with a book version of Superman. It is the story of a giant metal man whose competition with a monster from space brings peace to Earth. It was made into the animated film *The Iron Giant* in 1999.

Prepare to Read

❶ Do Not Go Gentle into That Good Night ◆ Fern Hill ◆ The Horses ◆ The Rain Horse

Dylan Thomas (1914–1953)

Playful with language and exuberant about life, Thomas gained remarkable popularity in his lifetime. However, he also had a darker side, evident in his poems of death and the loss of childhood innocence.

A Young Poet Dylan Thomas was born in Swansea in southwestern Wales, an industrial city. However, he often visited his maternal grandfather's farm, which he describes in "Fern Hill." With the encouragement of his father, an English teacher, he became interested in poetry at an early age. Before turning twenty, he had already written—at least in early form—many of his best-known poems. As a teenager, he also produced source books of ideas that served as a basis for later works.

Journeys Abroad At the age of twenty-one, Thomas went to London, where he worked in journalism, broadcasting, and filmmaking for a number of years. In 1940, he published a collection of humorous stories about his childhood and youth, *Portrait of the Artist as a Young Dog*. In 1950, he made the first of four trips to the United States. Audiences here embraced him not only for his theatrical readings of his poems but also for the freshness and complexity of his poetic voice.

Though he continued to publish poetry, two of the later works for which he is best known are prose: Under Milkwood, a "play for voices," and A Child's Christmas in Wales, a memoir.

An Artist's Problems Although acclaimed at an early age, Thomas struggled with poverty and alcoholism through most of his adult life. He died while on tour in the United States, where he had planned to collaborate on an opera with Igor Stravinsky.

Ted Hughes (1930–1998)

Born in rural West Yorkshire, Hughes spent much of his youth hunting and fishing with his brother. These experiences contributed to his lifelong interest in the beauty and violence of nature, recurring themes in his work.

Hughes and His Father It would be a mistake, however, to ignore the violence of World War I as an influence on Hughes. He was born well after the war, but his father had had a traumatic experience in that conflict. He was among a handful of men to survive the destruction of his regiment. Hughes once said that as a child, he was strongly affected by his father's silence about this experience.

Hughes himself served in the Royal Air Force and then studied archaeology and anthropology at Pembroke College, Cambridge, where he met the American poet Sylvia Plath. He married Plath in 1956, but they later separated.

A Variety of Work Hughes is best known for his volumes of poetry *Hawk in the Rain*, *Crow*, and *Moortown*. In these and other works, he uses free verse and powerful, direct speech to express a yearning for a lost wholeness with the natural world. In exploring this theme, which appears in "Horses" and "The Rain Horse," he was strongly influenced by the prose and poetry of D. H. Lawrence.

Hughes was a versatile writer who, in addition to poetry and fiction, wrote books for children. He even wrote a play in a language he invented. One of his final publications was *Tales from Ovid* (1997), a translation of many verse stories from the Latin poet Ovid's *Metamorphoses*. Hughes was poet laureate of England from 1984 until his death.

TEACHING RESOURCES

The following resources can be used to enrich or extend the instruction for pp. 1204–1205.

Motivation

Interest Grabber Video, Tape 6

Background

Beyond Literature, Community Connection: Preservation of Wilderness Lands, p. 59 

Take It to the Net

Visit www.phschool.com for background and hotlinks for the selections.

Literary Analysis

Literary Analysis and Reading Transparencies, Voice, p. 118

Reading

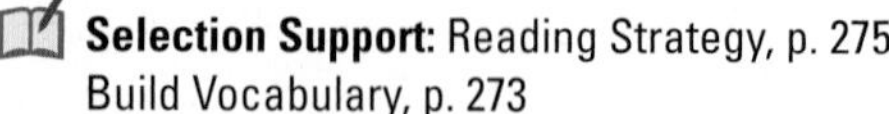

Selection Support: Reading Strategy, p. 275; Build Vocabulary, p. 273

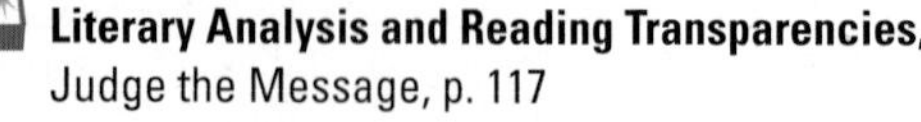

Literary Analysis and Reading Transparencies, Judge the Message, p. 117

BLOCK SCHEDULING: Resources marked with this symbol provide varied instruction during 90-minute blocks.

Preview

Connecting to the Literature

Even if you live in a city, nature is your home. In these poems and stories, the writers consider how sweet and strange a home nature can be.

❷ Literary Analysis

Voice

The **voice** of a poet is his or her "sound" on the page. A poet's voice is based on elements like word choice, sound devices, pace, attitude, and even patterns of vowels and consonants. These two poets have different voices, Thomas tumbling words out in a rush and Hughes "speaking" in separate little blips of images:

- *Thomas, in "Fern Hill"*: "All the sun long it was running, it was lovely, . . . "
- *Hughes, in "The Horses"*: "Not a leaf, not a bird"

Listen for the different voices of these poets as you read their poems.

Comparing Literary Works

Because they have different "voices," these two poets use different poetic forms and meters. To complement his tight, closed way of speaking, Hughes employs loose, unrhyming couplets and the open rhythms of free verse. In contrast, Thomas reigns in his headlong speech with tight poetic forms like the **villanelle**—a nineteen-line poem in which lines 1 and 3 of the opening stanza appear regularly throughout and the rhyme scheme is *aba aba aba aba aba abaa*. In reading these poets, compare the ways in which their voices relate to the forms and rhythms they use.

❸ Reading Strategy

Judging the Writer's Message

In **judging a writer's message,** you test what a writer says against your own experience and your past reading. For example, in "Do Not Go Gentle," Thomas says that the dying should fight against death. Does your experience or reading suggest that this is good advice? Use a chart like this one to record a poet's message and your evaluation of it.

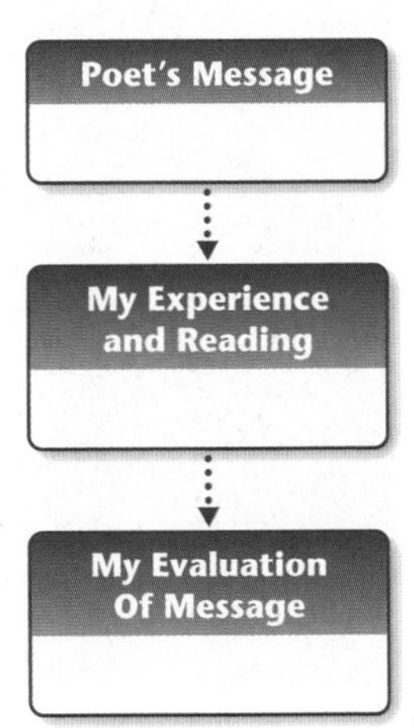

Vocabulary Development

grieved (grēvd) *v.* felt deep grief for; mourned (p. 1207)

transfiguring (trans fig´ yər iŋ) *adj.* changing or transforming, especially in a way that glorifies (p. 1213)

exasperated (eg zas´ pər āt´ id) *adj.* extremely annoyed (p. 1213)

nondescript (nän´ di skript´) *adj.* lacking identifying characteristics; bland (p. 1214)

malevolent (mə lev´ ə lənt) *adj.* wishing harm to others (p. 1218)

❷ Literary Analysis

Voice

- Tell students that just as each of them has a different way of communicating with words, every poet has an individual voice.
- Read the instruction about voice together as a class and call students' attention to the examples from the poems.
- Use the instruction for Comparing Literary Works to introduce students to the various poetic devices poets use to create their voice.
- Use the Voice transparency in **Literary Analysis and Reading Transparencies,** p. 118, to help students connect voice with word choice, diction, and rhythm.

❸ Reading Strategy

Judging the Writer's Message

- Tell students that they can judge a writer's message by comparing it with their own experience or with what they have learned through other reading.
- Have students set up Message organizers to help them evaluate the message of each poet and poem.
- Refer students to the Judging the Message transparency, p. 117 in **Literary Analysis and Reading Transparencies,** to see how a reader might judge Thomas's message in "Do Not Go Gentle into That Good Night."

Vocabulary Development

- Pronounce each vocabulary word for students, and read the definition as a class. Have students identify any words with which they are already familiar.

CUSTOMIZE INSTRUCTION FOR UNIVERSAL ACCESS

For Less Proficient Readers	For English Learners	For Advanced Readers
Students will benefit from listening to both Thomas poems on audiocassette or CD. You may also want to get recordings of Thomas reading his own poems, which are often available in the library.	Have students study the vocabulary words. Then, ask: When you **grieved** for the loss of your pet, did you feel sad or happy? Would you be more likely to be **exasperated** at a friend who was late meeting you or at a friend winning a spelling bee? Would you expect a **nondescript** person to wear bright colors?	Ask students to research the lives of Thomas and Hughes to discover family influences on the poets' work. For example, Thomas was introduced to the natural world at his grandfather's farm, while the ideas and attitudes Hughes learned from his brother and his father influenced his poetry.

 ***E-Teach***

Visit E-Teach at www.phschool.com for teachers' essays on how to teach, with questions and answers.

TEACH

Step-by-Step Teaching Guide for pp. 1206–1220

❶ About the Selection

The speaker urges his father, identified in the last stanza, to resist death, to not "go gentle into that good night." In stanzas 2–5, he offers examples of different kinds of people who were moved to "rage against the dying of the light," suggesting that the urge to resist death is as much a part of the human condition as death itself.

❷ Background

Art

Fishermen at Sea off the Needles, by J. M. W. Turner

J. M. W. Turner is one of the most celebrated English landscape painters of the Romantic era. The dramatic sky seen in *Fisherman at Sea* is a hallmark of Turner's style, characterized by dramatic lighting. Use these questions for discussion:

1. What message about nature does this painting convey? In what way is this similar to the poem's message?
   Answer: The painting suggests that nature is mighty and has the power to destroy human lives; the poem deals with the human struggle against nature's destructive power in the form of death.
2. What elements in the painting convey the power of nature?
   Answer: The dark, ominous sky, the buffeting waves, and the smallness of the human figures.

❸ ▶Critical Viewing

Answer: The boat may represent the soul, which struggles to stay afloat as it resists the forces of the dark and powerful sea, which represents death.

❶ Do Not Go Gentle into That Good Night

Dylan Thomas

❷

Fisherman at Sea off the Needles, J. M. W. Turner, Tate Gallery

❸ ▲ **Critical Viewing** In what ways is the main boat in this painting an apt image of the soul's struggle against the "good night"? **[Analyze]**

TEACHING RESOURCES

The following resources can be used to enrich or extend the instruction for pp. 1206–1220.

Literary Analysis

Selection Support: Literary Analysis, p. 276

Listening to Literature Audiocassettes, Side 28 ■

Listening to Literature Audio CDs, CDs 16 and 17 ■

Extension

Fine Arts Transparencies, Volume 1, Transparency 17 (Display Van Gogh's *Wheat Field With Cypresses* and have students compare the painting to the "green and golden" imagery of "Fern Hill.")

■ **BLOCK SCHEDULING:** Resources marked with this symbol provide varied instruction during 90-minute blocks.

Do not go gentle into that good night,
Old age should burn and rave at close of day;
Rage, rage against the dying of the light.

Though wise men at their end know dark is right,
Because their words had forked no lightning they
Do not go gentle into that good night.

Good men, the last wave by, crying how bright
Their frail deeds might have danced in a green bay,
Rage, rage against the dying of the light.

Wild men who caught and sang the sun in flight,
And learn, too late, they grieved it on its way,
Do not go gentle into that good night.

Grave men, near death, who see with blinding sight
Blind eyes could blaze like meteors and be gay,
Rage, rage against the dying of the light.

And you, my father, there on the sad height,
Curse, bless, me now with your fierce tears, I pray.
Do not go gentle into that good night.
Rage, rage against the dying of the light.

Literary Analysis

Voice and Villanelle In lines 4–15, how does the last line of each stanza stop the movement of the poem?

grieved (grēvd) *v.* felt deep grief for; mourned

Review and Assess

Thinking About the Selection

1. **(a) Recall:** What is the "good night" mentioned in the title of "Do Not Go Gentle into That Good Night"? **(b) Infer:** What specific event is Thomas facing in the poem?
2. **(a) Recall:** Where in the poem does the word *grave* appear? **(b) Analyze:** What double meaning does the word have?
3. **(a) Recall:** What are four types of men Thomas describes in the poem? **(b) Infer:** Does Thomas suggest that each has regrets as he comes to the end of his life? Explain.
4. **(a) Recall:** What advice does the speaker give in lines 3, 9, 15, and 19? **(b) Interpret:** Considering the speaker's advice in these lines, why do you think he refers to the night as "good"?
5. **Evaluate:** Would this poem have been better if Thomas had chosen to work with a less restrictive form than villanelle? Why or why not?
6. **Take a Position:** Should people respond to death and life as intensely as Thomas does in this poem? Why or why not?

4 Literary Analysis

Voice and Villanelle

- After students have read the poem, have them reread the first stanza. Ask what Thomas is referring to in the following phrases: "that good night," "close of day," and "the dying of the light."
  Answer: Thomas is referring to death.
- Ask students the Literary Analysis question on p. 1207: In lines 4–15, how does the last line of each stanza stop the movement of the poem?
  Answer: Thomas ends each stanza with one of two dramatic imperatives: "Rage" (repeated in stanzas 1, 3, and 5) and "Do not go gentle" (repeated in stanzas 2 and 4).

Answers for p. 1207

Review and Assess

1. **(a)** The "good night" is death. **(b)** Thomas is facing the approaching death of his father.
2. **(a)** *Grave* appears at the beginning of the fifth stanza. **(b)** The word means both "very serious" and a place where people are buried after death.
3. **(a)** Thomas describes "wise men," "good men," "wild men," and "grave men." **(b)** Yes, Thomas describes each kind of man as wishing he had done more, or had more success, and so forth.
4. **(a)** The poet tells his father to "Rage," and "Do not go gentle." **(b)** Students may suggest that the word *good* is used ironically or as part of the phrase *good night,* meaning "farewell."
5. Students may say that the poet's message is well served by the repetitive form of the villanelle.
6. Students may express varying views about accepting or resisting death. Point out that Thomas's poem is not clear about how a dying person is to resist death.

CUSTOMIZE INSTRUCTION FOR UNIVERSAL ACCESS

For Special Needs Students	For Less Proficient Readers	For Advanced Readers
Before they read, ask students how they might interpret the exhortation in the title "Do Not Go Gentle into That Good Night." What does "going gentle" represent? What does "that good night" represent? As students read the poem, ask them to identify the meaning of "close of day," "dark is right," and so forth.	To help students grasp the message of Dylan Thomas's poetry, emphasize that in each of the stanzas 2 through 5, Thomas names a different type of person, describes a regret that people of that type might have at the end of life, and urges people of that type to resist death. Have students chart these three elements in each of these four stanzas.	On the basis of the poem and the biographical information about the poet, ask students to speculate on which of the four kinds of men—wise, good, wild, grave—Thomas might have considered himself to be. Ask students to justify their choices.

5 About the Selection

From the perspective of adulthood, the speaker recalls the carefree and magical days he spent on a farm during his childhood—days when "Time let me play and be / Golden in the mercy of his means." At the end of the poem, the poet contrasts his former innocence with his present knowledge of the tyranny of time. He now knows that during childhood, "Time held me green and dying / Though I sang in my chains like the sea."

6 Literary Analysis

Voice

- Ask students what they think Thomas's view of nature is as they read the first three stanzas of the poem.
  Answer: Thomas views nature as surrounding him with beauty and lushness, particularly when he was a child.
- Ask students the Literary Analysis question on p. 1208: What is the contrast between Thomas's way of tumbling words out and the stanzas he uses?
  Possible response: The structure of the poem does not "tumble." It is organized into six stanzas with the same number of lines, and the same type of indenting. Thomas worked very hard to make it look as if the poem "just happened."

5 Fern Hill

Dylan Thomas

Now as I was young and easy under the apple boughs
About the lilting house and happy as the grass was green,
    The night above the dingle starry,
        Time let me hail and climb
    Golden in the heydays of his eyes,
And honored among wagons I was prince of the apple towns
And once below a time I lordly had the trees and leaves
        Trail with daisies and barley
    Down the rivers of the windfall light.

And as I was green and carefree, famous among the barns
About the happy yard and singing as the farm was home,
    In the sun that is young once only,
        Time let me play and be
6   Golden in the mercy of his means,
And green and golden I was huntsman and herdsman, the calves
Sang to my horn, the foxes on the hills barked clear and cold,
        And the sabbath rang slowly
    In the pebbles of the holy streams.

All the sun long it was running, it was lovely, the hay
Fields high as the house, the tunes from the chimneys, it was air
    And playing, lovely and watery
        And fire green as grass.
    And nightly under the simple stars
As I rode to sleep the owls were bearing the farm away,
All the moon long I heard, blessed among stables, the nightjars[1]
    Flying with the ricks,[2] and the horses
        Flashing into the dark.

And then to awake, and the farm, like a wanderer white
With the dew, come back, the cock on his shoulder; it was all

Literary Analysis
Voice What is the contrast between Thomas's way of tumbling words out and the stanzas he uses?

1. **nightjars** *n.* common nocturnal birds, named for the whirring sound that the male makes.
2. **ricks** *n.* haystacks.

ENRICHMENT: Literature Connection

Literary Criticism

Read the following quotations to students or write them on the board:

> "[Dylan Thomas attempts] to express his highly intuitive, indeed mystical sense of reconciliation of opposites—life and death, beauty and horror, growth and decay. . . ."—William Vaughn Moody and Robert Morse Lovett
>
> "Thomas is a poet who takes care of the sound and lets the sense take care of itself."—Robert Graves

Ask students to respond to these two evaluations, based on what they have read in the poems. Tell students to explain whether they agree or disagree with the statements, using details from the poems to justify their opinions.

Shining, it was Adam and maiden,
The sky gathered again
And the sun grew round that very day.
So it must have been after the birth of the simple light
In the first, spinning place, the spellbound horses walking warm
Out of the whinnying green stable
On to the fields of praise.

And honored among foxes and pheasants by the gay house
Under the new made clouds and happy as the heart was long,
In the sun born over and over,
I ran my heedless ways,
My wishes raced through the house-high hay
And nothing I cared, at my sky blue trades, that time allows
In all his tuneful turning so few and such morning songs
Before the children green and golden
Follow him out of grace,

Nothing I cared, in the lamb white days, that time would take me
Up to the swallow thronged loft by the shadow of my hand,
In the moon that is always rising,
Nor that riding to sleep
I should hear him fly with the high fields
And wake to the farm forever fled from the childless land.
❼ Oh as I was young and easy in the mercy of his means,
Time held me green and dying
Though I sang in my chains like the sea.

Reading Strategy
Judging the Writer's Message Is Thomas right in suggesting that a person can "wake" one day to realize that childhood has "forever fled"? Why or why not?

Review and Assess

Thinking About the Selection

1. **Respond:** Does your childhood seem like a distant memory, or are your early experiences still vivid in your mind? Explain.
2. **(a) Recall:** Which two colors does the speaker use to describe himself in his youth? **(b) Analyze:** How would you describe his feelings about his childhood?
3. **(a) Recall:** Paraphrase the final stanza. **(b) Interpret:** How does the mood change in this stanza? **(c) Infer:** What is the reason for this shift?
4. **Interpret:** What is the meaning of lines 53–54?
5. **Draw Conclusions:** What does this poem suggest about Thomas's attitude toward the different stages of life?
6. **Classify:** Into what important stages would you divide human life? Explain.

CUSTOMIZE INSTRUCTION FOR UNIVERSAL ACCESS

For Special Needs Students	For Less Proficient Readers	For Gifted/Talented Students
Have students listen to a recording of the poem on either audiocassette or CD. Ask them to pay attention to the pacing, the pronunciation of words, and the ideas they get from listening. Then, ask volunteers to read individual stanzas aloud.	Draw students' attention to Thomas's use of the words *green* and *golden* in lines 2, 5, 10, 14, 15, 22, 35, 44, and 53. Encourage them to comment on the meaning and significance of these two colors to the poet. Then, ask students which colors they would use if they were to write a poem about themselves at some point in their life.	Ask students what metaphor Thomas uses in stanza 4. That is, to what does he compare each new day to which he awakens? (The poet compares each new day to the first day of creation. "Adam and maiden" represent Adam and Eve.)

❼ Reading Strategy

Judging the Writer's Message

- Ask students to find examples of words and phrases the speaker uses to suggest that he will not always have as much time to experience the beauty in nature as he once had.
  Possible responses: "I ran my heedless ways," "time allows . . . so few and such morning songs," "I should hear him fly with the high fields," and "And wake to the farm forever fled from the childless land" suggest that the speaker's childhood will end.
- Ask students the Reading Strategy question on p. 1209: Is Thomas right in suggesting that a person can "wake" one day to realize that childhood has "forever fled"? Why or why not?
  Possible response: Yes, often one does not realize the value of a particular time in one's life until it suddenly is no longer there.

Answers for p. 1209

Review and Assess

1. Students' reflections on their childhoods will vary.
2. **(a)** The speaker uses the colors green and golden to describe himself in his youth. **(b)** He feels that his childhood was a charmed, mythical time.
3. **(a)** I cared nothing about the passage of time when I was younger. One day I woke up and my childhood had fled. I realized that even as I felt young and immortal, I was already approaching death. **(b)** The mood changes from one of joy and celebration to one of sadness and loss. **(c)** These lines reflect the speaker's adult awareness of mortality.
4. Within the "chains," or limitations, imposed by time, Thomas the child lived with boundless energy and joy.
5. Thomas celebrates the ignorance of childhood but with the knowledge of adult years.
6. Students may suggest childhood, adolescence, young adulthood, middle age, and old age.

8 About the Selection

The speaker vividly describes an encounter with nature as well as the sense of awe that accompanied it. He hopes that the image of these stalwart horses will remain with him through the years.

9 Literary Analysis

Voice

- Ask students to identify the personification in the first stanza. What is being personified, and how?
  Answer: The phrase "evil air" is personification, because it gives air a human quality. The poet calls the air evil because it is cold and still.
- Ask students to paraphrase the second stanza as if they were writing a prose description.
  Possible response: I could not see a leaf on a tree, and could not hear a single bird. My surroundings seemed to be a group of statues made of frost. I came out into the open above the wood.
- Ask students the Literary Analysis question on p. 1210: How do the stanzas in this poem suggest Hughes's style of "speaking" in short bursts of images?
  Answer: Hughes captures a place or a feeling in a few words, sometimes only two or three, as in "Not a leaf," "not a bird," "ten together," "Megalith-still."

10 Literary Analysis

Voice

- Remind students that alliteration is the repetition of the same consonant sound at the beginnings of words or in accented syllables.
- Ask students to find two examples of alliteration in stanzas four and five. Have them describe how each example combines with Hughes's style of speaking to help create his voice.
  Answer: The repetition of /h/ in "Halved the sky ahead. And I saw the horses: / Huge in the dense gray" and the repetition of /m/ in "Megalith-still. They breathed, making no move." The alliteration helps reinforce Hughes's short, complete images, part of his voice.

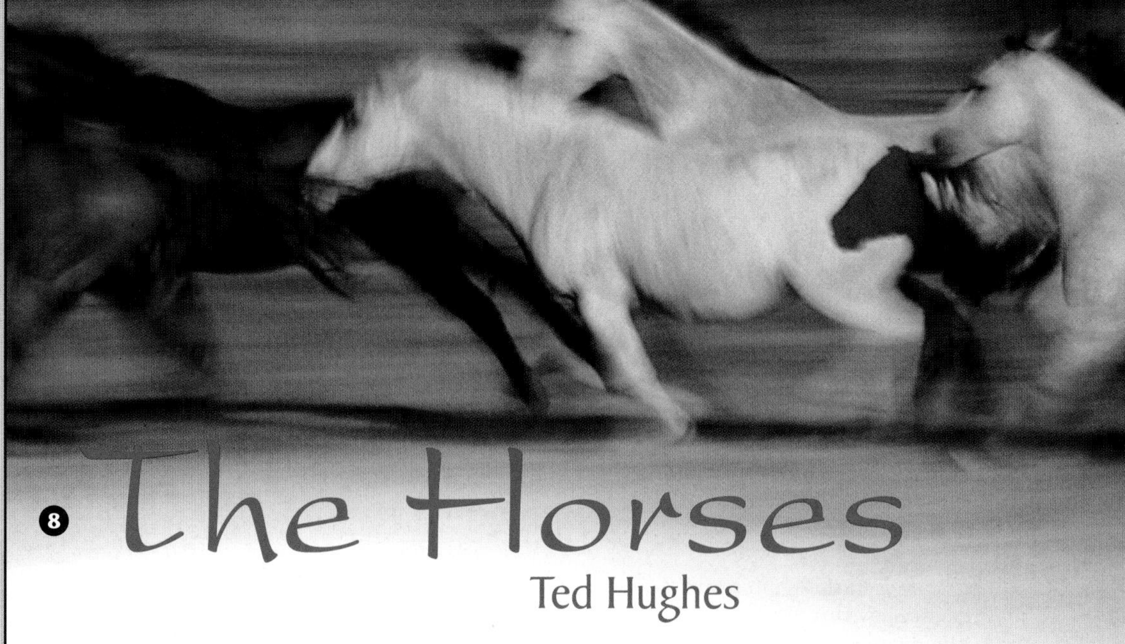

8 The Horses

Ted Hughes

Background

Although both Thomas and Hughes wrote of nature, they approached it differently. Thomas was fascinated by nature's double face, life and death, as demonstrated in the line "Time held me green and dying" from "Fern Hill." Hughes was often closely attuned to nature's violence, as in "The Rain Horse," or to its remote, primitive, nonhuman beauty, as in "The Horses."

9

I climbed through woods in the hour-before-dawn dark.
Evil air, a frost-making stillness,

Not a leaf, not a bird—
A world cast in frost. I came out above the wood

Where my breath left tortuous statues in the iron light.
But the valleys were draining the darkness

10

Till the moorline—blackening dregs of the brightening gray—
Halved the sky ahead. And I saw the horses:

Huge in the dense gray—ten together—
Megalith-still.[1] They breathed, making no move,

Literary Analysis
Voice How do the stanzas in this poem suggest Hughes's style of "speaking" in short bursts of images?

1. **Megalith-still** still as the huge stones left by ancient peoples, such as those at Stonehenge.

ENRICHMENT: Science Connection

Horses

Although the horses in both Ted Hughes's poem and short story symbolize the timeless and untamed energies of nature, horses are in fact domesticated animals, as are dogs, cats, cows, and sheep. Encourage interested students to learn about the history and "family tree" of the domestic horse—whose scientific name is *Equus caballus*—and share their findings with the class. Among the questions students might research are: When did people first domesticate the horse? Which species represent the horse's wild "cousins"? Where in the world are there populations of domestic horses that have reverted to living in the wild?

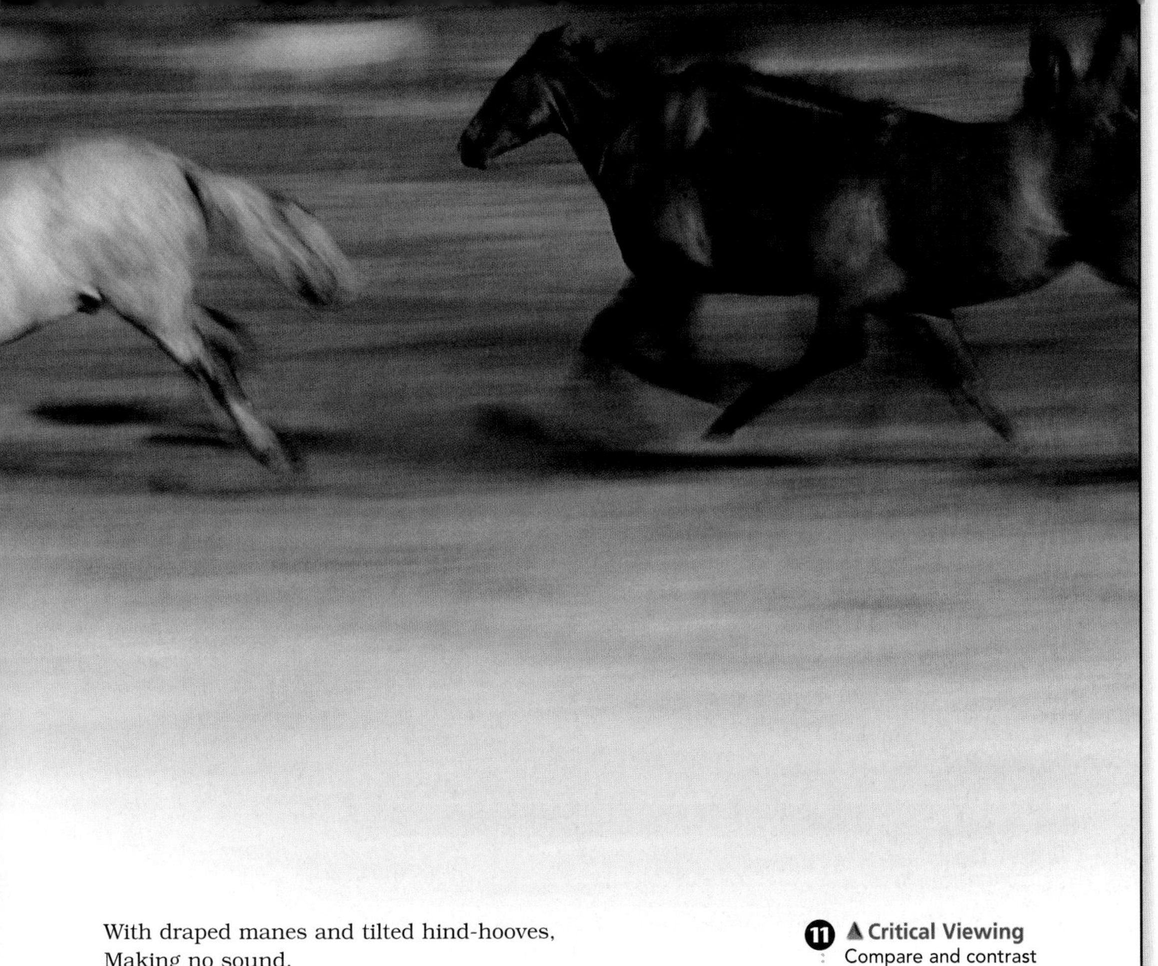

With draped manes and tilted hind-hooves,
Making no sound.

I passed: not one snorted or jerked its head.
Gray silent fragments
Of a gray silent world.

I listened in emptiness on the moor-ridge.
The curlew's[2] tear turned its edge on the silence.

Slowly detail leafed from the darkness. Then the sun
Orange, red, red erupted

Silently, and splitting to its core tore and flung cloud,
Shook the gulf open, showed blue,

11 ▲ **Critical Viewing** Compare and contrast the horses in the poem with those in the picture. **[Compare and Contrast]**

12  **Reading Check** What are the horses doing when Hughes sees them?

2. curlew's (kur´ lo͞o) *n.* of a large, brownish wading bird with long legs.

11 ▶ **Critical Viewing**

Answer: The horses in the photo are running, while the horses in the poem are still. Both convey power but in different ways—the horses in the photo convey released energy, whereas those in the poem are filled with tension and potential energy.

12 **Reading Check**

Answer: The horses are standing as still as stone statues.

13 Reading Strategy

Judging the Writer's Message (p. 1212)

- Ask what the speaker is doing in line 34.
  Answer: The speaker is going about his life, the years are passing, he lives in a place with crowded streets and many faces.
- Ask students the Reading Strategy question on p. 1212: Can a memory of something seen in nature stay with a person for years, as Hughes suggests in lines 34–35?
  Possible response: Students may say that they have memories from their childhood and that some are very vivid.

CUSTOMIZE INSTRUCTION FOR UNIVERSAL ACCESS

For Special Needs Students	For Less Proficient Readers	For Gifted/Talented Students
Students may want to write their own horse poems and collect photos and illustrations of this animal from magazines and other sources. Point out that Hughes describes the horses as seen at dawn and just after sunrise. They might want to write a poem or draw an illustration of horses in bright sunlight, at night, in the rain or snow, or in a barn.	Have students use the Voice transparency on p. 118 of **Literary Analysis and Reading Transparencies** as a model and add their own entries to each of the circles. For example, under Word Choice, they might add *snorted, erupted,* and *splitting.*	Students may want to draw or make sculptures of the group of horses as they envision the animals from the poet's description.

Answers for p. 1212

Review and Assess

1. Students should offer reasons to explain their choices.
2. **(a)** The poem is set in the woods at dawn in an earlier time in the speaker's life. **(b)** The dramatic sunrise midway through the poem reflects the speaker's dramatic discovery of the horses and the dramatic shift in his perception of them.
3. **(a)** The speaker sees the horses twice. **(b)** In the first, predawn sighting, the horses appear gray and stonelike, whereas in the second sighting, they "steam" and "glisten" in the morning light. In both sightings, the horses are powerful, mysterious, silent, and still.
4. **(a)** The speaker walks up through a woodland area just before dawn, then as the sun rises he turns and walks back down the way he came. He sees the horses on each journey, both up and down. **(b)** The poem suggests that nature is beautiful, powerful, mysterious, and timeless.
5. **(a)** The speaker wants to retain the memory of his encounter with the horses. **(b)** He may find solace in the peacefulness of the scene when he is surrounded by the "din of the crowded streets."
6. Students may say that by affirming the mystery and significance in nature, the poem provides convincing arguments for controlling development.

And the big planets hanging—
I turned

Stumbling in the fever of a dream, down towards
The dark woods, from the kindling tops.

And came to the horses.
                    There, still they stood,
But now steaming and glistening under the flow of light,

Their draped stone manes, their tilted hind-hooves
Stirring under a thaw while all around them

The frost showed its fires. But still they made no sound.
Not one snorted or stamped,

Their hung heads patient as the horizons,
High over valleys, in the red leveling rays—

In din of the crowded streets, going among the years, the faces,
May I still meet my memory in so lonely a place

Between the streams and the red clouds, hearing curlews,
Hearing the horizons endure.

Reading Strategy
Judging the Writer's Message Can a memory of something seen in nature stay with a person for years, as Hughes suggests in lines 34–35?

Review and Assess

Thinking About the Selection

1. **Respond:** What kind of place or scene would you like to remember later, "going among the years"? Why?
2. **(a) Recall:** What is the setting of the poem, its time and place? **(b) Evaluate:** How does this setting heighten the impact of events in the poem?
3. **(a) Recall:** How many times does the speaker sight the horses? **(b) Compare and Contrast:** Compare and contrast the horses in the different sightings.
4. **(a) Recall:** What actually occurs during the course of the poem? **(b) Draw Conclusions:** What view of nature do the descriptions and actions in the poem suggest? Explain.
5. **(a) Recall:** What wish does the speaker make at the end of the poem? **(b) Evaluate:** In what ways might the speaker—or anyone—draw solace from a scene like this in the future?
6. **Make a Judgment:** Does this poem provide a good argument for protecting nature against development? Explain.

ENRICHMENT: Literature Connection

Ted Hughes

Hughes's early life in Yorkshire was partial inspiration for his becoming a poet. He told a writer once that he "began writing poems in adolescence, when it dawned upon him that his earlier passion for hunting animals in his native Yorkshire ended either in the possession of a dead animal, or at best a trapped one. He wanted to capture not just live animals, but the aliveness of animals in their natural state: their wildness, . . . the fox-ness of the fox and the crow-ness of the crow."

Some critics suggest that Hughes's concentration on animals in his poetry was a way of examining the position of man in nature—a position of alienation. Animals symbolize, according to these critics, the "instinctive power of nature that he finds lacking in human society."

Hughes lived on and worked his own farm later in his life. His collection *Moortown* is a group of poems about his experiences as a farmer.

14 The Rain Horse

Ted Hughes

As the young man came over the hill the first thin blowing of rain met him. He turned his coat-collar up and stood on top of the shelving rabbit-riddled hedgebank, looking down into the valley.

He had come too far. What had set out as a walk along pleasantly-remembered tarmac[1] lanes had turned dreamily by gate and path and hedge-gap into a cross-ploughland trek, his shoes ruined, the dark mud of the lower fields inching up the trouser legs of his gray suit where they rubbed against each other. And now there was a raw, flapping wetness in the air that would be downpour again at any minute. He shivered, holding himself tense against the cold.

15 This was the view he had been thinking of. Vaguely, without really directing his walk, he had felt he would get the whole thing from this point. For twelve years, whenever he had recalled this scene, he had imagined it as it looked from here. Now the valley lay sunken in front of him, utterly deserted, shallow, bare fields, black and sodden as the bed of an ancient lake after the weeks of rain.

Nothing happened. Not that he had looked forward to any very transfiguring experience. But he had expected something, some pleasure, some meaningful sensation, he didn't quite know what.

So he waited, trying to nudge the right feelings alive with the details—the surprisingly familiar curve of the hedges, the stone gate-pillar and iron gatehook let into it that he had used as a target, the long bank of the rabbit-warren on which he stood and which had been the first thing he ever noticed about the hill when twenty years ago, from the distance of the village, he had said to himself "That looks like rabbits."

Twelve years had changed him. This land no longer recognized him, and he looked back at it coldly, as at a finally visited home-country, known only through the stories of a grandfather; felt nothing but the dullness of feeling nothing. Boredom. Then, suddenly, impatience, with a whole exasperated swarm of little anxieties about his shoes,

transfiguring (trans fig′ yər iŋ) *adj.* changing or transforming, especially in a way that glorifies

exasperated (eg zas′ pər āt′ id) *adj.* extremely annoyed

16 **Reading Check**

In what way has the young man changed since the last time he was in this place?

1. **tarmac** material used for paving.

14 About the Selection

In a story laden with symbolism, the weather and a rogue horse conspire to make a man miserable and frightened as he visits the farmland where he grew up. The man has come to the scene seeking to recapture an image that he held in his imagination from the past. Instead he finds himself in an unfamiliar, hostile landscape that threatens his very life as well as his lost memories.

15 Critical Thinking

Infer

- Have students read the third paragraph and note the expectations of the man: ". . . he had imagined it as it looked from here." Then, have them read the description of the way the valley looks now and infer what it looked like twelve years ago.
  Possible response: The valley may have been full of life, with hedges and gates, crops in full bloom, and the hills full of color.
- Ask students to compare the man's feelings about the valley twelve years ago and his feelings about it now.
  Answer: Twelve years ago the scene gave him pleasure; now it leaves him cold and bores him.

16 Reading Check

Answer: The man is no longer comfortable in the natural world.

CUSTOMIZE INSTRUCTION FOR UNIVERSAL ACCESS

For English Learners	For Less Proficient Readers	For Gifted/Talented Students
Ask students to find other examples of alliteration on p. 1212. Which sound is repeated many times on this page? Ask them for examples. (The sound of *s* blends, particularly *st*, is repeated. "There, still they stood, / But now steaming and glistening"; "But still they made no sound. / Not one snorted or stamped.")	Have students read the sentence in the middle of p. 1213 that begins, "Now the valley lay sunken . . ." Ask them to compare the writing here with the short, sharp images Hughes writes in "The Horses." How are they similar?	Encourage students to write about an experience they have had in returning to a place they once knew, as the man returns to a farm where he spent time in his childhood. Perhaps students lived in a different home when they were younger, or vacationed in a place to which they returned only recently.

17 Literary Analysis

Voice

- Ask students to identify the two metaphorical descriptions of the rain in this passage. To what is the rain compared?
  Answer: "Spitting rain" and "the rain pulling up out of the distance, dragging its gray broken columns, . . ." both compare the rain to a creature that can spit and move of its own volition.
- Ask what the metaphors tell the reader about the meaning of the rain in this character's mind.
  Possible response: The young man experiences the rain as very unpleasant and actively hostile to him.

18 Reading Strategy

Judging the Writer's Message

- Have students describe the man's response to the situation in which he has found himself.
  Answer: He is angry with himself and with the land for putting him in a position in which he feels outcast, old, stiff, and stupid.
- Ask students what they think the writer's message is in the first of the two paragraphs in the passage.
  Answer: The natural world is not always a welcoming place for humans.
- Ask students the Reading Strategy question on p. 1214: Do you think the idea that the horse might be "up to no good" comes from the young man, from Hughes, or from both of them? Explain.
  Possible response: The idea comes from both the young man and the writer. It comes from the young man in the sense that it reflects his unease in his surroundings. It comes from Hughes in the sense that it reflects Hughes's concern with a power in nature separate from human concerns.

and the spitting rain and his new suit and that sky and the two-mile trudge through the mud back to the road.

It would be quicker to go straight forward to the farm a mile away
17 in the valley and behind which the road looped. But the thought of meeting the farmer—to be embarrassingly remembered or shouted at as a trespasser—deterred him. He saw the rain pulling up out of the distance, dragging its gray broken columns, smudging the trees and the farms.

A wave of anger went over him: anger against himself for blundering into this mud-trap and anger against the land that made him feel so outcast, so old and stiff and stupid. He wanted nothing but to get
18 away from it as quickly as possible. But as he turned, something moved in his eye-corner. All his senses startled alert. He stopped.

Over to his right a thin, black horse was running across the ploughland towards the hill, its head down, neck stretched out. It seemed to be running on its toes like a cat, like a dog up to no good.

Reading Strategy
Judging the Writer's Message Do you think the idea that the horse might be "up to no good" comes from the young man, from Hughes, or from both of them? Explain.

From the high point on which he stood the hill dipped slightly and rose to another crested point fringed with the tops of trees, three hundred yards to his right. As he watched it, the horse ran up to that crest, showed against the sky—for a moment like a nightmarish leopard—and disappeared over the other side.

For several seconds he stared at the skyline, stunned by the unpleasantly strange impression the horse had made on him. Then the plastering beat of icy rain on his bare skull brought him to himself. The distance had vanished in a wall of gray. All around him the fields were jumping and streaming.

Holding his collar close and tucking his chin down into it he ran back over the hilltop towards the town-side, the lee-side, his feet sucking and splashing, at every stride plunging to the ankle.

This hill was shaped like a wave, a gently rounded back lifting out of the valley to a sharply crested, almost concave front hanging over the river meadows towards the town. Down this front, from the crest, hung two small woods separated by a fallow field. The near wood was nothing more than a quarry, circular, full of stones and bracken,[2] with a few thorns and nondescript saplings, foxholes and rabbit holes. The other was rectangular, mainly a planting of scrub oak trees. Beyond the river smoldered the town like a great heap of blue cinders.

nondescript (nän´ di skript´) *adj.* lacking identifying characteristics; bland

He ran along the top of the first wood and finding no shelter but the thin, leafless thorns of the hedge, dipped below the crest out of the wind and jogged along through thick grass to the wood of oaks. In blinding rain he lunged through the barricade of brambles at the wood's edge. The little crippled trees were small choice in the way of shelter, but at a sudden fierce thickening of the rain he took one at random and crouched down under the leaning trunk.

Still panting from his run, drawing his knees up tightly, he watched the bleak lines of rain, gray as hail, slanting through the

2. **bracken** Large, coarse ferns.

ENRICHMENT: Literature Connection

Writers' Attitudes Toward Nature

Is nature an arena of bloody competition, "red in tooth and claw," as Tennyson writes? Is it something in which we can trust, as Wordsworth suggests: "Nature never did betray / The heart that loved her"? The answer is that different poets "see" different things in the natural world.

Like Hughes, Dylan Thomas was fascinated by nature's double face: life and death. He refers to both creation and destruction in the title of one of his most famous poems, "The Force That Through the Green Fuse Drives the Flower." The color green suggests life and vitality, but the word *fuse*—a figure of speech for the flower's stem—suggests a bomb's fuse. In "Fern Hill," the double face of nature is also evident: "Time held me green and dying." Through most of the poem, however, Thomas stresses nature's sweet greenness, associated with childhood.

boughs into the clumps of bracken and bramble. He felt hidden and safe. The sound of the rain as it rushed and lulled in the wood seemed to seal him in. Soon the chilly sheet lead of his suit became a tight, warm mold, and gradually he sank into a state of comfort that was all but trance, though the rain beat steadily on his exposed shoulders and trickled down the oak trunk on to his neck.

All around him the boughs angled down, glistening, black as iron. From their tips and elbows the drops hurried steadily, and the channels of the bark pulsed and gleamed. For a time he amused himself calculating the variation in the rainfall by the variations in a dribble of water from a trembling twig-end two feet in front of his nose. He studied the twig, bringing dwarfs and continents and animals out of its scurfy bark. Beyond the boughs the blue shoal of the town was rising and falling, and darkening and fading again, in the pale, swaying backdrop of rain.

He wanted this rain to go on forever. Whenever it seemed to be drawing off he listened anxiously until it closed in again. As long as it lasted he was suspended from life and time. He didn't want to return to his sodden shoes and his possibly ruined suit and the walk back over that land of mud.

All at once he shivered. He hugged his knees to squeeze out the cold and found himself thinking of the horse. The hair on the nape of his neck prickled slightly. He remembered how it had run up to the
19 crest and showed against the sky.

He tried to dismiss the thought. Horses wander about the countryside often enough. But the image of the horse as it had appeared against the sky stuck in his mind. It must have come over the crest just above the wood in which he was now sitting. To clear his mind, he twisted around and looked up the wood between the tree stems, to his left.

At the wood top, with the silvered gray light coming in behind it, the black horse was standing under the oaks, its head high and alert, its ears pricked, watching him.

A horse sheltering from the rain generally goes into a sort of stupor, tilts a hind hoof and hangs its head and lets its eyelids droop, and so it stays as long as the rain lasts. This horse was nothing like that. It was watching him intently, standing perfectly still, its soaked neck and flank shining in the hard light.

He turned back. His scalp went icy and he shivered. What was he to do? Ridiculous to try driving it away. And to leave the wood, with the rain still coming down full pelt, was out of the question. Meanwhile the idea of being watched became more and more unsettling until at last he had to twist around again, to see if the horse had moved. It stood exactly as before.

This was absurd. He took control of himself and turned back deliberately, determined not to give the horse one more thought. If it wanted to share the wood with him, let it. If it wanted to stare at him, let it. He was nestling firmly into these resolutions when the ground shook and he heard the crash of a heavy body coming down the

Literary Analysis

Voice What does the brief length of the paragraphs in this section of the story suggest about the young man's state of mind?

 **Reading Check**

In what way does the horse behave differently from other horses that shelter from the rain?

19 Literary Analysis

Voice

- Have students summarize the young man's behavior and emotions in this passage.
  Answer: The man first wishes the rain would go on forever and hide him from the real world. Then, he realizes how cold it is and thinks again of the horse. Next, he tries to think of a justification for the horse's acting the way it does. Finally, he looks around and finds the horse watching him.
- Ask students the Literary Analysis question on p. 1215: What do the brief paragraphs in this section of the story suggest about the young man's state of mind?
  Answer: They suggest that he is unsettled, jumping back and forth among ideas of what to do.

20 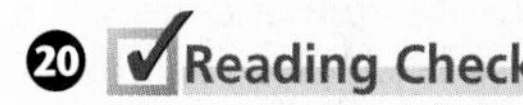

Answer: This horse watches the man intently. It is neither in a sleepy state nor are its eyelids drooping.

CUSTOMIZE INSTRUCTION FOR UNIVERSAL ACCESS

For Special Needs Students	For Less Proficient Readers
Help students note the importance of the weather in this story, as a presence carrying physical, psychological, and emotional weight. Have them keep a notebook of descriptions of the rain, starting with the first line of the story on p. 1213, and the sentence a little farther down, "And now there was a raw, flapping wetness in the air that would be downpour again at any moment." Tell students that good writers are able to describe the same phenomenon in a variety of ways.	Help students infer what kind of town the young man sees at the bottom of the valley. Point them to the descriptions on pp. 1214 and 1215: "Beyond the river smoldered the town like a great heap of blue cinders" and "Beyond the boughs the blue shoal of the town was rising and falling. . . ." (Students may suggest that it is an industrial town, with smoke, industry, and pollution.)

21 Reading Strategy

Judging the Writer's Message

- Ask students what the man's first thought is as the horse seems to charge him and he trips and falls. Answer: The man thinks that he must be careful not to get leaf mold on his suit.
- Ask why this thought is symbolic of the man's place in this valley. Answer: The man's fear for his suit, rather than his safety or even life, shows that his values are no longer tied to the natural world.
- Ask students the Reading Strategy question on p. 1216: How do the young man's experiences with the horse relate to the earlier statement that "This land no longer recognized him"? Answer: The man no longer feels a part of this land, even though he grew up here. The experiences with the horse make him feel that he is no longer recognized as being welcome here.

22 Literary Analysis

Voice

- Ask students what explanations the man suggests to himself for the horse's attacking him. Answer: The man thinks the horse is mad, has a brain abscess, is spiteful, or is affected by the rain.
- Ask what is ironic about the statements, "The horse was evidently mad . . ." and "Rain sometimes puts creatures into queer states." Possible response: These statements are ironic because both of these things could just as easily be true of the man.

wood. Like lightning his legs bounded him upright and about face. The horse was almost on top of him, its head stretching forwards, ears flattened and lips lifted back from the long yellow teeth. He got one snapshot glimpse of the red-veined eyeball as he flung himself backwards around the tree. Then he was away up the slope, whipped by oak twigs as he leapt the brambles and brushwood, twisting between the close trees till he tripped and sprawled. As he fell the warning flashed through his head that he must at all costs keep his suit out of the leaf-mold, but a more urgent instinct was already
21 rolling him violently sideways. He spun around, sat up and looked back, ready to scramble off in a flash to one side. He was panting from the sudden excitement and effort. The horse had disappeared. The wood was empty except for the drumming, slant gray rain, dancing the bracken and glittering from the branches.

He got up, furious. Knocking the dirt and leaves from his suit as well as he could he looked around for a weapon. The horse was evi-
22 dently mad, had an abscess on its brain or something of the sort. Or maybe it was just spiteful. Rain sometimes puts creatures into queer states. Whatever it was, he was going to get away from the wood as quickly as possible, rain or no rain.

Reading Strategy Judging the Writer's Message How do the young man's experiences with the horse relate to the earlier statement that "this land no longer recognized him"?

Since the horse seemed to have gone on down the wood, his way to the farm over the hill was clear. As he went, he broke a yard length of wrist-thick dead branch from one of the oaks, but immediately threw it aside and wiped the slime of rotten wet bark from his hands with his soaked handkerchief. Already he was thinking it incredible that the horse could have meant to attack him. Most likely it was just going down the wood for better shelter and had made a feint[3] at him in passing—as much out of curiosity or playfulness as anything. He recalled the way horses menace each other when they are galloping around in a paddock.

The wood rose to a steep bank topped by the hawthorn hedge that ran along the whole ridge of the hill. He was pulling himself up to a thin place in the hedge by the bare stem of one of the hawthorns when he ducked and shrank down again. The swelling gradient of fields lay in front of him, smoking in the slowly crossing rain. Out in the middle of the first field, tall as a statue, and a ghostly silver in the under-cloud light, stood the horse, watching the wood.

He lowered his head slowly, slithered back down the bank and crouched. An awful feeling of helplessness came over him. He felt certain the horse had been looking straight at him. Waiting for him? Was it clairvoyant?[4] Maybe a mad animal can be clairvoyant. At the same time he was ashamed to find himself acting so inanely, ducking
 and creeping about in this way just to keep out of sight of a horse. He tried to imagine how anybody in their senses would just walk off home. This cooled him a little, and he retreated farther down the

3. **feint** Pretend attack.
4. **clairvoyant** Having the supernatural ability to see what is not present or to read minds.

wood. He would go back the way he had come, along under the hill crest, without any more nonsense.

The wood hummed and the rain was a cold weight, but he observed this rather than felt it. The water ran down inside his clothes and squelched in his shoes as he eased his way carefully over the bedded twigs and leaves. At every instant he expected to see the prick-eared black head looking down at him from the hedge above.

At the woodside he paused, close against a tree. The success of this last manoeuvre was restoring his confidence, but he didn't want to venture out into the open field without making sure that the horse was just where he had left it. The perfect move would be to withdraw quietly and leave the horse standing out there in the rain. He crept up again among the trees to the crest and peeped through the hedge.

The gray field and the whole slope were empty. He searched the distance. The horse was quite likely to have forgotten him altogether and wandered off. Then he raised himself and leaned out to see if it had come in close to the hedge. Before he was aware of anything the ground shook. He twisted around wildly to see how he had been caught. The black shape was above him, right across the light. Its
24 whinnying snort and the spattering whack of its hooves seemed to be actually inside his head as he fell backwards down the bank, and leapt again like a madman, dodging among the oaks, imagining how the buffet would come and how he would be knocked headlong. Halfway down the wood the oaks gave way to bracken and old roots and stony rabbit diggings. He was well out into the middle of this before he realized that he was running alone.

Gasping for breath now and cursing mechanically, without a thought for his suit he sat down on the ground to rest his shaking legs, letting the rain plaster the hair down over his forehead and watching the dense flashing lines disappear abruptly into the soil all around him as if he were watching through thick plate glass. He took deep breaths in the effort to steady his heart and regain control of himself. His right trouser turn-up was ripped at the seam and his suit jacket was splashed with the yellow mud of the top field.

Obviously the horse had been farther along the hedge above the steep field, waiting for him to come out at the woodside just as he had intended. He must have peeped through the hedge—peeping the wrong way—within yards of it.

However, this last attack had cleared up one thing. He need no longer act like a fool out of mere uncertainty as to whether the horse was simply being playful or not. It was definitely after him. He picked

Literary Analysis
Voice Through the use of such phrases as "whinnying snort" and "spattering whack," does Hughes create a voice that is distant or engaged, slow or rapid? Explain.

25 

What happens when the horse attacks the young man?

23 Critical Thinking

Make Judgments

- Ask students how the man feels at this point in his encounter with the horse.
  Answer: The man feels helpless but also ashamed. Why would anyone in his right senses act the way he is acting, hiding from a horse?
- Have students speculate on what the young man means by deciding to go another direction, "without any more nonsense."
  Answer: The man feels that it is nonsense that he should be threatened by a horse, a domesticated animal.

24 Literary Analysis

Voice

- Have students skim the story to find the encounters between the man and the horse. Have them summarize them in brief statements that show the progression of the encounters.
- Lead students to see that in the first encounter the man just sees the horse running in the distance; in the second encounter he finds the horse watching him, followed by an attack; in the third encounter he escapes an attack that takes place before he can spot the horse.
- Ask students how they would describe the progression of encounters.
  Possible response: In each encounter the horse gets closer and potentially more dangerous.
- Ask students the Literary Analysis question on p. 1217: Through the use of such phrases as "whinnying snort" and "spattering whack," does Hughes create a voice that is distinct or engaged, slow or rapid? Explain.
  Answer: The voice in this passage is fast-paced and engaged, reflecting the intense physical action that is taking place.

25 Reading Check

Answer: The man runs and tries to get out of the way.

CUSTOMIZE INSTRUCTION FOR UNIVERSAL ACCESS

For English Learners	For Advanced Readers
Have students fill out a graphic organizer like the Voice transparency on p. 118 of **Literary Analysis and Reading Transparencies,** using this story as the subject. Have them enter examples of words made by the writer that communicate the sense of menace and estrangement that the young man feels, as well as examples of the diction and rhythm Hughes uses, some of which will probably remind them of Hughes's poetry.	Ted Hughes was the poet laureate of England when he died. Students may want to do research to see what a poet laureate does, both in England and in the United States. They may also find out who the current laureate of the United States is and bring in some of his or her poetry to read.

26 Reading Strategy

Judging the Writer's Message

- Ask students if they think the horse is real or a creation of the man's imagination.
  Possible responses: The horse is real and is trying simply to get the man out of its territory. The horse is not real but a part of the man's extreme discomfort with the place he is in.
- Ask students the Reading Strategy question on p. 1218: Do you view a horse as a powerful force of nature, as Hughes seems to do in the paragraph beginning, "Now he noticed . . ."? Why or why not?
  Possible response: The horse is a powerful force of nature, even though it is domesticated, because it is a large animal and is still more tied to the natural world than humans are.

27 Vocabulary Development

Latin Root *-vol-*

- Ask students to read the paragraph that contains the vocabulary word *malevolent* and try to determine its meaning without looking at the margin note.
- Tell students that *malevolent* comes from the Latin prefix *mal-*, meaning "bad," and the root *-vol-*, meaning "to wish." Ask why Hughes uses the word in this context of the story.
  Answer: The young man thinks the horse has malevolent intentions toward him.
- Have students think of other words that contain the root *-vol-* or use a dictionary to find examples.
  Possible response: Words that contain the root *-vol-* include *voluntary, volunteer,* and *volition.*

up two stones about the size of goose eggs and set off towards the bottom of the wood, striding carelessly.

A loop of the river bordered all this farmland. If he crossed the little level meadow at the bottom of the wood, he could follow the three-mile circuit, back to the road. There were deep hollows in the river-bank, shoaled with pebbles, as he remembered, perfect places to defend himself from if the horse followed him out there.

The hawthorns that choked the bottom of the wood—some of them good-sized trees—knitted into an almost impassable barrier. He had found a place where the growth thinned slightly and had begun to lift aside the long spiny stems, pushing himself forward, when he stopped. Through the bluish veil of bare twigs he saw the familiar shape out in the field below the wood.

But it seemed not to have noticed him yet. It was looking out across the field towards the river. Quietly, he released himself from the thorns and climbed back across the clearing towards the one side of the wood he had not yet tried. If the horse would only stay down there he could follow his first and easiest plan, up the wood and over the hilltop to the farm.

Now he noticed that the sky had grown much darker. The rain was heavier every second, pressing down as if the earth had to be flooded before nightfall. The oaks ahead blurred and the ground drummed. He began to run. And as he ran he heard a deeper sound running with him. He whirled around. The horse was in the middle of the clearing. It might have been running to get out of the terrific rain except that it was coming straight for him, scattering clay and stones,
26 with an immensely supple and powerful motion. He let out a tearing roar and threw the stone in his right hand. The result was instantaneous. Whether at the roar or the stone the horse reared as if against a wall and shied to the left. As it dropped back on its fore-feet he flung his second stone, at ten yards' range, and saw a bright mud blotch suddenly appear on the glistening black flank. The horse surged down the wood, splashing the earth like water, tossing its long tail as it plunged out of sight among the hawthorns.

Reading Strategy
Judging the Writer's Message Do you view a horse as a powerful force of nature, as Hughes seems to do in the paragraph beginning, "Now he noticed . . ."? Why or why not?

He looked around for stones. The encounter had set the blood beating in his head and given him a savage energy. He could have
27 killed the horse at that moment. That this brute should pick him and play with him in this malevolent fashion was more than he could bear. Whoever owned it, he thought, deserved to have its neck broken for letting the dangerous thing loose.

malevolent (mə lev′ ə lent) *adj.* wishing harm to others

He came out at the woodside, in open battle now, still searching for the right stones. There were plenty here, piled and scattered where they had been ploughed out of the field. He selected two, then straightened and saw the horse twenty yards off in the middle of the steep field, watching him calmly. They looked at each other.

"Out of it!" he shouted, brandishing his arm. "Out of it! Go on!" The horse twitched its pricked ears. With all his force he threw. The stone soared and landed beyond with a soft thud. He re-armed and

ENRICHMENT: Social Studies Connection

Community Activism

While students may agree with Ted Hughes's message that many people in the modern world feel cut off from nature, they are also likely to agree that many citizens are taking action to protect Earth's environment and animal habitat and to raise awareness about environmental issues. Encourage students to report on environmental projects and activities in which they have participated or about which they have heard from others. Also, have students use newspapers, bulletins, and other local resources to learn of additional hands-on projects and educational programs in their community. Students might compile their findings into a directory of community events focusing on nature and the environment.

threw again. For several minutes he kept up his bombardment without a single hit, working himself into a despair and throwing more and more wildly, till his arm began to ache with the unaccustomed exercise. Throughout the performance the horse watched him fixedly. Finally he had to stop and ease his shoulder muscle. As if the horse had been waiting for just this, it dipped its head twice and came at him.

28 He snatched up two stones and roaring with all his strength flung the one in his right hand. He was astonished at the crack of the impact. It was as if he had struck a tile—and the horse actually stumbled. With another roar he jumped forward and hurled his other stone. His aim seemed to be under superior guidance. The stone struck and rebounded straight up into the air, spinning fiercely, as the horse swirled away and went careering down towards the far bottom of the field, at first with great, swinging leaps, then at a canter,[5] leaving deep churned holes in the soil.

It turned up the far side of the field, climbing till it was level with him. He felt a little surprise of pity to see it shaking its head, and once it paused to lower its head and paw over its ear with its fore-hoof as a cat does.

"You stay there!" he shouted. "Keep your distance and you'll not get hurt."

And indeed the horse did stop at that moment, almost obediently. It watched him as he climbed to the crest.

The rain swept into his face and he realized that he was freezing, as if his very flesh were sodden. The farm seemed miles away over the dreary fields. Without another glance at the horse—he felt too exhausted to care now what it did—he loaded the crook of his left arm with stones and plunged out on to the waste of mud.

He was half-way to the first hedge before the horse appeared, silhouetted against the sky at the corner of the wood, head high and attentive, watching his laborious retreat over the three fields.

The ankle-deep clay dragged at him. Every stride was a separate, deliberate effort, forcing him up and out of the sucking earth, burdened as he was by his sogged clothes and load of stone and limbs that seemed themselves to be turning to mud. He fought to keep his breathing even, two strides in, two strides out, the air ripping his lungs. In the middle of the last field he stopped and looked around. The horse, tiny on the skyline, had not moved.

At the corner of the field he unlocked his clasped arms and dumped the stones by the gatepost, then leaned on the gate. The farm was in front of him. He became conscious of the rain again and suddenly longed to stretch out full-length under it, to take the cooling, healing drops all over his body and forget himself in the last wretchedness of the mud. Making an effort, he heaved his weight over the gate-top. He leaned again, looking up at the hill.

5. **canter** gait like a slow gallop.

Reading Strategy
Judging the Writer's Message How do the actions and attitudes of the young man in this story differ from those of the speaker in the poem "Horses"?

29 **Reading Check**
How does the young man defend himself against the horse?

CUSTOMIZE INSTRUCTION FOR UNIVERSAL ACCESS

For Special Needs Students	For Less Proficient Readers	For Advanced Readers
Students may enjoy reading the book *James Herriot's Yorkshire* by James Herriot, the Yorkshire vet, and Derry Brabbs, a photographer. Have them find photographs in the book that they imagine might look much like the scene in the story, but with a continual downpour occurring. Do they find this kind of environment attractive?	Have students compare the writer's description of the weather with that of the horse. Ask them to read the paragraph on p. 1218: "Now he noticed that the sky had grown much darker." Do students think that the man links the weather and the horse in his mind?	Have students write an essay on whether the man's actions can be seen as a victory over the horse or as a loss of connection with the natural world. Do they share Hughes's pessimistic message about the alienation of modern human beings from nature?

28 Reading Strategy
Judging the Writer's Message

- Ask students what the young man does as the horse continues to charge him.
  Answer: He throws stones at the horse and then runs away from it.
- Ask students why they think the horse brushes its forehoof over its ear.
  Answer: The man has hit it with one of his stones and injured it.
- Ask students the Reading Strategy question on p. 1219: How do the actions and attitudes of the young man in this story differ from those of the speaker in the poem "Horses"?
  Answer: The speaker in the poem has great respect for the horses he sees and does not intrude upon them. The man in this story hates the horse and tries to force it to leave him alone.

29  Reading Check
Answer: The man throws stones at the horse.

30 Reading Strategy
Judging the Writer's Message (p. 1220)

- Ask students what they think the references to the man's heart and brain in the last paragraph symbolize.
  Possible response: The references are symbolic of the man's having lost his feelings for and understanding of the natural world over the years.
- Ask students the Reading Strategy question on p. 1220: Do you agree that it is bad to feel cut off from nature, as Hughes seems to suggest in this story?
  Possible answer: Influenced by the vivid experiences of the man, students may agree that it is bad to be cut off from nature.

ASSESS

Answers for p. 1220

Review and Assess

1. Students may say that the behavior of the horse in this story is not typical.
2. **(a)** The man feels that the land no longer recognizes him. He may also mean that he no longer recognizes the land. **(b)** The rain makes him physically uncomfortable, ruins his good clothing, and provides a barrier between him and the landscape.
3. **(a)** The horse follows him, seems to watch him, and charges at him several times. The man finally gets away by pelting the horse with stones and then running to the gate. **(b)** The man feels hostile toward nature, just as the horse behaves in a hostile manner toward him.
4. **(a)** Students may suggest that the horse is not real. The best evidence for this is the story's title, which suggests that the appearance of the horse is somehow connected with the weather that makes the man feel so unwelcome. Some students may say that if the horse is real, the threat it presents is magnified by the man. **(b)** In beating back nature's forces, the man has lost the part of himself that is in tune with the natural world.
5. The speaker of "The Horses" is inspired by the wildness of the scene and the self-sufficiency of the horses he encounters. He hopes to carry the awe he feels throughout life. The protagonist of "The Rain Horse" is returning to a scene from memory and finds it disappointing. He feels threatened, rather than inspired, by the horse, even before it attacks him.
6. Students may say that many people are indeed out of touch with nature as more and more of the natural world disappears every year.

Rain was dissolving land and sky together like a wet water-color as the afternoon darkened. He concentrated raising his head, searching the skyline from end to end. The horse had vanished. The hill looked lifeless and desolate, an island lifting out of the sea, awash with every tide.

Under the long shed where the tractors, plough, binders and the rest were drawn up, waiting for their seasons, he sat on a sack thrown over a petrol drum, trembling, his lungs heaving. The mingled smell of paraffin, creosote,[6] fertilizer, dust—all was exactly as he had left it twelve years ago. The ragged swallows' nests were still there tucked in the angles of the rafters. He remembered three dead foxes hanging in a row from one of the beams, their teeth bloody.

30 The ordeal with the horse had already sunk from reality. It hung under the surface of his mind, an obscure confusion of fright and shame, as after a narrowly-escaped street accident. There was a solid pain in his chest, like a spike of bone stabbing, that made him wonder if he had strained his heart on that last stupid burdened run. Piece by piece he began to take off his clothes, wringing the gray water out of them, but soon he stopped that and just sat staring at the ground, as if some important part had been cut out of his brain.

Reading Strategy
Judging the Writer's Message Do you agree that it is bad to feel cut off from nature, as Hughes seems to suggest in this story?

6. **petrol . . . paraffin, creosote** (krē´ ə sōt´) Petrol is gasoline; paraffin, wax; creosote, an oily liquid made from tar and used to preserve wood.

Review and Assess

Thinking About the Selection

1. **Respond:** Did the behavior of the horse surprise you? Explain.
2. **(a) Recall:** What effect has a twelve-year absence had on the man's relationship with this landscape? **(b) Infer:** What effect does the rain have on his mood and, specifically, on his feelings toward the landscape?
3. **(a) Recall:** Briefly summarize the man's interactions with the horse. **(b) Connect:** Is there a link between the behavior of the horse and the man's feelings about the landscape? Explain.
4. **(a) Make a Judgment:** Has the man been imagining the horse or, if the horse is real, the threat that it poses? Explain your opinion. **(b) Interpret:** What is the meaning of the last line of the story?
5. **Compare and Contrast:** Compare and contrast the attitudes toward nature of the speaker in "The Horses" and of the main character in "The Rain Horse."
6. **Speculate:** Do you think that many people today are out of touch with nature? Why or why not?

ASSESSMENT PRACTICE: Writing Skills

Style (For more practice, see Test Preparation Workbook, p. 59.)

Many tests require students to recognize stylistic devices and effective language. Use this sample item after students read pp. 1208–1209.

The mood of this poem can best be described as ______.

A optimistic
B depressed
C religious
D dreamlike

Review with students the definition of mood and lead them through the possible answers. Make sure students recognize that the question asks about the overall mood of the poem, not the mood in a particular stanza. Students should determine that the correct answer is *D*. The vivid, often surreal imagery contributes strongly to the poem's dreamlike quality.

Review and Assess

Literary Analysis

Voice

1. Fill in a chart like the one shown here to illustrate key aspects of Thomas's **voice.**

Quality	Examples
Tumbles out words in a rush	
Shows an attitude of wonder about life	
Uses complex poetic forms	

2. Devise and fill in a similar chart for Hughes, listing these qualities: Speaks in blips and pulses; feels awe toward nature; uses free verse; bunches together words of one syllable.
3. Identify the voice in these lines as belonging to Hughes or Thomas, and explain your choice: "Dawn—a smoldering fume of dry frost, / Sky—edge of red-hot iron."

Comparing Literary Works

4. Given Hughes's poetic voice, do you think he would have chosen a form like the **villanelle** to address his dying father? Why or why not?
5. Why are the unrhymed couplets of "The Horses" unsuited to Thomas's aim in "Fern Hill"—to convey the rushing wonder of childhood?
6. If Thomas had written about the experience Hughes describes in "The Horses," how might the poem have been different?

Reading Strategy

Judging the Writer's Message

7. In "Fern Hill," Thomas suggests that children are carefree, with no awareness of death. Do you **judge this message** to be true? Explain.
8. In "The Horses" and "The Rain Horse," Hughes seems to be saying that people who live in cities are cut off from nature. Do you think this is necessarily true? Explain.

Extend Understanding

9. **Social Studies Connection:** Explain a possible link between the Industrial Revolution (the rise of factories and the decline of traditional farming life) and the theme of "The Rain Horse."

Quick Review

A writer's **voice,** his or her "sound" on the page, includes elements like word choice, sound devices, phrasing, pace, and attitude.

A **villanelle** is a nineteen-line poem in which lines 1 and 3 of the opening stanza alternate as endings of the next four stanzas and appear together at the end of the final stanza. The rhyme scheme of the villanelle is *aba aba aba aba aba abaa.*

To **judge a writer's message** test what a writer says against your own ideas and experiences.

Take It to the Net

www.phschool.com

Take the interactive self-test online to check your understanding of these selections.

Answers for p. 1221

Review and Assess

1. Thomas: **Quality:** Tumbles out words in a rush; **Examples:** "Now as I was young and easy under the apple boughs / About the lilting house and happy as the grass was green." **Quality:** Shows an attitude of wonder about life; **Example:** "Time let me play and be / Golden in the mercy of his means." **Quality:** Uses complex poetic forms; **Example:** Villanelle form of "Do Not Go Gentle into That Good Night."
2. Hughes: **Quality:** Speaks in blips and pulses; **Examples:** "Not a leaf, not a bird—"; "I passed: not one snorted or jerked its head. / Gray silent fragments / Of a gray silent world." **Quality:** Feels awe toward nature; **Example:** "Till the moorline—blackening dregs of the brightening gray— / Halved the sky ahead. And I saw the horses." **Quality:** Uses free verse; **Example:** "Slowly detail leafed from the darkness. Then the sun / Orange, red, red erupted." **Quality:** Bunches together words of one syllable; **Example:** "Not a leaf, not a bird— / A world cast in frost."
3. The words probably belong to Hughes because of the brief, short ideas, the dashes for pauses, and the one-syllable words.
4. Hughes would probably not have chosen a form like the villanelle because the repetitiveness of the form might make his "bursts" monotonous.
5. Students may say that the disconnection of unrhymed couplets from one another would not have allowed Thomas to offer the overflowing images that his more formally unified structure allows. They may also note that Thomas's rhyme keeps his overflow from becoming chaotic, where Hughes's unrhymed form would not.
6. Students may say that Thomas would have filled the poem with many more images, all tumbling over themselves.
7. Students may agree that young people don't seem to feel their own mortality as much as adults do.

continued

Answers continued

8. Students may suggest that the natural world has largely been shut out of cities and that people who were once in touch with the natural world might be more aware of this loss than other people.
9. The Industrial Revolution replaced individual farms and businesses with factories. Both Hughes selections reflect a city dweller's perception that he has forgotten how it feels to live in the natural world.

ENRICHMENT: Further Reading

Other Works by the Authors

Other Works by Dylan Thomas

"Poem in October"
"The Force That through the Green Fuse Drives the Flower"

Other Works by Ted Hughes

Moortown
Crow
The Iron Giant

EXTEND

Answers for p. 1222

❶ Vocabulary Development

Word Analysis

1. voluntary—in accord with one's wishes
2. volunteer—one who does something because he or she wishes to do so, not because he or she is ordered to do so
3. benevolent—wishing well

Spelling Strategy

1. grieved
2. traceable

Fluency: Sentence Completion

exasperated; nondescript; malevolent; grieved; transfiguring

❷ Grammar and Style

1. As the young man came over the hill, the first thin blowing of rain met him.
2. When he had recalled this scene in the past, he had imagined it as it looked from here.
3. Since the horse seemed to have gone on down the wood, his way to the farm over the hill was clear.
4. As he fell, the warning flashed through his head that he must keep his suit out of the leaf-mold.
5. As if the horse had been waiting for just this, it dipped its head twice and came at him.

Writing Application

Have students exchange their paragraphs with partners to check for correct usage of adverb clauses.

Integrate Language Skills

❶ Vocabulary Development Lesson

Word Analysis: Latin Root *-vol-*

The Latin root *-vol-* means "to wish" or "to use one's will." In *malevolent,* it means "wishing harm." Knowing the meaning of this root, define each word.

1. voluntary 2. volunteer 3. benevolent

Spelling Strategy

When forming the past tense of a verb that ends in a silent *e*, drop the *e* before adding *-ed: exasperate* + *-ed* = *exasperated*. In general, drop the final *e* whenever adding an ending that begins with a vowel. Some exceptions occur when the root ends in *ce* or *ge*. On your paper, add the ending indicated to each word.

1. grieve + *-ed* 2. trace + *-able*

Fluency: Sentence Completion

Review the vocabulary list on page 1205. Then, in your notebook, write the word from the vocabulary list that best fits in each blank. Use each word only once.

At first, the young man was merely __?__ as he walked over the wet ground. His clothes were soaked, and the meadow looked dull and __?__. Then, suddenly, a __?__ horse appeared and tried to attack him. As he thought about the experience later, he __?__; nature, once friendly toward him, had become hostile. Although he expected his experience to be a(n) __?__ one, his flight from the "rain horse"was a disturbing experience.

❷ Grammar and Style Lesson

Sentence Beginnings: Adverb Clauses

Adverb clauses are subordinate clauses that modify verbs, adverbs, or adjectives. They answer the questions *when, why,* or *under what conditions*. Both Thomas and Hughes add variety to their writing by using adverb clauses to begin sentences.

> As I rode to sleep the owls were bearing the farm away, . . . (answers the question *when?*)

Practice Using a conjunction like *as, as if, after, because, when,* or *since,* combine each sentence pair into a single sentence beginning with an adverb clause. If necessary, replace nouns with pronouns.

1. The young man came over the hill. The first thin blowing of rain met him.
2. He had recalled this scene in the past. He had imagined it as it looked from here.
3. The horse seemed to have gone on down the wood. His way to the farm over the hill was clear.
4. He fell. The warning flashed through his head that he must keep his suit out of the leaf-mold.
5. The horse had been waiting for just this. It dipped its head twice and came at him.

Writing Application Write a paragraph about an encounter with an animal. To add variety to your paragraph and to describe events clearly, link ideas by using adverb clauses at the beginning of at least two sentences.

WG *Prentice Hall Writing and Grammar Connection: Chapter 19, Section 3*

1222 ◆ A Time of Rapid Change (1901–Present)

TEACHING RESOURCES

The following resources can be used to enrich or extend the instruction for pp. 1222–1223.

Vocabulary

- **Selection Support:** Build Vocabulary, p. 273
- **Vocabulary and Spelling Practice Book** (Use this booklet for skills enrichment.) ■

Grammar

- **Selection Support:** Grammar and Style, p. 274
- WG **Writing and Grammar,** Diamond Level, p. 458 ■

Writing

- WG **Writing and Grammar,** Diamond Level, p. 310
- **Writing and Grammar iText CD-ROM**

■ **BLOCK SCHEDULING:** Resources marked with this symbol provide varied instruction during 90-minute blocks.

❸ Writing Lesson

Parody of a Poet's Voice

Dylan Thomas and Ted Hughes wrote in distinctive voices. Choose one of these voices and write a poem in which you parody or imitate the author's style for a humorous effect.

Prewriting Review the characteristics of the voice you are parodying. Then, use a chart like this one to note the characteristics of the voice, ways in which you can exaggerate them, and a slightly ridiculous subject to which you can apply them.

Model: Analyzing Voice for Parody

Thomas's Voice	Ways of Exaggerating	Ridiculous Subject
1. tumbling, rushing words	make even faster	taking a math test
2.		

Drafting Consider using the poet's own forms, rhythms, and words as a basis for your parody. Then, make substitutions that exaggerate the characteristics of the voice and refocus the poem on the ridiculous subject.

Revising Read your poem aloud to several classmates. If they cannot identify the poet whose voice you are parodying, be sure you have included—in exaggerated form—all the main features of that poet's voice.

WG *Prentice Hall Writing and Grammar Connection: Chapter 14, Section 2*

❹ Extension Activities

Listening and Speaking Listen to a recording of Dylan Thomas reading his poetry. Then, imitating Thomas's reading style, perform your own **oral interpretation** of one of the poems. Focus on these elements:

- Pronunciation, saying words correctly
- Enunciation, speaking words clearly
- Pacing, slowing down or speeding up
- Volume, speaking loudly or softly

After your performance, lead the class in a discussion of Thomas's reading style.

Research and Technology With two classmates, give a **panel presentation** on the nature poetry of Dylan Thomas, Ted Hughes, and D.H. Lawrence. Each person can research a poet, using the poet's books, critical works about him, and Web sites. Present information on each poet and discuss their similarities and differences. Then, answer audience questions. **[Group Activity]**

 ***Take It to the Net*** www.phschool.com

Go online for an additional research activity using the Internet.

ASSESSMENT RESOURCES

The following resources can be used to assess students' knowledge and skills.

Selection Assessment

- **Formal Assessment,** Selection Test, pp. 283–285
- **Open Book Test,** pp. 174–176
- **Got It! Assessment Videotapes,** Tape 6
- **Test Bank Software**

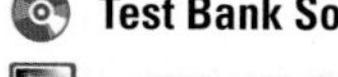 ***Take It to the Net***

Visit www.phschool.com for self-tests and additional questions on the selections.

- **Workbook**
- **Skill Book**
- **Transparencies**
- **CD-ROM**

❸ Writing Lesson

- Read examples of literary parodies to students.
- Help students brainstorm ideas for poem parodies as well as examples of exaggeration they can use in their poems.
- Use the Writing Lesson to guide students in writing a parody.
- Ask volunteers to read their parodies to the class. Ask listeners to identify the writer or the poem being parodied.

❹ Listening and Speaking

- Divide students into groups, each group to work on a specific poem.
- After students have listened to Thomas's recording, have them discuss his style.
- Have students apply elements of pronunciation, enunciation, and pacing to their own oral interpretations.

CUSTOMIZE INSTRUCTION For Universal Access

To address different learning styles, use the activities suggested in the **Extension Activities** booklet, p. 59.

- For Intrapersonal and Verbal/Linguistic Learners, use Activity 5.
- For Verbal/Linguistic Learners, use Activity 6.
- For Visual/Spatial and Logical/Mathematical Learners, use Activity 7.

An Arundel Tomb ✦ The Explosion ✦ On the Patio ✦ Not Waving but Drowning

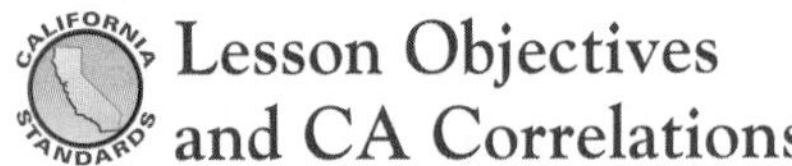

Lesson Objectives and CA Correlations

1. **To analyze and respond to literary elements**
   - Literary Analysis: Free Verse and Meter **R 3.3**
   - Comparing Literary Works **R 3.4**
2. **To read, comprehend, analyze, and critique a poem**
   - Reading Strategy: Reading in Sentences
   - Reading Check Questions
   - Review and Assess Questions
3. **To develop word analysis skills, fluency, and systematic vocabulary**
   - Vocabulary Development Lesson: Latin Root *-fid-* **R 1.1**
4. **To understand and apply written and oral language conventions**
   - Spelling Strategy **LC 1.2**
   - Grammar and Style Lesson: Sequence of Tenses **LC 1.1**
5. **To understand and apply appropriate writing and research strategies**
   - Writing Lesson: Reflective Essay **W 1.1, 1.5, 1.9, 2.3**
   - Extension Activity: Slide Show **W 1.7, 2.6**
   - Assessment Practice (ATE)
6. **To understand and apply listening and speaking strategies**
   - Extension Activity: Eulogy **LS 1.4**

STEP-BY-STEP TEACHING GUIDE	PACING GUIDE
PRETEACH	
Motivate Students and Provide Background	
Use the Motivation activity (ATE p. 1224)	5 min.
Read and discuss author and background features (SE/ATE pp. 1224, 1226) [A]	5 min.
Introduce the Concepts	
Introduce the Literary Analysis and Reading Strategy (SE/ATE p. 1225) [A]	15 min.
Pronounce the vocabulary words and read their definitions (SE p. 1225)	5 min.
TEACH	
Monitor Comprehension	
Informally monitor comprehension by circulating while students read independently or in groups [A]	15 min.
Monitor students' comprehension with the Reading Check notes (SE/ATE p. 1227)	as students read
Develop vocabulary with Vocabulary notes (SE pp. 1227, 1232; ATE p. 1227)	as students read
Develop Understanding	
Develop students' understanding of free verse and meter with the Literary Analysis annotations (SE pp. 1227, 1228, 1229; ATE pp. 1226, 1228) [A]	5 min.
Develop students' ability to read in sentences with the Reading Strategy annotations (SE p. 1231; ATE pp. 1227, 1231)	5 min.
ASSESS	
Assess Mastery	
Assess students' mastery of the Reading Strategy and Literary Analysis by having them answer the Review and Assess questions (SE/ATE p. 1233)	20 min.
Use one or more of the print and media Assessment Resources (ATE p. 1235) [A]	up to 45 min.
EXTEND	
Apply Understanding	
Have students complete the Vocabulary Development Lesson and the Grammar and Style Lesson (SE p. 1234) [A]	20 min.
Apply students' knowledge of transitions used to make comparisons using the Writing Lesson (SE/ATE p. 1235) [A]	45 min.
Apply students' understanding using one or more of the Extension Activities (SE p. 1235)	20–90 min.

[A] **ACCELERATED INSTRUCTION:** Use the strategies and activities identified with an [A].

UNIVERSAL ACCESS
● = Below-Level Students
▲ = On-Level Students
■ = Above-Level Students

Time and Resource Manager

Reading Level: Challenging, Average, Average, Easy
Average Number of Instructional Days: 4

RESOURCES		
PRINT	**TRANSPARENCIES**	**TECHNOLOGY**
• **Beyond Literature,** Cross-Curricular Connection: Social Studies, p. 60 ▲ ■		• **Interest Grabber Video,** Tape 6 ● ▲ ■
• **Selection Support Workbook:** ● ▲ ■ Literary Analysis, p. 280 Reading Strategy, p. 279 Build Vocabulary, p. 277	• **Literary Analysis and Reading Transparencies,** pp. 119 and 120 ● ▲ ■	
		• **Listening to Literature** ● ▲ ■ Audiocassettes, Side 29 Audio CDs, CD 17
• **Literatura en español** ● ▲ • **Literary Analysis for Enrichment** ■		
• **Formal Assessment:** Selection Test, pp. 286–288 ● ▲ ■ • **Open Book Test,** pp. 177–179 ● ▲ ■ • **Performance Assessment and Portfolio Management,** p. 11 ● ▲ ■ • PRENTICE HALL ASSESSMENT SYSTEM ● ▲ ■	• PRENTICE HALL ASSESSMENT SYSTEM ● ▲ ■ Skills Practice Answers and Explanations on Transparencies ● ▲ ■	• **Test Bank Software** ● ▲ ■ • **Got It! Assessment Videotapes,** Tape 6 ● ▲
• **Selection Support Workbook:** ● ▲ ■ Grammar and Style, p. 278 • **Writing and Grammar,** Diamond Level ● ▲ ■ • **Extension Activities,** p. 60 ● ▲ ■	• **Daily Language Practice Transparencies** ● ▲ • **Writing Models and Graphic Organizers on Transparencies,** pp. 5–12 ● ▲ ■	• **Writing and Grammar iText CD-ROM** ● ▲ ■ ***Take It to the Net*** www.phschool.com

BLOCK SCHEDULING: Use one 90-minute class period to preteach the selections and have students read them. Use a second 90-minute class period to assess students' mastery of skills and have them complete one of the Extension Activities.

PRETEACH

Step-by-Step Teaching Guide for pp. 1224–1225

Motivation

Invite volunteers to use body language to convey an emotion and encourage the rest of the class to guess the emotion. Discuss why body language is such a powerful tool in communication. Ask students to make a list of situations in which it is important to read body language (for example, when caring for a child, when interacting with someone who is angry or upset). Tell students to watch for examples of "telling" body language in the following poems.

Interest Grabber Video

As an alternative, play "'Not Waving but Drowning': Reading and Student Response" on Tape 6 to engage student interest.

❶ More About the Authors

Philip Larkin

When Philip Larkin was offered the position of England's poet laureate in 1984, he turned it down, saying he had not published anything since 1974. The post went to Ted Hughes. Larkin's critical influence on British poetry helped to gain notice and eventual acceptance of Stevie Smith's poetry.

Peter Redgrove

Peter Redgrove's vision was informed by his background in biology, chemistry, and other scientific fields. He blends his knowledge of the natural sciences with his own exhilarating vision of the world of nature.

Stevie Smith

Stevie Smith's radio broadcasts of her poems were popular in the 1960s, and her public readings were well attended. Public interest in her was extended by Hugh Whitemore's play *Stevie* (1977), which he later adapted as a film.

Prepare to Read

❶ An Arundel Tomb ◆ The Explosion ◆ On the Patio ◆ Not Waving but Drowning

Philip Larkin (1922–1985)

Philip Larkin turned what could have been a discouragement into a reason for developing poetic skill and emotional restraint. As a child in Coventry, England, his home life was dominated by a father who held him accountable to rigid standards. Larkin escaped from these pressures by building a private childhood world rich in creativity and imagination.

Deprivation Versus Daffodils Reflecting on his life, Larkin metaphorically explained how he drew inspiration from his difficult experiences when he told an interviewer, "Deprivation is for me what daffodils were for Wordsworth."

Although Larkin also developed a lifelong interest in jazz, which he came to love "even more than poetry," it was his clear-eyed, honest poetry, combining conversational language with well-crafted forms, that won him international fame. His poetry speaks of day-to-day realities, sometimes discouragingly, but is quietly haunted by realities beyond everyday life.

Peter Redgrove (1932–2003)

Like William Blake, a visionary poet with whom he is sometimes compared, Peter Redgrove does not fit into the usual categories. He lived at a distance from the literary hub of London—in Falmouth, Cornwall, the southwestern tip of England. Redgrove lived at an imaginative distance from London as well, rejecting the drab, everyday qualities so prevalent in many post-World War II British poems.

Transformation Through Imagination In his poetry, novels, television scripts, and nonfiction works, Redgrove celebrates our power to reimagine and transform our lives. His rich visual imagery reflects a heightened awareness that borders on the mystical as he speaks for stones or sees the world through the eyes of a wandering dog.

Redgrove's poems have been widely acclaimed in England, and he was the recipient of the 1997 Queen's Medal for Poetry.

Stevie Smith (1902–1971)

Stevie Smith's poems, cannot be easily classified. They are modeled, however, on familiar forms—hymns, popular songs, and nineteenth-century British and American poems. Using simple forms and language, she often evokes despair, perhaps relying on the poetic statement of bleak feelings to cleanse or banish them from life.

The author of this unusual body of work was born Florence Margaret Smith in Hull, Yorkshire. Due to her mother's ill health, she was raised mostly by her beloved Auntie Lion, with whom she continued to live in a Northern London suburb even as an adult. While working for a magazine, Smith wrote three novels and nine collections of poems.

Poems and Doodles Smith's poems can be humorous, macabre, surprising, and childlike, and she often illustrates them with sketches or doodles that echo her playful rhythms.

Some critics suggest that her work cunningly satirizes conventional forms of poetic expression, such as the hymn and the nursery rhyme, and adds dark new depths and keen irony to these traditional forms.

TEACHING RESOURCES

The following resources can be used to enrich or extend the instruction for pp. 1224–1225.

Motivation

Interest Grabber Video, Tape 6

Background

Beyond Literature, p. 60

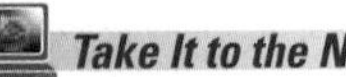

Take It to the Net

Visit www.phschool.com for background and hotlinks for the selections.

Literary Analysis

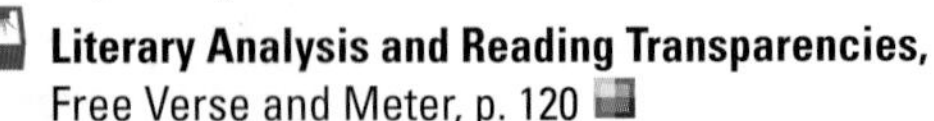

Literary Analysis and Reading Transparencies, Free Verse and Meter, p. 120

Reading

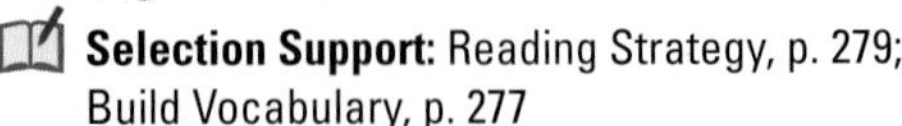

Selection Support: Reading Strategy, p. 279; Build Vocabulary, p. 277

Literary Analysis and Reading Transparencies, Read in Sentences, p. 119

BLOCK SCHEDULING: Resources marked with this symbol provide varied instruction during 90-minute blocks.

Preview

Connecting to the Literature

Body language can reveal deep emotions. In each of these poems, a gesture holds a clue to the meaning.

❷ Literary Analysis

Free Verse and Meter

Free verse is poetry without regular end rhymes or the regular rhythms called **meter.** Widely used today, free verse has lines of varying lengths and an invented rhythm that suits the meaning. Redgrove uses free verse in "The Patio."

In contrast, Larkin uses regular meters that are classified by the stresses in each foot, or group of syllables, and the number of feet per line, as follows:

- **iamb**—foot with an unstressed and stressed syllable (˘ ´)
- **trochee**—foot with a stressed and unstressed syllable (´ ˘)
- **tetrameter**—verse with four feet per line

"An Arundel Tomb" uses **iambic tetrameter** with variations:

The earl and countess lie in stone, . . .

"The Explosion" uses **trochaic tetrameter** (with some lines of iambic tetrameter):

Shadows pointed towards the pithead: . . .

Stevie Smith adapts the **ballad stanza,** which usually alternates four- and three-beat lines and has a rhyme scheme of *abab* or *abcb*. Smith uses the scheme *abcb*—though "moaning" and "drowning" do not rhyme exactly—but her free rhythms include lines with one to six beats.

Comparing Literary Works

The rhythm of these poems adds to their **dramatic structure**—their use of contrasts to build toward a climax. Compare the ways in which these poems achieve such a climax.

❸ Reading Strategy

Reading in Sentences

To understand a poem, **read in sentences:** Pause with punctuation, rather than automatically stopping at the ends of lines. As a reminder, mark the ends of lines in a copy of the poem with signs like these.

Sign	Means
	Continue without pause
	Pause for comma, dash, or semicolon and continue
	Full stop for period

Vocabulary Development

effigy (ef′ i jē) *n.* portrait or statue of a person (p. 1227)

supine (so͞o′ pīn′) *adj.* lying on the back (p. 1227)

fidelity (fə del′ ə tē) *n.* faithfulness (p. 1227)

larking (lärk′ iŋ) *n.* free-spirited, whimsical fun (p. 1232)

CUSTOMIZE INSTRUCTION FOR UNIVERSAL ACCESS

For Less Proficient Readers	For English Learners	For Advanced Readers
If students have difficulty understanding a poem because they continue to stop at the end of lines, suggest that they type the poem on a computer. They should type it as if it were a story, not a poem. Then have them reread it. They should understand it better now.	Have students use the vocabulary words in sentences and answer questions about each one. Where have they seen an effigy on the news or at sports events? How would they demonstrate being in a supine position? When have they experienced or demonstrated fidelity with regard to a person or an animal?	The biographical information for Peter Redgrove says that he has written poems that speak for stones or that see the world through the eyes of a dog. Ask students to write a poem about something in the natural world, such as a tree or a lion. How would they see the world through the eyes of a lion?

❷ Literary Analysis

Free Verse and Meter

- Point out to students that some poets write without a definite meter while others write in strict metrical form.
- Read the instruction about free verse and meter as a class and call students' attention to the examples from the selections.
- Use the instruction for Comparing Literary Works to help students learn how to unite the rhythm and dramatic structure of a poem.
- Use the Free Verse and Meter transparency on p. 120 of **Literary Analysis and Reading Transparencies** to demonstrate for students how to scan examples of iambic tetrameter and trochaic tetrameter.

❸ Reading Strategy

Reading in Sentences

- Have a volunteer read aloud the first five or ten lines of the biographical information about Philip Larkin on p. 1224. Instruct the student to pause at the end of each line, not at punctuation. Ask students if they understood what they just heard.
- Point out that one of the reasons they often do not understand poetry is that they read it this way. Poets use the same punctuation that prose writers do, and usually they use it for the same reasons. A comma means pause; a period means stop. If students read poetry as if it were prose, that will eliminate many of their comprehension problems.
- Introduce students to the symbols they can use at the end of poetic lines to help them read in sentences.

Vocabulary Development

- Pronounce each vocabulary word for students, and read the definitions as a class. Have students identify any words with which they are already familiar.

E-Teach

Visit E-Teach at www.phschool.com for teachers' essays on how to teach, with questions and answers.

TEACH

Step-by-Step Teaching Guide for pp. 1226–1232

CUSTOMIZE INSTRUCTION
For Musical/Rhythmic Learners

Have students read aloud excerpts from two or more of the works. They can then lead a discussion about how the various voices differ from one another.

❶ About the Selections

Both of these poems deal with death and its effect on those who survive. In "An Arundel Tomb," Larkin points out an amusing misconception on the part of the tomb's visitors: Whereas those who view the effigy are comforted by the thought of love's enduring through the centuries, the actual couple buried in the tomb had no intention of conveying such a message or serving as such an ideal.

In "The Explosion," Larkin vividly depicts the fatal suddenness of a coal mine's explosion and how it affects the town's women—the survivors.

❷ Literary Analysis

Free Verse and Meter

- Have students read the first stanza aloud. Ask them how many metrical feet each line of the poem contains.
  Answer: four
- Ask students to identify the stressed words or syllables in the first two lines of the poem.
  Answer: Side by side their faces blurred, / The earl and countess lie in stone
- Ask students the Literary Analysis question on p. 1227: How do the meters of lines 1 and 2 differ?
  Answer: The first line is trochaic tetrameter, and the second line is iambic tetrameter.

❶ AN ARUNDEL TOMB

Philip Larkin

Tombstones of Tiberius Julius Rufus and his son Petronius Rufus and their wives.

Background

The inspiration for "An Arundel Tomb" was a stone monument in Chichester Cathedral, Sussex, near the site of the ancient Roman town of Arundel. The monument is a fourteenth-century table tomb (similar to the ancient Roman tombstones shown here). On it lie the effigies of Richard Fitzalan, thirteenth Earl of Arundel, and his second wife, Eleanor, holding hands (as the couple do on the Roman tombstones). Today, visitors to the cathedral can see the tomb itself and a copy of Larkin's poem inspired by the tomb.

Side by side, their faces blurred,
The earl and countess lie in stone,
Their proper habits vaguely shown
As jointed armor, stiffened pleat,
And that faint hint of the absurd—
The little dogs under their feet.

TEACHING RESOURCES

The following resources can be used to enrich or extend the instruction for pp. 1226–1232.

Literary Analysis

Selection Support: Literary Analysis, p. 280

Reading

Listening to Literature Audiocassettes, Side 29

Listening to Literature Audio CDs, CD 17

BLOCK SCHEDULING: Resources marked with this symbol provide varied instruction during 90-minute blocks.

Such plainness of the pre-baroque
Hardly involves the eye, until
It meets his left-hand gauntlet,[1] still
Clasped empty in the other; and
One sees, with a sharp tender shock,
His hand withdrawn, holding her hand.

They would not think to lie so long.
Such faithfulness in effigy
Was just a detail friends would see:
A sculptor's sweet commissioned grace
Thrown off in helping to prolong
The Latin names around the base.

They would not guess how early in
Their supine stationary voyage
The air would change to soundless damage,
Turn the old tenantry[2] away;
How soon succeeding eyes begin
To look, not read. Rigidly they

3

Persisted, linked, through lengths and breadths
Of time. Snow fell, undated. Light
Each summer thronged the glass. A bright
Litter of birdcalls strewed the same
Bone-riddled ground. And up the paths
The endless altered people came,

Washing at their identity.
Now, helpless in the hollow of
An unarmorial age, a trough
Of smoke in slow suspended skeins[3]
Above their scrap of history,
Only an attitude remains:

Time has transfigured them into
Untruth. The stone fidelity
They hardly meant has come to be
4
Their final blazon,[4] and to prove
Our almost-instinct almost true:
What will survive of us is love.

1. **gauntlet** armored glove.
2. **tenantry** peasants farming the nobles' land.
3. **skeins** loosely coiled bunches of thread or yarn.
4. **blazon** coat of arms; a noble family's symbol.

5 ◀ Critical Viewing Do engraved images and messages such as the ones on these tombstones always become an "untruth" in relation to life—as Larkin's poem seems to claim? Explain. **[Relate]**

Literary Analysis
Free Verse and Meter
How do the meters of lines 1 and 2 differ?

effigy (ef´ i jē) *n.* portrait or statue of a person

supine (so͞o´ pīn´) *adj.* lying on the back

fidelity (fə del´ ə tē) *n.* faithfulness

6 ✓ Reading Check
How did the sculptor portray the earl and countess on their tomb?

3 Reading Strategy

Reading in Sentences

- Have students read the fourth stanza of the poem and determine how many sentences it contains.
  Answer: one
- Now have students read the fifth stanza and identify the number of sentences it contains. Ask them if all the sentences both begin and end in the fifth stanza.
  Answer: There are three complete sentences, plus two partial sentences, one of which begins in the previous stanza, and one that ends in the next stanza.
- After reading the short sentences in stanza five, have students summarize what has happened near the tomb over time.
  Possible response: It snows year after year. The light grows brighter each summer. Birds sing nearby each year.

4 Vocabulary Connection

Latin Root *-fid-*

- Tell students that the word *fidelity* comes from the Latin root *-fid-*, which means "faith." Ask them how the word in the poem is related to the root.
  Answer: The word *fidelity* means "faithfulness," and the poem suggests that the sculpture shows an enduring fidelity between the two people that did not really survive their deaths.
- Ask students to name other words with the same root as *fidelity*.
  Possible responses: Students may cite *confidence, infidelity.*

5 ▶ Critical Viewing

Answer: Students may say that an engraved image always becomes an "untruth" because later viewers can never see the original image as it was seen by people of the time. Other students may say that the passage of time offers new opportunities to see more truly.

6 ✓ Reading Check

Answer: The sculptor portrayed the two people holding hands.

CUSTOMIZE INSTRUCTION FOR UNIVERSAL ACCESS

For Special Needs Students	For Less Proficient Readers	For English Learners
Have students determine how many sentences are in the first stanza (only one). Then, have them use the end-of-line traffic signs to mark the first stanza of the poem to show how to read it. (Pause sign following lines 1, 2, 4, and 5; Continue sign after line 3; Full Stop sign at the end of line 6.)	Help students determine the rhyme scheme for the poem. Have them start by writing the final words in the six lines of the first stanza, one under the other (*blurred, stone, shown, pleat, absurd, feet*). Then, have them assign a rhyme scheme to the words based on their rhymes (abb cac).	"An Arundel Tomb" is difficult to follow even for experienced readers. Work with students to paraphrase what is being described as the poem progresses.

7 Literary Analysis

Free Verse and Meter

- Ask students to read the first stanza for meaning. Ask if the description of the slagheap sleeping in the sun makes the reader see the scene as peaceful.
  Answer: Both the title and the first stanza use the word *explosion*, which suggests that despite the sleeping slagheap, something violent will happen in the poem.
- Now ask students to read the first stanza again, this time being aware of the rhythm and meter. Ask them the Literary Analysis question on p. 1228: What is the meter of the lines in the first stanza? Explain.
  Answer: Trochaic tetrameter: There are four metrical feet, and each foot (except the very last) consists of a stressed syllable followed by an unstressed syllable.

8 Literary Analysis

Free Verse, Meter, and Dramatic Structure

- Have students speculate on why Larkin uses a regular meter throughout much of his poem.
  Possible response: The regular meter creates a sense of ceremony appropriate for a tragedy.
- Ask students the Literary Analysis question on p. 1229: Why do you think that at the climax of the poem, the line describing the "unbroken" eggs breaks the metrical pattern?
  Possible response: The poem builds to a climax, a stopping point. A line that breaks the previous rhythm reflects the relation of the climax to the preceding ideas and events.

The EXPLOSION

Philip Larkin

On the day of the explosion
Shadows pointed towards the pithead:
In the sun the slagheap slept.

Down the lane came men in pitboots
Coughing oath-edged talk and pipe-smoke,
Shouldering off the freshened silence.

One chased after rabbits; lost them;
Came back with a nest of lark's eggs;
Showed them; lodged them in the grasses.

So they passed in beards and moleskins,[1]
Fathers, brothers, nicknames, laughter,
Through the tall gates standing open.

Literary Analysis
Free Verse and Meter
What is the meter of the lines in the first stanza? Explain.

1. **moleskins** garments, especially trousers, of heavy cotton.

ENRICHMENT: Literature Connection

Meter and Free Verse

The iamb is a metrical foot consisting of one unstressed syllable followed by a stressed syllable. The word comes from the Greek *iambos*, which means "lame." You can hear the gait of a limping person in the meter of the foot. The iamb is the most frequently used foot in English poetry; it is thought to mimic the natural rhythm of the language.

A trochee is a metrical foot consisting of a stressed syllable followed by an unstressed syllable. The word comes from the Greek *trokhaios*, meaning "running."

Larkin uses trochaic tetrameter (tetrameter is verse with four feet to a line) in "The Explosion" and iambic tetrameter in "An Arundel Tomb."

Free verse is rhymed or unrhymed poetry without any of the regular rhythms called meter. Free verse has lines of different lengths and an invented rhythm that suits its meaning. Smith and Redgrove use varying free-verse rhythms to reinforce their meanings.

At noon, there came a tremor; cows
Stopped chewing for a second; sun,
Scarfed as in a heat-haze, dimmed.

The dead go on before us, they
Are sitting in God's house in comfort,
We shall see them face to face—

Plain as lettering in the chapels
It was said, and for a second
Wives saw men of the explosion

Larger than in life they managed—
Gold as on a coin, or walking
Somehow from the sun towards them,

8 One showing the eggs unbroken.

Literary Analysis
Free Verse, Meter, and Dramatic Structure Why do you think that at the climax of the poem, the line describing the "unbroken" eggs breaks the metrical pattern?

Review and Assess

Thinking About the Selections

1. **Respond:** Do you find it easy to visualize what these poems describe? Why or why not?
2. **(a) Recall:** Describe the sculptured couple on whom the poet focuses in "An Arundel Tomb." **(b) Interpret:** What does the poet mean by stating that this couple has made a "supine stationary voyage"?
3. **(a) Recall:** In "An Arundel Tomb," what detail of the monument catches the speaker's eye? **(b) Interpret:** Referring to this detail, explain why "Time has transfigured" the couple "into / Untruth."
4. **(a) Recall:** What disaster occurs in "The Explosion"? **(b) Connect:** What two things in the poem last "for a second"? **(c) Interpret:** What is the meaning of the final gesture in the poem?
5. **(a) Compare and Contrast:** Compare and contrast the ways in which each poem comments on the assertion that "What will survive of us is love." **(b) Compare and Contrast:** In what way does a gesture offer a clue to the meaning of each of these poems **(c) Draw Conclusions:** Do these poems show the same optimism or pessimism about life? Explain.
6. **Speculate:** What gives the imagination the power to range over centuries or zero in on an instant, as it does in these poems?

CUSTOMIZE INSTRUCTION FOR UNIVERSAL ACCESS

For Special Needs Students	For Less Proficient Readers
Have students outline the events in "The Explosion" and tell which stanzas describe each one. (Stanza one is the exposition, setting time and place. Stanzas two through eight are the rising action: The men walk to the mine as they do every day, laughing and talking. Time passes and the explosion occurs. More time passes and the villagers are sitting in the chapel during the funeral. The wives see the men as if they were still alive. The climax occurs when the wives see the unbroken eggs.)	Have students note the change in meter between the fourth and fifth stanzas in "The Explosion." Ask them to identify the shift in meter and to speculate on why the poet made this choice. (The first four stanzas are written in trochaic tetrameter. The fifth stanza is written in iambic tetrameter.) The event that occurs in stanza five kills the miners and interrupts the lives of the survivors, and the poet emphasizes this by interrupting the regular rhythm.

Answers for p. 1229

Review and Assess

1. Students may say that "An Arundel Tomb" is not particularly easy to visualize but that "The Explosion" is.
2. **(a)** The couple lie side by side, his left hand free of his glove and holding one of hers. **(b)** Students may say that in death people may lie supine, without moving, yet be on a "voyage" to another physical state.
3. **(a)** The detail of the couple holding hands catches the eye. **(b)** The gesture was put in by the sculptor for artistic reasons; the couple might have considered it a detail for their friends to see. It is not true, however, that their loyalty to each other survives, since they are dead, nor did anyone intend the gesture as a message to future generations.
4. **(a)** A mine explosion occurs in the poem. **(b)** Cows stopped chewing for a second when the explosion occurred; the wives saw their husbands walking toward them for a second. **(c)** The final gesture—the display of the unbroken eggs—is an affirmation of what has been lost and makes present what is irrecoverably gone.
5. **(a)** "An Arundel Tomb" suggests that people in the present want to remember people in the past in comfortable and conventional terms. "The Explosion" suggests that the survivors will remember their husbands, fathers, and brothers with love. **(b)** The hand-holding of the effigies and the envisioning of the dead men as they lived both convey love's triumph over death. **(c)** The second poem is more pessimistic than the first; we know that the men are lost and the eggs broken, but we may take some comfort in the symbolic survival of the noble couple's love.
6. Students may say that the ability to search for and perceive deeper meanings gives the imagination its power.

❾ About the Selections

Both poems use images of water but in strikingly different ways. "On the Patio" uses the image of the poet draining a glass and allowing the thunderstorm to refill it as a symbol of a person willing to be open to nature and its bounty, someone who wants to get the most out of life, "draining" life's glass and coming back for a "refill." "Not Waving but Drowning" uses the water that drowned a man as a symbol of the coldness and isolation that plagued him his whole life—and finally led to his death.

❿ Background

Art

Blue Rain, by Ross M. Horowitz

This photograph suggests the wild profusion of rain during a thunderstorm as described by Peter Redgrove in "On the Patio." It is easy to imagine this rain filling up a glass left out in a thunderstorm. Use these questions for discussion:

1. The poet refers to the "cloud . . . transferring its might into a glass." What elements of this photograph convey that "might"?
   Answer: The slanting lines of the rain and the sheer profusion of the dotlike raindrops convey the sense of an explosion, a huge force that cannot be contained.
2. Imagine drinking a glass full of the rain in this photograph. What emotions might you feel and why?
   Answer: It might be exhilarating, joyful, or even a little frightening to drink the results of such a powerful, explosive event.

⓫ ▶Critical Viewing

Answer: Students should focus on the strong visual elements of the photograph: the slanting lines of the falling rain and the explosive profusion of the fallen drops.

❿

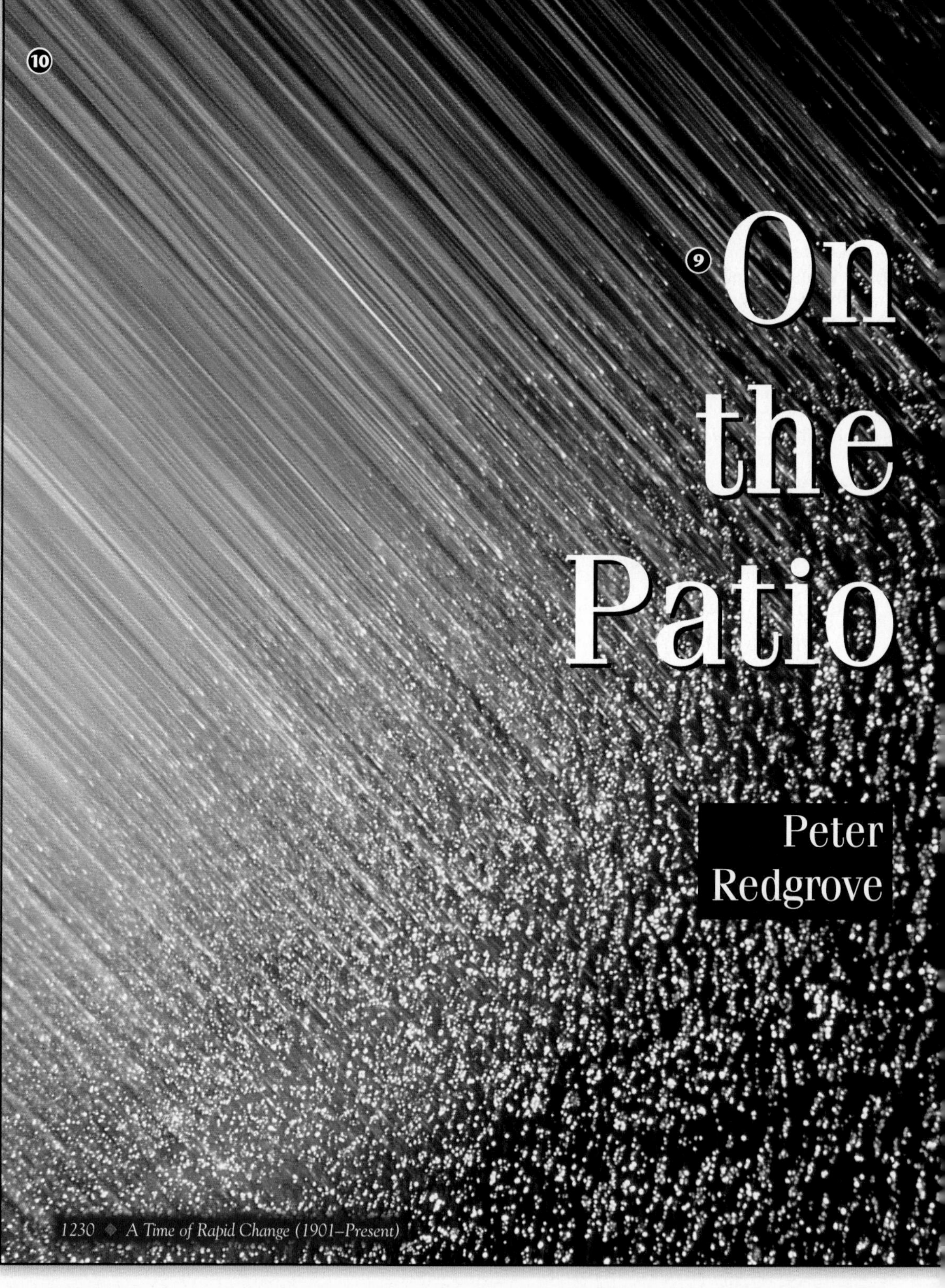

❾ On the Patio

Peter Redgrove

ENRICHMENT: Science Connection

Body Language

Scientists have discovered much about the role of body language in communication and how it differs from one culture to another. For example, people from Latin American and Arab cultures generally stand closer together when they talk than do people from the United States. In addition, people from Japanese and Native American cultures consider it disrespectful to look a person in the eye in some situations.

Poets have long recognized the importance of body language. Each of these poems includes a gesture that "comments" on what is happening. In Larkin's "Explosion," wives who are remembering an explosion that killed their husbands imagine one man holding miraculously "unbroken" eggs in his outstretched hand. Smith, in "Not Waving but Drowning," shows how a misinterpreted gesture can tell the story of a person's life. Meanwhile, Redgrove sums up a whole attitude toward life in a single gesture.

A wineglass overflowing with thunderwater
Stands out on the drumming steel table

Among the outcries of the downpour
Feathering chairs and rethundering on the awnings.

How the pellets of water shooting miles
Fly into the glass of swirl, and slop

Over the table's scales of rust
Shining like chained sores,

12 Because the rain eats everything except the glass
Of spinning water that is clear down here

But purple with rumbling depths above, and this cloud
Is transferring its might into a glass

In which thunder and lightning come to rest,
The cloud crushed into a glass.

Suddenly I dart out into the patio,
Snatch the bright glass up and drain it,

Bang it back down on the thundery steel table for a refill.

Reading Strategy
Reading in Sentences As you read the poem, at the end of which lines should you come to a full stop? Explain.

Review and Assess

Thinking About the Selection

1. **Respond:** How do you respond to the final line of the poem? Why?
2. **(a) Recall:** Describe the scene depicted in "On the Patio."
   (b) Connect: How do the images in the poem link what occurs above with what occurs below?
3. **(a) Recall:** At the end of the poem, what does the speaker do?
   (b) Interpret: What is the meaning of the speaker's final gesture?
4. **Speculate:** Why do natural phenomena like thunder and rain inspire heightened feelings, such as intoxication or gloom?

11 ◀ **Critical Viewing** Does this photograph convey the power of the "thunderwater" in the poem? Explain your answer. **[Evaluate]**

12 Reading Strategy

Reading in Sentences

- Have students take turns reading the poem aloud. Then, have them mark the poem with Pause and Continue end-of-line traffic signs. (Pause signs follow lines 8, 13, 15, and 16. Continue signs follow lines 1–3, 5–7, and 9–12.)
- Ask students why they might have to read lines 5–14 more than once to grasp the meaning.
  Answer: This part of the poem has few pauses and the ideas continue for many lines.
- Ask students the Reading Strategy question on p. 1231: As you read the poem, at the end of which lines would you come to a full stop? Explain.
  Answer: Students should say at the end of lines 4, 14, and 17, because these lines are punctuated by periods.

Answers for p. 1231

Review and Assess

1. Students may say that they feel that the speaker's gesture is a way of communicating with the thunderstorm and they like the poet's action.
2. **(a)** A wineglass has been left out on a table on a patio during a thunderstorm and is filling up with water. **(b)** The images concern both the violent descent of the rain from the clouds and its local effects on the patio.
3. **(a)** He drinks the glass of rainwater and puts it back to fill up again. **(b)** The gesture symbolizes the speaker's getting the most that life has to offer.
4. Students may say that nature's phenomena can envelop human beings so that they feel a part of the natural world, a feeling that many people would find intoxicating.

CUSTOMIZE INSTRUCTION FOR UNIVERSAL ACCESS

For Special Needs Students	For English Learners
This poem's long sentences may present problems for students. Using the images and the punctuation, work with students to understand the basic progression of the poem. Artistic students might want to illustrate one of the images in the poem, for example the rain drumming on the steel table and rethundering on the awnings, or the cloud that spawns the thunder and lightning coming to rest by being crushed into a glass.	Have students note the sensory imagery in the poem. Ask them to find examples of images that appeal particularly to the sense of sight and sound. (Examples: sound images in lines 1–4, sight images in lines 9–12)

ASSESS

Answers for p. 1232

Review and Assess

1. Students' suggestions will vary. For example, a diner signaling for the check in a restaurant might be given more water.
2. **(a)** They say the water must have been too cold for him. **(b)** They say they thought he was waving and that he always loved "larking," having a good time. They do not understand that all his life he was not waving or being playful, but really drowning, isolated from the rest of them. **(c)** The dead man says that all his life he was unable to cope with the circumstances of his life.
3. The poet uses a single event to make an observation about how people misunderstand others for an entire lifetime.

Nobody heard him, the dead man,
But still he lay moaning:
I was much further out than you thought
And not waving but drowning.

Poor chap, he always loved larking
And now he's dead
It must have been too cold for him his heart gave way,
They said.

Oh, no no no, it was too cold always
(Still the dead one lay moaning)
I was much too far out all my life
And not waving but drowning.

larking (lärk′ iŋ) *n.* free-spirited, whimsical fun

Review and Assess

Thinking About the Selection

1. **Respond:** When have you seen a gesture completely misinterpreted, as in "Not Waving but Drowning"?
2. **(a) Recall:** What do "They" say about "the dead man"? **(b) Interpret:** How do "They" misinterpret the gesture and whole life of "the dead man"? **(c) Draw Conclusions:** What might "the dead man" mean when he moans, "I was much too far out all my life"?
3. **Generalize:** Using this poem as an example, explain how poetry reveals the extraordinary in the ordinary.

ASSESSMENT PRACTICE: Writing Skills

Style **(For more practice, see Test Preparation Workbook, p. 60.)**

Many tests require students to recognize stylistic devices and effective language. Use this sample item.

One chased after rabbits; lost them;
Came back with a nest of lark's eggs;
Showed them; lodged them in the grasses.

Which of the following appears in these lines?

A parallel structure
B subject-verb disagreement
C personification
D dangling modifier

Review with students the definitions of each of the choices. Knowing that parallel structure is the repetition of a basic grammatical pattern should lead students to the correct answer, *A*.

Review and Assess

Literary Analysis

Free Verse and Meter

1. Use a chart like this one to analyze Larkin's use of **iambic** and **trochaic tetrameter** in his two poems. Note the pattern of stresses in each line, using (´) to indicate stressed syllables and (˘) to indicate unstressed ones.

"An Arundel Tomb"	"The Explosion"
Their proper habits vaguely shown	It was said, and for a second
As jointed armor, stiffened pleat, . . .	Wives saw men of the explosion . . .

2. (a) How does Larkin change the meter of "The Explosion" in lines 13–14 and 25? (b) Why do you think he introduces these changes?
3. How do the **free-verse** lines in "On the Patio" reflect the setting?
4. (a) Identify a line with one beat and a line with six beats in the modified **ballad stanza** of "Not Waving." (b) How do these contrasting line lengths stress the finality of death?

Comparing Literary Works

5. Review the **dramatic structure** of "The Explosion," "On the Patio," and "Not Waving." How does the climax in each poem repeat and transform an earlier image or phrase?
6. Show how the drama in "An Arundel Tomb" and in "Not Waving but Drowning" is based on contrasts between appearance and reality.
7. Which poem ends in the most dramatic gesture? Explain.

Reading Strategy

Reading in Sentences

8. When you **read in sentences,** where do you pause at the end of the lines in "The Explosion" and where do you stop?
9. (a) Which lines in "On the Patio" require a full stop at the end? Why? (b) Which sentence in the poem describes a scene, which elaborates on the scene, and which describes an action?

Extend Understanding

10. **Performing Arts Connection:** Which poem could best be conveyed by a pantomime, a series of silent gestures? Why?

Quick Review

Free verse is poetry without regular end rhymes or the regular rhythms called **meter.**

A metric **foot** is a group of syllables with a pattern of stresses. Examples of feet are the **iamb** (unstressed, stressed) and the **trochee** (stressed, unstressed). A line in **tetrameter** has four metric feet.

A **ballad stanza** usually alternates four- and three-beat lines and has a rhyme scheme of *abab* or *abcb*.

Dramatic structure in a poem is the use of contrasts to build to an effective climax.

To **read a poem in sentences,** pause as punctuation indicates but do not automatically stop at the end of each line.

 ***Take It to the Net***

www.phschool.com

Take the interactive self-test online to check your understanding of these selections.

FURTHER READING

Other Works by the Authors

Other Works by Philip Larkin

The Collected Poems

Other Works by Peter Redgrove

Man Named East and Other New Poems

Other Works by Stevie Smith

Novel on Yellow Paper

Answers for p. 1233

Review and Assess

1. "An Arundel Tomb"

Thĕir próper̆ hábĭts vágŭely
shówn
Ăs jóintĕd ármŏr, stíffenĕd
pléat, . . .

"The Explosion"

Ít wăs sáid, ănd fór ă sécon̆d
Wíves săw mén ŏf thé
ĕxplósiŏn . . .

2. **(a)** In lines 13, 14, and 25, the poet changes from trochaic tetrameter to iambic tetrameter. **(b)** In lines 13–14, the change in meter represents the break in the town's life caused by the explosion. In line 25, the break in rhythm slows the last line in a sudden and dramatic way, emphasizing the image.

3. The free-verse lines of "On the Patio" convey the continuous drumming of the rain.

4. **(a)** Line 8 has one beat and line 7 has six beats. **(b)** After the failure to rescue the man, there is nothing more to say.

5. The climactic line in "The Explosion" repeats the image of the eggs, transforming them into a vision of what is gone. The final image in "On the Patio" shows the man banging his glass on the table, repeating and transforming the image of the "drumming steel table" banged on by the rain. The final image of a man "not waving but drowning" in Stevie Smith's poem repeats an opening image, its meaning reinforced by the second stanza.

6. In "An Arundel Tomb," the faithfulness suggested by the figures on the tomb is revealed to be false; it was the creation of the artist. In "Not Waving but Drowning," the man appeared to others to be fun loving (waving), while he was in reality isolated and cut off (drowning).

7. Students may say that showing the eggs is the most dramatic because it is supernatural.

8. Readers should pause at the end lines punctuated with a comma, a semicolon, or a colon and come to a stop at the end of lines ending with with a period.

continued

Answers continued

9. **(a)** Lines 4, 14, and 17 require a full stop at the end. These lines complete sentences. **(b)** The first sentence describes a scene, the second sentence elaborates on that scene, and the third sentence describes an action.

10. Students may suggest "Not Waving but Drowning" for its simplicity.

EXTEND

Answers for p. 1234

❶ Vocabulary Development

Word Analysis

1. infidels
2. fidelity
3. bona fides
4. fiduciary

Concept Development: Antonyms

1. b
2. b
3. a
4. c

Spelling Strategy

1. merge
2. correct
3. collage
4. correct

❷ Grammar and Style

1. He uses the present tense.
2. By reading in the present tense, we imagine ourselves in the poet's place, looking at the sculpture.
3. The sentence that begins in line 24 begins the poet's use of past tense.
4. Larkin uses the present perfect tense in lines 37–39.
5. Possible response: The change in tense in the sixth stanza of "The Explosion" serves to change the setting from the village to the church.

Writing Application

Students' poems will vary.

Integrate Language Skills

❶ Vocabulary Development Lesson

Word Analysis: Latin Root *-fid-*

The word *fidelity* means "faithfulness." It contains the root *-fid-*, which comes from the Latin word *fides*, meaning "faith." This root appears in the terms from economics, political science, and history that appear below. Use these terms to complete the sentences following. Then, verify your answers by using a dictionary.

fiduciary fidelity infidels bona fides

1. To Renaissance Christians, the Islamic Turks were ___?___.
2. Under feudalism, vassals pledged their ___?___ to an overlord.
3. Banks require loan applicants to produce ___?___.
4. An orphan who inherited money might have a ___?___ guardian.

Concept Development: Antonyms

Select the letter of the antonym, the word opposite in meaning, of each numbered word.

1. effigy: (a) scarecrow, (b) original, (c) likeness
2. supine: (a) bright, (b) upright, (c) cowardly
3. fidelity: (a) disloyalty, (b) cowardice, (c) faithfulness
4. larking: (a) mischief, (b) bird-watching, (c) toil

Spelling Strategy

The sound *j* as the final consonant sound of an English word is almost always spelled with the letter *g*, as in *effigy*. Some exceptions to this rule are words from other languages, like *ouija board*.

On your paper, correct any misspelled words:

1. merje 2. elegy 3. collaje 4. raja

❷ Grammar and Style Lesson

Sequence of Tenses

The poets featured in this section use different **verb tenses** to show the relationship of events in time. The **present tense** indicates events in the present or ongoing conditions. The **past tense** shows events that occurred and ended in the past. The **present perfect tense** shows events that began in the past and have continued into the present.

Present Tense: The earl and countess lie in stone. . . .

Past Tense: Rigidly they / / Persisted, linked . . .

Present Perfect Tense: Time has transfigured them . . .

Looking at Style Answer these questions:

1. What tense does Larkin use in lines 1–10 of "An Arundel Tomb"?
2. How does this tense draw you into the poem?
3. Where in the poem does Larkin shift to the past tense?
4. Where does he use the present perfect tense to express a key idea?
5. What is the effect of the change in tenses in "The Explosion"?

Writing Application Write a poem in free verse or meter, using the present, past, and present perfect tenses to convey a message about time.

WG Prentice Hall Writing and Grammar Connection: Chapter 21, Section 2

TEACHING RESOURCES

The following resources can be used to enrich or extend the instruction for pp. 1234–1235.

Vocabulary

- **Selection Support:** Build Vocabulary, p. 277
- **Vocabulary and Spelling Practice Book** (Use this booklet for skills enrichment.)

Grammar

- **Selection Support:** Grammar and Style, p. 278
- **Writing and Grammar,** Diamond Level, p. 532
- **Daily Language Practice Transparencies**

Writing

- **Writing and Grammar,** Diamond Level, p. 106
- **Writing Models and Graphic Organizers on Transparencies,** pp. 5–12
- **Writing and Grammar iText CD-ROM**

BLOCK SCHEDULING: Resources marked with this symbol provide varied instruction during 90-minute blocks.

❸ Writing Lesson

Reflective Essay

The poets in this section explore the deeper meanings of apparently ordinary sights and events, like a person waving or rain falling on a patio. Write a reflective essay that reveals an apparently ordinary event or sight to be extraordinary.

Prewriting Recall an everyday sight or event that stirs strong emotions in you. Jot down the ideas, feelings, and comparisons it inspires. For further inspiration, review the comparisons in these poems.

Drafting Begin by describing the event or sight. Then, referring to your notes, weave in the deeper meanings it suggests. Use transitions to introduce comparisons you make. Conclude by briefly summarizing the meanings you have discovered.

Revising Have classmates evaluate whether you demonstrated the extra-ordinary within the ordinary. If not, add vivid comparisons introduced by transitions.

Model: Using Transitions to Make Comparisons

The plastic bag was ~~weird.~~ *like a misshapen leaf from a tree that never existed. . . .*

Transitions help readers understand comparisons. Other transitions that show comparisons include *as* and *similar to.*

WG *Prentice Hall Writing and Grammar Connection: Chapter 6, Section 3*

❹ Extension Activities

Research and Technology With a team, create a **slide show** about medieval tomb statuary to help your classmates better understand "An Arundel Tomb." Use strategies like these:

- Make transparencies and photocopies of images to be shown.
- Record information about the statues on note cards.

Use your notes to prepare a script explaining how each work relates to the Arundel tomb. Then, use an overhead projector to show the transparencies in a predetermined sequence. **[Group Activity]**

Listening and Speaking Referring to "The Explosion," write and deliver a **eulogy**—a memorial speech—in honor of the miners who died. Use devices like these in your speech: *rhetorical questions*, asked to emphasize a point, not to receive an answer; and *figurative language*, like Larkin's comparison of the men to "Gold as on a coin."

Take It to the Net www.phschool.com

Go online for an additional research activity using the Internet.

Lesson Support for p. 1235

❸ Writing Lesson

- Tell students that ordinary events can inspire prose writing as well as poetry.
- Encourage students to think of an ordinary event, sight, or feeling that they feel strongly about.
- Use the Writing Lesson to guide students in developing their essays. You may wish to display the Reflective Essay transparencies in **Writing Models and Graphic Organizers on Transparencies,** pp. 5–12.
- Use the Reflective Composition rubric in **Performance Assessment and Portfolio Management,** p. 11, to evaluate students' essays.

❹ Listening and Speaking

- Define *eulogy* for students, and encourage them to reread the poem and list things they would remember about the group of miners who died in "The Explosion."
- Help students construct rhetorical questions and examples of figurative language for their eulogies.
- Ask volunteers to read their eulogies to the class for comment.

CUSTOMIZE INSTRUCTION For Universal Access

To address different learning styles, use the activities suggested in the **Extension Activities** booklet, p. 60.

- For Visual/Spatial Learners, use Activity 5.
- For Intrapersonal and Verbal/Linguistic Learners, use Activity 6
- For Interpersonal Learners, use Activity 7.

ASSESSMENT RESOURCES

The following resources can be used to assess students' knowledge and skills.

Selection Assessment

- **Formal Assessment:** Selection Test, pp. 286–288
- **Open Book Test,** pp. 177–179
- **Got It! Assessment Videotapes,** Tape 6
- **Test Bank Software**
- ***Take It to the Net***
  Visit www.phschool.com for self-tests and additional questions on the selections.

Writing Rubric

- **Performance Assess. and Portfolio Mgmt.,** p. 11

PRENTICE HALL ASSESSMENT SYSTEM

- **Workbook**
- **Skill Book**
- **Transparencies**
- **CD-ROM**

B. Wordsworth

Lesson Objectives and CA Correlations

1. **To analyze and respond to literary elements**
    - Literary Analysis: First-Person Narrator **R 3.1**
    - Connecting Literary Elements: Characterization **R 3.3**
2. **To read, comprehend, analyze, and critique a short story**
    - Reading Strategy: Responding to Characters
    - Reading Check Questions
    - Review and Assess Questions
3. **To develop word analysis skills, fluency, and systematic vocabulary**
    - Vocabulary Development Lesson: Forms of *patron* **R 1.1**
4. **To understand and apply written and oral language conventions**
    - Spelling Strategy **LC 1.2**
    - Grammar and Style Lesson: Pronoun Case in Compound Constructions **LC 1.1**
5. **To understand and apply appropriate writing and research strategies**
    - Writing Lesson: Account of a Remarkable Person **W 1.1, 1.9, 2.1**
    - Extension Activity: Classroom Exhibit **W 1.7**
    - Assessment Practice (ATE)
6. **To understand and apply listening and speaking strategies**
    - Extension Activity: Multimedia Tour **LS 1.10, 2.4**

STEP-BY-STEP TEACHING GUIDE	PACING GUIDE
PRETEACH	
Motivate Students and Provide Background	
Use the Motivation activity (ATE p. 1236)	5 min.
Read and discuss author and background features (SE/ATE pp. 1236, 1238) [A]	5 min.
Introduce the Concepts	
Introduce the Literary Analysis and Reading Strategy (SE/ATE p. 1237) [A]	15 min.
Pronounce the vocabulary words and read their definitions (SE p. 1237)	5 min.
TEACH	
Monitor Comprehension	
Informally monitor comprehension by circulating while students read independently or in groups [A]	20 min.
Monitor students' comprehension with the Reading Check notes (SE/ATE pp. 1239, 1241, 1243)	as students read
Develop vocabulary with Vocabulary notes (SE pp. 1238, 1242)	as students read
Develop Understanding	
Develop students' understanding of first-person narrator with the Literary Analysis annotations (SE pp. 1238, 1243, 1244; ATE pp. 1238, 1240, 1243) [A]	5 min.
Develop students' ability to respond to a character with the Reading Strategy annotations (SE/ATE pp. 1240, 1241)	5 min.
ASSESS	
Assess Mastery	
Assess students' mastery of the Reading Strategy and Literary Analysis by having them answer the Review and Assess questions (SE/ATE p. 1245)	15 min.
Use one or more of the print and media Assessment Resources (ATE p. 1247) [A]	up to 45 min.
EXTEND	
Apply Understanding	
Have students complete the Vocabulary Development Lesson and the Grammar and Style Lesson (SE p. 1246) [A]	20 min.
Apply students' knowledge of using details as support using the Writing Lesson (SE/ATE p. 1247) [A]	45 min.
Apply students' understanding using one or more of the Extension Activities (SE p. 1247)	20–90 min.

ACCELERATED INSTRUCTION:
Use the strategies and activities identified with an [A].

UNIVERSAL ACCESS
● = Below-Level Students
▲ = On-Level Students
■ = Above-Level Students

Time and Resource Manager

Reading Level: Average
Average Number of Instructional Days: 4

RESOURCES		
PRINT	**TRANSPARENCIES**	**TECHNOLOGY**
• **Beyond Literature,** Career Connection: Astronomer, p. 61 ▲ ■		• **Interest Grabber Video,** Tape 6 ● ▲ ■
• **Selection Support Workbook:** ● ▲ ■ Literary Analysis, p. 284 Reading Strategy, p. 283 Build Vocabulary, p. 281	• **Literary Analysis and Reading Transparencies,** pp. 121 and 122 ● ▲ ■	
		• **Listening to Literature** ● ▲ ■ Audiocassettes, Side 29 Audio CDs, CD 17
• **Literatura en español** ● ▲ • **Literary Analysis for Enrichment** ■		
• **Formal Assessment:** Selection Test, pp. 289–291 ● ▲ ■ • **Open Book Test,** pp. 181–183 ● ▲ ■ • PRENTICE HALL ASSESSMENT SYSTEM ● ▲ ■	• PRENTICE HALL ASSESSMENT SYSTEM ● ▲ ■ Skills Practice Answers and Explanations on Transparencies ● ▲ ■	• **Test Bank Software** ● ▲ ■ • **Got It! Assessment Videotapes,** Tape 6 ● ▲
• **Selection Support Workbook:** ● ▲ ■ Grammar and Style, p. 282 • **Writing and Grammar,** Diamond Level ● ▲ ■ • **Extension Activities,** p. 61 ● ▲ ■	• **Daily Language Practice Transparencies** ● ▲	• **Writing and Grammar iText CD-ROM** ● ▲ ■ ***Take It to the Net*** www.phschool.com

BLOCK SCHEDULING: Use one 90-minute class period to preteach the selection and have students read it. Use a second 90-minute class period to assess students' mastery of skills and have them complete one of the Extension Activities.

PRETEACH

Step-by-Step Teaching Guide for pp. 1236–1237

Motivation

Ask students to define *poet* and *poem.* Elicit the broader meanings of *poet* (someone who has profound insights into the world and who expresses these insights in meaningful, provocative writing) and *poem* (an expression of beauty or deep feeling in words). Tell students that the main character in this story will help them further define the concept of a poet or a poem.

Interest Grabber Video

As an alternative, play "'B. Wordsworth': Homelessness" on Tape 6 to engage student interest.

❶ More About the Author

Naipaul also writes nonfiction, including a report on a journey he took through the United States, apparently seeking connections between the American South and his own Trinidadian culture. Along with the issue of race, Naipaul considered features of southern Americana such as country and western music, conservative Christianity, and the ongoing obsession with Elvis Presley.

V. S. Naipaul was awarded the 2001 Nobel Prize for Literature.

Prepare to Read

❶ B. Wordsworth

V. S. Naipaul (b. 1932)
V. S. Naipaul, who grew up in Trinidad, has earned a reputation as a brilliant writer of fiction and nonfiction books about colonialism, exile, and issues of identity in the contemporary world. He has also stirred up controversy, and some writers have accused him of taking a snobbish attitude toward Third World cultures.

A "Many-Sided Background" Naipaul, whose family came from India, was born in Trinidad, then a part of the British West Indies. There, he grew up in the Hindu culture and attended British schools. These experiences, combined with living in England and traveling all over the world, make up what Naipaul calls his "many-sided background."

In his book of autobiographical writings, *Finding the Center: Two Narratives* (1984), Naipaul recounts how his grandfather came to Trinidad as an indentured laborer. Life for such Asian Indian immigrants was certainly better than it was for the Africans enslaved in the West Indies two hundred years previously. However, the terms of indenture were not always strictly followed, and members of the Indian community faced many frustrations as a result. The next generation fared somewhat better; Naipaul's father became a popular journalist with the main Trinidadian newspaper.

Explorations in Writing Even as a student, Naipaul shared his father's talent for writing, and he won a scholarship to Oxford University. While in his final year there, he learned that his father had died. At this point, Naipaul's family wanted him to return and settle in Trinidad, but he decided to remain in Britain. He soon found work in London writing about the West Indies for radio.

Far from home, he began to write stories that drew on his memories of Trinidad. Those early stories, including "B. Wordsworth," were eventually collected in *Miguel Street* (1959). In these tales, a young narrator describes the comic and absurd elements of growing up in the West Indies. Although the narrator is about Naipaul's age, he is also quite different from Naipaul. He lives alone with his mother, unlike Naipaul, who lived with an extended family. Naipaul made some of these changes out of a need to simplify. To gain a full perspective of the community, he also created a "narrator more in tune with the life of the street than I had been."

"Fiction Never Lies" *A House for Mr. Biswas* (1961) combines the comic perspective of his early tales with poignant and universal themes to tell the story of a man similar to his father. Naipaul returned to his own youth in the novelistic memoir *A Way in the World* (1994). In justifying his choice of fictional accounts over autobiography, Naipaul explains that "an autobiography can distort, facts can be realigned. But fiction never lies. It reveals the writer totally."

Reports on Rootlessness Naipaul is drawn to writing about people living on the margins of the modern world, people who have to struggle against rootlessness and cope with sweeping change. His 1971 novel *In a Free State*, about self-exiles who meet in Africa, won Britain's prestigious Booker Prize.

Relationship With India Naipaul's preoccupation with exile and cultural identity no doubt arises from his own complex relationship with India, the country of his heritage. He has written several nonfiction books about India, including *India: An Area of Darkness* (1965), *India: A Wounded Civilization* (1977), and *India: A Million Mutinies Now* (1990). These works reflect his changing attitudes toward a civilization that shaped his family.

TEACHING RESOURCES

The following resources can be used to enrich or extend the instruction for pp. 1236–1237.

Motivation

Interest Grabber Video, Tape 6

Background

Beyond Literature, Career Connection: Astronomer, p. 61 

Take It to the Net

Visit www.phschool.com for background and hotlinks for "B. Wordsworth."

Literary Analysis

Literary Analysis and Reading Transparencies, First-Person Narrator, p. 122

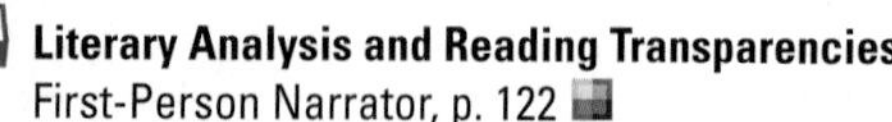

Reading

Selection Support: Reading Strategy, p. 283; Build Vocabulary, p. 281

Literary Analysis and Reading Transparencies, Respond to Character, p. 121

BLOCK SCHEDULING: Resources marked with this symbol provide varied instruction during 90-minute blocks.

Preview

Connecting to the Literature

Your name is an important part of your identity. Be alert to the importance of names in this story, whose title is a famous poet's name that a character has adapted for himself.

❷ Literary Analysis

First-Person Narrator

The point of view from which a story is told determines how you see and understand what occurs.

- A **first-person narrator** participates in the events of the story and refers to himself or herself as "I" or to his or her group or family as "we." This type of narrator shares his or her own thoughts and feelings about events.
- A **third-person narrator** is outside the action, refers to the characters as "he" or "she," and reveals the thoughts and feelings of several characters.

In "B. Wordsworth," Naipaul uses a first-person narrator to re-create Trinidad in the 1940s:

> At about ten an Indian came in his dhoti and white jacket, and <u>we</u> poured a tin of rice into the sack he carried on his back.

When reading, remember that the narrator is not the same person as the author, and ask yourself how the narrator's perspective affects the story.

Connecting Literary Elements

Naipaul's use of a first-person narrator affects the **characterization** of the two main people in this story, their development as fictional characters. You learn about the narrator through what he says, does, and thinks. However, because you see B. Wordsworth through the narrator's eyes, you can only guess what he thinks. As you read, compare your reactions to B. Wordsworth with the narrator's boyish responses.

❸ Reading Strategy

Responding to Characters

You will become more involved in a story by **responding to characters,** noting your reactions to their words, actions, and thoughts. Use a chart like this one to record these personal responses as you read.

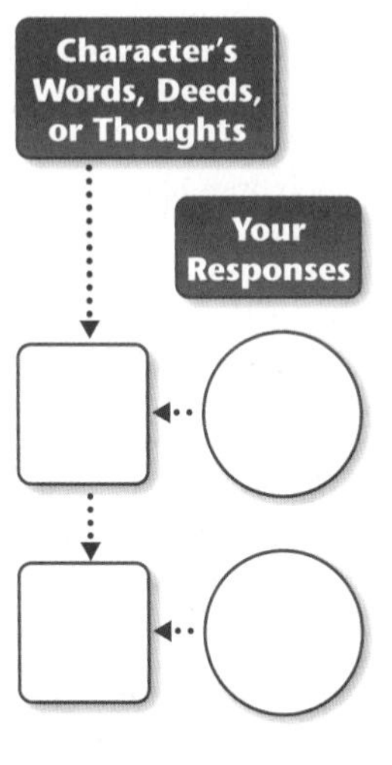

Vocabulary Development

rogue (rōg) *n.* wandering beggar or tramp; scoundrel (p. 1238)

patronize (pā′ trən īz′) *v.* to be a customer of a particular merchant or store (p. 1242)

distill (di stil′) *v.* to obtain the essential part (p. 1242)

keenly (kēn′ lē) *adv.* sharply; intensely (p. 1243)

❷ Literary Analysis

First-Person Narrator

- Remind students that that they have just read selections by third-person narrators.
- Read the instruction about first-person narrator together as a class and call students' attention to the example from the story.
- Use the instruction for Connecting Literary Elements to remind students that readers learn about characters in a first-person narration only through the perspective of the narrator.
- Use the First-Person Narrator transparency on p. 122 of **Literary Analysis and Reading Transparencies** to demonstrate for students how they can keep track of a first-person narration with a graphic organizer.

❸ Reading Strategy

Responding to Characters

- Tell students that readers become more involved in literature when they respond to the characters.
- Remind students that they can learn about characters through their words, actions, or thoughts.
- Instruct students to set up a graphic organizer like the one on this page, or like the example on the Responding to Character transparency on p. 121 of **Literary Analysis and Reading Transparencies,** to record their responses to "B. Wordsworth."

Vocabulary Development

- Pronounce each vocabulary word for students, and read the definitions as a class. Have students identify any words with which they are already familiar.

CUSTOMIZE INSTRUCTION FOR UNIVERSAL ACCESS

For Less Proficient Readers	For English Learners	For Advanced Readers
Ask students to discuss what it means to be "snobbish" about ideas, people, or events. Have them look up the word in a dictionary and then give examples from their own experience. In their discussion, have students consider: How is being snobbish hurtful to others? How might it be a defense of one's own culture?	Invite students to look up the meanings of some of the words used in the biographical material on p. 1236, to use as a guide when they read the story. Examples are *colonialism, exile, indentured, immigrant, perspective, rootlessness,* and *identity.* Have them think about how the meaning of each word is reflected in the story.	Have students write a critical appraisal of Naipaul's words from p. 1236: ". . . an autobiography can distort, facts can be realigned. But fiction never lies. It reveals the writer totally." Ask if this statement meshes with their view of the difference between autobiography and fiction.

 **E-Teach**

Visit E-Teach at www.phschool.com for teachers' essays on how to teach, with questions and answers.

TEACH

Step-by-Step Teaching Guide for pp. 1238–1244

CUSTOMIZE INSTRUCTION
For Musical/Rhythmic Learners

Encourage students to find recorded examples of British and West Indian accents. Have them prepare dramatic readings of some of the story's dialogue, contrasting the narrator's voice with B. Wordsworth's.

❶ About the Selection

This story expresses the pain of life in colonial society by dramatizing the ways a Trinidadian poet is kept from success. An innocent narrator—a young boy—at first takes the poet at face value, noticing only his wondrous way of appreciating life's beauty. Gradually, however, the boy realizes the ways the poet's life has been limited so that his ability to produce written work has been stunted. By the story's end, the boy is brought to tears not only by the poet's approaching death but also by society's restrictions and life's tragedy: "I . . . ran home crying, like a poet, for everything I saw."

❷ Literary Analysis

First-Person Narrator

- Ask students to read the introduction and the first paragraph of the story and to describe the setting.
  Answer: The setting is a very poor immigrant Indian community in Trinidad.
- Have students determine the point of view of the story and tell how they know.
  Answer: The point of view is first-person. The narration is told from the "I" point of view.
- Ask students the Literary Analysis question on p. 1238: What is your impression of the narrator? Explain.
  Possible response: The narrator is young (he goes to school), obedient (he responds quickly when the stranger asks to come in the yard), and observant (he describes the people in his community).

❶ 

B. Wordsworth

V. S. Naipaul

Background

This story is set in Trinidad, probably in the 1940s. Trinidad, which became independent in 1962, had been a British colony since 1802. From 1845 to 1917, it had received indentured workers emigrating from India. Naipaul's grandfather had been such a worker, borrowing money for passage and laboring for years to pay off the debt. With a diverse population and with the culture of Britain, the colonial power, held up as "superior," cultural identity and names were key issues in Trinidad.

❷ Three beggars called punctually every day at the hospitable houses in Miguel Street. At about ten an Indian came in his dhoti[1] and white jacket, and we poured a tin of rice into the sack he carried on his back. At twelve an old woman smoking a clay pipe came and she got a cent. At two a blind man led by a boy called for his penny.

Sometimes we had a rogue. One day a man called and said he was hungry. We gave him a meal. He asked for a cigarette and wouldn't go until we had lit it for him. That man never came again.

The strangest caller came one afternoon at about four o'clock. I had come back from school and was in my home-clothes. The man said to me, "Sonny, may I come inside your yard?"

He was a small man and he was tidily dressed. He wore a hat, a white shirt and black trousers.

I asked, "What you want?"

He said, "I want to watch your bees."

We had four small gru-gru palm trees[2] and they were full of uninvited bees.

I ran up the steps and shouted, "Ma, it have a man outside here. He say he want to watch the bees."

rogue (rōg) *n.* wandering beggar or tramp; scoundrel

Literary Analysis
First-Person Narrator What is your impression of the narrator? Explain.

1. **dhoti** (dō′ tē) traditional loincloth worn by Hindu men.
2. **gru-gru** (gro͞o′ gro͞o′) **palm trees** West Indian palms that yield edible nuts.

TEACHING RESOURCES

The following resources can be used to enrich or extend the instruction for pp. 1238–1244.

Literary Analysis
Selection Support: Literary Analysis, p. 284

Reading
Listening to Literature Audiocassettes, Side 29
Listening to Literature Audio CDs, CD 17 

BLOCK SCHEDULING: Resources marked with this symbol provide varied instruction during 90-minute blocks.

My mother came out, looked at the man and asked in an unfriendly way, "What you want?"

The man said, "I want to watch your bees."

His English was so good, it didn't sound natural, and I could see my mother was worried.

She said to me, "Stay here and watch him while he watch the bees."

The man said, "Thank you, Madam. You have done a good deed today."

He spoke very slowly and very correctly as though every word was costing him money.

We watched the bees, this man and I, for about an hour, squatting near the palm trees.

The man said, "I like watching bees. Sonny, do you like watching bees?"

I said, "I ain't have the time."

He shook his head sadly. He said, "That's what I do, I just watch. I can watch ants for days. Have you ever watched ants? And scorpions, and centipedes, and congorees[3]—have you watched those?"

I shook my head.

I said, "What you does do, mister?"

He got up and said, "I am a poet."

I said, "A good poet?"

He said, "The greatest in the world."

"What your name, mister?"

"B. Wordsworth."

"B for Bill?"

3 "Black. Black Wordsworth. White Wordsworth[4] was my brother. We share one heart. I can watch a small flower like the morning glory and cry."

I said, "Why you does cry?"

"Why, boy? Why? You will know when you grow up. You're a poet, too, you know. And when you're a poet you can cry for everything."

I couldn't laugh.

He said, "You like your mother?"

"When she not beating me."

4

Man From the Village, Carlton Murrell

5 ▲ Critical Viewing
How does the attitude of the man in the painting compare with that of B. Wordsworth? **[Compare and Contrast]**

3. **congorees** (käŋ′ gər ēz) Conger or Congo eels; large, scaleless eels found in the warm waters of the West Indies.
4. **White Wordsworth** English Romantic poet William Wordsworth (1770–1850).

6  Reading Check
How does the narrator meet B. Wordsworth?

3 Background

Meaning of Name "B. Wordsworth"

William Wordsworth was a romantic poet who also loved nature. Students may want to draw further parallels between the "brothers" by reading W. Wordsworth's poem "The World Is Too Much with Us," p. 675.

4 Background

Art

Man From the Village, by Carlton Murrell

Murrell was born in Bridgetown, Barbados, in 1945 and now lives in Brooklyn, New York. This painting was done by the artist on one of his yearly trips to Barbados. One night, Murrell saw this retired fisherman and was struck by the man's dignity, in spite of his obvious poverty.

Use these questions for discussion:

1. How is this man's relationship to his village like that of B. Wordsworth's? How is it different?
   Answer: Both figures are shaped by their environments, but B. Wordsworth departs from his environment through his careful, educated speech and poetic aspirations.
2. What characteristics of this man suggest the character of B. Wordsworth?
   Answer: The man in the painting suggests a quiet dignity despite his impoverished surroundings.

5 ▶Critical Viewing

Possible response: Both B. Wordsworth and the man in the painting have a quiet dignity, a serene air, and a strong relationship to their environments.

6 Reading Check

Answer: B. Wordsworth asks to come into the narrator's yard to watch the bees.

CUSTOMIZE INSTRUCTION FOR UNIVERSAL ACCESS

For Special Needs Students	For Less Proficient Readers	For English Learners
Have students reread the Background on p. 1238 and speculate on what effect the British colonization might have had on Trinidadians. Also have them guess why a poet of Trinidad might name himself "Black Wordsworth," the so-called brother of the British poet "White Wordsworth."	Students may want to rephrase the dialect of the young narrator into Standard English. For example, what would be the "translations" for "What you want?" "I ain't have the time" and "What you does do, mister?"	Help students find recorded examples of British and West Indian accents. Then, encourage them to prepare dramatic readings of parts of the story's dialogue, contrasting the narrator's and B. Wordsworth's ways of speaking.

7 Reading Strategy

Responding to Characters

- After students have read the passage, ask them how the narrator tries to protect B. Wordsworth's feelings from his mother's response.
  Answer: The narrator says his mother doesn't have four cents, not that she will have B. Wordsworth taken away.
- Ask students the Reading Strategy question on p. 1240: What is your response to the mother's angry words?
  Possible response: Since students learned on the previous page that his mother beats the narrator, they probably don't have much sympathy for her and will respond negatively to her words.

8 Literary Analysis

First-Person Narrator

- Ask students to read the two paragraphs in this passage and to identify the sensory details.
  Answer: The narrator describes B. Wordsworth's yard in terms of the trees, then describes the taste and the physical feeling of eating mangoes.
- Have students compare these two paragraphs with previous passages that present the narrator's dialogue. What difference do they see?
  Answer: The dialogue is written in dialect, and the narration is written in Standard English.
- Ask students what this difference in style suggests about the narrator.
  Possible response: The change in style suggests that the narrator grew up using the dialect of his culture and then learned Standard English, perhaps in a colonial school or in England.

He pulled out a printed sheet from his hip-pocket and said, "On this paper is the greatest poem about mothers and I'm going to sell it to you at a bargain price. For four cents."

I went inside and I said, "Ma, you want buy a poetry for four cents?"

7 My mother said, "Tell that blasted man I haul his tail away from my yard, you hear."

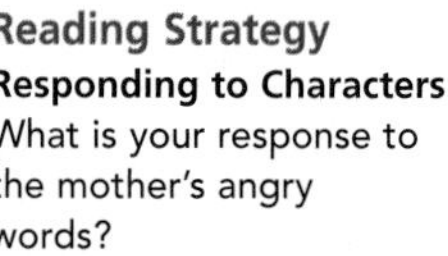

Reading Strategy
Responding to Characters What is your response to the mother's angry words?

I said to B. Wordsworth, "My mother say she ain't have four cents."

B. Wordsworth said, "It is the poet's tragedy."

And he put the paper back in his pocket. He didn't seem to mind.

I said, "Is a funny way to go round selling poetry like that. Only calypsonians[5] do that sort of thing. A lot of people does buy?"

He said, "No one has yet bought a single copy."

"But why you does keep on going round, then?"

He said, "In this way I watch many things, and I always hope to meet poets."

I said, "You really think I is a poet?"

"You're as good as me," he said.

And when B. Wordsworth left, I prayed I would see him again.

About a week later, coming back from school one afternoon, I met him at the corner of Miguel Street.

He said, "I have been waiting for you for a long time."

I said, "You sell any poetry yet?"

He shook his head.

He said, "In my yard I have the best mango tree in Port-of-Spain.[6] And now the mangoes are ripe and red and very sweet and juicy. I have waited here for you to tell you this and to invite you to come and eat some of my mangoes."

He lived in Alberto Street in a one-roomed hut placed right in the center of the lot. The yard seemed all green. There was the big mango tree. There was a coconut tree and there was a plum tree. The place

8 looked wild, as though it wasn't in the city at all. You couldn't see all the big concrete houses in the street.

He was right. The mangoes were sweet and juicy. I ate about six, and the yellow mango juice ran down my arms to my elbows and down my mouth to my chin and my shirt was stained.

My mother said when I got home, "Where you was? You think you is a man now and could go all over the place? Go cut a whip for me."

She beat me rather badly, and I ran out of the house swearing that I would never come back. I went to B. Wordsworth's house. I was so angry, my nose was bleeding.

---

5. **calypsonians** (kə lip sō′ nē ənz) those who sing calypso songs; the characteristic satirical street singers of Trinidad.
6. **Port-of-Spain** seaport capital of Trinidad and Tobago.

ENRICHMENT: Social Studies Connection

Trinidad

Today the name of the country in which this story is set is Trinidad and Tobago. The country is made up of two islands in the Caribbean near the northeast coast of South America. The island of Trinidad makes up about 95 percent of the land area of Trinidad and Tobago, and 95 percent of the country's people live there. Trinidadians of African and Indian descent make up about 80 percent of the population. The rest of the people are of European, Chinese, or mixed European and African background.

English is the country's official language, though French, Spanish, and Hindi (an Indian language) are also spoken. Trinidad English is an island form of English influenced by both French and Spanish. The literacy rate in Trinidad is 98 percent and almost all adults can read and write.

B. Wordsworth said, "Stop crying, and we will go for a walk."

I stopped crying, but I was breathing short. We went for a walk. We walked down St. Clair Avenue to the Savannah and we walked to the race-course.

B. Wordsworth said, "Now, let us lie on the grass and look up at the sky, and I want you to think how far those stars are from us."

9 I did as he told me, and I saw what he meant. I felt like nothing, and at the same time I had never felt so big and great in all my life. I forgot all my anger and all my tears and all the blows.

When I said I was better, he began telling me the names of the stars, and I particularly remembered the constellation of Orion the Hunter,[7] though I don't really know why. I can spot Orion even today, but I have forgotten the rest.

Then a light was flashed into our faces, and we saw a policeman. We got up from the grass.

The policeman said, "What you doing here?"

B. Wordsworth said, "I have been asking myself the same question for forty years."

We became friends, B. Wordsworth and I. He told me, "You must never tell anybody about me and about the mango tree and the coconut tree and the plum tree. You must keep that a secret. If you tell anybody, I will know, because I am a poet."

I gave him my word and I kept it.

I liked his little room. It had no more furniture than George's front room,[8] but it looked cleaner and healthier. But it also looked lonely.

One day I asked him, "Mister Wordsworth, why you does keep all this bush in your yard? Ain't it does make the place damp?"

10 He said, "Listen, and I will tell you a story. Once upon a time a boy and girl met each other and they fell in love. They loved each other so much they got married. They were both poets. He loved words. She loved grass and flowers and trees. They lived happily in a single room, and then one day, the girl poet said to the boy poet, 'We are going to have another poet in the family.' But this poet was never born, because the girl died, and the young poet died with her, inside her. And the girl's husband was very sad, and he said he would never touch a thing in the girl's garden. And so the garden remained, and grew high and wild."

I looked at B. Wordsworth, and as he told me this lovely story, he seemed to grow older. I understood his story.

We went for long walks together. We went to the Botanical Gardens and the Rock Gardens. We climbed Chancellor Hill in the late afternoon and watched the darkness fall on Port-of-Spain, and watched the lights go on in the city and on the ships in the harbor.

7. **constellation of Orion** (ō rī´ ən) **the Hunter** group of stars named after a mythological giant who was killed accidentally by the goddess of hunting, Diana.

8. **George's front room** George is a character in one of the companion stories in Naipaul's book, *Miguel Street*.

Reading Strategy
Responding to Characters
How does the way in which B. Wordsworth treats the angry and crying narrator affect your response to Wordsworth?

11  **Reading Check**
What does B. Wordsworth do when the narrator, angry and crying, comes to see him?

9 Reading Strategy

Responding to Characters

- Ask students what condition the narrator is in after his mother has beaten him.
  Answer: He is angry and crying. His nose is bleeding and he is breathing in short gasps.
- Ask students why they think B. Wordsworth does not deal with the issue of the mother's beating of the narrator but merely tries to comfort the narrator.
  Answer: B. Wordsworth has less power than the mother and realizes he can do nothing about her violence. What he can do is try to give the narrator some experiences to strengthen him psychologically.
- Ask students the Reading Strategy question on p. 1241: How does the way in which B. Wordsworth treats the narrator affect your response to Wordsworth?
  Answer: Readers feel grateful to Wordsworth for trying to comfort the boy by giving him information about the heavens that helps him forget his beating.

10 Reading Strategy

Responding to Character

- Ask students to read the passage and identify the kind of literature it reminds them of.
  Answer: The form of the story is similar to that of a fairy tale, especially the "Once upon a time . . ." form.

Monitor Progress Ask students how this story makes them feel about B. Wordsworth.
Possible response: Some students may feel sympathetic to one who has experienced such a tragic loss; others may think, based on the fairy-tale similarity, that B. Wordsworth has made up the story for some reason.

11 Reading Check

Answer: B. Wordsworth shows the narrator the heavens and identifies the constellations for him.

CUSTOMIZE INSTRUCTION FOR UNIVERSAL ACCESS

For Less Proficient Readers	For Gifted/Talented Students	For Advanced Readers
Ask students to list the characteristics of B. Wordsworth that they have learned about so far in the story that would make him a good poet. (He is observant and likes to watch things going on such as bees and the constellations; he is sensitive to the importance of words; he is a good storyteller; he is open to emotions; and so on.)	Have students note the exchange between the policeman and B. Wordsworth. Ask them why this exchange is humorous and what they think it means. (The policeman is asking a literal question about what the two people are doing in the park. B. Wordsworth answers it as though the policeman had asked a philosophical question.)	Students may want to do some research into constellations and present their findings to the class. Are the constellations students can see the same ones, or different ones, from those seen in the Caribbean? Which constellations are visible in the night sky at the time when students are reading this story?

⓬ Background

Art

The Red House, by Carlton Murrell

Murrell returns to his native Barbados once or twice a year and tries to document a way of life that is rapidly changing. *The Red House* is a painting of a chattel house, the type of residence that is being phased out in the islands. This painting conveys the colors, scenery, and mood of a tropical culture. Use the following question for discussion:

- Which character in the story might live in this house?
  Possible responses: The cramped, narrow house could be the home of the narrator and his mother, who seem to live in a rather confined world until B. Wordsworth offers the narrator a broader view. The private, mysterious world of the house evokes B. Wordsworth's unique and special world.

⓭ ▶Critical Viewing

Answer: The house looks similar to the one-room hut described by the narrator. However, there appears to be another house just behind it, and the yard is not nearly as full of trees as in the description; and the only identifiable trees are the palm trees.

⓮ Critical Thinking

Analyze

- Ask students what two characteristics of B. Wordsworth's behavior the narrator describes in this passage.
  Answer: Wordsworth does everything as though he were doing it for the first time, and he does everything as though he were performing some church rite.
- Ask students to analyze these behaviors by describing them in their own words, and then tell how the characteristics might be important ones for a poet to have.
  Possible response: The first behavior suggests that everything is always new to Wordsworth, and the second behavior suggests that the character has a very spiritual approach to life. Both characteristics would be important to a poet.

⓬

⓮ He did everything as though he were doing it for the first time in his life. He did everything as though he were doing some church rite.

He would say to me, "Now, how about having some ice cream?"

And when I said, yes, he would grow very serious and say, "Now, which café shall we patronize?" As though it were a very important thing. He would think for some time about it, and finally say, "I think I will go and negotiate the purchase with that shop."

The world became a most exciting place.

One day, when I was in his yard, he said to me, "I have a great secret which I am now going to tell you."

I said, "It really secret?"

"At the moment, yes."

I looked at him, and he looked at me. He said, "This is just between you and me, remember. I am writing a poem."

"Oh." I was disappointed.

He said, "But this is a different sort of poem. This is the greatest poem in the world."

The Red House, Carlton Murrell

I whistled.

He said, "I have been working on it for more than five years now. I will finish it in about twenty-two years from now, that is, if I keep on writing at the present rate."

"You does write a lot, then?"

He said, "Not any more. I just write one line a month. But I make sure it is a good line."

I asked, "What was last month's good line?"

He looked up at the sky, and said, *"The past is deep."*

I said, "It is a beautiful line."

⓯ B. Wordsworth said, "I hope to distill the experiences of a whole month into that single line of poetry. So, in twenty-two years, I shall have written a poem that will sing to all humanity."

I was filled with wonder.

⓭ ▲ **Critical Viewing** Do you think this could be B. Wordsworth's house? Why or why not? **[Connect]**

patronize (pā´ trən īz´) *v.* to be a customer of a particular merchant or store

distill (di stil´) *v.* to obtain the essential part

ENRICHMENT: Music Connection

Calypso

When asked what he does for a living, B. Wordsworth says that he sings calypsos. Calypso is a type of music that originated on the island of Trinidad and combines features of African and Spanish music with American jazz and blues. Calypso is often sung in French Creole dialect as well as in English. The songs are accompanied by such instruments as maracas—rattles traditionally made of dried gourds containing loose seeds; the cuatro—a stringed instrument; and guitars, flutes, and saxophones. Calypso songs may also be accompanied by drums made from steel oil containers and played with sticks. The lyrics convey a variety of messages as each expresses the personal point of view of the singer-poet. The calypso season mentioned by B. Wordsworth takes place during carnival time, which begins in January and ends at the start of Lent.

Our walks continued. We walked along the sea-wall at Docksite one day, and I said, "Mr. Wordsworth, if I drop this pin in the water, you think it will float?"

He said, "This is a strange world. Drop your pin, and let us see what will happen."

The pin sank.

I said, "How is the poem this month?"

But he never told me any other line. He merely said, "Oh, it comes, you know. It comes."

Or we would sit on the sea-wall and watch the liners come into the harbor.

But of the greatest poem in the world I heard no more.

I felt he was growing older.

"How you does live, Mr. Wordsworth?" I asked him one day.

He said, "You mean how I get money?"

When I nodded, he laughed in a crooked way.

He said, "I sing calypsoes in the calypso season."

"And that last you the rest of the year?"

"It is enough."

"But you will be the richest man in the world when you write the greatest poem?"

He didn't reply.

One day when I went to see him in his little house, I found him lying on his little bed. He looked so old and so weak, that I found myself wanting to cry.

He said, "The poem is not going well."

He wasn't looking at me. He was looking through the window at the coconut tree, and he was speaking as though I wasn't there. He said, "When I was twenty I felt the power within myself." Then, almost in front of my eyes, I could see his face growing older and more tired. He said, "But that—that was a long time ago."

And then—I felt it so keenly, it was as though I had been slapped by my mother. I could see it clearly on his face. It was there for everyone to see. Death on the shrinking face.

He looked at me, and saw my tears and sat up.

He said, "Come." I went and sat on his knees.

He looked into my eyes, and he said, "Oh, you can see it, too. I always knew you had the poet's eye."

He didn't even look sad, and that made me burst out crying loudly.

He pulled me to his thin chest, and said, "Do you want me to tell you a funny story?" and he smiled encouragingly at me.

But I couldn't reply.

He said, "When I have finished this story, I want you to promise that you will go away and never come back to see me. Do you promise?"

I nodded.

Literary Analysis

First-Person Narrator and Characterization What do you know about B. Wordsworth's ambitious plan that the narrator does not seem to know?

keenly (kēn′ lē) *adv.* sharply; intensely

 **Reading Check**

What does the narrator suddenly realize is going to happen to B. Wordsworth?

⓯ Literary Analysis

First-Person Narrator and Characterization

- Ask students how B. Wordsworth describes his poem-writing habits.
  Answer: He says he writes one line a month but makes sure that it is a good line.
- Have students speculate on why B. Wordsworth says he will finish the poem in twenty-two years.
  Possible response: He wants to give himself enough time to be sure to finish the poem, but he does not really know how many years it will take him.
- Ask students the Literary Analysis question on p. 1243: What do you know about B. Wordsworth's ambitious plan that the narrator does not seem to know?
  Answer: The poet will never finish his poem. Perhaps he is not even writing it.

⓰ Reading Check

Answer: The narrator realizes that B. Wordsworth is going to die.

⓱ Literary Analysis

First-Person Narrator (p. 1244)

- Have students speculate on what the narrator means by the last sentence of the story.
  Possible response: The narrator means that he has absorbed the characteristics of the poet from B. Wordsworth and will become a poet himself.
- Have students answer the Literary Analysis question on p. 1244: How would the story be different if it were told by a third-person narrator? Explain.
  Possible responses: Through the first-person narration, readers see B. Wordsworth through the boy's eyes; they identify with the narrator's growth and with his loss of innocence; they feel the difference between the narrator now and the narrator as a small boy. This would have not been the case if the story had been told from a more distant third-person point of view.

CUSTOMIZE INSTRUCTION FOR UNIVERSAL ACCESS

For Special Needs Students	For Less Proficient Readers	For English Learners
Have partners take turns presenting passages of the story that include dialogue between the narrator and B. Wordsworth. How would each student reading the narrator change his or her voice to show the difference between the narrator as a young boy and the narrator as the person telling the story?	Ask students whether they have ever learned B. Wordsworth's real name. Then, ask them to see if they learn it before the end of the story. Have them discuss what the writer might be trying to express by not letting readers know the poet's true name.	Have students study the vocabulary words and use them in written sentences. Ask them to suggest related words for *patronize* and *distill*. (Students may cite *patron, patronizing, patronage, distilling, distilled, distillation.*)

ASSESS

Answers for p. 1244

Review and Assess

1. Students might refer to aspects of nature, relationships with people, or favorite types of entertainment.
2. **(a)** He says he wants to watch the bees. **(b)** The other visitors want to be given something—food, money, a cigarette. B. Wordsworth just wants to look, which won't cost the boy and his mother anything.
3. **(a)** Black **(b)** Possible response: The boy has the ability to see and feel, which is what poets do.
4. He finds the world constantly surprising and delightful, which is a good emotion for a poet.
5. **(a)** Students may say that the "story" is a tragedy that actually happened to B. Wordsworth; this explains why his garden grows wild. **(b)** By maintaining the pretense of "once upon a time," B. Wordsworth may be protecting the boy (or himself) from confronting a deep personal pain.
6. **(a)** He wants to nurture another young poet and possibly have an admiring audience for himself. **(b)** He gains a friend. He learns that there is more to life than being beaten by his mother. He "gets in touch with his emotions"—in other words, he becomes a poet too.
7. Answers will vary. Students should take into account the fact that B. Wordsworth's identification of himself with "White Wordsworth" is an acknowledgment of the importance—for good or for ill—of British culture on the island.

He said, "Good. Well, listen. That story I told you about the boy poet and the girl poet, do you remember that? That wasn't true. It was something I just made up. All this talk about poetry and the greatest poem in the world, that wasn't true, either. Isn't that the funniest thing you have heard?"

But his voice broke.

I left the house, and ran home crying, like a poet, for everything I saw.

17 I walked along Alberto Street a year later, but I could find no sign of the poet's house. It hadn't vanished, just like that. It had been pulled down, and a big, two-storied building had taken its place. The mango tree and the plum tree and the coconut tree had all been cut down, and there was brick and concrete everywhere.

It was just as though B. Wordsworth had never existed.

Literary Analysis
First-Person Narrator How would the story be different if it were told by a third-person narrator? Explain.

Review and Assess

Thinking About the Selection

1. **Respond:** When the narrator is with B. Wordsworth, the world becomes "a most exciting place." What simple things make the world "exciting" for you? Why?
2. **(a) Recall:** What reason does B. Wordsworth give for wanting to come into the boy's yard? **(b) Compare and Contrast:** How is B. Wordsworth different from the other visitors who are described?
3. **(a) Recall:** What does the *B* in B. Wordsworth's name stand for? **(b) Interpret:** What does B. Wordsworth mean when he calls the boy "a poet"?
4. **Draw Conclusions:** B. Wordsworth "did everything as though he were doing it for the first time." In what way does this make B. Wordsworth "a poet"?
5. **(a) Infer:** What does the story of the boy poet and the girl poet suggest about B. Wordsworth? **(b) Interpret:** Why does he tell the boy that the story is untrue?
6. **(a) Infer:** What do you think B. Wordsworth's motivation is for spending time with the boy? **(b) Draw Conclusions:** What does the boy gain from knowing B. Wordsworth?
7. **Make a Judgment:** Do you think that B. Wordsworth's choice of a name shows (a) the harmful effects of colonialism on the identity and self-worth of colonized peoples, (b) the pride that colonized peoples can assert, or (c) a combination of both? Explain your answer.

ASSESSMENT PRACTICE: Writing Skills

Strategy **(For more practice, see Test Preparation Workbook. p. 61.)**

Many tests require students to apply revision strategies to a given passage. Use this sample test item.

One day a man called and said he was hungry.

Without changing the meaning of the sentence, the words "late in the afternoon" can be inserted in each of the following locations EXCEPT ___.

A before *One* **C** after *called*
B after *day* **D** after *hungry*

Explain that the way to answer a question of this type is to use the phrase in each of the possible locations. The correct choice is *D*. If the phrase were added after *hungry*, the sentence would mean that the man was hungry late in the afternoon, not that he called at that time.

Review and Assess

Literary Analysis

First-Person Narrator

1. Cite two pieces of evidence that indicate that the story is told by a **first-person narrator** rather than a **third-person narrator.**
2. Fill in a chart like this one to show how parts of the story might be different if B. Wordsworth were the first-person narrator.

Narrator	Characters' First Meeting	Knowledge of B. Words-worth's Past	B. Words-worth's Death	Mystery About B. Wordsworth
Boy				
B. Wordsworth				

3. (a) How is the narrator's voice different from the boy's dialogue? (b) Explain how this difference suggests B. Wordsworth's effect on the boy.

Connecting Literary Elements

4. Explain how a detail from each of the following categories adds to the **characterization** of B. Wordsworth: (a) what the narrator says about him, (b) what he says, (c) his name.
5. What do you learn about B. Wordsworth indirectly through his way of dealing with the narrator's anger?
6. Does the characterization of B. Wordsworth show that an author can develop a character in ways that escape a first-person narrator's awareness? Explain.

Reading Strategy

Responding to Characters

7. To which of the two main characters do you **respond** more strongly? Explain.
8. What is your response to B. Wordsworth's belief that it is possible and desirable to "cry for everything"? Explain.

Extend Understanding

9. **Psychology Connection:** What importance, if any, do role models like B. Wordsworth have in a young person's development? Explain.

Quick Review

A **first-person narrator** participates in the events of the story and refers to himself or herself as "I."

A **third-person narrator** does not take part in the story and refers to characters as "he" or "she."

Characterization, the process by which a writer develops a character, includes what a character says, does, and thinks, as well as the reaction of other characters to him or her.

To **respond to a character,** note your personal reactions to a character's words, thoughts, and actions.

Take It to the Net

www.phschool.com

Take the interactive self-test online to check your understanding of the selection.

Answers for p. 1245

Review and Assess

1. A first-person narrator participates in the events of the story and refers to himself or herself as "I." A first-person narrator shares his or her own thoughts and feelings but not those of the other characters.
2. *Boy:* **Characters' First Meeting:** tidily dressed man wants to come into yard and watch bees; **Knowledge of B. Wordsworth's Past:** Revealed gradually by B. Wordsworth; **B. Wordsworth's Death:** Narrator surprised to learn that B. Wordsworth is dying; **Mystery About B. Wordsworth:** Narrator shattered by learning that much of what B. Wordsworth has told him is not true; ***B. Wordsworth:*** **Characters' First Meeting:** B. Wordsworth always on the lookout for interesting things to watch; **Knowledge of B. Wordsworth's Past:** Character would perhaps reveal some things about his past; **B. Wordsworth's Death:** Readers would have information about how character felt about his death; **Mystery About B. Wordsworth:** Character would perhaps reveal himself to reader and perhaps not.
3. **(a)** The narrator's voice is an adult voice and also uses Standard English. The boy's voice is a child's voice and also uses Trinidadian English, or dialect. **(b)** The boy may have been inspired by B. Wordsworth to get a formal education.
4. **(a)** The narrator describes him as tidily dressed. **(b)** The character describes himself as a poet. **(c)** The character reveals that he wishes for the talent, background, and success of the British poet William Wordsworth.
5. B. Wordsworth is a sensitive and compassionate character who tries to comfort a boy who has been beaten.
6. Possible response: Yes, we understand B. Wordsworth's failure and frailty through what the boy reveals, though the boy does not see them as such. Thus, the author succeeds in developing his character beyond the narrator's awareness.

continued

ENRICHMENT: Further Reading

Other Works by V. S. Naipaul

Miguel Street

Finding the Centre

A Way in the World

A House for Mr. Biswas

Take It to the Net

Visit www.phschool.com for more information about V. S. Naipaul.

Answers continued

7. Some students will identify with the boy because of his appreciation of an older mentor. Others will identify with B. Wordsworth because of his poetic character or his status as an outsider.
8. Some students may think the character means that it is always possible to be aware that life is transitory.
9. Students may say that role models show a younger person what it is possible to do with one's life.

EXTEND

Answers for p. 1246

❶ Vocabulary Development

Word Analysis

1. patron
2. patronage
3. patronize

Spelling Strategy

1. quietly
2. shrilly
3. romantically

Fluency: Clarification

1. Such a poet would be more likely to describe details.
2. No, a 1,000-page novel would expand meaning.
3. No, a rogue goes his or her own way.
4. You would patronize a snack bar.

❷ Grammar and Style

1. The poet and I shared a mango.
2. We watched the bees, this man and I, for about an hour.
3. It was a secret between him and me.
4. It was as if the stars glowed for him and me.
5. A calypsonian sang my friend and me a song.

Writing Application

Sample response: I remembered how he and I would watch the ships in the harbor. It was a meaningful experience for him and me. I wished I could still visit him and that he would tell me about his poetry.

Integrate Language Skills

❶ Vocabulary Development Lesson

Word Analysis: Forms of *patron*

Patronize means "to be a customer" or "to be kind but in a snobbish way." The word, with its hint of power, comes from a Latin root meaning "protector," "defender," or "father." Its various forms reflect this meaning. A *patron* of the arts is "a person of wealth and power who supports artists." *Patronage* refers to both "business given to a store," and "the power to grant favors in order to gain political advantage."

On your paper, complete each sentence using one of the following words:

patronize patron patronage

1. A __?__ of the arts, she gave generously to the orchestra.
2. Some believe that __?__ leads to corruption in politics.
3. I always __?__ that fruit store.

Spelling Strategy

When adding the suffix *-ly*, do not change the end of the word except in three situations. For words that end in two *l's*, drop one *l* (*full, fully*). For words that end in a consonant + *-le*, drop the *e* (*able, ably*). For many adjectives with two or more syllables that end in *-c*, add *-ally* (*intrinsic, intrinsically*). In your notebook, add *-ly* to each of the following adjectives.

1. quiet 2. shrill 3. romantic

Fluency: Clarification

Explain answers to these questions:

1. Would a *keenly* observant poet describe or gloss over details?
2. Can a 1,000-page novel *distill* meaning?
3. Does a *rogue* promote society's rules?
4. Would you *patronize* a forest or a snack bar?

❷ Grammar and Style Lesson

Pronoun Case in Compound Constructions

For compound constructions, use the **case**—nominative or objective form—that would be correct if the pronoun were used alone.

Nominative Case: We became friends, B. Wordsworth and I. (appositive of subject, *we*)

Objective Case: This is just between you and me . . . (object of the preposition *between*)

Practice In your notebook, write each sentence using the correct pronoun or pronouns.

1. The poet and (I, me) shared a mango.
2. We watched the bees, this man and (I, me), for about an hour.
3. It was a secret between (he, him) and (I, me).
4. It was as if the stars glowed for (he, him) and (I, me).
5. A calypsonian sang my friend and (I, me) a song.

Writing Application Write a paragraph in which the narrator of the story reflects on B. Wordsworth after B. Wordsworth's death. In your paragraph, use the nominative and objective cases of pronouns once each in compound constructions.

WG Prentice Hall Writing and Grammar Connection: Chapter 22, Section 1

TEACHING RESOURCES

The following resources can be used to enrich or extend the instruction for pp. 1246–1247.

Vocabulary

- **Selection Support:** Build Vocabulary, p. 281
- **Vocabulary and Spelling Practice Book** (Use this booklet for skills enrichment.)

Grammar

- **Selection Support:** Grammar and Style, p. 282
- **Writing and Grammar,** Diamond Level, p. 564 ■
- **Daily Language Practice Transparencies**

Writing

- **Writing and Grammar,** Diamond Level, p. 102 ■
- **Writing and Grammar iText CD-ROM**

■ **BLOCK SCHEDULING:** Resources marked with this symbol provide varied instruction during 90-minute blocks.

❸ Writing Lesson

Account of a Remarkable Person

The narrator of Naipaul's story will never forget the remarkable B. Wordsworth. Write an account of a remarkable person you have met, using yourself as a first-person narrator.

Prewriting Choose a subject. Then, jot down traits that make your subject remarkable. Select a scene involving you and the subject that reveals this person's memorable personality.

Drafting As a first-person narrator, write an account of the scene. Like Naipaul, characterize your subject using your reactions and your subject's words and actions.

Revising Show your account to several classmates to see whether your subject's remarkable qualities have come through. If not, replace vague adjectives with precise ones and add dialogue that conveys the flavor of the subject's personality.

Model: Adding Precise Details as Support

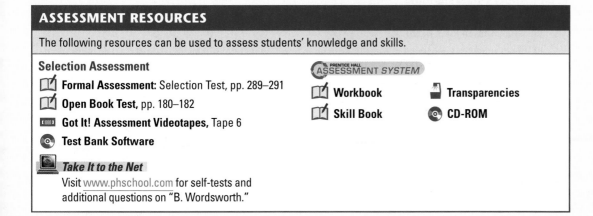

resonant *lilting*

Mrs. Walcott's ~~pleasant~~ voice and Jamaican accent made everything she said sound ~~true~~. *like a melody. On that occasion, she declared, "Hear the sounds behind the sounds."*

The writer replaces vague language with precise adjectives and a simile and adds a vivid quotation.

 *Prentice Hall Writing and Grammar Connection: Chapter 6, Section 2*

❹ Extension Activities

Listening and Speaking With a team, create a **multimedia tour** of Trinidadian calypso festivals. Include elements like these:

- Recordings of calypso singers
- Slides showing festivals
- T-shirts with stage names of singers, like Lord Melody
- Demonstrations of instruments, like the *shak-shak* (maraca)

Arrange the elements you choose so that they will be most effective. Then, share your tour with the class. **[Group Activity]**

Research and Technology Research British colonialism in the West Indies. Then, design a **classroom exhibit** that reflects British influence on this region. Use the organization of your research notes to structure the exhibit. For example, if you date your note cards by decade, arrange your exhibit by decade. Caption items clearly, produce a map of the exhibit, and open your exhibit to the class.

 www.phschool.com

Go online for an additional research activity using the Internet.

Lesson Support for p. 1247

❸ Writing Lesson

- Have students list the traits for the remarkable person they choose as the subject for their account.
- Remind students as they prepare to write that they will use the first-person point of view.
- Use the Writing Lesson to guide students in developing their account.

❹ Listening and Speaking

- Divide the class into groups to create different portions of the multimedia tour.
- Guide each group in the research and collection they are doing and then have groups meet together to coordinate the presentation.
- After students have presented their performance in the classroom, encourage them to talk to other teachers about presenting their tour throughout the school.

CUSTOMIZE INSTRUCTION For Universal Access

- To address different learning styles, use the activities suggested in the **Extension Activities** booklet, p. 61.
- For Verbal/Linguistic and Logical/Mathematical Learners, use Activity 5.
- For Visual/Spatial Learners, use Activity 6.
- For Verbal/Linguistic and Interpersonal Learners, use Activity 7.

ASSESSMENT RESOURCES

The following resources can be used to assess students' knowledge and skills.

Selection Assessment

- **Formal Assessment:** Selection Test, pp. 289–291
- **Open Book Test,** pp. 180–182
- **Got It! Assessment Videotapes,** Tape 6
- **Test Bank Software**

Take It to the Net

Visit www.phschool.com for self-tests and additional questions on "B. Wordsworth."

- **Workbook**
- **Skill Book**
- **Transparencies**
- **CD-ROM**

The Train From Rhodesia

Lesson Objectives and CA Correlations

1. **To analyze and respond to literary elements**
   - Literary Analysis: Conflict and Theme **R 3.2**
   - Connecting Literary Elements: Implied Theme **R 3.1**
2. **To read, comprehend, analyze, and critique a short story**
   - Reading Strategy: Reading Between the Lines
   - Reading Check Questions
   - Review and Assess Questions
3. **To develop word analysis skills, fluency, and systematic vocabulary**
   - Vocabulary Development Lesson: Greek Prefix *a-* **R 1.1, 1.2**
4. **To understand and apply written and oral language conventions**
   - Spelling Strategy **LC 1.2**
   - Grammar and Style Lesson: Nominative Absolutes **LC 1.1**
5. **To understand and apply appropriate writing and research strategies**
   - Writing Lesson: Analysis of Storytelling Technique **W 1.1, 1.9, 2.2**
   - Extension Activity: Historical Report **W 1.8, 2.4**
   - Assessment Practice (ATE)
6. **To understand and apply listening and speaking strategies**
   - Extension Activity: Debate **LS 1.5**

STEP-BY-STEP TEACHING GUIDE	PACING GUIDE
PRETEACH	
Motivate Students and Provide Background	
Use the Motivation activity (ATE p. 1248)	5 min.
Read and discuss author and background features (SE/ATE pp. 1248, 1250, 1252) [A]	5 min.
Introduce the Concepts	
Introduce the Literary Analysis and Reading Strategy (SE/ATE p. 1249) [A]	15 min.
Pronounce the vocabulary words and read their definitions (SE p. 1249)	5 min.
TEACH	
Monitor Comprehension	
Informally monitor comprehension by circulating while students read independently or in groups [A]	15 min.
Monitor students' comprehension with the Reading Check notes (SE/ATE pp. 1251, 1253)	as students read
Develop vocabulary with Vocabulary notes (SE pp. 1251, 1253, 1254)	as students read
Develop Understanding	
Develop students' understanding of conflict and theme with the Literary Analysis annotations (SE p. 1253; ATE pp. 1251, 1253) [A]	5 min.
Develop students' ability to read between the lines with the Reading Strategy annotations (SE/ATE pp. 1251, 1253)	5 min.
ASSESS	
Assess Mastery	
Assess students' mastery of the Reading Strategy and Literary Analysis by having them answer the Review and Assess questions (SE/ATE p. 1255)	20 min.
Use one or more of the print and media Assessment Resources (ATE p. 1257) [A]	up to 45 min.
EXTEND	
Apply Understanding	
Have students complete the Vocabulary Development Lesson and the Grammar and Style Lesson (SE p. 1256) [A]	20 min.
Apply students' knowledge of transitions used to make connections using the Writing Lesson (SE/ATE p. 1257) [A]	45 min.
Apply students' understanding using one or more of the Extension Activities (SE p. 1257)	20–90 min.

ACCELERATED INSTRUCTION:
Use the strategies and activities identified with an [A].

UNIVERSAL ACCESS
● = Below-Level Students
▲ = On-Level Students
■ = Above-Level Students

Time and Resource Manager

Reading Level: Easy
Average Number of Instructional Days: 4

RESOURCES		
PRINT	**TRANSPARENCIES**	**TECHNOLOGY**
• **Beyond Literature,** Cross-Curricular Connection: Social Studies, p. 62 ▲ ■		• **Interest Grabber Video,** Tape 6 ● ▲ ■
• **Selection Support Workbook:** ● ▲ ■ Literary Analysis, p. 288 Reading Strategy, p. 287 Build Vocabulary, p. 285	• **Literary Analysis and Reading Transparencies,** pp. 123 and 124 ● ▲ ■	
		• **Listening to Literature** ● ▲ ■ Audiocassettes, Side 29 Audio CDs, CD 17
• **Literatura en español** ● ▲ • **Literary Analysis for Enrichment** ■		
• **Formal Assessment:** Selection Test, pp. 292–294 ● ▲ ■ • **Open Book Test,** pp. 184–186 ● ▲ ■ • PRENTICE HALL ASSESSMENT SYSTEM ● ▲ ■	• PRENTICE HALL ASSESSMENT SYSTEM ● ▲ ■ Skills Practice Answers and Explanations on Transparencies ● ▲ ■	• **Test Bank Software** ● ▲ ■ • **Got It! Assessment Videotapes,** Tape 6 ● ▲
• **Selection Support Workbook:** ● ▲ ■ Grammar and Style, p. 286 • **Writing and Grammar,** Diamond Level ● ▲ ■ • **Extension Activities,** p. 62 ● ▲ ■	• **Daily Language Practice Transparencies** ● ▲	• **Writing and Grammar iText CD-ROM** ● ▲ ■ ***Take It to the Net*** www.phschool.com

BLOCK SCHEDULING: Use one 90-minute class period to preteach the selection and have students read it. Use a second 90-minute class period to assess students' mastery of skills and have them complete one of the Extension Activities.

PRETEACH

Step-by-Step Teaching Guide for pp. 1248–1249

Motivation

Ask students to think of a moment in their own lives when a person they had admired, trusted, or loved said or did something that shocked them or caused them to think differently about the person. Point out that the moment of revelation might have been a minor incident, but one that revealed a great character flaw. Read this passage from the story aloud: "But how could you, she said. He was shocked by the dismay of her face. Good heavens, he said, what's the matter?" Have students use these lines to predict what might be wrong between the two characters. Then, have them read the story to find out.

Interest Grabber Video

As an alternative, play "'The Train from Rhodesia': Apartheid" on Tape 6 to engage student interest.

❶ Background

More About the Author

Nadine Gordimer was born into a white, middle-class family in South Africa. Her parents were Jewish immigrants—her father was from Lithuania (part of the Soviet Union when he left) and her mother, from England. She was educated at a convent school and began writing at age nine. She was a voracious reader, and it was her reading that introduced her to the world outside of South Africa.

Gordimer's purpose has always been to show the effects of apartheid on both society and individuals. She understands that everyone suffers when injustice exists.

While she tries to avoid the celebrity that goes with international fame, Gordimer's continued success, numerous awards, and continued lecturing keep her in the public eye. Today, she is the acknowledged "doyenne of South African letters" and has seen the end of the system against which she wrote.

Prepare to Read

❶ The Train from Rhodesia

Nadine Gordimer (b. 1923)

The fiction of Nadine Gordimer has been shaped by her life in South Africa and by her firm opposition to the former government's policy of apartheid, an institutional form of racial separation and prejudice. Initially honored for her short fiction, Gordimer says that, in time, she found the short story "too delicate for what I have to say." In her longer works, as well as in her short stories, she has had a great deal to say about racial division and its harmful effects on oppressed and oppressor alike. The South African government responded by banning some of her work. Nevertheless, Gordimer has built an international reputation as a writer.

Small Town Origins Gordimer was born in Springs, South Africa, a small town near Johannesburg. Her mother took her out of the local private school when she was eleven. From then until she was sixteen, she "read tremendously" and wrote much fiction. She published her first adult short story, "Come Again Tomorrow," when she was fifteen. She continued to write short stories during her year of study at the University of Witwatersrand.

Literary Success *The Soft Voice of the Serpent* (1952) was the first collection of her stories to be published in the United States. Following the critical success of that book, Gordimer's stories appeared in such leading American magazines as *The New Yorker*, *The Atlantic Monthly*, and *Harper's Magazine*. These stories often describe the entrapment of whites who inherited political and economic power in the closed society of South Africa under apartheid. Frequently, as in "The Train from Rhodesia," she builds a tale around a fleeting but sharply focused moment of insight.

Although politics is a perpetual concern of Gordimer's, she does not turn fiction into sermonizing. A reviewer in *The Times Literary Supplement* noted that Gordimer "is never guilty of pushing her characters to the sideline in order to make an overt political point—a fact which, paradoxically, enables her to demonstrate South Africa's political oddities more exactly." Even though the regime of apartheid that Gordimer criticized ended in 1991, the truths that she uncovered through her characters endure.

Compassionate Observer In all her fiction—including such novels as *A Guest of Honor* (1970), *The Conservationist* (1974), and *Burger's Daughter* (1979)—Gordimer shows an ability to write from different vantage points. She portrays with insight Anglos (South Africans of English ancestry), Afrikaners (South Africans of Dutch ancestry), and black South Africans, describing her characters in a variety of economic and social settings. She writes as a compassionate observer of the human condition. In lyric tones, yet without sentimentality, she pictures the South African scene with awareness and humanity, stressing themes of understanding, honesty, and forgiveness.

"Luminous Symbol" Until she was thirty, Gordimer had never been outside South Africa. Since then, however, she has traveled widely and lectured in a number of top United States universities, including Princeton, Columbia, and the University of Michigan. She has also won a great many literary awards, including the Nobel Prize for Literature in 1991. Called by one observer "a luminous symbol of at least one white person's understanding of the black man's burden," she is without doubt one of the leading novelists writing in English.

TEACHING RESOURCES

The following resources can be used to enrich or extend the instruction for pp. 1248–1249.

Motivation

Interest Grabber Video, Tape 6

Background

Beyond Literature, p. 62

Take It to the Net

Visit www.phschool.com for background and hotlinks for "The Train from Rhodesia."

Literary Analysis

Literary Analysis and Reading Transparencies, Conflict and Theme, p. 124

Reading

Selection Support: Reading Strategy, p. 287; Build Vocabulary, p. 285

Literary Analysis and Reading Transparencies, Reading Between the Lines, p. 123

BLOCK SCHEDULING: Resources marked with this symbol provide varied instruction during 90-minute blocks.

Preview

Connecting to the Literature

You may have seen a single lie ruin a whole friendship. When an entire society is based on lies that are told to justify injustice, these lies can spoil even the happiest of times, as the couple in the story discovers.

❷ Literary Analysis

Conflict and Theme

Writers dramatize their **themes,** or central insights, by showing characters in the midst of a **conflict,** an inner or outer struggle. In a simple story, the conflict between a good character and a bad one suggests a simple theme: Good will triumph over evil. In more complex stories, however, these generalizations may apply:

- Conflicts reflect tangled contradictions in life, not simple choices or clear lessons.
- Themes may take the form of implied questions to which various characters offer various answers.
- Conflicts need not be resolved. Instead, a story may deepen a conflict, reformulate it, or replace it with a new conflict.

As you read, determine what questions or problems are posed by the conflict in "The Train from Rhodesia."

Connecting Literary Elements

A conflict in a story may powerfully dramatize a theme, yet the story may never state that theme directly. Through conflicts, images, symbols, and other devices, a writer may establish an **implied theme.** As you form your interpretation of the theme of Gordimer's story, consider what she gains by stating it indirectly rather than directly.

❸ Reading Strategy

Reading Between the Lines

Writers do not always describe the details of a situation. Even characters may appear to be unaware of the reasons for their own reactions. When you encounter gaps in a writer's explicit explanations, **read between the lines**—deduce the details or connections that the writer is indicating. Use a chart like the one shown to help you read between the lines of this story.

Passage

The mane of the lion figurine shows "that the artist had delight in the lion."

What Is Missing

A direct statement of the figurine's effect on the young woman

What Is Implied

The young woman is moved by the truth of the figurine and by the joyful vision of the artist who created it.

Vocabulary Development

impressionistic (im presh′ ən is′ tik) *adj.* conveying a picture through quickly sketched suggestions of details (p. 1251)

elongated (ē lôŋ′ gāt′ id) *adj.* lengthened; stretched (p. 1251)

segmented (seg′ ment id) *adj.* divided into joined parts (p. 1253)

splaying (splā′ iŋ) *v.* spreading out (p. 1253)

atrophy (a′ trə fē) *v.* waste away (p. 1254)

❷ Literary Analysis

Conflict and Theme

- Tell students that as they read "The Train from Rhodesia" they will be focusing on issues of conflict and theme. Explain to students that, while a theme can often be as simple as the struggle between good and evil, many stories are more complex. Review the list of characteristics of more complex stories found on p. 1249.
- Have students consider the way in which Gordimer develops her theme through the course of the story. Does she reveal the theme explicitly? If not, why not? What might she accomplish by her technique?

❸ Reading Strategy

Reading Between the Lines

- Explain to the students that authors' description of characters and situations often leave important information unstated. In such cases, it is critical to *read between the lines*—that is, deduce the details or connections that have gone unstated.
- Explain to students how to use the chart to help them organize their deductive reasoning, discussing the example provided. Use the Reading Between the Lines transparency on p. 123 of **Literary Analysis and Reading Transparencies** to model this skill.

Vocabulary Development

- Pronounce each vocabulary word for students, and read the definitions as a class. Have students identify any words with which they are already familiar.

CUSTOMIZE INSTRUCTION FOR UNIVERSAL ACCESS

For Less Proficient Readers	For English Learners	For Advanced Readers
To prepare students to read the story, use the Conflict and Theme transparency, p. 124 of **Literary Analysis and Reading Transparencies.** This will introduce them to the conflict and theme in Gordimer's tale. Then, have students look for these elements as they read the story.	English language learners might be confused by the lack of quotation marks surrounding dialogue in the story. Encourage them to look for speaker tags to identify who is speaking.	Advanced readers can be challenged to read between the lines to identify the role of the train in the story. Point out that the railroads were built with native African labor for the social and economic convenience of the European colonists. Have these students interpret the symbolic function of the train in the story.

 ***E-Teach***

Visit E-Teach at www.phschool.com for teachers' essays on how to teach, with questions and answers.

TEACH

Step-by-Step Teaching Guide for pp. 1250–1254

CUSTOMIZE INSTRUCTION
For Interpersonal Learners

Interpersonal learners might benefit by imagining themselves in the place of the young woman on the train. Encourage them to jot down thoughts she might have as the conflict with her husband intensifies.

1 About the Selection

The story "The Train from Rhodesia" illustrates how a moment in time can change and define a life. Though the incident described takes only an instant, it is an instant that not only shapes a marriage, but reflects the social and political situation of a whole country. On the surface, the incident is nothing more than a bargain sought and made over a carving, but below that surface, basic emotions stir, struggle, and finally emerge for a brief moment of both despair and clarity.

2 Critical Thinking

Analyze

- Have students discuss the image of the train based on the details in the text.
- Ask students how this image of the train reflects its impact on the people waiting for it.
  Possible response: The train is described as powerful and threatening, reflecting the tremendous impact it can have on the lives of those waiting.

3 Critical Thinking

Infer

- Have students rephrase the image of the children's feet in their own words.
- Urge students to reflect on how this image of the children's feet reveals the writer's feelings about apartheid.
  Answer: The fact that their feet leave no imprint shows that the writer feels the African children are erased from their own land; they have little opportunity to develop as individuals and leave a mark.

1 The Train from Rhodesia

Nadine Gordimer

Background

This story is set at a time when South Africa and Rhodesia (now Zimbabwe) enforced policies of racial separation, called apartheid in South Africa, ensuring the continued privileges of a white minority and its domination over the black majority.

2 The train came out of the red horizon and bore down toward them over the single straight track.

The stationmaster came out of his little brick station with its pointed chalet roof, feeling the creases in his serge uniform in his legs as well. A stir of preparedness rippled through the squatting native vendors waiting in the dust; the face of a carved wooden animal, eternally surprised, stuck out of a sack. The stationmaster's barefoot children wandered over. From the gray mud huts with the untidy heads that stood within a decorated mud wall, chickens, and dogs with their skin stretched like parchment over their bones, followed the piccanins[1] down to the track. The flushed and perspiring west cast a reflection, faint, without heat, upon the station, upon the tin shed marked "Goods," upon the walled kraal,[2] upon the gray tin house of the stationmaster and upon the sand, that lapped all around, from sky to sky, cast little rhythmical cups of shadow, so that the sand became the
3 sea, and closed over the children's black feet softly and without imprint.

The stationmaster's wife sat behind the mesh of her veranda. Above her head the hunk of a sheep's carcass moved slightly, dangling in a current of air.

They waited.

The train called out, along the sky; but there was no answer; and the cry hung on: I'm coming . . . I'm coming . . .

The engine flared out now, big, whisking a dwindling body behind it; the track flared out to let it in.

Creaking, jerking, jostling, gasping, the train filled the station.

1. **piccanins** *n.* native children.
2. **kraal** (kräl) *n.* fenced-in enclosure for cattle or sheep.

TEACHING RESOURCES

The following resources can be used to enrich or extend the instruction for pp. 1250–1254.

Literary Analysis

- **Selection Support:** Literary Analysis, p. 288
- **Literary Analysis and Reading Transparencies,** p. 124

Reading

- **Listening to Literature Audiocassettes,** Side 29
- **Listening to Literature Audio CDs,** CD 17

BLOCK SCHEDULING: Resources marked with this symbol provide varied instruction during 90-minute blocks.

Here, let me see that one—the young woman curved her body further out of the corridor window. Missus? smiled the old boy, looking at the creatures he held in his hand. From a piece of string on his gray finger hung a tiny woven basket; he lifted it, questioning. No, no, she urged, leaning down toward him, across the height of the train, toward the man in the piece of old rug; that one, that one, her hand commanded. It was a lion, carved out of soft dry wood that looked like spongecake; heraldic, black and, white, with impressionistic detail burnt in. The old
4 man held it up to her still smiling, not from the heart, but at the customer. Between its Vandyke[3] teeth, in the mouth opened in an endless roar too terrible to be heard, it had a black tongue. Look, said the young husband, if you don't mind! And round the neck of the thing, a piece of fur (rat? rabbit? meerkat?); a real mane, majestic, telling you somehow that the artist had delight in the lion.

impressionistic (im presh′ ən is′ tik) *adj.* conveying a picture through quickly sketched suggestions of details

5 All up and down the length of the train in the dust the artists sprang, walking bent, like performing animals, the better to exhibit the fantasy held toward the faces on the train. Buck, startled and stiff, staring with round black and white eyes. More lions, standing erect, grappling with strange, thin, elongated warriors who clutched spears and showed no fear in their slits of eyes. How much, they asked from the train, how much?

elongated (i lôŋ′ gāt′ id) *adj.* lengthened; stretched

6 Give me penny, said the little ones with nothing to sell. The dogs went and sat, quite still, under the dining car, where the train breathed out the smell of meat cooking with onion.

Reading Strategy
Reading Between the Lines What does the behavior of the dogs suggest about the community around the train station?

A man passed beneath the arch of reaching arms meeting gray-black and white in the exchange of money for the staring wooden eyes, the stiff wooden legs sticking up in the air; went along under the voices and the bargaining, interrogating the wheels. Past the dogs; glancing up at the dining car where he could stare at the faces, behind glass, drinking beer, two by two, on either side of a uniform railway vase with its pale dead flower. Right to the end, to the guard's van, where the stationmaster's children had just collected their mother's two loaves of bread; to the engine itself, where the stationmaster and the driver stood talking against the steaming complaint of the resting beast.

The man called out to them, something loud and joking. They turned to laugh, in a twirl of steam. The two children careered over the sand, clutching the bread, and burst through the iron gate and up the path through the garden in which nothing grew.

Passengers drew themselves in at the corridor windows and turned into compartments to fetch money, to call someone to look. Those sitting inside looked up: suddenly different, caged faces, boxed in, cut

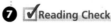

7 
Reading Check
What attracts the interest of the young woman on the train?

3. **Vandyke** (van dīk′) *adj.* tapering to a point, like a Vandyke beard.

4 Reading Strategy
Reading Between the Lines

- Remind students that they can often deduce details and implications not explicitly stated in the text by thinking about the details that are given.
- Ask students to interpret the meaning of the bracketed sentence. Ask: What is the difference between smiling "from the heart" and "at the customer"?
  Answer: Students should note that a smile "at the customer" denotes courtesy rather than warmth or emotional feeling.

5 Literary Analysis
Conflict and Theme

- Remind students that as they read they will be analyzing the relationships between conflict and theme.
- Have students read the bracketed paragraph. Then, ask them what conflict is suggested by the contrast between the "bent" artists, moving like performing animals, and the "elongated" statues of lion-hunting warriors?
  Answer: The artists are treated like animals in a zoo or circus, while the carved warriors carry themselves with nobility and pride, a pride the Europeans no longer allow the Africans to feel.

6 Reading Strategy
Reading Between the Lines

- Have students read the bracketed paragraph and then describe the behavior of the dogs.
- Then, ask them the Reading Strategy question on p. 1251: What does the behavior of the dogs suggest about the community around the train station?
  Answer: The dogs' behavior suggests that the hungry community waits with bated breath for the passengers to spend money there, just as the hungry dogs wait silently for food to fall their way from the train. The silence of the dogs suggests that they expect to be chased away if they bark, just as the behavior of the vendors suggests that they do not expect to be treated with respect.

7 Reading Check

Answer: A carving of a lion attracts the young woman's attention.

CUSTOMIZE INSTRUCTION FOR UNIVERSAL ACCESS

For Gifted/Talented Students	For Advanced Readers
Have students perform the incident in this story as a dramatic scene. Students may choose to use language consistent with the characters and setting of the story, or they might adapt the conflict to more contemporary language.	Have students read the story independently at their own pace. Then, allow time for them to visit www.phschool.com to find out more about Nadine Gordimer and the historical context in which she wrote.

❽ Background

Apartheid

Though the Boers (South Africans of Dutch descent) had been in South Africa for three hundred years, the political policy of apartheid did not exist until 1948. It was directed not only at blacks, but also at those of any nonwhite race, as Indian and Pakistani immigrants flooded into South Africa after the British pulled out of India.

While apartheid created a separation between white and nonwhite society, it also created such laws as the Promotion of Bantu Self-Government Act and Bantu Homelands Citizenship Act, creating independent, self-governing nations for black Africans. This was in part a reaction to the massive immigration of blacks from elsewhere in Africa, who came to South Africa looking for what were comparatively high-paying jobs. However, the dependence of the South African economy on nonwhite labor made it difficult for the government to carry out its policy of separate development.

Although the government had the power to suppress criticism, opposition to apartheid always existed in South Africa. While the Boers (also called Afrikaners) made up a majority of the white population (about 60 percent), they were not the only whites. And even some Boers were critical of the policy.

Efforts to enforce the speaking of Afrikaans (the Dutch-based language of the Boers) led to the Soweto riots in 1976, and some white politicians began to call for the establishment of racial equality.

In 1990 and 1991, after years of violent struggle involving government forces, pro-apartheid groups, and anti-apartheid forces, the government of South African president F. W. de Klerk repealed most of the social legislation that provided the basis for apartheid. In 1993, a new constitution enfranchised blacks and other racial groups, and all-race national elections were held in 1994. In that year, Nelson Mandela, a leader of the anti-apartheid African National Congress, was elected the country's first black president.

off, after the contact of outside. There was an orange a piccanin would like. . . . What about that chocolate? It wasn't very nice. . . .

A young girl had collected a handful of the hard kind, that no one liked, out of the chocolate box, and was throwing them to the dogs, over at the dining car. But the hens darted in, and swallowed the chocolates, incredibly quick and accurate, before they had even dropped in the dust, and the dogs, a little bewildered, looked up with their brown eyes, not expecting anything.

—No, leave it, said the girl, don't take it. . . .

Too expensive, too much, she shook her head and raised her voice to the old boy, giving up the lion. He held it up where she had handed it to him. No, she said, shaking her head. *Three-and-six?*[4] insisted her husband, loudly. Yes baas! laughed the boy. Three-and-six?—the young man was incredulous. Oh leave it—she said. The young man stopped. Don't you want it? he said, keeping his face closed to the boy. No, never mind, she said, leave it. The old native kept his head on one side, looking at them sideways, holding the lion. Three-and-six, he murmured, as old people repeat things to themselves.

The young woman drew her head in. She went into the coupé[5] and sat down. Out of the window, on the other side, there was nothing; sand and bush; a thorn tree. Back through the open doorway, past the figure of her husband in the corridor, there was the station, the voices, wooden animals waving, running feet. Her eye followed the funny little valance of scrolled wood that outlined the chalet roof of the station; she thought of the lion and smiled. That bit of fur round the neck. But the wooden buck, the hippos, the elephants, the baskets that already bulked out of their brown paper under the seat and on the luggage rack! How will they look at home? Where will you put them? What will they mean away from the places you found them? Away from the unreality of the last few weeks? The man outside. But he is not part of the unreality; he is for good now. Odd . . . somewhere there was an idea that he, that living with him, was part of the holiday, the strange places.

Outside, a bell rang. The stationmaster was leaning against the end of the train, green flag rolled in readiness. A few men who had got down to stretch their legs sprang on to the train, clinging to the observation platforms, or perhaps merely standing on the iron step, holding the rail; but on the train, safe from the one dusty platform, the one tin house, the empty sand.

There was a grunt. The train jerked. Through the glass the beer drinkers looked out, as if they could not see beyond it. Behind the flyscreen, the stationmaster's wife sat facing back at them beneath the darkening hunk of meat.

Literature in context — History Connection

❽ *Apartheid*

In Gordimer's story, the interactions between white passengers and black vendors reflect the social regime called apartheid ("apartness" in the language of Dutch South Africans). Under apartheid in South Africa, blacks were restricted to living in certain areas. To travel through a white area, they were required to carry passes—even if they worked every day in such areas. Public places—such as schools, restaurants, and hotels—were segregated by law. Whites lived as privileged rulers in the country. Blacks lived for the most part in poverty, stripped of political power. It was only in the closing decades of the twentieth century that blacks, after violent struggles, gained political rights in South Africa and Rhodesia.

---

4. **three-and-six** three shillings and sixpence.
5. **coupé** (ko͞o pā′) n. half-compartment at the end of a train, with seats on only one side.

ENRICHMENT: Social Studies Connection

Local Trains

Point out that the social and economic activity of the town in the story seems centered on the train station. Explain that in many areas, trains are the main mode of transportation. Africa, especially, has a poor road system due to problems of topography and climate. In the south, where the story is set, railroad development has been vital to the economy. Ask students if their community is served by a railroad, or if it was in the past. If so, have them explore how the coming of the railroad affected the community and, if it has stopped running, how its passing affected the area.

There was a shout. The flag drooped out. Joints not yet coordinated, the segmented body of the train heaved and bumped back against itself. It began to move; slowly the scrolled chalet moved past it, the yells of the natives, running alongside, jetted up into the air, fell back at different levels. Staring wooden faces waved drunkenly, there, then gone, questioning for the last time at the windows. Here, one-and-six baas!—As one automatically opens a hand to catch a thrown ball, a man fumbled wildly down his pocket, brought up the shilling and sixpence and threw them out; the old native, gasping, his skinny toes splaying the sand, flung the lion.

segmented (seg′ ment id) *adj.* divided into joined parts

splaying (splā′ iŋ) *v.* spreading out

The piccanins were waving, the dogs stood, tails uncertain, watching the train go: past the mud huts, where a woman turned to look, up from the smoke of the fire, her hand pausing on her hip.

The stationmaster went slowly in under the chalet.

The old native stood, breath blowing out the skin between his ribs, feet tense, balanced in the sand, smiling and shaking his head. In his opened palm, held in the attitude of receiving, was the retrieved shilling and sixpence.

9 The blind end of the train was being pulled helplessly out of the station.

Reading Strategy
Reading Between the Lines What does the writer's choice of the words *blind, pulled,* and *helplessly* suggest about the fate of those on the train?

The young man swung in from the corridor, breathless. He was shaking his head with laughter and triumph. Here! he said. And waggled the lion at her. One-and-six!

What? she said.

He laughed. I was arguing with him for fun, bargaining—when the train had pulled out already, he came tearing after. . . . One-and-six baas! So there's your lion.

She was holding it away from her, the head with the open jaws, the pointed teeth, the black tongue, the wonderful ruff of fur facing her. She was looking at it with an expression of not seeing, of seeing something different. Her face was drawn up, wryly, like the face of a discomforted child. Her mouth lifted nervously at the corner. Very slowly, cautious, she lifted her finger and touched the mane, where it was joined to the wood.

But how could you, she said. He was shocked by the dismay of her face.

Good heavens, he said, what's the matter?

10 If you wanted the thing, she said, her voice rising and breaking with the shrill impotence of anger, why didn't you buy it in the first place? If you wanted it, why didn't you pay for it? Why didn't you take it decently, when he offered it? Why did you have to wait for him to run after the train with it, and give him one-and-six? One-and-six!

She was pushing it at him, trying to force him to take it. He stood astonished, his hands hanging at his sides.

But you wanted it! You liked it so much? —It's a beautiful piece of work, she said fiercely, as if to protect it from him.

You liked it so much! You said yourself it was too expensive—

Literary Analysis
Conflict and Theme What does the conflict between the husband and wife suggest about the way in which racism poisons perception?

11 ✔**Reading Check**
What finally happens with the lion?

9 Reading Strategy
Reading Between the Lines

- Ask students to compare this description of the train with that at the beginning of the story.
  Answer: Students may note that while the opening description suggested a sense of the power of the train, this reference suggests weakness and passivity.
- Ask students the Reading Strategy question on p. 1253: What does the writer's choice of the words *blind, pulled,* and *helplessly* suggest about the fate of those on the train?
  Answer: It reinforces the notion that the characters are at the mercy of historical forces outside their control.

10 Literary Analysis
Conflict and Theme

- Ask students why the wife is angry.
  Possible response: She feels that her husband has not behaved decently in taking advantage of the artist.
- Then, ask the Literary Analysis question on p. 1253: What does the conflict between the husband and the wife suggest about the way in which racism poisons perception?
  Answer: The husband's racism will not allow him to see the vendor as someone he should treat with respect, or to see the statue as a work of art with a more-than-monetary value.

11 ✔Reading Check

Answer: The husband finally buys the lion, but at a reduced price, and in doing so demeans the artist.

CUSTOMIZE INSTRUCTION FOR UNIVERSAL ACCESS

For Less Proficient Readers	For Special Needs Students	For Advanced Readers
Have students assume the role of a friend to the lady on the train. Then, have them write her a letter giving her advice about her new feelings of "shame" and "weariness."	Have students perform a short skit reenacting the implications of the bygone glory of the native African cultures suggested by the statues as compared with the vendors' present circumstances. Have one student play a proud, traditional African and another play the role of one of the present-day vendors.	After students have finished reading the story, have them write an essay presenting their views as to whether the story is pessimistic or optimistic about the relations of blacks and whites in Southern Africa. Instruct them to use specific passages to support their arguments.

ASSESS

Answers for p. 1254

Review and Assess

1. **(a)** The local African artists, vendors, children, and dogs come to meet the train. **(b)** The interactions reflect the insensitive attitude of the wealthy toward the poor.
2. **(a)** The lion impresses the woman because its details show that the artist had delight in the lion. **(b)** The woman is angry because her husband will enter the bargain only if he can best his social inferior, not simply to acquire something he wants or values.
3. **(a)** The woman has learned that her new husband is still really a stranger to her and has characteristics she cannot admire. The young man has learned little more than that he does not understand his new bride.
(b) Possible response: The welfare of the marriage depends upon whether the young woman is able to communicate her convictions to her husband. If she doesn't, she will remain isolated and lonely, and her husband will probably never understand why she becomes moody.
4. Students may respond that the train and station symbolize Africa. Others may feel it represents the point of connection between peoples.
5. Students may agree that social elements such as race, economic status, dress, or accomplishment often shape people's attitudes and perceptions.

Oh *you*—she said, hopeless and furious. *You* . . . . She threw the lion onto the seat.

He stood looking at her.

She sat down again in the corner and, her face slumped in her hand, stared out of the window. Everything was turning around inside her. One-and-six. One-and-six. One-and-six for the wood and the carving and the sinews of the legs and the switch of the tail. The mouth open like that and the teeth, the black tongue, rolling, like a wave. The mane round the neck. To give one-and-six for that. The heat of shame mounted through her legs and body and sounded in her ears like the sound of sand pouring, pouring, pouring. She sat there, sick. A weariness, a tastelessness, the discovery of a void made her hands slacken their grip, atrophy emptily, as if the hour was not worth their grasp. She was feeling like this again. She had thought it was something to do with singleness, with being alone and belonging too much to oneself.

atrophy (a´ trə fē) *v.* waste away

She sat there not wanting to move or speak, or to look at anything, even; so that the mood should be associated with nothing, no object, word or sight that might recur and so recall the feeling again. . . . Smuts blew in grittily, settled on her hands. Her back remained at exactly the same angle, turned against the young man sitting with his hands drooping between his sprawled legs, and the lion, fallen on its side in the corner.

The train had cast the station like a skin. It called out to the sky, I'm coming, I'm coming; and again, there was no answer.

Review and Assess

Thinking About the Selection

1. (a) **Recall:** Who comes to meet the train from Rhodesia?
(b) **Infer:** What does the interaction between these people and the passengers indicate about the story's theme?
2. (a) **Analyze:** Why does the lion impress the young woman?
(b) **Interpret:** Why is the young woman angry when her husband bargains for and obtains the lion at a low price?
3. (a) **Draw Conclusions:** What have the husband and the wife discovered about each other by the end of the story?
(b) **Speculate:** How might their marriage fare, given this episode? Explain.
4. **Interpret:** What do you think the train and the station symbolize in this story?
5. **Apply:** In the story, social assumptions about whites bargaining with black vendors prevent a man from seeing the true value of a statue. In your own experience, do social assumptions often cloud people's perceptions? Explain.

ASSESSMENT PRACTICE: Writing Skills

Organization (For more practice, see Test Preparation Workbook, p. 62.)

Many tests ask students questions about a text's organization. Use the following sample item to teach students how to recognize patterns of organization within a paragraph. Have students read the fourth paragraph on p. 1251.

Which of the following best expresses how the description in this paragraph is organized?

A spatially, from the sky to the ground
B from a general overview of the scene to specific details
C spatially, from one end of the train to the other
D from specific details to a general overview of the scene

Lead students to recognize that the description is arranged in spatial order. The description moves along with the man, who begins walking at the beginning of the passenger cars and ends at the engine. Students should determine that the correct answer is *C*.

Review and Assess

Literary Analysis

Conflict and Theme

1. Why does a **conflict** erupt between the young woman and her husband when he buys the lion at such a low price?
2. (a) How does the shame that the young woman feels reveal an inner conflict, one in which she struggles with herself? (b) Why might she explain her inner "void" differently from the way she once did?
3. To define the **theme** of the story, explain what questions the woman's conflicts raise about her society.

Connecting Literary Elements

4. Use a chart like the one shown to explain how the images in the description of the arrival of the train establish the **implied theme.**

Detail
"the sand . . . closed over the children's black feet . . . without imprint."
Implication
Blacks in the area lead anonymous, vanishing lives.
Link to Theme
Whites deny or suppress what is of value in the lives of blacks in the area.

5. Analyze the argument between the woman and the man. (a) What different connections does each see between "liking," "wanting," and "buying"? (b) How does this argument help establish the theme?
6. The woman does not effectively articulate her viewpoint. (a) What does this inability suggest about the problem she faces? (b) Why might requiring the reader to interpret her point add to the effectiveness of the story?

Reading Strategy

Reading Between the Lines

7. What conflict is suggested by the contrast between the "bent" artists and the "elongated" statues of lion-hunting warriors?
8. What attitude toward beauty is implied in the lines "One-and-six. One-and-six for the wood and the carving and the sinews. . . ."?

Extend Understanding

9. **Visual Arts Connection:** Contrast the lion in the story with a toy animal you might find in an American souvenir shop. What does this contrast suggest about the cultures in which the figures originate?

Quick Review

Writers dramatize **themes,** or central insights or questions, by showing characters in the midst of a **conflict,** an inner or outer struggle.

Writers often establish an **implied theme** through conflicts, images, symbols, and other devices.

Read between the lines to understand details and connections that a writer only suggests.

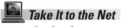

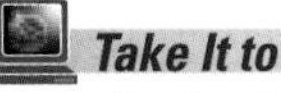
Take It to the Net

www.phschool.com

Take the interactive self-test online to check your understanding of the selection.

Answers for p. 1255

Review and Assess

1. The woman is horrified by her new husband's exploitation of the poor artist. The young husband is baffled by his wife's reaction.
2. **(a)** The bride struggles with a feeling of isolation and emptiness. **(b)** In the past she felt lonely because she was single. Now she must face up to dismay at the gulf between the poor and the well-to-do.
3. The theme is that some people respect other cultures, and some do not. The woman's conflict raises questions about how she can help change wrong attitudes and how she can remain in a society whose attitudes she does not share.
4. **Detail:** the people don't get off the train; **Implication:** the train separates those inside from those outside; **Link to Theme:** people are separated by their attitudes toward cultural differences. **Detail:** the young woman curves further out the window; **Implication:** she is reaching out, trying to make contact; **Link to Theme:** some people react differently to cultural differences.
5. **(a)** While the man believes that "liking" and "wanting" should be satisfied by "buying" whenever possible and as economically as possible, the woman believes this is wrong when it means taking advantage of another person. **(b)** The argument raises the core issues of the theme. Is it right to take advantage of someone's poverty?
6. **(a)** Her inability to articulate her viewpoint suggests that she will not be able to resolve the conflict with her husband, unless she learns how to both define and communicate her objections. **(b)** It draws the reader into the situation, making the reader recognize and identify with the woman's reaction.

continued

Answers continued

7. It contrasts a past in which people stood tall and battled physical enemies (not attitudes), with a present in which people are no longer proud hunters, or even proud artists, but beggars who rely on the passing train.
8. It shows that the husband values the bargain more than the beauty.
9. Students may respond that the lion in the story is beautifully hand-carved, showing respect for the lions of Africa. Plastic toys made in America are often romanticized, sentimental versions, and mass produced.

EXTEND

Answers for p. 1256

❶ Vocabulary Development

Word Analysis

1. Atypical: Not conforming to type; unusual or irregular.
2. Amorphous: Lacking definite form; shapeless
3. Asymmetrical: Having no balance or symmetry
4. Anaerobic: Capable of living without free oxygen

Fluency: Context

Have students exchange their diary entries with partners to check that all vocabulary words are used.

Spelling Strategy

1. journeying
2. boyish
3. essayist
4. worrying
5. grayish
6. simplifying

❷ Grammar and Style

1. green flag rolled in readiness.
2. joints not yet coordinated.
3. his skinny toes splaying the sand,
4. her voice rising and breaking with the shrill impotence of anger,
5. her face slumped in her hand,

Writing Application

Possible response: The young couple's new home, furnishings sparkling with newness, was in a gracious old building, its walls faded with age. She would put the buck on the shelf over her new husband's desk, its drawers overflowing with his business correspondence.

Integrate Language Skills

❶ Vocabulary Development Lesson

Word Analysis: Greek Prefix *a-*

The word *atrophy* means "waste away." It combines the Greek prefix *a-*, meaning "without" or "not," with a word that means "to feed." *Atrophy* names what happens when something, such as a muscle or a skill, is *not* nourished.

The prefix *a-* acts like a negative sign, contradicting the root to which it is affixed. It appears in many words related to science, mathematics, and the social sciences. If the root word to which it is joined begins with a vowel (or sometimes with an *h*), the prefix *a-* becomes *an-*.

Define each of the following words, consulting your dictionary as needed:

1. atypical
2. amorphous
3. asymmetrical
4. anaerobic

Fluency: Context

In the role of the woman in the story, write a diary entry about the incident at the station. Use all the words from the vocabulary list on page 1249 in your entry.

Spelling Strategy

To add *-ist*, *-ing*, or *-ish* to a word that ends in *y*, retain the *y* and simply add the suffix. The word *splay*, for example, retains its final *y*, to become *splaying*. Add the suffix *-ist*, *-ing*, or *-ish* to form another English word from each of the words listed.

1. journey
2. boy
3. essay
4. worry
5. gray
6. simplify

❷ Grammar and Style Lesson

Nominative Absolutes

Gordimer piles up details to add immediacy to her descriptions of the bustle at a train station when a train pulls in. She often uses **nominative absolutes,** phrases consisting of a noun or pronoun modified by a participial phrase. A nominative absolute is not grammatically linked with any single word in the sentence. Instead, it adds additional details about the topic of the sentence.

Example: The old native stood, breath blowing out the skin between his ribs. . . .

Practice Identify the nominative absolute in each sentence.

1. The stationmaster was leaning against the end of the train, green flag rolled in readiness.
2. Joints not yet coordinated, the segmented body of the train . . . bumped back against itself.
3. . . . the old native, gasping, his skinny toes splaying the sand, flung the lion.
4. If you wanted the thing, she said, her voice rising and breaking with the shrill impotence of anger, why didn't you buy it in the first place?
5. She sat down again in the corner and, her face slumped in her hand, stared out of the window.

Writing Application Write a description of the new couple's home, including the artifacts they have collected while on their honeymoon, using three nominative absolutes. Underline each nominative absolute in your description.

WG Prentice Hall Writing and Grammar Connection: Chapter 19, Section 2

TEACHING RESOURCES

The following resources can be used to enrich or extend the instruction for pp. 1256–1257.

Vocabulary

- **Selection Support:** Build Vocabulary, p. 285
- **Vocabulary and Spelling Practice Book** (Use this book for skills enrichment.)

Grammar

- **Selection Support:** Grammar and Style, p. 286
- **Writing and Grammar,** Diamond Level, p. 446
- **Daily Language Practice Transparencies** ■

Writing

- **Writing and Grammar,** Diamond Level, p. 315
- **Writing and Grammar iText CD-ROM** ■

■ **BLOCK SCHEDULING:** Resources marked with this symbol provide varied instruction during 90-minute blocks.

❸ Writing Lesson

Analysis of Storytelling Technique

Gordimer suggests the central problem of her story by weaving together parts of conversation and half-glimpsed events. Write an analysis of her use of imagery and dialogue, explaining how they serve indirectly to establish her theme.

Prewriting Review the story, noting passages in which a description, an event, or an utterance adds a particular mood or suggests a parallel with social circumstances.

Drafting Discuss story elements in logical order. Relate imagery and dialogue to the theme. Conclude your essay by discussing the overall effect of Gordimer's technique.

Revising Review your draft, circling areas in which you link ideas. Add transitions, such as *in addition*, *by contrast*, *despite*, and *furthermore*, to clarify connections.

Model: Clarifying Connections With Transitions

When the girl throws candies out the window, she intends them for the dogs. *Instead, as Gordimer describes it, "the* ~~"The~~ hens darted in, and swallowed the chocolates." *In this image,* Gordimer anticipates her main character's difficulty.

Added transitions strengthen the connections between ideas.

Prentice Hall Writing and Grammar Connection: Chapter 14, Section 3

❹ Extension Activities

Listening and Speaking With a group, hold a **debate** on this proposition: *One should always pay a fair price for a thing.* Use the following strategies:

- **Inductive arguments:** general conclusions drawn from particular instances
- **Deductive arguments:** conclusions drawn by applying general premises to a specific case

Hold your debate in class. **[Group Activity]**

Research and Technology Research and write a brief **historical report** on South Africa. In your word-processor draft, incorporate charts, spreadsheets, and other informative graphics.

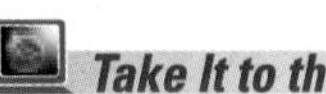

Take It to the Net www.phschool.com

Go online for an additional research activity using the Internet.

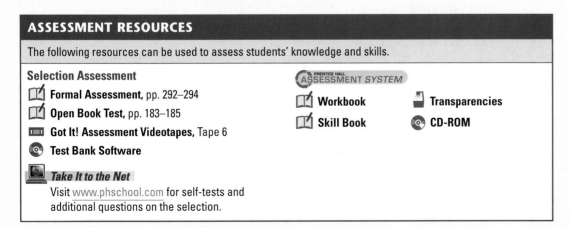

ASSESSMENT RESOURCES

The following resources can be used to assess students' knowledge and skills.

Selection Assessment

- **Formal Assessment,** pp. 292–294
- **Open Book Test,** pp. 183–185
- **Got It! Assessment Videotapes,** Tape 6
- **Test Bank Software**

Take It to the Net

Visit www.phschool.com for self-tests and additional questions on the selection.

PRENTICE HALL ASSESSMENT SYSTEM

- **Workbook**
- **Skill Book**
- **Transparencies**
- **CD-ROM**

Lesson Support for p. 1257

❸ Writing Lesson

- Tell students a critical response is a piece of nonfiction writing that presents a reaction to, or an analysis of, a literary work. An effective response to literature usually:

  identifies the work or works being discussed

  supports the writer's interpretations with precise examples, citations or quotations.

  is organized clearly and effectively

  offers an opinion, a judgment, or an evaluation based on close scrutiny of specific elements.
- Model a brief critical response for the students based on the first paragraph of "The Train from Rhodesia."

❹ Listening and Speaking

- Divide the students into three groups.
- Tell one group of students to research the history of South Africa on the Internet.
- Suggest that the second group request current information from the United Nations.
- Tell the third group how to contact the South African embassy in Washington to request information.
- Have each group write a brief report on their findings.

CUSTOMIZE INSTRUCTION For Universal Access

To address different learning styles, use the following activities suggested in the **Extension Activities** booklet, p. 62.

- For Visual/Spatial Learners, use Activity 5.
- For Logical/Mathematical and Visual/Spatial Learners, use Activity 6.
- For Interpersonal and Visual/Spatial and Verbal/Linguistic Learners, use Activity 7.

from Midsummer XXIII ✦ *from* Omeros, *from* Chapter XXVIII ✦ From Lucy: Englan' Lady

Lesson Objectives and CA Correlations

1. **To analyze and respond to literary elements**
   - Literary Analysis: Theme and Context **R 3.7**
   - Comparing Literary Works **R 3.3**
2. **To read, comprehend, analyze, and critique a poem**
   - Reading Strategy: Applying Background Information **R 3.7**
   - Reading Check Questions
   - Review and Assess Questions
3. **To develop word analysis skills, fluency, and systematic vocabulary**
   - Vocabulary Development Lesson: Latin Root *-duc-* **R 1.1, 1.2**
4. **To understand and apply written and oral language conventions**
   - Spelling Strategy **LC 1.2**
   - Grammar and Style Lesson: Commonly Confused Words: *affect* and *effect* **LC 1.1**
5. **To understand and apply appropriate writing and research strategies**
   - Writing Lesson: Script for the Multimedia Presentation of a Poem **W 1.1, 1.9, 2.6**
   - Extension Activity: Caribbean Culture Festival
   - Assessment Practice (ATE)
6. **To understand and apply listening and speaking strategies**
   - Extension Activity: Recitation **LS 1.9, 2.5**

STEP-BY-STEP TEACHING GUIDE	PACING GUIDE
PRETEACH	
Motivate Students and Provide Background	
Use the Motivation activity (ATE p.1258)	5 min.
Read and discuss author and background features (SE/ATE pp. 1258, 1260) [A]	5 min.
Introduce the Concepts	
Introduce the Literary Analysis and Reading Strategy (SE/ATE p. 1259) [A]	15 min.
Pronounce the vocabulary words and read their definitions (SE p. 1259)	5 min.
TEACH	
Monitor Comprehension	
Informally monitor comprehension by circulating while students read independently or in groups [A]	10 min.
Monitor students' comprehension with the Reading Check notes (SE/ATE pp. 1263, 1265)	as students read
Develop vocabulary with Vocabulary notes (SE p. 1261)	as students read
Develop Understanding	
Develop students' understanding of theme and context with the Literary Analysis annotations (SE p. 1263; ATE pp. 1260, 1263) [A]	5 min.
Develop students' ability to apply background information with the Reading Strategy annotation (ATE p. 1260)	5 min.
ASSESS	
Assess Mastery	
Assess students' mastery of the Reading Strategy and Literary Analysis by having them answer the Review and Assess questions (SE/ATE p. 1267)	15 min.
Use one or more of the print and media Assessment Resources (ATE p. 1269) [A]	up to 45 min.
EXTEND	
Apply Understanding	
Have students complete the Vocabulary Development Lesson and the Grammar and Style Lesson (SE p. 1268) [A]	20 min.
Apply students' knowledge of following script format using the Writing Lesson (SE/ATE p. 1269) [A]	45 min.
Apply students' understanding using one or more of the Extension Activities (SE p. 1269)	20–90 min.

[A] **ACCELERATED INSTRUCTION:** Use the strategies and activities identified with an [A].

UNIVERSAL ACCESS
● = Below-Level Students
▲ = On-Level Students
■ = Above-Level Students

Time and Resource Manager

Reading Level: Challenging, Challenging, Average
Average Number of Instructional Days: 4

RESOURCES		
PRINT	**TRANSPARENCIES**	**TECHNOLOGY**
• **Beyond Literature,** Cross-Curricular Connection: Social Studies, p. 63 ▲ ■		• **Interest Grabber Video,** Tape 6 ● ▲ ■
• **Selection Support Workbook:** ● ▲ ■ Literary Analysis, p. 292 Reading Strategy, p. 291 Build Vocabulary, p. 289	• **Literary Analysis and Reading Transparencies,** pp. 125 and 126 ● ▲ ■	
		• **Listening to Literature** ● ▲ ■ Audiocassettes, Side 29 Audio CDs, CD 17
• **Literatura en español** ● ▲ • **Literary Analysis for Enrichment** ■	• **Fine Art Transparencies, Volume 1,** Transparency 9 ● ▲ ■	
• **Formal Assessment:** Selection Test, pp. 295–297 ● ▲ ■ • **Open Book Test,** pp. 186–188 ● ▲ ■ • PRENTICE HALL ASSESSMENT SYSTEM ● ▲ ■	• PRENTICE HALL ASSESSMENT SYSTEM ● ▲ ■ Skills Practice Answers and Explanations on Transparencies ● ▲ ■	• **Test Bank Software** ● ▲ ■ • **Got It! Assessment Videotapes,** Tape 6 ● ▲
• **Selection Support Workbook:** ● ▲ ■ Grammar and Style, p. 290 • **Writing and Grammar,** Diamond Level ● ▲ ■ • **Extension Activities,** p. 63 ● ▲ ■	• **Daily Language Practice Transparencies** ● ▲	• **Writing and Grammar iText CD-ROM** ● ▲ ■ ***Take It to the Net*** www.phschool.com

BLOCK SCHEDULING: Use one 90-minute class period to preteach the selections and have students read them. Use a second 90-minute class period to assess students' mastery of skills and have them complete one of the Extension Activities.

PRETEACH

Step-by-Step Teaching Guide for pp. 1258–1259

Motivation

To prepare students for these poems about West Indians adapting to European culture, have them share memories of times they visited a place very different from their own home—a different country, region, or neighborhood unlike the place they live. What differences did they find in the way people talked, dressed, ate, and behaved? How did they cope? The conditions they experienced are the context of their story. Then, ask whether they enjoyed their visit, and why. Tell them that what they got out of their trip could be the theme of their story.

Interest Grabber Video

As an alternative, play "*Midsummer,* XXIII: Derek Walcott on the Music and Rhythm of Writing" on Tape 6 to engage student interest.

❶ Background

More About the Authors

Derek Walcott

The experience of growing up on the isolated volcanic island of St. Lucia, an ex-British colony, has had a strong influence on Walcott's life and work. Walcott has been an assiduous traveler to other countries but has always, not least in his efforts to create an indigenous drama, felt himself deeply rooted in Caribbean society, with its cultural fusion of African, Asian, and European elements.

James Berry

In postwar London, while working days, James Berry took night classes to educate himself. He trained to become a telegraphist, which was his occupation for many years. In 1976 he published *Bluefoot Traveler,* a book of black British poetry. Since his early days in England, Berry has remained an active campaigner on behalf of black people and has helped to promote young black writers in particular.

Prepare to Read

❶ *from* Midsummer, XXIII ◆ *from* Omeros, *from* Chapter XXVIII ◆ From Lucy: Englan' Lady

Derek Walcott (b. 1930)

Nobel Prize-winner Derek Walcott, one of the most renowned contemporary poets writing in English, has roots in two worlds. Both of his grandmothers were descended from enslaved Africans, and both of his grandfathers were white colonials. Throughout his life, Walcott has reflected upon his contrasting heritages. These reflections propel his poems, which may carry the reader from tropical Trinidad to ancient Greece to Shakespeare's England, sometimes in a single line of poetry.

Early Success Walcott, born on the Caribbean Island of St. Lucia, graduated from the University of the West Indies. He published the first of his many books of poetry, *Twenty-five Poems,* when he was just a teenager. Subsequent collections include *The Gulf* (1970), *Sea Grapes* (1976), *Collected Poems 1948–1984* (1986), and *Tiepolo's Hound* (2000).

In 1959, Walcott, also an accomplished playwright, founded the Trinidad Theatre Workshop. His play *Dream on Monkey Mountain* won an Obie in 1971. More recently, Walcott collaborated with songwriter and composer Paul Simon on a Broadway musical, *The Capeman* (1997).

High Honors Walcott's 1990 book *Omeros,* which draws on the epics of the ancient Greek poet Homer, ensured him the Nobel Prize for Literature in 1992. The Swedish Academy, when granting the award, concluded that "West Indian culture has found its great poet." Such a role entails responsibilities, and Walcott's poetry often reflects on the traditions to which he belongs.

James Berry (b. 1925)

Born in a small village on the island of Jamaica and now living in Britain, James Berry draws from his many varied experiences to infuse English poetry with vivid fresh language. His work combines imagery and rhythms from his rural West Indian background with the snap and style of urban London.

Experiences of Poverty Berry's childhood experiences of poverty are all too typical in the West Indies. He had to leave school at age fourteen to help support his family. During World War II, he traveled to the United States to find work. After living in several places, including Harlem, he returned to Jamaica, discouraged by the prejudice he encountered in the States. In 1948, Berry left for England, where he began to write.

Crossing the Gaps In both prose and in poetry, Berry tells the stories of people whom history usually ignores. His books include *A Thief in the Village,* a collection of stories for children that was a Coretta Scott King Honor Book in 1989. He has also written a novel, *Ajeemah and His Son,* a story from the days of slavery. His poetry makes musical use of both English and the Creole language of his native island. Collections include *Fractured Circles* (1979) and *Lucy's Letters and Loving* (1982). In whatever form Berry writes, he works to cross the gaps between cultures and races. Lucy's simple, wise commentary on the Queen in "From Lucy: Englan' Lady" shows how powerful the results can be.

TEACHING RESOURCES

The following resources can be used to enrich or extend the instruction for pp. 1258–1259.

Motivation

Interest Grabber Video, Tape 6

Background

Beyond Literature, p. 63

Take It to the Net

Visit www.phschool.com for background and hotlinks for the selections.

Literary Analysis

Literary Analysis and Reading Transparencies, Theme and Context, p. 126

Reading

Selection Support: Reading Strategy, p. 291; Build Vocabulary, p. 289

Literary Analysis and Reading Transparencies, Applying Background Information, p. 125

BLOCK SCHEDULING: Resources marked with this symbol provide varied instruction during 90-minute blocks.

Preview

Connecting to the Literature

The language that you speak is part of you, but what makes it yours? Are some ways of speaking it more truly yours—more natural to you—than others? These poets explore some of the different "languages" that make up English. They also demonstrate how a poet makes a language his or her own.

❷ Literary Analysis

Theme and Context

Understanding the **context** of a work—the historical moment in which it originates—can help you better appreciate its **theme**—the central issue it explores. The themes of the poems given here are general: the responsibilities of an artist and the burden of a social role. Their context, though, is the meeting of two specific cultures—British and Caribbean. Note the forms that this encounter takes, whether as a dialogue or as a collision.

Comparing Literary Works

In these poems, Walcott and Berry consider and address the literary tradition in which they write. Each in his own way both pledges allegiance to this tradition and questions it. Their techniques for engaging with the tradition include the following:

- **Allusions**—brief references to literary works, people, or events. An allusion implies that the writer and the reader "own" a common culture.
- **Political critique of art**—examination of the political implications of art. Such critique often questions the "ownership" of art, raising the question of who produces, judges, and learns to appreciate it.

Compare the ways in which these poets address and expand their traditions.

❸ Reading Strategy

Applying Background Information

Sometimes you must **apply background information** to understand a poem. For example, to understand Walcott's response to the Brixton riots in *Midsummer*, XXIII, it is useful to know that the riots erupted in London among Caribbean immigrants. Use a chart like the one shown to help you apply background information to these poems. (You will find such information in footnotes and in the Background feature, page 1260.)

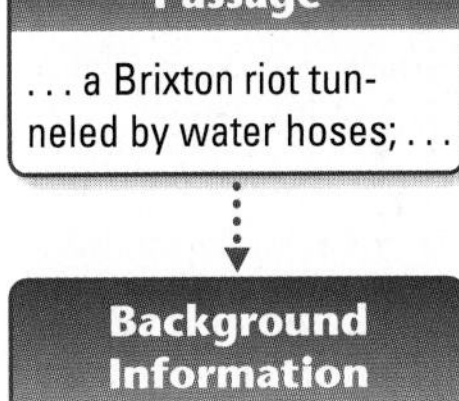

Passage
. . . a Brixton riot tunneled by water hoses; . . .
Background Information
Residents of the South London district of Brixton rioted in April 1981.
Interpretation
"Tunneled by water hoses": The police sprayed rioters with high-pressure water from fire-hoses to disperse them.

Vocabulary Development

antic (an′ tik) *adj.* odd and funny; silly (p. 1261)

rancor (raŋ′ kər) *n.* continuing, bitter hate or ill will (p. 1261)

eclipse (i klips′) *n.* dimming or extinction of power or glory (p. 1261)

inducted (in duk′ tid) *v.* brought formally into an organization (p. 1261)

❷ Literary Analysis

Theme and Context

- Tell students that in these readings they will be focusing on the relationship of theme and context.
- While the theme of a work—the central issue it explores—may concern human beings generally, knowledge of the context of a work is often helpful in understanding how the theme is being presented.
- In these works, students will be learning about the encounter of different cultures with one another. This encounter provides an important element of the context of the works. Have students pay close attention to the cross-cultural implications of these works.
- Both Walcott and Berry are responding to the specific traditions in which they were writing. Tell students to be on the lookout for ways that each relates to the tradition in which he is working.

❸ Reading Strategy

Applying Background Information

- Explain to students that background information is sometimes critical for the complete understanding and appreciation of a poem.
- Explain the use of the chart to help students apply background information to the interpretation of these poems.

Vocabulary Development

- Pronounce each vocabulary word for students, and read the definitions as a class. Have students identify any words with which they are already familiar.

CUSTOMIZE INSTRUCTION FOR UNIVERSAL ACCESS

For Less Proficient Readers	For English Learners	For Advanced Readers
Some students may have difficulty with the plant imagery, shifting speakers, and time shifts in the excerpt from Walcott's *Omeros*. Explain these aspects of the poem before students read. After they read, use the annotations accompanying the poem to guide students.	Some students may respond strongly to the themes of these selections. Ask students whether Caribbean immigrants are better off shedding their culture and adapting fully to their new British home, or whether there is value in holding on to traditions. Organize a debate about the issue.	Have students create an outline of causes-and-effects for the Brixton riot of 1981. Ask students to explain how their outlines create a context for understanding Derek Walcott's work.

E-Teach

Visit E-Teach at www.phschool.com for teachers' essays on how to teach, with questions and answers.

TEACH

Step-by-Step Teaching Guide for pp. 1260–1266

❶ About the Selection

Derek Walcott wrestles with his conflicting loyalties as a black Caribbean poet accepted in white British society.

❷ Literary Analysis

Theme and Context

- Remind students that they should be focusing on the relationship between theme and context as they read the poem.
- Ask students how Walcott develops both a specific context and the beginning of a universal theme in the first five lines of the poem.
  Answer: His description of the Brixton riot establishes a specific context, while lines 4–5 express a universal theme about the human longing for light and a meaningful life.

❸ Reading Strategy

Apply Background Information

- Remind students that they need to be on the lookout for contextual background information in order to fully understand the poem.
- Ask students what relevance these references to the Boer War and apartheid have to the context and theme of the poem.
  Answer: Walcott suggests that the condition of blacks in England today has some resemblances to that under apartheid.

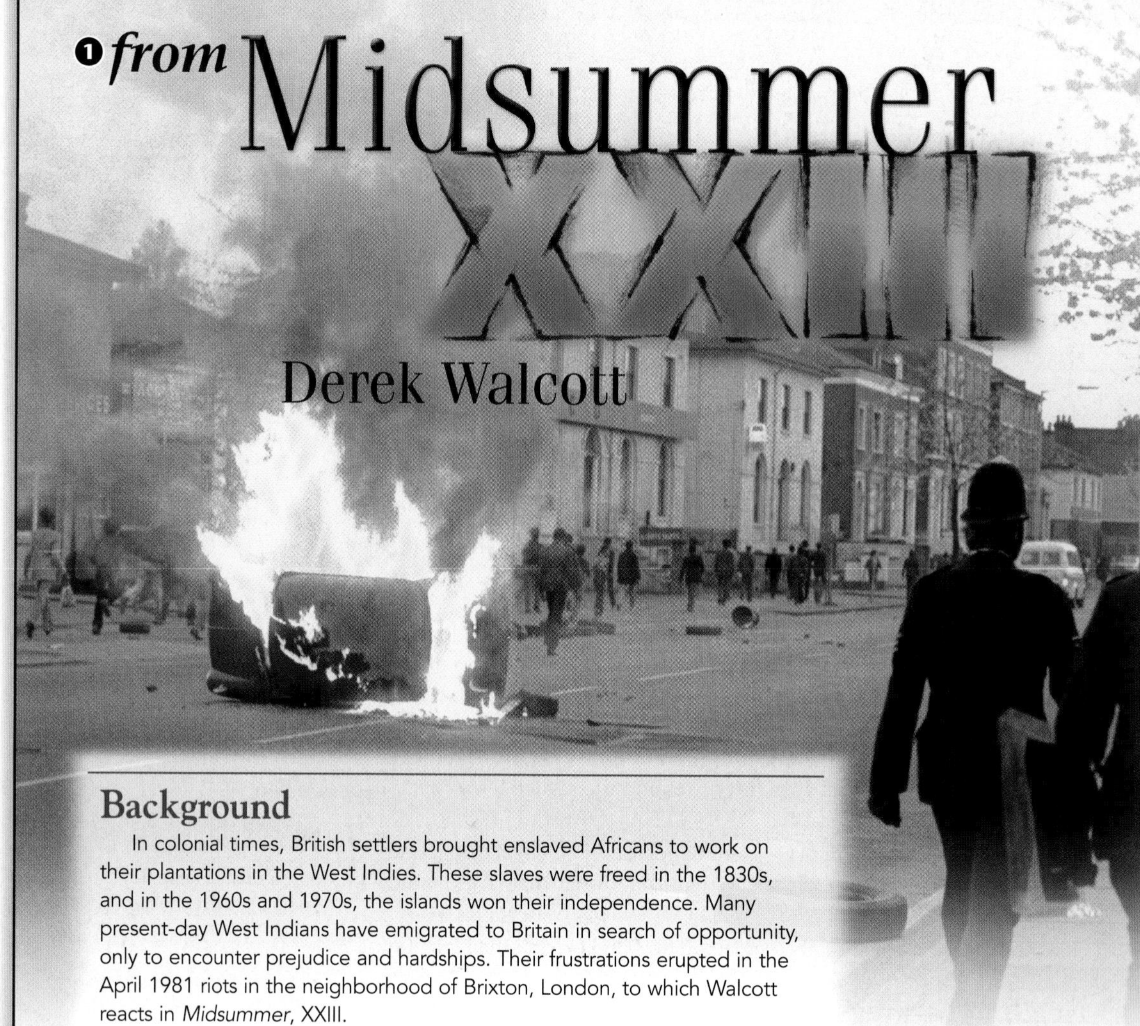

❶ *from* Midsummer XXIII

Derek Walcott

Background

In colonial times, British settlers brought enslaved Africans to work on their plantations in the West Indies. These slaves were freed in the 1830s, and in the 1960s and 1970s, the islands won their independence. Many present-day West Indians have emigrated to Britain in search of opportunity, only to encounter prejudice and hardships. Their frustrations erupted in the April 1981 riots in the neighborhood of Brixton, London, to which Walcott reacts in *Midsummer*, XXIII.

With the stampeding hiss and scurry of green lemmings,
midsummer's leaves race to extinction like the roar
of a Brixton riot tunneled by water hoses;
they seethe towards autumn's fire—it is in their nature,
being men as well as leaves, to die for the sun.

The leaf stems tug at their chains, the branches bending
like Boer cattle under Tory whips that drag every wagon
nearer to apartheid.[1] And, for me, that closes

1. **Boer** (bōr) **cattle . . . apartheid** In the 1600s, the Boers, people of Dutch descent, colonized South Africa, where apartheid (racial segregation) was later practiced. The Tories held power in Britain when it won control of South Africa in the Boer War (1899–1902).

TEACHING RESOURCES

The following resources can be used to enrich or extend the instruction for pp. 1260–1266.

Literary Analysis

Selection Support: Literary Analysis, p. 292 ■

Reading

Listening to Literature Audiocassettes, Side 29 ■

Listening to Literature Audio CDs, CD 17 ■

Extension

Fine Art Transparencies, Volume 1, Transparency 9 (Have students discuss the artistic traditions reflected in Michael Cummings's *African Jazz Series #5.* Note that, like Cummings, Walcott and Berry look to varied traditions in their work.)

■ **BLOCK SCHEDULING:** Resources marked with this symbol provide varied instruction during 90-minute blocks.

the child's fairy tale of an antic England—fairy rings,
thatched cottages fenced with dog roses,
a green gale lifting the hair of Warwickshire.
I was there to add some color to the British theater.
"But the blacks can't do Shakespeare, they have no experience."
This was true. Their thick skulls bled with rancor
when the riot police and the skinheads exchanged quips
you could trace to the Sonnets,[2] or the Moor's eclipse.[3]
Praise had bled my lines white of any more anger,
and snow had inducted me into white fellowships,
while Calibans[4] howled down the barred streets of an empire
that began with Caedmon's raceless dew,[5] and is ending
in the alleys of Brixton, burning like Turner's ships.[6]

antic (an´ tik) *adj.* odd and funny; silly

rancor (raŋ´ kər) *n.* continuing, bitter hate or ill will

eclipse (ē klips´) *n.* dimming or extinction of power or glory

inducted (in dukt´ id) *v.* brought formally into an organization

2. **the Sonnets** William Shakespeare's sequence of 154 sonnets, noted for their passionate, often witty inquiries into love and rivalry.
3. **the Moor's eclipse** In Shakespeare's *Othello,* Othello the Moor (a black North African) is destroyed by the scheming of his white lieutenant, Iago.
4. **Calibans** Caliban is a deformed creature in Shakespeare's play *The Tempest.* Enslaved by the enchanter Prospero, Caliban has been interpreted as a native who rebels against his island's "colonizer," Prospero.
5. **Caedmon's** (kad´ mənz) **raceless dew** poetry written by the earliest known English poet, Caedmon (seventh century).
6. **Turner's ships** British artist J. M. W. Turner (1775–1851) rendered atmospheric oil paintings of, among other subjects, ships burning in battle.

Review and Assess

Thinking About the Selection

1. **(a) Recall:** Toward what are midsummer's leaves racing? **(b) Interpret:** What mood does this race create for the poem?
2. **(a) Recall:** What event "closes" for the speaker "the child's fairy tale of an antic England"? **(b) Infer:** Why is this event disillusioning? **(c) Connect:** Why does Walcott's reason for being in England at the time make the event especially significant for him?
3. **(a) Draw Conclusions:** What does the speaker mean when he says that the "empire / . . . is ending / in the alleys of Brixton"? **(b) Connect:** What common idea or pattern connects the midsummer leaves, Walcott's disillusionment, and the crisis in England?
4. **Infer:** Judging by the poem, has Walcott come to terms with belonging to both black and white traditions? Explain.
5. **Make a Judgment:** Do you think black artists such as Walcott should withdraw from "white fellowships" to protest racial injustices? Explain.

CUSTOMIZE INSTRUCTION FOR UNIVERSAL ACCESS

For Less Proficient Readers	For English Learners	For Advanced Readers
Help students understand the context of the poem by explaining to them aspects of the colonial legacy it reflects. You may wish to point out that the West Indians were once ruled by the British; that West Indian immigration to Britain is an aftereffect of the colonial days; that the riots are a response to continuing oppression.	Help students appreciate the subtleties of the mixed cultural references and characteristics of the poem. Point out, for example, that the educated style, the references to Shakespeare, and the use of *they* and *their* suggest a British person. On the other hand, the angry descriptions of British oppression suggest a West Indian.	Louis James writes that in *Midsummer,* Derek Walcott tries "to reconcile his divided heritage." Have students show in an essay how Walcott makes this attempt in *Midsummer,* XXIII.

Answers for p. 1261

Review and Assess

1. **(a)** The leaves are racing to extinction. **(b)** Students may respond that it suggests a frenzied, deeply disturbed mood.
2. **(a)** The violence of the Brixton riots ends the speaker's romantic picture of England. The riots show that Britain is a troubled, divided and violent society. **(b)** The event is disillusioning because its violence contrasts with the innocence of fairy tales and suggests that England is not truly open to West Indians like Walcott. **(c)** Walcott was participating in a theatrical project, a sign of British acceptance of West Indians; the riots expose a more brutal truth about West Indians' place in Britain. Walcott must have come to question his role in the theater if such tokenism ("to add a touch of color to the British theater") served to mask the injustice exposed by the riots.
3. **(a)** West Indians were once ruled by the British, and West Indian immigration to Britain is an aftereffect or even continuation of the empire; the riots show, though, that the empire has failed to unite people but instead is torn apart by internal conflict. **(b)** The leaves are dead or dying. Walcott's innocence dies with them, and the crisis in England is a dramatic enactment of the empire's end.
4. The two societies battle within him—the educated style evokes the British tradition; the angry descriptions of British oppression suggest a West Indian perspective. The speaker seems torn between identifying with his oppressed countrymen and enjoying the praise and acceptance of British critics.
5. Some students may agree that black artists should reject white patronage. Other students may feel that artists may do more to reduce injustice by maintaining ties with whites.

❹ About the Selection

This excerpt from Chapter XXVIII of Walcott's epic poem focuses on the painful legacies of the trade that brought enslaved Africans to America and the Caribbean. A West African griot, or storyteller, describes the Africans' experiences on the slave ships, and another speaker then comments on the legacy of those experiences.

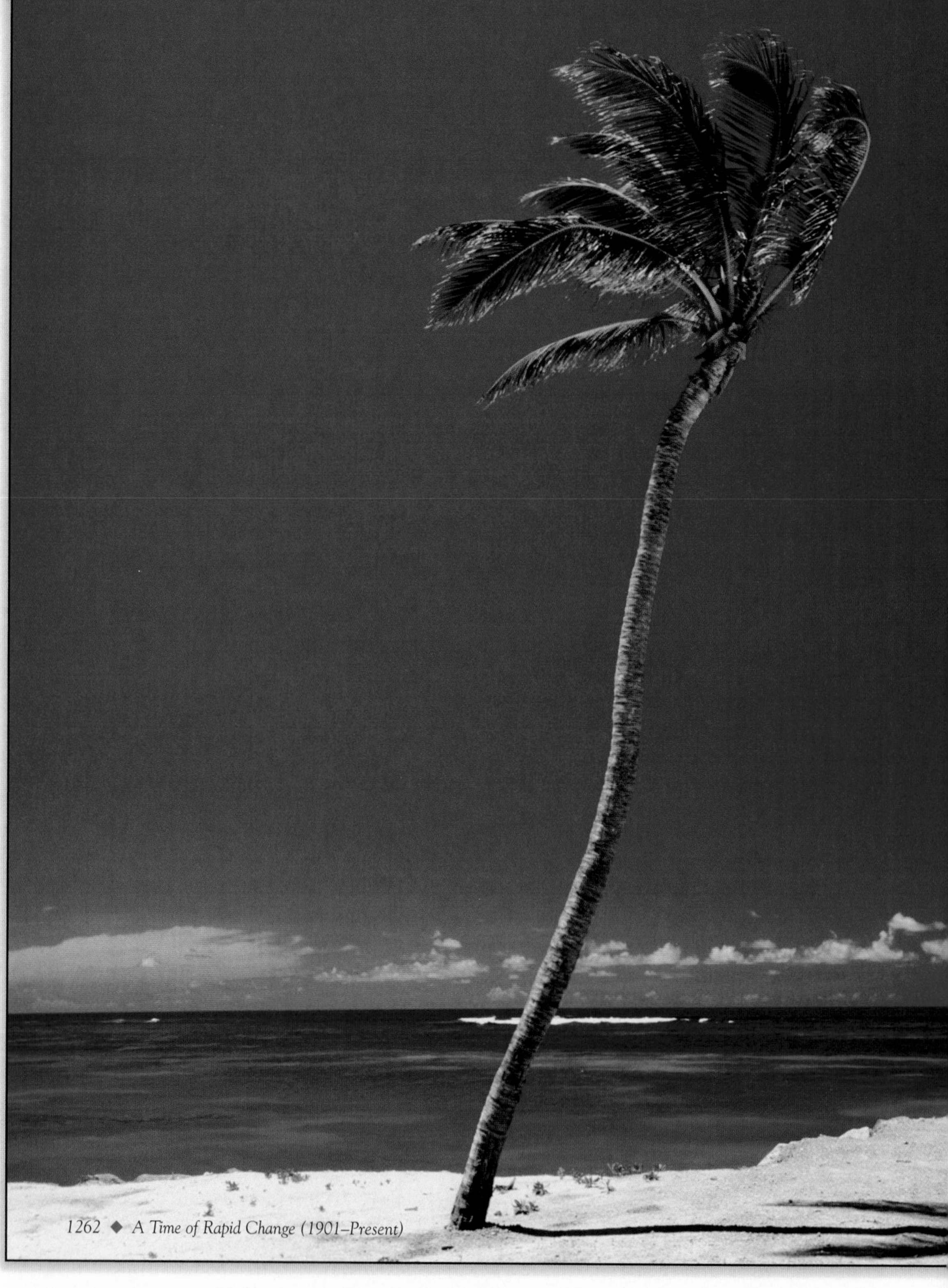

ENRICHMENT: Social Studies Connection

The Bight of Benin

A bight is a bay formed by a curve in a coastline. The Bight of Benin is one of two bays on the West Coast of Africa that together form the Gulf of Guinea. The land along the Bight of Benin was once home to the great Kingdom of Benin, which existed from the thirteenth to the nineteenth centuries. The residents of Benin were great traders, and their king ruled from an affluent court known for its beautiful brass and bronze sculptures. The first Europeans to visit Benin were the Portuguese in 1472. The king of Benin actually sent armies to raid rival villages to capture slaves to sell to European traders.

Today Benin is a small country in West Africa located between Nigeria and Togo. It was once known as Dahomey. Benin is one of the poorest countries in West Africa, and most people there are subsistence farmers. Their crops include palm kernels, yams, and peanuts.

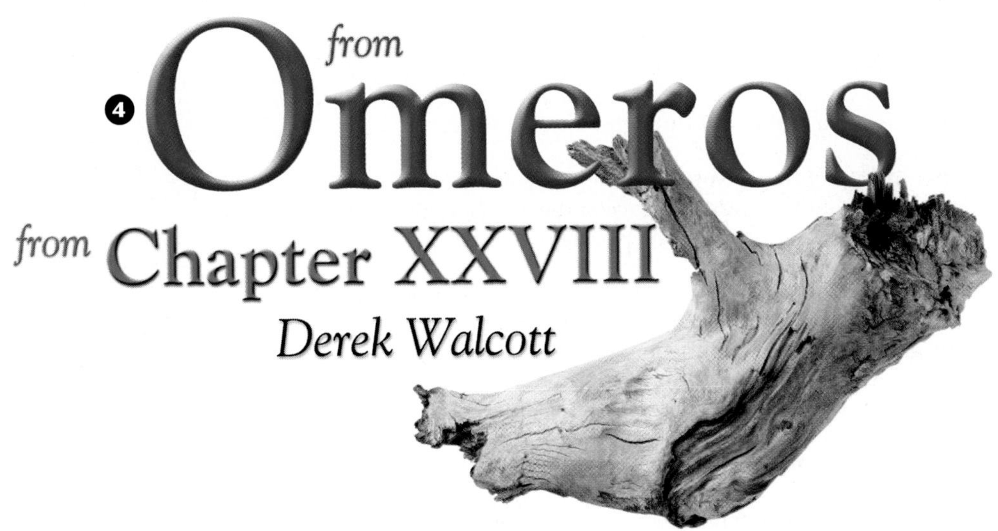

from Omeros
from Chapter XXVIII
Derek Walcott

Now he heard the griot[1] muttering his prophetic song
of sorrow that would be the past. It was a note, long-drawn
and endless in its winding like the brown river's tongue:

"We were the color of shadows when we came down
with tinkling leg-irons to join the chains of the sea,
for the silver coins multiplying on the sold horizon,

and these shadows are reprinted now on the white sand
of antipodal[2] coasts, your ashen ancestors
from the Bight of Benin, from the margin of Guinea.[3]

There were seeds in our stomachs, in the cracking pods
of our skulls on the scorching decks, the tubers[4]
withered in no time. We watched as the river-gods

changed from snakes into currents. When inspected,
our eyes showed dried fronds[5] in their brown irises,
and from our curved spines, the rib-cages radiated

like fronds from a palm-branch. Then, when the dead
palms were heaved overside, the ribbed corpses
floated, riding, to the white sand they remembered,

1. **griot** (grē´ ō) *n.* in West African cultures, a poet/historian/performer who preserves and passes on the oral tradition.
2. **antipodal** (an tip´ ə dəl) *adj.* situated on opposite sides of the earth.
3. **the Bight** (bīt) **of Benin** (be nēn´) . . . **Guinea** (gin´ ē) area of west central Africa that came to be known as the Slave Coast.
4. **tubers** (to͞ob´ ərz) *n.* thick, fleshy parts of underground stems, such as potatoes.
5. **fronds** (frändz) *n.* leaves of a palm; also the leaflike parts of seaweed.

Literary Analysis
Theme and Context
What two diverse contexts does Walcott invoke by having a griot speak in an epic?

Reading Check
To what does the griot compare the enslaved people?

5 Literary Analysis
Theme and Context

- Recall for students the characteristics of an epic poem. An epic is a long narrative poem, often derived from an oral tradition, that recounts the story of a hero and reflects the values of a culture.
- Have students read the first stanza. Then, ask them the Literary Analysis question on p. 1263: What two diverse contexts does Walcott invoke by having a griot speak in an epic?
  Answer: He invokes the oral traditions of both the griot and the western European tradition of epic going back to Homer. A griot is a traveling poet, musician, or entertainer from North and West Africa, whose duties include the recitation of tribal and family histories.

6 Critical Thinking
Infer

- Read aloud the first two stanzas of the poem. Ask students to identify how many people are speaking in these stanzas.
- Then, have students explain when the poem switches from one speaker to another.
  Answer: In the first stanza of the poem, the first speaker introduces the griot, or West African storyteller. The griot tells the story of slavery from lines 4–24. Later, the first speaker will return to sum up the meaning of the story the griot has told.

7 Reading Check

Answer: The griot compares the enslaved people to shadows and palm trees.

CUSTOMIZE INSTRUCTION FOR UNIVERSAL ACCESS

For Less Proficient Readers	For Gifted/Talented Students	For Advanced Readers
Have students research what happened to the Ashanti and other African cultures transplanted to the Caribbean. Then, have them write a report on their findings.	Have students perform the incident in this story as a role play. Suggest that one of the students play the role of griot in narrating the story, while other students find creative ways of depicting the events related in the poem.	Have students research and prepare a festival of Caribbean culture. Suggest that they focus on the language, food, and music of Jamaica, St. Lucia, and other countries in the region.

Answers for p. 1264

Review and Assess

1. Students may mention the "brown river's tongue," the "tinkling leg irons," the "chains of the sea," and the "silver coins multiplying on the sold horizon."
2. **(a)** The griot recalls the voyage of the Africans from the Slave Coast to the Caribbean. **(b)** The plant imagery is first used to describe the bodies of enslaved Africans. Then, the image of driftwood on the waves in the present is presented as an invitation to remember the enslaved Africans of the past.
3. **(a)** The different tribes, even families, were split up, separated from each other. **(b)** Each man "was a nation in himself" because he was separated from his tribe, from his family, and from his friends.
4. **(a)** Born from extreme deprivation was a kind of "grace" that taught the enslaved how to endure. **(b)** According to the poem, Africans drew on and enhanced their inner strength and grace out of necessity.
5. Students may respond that Walcott's main aim is to better understand the origins of the Africans' present situation by dramatizing their past experiences. He does not dwell on the details of the enslaved people's suffering but instead shows how their fate led to the present.
6. Students may respond that Walcott has used the power of poetry to effectively portray the slaves' suffering through such imagery as "the cracking pods / of our skulls on the scorching decks," "the ribbed corpses floated," and "the bolt rammed home its echo."

to the Bight of Benin, to the margin of Guinea.
So, when you see burnt branches riding the swell,
trying to reclaim the surf through crooked fingers,

after a night of rough wind by some stone-white hotel,
past the bright triangular passage of the windsurfers,
remember us to the black waiter bringing the bill."

But they crossed, they survived. There is the epical splendor.
Multiply the rain's lances, multiply their ruin,
the grace born from subtraction as the hold's iron door

rolled over their eyes like pots left out in the rain,
and the bolt rammed home its echo, the way that thunder-
claps perpetuate their reverberation.

So there went the Ashanti one way, the Mandingo another,
the Ibo another, the Guinea.[6] Now each man was a nation
in himself, without mother, father, brother.

---

6. **the Ashanti** (ə shan´ tī) . . . **the Mandingo** (man diŋ´ gō) . . . **the Ibo** (ē´ bō´) . . . **the Guinea** (gin´ ē) names of West African peoples.

Review and Assess

Thinking About the Selection

1. **Respond:** What sights connect you to a larger past, as the burnt branches connect the speaker to the past in the poem?
2. **(a) Recall:** What event does the griot describe in lines 4–24 of this excerpt from *Omeros*? **(b) Analyze:** How does the griot use plant imagery to link past and present?
3. **(a) Recall:** What happens to members of the different West African peoples once they are brought across the sea? **(b) Interpret:** What does Walcott mean when he says, "Now each man was a nation / in himself"?
4. **(a) Interpret:** What might Walcott mean by "the grace born from subtraction" (line 27)? **(b) Draw Conclusions:** According to the poem, what positive result does the slave trade have?
5. **Draw Conclusions:** Would you say that Walcott's main aim is to dramatize past experiences or to better understand the origins of the present? Explain.
6. **Make a Judgment:** In this excerpt, does Walcott pass too quickly over the suffering inflicted by the slave trade? Explain.

ENRICHMENT: Social Studies

The Ashanti

The Ashanti, or Asante, are a West African group united by a common language. Many Ashanti still inhabit areas of Ghana, Togo, and the Ivory Coast in West Africa today. They live by farming and the trading of handmade crafts.

The Ashanti established a powerful, wealthy empire built on trade in Central Guinea during the seventeenth and eighteenth centuries. When English officials visited the Ashanti capital of Kumasi in 1817, they were amazed to find long, wide streets and a great city. One of the officials wrote: "An area of nearly a mile in circumference was crowded with magnificence and novelty. The king, his chiefs, and captains, were splendidly dressed and were surrounded by attendants of every kind. More than a hundred bands broke into music on our arrival."

Have students discuss their reactions to this vivid description of a nineteenth-century African city. Did they find the wealth and culture of the Ashanti city surprising? Why or why not?

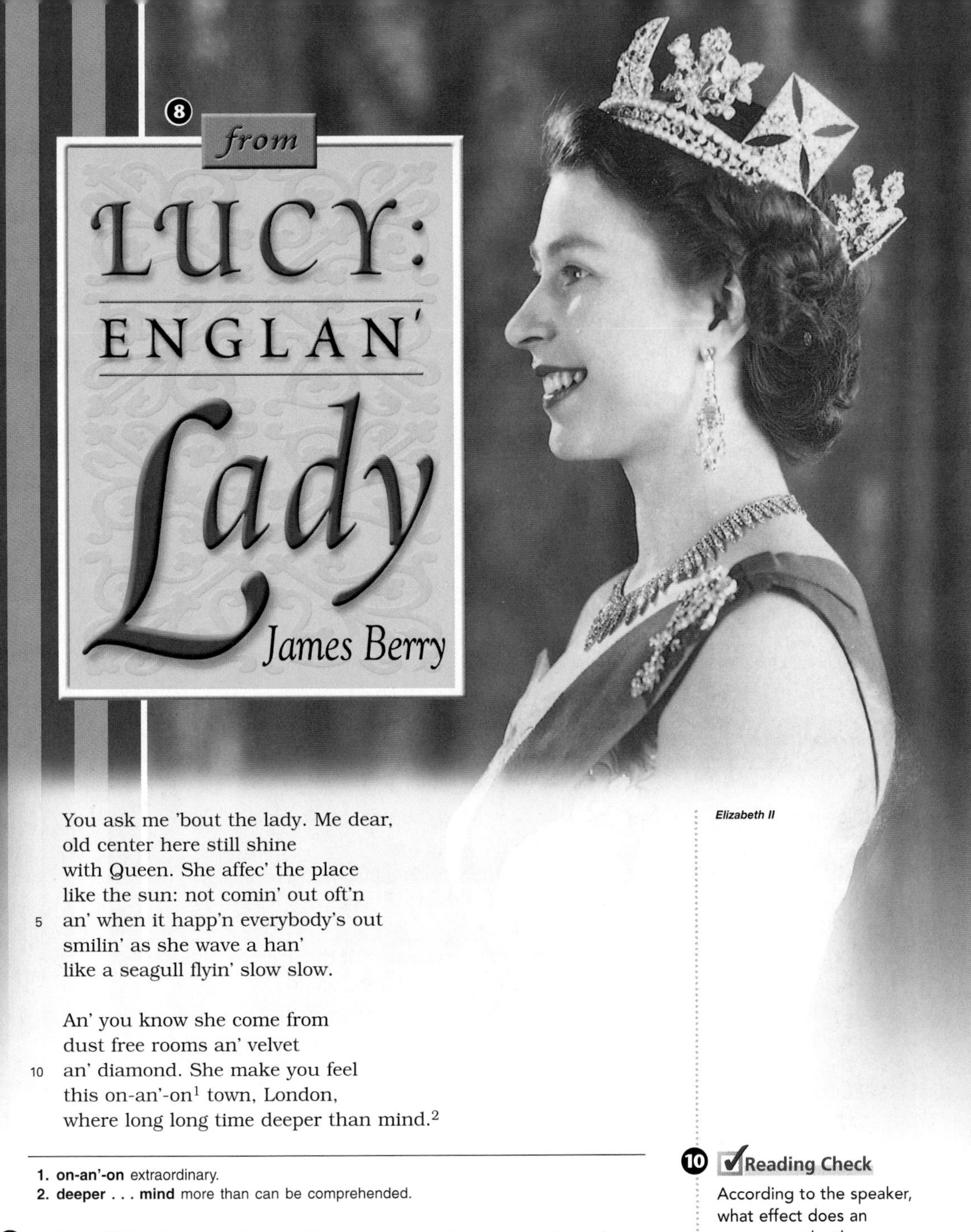

8 from

LUCY: ENGLAN' Lady

James Berry

Elizabeth II

You ask me 'bout the lady. Me dear,
old center here still shine
with Queen. She affec' the place
like the sun: not comin' out oft'n
an' when it happ'n everybody's out
smilin' as she wave a han'
like a seagull flyin' slow slow.

An' you know she come from
dust free rooms an' velvet
an' diamond. She make you feel
this on-an'-on[1] town, London,
where long long time deeper than mind.[2]

1. **on-an'-on** extraordinary.
2. **deeper . . . mind** more than can be comprehended.

9 ▲ **Critical Viewing** Does Queen Elizabeth show the "strain keepin' good graces" referred to in the poem? Explain. **[Analyze]**

10 ✔ **Reading Check**

According to the speaker, what effect does an appearance by the Queen have?

8 About the Selection

In this poem a Jamaican immigrant woman living in London expresses her thoughts about Queen Elizabeth in a letter to a friend back home. In Jamaican dialect, she wonders, in a half-amused, bittersweet tone, whether the queen doesn't find her life as a royal celebrity lonely.

9 ▶ Critical Viewing

Answer: Students may say that the queen's posture in this photo looks stiff and that her smile looks frozen and artificial, reflecting the "strain" referred to in the poem.

10 ✔ Reading Check

Answer: The effect is like the sun.

CUSTOMIZE INSTRUCTION FOR UNIVERSAL ACCESS

For Special Needs Students	For Less Proficient Readers	For English Learners
Have students read along with **Listening to Literature Audio-cassettes,** Side 29, in order that they may appreciate the musicality of the Jamaican dialect. Students will often find it easier to compre-hend the dialect when they hear the words spoken.	Have students write a letter to Lucy giving her some recent news about the queen and other members of Britain's royal family. Suggest that they respond to some of the ideas she expresses in her letter.	Have students perform Berry's dialect poem for the class. In rehearsing, have them follow the poet's own advice for reading a poem in Jamaican dialect: "Feel out the rhythm . . . then express it with your own easy natural voice."

ASSESS

Answers for p. 1266

Review and Assess

1. **(a)** The speaker lives in London. **(b)** Leela has not been to London. Lucy takes pains to describe the streets, the buildings, the feeling tone of the old city, and, more significantly, an appearance of Queen Elizabeth . . . an event witnessed by most visitors to London. **(c)** It appears Leela is curious to know if Lucy has met the queen.
2. **(a)** Lucy compares the appearance of the queen to the infrequent (in London) appearance of the sun. **(b)** The queen embodies the extraordinary qualities of London and the English heritage.
3. **(a)** Lucy feels the queen must suffer feelings of loneliness and isolation brought about by always being on display. **(b)** Lucy brings the queen back to human size when she observes "mus' be hard strain keepin' good graces for all hypocrite faces." At the same time, this observation makes Lucy seem as if she observes life from the center of things because it shows her equipped to judge the condition of anyone, even the queen.
4. Students may respond that Lucy might feel sorry for American celebrities who lead public lives similar to the queen's.
5. Students may respond that by using dialect, Berry has made Lucy both a genuine Jamaican and an outsider in London, even though she lives there.

An' han's after han's[3] die away,
makin' streets, putt'n' up bricks,
a piece of brass, a piece of wood
an' plantin' trees: an' it give
a car a halfday job gett'n' through.

An' Leela, darlin', no, I never
meet the Queen in flesh. Yet
sometimes, deep deep, I sorry for her.
Everybody expec' a show
from her, like she a space touris'
on earth. An' darlin', unless
you can go home an' scratch up[4]
you' husban', it mus' be hard
strain keepin' good graces for
all hypocrite faces.

Anyhow, me dear, you know what
ole time people say,
"Bird sing sweet for its nest."[5]

---

3. **han's after han's** many generations.
4. **scratch up** lose your temper at.
5. **"Bird . . . nest"** Jamaican proverb, referring to the nightingale's habit of singing loudest near its nest. It means, "Those closest to home are the most contented."

Review and Assess

Thinking About the Selection

1. **(a) Recall:** Where does the speaker of the poem live? **(b) Infer:** Has Leela, the person whom the speaker addresses, ever been there? Explain how you know. **(c) Infer:** About what does Leela appear to be curious?
2. **(a) Recall:** To what does Lucy compare the appearance of the Queen? **(b) Interpret:** Why does the Queen make Lucy "feel" the full extent of London?
3. **(a) Summarize:** What problems does Lucy think the Queen has as a result of her position? **(b) Analyze:** In what way do Lucy's perceptions bring the Queen back to human size and, at the same time, make Lucy seem as if she observes life from the center of things?
4. **Apply:** How might Lucy respond to a contemporary American celebrity? Explain.
5. **Evaluate:** Is Berry's use of Jamaican dialect effective in creating a distinctive, authentic voice for Lucy? Explain.

ASSESSMENT PRACTICE: Writing Skills

Style **(For more practice, see Test Preparation Workbook, p. 63.)**

Many tests require students to recognize stylistic devices and effective language. Use the following sample item to show students how to recognize the tone of a poem. Have students read p. 1261 before answering this question.

With the stampeding hiss and scurry of green lemmings, / midsummer's leaves race to extinction like the roar/ of a Brixton riot tunneled by water hoses; / they seethe towards autumn's fire . . .

The tone in this passage can *best* be described as one of —

A hopelessness
B urgency
C acceptance
D humor

Point out the violent images in this passage: "stampeding hiss," "the roar of a Brixton riot." By considering the poem's diction, students should determine that the correct answer is *B*.

Review and Assess

Literary Analysis

Theme and Context

1. Explain how the **context** of *Midsummer*—a clash between cultures—ignites a conflict in the poet's mind.
2. The excerpt from *Omeros* tells in epic style how blacks, including Walcott's ancestors, arrived in the Caribbean. In what way is Walcott's **theme** a response to a context?
3. (a) What general concern about social roles does Berry explore in "From Lucy: Englan' Lady"? (b) Explain how his choice of speaker makes his presentation of this theme effective.

Comparing Literary Works

4. (a) Compare Walcott's use of **allusions** in *Midsummer* and *Omeros* with Berry's in "From Lucy." Use a chart like the one shown.

Allusion	Literary/ Scholarly?	News/ Popular Trends?	Folksy?
"'Bird sing sweet for its nest.'"			Yes: It is a country proverb.

(b) What do the poets' use of allusions suggest about their respective places in the British literary tradition?

5. (a) Compare the **political critiques** implied by Walcott's choice of speaker in *Omeros* and by Berry's choice of speaker in "From Lucy." (b) Judging by *Midsummer* and "From Lucy," how would each poet answer the question, Who owns English literature?

Reading Strategy

Applying Background Information

6. Walcott expresses the conflict of a divided heritage in *Midsummer*. How does he deal with that heritage in the excerpt from *Omeros*?
7. How does Berry's background and his residence in London help explain the word choice and subject matter of "From Lucy"?

Extend Understanding

8. **Cultural Connection:** Do you think the media exclude speakers who, like those in Berry's and Walcott's poems, offer a fresh, alternative perspective on events? Explain.

Quick Review

A **theme** is the central issue raised by a literary work.

A theme can be better understood by appreciating its **context,** the historical moment in which it originates.

Allusions are brief references without explanation to people, events, and other literary works.

A **political critique of art** is the examination of the historical and political implications of a work of art.

To **apply background information** about a literary work, consider its author or its context in order to understand it.

Take It to the Net

www.phschool.com

Take the interactive self-test online to check your understanding of these selections.

Answers for p. 1267

Review and Assess

1. As a beneficiary of Britain's literary admiration, Walcott feels disloyal to his countrymen in light of the Brixton riots.
2. Walcott's theme responds to the immediate context of a black waiter bringing a bill in "some stone-white hotel."
3. **(a)** Berry suggests that social roles like the queen's mask emotional realities. **(b)** By choosing a poor immigrant to describe London and the queen to a friend and confidant back home, Berry brings the queen's possible problems "down to Earth."
4. **(a)** Possible response: Walcott's allusion ". . . like Boer cattle under Tory whips that drag every wagon nearer to apartheid" is historical and scholarly. Berry's allusion to a "space touris' / on earth" is to popular literature (science fiction) and so sounds folksy when applied to the queen. **(b)** Walcott's literary references suggest that he uses the resources of the tradition fully. Berry, by contrast, uses folksy turns of phrase as an alternative to traditional allusions, challenging the ability of the tradition to represent certain experiences or perspectives.
5. **(a)** Walcott's choice of a griot as speaker in *Omeros* and Berry's choice of a West Indian immigrant in "From Lucy" suggest that both poets believe that the traditional resources of English-language literature are not sufficient to express certain viewpoints or tell certain stories. In this way, both suggest that traditional English-language literature excludes certain perspectives or is dominated by white perspectives. **(b)** Walcott might say that any writer can own English literature provided he or she reworks its traditions to fit his or her own experiences, as Walcott has done. Berry might say that any reader can own English literature, as long as he or she can read past standard opinions of that literature to see the human truth it expresses (as Lucy sees past standard ideas of the queen to find a human truth).

continued

Answers continued

6. In *Omeros,* Walcott uses a traditional African speaker to account for how blacks such as Walcott's ancestors arrived in the Caribbean.
7. Berry himself grew up in poverty in a small village in Jamaica. In 1948 he left for England, where he enjoyed the excitement and personal freedom of urban London. These factors are reflected in the speaker's voice in "From Lucy."
8. Students may respond that some media exclude speakers who offer a fresh perspective, while others regularly spotlight such participants.

EXTEND

Answers for p. 1268

❶ Vocabulary Development

Word Analysis

1. Conduct— to direct the course of; to manage or control; to lead or guide
2. Deduce—to lead to a conclusion or insight
3. Ductile—easily molded or shaped, easily led

Spelling Strategy

1. stack, realistic
2. frantic, park

Concept Development: Synonyms

1. c
2. e
3. d
4. c

❷ Grammar and Style

1. effect
2. affected
3. effected
4. affected
5. affect

Writing Application

Sample response: Walcott's background has affected the kind of poetry he writes.

The kind praises of the British critics affected his first views of British society as a whole. The Brixton riots, however, had the effect of making him revise his initial impressions.

Integrate Language Skills

❶ Vocabulary Development Lesson

Word Analysis: Latin Root *-duc-*

The word *inducted,* which means "led into a group," is formed from the Latin root *-duc-*, meaning "to lead." The root also appears in many scientific terms. Explain how this root contributes to the definition of each of the following words.

1. conduct 2. deduce 3. ductile

Spelling Strategy

The hard final *c* sound in an adjective is usually made by the letter *c* alone, as in the word *antic*. Add the correct ending to each italicized word.

1. Your plan to complete that *sta*__ of homework in an hour is hardly *realist*__.
2. I was *frant*__ when I discovered there was no place to *par*__ at the mall.

Concept Development: Synonyms

Synonyms are pairs of words that share nearly the same meaning. In your notebook, write the letter of the word that is a synonym of the word from the vocabulary list on page 1259.

1. rancor: (a) joyfulness, (b) musicality (c) hatred, (d) frustration, (e) sweetness
2. inducted: (a) anticipated, (b) concluded, (c) lost, (d) generalized, (e) initiated
3. antic: (a) oppositional, (b) dangerous, (c) herbivorous, (d) zany, (e) disappointing
4. eclipse: (a) outburst, (b) conflagration, (c) extinction (d) omission, (e) tumult

❷ Grammar and Style Lesson

Commonly Confused Words: *affect* and *effect*

Two commonly confused words are *affect* and *effect*. Though their meanings are related, they are quite different. ***Affect*** is most often a verb meaning "to influence." It can also be a noun meaning "mood; feeling" or a verb meaning "to put on; to make a pretense of being or having." ***Effect*** is most often a noun meaning "result." It can also be a verb meaning "bring about."

Verb: How will this change affect you?

Noun: What is the effect of the change?

In most cases, you can avoid confusing these words by deciding whether you want a verb meaning "to influence" (*affect*) or a noun meaning "result" (*effect*).

Practice Choose the correct word to complete each sentence.

1. Berry's stay in Harlem had a direct (affect, effect) on his ideas about prejudice.
2. Walcott's background has (effected, affected) the kind of poetry he writes.
3. Berry's poetry has (effected, affected) changes in West Indians' outlook.
4. Was Walcott more (effected, affected) by the Brixton riot than Berry was?
5. Readers respond strongly to Lucy's kindly (effect, affect).

Writing Application Write a paragraph based on one of the sentences above, using the words *affect* and *effect* twice.

WG Prentice Hall Writing and Grammar Connection: Chapter 25, Section 2

TEACHING RESOURCES

The following resources can be used to enrich or extend the instruction for pp. 1268–1269.

Vocabulary

- **Selection Support:** Build Vocabulary, p. 289
- **Vocabulary and Spelling Practice Book,** (Use this book for skills enrichment.)

Grammar

- **Selection Support:** Grammar and Style, p. 290
- **Writing and Grammar,** Diamond Level, p. 646
- **Daily Language Practice Transparencies** ■

Writing

- **Writing and Grammar,** Diamond Level, p. 792
- **Writing and Grammar iText CD-ROM** ■

■ **BLOCK SCHEDULING:** Resources marked with this symbol provide varied instruction during 90-minute blocks.

❸ Writing Lesson

Script for the Multimedia Presentation of a Poem

In their poems, Walcott and Berry conjure up vivid scenes and lively speakers. Plan a multimedia presentation of one of their poems. Prepare a script describing the audiovisual aids that will bring out the imagery, rhythms, and spirit of the work.

Prewriting Choose one of the poems, and make a list of photographs, artwork, music, video clips, and sound effects that will highlight its theme and images.

Drafting Draft your script, clearly showing the line-by-line relationship between the text and the sounds and images you will use. Match strong audiovisual effects with the central ideas in the poem.

Model: Following Script Format

SPEAKER: She affec' the place
[VISUAL: video slide of bright sun in sky]
like the sun: not comin' out oft'n
[VISUAL: sky dissolves into photo of crowd]
[AUDIO: fade in sound of happy crowd cheering]
an' when it happ'n everybody's out

Bracketed directions clearly convey the timing of audiovisual effects with the reading of the poem.

Revising Make sure that the format of your script is clear and easy to follow. Adjust the script to achieve the clearest, strongest arrangement of multimedia elements.

WG *Prentice Hall Writing and Grammar Connection: Chapter 28, Section 3*

❹ Extension Activities

Listening and Speaking Prepare a **recitation** of Berry's poem, with special attention to the oral interpretation of the speaker's dialect.

- Prepare by listening to recorded examples of West Indian speech or by consulting with West Indians in your community.
- Follow Berry's own advice for reading a dialect poem: "Feel out the rhythms. . . . Then express it with your own easy natural voice."

Deliver your reading before the class.

Research and Technology With a group, prepare a **Caribbean culture festival.** Showcase the language, food, and music of Jamaica, St. Lucia, and other islands in the region. Provide informational note cards or audiotapes for the various exhibits, as well as a detailed map of the festival. **[Group Activity]**

Take It to the Net www.phschool.com

Go online for an additional research activity using the Internet.

Lesson Support for p. 1269

❸ Writing Lesson

- With students, analyze the poem to select which medium will produce the best presentation.
- Review the script format with the class.
- Tell the class to decide what audiovisual aids they will use for the presentation. Explain to students they will need to limit the amount of material.
- Divide the class into four groups. Ask group 1 to find the visuals, group 2 to obtain the music, group 3 to write the script, and group 4 to produce the presentation.
- Have the class present the material and describe their efforts.

❹ Listening and Speaking

- Divide the class into three groups. Have each group select a reader. Each reader is to read one stanza.
- The other students should comment on whether their reader has captured Berry's rhythm and meaning in their reading.

CUSTOMIZE INSTRUCTION
For Universal Access

To address different learning styles, use the following activities suggested in the **Extension Activities** booklet, p. 63.

- For Musical/Rhythmic Learners, use Activity 5.
- For Visual/Spatial Learners, use Activity 6.
- For Interpersonal and Verbal/Linguistic Learners, use Activity 7.

ASSESSMENT RESOURCES

The following resources can be used to assess students' knowledge and skills.

Selection Assessment

- **Formal Assessment,** pp. 295–297
- **Open Book Test,** pp. 186–188
- **Got It! Assessment Videotapes,** Tape 6
- **Test Bank Software**

Take It to the Net
Visit www.phschool.com for self-tests and additional questions on the selections.

PRENTICE HALL ASSESSMENT SYSTEM

- **Workbook**
- **Skill Book**
- **Transparencies**
- **CD-ROM**

A Devoted Son

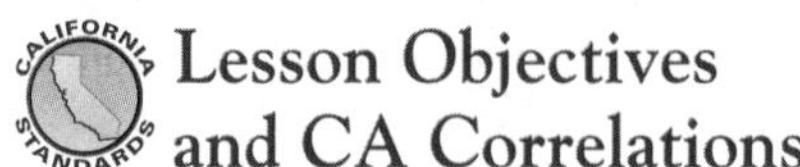

Lesson Objectives and CA Correlations

1. **To analyze and respond to literary elements**
   - Literary Analysis: Static and Dynamic Characters **R 3.1**
   - Connecting Literary Elements: Characters as Symbols **R 3.3**
2. **To read, comprehend, analyze, and critique a short story**
   - Reading Strategy: Evaluating Characters' Decisions **R 3.2**
   - Reading Check Questions
   - Review and Assess Questions
3. **To develop word analysis skills, fluency, and systematic vocabulary**
   - Vocabulary Development Lesson: Latin Root *-fil-* **R 1.1, 1.2**
4. **To understand and apply written and oral language conventions**
   - Spelling Strategy **LC 1.2**
   - Grammar and Style Lesson: Sentence Variety **LC 1.1**
5. **To understand and apply appropriate writing and research strategies**
   - Writing Lesson: Proposal for a Program for the Elderly **W 1.1, 1.3, 1.4, 1.6, 1.9**
   - Extension Activity: Social Services Report **W 1.6, 1.8**
   - Assessment Practice (ATE)
6. **To understand and apply listening and speaking strategies**
   - Extension Activity: Role Play **LS 1.7, 1.8**

STEP-BY-STEP TEACHING GUIDE	PACING GUIDE
PRETEACH	
Motivate Students and Provide Background	
Use the Motivation activity (ATE p. 1270)	5 min.
Read and discuss author and background features (SE/ATE pp. 1270, 1272) [A]	5 min.
Introduce the Concepts	
Introduce the Literary Analysis and Reading Strategy (SE/ATE p. 1271) [A]	15 min.
Pronounce the vocabulary words and read their definitions (SE p. 1271)	5 min.
TEACH	
Monitor Comprehension	
Informally monitor comprehension by circulating while students read independently or in groups [A]	30 min.
Monitor students' comprehension with the Reading Check notes (SE/ATE pp. 1273, 1277, 1279, 1281)	as students read
Develop vocabulary with Vocabulary notes (SE pp. 1273, 1276; ATE p. 1273)	as students read
Develop Understanding	
Develop students' understanding of static and dynamic characters with the Literary Analysis annotations (SE/ATE pp. 1276, 1277, 1280, 1281) [A]	5 min.
Develop students' ability to evaluate characters' decisions with the Reading Strategy annotations (SE pp. 1272, 1274, 1277, 1279, 1280; ATE pp. 1273, 1274, 1277, 1279, 1280)	5 min.
ASSESS	
Assess Mastery	
Assess students' mastery of the Reading Strategy and Literary Analysis by having them answer the Review and Assess questions (SE/ATE p. 1283)	15 min.
Use one or more of the print and media Assessment Resources (ATE p. 1285) [A]	up to 45 min.
EXTEND	
Apply Understanding	
Have students complete the Vocabulary Development Lesson and the Grammar and Style Lesson (SE p. 1284) [A]	20 min.
Apply students' knowledge of connotations using the Writing Lesson (SE/ATE p. 1285) [A]	45 min.
Apply students' understanding of the story using one or more of the Extension Activities (SE p. 1285)	20–90 min.

ACCELERATED INSTRUCTION:
Use the strategies and activities identified with an [A].

UNIVERSAL ACCESS
● = Below-Level Students
▲ = On-Level Students
■ = Above-Level Students

Time and Resource Manager

Reading Level: Average
Average Number of Instructional Days: 4

RESOURCES		
PRINT	**TRANSPARENCIES**	**TECHNOLOGY**
• **Beyond Literature,** Cross-Curricular Connection: Physical Education, p. 64 ▲ ■		• **Interest Grabber Video,** Tape 6 ● ▲ ■
• **Selection Support Workbook:** ● ▲ ■ Literary Analysis, p. 296 Reading Strategy, p. 295 Build Vocabulary, p. 293	• **Literary Analysis and Reading Transparencies,** pp. 127 and 128 ● ▲ ■	
		• **Listening to Literature** ● ▲ ■ Audiocassettes, Side 30 Audio CDs, CD 18
• **Literatura en español** ● ▲ • **Literary Analysis for Enrichment** ■		
• **Formal Assessment:** Selection Test, pp. 298–300 ● ▲ ■ • **Open Book Test,** pp. 190–192 ● ▲ ■ • PRENTICE HALL ASSESSMENT SYSTEM ● ▲ ■	• PRENTICE HALL ASSESSMENT SYSTEM ● ▲ ■ Skills Practice Answers and Explanations on Transparencies ● ▲ ■	• **Test Bank Software** ● ▲ ■ • **Got It! Assessment Videotapes,** Tape 6 ● ▲
• **Selection Support Workbook:** ● ▲ ■ Grammar and Style, p. 294 • **Writing and Grammar,** Diamond Level ● ▲ ■ • **Extension Activities,** p. 64 ● ▲ ■	• **Daily Language Practice Transparencies** ● ▲	• **Writing and Grammar iText CD-ROM** ● ▲ ■ ***Take It to the Net*** www.phschool.com

BLOCK SCHEDULING: Use one 90-minute class period to preteach the selection and have students read it. Use a second 90-minute class period to assess students' mastery of skills and have them complete one of the Extension Activities.

PRETEACH

Step-by-Step Teaching Guide for pp. 1270–1271

Motivation

Ask students what they know of care for the elderly in the United States today. Ask: To what extent are children responsible for their parents' care in their later years? What problems arise from this intergenerational interaction? Tell students that in this story a conflict arises over a son's attempts to control his elderly father's diet and medical care at the end of his life. Have students reevaluate their opinions on this subject after they have read the story.

Interest Grabber Video

As an alternative, play "'A Devoted Son': Daily Life in India" on Tape 6 to engage student interest.

❶ Background

More About the Author

Desai's work is part of a new style of writing to come out of India, which is not nearly as conservative as Indian writing has been in the past. One concern evident in her work, especially the novel *Baumgartner's Bombay*, is cultural estrangement and dividedness. Desai grew up during World War II and could see the anxiety her German mother was experiencing about her family in Germany. After the war, when she realized the Germany she had known was devasted, her mother never returned there. Desai herself did not visit Germany until she was an adult.

Prepare to Read

❶ A Devoted Son

Anita Desai (b. 1937)

Anita Desai's father was Indian and her mother, German. This unusual heritage may have contributed to her understanding of people from many different cultures. She displays this understanding in finely crafted novels and short stories about conflicts among characters of different generations and backgrounds. These works of fiction have gained her a reputation as one of the most gifted Indian novelists writing in English.

A Diverse Heritage Desai was born in the northern Indian town of Mussoorie, located at the foot of the Himalaya Mountains. She grew up in a large house in the old section of Delhi, India's capital city. "There were a great many books in the house and we were all bookworms," Desai recalls.

Choosing a Language Because of its unique heritage, Desai's family spoke three languages: Hindi, English, and German. Desai first learned English at school. When asked why she chose to write in it, Desai explained "it had a tremendous effect that the first thing you saw written and the first thing you ever read was English. It seemed to me the language of books. I just went on writing it because I always wanted to belong to this world of books."

Desai was part of a new development in Indian literature—the Indian writing in English. Writing literature is itself in tension with traditional Indian culture. Desai points out that "at one time all literature was recited rather than read and that remains the tradition in India. It is still rather a strange act to buy a book and read it, an unusual thing to do."

Early Work and Recognition A precocious writer, Desai finished her first English story when she was seven and published for the first time when she was nine. After graduating from Delhi University, the newly married Desai joined the Writers Workshop in Calcutta. In 1963, she published her first novel, *Cry the Peacock*, a portrayal of the despair of a young married woman. This novel was followed by *Bye-Bye, Blackbird* (1968), *Fire on the Mountain* (1977), and *Clear Light of Day* (1980). This last novel, a study of complex family relationships, was nominated for England's prestigious Booker Prize. The critic Victoria Glendinning said of this work, "Quiet writing, like Anita Desai's, can be more impressive than stylistic fireworks." In many works, she uses this quiet power to explore the struggle of women in Indian culture with the roles imposed on them by tradition.

Teaching and Writing After winning success as a writer, Desai also pursued a teaching career. She has taught, for example, at Cambridge University in England and at Smith College in Massachusetts. She continues to publish, examining the gulf between reality and delusion in recent novels.

The Clash of Cultures Another theme of her work, evident in *Baumgartner's Bombay* (1989) and in *Journey to Ithaca* (1995), is the contrast between Indian and modern European perspectives. *Journey to Ithaca*, for example, features a European couple who travel to India on a quest for spiritual meaning. Her 1999 novel *Fasting, Feasting*, a runner-up for the Booker Prize, relates how a brother and sister accommodate, each in a different way, the pressures of their strict and traditional parents. The clash between modern and traditional Indian values is also addressed in "A Devoted Son," which first appeared in her collection of short stories *Games at Twilight* (1978).

TEACHING RESOURCES

The following resources can be used to enrich or extend the instruction for pp. 1270–1271.

Motivation

Interest Grabber Video, Tape 6

Background

Beyond Literature, p. 64

Take It to the Net

Visit www.phschool.com for background and hotlinks for "A Devoted Son."

Literary Analysis

Literary Analysis and Reading Transparencies, Static and Dynamic Characters, p. 128

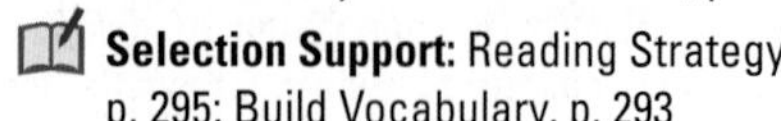

Selection Support: Reading Strategy p. 295; Build Vocabulary, p. 293

Reading

Literary Analysis and Reading Transparencies, Evaluating Characters' Decisions, p. 127

BLOCK SCHEDULING: Resources marked with this symbol provide varied instruction during 90-minute blocks.

Preview

Connecting to the Literature

The modern world, with its powerful technology and instantaneous communications, seems to make wishes come true. As "A Devoted Son" shows, though, one should be careful what one wishes for.

❷ Literary Analysis

Static and Dynamic Characters

Lifelike and believable characters in literature are often fluid—they change as the story unfolds. Some characters remain the same, however.

- **Static characters** are figures in a work who do not change. They may represent a social role or a particular attitude.
- **Dynamic characters** are figures who undergo a major change. The change may be one that they have chosen or one that is thrust upon them. Writers use such characters to develop truths about life or psychological insights.

In "A Devoted Son," only one character is dynamic. Consider whether this character is someone who embraces change or is someone who, despite preference and belief, is forced by events to change.

Connecting Literary Elements

Authors sometimes use characters as symbols to represent ideas or general attitudes. Static characters are particularly useful as symbols: Because they do not change, they can effectively represent one thing. When you read a story with many static characters, such as "A Devoted Son," consider whether the author is using these characters as symbols to represent specific cultural beliefs, traditional roles, or social trends.

❸ Reading Strategy

Evaluating Characters' Decisions

Like people in life, characters in literary works make choices. You can **evaluate characters' decisions** just as you would assess your own. When a character makes an important choice, use organized questioning to evaluate the decision and its effect on future actions. This organizer shows one approach you might apply.

Character's Decision
Rakesh decides to become a doctor.

Criteria
- Is decision right for character?
- Effect on other characters.
- Would I make a similar decision?

Evaluation

Vocabulary Development

exemplary (eg zem′ plə rē) *adj.* of that which should serve as a model (p. 1273)

filial (fil′ ē əl) *adj.* expected of a son or daughter (p. 1273)

encomiums (en kō′ mē əmz) *n.* formal expressions of great praise (p. 1273)

complaisant (kəm plā′ zənt) *adj.* agreeable; willing to please (p. 1273)

fathom (fa*th*′ əm) *v.* understand thoroughly (p. 1276)

CUSTOMIZE INSTRUCTION FOR UNIVERSAL ACCESS

For Less Proficient Readers	For English Learners	For Advanced Readers
Students may have difficulty with the many long, complicated sentences Desai uses. Read some of these passages aloud for students and help them interpret and analyze them.	Students may find much to identify with in this story of a clash between generations, in which the young embrace the modern world while older relatives cling to traditional ways. The issue of filial devotion may also be an important one for them. Involve students in discussions of these issues.	Encourage students to do their own research on different aspects of Indian society. In India, elderly parents often live with the family of one of their children. Organize students on a panel and have them discuss the potential advantages and conflicts of such an arrangement.

❷ Literary Analysis

Static and Dynamic Characters

- Tell students that as they read "A Devoted Son," they are going to be analyzing the ways in which Desai creates her characters.
- Note that one of the key ways in which writers create interest in a short story is to show a character at a moment of change or insight into his or her life. Some characters remain unchanged, however, and never examine their own assumptions and actions.

  Static characters are characters that do not change through the course of a work.

  Dynamic characters undergo a major change.
- Explain to students that authors sometimes use characters as symbols.
- Note that static characters are particularly useful as symbols because they do not change.
- Have students be on the lookout for static characters that are being used as symbols.

❸ Reading Strategy

Evaluating Characters' Decisions

- Point out to students that people are often judged by their decisions and that characters in fiction make decisions just as do people in real life. Tell students they should undertake to evaluate the decisions of the characters in the story as they read.
- Explain to students how they can use the chart to analyze characters' decisions.

Vocabulary Development

- Pronounce each vocabulary word for students, and read the definitions as a class. Have students identify any words with which they are already familiar.

 **E-Teach**

Visit E-Teach at www.phschool.com for teachers' essays on how to teach, with questions and answers.

TEACH

Step-by-Step Teaching Guide for pp. 1272–1282

CUSTOMIZE INSTRUCTION
For Bodily/Kinesthetic Learners

This story begins with an important act of filial devotion: a successful son's bowing down to touch his father's feet. As these students read, encourage them to notice how characters use body language and facial expressions to express their feelings for each other. Encourage students to choose a scene from the story to role-play. Together with a partner, have them role-play the scene for an audience of classmates, adding dialogue where necessary.

❶ About the Selection

In this ironically titled story, an Indian family sacrifices everything to send their son Rakesh to medical school. Rakesh's father is proud of his son's success and devotion—until the son begins applying his modern medical knowledge and devotion to a strict control of his aging father's diet. The father's decline in body and spirit, and his growing regret at the estrangement that a modern education has caused between his son and him, make for a poignant story with a universal theme of generational conflict.

❶ 

A Devoted Son

Anita Desai

Background

Since India won its independence from Britain in 1947, modernization has resulted in dramatic contrasts between old and new. In this story, Desai dramatizes the conflict between the traditional respect shown parents, symbolized in the custom of touching one's father's feet, with the modern education that parents ask their children to acquire.

When the results appeared in the morning papers, Rakesh scanned them barefoot and in his pajamas, at the garden gate, then went up the steps to the verandah where his father sat sipping his morning tea and bowed down to touch his feet.

"A first division, son?" his father asked, beaming, reaching for the papers.

"At the top of the list, papa," Rakesh murmured, as if awed. "First in the country."

Bedlam broke loose then. The family whooped and danced. The whole day long visitors streamed into the small yellow house at the end of the road to congratulate the parents of this *Wunderkind*,[1] to slap Rakesh on the back and fill the house and garden with the sounds and colors of a festival. There were garlands and halwa,[2] party clothes and gifts (enough fountain pens to last years, even a watch or two), nerves and temper and joy, all in a multicolored whirl of pride and great shining vistas newly opened: ❷ Rakesh was the first son in the family to receive an education, so much had been sacrificed in order to send him to school and then medical college, and at last the fruits of their sacrifice had arrived, golden and glorious.

To everyone who came to him to say "*Mubarak*, Varmaji, your son has brought you glory," the father said, "Yes, and do you know what is the first thing he did when he saw the results this morning? He came

Reading Strategy
Evaluating Characters' Decision What decision did the family make regarding Rakesh?

1. ***Wunderkind*** person who achieves remarkable success at an early age.
2. **halwa** (häl vä´) (also halva) Middle Eastern sweet confection made of sesame flour and honey.

TEACHING RESOURCES

The following resources can be used to enrich or extend the instruction for pp. 1272–1282.

Literary Analysis

Selection Support: Literary Analysis, p. 298

Reading

Listening to Literature Audiocassettes, Side 30

Listening to Literature Audio CDs, CD 18

 **BLOCK SCHEDULING:** Resources marked with this symbol provide varied instruction during 90-minute blocks.

and touched my feet. He bowed down and touched my feet." This moved many of the women in the crowd so much that they were seen to raise the ends of their saris and dab at their tears while the men reached out for the betel-leaves[3] and sweetmeats that were offered around on trays and shook their heads in wonder and approval of

3 such exemplary filial behavior. "One does not often see such behavior in sons any more," they all agreed, a little enviously perhaps. Leaving the house, some of the women said, sniffing, "At least on such an occasion they might have served pure *ghee*[4] sweets," and some of the men said, "Don't you think old Varma was giving himself airs? He needn't think we don't remember that he comes from the vegetable market himself, his father used to sell vegetables, and he has never seen the inside of a school." But there was more envy than rancor[5] in their voices and it was, of course, inevitable—not every son in that shabby little colony at the edge of the city was destined to shine as Rakesh shone, and who knew that better than the parents themselves?

exemplary (eg zem´ plə rē) *adj.* of that which should serve as a model

filial (fil´ ē əl) *adj.* expected of a son or daughter

And that was only the beginning, the first step in a great, sweeping ascent to the radiant heights of fame and fortune. The thesis he wrote for his M.D. brought Rakesh still greater glory, if only in select medical circles. He won a scholarship. He went to the USA (that was what his father learnt to call it and taught the whole family to say—not America, which was what the ignorant neighbors called it, but, with a grand familiarity, "the USA") where he pursued his career in the most prestigious of all hospitals and won encomiums from his American colleagues which were relayed to his admiring and glowing family. What was more, he came *back*, he actually returned to that small yellow house in the once-new but increasingly shabby colony, right at the end of the road where the rubbish vans tipped out their stinking contents for pigs to nose in and rag-pickers to build their shacks on, all steaming and smoking just outside the neat wire fences and well-tended gardens. To this Rakesh returned and the first thing he did on entering the house was to slip out of the embraces of his sisters and brothers and bow down and touch his father's feet.

encomiums (en kō´ mē əmz) *n.* formal expressions of great praise

As for his mother, she gloated chiefly over the strange fact that he had not married in America, had not brought home a foreign wife as all her neighbors had warned her he would, for wasn't that what all Indian boys went abroad for? Instead he agreed, almost without argument, to marry a girl she had picked out for him in her own village, the daughter of a childhood friend, a plump and uneducated girl, it was true, but so old-fashioned, so placid, so complaisant that she slipped into the household and settled in like a charm, seemingly too lazy and too good-natured to even try and make Rakesh leave home and set up independently, as any other girl might have done. What was more, she was pretty—really pretty, in a plump, pudding

complaisant (kəm plā´ zənt) *adj.* agreeable; willing to please

4 Reading Check

What has Rakesh accomplished?

---

3. **betel-leaves** leaves of a climbing evergreen shrub which are chewed in the East with betel nut parings and a little lime.
4. ***ghee*** clarified butter, often used in Indian cooking.
5. **rancor** bitter, lasting hate.

2 Reading Strategy

Evaluating Characters' Decisions (p. 1272)

- Read aloud the bracketed passage on p. 1272 to students and then ask them to rephrase the material in their own words.
- Ask students the Reading Strategy question on p. 1272: What decision did the family make regarding Rakesh?
  Answer: They decided to sacrifice everything in order to provide for his education.

Monitor Progress Ask how the family feels at the beginning of the story about their decision to make sacrifices to educate their son. Then, ask students if they think the family was doing the right thing. Have them give reasons for their answers.
Possible responses: At the beginning of the story the family feels that all of the sacrifices have been worth it, because Rakesh has brought honor and glory to them through his achievement. Some students may question the fairness of a family's sacrificing everything for the sake of one member.

3 Vocabulary Development

Latin Root *-fil-*

- Point out the word *filial* to students. Explain that the word contains the Latin root *-fil-*, meaning "son or daughter," and means "expected of a son or daughter."
- Have students suggest other words that contain this root and offer definitions of each word they suggest.
  Possible responses: Such words include *affiliate* and *affiliation.*

4 Reading Check

Answer: Rakesh has managed to gain scholarships for study abroad in the United States to complete his medical training.

CUSTOMIZE INSTRUCTION FOR UNIVERSAL ACCESS

For Less Proficient Readers	For English Learners	For Advanced Readers
Have students write an essay addressing similar conflicts between different generations in American society. They might wish to draw upon their own personal experience, or perhaps address questions regarding the challenges associated with the assimilation of immigrants from one generation to the next.	Given that the language and the ideas of this story are relatively accessible to English learners, it serves as a good opportunity for them to focus on their speaking and presentation skills. As students read the story, have them collect information and citations for an oral presentation.	Have students read the story independently at their own pace. Then, inform them that Desai has said that she is interested in discovering "the truth that is nine-tenths of the iceberg that lies submerged beneath the one-tenth visible portion we call Reality." Then, have them write an essay discussing this statement.

⑤ Reading Strategy

Evaluating Characters' Decisions

- As students continue reading the selection, have them consider what is motivating Rakesh's decisions.
- Then, ask them the Reading Strategy question on p. 1274: What seems to guide the decisions that Rakesh is making about his life?
  Possible responses: Students may say that Rakesh bases his decisions on his desire for success and his desire to please his parents. Others may see him as spineless and empty, doing everything just to fulfill his parents' expectations.

way that only gave way to fat—soft, spreading fat, like warm wax—after the birth of their first baby, a son, and then what did it matter?

⑤ For some years Rakesh worked in the city hospital, quickly rising to the top of the administrative organization, and was made a director before he left to set up his own clinic. He took his parents in his car—a new, sky-blue Ambassador with a rear window full of stickers and charms revolving on strings—to see the clinic when it was built, and the large sign-board over the door on which his name was printed in letters of red, with a row of degrees and qualifications to follow it like so many little black slaves of the regent.[6] Thereafter his fame seemed to grow just a little dimmer—or maybe it was only that everyone in town had grown accustomed to it at last—but it was also the beginning of his fortune for he now became known not only as the best but also the richest doctor in town.

However, all this was not accomplished in the wink of an eye. Naturally not. It was the achievement of a lifetime and it took up Rakesh's whole life. At the time he set up his clinic his father had grown into an old man and retired from his post at the kerosene dealer's depot at which he had worked for forty years, and his mother died

6. **regent** ruler; governor.

Reading Strategy
Evaluating Characters' Decisions What seems to guide the decisions that Rakesh makes about his life?

ENRICHMENT: Career Connection

Training for Physicians

The conflict in this story involves the sacrifices a family makes to send a son to medical school. Tell students that in the United States most students who wish to become physicians first complete four years of college, followed by four years of medical school. For the first two years, students study anatomy, physiology, pathology, and other related subjects. During the last two years students have a clinical internship, in which they work, under supervision, with patients. After graduating from medical school, most doctors then do a residency in a specialty such as emergency medicine, pediatrics, or surgery. This training may last two to seven years, during which time the physician must pass a state exam and obtain a license to practice medicine.

Invite a medical student, intern, or resident physician to speak to the class about their training and the sacrifices and rewards of their career.

soon after, giving up the ghost with a sigh that sounded positively happy, for it was her own son who ministered to her in her last illness and who sat pressing her feet at the last moment—such a son as few women had borne.

For it had to be admitted—and the most unsuccessful and most rancorous of neighbors eventually did so—that Rakesh was not only

6 ▼ **Critical Viewing**
How comfortable do you imagine it is for a man such as Rakesh or the businessman in the photograph to dwell among those less fortunate than himself? **[Speculate]**

6 ▶ **Critical Viewing**

Answer: Such people probably feel very uncomfortable, and perhaps guilty, about the contrasts between their own opportunities and comforts and those available to most other people in their society, especially if those other people are family members and childhood friends.

7 Literary Analysis

Static and Dynamic Characters

- Remind students of the difference between static and dynamic characters and ask them what hints the author gives in the indicated passage that the father may be a dynamic character.
  Answer: Varma's character is beginning to change as his health begins to deteriorate.
- Ask students the Literary Analysis question on p. 1276: In what ways is Rakesh's father changing? What events precede this change?
  Answer: His health is beginning to deteriorate, and with this he is also beginning to exhibit certain unusual and inexplicable behaviors. These changes were preceded by the death of his wife, and his retirement.

8 Critical Thinking

Analyze

- Have a volunteer read aloud the last paragraph on p. 1276 (which continues onto the next page). Ask students to describe Rakesh's actions.
- Then, ask students how Rakesh continues to show devotion to his father.
  Answer: Rakesh brings his father his tea in the man's favorite tumbler, sits on the old man's bed and reads to him, encourages him to spend his summer evenings outdoors, and even soothes him to sleep.

a devoted son and a miraculously good-natured man who contrived somehow to obey his parents and humor his wife and show concern equally for his children and his patients, but there was actually a brain inside this beautifully polished and formed body of good manners and kind nature and, in between ministering to his family and playing host to many friends and coaxing them all into feeling happy and grateful and content, he had actually trained his hands as well and emerged an excellent doctor, a really fine surgeon. How one man—and a man born to illiterate parents, his father having worked for a kerosene dealer and his mother having spent her life in a kitchen—had achieved, combined and conducted such a medley of virtues, no one could fathom, but all acknowledged his talent and skill.

fathom (fa*th*′ əm) *v.* understand thoroughly

7 It was a strange fact, however, that talent and skill, if displayed for too long, cease to dazzle. It came to pass that the most admiring of all eyes eventually faded and no longer blinked at his glory. Having retired from work and having lost his wife, the old father very quickly went to pieces, as they say. He developed so many complaints and fell ill so frequently and with such mysterious diseases that even his son could no longer make out when it was something of significance and when it was merely a peevish whim. He sat huddled on his string bed most of the day and developed an exasperating habit of stretching out suddenly and lying absolutely still, allowing the whole family to fly around him in a flap, wailing and weeping, and then suddenly sitting up, stiff and gaunt, and spitting out a big gob of betel-juice as if to mock their behavior.

Literary Analysis
Static and Dynamic Characters In what way is Rakesh's father changing? What events precede this change?

He did this once too often: there had been a big party in the house, a birthday party for the youngest son, and the celebrations had to be suddenly hushed, covered up and hustled out of the way when the daughter-in-law discovered, or thought she discovered, that the old man, stretched out from end to end of his string bed, had lost his pulse; the party broke up, dissolved, even turned into a band of mourners, when the old man sat up and the distraught daughter-in-law received a gob of red spittle right on the hem of her organza sari.[7] After that no one much cared if he sat up crosslegged on his bed, hawking and spitting, or lay down flat and turned gray as a corpse. Except, of course, for that pearl amongst pearls, his son Rakesh.

8 It was Rakesh who brought him his morning tea, not in one of the china cups from which the rest of the family drank, but in the old man's favorite brass tumbler, and sat at the edge of his bed, comfortable and relaxed with the string of his pajamas dangling out from under his fine lawn night-shirt, and discussed or, rather, read out the morning news to his father. It made no difference to him that his father made no response apart from spitting. It was Rakesh, too, who, on returning from the clinic in the evening, persuaded the old man to come out of his room, as bare and desolate as a cell, and take the

7. **organza sari** Saris are traditional garments worn by Indian women, consisting of lengths of cotton, silk, or other cloth wrapped around the waist and draped over one shoulder; organza is a sheer, stiffened fabric.

 **ENRICHMENT: Health Connection**

Dietary Issues

In this story a conflict arises over a son's attempts to control his father's diet, particularly the father's intake of fat and sugar. As societies become more affluent, people tend to consume fewer complex carbohydrates and more fats and animal proteins. In the United States, for example, about forty percent of the calories people consume come from fats and about twenty percent come from sugar. High consumption of foods containing saturated fats and cholesterol is related to an increase in heart disease.

Have some students research information about high-density lipoprotein (HDL), or "good cholesterol," and low-density lipoprotein (LDL), or "bad cholesterol," and report their findings to the class. Have other students research the low fat/ high carbohydrate "food pyramid" diet currently recommended by doctors as a healthy diet.

evening air out in the garden, beautifully arranging the pillows and bolsters on the divan in the corner of the open verandah. On summer nights he saw to it that the servants carried out the old man's bed onto the lawn and himself helped his father down the steps and onto the bed, soothing him and settling him down for a night under the stars.

All this was very gratifying for the old man. What was not so gratifying was that he even undertook to supervise his father's diet. One day when the father was really sick, having ordered his daughter-in-law to make him a dish of *soojie halwa* and eaten it with a saucerful of
9 cream, Rakesh marched into the room, not with his usual respectful step but with the confident and rather contemptuous stride of the famous doctor, and declared, "No more *halwa* for you, papa. We must be sensible, at your age. If you must have something sweet, Veena will cook you a little *kheer*,[8] that's light, just a little rice and milk. But nothing fried, nothing rich. We can't have this happening again."

The old man who had been lying stretched out on his bed, weak and feeble after a day's illness, gave a start at the very sound, the tone of these words. He opened his eyes—rather, they fell open with shock—and he stared at his son with disbelief that darkened quickly to reproach. A son who actually refused his father the food he craved? No, it was unheard of, it was incredible. But Rakesh had turned his back to him and was cleaning up the litter of bottles and packets on the medicine shelf and did not notice while Veena slipped silently out of the room with a little smirk that only the old man saw, and hated.

Halwa was only the first item to be crossed off the old man's diet.
10 One delicacy after the other went—everything fried to begin with, then everything sweet, and eventually everything, everything that the old man enjoyed.

The meals that arrived for him on the shining stainless steel tray twice a day were frugal to say the least—dry bread, boiled lentils, boiled vegetables and, if there were a bit of chicken or fish, that was boiled too. If he called for another helping—in a cracked voice that quavered theatrically—Rakesh himself would come to the door, gaze at him sadly and shake his head, saying, "Now, papa, we must be careful, we can't risk another illness, you know," and although the daughter-in-law kept tactfully out of the way, the old man could just see her smirk sliding merrily through the air. He tried to bribe his grandchildren into buying him sweets (and how he missed his wife now, that generous, indulgent and illiterate cook), whispering, "Here's fifty paise," as he stuffed the coins into a tight, hot fist. "Run down to the shop at the crossroads and buy me thirty paise worth of *jalebis*,[9] and you can spend the remaining twenty paise on yourself. Eh? Understand? Will you do that?" He got away with it once or twice but then was found out, the conspirator was scolded by his father and smacked by his mother and Rakesh came storming into the room, almost tearing his hair as he shouted through

8. ***kheer*** rice pudding traditionally served as a dessert in southern India.
9. ***jalebis*** Indian sweet made by frying a coil of batter and then soaking it in syrup.

Literary Analysis
Static and Dynamic Characters Does Rakesh's "rather contemptuous stride" show a change in his character? In what way is he still the ideal son in this scene?

Reading Strategy
Evaluating Characters' Decisions What does Rakesh seem to disregard in his decision about his father's diet? Is his choice wise? Explain.

11 
What does Rakesh change in his father's life?

9 Literary Analysis

Static and Dynamic Characters

- As students read the indicated passage, ask them again to consider Rakesh in terms of static and dynamic characters.
- Ask students the Literary Analysis question on p. 1277: Does Rakesh's "rather contemptuous stride" show a change in his character? In what way is he still the ideal son in this scene?
Possible responses: Although Rakesh is acting more assertively than in the past and seems less concerned about pleasing his father, he is still an ideal, devoted son because he wants to do everything possible to keep his father alive and healthy. He is willing to risk his father's anger in order to save his father's life.

10 Reading Strategy

Evaluating Characters' Decisions

- Have students pay particular attention to the father's reaction to his son's insistence that he change his diet.
- Ask students the Reading Strategy question on p. 1277: What does Rakesh seem to disregard in his decision about his father's diet? Is his choice wise? Explain.
Possible responses: Some students may feel Rakesh does the right thing because he is trying to keep his father alive; others may feel Rakesh makes a mistake by not allowing his father the small pleasures that mean so much to him and by alienating himself from the old man at the end of his life.

11 ✓Reading Check

Answer: Rakesh changes his father's diet, eliminating his favorite sweet and fried foods.

12 Background

Hinduism

To help explain the significance of the grazing cow in the photo on this page, tell students that over eighty percent of the Indian population practices the religion of Hinduism. Among the characteristics of Indian society traceable to Hinduism are the Indian caste system, the concepts of dharma, karma, and reincarnation, the practice of yoga, and the veneration of cows as sacred animals. For Hindus, the cow represents life because it provides for human beings in so many ways. Cows are honored and protected in Indian society, and, at one time, killing a cow was considered a capital offense.

13 ▶Critical Viewing

Answer: The billboard in English tells about computer courses that lead to a degree from an American university, which shows the appeal being made to young Indians to be modern and ambitious. The sign on the buildings advertises modern air travel in both English and Indian characters, but the Indian characters are fading. The cow is a sign of India's traditional Hindu religion, in which cows are considered sacred animals and are protected, rather than killed and eaten.

12

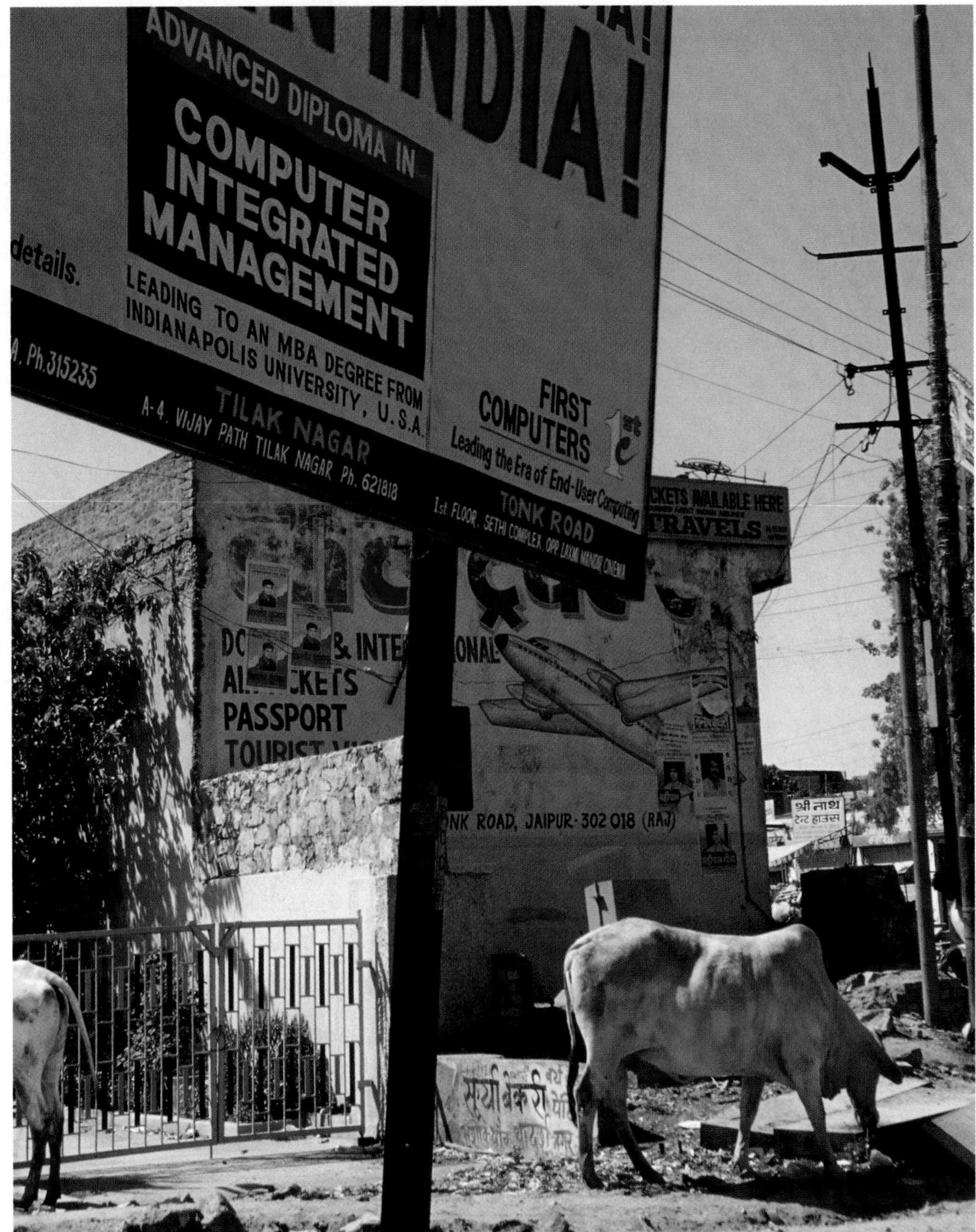

13 ▲**Critical Viewing** Identify three details in this photograph that illustrate the story's theme of ambition and the conflict between the modern and the traditional. **[Interpret]**

ENRICHMENT: Science Connection

Cholera and Typhoid Fever

Cholera, an infectious disease caused by drinking water that has been contaminated with bacteria, is widespread in India. The disease causes severe diarrhea, which leads to loss of body fluids and salts. If the fluids are not replaced promptly, the victim can lapse into a coma and die within twenty-four hours. Vaccines against the disease offer limited protections, and the best way to prevent the spread of disease in India is by cleaning up its supply of drinking water.

Typhoid fever is also caused by bacteria. It can be spread by food handlers who are carriers of the disease, one reason for requiring workers in restaurants to wash their hands. Typhoid can now be treated with antibiotics.

Have students research cholera and typhoid epidemics that have occurred in American history and find out whether any outbreaks still occur in the United States today.

compressed lips, "Now papa, are you trying to turn my little son into a liar? Quite apart from spoiling your own stomach, you are spoiling him as well—you are encouraging him to lie to his own parents. You should have heard the lies he told his mother when she saw him bringing back those *jalebis* wrapped up in filthy newspaper. I don't allow anyone in
14 my house to buy sweets in the bazaar, papa, surely you know that. There's cholera in the city, typhoid, gastroenteritis[10]—I see these cases daily in the hospital, how can I allow my own family to run such risks?" The old man sighed and lay down in the corpse position. But that worried no one any longer.

There was only one pleasure left in the old man now (his son's early morning visits and readings from the newspaper could no longer be called that) and those were visits from elderly neighbors. These were not frequent as his contemporaries were mostly as decrepit and helpless as he and few could walk the length of the road to visit him any more. Old Bhatia, next door, however, who was still spry enough to refuse, adamantly, to bathe in the tiled bathroom indoors and to insist on carrying out his brass mug and towel, in all seasons and usually at impossible hours, into the yard and bathe noisily under the garden tap, would look over the hedge to see if Varma were out on his verandah and would call to him and talk while he wrapped his *dhoti*[11] about him and dried the sparse hair on his head, shivering with enjoyable exaggeration. Of course these conversations, bawled across the hedge by two rather deaf old men conscious of having their entire households overhearing them, were not very satisfactory but Bhatia occasionally came out of his yard, walked down the bit of road and came in at Varma's gate to collapse onto the stone plinth built under the temple tree. If Rakesh was at home he would help his father down the steps into the garden and arrange him on his night bed under the tree and leave the two old men to chew betel-leaves and discuss the ills of their individual bodies with combined passion.

"At least you have a doctor in the house to look after you," sighed Bhatia, having vividly described his martyrdom to piles.

"Look after me?" cried Varma, his voice cracking like an ancient clay jar. "He—he does not even give me enough to eat."

"What?" said Bhatia, the white hairs in his ears twitching. "Doesn't give you enough to eat? Your own son?"

"My own son. If I ask him for one more piece of bread, he says no, papa, I weighed out the *ata* myself and I can't allow you to have more than two hundred grams of cereal a day. He *weighs* the food he gives me, Bhatia—he has scales to weigh it on. That is what it has come to."

"Never," murmured Bhatia in disbelief. "Is it possible, even in this evil age, for a son to refuse his father food?"

---

10. **cholera . . . typhoid, gastroenteritis** dangerous infectious diseases causing fever or intestinal problems.
11. ***dhoti*** cloth worn by male Hindus, the ends being passed through the legs and tucked in at the waist.

Reading Strategy
Evaluating Characters' Decisions What problems does Rakesh's decision to forbid his father sweets cause?

15 **Reading Check**
What does Varma complain about to his friend?

14 Reading Strategy
Evaluating Characters' Decisions

- Ask students if Rakesh's decision banning sweets from the bazaar is based on logic or emotion.
  Answer: Though his desire to protect his family involves some emotion, Rakesh's decision is based mainly on logic: Buying sweets from the bazaar carries some risk of diseases such as cholera, so there will be no sweets bought, no matter how happy they make his father.
- Then, ask students the Reading Strategy question on p. 1279: What problems does Rakesh's decision to forbid his father sweets cause?
  Answer: Rakesh's severe control of Varma's diet causes the relationship between father and son to deteriorate: Visits from Rakesh are no longer a pleasure for Varma.

15 Reading Check

Answer: Varma complains that his son does not give him enough to eat.

CUSTOMIZE INSTRUCTION FOR UNIVERSAL ACCESS

For Less Proficient Readers	For Gifted/Talented Students
Have students write a character sketch of Rakesh or his father at this point in the story. Have them include information about the appearance, opinions, and habits of the character.	Have students choose a scene from the story. Then have them role-play the scene for an audience of classmates, adding dialogue where necessary.

16 Literary Analysis

Static and Dynamic Characters

- Remind students of the difference between static and dynamic characters. Have them provide examples of each type from selections they have read in previous units.
- Then, ask them the Literary Analysis question on p. 1280: The narrator says Rakesh's character "now underwent a curious sea change." Which character has really changed and which one has stayed the same?
  Answer: The narrator's words are ironic, because in fact it is Varma who has changed, not only in terms of his health, but also psychologically, in his changed perception of his son.

17 Reading Strategy

Evaluating Characters' Decisions

- Ask students how Varma's evaluation of his decision to educate his son has changed. Then, ask students if their own evaluation of the decision has changed from the beginning of the story. Have them give reasons for their answer.
  Possible responses: Varma now regrets the decision to educate his son, because he believes his son has become heartlessly efficient and tyrannical as a result of his medical training and success. Students' own evaluations of the decision will vary.
- Then, ask the Reading Strategy question on p. 1280: What new view does this paragraph give of the family's decision to send Rakesh to medical school?
  Possible responses: Students may respond that at this point we see the purely clinical side of Rakesh's medical training outweighing the human side of his relationship with his father.

"Let me tell you," Varma whispered eagerly. "Today the family was having fried fish—I could smell it. I called to my daughter-in-law to bring me a piece. She came to the door and said no. . . ."

"Said no?" It was Bhatia's voice that cracked. A *drongo*[12] shot out of the tree and sped away. *"No?"*

"No, she said no, Rakesh has ordered her to give me nothing fried. No butter, he says, no oil. . . ."

16 "No butter? No oil? How does he expect his father to live?"

Old Varma nodded with melancholy triumph. "That is how he treats me—after I have brought him up, given him an education, made him a great doctor. Great doctor! This is the way great doctors treat their fathers, Bhatia," for the son's sterling personality and character now underwent a curious sea change. Outwardly all might be the same but the interpretation had altered: his masterly efficiency was nothing but cold heartlessness, his authority was only tyranny in disguise.

Literary Analysis
Static and Dynamic Characters The narrator says Rakesh's character "now underwent a curious sea change." Which character has really changed and which one has stayed the same?

17 There was cold comfort in complaining to neighbors and, on such a miserable diet, Varma found himself slipping, weakening and soon becoming a genuinely sick man. Powders and pills and mixtures were not only brought in when dealing with a crisis like an upset stomach but became a regular part of his diet—became his diet, complained Varma, supplanting the natural foods he craved. There were pills to regulate his bowel movements, pills to bring down his blood pressure, pills to deal with his arthritis and, eventually, pills to keep his heart beating. In between there were panicky rushes to the hospital, some humiliating experience with the stomach pump and enema, which left him frightened and helpless. He cried easily, shriveling up on his bed, but if he complained of a pain or even a vague, gray fear in the night, Rakesh would simply open another bottle of pills and force him to take one. "I have my duty to you papa," he said when his father begged to be let off.

Reading Strategy
Evaluating Characters' Decisions What new view does this paragraph give of the family's decision to send Rakesh to medical school?

"Let me be," Varma begged, turning his face away from the pills on the outstretched hand. "Let me die. It would be better. I do not want to live only to eat your medicines."

"Papa, be reasonable."

"I leave that to you," the father cried with sudden spirit. "Leave me alone, let me die now, I cannot live like this."

"Lying all day on his pillows, fed every few hours by his daughter-in-law's own hand, visited by every member of his family daily—and then he says he does not want to live 'like this,'" Rakesh was heard to say, laughing, to someone outside the door.

"Deprived of food," screamed the old man on the bed, "his wishes ignored, taunted by his daughter-in-law, laughed at by his grandchildren—*that* is how I live." But he was very old and weak and all anyone heard was an incoherent croak, some expressive grunts and cries of genuine pain. Only once, when old Bhatia had come to see him and they sat together under the temple tree, they heard him cry, "God is calling me—and they won't let me go."

---

12. *drongo* black bird with a long forked tail.

The quantities of vitamins and tonics he was made to take were not altogether useless. They kept him alive and even gave him a kind of strength that made him hang on long after he ceased to wish to hang on. It was as though he were straining at a rope, trying to break it, and it would not break, it was still strong. He only hurt himself, trying.

In the evening, that summer, the servants would come into his cell, grip his bed, one at each end, and carry it out to the verandah, there sitting it down with a thump that jarred every tooth in his head. In answer to his agonized complaints they said the doctor sahib had told them he must take the evening air and the evening air they would make him take—thump. Then Veena, that smiling, hypocritical pudding in a rustling sari, would appear and pile up the pillows under his head till he was propped up stiffly into a sitting position that made his head swim and his back ache.

"Let me lie down," he begged. "I can't sit up any more."

"Try, papa, Rakesh said you can if you try," she said, and drifted away to the other end of the verandah where her transistor radio vibrated to the lovesick tunes from the cinema that she listened to all day.

So there he sat, like some stiff corpse, terrified, gazing out on the lawn where his grandsons played cricket,[13] in danger of getting one of their hard-spun balls in his eye, and at the gate that opened onto the dusty and rubbish-heaped lane but still bore, proudly, a newly touched-up signboard that bore his son's name and qualifications, his own name having vanished from the gate long ago.

At last the sky-blue Ambassador arrived, the cricket game broke up in haste, the car drove in smartly and the doctor, the great doctor, all in white, stepped out. Someone ran up to take his bag from him, others to escort him up the steps. "Will you have tea?" his wife called,
18 turning down the transistor set. "Or a Coca-Cola? Shall I fry you some *samosas?*"[14] But he did not reply or even glance in her direction. Ever a devoted son, he went first to the corner where his father sat gazing, stricken, at some undefined spot in the dusty yellow air that swam before him. He did not turn his head to look at his son. But he stopped gobbling air with his uncontrolled lips and set his jaw as hard as a sick and very old man could set it.

"Papa," his son said, tenderly, sitting down on the edge of the bed and reaching out to press his feet.

Old Varma tucked his feet under him, out of the way, and continued to gaze stubbornly into the yellow air of the summer evening.

"Papa, I'm home."

Varma's hand jerked suddenly, in a sharp, derisive movement, but he did not speak.

"How are you feeling, papa?"

Literary Analysis
Static and Dynamic Characters Compare the father's character at the end of the story with that of the betel-juice spitter of earlier scenes.

 **Reading Check**
How does Varma respond to his son's treatment?

13. **cricket** open-air game played between two teams and utilizing a ball, bats, and wicket.
14. ***samosas*** triangular pastries fried in clarified butter or oil, containing spiced vegetables or meat.

18 Literary Analysis

Static and Dynamic Characters

- Have students offer a brief evaluation of the character of the betel-juice spitter from earlier in the story.
  Answer: He is peevish and irrational, using childish ploys to get attention.
- Then, ask students the Literary Analysis question on p. 1281: Compare the father's character at the end of the story with that of the betel-juice spitter of earlier scenes.
  Possible responses: After his initial sulks and irritable posing, he has now given up and truly withdrawn, which gives him more dignity. He now seems victimized by the rest of the family, and the reader feels sorry for him.

19 Reading Check

Answer: Varma resents his son's treatment of him, so he withdraws from Rakesh and all the other members of his family. His withdrawal from Rakesh is marked symbolically by his pulling his feet back to frustrate his son's attempt to demonstrate his "devotion."

Then Varma turned and looked at his son. His face was so out of control and all in pieces, that the multitude of expressions that crossed it could not make up a whole and convey to the famous man exactly what his father thought of him, his skill, his art.

"I'm dying," he croaked. "Let me die, I tell you."

"Papa, you're joking," his son smiled at him, lovingly. "I've brought you a new tonic to make you feel better. You must take it, it will make you feel stronger again. Here it is. Promise me you will take it regularly, papa."

Varma's mouth worked as hard as though he still had a gob of betel in it (his supply of betel had been cut off years ago). Then he spat out some words, as sharp and bitter as poison, into his son's face. "Keep your tonic—I want none—I want none—I won't take any more of—of your medicines. None. Never," and he swept the bottle out of his son's hand with a wave of his own, suddenly grand, suddenly effective.

His son jumped, for the bottle was smashed and thick brown syrup had splashed up, staining his white trousers. His wife let out a cry and came running. All around the old man was hubbub once again, noise, attention.

He gave one push to the pillows at his back and dislodged them so he could sink down on his back, quite flat again. He closed his eyes and pointed his chin at the ceiling, like some dire prophet, groaning, "God is calling me—now let me go."

Review and Assess

Thinking About the Selection

1. **Respond:** At the end of the story, with whom do you sympathize more—Rakesh or his father, Varma? Explain.
2. (a) **Recall:** What is the first thing Rakesh does when he sees his excellent exam results? (b) **Infer:** What values does Rakesh's behavior reflect?
3. (a) **Recall:** Name three things about which Rakesh and Varma come to disagree. (b) **Interpret:** How do these disagreements reflect the central conflict of the story?
4. (a) **Analyze:** Is the central conflict a struggle between two traditions or between a tradition and itself? Explain. (b) **Distinguish:** In what ways is this conflict specifically Indian and in what ways is it universal?
5. (a) **Evaluate:** Do you think Rakesh's behavior is truly devoted? Explain. (b) **Generalize:** What does this story suggest about the relationship between devotion and compassion?
6. **Make a Judgment:** Drawing on the story, explain how you think adult children should care for their parents.

ASSESS

Answers for p. 1282

Review and Assess

1. Many students may sympathize with the father because he is in such a weak, pitiable condition.
2. **(a)** Rakesh bowed down to touch his father's feet. **(b)** Rakesh's behavior reflects traditional values.
3. **(a)** Rakesh and Varma disagree about Varma's diet, whether Varma should be taken outside when he prefers to stay indoors, and whether or not Varma can lie down during the daytime. **(b)** These disagreements reflect the central conflict, because in order to adhere to his professional ethos, Rakesh ignores the traditional idea that he should respect his father's autonomy.
4. **(a)** Students may respond that the conflict lies between the Indian tradition of caring for one's parents and the medical tradition of caring for one's patients. It's the same traditional concept in both cases, but the Indian version acknowledges our emotional needs, and the medical version, at least as practiced by Rakesh, does not. **(b)** The conflict is specifically Indian in that Varma wants to eat a traditional diet. The generational conflict is universal.
5. **(a)** Some students may respond that Rakesh's behavior seems truly devoted. He cares for his father's health and provides what companionship he can. Others may say that Rakesh's medical training blinds him to his father's misery. **(b)** Students may respond that true devotion calls for a deep awareness of a person's suffering, coupled with the wish to relieve it.
6. The story clearly establishes that both devotion and compassion are called for in caring for parents.

ASSESSMENT PRACTICE: Writing Skills

Strategy (For more practice, see Test Preparation Workbook, p. 64.)

Many tests require students to apply revision strategies to a given passage. Use the following sample item to help students determine which sentence best fits in a given location.

The old man who had been lying on his bed, weak and feeble after a day's illness, gave a start at the sound, the tone of these words. He opened his eyes—rather, they fell open with shock—and he stared at his son with disbelief that darkened to reproach.

Which sentence would best be placed after the first sentence?

A It was almost eight o'clock in the evening.
B In the other room, children were arguing.
C The muscles of his entire body jerked, as if he had been struck by lightning.
D He thought he might have malaria.

The main idea of the passage is the old father's shock at his son's tone and words. Students should determine that the correct answer is *C*.

Review and Assess

Literary Analysis

Static and Dynamic Characters

1. Are Rakesh's mother and wife **static** or **dynamic characters**? Explain your classifications.
2. By the end of the story, what new perspective has Varma developed on his "devoted son"?
3. Compare Rakesh and Varma at the beginning, middle, and end the story. Which of the two is dynamic? Explain.
4. How does Desai use static and dynamic characters to reflect the fate of traditional beliefs in the modern world?

Connecting Literary Elements

5. Which character in the story most clearly symbolizes traditional roles in India? Why?
6. Use a chart like the one below to interpret Rakesh's actions.

7. (a) What is the effect of Rakesh's actions? (b) Draw a conclusion about what Rakesh symbolizes.
8. Are symbolic characters the same as stereotypes, depictions representing an entire group by a few exaggerated characteristics? Explain.

Reading Strategy

Evaluating Characters' Decisions

9. **Evaluate** Rakesh's decisions concerning his father's diet. Consider Rakesh's motives, the effect of his decisions on his father, and your own ideas of what is reasonable.
10. (a) Why does the family decide to make sacrifices for Rakesh's education? (b) Was this decision unwise? Explain.

Extend Understanding

11. **Cultural Connection:** Judging from the story, what attitudes toward the elderly prevail in India? Explain.

Quick Review

A **static character** is a figure in a literary work who does not change.

A **dynamic character** is a figure who undergoes a significant change.

To **evaluate a characters' decision,** analyze why it was made, determine its effects, and assess whether or not it was effective or wise.

 ***Take It to the Net***

www.phschool.com

Take the interactive self-test online to check your understanding of the selection.

Lesson Support for p. 1283

Review and Assess

1. Rakesh's mother and wife are static characters. They do not change in the course of the story.
2. By the end of the story, Varma regards Rakesh as logical, cold-hearted, even tyrannical.
3. In the beginning of the story, both Rakesh and Varma are traditional. However, by the middle, while Varma remains traditional, Rakesh is a combination of traditional and modern, owing to his education. By the end, Varma is hostile toward his son. Rakesh is now more modern than traditional.
4. Students may respond that Desai shows how traditional ideas of success promote westernization while Western ideals distort tradition ("devotion" becomes cold and disrespectful when filtered through Western ideas).
5. While Rakesh's mother and wife are traditional characters, they are peripheral characters in the story. Varma's character most clearly symbolizes traditional roles in India, because he does not adapt his views and habits until the very end of his life.
6. Possible response: Rakesh's going to medical school fits traditional ideals, while his regulating his father's diet fits modern ideals.
7. **(a)** Rakesh's actions as a young doctor returning to India bring pride and joy to his family. His actions as he cares for his aging father alienate him from his father and from India's social customs. **(b)** Students may reply that Rakesh symbolizes the struggle to grow with scientific advances without losing what is good in traditional values.
8. Possible response: Like a stereotype, a symbolic character may be created from exaggerated generalized characteristics. A symbolic character is used to show a truth about people's motives and conflicts. A stereotype, by contrast, is used to degrade people.

continued

Answers continued

9. In their responses, students should rank the relative importance they place on the following: Rakesh's father's health, his emotional well-being, and Rakesh's traditional obligation to his father.
10. **(a)** Rakesh's parents were proud people, who loved their son. **(b)** Some students may feel this was the right thing to do. Other students may conclude that it led to too much unhappiness.
11. Judging from the story, Indians believe the elderly should be treated according to their wishes.

EXTEND

Answers for p. 1284

❶ Vocabulary Development

Word Analysis

1. filiation—the condition or fact of being the child of a certain parent
2. affiliate—member; connected group (the "son" or "daughter" of a "parent" organization)
3. unaffiliated—not associated with a group (of a "son" or "daughter" without "parents")

Spelling Strategy

1. aquariums, aquaria
2. radiuses, radii
3. syllabuses, syllabi

Fluency: Context

1. encomiums
2. filial
3. exemplary
4. fathom
5. complaisant

❷ Grammar and Style

Sample answers:

1. Bedlam—whooping, dancing, an endless stream of visitors crowding into the house—broke loose then.
2. Rakesh's colleagues gave him kudos for his thesis.
3. To have graduated with top honors and then to return home to found a clinic was the achievement of a lifetime.
4. In the traditional Indian view, it was unthinkable that a son would refuse to provide his father with the food he craved.
5. Outwardly nothing had changed. The interpretation, however, had. Rakesh's authority was just tyranny.

Writing Application

Sample response: Rakesh's decision to go to medical school, to achieve great honor while there, and then to return to his humble town to set up practice filled his family with pride and their neighbors with envy and respect. Rakesh's hard-earned credentials did not pose a conflict until his father became elderly.

Integrate Language Skills

❶ Vocabulary Development Lesson

Word Analysis: Latin Root *-fil-*

The word *filial,* meaning "suitable to or due from a son or daughter," contains the Latin root *-fil-*, meaning "son or daughter." Explain how the root helps define each of these words.

1. filiation 2. affiliate 3. unaffiliated

Spelling Strategy

Nouns that end in *-um* and *-us* usually have Latin roots. In addition to regular plurals formed by adding *s* or *es,* these nouns have classical plurals in which *um* becomes *a* and *us* becomes *i*. For example, *encomium* becomes *encomia,* and *focus* becomes *foci*. In formal or technical contexts, the classical plural may be preferred. Give the two plurals for each of these nouns.

1. aquarium 2. radius 3. syllabus

Fluency: Context

Write the word from the vocabulary list on page 1271 that best fits in each sentence. Use the context suggested by the sentence to help you choose the correct word.

1. Rakesh won __?__ for his superior talents.
2. The faithful son felt that he had fulfilled his __?__ obligations.
3. Most of the neighbors considered Rakesh a(n) __?__ son.
4. Varma could not __?__ the change in his relationship with Rakesh.
5. Despite the effects of his actions, Rakesh could be described as __?__.

❷ Grammar and Style Lesson

Sentence Variety

Desai uses **sentence variety**—sentences of different lengths—to heighten drama and reinforce meaning. In the example, two short simple sentences are followed by a long simple sentence.

Example: Bedlam broke loose then. The family whooped and danced. The whole day long visitors streamed into the small yellow house at the end of the road to congratulate the parents of this *Wunderkind,* to slap Rakesh on the back and fill the house and garden with the sounds and colors of a festival.

In the example, the short sentences convey the suddenness of the eruption. The long sentence suggests a long day in which one conversation flows into another.

Practice Rewrite each item below, revising its length. Add details or break single sentences into parts, as necessary.

1. Bedlam broke loose then.
2. The thesis he wrote for his M.D. brought Rakesh still greater glory, if only in select medical circles.
3. It was the achievement of a lifetime. . . .
4. A son who actually refused his father the food he craved?
5. Outwardly all might be the same but the interpretation had altered: . . . his authority was only tyranny in disguise.

Writing Application Using varied sentences, write a paragraph evaluating Rakesh's decisions.

WG *Prentice Hall Writing and Grammar Connection: Chapter 19, Section 4*

TEACHING RESOURCES

The following resources can be used to enrich or extend the instructions for pp. 1284–1285.

Vocabulary

- **Selection Support:** Build Vocabulary, p. 293
- **Vocabulary and Spelling Practice Book,** (Use this book for skills enrichment.)

Grammar

- **Selection Support:** Grammar and Style, p. 294
- **Writing and Grammar,** Diamond Level, p. 468
- **Daily Language Practice Transparencies** ■

Writing

- **Writing and Grammar,** Diamond Level, p. 133
- **Writing and Grammar iText CD-ROM** ■

■ **BLOCK SCHEDULING:** Resources marked with this symbol provide varied instruction during 90-minute blocks.

❸ Writing Lesson

Proposal for a Program for the Elderly

As Anita Desai's story shows, "care" for the elderly may not always contribute to their happiness. Review the story for ways in which Rakesh fails to address his father's deepest needs. Then, write an illustrated proposal advocating a program in which students help elders while avoiding the mistakes of Rakesh's approach.

Prewriting Brainstorm with a group to establish the details of your program. For example, you might establish structured visits to seniors that include socializing and conducting oral-history interviews. Choose effective images to illustrate your proposal.

Drafting State the objectives of your program clearly, using active verbs with positive associations, like *broaden*, *teach*, and *serve*. Arrange images and text for the best effect.

Revising Exchange papers with a classmate, and review each other's proposals. Find and replace words or images that sour your positive tone.

Model: Revising to Improve Persuasive Impact

The factor that ~~differentiates~~ *puts* this program ~~from~~ *miles ahead of* others is the input of the elderly themselves.

More active, forceful phrasing enhances the persuasive effect of this sentence.

WG Prentice Hall Writing and Grammar Connection: Chapter 7, Section 4

❹ Extension Activities

Listening and Speaking Choose a scene from the story. With a partner, perform a **role play** of the scene. As you prepare, follow these performance tips:

- Practice improvising dialogue to add spontaneity to your role play.
- Explore some ways to extend the scene beyond the story.
- Write a brief narrated introduction to set the scene.

After rehearsing, perform your role play for classmates. **[Group Activity]**

Research and Technology Write a **social services report** comparing how India and the United States provide for their elderly. Use library and Internet reference sources to collect current data and reports. Based on your comparisons, draw a conclusion about needed improvements in both systems. Present your findings to the class, using graphs to illustrate your comparative statistics.

www.phschool.com

Go online for an additional research activity using the Internet.

❸ Writing Lesson

- Tell the students to develop an action plan they could implement to help seniors in their community. Tell them to state two or three major objectives for their program.
- Explain that associations that words have beyond their dictionary meaning, their connotations, create an emotional "music." Point out that properly phrased, the emotional content will help them sell their proposals.
- Tell the students that as they write their proposals they should be sure the emotional music of their words supports their message.

❹ Listening and Speaking

- Divide the class into three groups. Assign the beginning of the story to the first group, the middle to the second group, and the end of the story to the third group.
- Have each group write dialogue and extended activities for their part of the story.
- Tell the students to write the introduction for the part of the story that they will perform.

CUSTOMIZE INSTRUCTION For Universal Access

To address different learning styles, use the following activities suggested in the Extension Activities booklet, p. 64.

- For Intrapersonal Learners, use Activity 5.
- For Musical/Rhythmic Learners, use Activity 6.
- For Visual/Spatial and Interpersonal Learners, use Activity 7.

ASSESSMENT RESOURCES

The following resources can be used to assess students' knowledge and skills.

Selection Assessment

- **Formal Assessment,** pp. 298–300
- **Open Book Test,** pp. 189–191
- **Got It! Assessment Videotapes,** Tape 6
- **Test Bank Software**

Visit www.phschool.com for self-tests and additional questions on the selections.

Skill Book

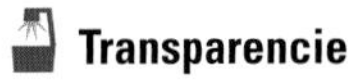

CD-ROM

E-Teach

Visit E-Teach at www.phschool.com for teachers' essays on how to teach, with questions and answers.

from We'll Never Conquer Space

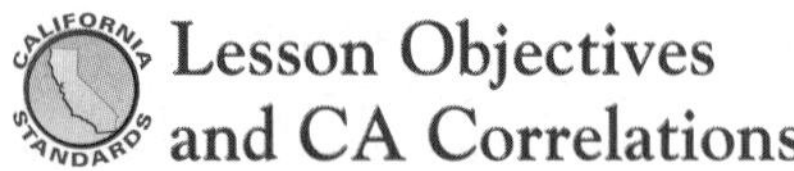

Lesson Objectives and CA Correlations

1. **To analyze and respond to literary elements**
   - Literary Analysis: Prophetic Essay **R 3.1**
   - Connecting Literary Elements: Analogies **R 1.3**
2. **To read, comprehend, analyze, and critique nonfiction**
   - Reading Strategy: Challenging the Text **R 2.6**
   - Reading Check Questions
   - Review and Assess Questions
3. **To develop word analysis skills, fluency, and systematic vocabulary**
   - Vocabulary Development Lesson: Latin Suffixes *-ible* and *-able* **R 1.1, 1.2**
4. **To understand and apply written and oral language conventions**
   - Spelling Strategy **LC 1.2**
   - Grammar and Style Lesson: Linking Verbs and Subject Complements **LC 1.1**
5. **To understand and apply appropriate writing and research strategies**
   - Writing Lesson: Analysis of an Argument **W 1.1, 1.9, 2.2**
   - Extension Activity: Museum Exhibit **W 1.6**
   - Assessment Practice (ATE)
6. **To understand and apply listening and speaking strategies**
   - Extension Activity: Panel Discussion **LS 1.8**

STEP-BY-STEP TEACHING GUIDE	PACING GUIDE
PRETEACH	
Motivate Students and Provide Background	
Use the Motivation activity (ATE p. 1286)	5 min.
Read and discuss author and background features (SE/ATE pp. 1286, 1288, 1293) [A]	5 min.
Introduce the Concepts	
Introduce the Literary Analysis and Reading Strategy (SE/ATE p. 1287) [A]	15 min.
Pronounce the vocabulary words and read their definitions (SE p. 1287)	5 min.
TEACH	
Monitor Comprehension	
Informally monitor comprehension by circulating while students read independently or in groups [A]	25 min.
Monitor students' comprehension with the Reading Check notes (SE/ATE pp. 1289, 1291, 1293)	as students read
Develop vocabulary with Vocabulary notes (SE pp. 1288, 1289, 1290, 1291, 1292, 1294; ATE p. 1289)	as students read
Develop Understanding	
Develop students' understanding of prophetic essay with the Literary Analysis annotations (SE/ATE p. 1290) [A]	5 min.
Develop students' ability to challenge the text with the Reading Strategy annotations (SE pp. 1289, 1290, 1294; ATE pp. 1289, 1290, 1293)	5 min.
ASSESS	
Assess Mastery	
Assess students' mastery of the Reading Strategy and Literary Analysis by having them answer the Review and Assess questions (SE/ATE p. 1295)	15 min.
Use one or more of the print and media Assessment Resources (ATE p. 1297) [A]	up to 45 min.
EXTEND	
Apply Understanding	
Have students complete the Vocabulary Development Lesson and the Grammar and Style Lesson (SE p. 1296) [A]	20 min.
Apply students' skill in analyzing a writer's assumptions using the Writing Lesson (SE/ATE p. 1297) [A]	45 min.
Apply students' understanding using one or more of the Extension Activities (SE p. 1297)	20–90 min.

ACCELERATED INSTRUCTION:
Use the strategies and activities identified with an [A].

UNIVERSAL ACCESS
● = Below-Level Students
▲ = On-Level Students
■ = Above-Level Students

Time and Resource Manager

Reading Level: Average
Average Number of Instructional Days: 4

RESOURCES		
PRINT	**TRANSPARENCIES**	**TECHNOLOGY**
• **Beyond Literature,** Cross-Curricular Connection: Science, p. 65 ▲ ■		• **Interest Grabber Video,** Tape 6 ● ▲ ■
• **Selection Support Workbook:** ● ▲ ■ Literary Analysis, p. 300 Reading Strategy, p. 299 Build Vocabulary, p. 297	• **Literary Analysis and Reading Transparencies,** pp. 129 and 130 ● ▲ ■	
		• **Listening to Literature** ● ▲ ■ Audiocassettes, Side 30 Audio CDs, CD 18
• **Literatura en español** ● ▲ • **Literary Analysis for Enrichment** ■		
• **Formal Assessment:** Selection Test, pp. 301–303 ● ▲ ■ • **Open Book Test,** pp. 192–194 ● ▲ ■ • PRENTICE HALL ASSESSMENT SYSTEM ● ▲ ■	• PRENTICE HALL ASSESSMENT SYSTEM ● ▲ ■ Skills Practice Answers and Explanations on Transparencies ● ▲ ■	• **Test Bank Software** ● ▲ ■ • **Got It! Assessment Videotapes,** Tape 6 ● ▲
• **Selection Support Workbook:** ● ▲ ■ Grammar and Style, p. 298 • **Writing and Grammar,** Diamond Level ● ▲ ■ • **Extension Activities,** p. 65 ● ▲ ■	• **Daily Language Practice Transparencies** ● ▲	• **Writing and Grammar iText CD-ROM** ● ▲ ■ ***Take It to the Net*** www.phschool.com

BLOCK SCHEDULING: Use one 90-minute class period to preteach the selection and have students read it. Use a second 90-minute class period to assess students' mastery of skills and have them complete one of the Extension Activities.

PRETEACH

Step-by-Step Teaching Guide for pp. 1286–1287

Motivation

Students may be familiar with such science-fiction films as *2001: A Space Odyssey* and the *Star Trek* television series in which space travel is a basic premise. Have students discuss the extent to which they believe that people will make themselves at home in space in their lifetime. Then, tell them that the essay they will read by a noted science-fiction writer may qualify some of the ideas they have about life in the Space Age.

Interest Grabber Video

As an alternative, play "'We'll Never Conquer Space': Space Exploration" on Tape 6 to engage student interest.

1 Background

More About the Author

In 1945, Clarke published a technical paper "Extra-Terrestrial Relays," laying down the principles of the satellite communication with satellites in geostationary orbits—a speculation that was realized twenty-five years later. His inventiveness has brought him numerous honors, such as the 1982 Marconi International Fellowship; a gold medal from the Franklin Institute; the Vikram Sarabhai Professorship of the Physical Research Laboratory, Ahmedabad; the Lindbergh Award; and a Fellowship of King's College, London.

Prepare to Read

1 *from* We'll Never Conquer Space

Arthur C. Clarke (b. 1917)

With more than one hundred million copies of his books in print worldwide, Arthur C. Clarke may be the most successful science-fiction writer of all time. The extensive appeal of his books is probably due to their distinctive combination of technical expertise and touches of poetry.

A Scientific Start As a child, Clarke's natural curiosity led him to explore science and space with unflagging enthusiasm. He created his own map of the moon based on observations he made with a homemade telescope. At the age of twelve, when he started to read a mass-circulation magazine called *Amazing Stories*, Clarke discovered science fiction, the genre in which he would have such success.

Imagining Satellites During World War II, Clarke's interest in scientific matters led to his service as a radar instructor in the Royal Air Force. At the end of the war, he drew on his wartime experience and his passion for space in an article for *Wireless World* magazine. The piece, entitled "Extra-Terrestrial Relays," explained how television and telephone signals could be bounced off relay stations—satellites—sent into orbit by rocket. Clarke described, in essence, the methods used today for television and other broadcasting.

Nearly twenty years later, in 1962, as if in answer to Clarke's prediction, the Communications Satellite Corporation (COMSAT) was authorized by Congress to manage commercial communication satellite systems. Clarke modestly commented that the article he had written in the 1940s had advanced telecommunications by "15 minutes." Many others, however, disagree with his humble assessment: They consider Clarke "the godfather of global communication."

A Writer's Perspective Since the early 1950s, Clarke has worked full time as a writer, producing more than seventy works of fiction and nonfiction. Among his most famous science-fiction novels are *Childhood's End* (1953) and *The City and the Stars* (1956).

One of his earliest stories, "The Sentinel" (1951), provided the germ of an idea for the epic film *2001: A Space Odyssey* (1968). As filmed by British director Stanley Kubrick, this poetic classic combines several different narratives, including the tale of a sentient, murderous computer named HAL 9000. Clarke has summarized the film as an exploration of "man's place in the pecking order of cosmic intelligence." While working on the film, Clarke was also writing a novel based on the same material. The novel was published a few months after the film was released. Many readers find that the novel helps explain some of the film's beautiful but opaque images.

Distant Yet Connected Since 1956, Clarke has lived in Colombo, Sri Lanka. Fascinated by the region's spectacular underwater realms, he became an avid scuba diver and undersea explorer. An extensive media center helps Clarke stay in touch with the larger world, pursuing his curiosity about new technological and scientific discoveries.

Exploration of the Possible Like his distinguished contemporaries Isaac Asimov and Ray Bradbury, Clarke has established credibility with his audience through an impressive command of science. But while his speculations are grounded in hard facts, he turns them to lyrical, romantic ends in his science-fiction works.

Challenging the notion that science fiction is escapism, Clarke has asserted that the genre is "virtually the only kind of writing that's dealing with real problems and possibilities. . . ."

TEACHING RESOURCES

The following resources can be used to enrich or extend the instruction for pp. 1286–1287.

Motivation

Interest Grabber Video, Tape 6

Background

Beyond Literature, p. 65

Take It to the Net

Visit www.phschool.com for background and hotlinks for "We'll Never Conquer Space."

Literary Analysis

Literary Analysis and Reading Transparencies, Prophetic Essay, p. 130

Reading

Selection Support: Reading Strategy, p. 299; Build Vocabulary, p. 297

Literary Analysis and Reading Transparencies, Challenging the Text, p. 129

BLOCK SCHEDULING: Resources marked with this symbol provide varied instruction during 90-minute blocks.

Preview

Connecting to the Literature

If you were to predict how technology will change your daily life in twenty-five years, you might work from a mix of guesses and facts. In this essay, Clarke uses all the science at his fingertips to make a prediction.

❷ Literary Analysis

Prophetic Essay

All of us make guesses about the future. In a **prophetic essay,** a writer makes bold, systematic predictions. A prophetic essay has these features:

- It is a brief work of nonfiction.
- It makes predictions about the future of a large collective, such as a nation, people, or planet.
- It may give warnings against complacency or pride, as the prophets in the Bible do.
- It uses ringing, memorable phrases to impress predictions on readers' memories or to reinforce warnings.

Notice how the predictions in the prophetic essay "We'll Never Conquer Space" also serve as a warning against overconfidence.

Connecting Literary Elements

Analogies are extended comparisons that help a reader grasp an idea by showing how it parallels a more familiar idea. Clarke uses a number of analogies to explain unfamiliar concepts. For example, he compares the situation of colonists in space with that of settlers on islands. As you read, notice how such analogies help you grasp abstract or hard-to-picture ideas by comparing those ideas with clear, understandable images.

❸ Reading Strategy

Challenging the Text

When you **challenge a text,** you critically question the statements it makes. You treat it like a friend you can argue with rather than like an authority whose words you must accept. When you read a provocative statement in this essay, ask yourself questions like those shown in the chart.

Provocative Statement

"We'll Never Conquer Space"

- Do Clarke's arguments fully support this sweeping claim?
- *Never* and *always* are unconditional, and statements using them can be proved wrong with a single counter-example. Is there such a counterexample to Clarke's claim?

Vocabulary Development

ludicrous (lo͞o′ di krəs) *adj.* absurd; ridiculous (p. 1288)

irrevocable (ir rev′ ə kə bəl) *adj.* unable to be undone or canceled (p. 1289)

instantaneous (in′ stən tā′ nē əs) *adj.* done or happening in an instant (p. 1290)

enigma (i nig′ mə) *n.* riddle; perplexing statement, person, or situation (p. 1291)

inevitable (in ev′ i tə bəl) *adj.* unavoidable; certain to happen (p. 1292)

zenith (zē′ nith) *n.* highest point of something, especially of the sky or celestial sphere (p. 1294)

❷ Literary Analysis

Prophetic Essay

- Explain to students that the story they will be reading is described as a "prophetic essay." Review the characteristics of such an essay given on p. 1287.
- Tell students to be prepared to analyze Clarke's prophecies in these terms.
- Explain to students that Clarke uses *analogies* to help his readers grasp unfamiliar ideas. *Analogies* are an effective means of accomplishing this because they compare unfamiliar ideas with more commonly known ones.

❸ Reading Strategy

Challenging the Text

- Explain to students that they will be asked to challenge the text as they read. Challenging the text entails questioning the assertions the text makes on a given point.
- Suggest that students can think of their encounter with the text as being similar to any encounter they may have with any person. Tell them that they need to question any provocative statement the text makes, just as they would of a person they might encounter.
- Use the Challenging the Text transparency in **Literary Analysis and Reading Transparencies,** p. 129, to demonstrate this skill.

Vocabulary Development

- Pronounce each vocabulary word for students, and read the definitions as a class. Have students identify any words with which they are already familiar.

CUSTOMIZE INSTRUCTION FOR UNIVERSAL ACCESS

For Less Proficient Readers	For English Learners	For Advanced Readers
Students may find some of the scientific ideas in this selection confusing. Encourage them to create a main idea and details chart for each section of the essay, breaking down Clarke's ideas and supporting details into manageable form.	Students learning English may have difficulty with some of the technical terms in the selection. Go over words and phrases such as *suspended animation, solar space, stellar space, solar system, galaxy,* and *light-year* to help students understand their meaning.	Have students work in pairs to discuss and evaluate the logic in Clarke's essay. When students have finished, have them present their evaluations to the class.

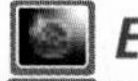 ***E-Teach***

Visit E-Teach at www.phschool.com for teachers' essays on how to teach, with questions and answers.

TEACH

Step-by-Step Teaching Guide for pp. 1288–1294

CUSTOMIZE INSTRUCTION
For Visual/Spatial Learners

These students may find it helpful to have an image or map of the galaxy at hand as they read. They can use the map to locate some of the stars and systems the writer mentions.

❶ About the Selection

In this essay, Arthur C. Clarke challenges the idea that we may ever truly "conquer" space. He stresses the improbability that humans will ever travel fast enough to make it possible to maintain a true connection with those left behind. The physical limitations on communication would separate humanity from itself, rendering the idea of "conquering" space meaningless.

❷ Reading Strategy

Challenging the Text (p. 1289)

- Have students read the bracketed paragraphs on page 1289. Remind them that they need to challenge the text. Have students suggest questions they can ask to challenge the text.
  Possible responses: Students may ask whether any recent scientific advances invalidate any of Clarke's assumptions or whether Clarke is correct in assuming that people today view space as conquerable.
- Ask them the Reading Strategy question on p. 1289: What event or trend could you use to challenge Clarke's statement that the world is "shrinking"?
  Possible responses: Students may argue that terrorist activity, civil war, and children in poverty all point to significant, perhaps unbridgeable, distances between people.

①*from*

We'll Never Conquer Space

Arthur C. Clarke

Background

Clarke wrote this essay in 1960, at the brink of the era of space exploration. Three years earlier, in 1957, *Sputnik* had become the first satellite launched into space. The year after Clarke wrote the essay, in 1961, Alan Shepard became the first American to enter space. Over the next sixteen years, human beings were to land on the moon (1969) and explore Mars via remote probes (1997). Yet Clarke's caution about the limits on the human conquest of space has yet to be tested.

Man will never conquer space. Such a statement may sound ludicrous, now that our rockets are already 100 million miles beyond the moon and the first human travelers are preparing to leave the atmosphere. Yet it expresses a truth which our forefathers knew, one we have forgotten—and our descendants must learn again, in heartbreak and loneliness.

ludicrous (lo͞o′ di krəs) *adj.* absurd; ridiculous

Our age is in many ways unique, full of events and phenomena which never occurred before and can never happen again. They distort our thinking, making us believe that what is true now will be true forever, though perhaps on a larger scale. Because we have annihilated distance on this planet, we imagine that we can do it once again. The facts are far otherwise, and we will see them more clearly if we forget the present and turn our minds towards the past.

To our ancestors, the vastness of the earth was a dominant fact controlling their thoughts and lives. In all earlier ages than ours, the world was wide indeed, and no man could ever see more than a tiny fraction of its immensity. A few hundred miles—a thousand, at the most—was

TEACHING RESOURCES

The following resources can be used to enrich or extend the instruction for pp. 1288–1294.

Literary Analysis

Selection Support: Literary Analysis, p. 300 ■

Reading

Listening to Literature Audiocassettes, Side 30 ■

Listening to Literature Audio CDs, CD 18 ■

■ **BLOCK SCHEDULING:** Resources marked with this symbol provide varied instruction during 90-minute blocks.

infinity. Only a lifetime ago, parents waved farewell to their emigrating children in the virtual certainty that they would never meet again.

And now, within one incredible generation, all this has changed. Over the seas where Odysseus wandered for a decade, the Rome-Beirut Comet whispers its way within the hour. And above that, the closer satellites span the distance between Troy and Ithaca[1] in less than a minute.

Psychologically as well as physically, there are no longer any remote places on earth. When a friend leaves for what was once a far
2 country, even if he has no intention of returning, we cannot feel that same sense of irrevocable separation that saddened our forefathers. 3
We know that he is only hours away by jet liner, and that we have merely to reach for the telephone to hear his voice.

In a very few years, when the satellite communication network is established, we will be able to see friends on the far side of the earth as easily as we talk to them on the other side of the town. Then the world will shrink no more, for it will have become a dimensionless point.

Forever Too Large

But the new stage that is opening up for the human drama will never shrink as the old one has done. We have abolished space here on the little earth; we can never abolish the space that yawns between the stars. Once again we are face to face with immensity and must accept its grandeur and terror, its inspiring possibilities and its dreadful restraints. From a world that has become too small, we are moving out into one that will be forever too large, whose frontiers will recede from us always more swiftly than we can reach out towards them.

Consider first the fairly modest solar, or planetary, distances which we are now preparing to assault. The very first Lunik[2] made a substantial impression upon them, traveling more than 200 million miles from the earth—six times the distance to Mars. When we have harnessed nuclear energy for spaceflight, the solar system will contract until it is little larger than the earth today. The remotest of the planets will be perhaps no more than a week's travel from the earth, while Mars and Venus will be only a few hours away.

This achievement, which will be witnessed within a century, might appear to make even the solar system a comfortable, homely place, with such giant planets as Saturn and Jupiter playing much the same role in our thoughts as do Africa or Asia today. (Their qualitative differences of climate, atmosphere and gravity, fundamental though they are, do not concern us at the moment.) To some extent this may

1. **Odysseus . . . Troy and Ithaca** Odysseus was the King of Ithaca and hero of Homer's *Odyssey.* Troy and Ithaca are the ancient cities marking the beginning and end of his wanderings across the Mediterranean Sea in the *Odyssey*. The Comet was an airplane, one of the fastest at the time the essay was written.
2. **Lunik** name given by American journalists to Luna I, an unmanned Soviet space probe of 1959.

Reading Strategy
Challenging the Text
What event or trend could you use to challenge Clarke's statement that the world is "shrinking"?

3 **irrevocable** (ir rev´ ə kə bəl) *adj.* unable to be undone or canceled

4 **Reading Check**
What effect does Clarke say technology is having on distances on Earth?

3 Vocabulary Development

Latin Suffixes *-ible* and *-able*

- Have students read the indicated sentence and ask them if they can determine the sense of the word *irrevocable* from the context.
- Note that they will find the words *incredible* and *irrevocable* in Clarke's essay. Explain that the suffixes of these words, *-ible* and *-able,* both mean "able to, or capable of." Something that is *incredible* is "not able to be believed." Something that is *irrevocable* is "not able to be altered." Note, however, that this suffix need not necessarily be associated with a negative term. For example, *credible* means "able to be believed."

4 Reading Check

Answer: Clarke argues that advances in technology are decreasing distances on Earth.

CUSTOMIZE INSTRUCTION FOR UNIVERSAL ACCESS

For Less Proficient Readers	For English Learners	For Advanced Readers
Have students write an e-mail message to Arthur C. Clarke responding to his message in "We'll Never Conquer Space." Have them tell him about a passage they liked or disliked and ask him any questions they may have.	If students are interested in rockets and space travel, suggest that they read a longer work on the topics, such as *The Rocket Boys.*	Have students form a small panel to discuss the implications of Clarke's essay. If Clarke is correct that space will never be conquered, what are the practical and philosophical uses of space exploration?

5 Reading Strategy
Challenging the Text

- Read aloud the bracketed passage to students. Have them summarize Clarke's comments on communication in space.
- Ask them the Reading Strategy question on p. 1290: Consider e-mail, invented after Clarke wrote the essay. How important is direct conversation in conducting business across a distance?
  Answer: Conversation is perhaps not as important as Clarke seems to think. People could conduct business over the long term, sending messages as they did in the days of the American frontier.

6 Literary Analysis
Prophetic Essay

- Ask students what warning the writer is giving readers in the bracketed paragraph.
  Answer: He is warning that the exploration of deep space will require a sacrifice of immediate communications that may prove too great a strain for human relations.
- Then, ask students the Literary Analysis question on p. 1290: In what way is Clarke's prediction of "a perpetual reminder of . . . limitations" like a prophet's warning against excessive pride?
  Possible responses: Students may reply that Clarke is asserting that humanity has grown overconfident on the basis of its previous technological accomplishments, and that this overconfidence predisposes people to have an unrealistic view of their future potential.

be true, yet as soon as we pass beyond the orbit of the moon, a mere quarter-million miles away, we will meet the first of the barriers that will separate the earth from her scattered children.

The marvelous telephone and television network that will soon enmesh the whole world, making all men neighbors, cannot be extended into space. It will never be possible to converse with anyone on another planet.

Do not misunderstand this statement. Even with today's radio equipment, the problem of sending speech to the other planets is almost trivial. But the messages will take minutes—sometimes hours—on their journey, because radio and light waves travel at the
5 same limited speed of 186,000 miles a second.

Twenty years from now you will be able to listen to a friend on Mars, but the words you hear will have left his mouth at least three minutes earlier, and your reply will take a corresponding time to reach him. In such circumstances, an exchange of verbal messages is possible—but not a conversation.

Even in the case of the nearby moon, the 2½ second time-lag will be annoying. At distances of more than a million miles, it will be intolerable.

Reading Strategy
Challenging the Text Consider E-mail, invented after Clarke wrote the essay. How important is direct conversation in conducting business across a distance?

"Time Barrier"

To a culture which has come to take instantaneous communication for granted, as part of the very structure of civilized life, this "time barrier" may have a profound psychological impact. It will be a
6 perpetual reminder of universal laws and limitations against which not all our technology can ever prevail. For it seems as certain as anything can be that no signal—still less any material object—can ever travel faster than light.

The velocity of light is the ultimate speed limit, being part of the very structure of space and time. Within the narrow confines of the solar system, it will not handicap us too severely, once we have accepted the delays in communication which it involves. At the worst, these will amount to 20 hours—the time it takes a radio signal to span the orbit of Pluto, the outermost planet.

Between the three inner worlds the earth, Mars, and Venus, it will never be more than 20 minutes—not enough to interfere seriously with commerce or administration, but more than sufficient to shatter those personal links of sound or vision that can give us a sense of direct contact with friends on earth, wherever they may be.

It is when we move out beyond the confines of the solar system that we come face to face with an altogether new order of cosmic reality. Even today, many otherwise educated men—like those savages who can count to three but lump together all numbers beyond four—cannot grasp the profound distinction between solar and stellar space. The first is the space enclosing our neighboring worlds, the planets; the second is that which embraces those distant suns, the stars, and it is literally millions of times greater.

instantaneous (in′ stən tā′ nē əs) *adj.* done or happening in an instant

Literary Analysis
Prophetic Essay In what way is Clarke's prediction of "a perpetual reminder of . . . limitations" like a prophet's warning against excessive pride?

ENRICHMENT: Science Connection
Artificial Satellites

Point out to students that there are over 2,000 artificial satellites orbiting the earth right now. There are six different types of satellites. (1) Earth-observation satellites take pictures of the earth that are then analyzed by computers to study the location of mineral and water deposits, the effects of pollution, and the spread of crop and forest disease. (2) Communications satellites, used primarily by television and telephone companies, receive radio signals and transmit them to other locations. (3) Scientific research satellites gather information about space, the planets, and Earth's atmosphere. (4) Weather satellites observe and relay information about weather patterns. (5) Navigation satellites aid vehicles on land, on sea, and in the air to determine their exact locations by sending out signals picked up by a transmitter on the vehicle. (6) Finally, military satellites are used for military purposes such as noting the location of weapons and the movement of troops.

There is no such abrupt change of scale in terrestrial affairs. To obtain a mental picture of the distance to the nearest star, as compared with the distance to the nearest planet, you must imagine a world in which the closest object to you is only five feet away—and then there is nothing else to see until you have traveled a thousand miles.

Many conservative scientists, appalled by these cosmic gulfs, have denied that they can ever be crossed. Some people never learn; those who 60 years ago scoffed at the possibility of flight, and ten (even five!) years ago laughed at the idea of travel to the planets, are now quite sure that the stars will always be beyond our reach. And again they are wrong, for they have failed to grasp the great lesson of our age—that if something is possible in theory, and no fundamental scientific laws oppose its realization, then sooner or later it will be achieved.

One day, it may be in this century, or it may be a thousand years from now, we shall discover a really efficient means of propelling our space vehicles. Every technical device is always developed to its limit (unless it is superseded by something better) and the ultimate speed for spaceships is the velocity of light. They will never reach that goal, but they will get very close to it. And then the nearest star will be less than five years' voyaging from the earth.

Our exploring ships will spread outwards from their home over an ever-expanding sphere of space. It is a sphere which will grow at almost—but never quite—the speed of light. Five years to the triple system of Alpha Centauri, 10 to the strangely-matched doublet Sirius A and B, 11 to the tantalizing enigma of 61 Cygni,[3] the first star suspected to possess a planet. These journeys are long, but they are not impossible. Man has always accepted whatever price was necessary for his explorations and discoveries, *and the price of Space is Time.*

Even voyages which may last for centuries or millennia will one day be attempted. Suspended animation has already been achieved in the laboratory, and may be the key to interstellar travel. Self-contained cosmic arks which will be tiny traveling worlds in their own right may be another solution, for they would make possible journeys of unlimited extent, lasting generation after generation.

The famous Time Dilation effect predicted by the Theory of Relativity,[4] whereby time appears to pass more slowly for a

7 ▼ Critical Viewing Does the suit worn by astronauts support Clarke's argument that space cannot be "conquered"? Explain. **[Make a Judgment]**

Astronaut Buzz Aldrin on moon near Lunar Module, during Apollo 11, NASA

enigma (e nig´ mə) *n.* riddle; perplexing statement, person, or situation

8 ✓Reading Check What barrier will space travel force people to confront?

3. **Alpha Centauri . . . 61 Cygni** Alpha Centauri is a system of three stars in the constellation of the Centaur; one of these, Proxima Centauri, is the star closest to Earth besides the sun. Sirius, known as the Dog Star, is the brightest star in Earth's sky; it is actually two stars orbiting each other, one of which (Sirius B), is only as big as the earth. 61 Cygni is a binary star in the constellation Cygnus, the Swan.
4. **Theory of Relativity** In physics, the theory that measurements of an object's physical properties will vary depending on the relative motion of the observer and the observed object: Only the speed of light is constant. One consequence of the theory is that time, as measured by an external observer, will slow down on an object moving close to the speed of light. In theory, a person traveling near the speed of light would age at a slower rate than a person traveling more slowly (the "Time Dilation effect" referred to by Clarke).

7 ▶ Critical Viewing

Possible responses: Students may respond that it supports Clarke's argument. The suit is bulky and surrounds the astronaut completely, adding to his or her isolation and limiting his or her ability to maneuver. "Conquering" space—that is, truly being at home there—in such a suit seems unlikely.

8 ✓Reading Check

Answer: Space travel will force people to confront the barrier posed by the speed of light.

CUSTOMIZE INSTRUCTION FOR UNIVERSAL ACCESS

For Special Needs Students	For Gifted/Talented Students
Have students view *2001: A Space Odyssey* and make an oral presentation to the class explaining the different issues the film posed. Are the concerns the film raises with respect to computer technology unrealistic? In what ways was Clarke's vision prophetic?	Have students construct a three-dimensional model using whatever materials they find appropriate to illustrate different points of Clarke's essay. For example, they may design something that gives an accessible representation of the relationships of distance and scale in space.

9 ▶Critical Viewing

Answer: Because the picture is on such a small scale, it doesn't give a sense of the distances in space. The photograph doesn't relate to anything we know, whereas Clarke's analogy to ocean islands is dramatic and convincing.

10 Reading Strategy

Challenging the Text (p. 1294)

- Have students read the indicated passage. Then, have them determine how the time lag in messages sent to another planet might affect conversations between people.
  Answers: Because receipt and reply would be separated by years, people would be simply transmitting history rather than messages.
- After reviewing the arguments about information lag, ask students the Reading Strategy question on p. 1294: In his arguments about information lag, what is Clarke assuming about the length of human life? Do you agree?
  Answers: Clarke is assuming that we will not extend our lifetimes appreciably. If we do, however, the lag in time in communications may mean far less to us than it would today.

traveler moving at almost the speed of light, may be yet a third. And there are others.

Looking far into the future, therefore, we must picture a slow (little more than half a billion miles an hour!) expansion of human activities outwards from the solar system, among the suns scattered across the region of the galaxy in which we now find ourselves. These suns are on the average five light-years apart; in other words, we can never get from one to the next in less than five years.

To bring home what this means, let us use a down-to-earth analogy. Imagine a vast ocean, sprinkled with islands—some desert, others perhaps inhabited. On one of these islands an energetic race has just discovered the art of building ships. It is preparing to explore the ocean, but must face the fact that the very nearest island is five years' voyaging away, and that no possible improvement in the technique of ship-building will ever reduce this time.

In these circumstances (which are those in which we will soon find ourselves) what could the islanders achieve? After a few centuries, they might have established colonies on many of the nearby islands and have briefly explored many others. The daughter colonies might themselves have sent out further pioneers, and so a kind of chain reaction would spread the original culture over a steadily expanding area of the ocean.

inevitable (in ev´ i tə bəl) *adj.* unavoidable; certain to happen

9 ▼ Critical Viewing Does this picture convey a sense of these immense distances as clearly as Clarke's prose? Explain. **[Analyze]**

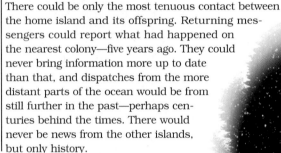

But now consider the effects of the inevitable, unavoidable time-lag. There could be only the most tenuous contact between the home island and its offspring. Returning messengers could report what had happened on the nearest colony—five years ago. They could
10 never bring information more up to date than that, and dispatches from the more distant parts of the ocean would be from still further in the past—perhaps centuries behind the times. There would never be news from the other islands, but only history.

Independent "Colonies"

All the star-borne colonies of the future will be independent, whether they wish it or not. Their liberty will be inviolably protected by Time as well as Space. They must go their own way and achieve their own destiny, with no help or hindrance from Mother Earth.

At this point, we will move the discussion on to a new level and deal with an obvious objection. Can we be sure that the velocity of light is indeed a limiting factor? So many "impassible" barriers have been shattered in the past; perhaps this one may go the way of all the others.

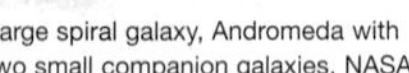

Large spiral galaxy, Andromeda with two small companion galaxies, NASA

ENRICHMENT: Science Connection

Space Station *Mir*

Clarke's mention of "self-contained cosmic arks" may bring to mind the Russian space station *Mir. Mir,* meaning "peace," was launched in February of 1986 by the former Soviet Union. It was a core module with two docking ports and four other hatches designed to hook up with laboratory modules. Scientists on *Mir* were able to study many aspects of space as well as the effects of long-term stays in space on humans—some of the crew members stayed on board for over a year at a time. During its years in orbit, *Mir* was constantly manned by first Soviet, and later Russian, cosmonauts. *Mir* would also serve as host to American astronauts visiting in the space shuttle. After a decade of service, *Mir* developed serious technical problems, including several power losses that would finally spell its demise in March of 2001. As *Mir* reentered Earth's atmosphere at speeds approaching that of sound, it left a fiery blaze in its trail.

We will not argue the point, or give the reasons why scientists believe that light can never be outraced by any form of radiation or any material object. Instead, let us assume the contrary and see just where it gets us. We will even take the most optimistic possible case and imagine that the speed of transportation may eventually become infinite.

Picture a time when, by the development of techniques as far beyond our present engineering as a transistor is beyond a stone axe, we can reach anywhere we please instantaneously, with no more effort than by dialing a number. This would indeed cut the universe down to size and reduce its physical immensity to nothingness. What would be left?

Everything that really matters. For the universe has two aspects—its scale, and its overwhelming, mind-numbing complexity. Having abolished the first, we are now face-to-face with the second.

What we must now try to visualize is not size, but quantity. Most people today are familiar with the simple notation which scientists use to describe large numbers; it consists merely of counting zeroes, so that a hundred becomes 10^2, a million, 10^6, a billion, 10^9 and so on. This useful trick enables us to work with quantities of any magnitude, and even defense budget totals look modest when expressed as \$5.76 x 10^9 instead of \$5,760,000,000.

The number of other suns in our own galaxy (that is, the whirlpool of stars and cosmic dust of which our sun is an out-of-town member, lying in one of the remoter spiral arms) is estimated at about 10^{11}—or written in full, 100,000,000,000. Our present telescopes can observe something like 10^9 other galaxies, and they show no sign of thinning out even at the extreme limit of vision.

There are probably at least as many galaxies in the whole of creation as there are stars in our own galaxy, but let us confine ourselves to those we can see. They must contain a total of about 10^{11} times 10^9 stars, or 10^{20} stars altogether. 1 followed by 20 other digits is, of course, a number beyond all understanding.

Before such numbers, even spirits brave enough to face the challenge of the light-years must quail. The detailed examination of all the grains of sand on all the beaches of the world is a far smaller task than the exploration of the universe.

And so we return to our opening statement. Space can be mapped and crossed and occupied without definable limit; but it can never be conquered. When our race has reached its ultimate achievements, and the stars themselves are scattered no more widely than the seed of Adam, even then we shall still be like ants crawling on the face of the earth. The ants have covered the world but have they conquered it—for what do their countless colonies know of it, or of each other?

11 ***Finding a Place in the World***

Clarke's essay poses the question, What is the place of humanity in the universe? With each shift in history, the literature of the British tradition has returned to this question—whether it is in the mingled yearnings for home and for the sea in the Anglo-Saxon poem "The Seafarer" (p. 16) or in Bede's definition of England as a homeland (p. 74) or in Milton's cosmic explorations in *Paradise Lost* (p. 468). Swift brought his satirical eye to the question in *Gulliver's Travels* (p. 514), finding that we are neither small enough (nor unreasonable enough) for Lilliput nor big enough (nor good enough) for Brobdingnag. Sydney Smith took on the issue in perhaps its smallest form: How physically comfortable can we be in the world? (see p. 900).

Many of these writers, like Clarke, uncover a kind of universal human homelessness—a way in which the world leaves us with persistent, unsatisfied desires or unanswered questions. By affirming this condition, these writers remind us of our limits. At the same time, they affirm a special kind of freedom—a freedom to challenge or to celebrate these limits and the life they define.

12  **Reading Check**

What second obstacle does Clarke see to truly conquering space?

11 Background

Finding a Place in the World

While Clarke's subject is largely informed by science, it is not entirely different from many of the other authors students have been studying throughout this text. Indeed, many of these authors share a common theme in assessing humanity's proper place in the scheme of things. Whether this theme may take the guise of England as a homeland, or Earth as our mother planet, there is a common concern for the question of home and homelessness.

12 Reading Check

Answer: The second challenge he sees to conquering space derives simply from the vast number of galaxies, and thus potential worlds to be explored.

ASSESS

Answers for p. 1294

Review and Assess

1. **(a)** Clarke points out that even radio waves travel too slowly to allow for a true "conversation" across the vast distances of space. Whatever communication there could be would have to be in a form more like messages, some of which would take years, decades, or even centuries to arrive. **(b)** Clarke thinks of conversation as being immediate, and messages as entailing delay. That delay, he feels, would mean the messages would be more like "history" than communication.
2. **(a)** Within a century, Clarke predicts we will be able to harness nuclear energy for spaceflight, and travel to the remotest planets in our solar system within a week's time, or to Mars and Venus within a few hours. **(b)** Clarke argues this would not help humans conquer space, because space is far too vast, and there are countless galaxies.
3. **(a)** For Clarke, conquering space is different from conquering Earth by dint of the sheer size of space, especially when measured against the life span of the human being. The closest we would come, in his view, would be by bridging space with generation after generation of explorers, with no one to whom any given expedition could report results. **(b)** Clarke feels that attempting to conquer space would divide human society.
4. Some students may respond that Clarke has made a compelling case for the impossibility of conquering space. Others may argue that Clarke bases his arguments on existing technology and existing science. Some may even challenge whether mankind is forever doomed to a short life span.
5. Some students may respond that Clarke would have a dampening effect on our pride and ambition. Others may feel his observations serve to help rein in excessive arrogance.

So it will be with us as we spread outwards from Mother Earth, loosening the bonds of kinship and understanding, hearing faint and belated rumors at second—or third—or thousandth-hand of an ever-dwindling fraction of the entire human race.

Though Earth will try to keep in touch with her children, in the end all the efforts of her archivists and historians will be defeated by time and distance, and the sheer bulk of material. For the number of distinct societies or nations, when our race is twice its present age, may be far greater than the total number of all the men who have ever lived up to the present time.

We have left the realm of human comprehension in our vain effort to grasp the scale of the universe; so it must always be, sooner rather than later.

When you are next outdoors on a summer night, turn your head towards the zenith. Almost vertically above you will be shining the brightest star of the northern skies—Vega of the Lyre,[5] 26 years away at the speed of light, near enough the point-of-no-return for us short-lived creatures. Past this blue-white beacon, 50 times as brilliant as our sun, we may send our minds and bodies, but never our hearts.

For no man will ever turn homewards from beyond Vega, to greet again those he knew and loved on the earth.

Reading Strategy
Challenging the Text
In his arguments about information lag, what is Clarke assuming about the length of human life? Do you agree?

zenith (zē′ nəth) *n.* highest point of something, especially of the sky or celestial sphere

5. **Vega of the Lyre** star in the northern constellation, Lyra, and the fourth brightest of the stars in Earth's night sky.

Review and Assess

Thinking About the Selection

1. **(a) Recall:** What reason does Clarke offer for claiming that a true conversation with someone on another planet is impossible? **(b) Classify:** What distinction does Clarke make between exchanging messages and having a conversation?
2. **(a) Recall:** What technological goal will be reached within a century, according to Clarke? **(b) Draw Conclusions:** Why would this achievement not help humans "conquer space"?
3. **(a) Compare and Contrast:** According to Clarke, how is conquering space different from conquering regions of the Earth? **(b) Infer:** What implications does Clarke think that conquering space would have for human society?
4. **Evaluate:** Has Clarke made a persuasive argument about the impossibility of conquering space? Explain.
5. **Apply:** If Clarke's warning about human limitations was taken seriously throughout our society, what effect might it have on human pride and ambition?

ASSESSMENT PRACTICE: Writing Skills

Strategy (For more practice, see Test Preparation Workbook, p. 65)

Tests often require students to apply revision strategies to passages in order to evaluate the appropriateness of a sentence. Use the following sample test item to give students practice:

Self-contained cosmic arks . . . may be another solution, for they would make possible journeys of unlimited extent, lasting generation after generation.

To add information about these spaceships, which of the following would be most suitable?

A Spacesuits have sophisticated air conditioning systems.
B Space travelers would need special training.
C These vessels would require heavy shielding against the dangerous solar radiation.
D Films and TV shows have been made about space travel.

The correct answer is *C*. The other choices are not specifically about the spaceships.

Review and Assess

Literary Analysis

Prophetic Essay

1. (a) Summarize the prediction that Clarke makes in this **prophetic essay.** (b) Identify two specific facts that support it.
2. (a) Choose two memorable phrases or sentences in the essay. (b) Explain how they add to the essay's persuasive power.
3. (a) Identify at least four strategies that Clarke uses to support his prophecy. (b) Explain which one you think is most effective.
4. Do you think Clarke's prophecy would have a good influence if it were taken to heart by people? Explain, describing the effect you think the prophecy might have on people's outlook.

Connecting Literary Elements

5. (a) What point does Clarke make with the **analogy** of an ocean sprinkled with islands? (b) What associations make the image of islands especially effective?
6. Use a chart like the one below to interpret the analogy that compares ants on Earth with humans exploring space.

Things Compared	Similarities Emphasized	What Is Explained

7. Evaluate Clarke's use of analogies. Does he use them to oversimplify complex issues or to make it easier to grasp difficult concepts? Explain.

Reading Strategy

Challenging the Text

8. Clarke states "Man has always accepted whatever price was necessary for his explorations. . . ." Write a few sentences **challenging** this statement, and decide whether or not you agree.
9. The word *may* can signal that an author is guessing rather than giving facts. Find and challenge one of Clarke's guesses.

Extend Understanding

10. **Science Connection:** How are scientific prophecies different from the predictions of popular culture, such as fortunetelling and astrology?

Quick Review

A **prophetic essay** is a brief work of nonfiction that makes bold predictions about the future.

An **analogy** is an extended comparison, often between a familiar and an unfamiliar idea or topic.

To deepen your understanding of a work, **challenge the text** by questioning the claims it makes.

Take It to the Net

www.phschool.com

Take the interactive self-test online to check your understanding of the selection.

Answers for p. 1295

Review and Assess

1. **(a)** Clarke predicts that man will not conquer space—that it is simply too vast. **(b)** According to Clarke, the speed of light is too slow to get the job done. Clarke argues that once we have "covered" space, we will be isolated in both space and time.
2. Possible response: **(a)** "When our race has reached its ultimate achievements, . . . even then we shall still be like ants crawling on the face of the earth." "For no man will ever . . . greet again those he knew and loved on earth." **(b)** The first sentence is effective because of its biblical connotations. The second sentence is powerful because it speaks of emotional distance.
3. **(a)** Clarke includes scientific information, describes the Lunik space probe, writes in memorable phrases and sentences, and uses comparisons to help the reader visualize the vastness of space. **(b)** Some students may respond that they find the scientific facts most convincing; others may be most convinced by the comparisons.
4. Students may see a good effect of Clarke's prophecy if it resulted in a renewed effort to improve life on this planet, since space offers no realistic hope of "escape."
5. **(a)** Clarke is illustrating how widely separated and isolated by both space and time space explorers will be. **(b)** Students may say that islands connote isolation and remoteness.
6. **Things Compared:** spread of ant colonies across Earth and the future spread of human colonies in space; **Similarities Emphasized:** Isolation of space colonies from one another would be like isolation of ant colonies from one another; **What Is Explained:** Human "civilization" in space would have as much unity as ant "civilization" on earth.
7. Students may say that when Clarke compares space to a vast ocean, and human space explorers to ants, he makes it easier to grasp difficult concepts.

continued

Answers continued

8. Students may respond that individuals have not always accepted whatever price was necessary for explorations.
9. Clarke is guessing when he says "One day, it may be in this century, or it may be a thousand years from now, we shall discover a really efficient means of propelling our space vehicles." Not only do we not know for a fact that such a development is imminent, but we may question whether his related claim—that technology always realizes what is theoretically possible—is necessarily true. In an age of scarce resources and of environmental and social awareness, people may choose to pursue other technologies besides those involved in space flight.
10. Scientific prophecies must employ the methodology of science.

EXTEND

Answers for p. 1296

❶ Vocabulary Development

Word Analysis

1. definable
2. resistible
3. combustible

Spelling Strategy

1. irregular
2. incapable
3. irresponsible

Concept Development: Synonyms

1. c
2. b
3. a
4. b
5. a
6. c

❷ Grammar and Style

1. Linking verb: "is"; subject complement: "in many ways unique."
2. Linking verb: "was"; subject complement: "wide indeed."
3. Linking verb: "was"; subject complement: "infinity."
4. Linking verb: "is"; subject complement: "almost trivial."
5. Linking verb: "is"; subject complement: "a far smaller task than the exploration of the universe."

Writing Application

1. A bird in the hand (linking verb) is (subject complement) worth two in the bush.
2. Where there's a will there (linking verb) 's (is) (subject complement) a way.
3. He who hesitates (linking verb) is (subject complement) lost.
4. Handsome (linking verb) is (subject complement) as handsome does.
5. All (linking verb) is (subject complement) fair in love and war.

Integrate Language Skills

❶ Vocabulary Development Lesson

Word Analysis: Latin Suffixes *-ible* and *-able*

The suffixes *-ible* and *-able* both mean "able to," "having qualities of," "worthy of," or "capable of." Something *incredible* is "not able to be believed." Something *irrevocable* is "not able to be altered." Change each word following into a related word that ends in *-ible* or *-able*.

1. define 2. resist 3. combustion

Spelling Strategy

The prefix *in-* or *im-*, meaning "not," changes to *ir-* when added to a word that begins with an *r*, as in the word *irrevocable*. Add the prefix *in-*, *im-*, or *ir-* to the following words:

1. regular 2. capable 3. responsible

Concept Development: Synonyms

Choose the letter of the word or words closest in meaning to the first word.

1. ludicrous: (a) frisky, (b) morbid, (c) absurd
2. irrevocable: (a) rapid, (b) unalterable, (c) fickle
3. instantaneous: (a) immediate, (b) faulty, (c) risky
4. enigma: (a) quotation, (b) riddle, (c) archive
5. inevitable: (a) unavoidable, (b) sudden, (c) direct
6. zenith: (a) depth, (b) revolution, (c) peak

❷ Grammar and Style Lesson

Linking Verbs and Subject Complements

Linking verbs, such as *seem* or *be*, connect the subject with words that complete the sentence. A **subject complement** is the noun, pronoun, or adjective that follows a linking verb and identifies or describes the subject.

Example: . . . the vastness of the earth (S) was (LV) a dominant fact (SC). . . .

The overuse of linking verbs can make writing dull. However, one effective stylistic use of this grammatical device is to make a vivid, surprising comparison, as when Clarke writes "A few hundred miles . . . was infinity."

Practice Identify the linking verb and the subject complement in each sentence.

1. Our age is in many ways unique, . . .
2. . . . the world was wide indeed, . . .
3. A few hundred miles . . . was infinity.
4. . . . the problem of sending speech to other planets is almost trivial.
5. The detailed examination of all the grains of sand on all the beaches of the world is a far smaller task than the exploration of the universe.

Writing Application Find five proverbs that use linking verbs, such as "Home is where the heart is." Explain why this grammatical structure is common in proverbs.

WG Prentice Hall Writing and Grammar Connection: Chapter 18, Section 3

TEACHING RESOURCES

The following resources can be used to enrich or extend the instruction for pp. 1296–1297.

Vocabulary

- **Selection Support:** Build Vocabulary, p. 297
- **Vocabulary and Spelling Practice Book,** (Use this book for skills enrichment.)

Grammar

- **Selection Support:** Grammar and Style, p. 298
- **Writing and Grammar,** Diamond Level, p. 426
- **Daily Language Practice Transparencies** ■

Writing

- **Writing and Grammar,** Diamond Level, p. 317
- **Writing and Grammar iText CD-ROM** ■

■ **BLOCK SCHEDULING:** Resources marked with this symbol provide varied instruction during 90-minute blocks.

❸ Writing Lesson

Analysis of an Argument

Arthur C. Clarke argues that space cannot be conquered. His argument depends on a few basic assumptions, such as his notion of what it means to "conquer" a domain. Write an essay in which you identify, analyze, and evaluate these assumptions.

Prewriting Briefly outline the points in Clarke's essay. For each, identify the assumptions that he makes about the universe or about society.

Drafting In your draft, analyze each of Clarke's assumptions in turn. Then, evaluate each in terms of plausibility, support by scientists, and any other factor that seems appropriate.

Revising Review your draft, circling passages in which you connect two of Clarke's ideas. Draw an arrow from each circled statement to a sentence that further analyzes these ideas. If you cannot find such a sentence, consider elaborating on the circled statement.

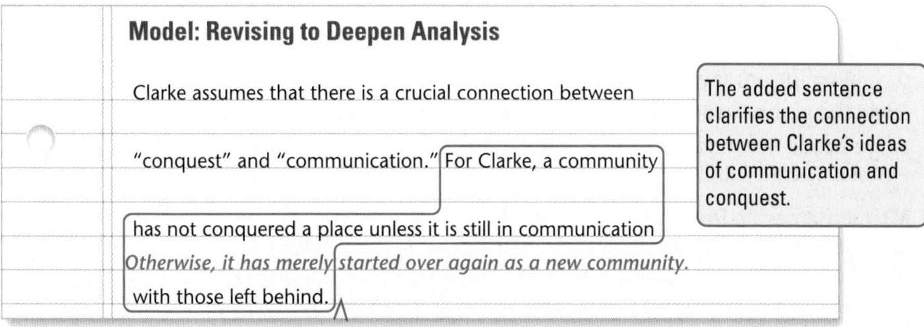

Model: Revising to Deepen Analysis
Clarke assumes that there is a crucial connection between
"conquest" and "communication." For Clarke, a community
has not conquered a place unless it is still in communication
Otherwise, it has merely started over again as a new community.
with those left behind.
The added sentence clarifies the connection between Clarke's ideas of communication and conquest.

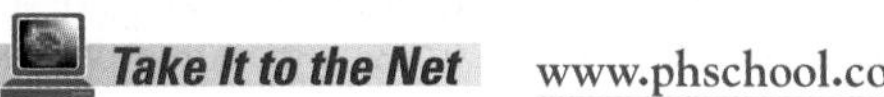

❹ Extension Activities

Listening and Speaking Hold a **panel discussion** about the implications of Clarke's essay, both for the future of space travel and for our idea of humanity's place in the cosmos. Panelists should follow these guidelines:

- Use technical language when appropriate.
- Use figurative language, including analogies, to explain unfamiliar concepts.

Hold your discussion before the class.
[Group Activity]

Research and Technology Construct a **museum exhibit** that dramatizes Clarke's ideas. Use a variety of research strategies to build an effective exhibit. For instance, you might contact a local university for advice and to arrange the taping of interviews with professors.

Take It to the Net www.phschool.com

Go online for an additional research activity using the Internet.

Lesson Support for p. 1297

❸ Writing Lesson

- Tell students a critical response is a piece of nonfiction writing that presents a reaction to, or an analysis of, a literary work. An effective response to literature usually:

  identifies the work or works being discussed;

  supports the writer's interpretations with precise examples, citations or quotations;

  is organized clearly and effectively;

  offers an opinion, a judgment, or an evaluation based on close scrutiny of specific elements.

- Model a critical response for the students based on one or two paragraphs from "We'll Never Conquer Space."

❹ Listening and Speaking

- Divide the class into two groups. Tell the first group to identify Clarke's technical examples. Tell the second group to find Clarke's figurative examples.
- Have each group identify a spokesperson for the panel, representing the technical and figurative arguments.

CUSTOMIZE INSTRUCTION For Universal Access

To address different learning styles, use the activities suggested in the **Extension Activities** booklet, p. 65.

- For Verbal/Linguistic and Visual/Spatial Learners, use Activity 5.
- For Visual/Spatial Learners, use Activity 6.
- For Logical/Mathematical Learners, use Activity 7.

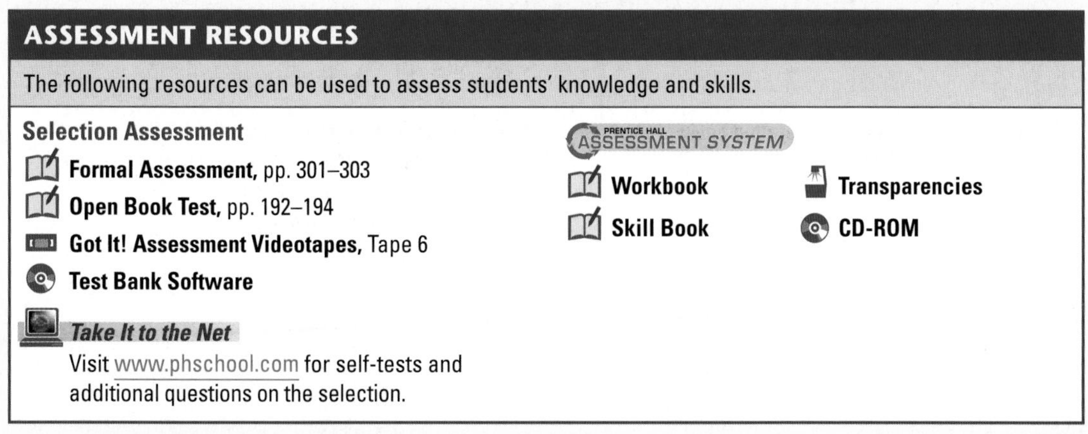

ASSESSMENT RESOURCES

The following resources can be used to assess students' knowledge and skills.

Selection Assessment

- **Formal Assessment,** pp. 301–303
- **Open Book Test,** pp. 192–194
- **Got It! Assessment Videotapes,** Tape 6
- **Test Bank Software**

Take It to the Net

Visit www.phschool.com for self-tests and additional questions on the selection.

PRENTICE HALL ASSESSMENT SYSTEM

- **Workbook**
- **Skill Book**
- **Transparencies**
- **CD-ROM**

Lesson Objectives

1. To write an evaluative essay
2. To identify and understand the author's style and purpose
3. To analyze these purposes to question the accessibility of modern poetry
4. To use writing strategies to generate ideas, plan, organize, evaluate, and revise writing

Prewriting

- Help students choose selections to analyze by having them fill in a chart listing poem titles and their accessibility level. Encourage them to review the selections to renew their familiarity with them.
- Have students explain their accessibility ratings using evidence from the works themselves. Encourage them to discern the author's purpose based on the imagery of the poem.
- When students have completed their charts and gathered support, encourage them to work with other students to formalize the focus of their essay. Ask students to add details they obtain from these meetings.

Writing About Literature

Evaluate Literary Trends

A poem like *Beowulf* was intended to reach an entire community—to thrill, instruct, and dazzle any Anglo-Saxon who heard it sung. Is it still possible for one poem to appeal to everyone? Many modern poets write poems rich in ambiguity and nuance as they explore the complexities of contemporary life. Some critics feel that, as a result, modern poetry has become too obscure and difficult to reach a large body of readers. Following the assignment outlined in the yellow box, write an essay in which you present your own views about the accessibility of poetry.

Assignment: The Audience for Modern Poetry

How accessible should poetry be? Write an essay in which you consider the reasons that many modern poets create complex and challenging works that require multiple readings. Then, provide an evaluation of the role that accessibility or community should play in shaping a poet's voice.

Criteria:

- Include a thesis statement that addresses the role of accessibility in modern poetry.
- Analyze several modern poems, including examples of easily accessible poetry as well as more challenging poems.
- Approximate length: 1,500 words

Prewriting

Find a focus. Begin by evaluating some of the poems you have read in this unit. Answer the questions below and fill in a chart like the one shown to help you organize your thoughts.

- Does the author's style include nuance (subtle shades of meaning) and ambiguity (words and ideas that may be interpreted in a variety of ways)? How?
- Do the nuances and ambiguities reflect aspects of a subject or feeling, or are they simply used for effect?
- Does the author use allusions (brief, unexplained literary references)?
- What needs of readers can this poem satisfy? What purpose of the writer's does it fulfill?

Model: Gathering Details for an Evaluation

Poem	Accessibility (1 = very accessible; 5 = very obscure)	Author's Purpose	Reader's Needs
Midsummer, XXIII Walcott	4	The complexity of the poem helps Walcott explore ambiguous feelings about his identity.	It does not fill a need for easy answers. It does enhance our perceptions of social problems and make us question the role of literature in life.

Gather support. As you form an opinion of a poem, jot it down and copy one or two lines or images from the poem that support it.

Compare evaluations. The topic of this essay is readers' reactions, so you may want to discuss your chosen poems in a group. Make generalizations based on the group's responses.

Read to Write

Do not limit your review to poems you remember enjoying. When you reread and analyze a poem, you may discover that your opinion of it is very different from your first impression.

TEACHING RESOURCES

The following resources can be used to enrich or extend the instruction for pp. 1298–1299.

Writing and Grammar, Diamond Level, Chapter 14, pp. 309–329

Writing and Grammar iText CD-ROM

Students can use the following tools as they complete their evaluative essays:

- Cause and Effect Model
- Topic Bank
- Editing Tools

Drafting

Organize. Make an outline to help you find the basic organization of your essay. Use each major heading to write several paragraphs relating to that single topic. You may find it useful to create a fairly detailed outline in which you break down major headings into subheadings. When you draft from a detailed outline, you might write a complete paragraph for each subheading, with each detail beneath the subheading developed into a sentence.

Conclude effectively. In your concluding paragraph, review and tie together the ideas you have discussed in the body of your essay. Finish your essay with a strong statement about the importance of accessibility to modern poetry.

Write to Learn
An outline can guide your first draft, but feel free to add ideas that occur to you while you write. Later, when you revise, make sure that your added ideas are coherent and relevant.

Model: Tying Together Points in an Effective Conclusion

Eliot's and Walcott's references are obscure. Their sentiments are ambiguous, a mixture of irony, guilt, and detachment. These features alone would discourage the majority of readers. In addition, both writers emphasize their inability to belong fully to a community. Yet, as I have argued, if their predicament is the predicament of the modern individual, then we need poetry like Eliot's and Walcott's to let us know we are not alone. That knowledge is itself a kind of community.

A clear, memorable concluding sentence ties together the writer's ideas.

Revising and Editing

Review content: Assess emotional language. Your opinions should be expressed in logical, careful language. Eliminate unsupportable superlatives—for example, *completely without value*—and strengthen opinions that seem weak or vague.

Review style: Avoid ambiguity. Poetry may or may not benefit from ambiguity, but essay writing needs to be clear. Replace statements that are vague or could be interpreted more than one way.

Unclear: Modern poetry is complicated because of life.
Clear: Modern poetry's complexity reflects the confusion and chaos of modern life.

Write to Explain
In your essay, you may wish to include classmates' thoughts from a group discussion. Be sure to identify the source of any observation.

Publishing and Presenting

Plan a poetry reading. Hold a classroom or school poetry reading in which students read modern poems. Alternate these readings with student evaluations of the poems, adapted or abridged from your essays. Student readers should lead audience discussions of the poems and evaluations.

WG *Prentice Hall Writing and Grammar Connection: Chapter 14*

CUSTOMIZE INSTRUCTION FOR UNIVERSAL ACCESS

For Less Proficient Writers	For English Learners	For Advanced Writers
Work with students to evaluate the accessibility of poems in a chart format. Encourage students to voice their opinions of the author's purpose and to describe any stumbling blocks they might have encountered while reading the poetry. Tell students to use these verbal arguments in their essays.	Encourage students to use poetry from the unit to evaluate, but also to include pieces in their home language. Ask them to question whether the language has any impact on their understanding, or if poetry in general is complex and challenging. Have them address any similarities or differences in their essay.	Encourage students to share their final opinions with other students. While comparing evaluations, have students consider what types of elements in poetry will make it more accessible to one group of people while leaving others in the dark. What similarities in literature (short stories, novels, plays) can students uncover?

Drafting

- Explain to students that an informal outline provides a way to organize the information they have collected during the prewriting stage.
- Remind students that the concluding statements of their essays will summarize their evaluation of the accessibility of poetry. In the model, Eliot's and Walcott's poetry is an example of the writer's belief that his sentiment is shared by many, explaining the need for their type of poetry. Tying the ideas together at the conclusion of the essay clarifies the evaluation of the topic.

Revising and Editing

- If students find that their explanation of opinions is lacking substance, they might want to try collecting more explicit evidence to replace any areas of ambiguity.
- Remind students that in an evaluative essay, the writer is allowing a reader to see his or her opinion through the writer's eyes. Include exact statements clarifying points that may lead to alternate interpretation.

Publishing and Presenting

- Suggest that students organize their poetry reading program, alternating the presentation of views on the accessibility of poetry with readings from modern poems. For example, read a modern poem, followed by an evaluative essay that is positive, then read another poem and an essay that suggests poetry is too inaccessible.
- Students should consider the audience for the readings when compiling essays. A classroom audience may be more at ease with complete readings of essays, while an abridged version may be more suitable for entire student body populations.

Lesson Objectives

1. To develop a multimedia report
2. To use writing strategies to generate ideas, plan, organize, evaluate, and revise the composition

Prewriting

- In small group discussion, have students share topic ideas.
- Point out that the topic for the report should be general enough so that media materials are readily available. Tell students that the media materials chosen should not overburden the report. The focus should remain the writing.
- Tell students to utilize school resources to locate needed audio-visual materials. In preparation for their reports, encourage students to identify and locate materials in advance of their outline preparation. Oftentimes, materials will take days to arrive or might be "lost in the system."
- Before students draft their reports, have them review the Rubric for Self-Assessment (p. 1303), so they know what is expected.

Writing WORKSHOP

Exposition: Multimedia Report

In a **multimedia report,** you organize words, images, and sounds into a coherent, informative, and lively presentation of a topic. In this workshop, you will assemble information into a developed multimedia script.

Assignment Criteria Your multimedia script should do the following:

- Combine words, images, and sound to present information and give the "flavor" of a topic
- Organize information in a clear, consistent manner
- Pace elements to create a coherent, even dramatic flow of sound, images, and information
- Use varied media (videos, audio recordings, spoken words, and so on) appropriate to each aspect of the topic
- Conclude with a strong, memorable ending

To preview the criteria on which your multimedia report may be assessed, see the Rubric on page 1303.

Prewriting

Choose a topic. The topic of your report must be one for which materials from several media are available. You might conduct a **media flip-through,** browsing magazines and television programs for a topic. Choose a topic that is of interest to your audience. If you do not have a specific audience in mind, choose a topic of general interest. Begin by giving your presentation a focus.

Example Focus: Zion Canyon National Park, yesterday and today

Select media materials appropriately. The media elements you choose must be varied and work well with your topic. The equipment needed to present them must also be available—old phonograph records, for instance, are useless without a turntable. Be aware that packing a script with too many elements—charts, images, sound effects, and audio clips—can lead to an unwieldy and potentially confusing presentation.

Collect relevant materials. Collect audiovisual materials for possible use. Depending on the topic, you may find what you need in libraries, on the Internet, or in a collection of your own.

Sketch an outline. First, outline your topic. Then, think of the audiovisual elements that will best explain, illustrate, or set a mood for each aspect of your topic. Do a rough storyboard indicating where you expect to incorporate the various media materials.

Selecting Material
Renaissance Portraits
I. Raphael
portraits show high individuality
VISUALS
-portrait of Baldassare Castiglione
AUDIO
-music that expresses courtliness
II. Later Renaissance Art
Titan (Venice)
VISUALS
-map showing Venice
AUDIO
-baroque music such as Vivaldi or Bach

TEACHING RESOURCES

The following resources can be used to enrich or extend the instruction for pp. 1300–1303.

Writing and Grammar, Diamond Level, Chapter 13, pp. 274–305

Performance Assessment and Portfolio Management, p. 14

Writing and Grammar iText CD-ROM
Students can use the following tools as they complete their multimedia reports:

- Topic Web Organizer
- Photo Story Board
- Unity and Coherence Revising Tool

Student Model

Before you begin drafting your script, read this student model and review the characteristics of a strong multimedia script.

Kate Vengraitis
Maplewood, NJ

Raphael's Art of the Portrait

Text	Audio and Video
[Cue AUDIO.] In the fifteenth and sixteenth centuries, art underwent a drastic change. [Cue VIDEO SLIDESHOW.] Each artist developed a unique style, sometimes blatantly trying to break the rules, other times creating innovative techniques. One common focus for Renaissance artists was the portrayal of individual personality. [Fade music.]	AUDIO: brass theme from Mussorgsky's *Pictures at an Exhibition.* VIDEO: Rapid dissolve from one slide to the next: Raphael's *Baldassare Castiglione* to Bronzio's *Portrait of a Young Man* to Titian's *Man with the Glove.*
[Cue SLIDE A.] In the Early Renaissance, portraits remained somewhat formal. By the High Renaissance, though, there is a clear focus on the personality of the subject, as in this portrait by Raphael. [Cue SLIDE B; pause.] In this portrait, *Baldassare Castiglione,* every detail helps communicate the subject's inner self. The background remains a stately neutral shade, free of decoration, appropriate for a man such as Baldassare Castiglione, the author of a handbook on genteel behavior.	SLIDE A: Timeline: Early / High Renaissance SLIDE B: Raphael's *Baldassare Castiglione.*
[Cue AUDIO.] The pose exhibits the man's elegant manner, his head and hands placed in the perfectly calm demeanor which a man of his stature would be expected to display. [Show SLIDE C; pause, then back to SLIDE B.]	AUDIO: selection from Bach's *The Well-Tempered Clavier.* SLIDE C: Detail of Castiglione's hands. SLIDE B
[Cue MUSIC.] [Cue VIDEO SLIDESHOW.] As this painting attests, Renaissance painters discovered complex ways to give insight into the individuality of their subjects.	AUDIO: Same as at opening. VIDEO SLIDESHOW: Same as at opening.

Dramatic theme music and a sampling of portraits establishes the tone and topic of the presentation.

Transitions and pauses keep the flow of the presentation smooth.

Kate chooses music to reflect the melancholy mood of this portrait.

Information is consistently organized, with each new main idea illustrated by a slide.

Both the audiovisual and textual parts of Kate's conclusion are strong and memorable.

CUSTOMIZE INSTRUCTION FOR UNIVERSAL ACCESS

For Less Proficient Writers	For English Learners	For Advanced Writers
Have students share their outlines with other classmates, asking for feedback on the flow of their outlines. Students should question whether the outlines provide a good basis for the topic description as well as an opportunity to tie the information together in a conclusive fashion.	Have students choose one general topic together. As a group and with a teacher, have them create an outline for a multimedia report, providing information on how to obtain audiovisual materials as well as how to organize images and sounds to make them effective for this particular topic.	Challenge students to pick a topic that requires more research, rather than a topic with which they are already familiar. Have them complete their outlines and share them with classmates for feedback.

Student Model

- Explain that the Student Model is a sample, and that reports may be longer.
- Discuss how the student supports her report using striking audio to offset the slides of gentler Renaissance artworks.
- Point out how Kate uses slide movement within the text to maintain direction and focus on the topic. Ask students why this helps preserve the integrity of her report.
  Possible response: The focus continues to be on the artwork. By continually changing visual cues, the reader/listener is intrigued and entertained while being informed.
- Discuss the organization of Kate's words and images in her report. This clear and well-thought-out presentation is easily understood.
- Ask the students why Kate has chosen to insert music to signal the introduction of Slide C.
  Possible responses: This signal allows the audience to take an audio cue as to the meaning behind the portrait.
- Finally, ask students what Kate does in her final transition.
  Possible response: She restates her topic and concludes her report with finality.

Real-World Connection

Multimedia Reports in the Real World

Tell students that multimedia reports surround our daily culture. Gone is the day when radio was the only source of news information. Today the television provides us with plenty of examples of multimedia. From news reports to commercials, each piece of airtime is carefully scripted to include just the right amount of music, video footage, and voiceover to engage viewers. Discuss in class how the use of multimedia reports influences opinion and thought in today's world. Have students discuss the impact of the six o'clock news and advertising. Ask students to bring examples of reports to class where the elements of multimedia work together to influence the population of television watchers.

Drafting

- Explain to students that their text is not ancillary to their report. It remains the most important part of the multimedia presentation.
- Suggest that students write the text first. The audio and video movements should be on small slips of paper or self-sticking notes. They can then move these slips around to see what order works best, and if the text order changes, the audio and video can follow suit. Encourage students to make a copy of their script with the audio and video slips taped down, so that they don't lose the organization.
- Ask students to share their drafts with a partner, asking if the format flows well to a strong, conclusive ending. Have students think of alternate ways to present information if the flow and variety are weak.
- Tell students that all the rehearsal in the world cannot compensate for faulty audio/visual equipment. Encourage students to double check that all equipment is functional prior to making presentations.

Revising

- Supply students with red and blue colored pencils and have them follow the instructions in the text.
- Tell students to anticipate nervousness in a multimedia presentation. Have the partner keep track of total presentation time when trouble areas are sorted out. Make sure if an assistant is being used for the presentation, he or she is aware of the cues to make transitions.
- Encourage students to follow the student example of removing audio to provide a better transition for the audience.

continued on p. 1303

Drafting

Write the text. Your narrated text is the glue that holds the elements of your presentation together. As you draft, follow your outline. Remember that your narration must clearly guide an audience by explaining the relevance of materials and creating transitions.

Select and position media sources. As you write the text, make final decisions on which sources to include.

- **Use script format.** Use a format such as that modeled on page 1301, to clearly coordinate narration with other elements.
- **Consider variety and flow.** As you choose audiovisual elements, focus on illustrating or setting the tone for each main point. Then, review your script to improve variety and pacing.

Prepare equipment. Assemble CD players, projectors, and any other equipment needed. Set media items such as CDs to the exact sections you will use. Enlist an assistant, or videotape your presentation.

Variety	
AVOID:	Photograph after photograph of the same scene
IMPROVEMENT:	A photograph of the scene, followed by a map showing its location
Pacing	
AVOID:	Ten minutes of the same music, interrupted by one minute of a different piece
IMPROVEMENT:	Two different pieces of music: One playing for a few minutes at the beginning, the other playing briefly in the middle, and then the opening theme repeated during the conclusion

Revising

Revise to improve media handling. Make sure your script will flow smoothly when you present it to an audience.

1. Give a partner a copy of your script. Then, give your presentation.
2. Have your partner star in red any places where you spoke too quickly, seemed to lose your place, or had trouble making the media work.
3. Work on the trouble areas. Practice reading until your pace is right and you are comfortable. Consider dropping a visual or two if necessary.

Model: Editing for Smooth Flow

(Cue AUDIO) The pose exhibits the man's elegant manner, his head and hands ☆~~(Show SLIDE C)~~ placed in the perfectly calm demeanor which a man of his stature would be expected to display. ~~(Show~~ SLIDE B) *(Show SLIDE C; pause, then back to*	AUDIO: selection from Bach's *Well-Tempered Clavier* SLIDE C: Detail of Castiglione's hands. SLIDE B: Raphael's *Baldassare Castiglione.* Full length.

Katie postpones showing Slide C to make her delivery smoother and to provide better pacing for the audience.

USING TECHNOLOGY IN WRITING

If students are using word processors for their script generation, encourage them to use different fonts or colors for the audio and video portions of their reports. This will make it easier for them to make revisions to their presentations as well as provide a clear-cut outline on the direction of their report for both the speaker and any audio/visual assistants.

Students can also use the organizing tools and revision checkers on **Writing and Grammar iText CD-ROM.**

Revise to strengthen transitions. If you have included many sounds and images, your audience may grow confused about where your presentation is going. Transitions indicate when you are moving to a new point.

Vague: . . . traffic congestion. Here, the situation improved dramatically.

Clear: . . . traffic congestion. *The next photo shows how* the situation improved dramatically *after strict driving restrictions were imposed.*

Compare the model and nonmodel. Why is the model an improvement?

Nonmodel	Model
(Cue SLIDE B: High Renaissance portrait) In the Early Renaissance, portraits remained somewhat formal. By the High Renaissance, though, there is a clear focus on the personality of the subject.	(Cue SLIDE A: Timeline) In the Early Renaissance, portraits remained somewhat formal. By the High Renaissance, though, there is a clear focus on the personality of the subject, as in this portrait by Raphael. (Cue SLIDE B: High Renaissance portrait)

Publishing and Presenting

Present your report. Make your final presentation to your class or another interested audience. Follow these suggestions:

- Have everything set up in the presentation area in advance.
- Speak slowly and confidently.
- Do not get flustered if you make a mistake. Keep a sense of humor.

WG *Prentice Hall Writing and Grammar Connection: Chapter 13*

Rubric for Self-Assessment

Evaluate your multimedia script using the following criteria and rating scale.

Criteria	Rating Scale Not very				Very
How interesting, varied, and appropriate are your media elements?	1	2	3	4	5
How well organized is your presentation of information?	1	2	3	4	5
How smoothly does the text lead into the various media elements?	1	2	3	4	5
How effective are the pacing and the transitions from one segment to the next?	1	2	3	4	5
How strong and memorable is your ending?	1	2	3	4	5

Revising (continued)

- Have students evaluate the first transitional model ("Vague" and "Clear") on the student page. Discuss how the changes affected their understanding of the text. Ask them what the next photo in this presentation may look like.
  Possible response: A clear highway with two car lengths between vehicles.
- Have students compare the Model and Nonmodel, identifying the changing direction of the report. Discuss how these changes affect the meaning to the listener and viewer.
  Answer: The text now correlates directly with the slides.
- Have students review their presentations to confirm media placement and strengthen transitions to create impact and meaning.

Publishing and Presenting

- Ask students to think about the audience they had in mind when they wrote their multimedia reports.
- Discuss ways in which different audiences would affect their presentations. How could they adopt changes to keep the effectiveness of their topic?

Assessment

- Review the assessment criteria in class.
- Before students proceed with self-assessment, have them score the Student Model in class, using one or more of the rubric categories, to help them see how to apply the criteria.
- The rubric on this page can be found on p. 14 of **Performance Assessment and Portfolio Management.**

TEST-TAKING TIP

Suggest to students that, on test items featuring a reading passage, they underline the main idea in the passage. Doing this will aid them in understanding a passage and will serve as a reminder of the main idea, while preventing them from getting bogged down in the details. Tell them that knowing the location of the main idea will help them assess the organization of a passage.

Lesson Objectives

1. To respond to bias in media with questions, challenges, or affirmations
2. To determine the point of view and/or perspective in a newscast
3. To identify images and use of the images to elicit emotions from the audience
4. To describe the reasons behind news bias and techniques used to report news

Taking It Apart

- Remind students to listen and look closely to the language as well as to audio and video in a newscast. Encourage students to make notes on the individual parts of the newscast as it is played out. Ask students to record a newscast so they can review the program and reevaluate, identify hidden subtleties, and confirm their evidence.
- After students complete the Activity on the student page, have them fill out the media feedback form. When they finish, have them discuss their answers as a class or in small groups.

Evaluating the Whole

- Ask students to identify two reasons why a newscast will present information in a biased manner. Possible response: Students may suggest that the station does not have all the information about the situation, or that there is a previous bias, such as involvement of a major contributor to the station or an advertiser in the story.
- Have students choose a news topic they recognize as biased. Have them evaluate the whole story, asking the questions on the student page. Suggest that they send their evaluations to the news station directly, asking for a response to their findings.

Listening and Speaking WORKSHOP

Analyzing Bias in News Media

One day, you turn on the television to discover that every channel is flooded with outraged accusations against a politician. On one channel, though, you happen to catch an expert explaining away the charges. The next day, the story seems to have vanished without a trace. You may have just been a witness to **media bias.**

The **news media** include all forms in which news and opinion are delivered to the public, from television to the Internet. **Bias** is an unacknowledged or concealed tendency to favor one side over another in a controversy. For instance, by presenting accusations against someone without giving equal time to his or her defense, the media show bias against the person. When following a news story, analyze the possible bias of reports.

Taking It Apart

While bias in the news may be subtle, there are certain techniques that critical viewers look out for:

- Emotionally charged language that suggests a point of view
- Hasty generalizations based on only a few cases
- Inflammatory images that elicit strong emotions from the audience
- Facts and images that reflect only one point of view
- The ordering of stories to emphasize or downplay the significance of a particular story

Evaluating the Whole

When analyzing a news story, ask yourself the following questions:

- What do you believe public response to the newscast will be? Who will benefit from this response?
- Was important information or an important perspective left out of the newscast? Why do you think this choice was made?
- Did the newscast use any elements indicating bias, such as inflammatory images or emotionally charged language?

Once you have detected bias in a news story, then you can critically weigh the information presented and form your own opinions.

Activity: View and Analyze Using a chart like the one shown, compare the coverage of the same news story on two different television stations. Use your comparison to help you detect bias.

	Media Source 1	Media Source 2
Charged language		
Generalizations		
Images		
Perspectives included		
Slot for story (first, last, middle / before or after commercial)		

CUSTOMIZE INSTRUCTION FOR UNIVERSAL ACCESS

For English Learners

Identify the meaning of the word *bias* as a group. Have students give examples of biased stories they have encountered. If possible, select a few news stories to show the students. Ask them to work alone to list any biases they notice in these stories. Make a list as students volunteer their findings to the class. Ask the students how this bias affects them. Ask the students to try to come up with reasons why this bias was used.

Assessment WORKSHOP

Strategy, Organization, and Style

On some tests, you may be asked to read a passage and answer questions about its organization and use of language. Use these strategies to help you answer such questions:

- Outline in logical order the events or ideas that the passage presents. Next to each item on your outline, write the number of the corresponding sentence or paragraph. Use the outline to help you answer questions about reordering the parts of the passage.
- Jot down a note summing up the purpose of the passage—to persuade readers to a given opinion or to inform them about a given topic. Refer to this note when answering questions about main ideas, supporting details, or sentences that do not belong.

Test-Taking Strategies

- Read the *entire* passage before answering questions.
- Eliminate any answers that clearly do not make sense.

Sample Test Item

Directions: Read the passage, and then answer the question that follows.

(1) Millions of people communicate over the Internet. (2) Some choose a custom-made home entertainment center. (3) Technology certainly has made the world seem smaller. (4) As communication technologies advance, consumers can choose among many devices designed to make their lives easier. (5) Many people carry cell phones.

1. Choose the sentence sequence that is most logical.

   A NO CHANGE
   B 4, 2, 5, 1, 3
   C 3, 1, 4, 2, 5
   D 1, 4, 2, 3, 5

Answer and Explanation

The correct answer is ***B***. It is the most logical because (4) is the topic sentence of the passage. Answers *A* and *D* are incorrect because each entails starting the paragraph with an isolated detail. Answer *C* is incorrect because it involves breaking up the list of examples that support the main idea, creating the impression that they support different ideas.

Practice

Directions: Read the passage, and then answer the questions that follow.

(1) It is time for everyone to realize that these laws make sense. (2) Several cities have enacted laws prohibiting the playing of boomboxes in public. (3) When will people learn to turn off those obnoxious boomboxes in public places? (4) Such laws have returned peace to city streets. (5) Too often citizens are assaulted by high-volume noise.

1. Choose the most logical sentence sequence:

   A 3, 5, 2, 4, 1
   B 1, 2, 3, 5, 4
   C 5, 3, 1, 2, 4
   D 4, 2, 1, 3, 5

2. Which of these sentences best summarizes the main idea of the passage?

   A Boomboxes are obnoxious.
   B More laws are needed to control the chaotic element in society.
   C Citizens need legal protections against noise in public places.
   D People are rude.

Lesson Objective

To recognize strategy, organization, and style in a sample test reading passage

Apply Reading Strategies

Explain to students that identifying key words and signal phrases in the sentences of a passage will help them put the sentences into a logical order.

Test-Taking Skills

- Tell students that a careful reading of the sentences is vital to finding the logical order of a passage.
- Have them read the sample test item, and ask them why sentence 4 is the topic sentence.
  Answer: It is more general, whereas the other sentences provide isolated details and supporting points.
- Remind them that they can often find the logical order of a passage by moving from the general to the particular.

Answers

1. The correct answer is *A*. It is the most logical because (3) introduces the topic or problem to the reader. Answer *B* is incorrect because it involves starting the passage with part of the solution to the problem. Answer *C* is incorrect because the sentences involving the solution and support for the solution are out of order. Answer *D* is incorrect because it begins with the solution without stating the problem.
2. The correct answer is *C*. Answer *B* and *D* are incorrect because they are not stated in the passage. Answer *A* is incorrect because it is a detail, not a summary of the passage.

TEACHING RESOURCES

The following resources can be used to enrich or extend the instruction for p. 1305.

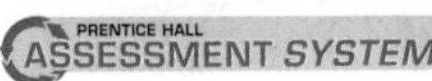

Workbook | **Transparencies**
Skill Book | **CD-ROM**

RESOURCES

Handbooks

Indexes

SUGGESTIONS FOR SUSTAINED READING

Following are some suggestions for longer works that will give you the opportunity to experience the fun of sustained reading. Each of the suggestions further explores one of the themes in this book. Many of the titles are included in the Prentice Hall Literature Library.

Unit One

Grendel

John Gardner

Once again we meet Beowulf's foe, but this time we get the story from Grendel's point of view. This retelling of the epic poem begins with the monster attacking Hrothgar's meadhall and men, and it ends right after his fight with Beowulf, as Grendel is about to die. *Grendel* is a funny, intriguing examination of the way we look at monsters, heroes, and the worlds that we create with both.

The Once and Future King

T. H. White

This novel is a magical retelling of the legend of Arthur—from the adventure-filled days of Arthur's youth to the golden age of Camelot to the final scene in which the old, broken king lies alone on the battlefield at Salisbury. In this unforgettable tale, the characters of the legend come to life, as they experience the wonders and horrors of magic, suffer victory and defeat in battle, and grapple with matters of love, betrayal, and honor.

Unit Two

Hamlet

William Shakespeare

One of Shakespeare's greatest tragedies, *Hamlet* is the tale of a young man forced to confront and question all that he formerly believed to be true. As the play begins, Prince Hamlet is mourning the death of his father, the King of Denmark. He must also accept the new marriage of his mother to his uncle, who now rules Denmark. As Hamlet struggles with these changes, the ghost of his father appears to him and tells Hamlet that he was poisoned by his brother. He urges Hamlet to avenge his murder. The revenge of Hamlet and its aftermath are the heart of the play.

The Tempest

William Shakespeare

This drama—a tale of magic, mystery, and love—takes place on what at first appears to be a deserted island. Prospero, his daughter Miranda, the spirit Ariel, and the man-monster Caliban inhabit the island. Through his magic and the aid of Ariel, Prospero is able to lure to the island a boat that carries his brother Antonio, who had dispossessed him of his throne. Prospero works his magic to arrive at a wonderful marriage for his daughter and the Prince of Naples and to reclaim his rightful title as the Duke of Milan.

Unit Three

Robinson Crusoe

Daniel Defoe

Defoe's *Robinson Crusoe* marked the beginning of the modern English novel. It is, however, a novel populated mostly by a single character. In 1659, Crusoe is shipwrecked on an island off the coast of South America and begins a twenty-eight-year stay on the island. Although specific history is not alluded to, Crusoe is very much a product of his time—he grew up during England's Civil War and the Restoration. Crusoe's attempts to create a decent society and improve his own moral character echo England's struggles to restore itself after the political turmoil of the Civil War.

Gulliver's Travels

Jonathan Swift

Swift's *Gulliver's Travels* is a children's story, a fantasy, a parody of travel books, and a sophisticated satire of English politics all in one. This masterpiece describes four voyages of Lemuel Gulliver, a ship's physician, to exotic lands. Gulliver begins in Lilliput, where the inhabitants are one twelfth the size of human beings. By the story's end, the playful elements have yielded to a bitter indictment of humankind's corruption of reason. Swift's unique combination of allegory—using settings, objects, or characters to stand for ideas and qualities beyond themselves—has made his work appealing to all audiences.

Suggested Titles Related to Thematic Units

Unit Four

Pride and Prejudice
Jane Austen

With her usual comic flair and common sense, Jane Austen explores the pressure on women to succeed in the marriage market. Mrs. Bennet, all too aware of this market's demands, shamelessly pursues marriage for each of her daughters. Although one of them, Elizabeth, is socially inferior to the arrogant Mr. Darcy, he loses his heart to her all the same. This victory of romance shows that feelings are at least as important as shrewd calculations of matchmakers. Austen's common sense prevails over pounds and shillings.

Emma
Jane Austen

Austen has great fun with her heroine Emma Woodhouse. Emma has appointed herself matchmaker for her community, meddling in almost everyone's affairs. Although her friend Mr. Knightly cautions her against the reckless pursuit of marital bliss for others, she learns the folly of her ways only through bitter experience. Also, she realizes almost too late that her frantic activity has led her to ignore her own happiness and the person best suited to guarantee it: the same Mr. Knightly who has been her loyal friend.

Unit Five

Wuthering Heights
Emily Brontë

The setting of *Wuthering Heights* is the wild and windy moors of northern Yorkshire. Central to the story is the romantic and brooding Heathcliff, a gypsy adopted into a family and mistreated by his foster brother. The story revolves around Heathcliff's thwarted love for Catherine and his revenge on those who mistreated him. By the end of the tale, Heathcliff's passion is spent, and happiness becomes possible for two of the younger members of the family, who are able to make a new beginning.

The Importance of Being Earnest
Oscar Wilde

Mocking the social conventions of the Victorian Era, *The Importance of Being Earnest* is one of the wittiest comedies ever written. Jack Worthing invents a mischievous younger brother named Ernest to allow him to adventure in London. Algernon Moncrieff appears at Jack's home assuming the identity of Ernest Worthing to meet Jack's attractive ward, Cecily Cardew. Both men have told their romantic interests that their names are Ernest because the women want to marry men named Ernest!

Unit Six

Heart of Darkness
Joseph Conrad

Conrad explores the human mind and the effects of colonialism in this great novel that has inspired many other writers. Conrad's narrator, the river steamer captain Marlow, tells a group of friends about an ominous journey into the heart of the African jungle. Mysterious, grotesque tales about the white ivory trader Kurtz pale in comparison with the reality Marlow finds when he meets the man. In Conrad's classic tale, the "heart of darkness" is both the human heart and the oppressive colonial system.

Pygmalion
George Bernard Shaw

Like his professor of phonetics, Henry Higgins, Shaw believed in the power of language to break down class barriers. In Shaw's play, the overbearing Higgins transforms Eliza Doolittle, a cockney flower girl, into an elegant woman. Neither character foresees, however, that falling in love may complicate the process of Eliza's transformation. Nearly half a century after it was written, Shaw's comedy became the basis of the enormously successful musical *My Fair Lady.*

A Passage to India
E. M. Forster

Forster's novel is a classic portrayal of clashing cultures. Adela Quested, a young British visitor to India, falsely accuses Aziz, a likable Indian doctor, of assaulting her on a tour of the Malabar Caves. As the British and Indian characters react to this accusation, the reader sees the cultural differences between them. Forster shows that in a colonial situation, these differences inevitably lead to misunderstandings.

GLOSSARY

abasement (ə bās′ mənt) *n.:* Condition of being put down or humbled
abated (ə bāt′ id) *v.:* Lessened
abrogated (ab′rō gāt′ id) *v.:* Repealed; annulled
absolution (ab′ sə lo͞o′ shən) *n.:* Act of freeing someone of a sin or of a criminal charge
acceded (ak sēd′ id) *v.:* Yielded (to); agreed
adjure (ə jo͝or′) *v.:* Appeal earnestly
admonish (ad män′ ish) *v.:* Advise; caution
adroitly (ə droit′ lē) *adv:* With physical or mental skill
adulterations (ə dul′ tər ā′ shənz) *n.:* Impurities; added ingredients that are improper or inferior
adversary (ad′ vər ser′ ē) *n.:* Opponent
adversity (ad vʉr′ sə tē) *n.:* Misfortune
affinities (ə fin′ i tēz) *n.:* Family connections; sympathies
affluence (af′ lo͞o əns) *n.:* Abundant wealth
aldermen (ôl′ dər mən) *n.:* Chief officers in a shire, or district
alters (ôl′ tərs) *v.:* Changes
amiable (ā′ mē ə bəl) *adj.:* Friendly
amorous (am′ ə res) *adj.:* Full of love
anachronism (ə nak′ rə niz′ əm) *n.:* Something out of its proper time in history
anarchy (an′ ər kē) *n.:* Absence of government; confusion, disorder, and violence
anatomize (ə nat′ ə mīz′) *v.:* Dissect in order to examine structure
antic (an′ tik) *adj.:* Odd and funny
aperture (ap′ ər chər′) *n.:* Opening
apothecary (ə päth′ ə kər′ ē) *n.:* pharmacist; druggist
appendage (ə pen′ dij) *n.:* Something added on
apprehension (ap′ rē hen′ shən) *n.:* Anxious feeling of foreboding; dread
approbation (ap′ rə bā′ shən) *n.:* Official approval, sanction, or commendation
arbiter (är′ bət ər) *n.:* Judge; umpire
arboreal (är bôr′ ē əl) *adj.:* Of, near, or among trees
artifice (ärt′ə fis) *n.:* Skill; skillful illusion
aspire (ə spīr′) *v.:* Rise high, yearn, or seek after
assault (ə sôlt′) *v.:* Violently attack
assay (a sā′) *v.:* try or attempt
assignations (as′ ig nā′ shənz) *n.:* Appointments to meet
asunder (ə sun′ dər) *adv.:* Into parts or pieces
atrophy (a′ trə fē) *v.:* Waste away
augment (ôg ment′) *v.:* Make greater; enlarge
august (ô gust′) *adj.:* Worthy of great respect
authenticity (ô′ thən tis′ ə tē) *n.:* Quality or state of being authentic; genuineness
avarice (av′ ər is) *n.:* Greed
averred (ə vʉrd′) *v.:* Stated to be true
avouches (ə vouch′ ez) *v.:* Asserts positively; affirms
balm (bäm) *n.:* Anything healing or soothing
barricaded (bar′ i kād′ id) *v.:* Blocked
blight (blīt) *n.:* Condition of withering
blithe (blī*th*) *adj.:* Cheerful
brazening (brā′ zən iŋ) *v.:* Daring boldly or shamelessly
breach (brēch) *n.:* Breaking open; the opening created by a break; failure to fullfill an agreement
cadence (kād′ əns) *n.:* Measured movement
cant (kant) *n.:* Insincere or meaningless talk
capital (kap′ ət əl) *n.:* Wealth in money or property
caprices (kə prē′ sis) *n.:* Whims
careered (kə rird′) *v.:* Rushed wildly
certify (sʉrt′ ə fī′) *v.:* Declare a thing true or accurate; verify; attest
chronicle (krän′ i kəl) *n.:* Historical record
churls (chʉrlz) *n.:* Farm laborers; peasants
circumscribed (sʉr′ kəm skrībd′) *adj.:* Limited; having a definite boundary
clamorous (klam′ ər əs) *adj.:* Noisy
combustible (kəm bus′ tə bəl) *adj.:* Capable of igniting and burning; flammable
commission (kə mish′ ən) *n.:* Authorization; act of giving authority to an individual
compassionate (kəm pash′ ən it) *adj.:* Sympathizing; pitying
complaisant (kəm plā′ zənt) *adj.:* Agreeable; willing to please
comprised (kəm prīzd′) *v.:* Consisted of; included or contained
confiscation (kän′ fis kā′ shən) *n.:* Official act of seizing private property
conflagration (kän′ flə grā′ shən) *n.:* Great fire
confounded (kən found′ id) *adj.:* Confused; bewildered; mixed together indiscriminately
conjecture (kən jek′ chər) *v.:* Guess
conquest (käŋ′ kwest′) *n.:* The winning of another's affection or submission
contention (kən ten′ shən) *n.:* Dispute; argument
contentious (kən ten′ shəs) *adj.:* Quarrelsome
contrite (kən trīt′) *adj.:* Willing to repent or atone
conviction (kən′ vik′ shən) *n.:* Belief; faith
copious (kō′ pē əs) *adj.:* Abundant; plentiful
countenance (koun′ tə nəns) *n.:* Face
covetousness (kuv′ət əs ness) *n.:* Greediness
coyness (koi′ nis) *n.:* Shyness; aloofness, often as part of a flirtation
credulity (krə do͞o′ lə tē) *n.:* Tendency to believe too readily
credulous (krej′ o͞o ləs) *adj.:* Tending to believe too readily
dauntless (dônt′ lis) *adj.:* Fearless; cannot be intimidated
decimation (des′ ə mā′ shun) *n.:* Destruction or killing of one in ten or of any large part of a group
defiantly (di fī′ ənt lē) *adv.:* Disobediently; with resistance
deign (dān) *v.:* condescend; lower oneself
depredation (dep′ rə dā′ shən) *n.:* Act or instance of robbing, plundering, or laying waste
derided (di rīd′ id) *v.:* Made fun of; ridiculed
derision (di rizh′ ən) *n.:* Contempt or ridicule
desolate (des′ ə lit) *adj.:* Deserted; forlorn
despotic (de spät′ ik) *adj.:* Tyrannical
destitute (des′ tə to͞ot) *adj.:* Lacking
devise (de vīz′) *v.:* work out or create; plan
diabolical (dī′ ə bäl′ i kəl) *adj.:* Evil
diffusive (di fyo͞o′siv) *adj.:* Tending to spread out
disabused (dis′ ə byo͞ozd′) *adj.:* Freed from false ideas
disaffection (dis′ ə fek′ shən) *n.:* Discontent; disillusionment
discerned (di zʉrnd′) *v.:* Recognized as separate or different
disconcerted (dis′ kən sʉrt′ əd) *adj.:* Embarrassed and confused
discoursing (dis kôrs′ iŋ) *v.:* Talking about; discussing
discreet (dis krēt′) *adj.:* Wise; prudent
discretion (di skresh′ ən) *n.:* Good judgment; prudence
dislocation (dis′ lō kā′ shən) *n.:* Condition of being out of place
dispensation (dis′ pən sā′ shən) *n.:* Religious system or belief
distemper (dis tem′ pər) *n.:* Infectious disease such as a plague
distill (di stil′) *v.:* Obtain the essential part
divert (də vʉrt′) *v.:* Amuse; entertain; distract
dominion (də min′ yən) *n.:* Rule or power to rule; a governed territory
dowry (dou′ rē) *n.:* Property that a woman brings to her husband at marriage
eclipse (ē klips′) *n.:* Dimming or extinction of fame or glory
efficacious (ef′ i kā′ shəs) *adj.:* Effective
efficacy (ef′ i kə sē) *n.:* Power to produce intended effects
effigy (ef′ i jē) *n.:* Portrait or statue of a person
elongated (ē lôŋ′ gāt′ id) *adj.:* Lengthened; stretched
eludes (ē lo͞odz′) *v.:* Avoids or escapes
emancipate (ē man′ sə pāt) *v.:* Free from slavery or oppression
embarked (em bärkt′) *v.:* Engaged in something, such as a conversation
embellishments (em bel′ ish mənts) *n.:* Decorative touches; ornamentation
encomiums (en kō′ mē əms) *n.:* Formal expressions of great praise
endurance (en do͝or′ əns) *n.:* Ability to last or continue
enigma (i nig′ mə) *n.:* Riddle; perplexing statement, person, or situation
enquiry (en kwīr′ ē) *n.:* Question; investigation
entreated (en trēt′ id) *v.:* Begged; pleaded
equivocate: (ē kwiv′ə kāt) *v.:* Use terms that have two or more meanings to mislead purposely or deceive
evanescence (ev′ ə nes′ əns) *n.:* Vanishing or tendency to vanish
exasperated (eg zas′ pər āt′ id) *adj.:* Extremely annoyed; out of patience
excrescence (eks kres′ əns) *n.:* Abnormal or disfiguring outgrowth
exemplary (eg zem′ plə rē) *adj.:* Serving as a model or example; of that which should be imitated
exonerate (eg zän′ ər āt′) *v.:* Free from a charge of guilt; declare or prove blameless
expedient (ek spē′ dē ənt) *n.:* Device used in an emergency

expiated (ēk′ spē āt′ id) *v.:* Atoned; made amends for, especially by suffering

expostulate (eks päs′ chə lāt′) *v.:* Reason earnestly with

extenuating (ek sten′ yo͞o āt′ iŋ) *adj.:* Lessening the seriousness of; excusing

fastidious (fas tid′ ē əs) *adj.:* Particular; difficult to please

fathom (fat*h*′ əm) *v.:* Understand thoroughly

fathomless (fat*h*′ əm lis) *adj.:* Too deep to be measured or understood

feigned (fānd) *v.:* Made a false show of; pretended

fervent (fʉr′ vənt) *adj.:* Having or showing great warmth of feeling

fidelity (fə del′ ə tē) *n.:* Faithfulness

filial (fil′ ē əl) *adj.:* Expected of a son or daughter

forage (fôr′ ij) *n.:* Food grazed for by animals

forfeited (fôr′ fit id) *v.:* Gave up, as a penalty

formidable (fôr′ mə də bəl) *adj.:* Causing fear or dread

fortitude (fôrt′ ə to͞od′) *n.:* Courage; strength to endure

fraudulent (frô′ jə lənt) *adj.:* Characterized by deceit or trickery

furrow (fʉr′ ō) *n.:* Narrow groove, such as that made in the ground by a plow

galled (gôld) *adj.:* Injured or made sore by rubbing or chafing

garnished (gär′ nisht) *adj.:* Decorated; trimmed

garrulous (gar′ ə ləs) *adj.:* Talkative

gaunt (gônt) *adj.:* Very thin and angular

gleaned (glēnd) *v.:* Collected bit by bit, as when gathering stray grain after a harvest

grandeur (grän′ jər) *n.:* Splendor; magnificence

gravity (grav′ i tē) *n.:* Seriousness

grieved (grēvd) *v.:* Caused to feel deep grief; mourned; felt deep grief for

grievous (grēv′ əs) *adj.:* Causing sorrow; hard to bear

guile (gīl) *n.:* Artful trickery; cunning

habituate (hə bich′ o͞o āt′) *v.:* Make used to

harbingers (här′ bin jərs) *n.:* Forerunners

harried (har′ ēd) *v.:* Harassed

hoary (hôr′ ē) *adj.:* White or gray with age

ignoble (ig nō′ bəl) *adj.:* Not noble; common

ignominy (ig′ nə min′ ē) *n.:* Humiliation; dishonor; disgrace

illumine (i lo͞o′ mən) *v.:* Light up

impediments (im ped′ə mənts) *n.:* Obstructions

imperial (im pir′ ē əl) *adj.:* Of an empire; having supreme authority

imperialism (im pir′ ē əl iz′əm) *n.:* Policy of forming an empire and securing economic power by conquest and colonization

imperturbable (im′ pər tʉr′ bə bəl) *adj.:* Calm; not easily ruffled

importuning (im′ pôr to͞on′ iŋ) *v.:* Pleading with

impressionistic (im presh′ ən is′ tik) *adj.:* Conveying a quick, overall picture

impudence (im′ pyo͞o dəns) *n.:* Lack of shame; rudeness

impulse (im′ puls′) *n.:* Force driving forward

inauspicious (in′ ô spish′əs) *adj.:* Not promising a good outcome; unfavorable

incitement (in sīt′ mənt) *n.:* Act of urging; encouragement

inconstancy (in kän′ stən sē) *n.:* Fickleness; changeableness

inconstantly (in kän′ stənt lē) *adv.:* Changeably; in a fickle way

incredulously (in krej′ o͞o ləs lē) *adv.:* In a manner expressing doubt or disbelief

inculcated (in kul′ kāt′ id) *v.:* Impressed upon the mind by frequent repetition

indignant (in dig′nənt) *adj.:* Outraged; filled with righteous anger

indissoluble (in′ di säl′ yo͞o bəl) *adj.:* Not able to be dissolved or undone

indolence (in′ də ləns) *n.:* Idleness; laziness

inducted (in dukt′ id) *v.:* Brought formally into an organization

inevitable (in ev′ i tə bəl) *adj.:* Unavoidable; certain to happen

infirmity (in fʉr′ mə tē) *n.:* Physical or mental defect; illness

ingenuous (in jen′ yo͞o əs) *adj.:* Naive; simple

inklings (iŋk′ liŋz) *n.:* Indirect suggestions; vague ideas

innumerable (i no͞o′ mər ə bəl) *adj.:* Too many to count

insensible (in sen′ sə bəl) *adj.:* Unable to feel or sense anything; numb

instantaneous (in′ stən tā′ nē əs) *adj.:* Done or happening in an instant

intemperance (in tem′ pər əns) *n.:* Lack of restraint

intermit (in′ tər mit′) *v.:* Stop for a time

internment (in tʉrn′ mənt) *n.:* Confinement, especially during war

interred (in tʉrd′) *v.:* Buried

intimidated (in tim′ ə dāt′ əd) *v.:* Made afraid; frightened

intrigues (in trēgz′) *v.:* Plots or schemes secretly or underhandedly

intrinsically (in trin′ sik lē) *adv.:* At its core; inherently; innately

invincible (in vin′ sə bəl) *adj.:* Unconquerable

irrevocable (ir rev′ ə kə bəl): *adj.:* Unable to be undone or canceled

judicious (jo͞o dish′ əs) *adj.:* Showing good judgment

keenly (kēn′ lē) *adv.:* Sharply; intensely

ken (ken) *n.:* Range of sight or knowledge

laity (lā′ i tē) *n.:* Those not initiated into the priesthood or other profession

lamentable (lam′ ən tə bəl) *adj.:* Distressing

languish (laŋ′ gwish) *v.:* Become weak; droop

languished (laŋ′ gwisht) *adj.:* Weakened; dulled

largesse (lär jes′) *n.:* Nobility of spirit

larking (lärk′ iŋ) *n.:* Free-spirited, whimsical fun

laudable (lôd′ ə bəl) *adj.:* Worthy of praise

liege (lēj) *n.:* Lord or king

litanies (lit′ən ēz) *n.:* Prayers in which a congregation repeats a fixed response; repetitive recitations

loathsome (lōt*h*′ səm) *adj.:* Disgusting

ludicrous (lo͞o′ di krəs) *adj.:* Absurd; ridiculous

malevolence (mə lev′ ə ləns) *n.:* Ill will; spitefulness

malevolent (mə lev′ ə lent) *adj.:* Wishing harm to others

malicious (mə lish′ əs) *adj.:* Deliberately harmful; destructive

malignity (mə lig′ nə tē) *n.:* Strong desire to harm others

massive (mas′ iv) *adj.:* Big and solid; bulky

maxim (maks′ im) *n.:* Briefly expressed general truth or rule of conduct

melancholy (mel′ ən käl′ ē) *adj.:* Sad; depressing

minions (min′ yənz) *n.:* Attendants or agents

mockeries (mäk′ ər ēz) *n.:* Ridicule; futile or disappointing efforts

monotonous (mə nät′ ən əs) *adj.:* Having little variation

mortal (môr′ təl) *adj.:* Of that which must eventually die

multitudinous: (mul′ tə to͞od′ ′n əs) *adj.:* Existing in great numbers

munificence (myo͞o nif′ə səns) *n.:* Lavish generosity

nocturnal (näk tʉr′ nəl) *adj.:* Occurring at night

nondescript (nän′ di skript′) *adj.:* Lacking identifying characteristics; bland

nuisance (no͞o′ səns) *n.:* act, thing, or condition causing trouble

obdurate (äb′ do͞or it) *adj.:* Stubborn; unyielding

obliquely (ə blēk′ lē) *adv.:* At a slant; indirectly

obliterate (ə blit′ ə rāt) *v.:* Destroy utterly

obscure (əb skyo͞or′) *adj.:* Not easily seen; not generally known

obstinate (äb′ stə nət) *adj.:* Stubborn; dogged; mulish

odious (ō′ dē əs) *adj.:* Hateful; disgusting

officious (ə fish′ əs) *adj.:* Meddlesome

omniscient (äm nish′ ənt) *adj.:* Having infinite knowledge; knowing all things

ordeal (ôr dēl′) *n.:* Difficult or painful experience that tests one

pallor (pal′ ər) *n.:* Lack of color; paleness

palpable (pal′ pə bəl) *adj.:* Capable of being touched or felt

paltry (pôl′ trē) *adj.:* Practically worthless; insignificant

patronize (pā′ trə nīz) *v.:* To be a customer of a particular merchant or store

penury (pen′ yo͞o rē) *n.:* Poverty

peril (per′ əl) *n.:* Exposure to harm

pernicious (pər nish′ əs) *adj.:* Causing serious injury; deadly

persistent (pər sis′ tənt) *adj.:* Continuing without letup

perturbation (pʉr′ tər bā′ shən) *n.:* Disturbance

phantasm (fan′ taz′ əm) *n.:* Supernatural form or shape; ghost; figment of the mind

piety (pī′ ə tē) *n.:* Devotion to sacred duties

platitude (plat′ ə to͞od′) *n.:* Statement lacking originality

plebeian (plē bē′ ən) *adj.:* Common; not aristocratic

portals (pôr′ təlz) *n.:* Doors; gateways

prating (prāt iŋ) *n.:* Chatter

predominance (prē däm′ ə nəns) *n.:* Superiority

prefiguring (prē fig′ yer iŋ) *v.:* Resembling and so suggesting beforehand

prenatal (prē nāt′ əl) *adj.:* Before birth

preponderates (prē pän´ də rāts´) *v.:* Dominates; causes the arm of a balance scale to tip downward
presumption (prē zump´ shən) *n.:* Audacity; tending to assume certain things
prevarication (pri var´ i kā´ shən) *n.:* Evasion of truth
prime (prīm) *n.:* Best stage of a thing or process
pristine (pris tēn´) *adj.:* Original; unspoiled
procured (prō kyoord´) *v.:* Obtained
prodigal (präd´ i gəl) *adj.:* Recklessly wasteful
prodigious (prō´dij´ əs) *adj.:* Enormous
profanation (präf ə nā´ shən) *n.:* Action showing disrespect for something sacred
profuse (prō fyo͞os´) *adj.:* Abundant; pouring out
promontories (präm´ ən tôr´ ēz) *n.:* Parts of high land sticking out into the sea or other body of water
propagators (präp´ ə gāt´ ərz) *n.:* Those who cause something to happen or to spread
propitiate (prə pish´ ē āt) *v.:* Win the goodwill of; appease
prostrate (präs´ trāt) *adj.:* Defenseless; in a prone or lying position
purge (purj) *v.:* Purify; cleanse
rancor (raŋ´ kər) *n.:* Ill will
ransacked (ran´ sakt´) *v.:* Searched through for plunder; pillaged; robbed
rapture (rap´ chər) *n.:* Joy; great pleasure
rapturous (rap´ chər us) *adj.:* Ecstatic
ravaged (rav´ ijd) *v.:* Destroyed
recompense (rek´əm pens´) *n.:* Reward; payment in return for something
redress (ri dres´) *n.:* Compensation, as for a wrong
refractory (ri frak´ tər ē) *adj.:* Hard to manage; stubborn
remnant (rem´ nənt) *n.:* What is left over
remonstrated (ri män´ strāt id) *v.:* Objected strongly
reparation (rep´ ə rā´ shən) *n.:* Something making up for wrong or injury
requiem (rek´ wē əm) *n.:* Musical composition honoring the dead
requisites (rek´wə zits) *n.:* Things necessary for a given purpose
requisitioned (rek´ wə zish´ ənd) *v.:* Requested or applied for with a formal written order
retaliate (ri tal´ ē āt´) *v.:* Return an injury or wrong
reticent (ret´ ə sənt) *adj.:* Silent; reserved
retort (ri tôrt´) *v.:* Respond with a clever answer or wisecrack
reverence (rēv´ər əns) *n.:* Deep respect
reverently (rev´ ər ənt lē) *adv.:* With deep respect or awe
righteous (rī´chəs) *adj.:* Acting in a just, upright manner; doing what is right
rogue (rōg) *n.:* Scoundrel; wandering beggar
roused (rouzd) *v.:* Stirred up; risen from cover
rue (ro͞o) *n.:* Sorrow; regret
sanction (saŋk´ shən) *n.:* Authorized approval or permission
sanguine (saŋ´ gwin) *adj.:* Confident; cheerful
satiety (sə tī´ ə tē) *n.:* State of being filled to excess
schism (siz´ əm) *n.:* Division of a group into factions
scope (skōp) *n.:* Range of perception or understanding
scruple (skro͞o´ pəl) *n.:* Hesitation caused by one's conscience or principles; uneasy feeling; qualm
segmented (seg´ ment id) *adj.:* Separated into parts
semblance (sem´ bləns) *n.:* Appearance; image
senility (si nil´ə tē) *n.:* Mental and physical decay due to old age
sentinel (sen´ ti nəl) *n.:* Person or animal that guards or watches over
sequestered (si kwes´ tərd) *v.:* Kept apart from others
sinuous (sin´ yo͞o əs) *adj.:* Bending; winding
skeptical (skep´ ti kəl) *adj.:* Doubting; not easily persuaded
sloth (slôth) *n.:* Laziness; idleness
sojourn (sō´ jurn) *v.:* Stay for a while
solace (säl´ is) *n.:* Comfort; relief
solicitous (sə lis´ ə təs) *adj.:* Showing care or concern
solicitude (sə lis´ ə to͞od´) *n.:* Care; concern
sordid (sôr´ did) *adj.:* Unclean; dirty
sovereign (säv´ rən) *adj.:* Supreme in power, rank, or authority
sovereignty (säv´ rən tē) *n.:* Supreme political authority
specious (spē´ shəs) *adj.:* Deceptively attractive or valid; false
spectral (spek´ trəl) *adj.:* Ghostly
speculation (spek´ yo͞o lā´ shən) *n.:* Train of thought on a subject, especially one using hypotheses or guesses
splaying (splā´ iŋ) *v.:* Spreading
squalid (skwäl´ id) *adj.:* Miserably poor; wretched
stagnant (stag´ nənt) *adj.:* Motionless; stale
stature (stach´ ər) *n.:* Height of a person standing; development, growth, or level of achievement
stead (sted) *n.:* Position of a person as filled by a replacement or substitute
stealthy (stel´ thē) *adj.:* Sly; furtive
stoic (stō´ ik) *n.:* Person indifferent to joy, grief, pleasure, or pain
stranded (stran´ did) *v.:* Forced into shallow water or onto a beach; left helpless
stringent (strin´ jənt) *adj.:* Strict
sublime (sə blīm´) *adj.:* Inspiring awe through greatness or beauty
sublimity (sə blim´ ə tē) *n.:* Quality of being majestic or noble
subsequently (sub´ si kwənt lē) *adv.:* At a later time
succor (suk´ ər) *v.:* Help; aid; relieve
suffused (sə fyo͞ozd´) *v.:* Spread throughout
sullen (sul´ ən) *adj.:* Gloomy; dismal
sundry (sun´ drē) *adj.:* Various; miscellaneous
supine (so͞o pin´) *adj.:* Lying on the back
suppliant (sup´ lē ənt) *adj.:* Beseeching prayerfully; imploring
supplication (sup´ lə kā´ shən) *n.:* Act of praying or pleading
surmise (sər mīz´) *n.:* Guess; assumption
symmetry (sim´ ə trē) *n.:* Balanced form; the beauty resulting from such balance
tarry (tar´ ē) *v.:* Delay or linger
teeming (tēm´ iŋ) *adj.:* Filled to overflowing
temperate (tem´ pər it) *adj.:* Mild
tempests (tem´ pists) *n.:* Storms
tempestuous (tem pes´ cho͞o əs) *adj.:* Turbulent; violently stormy
terrestrial (tə res´ trē əl) *adj.:* Relating to Earth or to things of this world
timorous (tim´ ər əs) *adj.:* Timid
topographical (täp´ə graf´ i kəl) *adj.:* Relating to a map of the surface features of a region, including its elevations, rivers, mountains, and so on
torrid (tôr´ id) *adj.:* Very hot; scorching
tranquil (tran´ kwil) *adj.:* Calm; serene
transcendent (tran sen´ dənt) *adj.:* Surpassing; beyond all limits
transfiguring (trans fig´ yər iŋ) *adj.:* Changing the appearance of a thing or person, especially so as to glorify it
transgress (trans gres´) *v.:* Violate a law or command
transient (tran´ shənt) *adj.:* Temporary; passing through quickly
treachery (trech´ ər ē) *n.:* Betrayal of trust, faith, or allegiance
treasons (trē´ zenz) *n.:* Betrayals of one's country or oath of loyalty
trepidation (trep´ ə dā´ shən) *n.:* Trembling
trifles (trī´ fəlz) *n.:* Things of little value or importance; trivial matters
tumid (to͞o´ mid) *adj.:* Swollen
tumult (to͞o´ mult´) *n.:* Noisy commotion
turbid (tur´ bid) *adj.:* Muddy or cloudy; stirred up; confused
uncanny (un kan´ ē) *adj.:* Mysterious; hard to explain
ungenial (un jēn´ yəl) *adj.:* Unfriendly
upbraidings (up brād´ iŋz) *n.:* Stern words of disapproval; scoldings
vales (vāls) *n.:* Valleys; hollows; depressed stretches of ground
valor (val´ ər) *n.:* Marked courage or bravery
venerable (ven´ ər ə bəl) *adj.:* Commanding respect by virtue of age, character, or rank
vernal (vurn´ əl) *adj.:* Relating to spring
vestige (ves´ tij) *n.:* Trace; remaining bit
vindication (vin´ də kā´ shən) *n.:* Act of providing justification or support for
vintage (vin´ tij) *n.:* Wine of fine quality
visage (viz´ ij) *n.:* Person's face or expression
wan (wän) *adj.:* Sickly; pale
waning (wān´ iŋ) *v.:* Gradually becoming dimmer
winsome (win´ səm) *adj.:* Having a charming, attractive appearance or manner
winsomeness (win´ səm niss) *n.:* Charm; winning quality
writhing (rīth´ iŋ) *adj.:* Making twisting or turning motions
zenith (zē´ nith) *n.:* Highest point of something, especially of the sky or celestial sphere

LITERARY TERMS HANDBOOK

ALLEGORY An *allegory* is a literary work with two or more levels of meaning—a literal level and one or more symbolic levels. The events, settings, objects, or characters in an allegory—the literal level—stand for ideas or qualities, such as goodness, tyranny, salvation, and so on. Allegorical writing was common in the Middle Ages. Spenser revived the form in *The Faerie Queene,* and John Bunyan revived it yet again in *The Pilgrim's Progress.* Some modern novels, such as George Orwell's *Animal Farm,* can be read as allegories.

ALLITERATION *Alliteration* is the repetition of initial consonant sounds in accented syllables. Coleridge uses the alliteration of both *b* and *f* sounds in this line from *The Rime of the Ancient Mariner*:

> The fair breeze blew, the white foam flew.

Especially in poetry, alliteration is used to emphasize and to link words, as well as to create musical sounds.

See also Anglo-Saxon Poetry.

ALLUSION *Allusion* is a reference to a well-known person, place, event, literary work, or work of art.

AMBIGUITY *Ambiguity* is the effect created when words suggest and support two or more divergent interpretations. Ambiguity may be used in literature to express experiences or truths that are complex or even contradictory. For instance, the title of Elizabeth Bowen's short story "The Demon Lover," on page 1032, is ambiguous: It can refer either to the main character, who is a lover of a "demon" (a past love that she has not resolved), to the past that haunts her, or to her demonic lover, a ghost who haunts her. This ambiguous use of words reflects a larger ambiguity in the story.

See also Irony.

ANALOGY An *analogy* is an extended comparison of relationships. It is based on the idea or insight that the relationship between one pair of things is like the relationship between another pair. Unlike a metaphor, another form of comparison, an analogy involves an explicit comparison, often using the word *like* or *as.*

See also Metaphor *and* Simile.

ANAPEST *See* Meter.

ANGLO-SAXON POETRY The rhythmic poetry composed in the Old English language before A.D. 1100 is known as *Anglo-Saxon poetry.* It generally has four accented syllables and an indefinite number of unaccented syllables in each line. Each line is divided in half by a caesura, or pause, and the halves are linked by the alliteration of two or three of the accented syllables. The following translation from "Wulf and Eadwacer" shows the alliteration and caesuras used in Anglo-Saxon poetry:

> I waited for my Wulf // with far-Wandering yearnings,
> When it was rainy weather // and I sat weeping.

Anglo-Saxon poetry was sung or chanted to the accompaniment of a primitive harp; it was not written but was passed down orally.

See also Alliteration, Caesura, *and* Kenning.

ARCHETYPAL LITERARY ELEMENTS *Archetypal literary elements* are patterns in literature found around the world. For instance, the occurrence of events in threes is an archetypal element of fairy tales. Certain character types, such as mysterious guides, are also archetypal elements of such traditional stories. According to some critics, these elements express in symbolic form truths about the human mind.

ASSONANCE *Assonance* is the repetition of vowel sounds in stressed syllables containing dissimilar consonant sounds. Robert Browning uses assonance in this line in "Andrea del Sarto":

> Ah, but man's reach should exceed his grasp. . . .

The long *e* sound is repeated in the words *reach* and *exceed.* The syllables containing these sounds are stressed and contain different consonants: *r-ch* and *c-d.*

See also Consonance.

BALLAD A *ballad* is a song that tells a story, often about adventure or romance, or a poem imitating such a song. Most ballads are divided into four- or six-line stanzas, are rhymed, use simple language, and depict dramatic action. Many ballads employ a repeated refrain. Some use incremental repetition, in which the refrain is varied slightly each time it appears.

BLANK VERSE *Blank verse* is unrhymed poetry usually written in iambic pentameter (see Meter). Occasional variations in rhythm are introduced in blank verse to create emphasis, variety, and naturalness of sound. Because blank verse sounds much like ordinary spoken English, it is often used in drama, as by Shakespeare, and in poetry. The following lines come from Wordsworth's blank-verse poem "Lines Composed a Few Miles Above Tintern Abbey," on page 666:

> For thou | art with | me here | upon | the banks
> Of this | fair riv | er; thou | my dear | est Friend

See also Meter.

CAESURA A *caesura* is a natural pause in the middle of a line of poetry. In Anglo-Saxon poetry, a caesura divides each four-stress line in half and thus is essential to the rhythm.

See also Anglo-Saxon Poetry.

CARPE DIEM A Latin phrase, *carpe diem* means "seize the day" or "make the most of passing time." Many great literary works have been written with the *carpe diem* theme.

CHARACTER A person (though not necessarily a human being) who takes part in the action of a literary work is known as a character. Characters can be classified in different ways. A character who plays an important role is called a *major character.* A character who does not is called a *minor character.* A character who plays the central role in a story is called the *protagonist.* A character who opposes the protagonist is called the *antagonist.* A *round character* has many aspects to his or her personality. A *flat character* is defined by only a few qualities. A character who changes is called *dynamic*; a character who does not change is called *static.*

See also Characterization.

CHARACTERIZATION *Characterization* is the act of creating and developing a character. A writer uses *direct characterization* when he or she describes a character's traits explicitly. Writers also use *indirect characterization.* A character's traits can be revealed indirectly in what he or she says, thinks, or does; in a description of his or her appearance; or in the statements, thoughts, or actions of other characters.

See also Character.

CLIMAX The *climax* is the high point of interest or suspense in a literary work. Often, the climax is also the crisis in the plot, the point at which the protagonist changes his or her understanding or situation. Sometimes, the climax coincides with the *resolution,* the point at which the central conflict is ended.

See also Plot.

COMEDY A *comedy* is a literary work, especially a play, that has a happy ending. A comedy often shows ordinary characters in conflict with their society. Types of comedy include *romantic comedy,* which involves problems among lovers, and the *comedy of manners,* which satirically challenges the social customs of a sophisticated society. Comedy is often contrasted with tragedy, in which the protagonist meets an unfortunate end.

See also Drama *and* Tragedy.

CONCEIT A *conceit* is an unusual and surprising comparison between two very different things. This special kind of metaphor or complicated analogy is often the basis for a whole poem. During the Elizabethan Age, sonnets commonly included Petrarchan conceits. *Petrarchan conceits* make extravagant claims about the beloved's beauty or the speaker's suffering, with comparisons to divine beings, powerful natural forces, and objects that contain a given quality in the highest degree. Spenser uses a Petrarchan conceit when he claims in Sonnet 1, on page 236, that the "starry light" of his beloved's eyes will make his book happy when she reads it.

Seventeenth-century *metaphysical* poets used elaborate, unusual, and highly intellectual conceits, as in the conceit of the compass in John Donne's "A Valediction: Forbidding Mourning," on page 424.

See also Metaphor.

CONFLICT A *conflict* is a struggle between opposing forces. Sometimes, this struggle is internal, or within a character. At other times, the struggle is external, or between the character and some outside force. The outside force may be another character, nature, or some element of society such as a custom or a political institution. Often, the conflict in a work combines several of these possibilities.

See also Plot.

CONNOTATION *Connotation* refers to the associations that a word calls to mind in addition to its dictionary meaning. For example, the words *home* and *domicile* have the same dictionary meaning. However, the first has positive connotations of warmth and security, whereas the second does not.

See also Denotation.

CONSONANCE *Consonance* is the repetition of final consonant sounds in stressed syllables containing dissimilar vowel sounds. Samuel Taylor Coleridge uses consonance in these lines from *The Rime of the Ancient Mariner,* on page 686:

> a frightful fie*nd* / Doth close behi*nd* him tread.

Fiend and the stressed syllable in *behind* have the same final consonant sounds but different vowel sounds.

See also Assonance.

COUPLET A *couplet* is a pair of rhyming lines written in the same meter. A *heroic couplet* is a rhymed pair of iambic pentameter lines. In a *closed couplet,* the meaning and grammar are completed within the two lines. These lines from Alexander Pope's *An Essay on Criticism* are a closed heroic couplet:

> True ease in writing comes from art, not chance,
> As those move easiest who have learned to dance.

Shakespearean sonnets usually end with heroic couplets.

See also Sonnet.

DACTYL See Meter.

DENOTATION *Denotation* is the objective meaning of a word—that to which the word refers, independent of other associations that the word calls to mind. Dictionaries list the denotative meanings of words.

See also Connotation.

DIALECT *Dialect* is the form of a language spoken by people in a particular region or group. Dialects differ from one another in grammar, vocabulary, and pronunciation. Robert Burns used a Scots dialect in poems like "Auld Lang Syne":

> Should auld acquaintance be forgot,
> And never brought to min'?
> Should auld acquaintance be forgot,
> And days o' auld lang syne?

DIALOGUE *Dialogue* is a conversation between characters. Writers use dialogue to reveal character, to present events, to add variety to narratives, and to interest readers. Dialogue in a story is usually set off by quotation marks and paragraphing. Dialogue in a play script generally follows the name of the speaker.

DIARY A *diary* is a personal record of daily events, usually written in prose. Most diaries are not written for publication; sometimes, however, interesting diaries or diaries written by influential people are published. One example of a published diary is that of Samuel Pepys, a selection from which appears on page 496.

See also Journal.

DICTION *Diction* is a writer's word choice. It can be a major determinant of the writer's style. Diction can be described as formal or informal, abstract or concrete, plain or ornate, ordinary or technical.

See also Style.

DIMETER *See* Meter.

DRAMA A *drama* is a story written to be performed by actors. It may consist of one or more large sections, called acts, which are made up of any number of smaller sections, called scenes.

Drama originated in the religious rituals and symbolic reenactments of primitive peoples. The ancient Greeks, who developed drama into a sophisticated art form, created such dramatic forms as tragedy and comedy.

The first dramas in England were the miracle plays and morality plays of the Middle Ages. Miracle plays told biblical stories. Morality plays, such as *Everyman*, were allegories dealing with personified virtues and vices. The English Renaissance saw a flowering of drama in England, culminating in the works of William Shakespeare, who wrote many of the world's greatest comedies, tragedies, histories, and romances. During the Neoclassical Age, English drama turned to satirical comedies of manners that probed the virtues of upper-class society. In the Romantic and Victorian ages, a few good verse plays were written, including Percy Bysshe Shelley's *The Cenci* and *Prometheus Unbound*. The end of the nineteenth and beginning of the twentieth centuries saw a resurgence of the drama in England and throughout the English-speaking world. Great plays of the Modern period include plays by Bernard Shaw, Christopher Fry, T. S. Eliot, Harold Pinter, and Samuel Beckett.

DRAMATIC MONOLOGUE A *dramatic monologue* is a poem in which an imaginary character speaks to a silent listener. During the monologue, the speaker reveals his or her personality, usually at a moment of crisis. Robert Browning's "My Last Duchess," on page 836, is a dramatic monologue.

ELEGY An *elegy* is a solemn and formal lyric poem about death. It may mourn a particular person or reflect on a serious or tragic theme, such as the passing of youth or beauty. See Thomas Gray's "Elegy Written in a Country Churchyard," on page 570.

See also Lyric Poem.

END-STOPPED LINE An *end-stopped* line is a line of poetry concluding with a break in the meter and in the meaning. This pause at the end of a line is often punctuated by a period, comma, dash, or semicolon. These lines from "Away, Melancholy," by Stevie Smith, are end-stopped:

> Are not the trees green,
> The earth as green?
> Does not the wind blow,
> Fire leap and the rivers flow?

See also Run-on Line.

EPIC An *epic* is a long narrative poem about the adventures of gods or of a hero. *Beowulf*, on page 38, is a *folk epic*, one that was composed orally and passed from storyteller to storyteller. The ancient Greek epics attributed to Homer—the *Iliad* and the *Odyssey*—are also folk epics. The *Aeneid*, by the Roman poet Virgil, and *The Divine Comedy*, by the Italian poet Dante Alighieri, are examples of literary epics from the Classical and Medieval periods, respectively. John Milton's *Paradise Lost*, a selection from which appears on page 468, is also a literary epic. Milton's goal in creating *Paradise Lost* was to write a Christian epic similar in form and equal in value to the great epics of antiquity. An epic presents an encyclopedic portrait of the culture in which it was produced.

Epic conventions are traditional characteristics of epic poems, including an opening statement of the theme; an appeal for supernatural help in telling the story (an invocation); a beginning *in medias res* (Latin: "in the middle of things"); catalogs of people and things; accounts of past events; and descriptive phrases.

See also Kenning.

EPIGRAM An *epigram* is a brief statement in prose or in verse. The concluding couplet in an English sonnet may be epigrammatic. An essay may be written in an epigrammatic style.

EPIPHANY *Epiphany* is a term introduced by James Joyce to describe a moment of insight in which a character recognizes a truth. In Joyce's "Araby," on page 1147, the boy has an epiphany when he sees the falsity of his dream.

EPITAPH An *epitaph* is an inscription written on a tomb or burial place. In literature, epitaphs include serious or humorous lines written as if intended for such use, like the epitaph in Thomas Gray's "Elegy Written in a Country Churchyard," on page 570.

See Epic.

ESSAY An *essay* is a short nonfiction work about a particular subject. Essays are of many types but may be classified by tone or style as formal or informal. Addison's breezy style and tongue-in-cheek descriptions make "The Aims of *The Spectator*," on page 592, an instance of an informal essay. An essay is often classed by its main purpose as descriptive, narrative, expository, argumentative, or persuasive.

EXTENDED METAPHOR *See* Metaphor.

FICTION *Fiction* is prose writing about imaginary characters and events. Some writers of fiction base their stories on real events, whereas others rely solely on their imaginations.

See also Narration and Prose.

FIGURATIVE LANGUAGE *Figurative language* is writing or speech not meant to be interpreted literally. Poets and other writers use figurative language to paint vivid word pictures, to make their writing emotionally intense and concentrated, and to state their ideas in new and unusual ways.

Among the figures of speech making up figurative language are hyperbole, irony, metaphor, metonymy, oxymoron, paradox, personification, simile, and synecdoche.

See also the entries for individual figures of speech.

FOLKLORE The stories, legends, myths, ballads, riddles, sayings, and other traditional works produced orally by illiterate or semiliterate peoples are known as *folklore*. Folklore influences written literature in many ways. The beheading contest in *Sir Gawain and the Green Knight*, on page 162, is an example of folklore.

FOOT *See* Meter.

FREE VERSE *Free verse* is poetry not written in a regular, rhythmical pattern, or meter. Instead of having metrical feet and lines, free verse has a rhythm that suits its meaning and that uses the sounds of spoken language in lines of different lengths. Free verse has been widely used in twentieth-century poetry. An example is "The Galloping Cat," by Stevie Smith:

> All the same I
> Intend to go on being
> A cat that likes to
> Gallop about doing good
> So
> Now with my bald head I go,
> Chopping the untidy flowers down, to and fro.

GOTHIC *Gothic* is a term used to describe literary works that make extensive use of primitive, medieval, wild, mysterious, or natural elements. Gothic novels, such as Mary Wollstonecraft Shelley's *Frankenstein*, the Introduction to which appears on page 650, often depict horrifying events set in gloomy castles.

HEPTAMETER *See* Meter.

HEXAMETER *See* Meter.

HYPERBOLE *Hyperbole* is a deliberate exaggeration or overstatement. In "Song," on page 422, John Donne uses this figure of speech:

> When thou sigh'st, thou sigh'st not wind,
> but sigh'st my soul away

See also Figurative Language.

IAMBIC PENTAMETER *See* Meter.

IMAGE An *image* is a word or phrase that appeals to one or more of the senses—sight, hearing, touch, taste, or smell. In a famous essay on *Hamlet*, T. S. Eliot explained how a group of images can be used as an "objective correlative." By this phrase, Eliot meant that a complex emotional state can be suggested by images that are carefully chosen to evoke this state.

See also Imagery.

IMAGERY *Imagery* is the descriptive language used in literature to re-create sensory experiences. Imagery enriches writing by making it more vivid, setting a tone, suggesting emotions, and guiding readers' reactions.

IRONY *Irony* is the general name given to literary techniques that involve surprising, interesting, or amusing contradictions. In *verbal irony*, words are used to suggest the opposite of their usual meaning. In *dramatic irony*, there is a contradiction between what a character thinks and what the reader or audience knows to be true. In *irony of situation*, an event occurs that directly contradicts expectations.

JOURNAL A *journal* is a daily autobiographical account of events and personal reactions. Daniel Defoe adapted this form to fictional use in *A Journal of the Plague Year*, an excerpt from which appears on page 503.

See also Diary.

KENNING A *kenning* is a metaphorical phrase used in Anglo-Saxon poetry to replace a concrete noun. In "The Seafarer," on page 16, the cuckoo is called "summer's sentinel" and the sea, "the whale's home."

See also Anglo-Saxon Poetry *and* Epic.

LEGEND A *legend* is a widely told story about the past that may or may not be based in fact. A legend often reflects a people's identity or cultural values, generally with more historical truth than that in a myth. English legends include the stories of King Arthur (retold in *Morte d'Arthur,* a selection from which appears on page 176) and Robin Hood.

See also Myth.

LYRIC POEM A *lyric poem* is a poem expressing the observations and feelings of a single speaker. Unlike a narrative poem, it presents an experience or a single effect, but it does not tell a full story. Types of lyric poems include the elegy, the ode, and the sonnet.

METAPHOR A *metaphor* is a figure of speech in which one thing is spoken of as though it were something else, as in "death, that long sleep." Through this identification of dissimilar things, a comparison is suggested or implied.

An *extended metaphor* is developed at length and involves several points of comparison. A mixed metaphor occurs when two metaphors are jumbled together, as in "The thorns of life rained down on him."

A *dead metaphor* is one that has been so overused that its original metaphorical impact has been lost. Examples of dead metaphors include "the foot of the bed" and "toe the line."

See also Figurative Language.

METAPHYSICAL POETRY The term *metaphysical poetry* describes the works of such seventeenth-century English poets as Richard Crashaw, John Donne, George Herbert, and Andrew Marvell. Characteristic features of metaphysical poetry include intellectual playfulness, argument, paradoxes, irony, elaborate and unusual conceits, incongruity, and the rhythms of ordinary speech. Examples of metaphysical poems in this textbook include Donne's "Song," on page 450, and Marvell's "To His Coy Mistress," on page 446.

METER *Meter* is the rhythmical pattern of a poem. This pattern is determined by the number and types of stresses, or beats, in each line. To describe the meter of a poem, you must scan its lines. Scanning involves marking the stressed and unstressed syllables, as follows:

Ĭ wéen | thăt, whén | thĕ gráve's | dărk wáll
Dĭd fírst | hĕr fórm | rĕtáin,
Thĕy thóught | thĕir héarts | cŏuld né'er | rĕcáll
Thĕ líght | ŏf jóy | ăgáin.
—Emily Brontë, "Song"

As you can see, each stressed syllable is marked with a slanted line (´) and each unstressed syllable with a horseshoe symbol (˘) . The stresses are then divided by vertical lines into groups called feet. The following types of feet are common in English poetry:

1. *Iamb:* a foot with one unstressed syllable followed by one stressed syllable, as in the word *afraid*
2. *Trochee:* a foot with one stressed syllable followed by one unstressed syllable, as in the word *heather*
3. *Anapest:* a foot with two unstressed syllables followed by one stressed syllable, as in the word *disembark*
4. *Dactyl:* a foot with one stressed syllable followed by two unstressed syllables, as in the word *solitude*
5. *Spondee:* a foot with two stressed syllables, as in the word *workday*
6. *Pyrrhic:* a foot with two unstressed syllables, as in the last foot of the word *unspeak | ably*
7. *Amphibrach:* a foot with an unstressed syllable, one stressed syllable, and another unstressed syllable, as in the word *another*
8. *Amphimacer:* a foot with a stressed syllable, one unstressed syllable, and another stressed syllable, as in *up and down*

A line of poetry is described as *iambic, trochaic, anapestic,* or *dactylic* according to the kind of foot that appears most often in the line. Lines are also described in terms of the number of feet that occur in them, as follows:

1. *Monometer:* verse written in one-foot lines:

   Sóund thĕ Flúte!
   Nów ĭt's múte.
   Bírds dĕlíght
   Dáy ănd Níght.
   —William Blake, "Spring"

2. *Dimeter:* verse written in two-foot lines:

   Ŏ Róse | thŏu ărt síck.
   Thĕ ĭnvís | ĭblĕ wórm.
   Thăt flíes | ĭn thĕ níght
   Ĭn thĕ hów | lĭng stórm:
   Hăs fóund | ŏut thy̆ béd
   Ŏf crím | sŏn jóy: . . .
   —William Blake, "The Sick Rose"

3. *Trimeter:* verse written in three-foot lines:

   Ĭ wént | tŏ thĕ Gárd | ĕn ŏf Lóve
   Ănd sáw | whăt Ĭ név | ĕr hăd séen:
   Ă Cháp | ĕl wăs búilt | ĭn thĕ mídst,
   Whĕre Ĭ úsed | tŏ pláy | ŏn thĕ gréen.
   —William Blake, "The Garden of Love"

4. *Tetrameter:* verse written in four-foot lines:

   Ĭ wánd | ĕr thró' | ĕach chárt | ĕr'd stréet
   Néar whĕre | thĕ chárt | ĕr'd Thámes |
   dŏes flów

And mark | in ev | ery face | I meet
Marks of | weakness, | marks of | woe.

—William Blake, "The Little Black Boy"

A six-foot line is called a *hexameter.* A line with seven feet is a *heptameter.*

A complete description of the meter of a line tells both how many feet there are in the line and what kind of foot is most common. Thus, the stanza from Emily Brontë's poem, quoted at the beginning of this entry, would be described as being made up of alternating iambic tetrameter and iambic trimeter lines. Poetry that does not have a regular meter is called *free verse.*

See also Free Verse.

METONYMY *Metonymy* is a figure of speech that substitutes something closely related for the thing actually meant. In the opening line of "The Lost Leader," Robert Browning says, "Just for a handful of silver he left us," using "silver" to refer to money paid for a betrayal.

See also Figurative Language.

MIRACLE PLAY See Drama.

MOCK EPIC A *mock epic* is a poem about a trivial matter written in the style of a serious epic. The incongruity of style and subject matter produces comic effects. Alexander Pope's *The Rape of the Lock,* on page 532, is a mock epic.

See also Epic.

MODERNISM *Modernism* describes an international movement in the arts during the early twentieth century. Modernists rejected old forms and experimented with the new. Literary Modernists—such as James Joyce, W. B. Yeats, and T. S. Eliot—used images as symbols. They presented human experiences in fragments, rather than as a coherent whole, which led to new experiments in the forms of poetry and fiction.

MONOLOGUE A *monologue* is a speech or performance given entirely by one person or by one character.

See also Dramatic Monologue *and* Soliloquy.

MOOD *Mood,* or *atmosphere,* is the feeling created in the reader by a literary work or passage. Mood may be suggested by the writer's choice of words, by events in the work, or by the physical setting. Nadine Gordimer begins "The Train from Rhodesia," on page 1250, with a description of the hot, sandy train station that sets a mood mixing boredom and confinement with the eager expectation of the train.

See also Setting *and* Tone.

MORALITY PLAY *See* Drama.

MYTH A *myth* is a fictional tale, originally with religious significance, that explains the actions of gods or heroes, the causes of natural phenomena, or both. Allusions to characters and motifs from Greek, Roman, Norse, and Celtic myths are common in English literature. In addition, mythological stories are often retold or adapted.

See also Legend.

NARRATION *Narration* is writing that tells a story. The act of telling a story is also called narration. The *narrative,* or story, is told by a character or speaker called the *narrator.* Biographies, autobiographies, journals, reports, novels, short stories, plays, narrative poems, anecdotes, fables, parables, myths, legends, folk tales, ballads, and epic poems are all narratives, or types of narration.

See also Point of View.

NARRATIVE POEM A *narrative poem* is a poem that tells a story in verse. Three traditional types of narrative poems include ballads, epics, and metrical romances.

NATURALISM *Naturalism* was a literary movement among writers at the end of the nineteenth century and during the early decades of the twentieth century. The Naturalists depicted life in its grimmer details and viewed people as hopeless victims of natural laws.

See also Realism.

NEOCLASSICISM *Neoclassicism* was a literary movement of the late seventeenth and the eighteenth centuries in which writers turned to classical Greek and Roman literary models and standards. Like the ancients, Neoclassicists, such as Alexander Pope, stressed order, harmony, restraint, and the ideal. Much Neoclassical literature dealt with themes related to proper human conduct. The most popular literary forms of the day—essays, letters, early novels, epigrams, parodies, and satires—reflected this emphasis.

See also Romanticism.

NOVEL A *novel* is an extended work of fiction that often has a complicated plot, many major and minor characters, a unifying theme, and several settings. Novels can be grouped in many ways, based on the historical periods in which they are written (such as Victorian), on the subjects and themes that they treat (such as Gothic or regional), on the techniques used in them (such as stream of consciousness), or on their part in literary movements (such as Naturalism or Realism). Among the early novels were Samuel Richardson's *Pamela* and *Clarissa* and Henry Fielding's *Tom Jones.* Other classic English novels include Jane Austen's *Pride and Prejudice,* Sir Walter Scott's *Waverley,* Charles Dickens's *David Copperfield,* and George Eliot's *The Mill on the Floss.* Major twentieth-century novelists include James Joyce, Virginia Woolf, D. H. Lawrence, Henry James, Graham Greene, and Patrick White. A *novella*—for example, Joseph Conrad's *Heart of Darkness*—is not as long as a novel but is longer than a short story.

OBJECTIVE CORRELATIVE *See* Image.

OCTAVE *See* Stanza.

ODE An *ode* is a long, formal lyric poem with a serious theme. It may have a traditional structure with stanzas grouped in threes, called the *strophe*, the *antistrophe*, and the *epode*. Odes often honor people, commemorate events, or respond to natural scenes.

See also Lyric Poem.

ONOMATOPOEIA *Onomatopoeia* is the use of words that imitate sounds. Examples of such words are *buzz, hiss, murmur,* and *rustle*. Onomatopoeia is used to create musical effects and to reinforce meaning.

ORAL TRADITION *Oral tradition* is the body of songs, stories, and poems preserved by being passed from generation to generation by word of mouth. Among the many materials composed or preserved through oral tradition in Great Britain are *Beowulf,* on page 38, and the folk ballads on pages 194–200. In his *Morte d'Arthur,* a selection from which begins on page 176, Sir Thomas Malory drew on Arthurian legends from the oral tradition. Shakespeare drew on materials from the oral tradition to create the sprites and fairies of *A Midsummer Night's Dream* and the witches of *Macbeth,* on page 300. Folk epics, ballads, myths, legends, folk tales, folk songs, proverbs, and nursery rhymes are all products of the oral tradition.

See also Ballad, Folklore, Legend, *and* Myth.

OXYMORON An *oxymoron* is a figure of speech that fuses two contradictory ideas, such as "freezing fire" or "happy grief," thus suggesting a paradox in just a few words.

See also Figurative Language *and* Paradox.

PARABLE A *parable* is a short, simple story from which a moral or religious lesson can be drawn. The most famous parables are those in the New Testament, an example of which appears on page 279.

PARADOX A *paradox* is a statement that seems to be contradictory but that actually presents a truth. In "Love's Growth," John Donne presents the following paradox:

> Methinks I lied all winter, when I swore
> My love was infinite, if spring make it more.

Because a paradox is surprising or even shocking, it draws the reader's attention to what is being said.

See also Figurative Language *and* Oxymoron.

PARODY A *parody* is a humorous imitation of another work or of a type of work. For instance, Chaucer parodies the grand style of an epic poem in "The Nun's Priest's Tale" from *The Canterbury Tales* on page 119 by applying that style to trivial incidents.

PASTORAL *Pastoral* refers to literary works that deal with the pleasures of a simple rural life or with escape to a simpler place and time. The tradition of pastoral literature began in ancient Greece with the poetic idylls of Theocritus. The Roman poet Virgil also wrote a famous collection of pastoral poems, the *Eclogues*.

During the European Renaissance, pastoral writing became quite popular. Two famous examples are *The Countess of Pembroke's Arcadia,* by Sir Philip Sidney, and Christopher Marlowe's "The Passionate Shepherd to His Love," on page 245.

Today, the term *pastoral* is commonly applied to any work in which a speaker longs to escape to a simpler rural life. By this definition, both William Wordsworth's "The World Is Too Much With Us," on page 675, and William Butler Yeats's "The Lake Isle of Innisfree," on page 968, are pastoral poems.

PENTAMETER *See* Meter.

PERSONIFICATION *Personification* is a figure of speech in which a nonhuman subject is given human characteristics. Percy Bysshe Shelley uses personification in these lines:

> Swiftly walk o'er the western wave,
> Spirit of the Night!

Effective personification of things or ideas makes their qualities seem unified, like the characteristics of a person, and their relationship with the reader seem closer.

See also Figurative Language *and* Metaphor.

PLOT *Plot* is the sequence of events in a literary work. The two primary elements of any plot are characters and a conflict. Most plots can be analyzed into many or all of the following parts:

1. The *exposition* introduces the setting, the characters, and the basic situation.
2. The *inciting incident* introduces the central conflict.
3. During the *development,* the conflict runs its course and usually intensifies.
4. At the *climax,* the conflict reaches a high point of interest or suspense.
5. The *denouement* ties up loose ends that remain after the climax of the conflict.
6. At the *resolution,* the story is resolved and an insight is revealed.

There are many variations on the standard plot structure. Some stories begin *in medias res* ("in the middle of things"), after the inciting incident has already occurred. In some stories, the expository material appears toward the middle, in flashbacks. In many stories, there is no denouement. Occasionally, the conflict is left unresolved.

POETRY *Poetry* is one of the three major types, or genres, of literature, the others being prose and drama. Poetry defies simple definition because there is no single characteristic that is found in all poems and not found in all nonpoems.

Often, poems are divided into lines and stanzas. Poems

such as sonnets, odes, villanelles, and sestinas are governed by rules regarding the number of lines, the number and placement of stressed syllables in each line, and the rhyme scheme. In the case of villanelles and sestinas, the repetition of words at the ends of lines or of entire lines is required. (An example of a sestina, Seamus Heaney's "Two Lorries," appears on page 1107. An example of a villanelle, Dylan Thomas's "Do Not Go Gentle into That Good Night," appears on page 1206.) However, some poems are written in free verse. Most poems make use of highly concise, musical, and emotionally charged language. Many also use imagery, figurative language, and devices of sound like rhyme.

Types of poetry include *narrative poetry* (ballads, epics, and metrical romances); *dramatic poetry* (dramatic monologues and dramatic dialogues); *lyrics* (sonnets, odes, elegies, and love poems); and *concrete poetry* (a poem presented on the page in a shape that suggests its subject).

POINT OF VIEW The perspective, or vantage point, from which a story is told is its *point of view.* If a character within the story narrates, then it is told from the *first-person point of view.* If a voice from outside the story tells it, then the story is told from the *third-person point of view.* If the knowledge of the storyteller is limited to the internal states of one character, then the storyteller has a *limited point of view.* If the storyteller's knowledge extends to the internal states of all the characters, then the storyteller has an *omniscient point of view.*

PROSE *Prose* is the ordinary form of written language and one of the three major types of literature. Most writing that is not poetry, drama, or song is considered prose. Prose occurs in two major forms: fiction and nonfiction.

PYRRHIC *See* Meter.

QUATRAIN *See* Stanza.

REALISM *Realism* is the presentation in art of details from actual life. During the last part of the nineteenth century and the first part of the twentieth, Realism enjoyed considerable popularity among writers in the English-speaking world. Novels often dealt with grim social realities and presented realistic portrayals of the psychological states of characters.

REFRAIN A *refrain* is a regularly repeated line or group of lines in a poem or song.

See also Ballad.

REGIONALISM *Regionalism* is the tendency to confine one's writing to the presentation of the distinct culture of an area, including its speech, customs, and history. For example, the Brontës wrote about Yorkshire, Thomas Hardy wrote about Dorset and Wessex, and D. H. Lawrence wrote about Nottinghamshire.

RHYME *Rhyme* is the repetition of sounds at the ends of words. End rhyme occurs when rhyming words appear at the ends of lines. *Internal rhyme* occurs when rhyming words fall within a line. *Exact rhyme* is the use of identical rhyming sounds, as in *love* and *dove. Approximate,* or *slant, rhyme* is the use of sounds that are similar but not identical, as in *prove* and *glove.*

RHYME SCHEME *Rhyme scheme* is the regular pattern of rhyming words in a poem or stanza. To indicate a rhyme scheme, assign a different letter to each final sound in the poem or stanza. The following lines from Charlotte Brontë's "On the Death of Anne Brontë" have been marked:

There's little joy in life for me, *a*
And little terror in the grave; *b*
I've lived the parting hour to see *a*
Of one I would have died to save. *b*

RHYTHM *See* Meter.

ROMANCE A *romance* is a story that presents remote or imaginative incidents rather than ordinary, realistic experience. The term *romance* was originally used to refer to medieval tales of the deeds and loves of noble knights and ladies. These early romances, or tales of chivalry and courtly love, are exemplified by *Sir Gawain and the Green Knight,* on page 162, and by the extract from Malory's *Morte d'Arthur,* on page 176. During the Renaissance in England, many writers, such as Edmund Spenser in *The Faerie Queene,* drew heavily on the romance tradition. From the eighteenth century on, the term *romance* has been used to describe sentimental novels about love.

ROMANTICISM *Romanticism* was a literary and artistic movement of the eighteenth and nineteenth centuries. In reaction to Neoclassicism, the Romantics emphasized imagination, fancy, freedom, emotion, wildness, the beauty of the untamed natural world, the rights of the individual, the nobility of the common man, and the attractiveness of pastoral life. Important figures in the Romantic Movement included William Wordsworth, Samuel Taylor Coleridge, Percy Bysshe Shelley, John Keats, and George Gordon, Lord Byron.

RUN-ON LINE A *run-on line* is a line that does not contain a pause or a stop at the end. It ends in the middle of a statement and a grammatical unit, and the reader must read the next line to find the end of the statement and the completion of the grammatical unit. The beginning of Molly Holden's "The Double Nature of White" illustrates the run-on line:

White orchards are the earliest, stunning
the spirit resigned to winter's black, white thorn
sprays first the bare wet branches of the hedge.

See also End-Stopped Line.

SATIRE *Satire* is writing that ridicules or holds up to contempt the faults of individuals or groups. Satires include Jonathan Swift's prose work *Gulliver's Travels,* on page 514, and Alexander Pope's poem *The Rape of the Lock,* on page 532. Although a satire is often humorous, its purpose is not simply to make readers laugh but also to correct the flaws and shortcomings that it points out.

SCANSION *Scansion* is the process of analyzing the metrical pattern of a poem.

See also Meter.

SERMON A *sermon* is a speech offering religious or moral instruction. For example, the Sermon on the Mount, on page 278, given by Jesus on a mountain in Galilee, contains the basic teachings of Christianity.

SESTET *See* Stanza.

SETTING The *setting* is the time and place of the action of a literary work. A setting can provide a backdrop for the action. It can be the force that the protagonist struggles against and thus the source of the central conflict. It can also be used to create an atmosphere. In many works, the setting symbolizes a point that the author wishes to emphasize.

See also Mood *and* Symbol.

SHORT STORY A *short story* is a brief work of fiction. The short story resembles the longer novel, but it generally has a simpler plot and setting. In addition, a short story tends to reveal character at a crucial moment, rather than to develop it through many incidents.

SIMILE A *simile* is a figure of speech that compares two apparently dissimilar things using *like* or *as.* Christina Rossetti uses simile in "Goblin Market" to describe two sisters:

> Like two blossoms on one stem,
> Like two flakes of new-fallen snow,
> Like two wands of ivory
> Tipped with gold for awful kings.

By comparing apparently dissimilar things, the writer of a simile surprises the reader into an appreciation of the hidden similarities of the things being compared.

See also Figurative Language.

SOLILOQUY A *soliloquy* is a long speech in a play or in a prose work made by a character who is alone and thus reveals private thoughts and feelings to the audience or reader. William Shakespeare opens Act III of *Macbeth,* on page 337, with a soliloquy in which Banquo speculates on Macbeth's reaction to the witches' prophecy.

See also Monologue.

SONNET A sonnet is a fourteen-line lyric poem with a single theme. Sonnets are usually written in iambic pentameter. The *Petrarchan,* or *Italian sonnet,* is divided into two parts, an eight-line octave and a six-line sestet. The octave rhymes *abba abba,* while the sestet generally rhymes *cde cde* or uses some combination of *cd* rhymes. The octave raises a question, states a problem, or presents a brief narrative, and the sestet answers the question, solves the problem, or comments on the narrative.

The *Shakespearean,* or *English, sonnet* has three four-line quatrains plus a concluding two-line couplet. The rhyme scheme of such a sonnet is usually *abab cdcd efef gg.* Each of the three quatrains usually explores a different variation of the main theme. Then, the couplet presents a summarizing or concluding statement.

See also Lyric Poem *and* Sonnet Sequence.

SONNET SEQUENCE A *sonnet sequence* is a series or group of sonnets, most often written to or about a beloved. Although each sonnet can stand alone as a separate poem, the sequence lets the poet trace the development of a relationship or examine different aspects of a single subject. Examples of sonnet sequences are Sir Philip Sidney's *Astrophel and Stella,* Edmund Spenser's *Amoretti,* and Elizabeth Barrett Browning's *Sonnets from the Portuguese.*

See also Sonnet.

SPEAKER The *speaker* is the imaginary voice assumed by the writer of a poem; the character who "says" the poem. This character is often not identified by name but may be identified otherwise. For example, the title of William Blake's poem "The Chimney Sweeper," on page 643, identifies the speaker, a child who gives an account of his life.

Recognizing the speaker and thinking about his or her characteristics are often central to interpreting a lyric poem. In Blake's poem, for instance, the speaker's acceptance of his oppressive life is offered for the reader's evaluation.

See also Point of View.

SPONDEE *See* Meter.

SPRUNG RHYTHM The term *sprung rhythm* was used by Gerard Manley Hopkins to describe the idiosyncratic meters of his poems. The rhythm is quite varied and contains such violations of traditional metrical rules as several strong stresses in a row or feet containing more than two weak stresses.

STANZA A *stanza* is a group of lines in a poem, which is seen as a unit. Many poems are divided into stanzas that are separated by spaces. Stanzas often function like paragraphs in prose. Each stanza states and develops one main idea.

Stanzas are commonly named according to the number of lines found in them, as follows:

1. *Couplet:* a two-line stanza
2. *Tercet:* a three-line stanza
3. *Quatrain:* a four-line stanza
4. *Cinquain:* a five-line stanza
5. *Sestet:* a six-line stanza

6. *Heptastich:* a seven-line stanza
7. *Octave:* an eight-line stanza

See also Sonnet.

STYLE *Style* is a writer's typical way of writing. Determinants of a writer's style include formality, use of figurative language, use of rhythm, typical grammatical patterns, typical sentence lengths, and typical methods of organization. John Milton is noted for a grand, heroic style that contrasts with John Keats's rich, sensory style and with T. S. Eliot's allusive, ironic style.

See also Diction.

SUBLIME The *sublime* is an effect created in literature when a writer confronts a power or mystery in nature that exceeds human understanding. The effect is achieved by representing the infinite or endless in sensory terms, as when Byron characterizes the inexhaustible power of the ocean in the "Apostrophe to the Ocean" in *Childe Harold's Pilgrimage,* on page 720.

SYMBOL A *symbol* is a sign, word, phrase, image, or other object that stands for or represents something else. Thus, a flag can symbolize a country, a spoken word can symbolize an object, a fine car can symbolize wealth, and so on. In literary criticism, a distinction is often made between traditional or conventional symbols—those that are part of our general cultural inheritance—and personal symbols—those that are created by particular authors for use in particular works. For example, the lamb in William Blake's poem "The Lamb," on page 640, is a conventional symbol for peace, gentleness, and innocence. However, the tiger in Blake's poem "The Tyger," on page 641, is not a conventional or inherited symbol. Blake created this symbol specifically for this poem.

Conventional symbolism is often based on elements of nature. For example, youth is often symbolized by greenery or springtime, middle age by summer, and old age by autumn or winter. Conventional symbols are also borrowed from religion and politics. For example, a cross may be a symbol of Christianity, or the color red may be a symbol of Marxist ideology.

SYNECDOCHE *Synecdoche* is a figure of speech in which a part of something is used to stand for the whole. In the preface to his long poem entitled *Milton,* William Blake includes these lines: "And did those feet in ancient time / Walk upon England's mountains green?" The "feet" stand for the whole body, and "England's mountains green" stand for England.

See also Figurative Language.

TETRAMETER *See* Meter.

THEME *Theme* is the central idea, concern, or purpose in a literary work. In an essay, the theme might be directly stated in what is known as a thesis statement. In a serious literary work, the theme is usually expressed indirectly rather than directly. A light work, one written strictly for entertainment, may not have a theme.

TONE *Tone* is the writer's attitude toward the readers and toward the subject. It may be formal or informal, friendly or distant, personal or pompous. For example, John Keats's tone in his poem "On First Looking into Chapman's Homer," on page 746, is earnest and respectful, while James Boswell's tone in *The Life of Samuel Johnson,* which begins on page 554, is familiar and engaging.

See also Mood.

TRADITION In literary study and practice, a *tradition* is a past body of work, developed over the course of history. A literary tradition may be unified by form (the tradition of the sonnet), by language (literature in English), or by nationality (English literature). A tradition develops through the acknowledgment of works, forms, and styles as classic. It also develops through critical reappraisals, as when T. S. Eliot, in the early twentieth century, elevated seventeenth-century poet John Donne out of the shadows of critical obscurity and disfavor. Writers participate in a tradition if only by following conventions about the suitable forms and subjects for literature. They make conscious use of the tradition when they use references, stories, or forms from old literature to give authority to their work. For example, John Milton uses the classical form of the epic in *Paradise Lost,* page 468, to retell the biblical story of the Fall. Writers may also break from a tradition, as when Wordsworth rejects elevated poetic language in favor of conversational speech in poems such as "London, 1802," page 676. A tradition may also be used to question itself. For example, Derek Walcott in the extract from *Midsummer,* page 1260, uses references to Shakespeare's works to question the extent to which he, a black poet, can participate in a tradition largely maintained by white society for white society.

TRAGEDY *Tragedy* is a type of drama or literature that shows the downfall or destruction of a noble or outstanding person, traditionally one who possesses a character weakness called a *tragic flaw.* Macbeth, for example, is a brave and noble figure led astray by ambition. The *tragic hero* is caught up in a sequence of events that inevitably results in disaster. Because the protagonist is neither a wicked villain nor an innocent victim, the audience reacts with mixed emotions—both pity and fear, according to the Greek philosopher Aristotle, who defined tragedy in the *Poetics.* The outcome of a tragedy, in which the protagonist is isolated from society, contrasts with the happy resolution of a comedy, in which the protagonist makes peace with society.

See also Comedy *and* Drama.

TRIMETER *See* Meter.

TROCHEE *See* Meter.

The Writing Process

A polished piece of writing can seem to have been effortlessly created, but most good writing is the result of a process of writing, rethinking, and rewriting. The process can roughly be divided into stages: prewriting, drafting, revising, editing, proofreading, and publishing.

It is important to remember that the writing process is one that moves backward as well as forward. Even while you are moving forward in the creation of your composition, you may still return to a previous stage—to rethink or rewrite.

Following are stages of the writing process, with key points to address during each stage.

Prewriting

In this stage, you plan out the work to be done. You prepare to write by exploring ideas, gathering information, and working out an organization plan. Following are the key steps to take at this stage.

Step 1: Analyze the writing situation. Start by clarifying your assignment, so that you know exactly what you are supposed to do.

- ***Focus your topic.*** If necessary, narrow the topic—the subject you are writing about—so that you can write about it fully in the space you have.
- ***Know your purpose.*** What is your goal for this paper? What do you want to accomplish? Your purpose will determine what you include in the paper.
- ***Know your audience.*** Who will read your paper influences what you say and how you say it.

Step 2: Gather ideas and information. You can do this in a number of ways:

- ***Brainstorm.*** When you brainstorm, either alone or with others, you come up with possible ideas to use in your paper. Not all of your ideas will be useful or suitable. You will need to evaluate them later.
- ***Consult other people about your subject.*** Speaking informally with others may suggest an idea or an approach you did not see at first.
- ***Make a list of questions about your topic.*** When your list is complete, find the answers to your questions.
- ***Do research.*** Your topic may require information that you do not have, so you will need to go to other sources to find information. There are numerous ways to find information on a topic.

The ideas and information you gather will become the content of your paper. Not all of the information you gather will be needed. As you develop and revise your paper, you will make further decisions about what to include and what to leave out.

Drafting

When you draft, you put down your ideas on paper in rough form. Working from your prewriting notes and your outline or plan, you develop and present your ideas in sentences and paragraphs.

Organize. First, make a rough plan for the way you want to present your information. Sort your ideas and notes. Decide what goes with what and which points are the most important. You can make an outline to show the order of ideas, or you can use some other organizing plan that works for you.

There are many ways in which you can organize and develop your material. Use a method that works for your topic. Following are common methods of organizing information in the development of a paper:

- ***Chronological Order*** In this method, events are presented in the order in which they occurred. This organization works best for presenting narrative material or explaining in a "how-to" format.
- ***Spatial Order*** In spatial order, details are presented as seen in space; for example, from left to right, top to bottom, or from foreground to background. This order is good for descriptive writing.
- ***Order of Importance*** This order helps readers see the relative importance of ideas. You present ideas from the most to least important or from the least to most important.
- ***Main Idea and Details*** This logical organization works well to support an idea or opinion. Present each main idea, and back it up with appropriate support.

Once you have chosen an organization, begin writing your draft. Do not worry about getting everything perfect at the drafting stage. Concentrate on getting your ideas down.

Write your draft in a way that works for you. Some writers work best by writing a quick draft—putting down all their ideas without stopping to evaluate them. Other writers prefer to develop each paragraph carefully and thoughtfully, making sure that each main idea is supported by details.

As you are developing your draft, keep in mind your purpose and your audience. These determine what you say and how you say it.

Do not be afraid to change your original plans during drafting. Some of the best ideas are those that were not planned at the beginning. Write as many drafts as you like, until you are happy with the results.

Develop an Essay Most papers, regardless of the topic, are developed with an introduction, a body, and a conclusion. Here are tips for developing these parts:

Introduction In the introduction to a paper, you want to engage your readers' attention and let them know the purpose of your paper. You may use the following strategies in your introduction:

- Startle your readers.
- Take a stand.
- Use an anecdote.
- Quote someone.

Body of the Paper In the body of your paper, you present your information and make your points. Your organization is an important factor in leading readers through your ideas. Elaborating on your main ideas is also important. Elaboration is the development of ideas to make your written work precise and complete. You can use the following kinds of details to elaborate your main ideas:

- Facts and statistics
- Anecdotes
- Sensory details
- Examples
- Explanations and definitions
- Quotations

Conclusion The ending of your paper is the final impression you leave with your readers. Your conclusion should give readers the sense that you have pulled everything together. Following are some effective ways to end your paper:

- Summarize and restate.
- Ask a question.
- State an opinion.
- Tell an anecdote.
- Call for action.
- Provide an insight.

Revising

Once you have a draft, you can look at it critically or have others review it. This is the time to make changes—on many levels. Revising is the process of reworking what you have written to make it as good as it can be.

Revising Your Overall Structure Start by examining the soundness of your structure, or overall organization. Your ideas should flow logically from beginning to end. You may strengthen the structure by reordering paragraphs or by adding information to fill in gaps.

Revising Your Paragraphs Next, examine each paragraph in your writing. Consider the way each sentence contributes to the point of the paragraph. As you evaluate your draft, rewrite or eliminate any sentences that are not effective.

Revising Your Sentences When you study the sentences in your draft, check to see that they flow smoothly from one to the next. Look to see that you have avoided the pattern of beginning most of your sentences in the same way, and vary your sentence length.

Revising Your Word Choice The final step in the process of revising your work is to analyze your choice of words. Consider the connotations, or associations each word suggests, and make sure that each word conveys the exact meaning you intended. Also, look for the repetition of words, and make revisions to polish your writing.

Peer Review After you have finished revising your draft, work with one or more classmates to get a fresh perspective on your writing. First, have your reviewer look at one element of your writing, and ask your reviewer a specific question to get the most focused feedback possible. Weigh the responses you receive, and determine which suggestions you want to incorporate in your draft.

Editing

When you edit, you look more closely at the language you have used to ensure that the way you expressed your ideas is the most effective.

- Replace dull language with vivid, precise words.
- Cut or change unnecessary repetition.
- Cut empty words and phrases—those that do not add anything to the writing.
- Check passive voice. Usually, active voice is more effective.
- Replace wordy expressions with shorter, more precise ones.

Proofreading

After you finish your final draft, proofread it, either on your own or with the help of a partner.

It is useful to have both a dictionary and a usage handbook available to help you check that your work is correct. Here are the tasks in proofreading:

- Correct errors in grammar and usage.
- Correct errors in punctuation and capitalization.
- Correct errors in spelling.

Publishing

Now your paper is ready to be shared with others. Consider sharing your writing with classmates, family, or a wider audience.

THE MODES OF WRITING

Writing is a process that begins with the exploration of ideas and ends with the presentation of a final draft. Often, the types of writing are grouped into modes according to form and purpose.

The modes addressed in this handbook are

- Narration
- Description
- Persuasion
- Exposition
- Research Writing
- Response to Literature
- Writing for Assessment
- Workplace Writing

NARRATION

Whenever writers tell any type of story, they are using **narration.** Although there are many kinds of narration, most narratives share certain elements, such as characters, a setting, a sequence of events, and, often, a theme. Following are some types of narration:

Autobiographical Writing Autobiographical writing tells a true story about an important period, experience, or relationship in the writer's life. An autobiographical narrative can be as simple as a description of a recent car trip or as complex as the entire story of a person's life. Effective autobiographical writing includes

- A series of events that involve the writer as the main character
- Details, thoughts, feelings, and insights from the writer's perspective
- A conflict or an event that affects the writer
- A logical organization that tells the story clearly
- Insights that the writer gained from the experience

A few types of autobiographical writing are autobiographical incidents, personal narratives, autobiographical narratives or sketches, reflective essays, eyewitness accounts, anecdotes, and memoirs.

Short Story A short story is a brief, creative narrative—a retelling of events arranged to hold a reader's attention. Most short stories include

- Details that establish the setting in time and place
- A main character who undergoes a change or learns something during the course of the story
- A conflict or a problem to be introduced, developed, and resolved
- A plot, the series of events that make up the action of the story
- A theme or generalization about life

A few types of short stories are realistic stories, fantasies, historical narratives, mysteries, thrillers, science-fiction stories, and adventure stories.

DESCRIPTION

Descriptive writing is writing that creates a vivid picture of a person, place, thing, or event. Descriptive writing can stand on its own or be part of a longer work, such as a short story. Most descriptive writing includes

- Sensory details—sights, sounds, smells, tastes, and physical sensations
- Vivid, precise language
- Figurative language or comparisons
- Adjectives and adverbs that paint a word picture
- An organization suited to the subject

Some examples of descriptive writing include description of ideas, observations, travel brochures, physical descriptions, functional descriptions, remembrances, and character sketches.

PERSUASION

Persuasion is writing or speaking that attempts to convince people to accept a position or take a desired action. When used effectively, persuasive writing has the power to change people's lives. As a reader and a writer, you will find yourself engaged in many forms of persuasion. Here are a few of them:

Persuasive Essay A persuasive essay presents your position on an issue, urges your readers to accept that position, and may encourage them to take an action. An effective persuasive essay

- Explores an issue of importance to the writer
- Addresses an issue that is arguable
- Uses facts, examples, statistics, or personal experiences to support a position
- Tries to influence the audience through appeals to the readers' knowledge, experiences, or emotions
- Uses clear organization to present a logical argument

Persuasion can take many forms. A few forms of persuasion include editorials, position papers, persuasive speeches, grant proposals, advertisements, and debates.

Advertisements An advertisement is a planned communication meant to be seen, heard, or read. It attempts to persuade an audience to buy a product or service, accept an idea, or support a cause. Advertisements may appear in printed form—in newspapers and magazines, on billboards, or as posters or flyers. They may appear on radio or television, as commercials or public-service announcements. An effective advertisement includes

- A memorable slogan to grab the audience's attention
- A call to action, which tries to rally the audience to do something
- Persuasive and/or informative text
- Striking visual or aural images
- Details that provide such information as price, location, date, and time

Several common types of advertisements are public-service announcements, billboards, merchandise ads, service ads, online ads, product packaging, and political campaign literature.

EXPOSITION

Exposition is writing that informs or explains. The information you include in expository writing is factual or based on fact. Effective expository writing reflects a well-thought-out organization—one that includes a clear introduction, body, and conclusion. The organization should be appropriate for the type of exposition you are writing. Here are some types of exposition:

Comparison-and-Contrast Essay A comparison-and-contrast essay analyzes the similarities and differences between two or more things. You may organize your essay either point by point or subject by subject. An effective comparison-and-contrast essay

- Identifies a purpose for comparison and contrast
- Identifies similarities and differences between two or more things, people, places, or ideas
- Gives factual details about the subjects being compared
- Uses an organizational plan suited to its topic and purpose

Types of comparison-and-contrast essays are product comparisons, essays on economic or historical developments, comparison and contrast of literary works, and plan evaluations.

Cause-and-Effect Essay A cause-and-effect essay examines the relationship between events, explaining how one event or situation causes another. A successful cause-and-effect essay includes

- A discussion of a cause, event, or condition that produces a specific result
- An explanation of an effect, outcome, or result
- Evidence and examples to support the relationship between cause and effect
- A logical organization that makes the explanation clear

Some appropriate subjects for cause-and-effect essays are science reports, current-events articles, health studies, historical accounts, and cause-and-effect investigations.

Problem-and-Solution Essay A problem-and-solution essay describes a problem and offers one or more solutions to it. It describes a clear set of steps to achieve a result. An effective problem-and-solution essay includes

- A clear statement of the problem, with its causes and effects summarized for the reader
- The most important aspects of the problem
- A proposal of at least one realistic solution
- Facts, statistics, data, or expert testimony to support the solution
- Language appropriate to the audience's knowledge and ability levels
- A clear organization that makes the relationship between problem and solution obvious

Some types of issues that might be addressed in a problem-and-solution essay include consumer issues, business issues, time-management issues, and local issues.

RESEARCH WRITING

Research writing is based on information gathered from outside sources, and it gives a writer the power to become an expert on any subject. A research paper—a focused study of a topic—helps writers explore and connect ideas, make discoveries, and share their findings with an audience. Effective research writing

- Focuses on a specific, narrow topic, which is usually summarized in a thesis statement
- Presents relevant information from a wide variety of sources
- Structures the information logically and effectively
- Identifies the sources from which the information was drawn

Besides the formal research report, there are many other specialized types of writing that depend on accurate and insightful research, including multimedia presentations, statistical reports, annotated bibliographies, and experiment journals.

Documented Essay A documented essay uses research gathered from outside sources to support an idea. What distinguishes this essay from other categories of research is the level and intensity of the research. In a documented essay, the writer consults a limited number of sources to elaborate an idea. In contrast, a formal research paper may include many more research sources. An effective documented essay includes

- A well-defined thesis that can be fully discussed in a brief essay
- Facts and details to support each main point
- Expert or informed ideas gathered from interviews and other sources
- A clear, coherent method of organization
- Full internal documentation to show sources of information

Subjects especially suited to the documented essay format include health issues, current events, and cultural trends.

Research Paper A research paper presents and interprets information gathered through an extensive study of a subject. An effective research paper has

- A clearly stated thesis statement
- Convincing factual support from a variety of outside sources, including direct quotations whose sources are credited
- A clear organization that includes an introduction, body, and conclusion
- A bibliography, or works-cited list, that provides a complete listing of research sources

Some research formats you may encounter include lab reports, annotated bibliographies, and multigenre research papers.

RESPONSE TO LITERATURE

When you write a **response-to-literature essay,** you give yourself the opportunity to discover *what, how,* and *why* a piece of writing communicated to you. An effective response

- Contains a reaction to a poem, story, essay, or other work of literature
- Analyzes the content of a literary work, its related ideas, or the work's effect on the reader
- Presents a thesis statement to identify the nature of the response
- Focuses on a single aspect of the work or gives a general overview
- Supports opinion with evidence from the work addressed

The following are just a few of the ways you might respond in writing to a literary work: reader's response journals, character analyses, literary letters, and literary analyses.

WRITING FOR ASSESSMENT

One of the most common types of school **assessment** is the written test. Most often, a written test is announced in advance, allowing you time to study and prepare. When a test includes an essay, you are expected to write a response that includes

- A clearly stated and well-supported thesis or main idea
- Specific information about the topic derived from your reading or from class discussion
- A clear organization

In your school career, you will probably encounter questions that ask you to address each of the following types of writing: explain a process; defend a position; compare, contrast, or categorize; and show cause and effect.

WORKPLACE WRITING

Workplace writing is probably the format you will use most after you finish school. It is used in offices, factories, and by workers on the road. Workplace writing includes a variety of formats that share common features. In general, workplace writing is fact-based writing that communicates specific information to readers in a structured format. Effective workplace writing

- Communicates information concisely to make the best use of both the writer's and the reader's time
- Includes a level of detail that provides necessary information and anticipates potential questions
- Reflects the writer's care if it is error-free and neatly presented

Some common types of workplace writing include business letters, memorandums, résumés, forms, and applications.

Summary of Grammar

Nouns A **noun** names a person, place, or thing. A **common noun,** such as *country,* names any one of a class of people, places, or things. A **proper noun,** such as *Great Britain,* names a specific person, place, or thing.

Pronouns Pronouns are words that stand for nouns or for words that take the place of nouns. **Personal pronouns** refer to the person speaking; the person spoken to; or the person, place, or thing spoken about.

	Singular	*Plural*
First Person	I, me, my, mine	we, us, our, ours
Second Person	you, your, yours	you, your, yours
Third Person	he, him, his, she, her, hers, it, its	they, them, their, theirs

A **reflexive pronoun** ends in *-self* or *-selves* and names the person or thing receiving an action when that person or thing is the same as the one performing the action.

> I pray you, school *yourself.* (Shakespeare, p. 355)

An **intensive pronoun** also ends in *-self* or *-selves.* It adds emphasis to a noun or pronoun.

> The raven *himself* is hoarse
> That croaks the fatal entrance of Duncan
> Under my battlements. (Shakespeare, p. 300)

Demonstrative pronouns—such as *this, that, these,* and *those*—single out specific people, places, or things.

A **relative pronoun** begins a subordinate clause and connects it to another idea in the sentence.

> Annoyed, she picked up the letter, which bore no stamp. (Bowen, p. 1032)

Interrogative pronouns are used to begin questions.

> Who casts not up his eye to the sun when it rises? (Donne, p. 428)

Indefinite pronouns refer to people, places, or things, often without specifying which ones.

> Nought's had, all's spent,
> Where our desire is got without content: . . .
> (Shakespeare, p. 337)

Verbs A **verb** is a word or group of words that expresses an action, a condition, or the fact that something exists, while indicating the time of the action, condition, or fact. An **action verb** tells what action someone or something is performing. An action verb is **transitive** if it directs action toward someone or something named in the same sentence.

> *Gather* ye rosebuds while ye may, . . .
> (Herrick, p. 449)

An action verb is **intransitive** if it does not direct action toward something or someone named in the same sentence.

> The thought *served* as a challenge.
> (Woolf, p. 1158)

A **linking verb** expresses the subject's condition by connecting the subject with another word.

> But after some time that order was more necessary, . . . (Defoe, p. 503)

Helping verbs are verbs added to another verb to make a single verb phrase. They indicate the time at which an action takes place or whether it actually happens, could happen, or should happen.

> Nothing but an extreme love of truth *could have* hindered me from concealing this part of my story. (Swift, p. 514)

Adjectives An **adjective** is a word used to describe what is named by a noun or pronoun or to give a noun or pronoun a more specific meaning. Adjectives answer these questions:

> What kind? *purple* hat, *happy* face
> Which one? *this* bowl, *those* cameras
> How many? *three* cars, *several* dishes
> How much? *less* attention, *enough* food

The **articles** *the, a,* and *an* are adjectives. *An* is used before a word beginning with a vowel sound. *This, that, these,* and *those* are used as **demonstrative adjectives** when they appear directly before a noun.

> Perchance he for whom *this* bell tolls may be so ill as *that* he knows not it tolls for him. . . .
> (Donne, p. 429)

A noun may sometimes be used as an adjective:

> *language* lesson   *chemistry* book

Adverbs An **adverb** is a word that modifies a verb, an adjective, or another adverb. Adverbs answer the questions *where, when, how,* or *to what extent.*

> She will answer *soon.* (modifies verb *will answer*)
> I was *extremely* sad. (modifies adjective *sad*)
> You called *more* often than I. (modifies adverb *often*)

Prepositions A preposition is a word that relates a noun or pronoun that appears with it to another word in the sentence. It can indicate relations of time, place, causality, responsibility, and motivation. Prepositions are almost always followed by nouns or pronouns.

around the fire   *for* us
in sight   *till* sunrise

Conjunctions A conjunction is used to connect other words or groups of words.

Coordinating conjunctions connect similar kinds or groups of words:

bread *and* wine
brief *but* powerful

Correlative conjunctions are used in pairs to connect similar words or groups of words:

both Luis *and* Rosa
neither you *nor* I

Subordinating conjunctions indicate the connection between two ideas by placing one below the other in rank or importance:

The Count your master's known munificence
Is ample warrant *that* no one just pretense
Of mine for dowry will be disallowed; . . .
(Browning, p. 836)

Interjections An **interjection** is a word or phrase that expresses feeling or emotion and functions independently of a sentence.

Ah, love, let us be true
To one another! . . . (Arnold, p. 884)

Sentences A **sentence** is a group of words with a subject and predicate, expressing a complete thought.

Phrases A **phrase** is a group of words without a subject and verb that functions as one part of speech. A **prepositional phrase** is a group of words that includes a preposition and a noun or pronoun.

before dawn   *as a result of* the rain

An **adjective phrase** is a prepositional phrase that modifies a noun or pronoun.

The space of sky above us was the color *of ever-changing violet.* . . . (Joyce, p. 1147)

An **adverb phrase** is a prepositional phrase that modifies a verb, an adjective, or an adverb.

Arsat came through the doorway *with noiseless steps.* . . . (Conrad, p. 1134)

An **appositive phrase** is a noun or pronoun with modifiers, placed next to a noun or pronoun to add information and details.

How soon hath Time, *the subtle thief of youth,*
Stolen on his wing my three and twentieth year!
(Milton, p. 464)

A **participial phrase** is a participle that is modified by an adjective or adverb phrase or that has a complement (a group of words that completes the participle's meaning). The entire phrase acts as an adjective.

The boy gazed at his uncle from those big, hot, blue eyes, *set rather close together.*
(Lawrence, p. 1176)

A **gerund** is a noun formed from the present participle of a verb (ending in *-ing*). A **gerund phrase** is a gerund with modifiers or a complement (words that complete its meaning), all acting together as a noun.

Neither can we call this *a begging of misery* or *a borrowing of misery* . . . (Donne, p. 428)

An **infinitive phrase** is an infinitive with modifiers, complements (words completing its meaning), or a subject, all acting together as a single part of speech.

. . . let baser things devise *To die in dust* . . .
(Spenser, p. 238)

Clauses A **clause** is a group of words with its own subject and verb. An **independent clause** can stand by itself as a complete sentence. A **subordinate clause** cannot stand by itself as a complete sentence.

Mr. Thomas Davies the actor, *who then kept a bookseller's shop in Russell Street, Covent Garden,* told me that Johnson was very much his friend. . . . (Boswell, p. 554)

An **adjective clause** is a subordinate clause that modifies a noun or pronoun by telling *what kind* or *which one.*

. . . coffins were not to be had for the prodigious numbers *that fell in such a calamity as this.*
(Defoe, p. 503)

Subordinate adverb clauses modify verbs, adjectives, adverbs, or verbals by telling *where, when, in what way, to what extent, under what condition,* or *why.*

As soon as I saw the dead man I sent an orderly to a friend's house nearby. . . . (Orwell, p. 1018)

Subordinate noun clauses act as nouns.

To confirm *what I have now said,* . . . I shall here insert a passage which will hardly obtain belief.
(Swift, p. 514)

Summary of Capitalization and Punctuation

Capitalization

Capitalize the first word in sentences, interjections, and complete questions. Also, capitalize the first word in a quotation if the quotation is a complete sentence.

> I asked, "What do you want?" (Naipaul, p. 1238)

Capitalize all proper nouns and adjectives.

> Trinidadian   Thames River

Capitalize titles showing family relationships when they refer to a specific person unless they are preceded by a possessive noun or pronoun.

> Uncle Oscar   Mangan's sister

Capitalize the first word and all other key words in the titles of books, periodicals, poems, stories, plays, songs, and other works of art.

> *Frankenstein*   "Shooting an Elephant"

Punctuation

End Marks Use a **period** to end a declarative sentence, an imperative sentence, an indirect question, and most abbreviations.

> This tale is true, and mine. ("The Seafarer," p. 16)
>
> Let me not to the marriage of true minds
> Admit impediments. (Shakespeare, p. 255)
>
> At last she spoke to me. (Joyce, p. 1147)
>
> Mrs. Drover (Bowen, p. 1032)

Use a **question mark** to end an interrogative sentence.

> Sent he to Macduff? (Shakespeare, p. 300)

Use an **exclamation mark** after an exclamatory sentence, a forceful imperative sentence, or an interjection expressing strong emotion.

> "Hold off! unhand me, graybeard loon!" (Coleridge, p. 686)

Commas Use a **comma** before the conjunction to separate two independent clauses in a compound sentence.

> My heart aches, and a drowsy numbness pains
> My sense, . . . (Keats, p. 750)

Use commas to separate three or more words, phrases, or clauses in a series.

> Daffodil came in first, Lancelot second, Mirza third. (Lawrence, p. 1176)

Use commas to separate adjectives unless they must stay in a specific order.

> His *big, soft* eyes stared. . . . (Conrad, p. 1134)
>
> And *each slow* dusk a drawing-down of blinds. (Owen, p. 1053)

Use a comma after an introductory word, phrase, or clause.

> *When I nodded,* he laughed in a crooked way. (Naipaul, p. 1238)

Use commas to set off nonessential expressions.

> "Only you'd have to promise, *honor bright, uncle,* not to let it go beyond us three." (Lawrence, p. 1176)

Use commas with places, dates, and titles.

> Coventry, England
>
> September 1, 1939
>
> Reginald Farrars, M. P.

Use commas after items in addresses, after the salutation in a personal letter, after the closing in all letters, and in numbers of more than three digits.

> Hull Crescent, Dorchester
>
> Dear Randolph,
>
> Yours faithfully,
>
> 9,744

Use a comma to indicate words left out of parallel clauses, to set off a direct quotation, and to prevent a sentence from being misunderstood.

> In Tennyson's poetry, I admire the music; in Browning's, the sentiments.
>
> "Well—I suppose," she said slowly and bitterly, "it's because your father has no luck." (Lawrence, p. 1176)

Semicolons Use a **semicolon** to join independent clauses that are not already joined by a conjunction.

> The tone of her voice was not encouraging; she seemed to have spoken to me out of a sense of duty. (Joyce, p. 1147)

Use semicolons to avoid confusion when independent clauses or items in a series already contain commas.

> The Emperor concluded me to be drowned, and that the enemy's fleet was approaching in a hostile manner; but he was soon eased of his fears; for,

the channel growing shallower every step I made, I came in a short time within hearing, . . . (Swift, p. 514)

Colons Use a **colon** before a list of items following an independent clause.

Notable Victorian poets include the following: Tennyson, Browning, Arnold, Housman, and Hopkins.

Use a colon to introduce a formal or lengthy quotation.

And on the pedestal these words appear: "My name is Ozymandias, king of kings: . . ." (Shelley, p. 732)

Use a colon to introduce an independent clause that summarizes or explains the sentence before it.

The third day of the illness was critical: they were waiting for a change. (Lawrence, p. 1176)

Quotation Marks A **direct quotation** represents a person's exact speech or thoughts and is enclosed within quotation marks.

"If I go," I said, "I will bring you something." (Joyce, p. 1147)

An **indirect quotation** reports only the general meaning of what a person said or thought and does not require quotation marks.

Mother said he never considered me. (Bowen, p. 1032)

Always place a comma or a period inside the final quotation mark.

"We will each write a ghost story," said Lord Byron. . . . (Shelley, p. 650)

Always place a question mark or an exclamation mark inside the final quotation mark if the end mark is part of the quotation; if it is not part of the quotation, place it outside the final quotation mark.

The man said to me, "Sonny, may I come inside your yard?" (Naipaul, p. 1238)

Use single quotation marks for a quotation within a quotation.

"Lying all day on his pillows, . . . and then he says he does not want to live 'like this,'" Rakesh was heard to say. . . . (Desai, p. 1272)

Italicize the titles of long written works, movies, television and radio shows, lengthy works of music, paintings, and sculpture. Also, italicize foreign words not yet accepted into English and words you wish to stress.

If you are writing by hand or working in some other format that does not allow you to italicize text, underline such titles and words.

Howards End　　60 Minutes

Guernica　　déjà vu

Use quotation marks around the titles of short written works, episodes in a series, songs, and titles of works mentioned as parts of collections.

"The Lagoon"　　"Boswell Meets Johnson"

Parentheses Use **parentheses** to set off asides and explanations only when the material is not essential or when it consists of one or more sentences.

My eyes were often full of tears (I could not tell why) and at times a flood from my heart seemed to pour itself out into my bosom. (Joyce, p. 1147)

Hyphens Use a **hyphen** with certain numbers, after certain prefixes, with two or more words used as one word, with a compound modifier, and within a word when a combination of letters might otherwise be confusing.

twenty-nine　　re-create
pre-Romantic　　brother-in-law

Apostrophe Add an **apostrophe** and an *s* to show the possessive case of most singular nouns and of plural nouns that do not end in *-s* or *-es*.

Blake's poems　　the mice's whiskers

Add an apostrophe to show the possessive case of plural nouns ending in *-s* and *-es*.

the girls' songs　　the Ortizes' car

Use an apostrophe in a contraction to indicate the position of the missing letter or letters.

His English was so good, it *didn't* seem natural. . . . (Naipaul, p. 1238)

Use an apostrophe and an *-s* to write the plurals of numbers, symbols, letters, and words used to name themselves.

5's and 20's　　no *if's* or *but's*
five *a's*

Glossary of Common Usage

among, between

Among is generally used with three or more items. *Between* is generally used with only two items.

> *Among* Chaucer's characters, my favorite has always been the Wife of Bath.

> The ballad "Get Up and Bar the Door" consists largely of a dialogue *between* a man and his wife.

amount, number

Amount refers to quantity or a unit, whereas *number* refers to individual items that can be counted. *Amount* generally appears with a singular noun, and *number* appears with a plural noun.

> The *amount* of attention that great writers have paid to the Faust legend is remarkable.

> A considerable *number* of important English writers have been fascinated by the legend of King Arthur.

as, because, like, as to

To avoid confusion, use *because* rather than *as* when you want to indicate cause and effect.

> *Because* the narrator of Joyce's "Araby" is infatuated with Mangan's sister, he cannot see that he is driven by vanity.

Do not use the preposition *like* to introduce a clause that requires the conjunction *as.*

> *As* we might expect in a story by Joseph Conrad, there are two narrators in "The Lagoon."

The use of *as to* for *about* is awkward and should be avoided.

bad, badly

Use the predicate adjective *bad* after linking verbs such as *feel, look,* and *seem.* Use *badly* when an adverb is required.

> In "My Last Duchess," the Duke of Ferrara does not seem to feel *bad* about the death of his wife.

> The announcement of Lady Macbeth's death *badly* unnerves Macbeth.

because of, due to

Use *due to* if it can logically replace the phrase *caused by.* In introductory phrases, however, *because of* is better usage than *due to.*

> The classical allusions in *Paradise Lost* may be *due to* the poet's ambition to imitate the epics of Homer and Virgil.

> *Because of* the expansion of the reading public, eighteenth-century writers became less dependent on wealthy patrons.

compare, contrast

The verb *compare* can involve both similarities and differences. The verb *contrast* always involves differences. Use *to* or *with* after compare. Use *with* after contrast.

> Denise's report compared Shelley's style in "To a Skylark" *with* that of Keats in "Ode to a Nightingale."

> In Conrad's "The Lagoon," Arsat's point of view in the narration of his "story within a story" contrasts *with* the more detached third-person point of view that the author uses for the rest of the tale.

continual, continuous

Continual means "occurring again and again in succession," while *continuous* means "occurring without interruption."

> In "The Seafarer," the speaker describes *continual* hailstorms at sea.

> The white-hot fervor of "Ode to the West Wind" suggests that Shelley wrote the poem in a single *continuous* burst of inspiration.

different from, different than

The preferred usage is *different from.*

> In its simple, precise language, Housman's style is *different from* that of many other Victorian poets, including Tennyson and Hopkins.

farther, further

Use *farther* when you refer to distance. Use *further* when you mean "to a greater degree" or "additional."

> Although the sexton tries to persuade him to go no *farther,* Defoe is determined to enter the churchyard.

Boswell *further* illustrates Johnson's conversation by quoting his opinions of Sheridan and Derrick.

fewer, less

Use *fewer* for things that can be counted. Use *less* for amounts or quantities that cannot be counted.

Wordsworth uses *fewer* end-stopped lines than Pope does.

At the beginning of Luke's parable, the prodigal son shows *less* respect for the father than the older son does.

just, only

Only should appear directly before the word it modifies. *Just*, used as an adverb meaning "no more than," also belongs directly before the word it modifies.

The form of the villanelle allows a poet to use *just* two rhymes.

John Keats was *only* twenty-four when he wrote some of his greatest poems.

lay, lie

Lay is a transitive verb meaning "to set or put something down." Its principal parts are *lay, laying, laid, laid.*
Lie is an intransitive verb meaning "to recline." Its principal parts are *lie, lying, lay, lain.*

Coleridge implies that the mariner's reckless act of killing the albatross *lays* a curse on the crew.

As Paul *lies* dead at the end of D. H. Lawrence's story, his Uncle Oscar sadly comments that the boy may be better off.

plurals that do not end in *-s*

The plurals of certain nouns from Greek and Latin are formed as they were in their original language. Words such as *data, criteria, media,* and *phenomena* are plural and should be treated as such. Each has its own distinctive singular form: *datum, criterion, medium, phenomenon.*

Are the electronic *media* of the twentieth century contributing to the death of literature?

raise, rise

Raise is a transitive verb that usually takes a direct object. *Rise* is intransitive and never takes a direct object.

In "Musée des Beaux Arts," W. H. Auden *raises* the question of our insensitivity to suffering.

In Tennyson's poem, when Lancelot passes, the Lady of Shallot *rises* from her loom and paces.

that, which, who

Use the relative pronoun *that* to refer to things. Use *which* only for things and *who* only for people. Use *that* when introducing a subordinate clause that singles out a particular thing or person.

The contemporary poems *that* I most enjoy reading are James Berry's.

Which is usually used to introduce a subordinate clause that is not essential to identifying the thing or person in question:

"Fern Hill," *which* reflects Dylan Thomas's brilliant ability to evoke emotional response, plays on the connotations of words.

Who can be used to introduce either essential or nonessential subordinate clauses:

Two writers *who* helped redefine the essay are Addison and Steele. (essential)

Addison and Steele, *who* were close friends for most of their lives, had very different personalities and careers. (nonessential)

when, where

Do not directly follow a linking verb with *when* or *where*. Also, be careful not to use *where* when your context requires *that.*

Evaluation is ~~when you make~~ *the process of making* a judgment about the quality or value of something.

Sandy read ~~where~~ *that* after the Brownings eloped to Italy, they spent most of their married life in Florence.

who, whom

Remember to use *who* only as a subject in clauses and sentences and *whom* only as an object.

V. S. Naipaul, *who* wrote "B. Wordsworth," has also written some well-received novels.

V. S. Naipaul, *whom* many critics have praised as one of the best contemporary writers in English, was born and raised in Trinidad.

Introduction to the Internet

The Internet is a series of networks that are interconnected all over the world. The Internet allows users to have almost unlimited access to information stored on the networks. Dr. Berners-Lee, a physicist, created the Internet in the 1980s by writing a small computer program that allowed pages to be linked together using key words. The Internet was mostly text-based until 1992, when a computer program called the NCSA Mosaic (National Center for Supercomputing Applications) was created at the University of Illinois. This program was the first Web browser. The development of Web browsers greatly eased the ability of the user to navigate through all the pages stored on the Web. Very soon, the appearance of the Web was altered as well. More appealing visuals were added, and sound, too, was implemented. This change made the Web more user-friendly and more appealing to the general public.

Using the Internet for Research

Key Word Search

Before you begin a search, you should identify your specific topic. To make searching easier, narrow your subject to a key word or a group of key words. These are your search terms, and they should be as specific as possible. For example, if you are looking for the latest concert dates for your favorite musical group, you might use the band's name as a key word. However, if you were to enter the name of the group in the query box of the search engine, you might be presented with thousands of links to information about the group that is unrelated to what you want to know. You might locate such information as band member biographies, the group's history, fan reviews of concerts, and hundreds of sites with related names containing information that is irrelevant to your search. Because you used such a broad key word, you might need to navigate through all that information before you could find a link or subheading for concert dates. In contrast, if you were to type in "Duplex Arena and [band name]," you would have a better chance of locating pages that contain this information.

How to Narrow Your Search

If you have a large group of key words and still do not know which ones to use, write out a list of all the words you are considering. Once you have completed the list, scrutinize it. Then, delete the words that are least important to your search, and highlight those that are most important.

These **key search connectors** can help you fine-tune your search:

AND: Narrows a search by retrieving documents that include both terms. For example: *baseball* AND *playoffs*

OR: Broadens a search by retrieving documents including any of the terms. For example: *playoffs* OR *championships*

NOT: Narrows a search by excluding documents containing certain words. For example: *baseball* NOT *history of*

Tips for an Effective Search

1. Remember that search engines can be case-sensitive. If your first attempt at searching fails, check your search terms for misspellings and try again.
2. If you are entering a group of key words, present them in order from the most important to the least important key word.
3. Avoid opening the link to every single page in your results list. Search engines present pages in descending order of relevancy. The most useful pages will be located at the top of the list. However, read the description of each link before you open the page.
4. Some search engines provide helpful tips for specializing your search. Take the opportunity to learn more about effective searching.

Other Ways to Search

Using Online Reference Sites How you search should be tailored to what you are hoping to find. If you are looking for data and facts, use reference sites before you jump onto a simple search engine. For example, you can find reference sites to provide definitions of words, statistics about almost any subject, biographies, maps, and concise information on many topics. Here are some useful online reference sites:

Online libraries

Online periodicals

Almanacs

Encyclopedias

You can find these sources using subject searches.

Conducting Subject Searches As you prepare to go online, consider your subject and the best way to find information to suit your needs. If you are looking for general information on a topic and you want your search results to be extensive, consider the subject search indexes on most search engines. These indexes, in the form of category and subject lists, often appear on the first page of a search engine. When you click on a specific highlighted word, you will be presented with a new screen containing subcategories of the topic you chose.

Evaluating the Reliability of Internet Resources

Just as you would evaluate the quality, bias, and validity of any other research material you locate, check the source of information you find online. Compare these two sites containing information about the poet and writer Langston Hughes:

Site A is a personal Web site constructed by a college student. It contains no bibliographic information or links to sites that he used. Included on the site are several poems by Langston Hughes and a student essay about the poet's use of symbolism. It has not been updated in more than six months.

Site B is a Web site constructed and maintained by the English Department of a major university. Information on Hughes is presented in a scholarly format, with a bibliography and credits for the writer. The site includes links to other sites and indicates new features that are added weekly.

For your own research, consider the information you find on Site B to be more reliable and accurate than that on Site A. Because it is maintained by experts in their field who are held accountable for their work, the university site will be a better research tool than the student-generated one.

Tips for Evaluating Internet Sources

1. Consider who constructed and who now maintains the Web page. Determine whether this author is a reputable source. Often, the URL endings indicate a source.
   - Sites ending in *.edu* are maintained by educational institutions.
   - Sites ending in *.gov* are maintained by government agencies (federal, state, or local).
   - Sites ending in *.org* are normally maintained by nonprofit organizations and agencies.
   - Sites ending in *.com* are commercially or personally maintained.
2. Skim the official and trademarked Web pages first. It is safe to assume that the information you draw from Web pages of reputable institutions, online encyclopedias, online versions of major daily newspapers, or government-owned sites produce information as reliable as the material you would find in print. In contrast, unbranded sites or those generated by individuals tend to borrow information from other sources without providing documentation. As information travels from one source to another, it could have been muddled, misinterpreted, edited, or revised.
3. You can still find valuable information in the less "official" sites. Check for the writer's credentials, and then consider these factors:
   - Do not be misled by official-looking graphics or presentations.
   - Make sure that the information is updated enough to suit your needs. Many Web pages will indicate how recently they have been updated.
   - If the information is borrowed, notice whether you can trace it back to its original source.

Respecting Copyrighted Material

Because the Internet is a relatively new and quickly growing medium, issues of copyright and ownership arise almost daily. As laws begin to govern the use and reuse of material posted online, they may change the way that people can access or reprint material.

Text, photographs, music, and fine art printed online may not be reproduced without acknowledged permission of the copyright owner.

Writing Criticism

Literary criticism involves studying, analyzing, interpreting, and evaluating works of literature. It can be as brief as an answer to a question or as lengthy as an essay or a book. Following are examples of three types of criticism.

Three Types of Criticism

Analysis You are frequently asked to analyze, or break down into parts and examine, a passage or a work. Often you must support your analysis with specific references to the text. In this brief analysis, the writer uses words from the question to write a topic sentence and embeds quotations from the text as support.

Question In "Heat" by H. D., how does the speaker create the impression that heat is almost a solid substance?

Answer The speaker in "Heat" uses repetition and imagery to convey the impression that heat is almost a solid substance. By repeating the word *heat* in each of the three stanzas, the speaker emphasizes its physical presence. Further, the speaker uses images that appeal to the sense of touch in describing heat as if it were a substance. In the first stanza, the speaker asks the wind to "cut apart the heat," and in the third stanza, to "plow through it."

Biographical Criticism Critics who take a biographical approach use information about a writer's life to explain his or her work. In this passage of biographical criticism, Kenneth Silverman explains Edgar Allan Poe's preoccupation with death as Poe's response to the early death of his mother, Eliza.

> Much of his later writing, despite its variety of forms and styles, places and characters, is driven by the question of whether the dead remain dead. . . . The most persuasive and coherent explanation, . . . comes from the modern understanding of childhood bereavement. . . . [C]hildren who lose a parent at an early age, as Edgar lost Eliza Poe, . . . invest more feeling in and magnify the parent's image. . . . The young child . . . cannot comprehend the finality of death. . . .

Historical Criticism Using this approach, a critic explains how an author's work responds to the events, circumstances, or ideas of the author's historical era. In the following passage of historical criticism, Jean H. Hagstrum shows how William Blake's character Urizen symbolizes the Enlightenment ideas of Newton, Locke, and Bacon that Blake detested.

> Urizen is also an active force. Dividing, partitioning, dropping the plummet line, applying Newton's compasses to the world, he creates abstract mathematical forms. Like Locke, he shrinks the senses, narrows the perceptions, binds man to natural fact. Like Bacon, he creates the laws of prudence and crucifies passion.

Using Ideas From Research

Below are three common methods of incorporating the ideas of other writers into your work. Choose the most appropriate style by analyzing your needs in each case. In all cases, you must credit your source.

- **Direct Quotation:** Use quotation marks to indicate the exact words.
- **Paraphrase:** To share ideas without a direct quotation, state the ideas in your own words.
- **Summary:** To provide information about a large body of work, identify the writer's main idea.

Avoiding Plagiarism

Whether you are presenting a formal research paper or an opinion paper on a current event, be careful to give credit for any ideas or opinions that are not your own. Presenting someone else's ideas, research, or opinion as your own—even if you have rephrased it in different words—is plagiarism, the equivalent of academic stealing, or fraud.

You can avoid plagiarism by synthesizing what you learn: Read from several sources, and let the ideas of experts help you draw your own conclusions and form your own opinions. When you choose to use someone else's ideas or work to support your view, credit the source of the material.

Preparing a Manuscript

The presentation of your written work is important. Your work should be neat, clean, and easy to read. Follow your teacher's directions for placing your name and class, along with the title and date of your work, on the paper.

Research Papers

Most formal research papers have these features:

- Title Page
- Table of Contents or Outline
- Works-Cited List or Bibliography

Citing Sources

In research writing, cite your sources. In the body of your paper, provide a footnote, an endnote, or an internal citation, identifying the sources of facts, opinions, or quotations. At the end of your paper, provide a bibliography or a works-cited list, a list of all the sources you cite. Follow an established format, such as Modern Library Association (MLA) Style.

Works-Cited List (MLA Style)

A works-cited list must contain accurate information sufficient to enable a reader to locate each source you cite. The basic components of an entry are as follows:

- Name of the author, editor, translator, or group responsible for the work
- Title
- Place and date of publication
- Publisher

For print materials, the information required for a citation generally appears on the copyright and title pages of a work. For the format of works-cited list entries, consult the examples at right and in the chart on page R31.

Internal Citations (MLA Style)

An internal citation briefly identifies the source from which you have taken a specific quotation, factual claim, or opinion. It refers the reader to one of the entries on your works-cited list. An internal citation has the following features:

- It appears in parentheses.
- It identifies the source by the last name of the author, editor, or translator.
- It gives a page reference, identifying the page of the source on which the information cited can be found.

Punctuation An internal citation generally falls outside a closing quotation mark but within the final punctuation of a clause or sentence. For a long quotation set off from the rest of your text, place the citation at the end of the excerpt without any punctuation following.

Special Cases

- If the author is an organization, use the organization's name, in a shortened version if necessary.
- If you cite more than one work by the same author, add the title or a shortened version of the title.

Sample Works-Cited Lists

Carwardine, Mark, Erich Hoyt, R. Ewan Fordyce, and Peter Gill. *The Nature Company Guides: Whales, Dolphins, and Porpoises.* New York: Time-Life Books, 1998.

Whales in Danger. "Discovering Whales." 18 Oct. 1999. <http://whales.magna.com.au/DISCOVER>

Neruda, Pablo. "Ode to Spring." *Odes to Opposites.* Trans. Ken Krabbenhoft. Ed. and illus. Ferris Cook. Boston: Little, Brown and Company, 1995.

The Saga of the Volsungs. Trans. Jesse L. Byock. London: Penguin Books, 1990.

An anonymous work is listed by title.

Both the title of the work and of the collection in which it is found are listed.

Sample Internal Citations

It makes sense that baleen whales such as the blue whale, the bowhead whale, the humpback whale, and the sei whale (to name just a few) grow to immense sizes (Carwardine, Hoyt, and Fordyce 19–21). The blue whale has grooves running from under its chin to partway along the length of its underbelly. As in some other whales, these grooves expand and allow even more food and water to be taken in (Ellis 18–21).

Author's last name

Page numbers where information can be found

MLA Style for Listing Sources

Book with one author	Pyles, Thomas. *The Origins and Development of the English Language.* 2nd ed. New York: Harcourt Brace Jovanovich, Inc., 1971.
Book with two or three authors **Book with an editor**	McCrum, Robert, William Cran, and Robert MacNeil. *The Story of English.* New York: Penguin Books, 1987. Truth, Sojourner. *Narrative of Sojourner Truth.* Ed. Margaret Washington. New York: Vintage Books, 1993.
Book with more than three authors or editors	Donald, Robert B., et al. *Writing Clear Essays.* Upper Saddle River, NJ: Prentice-Hall, Inc., 1996.
Single work from an anthology	Hawthorne, Nathaniel. "Young Goodman Brown." *Literature: An Introduction to Reading and Writing.* Ed. Edgar V. Roberts and Henry E. Jacobs. Upper Saddle River, NJ: Prentice-Hall, Inc., 1998. 376–385. [Indicate pages for the entire selection.]
Introduction in a published edition	Washington, Margaret. Introduction. *Narrative of Sojourner Truth.* By Sojourner Truth. New York: Vintage Books, 1993, pp. v–xi.
Signed article in a weekly magazine	Wallace, Charles. "A Vodacious Deal." *Time,* 14 Feb. 2000: 63.
Signed article in a monthly magazine	Gustaitis, Joseph. "The Sticky History of Chewing Gum." *American History,* Oct. 1998: 30–38.
Unsigned editorial or story	"Selective Silence." Editorial. *Wall Street Journal,* 11 Feb. 2000: A14. [If the editorial or story is signed, begin with the author's name.]
Signed pamphlet	[Treat the pamphlet as though it were a book.]
Pamphlet with no author, publisher, or date	*Are You at Risk of Heart Attack?* n.p. n.d. [n.p. n.d. indicates that there is no known publisher or date]
Filmstrips, slide programs, and videotape	*The Diary of Anne Frank.* Dir. George Stevens. Perf. Millie Perkins, Shelley Winters, Joseph Schildkraut, Lou Jacobi, and Richard Beymer. Twentieth Century Fox, 1959.
Radio or television program transcript	"The First Immortal Generation." *Ockham's Razor.* Host Robyn Williams. Guest Damien Broderick. National Public Radio. 23 May 1999. Transcript.
Internet	*National Association of Chewing Gum Manufacturers.* 19 Dec. 1999 <http://www.nacgm.org/consumer/funfacts.html> [Indicate the date you accessed the information. Content and addresses at Web sites change frequently.]
Newspaper	Thurow, Roger. "South Africans Who Fought for Sanctions Now Scrap for Investors." *Wall Street Journal,* 11 Feb. 2000: A1+ [For a multipage article, write only the first page number on which it appears, followed by a plus sign.]
Personal interview	Smith, Jane. Personal interview. 10 Feb. 2000.
CD (with multiple publishers)	Simms, James, ed. *Romeo and Juliet.* By William Shakespeare. CD-ROM. Oxford: Attica Cybernetics Ltd.; London: BBC Education; London: HarperCollins Publishers, 1995.
Signed article from an encyclopedia	Askeland, Donald R. (1991). "Welding." *World Book Encyclopedia.* 1991 ed.

Index of Authors and Titles

Page numbers in *italics* refer to biographical information.

Index of Skills

Literary Analysis

Reading Strategies

Grammar and Style

Vocabulary

Critical Thinking and Viewing

Writing Applications

Writing Strategies

Listening and Speaking

Research and Technology

Index of Features

Literature in Context

A Closer Look

Writing Workshops

Listening and Speaking Workshops

Assessment Workshops

ACKNOWLEDGMENTS (CONTINUED)

Curtis Brown Ltd., London "Be Ye Men of Valor" (retitled Wartime Speech), BBC London, May 19, 1940, from *Blood, Toil, Tears and Sweat: The Speeches of Winston Churchill* edited and with and introduction by David Cannadine. Speeches Copyright © 1989 by Winston Churchill MP. All rights reserved.

Harlan Davidson, Inc./Forum Press, Inc. Excerpt from "Book I" of *Utopia* by Thomas More, edited and translated by H. V. S. Ogden, pp. 21, 22 (Crofts Classics Series). Copyright © 1949 by Harlan Davidson, Inc.

Doubleday, a division of Random House, Inc. "Haiku" from *An Introduction to Haiku* by Harold G. Henderson, copyright © 1958 by Harold G. Henderson. Used by permission of Doubleday, a division of Random House, Inc.

Faber and Faber Limited "The Chimney Sweeper" from *The Poetical Works of William Blake,* edited by John Sampson. Excerpt from the Introduction from *The North Ship* by Philip Larkin. Copyright © 1966 by Philip Larkin. "The Rain Horse" by Ted Hughes from *Wodwo.* Copyright © 1967. "The Horses" from *The Hawk in the Rain* by Ted Hughes. Copyright © 1957, 1960 by Ted Hughes.

Faber and Faber Limited and Farrar, Straus & Giroux, Inc. From *Station Island* by Seamus Heaney. Copyright © Seamus Heaney, 1984. First published in 1984 by Faber and Faber Limited.

Farrar, Straus & Giroux, Inc. "Follower" from *Poems 1965–1975* by Seamus Heaney. Copyright © 1980 by Seamus Heaney. *Midsummer,* XXIII, from *Collected Poems 1948–1984* by Derek Walcott. Copyright © 1986 by Derek Walcott. From Chapter XXVIII of *Omeros* by Derek Walcott. Copyright © 1990 by Derek Walcott. "An Arundel Tomb" by Philip Larkin from *Collected Poems.* Copyright © 1988, 1989 by the Estate of Philip Larkin. "Two Lorries" from *The Spirit Level* by Seamus Heaney. Copyright © 1996 by Seamus Heaney. "The Prologue" from *Gilgamesh: A New Rendering in English Verse* by David Ferry. Copyright © 1992 by David Ferry. "The Explosion" from *Collected Poems* by Philip Larkin. Copyright © 1988, 1989 by the Estate of Philip Larkin.

Forum for Peace and Reconcilliation, c/o Mr. Walter Kirwan "Opening Address for The Forum for Peace and Reconciliation," by Judge Catherine McGuinness, from www.lrlgov.ie/iveagh/anglorish/forum/inaug.html.

Harcourt, Inc. "L'Invitation au Voyage" by Charles Baudelaire, translated by Richard Wilbur from *Things of This World,* copyright © 1956 and renewed 1984 by Richard Wilbur. Excerpt from William Wordsworth and Samuel Coleridge by George Meyer from *Major British Writers: Enlarged Edition, II,* edited by G. B. Harrison, Charles W. Dunn, et al. Copyright, 1954, © 1959, by Harcourt, Inc. All rights reserved. "Three excerpts from George Gordon, Lord Byron" by Northrop Frye from *Major British Writers: Enlarged Edition, II,* edited by G.B. Harrision, Charles W. Dunn, et al. Copyright, 1954, © 1959, by Harcourt, Inc. All rights reserved.

Harcourt, Inc., the Executors of the Virginia Woolf Estate, and The Society of Authors "The Lady in the Looking Glass: A Reflection" from *A Haunted House and Other Short Stories* by Virginia Woolf, copyright 1944 and renewed 1972 by Harcourt, Inc. Reprinted by permission of Harcourt, Inc.

Harcourt, Inc., and Faber and Faber Ltd. "The Hollow Men," "Preludes" and "Journey of the Magi" from *Collected Poems 1909–1962* by T. S. Eliot, copyright 1936 by Harcourt, Inc., copyright © 1964, 1963 by T. S. Eliot. Reprinted by permission.

Harcourt, Inc., and A. M. Heath & Co. Ltd. "Shooting an Elephant" from *Shooting an Elephant and Other Essays* by George Orwell, copyright © by George Orwell, 1936, by permission of Mark Hamilton as the Literary Executor of the Estate of the Late Sonia Brownell Orwell and Martin Secker and Warburg Ltd.

HarperCollins Publishers, Inc., and William Heinemann Ltd. "A Devoted Son" from *Games at Twilight and Other Stories* by Anita Desai. Copyright © 1978 by Anita Desai. Reprinted by permission of HarperCollins Publishers, Inc.

HarperCollins Publishers Ltd., U.K. "The Rights We Enjoy, the Duties We Owe" reprinted by permission of Fourth Estate, Ltd., from *New Britain: My Vision of a Young Country* by Tony Blair © 1996 by The Office of Tony Blair. Used by permission.

David Higham Associates Limited "On the Patio" from *Poems 1954–1987* by Peter Redgrove. Copyright © Peter Redgrove, 1959, 1961, 1963,1966, 1972, 1973, 1975, 1977, 1979, 1981, 1985, 1986, 1987. All rights reserved.

Henry Holt and Company, Inc., and The Society of Authors "When I Was One-and-Twenty" from *The Collected Poems of A. E. Housman* by A. E. Housman. Copyright 1939, 1940, © 1965 by Henry Holt and Company, Inc., © 1967 by Robert E. Symons. Used by permission of Henry Holt and Company, Inc.

International Publishers Co. Excerpt from "English Poets" from *Illusion and Reality* by Christopher Caudwell. Copyright © 1937, by Executor of the Estate of Christopher Caudwell. All rights reserved.

John Johnson Ltd. "Eve's Apology" from *The Poems of Shakespeare's Dark Lady: Salve Deus Judaeorum* by Emilia Lanier, introduced by A. L. Rowse. Reprinted by permission of John Johnson Ltd. for Dr. A. L. Rowse.

Alfred A. Knopf, Inc., a division of Random House, Inc. "The Demon Lover" from *The Collected Stories of Elizabeth Bowen* by Elizabeth Bowen, copyright © 1981 by Curtis Brown Ltd., Literary Executors of the Estate of Elizabeth Bowen. Used by permission of Alfred A. Knopf, a division of Random House, Inc.

George P. Landow "The Victorian Web Overview" by George P. Landow from www.stg.brown.edu. Used by permission.

Hal Leonard Publishing Corporation "New Beginning," words and music by Tracy Chapman. © 1996 EMI April Music Inc. and Purple Rabbit Music. All rights controlled and administered by EMI April Music Inc. All rights reserved. International copyright secured. Used by permission.

L. R. Lind From *Ovid: Tristia* translated by L. R. Lind. Published by The University of Georgia Press. All rights reserved. Copyright © 1975 by L. R. Lind.

Little, Brown and Company From "A World Lit Only By Fire'" by William Manchester from *The House of the Spirits.* © 1985 by Alfred A. Knopf, Inc.

Dr. Peter F. Morgan "Early Reviews of Wordsworth" from *Jeffreys' Criticism* by Francis Jeffrey, edited by Peter F. Morgan. Copyright © 1983 Peter F. Morgan. Used by permission.

ACKNOWLEDGMENTS (CONTINUED)

The National Gallery, London "The Gallery's Role and Objectives" by The National Gallery Department Office, from *The Gallery's Roles and Objectives.*

New American Library, a division of Penguin Putnam, Inc. From *Beowulf* by Burton Raffel, translator. Translation copyright © 1963 by Burton Raffel. Afterword © 1963 by New American Library. Used by permission.

New Beacon Books Ltd. From "Lucy: Englan' Lady" from *Lucy's Letters and Loving* by James Berry. © 1982 by James Berry.

New Directions Publishing Co. "Not Waving but Drowning" from Stevie Smith, from *The Collected Poems of Stevie Smith.* Copyright © 1972 by Stevie Smith. "Far Corners of the Earth" by Tu Fu, translated by David Hinton, from *The Selected Poems of Tu Fu.* Copyright ©1989 by David Hinton. "Anthem for Doomed Youth" by Wilfred Owen, from *The Collected Poems of Wilfred Owen,* edited by C. Day Lewis. Copyright © Chatto & Windus Ltd. 1946, 1963.

New Directions Publishing Corporation and David Higham Associates Ltd. "Do Not Go Gentle Into That Good Night" by Dylan Thomas, from *The Poems of Dylan Thomas.* Copyright © 1952 by The Trustees for the Copyrights of Dylan Thomas. "Fern Hill" by Dylan Thomas, from *The Poems of Dylan Thomas.* Copyright © 1945 by The Trustees for the Copyrights of Dylan Thomas. Reprinted by permission of New Directions Publishing Corporation, and David Higham Associates Ltd.

Newmarket Press From *The Sense and Sensibility Screenplay & Diaries* by Emma Thompson, published by Newmarket Press. Copyright © 1995 Columbia Pictures Industries, Inc. All rights reserved. Reprinted by permission of Newmarket Press, 18 East 48th Street, New York, NY 10017.

News International Syndication Articles "Death of a King" and "The New Queen" reprinted from Times Newspapers Limited, 7 February 1952. Copyright © Times Newspapers Limited, 1952.

North Point Press, a division of Farrar, Straus & Giroux, Inc. "Testament" by Bei Dao from A *Splintered Mirror: Chinese Poetry From the Democracy Movement* translated by Donald Finkel. Translation copyright © 1991 by Donald Finkel. Reprinted by permission of North Point Press, a division of Farrar, Straus & Giroux, Inc.

W. W. Norton & Company, Inc. From *Beowulf: A New Verse Translation* by Seamus Heaney. Copyright © 2000 by Seamus Heaney. "Outside History" from *Outside History: Selected Poems, 1980–1990* by Eavan Boland. Copyright © 1990 by Eavan Boland. From *Sir Gawain and the Green Knight: A New Verse Translation* by Marie Borroff, translator. Copyright © 1967 by W. W. Norton & Company, Inc. All rights reserved. Used by permission of W. W. Norton & Company, Inc.

Oxford University Press, London "God's Grandeur," "Pied Beauty," and "Spring and Fall" from *Poems of Gerard Manley Hopkins,* 4th edition, edited by W. H. Gardner and N. H. MacKenzie. "The Lamb," "The Chimney Sweeper," and "Infant Sorrow" from *The Poetical Works of William Blake* edited by John Sampson. Sonnet 43 from *The Poetical Works of Elizabeth Barrett Browning,* Oxford Edition. "To Althea" and "To Lucasta, on Going to the Wars" from *The Poems of Richard Lovelace,* edited by C. H. Wilkinson, copyright © 1953. "Kubla Khan" and "The Rime of the Ancient Mariner" from *The Poems of Samuel Taylor Coleridge.* Lines from "In Memoriam, A. H. H.," "The Lady of Shalott," lines from "The Princess," and "Ulysses" from *Alfred Tennyson: Poetical Works.* "To the Virgins, to Make Much of Time" from *The Poems of Robert Herrick* edited by L. C. Martin. From "The Life of Samuel Johnson" in *Boswell's Life of Johnson* by James Boswell, edited by C. B. Tinker. "Sonnet 31" and "Sonnet 39" from *The Poems of Sir Philip Sidney* edited by William A. Ringler, Jr. "The Passionate Shepherd to His Love" from *Marlowe's Poems,* edited by Roma Gill, Volume 1, © Roma Gill 1987, Clarendon Press, Oxford. Reprinted by permission of the publisher, Oxford University Press. "Sonnet 1" and "Sonnet 75" from *The Poetical Works of Edmund Spenser* edited by J. C. Smith and E. de Selincourt. "On Making an Agreeable Marriage" from *Jane Austen's Letters,* collected and edited by Deirdre Le Faye, copyright Deirdre Le Faye 1995. "The Middle Ages: 1000 Years of Darkness? No!" by H.W.C. Davis from *Medieval Europe.* "A Valuable Resource" by Jon Silkin from *Out of Battle: The Poetry of the Great War.* Copyright © Jon Silkin 1972. First published 1972. First issued as an Oxford University Press Paperback 1978.

Oxford University Press, Inc. From "The Wanderer," translated by Charles W. Kennedy, from *An Anthology of Old English Poetry.* Copyright © 1960 by Charles W. Kennedy. Used by permission of Oxford University Press, Inc.

Penguin Books Ltd. "How Siegfried Was Slain" from *The Nibelungenlied* translated by A. T. Hatto (Penguin Classics, Revised Edition, 1969), copyright © A. T. Hatto, 1965, 1969. From *A History of the English Church and People* by Bede, translated by Leo Sherley-Price, revised by R. E. Latham (Penguin Classics 1955, Revised edition 1968). Copyright © Leo Sherley-Price, 1955, 1968. "The Nun's Priest's Tale" and "The Prologue" to *The Canterbury Tales* by Geoffrey Chaucer, translated by Nevill Coghill (Penguin Classics 1951, Fourth revised edition 1977), copyright © 1951 by Nevill Coghill. Copyright © Nevill Coghill, 1958, 1960, 1975, 1977. Reprinted by permission of Penguin Books Ltd. "Melting Snow" by Kobayashi Issa (18 lines) from *The Penguin Book of Japanese Verse,* translated by Geoffrey Bownas and Anthony Thwaite (Penguin Books, 1964) Translation copyright © Geoffrey Bownas and Anthony Thwaite, 1964. Used by permission.

Phoebe Phillips Editions Excerpt from *The Anglo-Saxon Chronicle,* translated and collated by Anne Savage. Copyright © 1983 by Phoebe Phillips. All rights reserved.

Random House, Inc., and Curtis Brown Ltd. "In Memory of W. B. Yeats" from *W. H. Auden: Collected Poems* by W. H. Auden, edited by Edward Mendelson. "Musée des Beaux Arts" from *W. H. Auden: Collected Poems* by W. H. Auden, edited by Edward Mendelson. Copyright © 1939 by W. H. Auden. All rights reserved. Copyright 1940 and renewed 1968 by W. H. Auden. Used by permission of Random House, Inc., and Curtis Brown Ltd.

Random House, Inc., and Faber and Faber Ltd. "Not Palaces" from *Selected Poems* by Stephen Spender, copyright 1964 by Stephen Spender. In the UK, from *Collected Poems, 1928–1985.* Copyright © 1986 by Stephen Spender. Copyright 1934 by The Modern Library, Inc., and renewed 1962 by Stephen Spender. Used by permission of Random House, Inc., and Faber and Faber Ltd.

ACKNOWLEDGMENTS (CONTINUED)

Random House, Inc., and Methuen Publishing Ltd. From *A Man For All Seasons* by Robert Bolt, published by Heinemann Educational Books. Copyright © 1960, 1962 by Robert Bolt; copyright renewed 1988, 1990 by Robert Bolt. Reprinted by permission of Random House, Inc., and Methuen Publishing Ltd.

Marian Reiner, Literary Agent "Haiku" by Yosa Buson from *More Cricket Songs: Japanese Haiku,* translated by Harry Behn. Copyright © 1971 by Harry Behn.

Scovil Chichak Galen Literary Agency, Inc. "We'll Never Conquer Space" by Arthur C. Clarke, from *Science Digest,* June 1960. Copyright © 1960 by Popular Mechanics Company. Reprinted by permission of the author and the author's agents, Scovil Chichak Galen Literary Agency, Inc.

Scribner, a division of Simon & Schuster, Inc., and A.P. Watt Ltd. "The Second Coming" from *The Poems of W.B. Yeats: A New Edition*, edited by Richard J. Finneran. Copyright © 1924 by Macmillan Publishing Company, copyright renewed © 1952 by Bertha Georgie Yeats. "Sailing to Byzantium," from *The Poems of W. B. Yeats: A New Edition*, edited by Richard J. Finneran. Copyright © 1928 by Macmillan Publishing Company, copyright renewed © 1956 by Georgie Yeats. Reprinted with the permission of Scribner, a division of Simon & Schuster, Inc.

Simon & Schuster, Inc., and Jonathan Clowes Ltd. "No Witchcraft for Sale," reprinted with the permission of Simon & Schuster and Jonathan Clowes Ltd. from *African Short Stories* by Doris Lessing. Copyright © 1951, 1953, 1954, 1957, 1958, 1962, 1963, 1964, 1965, 1972, 1981 by Doris Lessing.

Estate of Ann Stanford c/o Rosanna Norton "The Wife's Lament" by Ann Stanford from *The Women Poets in English: An Anthology.* Copyright © 1972 by Ann Stanford. Used by permission.

Taylor & Francis Lines from "An Essay on Man" and Canto III and lines from Canto V from *The Rape of the Lock,* reprinted from *The Poems of Alexander Pope*, edited by John Butt. Published by Methuen & Co., Ltd., London. Used by permission.

University of California Press "You Know the Place: Then" from *Sappho: A New Translation* by Mary Barnard. Copyright © 1958 The Regents of the University of California; © renewed 1984 Mary Barnard. "The Diameter of the Bomb," translated by Chana Bloch, from *The Selected Poetry of Yehuda Amichai,* translated/edited by Chana Bloch and Stephen Mitchell. Translation copyright © 1996 by The Regents of the State of California. Used by permission.

University of Chicago Press From *The Iliad of Homer,* translated by Richmond Lattimore. Copyright © 1951, The University of Chicago. "Oedipus the King" by Sophocles from *The Complete Greek Tragedies,* Grene & Lattimore, eds., pp. 11–17. Used by permission.

University of Texas Press "Sonnet LXXXIX" and "Sonnet LXIX" from *100 Love Sonnets: Cien Sonetos de Amore,* by Pablo Neruda, translated by Stephen Tapscott. Copyright © 1959 by Pablo Neruda and Fundacion Pablo Neruda. Copyright © 1986 by the University of Texas Press. Used by permission of University of Texas Press.

University of Wisconsin Press Excerpts from "The Defense of Poesey" from *Sir Philip Sidney: Selected Prose and Poetry,* edited by Robert Kimbrough. Copyright © 1969, 1983 Robert Kimbrough.

Viking Penguin, Inc., a division of Penguin Putnam, Inc., and Barbara Levy Literary Agency "Wirers" from *Collected Poems of Siegfried Sassoon* by Siegfried Sassoon. Copyright 1918, 1920 by E.P. Dutton. Copyright 1936, 1946, 1947, 1948 by Siegfried Sassoon. Used by permission of Viking Penguin, a division of Penguin Putnam, Inc. and Barbara Levy Literary Agency for George Sassoon.

Viking Penguin, a division of Penguin Putnam, Inc., and David Higham Associates Ltd. "A Shocking Accident," copyright © 1957 by Graham Greene. In the USA from *Collected Stories of Graham Greene* by Graham Greene. In England from *Twenty-One Stories* by Graham Greene. Used by permission of Viking Penguin, a division of Penguin Putnam Inc. and David Higham Associates Ltd.

Viking Penguin, Inc., a division of Penguin Putnam, Inc. "Araby" from *Dubliners* by James Joyce, copyright 1916 by B. W. Heubsch. Definitive text copyright © 1967 by The Estate of James Joyce. "The Book of Sand" from *Collected Fictions* by Jorge Luis Borges, translated by Andrew Hurley, copyright © 1998 by Maria Kodama; translation copyright © 1998 by Penguin Putnam, Inc. "The Train from Rhodesia," copyright 1952 by Nadine Gordimer, from *Selected Stories* by Nadine Gordimer. Used by permission of Viking Penguin, a division of Penguin Putnam, Inc.

Viking Penguin, Inc., a division of Penguin Putnam, Inc., and The Bodley Head, c/o of Random House Group Ltd. "The Distant Past," from *Angels at the Ritz and Other Stories* by William Trevor, copyright © 1975 by William Trevor. Published in England by The Bodley Head. Used by permission of Viking Penguin, a division of Penguin Putnam, Inc. and The Random House Group Ltd.

Viking Penguin, Inc., a division of Penguin Putnam, Inc., and Laurence Pollinger Ltd. "The Rocking-Horse Winner," copyright © 1933 by the Estate of D. H. Lawrence, renewed © 1961 by Angelo Ravagli and C. M. Weekley, Executors of the Estate of Frieda Lawrence, from *Complete Short Stories of D.H. Lawrence* by D.H. Lawrence.

Wake Forest University Press "Carrick Revisited" from *Selected Poems of Louis MacNeice,* edited by Michael Longley. © Wake Forest University Press, 1990. Reprinted by permission of Wake Forest University Press.

Estate of Arthur Waley c/o John Robinson Excerpts from *The Analects of Confucius,* translated and annotated by Arthur Waley. Copyright © 1938 by George Allen and Unwin Ltd.

Warner Bros. Publications Inc. "Cromwell: The Movie" by Ken Hughes from *Cromwell* (1970: movie). Copyright © 1970.

Warner/Chappell Music, Inc., A Division of Warner Brothers Music "Freeze Tag" written by Suzanne Vega. Song copyright © 1985 by Waifersongs Ltd. And AGF Music Ltd. (ASCAP).

Yale University Press "The Seafarer" from *Poems from the Old English,* translated by Burton Raffel. Copyright © 1960, 1964; renewed 1988, 1922 by The University of Nebraska Press. Copyright © 1994 by Burton Raffel. Used by permission.

Note: Every effort has been made to locate the copyright owner of material reprinted in this book. Omissions brought to our attention will be corrected in subsequent printings.

CREDITS

Cover and Title Page: *Salisbury Cathedral from the Bishop's Grounds,* 1823, John Constable, Victoria & Albert, London/Art Resource, NY; **vi:** Werner Forman Archive, Viking Ship Museum, Bygdoy, Oslo, Art Resource, NY; **viii:** Chad Ehlers, 1987/PNI; **ix:** Board of Trustees of the Armouries/Geoff Dann/© Dorling Kindersley; **x, xi:** Corel Professional Photos CD-ROM™; **xii:** © R. J. Erwin/Photo Researchers, Inc.; **xiv:** Greek vase, terracotta, c. 460 B.C. Attributed to the Orchard Painter, Column Krater (called the "Orchard Vase"), Side A: *Women Gathering Apples,* The Metropolitan Museum of Art, Rogers Fund, 1907 (07.286.74); **xv:** Culver Pictures, Inc.; **xvi:** *Antea* (Portrait of a Lady), Parmigianino, Museo Nazionale di Capodimonte, Naples/Scala/Art Resource, NY; **xix:** NASA/Omni-Photo Communications, Inc.; **1:** The Bodleian Library, Oxford; **2:** (m.) Michael Nicholson/CORBIS; **2:** (t.l.) Richard Nowitz/CORBIS; **2:** (b.) Scala/Art Resource, NY; **2:** (t.r.) The Granger Collection, New York; **3:** (m.) *The Murder of Thomas Becket,* English illuminated psalter, c. 1200, The Granger Collection, New York; **3:** (t.) Superstock; **3:** (b.) Art Resource, NY; **5:** Viking sword, iron, copper, and silver, The Metropolitan Museum of Art, Rogers Fund, 1955, © Copyright 1980, 1987 by The Metropolitan Museum of Art; **6:** Erich Lessing/Art Resource, NY; **8:** British Museum, London, UK/The Bridgeman Art Library, London/New York; **9:** The Granger Collection, New York; **10:** *Sketch of Robin Hood,* 1852, Richard Dadd, Yale Center for British Art, Paul Mellon Collection; **13:** *Arrival of William at Penvesy* (detail from Bayeux Tapestry), Giraudon/Art Resource, NY; **14:** The Granger Collection, New York; **16:** The Bodleian Library, Oxford; **18:** Digital Imagery © Copyright 2001 PhotoDisc, Inc.; **22:** *Wreck of a Transport Ship,* Joseph Mallord William Turner/The Bridgeman Art Library, London/New York; **25:** *Susanna in Bath* (detail), Albrecht Altdorfer, *Wasserholendes Mädchen,* München, Alte Pinakothek, Munich. Photo: Blauel/ Artothek; **30:** The Granger Collection, New York; **32:** Corel Professional Photos CD-ROM™; **33:** CORBIS; **34:** (t.) Fan mounted as an album leaf: *Evening in Spring Hills,* ink and color on silk. H. 9-3/4 in. W. 10-1/4 in. (24.8 x 26.1 cm.) Chinese, The Metropolitan Museum of Art, Gift of John M. Crawford, Jr., in honor of Alfreda Murck, 1986 (1986.493.1). Photograph © 1987 The Metropolitan Museum of Art; **34:** (b.) Cliché Bibliothèque nationale de France, Paris; **35:** *Beowulf on the Funeral Pyre,* Rockwell Kent, The Granger Collection, New York; **36:** Statens Historiska Museet, Stockholm, Werner Forman Archive/Art Resource, NY; **38:** Courtesy of the Trustees of British Library; **42:** Werner Forman Archive, Viking Ship Museum, Bygdoy, Oslo, Art Resource, NY; **44:** Werner Forman Archive, Statens Historiska Museet, Stockholm, Art Resource, NY; **46:** Art Resource, NY; **49:** *Golden Horn* (detail), The National Museet, Copenhagen, Photo by Lennart Larsen; **50:** Silver pendant showing the helmet of the Vendel, 10th century, Swedish-Ostergotland, Viking Werner Forman Archive, Statens Historiska Museet, Stockholm, Art Resource, NY; **53:** The Granger Collection, New York; **54:** *The Dragon* for "The High Kings," George Sharp, Courtesy of the artist; **55:** Werner Forman Archive, National Museum, Copenhagen, Art Resource, NY; **56:** Gilt-bronze winged dragon-bridle mounting, 8th century, Swedish Artifact, Statens Historiska Museet, Stockholm, Werner Forman Archive/Art Resource, NY; **58:** Head of carved post from the ship burial at Oseberg, Werner Forman Archive/Art Resource, NY; **64:** Impression from a Sumerian cylinder seal of about 2750 B.C.: *Hero and Animals,* The Granger Collection, New York; **66:** © British Museum; **68:** British Museum, London, UK/Bridgeman Art Library, London/New York; **70:** CORBIS-Bettmann; **71:** *Four Kings of England* (left to right): Henry II, Richard I, John, Henry III, from *Historia Anglorum,* 13th c. Roy 14 C VII f. 9. British Library, London, Great Britain, Bridgeman/Art Resource, NY; **72:** Snark/Art Resource, NY; **75:** The Bodleian Library, Oxford; **77:** Courtesy of the Trustees of British Library; **90:** Image Select/Art Resource, NY; **92:** © Dorling Kindersley; **97:** *The Yeoman,* Arthur Szyk for *The Canterbury Tales,* The George Macy Companies; **99:** *The Monk,* Arthur Szyk for *The Canterbury Tales,* The George Macy Companies; **102:** *The Student,* Arthur Szyk for *The Canterbury Tales,* The George Macy Companies; **106:** *The Wife of Bath,* Arthur Szyk for *The Canterbury Tales,* The George Macy Companies; **111:** *The Pardoner,* Arthur Szyk for *The Canterbury Tales,* The George Macy Companies; **113:** Digital Imagery © Copyright 2001 PhotoDisc, Inc.; **121:** Courtesy of the Trustees of British Library; **124:** *The Nun's Priest,* detail from the Ellesmere Manuscript, Chaucer's *The Canterbury Tales,* The Huntington Library, San Marino, California; **128:** *Woman Feeding Chickens,* from an Italian manuscript (c. 1385), Österreichische National Bibliothek, Vienna; **131:** *Chaucer Reciting* Troilus and Cressida *Before a Court Gathering* (Frontispiece), Corpus Christi College; **143:** *The Pardoner,* Arthur Szyk for *The Canterbury Tales,* The George Macy Companies; **147, 149:** Lambeth Palace Library, London, UK/Bridgeman Art Library, London/New York; **154:** Corel Professional Photos CD-ROM™; **156:** © Hulton Getty/Archive Photos; **159:** *St. George and the Dragon,* c. 1506, Raphael, oil on panel, 11-1/8 x 8-1/2" © Board of Trustees, National Gallery of Art, Washington, D.C. Andrew W. Mellon Collection; **160:** The Granger Collection, New York; **165:** *Three Knights Returning from a Tournament.* French miniature from "Recueil de Traités de Dévotion." Ms. 137/1687, fol. 144 r.c.1371–78, Giraudon/Art Resource, NY; **169:** *Gawain Receiving the Green Girdle,* Fritz Kredel, Woodcut, from John Gardner, *The Complete Works of the Gawain Poet,* © 1965, The University of Chicago; **173:** The Bodleian Library, Oxford; **177:** *King Arthur's Round Table and the Holy Grail,* Art Resource, NY; **180:** *The Nine Heroes Tapestries:* Christian Heroes: Arthur (detail). Probably Nicolas Bataille, Paris, The Metropolitan Museum of Art; **182:** Bettmann/CORBIS; **188:** The Granger Collection, New York; **190:** Nicholas Sapieha/Stock, Boston; **194:** © Michael Giannechini/Photo Researchers, Inc.; **196:** The Granger Collection, New York; **198:** *Veronica Veronese,* Dante Gabriel Rossetti, Delaware Art Museum, Samuel and Mary Bancroft Memorial Collection; **204:** Silver Burdett Ginn; **207:** The Granger Collection, New York; **210:** *Siegfried's Death,* Handschriftenabteilung, Staatsbibliothek Preussischer Kulturbesitz, Berlin, photo Bildarchiv Preussicher Kulturbesitz; **214:** PhotoEdit; **220–221:** *The Peasant's Wedding,* Pieter Brueghel. Photo by Erich Lessing/Art Resource, NY; **222:** (b.r.) *William Shakespeare,* Martin Droeshout, The Granger Collection, New York; **222:** (t.r.) National Portrait Gallery, London/Superstock; **222:** (t.l., b.l.) The Granger Collection, New York; **223:** (t.) *The Defeat of the Spanish Armada,* 1588, The Granger Collection, New York; **223:** (m.) The Granger Collection, New York; **223:** (b.l.) Library of Congress/CORBIS; **223:** (b.r.) Scala/Art Resource, NY; **224:** The Granger Collection, New York; **225:** *The Launching of Fireships Against the Spanish Armada* (detail), National Maritime Museum, Greenwich, England; **226:** (t.) National Trust/Art Resource, NY; **226:** (b.) National Portrait Gallery, London/Superstock; **227:** Art Resource, NY; **228:** *The Hireling Shepherd,* William Holman Hunt © Manchester City Art Galleries; **229:** The Granger Collection, New York; **231:** CORBIS-Bettmann; **233:** *The Sonnet,* William Mulready, Victoria and Albert Museum/ Art Resource NY; **234:** (r.) *Sir Philip Sidney* (detail), c. 1576, artist unknown, by courtesy of the National Portrait Gallery, London; **234:** (l.) The Granger Collection, New York; **236, 237, 238:** Corel Professional Photos CD-ROM™; **239:** Chad Ehlers, 1987/PNI; **244:** (l., r.) The Granger Collection, New York; **250:** *William Shakespeare* (detail), artist unknown, by courtesy of the National Portrait Gallery, London; **252:** *Autumn,* 1865, Frederick Walker, Victoria & Albert Museum, London/Art Resource, NY; **255:** Corel Professional Photos CD-ROM™; **260:** *Portrait of Laura,* Biblioteca Laurenziana, Firenze, Scala/Art Resource, NY; **261:** The Granger Collection, New York; **262:** Sergio Larrain/Magnum Photos, Inc.; **263:** (m.) *King James I of England,* John DeCritz the Elder, Galleria Platina, Palazzo Pitti, Florence, Italy, Scala/Art Resource, NY; **263:** (l.) *King Henry VIII of England,* after Hans Holbein, oil on copper, c. 1536, The Granger Collection, New York; **263:** (r.) *Queen Elizabeth I of England in Coronation Robes,* unknown artist, The Granger Collection, New York; **264:** (l.) The Granger Collection, New York; **264:** (r.) North Wind Picture Archives; **266:** *Gardens at Llanerch,* Denbighshire, c. 1662–72, British School, 17th c., oil on canvas, 45 x 59-3/4 in. (114.1 x 151.7 cm) B1976.7.115. Yale Center for British Art, New Haven, Connecticut, Paul Mellon Collection; **268:** Portrait of Queen Elizabeth I, Bridgeman/Art Resource, NY; **270:** "Dangers Averted"

CREDITS

medal, celebrating the defeat of the Spanish Armada, c. 1589, gold cast and chased by Nicholas Hilliard (1537–1619), Fitzwilliam Museum, University of Cambridge/Bridgeman Art Library, London/New York; **274:** Digital Imagery © Copyright 2001 PhotoDisc, Inc.; **276:** By permission of the Folger Shakespeare Library, Washington, D.C.; **279:** Digital Imagery © Copyright 2001 PhotoDisc, Inc.; **284, 285:** Photofest; **288:** AP/Wide World Photos; **289:** The Globe Theatre, London, The Granger Collection, New York; **290:** Board of Trustees of the Armouries/Geoff Dann/© Dorling Kindersley; **291:** AP/Wide World Photos/Rota; **291:** (inset) AP/Wide World Photos/Max Nash; **292:** AP/Wide World Photos/Stefan Rousseau; **293:** (t.) Photograph by Cylla von Tiedemann. Courtesy of the Stratford Festival Archives; **293** (b.), **294** (t., b.), **295:** Photofest; **296:** *William Shakespeare* (detail), artist unknown, by courtesy of the National Portrait Gallery, London; **298:** (l.) *Scene from Macbeth* (detail), Cattermole, by permission of the Folger Shakespeare Library, Washington, D.C.; **298:** (r.) © Darren Robb/Stone; **300:** Corel Professional Photos CD-ROM™; **302:** *The Three Witches*, 1783, Henry Fuseli, oil on canvas, 65 x 91.5 cm, Kunsthaus Zürich © 1997 copyright Kunsthaus Zürich. All rights reserved.; **306:** *Macbeth and the Witches*, Clarkson Stanfield, © Leicester City Museums Service, Art Galleries and Records Service; **308:** © Darren Robb/Stone; **310:** Anne Van De Vaeken/The Image Bank; **313:** *Ellen Terry (as Lady Macbeth)*, 1889, oil on canvas 87 x 45", Tate Gallery on loan to National Portrait Gallery, London, Art Resource, NY; **321:** Hans Neleman/ The Image Bank; **325:** Photofest; **328:** The Pierpont Morgan Library, Art Resource, NY; **330:** *Lady Macbeth Seizing the Daggers*, Henry Fuseli, The Tate Gallery, London/Art Resource, NY; **337:** Board of Trustees of the Armouries/Geoff Dann/© Dorling Kindersley; **342:** e.t. archive; **345:** The Granger Collection, New York; **347:** *Scene from Macbeth*, Cattermole, by permission of the Folger Shakespeare Library, Washington, D.C.; **355:** Earl & Nazima Kowall/CORBIS; **356:** e.t. archive; **363:** The Granger Collection, New York; **369:** Corel Professional Photos CD-ROM™; **375:** © Dorling Kindersley; **376:** *Lady Macbeth Sleepwalking*, Henry Fuseli, Louvre, Paris, Scala/Art Resource, NY; **380:** Steve Mohlenkamp/ Index Stock Photography, Inc.; **382:** Courtesy of the Library of Congress; **384:** Courtesy of the Stratford Festival Archives; **392:** Photofest; **397:** Vatican Museum/Scala/Art Resource, NY; **400:** David Young-Wolff/PhotoEdit; **406–407, 408:** (t.l., b.l.) The Granger Collection, New York; **408:** (t.r.) CORBIS-Bettmann; **408:** (b.r.) Dave G. Houser/CORBIS; **409:** (m.r.) *Mrs. Siddons, the actress (1755–1831)*, c. 1783–85 by Thomas Gainsborough (1727–88), National Gallery, London/Bridgeman Art Library, London/New York; **409:** (t.) Marylebone Cricket Club, London/Bridgeman Art Library, London/New York; **409:** (m.l., b.) The Granger Collection, New York; **410:** *Execution of Charles I, 30 January 1649*, Weesop, The Granger Collection, New York; **415:** *Marriage à la Mode: The Marriage Contract*, 1743, William Hogarth. Reproduced by courtesy of the Trustees, National Gallery of Art, London; **416:** Historical Picture Archive/CORBIS; **417:** *View of the River Dee*, c. 1761 (oil on canvas) by Richard Wilson (1714–82), National Gallery, London/Bridgeman Art Library, London/New York; **419:** *A Musical Garden Party* (detail), colored silk on canvas, very fine tent stitch. H. 13 in. W. 20-1/2 in. Metropolitan Museum of Art, Gift of Irwin Untermyer, 1964. (64.101.1314). Photograph copyright © 1991 by the Metropolitan Museum of Art; **420:** The Granger Collection, New York; **422:** *Fair Is My Love*, 1900 (oil on canvas) by Edwin A. Abbey (1852–1911) Harris Museum and Art Gallery, Preston, Lancashire, UK/Bridgeman Art Library, London/ New York; **423:** Digital Imagery © Copyright 2001 PhotoDisc, Inc.; **425:** Corel Professional Photos CD-ROM™; **426:** *Sir Thomas Aston at the Deathbed of His Wife*, John Souch © Manchester City Art Galleries; **428:** Romilly Lockyer/ The Image Bank; **434:** The Granger Collection, New York; **436:** Joel Greenstein/Omni-Photo Communications, Inc.; **438:** *Portrait of Mrs. Richard Brinsley Sheriden*, Thomas Gainsborough, Andrew W. Mellon Collection © Board of Trustees, National Gallery of Art, Washington; **440:** Digital Imagery © Copyright 2001 PhotoDisc, Inc.; **444:** (t., m.) The Granger Collection, New York; **444:** (b.) New York Public Library; **446:** *The Interrupted Sleep*, oil on canvas. Oval 29-1/2 x 25-1/2 in., François Boucher, The Metropolitan Museum of Art, The Jules Bache Collection, 1949. (49.7.46) Photograph © 1984 The Metropolitan Museum of Art; **454–455:** Jules Zalon/The Image Bank; **456:** Jane Bowr/Camera Press London/Globe Photos; **457:** Corel Professional Photos CD-ROM™; **458:** AP/Wide World Photos; **459:** *Whitehall, January 30th, 1649 (Execution of Charles I)*, Ernest Crofts, Forbes Magazine Collection, Bridgeman/Art Resource, NY; **460:** CORBIS-Bettmann; **462:** Bildarchiv Preussischer Kulturbesitz; **463:** Chris Helli-er/CORBIS; **464:** Digital Imagery © Copyright 2001 PhotoDisc, Inc.; **466:** The Granger Collection, New York; **468, 471, 473:** Courtesy of the Trustees of British Library; **474:** Digital Imagery © Copyright 2001 PhotoDisc, Inc.; **480:** The Granger Collection, New York; **482:** Bildarchiv Preussischer Kulturbesitz; **484–485:** Fitzwilliam Museum, Cambridge; **490, 492:** Photofest; **493, 494** (l., r.): The Granger Collection, New York; **496:** Last page of Samuel Pepys's Diary, 31 May 1669, Pepys Library, Magdalene College, Cambridge, England; **498:** The Granger Collection, New York; **501:** *The Great Fire*, 1666, coloured engraving by Marcus Willemsz Doornik (17th century), Guildhall Library, Corporation of London/Bridgeman Art Library, London/New York; **504:** Courtesy of the Trustees of British Library; **507, 512, 516, 519, 523, 528:** The Granger Collection, New York; **530:** Corel Professional Photos CD-ROM™; **533:** *The Barge* (detail), 1895–1896, Aubrey Beardsley from "The Rape of the Lock," Smithers, 1896 from *The Best of Beardsley,* collected and edited by R.A. Walker, ©1948 by The Bodley Head. Published in the U.S.A. by Excalibur Books, plate 63; **534:** *The Rape of the Lock*, 1895–1896, Aubrey Beardsley, from "The Rape of the Lock," Smithers, 1896 from *The Best of Beardsley,* collected and edited by R.A. Walker, ©1948 by The Bodley Head. Published in the U.S.A. by Excalibur Books, plate 64; **535:** Digital Imagery © Copyright 2001 PhotoDisc, Inc.; **539:** *The Battle of the Beaux and the Belles*, drawing for the eighth illustration from *The Rape of the Lock* by Alexander Pope (1688–1744) pub. by Leonard Smithers, 1896 (pen & ink on paper) by Aubrey Beardsley (1872–98), The Barber Institute of Fine Arts, University of Birmingham/Bridgeman Art Library, London/New York; **540:** Historical Picture Archive/CORBIS; **546** (r., l.), **549:** The Granger Collection, New York; **557:** © British Museum; **568:** (l., r.) The Granger Collection, New York; **570, 574:** Lenore Weber/Omni-Photo Communications, Inc.; **576:** *Cottage and Pond, Moonlight*, Thomas Gainsborough, Art Resource, NY/Victoria and Albert Museum, London; **578, 582:** Digital Imagery © Copyright 2001 PhotoDisc, Inc.; **583:** AP/ Wide World Photos; **584:** The Granger Collection, New York; **585:** *Girl Writing by Lamplight*, c. 1850, by William Henry Hunt (1790–1864), The Maas Gallery, London/Bridgeman Art Library, London/New York; **586:** (l., r.) The Granger Collection, New York; **588, 593:** Corel Professional Photos CD-ROM™; **598:** Bob Kramer/Stock, Boston; **600:** Mary Kate Denny/PhotoEdit/PNI; **601:** John Barrett/Globe Photos; **604:** Flip Chalfant/ The Image Bank; **610–611:** *Two Men Observing the Moon*, Caspar David Friedrich, oil on canvas, 35 x 44.5 cm, (1819–1820), Staatl, Kunstsammlungen, Neue Meister, Dresden, Germany, Erich Lessing/Art Resource, NY; **612:** (t., b., m.r.) The Granger Collection, New York; **612:** (m.l.) Corel Professional Photos CD-ROM™; **613:** (t.l.) © Barson Collection/ Archive Photos, **613** (t.r., b.), **614:** The Granger Collection, New York; **616:** *Power loom weaving*, 1834 (engraving) by Thomas Allom (1804–72) (after), Private Collection/Bridgeman Art Library, London/New York; **617:** *Tea Time*, David Emil, Christie's, London/ SuperStock; **618:** © Hulton/Archive; **621:** *Sketch for Hadleigh Castle*, John Constable, Oil on canvas, c. 1829, The Granger Collection, New York; **623:** *Hummingbird Hunters*, 1884, James Farrington Gookins, Collection of the Shelden Swope Art Museum, Terre Haute, Indiana; **624:** (l.) *Robert Burns*, A. Nasmyth, by courtesy of the National Portrait Gallery, London; **624:** (r.) The Granger Collection, New York; **626:** © R. J. Erwin/Photo Researchers, Inc.; **629:** *The Bow*, Talbot Hughes, Warrington Museum & Art Gallery, Great Britain, Bridgeman/Art Resource, NY; **630:** Digital Imagery © Copyright 2001 PhotoDisc, Inc.; **633:** *The Village Wedding*, (detail), by Sir Luke Fildes (1844–1927), Christopher Wood Gallery, London/Bridgeman Art

Library, London/New York; **638:** The Granger Collection, New York; **640:** From a Manuscript of "The Lamb" by William Blake, Lessing J. Rosenwald Collection, Courtesy of the Library of Congress, Washington, D.C.; **641:** *The Tyger*, A Page from "Songs of Innocence and Experience," William Blake, The Metropolitan Museum of Art, Rogers Fund, 1917 © Copyright 1984 by The Metropolitan Museum of Art; **643:** © Archive Photos; **648:** *Mary Shelley* (detail), c. 1840, Richard Rothwell, by courtesy of the National Portrait Gallery, London; **650–651:** *A View of Chamonix and Mt. Blanc*, Ludwig Ferdinand Schnorr von Carolsfeld, Austrian Gallery, Vienna; **653:** © Belinda Wright/DRK Photo; **659:** *Elizabeth Beale Bordley*, c. 1797, Gilbert Stuart, oil on canvas, 29-1/4 x 24", 1886.2, courtesy of the Museum of American Art of the Pennsylvania Academy of the Fine Arts, Philadelphia. Bequest of Elizabeth Mifflin; **660:** CORBIS-Bettmann; **661:** *The Wanderer Over the Sea of Clouds*, 1818, by Caspar-David Friedrich (1774–1840), Kunsthalle, Hamburg/Bridgeman Art Library, London/New York; **662:** The Granger Collection, New York; **664:** © Colin Raw/Stone; **666:** The Granger Collection, New York; **669:** Digital Imagery © Copyright 2001 PhotoDisc, Inc.; **670:** *Tintern Abbey*, J.M.W. Turner, © British Museum; **673:** *Storming of the Bastille, 14 July 1789*, Anonymous, Chateau de, Versailles, France/Art Resource, NY; **675:** Corel Professional Photos CD-ROM™; **684:** *Samuel Taylor Coleridge* (detail), by courtesy of the National Portrait Gallery, London; **686:** Engraving by Gustave Doré for "The Rime of the Ancient Mariner" by Samuel Taylor Coleridge ©1970 by Dover Publications, Inc.; **689:** Engraving by Gustave Doré for "The Rime of the Ancient Mariner" by Samuel Taylor Coleridge ©1970 by Dover Publications, Inc.; **691:** The Granger Collection, New York; **695:** Engraving by Gustave Doré for "The Rime of the Ancient Mariner" by Samuel Taylor Coleridge ©1970 by Dover Publications, Inc.; **699:** Engraving by Gustave Doré for "The Rime of the Ancient Mariner" by Samuel Taylor Coleridge ©1970 by Dover Publications, Inc.; **702:** The Granger Collection, New York; **705:** Digital Imagery © Copyright 2001 PhotoDisc, Inc.; **710:** *Box and Cover*, Ming Dynasty, first half of 16th century, lacquer, black; mother-of-pearl; wood; fabric. H. 4 in. The Seattle Art Museum, Gift of Mr. and Mrs. Louis Brechemin. Photo by Paul Macapia; **716:** Culver Pictures, Inc.; **716:** "Lord Byron, shaking the dust of England from his shoes," from *The Poet's Corner*, pub. by William Heinemann, 1904 (engraving) by Max Beerbohm (1872–1956), Central Saint Martins College of Art and Design/ Bridgeman Art Library, London/New York; **718:** *In the Garden* (detail), c. 1889, Thomas Wilmer Dewing, oil on canvas, 20-5/8 x 35", National Museum of American Art, Washington, D.C./Art Resource, NY; **720–721:** *Shipwreck*, J.C.C. Dahl, Munich Neue Pinakothek/ Kavaler/Art Resource, NY; **722:** Corel Professional Photos CD-ROM™; **730:** The Granger Collection, New York; **732:** © Diane Rawson/Photo Researchers, Inc.; **734–735:** © David Sutherland/ Stone; **739:** *Cloud Study*, 1821, John Constable, Yale Center for British Art, Paul Mellon Collection; **744:** The Granger Collection, New York; **746:** Courtesy of the Trustees of British Library; **749:** *John Keats*, 1821, Joseph Severn, by courtesy of the National Portrait Gallery, London; **751:** *Small Bird On a Flowering Plum Branch*, attributed to Ma Lin, The Goto Museum; **754:** Greek vase, terracotta, c. 460 B.C. Attributed to the Orchard Painter, Column Krater (called the "Orchard Vase"), Side A: *Women Gathering Apples*, The Metropolitan Museum of Art, Rogers Fund, 1907, (07.286.74); **760:** *Lady Lilith*, 1868, Dante Gabriel Rossetti, Delaware Art Museum, Wilmington, DE, USA/Bridgeman Art Library, London/New York; **761:** CORBIS-Bettmann; **762:** *Kobayashi Issa*, Heibonsha/Pacific Press Service; **763:** (l.) *Crows Taking Flight through Spring Haze* (1782–1846), hanging scroll, Edo period, dated 1841; Toyama Kinenkan, Saitama prefecture, Okada Hanko, Foundation Toyama Memorial Museum; **763:** (r.) Yosa Buson, Heibonsha/ Pacific Press Service; **765:** *Forging the Anchor*, 1831, by William James Muller (1812–45), City of Bristol Museum and Art Gallery/ Bridgeman Art Library, London/New York; **766:** (all) The Granger Collection, New York; **768:** *The Workshops at the Gobelins*, 1840, by Jean-Charles Develly (1783–1849), Musée Carnavalet, Paris, France/Giraudon/Bridgeman Art Library, London/New York; **771:** Brown Brothers; **773:** SIPA Press; **778:** (l.) *Jane Austen* (detail), c. 1801—C. Auston, by courtesy of the National Portrait Gallery, London; **778:** (r.) The Granger Collection, New York; **780:** *Marriage à la Mode: The Marriage Contract*, 1743, William Hogarth, reproduced by courtesy of the Trustees, National Gallery of Art, London; **785:** Digital Imagery © Copyright 2001 PhotoDisc, Inc.; **790:** Photofest; **793:** Globe Photos; **796:** Walter Hodges/Tony Stone Images; **802–803:** *The Railway Station*, 1862, by William Powell Frith (1819–1909), Royal Holloway and Bedford New College, Surrey/Bridgeman Art Library, London/New York; **804:** (b.) The Granger Collection, New York; **804:** (t.r.) Library of Congress/CORBIS; **804:** (t.m.) Illustrated London News/CORBIS; **804:** (t.l.) © British Museum; **805:** (t.l.) *The Mad Tea Party* from First Edition of *Alice's Adventures*, Sir John Tenniel, The Granger Collection, New York; **805:** (t.r.) The Granger Collection, New York; **805:** (b.) Gary J. Shulfer; **805:** (m.) The Granger Collection, New York; **806:** The Royal Collection © Her Majesty Queen Elizabeth II; **807:** Hulton-Deutsch Collection/ CORBIS; **809:** *Day Dream*, 1880, Dante Gabriel Rosetti, Victoria & Albert Museum, London, UK/The Bridgeman Art Library, London/New York; **811:** *Bayswater Omnibus*, G.W. Joy, Museum of London; **813:** *Edwardian London*, 1901, by Eugene Joseph McSwiney (1866–1912), Christopher Wood Gallery, London/Bridgeman Art Library, London/New York; **815:** *Faustine*, 1904, Maxwell Armfield, Musée d'Orsay, Paris, France/Erich Lessing/Art Resource, NY; **816:** *Alfred Lord Tennyson* (detail), c. 1840, S. Laurence, by courtesy of the National Portrait Gallery, London; **818:** *The Stages of Life*, c. 1835 (oil on canvas) by Caspar-David Friedrich (1774–1840), Museum der Bildenden Kunste, Leipzig/Bridgeman Art Library, London/New York; **821:** Superstock; **824:** Digital Imagery © Copyright 2001 PhotoDisc, Inc.; **829:** Jean-Auguste-Dominique Ingres, *Ulysses*, 1827, Chester Dale Collection. Photograph © Board of Trustees, National Gallery of Art, Washington; **834:** (l., r.) The Granger Collection, New York; **836:** *Antea* (Portrait of a Lady), Parmigianino, Museo Nazionale di Capodimonte, Naples/Scala/Art Resource, NY; **839:** Culver Pictures, Inc.; **840:** *Italian Ruins*, John Claude Nattes, Victoria and Albert Museum/Art Resource, NY; **842:** Corel Professional Photos CD-ROM™; **848:** ©The Stock Market/Tibor Bognar; **849:** CORBIS-Bettmann; **851:** *Marine*, Marcel Mouillot, Galerie d'Art Moderne, Nancy/Art Resource, NY; **852:** CORBIS-Bettmann; **853:** *Music and Literature*, 1878, William M. Harnett, oil on canvas, 24 x 32-1/8" Albright-Knox Art Gallery, Buffalo, New York, Gift of Seymour H. Knox, 1941; **854:** (l., r.) The Granger Collection, New York; **856:** Illustration from *The Oxford Illustrated Dickens;* **857:** *Dickens's Dream*, Robert William Buss/ Bridgeman Art Library, London/New York; **858:** © Hulton Getty/Archive Photos; **860–861:** The Granger Collection, New York; **867:** Springer/CORBIS-Bettmann; **870:** *Rochester and Jane Eyre*, Frederick Walker, Private Collection/ Bridgeman Art Library, London/New York; **876–877:** *The Return of the Troops from the Crimea, Boulevard des Italiens, in front of the Hanover Pavilion, December 1855*, c. 19th century/Emmanuel Masses/Musée Carnavalet, Paris, France, Roger-Viollet Paris/Bridgeman Art Library, London/ New York; **879:** *Portrait of Koutouzov, Prince of Smolensk*, George Dawe, Hermitage, St. Petersburg, Russia/Giraudon/Art Resource, NY; **880:** *L. N. Tolstoi*, I. E. Repin, Sovfoto/Eastfoto; **881:** e.t. archive; **882:** (l.) *Matthew Arnold* (detail), 1888, G. J. Watts, by courtesy of the National Portrait Gallery, London; **882:** (r.) *Rudyard Kipling* (detail), 1899, P. Burne Jones, by courtesy of the National Portrait Gallery, London; **884:** Andrea Pistolesi/The Image Bank; **886:** The Granger Collection, New York; **887:** Private Collection/Bridgeman Art Library, London/New York; **889:** Culver Pictures, Inc.; **894:** Private Collection/Bridgeman Art Library, London/New York; **896:** *Woman Begging at Clonakilty*, James Mahony, The Illustrated London News, 1847. Photo by Grace Davies/Omni-Photo Communications, Inc.; **898:** Private Collection/ Bridgeman Art Library, London/New York; **900–901:** Culver Pictures, Inc.; **910–911:** © Joe Cornish/Stone; **913, 914:** Derek Speirs/Report Ltd; **915:** *Past and Present* (no. 2), Augustus Leopold Egg, Tate Gallery, London/Art Resource, NY; **916:** (l.) The Granger Collection, New York; **916:** (r.) *Thomas Hardy* (detail), R. G. Eres, by courtesy of the National Portrait

CREDITS

Gallery, London; **918:** *My Sweet Rose*, John William Waterhouse, Roy Miles Gallery, London/ Bridgeman/ Art Resource, NY; **921:** © Gregory K. Scott/Photo Researchers, Inc.; **923:** Lenore Weber/Omni-Photo Communications, Inc.; **924:** Digital Imagery © Copyright 2001 PhotoDisc, Inc.; **928:** (l.) *Gerard Manley Hopkins* (detail), 1859, A. E. Hopkins, by Courtesy of the National Portrait Gallery, London; **928:** (r.) The Granger Collection, New York; **930:** *Bird's Nest*, Ros W. Jenkins, Warrington Museum and Art Gallery, Bridgeman/Art Resource, NY; **933:** CORBIS-Bettmann; **938:** Corel Professional Photos CD-ROM™; **939:** Erich Lessing/Art Resource, NY; **942:** Jeff Greenberg/PhotoEdit; **950–951:** *The City Rises*, 1911 (tempera on card), Umberto Boccioni (1882–1916), Jesi Collection, Milan/Bridgeman Art Library, London/ New York; **952:** (b.l.) Imperial War Museum, London; **952:** (t.) Corel Professional Photos CD-ROM™; **952:** (b.r.) CORBIS-Bettmann; **952:** (b.m.) The National Archives/CORBIS; **953:** (r.) © Peter Marlow/Sygma; **953:** (l.) NASA; **953:** (m.) Michael St. Maur Shell/CORBIS; **954:** *Prado, Madrid, Spain*, Fitzwilliam Museum, University of Cambridge, UK/The Bridgeman Art Library, London/New York; **955:** Musée de Verdun/Luc Joubert/Tallandier; **956:** Culver Pictures, Inc.; **957:** Domenica del Corriere/ET Archive, London/SuperStock; **959:** David Hockney, *The Crossword Puzzle*, Minneapolis, Jan. 1983, photographic collage, 33 x 46", © David Hockney; **960:** Martin Jones/CORBIS; **963:** *The Children Enter the Palace of Luxury*, probably from "The Bluebird" by Maeterlinck, 1911 (oil on card) by Frederick Cayley Robinson (1862–1927), The Fine Art Society, London/ Bridgeman Art Library, London/New York; **964:** The Granger Collection, New York; **966:** *Her Signal*, c. 1892, Norman Garstin (1847–1926), The Royal Cornwall Museum, Truro/Bridgeman Art Library, London/New York; **969:** Dennis Stock/Magnum Photos, Inc.; **971:** Peter Johnson/CORBIS; **973:** *Ravenna: City and Port of Classis.* Mosaic, late 6th century A.D. from Basilicia of St. Apollinare Nuovo., The Granger Collection, New York; **978:** *T. S. Eliot* (detail), 1888–1965, Sir Gerald Kelly, National Portrait Gallery, Smithsonian Institution, Art Resource, New York; **980:** Chuck Carlton/Index Stock Photography, Inc.; **991:** Digital Imagery © Copyright 2001 PhotoDisc, Inc.; **996:** (t.l.) CORBIS-Bettmann; **996:** (t.r.) *Louis MacNeice* (detail), H. Loster, by Courtesy of the National Portrait Gallery, London; **996** (b.), **998:** The Granger Collection, New York; **1002:** *The Fall of Icarus*, Pieter Brueghel, Musées Royaux des Beaux-Arts de Belgique, Bruxelles; **1004–1005:** Simon Wilkinson/The Image Bank; **1007:** Richard Nowitz/CORBIS; **1013:** © Kim Sayer/CORBIS; **1014:** Jeremy Homer/CORBIS; **1016:** The Granger Collection, New York; **1018:** © Gregory C. Dimijian/Photo Researchers, Inc.; **1021:** Art Resource, NY; **1024–1025:** © Orwell Archive; **1030:** Alfred A. Knopf; **1034:** Digital Imagery © Copyright 2001 PhotoDisc, Inc.; **1037:** *Ox House, Shaftesbury*, 1932, John R. Biggs, wood engraving; **1042:** *Thrust*, 1959, Adolph Gottlieb, The Metropolitan Museum of Art, George A. Hearn Fund, 1959, photography by Malcolm Varon, © 1987/1989 Copyright by the Metropolitan Museum of Art, © Adolph and Esther Gottlieb Foundation/Licensed by VAGA, New York, NY; **1043:** Inge Morath/Magnum Photos, Inc.; **1044:** *Anna Akhmatova* (detail), N. I. Altman, The Granger Collection, New York; **1045:** *Anna Akhmatova*, N. I. Altman, The Granger Collection, New York; **1046:** Dorothy Alexander; **1047:** *A Balloon Site*, Coventry, 1940, Dame Laura Knight, Imperial War Museum, London; **1048:** (t.l., t.r.) The Granger Collection, New York; **1048:** (b.l.) *Siegfried Sassoon* (detail), Bassano, by Courtesy of the National Portrait Gallery, London; **1048:** (b.r.) The Granger Collection, New York; **1050, 1052:** Photri; **1053:** The Granger Collection, New York; **1054:** © S.C. Fried/Photo Researchers, Inc.; **1056:** CORBIS-Bettmann; **1062:** (l.) *Winston Churchill* (detail), National Portrait Gallery, Smithsonian Institution, Washington, D.C./Art Resource, NY; **1062:** (r.) The Granger Collection, New York; **1064:** Snark/Art Resource, NY; **1070:** Culver Pictures, Inc.; **1076:** Hulton Getty/Tony Stone Worldwide; **1078:** *Hillside in Wales* (detail), L.S. Lowry, The Tate Gallery, London/Art Resource, New York; **1080, 1082:** Digital Imagery © Copyright 2001 PhotoDisc, Inc.; **1088:** Mark Gerson Photography; **1091:** Nicholas Devore/Bruce Coleman, Inc.; **1092–1093:** Michael St. Maur/CORBIS; **1096:** (l.) The Granger Collection, New York; **1096:** (r.) Patrick Ward/Stock, Boston; **1102:** (l.) Thomas Victor; **1102:** (r.) The Irish Times; **1104–1105:** D'Lynn Waldron/The Image Bank; **1109:** *Starry Night over the Rhone River*, Vincent van Gogh, Musée d'Orsay, Paris, France/Art Resource, NY; **1114:** Thomas Victor; **1116:** Peter Dublin/Stock, Boston; **1119:** Terry Madison/The Image Bank; **1126:** Digital Imagery © Copyright 2001 PhotoDisc, Inc.; **1128:** © Richard Smith/Sygma; **1130:** AP/Wide World Photos; **1131:** *The Snack Bar*, 1930, Edward Burra, Tate Gallery, London/Art Resource, NY; **1132:** (r.) The Granger Collection, New York; **1132:** (l.) *Joseph Conrad* (detail), Walter Tittle, by Courtesy of the National Portrait Gallery, London; **1135:** Dieter & Mary Plage/Bruce Coleman, Inc.; **1137:** Digital Imagery © Copyright 2001 PhotoDisc, Inc.; **1140–1141:** Michael Freidel/Woodfin Camp & Associates; **1144:** Tony Arruza/CORBIS; **1149:** *St. Patrick's Close*, Walter Osborne, National Gallery of Ireland; **1151:** Digital Imagery © Copyright 2001 PhotoDisc, Inc.; **1156:** (l.) The Granger Collection, New York; **1156:** (r.) Photo by Jerry Bauer; **1159:** *The Garden of Love*, Walter Richard Sickert, Fitzwilliam Museum, Cambridge; **1160:** © Stephen Johnson/Stone; **1162, 1164:** Digital Imagery © Copyright 2001 PhotoDisc, Inc.; **1166:** The Granger Collection, New York; **1168:** Culver Pictures, Inc.; **1174:** (l.) *D. H. Lawrence* (detail), Jan Juta, by Courtesy of the National Portrait Gallery, London; **1174:** (r.) The Granger Collection, New York; **1177:** CORBIS-Bettmann; **1183:** Culver Pictures, Inc.; **1186–1187:** Aaron Horowitz/CORBIS; **1191:** Hans Neleman/The Image Bank; **1201:** Steve Dunwell/The Image Bank; **1202:** Susan Meiselas/Magnum Photos, Inc.; **1203:** *Political World*, © Kenneth Eward/BioGrafz—Science Source/Photo Researchers, Inc.; **1204:** (l.) CORBIS-Bettmann; **1204:** (r.) Thomas Victor; **1206:** *Fishermen at Sea off the Needles*, J.M.W. Turner, Tate Gallery (on loan)/e.t. archive; **1208:** Digital Imagery © Copyright 2001 PhotoDisc, Inc.; **1210–1211:** Dann Coffey/The Image Bank; **1213:** © J. B. Lafitte/Photo Researchers, Inc.; **1217:** © Jim Ballard/Stone; **1224:** (b.) Nicolas Elder/Globe Photos; **1224:** (t.) *Philip Larkin* (detail), Humphrey Ocean, by Courtesy of the National Portrait Gallery, London; **1224:** (m.) *Stevie Smith* (detail), Godfrey Argent, by Courtesy of the National Portrait Gallery, London; **1226:** Tombstones of Tiberius Julius Rufus and his son, Petronius Rufus, and their wives, Erich Lessing/Art Resource, NY; **1230:** Ross M. Horowitz/The Image Bank; **1236:** Ian Berry/Magnum Photos, Inc.; **1239:** *Man from the Village*, Carlton Murrell, Courtesy of the artist; **1240:** Digital Imagery © Copyright 2001 PhotoDisc, Inc.; **1242:** *The Red House*, Carlton Murrell, Courtesy of the artist; **1248:** Thomas Victor; **1250:** © Richard A Cooke III/Stone; **1258:** (r.) Camera Press/Globe Photos; **1258:** (l.) Eugene Richards/Magnum Photos, Inc.; **1260:** © Bettmann/CORBIS; **1262, 1263:** Digital Imagery © Copyright 2001 PhotoDisc, Inc.; **1265:** UPI/CORBIS-Bettmann; **1270:** Thomas Victor; **1274–1275:** Dinodia/Omni-Photo Communications, Inc.; **1278:** Grace Davies/ Omni-Photo Communications, Inc.; **1286:** UPI/Corbis-Bettmann; **1288, 1291, 1292:** NASA/Omni-Photo Communications, Inc.; **1293:** Digital Imagery © Copyright 2001 PhotoDisc, Inc.; **1300:** Pearson Education/PH School